Canadian Libel and Slander Actions

Canadian Libel and Slander Actions

ROGER D. McCONCHIE

Member of the Bars of
British Columbia and Alberta

DAVID A. POTTS

Member of the Bar of
Ontario

IRWIN
LAW

Canadian Libel and Slander Actions
© Irwin Law Inc., 2004

Published in 2004 by

Irwin Law Inc.
Suite 501
347 Bay Street
Toronto, ON
M5H 2R7
www.irwinlaw.com

ISBN: 1-55221-056-1

National Library of Canada Cataloguing in Publication

McConchie, Roger D.
    Canadian libel & slander actions / Roger McConchie, David Potts.

Includes bibliographical references and index.

ISBN 1-55221-056-1

    1. Libel and slander—Canada. I. Potts, David A. (David Anthony) II. Title.
III. Title: Canadian libel and slander actions.

KE1246.M33 2004   346.7103'4   C2004-904240-5
KF1266.M33 2004

The publisher acknowledges the financial support of the Government of Canada through the Book Publishing Industry Development Program (BPIDP) for our publishing activities. The publisher also acknowledges the Government of Ontario through the Ontario Media Development Corporation's Ontario Book Initiative.

Printed and bound in Canada

1 2 3 4 5   08 07 06 05 04

Summary Table of Contents

Detailed Table of Contents

chapter six:
Notice of Intended Action and Limitation Defences *61*

chapter ten:
Security for Costs Under Defamation Statutes

chapter twenty-one:

Justification

chapter twenty-two:

Consent

chapter twenty-five:
Pre-trial Disposition of Claims and Defences   *645*

chapter twenty-six:
Discovery of Documents   *673*

chapter twenty-nine:
Charge and Questions to the Jury   *817*

chapter thirty-two:
Related Causes of Action   *899*

Dedication:

For my wife, Rosa Maria McConchie
– R.D.M.

For Cheryl, Jason, Taylor, Stuart and Simon, and Cheesecake.
– D.A.P.

Acknowledgements

I would like to express my profound thanks to my former secretary and assistant, Donna Hesse, for her diligence and patience over the years in creating, assembling and collating the many drafts involved in preparing this book and facilitating the flow of information to the publisher. I also received invaluable cooperation from Library Services Manager Anne Beresford, Technicians Andy Froese and Nancy Souvestre, and Assistant Librarian Frances Wong at my former firm, Borden Ladner Gervais LLP. Carmen Marolla, a litigation paralegal, provided valuable assistance in developing the underlying material for many chapters.

I must also mention lawyers Allison Foord, Fred Kozak, Paul Eastwood, Brian MacLeod Rogers, and Patrick G. Foy, Q.C. who offered helpful comments during the latter stages of this project.

Needless to say, any errors which survive in this work despite the kind assistance and input I received are my responsibility.

Roger D. McConchie

* * * * *

I would first like to thank Linda F. Haney, for her enthusiasm, organizational genius, and supervision of this project. Her invaluable suggestions contributed immeasurably to this book.

Jeffrey Miller, our publisher, and Jo Roberts, our editor, provided support and assistance throughout the project. Steve Wallace and Michael Maehle of Osgoode Hall Law School assisted quickly and cheerfully in retrieving cases from the deepest recesses of the Great Library.

Mr. Justice Colin Campbell, Mr. Justice Dennis Lane, and Mr. Justice James Carnwath all of the Ontario Superior Court of Justice provided invaluable advice for the chapter on Jury Charge.

And finally I want to acknowledge the Honourable Charles Dubin, former Chief Justice of Ontario, for his insightful observations and comments, but also for the pleasure of learning from one of Canada's pre-eminent libel specialists.

David A. Potts

INTRODUCTION:

The Special Nature of Defamation Litigation

The gist of the cause of action for libel or slander is injury to reputation. In the common law provinces and three northern territories, the tort is firmly rooted in centuries of English jurisprudence and is largely unaltered by statute.

The issues in defamation litigation invariably transcend the private interests of the parties. Libel and slander lawsuits involve a clash between two fundamental democratic values — protection of reputation and freedom of expression. In many defamation lawsuits, the Court is required to engage in a delicate balancing exercise, the results of which may have broad implications for the way our democracy operates.

In the leading Canadian case, the 1995 ruling of the Supreme Court of Canada in *Hill* v. *Church of Scientology of Toronto*, [1995] 2 S.C.R. 1130, Cory J. emphasized the clash of values in libel litigation:

> ¶100 There can be no doubt that in libel cases the twin values of reputation and freedom of expression will clash. As Edgerton J. stated in *Sweeney* v. *Patterson*, 128 F.2d 457 (D.C. Cir. 1942) at p. 458, certiorari denied 317 U.S. 678 (1942), whatever is "added to the field of libel is taken from the field of free debate."

> ¶101 Much has been written of the great importance of free speech. Without this freedom to express ideas and to criticize the operation of institutions and the conduct of individual members of government agencies, democratic forms of government would wither and die. ... More recently, in *Edmonton Journal*, [1989] 2 S.C.R. 1326 ... it was said:

> > It is difficult to imagine a guaranteed right more important to a democratic society than freedom of expression. Indeed a democracy cannot exist without that freedom to express new ideas and to put forward

opinions about the functioning of public institutions. The concept of free and uninhibited speech permeates all truly democratic societies and institutions. The vital importance of the concept cannot be over-emphasized.

¶102 However, freedom of expression has never been recognized as an absolute right. Duff C.J.C. emphasized this point in *Re Alberta Legislation*, [1938] S.C.R. 100 at 107:

> The right of public discussion is, of course, subject to legal restrictions; those based upon considerations of decency and public order, and others conceived for the protection of various private and public interests with which, for example, the law of defamation and sedition are concerned. In a word, *freedom of discussion means ... "freedom governed by law."* [Emphasis added.]

¶107 The other value to be balanced in a defamation action is the protection of the reputation of the individual. Although much has very properly been said and written about the importance of freedom of expression, little has been written of the importance of reputation. Yet, to most people, their good reputation is to be cherished above all. A good reputation is closely related to the innate worthiness and dignity of the individual. It is an attribute that must, just as much as freedom of expression, be protected by society's laws. In order to undertake the balancing required by this case, something must be said about the value of reputation.

¶108 Democracy has always recognized and cherished the fundamental importance of an individual. That importance must, in turn, be based upon the good repute of a person. It is that good repute which enhances an individual's sense of worth and value. False allegations can so very quickly and completely destroy a good reputation. A reputation tarnished by libel can seldom regain its former luster. A democratic society, therefore, has an interest in ensuring that its members can enjoy and protect their good reputation so long as it is merited.

After the *Canadian Charter of Rights and Freedoms* came into force in 1982, libel litigants have expected to see changes in the balancing process as a result of the guarantee of freedom of expression contained in section 2(b).

Although *Hill v. Scientology*, [1995] 2 S.C.R. 1130, held that the constitutional liberties guaranteed by the *Canadian Charter of Rights and Freedoms* do not apply directly to libel litigation between private parties where government legislation, regulations, or actions are not implicated, *Charter* values were held to apply to the common law, which must therefore be interpreted and applied in a manner which is consistent with those *Charter* values. Accordingly, in any defamation lawsuit, it is open to the litigants to argue that the court, when balancing reputation against freedom of expression, should exercise its inherent jurisdiction to make incremental changes to modify or extend the common law to accommodate current social and political conditions.

Against the background of a clash between two fundamental democratic values, every potential defamation litigant must confront two basic questions. Assuming the expression does in fact refer to the potential plaintiff, the two basic questions are:

i)   Is the expression defamatory?
ii)   If it is defamatory, is the expression defensible?

Normally, the first is easily answered; the second, however, often raises complex issues of fact and law. In Canada, the threshold for finding that expression concerning an identifiable individual is defamatory is quite low — it need only lower that person in the estimation of right-thinking persons generally. Almost any disparaging remark could meet this test, which is therefore ideally suited to be administered by a jury. It requires no special legal skill. A lay person is as well qualified as a lawyer or judge — some would say better qualified — to say whether expression is defamatory.

Once expression is determined to be defamatory, defamation law affords the potential plaintiff several powerful presumptions. Here libel cases differ from much other civil litigation, where the plaintiff ordinarily carries the burden of proof on issues of liability and damages.

Once a plaintiff has shown that the expression is defamatory, the law presumes that it is false, that it is malicious, and that it has caused compensable injury to the plaintiff's reputation. Theoretically, presenting a plaintiff's libel case at trial could be as simple as proving the publication by filing the newspaper article, broadcast, or other publication in evidence as an exhibit, calling testimony to prove that the contents concern the plaintiff, and then closing the plaintiff's case without calling any testimony from the plaintiff. Needless to say, this simplistic approach is rarely seen. Substantial damages are unlikely to be awarded unless a plaintiff testifies.

The defendant has a variety of defences available, including traditional defences such as truth, fair comment, and privilege, both absolute and qualified. In a recent development, the defendant can now plead her own defamatory meaning and plead that the meaning is true. In the United

Kingdom, the House of Lords has developed a new privilege which in effect protects statements made in matters of public interest. That new privilege may well be in the process of migrating to Canada.

If these defences fail, the defendants may rely upon a range of pleas in mitigation of damages, both statutory and common law, including but not limited to pleading of apologies, absence of malice, and even the general bad reputation of the plaintiff.

Even to the most experienced libel lawyer there rarely appears to be a bright line between defensible and indefensible expression. To borrow words from Bulfinch's *Mythology*, the common law of defamation is a labyrinth "with numberless winding passages and turnings opening into one another, and seeming to have neither beginning nor end … so artfully contrived that whoever was enclosed in it could by no means find his way out unassisted." Even the most familiar defamation defences — justification (truth), fair comment, and privilege — lay many traps for the unwary litigant wending his or her way through this area of law.

Southin J.A. gives an explanation for the complexity of defamation law in *Baumann* v. *Turner* (1993), 105 D.L.R. (4th) 37 (B.C.C.A.) at 38:

> As Russell L.J., as he then was, remarked in *Broadway Approvals Ltd.* v. *Odhams Press Ltd.*, [1965] 2 All E.R. 523 at 540, the law of libel has characteristics of complexity and subtlety. These characteristics, when analyzed, are not only logical but also assist in maintaining the balance between, on the one hand, the private right to a reputation unsullied by calumny and, on the other hand, the public right of free and vigorous discussion which underlies the complex defence of fair comment.

One object of this book is to provide a road map through this labyrinth and to describe the common traps which lie in wait. In subsequent chapters, we discuss the special characteristics of modern Canadian defamation litigation. These include the following:

i)   Defamation pleadings are of vital importance. Lawsuits may be won or lost depending on the skill with which a litigant prepared his or her statement of claim, statement of defence, or reply to the statement of defence.

ii) The defamation pleadings will often be rigorously construed, resulting in serious constraints on the scope of discovery of documents or oral examination for discovery. They may also impose severe limitations on the evidence that may be lead at trial by either party.

iii) The conduct of the defendant and his or her legal counsel before, during, and after publication of the defamatory expression will come under a microscope at trial. Conduct on any appeal through to and including the entry of final judgment may also be relevant to determination of liability and quantum of damages.

iv) The posture of the parties may influence the award of damages, particularly because injury to reputation is usually intangible and not reflected in demonstrable financial losses by the plaintiff. If a plaintiff appears to be a venal golddigger, bent solely on extracting money from the defendant, a jury is unlikely to be sympathetic. If the conduct of a plaintiff or defendant has been improper before or during the litigation, the jury may find that conduct has aggravated the damages.

v) If a defendant maintains a plea that the defamatory expression is true, he or she may have to pay a price in the form of an increased award of damages if that defence is not established. This is particularly risky where a defendant engages in a hostile cross-examination of a defamation plaintiff at trial, increasing the public hurt and humiliation flowing from the defamatory expression.

vi) Any repetition of the libel and any disparaging comments about the plaintiff by the defence after the commencement of the lawsuit may also be held to aggravate the plaintiff's damages, even if the plaintiff does not bring a separate claim for defamation relating to the republication of the new disparaging remarks.

vii) Each libel case is unique. The assessment of damages and negotiation of settlement is often more difficult than in other civil cases involving personal injury; and a judge sitting without a jury may be more reluctant to be guided by other defamation damage awards than in personal injury cases.

viii) The "trilogy" cap imposed by the Supreme Court of Canada on general damages in personal injury cases does not apply to general or aggravated damages in defamation litigation. This also makes the assessment of damages more difficult and increases the exposure of defendants and their insurers.

ix) Special costs are more likely to be awarded to a successful plaintiff because of the intense scrutiny of the defendant's conduct typically performed in defamation litigation.

It is well accepted that defamation litigation pits individual reputation against freedom of expression. However, it is also true that in many cases it pits reputation against reputation. Particularly in the case of libel in the mass media, a lawsuit often calls into question the professional integrity and competence of the defendant journalist. This tends to raise the stakes considerably because libel trials and verdicts often attract significant publicity.

Emotion often plays a disproportionate role in libel litigation. Individual emotions on both sides frequently run very high. In many cases, an individual libel plaintiff will alternate between extremes of anger, anxiety, and depression, sometimes making it difficult for legal counsel to obtain consistent, informed, and thoughtful instructions. On the other hand, the plaintiff's emotional state sometimes works to the advantage of a libel defendant who is prepared to acknowledge his or her error. If a prompt, sincere, and effective retraction and apology can assuage a plaintiff's outrage, a defamation complaint may quickly be put to rest.

The damage caused by defamatory expression is often difficult to measure in monetary terms. The damage may be invisible to the eye. Unlike motor vehicle accident victims, the jury will not see a plaintiff slumped in a wheelchair, missing a limb, or physically scarred. The size of a damage award may instead depend on careful testimony about psychological and emotional injury and distress, often given by a series of witnesses who have observed the plaintiff since publication or broadcast of the libel. Presenting evidence of damage will tax the skill of plaintiff's counsel.

All of the above factors contribute to another distinguishing feature of defamation litigation. Except in the most straightforward cases, libel lawsuits tend to be enormously expensive both for the plaintiff and for the defence. This arises not only from the complexity of the law and the special care that must be paid to the conduct of the litigation, but also because of the ongoing thorough investigation of facts relevant to issues of malice and the conduct of the parties throughout the litigation.

In this age of globalization, a defamation litigant in Canada confronts many uncertainties arising from the fact that the defamatory expression may have been published or broadcast in multiple jurisdictions. As we discuss in later chapters, even within Canada there are some material differences in the law between the provinces as regards fair comment, justification, and preconditions to litigation. This is partly explained by the division of powers between Ottawa and the provinces. Civil defamation law is a matter of "Property and Civil Rights," a legislative subject assigned to the provinces by section 92(13) of the *Constitution Act, 1867* (U.K.), 30 & 31 Vict. c. 3, reprinted in R.S.C. 1985 App. II, No. 5 [formerly the *British North American Act*] and delegated to the Yukon, Northwest Territories, and Nunavut by the federal Parliament [*Yukon Act*, R.S.C. 1985, c. Y-2, s. 2/7(h); *Northwest Territories Act*, R.S.C. 1985 c. N.-27, s. 2/6(h); *Nunavut Act*, S.C. 1993 c. 28, s. 23(1)(L)].

If there is no Supreme Court of Canada decision governing a point, it is vital for defamation counsel to identify the leading decisions in the province where the action is brought before examining cases from other jurisdictions. Decisions from other commonwealth jurisdictions must be treated with caution for similar reasons. In many of those jurisdictions, the common law may also have been modified or codified by statute.

The following chapters will highlight, wherever possible, the differences in the common law and the statutory regimes which prevail in each of the provinces and the northern territories.

CHAPTER ONE

Libel and Slander

A. INTRODUCTION

The law of defamation concerns the torts of libel and slander.

At common law, libel is defamatory expression in writing or some other non-transitory form. Slander is an oral statement or some other form of transitory expression.

Bell v. *Intertan Canada Limited*, 2002 SKQB 446, per Matheson J. at para. 20.

Brule v. *Chmilar* (2000), 256 A.R. 168 (Q.B.) per Gallant J. at para. 59:

> A libel involves material exhibited in written or other concrete form, such as in film, pictures or statues. Slanders are defamations which have been spoken or embodied in some transitory form.

MacArthur v. *Meuser* (1997), 146 D.L.R. (4th) 125 (Ont. Gen. Div.) per Adams J. at para. 30 [aff'd (2000), 188 D.L.R. (4th) 191 (Ont. C.A.)] citing *Willows* v. *Williams* (1950), 2 W.W.R. (N.S.) 657 (Alta. S.C. (T.D.)) where Egbert J. stated at 658:

> In libel the defamatory statement is made in some visible and permanent form, and in slander it is made in spoken words, or in some other transitory form.

St. Elizabeth Home Society v. *Hamilton (City)*, [2001] O.J. No. 2597 per Harris J. at paras. 12–13 (S.C.J.).

Emonts v. *McKeever*, [1992] O.J. No. 1467 (Gen Div) per Goodearle J.

In *Varner* v. *Morton* (1919), 46 D.L.R. 597 (N.S.S.C.), Harris C.J. stated at 601:

> In the case of *Miller* v. *Donovan* (1896), 16 Misc. N.Y. 463, Geigerich J. gave
> a definition of libel which seems quite comprehensive enough to include the
> present case. It was, p. 454:
>
> > ... A malicious publication by writing, printing, picture, effigy, sign, or
> > otherwise than by mere speech ...

Republication of spoken words in a newspaper constitutes a libel.

> *Warner* v. *Earp* (1988) 38 O.R. (3d) 138 per Eberle J. at 140 (H.C.J.).

One court held that it would have treated telephone messages left by the
defendant on a tape machine as libels, not slanders, if the matter had been
so pleaded.

> *Fitzpatrick-Smith* v. *Jacobson*, [2000] O.T.C. 142 per Low J. at paras. 46, 47
> (S.C.J.).

Canadian case law has uniformly treated electronic communications on the
Internet as libel. See Chapter 6, "Notice of Intended Action and Limitation
Defences."

B. ORIGINS OF THE DISTINCTION

The source of the distinction between libel and slander is discussed in *Hill*
v. *Church of Scientology of Toronto*, [1995] 2 S.C.R. 1130, where Cory J. states
at paragraph 115:

> It was not until the late 17th century that the distinction between libel and
> slander was drawn by Chief Baron Hale in *King* v. *Lake* (1679), Hardres 470,
> 145 E.R. 552, where it was held that words spoken, without more, would not
> be actionable, with a few exceptions. Once they were reduced to writing,
> however, malice would be presumed and an action would lie.

The distinction has been described as an "historical accident arising out of
old and long forgotten jurisdictional conflicts."

> *R.* v. *Stevens*, [1993] M.J. No. 312, per Giesbrecht Prov. Ct. J. at para. 200 (Prov.
> Ct. (Crimn. Div.)) [aff'd, [1995] 4 W.W.R. 153 (Man. C.A.)], referring to *Thor-
> ley* v. *Lord Karry* (1812), 4 Taunt. 355 where Mansfield C.J. stated at 364:
>
> > ... the distinction has been made between written and spoken slander
> > as far back as Charles the Second's time, and the difference has been
> > recognized by the Courts for at least a century back.

An Ontario court has noted that slander originated in the common law courts and the libel action had its origins in the Court of Star Chamber "arising from the power and usefulness of print in seditious activity."

> *Fitzpatrick-Smith* v. *Jacobson*, [2000] O.T.C. 142, per Low J. at para. 46 (S.C.J.):
>
>> The difference in damages available for a libel action from those available for slander (other than those actionable *per se* at common law) could historically be rationalized in the relative power of the written word over the spoken. The written word has permanence and reproduceability. Its power to do harm is therefore far greater than that of the spoken word, which is evanescent. That distinction, however, breaks down when media are employed which give as much permanence and reproduceability to the spoken word as to the written…. In a communications environment where the spoken word can be captured, preserved and reproduced an indefinite number of times, distinctions between the sense used to receive a communication, that is the sense of sight as opposed to the sense of hearing, is less meaningful than the distinction between a communication which is permanent as opposed to one which is transitory. Cardozo J. in *Ostrowe* v. *Lee* (1931), 256 N.Y. 175 N.E. 505 at 506 remarked, "what gives the sting to the writing is its permanence of form. The spoken word dissolves, but the written one abides and 'perpetuates the scandal.'" The same conclusion was reached in *Farrell* v. *St. John's Publishing Co.* (1982), 35 Nfld. & P.E.I.R. 181 (reversed on other grounds). There, Mahoney J. held (at 201) that "any publication of defamatory matter in permanent form is a libel at common law." In England, the principle is recognized in the *Defamation Act*.

C. DAMAGES

Libel is actionable per se at common law and damages are presumed.

> *Campbell* v. *Cartmell* (1999), 104 O.T.C. 349 per Himel J. at para. 31 (S.C.J.).

At common law, slander is generally not actionable without proof of special damages.

> *Bell* v. *Intertan Canada Limited*, 2002 SKQB 446, per Matheson J. at para. 21.
>
> *St. Elizabeth Home Society* v. *Hamilton (City)*, [2001] O.J. No. 2597, per Harris J. at para. 13 (S.C.J.).

Mian v. Mahdi, [1995] O.J. No. 1722 per Dunnet J. at para. 53 (Gen. Div.).

Maher v. K Mart Canada Ltd. (1990), 84 Nfld. & P.E.I.R. 271, per Puddester J. at para. 38 (Nfld. S.C. (T.D.)).

Pootlas v. Pootlas (1999), 63 B.C.L.R. (3d) 305 per Burnyeat J. at 327–28 (S.C.).

If the slander is actionable per se, however, the plaintiff is not required to prove special damages. The case law has defined a number of categories of slander actionable per se:

i)   Imputations calculated to disparage the plaintiff in the way of his or her work, business, office, trade, calling, or profession;
ii)   Imputations that the plaintiff committed a criminal offence;
iii)   Imputations that the plaintiff suffers from a loathsome or contagious disease;
iv)   Imputations of unchastity to a woman.

Bell v. Intertan Canada Limited, 2002 SKQB 446, per Matheson J. at para. 22.

Minchin v. Samis (1913), 12 D.L.R. 137 (C.A.), cited with approval in *Mack v. North Hills News Ltd.* (1964), 44 D.L.R. (2d) 147 per Kirby J. at 155 (Alta. S.C. (T.D.)).

Lupee v. Hogan (1920), 47 N.B.R. 492 at 501.

Lawson v. Thompson (1968), 1 D.L.R. (3d) 270 per Seaton J. at 273 (B.C.S.C.), aff'd (1969), 5 D.L.R. (3d) 550 (B.C.C.A.).

Brown v. Cole, [1996] B.C.J. No. 2046 (S.C.) per Holmes J., varied (1998), 61 B.C.L.R. (3d) 1 (C.A.), leave to appeal to S.C.C. refused, [1998] S.C.C.A. No. 614.

1) Ontario

In Ontario, the *Libel and Slander Act*, R.S.O. 1990, c.L.12 provides in section 16:

In an action for slander for words calculated to disparage the plaintiff in any office, profession, calling, trade or business held or carried on by the plaintiff at the time of the publication thereof, it is not necessary to allege or prove special damage, whether or not the words are spoken of the plaintiff in the way of the plaintiff's office, profession, calling, trade or business, and the plaintiff may recover damages without averment or proof of special damage.

D. DISTINCTION ELIMINATED BY STATUTE

The distinction between libel and slander has been eliminated, however, in Alberta, where the *Defamation Act*, R.S.A. 2000, c. D-6, defines "defamation" in section 1(b) to mean "libel or slander," and provides in section 2:

2(1) An action lies for defamation.

(2) When defamation is proved, damage shall be presumed.

Brule v. *Chmilar* (2000), 256 A.R. 168 per Gallant J. at para. 59 (Q.B.), discussing ss.1(b) and 2 of the *Defamation Act.*

Equivalent provisions eliminating the distinction between libel and slander are found in the defamation statutes of Manitoba, New Brunswick, Newfoundland, the Northwest Territories, Nova Scotia, Prince Edward Island, and the Yukon Territory.

Manitoba, *Defamation Act*, R.S.M. 1987, c. D20, s.1 "defamation," s.2.

New Brunswick, *Defamation Act*, R.S.N.B. 1973, s.1 "defamation," s.2.

Newfoundland, *Defamation Act*, R.S.N. 1990, c. D-3, s.2(b), "defamation," s.3.

Northwest Territories, *Defamation Act*, R.S.N.W.T. 1988, c. D-1, s.1 "defamation," s.2.

Nova Scotia, *Defamation Act*, R.S.N.S. 1989, c. 122, s.2(b), "defamation," s.3.

Prince Edward Island, *Defamation Act*, R.S.P.E.I. 1988, c. D-5, s.1(b), "defamation," s.2.

Yukon, *Defamation Act*, R.S.Y.T. 1986, c. 41, s.1 "defamation," s.2.

E. SPECIAL PROVISIONS CONCERNING BROADCASTS

The defamation statutes in British Columbia and Ontario provide that defamatory words in a broadcast constitute libel.

British Columbia, *Libel and Slander Act*, R.S.B.C. 1996, c. 263, s.2.

Ontario, *Libel and Slander Act*, R.S.O. 1990, c. L.12, s.2.

CHAPTER TWO:

Defamation Actions to Avoid

Although the legal presumptions of falsity and damages might be regarded as favouring a defamation plaintiff, it is often unwise to undertake libel litigation unless there is no other way for the plaintiff to vindicate his or her reputation, the libel is demonstrably false, and there appear to be no viable defences to a libel lawsuit.

Literature, history, and current affairs reveal many examples of libel litigation folly. The United Kingdom offers particularly cogent examples of lawsuits that have backfired on plaintiffs.

Several categories to avoid are discussed below.

A. THE "HIGHWAYMAN"

In eighteenth-century England, during the reign of Queen Anne, a plaintiff brought an action for slander against someone who had said of him, "He is a highwayman." The defendant pleaded truth and succeeded on this defence at trial. Following the jury verdict, the plaintiff was arrested before he could leave the court, committed to Newgate jail, convicted at the next sessions of the criminal court, and hanged. In the words of Chief Justice Holt, "people ought to advise well before they bring such actions." The "highwayman" case is mentioned by the learned Chief Justice Holt in *Johnson* v. *Browning* (1705), 6 Modern Reports 217, 87 E.R. 969, and discussed in *Their Good Names*, by H. Montgomery Hyde, (London: Hamish Hamilton, 1970), at page 2.

B. OSCAR WILDE

Another ill-advised libel lawsuit was tried in 1895 when Oscar Wilde imprudently prosecuted the Marquis of Queensbury for criminal libel.

Wilde purported to be outraged by Lord Queensbury's statement that Wilde was "posing as a sodomite." The only witness who testified was Wilde who admitted on cross-examination that, among other things, he had "become intimate with a young lad" who sold newspapers from a kiosk on a public pier. Oscar Wilde withdrew his prosecution and consented to a directed verdict acquitting Lord Queensbury. Mr. Justice Collins told the jury that justification was proved, and that it was true in substance and in fact that Wilde had "posed" as a sodomite, and that the statement was published in such a manner as to be for the public benefit. After the acquittal of Lord Queensbury, Wilde was arrested later the same day, charged with gross indecency, convicted, and eventually sent to prison for two years. See *Their Good Names*, above, and H. Montgomery Hyde's *Famous Trials, Seventh Series: Oscar Wilde*, (Middlesex: Penguin, 1962).

C. JONATHAN AITKEN

Announcing his libel lawsuit against the *Guardian* newspaper and Granada Television from Conservative Central Office in London, on 10 April 1995, Cabinet Minister Jonathan Aitken said: "If it falls to me to start a fight to cut out the cancer of bent and twisted journalism in our country with the simple sword of truth and the trusty shield of British fair play, so be it. I am ready for the fight." Aitken sued over reports investigating his links with the Saudi Royal Family. On 20 June 1997 his libel action was dismissed after the defence proved beyond doubt that he had lied to the High Court during the eleven-day trial. The defendants produced documents showing Aitken had fabricated an alibi to contradict the media allegations.

On 7 December 1998 the former Cabinet minister was committed for trial at the Old Bailey to face charges of perjury and conspiracy to pervert the course of justice arising from the collapse of his libel action. Following his guilty plea to the perjury charge in June 1999, Aitken was sent for a brief period to Elmley Prison on the Isle of Sheppey, Kent, following which he was released on house arrest with electronic monitoring, with debts for costs estimated to exceed £1 million.

D. LORD ARCHER

In July 2001, Jeffrey Archer was found guilty and sentenced to four years in prison for perjury and attempting to obstruct justice. He was found to have lied in his successful libel case in 1987 against the *Daily Star* newspaper in which he had been awarded the equivalent of $1.1 million CDN in damages. The presiding judge at the perjury trial, Mr. Justice Humphrey Potts, said: "Sentencing you, Lord Archer, gives me no pleasure at all." But, he said "these charges represent as serious an offence of perjury as I have had experience of and have been able to find in the books."

Even Lord Archer's wife remarked on his talent for "inaccurate precis."

The *Daily Star* subsequently filed legal proceedings to recover the damages, costs, and interest.

Araminta Wordsworth, "He has got what he deserved" *National Post* (20 July 2001), A3.

E. McLIBEL

Corporate plaintiffs and impecunious lay litigant defendants may be a recipe for counterproductive libel litigation, even where the plaintiff is awarded damages and the ruling of the court expressly recognizes the importance of protecting commercial reputation.

Whatever the underlying merits of the libel complaint, the plaintiff may be depicted in continuing publicity releases by friends of the defendants on the Internet and in other media of communications as a corporate bully who ruthlessly deploys unlimited financial and legal resources to snuff out legitimate criticism. If the defendants are able to marshall support from like-minded individuals or groups, the Web community may mobilize to create web sites that republish and aggravate the original defamatory expression, often in jurisdictions far beyond the reach of the judicial remedies that might be obtained by the plaintiff.

Moreover, by filing a lawsuit in public court files, the plaintiff may give the news media an opportunity to repeat the defendants' original charges with virtually complete immunity, thereby ensuring that they reach a far wider audience than the defendants could have ever expected.

Consider the controversy over the libel action by McDonald's against two unemployed consumer activists, which became the longest libel trial in English history. Not only was this libel action covered by the press, it was the subject of considerable discussion on the Internet, including a web site developed by the opponents of McDonald's, which appeared to be designed entirely to ridicule McDonald's and advance further criticism. McDonald's, during a trial which spanned two years and occupied 313 hearing days, reaped enormous negative publicity and a modest verdict of £60,000. Following an appeal by the defendants, which consumed twenty-two hearing days, the damages were reduced to £40,000.

<www.McSpotlight.org/debate/mcds/> accessed 19 February 2004.

<www.McLibel.com> accessed 19 February 2004.

McDonalds Corp. v. Steel, [1995] 3 All E.R. 615, varied, [1999] E.W.J. No. 2173 (C.A.).

Guided by the experience of McDonald's, a prospective libel plaintiff may give very careful consideration to the implications of achieving victory in court, but losing the public relations battle in what one writer has described as "the second arena."

Bruce W. Sanford, *Libel and Privacy*, 2d ed., "The Second Arena: Winning the Battle, Losing the War" (Englewood Cliffs, NJ: Prentice Hall Law & Business, 1991) at pp. 694–96.

F. "QUICKSAND" CASES

This type of libel action takes many forms, but typically arises out of squabbles between commercial competitors, rival media outlets, or disputes within charities, ethnic communities, academic institutions, or trade unions.

The pleadings in these lawsuits are often lengthy compilations of charges, counter-charges, amended charges, and amended counter-charges, which grow as the parties recall or imagine grievances. They reflect the long-standing history of mutual rancor and loathing which has festered between the parties.

These lawsuits frequently bog down in a costly quagmire of discoveries and interlocutory proceedings about peripheral issues. If such lawsuits ever reach the first day of trial, the litigants may discover the court has little sympathy for either side.

The interchange of abusive articles had gone on for some years and each lady published her own side and each sought to provoke the other. The whole episode is quite devoid of significance, and, the parties having taken to their respective newspapers to redress their grievance, must be left to the consequences of their respective acts.

Falk v. Smith, [1941] O.R. 17 at 20 (C.A.) per Middleton J.A.

G. TACTICAL LIBEL LITIGATION

These libel claims are often added to wrongful dismissal lawsuits, takeover battles, and messy disputes between shareholders and boards of directors.

They have little to do with the central dispute between the parties. They are instituted as a means of threatening, pressuring, or diverting the attention of the opposing party. The object of the plaintiff is generally transparent to most outsiders, including juries sitting in judgment when the claim reaches trial.

CHAPTER THREE:

Should You Sue?

A. THE BASIC QUESTION

When you are attacked by the media, your competitors, or members of the public, should you sue for libel? Assuming that the elements of the plaintiff's case exist and that there are no defences, what other factors should be considered?

B. WHY SUE?

If the real answer is vengeance or money, a libel action is probably not warranted. Usually, a libel action should only be instituted if the primary objective is to vindicate the plaintiff's reputation.

C. OTHER OPTIONS

Is a libel action the only method of achieving the particular objective or can that be accomplished by an apology, retraction, or by writing rebuttal articles or letters to the editor? If a request for an apology has been spurned by a defamer, the plaintiff can proceed with a libel action with greater equanimity. In the preliminary letter to the defendant, a demand for payment of damages should normally be avoided; it may be viewed as "golddigging."

This does not mean that a libel action may not have important long-term financial implications. The destruction of a reputation may mean the end of a corporation or a career. But a libel action should be not be viewed as an accounting exercise in which you can precisely weigh the cost of the lawsuit against the amount of money that is likely to be recovered in damages.

D. WIDER CONSIDERATIONS

Thought must be given to various other factors before proceeding with a libel action.

- If the defamer is a disreputable publication or person, the defamatory statement might simply be treated with contempt, to avoid further republication.
- Determine the extent and location of the publication's circulation. In the age of global business and international communications, reputation may also be far-reaching.
- Determine the extent of the damage or at least the extent of the potential reaction in as concrete terms as possible. Record all calls about the libel made by the claimant's customers, suppliers, financial institutions, or others to assist in determining the impact of the libel. The plaintiff should be asked to keep notes of every time someone refers to the libel, and the impact it has on his or her life. These notes have several uses:
  - i) they ensure that events have been recorded while fresh in the plaintiff's mind;
  - ii) they will help in the decision whether to bring proceedings; and
  - iii) they will demonstrate in a concrete fashion the damage that the plaintiff has suffered.
- The solicitor should review in considerable detail the economic, emotional, and social impact that the plaintiff has claimed to suffer.
- The plaintiff should also be asked to reconstruct the circumstances of, and her detailed reaction to, her first exposure to the libel.
- Consider that libel actions are often heard by juries, which may compound the uncertainty inherent in the litigation process.
- Ensure that the plaintiff has no skeletons in her closet, as they can emerge at awkward moments.
- The institution of a libel action may give the libel greater circulation than it otherwise would have received had it been ignored.
- The plaintiff should carefully consider the optics of instituting or failing to institute libel proceedings. Will she be viewed as a bully? Will people consider her failure to institute libel proceedings as an admission of the truth of the libel? Will people consider that she had no other choice?

Mr. Justice Sharpe, in *The Last Day, The Last Hour: The Currie Libel Trial*, (Toronto: Carswell, 1988), graphically describes the conflicting pressures facing a plaintiff in a libel action. Sir Arthur Currie, the plaintiff, was the commander of the Canadian Corps in World War I. In 1927 the *Port Hope Evening Guide* published articles which accused Currie of needlessly wasting lives in the last weeks of the war.

At the time Currie was under constant pressure from his friends to drop the lawsuit. Just before he returned to the family home in Strathroy he seemed disposed to accept a full and complete retraction. He wrote to Montgomery "I sometimes think that the very fact that I entered an action against the paper achieved a good deal of what I might hope to gain by prosecuting the matter to an end" [at p. 66].

Currie continued to receive advice as to the wisdom of suing right up to the eve of trial. Tilley [his counsel], was not the only one to tell him that the suit might be a mistake. Many others agreed that the risks of a trial outweighed the possible benefits. Perhaps they were less certain than Currie seemed to be about the outcome. Certainly the trial would attract enormous publicity and provide Preston [the defendant] and others with a platform they could not otherwise hope for [at p. 71].

Walter Gow, a prominent Toronto lawyer, who had served as Deputy Minister of the Overseas Military Forces in London and who had been in Mons on Armistice Day, wrote to Currie offering his assistance but adding "I deplore the fact that you felt it necessary to put [Preston] in the limelight which I am afraid is exactly what he desires. It is a pity to dignify a man of Preston's type by bringing an action against him, but I can only assume as I do that you are driven to it and no other course seemed feasible" [at p. 71].

But not everyone urged caution on Currie. One old soldier wrote "It is about time that you got after some of the dirt throwers." Cy Peck, who at that time was a member of the Legislative Assembly of British Columbia wrote to encourage Currie. Peck had defended Currie's name years before in the House of Commons against the charges made by Sam Hughes. Acknowledging that many thought the libel action a mistake, Peck stated "Of course it isn't them that is being attacked. For myself I think there is a limit to this sort of thing — a time when one has got to give up taking everything lying down. This is a kind of supine philosophy now-a-days which deprecates making a fight about anything or against anything. 'Take no notice of it,' they say, that be a damned motto for a full-blooded man [at pp. 74–75]."

Currie did proceed to trial, won and was awarded $5,000 in damages by a jury.

E. REPUTATION MANAGEMENT ISSUES

Having reviewed these factors, the plaintiff's solicitor may want to consider several other matters.

1) Does the Complaint Go to the Core or the Margin of your Client's Reputation?

While everyone's reputation has certain common elements, there may be individual differences which warrant this analysis. For example, an attack on a lawyer's honesty and integrity go to the root of his reputation, while an allegation of manual clumsiness would not. Conversely, an allegation of clumsiness would go to the root of a surgeon's reputation, whereas allegations about his or her capacity to appreciate fine art might not be as important. Frequently libel lawsuits are instituted about allegations that only go to the margin of the plaintiff's reputation, and therefore are unlikely to be warranted.

Moreover, it may be unwise to institute libel proceedings over issues which involve a difference of opinion as opposed to factual inaccuracies. For example, a charity may be accused of not fulfilling its mandate effectively. This allegation involves a dispute about the merits of the particular charity's approach and whether or not such an approach is efficacious. On the other hand, an allegation that a charity is a "front" for a profit organization, or misuses its funds, or solicits funds improperly, goes to the root and the core of the charity's reputation and may result in the revocation of its license and the end of donations. This type of allegation should be pursued with vigour.

2) How Clear and Simple Is the Libel?

The libel should usually be capable of being summed up in a few words or a sentence. If it is any more complicated, the plaintiff may have difficulty persuading others that the impugned expression is actionable.

3) What Is the Reputational Status of the Plaintiff?

If a continuum were drawn with Mother Teresa at one end and Hitler at the other, where would the plaintiff be found? Like most human beings, probably somewhere in between. However, it is useful to pose this question since if the plaintiff is close to Mother Teresa, there may be no need for a libel action; on the other hand, if they are closer to Hitler, it may be to no avail.

4) Reputational Momentum

Is the plaintiff's reputation rising or falling at the time the statements were made? What impact, if any, does the statement have on that momentum? If a plaintiff is able to maintain upward reputational momentum in spite of an attack on his reputation, it may be unnecessary to bring a libel action. Conversely, if his reputation is already plummeting, he may have a hard time arguing that it was damaged by the particular statement. This analysis is usually only possible for well known individuals.

5) Reputational Pressure Points

While it may seem unconventional, the plaintiff's counsel should focus not solely on the words that were said, but also on their impact on the plaintiff. Naturally, in many cases it will be impossible to precisely calibrate the impact. However, the analysis should be made to determine whether it is worth proceeding. An example will illustrate this point.

Assume a well known neurosurgeon comes into your office and claims that she has been libeled in a newspaper by a former patient who made allegations about the quality of her work. The libel is probably very clear, and on its face, there might seem to be no option but to sue. However, one might consider the impact on the potential plaintiff's reputational pressure points. In the case of a neurosurgeon, they are:

i)   the College of Physicians and Surgeons;
ii)   the hospital at which the doctor works;
iii) the specialist peers of the doctor;
iv)   the consulting or referring physicians the doctor relies upon for referrals; and
v)   the doctor's patients.

It is often useful in this situation to enquire with the prospective plaintiff what has been the impact of the statement on these particular pressure points. This may assist the potential plaintiff in determining whether or not to proceed with a lawsuit.

6) When There Is No Choice But To Sue For Libel

Sometimes, regardless of the potential obstacles, the plaintiff has no option but to sue.

i)   The plaintiff's life is crumbling around him as a result of this libel.

ii)   The libel caused immediate and serious damage, and if not dealt with, will leave an indelible stain on the individual or the corporation's reputation.

iii)   The damage is (though not necessarily) tangible in the form of financial loss and loss of employment and professional opportunities.

iv)   The libel goes to the root of the plaintiff's reputation.

v)   The defendant spurns a request for an apology.

vi)   The libel is published in a very influential media outlet or by a very influential defendant, or to important customers or clients of the plaintiff, and failure to sue will probably be interpreted as an admission of its truth.

CHAPTER FOUR:

Response to a Lawsuit

A. FIRST STEPS

The first thing a defendant must bear in mind is that the entirety of the defendant's conduct, from the time the libel was published down to the close of trial, may be taken into account by the court.

Baxter v. *Canadian Broadcasting Corporation* (1979), 28 N.B.R. (2d) 114, 63 A.P.R. 114 at 162, para. 58 (Q.B. (T.D.)).

Hill v. *Church of Scientology of Toronto*, [1995] 2 S.C.R. 1130 at para. 182.

Leenen v. *Canadian Broadcasting Corporation* (2000), 48 O.R. (3d) 656 at paras. 143, 163, 205 (S.C.J.), aff'd (2001), 54 O.R. (3d) 612, leave to appeal to S.C.C. refused, [2001] S.C.C.A. No. 432.

A defendant who learns of a libel complaint or a libel lawsuit would be wise to involve his or her legal counsel immediately. The defendant should also give immediate notice to his or her insurer, who should be kept informed in a timely manner of steps being taken by the defendant to respond.

When served with legal process, a prudent defendant will note precisely the time, date, and manner that process was served. Because of the strict time limits under certain provincial defamation statutes for minimizing the defendant's liability for damages by publication of a correction, retraction, or apology, a defendant may not have much time to conduct an investigation to facilitate a decision on these matters. There is also often very little time to obtain detailed information about the alleged libel; the material originally relied upon and still available to support the expression at issue; and the evidence, including witnesses who can testify to the truth of the publication.

During the investigation process, careful consideration should be given to the need to protect the claim for solicitor-client privilege for any communications generated by the defendant or its employees or agents.

A prudent defendant will treat the libel complainant and his or her legal counsel in a polite and considerate manner. Unless his or her legal counsel advises otherwise, the defendant should promptly acknowledge the receipt of the libel complaint or the service of legal process as the case may be. Respectful and courteous conduct by the defendant and by defence counsel at the initial stages of a libel claim might well have a beneficial impact not only on subsequent settlement negotiations but also on the position of the defendant with respect to issues of malice and damages when they arise at trial.

Defendants may also investigate the desirability of a proactive media relations strategy. Astute public relations advisors, employed either in-house by the defendant or by external consulting firms, may assist in tailoring measures to project a positive (and truthful) image of the defendant to journalists, clients, employees, investors, and government without exacerbating the plaintiff's damages claim by repeating the libel or doing something else that smacks of malice. Given the increasing importance of the Internet as a medium of communications, moreover, increased attention should be given by business defendants to the risk to the defendants' reputation if the business is sued for defamation. The maxim "an ounce of prevention is worth a pound of cure" is perfectly applicable.

It is typically easier to persuade a libel plaintiff to settle on a reasonable basis before the lawsuit is filed or during the early stages of the lawsuit. A plaintiff who has already made a significant investment in legal fees or is poised to commence the trial might be reluctant to forego the option of a public court verdict which would clearly and unmistakably vindicate his or her reputation.

If the defendant knows that the defamatory expression is erroneous, the crucial question facing a defendant will often be whether or not to correct, retract, or apologize. Unless a defendant receives legal advice to the contrary, priority should be given to the subject of issuing an appropriate apology, retraction, or clarification. This course of action is typically advisable even if a settlement cannot be reached with a plaintiff. Publication of a correction, retraction, or apology may have a substantial mitigating effect on damages or in exceptional circumstances may prevent the plaintiff from recovering any sum whatsoever. If a retraction and apology is clear, unequivocal, and convincing, it may also go a long way to persuading the plaintiff to come to the settlement table and make a reasonable compromise.

B. INVESTIGATING LIABILITY AND DETERMINING RESPONSE

With the assistance of legal counsel, a defendant confronted with a libel complaint or libel lawsuit should meticulously take steps to investigate his or her potential liability and to determine the appropriate response to the plaintiff's complaint or lawsuit. Such steps may include the following:

1) Identify the expression which is of concern, and any related expression.

Libel complainants sometimes fail to state precisely what concerns them. Unless the defendant knows the precise expression which has offended the complainant, it may be difficult to assess the defendant's potential liability and to determine the appropriate response. It is therefore usually important to commit the complainant (or plaintiff) in writing to identifying the expression complained of. This will guide subsequent decisions by the defendant concerning the desirability of a retraction or apology, or the form and nature of any defence pleaded in the litigation.

Care should be taken, however, not to prejudice any libel notice defences which might otherwise be potentially available under the provincial defamation statutes by provoking the plaintiff into curing a defective libel notice within a limitation period.

2) What is the probable impact of the expression?

If the expression is likely to have a serious or lasting impact on the plaintiff's reputation, or his or her revenue or profitability and future prospects, the more likely it is that the plaintiff will carry the libel case forward in the courts. On the other hand, if the impact of the defamation is likely to be temporary or slight, the plaintiff might regard a correction, retraction, or apology, or even counterspeech, as an adequate remedy.

3) Is the expression of and concerning the plaintiff?

If the plaintiff is not expressly identified in the expression complained of, a defendant should carefully investigate the background facts and explore with the complainant why, and on what reasoning, it is argued that his or her reputation has been injured. If only a small circle of people would understand the defamatory expression to relate to the plaintiff, a defendant may expect a plaintiff to think twice before filing a libel lawsuit which might attract press publicity, thereby expanding the adverse impact of the libellous expression. A correction, retraction, or apology published to a select group of recipients might then be in order.

4)   Is the expression defamatory of the individual?

This requires a two question test. Both must be answered "yes" for the plaintiff to have a cause of action for libel:

   a)   First, is the expression capable, as a matter of law, of being defamatory?
   b)   If so, is the expression defamatory in fact?

Legal research can help provide the answer to question (a) and ought to be undertaken quickly, promptly, and thoroughly. This research will typically extend to synonyms of the words complained of. If a similar expression has never been the subject of libel litigation, a prospective plaintiff may be deterred by the novelty factor. Question (b) is a typically a matter of judgment for counsel, although in cases close to the line a test "jury" might be assembled by counsel and asked for their reaction.

5)   If the expression is defamatory, has it been published to a third party other than the individual and, if so, to whom, and in what form?

Publication to someone other than the plaintiff is an essential ingredient of the cause of action for defamation. Admittedly, publication to solely one individual will support a theoretical cause of action. However, prospective libel plaintiffs are unlikely to bring forward litigation unless there has been significant damage, which typically is not the case where publication is limited in scope.

6)   If the defamatory expression has been published to a third party, who is the author of the expression, where is the author located now, and where was the author located when the expression was published?

These questions are material to the potential strength of the defendant's position. Further, a defendant bears the burden of proving the truth of defamatory expression where a defence of justification is raised. The availability of the author to testify to the truth of his or her expression is a factor to be taken into account by a defendant engaged in determining whether or not to surrender and apologize or whether to mount a real defence. A prudent defendant should know whether the witness is outside the jurisdiction where litigation is likely to be brought and will investigate the likelihood of that individual voluntarily attending as a witness at trial.

7)   Who authorized, encouraged, or incited the defamatory expression? Where are they located now? Where were they located when they did so?

These questions are material to the potential liability of a defendant. The answers also bear on the availability of testimonial evidence that might support a substantive libel defence. If the individuals involved are in a foreign jurisdiction, their willingness to travel to the litigation forum should be ascertained.

8) Who was involved in transmitting or disseminating the defamatory expression from its author through to the third parties? Precisely what role did they play? What knowledge did they have of the defamatory nature of the expression? Where are they located now, and where were they located when they were involved in transmitting or disseminating the defamatory expression?

9) What defences may be open to those who have potential legal responsibility for the defamatory expression? Consider truth, fair comment, qualified privilege, absolute privilege, innocent dissemination, consent, and limitations.

10) Have the potential defendants been guilty of malice, which would defeat fair comment or qualified privilege?

11) If libel litigation is a real option, identify each country, province, or state in which the defamatory expression was published; identify each country, province, or state in which the individual's reputation may be affected; identify each country, province, or state in which each potential defendant is currently active; and identify the courts which are likely as a matter of private and international law to have jurisdiction to entertain a libel action arising from the expression.

12) Identify the countries, provinces, or states in which the potential defendants may have assets, and determine the likelihood that they would enforce a libel judgment from another country, province, or jurisdiction to hear the libel action. If the individual decides to sue, ensure that an appropriate decision is made with respect to defending the lawsuit and attorning to the jurisdiction where the litigation is brought.

The foregoing list is not, of course, intended to be exhaustive. The extent and degree of investigation by the defence will always depend on the circumstances of each case and a perceptive assessment of the real issues raised by the libel complaint.

CHAPTER FIVE:

Injunctions

A. SPECIAL RULES APPLY

At the outset of defamation litigation, a plaintiff may give high priority to preventing further publication of the defamatory expression. In this regard, a number of issues arise for consideration:

i) Will the court grant injunctive relief before trial?
ii) Should an application for an interlocutory injunction be made *ex parte* or with notice to the opposing party?
iii) Will the trial court grant a permanent injunction?

Although a large body of case law addresses these issues, the basic principles governing the exercise of the judicial discretion to enjoin defamatory expression are conveniently expressed in the following leading cases:

Bonnard v. Perryman, [1891] 2 Ch. 269 (C.A.).

Canada Metal Co. Ltd. et al. v. Canadian Broadcasting Corp. et al. (1974), 44 D.L.R. (3d) 329 (Ont. H.C.J.), aff'd (1975), 55 D.L.R. (3d) 42 (Ont. Div. Ct.).

Rapp v. McClelland & Stewart Ltd. (1981), 34 O.R. (2d) 452 (H.C.J.).

Canadian Human Rights Commission v. Canadian Liberty Net, [1998] 1 S.C.R. 626.

The fundamental rule is that a court will exercise its jurisdiction reluctantly. At the pretrial stage, a court is extremely cautious about enjoining free speech. Interlocutory injunctions will be granted only in exceptional circumstances, where the words complained of are unarguably defamatory and where a jury verdict dismissing the action would clearly be perverse.

The ordinary test for the grant of an interlocutory injunction does not apply to defamation litigation. That ordinary test has three stages:

i)   Is there a serious question to be tried?

ii)   Would the applicant suffer irreparable harm if the application were refused? and

iii)   Which of the parties would suffer greater harm from granting or refusal of the injunction pending a decision on the merits?

In defamation litigation, the third stage, the "balance of convenience," plays virtually no role in the determination by the court whether "prior restraint" of freedom of expression is warranted.

After a trial verdict for the plaintiff, a permanent injunction may issue if the court is satisfied that the defamation is injurious to the plaintiff and there is reason to apprehend further publication by the defendant.

> *Safeway Stores Ltd.* v. *Harris*, [1948] 4 D.L.R. 188 (Man. K.B.) varied, [1948] 4 D.L.R. 187 (Man. C.A.).

The jurisprudence is discussed in detail below.

B. INJUNCTIVE RELIEF BEFORE TRIAL

1) *Bonnard v. Perryman*

The leading case is *Bonnard* v. *Perryman*, [1891] 2 Ch 269 (C.A.), where the Court of Appeal set aside an interlocutory injunction granted by North J. of the High Court to restrain the publisher of a weekly newspaper from further "selling, circulating, or delivering or communicating to any person or persons, or permitting to be sold or circulated, or delivered or communicated, to any person or persons" copies of an article critical of the plaintiffs and their business activities.

In the Court of Appeal, Lord Coleridge C.J. (Lord Esher M.R., and Lindley, Bowen, and Lopes LL.J. concurring) confirmed the existence of a jurisdiction to grant an interlocutory injunction in a defamation case and reviewed the origins of that jurisdiction, at pages 263–64:

> Prior to the *Common Law Procedure Act*, 1854, neither Courts of Law nor Courts of Equity could issue injunctions in such a case as this: not Courts of Equity, because cases of libel could not come before them; not Courts of Law, because prior to 1854 they could not issue injunctions at all. But the 79th and 82nd sections of the *Common Law Procedure Act*, 1854, undoubtedly conferred on the Courts of Common Law the power, if a fit case should arise, to grant injunctions at any stage of a cause in all personal actions of contract or tort, with no limitation. This power was, by the *Judicature Act, 1873*, conferred

upon the Chancery Division of the High Court. Nevertheless, although the power had existed since 1854, there was no reported instance of its exercise by a Court of Common Law until *Saxby v. Easterbrook* [3 C.P.D. 339], which was decided in 1878. In that case the injunction was not applied for, nor, of course, granted, till after a verdict and judgment had ascertained the publication to be a libel. That case was acquiesced in; and about the same time the Chancery Division began, and it has since continued to assert the jurisdiction, which has been questioned before us, of granting injunctions on the interlocutory application of one of the parties to an action for libel … and we do not doubt upon the true construction of the statues and upon authority, that as a matter of jurisdiction, Mr. Justice North's order might lawfully be made.

Discussing the criteria which should guide the exercise of the jurisdiction, Lord Coleridge C.J. emphasized the special considerations which apply where the right to freedom of expression comes into conflict with the right to protection of individual reputation, stating at page 284:

But it is obvious that the subject-matter of an action for defamation is so special as to require exceptional caution in exercising the jurisdiction to interfere by injunction before the trial of an action to prevent an anticipated wrong. The right of free speech is one which it is for the public interest that individuals should possess, and, indeed, that they should exercise without impediment, so long as no wrongful act is done; and, unless an alleged libel is untrue, there is no wrong committed; but on the contrary, often a very wholesome act is performed in the publication and repetition of an alleged libel. Until it is clear that an alleged libel is untrue, it is not clear that any right at all has been infringed; and the importance of leaving free speech unfettered is a strong reason in cases of libel for dealing most cautiously and warily with the granting of interim injunctions. We entirely approve of and desire to adopt as our own, the language of Lord Esher, M.R, in *Coulson v. Coulson*, 3 Times L.R. 846 — "To justify the Court in granting an interim injunction it must come to a decision upon the question of libel or no libel, before the jury have decided whether it was a libel or not. Therefore the jurisdiction was of a delicate nature. It ought only to be exercised in the clearest cases, where any jury would say that the matter complained of was libellous, and where, if the jury did not so find, the Court would set aside the verdict as unreasonable." In the particular case before us, indeed, the libellous character of the publication is beyond dispute, but the effect of it upon the Defendant can be finally disposed of only by a jury, and we cannot feel sure that the defence of justification is one which, on the facts which may be before them, the jury may find to be wholly unfounded; nor can we tell what may be the damages recoverable.

A modern statement of the rationale for the rule in *Bonnard* v. *Perryman* is found in *Holley* v. *Smyth*, [1998] 1 All E.R. 853, where Auld L.J. stated at page 861 (C.A.):

> From the earliest days of the courts' consideration of their power to grant interlocutory relief in libel cases they seem to have been guided by two associated notions, one of high principle and one of principle and practicality. The first is the importance of protecting the individual's right to free speech. The second is an acknowledgment that the judges should not, save in the clearest case, usurp the jury's role by restraining at the interlocutory stage publication of a statement that the jury might later find to be no libel or true or otherwise defensible. Sometimes the second notion is expressed in the form that a judge should not interfere at the interlocutory stage unless the evidence before him so clearly establishes a culpable libel that he is confident that he would have to set aside a contrary verdict of the jury as perverse.

The rule in *Bonnard* v. *Perryman* has been applied in many other English decisions, including:

Khashoggi v. *IPC Magazines Ltd.*, [1986] 3 All E.R. 577 per Donaldson M.R. at 581 (C.A.):

> The point is that *Bonnard* v. *Perryman*, apart from its reference to freedom of speech, is based on the fact that the courts should not step in to defend a cause of action in defamation if they think that this is a case in which the plea of justification might, not would, succeed.

Herbage v. *Pressdram Ltd.*, [1984] 2 All E.R. 769 per Griffiths L.J. at 771 (C.A.):

> ... no injunction will be granted if the defendant raises the defence of justification. This is a rule so well-established that no elaborate citation of authority is necessary. It can be traced back to the leading case of *Bonnard* v. *Perryman*. ... These principles have evolved because of the value the court has placed on freedom of speech and I think also on the freedom of the press, when balancing it against the reputation of a single individual who, if wrong[ed], can be compensated in damages.

Fraser v. *Evans*, [1969] 1 All E.R. 8 per Lord Denning M.R. at 10 (C.A.):

> The court will not restrain the publication of an article, even though it is defamatory, when the defendant says that he intends to justify it or to make fair comment on a matter of public interest. This has been established for many years since *Bonnard* v. *Perryman* ([1891] 2 Ch

269, [1891-4] All ER Rep 965). The reason sometimes given is that the defences of justification and fair comment are for the jury, which is the constitutional tribunal, and not for the judge; but a better reason is the importance of the public interest that the truth should out. ... There is no wrong done if it [the alleged libel] is true, or if it is fair comment on a matter of public interest. The court will not prejudice the issue by granting an injunction in advance of publication.

The future development of English jurisprudence is likely to be affected by section 12(3) of the *Human Rights Act, 1998*, which provides:

No such relief [relief affecting the exercise of a Convention right to freedom of expression] is to be granted so as to restrain publication before trial unless the court is satisfied that the applicant is likely to establish that publication should not be allowed.

See *Cream Holdings Ltd.* v. *Banerjee,* [2003] E.W.C.A. Civ. 103, per Simon Brown L.J. at paras. 1–2 [application for injunctive relief to restrain further newspaper publication of material allegedly involving breaches of confidentiality].

2) Canadian Jurisprudence

The rule in *Bonnard* v. *Perryman* is also firmly established in Canadian jurisprudence.

a) *Canada Metal Co. Ltd. et al. v. Canadian Broadcasting Corp. et al.*

The subject of "prior restraint" of defamatory expression before trial was canvassed in detail in *Canada Metal Co. Ltd. et al.* v. *Canadian Broadcasting Corp. et al.*, where first the Ontario High Court, and later the Divisional Court, adopted the rule in *Bonnard* v. *Perryman* in the course of setting aside an *ex parte* injunction which prohibited the defendant from airing a television program about the plaintiffs.

The course of proceedings in *Canada Metal Co. Ltd. et al.* v. *Canadian Broadcasting Corp.et al* was as follows:

The High Court Decision

On 15 February 1974, Holland J. of the High Court granted an application by the defendants to dissolve the *ex parte* injunction. [*Canada Metal Co. Ltd. et al.* v. *Canadian Broadcasting Corp. et al.* (1974), 44 D.L.R. (3d) 329 (Ont. H.C.J.)] The learned judge began his analysis of the law by stating at page 344:

In deciding a matter such as this the Court should always bear in mind the principle of freedom of the press. This principle, fortunately, has always existed in Canada, and this existence is specifically recognized by s. 1 of the *Canadian Bill of Rights*. One must bear in mind that this particular programme, a so-called public affairs programme, dealt generally with an area of considerable public concern. This freedom of the press is, of course, a freedom governed by law and is not a freedom to make untrue defamatory statements: see *Reference re Alberta Statutes*, [1938] S.C.R. 100 at p. 133, [1938] 2 D.L.R. 81 at p. 107 [affirmed [1938] 4 D.L.R. 433, [1939] A.C. 117, [1938] 3 W.W.R. 337].

Holland J. then distilled the principles established in *Bonnard* v. *Perryman* and related authorities as follows [at page 344]:

The Court in a case of this type will only interfere with a publication of an alleged libel in the very clearest of cases. The Court must be satisfied that the words are beyond doubt defamatory, are clearly untrue so that no defence of justification would succeed and, where such defence may apply, are not fair comment on true or admitted facts.

Interim Injunction Pending Appeal

Pending disposition of the plaintiffs' application to the Divisional Court for leave to appeal, Cromarty J. of the High Court granted a further interim injunction.

Canada Metal Co. Ltd. et al. v. *Canadian Broadcasting Corp. et al.* (1975), 44 D.L.R. (3d) 329, Editorial Note.

Leave to Appeal

On 27 March 1974, O'Leary J. of the High Court granted leave to appeal [(1975), 44 D.L.R. (3d) 481] and continued the interim injunction granted by Cromarty J., stating at page 483:

As was stated by Mr. Justice Holland, the Court in a case of this kind will only interfere with the publication of an alleged libel in the clearest of cases. Before doing so the Court must be satisfied that any jury would say the matter complained of was libellous and that if the jury did not so find the Court would set aside the verdict as unreasonable. The Court must also be satisfied that in all probability the alleged libel was untrue.

O'Leary J. described the issues on the pending appeal in the following terms at pages 485–86:

All parties seem to be in agreement that the matters in issue in this action, freedom of speech on the one hand, and the right to be protected against libel on the other, are of substantial importance. I agree that the problem is an important one and accordingly, leave to appeal from the orders of Mr. Justice Holland is granted.

As mentioned earlier, the plaintiffs allege there are 14 libellous accusations contained in the said documentary. Certainly, there may well be substance to many if not all the complaints raised by the plaintiffs. In order that the purpose of the appeal to the Divisional Court will not be frustrated by further publication before the appeal is heard of the material complained of, an injunction is hereby granted until the Divisional Court has rendered its decision, restraining the defendants and their officers, servants, employees and agents and any other person with knowledge of this order from broadcasting or otherwise disseminating and from advertising or otherwise publicizing any part or portion of the script of the programme "Dying of Lead" that refers directly or by implication to the plaintiffs or either of them. ...

Appeal Dismissed

On 20 May 1975, the Divisional Court dismissed the appeal [(1975) 55 D.L.R. (3d) 42 (Ont. Div. Ct.)]. Stark J., speaking also for Zuber and Reid JJ., stated at pages 42–43:

This Court is unanimously of the opinion that the appeal from the order of Holland J., must be dismissed for the reasons given by him. We would merely like to add this.

The granting of injunctions to restrain publication of alleged libels is an exceptional remedy granted only in the rarest and clearest of cases. That reluctance to restrict in advance publication of words spoken or written is founded, of course, on the necessity under our democratic system to protect free speech and unimpeded expression of opinion. The exceptions to this rule are extremely rare.

For at least one hundred years and certainly since the leading cases of *William Coulson & Sons* v. *James Coulson & Co.* (1887), 3 T.L.R. 846, and *Collard* v. *Marshall*, [1892] 1 Ch. 571, and perhaps above all, in the leading case of *Bonnard* v. *Perryman*, [1891] 2 Ch. 269, it has been universally and consistently held by British and Canadian Courts that such an interim injunction will never be granted where the defendant expresses his intention to justify unless the words in question are so clearly defamatory and so obviously impossible to justify that the verdict of a jury accepting a plea of justification as a defence would of necessity have to be set aside as a perverse finding on appeal. That is not this case. Some of the words in the broadcast here are admittedly capable of defamatory meanings, but they are not all so clearly defamatory that a jury could not decline to accept all or some of the many allegations made by the plaintiff; and certainly the issue of justification in this case is a triable and disputable issue, not one which can be decided at this stage and clearly one which must go to the jury.

b) Subsequent Canadian Decisions

The principles expressed in *Bonnard* v. *Perryman* and *Canada Metal Co. Ltd. et al.* v. *Canadian Broadcasting Corp. et al.* have been applied or mentioned with approval in many decisions, including:

Canadian Human Rights Commission v. *Canadian Liberty Net*, [1998] 1 S.C.R. 626, per Bastarache J. at para. 46.

R.T. Investment Counsel Inc. v. *Werry* (1999), 46 B.L.R. (2d) 66 per Holmes at 70, para. 16 (B.C.S.C.).

Dr. A. v. *Mr. C.* (1994), 113 D.L.R. (4th) 726 per Esson C.J.S.C. at 732 (B.C.S.C.).

Cameron & Johnstone Ltd. v. *810202 Ontario Inc. (c.o.b. Princess Bingo)*, [1994] O.J. No. 1809 per Fedak J. at paras. 24, 34 (Gen. Div.) [injunction refused].

Lasik Vision Canada Inc. v. *TLC Vancouver Optometric Group Inc.*, [1999] B.C.J. No. 2834 per Macaulay J. at paras. 21–23 (S.C.), [the defences included truth, fair comment, and qualified privilege, and the expression at issue was not admittedly defamatory].

Rust Check Canada Inc. v. *Young* (1988), 47 C.C.L.T. 279 (Ont. H.C.J.) [slander of goods] where Watt J. stated *inter alia* at 309:

> It would also appear that the prior restraint imposed by an interlocutory injunction will not be imposed where it is at all doubtful whether that of which complaint is made is libellous, as there is a considerable public interest in the publication of the truth. For example, see *Liverpool Household* v. *Smith* (1887), 37 Ch. Div. 170 (C.A.); *Fraser* v. *Evans*, [1969] 1 Q.B. 349, 360–1; and, *Church of Scientology of California* v. *Reader's Digest Services*, [1981] N.S.W.L.R. 344.

Wescan Glass Industries (Can.) Inc. v. *National Glass Ltd.*, [1985] B.C.J. No. 1087 (S.C.), per Ruttan J. [injunction against business competitor refused].

Meier v. *Canadian Broadcasting Corporation* (1981), 19 C.P.C. 315 per McKenzie J. at 316 (B.C.S.C.).

Rapp v. *McClelland & Stewart Ltd.* (1981), 34 O.R. (2d) 452 per Griffiths J. at 455 (H.C.J.).

c) *Rapp* v. *McClelland & Stewart Ltd.*

In *Rapp* v. *McClelland & Stewart Ltd.* (1981), 34 O.R. (2d) 452 (H.C.J.), the plaintiffs sought an interlocutory injunction until trial restraining the defendants from printing, publishing, or distributing a nonfiction book which contained certain references to the plaintiff.

After reviewing *Canada Metal Co Ltd.*, above, including the lengthy passage in that judgment from *Bonnard* v. *Perryman*, Griffiths J. of the Ontario High Court of Justice defined the test for granting an interlocutory injunction in the following terms at pages 455–56:

> … the test for determining whether an interim injunction should issue involves not only a consideration of the likelihood of the defendant proving justification at trial, but also whether a jury will inevitably come to the conclusion that the words, however false, are also defamatory of the plaintiff.
>
> The guiding principle then is, that the injunction should only issue where the words complained of are so manifestly defamatory that any jury verdict to the contrary would be considered perverse by the Court of Appeal. To put it another way where it is impossible to say that a reasonable jury must inevitably find the words defamatory the injunction should not issue.
>
> … *American Cyanamid* … has not affected the well-established principle in cases of libel that an interim injunction should not be granted unless the jury would inevitably come to the conclusion that the words were defamatory.

Rapp v. *McClelland & Stewart Ltd.* has been cited with approval in a number of decisions involving applications for interlocutory injunctions to restrain defamatory expression, including:

> *Coltsfoot Publishing Ltd.* v. *Harris* (1999), 43 C.P.C. (4th) 282 per Saunders J. at para. 26 (N.S.S.C.).

> *Daishowa Inc.* v. *Friends of the Lubicon* (1995), 30 C.R.R. (2d) 26 (Ont. Gen. Div.), per Kitely J. at para. 213

> *Maritime Telegraph & Telephone Co.* v. *O'Hara*, [1989] N.S.J. No. 281 per Kelly J. (S.C.).

d) *Canadian Human Rights Commission* v. *Canadian Liberty Net*

The decision in *Canadian Human Rights Commission* v. *Canadian Liberty Net*, [1998] 1 S.C.R. 626 addressed, *inter alia*, the proper exercise of the interlocutory injunctive power in the Federal Court of Canada in relation to the hate speech provision in section 13(1) of the *Canadian Human Rights Act*, R.S.C. 1985, c. H-6, which reads:

It is a discriminatory practice for a person or a group of persons acting in concert to communicate telephonically or to cause to be so communicated, repeatedly, in whole or in part by means of the facilities of a telecommunication undertaking within the legislative authority of Parliament, any matter that is likely to expose a person or persons to hatred or contempt by reason of the fact that that person or those persons are identifiable on the basis of a prohibited ground of discrimination.

A key issue before the Supreme Court of Canada in *Canadian Human Rights Commission* v. *Canadian Liberty Net* was the applicability of the standard three-part test for the issuance of interlocutory injunctions prescribed in *American Cyanamid Co.* v. *Ethicon Inc.*, [1975] A.C. 396 (F.C.T.D.) and adopted in *RJR-MacDonald Inc.* v. *Canada (Attorney General)*, [1994] 1 S.C.R. 311. That standard test, as explained by Sopinka and Cory JJ. in *RJR-MacDonald* at para. 43, is as follows:

> First, a preliminary assessment must be made of the merits of the case to ensure that there is a serious question to be tried. Secondly, it must be determined whether the applicant would suffer irreparable harm if the application were refused. Finally, an assessment must be made as to which of the parties would suffer greater harm from the granting or refusal of the remedy pending a decision on the merits.

Bastarache J. (L'Heureux-Dubé and Gonthier concurring), concluded that the *Cynamid/RJR-MacDonald* test should not be applied to restrict free speech and referred with approval to the jurisprudence relating to interlocutory injunctions in defamation actions, stating at pages 665–68:

> ¶47 In my view, the *Cyanamid* test, even with these slight modifications, is inappropriate to the circumstances presented here. The main reason for this is that *Cyanamid*, as well as the two other cases mentioned above, involved the commercial context in which the criteria of "balance of convenience" and "irreparable harm" had some measurable meaning and which varied from case to case. Moreover, where expression is unmixed with some other commercial purpose or activity, it is virtually impossible to use the second and third criteria without grievously undermining the right to freedom of expression contained in s. 2(b) of the *Charter*. The reason for this is that the speaker usually has no tangible or measurable interest other than the expression itself, whereas the party seeking the injunction will almost always have such an interest. This test developed in the commercial context stacks the cards against the non-commercial speaker where there is no tangible, immediate utility arising from the expression other than the freedom of expression itself.

¶48 The inappropriateness of the *Cyanamid* test is confirmed by the jurisprudence relating to injunctions against allegedly defamatory statements, in both England and Canada. In both countries, the *Cyanamid* test has been rejected for injunctions against dissemination of defamatory statements. Although defamation does not possess precisely the same characteristics as discriminatory hate speech, it is a much closer analogy than restraining commercial activity, even where that commercial activity includes a speech element. Defamation typically involves damage to only one person's reputation and not an entire group. On the other hand, given the widespread circulation of many defamatory statements in the press and the crystallized damage which a defamatory statement may have, compared with the slow, insidious effect of a relatively isolated bigoted commentary, the two are not necessarily substantially different in terms of the "urgency" requirement. Certainly from the point of view of the rights of the speaker, bigotry and defamation cases both represent potentially low- or no-value speech and are in that sense, extremely similar. It is therefore helpful to look at the approach to injunctions in cases of defamatory speech to determine how "urgency" should be defined in the context of s. 13(1) of the *Human Rights Act*.

Bastarache J. referred to a leading Canadian textbook on the subject of injunctions:

> ¶49 In his treatise *Injunctions and Specific Performance* (2nd ed. 1992, (loose-leaf)), Robert Sharpe says the following, at paras. 5.40-5.70 (pp. 5.2–5.4):

> > There is a significant public interest in the free and uncensored circulation of information and the important principle of freedom of the press to be safeguarded … .

> > The well-established rule is that an interlocutory injunction will not be granted where the defendant indicates an intention to justify [i.e. prove the truth of] the statements complained of, unless the plaintiff is able to satisfy the court at the interlocutory stage that the words are both clearly defamatory and impossible to justify.

> > … it seems clear that the rule is unaffected by the *American Cyanamid* case and that the balance of convenience is not a factor.

Bastarache J. then proceeded to address certain more recent English authorities which have re-affirmed the rule in *Bonnard* v. *Perryman*, stating at pages 666–67:

> One of the leading English authorities has a close affinity to the *Human Rights Act* in that it was a statutory prohibition on certain expression. *Herbage* v. *Pressdram Ltd.*, [1984] 1 W.L.R. 1160, involved the application of the *Reha-*

bilitation of Offenders Act 1974, which had been enacted by Parliament to prevent indefinite reference to an individual's criminal history, after the individual had served his or her sentence. Based on that specific legislative intention, contended the applicant, an injunction should be issued. Griffiths L.J. (on behalf of himself and Kerr L.J. on a two-judge panel) rejected that approach (at p. 1163):

> If the court were to accept this argument, the practical effect would I believe be that in very many cases the plaintiff would obtain an injunction, for on the *American Cyanamid* principles he would often show a serious issue to be tried, that damages would not be realistic compensation, and that the balance of convenience favoured restraining repetition of the alleged libel until trial of the action. It would thus be a very considerable incursion into the present rule which is based on freedom of speech.

Bastarache J. explicitly endorsed the decision of the Ontario High Court in *Rapp v. McClelland*, above. He also noted that *Rapp v. McClelland* has been imported into the law of Quebec making the rule in *Bonnard v. Perryman* truly national in its application, stating at pages 667–68:

> This passage [Author's Notes from *Rapp v. McClelland* — above p. 43] has recently been cited with approval in the Quebec Court of Appeal in *Champagne v. Collège d'enseignement général et professionnel (CEGEP) de Jonquière*, [1997] R.J.Q. 2395. Rothman J.A., on this point speaking on behalf of Delisle and Robert JJ.A., went on to comment on the constitutional dimension of these common law approaches to the use of the injunctive power (at pp. 2402–3):
>
>> With the coming into force of the Canadian Charter and the Quebec Charter, these safeguards protecting freedom of expression and freedom of the press have become even more compelling.
>>
>> The common law authorities in Canada and the United Kingdom have suggested the guiding principle that interlocutory injunctions should only be granted to restrain in advance written or spoken words in the rarest and clearest of cases — where the words are so manifestly defamatory and impossible to justify that an action in defamation would almost certainly succeed. Given the value we place on freedom of expression, particularly in matters of public interest, that guiding principle has much to recommend it.

These cases indicate quite clearly that the *Cyanamid* test is not applicable in cases of pure speech and, therefore, the appellants are misguided in presuming that this test does apply. As Griffiths L.J. points out in *Herbage* v. *Pressdram*, *supra*, such a test would seldom, if ever, protect controversial speech. ...

Canadian Liberty Net has been cited in a number of recent decisions relating to interlocutory injunction applications in defamation cases.

> *Lasik Vision Canada Inc.* v. *TLC Vancouver Optometric Group Inc.*, [1999] B.C.J. No. 2834 per Macaulay J. at para. 3 (S.C.).

> *R.T. Investment Counsel Inc.* v. *Werry* (1999), 46 B.L.R. (2d) 66 per Holmes J. at 70, at para. 16 (B.C.S.C.).

> *Coltsfoot Publishing Ltd.* v. *Harris* (1999), 43 C.P.C. (4th) 282 per Saunders J. at 288–89, at para. 26 (N.S.S.C.).

e) Other Canadian Decisions Adopting the *Bonnard* v. *Perryman* Rule

Other Canadian decisions, although they do not refer expressly to *Bonnard* v. *Perryman*, *Canada Metal*, or *Rapp* v. *McClelland*, also support the rule in *Bonnard* v. *Perryman*. They include:

> *Doe* v. *Canadian Broadcasting Corporation* (1994), 86 B.C.L.R (2d) 202 (S.C.).

> *Simoni* v. *Blue Cross of Atlantic Canada* (1999), 184 Nfld. & P.E.I.R. 136 (Nfld. S.C.T.D.).

> *Sopréma Inc.* v. *New Brunswick Roofing Contractors Ass'n* (1996), 181 N.B.R. (2d) 223 (Q.B.(T.D.)).

In one case, the court assessed the merits of an application for an interlocutory injunction to restrain a publication by first applying the *Cyanamid* test but resorted to the *Canada Metal* test as a secondary check. It was held that although the plaintiff had framed its action as one for negligent misstatement, the principles in *Canada Metal* applied to the application for an interim injunction.

> *Bristol-Myers Squibb Canada Inc.* v. *Canadian Coordinating Office for Health Technology Assessment* (1998), 18 C.P.C. (4th) 178 per Chadwick J. at paras. 37–39 (Ont. Gen. Div.).

Courts occasionally apply the *American Cyanamid* test, appearing to overlook the special considerations that apply to interim restraints on defamatory expression.

> *Robertson* v. *Michaud*, [1995] N.B.J. No. 494 per Russell J. at para. 11 (Q.B. (T.D.)) [injunction refused on basis of *Cyanamid* test].

3) Interlocutory Injunctions Refused

The courts have refused to grant an interlocutory injunction for defamation:

i)   where there was an issue about the meaning of the words complained of.

   Rapp v. McClelland & Stewart Limited (1981), 34 O.R. (2d) 452 per Griffiths
   J. at 456 (H.C.J.) .

ii)   where the plaintiff did not know the words that the defendant intend-
      ed to publish.

   Liverpool Household Stores Assoc. v. Smith, [1887] 37 Ch. D. 170 per Cotton L.J. at 183 (C.A.).

   British Data Mgt. PLC v. Boxes Commercial Removals PLC, [1996] E.M.L.R.
   340 (C.A.)

iii) where the defendant swore that he would be able to justify the libel
      but the court was not satisfied that he would be able to do so.

   Fraser v. Evans, [1969] 1 All E.R. 8 at 10.

   Khashoggi v. IPC Magazines Ltd., [1986] 3 All E.R. 577 at 581.

   Herbage v. Pressdram Ltd., [1984] 2 All E.R. 769 at 771 (C.A.).

iv)   where the words complained of were published on a *prima facie* priv-
      ileged occasion.

   Quartz Hill Consol. Goldmining Co. v. Beall (1882), 20 Ch D. 501 (C.A.).

   Harakas v. Baltic Mercantile & Shipping Exchange Ltd., [1982] 1 W.L.R. 958.

v)   where damages would be an adequate remedy and there was no
      irreparable harm.

   Rapp v. McClelland & Stewart, above, at 456.

   Portal Gate Developments Inc. v. Ontario New Home Warranty Program,
   [2003] O.J. No. 3063 per Epstein J. at paras. 29, 35 (S.C.J.) [discussion of
   evidence necessary to establish irreparable harm; injunction against website rejected.]

4) Interlocutory Injunctions Granted

The British Columbia Court of Appeal reversed a lower court ruling and
granted an interim injunction against a broadcaster restraining further publication of statements about the plaintiff religious organization such as "rip-

off," "fraudulent," and "criminal." It was held that such an injunction met the test in *Bonnard* v. *Perryman*, where:

i) admittedly grossly defamatory allegations had been made in a series of radio broadcasts;

ii) the plaintiff tendered affidavits stating that those allegations were false;

iii) the defendant did not challenge the evidence of the plaintiff, either by cross-examination or by counter-affidavit; and

iv) the defendants, or some of them, had declared their intention to repeat or continue similar broadcasts.

Church of Scientology of British Columbia v. *Radio NW Ltd.*, [1974] 4 W.W.R. 173 per Branca J.A. at 177–78 (B.C.C.A.):

> In *Bonnard* there was affidavit material on behalf of the plaintiff-applicant that the allegations were false. The defendant filed an affidavit stating that the allegations were "true in substance and in fact" and that he would be "able to prove the same in the trial of the action by witnesses and cross-examination of the plaintiff and by other evidence." ...
>
> The difference between the procedure in the *Bonnard* case and in the instant case was that the affidavit of the defendant in the *Bonnard* case stated that all allegations were true and would be proven true.... [In the instant case] ... there was no material before the Court to suggest justification, privilege, qualified or otherwise, fair comment or other matters which might be a defence to an action for libel....
>
> ... The statements complained of are admittedly defamatory; it is sworn and not contradicted that additional programs will result in causing immediate, serious and irreparable injury to the appellant church; there is the threat of repetition.

And at page 179:

> In my judgment when once the appellant has proven the untruth of the allegations and thus proved an unlawful act and has in addition shown a probability of repetition of the untruthful allegations, then the question as to whether or not money can adequately compensate him and/or whether the balance of convenience weighs in favour of the respondents is of relatively little importance and an injunction must issue.

An injunction was granted restraining "watching and besetting" and picketing with signs bearing messages that were found to be "nothing more than a bitter attack by way of religious connotations on the church pastor which in turn [reflected] on the church and the majority of [its] membership." The signs conveyed no information, and the affidavit evidence did not show any reasonable justification. "They undoubtedly seriously interfere with the right of the majority of members to the enjoyment of attending church and worshipping there. At present and without more, they are a nuisance to those using the church."

Re Christ Church of China v. Lee (1983), 15 E.T.R. 272 (B.C.S.C.).

5) *Ex Parte* Applications

A plaintiff should not apply *ex parte* unless there is "genuine" or "extraordinary" urgency and it would be impractical to give notice to the opposing party.

Doe v. Canadian Broadcasting Corporation (1994), 86 B.C.L.R. (2d) 202, per Boyd J. at 207–8 (S.C.).

Maritime Telegraph and Telephone Co. v. O'Hara, [1989] N.S.J. No. 281 (S.C.), per Kelly J.

Where the plaintiff and the defendant are communicating through legal counsel, any application for an interim injunction should be brought with full and proper notice to the defendant.

Doe v. Canadian Broadcasting Corporation, above, at 207–8.

Where an *ex parte* injunction is granted, it should be only for such period of time as will enable notice to be served on those to be enjoined.

Maritime Telegraph & Telephone Co. v. O'Hara, [1989] N.S.J. No. 281 (S.C.), per Kelly J., citing *Griffin Steel Foundries Ltd. v. Canadian Association of Industrial, Mechanical and Allied Workers* (1977), 80 D.L.R. (3d) 634, per O'Sullivian J.A. at 639–40 (Man. C.A.).

If there was either no foundation or an insufficient foundation for characterizing the application as urgent at the time it was brought, and the non-urgent nature was not brought to the attention of the court when the *ex parte* order was sought, an interim *ex parte* injunction will be set aside.

Doe v. Canadian Broadcasting Corporation, above, at 208.

Normally, if the *ex parte* injunction is dissolved, it would still be possible for the plaintiff to apply for a new interim injunction on the basis of proper material.

Maritime Telegraph & Telephone Co. v. O'Hara, above.

A plaintiff who obtained an *ex parte* injunction where urgency cannot be demonstrated also risks being ordered to pay solicitor-client costs for the injunction to the person who was enjoined.

Leung v. Leung (1993), 77 B.C.L.R. (2d) 314 per Esson C.J.S.C. at 317 (S.C.).

It has been held that ordinarily, any *ex parte* injunction enjoining non-parties to a lawsuit would contemplate an undertaking by the plaintiff to the court that a lawsuit would be commenced immediately against those persons enjoined.

Coltsfoot Publishing Ltd. v. Harris (1999), 43 C.P.C. (4th) 282 per Saunders J. at para. 14 (N.S.S.C.).

6) Irrelevant Factors

a) Nature of the Defendant

The rule in *Bonnard v. Perryman* is not confined to publications by the news media.

Holley v. Smyth, [1998] 1 All E.R. 853 at 867

b) Motive of the Defendant

The rule in *Bonnard v. Perryman* applies regardless of the motive of the defendant, the threatened manner of publication, and the potential damage to the plaintiff.

Holley v. Smyth, above, Auld L.J. explained at 867:

> The media's motivation for publication is rarely restricted to the altruistic one of informing the public of matters in which it, the public, has an interest. There is usually the additional driving force of commercial self-interest, sometimes accompanied by obsessive vindictiveness and/or irresponsibility. Yet the authorities show that the presence of one or more of those factors does not deprive the media of the protection of the rule. Why then should those outside the media be subject to more stringent control because they may have a motive other than the pure one of disseminating truth? …
>
> There may be exceptions to the general rule, but neither the would-be libeler's motive nor the manner in which he threatens publication nor the potential damage to the plaintiff is normally a basis for making an exception.
>
> Motive is logically irrelevant to the defendant's entitlement to exercise his right of freedom of speech if what he has to say is or may be

true. In particular, English jurisprudence has rejected as candidates for exception motives of vindictiveness or pecuniary gain. The fact that Mr. Smyth has expressly made the implementation of his threat conditional on the plaintiffs' failure to pay the money he claims does not distinguish it from the authorities where motivation other than a simple desire to speak freely has been held to be irrelevant. It is a fallacy to attempt to distinguish it on the basis that Mr. Smyth's aim is not to exercise his right of freedom of speech, but to extract money from another as the price of silence. The subject matter of the application for interlocutory relief is his threat to speak freely, albeit that it is contingent on the plaintiffs not meeting his possibly justified demand. It is that threat, not the equally contingent offer to remain silent, that the plaintiffs seek to restrain. The fact that he may have expressly offered to remain silent if the plaintiffs met his demand does not, in my view, distinguish this case from the clearly implied threat to like effect in the *Crest Homes* case and the other two recent authorities to which I have referred. There is nothing unusual in an aggrieved person seeking what he considers to be his due by threatening to resort to the media if his claim is not met while hoping that it will not be necessary.

Crest Homes Ltd. v. *Ascott*, [1980] F.S.R. 369, per Lord Denning M.R. at 398 (C.A.).

Bestobell Paints Ltd. v. *Bigg*, [1975] F.S.R. 369 per Oliver J. at 435 (C.A.).

Al Fayed v. *The Observer Ltd.*, The Times, 14 July 1986, per Mann J.

7) Miscellaneous Relevant Factors

a) Timing

An interim injunction may be refused where the plaintiff has been dilatory in bringing the application or has, by other conduct, become disentitled to such relief.

Rust Check Canada Inc. v. *Young* (1988), 47 C.C.L.T. 279, per Watt J. at 310 (Ont. H.C.J.), citing *A. G.* v. *Sheffield Gas* (1853), 3 De G. M. & G. 304; *Greer* v. *Bristol Tanning* (1885), 2 R.P.C. 268; and *Dunlop* v. *Dunlop Rubber*, [1920] I.R. 280 at 292 (C.A.).

b) Adequacy of Damages

It has also been held that except in a case of manifest libel, the interim injunction should not issue where the wrong suffered by the plaintiff may be adequately compensated in damages.

Rapp v. *McClelland & Stewart Limited* (1981), 34 O.R. (2d) 452, per Griffiths
J. at 455 (H.C.J.), citing *Monson* v. *Tussauds Ltd.*, [1894] 1 Q.B. 671.

c) Imminent Publication

Coltsfoot Publishing Ltd. v. *Harris* (1999), 43 C.P.C. (4th) 282, per Saunders J.
at paras. 31–33 (N.S.S.C.):

> ¶31 The law is clear. Injunctions in the context of defamation will only
> lie in the clearest of cases where information that is obviously false and
> inevitably defamatory is about to be published.

Similarly, where commercially-published books or other publications have
already been put in circulation, an offer by the defendant to use its "best
efforts" to minimize the future publication of the alleged libel will likely
weigh against granting an interim injunction.

Rapp v. *McClelland & Stewart Limited* (1981), 34 O.R. (2d) 452 per Griffiths
J. at 456 (H.C.J.):

> Counsel for the defendants advises that the defendants are prepared to
> use their best efforts to instruct each store to black out the name of the
> plaintiff by black felt pen. As well, counsel for the defendants undertakes
> that no further books will be published or distributed by the defendants
> containing the name of the plaintiff. In my view this represents a very
> reasonable compromise and is an acceptable answer in the light of the
> very stringent onus placed upon the plaintiff in seeking this injunction.

d) Probable Efficacy

The decision whether or not to grant an injunction may be influenced by
the probable efficacy of such an order.

Robertson v. *Michaud*, [1995] N.B.J. No. 494 per Russell J. at para. 11 (Q.B.
(T.D.)):

> I cannot grant an injunction which will effectively protect people who
> live outside the jurisdiction of this Court.

Where books containing an allegedly defamatory passage about the plaintiff had been shipped by the defendant publisher to distributors, and a portion were outside the jurisdiction of the court, the court considered those
factors to weigh against an injunction.

Rapp v. *McClelland & Stewart Limited* (1981), 34 O.R. (2d) 452 per Griffiths
J. at 456 (H.C.J.).

e) Anonymous Speech

It has been held that a concern for freedom of speech is lessened where the allegedly defamatory statements are anonymous postings on Internet sites. Accordingly, a British Columbia court granted an *ex parte* interim injunction requiring the defendant to "forthwith remove the messages written and published on its Internet site" as identified in the motion.

Henry v. Stockhouse Media Corp., [1999] B.C.J. No. 3202 per Fraser J. at paras. 8 and 13 (S.C.):

> ¶8 I accept the high and stringent tests which the authorities lay down as to the granting of this kind of injunction. As to granting an injunction on an *ex parte* basis, the key is that the defendants are afforded no opportunity to say that the statements complained of are true. What has led me to the conclusion that the injunction should go is that the statements complained of are anonymous. Whoever WaveyDavey is, he or she feels free to throw around accusations of the most serious kind behind the cowardly screen of an alias. It seems to me that in these circumstances, the concern for the protection of free speech is lessened ... .

> ¶13 However, I consider it inappropriate to grant an injunction which will endure until trial, with the right in the defendants and the anonymous writers only to apply to set aside the injunction. It is my view that the injunction should be for as brief a period of time as is reasonable, with an obligation on the part of the plaintiffs to apply for the injunction to be extended.

The likelihood that defamatory expression will be republished before trial is an important factor. Evidence suggesting the expression is not likely to be repeated will weigh against an interlocutory injunction.

Lasik Vision Canada Inc. v. TLC Vancouver Optometric Group Inc., [1999] B.C.J. No. 2834, per Macaulay J. at para. 23 (S.C.) [injunction refused].

R.T. Investment Counsel Inc. v. Werry (1999), 46 B.L.R. (2d) 66, per Holmes J. at para. 18 (B.C.S.C.).

Soprema Inc. v. New Brunswick Roofing Contractors Ass'n (1996), 181 N.B.R. (2d) 223 per Russell J. at paras. 5–7 (Q.B. (T.D.)), citing Robert J. Sharpe, *Injunctions and Specific Performance*, 2d ed., (Aurora, ON: Canada Law Book) at 5.4, para. 5.60.

8) Scope of Injunctions

It was long the law of Ontario that a court will not generally restrain the publication of libels by interim injunction.

> The most that can be asked in any case is an injunction restraining the further publication of particular libels.
>
> *Meuneir* v. *Kilpatrick 1/85*, [1985] O.C.P. 109, per Kurisko L.J.S.C.O. (H.C.J.), citing *Natural Resources Security Co.* v. *"Saturday Night" Limited* (1910), 20 O.W.N. 9, per Middleton J. at 10.

It is unclear whether this is still the law in light of the scope of the injunction granted in *Canadian Tire Corp.* v. *Desmond*, [1972] 2 O.R. 60 at 62 (H.C.J.), where O'Driscoll J. issued an interlocutory injunction which restrained the defendant from "exhibiting any sign or sandwich board, or other printed or written material … containing any libelous statement of, or concerning the plaintiff company or the business."

> *Meuneir* v. *Kilpatrick 1/85*, [1985] O.C.P. 109 per Kurisko L.J.S.C.O. (H.C.J.), citing the conflict between *Canadian Tire*, above, and *Natural Resources Security Co.*, above, as a ground for granting leave to appeal.

9) Non-parties

The court has jurisdiction to grant an injunction binding on non-parties.

> *MacMillan Bloedel Ltd.* v. *Simpson*, [1996] 2 S.C.R. 1048 per McLachlin J. at 1064, para. 31.

The injunction may be worded to apply to anyone who has notice of the decision in appropriate circumstances.

> *Daishowa Inc.* v. *Friends of the Lubicon* (1998), 158 D.L.R. (4th) 699, per MacPherson J. at 746, para. 155 (Ont. Gen. Div.).

10) Consequences of Breach

Violation of both the letter and spirit of an injunction can be punishable as either contempt of court or as the *Criminal Code* offence of disobeying an order made by a court.

> *Canada Metal Co. Ltd.* v. *C.B.C. (No. 2)* (1974), 48 D.L.R. (3d) 641, 4 O.R. (2d) 585, 19 C.C.C. (2d) 218 (H.C.J.), rev'd on other grounds (1975), 59 D.L.R. (3d) 430, 8 O.R. (2d) 375, 23 C.C.C. (2d) 445 (C.A.); *Criminal Code*, R.S.C. 1985, c. C-46, s. 127(1), s. 718.

The procedure relating to civil contempt proceedings is often prescribed by the relevant court rules.

Calgary (City) Police Service v. *Wilde* (1999), 239 A.R. 197 (Q.B.) per Hawco J. [show cause hearing pursuant to rule 704 of the Alberta *Rules of Court*, defendant sentenced to imprisonment for a period of two weeks, sentence suspended as long as defendant complied with injunction, sentence suspended for two years].

Campbell v. *Cartmell* (1999), 104 O.T.C. 349 (S.C.J.), per Himel J. [motion at conclusion of trial for finding of contempt, r. 60.11 of *Rules of Civil Procedure*, R.R.O., Reg. 194, defendant fined $1,500].

The law relating to civil contempt by defiance of an injunction against defamatory speech is discussed in *Campbell* v. *Cartmell*, above, where Himel J. states at paragraphs 72–76:

¶72 Knowledge of the existence of an injunction is sufficient to obligate persons to obey it and the Order need not have been issued and entered in order to bind persons having knowledge of it: *Canada Metal, ibid.*, at p. 603.

¶73 An Order for an injunction must be implicitly observed and every diligence must be exercised to observe it to the letter. Respondents must not only obey the letter but also the spirit of the injunction: *Canada Metal, ibid.*, at p. 603.

¶74 Breach of an injunction is not excused because the person committing it had no direct intention to disobey the Order.

¶75 The absence of a contumacious intent is a mitigating factor, but it is not an exculpatory circumstance: *Re: Sheppard and Sheppard* (1976), 12 O.R. (2d) 4 (C.A.).

¶76 The defendant will be said to knowingly contravene the injunction if the evidence shows, beyond a reasonable doubt, that he knew what he was refrained from doing or understood that the injunction probably prohibited his contemplated course of action and was reckless as to whether it did or not. It is no defence for the defendant to be wilfully blind to the meaning of the injunction: *DiGiacomo* v. *DiGiacomo Canada Inc.* (1988), 20 C.P.R. (3d) 251 (Ont. H.C.) at p. 261–2.

A violation of an injunction may be prosecuted as an indictable offence under section 127(1) of the *Criminal Code*, which provides that every one who, without lawful excuse, disobeys a lawful order made by a court of justice ... is ... guilty of an indictable offence and liable for a term of imprisonment not exceeding two years.

11) Miscellaneous Interlocutory Injunctions

An Ontario court held that a plaintiff should not be required to prove that a defence of fair comment would inevitably fail where it was conceded that a sign carried by a defendant during "picketing" of the plaintiff's business premises was defamatory. In granting an interim injunction, the Court stated what it considered the appropriate test as follows:

> In my view the rights of the parties would be more fairly balanced if the plaintiff were entitled to an injunction in cases where the words are manifestly defamatory and the court, exercising its discretion cautiously with due regard for the high value we place on freedom of expression, is convinced, not that there is no reasonable possibility that there is a defence, but that it has been established that there is at least a substantial issue to be tried as to whether there is a defence of fair comment and that the other factors relevant to interlocutory injunctions such as the inadequacy of damages and the balance of convenience warrant an interlocutory injunction. To proceed otherwise would mean that plaintiffs who had strong but not inevitably successful cases would receive no adequate remedy where they proved at trial that they had been unjustifiably defamed.

> *Pilot Insurance Co. v. Jessome*, [1993] O.J. No. 172 (Gen. Div.), per D.S. Ferguson J., citing *Canadian Tire Corp. Ltd. v. Desmond*, [1972] 2 O.R. 60 at 61 (H.C.J.) [injunction granted: picket sign read "C.D.N. Tire cheated me will they cheat you"]

The court in *Pilot Insurance* held that the defence of fair comment "will likely fail at trial" [paragraph 40], and that "it is highly likely" that there will be a finding of malice at trial [paragraph 41]; that is, the plaintiffs "have a much stronger case" than the defendant [paragraph 42].

> *Rosemond Estates Inc. v. Levy*, [2003] O.J. No. 1748, per Spence J. at para. 32 (S.C.J.).

Plaintiffs have based their claims on other causes of action such as breach of confidence or conspiracy in an effort to circumvent the high hurdle imposed by *Bonnard v. Perryman*. Not surprisingly, judges have been cautious in granting injunctions in cases framed not in defamation but in injurious falsehood, which have the effect of restraining the publication of defamatory material. If the nature of the complaint is in substance a defamation action, then an injunction is unlikely to be granted.

It has been held that the statutory torts do not import a less stringent test for granting an interim injunction than allegations of defamation.

> *Lasik Vision Canada Inc.* v. *TLC Vancouver Optometric Group Inc.*, [1999] B.C.J. No. 2834, per Macaulay J. at para. 5 (S.C.) [claims under *Competition Act*, R.S.C. 1985, c. C-34, *Trade Practice Act*, R.S.B.C. 1996, c. 457].

> *Church of Scientology of California Inc.* v. *Readers Digest Services Pty Ltd.*, [1980] 1 N.S.W.L.R. 344 at 350–51.

However, plaintiffs have occasionally been successful in obtaining interlocutory relief by persuading the court that *Bonnard* v. *Perryman* does not apply because the claim is not, in reality, one in defamation. In *Gulf Oil (Great Britain) Ltd.* v. *Page*, [1987] Ch. 327 (C.A.), the plaintiff was granted an injunction where the cause of action was conspiracy to injure. Parker L.J. stated at pages 333–34:

> It is true that there is no wrong done if what is published is true provided that it is not published in pursuance of a combination, and even if it is, there is still no wrong unless the sole or dominant purpose of the combination and publication is to injure the plaintiff. If, however, there is both combination and purpose or dominant purpose to injure, there is a wrong done. When a plaintiff sues in conspiracy there is, therefore, a potential wrong even if it is admitted, as it is in the present case, that the publication is true and thus that there is no question of a cause of action in defamation. In such a case the court can, and in my view should, proceed on the same principles as it would in the case of any other tort.

> The prospect that this would open the floodgates and reverse the principle applicable in libel actions is, in my view, unreal. A plaintiff in an action against the author and publisher of an newspaper article, for example, might well establish a combination, but it appears to me that it would only be in the rarest case that sufficient evidence of a dominant purpose to injure could be made out to warrant the grant of interlocutory relief, and I have no doubt that the court would scrutinize with the greatest care any cause where a cause of action in conspiracy was joined to a cause of action in defamation and would require to be satisfied that such joinder was not merely an attempt to circumvent the rule in defamation.

12) Failed Applications

An application for an interim injunction which fails may nevertheless induce a court to direct that the action be dealt with expeditiously and that other procedural steps be taken to enhance the likelihood of an early trial date.

See *Simoni v. Blue Cross of Atlantic Canada* (1999), 184 Nfld. & P.E.I.R. 136 per Adam J. at para. 41 (Nfld. S.C. (T.D.)).

A court has imposed "conditions" on a defendant which are equivalent to an injunction where the defendant impliedly admitted, although asserting they were not engaged in tortious activity, that they may have been "intemperate."

Daishowa Inc. v. *Friends of the Lubicon* (1995), 30 C.P.R. (2d) 26, per Kitely J. at para. 357 (Ont. Gen. Div.) [reversed as to refusal to grant an interim injunction restricting secondary picketing: (1996), 27 O.R. (3d) 215, where the Divisional Court noted:

> In conclusion, Kitely J. did not grant an injunction restraining picketing or the threat of picketing in respect of Daishowa's customers. As a result of an admission by the Friends that they may have been intemperate, Kitely J. imposed conditions on the Friends. These conditions included: prohibiting references to a breach of the 1988 agreement and genocide; and, giving Daishowa copies of future correspondence addressed to Daishowa's customers.

13) Slander Not Actionable Per Se

On an application for an interim injunction, where proof of special damages is required, the court must be satisfied it has been incurred. It is not sufficient to adduce proof that the expression complained of is likely to cause damage, or even that it is calculated to do so.

Rust Check Canada Inc. v. *Young* (1988), 47 C.C.L.T. 279 per Watt J. at 299 (Ont. H.C.J.), citing *Gatley on Libel and Slander*, 8th ed., Philip Lewis ed., (London: Sweet & Maxwell, 1981) at 642–43.

14) Factors Relevant to Interlocutory Applications

Where the court dissolves an interim injunction, and a plaintiff indicates he or she intends to appeal that decision, the court may suspend the operation of its order temporarily to permit the defendant to take steps to obtain a stay from an appellate court.

Coltsfoot Publishing Ltd. v. *Harris* (1999), 43 C.P.C. (4th) 282, per Saunders J. at para. 39 (N.S.S.C.).

C. PERMANENT INJUNCTIONS

There may be circumstances where the principal relief sought by the plaintiff is a permanent injunction. A court clearly has jurisdiction to grant such an injunction.

Daishowa Inc. v. *Friends of the Lubicon* (1998), 158 D.L.R. (4th) 699, per MacPherson J. at 746, para. 154 (Ont. Gen. Div.).

Ferguson v. *Ferstay*, 2000 BCCA 592 per Rowles J.A. at paras. 25–26.

Wagner v. *Lim*, [1994] A.J. No. 637 per Egbert J. at para. 97 (Q.B.).

Webster v. *Webster*, [1997] B.C.J. No. 1952, per Rowles J.A. at paras. 2, 16 (C.A.).

A permanent injunction may be ordered where the court is satisfied the words are injurious to the plaintiff and there is reason to apprehend further publication by the defendant.

Kruger v. *Kay*, [1987] A.J. No. 37 (Q.B.) per Trussler J.

Safeway Stores Ltd. v. *Harris*, [1948] 4 D.L.R. 187 (Man. C.A.), aff'g [1948] 4 D.L.R. 187, per Williams C.J.K.B. at 20

Wagner v. *Lim*, [1994] A.J. No. 637 per Egbert J. at para. 97 (Q.B.).

It has been held that a permanent injunction is an exceptional remedy which should be ordered only in exceptional cases.

McKerron v. *Marshall*, [1999] O.J. No. 4048 per Reilly J. at para. 197 (S.C.J.):

> The mean-spirited focus of the defendant, to destroy [the plaintiff's] reputation and to end her career as a teacher, continued up to and including [the defendant's] final submissions. Failing such injunction, there is every reason to believe he may continue such efforts. Therefore, this Court intends to direct a permanent injunction restraining [the defendant], directly or by innuendo, publishing in any form, defamatory or disparaging comments about the plaintiff.

A court may decline to grant a permanent injunction where it is not satisfied by the evidence that a defendant will persist in making defamatory statements about the plaintiff.

R.E.G. v. *D.P.*, [1996] B.C.J. No. 1009, per Baker J. at para. 71 (S.C.).

L.E. v. W.P., [1998] B.C.J. No. 1250, per Collver J. at para. 75 (S.C.) ["… it would surprise me if filing of these reasons does not assist in stemming further [defamatory] speculation."].

In circumstances where a permanent injunction is denied, the court may grant leave to the plaintiff to renew an application by motion in the action if any further defamatory statements are made by the defendant at a later date.

R.E.G. v. D.P., [1996] B.C.J. No. 1009 per Baker J. at para. 72 (S.C.).

Where there was evidence before the court of a threat to continue publication of a slander actionable *per se*, a permanent injunction was ordered.

Tymofievich v. Miros, [1993] B.C.J. No. 1893, per Cooper J. at para. 26 (S.C.), aff'd [1994] B.C.J. No. 2606 (C.A.) [defendant informed plaintiff's lawyer that he intended to publish advertisements in a local newspaper seeking other persons who had business dealings with the plaintiff].

Campbell v. Cartmell, [1999] O.J. No. 3553 per Himel J. at paras. 59–60 (S.C.J.).

Where the defendants persisted in a defence of justification at trial, and continued to publish defamatory expression after commencement of the action, a permanent injunction was issued as part of the verdict to restrain the defendants from publishing or repeating the same or similar statements about the plaintiffs.

Wagner v. Lim (1994), 158 A.R. 241, per Egbert J. at para. 97 (Q.B.).

See also *Cameron v. Wilson-Haffenden*, [1986] B.C.J. No. 2616, per Bouck J. (S.C.) [The defendant "stated he intended to pursue this vendetta against the Plaintiff and the Federal Court after this trial, essentially using the same tactics."]

It may be necessary for a successful libel litigant to bring an application for additional injunctive relief if the defendant persists in publication of the libels after a verdict in favour of the plaintiff.

Hill v. Church of Scientology of Toronto, (1992) 7 O.R. (3d) 489 per Carruthers J. at 493–94 (Gen. Div.)

Hill v. Church of Scientology of Toronto, [1995] 2 S.C.R. 1130, per Cory J. at para. 201:

> On the very next day following the verdict, Scientology republished the libel in a press release delivered to the media. It then brought a motion to adduce fresh evidence which it stated would have a bearing "on the credibility and reputation of the plaintiff S. Casey Hill" which,

if presented at trial, "would probably have changed the result." Its actions were such that Hill was forced to bring an application for an injunction enjoining Scientology from republishing the libel. In his reasons for granting the injunction, Carruthers J. stated that he was forced to take that action because "no amount awarded on account of punitive damages would have prevented or will prevent the Church of Scientology from publishing defamatory statements about the plaintiff."

D. MANDATORY INJUNCTIONS

It is dubious whether a plaintiff is entitled to a mandatory injunction compelling a defendant news media organization to allow the plaintiff to preview a proposed article or broadcast to determine whether it is likely to be defamatory.

> *Doe v. Canadian Broadcasting Corporation* (1994), 86 B.C.L.R. (2d) 202, per Boyd J. at 215 (S.C.).

In a defamation verdict following a trial, an Alberta court ordered three defendants to write a letter of retraction to an official at Alberta Justice "to correct the record," although it declined to grant a permanent injunction restraining further publication of the expression complained of.

> *Kelly v. Low* (2000), 257 A.R. 279, per Lo Vecchio J. at para. 229 (Q.B.).

CHAPTER SIX:

Notice of Intended Action and Limitation Defences

A prospective defamation plaintiff confronts a minefield of limitations issues.

If the libel was published in a newspaper or a broadcast, defamation statutes in most provinces require that the plaintiff serve a notice of intended action on each prospective defendant within a relatively brief period. Those statutes almost invariably also prescribe a very short limitation period for filing such libel litigation. A prudent plaintiff will identify and diarize these special time limits relating to libels in the media. If the newspaper article or broadcast was distributed in more than one Canadian province, the plaintiff should identify and diarize the time limits applicable to each province.

If the defamatory expression was not published in a newspaper or broadcast, the requirement to serve a statutory notice of intended action will not apply to the prospective plaintiff. However, statutory limitation periods for filing defamation lawsuits differ from province to province. If the defamatory expression has been published in more than one province, a prudent plaintiff should identify and diarize each limitation period potentially applicable.

This chapter cannot address every nuance of provincial and territorial limitation law relating to libel litigation. Further, the law concerning limitation defences may change as a result of legislative amendment or new jurisprudence. Therefore the law on the subject of statutory notices and limitation periods should be reviewed each time a new defamation claim is being considered.

A. STATUTORY NOTICES OF INTENDED ACTION

Each Canadian province and territory except British Columbia and Saskatchewan prescribes in its defamation statute a very brief period within which a person who intends to institute an action for libel in a newspaper or in a radio or television broadcast must serve each prospective defendant with a written notice of intended legal action.

1) Saskatchewan and British Columbia

Saskatchewan requires that a notice of intention to sue for libel be given five days before filing a lawsuit against a daily newspaper, and fourteen days before filing a lawsuit against a weekly. There is no requirement relating to broadcasts.

> *Libel and Slander Act*, R.S.S. 1978, c. L-14, s. 15.

British Columbia does not require service of a notice of intention to sue for defamation. A plaintiff is merely obliged to let one clear day pass between publication of the libel in a newspaper or broadcast and the commencement of his or her litigation.

> *Libel and Slander Act*, R.S.B.C. 1996, c. 263, s. 5.

2) Six Weeks: Ontario

The shortest limitation period for service of a statutory notice of intended action is only six weeks. Section 5(1) of the Ontario *Libel and Slander Act*, R.S.O. 1990, c. L.12 provides:

> No action for libel in a newspaper or in a broadcast lies unless the plaintiff has, within six weeks after the alleged libel has come to the plaintiff's knowledge, given to the defendant notice in writing specifying the matter complained of, which shall be served in the same manner as a statement of claim or by delivering it to a grown-up person at the chief office of the defendant.

Section 5 applies only to newspapers printed and published in Ontario and to broadcasts from a station in Ontario.

> *Libel and Slander Act*, R.S.O. 1990, c. L.12, s. 7

The notice requirement in section 5(1) does not apply where the defamation is not found in a "newspaper" or "broadcast." Instead, the plaintiff is governed by the provisions of the *Limitation Act*, which do not require the plaintiff to provide notice beyond issuing a statement of claim.

> *Fotomaris v. Mantini-Atkinson*, [2002] O.J. No. 3202 per LaForme J. at paras. 12–19 (S.C.J.) [defamation alleged in a psychological assessment report].

It is not entirely clear whether section 5 would apply where a defamatory interview took place outside Ontario and was subsequently broadcast by a network throughout Canada including from an affiliate or network station in Ontario. A prudent plaintiff should give notice on the assumption such an interview will be considered a "broadcast from a station in Ontario" within the meaning of section 7.

> *Davies v. De Bane*, [1985] O.J. No. 363 per Potts J.

a) The Discoverability Principle

The phrase "after the libel has come to the plaintiff's knowledge" in section 5 has been interpreted as having an objective component. The six-week limitation period therefore starts to run when the plaintiff could have known of the libel with the exercise of reasonable diligence. It is therefore not necessary that a defendant seeking to rely on the six-week limitation period for notice prove actual knowledge of the libel by the plaintiff. Constructive knowledge is adequate.

> *Bhaduria v. Persaud* (1998), 40 O.R. (3d) 140 (Gen. Div.)

The six week period for giving notice is therefore subject to the concept of "discoverability," which is an important and well-established extension of the law relating to limitation periods. In *Misir v. Toronto Star Newspapers Limited* (1997), 105 O.A.C. 270, Laskin J.A. stated at paragraphs 14 and 15 (C.A.):

> Section 5(1), however, includes the element of discoverability. The six-week period for giving notice does not commence until the alleged libel has come to the point of knowledge ... The material before the Motions Judge does not disclose when Misir and Metro Orthopedic became aware of the publication of the May articles. On that ground alone the alleged libels in the May articles cannot be held to be barred by section 5(1) of the *Act*.
>
> Moreover, even if the Plaintiff had knowledge of the May articles when they were published, still they would not give effect to the limitation period ... Section 5(1) requires that the Plaintiff have knowledge of the alleged libel in May. Misir and Metro Orthopedic may have knowledge of the publication of the May article, but not of the libel. The May articles may have been defamatory, but they were not reasonably capable of defaming these plaintiffs until they were named in the September 30th article. Accordingly, the six week notice period for the May articles would not begin before the publication of the September 30th article.

Where the plaintiff is clearly identifiable in each of a series of twenty-three articles, there is no issue of discoverability relating to the fact she was not specifically named.

> *Merling v. Southam Inc. (c.o.b. Hamilton Spectator)* (2000), 183 D.L.R. (4th) 748, per McMurtry C.J.O. at para. 26 (Ont. C.A.).

In *Misir v. Toronto Star Newspapers Limited* (1997), 105 O.A.C. 270, Laskin J.A. stated at paragraph 16 (C.A.):

Indeed, had the plaintiffs given notice within six weeks of the publication of the May articles and issued their statement of claim before September 30, 1995, the defendants undoubtedly would have moved to dismiss the action because the articles did not refer to the plaintiffs. Thus, it seems to me that the trier of fact can look at the September 30 article to see to whom the previous eleven articles referred. A newspaper cannot avoid an action for libel by publishing a series of defamatory articles but only linking the plaintiffs to the defamation by identifying them in the last article. The English Court of Appeal came to a similar conclusion in *Hayward v. Thompson*, [1982] 1 Q.B. 47.

Applying these principles, the Ontario Court of Appeal held in *Misir* at paragraph 5 that the trier of fact would be entitled to find that the May articles were defamatory of the plaintiffs because of the publication of the September article.

The question of discoverability arose in another decision of the Ontario Court of Appeal: *Watson v. Southam Inc. (c.o.b. Hamilton Spectator)* (2000), 189 D.L.R. (4th) 695 (Ont. C.A.). After holding that "there is no doubt that the discoverability rule applies to Section 5(1)," Abella J.A. for the Court rejected defence submissions that the rule applied to preserve the cause of action in defamation against the defendant municipality on the particular facts of the case. In *Watson*, the plaintiffs claimed that the libel only came to their attention during the examination for discovery of one of the defendants in December 1994, when she denied having made a number of statements attributed to her in the newspaper articles and the plaintiffs realized that the defendant Regional Municipality of Hamilton-Wentworth had suppressed the fact that the female defendant had been misquoted. The Court of Appeal rejected this argument for several reasons [at paragraphs 57–61]:

i.   It was almost six months after the December 1994 discovery, namely in May 1995, that the plaintiffs filed motion material seeking to join the Regional Municipality of Hamilton-Wentworth as a defendant — well beyond the time limits in sections 5(1) and (6).

ii. The plaintiff Gallagher acknowledged that he knew in December 1994 that the Municipality might be liable, yet no action was brought against it until May 1995.

iii. The plaintiff Gallagher admitted at the time the notice letters were delivered and the statement of claim was issued (August 1994) he knew that he was at liberty to place the Municipality on notice of the alleged libel.

iv. The plaintiff Gallagher's affidavit in support of the motion to add the Municipality as a defendant conceded that he had not previously named the Municipality, not because he had no relevant knowledge, but because he intended to run for municipal office in November, 1994.

v. Finally, the plaintiff Gallagher admitted at trial that he made the statements attributed to him in a newspaper article dated 7 July 1994, confirming the action was not against the Municipality but against some of its employees.

Since there is a presumption of falsity when a libel has been published, the plaintiff cannot wait until the words are proved to be false.

Elliott v. Freisen (1982), 37 O.R. (3d) 409 (H.C.J.), aff'd (1984) ,45 O.R. (2d) 285 (C.A.).

Frisina v. Southam Press Ltd. (1980), 30 O.R. (2d) 65 (H.C.J.), aff'd (1981), 33 O.R. (2d) 287 (C.A.).

3) Three Months: Every Jurisdiction except Ontario, British Columbia, and Saskatchewan

Alberta's *Defamation Act*, R.S.A. 2000, c. D-6 stipulates that a statutory notice of intended action must be served within three months. Section 13 states:

13(1) No action lies unless the plaintiff has, within 3 months after the publication of the defamatory matter has come to the plaintiff's notice or knowledge, given to the defendant, in the case of a daily newspaper, 7, and in the case of any other newspaper or when the defamatory matter was broadcast, 14 days' notice in writing of the plaintiff's intention to bring an action, specifying the defamatory matter complained of.

(2) The notice shall be served in the same manner as a statement of claim.

The defamation statutes of Manitoba, New Brunswick, Newfoundland and Labrador, the Northwest Territories, Nova Scotia, Prince Edward Island, and the Yukon Territory contain notice provisions similar to Alberta's.

Manitoba, *Defamation Act*, R.S.M. 1987, c. D-20, ss.14(1), 14(2).

New Brunswick, *Defamation Act*, R.S.N.B. 1973, c. D-5, ss.13(1), 13(2).

Newfoundland and Labrador, *Defamation Act*, R.S.N. 1990, c. D-3, ss.16 (1), 16(2).

Northwest Territories, *Defamation Act*, R.S.N.W.T. 1988, c. D-1, ss.15(1), 15(2).

Nova Scotia, *Defamation Act*, R.S.N.S. 1989, c. 122, ss.18(1), 18(2).

Prince Edward Island, *Defamation Act*, R.S.P.E.I. 1988, c. D-5, ss.14(1), 14(2).

Yukon Territory, *Defamation Act*, R.S.Y.T. 1986, c. 41, ss.14(1), 14(2).

A Prince Edward Island court recently held that the libel notice requirement applied to an allegedly defamatory posting on an Internet web site which was not operated by a newspaper or broadcaster but rather by private individuals.

Gaiger v *Inn at Spry Point Inc.*, 2002 PEISCTD 60, per Deroches J. at paras. 32–33:

> ¶32 I would dismiss the defendant's defamation action. Section 14(10) of the *Defamation Act*, R.S.P.E.I. 1988,Ch. D-5 provides:
>
> > 14(1) No action lies unless the plaintiff has, within three months after the publication of the defamatory matter has come to his notice or knowledge, given to the defendant, in the case of a daily newspaper, five, and in the case of any other newspaper or where the defamatory matter was broadcast, fourteen days notice in writing of his intention to bring an action, specifying the language complained of.
> >
> > (2) The notice shall be served in the same manner as an originating notice.
>
> ¶33 There is no evidence of any notice being given to the plaintiffs in this case. In a case such as this where the claim for defamation is advanced in a counterclaim, I would read s. 14 as requiring the defendant to give notice to the plaintiffs (defendants by counterclaim). Also, I do not hold that the notice requirement applies only to newspapers or corporate broadcasting facilities. An examination of the purpose of the notice requirement leads me to conclude it should be applicable in all cases in which defamation is alleged as the basis for a claim.

There appears to be no Alberta jurisprudence which specifically interprets the phrase "after the publication of the defamatory matter has come to the plaintiff's notice or knowledge." However, when calculating the three-month limitation period, a prudent plaintiff should assume that it will begin to run, at the latest, when the plaintiff could reasonably have known of the libel with the exercise of reasonable diligence.

4) Purposes of the Statutory Notice of Intended Action

The notice requirements are intended to give the newspaper, broadcaster, or other person responsible for the libel an opportunity to correct, retract, or apologize for the defamatory expression. In this manner, the defendant may avoid or reduce the damages otherwise payable for publication of the libel. The plaintiff may also benefit because a prompt correction, retraction, or apology often constitutes a better remedy than damages.

Misir v. *Toronto Star Newspapers Limited* (1997), 105 O.A.C. 270 at 273 (C.A.).

Pitre v. *Jeffrey and Canadian Broadcasting Corporation* (1994), 119 Nfld. & P.E.I.R. 335 (P.E.I. S.C. (T.D.)).

Block v. *Winnipeg Sun* (1989), 59 Man. R. (2d) 302 at 304 (Q.B.).

Grossman v. *CFTO-TV Limited* (1982), 39 O.R. (2d) 498 per Cory J. at 501 (C.A.).

Frisina v. *Southam Press Inc.* (1981), 124 D.L.R. (3d) 340 at para. 12 (Ont. C.A.).

Paletta v. *Lethbridge Herald Company Limited* (1977), 2 Alta. L.R. (2d) 166, 2 A.R. 529 (S.C. (T.D.)).

Buro v. *Southam Press Limited*, [1974] 6 W.W.R 594 (Alta. S.C. (T.D.)).

Barber v. *Lupton* (1969), 71 W.W.R. 383 at 384 (Man. Q.B.).

Sentinel-Review Co. Ltd. v. *Robinson*, [1928] S.C.R. 258 at 261.

Culligan v. *Graphic Ltd.* (1917), 44 N.B.R. 481 at 502 (C.A.).

The notice requirement is also important because it enables the defendant to locate and preserve evidence when it is still fresh. Sources of information, including people interviewed, informants, notes, tapes, and other materials, are also more likely to be available if the defendant's investigation occurs shortly after publication.

Butler v. *Southam Inc.* (2000), 191 N.S.R. (2d) 158 at paras. 33–37 (S.C. (T.D.)), varied (on other grounds) (2001), 197 N.S.R. (2d) 97 at paras. 129–33 (C.A.).

Further, the notice provision may be of vital importance in relation to a series of articles. Timely notice of a complaint about one article may afford an opportunity to the newspaper or broadcaster to evaluate planned subsequent articles in the series in the light of that complaint, and either cancel them or obtain legal advice on further content.

Butler v. *Southam Inc.* (2001), 197 N.S.R. (2d) 97 at para. 133 (C.A.).

The Nova Scotia Court of Appeal has suggested that notices of intended action have a constitutional dimension arising from the fundamental clash in defamation lawsuits between the democratic values of protection of reputation and freedom of the press. In *Butler v. Southam Inc.* (2001), 197 N.S.R. (2d) 97 at paragraph 135 (C.A.), Cromwell J.A. approved the following passage from the decision of the judge in Chambers:

> [The statutory notice of action requirements] recognize that a defamation is a personal insult involving loss of reputation and esteem and other injury in a community and that the injury is immediate, upon publication, and provide a fair window of opportunity for the person claiming to be defamed to deal with the matter as he sees fit up to and including commencement of legal action. At the same time [the statutory notice of action requirement] acknowledges the freedom of the press by requiring timely notification of a defamation complaint for, to allow claims of this nature to exist for long periods of time such as for tort or contract claims without notification or commencement of legal proceedings would not only deprive a newspaper publisher of a full and fair defence but it would impose an unreasonable burden on its record keeping and on the memories of its writers and leave the publisher open to any number of unknown claimants with possible large damage claims without any ability to mitigate against such damages. To my mind such a situation would be most destructive to the operation of a daily newspaper and inconsistent with the principle of the freedom of the press. The Act, in effect, creates a reasonable balance between the interests of the press and those of a person alleging defamation.

5) Is the Libel Contained in a "Newspaper"?

A "newspaper" is defined by section 1(1) of the Ontario *Libel and Slander Act* to mean:

> ... a paper containing public news, intelligence, or occurrences, or remarks or observations thereon, or containing principally, advertisements, printed for distribution to the public and published periodically, or in parts or numbers, at least twelve times a year.

The Alberta *Defamation Act* defines "newspaper" somewhat differently in section 1(c) to mean:

> ... a paper containing news, intelligence, occurrences, pictures or illustrations, or remarks or observations thereon, printed for sale and published periodically, or in parts or numbers, at intervals not exceeding 31 days between the publication of any 2 of the papers, parts or numbers.

One difference between the Ontario and Alberta definitions of "newspaper" is the latter's requirement that the publication be printed "for sale." The current phenomenon of free newspapers means this difference is potentially of great significance. The scope of protection to newspapers afforded by Ontario's defamation legislation is much broader than Alberta's because it will protect free publications.

As does the Ontario statute, the Newfoundland and Labrador *Defamation Act* defines "newspaper" in section 2(c) in terms that do not require "sale":

> "Newspaper" means a paper containing public news, intelligence and occurrences or remarks or observations or containing only, or principally, advertisements, printed for distribution to the public and published periodically, or in parts or numbers, at least 12 times a year.

The definitions of "newspaper" in the defamation statutes of Manitoba, New Brunswick, the Northwest Territories, Nova Scotia, Prince Edward Island, the Yukon Territory, and Nunavut (which has adopted the Northwest Territories statute) is substantially the same as Alberta's:

> Manitoba, *Defamation Act*, R.S.M. 1987, c. D-20, s.1.
>
> New Brunswick, *Defamation Act*, R.S.N.B. 1973, c. D-5, s.1.
>
> Northwest Territories/Nunavut, *Defamation Act*, R.S.N.W.T. 1988, c. D-1, s.1.
>
> Nova Scotia, *Defamation Act*, R.S.N.S. 1989, c. 122, s.2(c) .
>
> Prince Edward Island, *Defamation Act*, R.S.P.E.I. 1988, c. D-5, s.1(c).
>
> Yukon Territory, *Defamation Act*, R.S.Y.T. 1986, c. 41, s.1.

Saskatchewan's *Libel and Slander Act* defines "newspaper" in section 2(a) to mean:

> ... a paper containing public news, intelligence or occurrences or remarks or observations thereon, printed for sale and published periodically or in parts or numbers at regular intervals not exceeding thirty-one days between the publication of any two of such papers, parts or numbers, and includes a paper printed in order to be made public weekly or oftener or at regular intervals not exceeding thirty-one days and containing only or principally advertisements.

It has been held that the Ontario definition of "newspaper" includes a confidential commercial report printed daily and issued to subscribers. It was also held such a publication was "printed for sale" within the meaning of the former Ontario definition of "newspaper," which has since been amended to remove the phrase "printed for sale."

Slattery v. R.G. Dun & Co. (1898), 18 P.R. 168 (Ont. H.C.).

Older case law concerning the meaning of "newspaper" must be treated with caution. For example, it has been held that a weekly publication of a union would not be a "newspaper" within the meaning of the Ontario statute. However, the definition of "newspaper" at the time of that decision contained the phrase "printed for sale."

Hebert v. *Jackson*, [1950] 2 D.L.R. 538 (Ont. H.C.); rev'd in part, [1951] 1 D.L.R. 13 (Ont. C.A.).

A publication for science fiction and fantasy fans has been held to be a "newspaper."

Weiss v. *Sawyer*, [2001] O.J. No. 4544 at 10 (S.C.J.), aff'd [2002] O.J. No. 3570 (C.A.).

In *Weiss* v. *Sawyer*, [2002] O.J. No. 3570 (C.A.), the Ontario Court of Appeal held that the on-line version of a publication was a "newspaper" within the meaning of Ontario's *Libel and Slander Act*, and that a newspaper is no less a newspaper because it appears in an on-line version. Writing for the court, Armstrong J.A. stated:

¶24 The Act defines a newspaper in part as a "paper" containing certain categories of information for distribution to the public. I think word "paper" is broad enough to encompass a newspaper, which is published on the Internet.

¶25 If I am wrong in my conclusion and the word "paper" is to be given a more restrictive meaning i.e. the substance upon which a newspaper is ordinarily printed, then arguably s. 5(1) is not available to the defendant. However, such a result would clearly be absurd. It would mean that if an action was commenced against a newspaper, without serving a s. 5(1) notice, it would be barred in relation to the newsprint publication but not so barred in relation to the online publication, unless of course it fell within the definition of "broadcast." The ordinary meaning rule of statutory interpretation articulated by Ruth Sullivan, in *Driedger on the Construction of Statutes*, 3rd ed. (Toronto: Butterworths Canada, 1994) at p. 7 is helpful:

(1) It is presumed that the ordinary meaning of a legislative text is the intended or most appropriate meaning. In the absence of a reason to reject it, the ordinary meaning prevails.

(2) Even where the ordinary meaning of a legislative text appears to be clear, the courts must consider the purpose and scheme of the legislation, and the consequences of adopting this meaning. They must take into account all relevant indicators of legislative meaning.

(3) In light of these additional considerations, the court may adopt an interpretation in which the ordinary meaning is modified or rejected. That interpretation, however, must be plausible, that is, it must be one the words are reasonably capable of bearing.

In my view, the purpose and scheme of the notice provision in the *Libel and Slander Act* are to extend its benefits to those who are sued in respect of a libel in a newspaper irrespective of the method or technique of publication. To use the words of Justice Lax, "a newspaper is no less a newspaper because it appears in an on-line version."

Consequently, statutory notices of intended action relating to defamatory statements in newspapers should also expressly refer to any publication on the newspaper's web site.

It has been held that the definition of "newspaper" in the Ontario *Libel and Slander Act* does not apply to:

i)   A promotional flyer.

> *Robinson v. Club Epiphany and Lounge*, [2001] O.J. No. 2102 (S.C.J.).

ii) A written assessment by a psychologist.

> *Fortomaris v. Mantini-Atkinson*, [2002] O.J. No. 3202 (S.C.J.)

iii) A fax transmission and an email to the editors of a magazine.

> *Weiss v. Sawyer*, [2002] O.J. No. 3570 (C.A.).

As noted above, only Ontario's *Libel and Slander Act* limits the application of the statutory notice of intended action requirement to newspapers printed and published in the province. A prudent plaintiff will therefore serve a statutory notice of intended action if there is any possibility that a publication containing defamatory expression will fall within the meaning of "newspaper" under any of the provincial definitions potentially applicable.

6) Is the Libel Contained in a "Broadcast"?

In Ontario's *Libel and Slander Act*, "broadcast" is defined in section 1(1) in the following terms:

> "Broadcasting" means the dissemination of writing, signs, signals, pictures and sounds of all kinds, intended to be received by the public either directly or through the medium of relay stations, by means of,
>
> (a) any form of wireless radioelectric communication utilizing Hertzian waves, including radiotelegraph and radiotelephone, or

(b)   cables, wires, fibre-optic linkages or laser beams,

and "broadcast" has a corresponding meaning; (*"radiodiffusion ou télédiffusion*," "*radiodiffuser ou télédiffuser*").

New Brunswick, the Northwest Territories, Nova Scotia, Prince Edward Island, the Yukon Territory, and Nunavut have not updated the definition of "broadcasting" in their defamation statutes to explicitly cover "cables, wires, fibre-optic linkages or laser beams" as Ontario has done.

New Brunswick, *Defamation Act*, R.S.N.B. 1973, c. D-5, s.1.

Northwest Territories/Nunavut, *Defamation Act*, R.S.N.W.T. 1988, c. D-1, s.1

Nova Scotia, *Defamation Act*, R.⸢ ⸣N.S. 1989, c. 122, s.2(c).

Prince Edward Island, *Defamation Act*, R.S.P.E.I. 1988, c. D-5, s.1(c).

Yukon Territory, *Defamation Act*, R.S.Y.T. 1986, c. 41, s.1.

The definition in the New Brunswick statute, for example, reads in section 1 as follows:

"Broadcasting" means the dissemination of any form of radioelectric communication, including radiotelegraph, radiotelephone and the wireless transmission of writing, signs, signals, pictures and sounds of all kinds by means of Hertzian waves.

The definition of "broadcasting" in Alberta's *Defamation Act* is unique. It reads in section 1(a):

"Broadcasting" means a transmission, emission or reception to the general public of signs, signals, writing, images, sounds or intelligence of any nature by means of electromagnetic waves of frequencies lower than 3000 gigahertz ...

Defamation Act, R.S.A. 2000, c. D-6, s. 1(a).

Saskatchewan's *Defamation Act* does not require a statutory notice of action with respect to libel contained in a broadcast. The statute does not contain a definition of "broadcast" or "broadcasting."

It has not yet been determined whether an on-line publication would fall within the definition of a "broadcast." In *Bahlieda* v. *Santa*, [2003] O.J. No. 1159 (S.C.J.), the Ontario Superior Court of Justice held on an application for summary judgment that placing material on the Internet, via a web site, constitutes "broadcasting" within the meaning of Ontario's *Libel and Slander Act*. Pierce J. stated at paragraph 52 that the notice period and short limitation period in the Ontario Court seek to ameliorate "widespread damage to reputation when a mass audience receives defamatory material" and that "the Internet, sometimes more than traditional broadcast media, reaches a mass audience." This decision was set aside on appeal to the Ontario Court of Appeal, however, in part because this was a genuine issue for trial and that the issue therefore should not have been determined on a summary judgment application: [2003] O.J. No. 4091 (C.A.). In *Weiss v. Sawyer*, [2002] O.J. No. 3570 (C.A.) at paragraph 26, the court declined to consider whether the on-line publication of a letter to the editor constituted a "broadcast" within the meaning of the *Libel and Slander Act* because of the court's finding that the publication was a "newspaper" and also because there was no evidence on the record to permit a determination whether the on-line publication fell within the statutory definition of "broadcast."

7) Failure to Serve A Notice of Intended Action

Failure to comply with the notice requirement is an absolute bar to a libel action in most provinces where the notice is required. This principle is illustrated in many decisions, including the following:

Siddiqui v. Canadian Broadcasting Corp. (2000), 50 O.R. (3d) 607 (C.A.), application for leave to appeal to S.C.C. dismissed, [2000] S.C.C.A. No. 664.

Watson v. Southam Inc. (c.o.b. Hamilton Spectator) (2000), 189 D.L.R. (4th) 695 at para. 50 (Ont. C.A.).

Merling v. Southam Inc. (c.o.b. Hamilton Spectator) (2000), 183 D.L.R. (4th) 748 (Ont. C.A.).

Misir v. Toronto Star Newspapers Limited (1997), 105 O.A.C. 270 at 273, per Laskin J.A. (C.A.).

Gallant v. Moncton Publishing Co. (1994), 146 N.B.R. (2d) 241 (C.A.).

Pitre v. Jeffrey and Canadian Broadcasting Corporation (1994), 119 Nfld. & P.E.I.R. 335 (P.E.I.S.C. (T.D.)).

Grossman v CFTO-TV Ltd. (1982), 39 O.R. (2d) 498 at 501 (C.A.), leave to appeal to S.C.C. refused 39 O.R. (2d) 498fn.

Frisina v. Southam Press Limited (1981), 33 O.R. (2d) 287 (C.A.), aff'g (1980). 30 O.R. (2d) 65 (H.C.J.).

Leslie v. Telegram Publishing Co. Ltd., [1955] 3 D.L.R. 317 (Ont. H.C.J.).

MCF Capital Inc. v. Canadian Broadcasting Corporation, [2003] M.J. No. 324, 2003 MBQB 205 per MacInnes J. at para. 30.

Although a court has no inherent power at law or in equity in any province to excuse noncompliance with the statutory requirement for a notice of intended action, a plaintiff who is met with the defence that his or her action is barred by this statutory requirement should investigate the availability of specific statutory relief.

For example, it has been held that a Nova Scotia court has a discretion within specified limits under section 3 of the *Limitation of Actions Act*, R.S.N.S. 1989, c. 258, to disallow the defence of failing to serve a notice of intended action prescribed by the *Defamation Act*, R.S.N.S. 1989, c. 122. This discretion is to be exercised when it is equitable to do so taking into account the degree to which the time limitation prejudices the plaintiff and the degree to which disallowance of the defence would prejudice the defendant. Whether the plaintiff has been diligent is an important aspect of this assessment.

MacIntyre v. *Canadian Broadcasting Corporation* (1985), 70 N.S.R. (2d) 129 (S.C.(A.D.)).

Butler v. *Southam Inc.* (2001), 197 N.S.R. (2d) 97 at paras. 125, 141 (C.A.).

A plaintiff who fails to serve a notice of intended action within the statutory time limits may face an interlocutory motion for judgment if he or she files suit for libel. In addition to the decisions cited above, see the following decisions:

Graye v. *Fillater* (1995), 25 O.R. (3d) 57 (Gen. Div.).

Stuarts Furniture and Appliances v. *No Frills Appliances & T.V. Limited* (1982), 40 O.R. (2d) 52 (H.C.J.).

Elliott v. *Freisen* (1982) 37 O.R. (2d) 409 (H.C.J.), aff'd (1984), 45 O.R. (2d) 285 (C.A.).

Leslie v. *Telegram Publishing Company Limited*, [1955] 3 D.L.R. 317 (Ont. H.C.J.).

Carter v. *Standard Limited* (1915), 30 D.L.R. 492 (N.B.S.C.).

8) Contents of the Notice

The defamation statutes of each jurisdiction (except the Yukon Territory) require that the plaintiff give notice of intended action "specifying the defamatory matter complained of." None of the defamation statutes prescribes a particular form of notice. Nevertheless, the courts have evolved tests of sufficiency.

The Supreme Court of Canada in *Sentinel-Review Company* v. *Robinson*, [1928] S.C.R. 258 put the matter very simply at page 259: "The notice is sufficient if the Plaintiffs' intention to sue is notified." A prudent plaintiff, however, will endeavor to draft the statutory notice of intended action with as much precision as possible in view of more recent jurisprudence.

The leading case is *Grossman* v. *CFTO-TV Limited* (1982), 39 O.R. (2d) 498 (C.A.), where Cory J.A. (as he then was) articulated a test of sufficiency at page 505:

> Does the notice identify the Plaintiff and fairly bring home to the publisher the matter complained of. Since the *Act* prescribes no particular form, the Court in answering this question can consider all the relevant circumstances.
>
> The longer and more frequent the broadcasts are, the greater the particularity that may be required of the notice. Similarly the more numerous the possible heads of complaint are, the more detailed the notice must be. The pleadings in a libel action are technical and they provide a wide variety of defences to a publisher. So long as the broadcaster is made clearly aware of the matter of which the plaintiff complains of, then there is no reason why the case, as defined by the pleadings, should not be determined on the merits.

The judgment of Cory J.A. in *Grossman* was explained in *Siddiqui* v. *Canadian Broadcasting Corporation* (2000), 50 O.R. (3d) 607 (C.A.), application for leave to appeal dismissed, [2000] S.C.C.A. No. 664, where Abella J.A. stated at pages 612–13:

> In *Grossman* v. *CFTO-TV Ltd.* (1982), 39 O.R. (2d) 498 at p. 505, 139 D.L.R. (3d) 618 (C.A.), Cory J.A. held that the s. 5(1) written notice must make a defendant "clearly aware" of the matter about which the plaintiff complains. There must, in other words, be more than technical compliance with the notice requirement.
>
> It is true that s. 5(1) does not stipulate what form a written notice must take, but it is also true that the section provides that the written notice must "specify" the matter complained of. This means that a defendant is entitled to know with clarity the essence of the case it has to meet and have an opportunity to meet it before an action for libel is commenced. The denial of sufficient particularity constitutes a denial of that opportunity. The issue in every case, therefore, is whether the written notice provides enough clear information for an appropriate response to be considered and taken.

See also *Young* v. *Toronto Star Newspapers Ltd.*, [2003] O.J. No 3100 per Rouleau J. at paras. 80–87 (S.C.J.).

In Ontario it will not be sufficient to merely set out an article in its entirety and say that it is "largely untrue and libelous" without identifying the part complained of:

> *Pohlman v. Herald Printing Company of Hamilton Limited* (1919), 45 O.L.R. 291 (C.A.).

A letter to the Canadian Broadcasting Corporation, which did not characterize a telecast as being defamatory, or employ the words "defamation," "defamatory," or similar words. did not satisfy the requirements of s. 14(1) of *The Defamation Act*, R.S.M. c. D-20.

> *MCF Capital Inc. v. Canadian Broadcasting Corporation*, [2003] M.J. No. 324, 2003 MBQB 205, per MacInnes J. at paras. 27–30 (Q.B.).

Certain courts in other provinces have held that the notice requirements ought to be interpreted liberally or beneficially to avoid depriving the plaintiff of her right of action.

> *Teeluck v. Cadogan Publishing Limited (c.o.b. Miramichi Leader)* (1998), 206 N.B.R. (2d) 224 at 234 (Q.B. (T.D.)).

> *A.U.P.E. v. Edmonton Sun* (1986), 49 Alta. L.R (2d) 141 (Q.B.).

> *Atlanticom Inc. v. Henley* (1986), 72 N.B.R. (2d) 162 (Q.B.).

> *England v. Canadian Broadcasting Corporation*, [1977] 3 W.W.R. 193 (N.W.T. S.C.).

> *Baxter v. Canadian Broadcasting Corporation and Malling* (1977), 19 N.B.R. (2d) 232 (S.C. (Q.B. Div.)).

> *Paletta v. Lethbridge Herald Company Limited* (1977), 2 Alta. L.R. (2d) 166, 2 A.R. 529 (S.C. (T.D.)).

> *Barber v. Lupton* (1969), 71 W.W.R. 383 (Man. Q.B.).

> *Charlton v. Albertan Publishing Company*, [1944] 2 W.W.R. 225 (Alta. S.C. (T.D.)).

A New Brunswick trial court has held that mere reference to dates of broadcasts is not adequate. However, the lower court's summary dismissal of the action on this ground was reversed by the New Brunswick Court of Appeal because the defence application could not be made until after a defence was filed, which had not occurred when the motion was heard. The appellate court also held that whether the specificity requirements have been met is to be determined taking into account the notice's content in light of the overall context in which it was given. The Court of Appeal also stated that courts have been loath to dismiss an action on account of inadequacy of notice except where it is clear there has been disregard for compliance with the statute.

> *Waugh v. C.B.C.* (2000), 224 N.B.R. (2d) 391 at paras. 8 and 14 (C.A.).

In *England v. Canadian Broadcasting Corporation*, [1979] 3 W.W.R. 193 at 221 (N.W.T.S.C.), the purported notice stated:

> The language complained of is all those statements broadcast on the said television programme concerning an inquest held by Walter England into the deaths of 31 people and the crash of a Panarctic Oil Company aircraft at Rea (*sic*) Point, in the North West (*sic*) Territories on October 30, 1974.

The court held at page 222 that the trend in the authorities is to deal with the substance and merit of the issues, not the form, and that this notice was sufficient.

9) Persons Entitled to Notice of Intended Action

All defendants implicated in the publication of defamatory expression in a newspaper or broadcast, including sources, advertisers, printers, interviewees, guests, and callers who have contributed directly or indirectly to the media publication, are entitled to the statutory notice under the Ontario *Libel and Slander Act*.

> *DeHeus v. Niagara (Region) Police Services*, [2001] O.J. No. 4201 (C.A.) [non-media defendants].

> *Weiss v. Sawyer*, [2001] O.J. No. 4544 at para. 5 (S.C.J.), aff'd [2002] O.J. No. 3570 at para. 15 (C.A.) [letter to editor of science fiction magazine].

> *Siddiqui v. Canadian Broadcasting Corporation* (2000), 50 O.R. (3d) 607 (Ont. C.A.), leave to appeal to S.C.C. denied, [2000] S.C.C.A. No. 664.

> *Watson v. Southam Inc. (c.o.b. Hamilton Spectator)* (2000), 189 D.L.R. (4th) 695 at paras. 50–55 [municipality sued vicariously for statements to defendant newspaper by employees].

> *Merling v. Southam Inc. (c.o.b. Hamilton Spectator)* (2000), 183 D.L.R. (4th) 748 (Ont. C.A.) [politicians quoted].

> *Boyer v. Toronto Life Publishing Company* (2000), 48 O.R. (3d) 383 (S.C.J.) [freelance writer and a source quoted in article].

> *Filion v. Canadian Broadcasting Corporation* (2000), 49 O.R. (3d) 364 (S.C.J.) [non-media defendants].

Hanover Nursing Home Limited v. *London and District Service Workers' Union Local 220*, [1999] O.J. No. 666, (1999) 91 O.T.C. 178 (Gen. Div.) [nursing home employee].

Bhaduria v. *Persaud* (1998), 40 O.R. (3d) 140 (Gen. Div.) [source quoted in newspaper].

McConnell v. *Moll*, [1997] O.J. No. 5371 (Gen. Div.) [school board source].

Cartwright v. *Pettkus*, [1996] O.J. No. 2767 (Gen. Div.) [writer of letter published in newspaper].

Emonts v. *McKeever*, [1992] O.J. 1467 [patron of phone-in radio show].

Proliege Development Corp. and the Tyrren Group Inc. v. *Ron Lenyk Harlequin Enterprises Limited (c.o.b. The Mississauga News), Steve Warburton and Steve Mahoney* (unreported decision of Mr. Justice Fitzpatrick released February 6, 1989) [person interviewed].

Greenpeace Foundation v. *Toronto Sun Publishing Co.* (1989), 69 O.R. (2d) 427 at 429 (H.C.J.) [freelance journalist].

Elliott v. *Freisen* (1982), 37 O.R. (2d) 409 (H.C.J.), aff'd (1984), 45 O.R. (2d) 285 (C.A.) [reporter].

Stuarts Furniture and Appliances et al. v. *No Frills Appliances & T.V. Limited et al.* (1982), 40 O.R. (2d) 52 (H.C.J.) [advertiser].

R.E. Knowles v. *Twentieth Century Publishing Company Limited et al.*, [1939] O.W.N. 403 (H.C.J.) [printer].

Redmond v. *Stacey* (1918), 14 O.W.N. 73 (H.C.) [a source].

It is settled law that section 5(1) of the Ontario *Libel and Slander Act* requires a plaintiff to give the statutory notice of intended action to non-publisher or non-media defendants. In *Watson* v. *Southam Inc. (c.o.b. Hamilton Spectator)* (2000), 189 D.L.R. (4th) 695 (Ont. C.A.), Abella J.A., writing the judgment of the court, stated:

> ¶51 The respondents argue, however, that there appears to be some dispute whether the requirement to give notice in s. 5(1) applies to non-publisher or non-media defendants. In *Knowles* v. *20th Century Publishing Co. Ltd.*, [1939] O.W.N. 403 (H.C.J.), for example, Godfrey J. held at p. 404 that: "all defendants are entitled to notice when the libel is contained in a newspaper."

> ¶52 Cory J.A. in *Grossman*, at p. 501, seemed to suggest that the notice requirement is meant only for publishers, when he said:

The purpose of the notice is to call the attention of the publishers to the alleged libellous matter. When it is received an investigation can be made, and if the publisher deems it appropriate, a correction, retraction or apology can be published. In this way the publisher can avoid or reduce the damages payable for the publication of a libellous statement.

But in *Grossman* there were only media defendants, leaving this case as a doubtful precedent for the conclusion that only media defendants are entitled to notice.

¶53 I see no principled basis for excluding any defendant from the benefit of the notice provision in s. 5(1) of the *Libel and Slander Act*. The purpose of the notice requirement is to give a defendant an independent opportunity to issue a retraction, correction, withdrawal or apology for allegedly defamatory statements, thereby mitigating potential damages. Whether the defendant is a media defendant appears to me to be irrelevant. The opportunity to mitigate damages should be available to all defendants.

¶54 Even as a potentially vicariously liable defendant, the Municipality was entitled to the same statutory protection as any other defendant, and was entitled to notice on its own behalf. No such notice was given. Since the failure to provide notice in a timely manner is an absolute bar, the claim against the Municipality should be dismissed.

In *Siddiqui* v. *Canadian Broadcasting Corp.* (2000), 50 O.R. (3d) 607 (C.A.), the court sustained a lower court order dismissing the libel action against five defendants on the grounds that they had not been served with a statutory notice of intended action prior to the issuance of the statement of claim. Those defendants included non-media individuals employed by a private charity and the manager of a private travel agency, all of whom were interviewed on camera for the CBC's broadcast documentary about the charity. Leave to appeal to the Supreme Court of Canada was refused, [2000] S.C.C.A. No. 664.

Libel plaintiffs who have not served non-media defendants as required by section 5(1) of the *Libel and Slander Act* have argued that the Court of Appeal decision in *Warner* v. *Earp* (1988), 38 O.R. (3d) 138 is authority for the proposition that non-media defendants are not covered by section 5(1). The same panel of the Court of Appeal that decided *Watson* v. *Southam*, above, ruled in *De Heus* v. *Niagara (Region) Police Services Board*, [2001] O.J. No. 4201 (C.A.), per Abella J.A., that:

Warner v. *Earp* (1998), 39 O.R. (3d) 138 (C.A.) does not deal with the notice requirement for non-media defendants and is therefore not inconsistent with this court's decision in *Watson* v. *Southam Inc.* (2000) 189 D.L.R. (4th) 695 (C.A.).

In *St. Elizabeth's Home Society* v. *Hamilton (City)*, [2002] O.J. No. 2690 (S.C.J.), the court noted that *Warner* v. *Earp* was a slander case, and stated at paragraph 8:

> *Warner* was a slander case. Section 5(1) deals with the prerequisites for an action for libel; it has nothing to do with slander.

The Divisional Court concluded that the law was correctly stated in *Watson* v. *Southam Inc.*, stating:

> ¶10 It would be our view that the principle of *stare decisis* is applicable. In that regard, this Court finds that the law in Ontario as to s. 5(1) of the SL Act is that as expressed by Abella J.A. in *Watson*. See the cases at p. 706 of *Watson* (para. 50) where Abella J.A. notes that "the failure to provide notice has been held to constitute an absolute bar to a defamation action." She discussed the policy reasons for the notice requirement being applicable to all defendants, media and non-media at p. 707 (para. 53). We would note as well that while *Brown* at p. 17–92 gives examples of defamation which could reach a large audience, some appear to involve slander as opposed to libel and one deals with the Internet, something of rather recent origin and application which may have therefore not have come to the (amending) attention of the Ontario Legislature. Rather the newspaper and broadcasting aspects can be seen from a policy point of view of addressing those incidents of libel where the potential for widespread dissemination is most apparent in practicality or reality, at least as of the last time the SL Act was looked at by the Ontario Legislature.

> ¶11 We would observe about s. 7 of the SL Act:

>> S. 7 subsection 5(1) and section 6 apply only to newspapers printed and published in Ontario and to broadcasts from a station in Ontario.

> In the context of the SL Act, we would view s. 7 as referring to the geographic location of the media as opposed to it excluding the media if it also is disseminated outside Ontario. In the subject case, the fact that the *Globe and Mail* newspaper is also printed and published outside of Ontario (as well as inside) would not take it outside the purview of s. 5(1). Nor would this fact, in our view, exempt the plaintiff here from giving notice to the defendants in this case.

Courts in Manitoba and Alberta have also held that non-media defendants are entitled to notice when the action is for libel in a newspaper or broadcast.

Borowski v. Hurst and Toronto Star Publishing Corporation (1984), 32 Man. R. (2d) 207 (Q.B.).

Paletta v. Lethbridge Herald Company Limited (1977), 2 Alta. L.R. (2d) 166 (S.C. (T.D.)).

The applicability of Alberta's notice requirement to non-media defendants may nevertheless be open to question. In *Barcan v Zorkin*, [1987] A.J. No. 575 (C.A.), the court concluded that whether the notice provision in then section 14 of the *Defamation* Act applied to certain defendants was an arguable question of fact and law. Speaking for the Court in allowing the plaintiff's appeal from a summary dismissal of his action, Stevenson J.A. stated:

> To conclude that these defendants are entitled to protection provided by the *Defamation Act*, it would be necessary to decide that each defendant was a proprietor or publisher of a newspaper, or an officer, servant or employee thereof. It would be necessary to find that this particular publication was a newspaper and that notice in writing had not been given.

This statement, on its face, appears to conflict with *Palleta*. However, the issue of the applicability of the notice requirements was not explicitly considered by the Court of Queen's Bench or the Court of Appeal, and *Paletta* is not mentioned in either judgment. However, it should also be noted that Alberta's statute contains the following provision for which there is no counterpart in the Ontario *Libel and Slander Act*:

> 12. Sections 13 to 17 [the notice requirement] apply only to actions for defamation against the proprietor or publisher of a newspaper or the owner or operator of a broadcasting station or an officer, servant or employee thereof in respect of defamatory matter published in that newspaper or broadcast from that station.

In earlier decisions in Manitoba and New Brunswick, courts have held that notice provisions do not apply to non-media defendants.

Mazatti v. Acme Products Limited, [1930] 3 W.W.R 43 (Man. Q.B.) [advertiser].

Underwood v. Roach (1908), 39 N.B.R. 27 (C.A.) [letter to the editor].

In *MCF Captial Inc. v. Canadian Broadcasting Corp.*, [2003] M.J. No. 324, 2003 MBQB 205, MacInnes J. held at paragraph 33 that there is no requirement in Manitoba for a libel notice to a defendant who is not the proprietor or publisher of a newspaper; or the owner operator of a broadcasting station; or of an officer, servant, or employee thereof. However, prior Manitoba cases are not mentioned.

In formulating the notice of intended action, a plaintiff should accurately identify the prospective defendants. Nevertheless, if there are misnomers, substantial compliance may be accepted by certain courts.

The Supreme Court of Canada held in *Knott v. Telegram Printing Company*, [1917] 3 W.W.R. 335, that there was substantial compliance where the notice of intended action had been addressed to "the Winnipeg Telegram Printing Company Limited" rather than to "The Telegram Printing Company Limited," the defendant's actual name. England J. stated at page 342:

> It reached the Defendant company and there is not the slightest room for question or doubt that it knew that it was intended for it. It was given the "opportunity to publish a full apology," which is the purpose of the statute to secure. The objection is as trivial as it is technical and to give it effect would be a travesty of justice.

In *Boyer v. Toronto Sun Life Publishing Company* (2000), 48 O.R. (3d) 383 (S.C.J.), Nordheimer J. rejected defence submissions that the notice of intended action must be "directed to" each of the defendants. In that case, the notice was addressed only to the corporate defendant Toronto Life, to the attention of one of the individual defendants, with copies of the letter being supplied for the other individual defendants. In his review of the case law that extended back more than a century, Nordheimer J. noted at paragraph 18:

> There is also nothing in the wording of s. 5(1) which says that the notice must be "directed" to the defendant. It simply requires that notice be given. Here, each of the individual defendants was given notice in one fashion or another of the plaintiff's complaint. Macfarlane and Dewar received their own copies of the letter. Duron received the original of the letter. None of the defendants have suggested that they did not receive notice or were unaware of the complaint of the plaintiff. It is also clear that the purpose of the section, which all of the authorities seem to agree is to provide the opportunity to correct, retract or apologize, was satisfied since a correction or clarification was offered by the solicitors for *Toronto Life*.

Other court decisions where technical objections by defendants have been unsuccessful include:

Charlton v. Albertan Publishing Co., [1944] 2 W.W.R. 225 (Alta. S.C. (T.D.)) [notice addressed to manager of company, not to company itself].

Elliott v. *Freisen* (1982), 37 O.R. (2d) 409 (H.C.J.), aff'd (1984), 45 O.R. (2d) 285 (C.A.), leave to appeal to S.C.C. refused, 3 May 1984 [notice addressed to "The Sudbury Star, Canadian Newspapers Company Limited, attention: John P. Freisen" instead of separate notices to Canadian Newspaper Company Limited and John P. Friesen].

Block v. *Winnipeg Sun* (1989), 59 Man. R. (2d) 302 (Q.B.) [notice given to the solicitor for the newspaper, who was also solicitor for the owner of the newspaper, was sufficient notice to the owner].

Nevertheless, it is recommended that a plaintiff take particular care in addressing his or her notice of intended action. In *Reis Lighting Products and Services* v. *Westcom Radio Group Ltd.*, [1996] M.J. No. 526, 113 Man. R. (2d) 129, the Manitoba Court of Appeal upheld a lower court decision striking out the action against WIC International Communications Ltd. and radio station manager Ralph Warrington. The notice had been sent to "Western Broadcasting Company Ltd" marked to the "attention" of Warrington.

It seems to be clear that notice to a reporter is not notice to the newspaper that employs the reporter.

Carter v. *Standard Limited* (1915), 30 D.L.R. 492 (N.B.S.C.).

10) Considerations Favouring Requirement of Notice to Nonmedia Defendants

It is submitted that there are good reasons for interpreting the statutory notice requirement in the Ontario *Libel and Slander Act* and equivalent provisions in the other provincial statutes as extending to non-media and non-publishing defendants where the defamatory expression is contained in a newspaper or broadcast. These include the following:

i) On principle, the statutory notice requirement should give everyone who may be jointly liable for the defamatory expression an equal opportunity and an equal incentive to correct, retract, or to apologize for the defamatory expression.

ii) Section 5(1) of the Ontario *Libel and Slander Act* speaks of notice to the "defendant," not notice to the proprietor or publisher of the newspaper or to the owner or operator of the broadcasting station. If the legislature had intended to create two classes of defendants for the purposes of section 5(1) — media and non-media — it ought to have expressed such an intention in clear language, particularly where one class would enjoy statutory protection and one would not.

iii)　It may be very difficult to discern the line dividing media defendants from non-media defendants. For example, is the writer of an op-ed piece that appears in a newspaper to be considered a media defendant or a non-media defendant? Would the answer turn on whether the newspaper paid for the op-ed piece? If the writer of an unpaid "op-ed" piece is a media defendant, why should a person who has written a letter to the editor not fall into the same class? What if the letter to the editor or an unpaid op-ed piece is professional journalist? What about the publisher of a newspaper who writes an op-ed piece or a letter to the editor of a publication whose editorials the publisher does not control?

iv)　If service of the statutory notice on a non-media defendant were to result in a decision by that defendant to withdraw and apologize for a defamatory accusation, that might assist the newspaper or broadcaster in assessing whether the circumstances of the case warrant a correction, retraction, or apology by the newspaper or broadcaster. If one objective of the statutory notice requirement is to encourage correction of defamatory mistakes so that damage is minimized, it makes sense to give the original source of the error an incentive to recant at an early opportunity.

v)　Freedom of speech is not restricted to one class of persons either at common law or in the jurisprudence under section 2(b) of the *Canadian Charter of Rights and Freedoms*. The statutory notice provisions are said to be one of libel law's mechanisms for balancing the conflicting rights to protection of reputation and to freedom of expression. It would be anomalous if this balancing mechanism discriminated between large media defendants and private individuals by favouring the former.

vi)　The law discourages a multiplicity of proceedings. In *Thomson v. Lambert*, [1938] 2 D.L.R. 545, the Supreme Court of Canada held that the gist of defamation is the publication of the defamatory matter and all those who participate in publishing and circulating it are liable as joint tortfeasors. The court held that liability for the false publication, whether of publisher, distributor, or vendor, is determinable in one action. Accordingly, a plaintiff who sued and took judgment against the distributors and vendors of a defamatory newspaper was not entitled to bring a subsequent lawsuit over the same defamatory matter against the newspaper's publishers. That would be an abuse of process. To be consistent with *Thomson v. Lambert*, the statutory requirement to serve notice of intended action should motivate a plaintiff to give notice to every defendant who is potentially liable for a newspaper publication or a broadcast, whether they are media or non-media. The plaintiff will not be entitled to bring separate lawsuits against the different classes of defendant. There is no reason to distinguish between the different classes of defendant at the notice stage.

vii) Many newspaper publications and broadcasts constitute an amalgam of expression authored by the media and by the non-media defendants. It will often be impossible for a jury to distinguish between the damages due to the particular part of the defamatory expression originating with the person interviewed, or some other identified or unidentified source, as opposed to the reporter, editor, or commentator who also participated in the publication or broadcast. If defendants might be jointly responsible to the plaintiff for damages caused by such expression, there should be a level playing field for the non-media and media defendants.

viii) It would be anomalous if newspaper publishers and broadcasters, who are usually well-positioned to seek pre-publication legal advice and who are more likely to detect a potential libel exposure, were permitted to enjoy a statutory protection from suit which is not available on similar terms to an individual source or interviewee. It would seem unreasonable that private individuals who have little knowledge or experience with defamation law and are therefore inherently more vulnerable should be deprived of defences available to the more sophisticated joint tortfeasor.

ix) In section 5(1) of the Ontario *Libel and Slander Act*, the notice requirement relates to "libel *in* a newspaper or in a broadcast" [emphasis added], not to libel *by* a newspaper or broadcast. As a simple matter of statutory construction, the conclusion reached by Abella J.A. in *Watson v. Southam Inc. (c.o.b. Hamilton Spectator)* (2000), 189 D.L.R. (4th) 695 (Ont. C.A.) that non-media defendants are covered by section 5(1) is eminently supportable.

x) Media defendants who do not receive a libel notice from the plaintiff might dispose of vital evidence before the non-media defendant is sued by the plaintiff. This evidence might consist of computer transcripts, notes of interviews with the non-media defendant, or audio or video tapes of statements made by the non-media defendant. The recollection of reporters who conducted the interviews with the non-media source may fade long before the non-media defendant realizes there is a need to preserve that evidence.

xi) Non-media defendants would remain vulnerable to libel litigation in Ontario for at least two years after publication. Media defendants, by contrast, benefit from a three-month limitation period, although they are more likely to have libel insurance coverage than an individual source. On this basis, discrimination which favours a commercial news media defendant over a private individual is unintelligible.

11) Pleadings Relating To Notice of Intended Action

It is open to question whether the plaintiff will be strictly limited to pleading in his or her statement of claim the stings of the libel identified in the notice.

Teeluck v. Cadogan Publishing Limited (c.o.b. Miramichi Leader), [1998] N.B.J. No. 454 (H.C.J.)

The plaintiff need not plead in the statement of claim that he or she has complied with the notice requirements of the *Libel and Slander Act*. A condition precedent need not be pleaded — the plaintiff must only set out the necessary and essential elements of the cause of action.

Canadian Plasmapheresis Centres Limited v. Canadian Broadcasting Corporation (1975), 8 O.R. (2d) 55 at 56 (H.C.J.) citing W.B. Williston & R.J. Rolls, *The Law of Civil Procedure* (Toronto: Butterworths, 1970), at 696.

Sentinel-Review Co. v. Robertson Estate, [1928] S.C.R. 258 at 261.

However, a defendant who wishes to defend on the basis of the plaintiff's failure to comply with the notice requirements must expressly plead such non-compliance in the statement of defence.

Elliott v. Freisen (1982), 37 O.R. (2d) 409 (H.C.J.), aff'd (1984) 45 O.R. (2d) 285 (C.A.).

Canadian Plasmapheresis Centres Limited v. Canadian Broadcasting Corporation (1975), 8 O.R. (2d) 55 at 58–59 (H.C.J.).

Sentinel Review Co. v. Robertson Estate,, [1928] S.C.R. 258 at 261–62.

12) Timing of Defence Motion to Dismiss for Non-compliance

A motion seeking to strike out a statement of claim for non-compliance with the notice requirement should be deferred until after the statement of defence has been delivered.

Waugh v. C.B.C. (2000), 224 N.B.R. (2d) 391 (C.A.).

Stark v. Toronto Sun Publishing Corporation (1983), 42 O.R. (2d) 791 at 793 (H.C.J.).

Lear Sales & Investment Corp. v. *F.P. Publications Ltd.*, [1976] A.J. No. 214 (S.C. (T.D.)).

Under the Ontario *Libel and Slander Act*, alleged non-compliance with both the statutory notice of intended action requirements and the limitations periods are properly dealt with as questions of law following the close of the pleadings.

Magnotta Winery Limited v. *Ziraldo* (1995), 25 O.R. (3d) 375 (Gen. Div.).

13) Service of Notice of Intended Action

Alberta, New Brunswick, Newfoundland and Labrador, the Northwest Territories, Nova Scotia, Ontario, Prince Edward Island, and the Yukon all require that the notice be served in the same manner as a statement of claim or an originating process.

In Ontario, section 5(1) of the *Libel and Slander Act* sets out two options for service of a notice on a corporate defendant:

i)   in the same manner as a statement of claim; or

ii) by delivering it to a grown-up person at the chief office of the defendant.

In Ontario, service on all defendants can be effected through the chief office of a corporate defendant publisher assuming there is legitimate reason to believe that there is a connection between the corporate publisher and the individual defendant.

> The delivery of the notices to the offices of the publication may constitute valid service of the notices on the individual defendants.

> *Boyer* v. *Toronto Life Publishing Company* (2000), 48 O.R. (3d) 383 at 385 (S.C.J.).

In *Boyer* the individual defendants asserted they had not been served with the notice required by section 5(1) of the Ontario *Libel and Slander Act* because the purported notice was contained in a letter addressed to the publication *Toronto Life* and the copies for the individual defendants were delivered by courier to the offices of *Toronto Life*. Rejecting the arguments that notice was defective, Nordheimer J. stated at pages 389–90:

> None of the defendants have suggested that they did not receive the notice or were unaware of the complaint of the plaintiff. It is also clear that the purpose of the section, on which all of the authorities seem to agree, is to provide the opportunity to correct, retract or apologize, which was satisfied, since the correction or clarification was offered by the solicitors for *Toronto Life* …

The notices reached the defendants and there is not the slightest room for question or doubt, and they knew that these notices were intended for them.

On the subject of the method of service, Nordheimer J. stated in *Boyer* at pages 390–391:

> It appears to me that there are two possible interpretations of this provision in s. 5(1). One is that only corporate defendants can be served through the second option. The other is that service on all defendants can be effected through the chief office of a corporate defendant publisher assuming there are legitimate reasons to believe that there is a connection between the corporate publisher and the individual defendants. The first interpretation takes the words used literally but results in an extremely technical, and I would say unfair, result. If all of the defendants are entitled to "equal access to the prescriptive shield offered by these sections," as stated by Goodearle J. in *Emonts v. McKeever*, supra, why should those defendants also not all be subject to both manners of service?
>
> The second interpretation of the section would result in the equal application of the section both in terms of its benefits and its obligations. It is also consistent with the effect of s. 8(1) of the Act which states:
>
> > 8(1). No defendant in an action for libel in a newspaper is entitled to the benefit of sections 5 and 6 unless the names of the proprietor and publisher and the address of the publication are stated either at the head of the editorials or on the front page of the newspaper.
>
> There does not seem to be any reason to deny all defendants the protection of ss. 5 and 6 of the Act from the failure of the publisher and proprietor to post their address unless it was intended that the address is one which might be used to give the required notice to all defendants.

Service of the notice on individual employees of a corporate defendant, however, is not service on the corporate defendant.

Watson v. Southam Inc. (c.o.b. Hamilton Spectator) (2000), 189 D.L.R. (4th) 695 at paras. 50–54 (Ont. C.A.).

14) Notice of Intended Action by Candidate for Public Office

Subsection 5(3) of the Ontario *Libel and Slander Act* provides:

> 5(3) This section does not apply to the case of a libel against any candidate for public office unless the retraction of the charge is made in a conspicuous manner at least five days before the election.

In *Merling v. Southam Inc. (c.o.b. Hamilton Spectator)* (2000), 183 D.L.R. (4th) 748 (Ont. C.A.), the court unanimously held that "This section" means subsection 5(2), not subsection 5(1) which concerns the notice of intended action for libel in a newspaper or broadcast. Per McMurtry C.J.O, at paragraphs 33–34:

¶33 If a candidate for public office was excepted from giving notice under s. 5(1) of the Libel and Slander Act then the publisher of the libel could not reasonably have knowledge of any need to publish a retraction. This interpretation defeats the intention of the legislature which was to inform the publisher of any alleged libellous matter so as to afford the publisher an opportunity to retract the material in a timely manner. As stated earlier, there is clearly a strong public interest component in providing the opportunity for a retraction during an election campaign.

¶34 Subsection 5(3) of the Libel and Slander Act clearly contemplates a retraction. A purposive interpretation of s. 5 strongly suggests that such a retraction contemplates the retraction referred to in s. 5(2). [Plaintiff limited to actual damages in certain circumstances.] The phrase "the retraction" in s. 5(3) must refer to the retraction in s. 5(2) or one would expect that the Legislature would have used the phrase "a retraction" instead.

This interpretation by the Ontario Court of Appeal is consistent with the explicit approach taken by the defamation statutes of the other Canadian jurisdictions, none of which give a candidate for public office any special rights in relation to a statutory requirement to serve a notice of intended action. Prior authority in Ontario, now overruled, suggested that a candidate for public office in Ontario was not obliged to serve a notice of intended action unless there was a retraction of the charges made in a conspicuous manner by the newspaper defendant at least five days before the election.

Wilson v. Taylor (1981), 15 C.C.L.T. 34 (Ont. H.C.J.).

15) Media Obligations

Newspapers and broadcasters will lose the benefit of the statutory notice of intended action and special limitation periods if they fail to comply with statutory requirements that they identify their owners and proprietors.

The Ontario *Libel and Slander Act*, for example, states in section 8 as follows:

(1) No defendant in an action for a libel in a newspaper is entitled to the benefit of sections 5 and 6 unless the names of the proprietor and pub-

lisher and the address of publication are stated either at the head of the editorials or on the front page of the newspaper.

(2) The production of a printed copy of a newspaper is admissible in evidence as *prima facie* proof of the publication of the printed copy and of the truth of the statements mentioned in subsection (1).

(3) Where a person, by registered letter containing his address and addressed to a broadcasting station, alleges that a libel against him has been broadcast from the station and requests the name and address of the owner or operator of the station or the names and addresses of the owner and the operator of the station, sections 5 and 6 do not apply with respect to an action by such person against such owner or operator for the alleged libel unless the person whose name and address are so requested delivers the requested information to the first-mentioned person, or mails it by registered letter addressed to him, within ten days from the date on which the first-mentioned registered letter is received at the broadcasting station.

Where a satirical magazine actively strived to preserve anonymity with respect to its proprietor and publisher, it was clearly arguable the magazine defendants would not have recourse to the limitation periods because they did not provide sufficient information pursuant to the requirement in section 8 of the Ontario *Libel and Slander Act*.

> *Hogan v. Great Central Publishing Ltd.* (1994), 16 O.R. (3d) 808 (Gen.Div.), per E. MacDonald J.

Comparable provisions are found in the other provincial statutes which require notice of intended action and stipulate abbreviated limitation periods. They each require that the name of the proprietor and publisher and address of the publication be "stated in a conspicuous place in the newspaper" and that the "names and addresses of the owner or operator of the station and of the officers, servants and employees of the station who were involved in the broadcast in respect of which the action is brought" be provided to the prospective plaintiff upon request.

> Alberta, *Defamation Act*, R.S.A. 2000, c. D-6, s.17.
> Manitoba, *Defamation Act*, R.S.M. 1987, c. D-20, s.18.
> New Brunswick, *Defamation Act*, R.S.N.B. 1973, c. D-5, s.18.
> Newfoundland and Labrador, *Defamation Act*, R.S.N. 1990, c. D-3, s.20 .
> Northwest Territories, *Defamation Act*, R.S.N.W.T. 1988, c. D-1, s.20.
> Nova Scotia, *Defamation Act*, R.S.N.S. 1989, c. 122, s.23.

Prince Edward Island, *Defamation Act*, R.S.P.E.I. 1988, c. D-5, s.19.

Yukon, *Defamation Act*, R.S.Y.T. 1986, c. 41, s.19.

There is no statutory presumption that the newspaper or broadcaster has complied with the statutory ownership notice. However, certain courts do not require strict compliance. Substantial compliance is sufficient.

Dingle v. World Newspapers Companies (1918), 57 S.C.R. 573.

Elliott v. Freisen (1984), 45 O.R. (2d) 285 (C.A.).

Scown v. Herald Publishing Company (1918), 56 S.C.R., 305 at 311.

Pohlman v. Herald Printing Company of Hamilton Limited (1919), 45 O.L.R. 291 [information appeared at foot of editorial page, not at head of editorial page as required by s. 7 of *Libel and Slander Act*, R.S.B.C. 1979, c. 234].

Some publications have nevertheless been found to be noncompliant:

Hermiston v. Robert Axford Holdings Inc. (1994), 120 D.L.R. (4th) 283 (Ont. Div. Ct.) [printing names of proprietor and publisher and address of publisher at bottom of editorial page rather than at head not substantial compliance with s. 8(1) of *Libel and Slander Act*, R.S.O. 1990, C. L.12]

Fulton v. West End Times Ltd. (1998) 45 B.C.L.R. (3d) 288 at 294

16) Interval between Notice and Action

Saskatchewan's *Libel and Slander Act* contains a simple notice requirement. It applies only to newspapers and it does not have a limitation component requiring that notice be given within a fixed period after knowledge of the publication comes to the attention of the plaintiff. Instead, the Act simply requires that notice be given five days before a lawsuit against a daily newspaper and fourteen days before a lawsuit against a weekly.

Libel and Slander Act, R.S.S. 1978, c. L-14, s. 15.

Most of the other provinces and territories also require an interval between notice of intended action and commencement of a libel lawsuit against newspapers and broadcasters. In Alberta, Manitoba, New Brunswick, Newfoundland and Labrador, and Nova Scotia, daily newspapers are entitled to seven days advance notice of a libel lawsuit. In Prince Edward Island and Saskatchewan, daily newspapers are entitled to five days notice. Fourteen days notice to daily newspapers must be given in the Northwest Territories and the Yukon Territory.

Newspapers other than dailies and broadcasters are entitled to fourteen days notice in the following provinces and territories.

Alberta, *Defamation Act*, R.S.A. 1980, c. D-6, s.13(1).
Manitoba, *Defamation Act*, R.S.M. 1987, c. D-20, s.14(1).
New Brunswick, *Defamation Act*, R.S.N.B. 1973, c. D-5, ss.13(1).
Newfoundland and Labrador, *Defamation Act*, R.S.N. 1990, c. D-3, s.16.
Northwest Territories, *Defamation Act*, R.S.N.W.T. 1988, c. D-1, s.15(1).
Nova Scotia, *Defamation Act*, R.S.N.S. 1989, c. 122, s.18(1).
Prince Edward Island, *Defamation Act*, R.S.P.E.I. 1988, c. D-5, s.14(1).
Yukon, *Defamation Act*, R.S.Y.T. 1986, c. 41, s.14(1).

Ontario is the only province that does not have a waiting period between service of the libel notice and commencement of the lawsuit.

B. LIMITATION DEFENCES FOR LIBEL AND SLANDER

Each province and territory has enacted statutes which bar or extinguish the cause of action for defamation after the lapse of a specified period of time.

Except for Alberta, British Columbia, and Manitoba, the defamation statute of each Canadian jurisdiction prescribes a special limitation period for lawsuits against newspapers or broadcasters (or both). In most instances, that limitation period is brief.

If a special limitation period for defamatory expression in a newspaper or broadcast does not apply, the limitation period will be in the general limitation of actions statute of each province.

What follows is a list of the current limitation periods for all defamation lawsuits, media or non-media, commencing with the shortest (three months) and ending with the longest (six years).

1) Three Months

The shortest limitation period is found in Ontario which requires that an action for libel in a newspaper or broadcast be commenced within three months after the defamatory matter "comes to the knowledge" of the person defamed.

Libel and Slander Act, R.S.O. 1990, c.L.12, s.6.

An action for a libel in a newspaper or in a broadcast shall be commenced within three months after the libel has come to the knowledge of the person defamed, but, where such an action is brought within that period, the action may include a claim for any other libel against the plaintiff by the defendant in the same newspaper or the same broadcasting station within a period of one year before the commencement of the action.

It appears that this three month limitation period will continue to apply after the *Limitations Act, 2003*, S.O. 2003 c. 24, Sched. B. came into force in Ontario on 1 January 2004. That statute provides that a

> limitation period set out in or under another Act that applies to a claim to which this Act applies is of no effect unless, (a) the provision establishing it is listed in the Schedule to this Act, or (b) the provision establishing it (i) is in existence on the day this Act comes into force, and (ii) incorporates by reference a provision listed in the Schedule to this Act.

The Schedule to the *Limitations Act, 2002* lists, *inter alia*, *Libel and Slander Act*, section 6 [s.19].

This three-month limitation has an objective component in the sense that actual knowledge on the part of the plaintiff need not be demonstrated by a defendant. The limitation period begins to run once the plaintiff, exercising reasonable diligence, could have known of the libel.

Bhaduria v. Persaud (1998), 40 O.R. (3d) 140 (Gen. Div.).

Larche v. Middleton (1989), 69 O.R. (2d) 400 (Ont. H.C.J.).

Hughes v. Board of Health for the Thunder Bay Health Unit, [1998] O.J. No. 5435 (Gen. Div.).

In *Gracey v. Thomson Newspapers Corp.*, (1991) 82 D.L.R. (4th) 244, the Ontario Court General Division permitted an amendment adding the Canadian Broadcasting Corporation and its reporters to existing libel litigation against Thomson Newspapers, Financial Times, and others, although the three-month limitation period against the CBC defendants had long expired. The CBC had been mistakenly sued in Federal Court where that defamation action had been struck out for lack of jurisdiction. Steele J. held at pages 250–251 that although limitation periods cannot be ignored, special circumstances justified adding new defendants in this case, as there had been no prejudice to the CBC defendants.

An action properly brought within Ontario's three-month limitation period may include a claim for any other libel by the same defendant newspaper or broadcaster within the year prior to the commencement of the lawsuit. An implied requirement, however, is that the plaintiff have served notice of intended action with respect to those other libels.

Frisina v. Southam Press Ltd. (1981), 124 D.L.R. (3d) 340 (Ont. C.A.).

Ontario, *Libel and Slander Act*, R.S.O. 1990, c. L.12, s.6.

Only newspapers printed and published in Ontario or broadcasts from a station in Ontario enjoy the benefit of the three-month limitation period.

Ontario, *Libel and Slander Act*, R.S.O. 1990, c. L12, s.7.

McConnell v. Moll, [1997] O.J. No. 5371 (Gen.Div.).

The three-month limitation period applies not only to the newspaper and broadcaster but also to any other defendant who was entitled to notice of intended action pursuant to section 5(1) of Ontario's *Libel and Slander Act*. This includes sources, interviewees, guests on television and radio programs, advertisers, freelance journalists, and anyone else who contributed to the newspaper publication or broadcast.

Hanover Nursing Home Ltd. v. London and District Service Worker's Union, Local 220 (1999), 91 O.T.C. 178 (Gen. Div.).

See also cases listed above under "Persons Entitled to Notice of Intended Action," section A(9).

2) Four Months

Newfoundland and Labrador prescribes a four-month limitation for an action against the proprietor or publisher of a newspaper, the owner or operator of a broadcasting station, or an officer, servant, or employee of the newspaper or broadcasting station, for defamation contained in the newspaper or broadcast.

Defamation Act, R.S.N. 1990, c. D-3, s.17

17. (1) An action against
(a)   the proprietor or publisher of a newspaper;
(b)   the owner or operator of a broadcasting station; or
(c)   an officer, servant or employee of the newspaper or broadcasting station,
for defamation contained in the newspaper or broadcast from the station shall be started within 4 months after the publication of the defamatory matter came to the notice or knowledge of the person defamed.

(2) An action brought and maintainable for defamation published within the period referred to in subsection (1) may include a claim for another defamation published against the plaintiff by the defendant in the same newspaper or from the same station within a period of 1 year before the start of the action.

On its face, this limitation period does not appear to apply to certain defendants who would be entitled to statutory notice of intended action: for example, interviewees, sources, guests, hotline callers, and advertisers are not mentioned.

As with the Ontario statute, section 2 of the Newfoundland and Labrador *Defamation Act* is subject to the implied requirement that notice of intended action has been given with respect to any earlier libels outside the four month period.

The phrase "after the publication of the defamatory matter came to the notice or knowledge of the person defamed" probably would be held to have an objective component. If that view is correct, the four month limitation period begins to run when the plaintiff could have known of the libel with the exercise of reasonable diligence.

> *Bhaduria* v. *Persaud* (1998), 40 O.R. (3d) 140 (Gen. Div.).

3) Six Months

New Brunswick, the Northwest Territories, Nova Scotia, Prince Edward Island, and the Yukon stipulate a six month limitation period for bringing a libel action against the proprietor or publisher of a newspaper, the owner or operator of a broadcasting station, or any officer, servant, or employee, for defamation contained in the newspaper or broadcast.

> New Brunswick, *Defamation Act*, R.S.N.B. 1973, c. D-5, s.14.
> Northwest Territories, *Defamation Act*, R.S.N.W.T. 1988, c. D-1, s.16.
> Nova Scotia, *Defamation Act*, R.S.N.S. 1989, c. 122, s.19.
> Prince Edward Island, *Defamation Act*, R.S.P.E.I. 1988, c. D-5, s.15.
> Yukon Territory, *Defamation Act*, R.S.Y.T. 1986, c. 41, s.15(1).

The New Brunswick provision, which is virtually identical to the provisions in the Northwest Territories, Nova Scotia, Prince Edward Island, and Yukon legislation, reads as follows in section 14:

> 14   An action against the proprietor or publisher of a newspaper, or the owner or operator of a broadcasting station, or any officer, servant or employee of such newspaper or broadcasting station, for defamation contained in the newspaper or broadcast from the station shall be commenced within six months after the publication of the defamatory matter has come to the notice or knowledge of the person defamed; but an action brought and maintainable for defamation published within that period may include a claim for any other defamation published against the plaintiff by the defendant in the same

newspaper or from the same station within a period of one year before the commencement of the action.

This provision does not, on its face, appear to extend to other persons who might have been entitled to receive notice of intended action, such as interviewees, guests, sources, or callers to radio hotline programs.

In Saskatchewan, an action against a newspaper must be brought within six months after the publication has come to the notice of the person defamed.

Libel and Slander Act, R.S.S. 1978, c. L-14, s.14.

14. An action for libel contained in a newspaper shall be commenced within six months after the publication thereof has come to the notice or knowledge of the person defamed, but where an action is brought and is maintainable for a libel published within that period, the action may include a claim for any other libel published against the plaintiff by the defendant in the same newspaper within a period of two years before the commencement of the action.

An argument that the six month limitation period in section 14 of the Saskatchewan statute runs from the date of damage instead of the date of publication has been rejected.

Reidy v. *Leader Star News Services*, 2001 SKQB 338, [2001] S.J. No. 444 (Q.B.).

In *Dickhoff* v. *Armadale Communications Ltd.*, [1993] S.J. No. 549 (C.A.), the court refused to permit a plaintiff to amend the style of cause to add another newspaper defendant outside the six month statutory limitation period, rejecting the plaintiff's submission that such an order was permitted by section 44(11) of the *Queen's Bench Act*, R.S.S. 1978, c. Q-1, which provided:

44(11) Notwithstanding that a limitation period has expired since the commencement of an action, the court may allow an amendment to the pleadings:

(a) asserting a new claim; or

(b) adding or substituting parties

provided that the claim asserted by the amendment, or by or against the new party, arose out of the same transaction or occurrence as the original claim and the court is satisfied that no party will suffer actual prejudice as a result of the amendment.

The Saskatchewan Court of Appeal held that although the same incidents giving rise to a news story may be reported in separate publications, each publisher's defences may differ because it is the publication that is the essence of a libel. Each publication is separate and leads to separate causes of action. "The story may be the same, but the publication is different."

The six month limitation periods discussed above probably contain an objective component, although there appears to be no case authority on point. If that view is correct, the six month limitation period begins to run when the plaintiff could have known of the libel with the exercise of reasonable diligence.

> *Bhaduria v. Persaud* (1998) 40 O.R. (3d) 140 (Gen. Div.).

4) One Year

In Nova Scotia, an action for slander must be brought within one year after the cause of action arose.

> *Limitation of Actions Act*, R.S.N.S. 1989, c. 258, s.2(1)(a), s.2(1)(e).
>
> 2(1) The actions mentioned in this Section shall be commenced within and not after the times respectively mentioned in such Section, that is to say:
> (a) actions for assault, menace, battery, wounding, imprisonment or slander, within one year after the cause of any such action arose; ...

At common law, a "cause of action" means all facts which give rise to a claim enforceable in an action. Every fact which is material to be proved to entitle the plaintiff to succeed, forms an essential part of a cause of action in tort.

> [T]he cause of action is said to accrue when the latest of the facts essential to the cause of action occurred.
>
> *Abbott-Smith v. Governors of University of Toronto* (1964), 45 D.L.R. (2d) 672 at 693 (N.S.S.C.), citing Geoffrey C. Cheshire, *Private International Law*, 6th ed. (Oxford: Clarendon Press, 1961 at 293; *Halsbury's Laws of England*, 3d ed., vol. 1 (London: Butterworths, 1952–64) at 6–7.

The jurisprudence recognizes two types of slander:

i)   slander which is actionable upon proof of damage;
ii)   slander actionable *per se*, that is to say without proof of damage.

Where defamatory expression is actionable *per se*, it is not necessary for the plaintiff to allege or to prove special damages.

> *Pootlass v. Pootlass* (1999), 63 B.C.L.R. (3d) 305, per Burnyeat J. at para. 13 (S.C.), citing *Allan v. Bushnell T.V. Co. Ltd.*, [1969] 2 O.R. 6 (C.A.); *LeBlanc v. L'Imprimerie Acadienne Ltée*, [1955] 5 D.L.R. 91 (N.B.S.C.).

On the other hand, in an action for slander which is not actionable per se, the plaintiff must allege and prove special damages.

> Pootlass v. Pootlass (1999), *ibid.* at para. 63, citing *Gibson v. McDougall* (1919), 17 O.W.N. 157 (H.C.); *Merkoff v. Pawluk*, [1931] 1 W.W.R. 669 (Alta. S.C. (T.D.)); *Brockley v. Maxwell*, [1949] 1 W.W.R. 1039 (B.C.S.C.); *Mengarelli v. Forrest*, [1972] 3 O.R. 397 (S.C. (Mast.)); *Johnson v. Jolliffe* (1981), 26 B.C.L.R. 176 (S.C.); *Robertson v. Robertson* (1932), 45 B.C.R. 460 (S.C.), *Ratcliffe v. Evans* (1892), 2 Q.B. 524 (C.A.).

> Special damages for the purposes of the law of defamation have been defined as any material or temporal loss which is either a pecuniary loss or is capable of being estimated in money. Special damages are not confined to business loss or loss of employment income. Rather, losses such as the loss of hospitality from friends providing such loss is capable of being estimated in money are also recoverable.

> Pootlass v. Pootlass, above, at para. 65

Slander actionable *per se* includes:

a) The imputation of a criminal offence.

> Pootlass v. Pootlass, above, at para. 13, citing *Mitchell v. Victoria Daily Times (No. 3)*, (1944), 60 B.C.R. 39 (S.C.), *Levi v. Reed* (1881), 6 S.C.R. 482, and *Cook v. Cook* (1875), 36 U.C.Q.B. 553 (Ont. C.A.). *Quaere* whether the crime must be one punishable by imprisonment: *Maher v. K Mart Canada Ltd.* (1990), 84 Nfld. & P.E.I.R. 271 (Nfld. S.C. (T.D.)), citing *Robertson v. Robertson*, [1921] 67 D.L.R. 496 (Alta. S.C. (T.D.)), *Lee v. Jones et al.* (1954), 1 D.L.R. 520 (Man. Q.B.).

b) The imputation that the plaintiff is unfit to practice the trade, business, or profession carried on or held by him or her at the time of publication.

> Viex Events Ltd. v. Abela, [1997] B.C.J. No. 3114 at para. 42 (S.C.).

> Brown v. Cole, [1996] B.C.J. No. 2046 at para. 89 (S.C.), varied (1998), 114 B.C.A.C., leave to appeal to S.C.C. dismissed, [1998] S.C.C.A. 614.

c) The imputation that the plaintiff is suffering from a contagious or infectious disease.

> Floyd v. Hiram Walker and Sons Limited and Duguid, [1957] O.R. 107 (H.C.J.), citing Richard O'Sullivan & Roland G. Brown, *Gatley on Slander*, 4th ed., (London: Sweet & Maxwell, 1953) at 48.

d) The imputation of adultery or unchastity to a woman or girl.

Floyd v. Hiram Walker and Sons Limited and Duguid, ibid.

A cause of action for slander *per se* arises immediately upon publication of the slander. On the other hand, the cause of action for slander which is not actionable *per se* will not arise until the plaintiff has sustained special damage. This distinction requires that a prospective plaintiff give close scrutiny to the nature of the defamatory imputation.

5) Two Years

Effective 1 January 2004, the Ontario limitation period for libel (other than libels governed by section 6 of the *Libel and Slander Act*) and for slander is the basic two year limitation period prescribed by section 4 of the *Limitations Act, 2002*, which reads:

Basic limitation period

4. Unless this Act provides otherwise, a proceeding shall not be commenced in respect of a claim after the second anniversary of the day on which the claim was discovered. 2002 c. 24, Sched. B, s. 4.

Section 5 of the *Limitations Act, 2002* provides:

Discovery

5.(1) A claim is discovered on the earlier of,
  (a) the day on which the person with the claim first knew,
      (i)   that the injury, loss or damage has occurred,
      (ii) that the injury, loss or damage was caused by or contributed to by an act or omission,
      (iii) that the act or omission was that of the person against whom the claim is made, and
      (iv) that, having regard to the nature of the injury, loss or damage, a proceeding would be an appropriate means to seem to remedy it; and
  (b) the day on which a reasonable person with the abilities and in the circumstances of the person with the claim first ought to have known of the matters referred to in clause (a).

Section 15 of the *Limitations Act, 2002* provides that no proceeding shall be commenced in respect of any element after the 15th anniversary of the day on which the act or omission on which the claim is based took place [2002], Sched. B. S. 15(2)].

The *Limitations Act, 2002* enacts substantial changes and prior jurisprudence in Ontario on limitations issues must therefore be considered in this context.

The Ontario limitation period for slander (but not libel) was previously two years. This was found in section 45(1) of the *Limitations Act*, R.S.O. 1990, c. L-15, which states:

> 45. (1) The following actions shall be commenced within and not after the times respectively hereinafter mentioned, …(i) an action upon the case for words, within two years after the words spoken;

a) Jurisprudence under section 45(1) of former *Limitations Act*, R.S.O. 1990, c. L-15

It has been held that the phrase "after the words spoken" imposes a rigid limitation period of two years for bringing a slander action in Ontario. It is immaterial whether the plaintiff learns of the defamatory expression within the two-year limitation period, whether the slander is of the type actionable only on proof of special damage, and if so, whether the only damage occurs more than two years after the words were spoken.

> *Floyd* v. *Hiram Walker & Sons Ltd. and Duguid* (1957), 7 D.L.R. (2d) 167.

> *Murphy* v. *Alexander*, [2001] O.J. No. 5465 at paras. 96–97 (S.C.J.).

6) The Discoverability Principle

The modern judicial approach to limitations periods prescribed by the former *Limitations Act*, R.S.O. 1990, suggested that the two-year limitation period under the Ontario statute for slander is subject to the "discoverability rule" which indicates that a limitation period begins to run when the material facts upon which the cause of action exists have or ought to have been discovered by the exercise of reasonable diligence. This discoverability rule has been held to apply to defamation actions and to delay the running of time in Ontario for an action for slander.

> *Larche* v. *Middleton* (1989), 69 O.R. (2d) 400 (H.C.J.), per Granger J. at 404–5.

> *Strong* v. *M.M.P.*, [1997] O.J. No. 2557, per Granger J. at parass 80–82 (Gen. Div.).

a) Other provinces

In Newfoundland and Labrador, the *Limitations Act*, S.N. 1995, c. L-16.1 provides in section 5 for a two-year limitation period for slander and libel:

> 5. Following the expiration of 2 years after the date on which the right to do so arose, a person shall not bring an action ...
>
> (d) for defamation other than defamation referred to in section 17 of the *Defamation Act.*

This two year limitation period applies to all defamation claims except those against the proprietor or publisher of a newspaper, the owner or operator of a broadcasting station, or an officer, servant, or employee of the newspaper or broadcasting station, for defamation contained in a newspaper or broadcast [see "Six Months" above, section A(3)]. The discoverability rule also applies to the Newfoundland and Labrador two year limitation period.

Similarly, defamation lawsuits in Saskatchewan against defendants other than newspapers are subject to a two-year limitation period prescribed by section 3 of the *Limitation of Actions Act*, R.S.S. 1978, c.L-15 in the following terms:

> 3(1) The following actions shall be commenced within and not after the times respectively hereinafter mentioned: within two years after the cause of action arose;
>
> (c) actions of defamation, whether libel or slander:
>
>   (i) within two years of publication of the libel or the speaking of the slanderous words; or
>
>   (ii) where special damage is the gist of the action within two years after the occurrence of the damage.

This Saskatchewan provision is subject to the discoverability rule. Moreover, the Saskatchewan limitation period for a cause of action for slander which is not actionable *per se* will not begin to run until the plaintiff has incurred special damage.

Alberta, British Columbia, and Manitoba do not have special limitations defences for the news media in their defamation statutes or in their limitations statutes. In each of those provinces, the general limitations statute provides for a two year limitation period with respect to a cause of action for defamation.

Alberta, *Limitation of Actions Act*, R.S.A. 2000, c.L-12, s.51(a).
British Columbia, *Limitation Act*, R.S.B.C. 1996, c.266, s.3 (2)(c).
Manitoba, *Limitations of Actions Act*, R.S.M. 1987, c. L-150, s.2 (1)(c).

The British Columbia provision, contained in section 3(2)(c) of the *Limitation Act*, reads:

3 (2) After the expiration of 2 years after the date on which the right to do so arose a person may not bring any of the following actions: ...
(c) for defamation;

The Manitoba limitation provision, contained in section 2(1) of the *Limitations of Actions Act*, reads:

2(1) The following actions shall be commenced within and not after the times respectively hereinafter mentioned: ...

(c) actions for defamation, within two years of the publication of the defamatory matter, or, where special damage is the gist of the action, within two years after the occurrence of such damage.

The Alberta limitation provision, contained in section 3(1) the *Limitation of Actions Act*, expressly incorporates a discoverability rule and reads:

3(1) Subject to section 11, if a claimant does not seek a remedial order within
(a) 2 years after the date on which the claimant first knew, or in the circumstances ought to have known,
    (i)   that the injury for which the claimant seeks a remedial order had occurred,
    (ii) that the injury was attributable to conduct of the defendant,
    (iii) that the injury, assuming liability on the part of the defendant warrants bringing a proceeding, or
(b) 10 years after the claim arose

whichever period expires first, the defendant, on pleading this Act as a defence, is entitled to immunity from liability in respect of the claim.

The Alberta *Limitations Act* was substantially amended in the 2000 general statute revisions. Alberta decisions concerning the previous defamation limitation in section 51 of the *Limitation of Actions Act*, R.S.A. 1980, c. L-15 must be considered in this context.

New Brunswick (with respect to non-media defendants who do not enjoy the special limitation period under the defamation statute) provides for a two-year limitation period in the following terms in section 4 of the *Limitation of Actions Act*, R.S.N.B. 1973, c. L-8:

> No action for assault, battery, wounding, seduction, imprisonment or defamation shall be commenced but within two years after the cause of action arose.

Prince Edward Island (with respect to non-media defendants who do not enjoy the special limitation period under the defamation statute) similarly provides for a two year limitation period in the following terms in section 2(1) of the *Statute of Limitations*, R.S.P.E.I. 1988, c. S-7:

> 2.(1) The following actions shall be commenced within and not after the times respectively hereinafter mentioned: …
>
> (c) actions of defamation, whether libel or slander, within two years of the publication of the libel or the speaking of the slanderous words or where special damage is the gist of the action, within two years after the occurrence of such damage.

The Prince Edward Island legislation expressly preserves the shorter limitation period against news media defendants in section 2(2) of the *Defamation Act*, R.S.P.E.I. 1988 c. D-5. The statute of limitations provides that the two-year limitation period does not extend to any action "where the time for bringing the action is by statute specially limited."

7) Six Years

In Nova Scotia, an action for libel against defendants who do not enjoy the special protection of the brief limitation periods expressed in the defamation statutes must be brought "within six years after the cause of action arose."

> *Limitation of Actions Act*, R.S.N.S. 1989, c. 258, s.2(1)(a), s.2(1)(e).
>
> 2 (1) The actions mentioned in this Section shall be commenced within and not after the times respectively mentioned in such Section, that is to say: …
>
> (e) … actions for libel … within six years after the cause of any such action arose;

In Ontario, the *Limitations Act, 2002*, S.O. 2002, c. 24 [in force 1 January 2004] has replaced the six year limitation period for libel (other than libels governed by section 6 of the *Libel and Slander Act*) formerly prescribed by section 45(1) of the *Limitation Act*, R.S.O. 1990, c. L-15. Under the 1990 statute, an action for libel is considered to be an "action upon the case" and is therefore subject to the six-year limitation period described in section 45(1):

> (1) The following actions shall be commenced within and not after the times respectively hereinafter mentioned, ...
>
> (g) an action ... upon the case other than for slander, within six years after the cause of action arose...

James v. Stonehocker, [2002] O.J. No. 3204 at para. 20 (S.C.J.).

It has been held that a libel published outside Ontario is subject to the ordinary limitation period for libel and not to the special abbreviated libel limitation period available to the Ontario media (three months) pursuant to that province's *Libel and Slander Act*.

Gouzenko v. Sinnot News Co. Ltd., [1972] 2 O.R. 296, per Wright J. at 300:

> When the Legislature is dealing with claims against newspapers within its jurisdiction, it obviously considers that action must be promptly brought, no doubt in order that it may be promptly disposed of [plaintiff's action dismissed, however, for want of prosecution].

8) Postponement of Limitation Period

In British Columbia, where material facts have been "wilfully concealed," it seems that the running of time for a defamation claim may be postponed until the identity of the defendant is known to the plaintiff and "those facts within [the plaintiff's] means of knowledge are such that a reasonable man ... having taken the appropriate advice ... would regard ... an action" as having "a reasonable prospect of success."

Safty v. Carey (1998), 110 B.C.A.C. 242.

Limitation Act, R.S.B.C. 1996, c. 263, s.6(3)(e).

It seems unlikely that "wilful concealment" could arise with respect to news media libels, except possibly as to the identity of an unnamed source of published information.

Pootlass v. Pootlass (1999), 63 B.C.L.R. (3d) 305, 32 C.P.C. (4th) 70 (S.C.).

Section 6 of the *Limitation Act* of British Columbia, which stipulates that the running of time with respect to the limitation period for "personal injury" may be postponed in certain circumstances, does not apply to a defamation action. The legislature has made separate provision for "defamation" and for "personal injury" in the statute.

Pootlass v. *Pootlass, ibid.*

Zanetti v. *Bonniehon Enterprises Ltd.*, [2003] B.C.J. No. 2162, 2003 BCCA 507, per Mackenzie J.A. for the court at para. 1.

Nevertheless, it appears that the British Columbia Supreme Court has accepted that the common law discoverability rule could apply to delay the running of time in appropriate circumstances.

Pootlass v. *Pootlass*, above, at paras. 54–56.

In New Brunswick, Newfoundland and Labrador, the Northwest Territories, Prince Edward Island, Saskatchewan, and the Yukon, defendants who cannot plead the special limitation periods available to the news media must rely on the ordinary two year limitation period prescribed by the general limitations statutes of those jurisdictions.

New Brunswick, *Limitations of Actions Act*, R.S.N.B. 1973, c. L-8, s.4.

Newfoundland and Labrador, *Limitation of Personal Actions Act*, R.S.N. 1990, c. L-15, s.2(4)(b).

Northwest Territories, *Limitation of Actions Act*, R.S.N.W.T. 1988, c. L-8, s.2(1)(c).

Prince Edward Island, *Statute of Limitations*, R.S.P.E.I. 1988, c. S-7, s.2(1)(c).

Saskatchewan, *Limitation of Actions Act*, R.S.S. 1978, c. L-15, s. 3(1)(c).

Yukon, *Limitation of Actions Act*, R.S.Y.T. 1986, s.2(1)(c).

Each of those limitations statutes (except New Brunswick and Newfoundland and Labrador) also provides, however, that where "special damage is the gist of the action," the two-year limitation period runs from "the occurrence of such damage."

Special damage is the "gist of the action" within the meaning of the limitations statutes of Manitoba, the Northwest Territories, Saskatchewan, Prince Edward Island, and the Yukon if the lawsuit is for slander which is not actionable *per se*.

Floyd v. *Hiram Walker and Sons Limited and Duguid*, [1957] O.R. 107 (H.C.I.)

9) Limitations Law is Substantive

The limitation periods prescribed by the various defamation and limitations statutes will probably be regarded as substantive rather than procedural in nature.

Tolofson v. Jensen, [1994] 3 S.C.R. 1022, (1994), 100 B.C.L.R. (2d) 1.

10) Special Limitation Periods

Libel plaintiffs must also take into account other special limitation periods including those protecting government employees. For example, section 7(1) of the *Public Authorities Protection Act*, R.S.O. 1990, c. P.38 creates a six month limitation period which applies where the defendants have acted within the scope of their statutory or other public duty or authority.

> *Croft v. Durham (Regional Municipality) Police Services Board* (1993), 15 O.R. (3d) 216 (Gen Div.).

> *Brown v. Pembroke (City) Police Services Board*, [2003] O.J. No. 2486 (C.A.) [endorsement].

11) Interlocutory Motion to Dismiss for Missed Limitation Period

A decision striking out an action as statute-barred cannot be sought by a defendant until after a defence has been filed and the issues of fact defined. The application of the limitations statute may depend on disputed findings of fact with respect to when the cause of action arose or the limitation period began to run. After a limitations defence has been raised in the pleadings, its effect may be dealt with by applications for summary relief under the relevant rules of court.

> *Bloomfield v. Rosthern Union Hospital Ambulance Board* (1990), 40 C.P.C. (2d) 38, 82 Sask. R. 310 (C.A.).

12) Internet Libel

A British Columbia court has rejected the proposition that every time some one accesses defamatory expression on the Internet, there is an actionable republication at least in circumstances where the webpage at issue was not modified since the original publication and the entity responsible in law for its contents held the belief the webpage had been shut down. The court reasoned that the interests of the British Columbia plaintiff were adequately protected by the discoverability principle expressed in section 6(4)(a) of the *Limitation Act*, R.S.B.C. 1996, c. 266.

> *Carter v B.C. Federation of Foster Parents Assn.*, [2004] B.C.J. No. 192, 2004 BCSC 137 per Taylor J. at para. 95:

95. In the realm of the Internet there is good reason for the application of s. 6(4)(a) in that a defamed person might be unaware of such comments long after they have been posted to a forum or chat room. But once aware, it is incumbent upon those affected by such comments to take steps to clear their name. They simply cannot let the defamation perpetuate itself without commencing their actions within the requisite time.

CHAPTER SEVEN:

Parties

A. INTRODUCTION

Defamation actions in Canada have been brought by and against individuals, trade unions, charities, trading corporations, professional regulatory bodies such as the College of Physicians and Surgeons, and government institutions such as municipalities, separate school boards, and police services boards.

This chapter provides a brief discussion of the question of legal capacity to sue or be sued for defamation. The law on this subject varies from province to province in part because of differences in legislation and in part because courts in different jurisdictions have reached different conclusions. It is impossible to address every nuance in this chapter. Prudent libel litigants and their legal counsel will closely study the law in their particular jurisdiction.

The issues addressed in this chapter overlap to some degree with issues discussed in Chapter 13, "Identification of the Plaintiff", Chapter 14, "Publication and Republication" and Chapter 30, "Damages."

B. STATUS

The status and immunity of defamation litigants are in large measure determined by the legal principles that apply to other tort claims.

An entity has the status to sue or be sued if it is recognized under the relevant statutory or common law as a natural or statutory person. A "natural person" is a living being, generally required to be of full age and mental competence, but it also includes alien citizens, nonresidents, convicts and accused persons, and in a representative capacity, mentally incompetent persons and infants. "Statutory" persons are nonliving entities recognized by law as possessing legal personalities separate and apart from their constituent members.

> *The International Assn. of Science and Technology for Development* v. *Hamza* (1995), 28 Alta. L.R. (3d) 125, per Conrad J.A. at 131 (C.A.):
>
> > ... In Alberta, corporations are deemed legal persons by virtue of s. 15(1) of the *Alberta Business Corporations Act*, S.A. 1981 c. B-15, which reads:
> >
> > > 15(1) A corporation has the capacity and, subject to this Act, the rights, powers and privileges of a natural person.
> >
> > Societies duly registered pursuant to the *Societies Act*, R.S.A. 1980, c. S-18, are deemed to be corporations and are thus granted the status of a statutory person pursuant to s. 10 of that Act which reads:
> >
> > > 10. From the date of the certificate of incorporation, the subscribers to the application and the other persons that from time to time become members of the society are a corporation and have all the powers, rights, and immunities vested by law in a corporation.

The Crown (federal and provincial) is also a statutorily recognized juridical person, as are foreign sovereigns and states.

> *The International Assn. of Science and Technology for Development* v. *Hamza, ibid.*

An office which is a creature of convention (not statute) cannot be sued. This would include the office of a provincial Premier. Accordingly, defamation plaintiffs should take care when drafting their pleadings to ensure that individual defendants are appropriately described in the style of cause.

> *The International Assn. of Science and Technology for Development* v. *Hamza, ibid.*, citing *Reference re Amendment of the Constitution of Canada (Nos. 1, 2, and 3)*, [1981] 1 S.C.R. 753, *R & W Such Holdings Ltd.* (1991), 126 A.R. 16 (Q.B.).

1) Deceased Persons

At common law, an action in tort does not survive an individual's death. No action in defamation could be brought on behalf of a deceased person. Accordingly, a defamation action by an individual could only be brought or maintained during his or her lifetime.

Allan Estate v. *Co-operators Life Insurance Co.*, [1999] 8 W.W.R. 328 per Lambert J.A. at para. 35 (B.C.C.A.).

George v. *Harris* (2001), 204 D.L.R. (4th) 218, per Epstein J. at para. 20 (Ont. S.C.J.), citing *Chamberlain* v *Williamson* (1814), 2 M.&S. 408 (Eng. K.B.).

Davie Estate v. *Yukon Territory Commissioner*, [1993] Y.J. No. 74 per Meredith J. at para. 10 (S.C.):

> I hold that damages for defamation do not survive the death of Mr. Davie and are not recoverable by his estate. For this reason alone, the defamation proceedings must be dismissed.

Small v. *Globe Printing Co.*, [1940] 2 D.L.R. 670 per Rose C.J.H.C. at 671 (Ont. S.C.J.) [plaintiff sued over defamation of deceased brother and deceased sister, claim dismissed].

This common law position has been partially modified by the enactment in most provinces of "survival of actions" legislation; however, such legislation generally does not provide for the survival of defamation claims.

Davie Estate v. *Yukon Territory Commissioner*, above, where Meredith J., in dismissing a defamation lawsuit, considered and rejected the argument that general or aggravated damages for defamation constituted a "pecuniary loss" within the meaning of section 5 of the *Survival of Actions Act*, R.S.Y. 1986, c. 166, which provides:

> Where a cause of action survives for the benefit of the estate of a deceased person, only damages that have resulted in actual pecuniary loss to the deceased person or the estate are recoverable and, without restricting the generality of the foregoing, the damages recoverable shall not include punitive or exemplary damages or damages for loss of expectation of life, for pain and suffering or for physical disfigurement.

Generally, the legislation specifically excludes libel and slander actions. This is the case in Ontario, where the *Trustee Act*, R.S.O. 1990, c. T.23, s. 38 provides in part:

> 38(1) Except in cases of libel and slander, the executor or administrator of any deceased person may maintain an action for all torts or injuries to the person or to the property of the deceased in the same manner and with the same rights and remedies as the deceased would, if living, have been entitled to do, and the damages when recovered shall form part of the personal estate of the deceased ... .

(2) Except in cases of libel or slander, if a deceased person committed or is by law liable for a wrong to another in respect of his or her person or to another person's property, the person wronged may maintain an action against the executor or administrator of the person who committed or is by law liable for the wrong.

Similar exclusions are contained in the legislation of the Northwest Territories, British Columbia, Alberta, Saskatchewan, Manitoba, and Newfoundland and Labrador.

Trustee Act, R.S.N.W.T. 1988, c. T-8, s.31.(1) ["except in the case of libel and slander"].

Estate Administration Act, R.S.B.C. 1996, c. 122, ss.59–61.

The Trustee Act, R.S.A. 2000, c. s. 32.

Survival of Actions Act, S.S. 1990–91.

Trustee Act, R.S.S. 1978, c. T-23, s.58.

The Trustee Act, R.S.M. 1987, c. T160, s.53.

Survival of Actions Act, R.S.N. 1990, c.-S32, ss.3, 11(a).

The survival of actions legislation in New Brunswick, Nova Scotia, and Prince Edward Island does not exclude libel or slander claims. The statutes provide that all causes of action subsisting against or vested in the deceased survive.

Survival of Actions Act, R.S.N.B. 1969, c. S-18, ss.1–3

Survival of Actions Act, R.S.N.S. 1989, c. 453, ss.2–4 [excludes cause of action for adultery or inducing spouse to leave or remain apart from spouse].

Survival of Actions Act, R.S.P.E.I. 1988, c. S-11, ss.1–4

General damages for presumed injury to reputation are not recoverable, however, under the New Brunswick, Nova Scotia, and Prince Edward Island legislation. Only damages that have resulted in actual pecuniary loss to the deceased or to the estate are recoverable. Under the New Brunswick statute, where the death occurred after January 1, 1993, "the damages recoverable may include punitive or exemplary damages in appropriate cases."

Survival of Actions Act, R.S.N.B., c. S-18, s.5.

Survival of Actions Act, R.S.N.S. 1989, c. 453, s.4.

Survival of Actions Act, R.S.P.E.I. 1988, c. S-11, s.5.

The courts have generally resisted efforts by family members to circumvent the common law position by claiming damages to themselves arising from defamation of deceased relatives.

Small v. Globe Printing Co., [1940] 2 D.L.R. 670, per Rose C.J.H.C. at 671 (Ont. H.C.J.) [plaintiff sued over defamation of deceased brother and deceased sister, claim dismissed].

Froese v. Canada Safeway Ltd., [1994] A.J. No. 1215, per Master Quinn at paras. 13, 15 (Q.B.):

13. In the present case neither Kenneth Froese or Kelsey Froese allege they have physical symptoms or that they have acquired a recognizable psychiatric illness as a result of the alleged defamation of Betty Froese. They complain of mental anguish, embarrassment and loss of financial and emotional support. Under the present state of the law it seems clear that such claims are not compensable ... .

15. As far as I can ascertain from the cases I have looked at and the cases reviewed in Linden I do not discern any trend in recent decisions suggesting the law is moving toward supporting claims by family members where another member of the family has been defamed ... .

2) Bankrupts

An undischarged bankrupt has status to bring a personal action for damages for defamation. The damages recovered in such an action are not vested in the bankruptcy trustee. The bankrupt's defamation claim is not affected by section 71 of the *Bankruptcy and Insolvency Act*, R.S.C. 1985, c. B-3.

Cherry v. Ivey (1982), 136 D.L.R. (3d) 381 [claim for slander] per Southey J. at 383–84 (Ont. H.C.J.), adopting *Wilson v. United Counties Bank, Ltd.*, [1920] A.C. 102 (H.L. Eng.), and approving *Egan v. Grayson* (1956), 8 D.L.R. (2d) 125 [claim for malicious prosecution] where McBride J. sitting in Bankruptcy stated at 128 (Alta. S.C. (T.D.)):

... [A]ny right of action for injury to his character and reputation remains vested in the bankrupt and does not pass to the trustee; the bankrupt may sue for damages for such injury in his own name, and if an award is made, it is purely personal to him and he keeps the amount awarded and the trustee cannot intercept it.

Re Holley (1986), 26 D.L.R. (4th) 230 [wrongful dismissal, mental distress] per Goodman J.A. for the Court at 242–45 (Ont. C.A.), approving *Cherry v. Ivey* and *Egan v. Grayson*, above.

Wallace v. *United Grain Growers Ltd. (c.o.b. Public Press)*, [1995] 9 W.W.R. 153 (Man. C.A.), varied, [1997] 3 S.C.R. 701 per Iacobucci J. (Lamer C.J. and Sopinka, Gonthier, Cory, and Major JJ. concurring) at para. 38:

> 38 The parties agreed that the claim for mental distress, loss of reputation and punitive damages is one that is personal in nature. Such a cause of action does not become the property of the trustee in bankruptcy and thus may be pursued by Wallace in his own right: *Re Holley* (1986), 59 C.B.R. (N.S.) 17 (Ont. C.A.).

If the defendant is bankrupt, the defamation plaintiff must address issues arising from section 69(3)(1) of the *Bankruptcy and Insolvency Act*, R.S.C. 1985, c. B-3 which provides:

> 69.(3)(1) Subject to subsection (2) and Sections 69.4 and 69.5, on the bankruptcy of any debtor, no creditor has any remedy against the debtor of the debtor's property, or shall commence or continue any action, execution or other proceedings, for the recovery of the claim provable in bankruptcy, until the trustee has been discharged.

It has been held that section 69(3)(1), applied in the context of Rule 11.01 of the Ontario *Rules of Court*, requires an Ontario court to stay defamation proceedings against a bankrupt until an "order to continue" the proceeding against the trustee in bankruptcy has been obtained and served. Such an "order to continue" may be obtained *nunc pro tunc*.

Murphy v. *Alexander*, [2001] O.T.C. 969, per Belleghem J. at paras. 100–5 (S.C.J.).

A defamation plaintiff is a creditor with a contingent claim against the bankrupt.

Murphy v. *Alexander*, *ibid.* at para. 103

Although an Ontario court is obligated under Rule 11.01 to stay the action until a motion is made to bankruptcy court once the *Rules* have been complied with, it has been held that the Ontario court may nevertheless make findings of fact which "may be of assistance to the Bankruptcy Court subsequently dealing with the issue of whether [the plaintiff's] claim is discharged upon [the defendant's] discharge or whether it remains a live issue between [the plaintiff and the defendant]." On this premise, the Ontario Superior Court of Justice in one case assessed not only the issue of liability but also the damages for which the bankrupt defendant would be liable to the plaintiff.

Murphy v. *Alexander, ibid.* at para. 106:

> Neither counsel referred me to a case which precludes me from making the findings of fact which may be helpful to the parties in determining whether, and if so how, to proceed. I have made a finding that [the bankrupt defendant] actionably defamed [the plaintiff] as a result of which [the plaintiff] sustained damages.

[Belleghem J. assessed damages at paras. 110–49.]

The bankrupt status of a defamation plaintiff may lead to an order that he or she post security for costs.

Kuntz v. *Darity*, [1989] B.C.J. No. 435 (C.A.) where Esson J.A., after referring with apparent approval to *Re Holley*, above, stated:

> Nevertheless, the fact of bankruptcy is one which has to be taken into consideration in deciding what is fair between these parties. It seems to me that, if the matter were to be allowed to go further, it would likely be necessary to require security for costs to be put up in some way because the position of an undischarged bankrupt is different from that of others.

3) Partners

There is very little Canadian jurisprudence on this subject. In an annotation to a reported decision nearly a century ago, it was suggested the both members of a two-member partnership could not be sued for a slander uttered by only one of the partners unless the other partner instructed him to utter it; i.e. the other partner desired and intended the publication.

Messervey v. *Simpson* (1912), 1 D.L.R. 532, per Robson J. at 533 (Man. K.B.), Annotation pp. 533–34.

In England, there is more recent authority which suggests that the question of liability for defamatory expression should involve an examination of the relevant legislation governing the rights and liabilities of partners.

Meekins v. *Henson*, [1964] 1 Q.B. 472, per Winn J. at 476 (Q.B.).

In British Columbia, the relevant legislation is the *Partnership Act*, R.S.B.C. 1996, c. 348, which provides in section 12:

Liability of firm

12 If, by any wrongful act or omission of any partner acting in the ordinary course of the business of the firm or with the authority of his or her part-

ners, loss or injury is caused to any person who is not a partner in the firm or any penalty is incurred, the firm is liable for that loss, injury or penalty to the same extent as the partner so acting or omitting to act.

It has been held, in the context of a defamation claim, that wording very similar to section 12 of the British Columbia *Partnership Act* which is found in section 10 of the *English Partnership Act, 1890*, equates the position of a partner in those respects with that of an employer or a principal. It deals only with such secondary liability.

Meekins v. Henson, ibid. at 477:

> Since no partner is the servant or employee of any other partner, or of the partnership, the ordinary doctrine of respondeat superior would not apply to raise such liability in the other partners as I have been speaking of. This provision produces, as I see it, a necessary equation of members of a partnership firm with employers for this purpose.

It has been suggested that liability may also arise independently of the statute, however, where a partner becomes actively involved in the publication of the defamatory expression, albeit the expression is directly published by another partner:

i)   Where the partners of the firm collectively decide that defamatory expression should be published; or

ii)   Where information is given by one partner to another in such terms or by such account that the first partner should forsee that the second partner would publish that information.

Meekins v. Henson, ibid. at 478

Where a publication for which each partner is responsible occurs on an occasion of qualified privilege, however, the malice of one partner does not taint the others.

Meekins v. Henson, ibid. at 480, approved on this point: *Egger v. Viscount Chelmsford*, [1965] 1 Q.B. 248, per Lord Denning at 263 (C.A.):

> The other cases are those where you have a group of persons, such as trustees or partners, who entrust one of themselves or their secretary with the writing of a letter. The occasion is privileged. One of the group is actuated by malice. The others are not. In such cases it has been held that each innocent member of the group is entitled to rely on the defence of qualified privilege, without being infected by the malice of the others.

If a partnership is defamed, all of the partners may sue for defamation. It has been held that if the partnership suffers damages because of defamatory expression directed at one of the partners, the firm is entitled to sue for defamation.

Le Fanu v. Malcomson (1848), 1 H.L. Cas. 637 at 669 (H.L. (Eng.).

Forster v. Lawson (1826), 3 Bing. 452.

4) Unincorporated Associations

An unincorporated association, other than a partnership, has no legal personality and therefore cannot sue or be sued in its own name for defamation.

Comeau v. Fundy Group Publications Ltd. (1981), 24 C.P.C. 251, per MacIntosh J. at paras. 6–14 (N.S.S.C. (T.D.)), adopting *Taff Vale Ry. Co.* v. *Amalg. Soc. of Ry. Servants*, [1901] A.C. 429 (H.L.), and citing *Halsbury's Laws of England* (4th ed), Vol. 28 at p. 18, Williston and Rolls, *Law of Civil Procedure*, Vol. 1 at p. 209, P.F. Carter-Ruck, *Libel and Slander* (1972) at 92, *Mercantile Marine Service Assn.* v. *Toms*, [1916] 2 K.B. 243 (C.A.) and *Hardie & Lane* v. *Chiltern*, [1928] 1 K.B. 663 (C.A.)

It has been held in Ontario that an unincorporated church is not an entity or person in law except to the extent of being able, through its trustees, to hold land and to sue and be sued in regard to its interest in such land by virtue of the *Religious Organizations' Lands Act*, R.S.O. 1980, c. 448. Accordingly, having no legal personality for any other purpose, the church could not sue for defamation.

Campbell v. Toronto Star Newspapers Ltd. (1990), 73 D.L.R. (4th) 190, per O'Leary J. for the Court at 192 (Ont. Div. Ct.).

The action for defamation must therefore be confined to the individuals who were responsible in law for the publication complained of. See Chapter 14, "Publication and Republication," section F, "Joint Liability."

5) For-profit Corporations

An incorporated business which provides goods or services has the status to sue for defamation.

Hiltz and Seamone Co. v. *Nova Scotia (Attorney General)* (1997), 164 N.S.R. (2d) 161 (S.C.), aff'd, [1999] 172 D.L.R. (4th) 488 (N.S.C.A.).

Ascot Holdings Ltd. v. *Wilkie* (1993), 49 C.P.R. (3d) 188 (B.C.S.C.).

Walker v. *CFTO Ltd.* (1987), 37 D.L.R. (4th) 224, per Robins J.A. for the Court at 233 (Ont. C.A.).

South Hetton Coal Co. Ltd. v. *North-Eastern News Ass'n Ltd.*, [1893] 1 Q.B. 133 (C.A.), approved *Derbyshire County Council* v. *Herald and Times Newspapers Ltd.*, [1993] A.C. 534 (H.L. (Eng.)).

McDonald's Corp. v. *Steel*, [1999] E.W.J. No. 2173, per Lord Justice Pill for the court at paras. 39–87 (Eng. C.A.).

A corporation also has the status to be named as a defendant in a defamation action and held liable in damages — either vicariously for the acts of its officers, employees, or agents, or in its own right as the publisher of defamatory expression.

Universal Weld Overlays Inc. v. *Shaben*, 2001 ABQB 1009 [defendant corporations Capitan Welding Technologies Inc. and Capitan Overlay Technologies Inc. ordered to pay $130,000 damages to plaintiffs].

Myers v. *Canadian Broadcasting Corp.* (2001), 6 C.C.L.T. (3d) 112 (Ont. C.A.), leave to appeal to S.C.C. refused, [2001] S.C.C.A. No. 433 [defendant corporation ordered to pay $350,000 damages].

Leenen v. *Canadian Broadcasting Corporation* (2001), 54 O.R. (3d) 612 (Ont. C.A.), leave to appeal to S.C.C. refused, [2001] S.C.C.A. No. 432 [defendant corporation ordered to pay $950,000 damages].

Fedele v. *Windsor Teachers Credit Union Ltd.*, [2000] O.J. No. 2755 (S.C.J.) [defendant credit union ordered to pay $15,000 damages].

Musgrave v. *Levesque Securities Inc.*, [2000] 50 C.C.E.L. (2d) 59 (N.S.S.C.) [damages of $20,000 assessed in favour of plaintiff].

Slack v. *Ad-Rite Associates Ltd.* (1998), 79 O.T.C. 46 (Gen. Div.) [damages of $1,000 payable by defendant].

Norman v. *Westcomm International Sharing Corp.* (1997), 46 O.T.C. 321 (Gen. Div.) [defendant ordered to pay damages in excess of $200,000].

Capitanescu v. *Universal Weld Overlays Inc.*, [1997] 10 W.W.R. 666 (Alta. Q.B.) [defendant ordered to pay $55,000 damages].

See the also the many other cases cited elsewhere in this book which involve corporations as defamation litigants, including Chapter 30, "Damages", "Corporate Damages."

The cases discussed in the Damages chapter support the principle that a corporation is not entitled to damages which can only be sustained by an individual, such as aggravated damages for hurt feelings.

a) No Corporate Veil

Individuals who publish defamatory expression are not protected by a corporate veil.

> *Lasik Vision Canada Inc.* v. *TLC Vancouver Optometric Group Inc.* (1999), 37 C.P.C. (4th) 380 per Macaulay J. at para. 25 (B.C.S.C.), citing, *inter alia, Gatley on Libel and Slander*, 9th ed., by P. Milmo & W.V.H. Rogers (London: Sweet & Maxwell, 1998) at 198.

The principle that a corporate employer may be held vicariously liable for defamatory expression published by an officer, director or employee does not relieve the individual tortfeasor of liability.

> *Decock* v. *Alberta* (2000), 186 D.L.R. (4th) 265 (Alta. C.A.) per Russell J.A. (Sulatycky J.A. concurring) at paras. 2, 22 [leave to appeal to S.C.C. granted 19 June 2000, appeal discontinued 17 January 2001, [2000] S.C.C.A. No. 301] [a case involving a claim in tort for negligence against Alberta Premier Ralph Klein and Alberta Health Minister Shirley McClellan]. Russell J.A. cites, *inter alia*, Ghislain Otis, "Personal Liability of Public Officials for Constitutional Wrongdoing: A Neglected Issue of Charter Application," (1996) 24 Man. L.J. 23 at 26–27, and *George* v. *Harris*, [1999] O.J. No. 639 at para. 33 (Gen. Div.), endorsed by the Ontario Supreme Court of Justice, Divisional Court at [1999] O.J. No. 3011, and states at 186 D.L.R. (4th) paras. 22, 24:
>
> > 22. It is a well-established principle of tort law that liability is firstly, personal. … No matter the role of the tortfeasor, liability will always fall "first and foremost" personally upon that individual. …
> >
> > 24. This principle of individual responsibility militates in favour of naming defendants personally. After all, it is the person who is alleged to have committed the tort. That said, since the function conferred or performed at the time of the commission of the alleged tort is essential to the determination of whether the Crown will also be liable, the official or office should be readily identified in the body of the pleadings.

6) Not-for-profit Organizations

Organizations with a charitable purpose which have been incorporated as societies or companies under provincial or federal legislation may sue or be sued for defamation.

Planned Parenthood Newfoundland/Labrador v. *Fedorik, et al.* (1982), 135 D.L.R. (3d) 714 (Nfld. S.C.T.D.) [plaintiff operated a birth control clinic, pre-natal and post-natal support groups, library, pregnancy testing, speaker's bureau, assistance in matters concerning human sexuality].

Care Canada v. *Canadian Broadcasting Corporation* (1999), 175 D.L.R. (4th) 743 (Ont. Div. Ct.).

Hunger Project v. *Council on Mind Abuse (C.O.M.A.) Inc.* (1995), 22 O.R. (3d) 29, per Macdonald J. at 39 (Gen. Div.):

> ... [A] corporation does have a business or charitable reputation ... Vindication of the plaintiff's reputation as a charitable organization was an important part of my damages award.

Chinese Empire Reform Association v. *Chinese Daily Newspaper Publishing Co.* (1907), 13 B.C.R. 141 per Morrison J. at 142 (C.A.):

> A non-trading corporation has the right to acquire property which may be the source of income or revenue. And the transaction of the business incidental thereto creates a reputation, rights and interests, in no essential respects different from that of an individual or a trading cor-poration. They may be enhanced or destroyed.

St. Michael's Extended Care Society v. *Frost*, [1994] 6 W.W.R. 718 (Alta. Q.B.) where Cawsey J. states at para. 30:

> St. Michael's is a not-for-profit body society operating a nursing home, auxiliary hospital, and senior's lodge in northeast Edmonton. It relies extensively on government and public funding to carry on its opera-tions and it has a reputation to protect. The Society's reputation for honesty, integrity, fairness and decency must of necessity play an important role in the performance of its duties and responsibilities. Defamation reflecting on its reputation would interfere with the per-formance of the Society's duties and responsibilities and would act to deter people from taking part in the Society's activities. It could also hinder the society in its efforts to raise money, both from government and private sources.

If a religious organization is incorporated it may sue or be sued for defamation.

Church of Scientology of Toronto v. *Globe & Mail Ltd. et al.* (1978), 84 D.L.R. (3d) 239 per Cory J. at 241 (Ont. H.C.J.):

Then authorities lead one to the conclusion that there can be no doubt of the right of a non-profit corporation to bring an action for libel or slander without proof of special damages which would affect it in its property or financial position or in the nature of its trade or calling. Where the trade or calling as here is one of "religion" the scope for injury in the trade or calling may be very broad indeed.

Rexdale Singh Sabha Religious Centre v. *Nagara Ltd. (c.o.b. Nagara Punjabi Weekly Newspaper)*, [2002] O.J. No. 2232 (S.C.J.) [plaintiff awarded $40,000 damages against corporate defendant].

7) Labour Unions

As a result of the constitutional division of legislative authority between the federal and provincial governments, labour relations are principally within the jurisdiction of the provinces. Pursuant to that jurisdiction, each province has enacted legislation governing collective bargaining and defining the legal status of unions.

Amalgamated Transit Union, Local 1374 v. *Independent Canadian Transit Union*, (1998), 63 B.C.L.R. (3d) 335, per Taylor J. at para. 21 (S.C.).

Constitution Act, 1867, ss. 92(13), 92(16).

Differences in provincial legislation and caselaw mean that whether or not a Canadian union has the legal capacity to sue or be sued for defamation depends on the jurisdiction where the suit is to be brought or defended.

The question of union status was reviewed in 2002 by the Supreme Court of Canada, where Iacobucci J. for the Court stated at para. 46:

[T]he world of labour relations in Canada has evolved considerably since the decision of this Court in *Orchard* v. *Tunney* [[1957] S.C.R. 436]. We now have a sophisticated statutory regime under which trade unions are recognized as entities with significant rights and obligations. As part of this gradual evolution the view has emerged that, by conferring these rights and obligations on trade unions, legislatures have intended, absent express legislative provisions to the contrary, to bestow on these entities the legal status to sue and be sued in their own name. As such, unions are legal entities at least for the purpose of discharging their function and performing their role in the field of labour relations. It follows from this that, in such a proceeding, a union may be held liable to the extent of its own assets.

Berry v. *Pulley*, [2002] S.C.J. No. 41, 2002 SCC 40 [group of pilots suing another group of pilots who were members of the same union].

This decision of the Supreme Court of Canada may have implications for the continued validity of certain provincial case law restrictions on the capacity of unions to sue or be sued for defamation in some Canadian jurisdictions.

A trade union with corporate status may sue and be sued in Nova Scotia. The same is true in Newfoundland and Labrador.

> *Comeau* v. *Fundy Group Publications Ltd.* (1981), 24 C.P.C. 251, per MacIntosh J. at para. 7 (N.S.S.C.(T.D.)), approving *O'Laughlin* v. *Halifax Longshoremen's Assn.* (1972), 3 N.S.R. (2d) 766 (S.C. (A.D.)), applying the provisions of the *Trade Union Act,* 1972 (Nova Scotia), c. 19.

> *United Food and Commercial Workers, Local 1252* v. *Cashin* (2002), 217 D.L.R. (4th) 620, per Roberts J.A. (Welsh J.A. concurring) at para. 109 (Nfld. C.A.).

If an umbrella labour organization has no corporate status under Nova Scotia legislation, but is merely an organization of trade unions with such status, it does not have the capacity to sue or be sued for defamation in Nova Scotia.

> *Comeau* v. *Fundy Group Publications Ltd.,* above, at para. 14 approving *O'Laughlin* v. *Halifax Longshoremen's Assn.,* above.

In British Columbia, unions have the status to sue in their own name for defamation despite the absence of a specific foundation for such a lawsuit within the *Labour Relations Code,* R.S.B.C. 1996, c. 244.

> *Re International Assn. of Bridge, Structural and Ornamental and Reinforcing Ironworkers (Local 97) and Campbell* (1997), 152 D.L.R. (4th) 547, per Macdonald J. at paras. 13–15 (B.C.S.C.):

> 13. I deal first with the "no status to sue" argument raised by Kieran and the Province [newspaper]. That argument arises out of the wording of s. 154 of the *Labour Relations Code,* S.B.C. ch 82, which provides that every trade union is a legal entity "for the purposes of the Code". Those purposes are listed in s. 2 of the Code, and do not include the maintenance of a suit for defamation. Since the plaintiff's capacity to do the things specifically authorized by the Code (e.g. collective bargaining) has not been damaged, these defendants argue that Local 97's claim must fail.

> 14. I reject that argument, and adopt the reasoning in *National Union of General and Municipal Workers* v. *Gillian and others,* [1946] 1 K.B. 81 (C.A.), which held that a trade union can sue in tort and maintain an action for defamation.

... if the persona juridicae is liable to be sued for infringing the rights of others, it must equally be able to sue to vindicate its own right (at pps. 86–7)

I can see no ground for excluding the action of defamation ...no reason why ... a trade union should be treated differently in law from a company ... (at p. 87)

A trade union ... stands in the same position. It, too, has its reputation. Why should it not be protected? (at p. 88)

See also *Pulp & Paper Workers of Canada* v. *Int. Brotherhood of Pulp, Sulphite and Paper Mill Workers* (1973), 37 D.L.R. (3d) 687 (B.C.S.C.), where the issue was not the status of the plaintiff union as a *persona juridica* but whether to succeed in a defamation lawsuit, a union must prove that the defamatory expression injuriously affected its property or financial position. Rae J. held at pages 702–75 that the union could succeed if it showed that it was defamed in the way of its business:

It is clear ... that the plaintiff trade union can maintain in its own name an action for libel in respect of words which tend to affect it injuriously in its financial position or in relation to its business. A lessening of subscriptions is such an injury. And where the words are calculated to injure the plaintiff's reputation in relation to its trade or business, the plaintiff is entitled to recover without proof of special damage: see *D. & L. Caterers, Ltd. et al* v. *D'Ajou*, [1945] 1 K.B. 363, see also the *South Hetton Coal* case, *supra*, at p. 139.

Unions also have the capacity to sue or be sued for defamation in Alberta.

Amalgamated Transit Union v. *Independent Canadian Transit Union*, [1997] 5 W.W.R. 662 (Alta. Q.B.), where Lutz J. noted at para. 16 that the defendant union had abandoned defences that the plaintiff unions did not have the capacity to sue in their own right.

The other defamation cases in British Columbia and Alberta involving unions as parties are too numerous to list here. It should also be noted that one of the largest aggregate defamation awards ever made in a common law jurisdiction in Canada involved plaintiff unions and their officers suing a defendant union and its officers for defamation.

Amalgamated Transit Union v. *Independent Canadian Transit Union*, *ibid*. The court awarded damages aggregating $705,000 to the libel plaintiffs as follows: to the plaintiff James Daley, $200,000 general damages plus $50,000 punitive damages; to the plaintiff Bruce Chalmers, $50,000 general damages plus $15,000 punitive damages; to the plaintiff Ron Sentell, $50,000 general damages plus $15,000 punitive damages; to the plaintiff Amalgamated Transit Union, $100,000 general damages plus $75,000 punitive damages; and to the plaintiff Local 1372, $100,000 general damages plus $50,000 punitive damages. The trial judge characterized the libels by the defendants as part of a raid by the defendant union on the plaintiff union, the defendant "groping for power with acts of predation (*sic*) of a magnitude rarely, if ever, seen in the labour movement in Canada. Those acts, verbal and written, often vitriolic, delivered directly and by innuendo, both between and during raids, culminated in yet another raid by ICTU on the Plaintiff Amalgamated Transit Union ("ATU") in 1989, and evidenced a sudden moderation from the outset of these proceedings."

In Ontario, however, it was held by the High Court of Justice that unions do not have the capacity to sue or be sued in their own name for defamation. No appeal was taken from that decision. The case appeared to turn on the application of Ontario legislation for which there was at the time no equivalent in any other Canadian province.

S.I.U. v. *Lawrence* (1977), 75 D.L.R. (3d) 357, per Osler J. at 361 (Ont. S.C.J.), applying *Nipissing Hotel Ltd. et al* v. *Hotel & Restaurant Employees & Bartenders Int'l Union et al*, [1963] 2 O.R. 169, 39 D.L.R. 675 (H.C.J.), and s. 3(2) of the *Rights of Labour Act*, R.S.O. 1970, c. 416 which reads:

> 3(2) A trade union shall not be made a party to any action in any court unless it may be so made a party irrespective of any of the provisions of this Act or of *The Labour Relations Act*

See also *Balanyk* v. *Greater Niagara General Hospital*, [1996] O.J. No. 1124 (Gen. Div.).

Kulyk v. *Toronto Board of Education*, [1996] O.J. No. 2972 (Gen. Div.).

Hanover Nursing Home Ltd. v. *London District Services Workers Union, Local 220*, [1999] O.J. No. 666 (Gen. Div.).

S.I.U. v. *Lawrence*, above, and other Ontario decisions denying unions the right to sue for defamation may need to be reconsidered in light of the decision of the Ontario Court of Appeal in *Professional Institute of the Public Service of Canada* v. *Canada (Attorney General)* (2002), 222 D.L.R. (4th) 438, where the court held (at page 448) that unions have the legal status to sue in their own names, at least for the purpose of discharging their functions in performing their roles in the field of labour relations. Gouge J.A. (at page

449) also rejected defence arguments that section 3(2) of the *Rights of Labour Act*, R.S.O. 1990, c. R.33, prohibits unions from suing in their own names in Ontario. Accordingly, the Court of Appeal reversed the motions judge and permitted the plaintiff unions to pursue litigation which challenged the federal legislation which authorizes the federal government and the R.C.M.P.

In his judgment, Gouge J.A. also stated (at paras. 25–27) that three propositions should be taken from the decision of the Supreme Court of Canada in *Berry* v. *Pulley,* 2002 SCC 40, where the Court reviewed the historical development of the legal status of trade unions:

> [25] First, absent clearly contrary intention, the legal status of trade unions to assert their rights in court, including common law rights, is now beyond question, at least in matters relating to their labour relations function and operations.

> [26] Second, while that legal status is founded in each case on the relevant provincial or federal labour legislation governing the union, it does not depend on any provision specific to that legislation. While variations exist among jurisdictions, the legal status accorded to trade unions derives not from specific provisions in any particular piece of legislation, but from the reality that, throughout Canada, the world of labour relations is governed by sophisticated statutory machinery which requires that unions have sufficient legal personality to play their role in that world. Thus legislatures must be taken to have impliedly conferred on unions the legal status necessary for them to do so.

> [27] Third, this recognition of the broadening legal status accorded to trade unions is a reflection of the extraordinary evolution over the last century of both their role and the complex labour relations regimes which now govern them and their activities. In order that unions be able to properly fulfill the functions now expected of them, courts must treat them as juridical entities.

The question of the right of union members to sue for defamation in a class action pursuant to Ontario Rule 75 was raised by the appeal from the High Court's decision in *S.I.U.* v. *Lawrence.* It was answered in the negative.

S.I.U. v. *Lawrence* (1979), 97 D.L.R. (3d) 324, per MacKinnon A.C.J.O. at 332, 335 (C.A.); leave to appeal to S.C.C. refused (1979), 97 D.L.R. (3d) 324n (S.C.C.).

The fact that a union formed under the legislation of another province has no status under the British Columbia *Labour Relations Code* does not mean it lacks capacity to sue or to be sued in the courts of British Columbia either in respect of matters unrelated to the British Columbia *Code*, generally, or in respect of recognition and enforcement of a foreign judgment granted in a jurisdiction where the foreign union does have such status.

> *Amalgamated Transit Union, Local 1374* v. *Independent Canadian Transit Union* (1998), 63 B.C.L.R. (3d) 335, per Taylor J. at paras. 36–38 (S.C.), citing *United Services Funds* v. *Richardson Greenshields of Canada Ltd.* (1987), 16 B.C.L.R. (2d) 187 (S.C.), *International Association of Science and Technology for Development* v. *Hamza*, [1995] 6 W.W.R. 75 (Alta. C.A.).

It has been held that where an action is brought and a judgment is obtained in the courts of another province of Canada, the parties to that action should usually have status to sue and to be sued in British Columbia on an application for recognition and enforcement of the foreign judgment, regardless of whether the parties would have such status for any other purposes.

> *Amalgamated Transit Union, Local 1374* v. *Independent Canadian Transit Union*, above, at para. 3, citing *United Services Funds* v. *Richardson Greenshields of Canada Ltd.*, above, *International Association of Science and Technology for Development* v. *Hamza*, above.

See also Chapter 13, "Identification of the Plaintiff", "Individual claims of defamation based on statements about a group."

8) Statutory Instruments

Federal or provincial statutes may confer powers on organizations or enterprises which fall short of full corporate status. These must be carefully examined to determine whether or not they confer a capacity to sue or to be sued for defamation.

9) Political Parties

There would seem to be no reason in principle why a political party, which is a legal entity by virtue of its incorporation as a company or society under provincial or federal legislation, should not be able to sue or be sued for defamation.

There are several recent reported decisions involving political parties sued for defamation. In those cases, the political party did not raise an issue about its capacity to be sued for defamation.

> *Re International Assn. of Bridge, Structural and Ornamental and Reinforcing Ironworkers (Local 97) and Campbell* (1997), 152 D.L.R. (4th) 547 (B.C.S.C.) [the

Liberal Party of British Columbia, at that time the provincial opposition party, was named as a defendant over a Liberal news release].

Reform Party of Canada v. *Western Union Insurance Co.* (1999), 16 C.C.L.I. (3d) 282 (B.C.S.C.), (2001) 87 B.C.L.R. (3d) 299 (C.A.) [political party sued for defamation sought insurance coverage in relation to that claim], where Huddart J.A. stated at 87 B.C.L.R. (3d) p. 301:

> In July, 1998, Senator E.M. Lawson sued the appellant for defamation he alleged occurred in an article on the scandals.html page located on the senate_reform.org website during the late spring of that year. The [Reform Party of Canada's] main website was reform.ca. It contained a link to the senate_reform site and to the page headed "Senate Scandals" where the allegedly defamatory comments were posted.

See also *Reform Fund of Canada* v. *Western Union Insurance Company* (11 February 2000), Calgary Registry 9901-15884 (Q.B.) [allegedly defamatory remarks about Senator Ghitter, subject of underlying action, were included in a fundraising letter].

An English court recently struck out a defamation action brought by the Referendum Party. The judge reasoned that a political party is analogous to a governmental body which cannot bring a defamation lawsuit as a result of the principle expressed in *Derbyshire County Council* v. *Herald and Times Newspapers Ltd.*, [1993] 1 All ER 1011 (H.L. (Eng.)) (see this chapter, "Municipal Bodies").

Goldsmith v. *Bhoyrul*, [1997] 4 All E.R. 268 where Buckley J. stated at 270–71 (Q.B.):

> … [T]he public interest in free speech and criticism in respect of those bodies putting themselves forward for office or to govern is also sufficiently strong to justify withholding the right to sue. Defamation actions or the threat of them would constitute unfettered free speech at the time on the topic when it is clearly in the public interest there should be none.

Nevertheless, the principle in *Goldsmith* v. *Bhoyrul*, above, does not bar a defamation lawsuit which names as a defendant an individual employee, officer, or member of a political party who publishes defamatory expression. It merely precludes naming the incorporated political party as a defendant.

There are few signs the Supreme Court of Canada is likely to move in the direction of *Derbyshire County Council* or *Goldsmith*. In its first decision in a defamation case since its landmark decision in *Hill* v. *Church of Scientology of Toronto*, [1995] 2 S.C.R. 1130, the Supreme Court of Canada ruled in December 2002 on the liability of an elected municipal councillor under Quebec law. Dismissing an appeal from a decision of the Quebec Court of Appeal exonerating the defendant councillor from liability for statements he made at a municipal council meeting, the Supreme Court of Canada nevertheless reiterated the importance of balancing freedom of expression against reputation. Although freedom of expression takes on "singular importance" in a defamation action against an elected municipal official, who is a conduit for the voice of his or her constituents, the right to reputation is also protected. Therefore, the Court unanimously held, "while elected officials may be quite free to discuss matters of public interest, they must act as would the reasonable person."

> *Prud'homme* v. *Prud'homme*, [2002] S.C.J. No. 86, 2002 SCC 85, per L'Heureux-Dubé and LeBel JJ. for the Court at paras. 42–44.

9) Government Defendants

The federal Crown may be held liable for defamation committed by an employee in circumstances where the employee would be held liable. Legislation has removed federal Crown immunity in this regard.

> *Crown Liability and Proceedings Act*, R.S.C. 1985, c. C-50, ss. 3, 10.

The immunity of the provincial Crown in each of the common law provinces has also been removed by legislation. For example, in Alberta the relevant legislation is the *Proceedings Against the Crown Act*, RSA 2000, c. P-25, sections 4–5.

Pursuant to the principle of individual responsibility for torts, a government minister or official may be personally named as a defendant to a defamation lawsuit. The principle of vicarious liability of an individual's employer for defamatory expression published in the course and scope of employment does not extinguish the individual's liability.

> *Decock* v. *Alberta* (2000), 186 D.L.R. (4th) 265, per Russell J.A. (Sulatycky J.A. concurring) at paras. 2, 22 (Alta. C.A.), leave to appeal to the S.C.C. granted, appeal discontinued, [2000] S.C.C.A. No. 301 [a case involving a claim in tort for negligence against Alberta Premier Ralph Klein and Alberta Health Minister Shirley McClellan]. Russell J.A. cites, *inter alia*, Ghislain Otis, "Personal Liability of Public Officials for Constitutional Wrongdoing: A Neglected Issue of Charter Application" (1996) 24 Man. L.J. 23 at 26–27, and *George* v. *Harris*, [1999] O.J. No. 639 at para. 33 (Gen. Div.), endorsed by the

Ontario Supreme Court of Justice, Divisional Court at [1999] O.J. No. 3011, and states at 186 D.L.R. (4th) para. 24:

> 24. This principle of individual responsibility militates in favour of naming defendants personally. After all, it is the person who is alleged to have committed the tort. That said, since the function conferred or performed at the time of the commission of the alleged tort is essential to the determination of whether the Crown will also be liable, the official or office should be readily identified in the body of the pleadings.

It has further been held that the question whether public officials should be immunized from personal liability, and if so, how, is one to be dealt with by the legislature. "Unless and until any legislative immunity from personal liability is prescribed for public officials, plaintiffs retain the option of naming these officials personally as defendants."

Decock v. Alberta, above.

10) Government Defendants

a) Municipalities

A municipal corporation may be held liable for defamatory statements made by one of its officers or servants in the course of his or her employment.

> *McKinnon v. Dauphin (Rural Municipality)*, [1996] 3 W.W.R. 127, per Clearwater J. at 145–46 (Man. Q.B.), adopting Ian MacF. Rogers, *The Law of Canadian Municipal Corporations*, looseleaf, vol. 2, 2d ed., (Toronto: Carswell, 1971) at 1426, para. 2572, [aff'd [1998] 1 W.W.R. 309 (Man. C.A.) per Huband J.A., who made no statement expressing agreement or disagreement with this principle].

> *McLay v. Bruce (County)* (1887), 14 O.R. 398, per Wilson C.J. at 404–5, 410–11 (H.C.), where he described the nature of the libel claim at 405:

> > The plaintiff's eighth paragraph of his statement of claim then sets out that the defendants published the said "accusations and charges hereinbefore made," in pamphlets, and in their minutes of council, which were then circulated throughout the country and elsewhere with the intent of injuring the plaintiff; which is plainly a charge of libel … .

> *Norman v. New Westminster (City)*, [1999] B.C.J. No. 433 (S.C.) [City ordered to pay $10,000 damages for defamatory expression published by Director of Planning].

A municipality cannot be held vicariously responsible, however, for the statements of an individual member of council who may say something of an inappropriate nature during the course of a council meeting, where there is nothing in the surrounding circumstances which would indicate that the member was speaking otherwise than for himself or herself.

> *McKinnon v. Dauphin (Rural Municipality)*, [1998] 1 W.W.R. 309, per Huband J.A. at 311 (Man. C.A.).

Elected municipal councillors may commit the tort of defamation in the performance of the duties of their office. "Because such a wrongful act cannot adequately be remedied at the polls, an effective sanction for it can be applied only by the courts."

> *Prud'homme v. Prud'homme*, [2002] S.C.J. No. 86, 2002 SCC 85, per L'Hereux-Dubé and LeBel JJ. at para. 16, on appeal from the Court of Appeal of Quebec, concerning the application of Quebec rules of civil liability for defamatory speech by a municipal councillor.

b) Police Boards

In British Columbia, a police officer was awarded damages against a police service board for wrongful dismissal including $50,000 aggravated and punitive damages, in part because "the public position [the board's representative] took in respect of the reasons for that abrupt dismissal, caused the plaintiff mental distress and loss of respect in the community."

> *Porter v. Tsewultan Police Service Board*, [2000] B.C.J. No. 1360, per Shabbits J. at para. 69 (S.C.).

11) Government Plaintiffs

a) Municipalities

In British Columbia, a municipal corporation has the capacity to sue for defamation.

> *Prince George (City) v. British Columbia Television System Ltd.* (1979), 95 D.L.R. (3d) 577, per Aikins J.A. (Craig J.A. concurring, Bull J.A. concurring in result in a separate judgment) at 579 (B.C.C.A.), applying the *Interpretation Act*, 1974 (B.C.), c. 42, s. 15 which provides: "Words in an enactment establishing a corporation shall be construed (a) to vest in the corporation power (i) to sue in its corporate name." Aikins J.A. stated at p. 582:
>
> > In my opinion, it is beyond question that municipal corporations have reputations. A cursory examination of the Municipal Act reveals the

great diversity of matters in respect of which municipalities may legislate and the diversity of activities in which such corporations may engage. The way in which a municipality legislates and the way in which it administers the legislation it enacts and conducts itself in relation to activities which it lawfully undertakes cannot but create a municipal reputation, be it good, bad or indifferent. I can see no basis in principle for holding that a municipal corporation, empowered by statute to sue in its corporate name, cannot maintain an action for libel. To hold otherwise would leave municipalities the helpless victims of all those who choose to publish untrue imputations which injure their reputations.

It is open to question whether the guarantee of freedom of expression contained in section 2(b) of the *Canadian Charter of Rights and Freedoms* would apply today to bar or limit in some fashion that capacity of a government body to sue for defamation.

In the United Kingdom, it has been held that a democratically elected government body, or in fact any government body, has no capacity to bring a defamation action. The House of Lords concluded that as it is of the highest importance that such be open to uninhibited public criticism, and that because the threat of civil actions would place an undesirable fetter on the freedom to express such criticism, it would be contrary to the public interest for institutions of central or local government to have any right at common law to maintain an action for damages for defamation.

Derbyshire County Council v. *Herald and Times Newspapers Ltd.*, [1993] A.C. 534, per Lord Keith at 550 (H.L. (Eng.)):

> A publication attacking the activities of the authority will necessarily be an attack on the body of councillors which represents the controlling party, or on the executives who carry on the day to day management of its affairs. If the individual reputation of any of these is wrongly impaired by the publication any of these can himself bring proceedings for defamation. Further, it is open to the controlling body to defend itself by public utterances and in debate in the council chamber.

In New South Wales, it has also recently been held that a democratically elected municipal council is not entitled to sue for defamation (but is entitled to sue for injurious falsehood in an appropriate case). This decision does not rule out personal lawsuits by individual council members.

Council of the Shire of Ballina v. *Ringland* (1994), 33 N.S.W.L.R. 680 (C.A.), per Gleeson C.J. (Kirby P. concurring; Mahoney J.A. dissenting on the defamation issue; Mahoney J.A. concurring, Kirby J.A. dissenting on the injurious false-hood issue) adopting *Derbyshire County Council* v. *Times Newspapers Ltd.*, above.

The United Kingdom and Australian authorities have not yet been considered in this context by a Canadian court.

b) Police boards

In Ontario, a court dismissed a defence application to strike a claim brought by the plaintiff, a police services board. The defendant's statements were held to be capable in law of being defamatory of the police services board.

> *Kenora (Town) Police Services Board* v. *Savino* (1995), 36 C.P.C. (3d) 46, per Stach J. at paras. 13–16 (Ont. Gen. Div.), referring to *Windsor Roman Catholic Separate School Board* v. *Southam, Inc.* (1984), 46 O.R. (2d) 231 (H.C.J.) and *Prince George* v. *British Columbia Television System Ltd.* (1979), 95 D.L.R. (3d) 577 (B.C.C.A.).

c) School boards

In Ontario, a "separate school board" incorporated under the Education Act is entitled to sue for defamation.

> *Windsor Roman Catholic Separate School Board* v. *Southam,* above, per DuPont J. at 235–36, following an extensive review of the authorities:

> > The Board's reputation for honesty, probity, fairness and decency must, of necessity, play an important role in the performance of its duties and responsibilities. Libels on its reputation would not only interfere in the performance of these duties and responsibilities, but would act to deter people from taking part in the Board itself. To deprive the Board of the expertise and skill of the leading members of the community could only further derogate from its responsibilities and duties.

C. IMMUNITIES

1) Diplomatic Immunity

Foreign diplomats cannot be sued for defamation unless the sending state waives the immunity or unless the defamation constitutes "an action relating to any professional or commercial activity exercised by the diplomatic agent ... outside his official function." The waiver by the sending state must be clear and unequivocal. There appears to be no reported case in the common law provinces where a sending state has waived the immunity to permit one of its diplomats to be sued in a Canadian court for defamation.

Foreign Missions and International Organizations Act, S.C. 1991, c. 41, ss.3, 4(1) (as am. by S.C. 1995, c. 5, s.25(1)(n)), which incorporates Articles 1, 22–24 and 27–40 of the *Vienna Convention on Diplomatic Relations*, [1966] Can. T.S. No. 29, Arts. Preamble, 4, 9, 32., Schedule 1. Article 31 provides in relevant part:

1. A diplomatic agent shall enjoy immunity from the criminal jurisdiction of the receiving State. He shall also enjoy immunity from its civil and administrative jurisdiction, except in the case of:

    ...

    (c) an action relating to any professional or commercial activity exercised by the diplomatic agent in the receiving State outside his official functions.

Laverty v. Laverty (1994), 32 C.P.C. (3d) 91 (Ont. Gen. Div.) [family law matter, USA refused to waive immunity].

This statutory immunity is a procedural bar. If it is raised, the action against the diplomat is not dismissed but merely stayed. It has been held, accordingly, that if the defendant at any time ceases to enjoy diplomatic immunity, the plaintiff may proceed with the action.

Ghosh v. D'Rozario, [1963] 1 Q.B. 106, per Davies L.J. at 118 (Eng. C.A.): However, the action is not at an end, but merely stayed. Should the defendant at any time cease to enjoy diplomatic immunity, it [i.e., the action] will be able to proceed.

This procedural bar also comes into effect if the defendant acquires his or her diplomatic status after publishing the defamatory expression and after the defamation litigation has commenced.

Ghosh v. D'Rozario, *ibid.* [action stayed once the defendant obtained diplomatic status even though he had already participated in the proceeding].

See *R. v. Yushko*, [1997] O.J. No. 284, per B.J. Young, Prov. J. at paras. 16–19 (Prov. Div.), adopting *Ghosh v. D'Rozario*.

2) Consular Immunity

Consular immunity is more limited than diplomatic immunity. A foreign consular officer enjoys statutory immunity only in respect of "acts performed in the exercise of consular functions."

Foreign Missions and International Organizations Act, S.C. 1991, c. 41, Schedule II, *Vienna Convention on Consular Relations*, Sch. II, Article 43.

Consular functions are defined in Article 5 of the statute. Only the sending state may waive this immunity.

3) Immunity of Foreign States

Defamation lawsuits against a foreign state and its functionaries are barred by the principle of sovereign immunity. This principle and its exceptions are incorporated into Canadian law by federal statute.

> *State Immunity Act*, R.S.C. 1985, c. S-18.

> *United States of America* v. *Friedland* (1999), 182 D.L.R. (4th) 614 at paras. 11, 28–29 (Ont. C.A.).

A foreign state includes "any sovereign or other head of the foreign state or of any political subdivision of the foreign state while acting as such in a public capacity," "any government of the foreign state or of any political sub-division of the foreign state, including any of its departments, and any agency of the foreign state," and "any political subdivision of the foreign state."

> *State Immunity Act*, R.S.C. 1985, c. S-18, s.2

An "agency of a foreign state" is any legal entity that is "an organ of the foreign state but that is separate from the foreign state." A "political subdivision" is a "province, state or other like political subdivision of a foreign state that is a federal state."

> *State Immunity Act*, R.S.C. 1985, c. S-18, s.2

It appears that the Court must apply Canadian and not foreign law to determine whether or not a party is an agency of a foreign state.

> *University of Calgary* v. *Colorado School of Mines*, [1996] 2 W.W.R. 596, per Kent J. at para. 21 (Alta. Q.B.), citing *Ferranti-Packard Ltd.* v. *Cushman Rentals Ltd.* (1980), 115 D.L.R. (3d) 691, per Reid J. at 693 (Ont. Div. Ct.).

Whether or not a particular institution is an agency of the foreign state, however, depends on the control which is exercised by that foreign state.

> *University of Calgary* v. *Colorado School of Mines*, ibid.

As in the case of diplomatic and consular immunity, this principle constitutes a procedural bar. A foreign state may waive its immunity. To be effective, such a waiver must be clear and unequivocal.

> *Re Canada Labour Code (sub. nom P.S.A.C. v. United States Defence Department)* (1988), 74 DLR (4th) 191 (Can. L.R.B.); aff'd [1990] 1 F.C. 332, rev'd on other grounds, [1992] 2 S.C.R. 50, 91 D.L.R. (4th) 449.

Section 4(4) of the *State Immunity Act* creates an exception to the general principle of sovereign immunity where the foreign state submits to the jurisdiction of the court by initiating proceedings in a court, and in consequence submits to the jurisdiction of the court "in respect of any ... counterclaim that arises ... out of the subject-matter of the proceedings initiated by the state."

State Immunity Act, R.S.C. 1985, c. S-18, s.4(4)

However, a defamed individual or corporation sued by a foreign state in a Canadian court generally will not be able to rely on section 4(4) to counterclaim in defamation against that foreign state or its functionaries.

The exception in section 4(4) of the *State Immunity Act* has been narrowly interpreted. Where the United States of America brought suit in the Ontario High Court against a Canadian resident for environmental cleanup costs in Colorado, a counterclaim in tort by the Canadian for damage to his business reputation was dismissed. It was held that the immunity of the United States was only waived in relation to a defensive counterclaim; not one which asserted tort claims that were independent of the proceeding initiated by the United States.

United States of America v. *Friedland* (1999), 182 D.L.R. (4th) 614 at 620 (Ont. C.A.), leave to appeal to the S.C.C. granted, [2000] S.C.C.A. No. 91 (appeal discontinued 30 August 2001).

A foreign state is not immune from the jurisdiction of Canadian courts in "any proceedings that relate to any commercial activity of the foreign state."

State Immunity Act, R.S.C. 1985, c. S-18, s.5

A "commercial activity" is "any particular transaction, act or conduct or any regular course of conduct that by reason of its nature is of a commercial character."

State Immunity Act, R.S.C. 1985, c. S-18, s.2

A foreign state is also not immune from the jurisdiction of a court in any proceedings that relate to "personal ... injury ... or any damage to or loss of property ... that occurs in Canada." It has been held, however, that this exemption from the principle of state immunity does not permit a plaintiff to bring an action for "mental distress, denial of liberty and damage to reputation." The expression "personal injury" in the exemption applies only to claims "arising out of a physical breach of personal integrity." Section 6(a) "could conceivably cover an overlapping area between physical harm and mental injury, such as nervous stress."

State Immunity Act, R.S.C. 1985, c. S-18, s.6

Schreiber v. *Canada (Attorney General)*, [2002] S.C.J. No. 63, 2002 SCC 62, per LeBel J. for the Court at para. 80.

In light of the 2002 decision of the Supreme Court of Canada in *Schreiber* v. *Canada*, above, a 1995 decision of the Alberta Court of Queen's Bench holding that a defamation action per se is a claim for "personal injury" is bad law on this point.

See *University of Calgary* v. *Colorado School of Mines*, [1996] 2 W.W.R. 596, per Kent J. at para. 36 (Alta. Q.B.).

4) Immunity of International Organizations

Defamation lawsuits against international organizations and their functionaries may be barred by an Order-in-Council made under the same federal statute which codifies diplomatic and consular immunities. This is a procedural bar.

Foreign Missions and International Organizations Act, S.C. 1991, c.41, s. 5, by virtue of which organizations specified in a federal Order in Council enjoy the immunities conferred by Schedule III, *Convention on the Privileges and Immunities of the United Nations* adopted by the General Assembly of the United Nations on 13 February 1946.

Attorney General of Canada v. *Lavigne* (1997), 145 D.L.R. (4th) 232 (Qc. C.A.) [importation of alcohol for use of ICAO staff, charges of illegal importation, held ICAO absolutely immune].

The procedural bar applies to claims based on vicarious liability.

Greco v. *Holy See (State of the Vatican City)*, [1999] O.J. No. 2467 (S.C.J.), varied on appeal, [2000] O.J. No. 5293 (S.C.J.).

There is a suggestion in certain jurisprudence, however, that the immunity enjoyed by international organizations should be constrained in a commercial context. If the international organization is involved in a purely commercial venture, and it is not one that has some state significance or one that is associated with acts of state, it may be open to a litigant to argue that the procedural immunities should not be made available for such conduct.

Gouvernement de la République démocratique du Congo c. *Venne*, [1969] 5 D.L.R. (3d) 128 (Qc. Q.B.), rev'd [1971] S.C.R. 997.

Zodiak International Products Inc. v. *Poland (Republic)*, [1977] C.A. 366 (Qc. C.A.).

It is beyond the scope of this book to explore the merits of this potential exemption from the absolute immunity enjoyed by sovereign states.

5) Individual Immunities Conferred by Statute

Certain forms of immunity for defamatory expression are conferred on individuals employed by government by federal and provincial statutes. These provisions must be carefully examined in the context of specific circumstances to determine whether the defamatory expression at issue falls within the scope of the immunity.

Nova Scotia (Labour Relations Board) v. *Future Inns Canada Inc.* (1999), 178 D.L.R. (4th) 202 per Pugsley J.A. at 221–23 (N.S.C.A.). Pugsley J.A. states at para. 56:

> Where a specific statutory immunity has been conferred … the immunity of Board members is clear respecting actions carried out in their capacity as Board members. The immunity is also clear respecting the actions of the Board when it acts in a Board capacity.

Pugsley J.A. continued at paras. 78, 85, and 95:

> 78. The critical issue …is whether the acts, or words (in the case of chairman Darby) of the appellants, forming the subject matter of the complaints in the statement of claim were performed, or said, in their capacity as a Board, or members of the Board.
>
> …
>
> 85. The claim advanced against chairman Darby involves, in my opinion, different considerations. He was not a member of either of the panels which participated in the decision to issue L.R.B. orders 4267 or 4284. Presumably, immunity is invoked as a result of responsibilities he assumed as chairman of the Board. We have not been directed to any provision in the Act or regulations, delegating authority to the chairman of the Board to speak to the media respecting the interpretation of Board orders. Whether the chairman of the Board should discuss with media the likelihood of litigants refusing to comply with Board orders is not a matter that I would consider as being without controversy. It is not, therefore, "plain and obvious" to me, that an action against chairman Darby should fail for these comments, pro-

vided it can be said that the statement of claim discloses a question "fit to be tried."

...

95. With respect to the claim against Chairman Darby, I am of the view that a question fit to be tried has been made out, and that it is not plain and obvious that Chariman Darby's statements are covered by the statutory immunity.

CHAPTER EIGHT:

Jurisdictional Issues

A. THE CONSTITUTIONAL AUTHORITY OVER DEFAMATION

Each provincial legislature has exclusive jurisdiction to make laws in relation to "Property and Civil Rights in the Province" and "Generally all Matters of a merely local or private Nature in the Province."

> *Constitution Act, 1867*, (U.K.) 30 & 31 Vict., c. 3, ss.92(13), 92(16).

Equivalent legislative jurisdiction has been delegated to the Yukon Territory and the Northwest Territories by the federal Parliament in Ottawa.

> *Yukon Act*, R.S.C. 1985, c. Y-2, s.17(h).

> *Northwest Territories Act*, R.S.C. 1985, c. N-27, s.16(h).

Libel and slander are common law torts over which the federal Parliament has no legislative competence.

> *Gracey v. Canadian Broadcasting Corporation*, [1991] 1 F.C. 739 (T.D.).

> *Cardinal v. Calliou*, [1999] A.J. No. 791 (Q.B.).

The common law, as modified by provincial and territorial legislation, therefore defines civil liability for defamation and related torts such as injurious falsehood.

B. THE COURT STRUCTURE

1) General Overview

The Supreme Court of Canada, which is at the pinnacle of the Canadian judicial system, will hear an appeal only if leave is obtained from that Court or from the appellate court whose decision is challenged. The Supreme Court of Canada is entitled to overrule its previous decisions but this power is used with restraint.

Below the Supreme Court of Canada, the Canadian court structure has three branches: the Federal Court, the provincial courts, and the territorial courts.

Each of the provinces has created a two-level superior court system pursuant to its constitutional jurisdiction to legislate for the constitution, maintenance, and organization of provincial courts, both of civil and criminal jurisdiction, including procedure in civil matters in those courts.

Constitution Act, 1867, above, s.92(14).

One level consists of the superior trial court which has original and inherent jurisdiction. The second level is the provincial appellate court.

Each province has also created an inferior trial court with limited statutory jurisdiction in civil matters. Often characterized as "small claims courts," whether or not they may hear civil suits for defamation depends on the jurisdiction conferred by the relevant provincial statutes.

The superior courts of the Northwest Territories and the Yukon Territory were established by the Parliament of Canada pursuant to its constitutional jurisdiction over those two northern territories. Each territory has a superior trial court and a superior appellate court.

Constitution Act, 1867, above, s.4.

Yukon Act, R.S.C. 1985, c. Y-2.

Northwest Territories Act, R.S.C. 1985, c. N-27, Part II.

2) The Federal Court

The Federal Court, which consists of the Federal Court Trial Division and the Federal Court of Appeal, was created by the federal Parliament of Canada pursuant to its constitutional jurisdiction to establish courts for the administration of federal laws.

Constitution Act, 1867, above, s.101.

The Federal Court has a very limited jurisdiction and largely deals with cases against the federal government and its agencies or reviews of federal tribunal decisions.

Constitution Act, 1867, above, ss.96–100.

Although the Federal Court has jurisdiction to hear defamation claims against the federal Crown itself, it has no jurisdiction over a defamation action between individuals.

> *Ochiichagwe'babigo'ining First Nation* v. *Beardy*, [1995] F.C.J. No. 1268 (T.D.).

> *Cardinal* v. *Calliou*, [1999] A.J. No. 791 (Q.B.).

Unlike the provincial superior courts, the Federal Court has no inherent jurisdiction. The parties cannot confer defamation jurisdiction upon the Federal Court by consent.

> *Puerto Rico* v. *Hernandez*, [1975] 1 S.C.R. 228.

> *New Brunswick (Electric Power Commissioners)* v. *Maritime Electric*, [1985] 2 F.C. 13 (F.C.A.).

> *Roberts* v. *Canada*, [1989] 1 S.C.R. 322.

The power of the federal Parliament to legislate with respect to the Federal Court is limited to areas strictly within the legislative jurisdiction of the Parliament of Canada. It cannot limit the jurisdiction of superior courts because it does not have legislative authority over them.

> *Law Society of British Columbia et al.* v. *Canada (A.G.)* (1980), 108 D.L.R. (3d) 753 (B.C.C.A.).

> *Shield* v. *Siksika Nation Indian Council Band No. 430* (1992), 159 A.R. 241 (Q.B.).

The jurisdiction of the Federal Court is determined by a three-prong test.

i)   There must be a statutory grant of jurisdiction by the Federal Parliament.
ii) There must be an existing body of federal law which is essential to the disposition of the case and which nourishes the statutory grant of jurisdiction.
iii) The law on which the case is based must be "a law of Canada" as the phrase is used in section 101 of the *Constitution Act, 1867*.

> *ITO-International Terminal Operators Ltd.* v. *Miida Electronics Inc.*, [1986] 1 S.C.R. 752 at 766.

The third test is satisfied if the dispute is to be determined on the basis of an existing federal statute.

> *Roberts* v. *Canada*, [1989] 1 S.C.R. 322.

A defamation claim based on provincial law does not fall within the jurisdiction of the Federal Court simply because it is intertwined with other claims made under the laws of Canada. There is currently no existing body of federal law concerning the torts of libel and slander and therefore an action for defamation is not based on a law of Canada as that phrase is used in section 101 of the *Constitution Act, 1867*.

The Federal Court has no jurisdiction over a defamation action against the Canadian Broadcasting Corporation, notwithstanding that the right to sue that entity is purportedly given by the *Broadcasting Act*, a federal statute.

Lougheed v. *Canadian Broadcasting Corporation* (1978), 86 D.L.R. (3d) 229 (Alta. Q.B.), varied (1979), 98 D.L.R. (3d) 264 (Alta. S.C.(A.D.)).

Smith v. *Canadian Broadcasting Corporation*, [1953] 1 D.L.R. 510 (Ont. H.C.J.).

Baton Broadcasting Ltd. v. *Canadian Broadcasting Corporation* (1965), 56 D.L.R. (2d) 215 (Ont. S.C.J.).

Bassett v. *Canadian Broadcasting Corporation* (1980), 116 D.L.R. (3d) 332.

Gracey v. *Canadian Broadcasting Corporation*, [1991] 1 F.C. 739 (T.D.).

The Canadian Broadcasting Corporation may be sued in defamation at common law without recourse to any statutory provision authorizing such action.

Bank of British Columbia v. *Canadian Broadcasting Corporation* (1992), 64 B.C.L.R. (2d) 166 (C.A.)

3) Small Claims Courts

In four of the common law provinces, defamation actions for damages below a modest monetary limit may be brought in the provincially-appointed inferior courts.

In New Brunswick, actions for libel and slander damages not exceeding $3,000 are required to be tried by a small claims judge.

Wilson v. *Maber*, (1998) 198 N.B.R. (2d) 247 (C.A.).

Rule 46.01(2).

Rule 75.01.

In Manitoba, Ontario, and Prince Edward Island, libel and slander actions within the monetary jurisdiction of the small claims court are tried in that court.

Suedfeld v. *Lancia*, [1993] O.J. No. 1693 (Ont. Ct. J. (Gen. Div. Sm. Cl.)).

Bhaduria v. *Standard Broadcasting Inc. (c.o.b. CFRB)*, [1996] O.J. No. 2853 (Gen. Div. Sm. Cl.).

Hasnu v. *Deshe Bedeshe Inc.*, [1998] O.J. No. 3493.

On the other hand, in Alberta, British Columbia, Newfoundland, Nova Scotia, Quebec, and Saskatchewan, the legislation creating small claims jurisdiction specifically excludes libel and slander claims.

Cohen v. Wilder, [1996] B.C.J. No. 856 (Prov. Ct. (Civ. Div.)).

Dawe v. Nova Collection Services (Nfld.) Ltd. (1998), 160 Nfld. & P.E.I.R. 266 (Nfld. Prov. Ct. (Sm. Cl.)).

C. COMPULSORY ARBITRATION

If the defamation claim arises from a collective agreement, and the relevant statute provides that such disputes must be resolved by arbitration, the court has no jurisdiction.

Weber v. Ontario Hydro (1995), 125 D.L.R. (4th) 583 (S.C.C.).

In *Weber*, McLachlin J. for the majority of the Supreme Court of Canada stated [at page 602] that:

> ... the task of the judge or arbitrator determining the appropriate forum for the proceedings centres on whether the dispute or difference between the parties arises out of the collective agreement. Two elements must be considered: the dispute and the ambit of the collective agreement.
>
> In considering the dispute, the decision-maker must attempt to define its "essential character," to use the phrase of LaForest J.A. in *Energy and Chemical Workers Union, Local 691 v. Irving Oil Ltd.* (1983), 148 D.L.R. (3d) 398, 47 N.B.R. (2d) 205 (C.A.). The fact that the parties are employer and employee may not be determinative. Similarly, the place of the conduct giving rise to the dispute may not be conclusive; matters arising from the collective agreement may occur off the workplace and conversely, not everything that happens on the workplace may arise from the collective agreement. ... In the majority of cases the nature of the dispute will be clear; either it had to do with the collective agreement or it did not. Some cases, however, may be less than obvious. The question in each case is whether the dispute, in its essential character, arises from the interpretation, application, administration or violation of the collective agreement.

Where defamatory statements are made by the defendant or its alleged agents or employees solely in relation to the plaintiff's employment by the defendant, it is unlikely the court will have jurisdiction.

Bergman v. Canadian Union of Public Employees, Local 608, [1999] B.C.J. No. 1242 (S.C.)

The fact that the plaintiff may seek relief against a person other than the employer may be irrelevant.

> *Giorno v. Pappas* (1999), 42 O.R. (3d) 626 (C.A.).

The fact that a dispute over defamatory expression is between an employer and a union is not determinative of whether or not an arbitrator has exclusive jurisdiction to hear the defamation claim. If the dispute falls outside the scope of normal employer/employee relations and the context of the collective agreement, the court has jurisdiction. There may also be circumstances where the regular courts retain a residual jurisdiction which is specifically exempted from the general rule in *Weber*.

> *Fording Coal Ltd.* v. *United Steelworkers of America, Local 7884* (1999), 169 D.L.R. (4th) 468 (B.C.C.A.).

A dispute centred on an employer's instigation of criminal proceedings against an employee, even for a workplace wrong, is not a dispute which in its essential character arises from the interpretation, application, administration, or violation of the collective agreement.

> *Piko* v. *Hudson's Bay Company* (1998), 41 O.R. (3d) 729 (C.A.).

D. THE PROVINCIAL SUPERIOR COURTS AND CONFLICTS OF LAWS

1) Jurisdiction *simpliciter*

Where a foreign defendant has a presence in another Canadian province or territory, the basic principle applied by Canadian courts is that a court may exercise jurisdiction over a defendant not present in the jurisdiction only if it has a "real and substantial connection" with the subject matter of the litigation.

> *Moran v. Pyle National (Canada) Ltd.*, [1975] 1 S.C.R. 393.
>
> *Tolofson v. Jensen*, [1994] 3 S.C.R. 1022.
>
> *Morguard Investments Ltd. v. De Savoye*, [1990] 3 S.C.R. 1077.
>
> *Hunt v. T&N PLC*, [1993] 4 S.C.R. 289.

Where the proposed foreign defendant has no presence in any Canadian province or territory, but rather in a foreign state, the assumption of jurisdiction by a Canadian court is governed by the three principles of "comity, order, and fairness."

Spar Aerospace Ltd. v. *American Mobile Satellite Corp.* (2002), 220 D.L.R. (4th) 54, per Lebel J. at para. 21 (S.C.C.).

Marren v. *Echo Bay Mines Ltd.*, 2003 BCCA 298 per Huddart J.A. at para. 14.

In *Spar Aerospace Ltd.* v. *American Mobile Satellite Corp.*, above, on appeal from the Court of Appeal for Quebec, the Supreme Court of Canada explained the real and substantial connection test as follows [per LeBel J. for a unanimous court]:

> ¶51 I agree with the appellants that *Morguard* and *Hunt* establish that it is a constitutional imperative that Canadian courts can assume jurisdiction only where a "real and substantial connection" exists: see La Forest J. in *Hunt* … at p. 328: "courts are required, by constitutional restraints, to assume jurisdiction only where there are real and substantial connections to that place." However, it is important to emphasize that *Morguard* and *Hunt* were decided in the context of interprovincial jurisdictional disputes. In my opinion, the two cases resulted in the enhancing or even broadening of the principles of reciprocity and speak directly to the context of interprovincial comity within the structure of the Canadian federation; see *Morguard*, supra, at p. 1109 and *Hunt*, supra, at p. 328

> ¶52 In *Morguard*, La Forest J. agreed with the flexible approach taken by Dickson J. (as he then was) with respect to the application of the "real and substantial connection" criterion in *Moran* v. *Pyle National (Canada) Ltd.*, [1975] 1 S.C.R. 393, and wrote at p. 1106:

>> At the end of the day, he rejected any rigid or mechanical theory for determining the situs of the tort. Rather, he adopted "a more flexible, qualitative and quantitative test," posing the question, as had some English cases there cited, in terms of whether it was "inherently reasonable" for the action to be brought in a particular jurisdiction, or whether, to adopt another expression, there was a "real and substantial connection" between the jurisdiction and the wrongdoing.

> He also delimited the decision to only address the modern interprovincial context (at p. 1098):

>> … there is really no comparison between the interprovincial relationships of today and those obtaining between foreign countries in the 19th century. Indeed, in my view, there never was and the courts made a serious error in transposing the rules developed for the enforcement of foreign judgments to the enforcement of judgments from sister-provinces. The considerations underlying the rules of comity apply

with much greater force between the units of a federal state, and I do not think it much matters whether one calls these rules of comity or simply relies directly on the reasons of justice, necessity and convenience to which I have already adverted.

After concluding that the real and substantial connection test was specially crafted to deal with the challenges posed by multiple jurisdictions within a federation, the Supreme Court of Canada in *Spar Aerospace* held that in any event the real and substantial connection test would be satisfied by proof that the reputation of the plaintiff had suffered damage in Quebec.

Spar Aerospace Ltd. v. *American Mobile Satellite Corp.*, above, at para. 56

It has been stated since the decision of the Supreme Court of Canada in *Spar Aerospace*, above, that the real and substantial connection test may in some instances lower the threshold for the taking of jurisdiction; that is, that this test is easier for a plaintiff to satisfy than a test involving the application of the three principles of comity, order, and fairness.

Marren v. *Echo Bay Mines Ltd.*, above, at para. 14.

It has been held that the real and substantial connection test is "not a prerequisite for the assertion of jurisdiction over defendants, even out-of-province defendants, that are present in the jurisdiction."

Incorporated Broadcasters Ltd. v. *Canwest Global Communications Corp.* (2003), 223 D.L.R. (4th) 627, per Rosenberg J.A. at para. 29 (Ont CA).

Presence-based jurisdiction permits jurisdiction over an extra-provincial defendant who is physically present within the territory of the court.

Muscutt v. *Courcelles* (2002), 213 D.L.R. (4th) 577, per Sharpe J.A. at para. 19 (Ont. C.A.).

Whatever the Supreme Court of Canada actually intended to say in *Spar Aerospace*, courts continue to apply the "real and substantial connection" test to claims against foreign defendants, including claims where injury to reputation within Canada is involved.

C.B. Distribution Inc. (*c.o.b. Upper Canada Malt Co.*) v. *BCB International Inc.*, [2003] O.J. No. 1583, per Sachs J. at para. 19 (S.C.J.) [defendant a customs broker based in Buffalo, New York].

Imagis Technologies Inc. v. *Red Herring Communications Inc.*, 2003 BCSC 366, per Pitfield J. at para. 14. [defendant a California company which publishes a magazine in print form and on the Internet].

Roth v. *Interlock Services Inc.*, 2003 BCSC 337 [all defendants were American residents. Defendant corporation was a Nevada corporation].

It seems that a tort may be regarded as having occurred in any country substantially affected by the defendant's activities or its consequences and the law which is likely to have been in the reasonable contemplation of the parties.

The term "real and substantial connection" has not yet been clearly defined, but foreseeability of injury to the plaintiff appears to be a relevant factor. This factor also comes into play in United States law where courts consider the foreseeability of injury to the plaintiff in his or her home state arising from defamatory statements in determining whether due process is violated.

Calder v. *Jones*, 465 U.S. 783 (1984).

The real and substantial connection test applies in a defamation context.

Olde v. *Capital Publishing Ltd. Partnership* (1997), 5 C.P.C. (4th) 94 (Ont. Gen. Div.), aff'd [1998] O.J. No. 237 (C.A.).

Bangoura v. *Washington Post*, [2004] O.J. No. 284, per Pitt J. at para.19 (S.C.).

Trizec Properties, Inc. v. *Citigroup Global Markets Canada, Inc.*, [2004] O.J. No. 323 per M.A. Sanderson J. at para. 28 (S.C.J.).

Where publication has occurred solely in a foreign jurisdiction, and any damage to the plaintiff's reputation must have been confined to that jurisdiction, there is no real and substantial connection to the domestic forum.

Caribbean Clear Beverages Corp. v. *Coopers & Lybrand Vancouver Ltd.*, [1998] B.C.J. No. 1608 (S.C.).

Where a broadcaster is aware, at the time of broadcast, that its signal would be picked up by cable and satellite companies in a Canadian province, and further broadcast in that Canadian province, the tort of defamation is committed within that province and its courts have jurisdiction.

Pindling v. *National Broadcasting Corp.* (1984), 49 O.R. (2d) 58 (H.C.J.).

It matters not whether defamatory expression crosses a border by means of the printed word, sound waves, or ether waves in so far as publication within the jurisdiction is concerned. The tort consists in making a third person understand actionable defamatory matter.

Jenner v. *Sun Oil Co. Ltd.*, [1952] O.R. 240 (H.C.J.).

A court's rule for service of process *ex juris* must be read to include the constitutional requirement of a real and substantial connection between the cause of action and the forum before the exercise of jurisdiction may be permitted.

Morguard Investments Ltd. v. *De Savoye*, [1990] 3 S.C.R. 1077 at 1109–20.

Dupont v. *Taronga Holdings Ltd.* (1986), 49 D.L.R. (4th) 353 (Qc. S.C.).

Marren v. *Echo Bay Mines Ltd.*, 2003 BCCA 298 per Huddart J.A. at para. 13

Muscutt v. *Courcelles* (2002), 213 D.L.R. (4th) 577 (Ont. C.A.) per Sharpe J.A. at para. 49

Provincial rules of court which permit service ex juris without court order are procedural and do not by themselves confer jurisdiction. It is not possible to reduce the real and substantial connection test to a fixed formula and a considerable measure of judgment is required in assessing whether the 'real and substantial connection' test has been met on the facts of a given case.

Muscutt v. *Courcelles*, *ibid.* at paras. 56–57:

> ¶56 The Supreme Court of Canada has insisted that the real and substantial connection test must be flexible. The court has not attempted to define the precise nature of the connection to the jurisdiction that is required and the court's language is ambiguous. While certain passages in *Morguard* suggest that the connection must be with the defendant, others suggest that the connection must be with the subject matter of the action or with the damages suffered by the plaintiff.

> ¶57 In his comment on *Morguard*, (1991) 70 Can. Bar Rev. 733 at p. 741, Professor Joost Blom observes that the court's language lends itself to two possible approaches: the "personal subjection" approach, and the "administration of justice" approach. Under the personal subjection approach, jurisdiction is legitimate if the defendant regularly lived or carried on business in the province, or if the defendant voluntarily did something that related to the province so as to make it reasonable to contemplate that he or she might be sued in the province. By contrast, under the administration of justice approach, the basis for assuming jurisdiction is broader than personal subjection. The forum need only meet a minimum standard of suitability, under which it must be fair for the case to be heard in the province because the province is a "reasonable place for the action to take place."

The Ontario Court of Appeal articulated a list of factors emerging from the case law which courts may take into account in determining whether the real and substantial connection test is met. These include:

i)   the connection between the forum and the plaintiff's claim;

ii)   the connection between the forum and the defendant;

iii)   unfairness to the defendant in assuming jurisdiction;

iv)   unfairness to the plaintiff in not assuming jurisdiction;

v)   the involvement of other parties to the suit;

vi)   the court's willingness to recognize and enforce an extraprovincial judgment rendered on the same jurisdictional basis;

vii)   whether the case is interprovincial or international in nature; and

viii)   comity and the standards of jurisdiction, recognition, and enforcement prevailing elsewhere

> *Muscutt v. Courcelles, ibid.* at paras. 76–100 (regarding factor ii):

> ¶83 *Moran v. Pyle* holds that conduct outside the territory may render the defendant subject to the jurisdiction of the forum where it is reasonably foreseeable that the defendant's conduct would result in harm within the jurisdiction. This foreseeability should be distinguished from a situation in which the wrongful act and injury occur outside the jurisdiction and the plaintiff returns and suffers consequential damage.

These factors were referred to with approval in the context of a defamation case involving a defendant magazine which published the allegedly defamatory expression in print form and on the Internet.

> *Imagis Technologies Inc. v. Red Herring Communications Inc.*, 2003 BCSC 366 per Pitfield J. at para. 41.

Such a requirement would be similar to the due process clause which applies in the United States.

> *International Shoe Co. v. Washington*, 326 U.S. 310 (1945).

Internet expression has come under scrutiny in the context of the real and substantial connection test. It has been held that:

> it would create a crippling effect on freedom of expression if, in every jurisdiction the world over in which access to the Internet could be achieved, a person who posts fair comment on a bulletin board could be hauled before the courts of each of those countries.

> *Braintech, Inc. v. Kostiuk* (1999), 171 D.L.R. (4th) 46 (B.C.C.A.), leave to appeal to S.C.C refused [1999] S.C.C.A. No. 236.

Accordingly, where there is no real and substantial connection between the parties before the domestic court and the foreign jurisdiction where a libel judgment was obtained, the domestic court will not enforce the foreign verdict.

> *Braintech, Inc. v. Kostiuk, ibid.*

In Australia, the High Court recently affirmed a lower court ruling and held that "publication" of defamatory articles occurs in Australia each time a person in that country downloads that material from an Internet website to her own computer. The High Court unanimously rejected the defence argument that the defamatory articles were published in New Jersey when they became available on the servers which the defendant maintained there. Accordingly, the lower court had jurisdiction *simpliciter* to try the claim.

Dow Jones & Co Inc. v. *Gutnick*, [2002] H.C.A. 56, aff'g [2001] V.S.C. 305. Gleeson C.J., McHugh, Gummow, and Hayne JJ. stated in a joint judgment:

> ¶26 Harm to reputation is done when a defamatory publication is comprehended by the reader, the listener, or the observer. Until then, no harm is done by it. This being so it would be wrong to treat publication as if it were a unilateral act on the part of the publisher alone. It is not. It is a bilateral act — in which the publisher makes it available and a third party has it available for his or her comprehension.

> ¶27 The bilateral nature of publication underpins the long-established common law rule that every communication of defamatory matter founds a separate cause of action ... That rule has found reflection from time to time in various ways in State legislation ... and it would be a large step now to depart from it.

> ¶44 In defamation, the same considerations that require rejection of locating the tort by reference only to the publisher's conduct, lead to the conclusion that, ordinarily, defamation is to be located at the place where the damage to reputation occurs. Ordinarily that will be where the material which is alleged to be defamatory is available in comprehensible form assuming, of course, that the person defamed has in that place a reputation which is thereby damaged. It is only when the material is in comprehensible form that the damage to reputation is done and it is damage to reputation which is the principal focus of defamation, not any quality of the defendant's conduct. In the case of material on the World Wide Web, it is not available in comprehensible form until downloaded on to the computer of a person who has used a web browser to pull the material from the web server. It is where that person downloads the material that the damage to reputation may be done. Ordinarily then, that will be the place where the tort of defamation is committed.

*Dow Jones & Co Inc.*v. *Gutnick,* above, was considered in *Harrods Limited* v. *Dow Jones & Company Inc.*, [2003] E.W.H.C. 1162 (Q.B.), where Eady J.

held [at paragraph 36] that publications had taken place within England in relation to a small number of hard copies of the *Wall Street Journal* received by English subscribers and "also to the apparently limited number of hits emanating from this jurisdiction on the relevant page of the web site." In *King v. Lewis & Ors.*, [2004] E.W.H.C. 168 (Q.B.), Eady J. at paragraph 15 explicitly approved the proposition that "the common law currently regards the publication of an Internet posting as taking place when it is downloaded" citing, *inter alia, Gutnick v. Dow Jones & Company Inc.*, above.

Gutnick was also considered and approved in *Bangoura v. Washington Post*, [2004] O.J. No. 284 (S.C.), where Pitt J. endorsed the plaintiff's submission that those who publish via the Internet are aware of the global reach of their publications and must consider the legal consequences in the jurisdicction of the subjects of their articles. The defendant has appealed *Bangoura*.

On the other hand, where a libel defendant submits to the jurisdiction of a foreign court, defends the defamation lawsuit on the merits through trial, and pursues in the foreign court an unsuccessful counterclaim for libel, a "real and substantial connection" between the defendant and the foreign court exists and the domestic court may recognize and enforce the foreign verdict.

Amalgamated Transit Union, Local 1374 v. Independent Canadian Transit Union (1998), 24 C.P.C. (4th) 203 (B.C.S.C.).

It has been held that a provincial superior court has jurisdiction to assess damages in respect of the publication of defamatory expression not only in the domestic forum but in other jurisdictions where the expression is the same. An action will lie for libel or slander published abroad if it is wrongful by the law of the jurisdiction where it occurred, as well as the domestic forum.

Hubert v. DeCamillas (1963), 41 D.L.R. (2d) 495 (B.C.S.C.).

Nevertheless, whether or not a plaintiff is entitled to effect service of the legal process on the defendant outside the domestic jurisdiction will depend on the relevant rules of court.

Gouzenko v. Martin (1981), 34 O.R. (2d) 394 (S.C.).

It has been suggested that the courts have recognized a limited form of "single publication" rule compelling a plaintiff to bring one lawsuit against all defendants in one court for damages arising from a publication where the defendants are "jointly concerned in a common enterprise."

Jeremy S. Williams, *The Law of Defamation in Canada* (Toronto: Butterworths, 1976) at 63.

Gouzenko v. *Martin* (1981), 34 O.R. (2d) 394 (S.C.).

By its nature, the tort of defamation requires that damages be assessed according to community standards and local considerations. An application for leave to serve *ex juris* may fail when the defamatory expression has been published solely in another jurisdiction.

Thatcher v. *Southam, Inc.* (1985), 42 Sask R. 272 (Q.B.).

Dickhoff v. *Armadale Communications Ltd.*, [1992] S.J. No. 383 (Q.B.).

Forwarding defamatory expression to a resident of the forum constitutes publication within the forum.

Wilson v. *Holt*, [1978] A.J. No. 58 (S.C. (T.D.)).

2) *Forum Non Conveniens*

The overriding consideration which must guide the court is whether some other forum is more convenient and appropriate for the pursuit of the action and for securing the ends of justice.

Amchem Products Inc. v. *British Columbia (Workers' Compensation Board)*, [1993] 1 S.C.R. 897.

There is no requirement for the domestic proceeding to be shown to be oppressive or vexatious in order for the defendant to obtain a stay. The loss of juridical advantage to a plaintiff opposing a stay application is simply a factor to be weighed with the other factors which are considered in identifying the appropriate forum. If a party seeks out a jurisdiction simply to gain a juridical advantage rather than by reason of a real and substantial connection of the case to the jurisdiction, that will normally be condemned as forum shopping. On the other hand, a party whose case has a real and substantial connection with a forum has a legitimate claim to the advantages that forum provides. The legitimacy of this claim is based on a reasonable expectation that in the event of litigation arising out of the transaction in question, those advantages will be available.

A Canadian court should only restrain the party invoking the jurisdiction of the foreign court if the latter assumes jurisdiction on a basis that is inconsistent with Canadian rules of private international law, and an injustice results to a litigant or would-be litigant in Canadian courts. The anti-suit injunction is directed not against the foreign court but against the parties so proceeding or threatening to proceed. An injunction will only be issued restraining a party who is amenable to the jurisdiction of the court against whom an injunction will be an effective remedy.

Where only a handful of defamatory magazines printed in a foreign jurisdiction were circulated in the domestic jurisdiction, and the plaintiff's only connection with the domestic jurisdiction was a temporary summer residence for several months a year, an Ontario court stayed libel proceedings against American defendants who would be able to shelter behind more restrictive libel laws in the United States. Granting the American defendants' application for a stay, the court stated:

> Persons expect their activities to be governed by the law of the place where they happen to be and that their legal benefits and responsibilities will be defined accordingly. It makes good sense at least in cases such as this where a very small portion of the publications were sold in Canada, to name the place where the majority of the sales took place as the one where the action should be tried.

> *Olde v. Capital Publishing Ltd. Partnership* (1997), 5 C.P.C. (4th) 94 (Ont. Gen. Div.), aff'd [1998] O.J. No. 237 (C.A.).

Perhaps because of the novelty of the Internet, it is not always safe to predict how a court will approach a stay application in respect of publication on a foreign website concerning an individual plaintiff resident in the domestic forum. Courts to date have tended to refuse stays where there is a possibility that the reputation of a plaintiff resident in the domestic forum might have been injured through the defamation having been viewed by someone in the domestic forum.

> *Kitakufe v. Oloya* (1998), 67 O.T.C. 315 (Gen. Div.).

> *Direct Energy Marketing Ltd. v. Hillson*, [1999] A.J. No. 695, 34 C.P.C. (4th) 200 (Alta. Q.B.).

> *Von Teichman v. Ottenschlager*, [2001] O.J. No. 3527 (S.C.J.).

> *Bangoura v. Washington Post*, [2004] O.J. No. 284, per Pitt J. at para.19 (S.C.).

See also:

> *Dow Jones & Co Inc. v. Gutnick*, [2002] H.C.A. 56, aff'g [2001] V.S.C. 305, per Gleeson C.J., McHugh, Gummow, and Hayne JJ. in a joint judgment at paras. 45–48.

> *Harrods Limited v. Dow Jones & Company Inc.*, [2003] E.W.H.C. 1162, per Eady J. at paras. 43–45 (Q.B.), *King v. Lewis & Ors.*, [2004] E.W.H.C. 168 (Q.B.).

The general guidelines that a court should apply on a stay application are as follows. In order to succeed in an application for a stay of proceedings, two conditions must be satisfied:

i)   The party applying for the stay (the defendant) must satisfy the court that there is another forum to whose jurisdiction he was amenable and in which justice can be done between the parties at substantially less inconvenience and expense.

ii) If the first condition is met, the plaintiff may still prevent a stay being granted if he can show that a stay would deprive him of a legitimate personal or juridical advantage which would be available to him by invoking the jurisdiction of the court where the stay is sought.

Cormie v. Western Report, [1990] B.C.J. No. 1759, 1990 BCCA CA010560.

Avenue Properties Ltd. v. *First City Development Corporation* (1987), 7 B.C.L.R. (2d) 45 (C.A.).

However, the court should not adopt an overly legalistic approach to these factors. It must always be remembered that the decision as to whether or not to decline jurisdiction is essentially a discretionary matter. What is at stake is, on the one hand, a plaintiff's right to bring her action in the forum of her choice and, on the other hand, the defendant's right not to be subjected to severe injustice by reason of those proceedings. The test thus involves a balancing of interests, the critical equation being between "any advantage to the plaintiff" and "any disadvantage to the defendant."

Castanho v. Brown & Root (U.K.) Ltd., [1980] 3 W.L.R. 991, [1981] 1 All E.R. 143 (H.L.), per Lord Scarman at 999–1000.

The principles to be applied by a court exercising its discretion in a *forum non conveniens* application are set out in *Avenue Properties Ltd.* v. *First City Development* (1986), above, at 50–52 by Madam Justice McLachlin of the British Columbia Court of Appeal, now of the Supreme Court of Canada. These may be summarized as follows:

i)   The decision to refuse or allow an application for a stay is discretionary.

ii) The plaintiff's choice of forum should not be lightly denied. He should not be required to travel outside the jurisdiction in order to present his case, particularly where he resides in the jurisdiction or where there is "... some other bona fide connection between the action and the jurisdiction in which it is sought to be brought."

iii)   The existence of two actions in different jurisdictions is not itself sufficient to invoke the court's jurisdiction to grant a stay.

iv)   A stay should not be granted if there is an apprehension of prejudice to one of the parties because of differences in rights, remedies, or procedures, in requiring the action to proceed in another forum.

The application of these principles to libel litigation is illustrated by *Irving* v. *Weiner*, [1992] B.C.J. No. 397, 1992 BCSC 3259, where the defendant federal Minister of Multiculturalism and Citizenship was alleged to have defamed the plaintiff in a press release stating that Canadians joined him "in expressing to [the plaintiff] our complete and utter rejection of his pseudo-historic theories and the web of myths and distortions by which he seeks to obscure the full horror and inhumanity of the Nazi regime." The statement was distributed by Canada newswire to media outlets in Canada and allegedly to other organizations. The Minister successfully moved to have the British Columbia lawsuit filed by Irving stayed in favour of Ontario. Noting that neither the plaintiff nor the defendant resided in British Columbia, that the costs of British Columbia litigation would far exceed the costs of the defendant in Ontario, and that Irving's travel costs to Ontario would be less than to British Columbia, the British Columbia Supreme Court reasoned that trying the action in Ontario would not deprive the plaintiff of any juridical advantage and that there were no significant differences between the defamation law of the two provinces as it related to this particular claim.

3) Where Did the Wrong Take Place?

As a general rule, the law to be applied in torts is the law of the place where the activity occurred; that is, the *lex loci delicti*. There are situations where an act occurs in one place but the consequences are directly felt elsewhere. In such cases, the issue of where the tort takes place itself raises thorny issues.

> *Tolofson* v. *Jensen*, [1994] 3 S.C.R. 1022, 100 B.C.L.R. (2d) 1.

In such a case, it may be that the consequences would be held to constitute the wrong.

> Difficulties may also arise where the wrong directly arises out of some transnational or interprovincial activity. There territorial considerations may become muted; they may conflict and other considerations may play a determining role.
>
> *Tolofson* v. *Jensen, ibid.*

The principle in *Tolofson* may be difficult to apply in the case of defamation arising from a publication involving multiple sales of publications in many jurisdictions. In such cases, where a very small portion of the publications were sold in Canada, an Ontario court has suggested that it would make sense for the court "to name the place where the majority of the sales took place as the one where the action should be tried, under the law thereof."

> *Olde v. Capital Publishing Ltd. Partnership* (1997), 5 C.P.C. (4th) 94 (Ont. Gen. Div.), aff'd, [1998] O.J. No. 237 (C.A.).

The British Columbia Supreme Court has rejected defence submissions that a plaintiff should be obliged to sue in a jurisdiction that has a connection to the cause of action where the law is most favourable to the defendants rather than in a jurisdiction that has a connection with the cause of action where the law is most favourable to the plaintiff.

> *Imagis Technologies Inc. v. Red Herring Communications Inc.*, 2003 BCSC 366, per Pitfield J. at para. 36

In the same case, the court rejected the argument by the defendants that a possible limitation on enforcement of a British Columbia libel judgment should be a factor causing the court not to assume jurisdiction in relation to the defendants. Once the court has concluded it can assume jurisdiction, enforcement of the judgment is not a factor to be considered again in the context of *forum non conveniens*.

> *Imagis Technologies Inc. v. Red Herring Communications Inc.*, ibid. [In this case, the defendants had suggested (but not lead evidence of the foreign law) that "a United States jurisdiction will not assist in the enforcement of a British Columbia judgment if that judgment is based upon legal principles that do not prevail in the United States so as to be inconsistent with the guarantee of free speech embodied in the United States Constitution." In this connection, the court stated, *inter alia*: "At the same time, fault and malice could be capable of proof by Imagis in the British Columbia action. Should that be done, a United States court might be persuaded that the judgment should be enforced as jurisdiction was properly assumed by British Columbia, and the evidence established liability in conformity with applicable American legal principles." The court added at para. 35: "Regardless, where it is alleged that a defamatory statement was published in British Columbia and a plaintiff has a reputation to protect in the province, the plaintiff is at liberty to decide whether it wishes to pursue judgment in this jurisdiction in order to have the benefit of a finding in its favour, whether or not any monetary damages may

be recovered as a consequence of that judgment. Frequently, financial compensation is but one benefit to be derived by a plaintiff from judgment in a defamation action."]

Several recent Ontario decisions also hold that pontential difficulties enforcing an Ontario libel verdict in the United States should not prevent a plaintiff from bringing an action in Ontario. A judgment may be of significant value in restoring a plaintiff's local reputation even if the U.S.A. courts refuse to enforce it.

> *Trizec Properties, Inc.* v. *Citigroup Global Markets Canada, Inc.*, [2004] O.J. No. 323, per M.A. Sanderson J. at para. 51 (S.C.J.).

> *Bangoura* v. *Washington Post*, [2004] O.J. No. 284, per Pitt J. at paras. 20–21 (S.C.).

E. RELIGIOUS COURTS

In some instances, the court has deferred to a religious court where the nature of the complaint would require the consideration of issues such as the supervising authority of religious officials, or other matters having to do with the application of religious laws.

> *Levitts Kosher Foods Inc.* v. *Levin* (1999), 175 D.L.R. (4th) 471 (Ont. H.C.J.).

> *Pederson* v. *Fulton* (1994), 111 D.L.R. (4th) 367 (Ont. Gen. Div.).

However, to justify a stay in favour of such a tribunal, the defendant must satisfy the court that continuance of the court action would work an injustice because it would be oppressive or vexatious or an abuse of the process of the court, and that the stay would not cause injustice to the plaintiff. It appears that a stay will not be ordered where the defamation claimant seeks an award of damages which can only be ordered and enforced by the court.

> *Gruner* v. *McCormack*, [2000] O.T.C. 143 (S.C.J.).

F. RECOGNITION AND ENFORCEMENT OF FOREIGN JUDGMENTS

The landmark decision of the Supreme Court of Canada in *Beals* v. *Saldanha*, 2003 SCC 72, held that the "real and substantial connection" test applies equally to the recognition of interprovincial judgments and to judgments rendered by courts outside Canada. Major J. (MacLachlin C.J., and Gonthier, Bastarache, Arbour and Deschamps JJ. concurring) described the test in the following terms (para. 32):

> The "real and substantial connection" test requires that a significant connection exist between the cause of action and the foreign court. Furthermore, a defendant can reasonably be brought within the embrace of a foreign jurisdiction's law where he or she has participated in something of significance or was actively involved in that foreign jurisdiction. A fleeting or relatively unimportant connection will not be enough to give a foreign court jurisdiction. The connection to the foreign jurisdiction must be a substantial one.

Although *Beals* did not involve a defamation claim, this decision of the Supreme Court of Canada clearly supports the earlier application of the "real and substantial connection" test to foreign defamation verdicts by the British Columbia Court of Appeal in *Braintech, Inc.* v *Kostiuk* and by the British Columbia Supreme Court in *A.T.U. Local 1384* v *I.C.T.U.* [see discussion above at pages 149 and 151 respectively].

On the subject of defences, *Beals* holds that a domestic defendant may resist enforcement of the foreign judgment on the following grounds:

a) Extrinsic fraud which mislead the foreign court into believing that it had jurisdiction over the cause of action [paragraphs 43–45];

b) Intrinsic fraud, going to the merits of the case, but limited to those facts the defendant could not have discovered and brought to the attention of the foreign court through the exercise of reasonable diligence [paragraphs 45–58];

c) A denial of natural justice. This applies where the foreign proceedings were contrary to Canadian notions of fundamental justice in terms of procedure or due process [paragraphs 59–70]; and

d) A defence of public policy. This applies if the foreign judgment is "contrary to the Canadian concept of justice" in the sense that the foreign law is "repugnant" or "contrary to [the Canadian] view of basic morality." [paragraphs 71–77]

With respect to defence (d), *Beals* appears to leave open the possibility that a foreign judgment would not be enforced if the damages awarded were so excessive as to "shock the conscience of the reasonable Canadian." Note that the test for Canadian appellate interference with Canadian trial awards for general or aggravated damages in defamation cases is whether they "shock the conscience" of the court [see Chapter 32, "Damages," page 551]. Major J. held for the majority in *Beals*, however, that the amount awarded by the Florida court in that case would not shock the conscience of the reasonable Canadian. It is not entirely clear the Florida award would have been unenforceable if it had been sufficiently excessive.

CHAPTER NINE:

Apologies and Retractions

A. INTRODUCTION

Many plaintiffs simply want a retraction and apology. There is often an "undoubted advantage to a plaintiff in the greater persuasive effect of having his or her reputation vindicated out of the defendant's mouth, rather than his or her own."

> *Murray Alter's Talent Associates Ltd.* v. *Toronto Star Newspapers Ltd.* (1995), 124 D.L.R. (4th) 105, per Borins J.A. at 118 (Ont. Div. Ct.), citing Fleming, "Retraction and Reply: Alternative Remedies for Defamation" (1978), 12 U.B.C.L. Rev. 15 at 25.

A timely retraction and apology may minimize the injury to the plaintiff. It may often be a better remedy than damages.

> *Grossman* v. *CFTO-TV Ltd.* (1982), 39 O.R. (2d) 498, per Cory JA at 501 (C.A.).

This expeditious remedy may be particularly attractive to a plaintiff where the initial publication has been to a limited group of people. Filing libel litigation often attracts media coverage. That may result in the publication of the defamatory expression more widely than the original publication by the defendant.

> *Tatum* v. *Limbrick*, [1994] B.C.J. No. 1471 per Edwards J. at para. 57 (S.C.).

A full and fair retraction coupled with a sincere and unequivocal apology often prevents litigation or brings a defamation lawsuit to an end at an early stage. If litigation nevertheless proceeds to trial, a retraction and apology may reduce the damages that would otherwise be awarded to the plaintiff. In the case of a newspaper or broadcast defendant, a proper retraction and apology may extinguish the possibility of the plaintiff recovering any damages other than actual pecuniary loss (if any).

If a defendant neglects or refuses to apologize, the result may be prolonged, inconvenient, and expensive litigation.

> *Leenen* v. *Canadian Broadcasting Corporation*, [2000] O.J. No. 3435, O.T.C. 672 (S.C.J.), aff'd (2001), 54 O.R. (3d) 612 (C.A.), leave to appeal to S.C.C.denied, [2001] S.C.C.A. No. 432, where Cunningham J., in the course of explaining his decision to award the plaintiff trial costs of $836,178 [in addition to the damages award of $950,000] stated at para. 4:
>
> > Litigation such as this is a high risk enterprise. … The plaintiff's offer to settle for an apology and a modest sum towards legal fees was very early on rejected by the defendants who, without any doubt, defended the action to the hilt. … That is their right as it is the right of any defendant who feels unjustifiably attacked. … Just as the plaintiff in this action took an enormous risk in prosecuting this claim, the defendants took an equal risk in adopting their scorched earth policy to the defence of the action.

The defendant's neglect or refusal to retract and apologize may in certain circumstances increase the damages. The court may draw an inference that the defendant published with actual malice, thereby aggravating the general damages or leading the court to make an award of punitive damages.

The adequacy and effect of apologies and retractions is addressed by the common law and by provincial defamation statutes. In some jurisdictions, the defamation statutes also contain provisions concerning related relief, such as the publication by the defendant of a rebuttal statement by the defamed person, or an "offer of amends" by the defendant. The statutes and jurisprudence differ somewhat from province to province, requiring litigants to treat court decisions from other jurisdictions with caution.

B. COMMON LAW CRITERIA FOR AN ADEQUATE APOLOGY AND RETRACTION

One of the best discussions of the criteria for an adequate apology for defamatory expression is found in the decision of Begbie C.J. in *Hoste* v. *Victoria Times Publishing Co.* (1889), 1 B.C.R. 365 at 366:

> That [the apology] is surely not sufficient. It is not the offer nor even the publication of an apology at all, but an offer to offer an apology.

And even in terms, it seems to reserve to the defendant a right of judging whether the plaintiff is reasonable in demanding any particular form e.g., it offers to make such an apology as the defendant thinks fit. Such an apology as merely 'beg your pardon', or 'sorry for it', is not sufficient in a case of libel. The defendant should admit that the charge was unfounded, that it was made without proper information, under an entire misapprehension of the real facts, etc., and that he regrets that it was published in his paper. Merely to say you are sorry, may mean that you are sorry because you have laid yourself open to an action, not that you repent having inflicted an unmerited wrong. A libel is an injury as well as an insult. The most proper apology cannot undo the irretrievable publication and dissemination of the slander, nor be regarded as a complete restitution, though it may properly be considered in damages. And that is what Lord Campbell's Act (a British libel statute) permits. You should not offer to make, but actually make and publish at once, and unconditionally, such an apology, expressing sorrow, withdrawing the imputation, rehabilitating the plaintiff's character as well as you can; not stipulating that the plaintiff is to accept it; not making any terms but publishing it in the interests of truth, and because you are anxious to undo whatever harm which may have accrued from a wrong which you find you have been the unconscious instrument of inflicting. Then in your statement of defence you can state what you have done. But a defendant in a libel case has no right to plead or refer to an apology, or bring it before the jury at all except under Lord Campbell's Act, which says that if the defendant, at the earliest opportunity publish an apology, he may plead that in mitigation of damages. That is the only authority I know for making any reference to an apology in the pleadings. It will be for the jury to say whether it was a reasonable and proper apology, and whether it is sufficient to absolve the defendant from any or how much of the damage the plaintiff has suffered. Obviously some libels may inflict an injury and loss that no apology or retraction by, or even remorse of, the wretched, miserable, libeller can wholly efface.

This decision has been cited with approval in a number of cases, including:

Amalgamated Transit Union v. *Independent Canadian Transit Union*, [1997] 5 W.W.R. 662 at 765 (Alta. Q.B.).

Brannigan v. *Seafarers International Union* (1963), 42 D.L.R. (2d) 249 at 257 (B.C.S.C.).

Carter v. *Gair* (1999), 170 D.L.R. (4th) 204 at 213 (B.C.C.A.).

Daley v. *Wallace* (1995), 44 C.P.C. (3d) 335 at 340 (Alta. Q.B.).

Dowding v. *Pacific West Equities* (1992), 63 B.C.L.R. (2d) 300 at 305 (S.C.).

Hunger Project v. *Council on Mind Abuse (C.O.M.A.) Inc.* (1995), 121 D.L.R. (4th) 734 at 737 (Ont. Gen. Div.).

Mitchell v. *Nanaimo District Teachers Association*, [1993] B.C.J. No. 386 per Hutchinson J. at para. 35 (S.C.), aff'd (1994), 94 B.C.L.R. (2d) 81 (C.A.).

Thompson v. *N.L. Broadcasting Ltd.* (1976), 1 C.C.L.T. 278 at 292–93 (B.C.S.C.).

Ungaro v. *Toronto Star Newspapers Ltd.* (1997), 144 D.L.R. (4th) 84 at 99 (Ont. Gen. Div.).

Vogel v. *Canadian Broadcasting Corporation*, [1982] 3 W.W.R. 97 at 160 (B.C.S.C.).

1) Legalistic Apologies

A defendant should avoid publishing an apology which cannot have much effect because it is expressed in excessively legalistic language or is otherwise vague or confusing.

Vogel v. *Canadian Broadcasting Corporation*, *ibid.* at 159–60.

2) Multiple Stings

In the case of multiple defamatory stings, the apology and retraction should express remorse for, and unequivocally withdraw, each defamatory imputation.

Brannigan v. *Seafarers International Union* (1963), 42 D.L.R. (2d) 249, per Hutcheson J. at 257 (B.C.S.C.).

3) Subject Matter of Apologies

Depending on the circumstances of the particular case, the defendant may need to apologize for:

i)   the literal meaning or innuendo meaning of the defamatory expression
ii)   the manner in which it was published
iii) the scope of publication
iv) his or her intention at the time of publication
v)   the nature of the injury caused to the plaintiff
vi) other matters arising from the original publication.

4) A Question for the Jury

The sufficiency or insufficiency of an apology is a question of a fact for the jury.

> *Dennis v. Southam Co. Ltd.*, [1955] 3 D.L.R. 346, per Beaubien J.A. at 348
> (Man. C.A.), citing W. Blake Odgers & Robert Ritson, *Odgers on Libel & Slander*, 6th ed. (London: Stevens, 1929) at 332, and *Doane v. Thomas,* [1922] 31
> B.C.R. 457 (C.A.).

The efficacy of an apology does not depend on what the defendant intended it to mean, but on the jury's finding as to what the ordinary reader might reasonably have taken an apology to mean.

> *Boushy v. Sarnia Gazette Publishing Co. Ltd.* (1980), 117 D.L.R. (3d) 171 per
> Southey J. at 175–76 (Ont. H.C.J.).

C. DISTINCTION BETWEEN AN APOLOGY AND A RETRACTION

Conceptually an "apology" and a "retraction" are different. An apology is a statement of remorse or regret for publishing defamatory expression and for its consequences in terms of injury or damage to the plaintiff. A retraction withdraws the defamatory imputation.

This distinction is expressed in certain provincial defamation statutes. For example, the Ontario *Libel and Slander Act* speaks variously of a "full and fair retraction" (section 5(2)), "a full apology" (section. 9(1)) and "a written apology" (section 22). In British Columbia, the concept of an apology is an element of a mitigation of damages provision (section 6) whereas the limitation of damages provision speaks of a "full and fair retraction." (section 7).

> *Ramsey v. Pacific Press, a Division of Southam Inc.*, [2000] B.C.J. No. 2422,
> 2000 BCSC 1551 at para. 60, per Taylor J.

> *Ungaro v. Toronto Star Newspaper Ltd.* (1997), 144 D.L.R. (4th) 84 at 97 (Ont.
> Gen. Div.), per Cavarzan J.

Courts are not always sensitive to the distinction between an apology and a retraction. In some decisions, the terms appear to be used interchangeably.

D. INADEQUATE APOLOGIES

1) Conditional or Hypothetical Apologies and Retractions

A conditional or hypothetical apology or retraction will normally not be considered adequate. An apology and retraction should be unequivocal.

Professor Williams, in an annotation to *Thompson v. NL Broadcasting Ltd.* (1976), 1 C.C.L.T. 278 at 279 (B.C.S.C.), provides useful observations about such apologies:

> The interesting feature of this case is the supposed apology. Lawyers for the plaintiff and defendant were unable to agree upon the appropriate form of an apology. The apology tendered by the defendant was unacceptable to the plaintiff and the defendant refused to publish the apology proffered by the plaintiff. What was actually published by the defendant and what he offered to publish constituted neither an apology nor a retraction and therefore served neither to mitigate damages nor to reduce them to actual damages.
>
> This decision is consistent with the authorities, such as *Lawson v. Burns (No. 2)* [(1976), 70 D.L.R. (3d) 735 (B.C.S.C.)] which require that there must be a genuine and frank withdrawal of the charges together with an expression of regret for those charges. An apology should not leave the impression of a reiteration of the original charge. The grudging way in which the defendant in his supposed apology stated "We are prepared to accept Mayor Thompson's answer" certainly aggravated the damages. The defendant implies that he will be the arbiter of whether a comment is justified. (This is an unfortunate tendency, which is commonly found among broadcasters and newspapers.) The hesitation and ambivalence with which this apology was delivered was undoubtedly the reason for the award of punitive damages. Furthermore, the implication that it was the wording rather than the substance of the comments, which was defamatory would be sufficient to incense a normal plaintiff. If a defendant intends to rely upon an apology it should be genuine and counsel will do a disservice to their clients if they allow them to persist in the idea that "if one says it in a clever enough way, they cannot take action." (*Cassell & Co. v. Broome*, [1972] 1 All E.R. 801 (H.L.)).

An apology by a defendant union was held to be inadequate where it did not unequivocally admit that a defamatory innuendo was unfounded or unequivocally express regret for its publication. The purported apology stated:

The Association [the Defendant] is concerned that your client [Plaintiff] appears to believe that the advertisement in question was directed at him personally. As indicated above, the Association assures your client that such was not the case. The Association does not believe that your client 'is the sort of person who would happily accept payment for doing nothing,' nor does it believe that he would 'arrogantly and blatantly disregard rules of polite conduct', nor does it believe that he is 'vulgar or greedy.' While the Association is of the view that none of these ideas could reasonably be taken from the material in question, it is sorry if your client has come to such a conclusion and it wishes to cause your client no distress.

Mitchell v. *Nanaimo District Teachers Assn.*, [1993] B.C.J. No. 386, per Hutchinson J. at paras. 35–37 (S.C.), aff'd (1994), 94 B.C.L.R. (2d) 81 (C.A.).

The conditional nature of an apology may render it insincere.

Amalgamated Transit Union v. *Independent Canadian Transit Union*, [1997] 5 W.W.R. 662, per Lutz J. at paras. 410, 412 (Alta. Q.B.), citing *Hoste* v. *Victoria Times Publishing Co.* (1889), 1 B.C.R. (Pt. 2) 365 at 366 (S.C.).

2) Evasive Apologies and Retractions

Evasive apologies were recently discussed in an article in the *National Post* newspaper:

In plain English: "His apology is really an evasion. It's a way of avoiding apologizing," Prof. Chambers explains.

Such apologies can actually add insult to injury by deflecting moral blame to the person at the receiving end, experts say.

Moral philosophers view apologies as an attempt to restore the "moral equilibrium" that was disturbed by an action.

"An apology is an attempt to set things back to the way they were before," says Michael McDonald, professor at the Centre for Applied Ethics at the University of British Columbia.

By implying that it was the other person who disturbed the moral equilibrium, an apology can aggravate the original insult.

"It's almost like saying you are to blame because you are being oversensitive about this," he says.

"His apology is really an evasion" *National Post* (25 January 2001) A1, A4.

Another form of evasive apology and retraction couples an innuendo that the plaintiff is somehow responsible for the defendant's misconduct (in

publishing the defamatory expression) with comments calculated to trivial-
ize the plaintiff's concerns about his or her reputation. Such an apology will
not be acceptable to the court. In one such case, the defendant's purported
expressions of apology were reported to be as follows:

> As far as I'm concerned I've done everything I possibly could to apologize for
> the incident and he [the plaintiff] in fact was the one doing something per-
> haps that he shouldn't have been doing.
>
> "Within 24 hours Ms. Hamilton-Brown issued a statement apologizing to
> Mr. Peters and his family for her comments.
>
> "Everybody and their dog" got a copy she said last night after a meeting
> with the Gondola Point council.
>
> "But that was not enough and the matter has resurfaced with the letter of
> intent [plaintiff's libel notice]
>
> "The whole thing to me seems ridiculous" she said.
>
> "The only thing I can say is that I apologized to Dr. Peters for the com-
> ment," she added. "I was hopeful that the apology, suggesting that he would
> never have done such a thing, would have sufficed. I apologized to every-
> body, and I do feel badly that I uttered those words after a very heated coun-
> cil meeting."

> *Peters* v. *Hamilton-Brown*, [2000] N.B.R (2d) (Supp.) No. 4, per McLellan J. at
> paras. 22–34 (Q.B.).

> See also *Kovlaske* v. *International Woodworkers of America - Canada, Local 1-
> 217*, [1999] B.C.J. No. 2326,per Loo J. at para. 59 (S.C.) citing *Brown* v. *Cole*,
> [1998] above:

>> ... the court found his remark that the plaintiff was "making a moun-
>> tain out of a molehill," an aggravating factor.

"A dishonest attempt to create something that might be put forward in
mitigation of damages and used as a feeble guise for a proper apology" may
assist the court in making a finding of actual malice against a defendant.

> *Platt* v. *Time International of Canada Ltd.*, [1964] 2 O.R. 21, per McRuer
> C.J.H.C. at 28 (H.C.J.), aff'd [1965] 1 O.R. 510n (C.A.).

3) Diluting or Voiding the Effect of an Apology

The content of the apology may dilute its force. Where a newspaper failed to
attribute the need for an apology to its own inadequate research before publication, but instead attributed it to information provided by the plaintiff, the
apology was held to be "somewhat ineffectual." The apology would have been

more effectual if the defendants, apprised of their error, had done further research to determine the truth, and then emphasized in the apology that it was further investigation that revealed the extent of the original mistake.

> *Prodor* v. *Canwest Publishers Limited*, [1996] B.C.J. No. 2504, per Collver J. at para. 62 (S.C.).

The conduct of a defendant subsequent to its publication of an apology may have the effect of diluting the apology and detracting from its sincerity.

> *Schultz* v. *Porter* (1979), 26 A.R. 61, per Waite J. at para. 11 (S.C.T.D.). [The defendant sent the plaintiff a letter purporting to be an apology. At trial, the defendant made an "incredible assertion in the witness box" that he believed in the truth of the defamatory imputation. The Court concluded the apology was "nothing more than a posture designed to avoid further difficulty and did not constitute an honest attempt to appease the plaintiff."]

Republication of the libel after an apology, for example, may permit the jury to make a finding of malice notwithstanding publication of an apology.

> *Teskey* v. *Canadian Newspapers Co. Ltd.* (1989), 68 O.R. (2d) 737 per Blair J.A. at 749 (C.A.)
>
> … [T]he trial judge … properly admitted into evidence four items published by the Free Press after the apology as evidence relating to malice and the aggravation of damages.
>
> *Platt* v. *Time Int'l of Canada Ltd.*, [1964] 2 O.R. 21 (H.C.J.), aff'd, [1965] 1 O.R. 510n [a libelous statement was partially repeated after the apology was tendered].

There may be circumstances where an apology, whether or not drafted by the defendant's legal counsel, is not issued in good faith – that is to show remorse and to correct the misstatements – but rather to repeat the assertions contained in the original defamatory publication. In such circumstances, the apology will not assist a defendant.

> *Jean* v. *Slyman*, [1990] B.C.J. No. 2044 (S.C.) per Cohen J. [characterizing the apology as "the attempted apology"].

The sincerity of an apology is not vitiated, however, merely because the defendant's lawyers initiate an investigation into the plaintiff's reputation after the commencement of litigation. "One would expect a law firm, properly approaching its responsibilities to its client, would have instituted such enquiry."

Munro v. *Toronto Sun Publishing Corporation* (1982), 39 O.R. (2d) 100 per Holland J. at para. 44 (H.C.J.).

D. MITIGATION OF DAMAGES BY APOLOGY AND RETRACTION AT COMMON LAW

An apology does not provide a general defence to liability. Nevertheless, the publication of an apology or retraction may mitigate the plaintiff's damages at common law, depending on its content, timing and other circumstances.

The common law principle that an apology may be considered in mitigation of damages continued even after the enactment of provisions in the provincial defamation statutes concerning retractions and apologies. Even if a defendant cannot satisfy the requirements of those statutory provisions, he or she is entitled to have an apology considered by the court.

> *Munro* v. *Toronto Sun Publishing Corporation, ibid.* at para. 66, approving Phillip Lewis, *Gatley on Libel and Slander*, 8th ed. (London: Sweet & Maxwell, 1981) at 589, paras. 1441–42.

> *Allan* v. *Bushnell T.V. Co. Ltd.*, [1969] 2 O.R. 6 (C.A.).

> *Tait* v. *New Westminster Radio Ltd.* (1984), 15 D.L.R. (4th) 115 at 119, 122–23 (B.C.C.A.). Hinkson J.A., after approving *Fritz* v. *Jim Pattison Broadcasting Ltd.* (6 October 1976), unreported, summarized [1976] W.W.D. 180 (B.C.) (Rae J.), *Smith* v. *Harrison* (1856), 1 F. & F. 565, 175 E.R. 845, and *Limon* v. *Bennett* (1900), 21 N.S.W.L.R. 164, stated at 122–23:

> > While a defence may involve certain requirements being met to give effect to it, a plea in mitigation does not involve meeting requirements but rather involves raising factors which may be taken into account.

> *Tedlie* v. *Southam Inc.*, [1950] 4 D.L.R. 415, per Montague J. at 425 (Man. K.B.) [apology not within statute, taken into account].

> *Hunter* v. *Fotheringham*, [1986] B.C.J. No. 2279 (S.C.).

> *Fisher* v. *Richardson*, [2002] B.C.J. No. 1017, 2002 BCSC 653 [apology adequately dealt with specific statements alleged to be defamatory and went to the recipients of the original defamatory letters].

It appears that it is open to a jury, at common law, to make a finding that an apology was so effective that it eliminated all damage the plaintiff might otherwise have suffered.

> *Alteman* v. *Ferguson*, [1919] 47 D.L.R. 618 (Man. C.A.).

However, even in cases where the defendant has made a full apology and retraction, the courts have recognized that the harm done by the defamatory statement is normally not completely ameliorated.

> *Associated Newspapers* v. *Dingle*, [1964] A.C. 371 per Lord Radcliffe at 399 (H.L.), stated that the jury or judge should allow for:
>
> > the sad truth that no apology, retraction or withdrawal can ever be guaranteed completely to undo the harm it [the libel] has done or the hurt it has caused ... .
>
> *Ley* v. *Hamilton* (1935), 153 L.T. 384 at 386 (H.L.) where Lord Atkin, quoted by Lord Diplock in *Broome* v. *Cassell & Co.*, [1972] A.C. 1027 at 1125 (H.L.) stated:
>
> > It is impossible to track the scandal to know what quarters the poison may reach.
>
> *Hoste* v. *Victoria Times Publishing Co.* (1889), 1 B.C.R. 365 (S.C.) where Begbie C.J.B.C. at 366 said the following:
>
> > A libel is an injury as well as an insult. The most proper apology cannot undo the irretrievable publication and dissemination of the slander nor be regarded as a complete restitution though it may properly be considered in damages.

A court has taken into account the publicity given by a defendant newspaper to the evidence at the trial which makes it abundantly clear to all reasonable persons that the defamatory accusations were groundless.

> *Bennett* v. *Sun Publishing Co.* (1972), 29 D.L.R. (3d) 423, per Anderson J. at 440 (B.C.S.C.).

By contrast, in assessing damages at trial, a court is not permitted to take into consideration the effect of its judgment as mitigating damages.

> *Bennett* v. *Sun Publishing Co. ibid.* at 440–41 (B.C.S.C.), citing *Associated Newspapers, Ltd.* v. *Dingle*, [1962] 2 All E.R. 737 at 750.

1) Effect of Failure to Apologize

A court assessing damages may take into account the defendant's failure to accept a plaintiff's offer to forgo court action in exchange for an apology. It may also take into account the defendant's refusal of an opportunity (even as late as the trial) to undertake to make an apology.

> *Viscount* v. *Atamanik*, [1998] B.C.J. No. 2530 per Errico J. at para. 14 (S.C.).

Walker v. CFTO Ltd. (1987), 37 D.L.R. (4th) 224 per Robins J.A. for the court at 238 (Ont. C.A.) [a jury's verdict effectively offered the defendant a chance to apologize and avoid significant liability in damages; the defendant declined the opportunity].

Tornberg v. Worrell, [1995] A.J. No. 1312, per Sulatycky J. at para. 45 (Q.B.).

R.G. v. Christison, [1997] 1 W.W.R. 641, per Wedge J. at paras. 144–46 (Sask. Q.B.).

The absence of an apology or a refusal to apologize may be a factor which increases or aggravates the plaintiff's general damages.

Hill v. Church of Scientology of Toronto, [1995] 2 S.C.R. 1130, per Cory J. at para. 191, citing Philip Lewis, *Gatley on Libel and Slander,* 8th ed. (London: Sweet & Maxwell, 1981) at 592–93, para. 1451.

Murphy v. Alexander, [2001] O.J. No. 5465, per Belleghem J. at para. 142 (S.C.J.):

> In assessing aggravated damages, considerations can include: whether there was a withdrawal of the libelous statement made by the defendant and an apology tendered …

Gestion Trans-Tek Inc. v. Lampel, [2001] O.J. No. 1207, per Wilkins J. at para. 51 (S.C.J.):

> No apology has ever been tendered and the plaintiff has been forced to trial to clear his name. In the circumstances, I am satisfied this is an appropriate situation for the Court to express its displeasure at his conduct and to make an award of aggravated damages in the amount of $10,000.

Bains v. Indo-Canadian Times Inc., [1995] 57 B.C.A.C. 90, per Donald J.A. (Goldie and Ryan JJ.A. concurring) at paras. 15, 27–34 (C.A.). [setting aside the award of punitive damages at trial without disturbing the trial judge's finding that damages were aggravated by the defendant's refusal to publish a proper apology and persistence in a plea of justification].

Platt v. Time International of Canada. Ltd. (1964), 44 D.L.R. (2d) 17 (Ont. H.C.J.), aff'd without written reasons (1964), 48 D.L.R. (2d) 508n (Ont. C.A.) [punitive damages awarded, taking into account, among other things, the absence of a proper retraction or apology].

Farrell v. St. John's Publishing Co. Ltd., [1986] N.J. No. 19 (Nfld. C.A.) per Morgan J.A. for the Court.

Wenman v. Pacific Press, [1991] B.C.J. No. 186, 1991 BCSC C891725 per Allan J.

Lawson v. Burns (1974), 56 D.L.R. (2d) 240, per Aikins J. at 258 (B.C.S.C.).

Barltrop v. Canadian Broadcasting Corporation (1978), 86 D.L.R. (3d) 61, per MacKeigan C.J.N.S. at 78–79 (N.S.S.C. (A.D.)) :

> The very factors which, if more pronounced, might have warranted punitive damages may, however, aggravate and increase the general damages. … So it is here. The prestige and apparent authority with which the defendant's programme falsely condemned the plaintiff, and its wide dissemination, without apology or explanation, … greatly magnified the derogatory impact on [the plaintiff's] reputation and pride.

Reichmann v. Berlin, [2002] O.J. No. 2732 per Sachs J. at para. 6 (S.C.J.).

Thomas v. Canadian Broadcasting Corporation, [1981] 4 W.W.R. 289, per Disbery J. at 340, 341–42 (N.W.T.S.C.).

Barcan v. Zorkin, [1991] 113 A.R. 381 (Q.B.) per Shannon J.

Vogel v. Canadian Broadcasting Corporation, [1982] 3 W.W.R. 97 (B.C.S.C.).

Safeway Stores Ltd. v. Harris, [1948] 4 D.L.R. 187, per McPherson C.J.M. at 195 (Man. K.B.).

Norman v. New Westminster (City), [1999] B.C.J. No. 433, per K. Smith J. at paras. 47–51 (S.C.):

> … the City Administrator prepared letters of apology … to be sent to all recipients of Mrs. Pynenburg's [defamatory] mailing. The letters were prepared with a line for her signature and his. She signed all of them except the letter of apology to Mr. Norman, which she refused to sign. It went to Mr. Norman under the signature of only the City Administrator. Her refusal to sign the letter to Mr. Norman is indicative of her state of mind toward him.

An unduly delayed apology may permit a finding of malice which aggravates damages or supports an award of punitive damages.

Campbell v. Cartmell, [1999] O.J. No. 3553, per Himel J. at paras. 4, 6 (S.C.J.), after citing Philip Lewis, *Gatley on Libel and Slander*, 8th ed. (London: Sweet & Maxwell, 1981) at 592–93.

A failure to apologize may also be taken into account by the court when fixing the scale of costs payable by the defendant.

R.G. v. Christison, [1997] 3 W.W.R. 604 (Sask. Q.B.) per Wedge J. at para. 9.

a) May Result in Punitive Damages

A refusal to apologize, combined with other factors, such as pleading justification, may even assist in supporting a finding of malice which leads to an award of punitive damages.

> *Thompson v. NL Broadcasting Ltd.* (1976), 1 C.C.L.T. 278, per Schultz J. at pp. 288–95 (B.C.S.C.).

> *Amalgamated Transit Union v. Independent Canadian Transit Union*, [1997] 5 W.W.R. 662, per Lutz J. at para. 413 (Alta. Q.B.), citing *Mercereau v. Hock*, [1930] 3 D.L.R. 159 (Sask. K.B.).

> *Platt v. Time International of Canada. Ltd.* (1964), 44 D.L.R. (2d) 17 (Ont. H.C.J.), aff'd without written reasons (1964), 48 D.L.R. (2d) 508n (Ont. C.A.) [punitive damages awarded, taking into account, among other things, the absence of a proper retraction or apology].

> *Hubert v. DeCamillas* (1963), 41 D.L.R. (2d) 495, per Aikins J. at 512, 514 (B.C.S.C.), citing *Ross v. Lamport* (1957), 9 D.L.R. (2d) 585 [where the Mayor of Toronto was assessed $25,000 damages for arrogantly defaming in newspapers a man who had appealed a refusal of a taxi licence, and for failing to apologize].

In certain circumstances, the failure of a defendant to apologize may legitimately be excused on the basis it would have required some repetition of the defamatory matter, thereby aggravating the situation.

> *Syms v. Warren* (1976), 71 D.L.R. (3d) 558, per Hamilton J. at 563 (Man. Q.B.).

2) Inadequate Apology May Result in Aggravation of Damages

The publication of an inadequate apology may aggravate the plaintiff's damages:

i)   where there is an unnecessary repetition, expressly or by implication, of the libelous statement.

> *Brannigan v. Seafarers International Union of Canada* (1963), 42 D.L.R. (2d) 249 per Hutcheson J. at 258 (B.C.S.C.), citing Harvey McGregor, *Mayne & McGregor on Damages*, 12th ed. (London: Sweet & Maxwell, 1961) at para. 894 [alleged apology, although ambiguous, bore interpretation plaintiff supported policies of communist party. Held: this was a "deliber-

ate and intended reiteration or emphasizing of the defamatory statement" that plaintiff was a communist or communist sympathizer].

Bennett v. Stupich (1981), 125 D.L.R. (3d) 743, per Mackoff J. at 752 (B.C.S.C.):

> In unnecessarily setting out the words in question in quotation marks, taken from the [plaintiff's] solicitor's letter, the defendant in so doing exacerbated the libel. By no stretch of the imagination can this be regarded as an apology.

ii) where there is an absence of any intention to withdraw or express regret for the statement or to rectify any harm done.

Hoste v. Victoria Times Publishing Co. (1889), 1 B.C.R. 365 (S.C.).

Brannigan v. Seafarers' International Union of Canada (1963), 42 D.L.R. (2d) 249 (B.C.S.C.).

iii) where the apology is framed in ironic or sarcastic terms.

Bennett v. Stupich (1981), above, at 751.

iv) where the apology implies or states that it was the literal wording rather than the substance of the defendant's statement that was defamatory.

Thompson v. NL Broadcasting Ltd. (1976), 1 C.C.L.T. 278 (B.C.S.C.) [see particularly the notations by Jeremy Williams at the beginning of the report].

It has been held that a false or insincere apology may aggravate damages.

Wiley v. Toronto Star Newspapers Ltd. (1988), 51 D.L.R. (4th) 439, per Mac-Farland J. at 449–50 (S.C.).

Brannigan v. Seafarers International Union of Canada (1963), 42 D.L.R. (2d) 249 per Hutcheson J. at 258 (B.C.S.C.) [apology was held to be a deliberate and intended reiteration of the defamatory matter].

Amalgamated Transit Union v. Independent Canadian Transit Union, [1997] 7 W.W.R. 696, per Lutz J. at para. 409 (Alta. Q.B.).

In assessing whether an inadequate apology has aggravated damages, the court may examine not only the content of the purported apology but the events which led to its formulation and publication.

Bennett v. Stupich (1981), above, at 751.

A well-intentioned albeit totally inept apology will not necessarily aggravate damages. Where the defendants genuinely wished to publish a proper and timely apology and retraction but did not do so because of ineptitude, inexperience, and lack of timely legal advice, the conduct of the defendants was not outrageous or malicious.

> *Fulton v. West End Times* (1998), 45 B.C.L.R. (3d) 288, per Holmes J. at paras. 37–38 (S.C.).

There may be situations where an apology to someone else aggravates the damages but these are likely to be rare.

> *Hodgson v. Canadian Newspapers Co.* (1998), 39 O.R. (3d) 235 per Lane J. at 405–6 (Gen. Div.), aff'd (2000), 189 D.L.R. (4th) 241 (Ont. C.A.), leave to appeal to S.C.C. denied, [2000] S.C.C.A. 465.

3) Location and Size of Apology and Retraction

The apology should normally be published in the same type and same location as the original defamatory article. A libel in headlines requires an apology in headlines.

> *Bennett v. Sun Publishing Co.* (1972), 29 D.L.R. (3d) 423 (B.C.S.C.) .

The plaintiff is entitled to have the apology and retraction given the same prominence as the original defamatory statement.

> *Jackson v. Australian Consolidated Press Limited*, [1966] 2 N.S.W.R. 775 (C.A.).

The circumstances will dictate whether the apology or retraction has to be printed in exactly the same page or in the same place.

> *Stieb v. The Vernon News*, [1947] 4 D.L.R. 397, per Macfarlane J. at 399 (B.C.S.C.) [apology appeared in the same position in the newspaper as the original article, but a little lower down in the column, at the foot of it].

> > The editors and publishers of the newspaper approached the matter in the practical spirit of correcting a mistake which they considered was unfortunate and with a view to inform their readers of the fact that a mistake had been made. As there was no malice in the original publication, so I think it is unnecessary that the apology should be abject. Too much of that sort of thing, as examples I can recall will illustrate, may become farcical and have the opposite effect.

> *Grabarevic v. Northwest Publications Ltd.* (1968), 67 D.L.R. (2d) 748 (B.C.C.A.).

> *Harvey v. Horizon Publications Ltd.* (1975), 61 D.L.R. (3d) 570 (B.C.S.C.).

Munro v. Toronto Sun Publishing Corp. (1982), 39 O.R. (2d) 100 (H.C.J.).

Murray Alter's Talent Associates Ltd. v. Toronto Star Newpapers Ltd. (1995), 124 D.L.R. (4th) 105 (Ont. Div. Ct.).

The English rules provide for the making of apologies by means of a statement in open court, which is protected by absolute privilege.

Watts v. Times Newspapers Ltd., [1995] E.W.J. No. 2882 at para. 28.

Under the British Columbia Supreme Court rule relating to an offer to settle, a plaintiff in an action for defamation who accepts an offer to settle, or takes money out of court (under Rule 21(18)), may apply to court (under Rule 37(36)) for leave to make a statement in open court in terms approved by the court. In practice, a plaintiff and defendant may agree that the plaintiff's statement will record the fact and content of an apology and retraction by the defendant.

4) Timing of Apology and Retraction

Whether or not an apology is considered timely will depend on the circumstances of the individual case.

i)   An apology one week after publication, even though the story was republished across Canada, was considered to be a prompt apology.

    Munro v. Toronto Sun Publishing Corp. above.

ii)   An apology two days after the libel was considered to be a prompt apology.

    Abraham v. Advocate, [1946] 2 W.W.R. 181 (P.C.)

iii) An apology which was published six weeks after a second broadcast was not acceptable timing.

    Thompson v. NL Broadcasting Ltd. (1976) 1 C.C.L.T. 278 (B.C.S.C.)

iv)   An apology five months after the libel was not acceptable timing.

    Brannigan v. Seafarers International Union (1963), 42 D.L.R. (2d) 249 (B.C.S.C.).

v)   An apology three years and eight months after the broadcast libel was too late to be a mitigating factor but was not an aggravating factor.

    Farrell v. Canadian Broadcasting Corporation (1987), 43 D.L.R. (4th) 667 at 681 (Nfld. C.A.), per Gushue J.A. [Goodridge C.J.N. concurring in separate reasons, Noel J. also concurring].

vi)   An apology not tendered until the fifth day of oral argument before the Court of Appeal was meaningless.

> *Hill v. Church of Scientology of Toronto*, [1995] 2 S.C.R. 1130 per Cory J. at 1207–8.

vii) An offer of an apology made six weeks after the defamatory publication was not at the "earliest opportunity."

> *Mitchell v. Nanaimo District Teachers Assn.*, [1993] B.C.J. No. 386 per Hutchinson J. at paras. 35–37 (S.C.).

viii) An apology not offered until the trial began was "not worth much … but perhaps every apology is worth something. On such a view one might be inclined to reduce a judgment for damages against [the defendant]. It would not be [a] great reduction."

> *Paul v. Van Hull* (1962), 36 D.L.R. (2d) 639, per Maybank J. at 661 (Man. Q.B.).

ix)   An apology offered during the defendant's cross-examination at trial two and a half years after the defamatory publication was "long over-due," in circumstances where a "reasonable and well intended investigation would have determined the plaintiff's innocence."

> *Kaniewski v. Key Property Management (1986) Inc.* (1992), 44 C.C.E.L. 136, per Kennedy J. at 147 (Ont. Gen. Div.).

x)   At trial, after the evidence was closed, the defendant sought to have his counsel apologize during the course of his address to the jury. "An apology at that stage if it had been permitted, and it was not, could hardly be inspired by a sincere desire to made amends and could only be motivated by a desire to escape from, or minimize the penalty a jury might impose."

> *Ross v. Lamport* (1957), 9 D.L.R. (2d) 585, per Roach J.A. at 590 (Ont. C.A.), new trial ordered, [1956] S.C.R. 366.

5) Scope of Publication of Apology and Retraction

The apology should be published as widely as the original defamatory statement so that the apology may as much as possible undo the harm caused by the libel.

> *Lafone v. Smith* (1858) 28 L.J. Ex. 33.

Where the defendant published its apology in its Toronto, Calgary, and Edmonton newspapers, passed it to a wire service it owned which supplied seventy-five newspapers, and referred to the apology in paid radio advertisements, it was held that the publication and republication of the apology were at least as complete and national in scope as the original publication.

Munro v. Toronto Sun Publishing Corporation (1982), 39 O.R. (2d) 100 per J. Holland J. at para. 42 (H.C.J.).

F. MITIGATION OF DAMAGES FOR NEWSPAPERS AND BROADCASTERS UNDER THE PROVINCIAL DEFAMATION ACTS

The provincial defamation statutes provide, with some variation, that the defendant may plead mitigating circumstances in an action for libel in a newspaper or other periodical publication, or in a broadcast.

British Columbia, *Libel and Slander Act*, R.S.B.C. 1996, c. 263, s.6.

Alberta, *Defamation Act*, R.S.A. 2000, c. D-6, s.15.

Saskatchewan, *Libel and Slander Act*, R.S.S. 1978, c. L-14, s.7.

Manitoba, *Defamation Act*, R.S.M. 1987, c. D-20, s.16.

Ontario, *Libel and Slander Act*, R.S.O. 1990, c. L.12, s.9.

New Brunswick, *Defamation Act*, R.S.N.B. 1973, c. D-5, s. 16(1).

Newfoundland and Labrador, *Defamation Act*, R.S.N. 1990, c. D-3, s.17.

Nova Scotia, *Defamation Act*, R.S.N.S. 1989, c. 122, s.21(1).

Prince Edward Island, *Defamation Act*, R.S.P.E.I. 1988, c..D-5, s.17(1).

Yukon Territory, *Defamation Act*, R.S.Y.T. 1986, c. 41, s. 17(1).

Northwest Territories, *Defamation Act*, R.S.N.W.T. 1988, c. D-1, s.18(1).

These provisions apply only to a "newspaper," "periodical," or "broadcast" as defined in the statute.

For example, the British Columbia *Libel and Slander Act* provides that in an action for libel in a newspaper or other periodical publication the defendant may plead in mitigation of damages that:

i)   the libel was published without actual malice and without gross negligence; and

ii)   before the commencement of the action, or at the earliest opportuni-
        ty afterwards, the defendant published or broadcast a full apology for
        the libel; or

iii)   if the newspaper or periodical publication in which the libel appeared
        is one ordinarily published at intervals exceeding one week, the
        defendant offered to publish the apology in a newspaper or other peri-
        odical publication to be selected by the plaintiff in the action.

The British Columbia statute also provides that in an action for libel in a
broadcast, the defendant may plead in mitigation of damages that:

i)   the libel was broadcast without actual malice and without gross neg-
        ligence and

ii)   before the commencement of the action, or at the earliest opportuni-
        ty afterwards, the defendant broadcast a full apology for the libel.

> British Columbia, *Libel and Slander Act*, R.S.B.C. 1996, c. 263, s.6.

In Alberta, the Yukon Territory, and the Northwest Territories, this mitigation provision applies only to actions for defamation against the proprietor or publisher of a newspaper or the owner or operator of a broadcasting
station or an officer, servant or employee thereof, in respect of defamatory
matter published in that newspaper or broadcast from that station.

> Alberta, *Defamation Act*, R.S.A. 2000, c. D-6, s.12.

> Yukon, *Defamation Act*, R.S.Y.T. 1986, c. 41, s.13.

> Northwest Territories, *Defamation Act*, R.S.N.W.T. 1988, c. D-1, s.14.

The onus of proof rests on the defendant to establish each element of the
statutory requirements.

> *Snider* v. *Calgary Herald*, [1985] 34 C.C.L.T. 27, per Miller A.C.J.Q.B. at para.
> 109 (Alta. Q.B.).

There is substantial jurisprudence concerning each of the elements of the
mitigation provisions.

1) "Without Actual Malice and Without Gross Negligence"

"Actual malice" is a term which relates to the actual state of mind or condition of the mind of the person who did the act. It implies some personal
hatred or ill will or wanton intention to injure and denotes a condition

which is directly imputable to the publisher concerned. The same considerations apply to the words "gross negligence."

Allan v. Bushnell T.V. Co. Ltd. (1969), 4 D.L.R. (3d) 212 per Schroeder J.A. at 220–21 (Ont. C.A.).

Popovich v. Lobay, [1937] 3 D.L.R. 713. (Man. C.A.) per Trueman J.A. [printer did not understand foreign language in which defamatory expression was published, apologized].

A publisher will be vicariously accountable, however, for the malice of its servants or agents.

Allan v. Bushnell T.V. Co. Ltd. (1969), above, at 221.

Where there is nothing analogous to a principal and agency relationship between a broadcaster and the third party news agency which supplied the erroneous information, the broadcaster is not tainted by the actual malice or gross negligence of that third party.

Allan v. Bushnell T.V. Co. Ltd., ibid. at 221.

2) "Before the Commencement of the Action, or at the Earliest Opportunity Afterwards"

An apology was not published at the earliest opportunity where a newspaper delayed eleven days from receipt of the notice of intention to sue.

Snider v. Calgary Herald, above, at para. 105:

> … it took two more days to talk to the publisher, five more days to hear from the Herald's solicitor, and then two more days to draft the apology. It does not appear to me that the senior staff at the Herald, or their solicitors, treated the matter very seriously even then, for it seems unreasonable that it would take nine more days after the untruths were recognized to get around to publishing the apology.

3) "The Defendant Published or Broadcast a Full Apology for the Libel"

A full apology requires a clear statement that there was no basis in fact for making the defamatory allegation. The apology should also adequately identify the original publication to which it relates.

Snider v. Calgary Herald, ibid. at para. 106.

A full apology under this section requires a "full and frank withdrawal of the charges or suggestions."

Kerr v. *Conlogue* (1992), 65 B.C.L.R. (2d) 70, per Sinclair Prowse J. (S.C.), citing *Hunter* v. *Fotheringham*, [1986] B.C.J. No. 2279 (S.C.)

Ramsey v. *Pacific Press, a Division of Southam Inc.*, [2000] B.C.J. No. 2422, 2000 BCSC 1551, where Taylor J. describes a "retraction/apology" at paras. 77–78:

> [77] A retraction/apology has three constituent parts.
>
> [78] It acknowledges the error, expresses regret for the error and expresses an apology for the erroneous statements. It must be understandable by a reasonable reader, not just the plaintiff, to be a full and unqualified apology and thus a full and fair retraction ... .

G. MITIGATION OF DAMAGES FOR ALL DEFENDANTS UNDER THE PROVINCIAL DEFAMATION ACTS

The defamation statutes also contain a provision permitting all defendants (not only the news media) to give evidence of an apology or offer of an apology in mitigation of damages.

Generally the statutes provide, with some provincial variations, that where the defendant has pleaded a denial of the alleged defamation only (or has suffered judgment by default or judgment has been given against him on a motion for judgment on the pleadings) he may give in evidence, in mitigation of damages, that he made or offered a written or printed apology to the plaintiff for the defamation before commencement of the action. If the action was commenced before there was an opportunity to make or offer the apology, he may plead that he did so as soon afterwards as he had an opportunity.

British Columbia, *Libel and Slander Act*, R.S.B.C. 1996, c. 263, s.10.

Alberta, *Defamation Act*, R.S.A. 2000, c. D-6, s. 4.

Saskatchewan, *Libel and Slander Act*, R.S.S. 1978, c. L-14, s.7.

Manitoba, *Defamation Act*, R.S.M. 1987, c. D-20, s.4.

Ontario, *Libel and Slander Act*, R.S.O. 1990, c. L.12, s.9.

New Brunswick, *Defamation Act*, R.S.N.B. 1973, c. D-5, s.4.

Nova Scotia, *Defamation Act*, R.S.N.S. 1989, c. 122, s.5.

Prince Edward Island, *Defamation Act*, R.S.P.E.I. 1988, c. D-5, s.4.

Newfoundland and Labrador, *Defamation Act*, R.S.N. 1990, c. D-3, s.5..

Yukon Territory, *Defamation Act*, R.S.Y.T. 1986, c. 41, s. 17(1).

Northwest Territories, *Defamation Act*, R.S.N.W.T. 1988, c. D-1, s.18(1).

Any apology offered or made pursuant to this provision must be a "full and frank withdrawal of the charges conveyed" and should be worded so that "an impartial person would consider it reasonably satisfactory in all the circumstances."

Carter v. *Gair* (1999) 170 D.L.R. (4th) 204 per Newbury J.A. at 213 (B.C.C.A.), quoting from *Risk Allah Bey* v. *Whitehurst* (1868), 18 L.T. 615 (Q.B.), and approving *Hunter* v. *Fotheringham*, [1986] B.C.J. No. 2279, and *Hoste* v. *Victoria Times Publishing Co.* (1889), 1 B.C.R. 365 (S.C.).

Where a defendant stipulated that the plaintiff was to accept their apology before they published it, the offer could be considered in mitigation of damages but its effect was minor where the defendant failed to carry through and publish the apology.

Carter v. *Gair, ibid.* at 213.

H. RESTRICTION OF DAMAGES FOR NEWSPAPERS AND BROADCASTERS UNDER THE PROVINCIAL DEFAMATION ACTS

The defamation statutes provide, with minor variations depending upon the province, that a plaintiff shall only recover special damages ("actual damages" in the British Columbia and Ontario statute) if:

i)   the defamatory matter was published in good faith,
ii)   there was reasonable ground to believe that it was for the public benefit [this requirement is not contained in the Ontario statute],
iii) it did not involve a criminal charge,
iv)   the publication took place in mistake or misapprehension of the facts,
v)   a "full and fair retraction" was published or broadcast, and
vi)   the retraction was published in as conspicuous a place and type as the defamatory matter, or in the case of a broadcast, as widely and as often [as stipulated in the statute].

British Columbia, *Libel and Slander Act*, R.S.B.C. 1996, c. 263, s.7.

Alberta, *Defamation Act*, R.S.A. 2000, c. D-6, s. 16(1).

Saskatchewan, *Libel and Slander Act*, R.S.S. 1978, c. L-14, s. 8(1).

Manitoba, *Defamation Act*, R.S.M. 1987, c. D-20, s.17.

Ontario, *Libel and Slander Act*, R.S.O. 1990, c. L.12, s.5(2).

New Brunswick, *Defamation Act*, R.S.N.B. 1973, c. D-5, s.17(1).

Nova Scotia, *Defamation Act*, R.S.N.S. 1989, c. 122, s.22(1).

Prince Edward Island, *Defamation Act*, R.S.P.E.I. 1988, c. D-5, s.18(1).

Newfoundland and Labrador, *Defamation Act*, R.S.N. 1990, c. D-3, s.19(1).

Yukon Territory, *Defamation Act*, R.S.Y.T. 1986, c. 41, s.18(1).

Northwest Territories, *Defamation Act*, R.S.N.W.T. 1988, c. D-1, s.19(1) .

These provisions apply only to defamatory expression in newspapers, periodicals, and broadcasts as defined in each statute.

Saskatchewan's provision does not apply to broadcasts. It is limited to libel in a "newspaper."

In essence, the eligible defendants are given the option of choosing between publishing a retraction or paying compensatory damages, which, at common law, are assessable without proof of actual damages.

Murray Alter's Talent Associates Ltd. v. *Toronto Star Newspapers Ltd.* (1995), 124 D.L.R. (4th) 105, per Borins J.A. at 118 (Ont. Div. Ct.).

The statutes of Alberta, Manitoba, New Brunswick, Nova Scotia, Prince Edward Island, the Yukon Territory, and the Northwest Territories also require that "a full apology" be published or broadcast with the "retraction."

The defendant must prove each of the elements of the statutory requirement.

Teskey v. *Canadian Newspapers Ltd.* (1989), 68 O.R. (2d) 737 at 744 (C.A.).

Ramsey v. *Pacific Press, a Division of Southam, Inc.*, [2000] B.C.J. No. 2422, 2000 BCSC 1551, at para. 62.

There is a considerable body of jurisprudence concerning these provisions.

1) "The Defamatory Matter was Published in Good Faith"

"Good faith" requires an honest belief in the truth of the matter published, formed on reasonable grounds. Proof that the defendant was not actuated by malice does not suffice. The defendant must exercise the care and vigilance of a prudent and conscientious person under similar circumstances. He or she must take all reasonable precautions to verify the truth of the statement before publication.

> *Teskey* v. *Canadian Newspapers Ltd.*, above, at 746, adopting the following statement by Mitchell J. in *Allan* v. *Pioneer Company*, 41 N.W. 936 at 939 (Minn. Sup. Ct. 1889), defining the meaning of the words "published in good faith" as they were used in the Minnesota section comparable to s. 5(2) of the Ontario *Libel and Slander Act*:

> > We may assume that the Act was designed to protect honest, and careful newspaper publishers. It is not to be presumed that the legislature intended to make so radical a change in the law of libel as to make mere belief in the truth of the article the test of good faith. If so, they have introduced a very dangerous principle, which virtually places the good name and reputation of the citizen at the mercy of the credulity or indifference of every reckless or negligent reporter. Good faith requires proper consideration for the character and reputation of the person whose character is likely to be injuriously affected by the publication. It requires of the publisher that he exercise the care and vigilance of a prudent and conscientious man, wielding, as he does, the great power of the public press. There must be an absence, not only of all improper motives, but of negligence, on his part. It is his duty to take all reasonable precautions to verify the truth of the statement, and to prevent untrue and injurious publications against others.

> *Ramsey* v. *Pacific Press, a Division of Southam, Inc.*, [2000] B.C.J. No. 2422, 2000 BCSC 1551, at paras. 67–69.

> *Ungaro* v. *Toronto Star Newspaper Ltd.* (1997), 144 D.L.R. (4th) 84, per Cavarzan J. at 95 (Ont. Gen. Div.).

A trial judge did not err in charging a jury that publishing an allegedly defamatory advertisement "with a complete disregard for whether it was a libel, whether it will harm somebody, is not publishing in good faith." These words are from the trial judgment in *Teskey* v. *Canadian Newspapers*, above at 746.

> *Teskey* v. *Canadian Newspapers*, above, at 748:

> > The opening line of the advertisement, containing the word "betrayal" should have rung an "alarm bell" as to its "potentially libellous" nature.

It was a "gross deviation of journalistic practice" to publish the advertisement without any investigation of the truth of the allegations it contained.

The requirement of good faith cannot be satisfied merely by some checking of the facts. A defendant must demonstrate that he or she exercised the care and vigilance of a prudent and conscientious individual.

Ungaro v. Toronto Star Newspaper Ltd. (1997), 144 D.L.R. (4th) 84 at 95 (Ont. Gen. Div.), where Cavarzan J. held that:

> In my view, Ms. Steed used the word "successfully" to characterize the outcome of Demarco's lawsuit against Ungaro, and I so find. She did not take all reasonable precautions to verify the truth of the statement. The checking done by Ms. Steed was inadequate in that it fell short of meeting the proper standard of care as outlined by Senator Doyle. To reiterate the words of Mitchell J. quoted above from *Allen v. Pioneer Co.*:
>
>> Good faith requires proper consideration for the character and reputation of the person whose character is likely to be injuriously affected by the publication. It requires of the publisher that he exercise the care and vigilance of a prudent and conscientious man, wielding, as he does, the great power of the public press. There must be an absence, not only of all improper motives, but of negligence, on his part.
>
> It is not sufficient that some checking of the facts was done. The Teskey case does not stand for the proposition that there must be a total failure to check facts in order to justify a finding of bad faith. In my view, it establishes a standard of reasonable care consistent with the standard articulated by Senator Doyle. That standard was not met in this case. I conclude, therefore, that the libellous statement was not published in good faith.
>
> Portions of the transcripts of the examination for discovery of Ellie Tesher, the editor of the Sunday Star, were read into the record at trial. She had read the article and had been involved in the decision to include it on the front page. She acknowledged that she had read the words complained of, that she understood their import, and that she did not ask that the facts alleged be checked before publication. She maintained that it was not part of her responsibilities to ensure that the facts were accurate. I agree with the submission by counsel for the

plaintiff that this reflects a lack of concern as well as being an admission of negligence.

Where a defendant failed to make inquiries although he suspected the source, he did not broadcast in good faith.

Ramsey v. *Pacific Press, a Division of Southam Inc.*, [2000] B.C.J. No. 2422, 2000 BCSC 1551 per Taylor J. at para. 68:

> Meisner failed to make inquiries about an information source that he himself had suspected. That suspicion, coupled with the knowledge of Ramsey's reputation despite his political differences with him, and the knowledge, as a public broadcaster of the effect of such an attribution to Ramsey shows that this editorial was not made in good faith.

The requirement of good faith will not be satisfied merely because the plaintiff believes that he was right in publishing the expression.

Bennett v. *Sun Publishing Co.* (1972), 29 D.L.R. (3d) 423 (B.C.S.C.), citing the headnote to *Halls* v. *Mitchell*, [1928] S.C.R. 125, where it states, *inter alia*, "It is not sufficient that the person making the statement believes, honestly and not without some ground, that the duty or interest exists."

2) "Reasonable Ground to Believe that it was for the Public Benefit"

[Note: this requirement is not contained in the Ontario *Libel and Slander Act*]

Where a broadcast attributed a politically controversial statement to a provincial cabinet minister who was facing a recall campaign in his own riding, there was reasonable ground to believe that the broadcast (if true) was for the public benefit.

Ramsey v. *Pacific Press*, above, at para. 70.

It has been held that in determining whether the publication was "for the public benefit," different considerations apply than when determining whether an occasion is one of qualified privilege. There is a benefit to the public in newspapers publishing notices and advertisements. That is of value to society as a whole, as is the publication of news.

Bordeleau v. *Bonnyville Nouvelle Ltd.*, [1993] 1 W.W.R. 634 (Alta. Q.B.) per Marshall J. [an advertisement congratulating the plaintiff on the impending arrival of her new baby (the plaintiff was not married and not pregnant) was for the public benefit].

3) "It Did Not Involve a Criminal Charge"

A defamatory editorial involved a criminal charge where it incorrectly named the plaintiff as the treasurer of a society and responsible for its financial transactions at a time for which it was convicted of the theft of charity funds.

> *Fulton* v. *West End Times Ltd.* (1998), 45 B.C.L.R. (3d) 288, per Holmes J. at para. 27 (S.C.).

4) "The Publication Took Place in Mistake or Misapprehension of the Facts"

The mistake must relate to the facts of the libel.

> *Teskey* v. *Canadian Newspapers Co. Ltd.* (1989), 68 O.R. (2d) 737 per Blair J.A. at 748 (C.A.), citing *LeBlanc* v. *L'Imprimerie Acadienne Ltée.*, [1955] 5 D.L.R. 91 (N.B.S.C.).

5) "A Full and Fair Retraction was Published or Broadcast"

In British Columbia, it was held that a retraction was not "full and fair" where a newspaper defendant did not make reasonable efforts to contact the plaintiff and obtain his input to the retraction, and where the newspaper did not contact knowledgeable, independent sources to obtain correct information about the plaintiff before the retraction. This resulted in an inadequate apology in part because it was qualified by the words "as far as we are aware."

> *Fulton* v. *West End Times Ltd.*, above, at 294:

> The defendant chose to run a qualified retraction regarding a possible association of the plaintiff to the Society. That was unfair to the plaintiff and [not] until it was stated the plaintiff had no association with the Nanaimo Commonwealth Holding Society could it be considered a full retraction.

A poorly drafted apology may not only be inadequate, it might also aggravate the plaintiff's damages.

> *Turco* v. *Dunlop*, [1998] B.C.J. No. 2711 at para 81 (S.C.).

Whether a retraction is "full" turns on whether a reasonable person would conclude that that retraction is a "full and frank withdrawal of the charges conveyed" and that it "admits that the charge was unfounded and made under a misapprehension of the real facts." It must be understandable by a reasonable person, not just the plaintiff, to be a full and unqualified retraction.

Ramsey v. *Pacific Press, a Division of Southam, Inc.*, [2000] B.C.J. No. 2422, 2000 BCSC 1551, per Taylor J. at paras. 72, 78.

Bennett v. *Stupich* (1981), 125 D.L.R. (3d) 743,per Mackof J. at 752 (B.C.S.C.) [rejecting a so-called "parliamentary form of apology" "wrapped in subtle qualification or ambiguity"].

At least if there is no evidence of personal malice between the defamer and the defamed, a "full and fair" apology does not require any element of "abjectness."

Ramsey v. *Pacific Press*, above, at para. 78.

A purported apology which merely constitutes an expression of regret at being caught up in a controversy for which the defendant is facing defamation proceedings is not a retraction or an apology within the meaning of the defamation statutes.

Ramsey v. *Pacific Press*, *ibid.* at para. 88.

Where a defendant's purported apology questions the plaintiff's intentions for taking defamation proceedings and attempts to shift responsibility to the plaintiff for the publication of the defamatory expression, it may be seen as evidence of an aggressive stance which prevents a finding that the apology is full and fair.

Ramsey v. *Pacific Press*, *ibid.* at paras. 90, 101:

> [101] ... [The defendant broadcaster] sought to blame [the plaintiff] for the predicament and explain himself out of the predicament he himself had created. I conclude that the December 16th editorial was neither an apology nor a retraction. Rather it consisted of [the defendant] pointing the finger of responsibility at others in the context of an aggressive assault upon [the plaintiff's] political views.

If the plaintiff stipulates the contents of a retraction and where it is to be published, he or she cannot later complain that the defendant did not satisfy the requirements of the statute.

Murray Alter's Talent Associates Ltd. v. *Toronto Star Newspapers Ltd.* (1995), 124 D.L.R. (4th) 105, per Borins J.A. at 126 (Ont. Div. Ct.).

The onus is on the defendant to publish a full and complete retraction. It has been held that a defendant cannot shift that onus to the plaintiff by imposing on him or her an obligation to advise and assist in drafting the apology.

> *Snider* v. *Calgary Herald* (1985), 34 C.C.L.T. 27 per Miller A.C.J.Q.B. at para. 112 (Alta. Q.B.).

The conduct of a defendant subsequent to the apology may dilute its apology and detract from its sincerity, thereby sabotaging the defendant's prior compliance with this element of the statutory requirements.

> *Teskey* v. *Canadian. Newspapers Co.* (1989), 68 O.R. (2d) 737, per Blair J.A. (C.A.)

The phrase "full and fair retraction" has been discussed in a number of cases, including:

i)   In *Teskey* v. *Cdn. Newspapers Co.*, above, at 721:

> The apology effectively withdraws the charge of unethical conduct on the part of the respondents, but its wording fell short of that which they consider to be "full and fair" when the apology stated:
>
> > "The Free Press has investigated this matter to our satisfaction and we are not aware of any evidence which would support such allegations."
>
> Blair J.A., speaking for the Court of Appeal, also recognized that a publisher may be "placed in a dilemma by the demand for a full retraction and the threat of a libel action" by a third party. Nevertheless he held:
>
> > "... The publisher's possible discomfort cannot, in my opinion, be an excuse for failure to make a full apology."
>
> *Teskey*, above at 749.

ii) In *Ungaro* v. *Toronto Star Newspapers Ltd.* (1997), 144 D.L.R. (4th) 84 (Ont. Gen. Div.), where Cavarzan J. held at 97–98 that the published retraction was inadequate because it left the impression that the plaintiff "was sued, though not successfully, for poor courtroom performance" when he was not sued for negligence.

iii) In *Wiley* v. *Toronto Star Newspapers Ltd.* (1988), 65 O.R. (3d) 31 (H.C.J.), MacFarland J. held at 37 that the "correction" was not a correction, compounded the error, and was never intended to be an apology. The content of the correction was factually incorrect and did nothing to alleviate the situation but could only have exacerbated it. [An appeal from this judgment to the Ontario Court of Appeal was dismissed May 29, 1990: 74 O.R. (2d) 100.] The imputation was that a Crown attorney deliberately or by incompetence had misled the police in an important case. The newspaper headline was incorrect as was that part of the story relating to it. The inaccuracies were admitted by the reporter who filed the story and the senior editor who was responsible for accuracy, but not until they were under cross-examination in the witness box at trial. "The question Mr. Sopinka asked of Mr. Wiley did not relate to whether or not there were reasonable and probable grounds for a case against Miss Nelles." "… [I]t was not full, not fair and not a retraction.":

> Even the purported retraction was incorrect. It is difficult to view the conduct of the newspaper in this case as anything other than plain sloppy or careless. They have been sloppy and careless in their publication about a professional man's heretofore unblemished reputation. Such conduct will not be tolerated by the courts.

The requirement relating to placement of an apology in a print publication is expressed various ways in the provincial defamation statutes:

i)   Alberta, Manitoba, New Brunswick, Newfoundland and Labrador, Northwest Territories, Nova Scotia, Prince Edward Island, the Yukon Territory:

> "in as conspicuous a place and type as was the alleged defamatory matter";

ii) Saskatchewan, Ontario:

> "in as conspicuous a place and type as was the alleged libel";

iii) British Columbia:

> "in as conspicuous a place and type as was the article complained of."

It appears there is no significant distinction, however, between the phrase "as was the alleged libel" and the phrase "as was the article complained of."

> *Murray Alter's Talent Associates Ltd. v. Toronto Star Newspapers Ltd.* (1995), 124 D.L.R. (4th) 105 per Borins J. at 116 (Ont. Div. Ct.):

> > It would appear that the purpose of replacing the words "article complained of" with the words "alleged libel" was not intended to affect the location of a published retraction, but was to use a proper legal word for less precise language, recognizing that defamatory matter may be expressed and conveyed in more ways than in, or by, an article.

It is clear that the intent of this requirement is that the retraction be published in a manner intended to attract the reader's attention. The act of placing a retraction in a location ordinarily read by those who might have read
the libel, set off and standing out from other materials on the page, headed
by the word "Correction" in bold type, achieves the attention-getting purpose of the legislation.

Murray Alter's Talent Associates Ltd. v. Toronto Star Newspapers Ltd., *ibid.* at 125.

The phrase "published in as conspicuous a place and type as was the
alleged libel" has been discussed in a number of decisions, including the
following:

i)   In *Bennett v. Sun Publishing Company Limited*, [1972] 4 W.W.R. 643
      (B.C.S.C.) the libel was contained in a prominent headline and
      accompanying story on the front page of the *Vancouver Sun* newspa-
      per. An apology and retraction were published in the lower left hand
      corner of the front page. Anderson J held at 660:

      As to the apology it was reasonably fair...but it should have been
      announced in headlines and placed in the right upper corner of the paper.
      I do not accept the ludicrous suggestion of counsel for the defendants that
      as newspapers did not carry headlines when the Libel and Slander Act was
      first enacted the requirement to publish an apology "in as conspicuous as
      place and type as the article complained of" should not be adhered to. The
      simple concept of "fair play" makes it incumbent on the publisher to apol-
      ogize in "headlines" if he had libeled in "headlines".

ii)   In *Munro v. Toronto Sun Publishing Corporation* (1982), 39 O.R. (2d)
      100 (H.C.J.), the libel was contained in a front page headline with the
      story printed on page 2 accompanied by another prominent headline.
      The defendants published an apology and retraction in the only edi-
      torial printed on the editorial page which was headed in large bold
      type "We were wrong." The same heading appeared at the bottom of
      the front page with a reference to the editorial page. Holland J. held
      this "clearly [met] the test of a full and abject apology and retraction"
      stating at p. 115:

      While the apology was not on the front page, I am not persuaded that any-
      thing turns on that. The apology can be said to be a blockbuster both as
      to content and the editorial form.

iii) In *Wiley v. Toronto Star Newspapers Ltd.* (1988), 65 O.R. (3d) 31
      (H.C.J.), the libel was published at the top of page A-2. It was very

prominently displayed – being five columns wide – under a headline in heavy black type which read: "Crown misled police, Nelles lawyer says." A retraction was published at the top right side of page A-3 which was only two columns wide; its headline was much smaller than that of the article alleged to be defamatory. MacFarland J. held the retraction did not satisfy the statute, stating at p. 40:

> A simple comparison of ex. 2 which is the defamatory article to ex. 7, the alleged "retraction," will show that the type used in the "retraction" was not nearly as large or as conspicuous as was the type used in the defamatory article. The headline of ex. 7 says only "Grange probe headline misleading" – there is no reference in the headline to which headline relating to the Grange Inquiry was misleading. At this time, nearly every edition of the newspaper contained a headline that related to the Grange Inquiry. There was nothing in the headline of ex. 7 which particularly drew the readers' attention to the fact that it was the headline in the defamatory article published August 21, 1984, which was "misleading." A reader of the newspaper who read only the headlines would be none the wiser. A reading of the article itself is required to determine which headline.

iv) In *Kerr* v. *Conlogue*, [1992] 4 W.W.R. 258 (B.C.S.C.), the defamatory expression was contained in the body of a full-page feature article published on the first page of the Arts and Entertainment section of *The Globe and Mail* newspaper. The article's headline did not libel the plaintiff. The retraction and apology appeared on page two of the first section of the newspaper and was entitled "Our Mistake." It consisted of two brief sentences. Sinclair Prowse J. (as she then was) found this did not satisfy the statute, stating at p. 277:

> … As has been noted, the defamatory article was on the front page of the Arts and Entertainment section of the Saturday *Globe and Mail* while the retraction was on the second page of an entirely different section of the paper.
>
> Given these circumstances, it can hardly be said that this retraction was published in as conspicuous a place and type as the article had been. This fact was dramatically demonstrated during these proceedings as many of the witnesses had read the article but had not read the apology or retraction.

v) In *Murray Alter's Talent Associates Ltd.* v. *Toronto Star Newspapers Ltd.* (1995), 124 D.L.R. (4th) 105 (Ont. Div. Ct.), the retraction was published in a box under the bold caption "Correction," within an article on a page in the fashion section of the newspaper that was similar in content to the article which contained the alleged defamatory expression. It was located in the very centre of the page, set off from the other material on the page by its caption and the surrounding box, where it stood out from the other material on the page. The Court found that it was intended to attract the attention of those who may have read the original article and complied with the statute. Borins J. stated at p. 124–25:

> ... the requirement that a retraction be published "in as conspicuous a place ... as was the alleged libel" does not require "an equivalence of the headlining and placement of the correction and the libelous story." In determining whether the statutory requirement has been satisfied, the court must begin with the location of the libel and then determine whether the publication of the retraction was in as conspicuous a place in the newspaper. On the basis of the various definitions of "conspicuous" set out on pp.18 and 19 of my reasons [ante p.120], it is my opinion that the meaning of that word which the legislature intended is "attracting attention". If, relative to the location of the libel, the retraction is published so that it is set off from other information on the page and thereby stands out so that it is obvious to the reasonable reader to whom it is intended, it is published in as "conspicuous a place ... as was the alleged libel." Thus, there are two elements to be considered – the location of the libel and, relative to that location, the location of the retraction. Had the Legislature intended that the retraction be published in the same location and type, and in the same manner, as the libel, it would have said so. It did not. It required, only, that the retraction be published in a manner intended to attract the same attention as the libel. This, of course, will be determined by the facts of each case.

In the same case, Steele J. concurred with Borins J. stating at 106:

> In my view, the retraction was more conspicuous than the libel ... I would stress the point that the retraction must be as conspicuous as the libel and not as conspicuous as the article in which the libel took place.

[Note: An important distinguishing fact in *Murray Alter's* is that the libel was contained in a story which was not about the plaintiff, who was also not mentioned in the headline. The plaintiff was only incidentally referred to late in the story.]

vi)   In *Harvey* v. *Horizon Publications Ltd.* (1975), 61 D.L.R. (3d) 570 (B.C.S.C.), the article alleged to be defamatotory was published on page 21 of *The Citizen* newspaper. The apology was published on page 1, in heavy black type, larger than the type on page 21 of the original report. Craig J. held at page 574 that the defendant had published an adequate apology.

7) Timing of Publication or Broadcast of Retraction

The Ontario *Libel and Slander Act* requires that the retraction be:

i)   published either in the next regular issue of the newspaper or in any regular issue and published within three days after the receipt of the [libel notice required by section 5(1)];

ii) broadcast either within a reasonable time or within three days after the receipt of the [libel notice required by section 5(1)].

> Ontario, *Libel and Slander Act*, R.S.O. 1990, c. L.12, s.5(2)(d)(i) and (ii).

Similar provisions are found in the other provincial defamation statutes.

A plaintiff may waive the three day requirement in the Ontario statute. If the plaintiff stipulates when the retraction is to be published, he or she cannot later complain of non-compliance with the statutory time periods.

> *Murray Alter's Talent Associates Ltd.* v. *Toronto Star Newspapers Ltd.* (1995), 124 D.L.R. (4th) 105, per Borins J.A. at 126 (Ont. Div. Ct.).

a) Candidates for Public Office

The defamation act provisions relating to mitigation of damages and restrictions of damages to pecuniary loss do not apply to defamation of a candidate unless the retraction is published or broadcast at least five days before the election (fifteen days in Saskatchewan). The statutes, with variations from province to province, stipulate which elected public offices are the subject of this exclusionary provision.

Section 5.3 of the Ontario *Libel and Slander Act* states that section 5 does not apply in the case of a libel against any candidate for public office unless a retraction of the charge is made in as conspicuous a manner, at least five days before the election.

> *Wilson* v. *Taylor* (1980), 118 D.L.R. (3d) 355 (Ont. H.C.J.).

The Ontario provision will not apply unless the plaintiff is a candidate for public office at the time of the publication.

> *Merling* v. *Southam Inc.* (*c.o.b. Hamilton Spectator*) (2000), 183 D.L.R. (4th) 748 (Ont. C.A.).

8) Consequences of Settlement Offers Involving an Apology and Retraction

It has been held that a plaintiff's offer to settle which offered to forgo damages, interest, and costs, to discontinue the defamation action and to provide a release, in exchange for a written retraction and apology by the defendant, fell within Ontario Rule 49.10. The plaintiff recovered damages of $25,000 at trial and it was accordingly held he was entitled to costs on a solicitor and client scale against the corporate defendant.

> *Hunger Project* v. *Council on Mind Abuse (C.O.M.A.) Inc.* (1995), 22 O.R. (3d) 29 per Macdonald J. at 39 (Gen. Div.).

> *Kaneff* v. *Ivanov* (1997), 36 O.T.C. 274 per Dyson J. (Gen. Div.), appeal dismissed, [1998] O.J. No. 5924 (C.A.).

> The Defendant had the opportunity immediately after the defamation to settle this case. Further, by letter of November 8, 1995 from the Plaintiff's solicitor the defendant received a most generous offer to settle the case by signing a sensitively drawn retraction and apology without any funds changing hands. ... Under the circumstances, I find this a case for an award of costs on a solicitor and client basis.

> *Mahoney* v. *Curwood Transport Ltd.* (1998), 26 C.P.C. (4th) 218, per Orsborn J. at 22 (Nfld. S.C. (T.D.)), adopting *Hunger Project*, above.

Where a plaintiff offered to settle for an "apology completely retracting the libellous statements as set out in the statement of claim and fully apologizing to the plaintiff in terms acceptable to the plaintiff or as approved by the trial judge," the provisions of Ontario Rule 49.10 applied and the plaintiff was entitled to solicitor and client costs. It appears that at least in this context, the trial judge may have a discretionary power to require the publication of an apology in a form acceptable to her or him.

> *Botiuk* v. *Toronto Free Press Publications Ltd.*, [1991] O.J. No. 1617 (Gen. Div.) per Carruthers J. [Plaintiff offered to settle for $400,000 plus apology, recovered judgment of $465,000 after trial] [affirmed as to costs, [1993] O.J. No. 239 at para. 29 (C.A.), rev'd on other grounds, [1995] 3 S.C.R. 31].

Where a binding settlement agreement is reached which includes an obligation to retract and apologize, the Court may order that it be performed under a rule of court that provides jurisdiction to make an order enforcing a settlement.

Cox v. *Armar International Inc.*, [1992] O.J. No. 1034 (Gen. Div.) per McWilliam J.

An Alberta court ordered an action stayed for fifteen days where the plaintiff offered to accept an apology and his costs. The court held that if the defendant within that period tendered an apology satisfactory to the plaintiff's solicitor, the action would be dismissed with costs payable to the plaintiff. If no apology was forthcoming, the action would proceed.

Todosichuk v. *MacLenahan*, [1946] 1 D.L.R. 557, per O'Connor J. at 559 (Alta. S.C. (T.D.)).

In determining whether a defendant's settlement offer was more favourable to the plaintiff than a defamation verdict after trial, it is relevant to consider (in favour of the plaintiff) that the defendants would not publish an apology or retraction and made their settlement offer conditional upon confidentiality.

Gouveia v. *Toronto Star Newspapers Ltd.* (1998) 75 O.T.C. 186, per Molloy J. (Gen. Div.).

Where a defendant newspaper offered to settle by paying damages and publishing a retraction and apology, and the plaintiff's action was dismissed at trial, the defendant was entitled to solicitor and client costs from the date of its settlement offer.

Iorfida v. *Macleod*, [1995] O.J. No. 2132, per Somers J. at para. 9 (Gen. Div.).

Bennett v. *Stupich* (1981), 125 D.L.R. (3d) 743, per Macfarlane J. at 751–52 (B.C.S.C.).

9) Plaintiff's Conduct Regarding Apologies and Retractions

A defamed plaintiff will often demand an apology and retraction before commencing litigation. However, the law does not require a person who has been defamed to draw the defendant's attention to the libel and invite it to expatiate and enlarge on the published account, nor is the plaintiff required to ask for an apology before bringing suit.

Grabarevic v. *Northwest Publications Ltd.* (1968), 67 D.L.R. (2d) 748, per Tysoe J.A. at 751 (B.C.C.A.).

Fortomaris v. Mantini-Atkinson, [2002] O.J. No. 3202 per LaForme J. at para. 18 (S.C.J.):

> ... [T]here is no common law obligation to request an apology or to draw the defendant's attention to the libel.

See also *Mychajluk v. Kolisnyk*, [1923] 4 D.L.R. 724, per Curran J. at 27 (Man. K.B.):

> It is true the plaintiff's solicitor did not before commencing action write a letter to defendants demanding retraction and apology, but the defendants were fully apprised of the complaint after action and it was their duty, if they wished to avoid further legal responsibility, to have at once retracted the article, apologized for its publication and offered to make amends.

The failure of a person defamed to ask for an apology, however, may in some circumstances help to show that his or her real object is not to vindicate his character but to make money out of the attack. The court must have careful regard to all the circumstances before arriving at such a conclusion.

Grabarevic v. Northwest Publications Ltd., above, at 751–52.

Where a newspaper became aware of its error without any communication from the plaintiff but did not do what was necessary to mitigate the wrong done the plaintiff, a court declined to draw an inference from the plaintiff's failure to demand a retraction or apology that he preferred the remedy of money to the immediate restoration of the plaintiff's reputation.

Grabarevic v. Northwest Publications Ltd., ibid. at 752.

Although there may be no legal obligation to do so, a plaintiff is often wise to communicate directly with a defendant, explaining the errors in the defamatory expression, and requesting a retraction and an apology.

Palmer School & Infirmary of Chiropractic v. City of Edmonton, [1921] 61 D.L.R. 93, per Hyndman J. at 94 (Alta. T.D.).

Murphy v. LaMarsh (1970), 13 D.L.R. (3d) 484 per Wilson C.J.S.C. at 492 (B.C.S.C.) [aff'd 18 D.L.R. (3d) 208 (B.C.C.A.), leave to appeal to S.C.C. denied, [1971] 214 S.C.R. ix]:

> This [holding a press conference when libel writ served] appears to me strange conduct for a man who thought he had been wronged and who might reasonably have considered at that stage the possibility that a

retraction might be made and his suit might be settled without further publicity.

If a defendant retracts and apologizes orally on the plaintiff's terms, but declines to provide a written version of the retraction and apology, a court will examine the entire circumstances to determine whether or not the plaintiff was justified in making the demand for a written apology.

Tatum v. *Limbrick*, [1994] B.C.J. No. 1471, per Edwards J. at para. 57 (S.C.) (action dismissed).

Where there have been without prejudice settlement negotiations in which the defendant has offered an apology conditional on settlement, the plaintiff should be cautious in cross-examining a defendant at trial on the subject of an offer of apology. It was held that where the plaintiff's cross-examination had the effect of placing without-prejudice communications partially into evidence, the defendant was entitled to complete the evidence on the subject by testifying about "minutes of apology" submitted by the defendant to the plaintiff and the plaintiff's response to that communication.

Amalgamated Transit Union v. *Independent Canadian Transit Union* (1995), 33 Alta. L. R. (3d) 317, per Lutz J. at paras. 18–28 (Q.B.).

Murray Alter's Talent Associates Ltd. v. *Toronto Star* (1995), 124 D.L.R. (4th) 105, per Borins J. at para. 39 (Ont. Div. Ct.):

> If a plaintiff stipulates the contents of a retraction and where and when it is to be published, it is my view that he or she cannot complain if the time of publication runs afoul of legislation enacted for the plaintiff's benefit.

A plaintiff's decision to widely circulate a written apology is not unreasonable and does not constitute contributory negligence on her part (in the sense that it may thereby disseminate the original libel more broadly). To have effect an apology should be public, not private. It would only be in the clearest instance of a very limited circulation of a defamation that notice of the apology could effectively be directed to a small, restricted number or group of persons.

Brown v. *Cole*, [1996] B.C.J. No. 2046, per Holmes J. at paras. 154–60 (S.C.), varied as to damages, otherwise affirmed without reference to this issue (1998), 61 B.C.L.R. (2d) 1 (C.A.), leave to appeal to S.C.C. denied, [1998] S.C.C.A. 614. Holmes J. stated at [1996] B.C.J. No. 2046 at para. 158:

It is true that many persons who had not heard of fraud allegations against the plaintiff were first informed by receipt of the information and apology letter [sent by the plaintiff]. That is unfortunate, but a necessary incident of reasonable measures taken by one defamed to try and rehabilitate his reputation. Far better knowledge of the fact of defamation, accompanied by proof of its untruthfulness, be coincident, than to incur the inevitable risk that in future old rumours might surface to again disparage the plaintiff.

10) Jurisdiction of Court to Compel an Apology and Retraction

Courts in Ontario, Manitoba, and British Columbia have held that a court has no jurisdiction to order the defendant to publish an apology.

Moore v. Canadian Newspapers Co. (1989), 60 D.L.R. (4th) 113, per Rosenberg J. at 116 (Div. Ct.) reversing a provincial court judgment requiring the publication of an apology and a retraction. [An order to publish an apology is an equitable remedy. A provincial court has no jurisdiction to grant equitable remedies under the *Courts of Justice Act*, 1984.]

Hunger Project v. Council on Mind Abuse (C.O.M.A.) Inc. (1995), 22 O.R. (3d) 29 per Macdonald J. at 33 (Gen. Div.), citing *Burnett v. R.* (1979), 94 D.L.R. (3d) 281 (H.C.J.) [where O'Driscoll J. stated at 288: "s. 5(2)(d) (of the Ontario *Libel and Slander Act*) speaks of a retraction but only as something a defendant has voluntarily done in order to mitigate damages." Claim for an apology in prayer for relief ordered struck out.]

Hasnu v. Deshe Bedeshe Inc., [1998] O.J. No. 3493, per P. Thomson J. at para. 39 (Gen. Div. (Sm. Cl. Ct.)).

Deborah Resources Ltd. v. McDonald's Restaurants of Canada Ltd., [1991] B.C.J. No. 2493, per Lamperson J. (S.C.):

Actions are commonly settled on terms that a court could not impose, e.g. an apology for libel … .

But see *Botiuk v. Toronto Free Press Publications Ltd.*, [1991] O.J. No. 1617 (Gen. Div.) where Carruthers J., in the context of an offer to settle for an apology and damages, stated:

…a trial judge has a discretionary power to require the publication of an apology in a form acceptable to her or him. Given an express desire on the part of the defendants in this case to make an apology, it is difficult for me to think that a trial judge would not have broken an impasse [on the content of the apology], assuming one existed, by accepting one position over the other or fashioning a compromise. [No apology was ordered in this case.]

In at least one instance, a jury attempted to order a defendant to write a letter of retraction. The trial judge refused to incorporate this portion of the jury's answers in the entered trial judgment.

Vancouver Industrial Electric Ltd. v. *Leone Industries Inc.*, [1999] B.C.J. No. 2444 (S.C.).

Where a plaintiff did not seek an apology in his statement of claim, a Manitoba court declined to include in its formal trial judgment a direction by the jury that a public apology be included in the judgment.

Laufer v. *Bucklaschuk* (1998), 128 Man. R. (2d) 156, per Hannsen J. at 158–59 (Q.B.), rev'd on unrelated grounds (1999), 1 D.L.R. (4th) 83 (Man. C.A.), leave to appeal to S.C.C. denied, [2000] S.C.C.A. No. 77.

An Alberta court ordered three defendants to write a letter of retraction to correct a defamatory publication made earlier to a department of the Alberta government. This relief was granted without reference to prior judicial authority.

Kelly v. *Low*, [2000] 257 A.R. 279, per LoVecchio J. at para. 229 (Q.B.).

A Prince Edward Island court held that an apology may be a form of equitable remedy available to a court in a defamation case. In these particular circumstances, the court did not make the order.

Ayangma v. *NAV Canada* (2000), 188 Nfld. & P.E.I.R. 65 per Webber J. at para. 122 (P.E.I.S.C. (T.D.)), varied without reference to this issue (2001), 203 D.L.R. (4th) 717 (P.E.I.S.C.(A.D.)0, application for leave to appeal to S.C.C. denied, [2001] S.C.C.A. No. 76..

An Ontario judge assessing damages (after the plaintiff took judgment in default of defence) ordered that the defendants pay general damages of $35,000 and punitive damages of $20,000 but went on to provide in her order that the punitive damages would not be payable if the defendants published, in a certain issue of a newspaper, an apology in the form set out in a schedule to the judgment. This provision in the order was set aside by consent, on appeal, without a statement of the appellate court's reasons.

Karas v. *Gegios*, [2002] O.J. No. 124 (C.A.) per Morden J.A. by endorsement. [See, [2001] O.J. No. 732 (S.C.J.) where the order concerning the apology is referred to in a subsequent judgment of Nordheimer J.]

11) Apology May Defame a Third party

The plaintiff should consider whether his or her apology could be defamatory of a third party.

Tracy v. Kemsley Newspapers Limited, unreported, 9 April 1954.

For example, where a defendant has identified the individual source of a defamatory allegation, publishing an apology that there is "no evidence to support" the defamatory allegation may lead to an inference that the source had lied.

Teskey v. Canadian Newspapers Co. Ltd. (1989), 68 O.R. (2d) 737 at 749 (C.A.).

The question whether an apology to a defamation plaintiff is published on a privileged occasion has been discussed in a number of recent decisions.

In one case a Singapore court held, in the particular circumstances before it, that an apology was published on a privileged occasion.

Overseas Chinese Banking Corp. v. Wright, [1994] 3 S.L.R. 760 at 786 (Sing. H.C.). [The defendant Mr. Wright was the author of a letter published in the *Business Times* which defamed the Overseas Chinese Banking Corp. The *Business Times* complied with the Bank's demand to publish an apology. Mr. Wright then sued both the Bank and the *Business Times* for libel on the apology. The court held that the apology was published on an occasion of qualified privilege.]

In another case, the English Court of Appeal held that an apology was not published on an occasion of qualified privilege.

Watts v. Times Newspapers Ltd., [1995] E.W.J. No. 2882 (C.A.) at para. 53.

A defendant cannot excuse his or her failure to make a full apology, however, on the ground that it might expose the defendant to a defamation lawsuit by a third party.

Teskey v. Cdn. Newspapers Co., above, at 748–49:

> The apology effectively withdraws the charge of unethical conduct on the part of the respondents, but its wording fell short of that which they consider to be "full and fair" when the apology stated:
>
> > "The Free Press has investigated this matter to our satisfaction and *we are not aware of* any evidence which would support such allegations."

… It may be that a publisher is placed in a dilemma by the demand for a full retraction and the threat of a libel action as *Gatley on Libel and Slander*, 8th ed. (1981), indicates at pp. 485–86:

> The publisher should take care in such circumstances not to defame a third party, though the occasion of a proper apology is arguably privileged.

The publisher's possible discomfort cannot, in my opinion, be an excuse for a failure to make a full apology.

12) Offer of Amends

Nova Scotia's *Defamation Act* provides that a defendant who has innocently published defamatory words may make an "offer of amends" to publish or join in the publication of a suitable correction of the words complained of, and a sufficient apology to the plaintiff.

Where copies of a document or record containing the defamatory words have been distributed by or with the knowledge of the defendant, the latter must also offer to take such steps as are reasonably practicable to notify persons to whom copies have been so distributed that the words are alleged to be defamatory of the plaintiff.

If the offer of amends is accepted by the plaintiff, the court is empowered to determine any dispute relating to fulfillment of the offer, and to order the defendant to pay the full legal costs of the plaintiff and any expenses reasonably incurred by the plaintiff in consequence of the defamatory publication.

Defamation Act, R.S.N.S. 1989, c. 122, s.16.

To establish that the words were published "innocently," the defendant must show either: (i) that he or she did not intend to publish them of and concerning the plaintiff, and did not know of circumstances by virtue of which they might be understood to refer to the plaintiff, or (ii) that the words were not defamatory on their face, and that the defendant did not know of circumstances by virtue of which they might be understood to be defamatory of the plaintiff.

The defendant must also show that he or she exercised all reasonable care in relation to the publication.

Defamation Act, R.S.N.S. 1989, c. 122, s.16

13) Rebuttal

The defamation statutes create an incentive for defendants to publish or broadcast a rebuttal by the plaintiff in certain circumstances.

A statutory defence of qualified privilege applies to fair and accurate reports published in a newspaper, or broadcast reports of public meetings or legislative proceedings. However, a defendant cannot rely on that qualified privilege if he or she has failed to comply with the plaintiff's request to publish or broadcast a "reasonable letter or statement of explanation or contradiction."

British Columbia, *Libel and Slander Act*, R.S.B.C. 1996, c. 263, s.4.

Alberta, *Defamation Act*, R.S.A. 1990, c. D-6, s.10(4).

Saskatchewan, *Libel and Slander Act*, R.S.S. 1978, c. L-14, s.10(3).

Manitoba, *Defamation Act*, R.S.M. 1987, c. D-20, s.10(4).

Ontario, *Libel and Slander Act*, R.S.O. 1990, c. L.12, s.3(7).

New Brunswick, *Defamation Act*, R.S.N.B. 1973, c. D-5, s.9(4).

Nova Scotia, *Defamation Act*, R.S.N.S. 1989, c. 122, s.13(6).

Prince Edward Island, *Defamation Act*, R.S.P.E.I. 1988, c..D-5, s.10(4).

Newfoundland and Labrador, *Defamation Act*, R.S.N. 1990, c..D-3, c. 63, s.12(4).

Yukon Territory, *Defamation Act*, R.S.Y.T. 1986, c. 41, s.10(4).

Northwest Territories, *Defamation Act*, R.S.N.W.T. 1988, c. D-1, s.11(4).

The plaintiff must set out the contradictions or explanations. A general demand for a full apology which does not particularize the plaintiff's complaint will not constitute compliance with the section. Nor does a request for a "retraction" constitute compliance with the section.

Hanson v. Nugget Publishers Ltd., [1927] 4 D.L.R. 791 (C.A.).

Khan v. Ahmed, [1957] 2 Q.B. 149.

Nowlan v. Moncton Publishing, [1952] 4 D.L.R. 808 (N.B.S.C. (A.D.)).

14) Pleading Other Defences

A defendant may be entitled to plead justification even if there has been an apology.

> *Dowding v. Pacific West Equities Ltd.* (1992), 63 B.C.L.R. (2d) 300, per MacDonald J. at 306 (S.C.).

> *New Era Home Appliances Ltd. v. Toronto Star Ltd.*, [1963] 1 O.R. 339, per Senior Master Marriott at 342 (S.C. (Mast.)).

It has been held that the fact of an apology is not an admission of liability for damages where the defence is qualified privilege.

> *McKinnon v. Dauphin (Rural Municipality)*, [1996] 3 W.W.R. 127, per Clearwater J. at para. 61 (Man. Q.B.), aff'd [1998] 1 W.W.R. 309 (Man. C.A.).

15) Apologies On-Line

In the old days of hard copy, publishers could recover defamatory books from distributors and either "pulp" them or paste inserts over offending material. Rarely was it possible for newspaper publishers to catch defamatory issues before distribution. Nevertheless, newspapers had a short shelf life. Access to old copies of newspapers in public libraries was difficult and time consuming. Even commercial clipping services did not claim comprehensive coverage on any subject.

With defamatory electronic material, a retraction and apology may be both more significant and more difficult. How does one retract material from electronic databases operated by independent third parties such as Compuserve, AmericaOnline, or Lexis , who may have obtained the original material under license?

As libel plaintiffs become alive to the implications of electronic databases, however, defendants may expect demands for permanent removal of defamatory material.

Contracts between newspapers or broadcasters and independent third party database operators may permit the original publisher to require the elimination of material which becomes the subject of a libel complaint.

If for any reason original defamatory expression is not removed from the electronic database, the apology and retraction may be hypertext linked, or attached in some other manner, to the original defamatory material.

Publishers probably should not assume that the search engines incorporated in their own sites or the popular search engines available via Netscape or Microsoft browsers will pull up both the apology and the defamatory material.

Publishers should also be aware that their apology and retraction may appear on the libel plaintiff's own web page. Phillip Environmental's home-page at one time contained the following posting dated November 30, 1995:

> Former Employee Retracts False Allegations.
>
> Phillip Environmental Inc. announced today that [the defendant], a former employee of the company, has retracted the allegations contained in a letter written by him to the Ministry of the Environment and Energy.
>
> [The defendant] sincerely apologizes to the shareholders, directors and management of Phillip Environmental Inc. for any harm that may have result-ed to the company and its shareholders from the publication of his letter beyond the environmental assessment process. [The defendant] wrote the let-ter solely to express his viewpoint to the Ministry of the Environment and Energy regarding the approval of a landfill. In regard to that approval process, the response by senior management of Phillip and the MOEE has satisfied [the defendant] that, with the terms and conditions which will be imposed by the Ministry on the landfill, the environmental assessment process is working in the public interest.

The Phillip Environmental web page informed its readers that the company "intends to continue its lawsuit for defamation against [the defendant] and any other parties who participated in the distribution of the letter."

There is no reported Canadian jurisprudence yet on the subject of online apologies.

CHAPTER TEN:

Security for Costs Under Defamation Statutes

The provincial defamation legislation on security for costs is not uniform across Canada. Consequently, decisions from one province may have little or no application in another province with different legislation.

A. SECURITY FOR COSTS LEGISLATION

Under the defamation legislation of British Columbia, Ontario, and Saskatchewan, a defendant may in certain situations apply for an order compelling the plaintiff to pay security for costs.

British Columbia, *Libel and Slander Act*, R.S.B.C. 1996, c. 262.

Ontario, *Libel and Slander Act*, R.S.O. 1990, c. L.12.

Saskatchewan, *Libel and Slander Act*, R.S.S. 1978, c. L-14.

The Ontario *Libel and Slander Act* contains separate security for costs provisions for libel and for slander. Section 12 contains the provisions referring to libel in a newspaper or in a broadcast:

(1) In an action for a libel in a newspaper or in a broadcast, the defendant may, at any time after the delivery of the statement of claim or the expiry of the time within which it should have been delivered, apply to the court for security for costs, upon notice and an affidavit by the defendant or his agent showing the nature of the action and of the defence, that the plaintiff is not possessed of property sufficient to answer the costs of the action in case judgment is given in favour of the defendant, that the defendant has a good defence on the merits and that the statements complained of were made in good faith, or that the grounds of action are trivial or frivolous, and the court may make an order for the

plaintiff to give security for costs, which shall be given in accordance with the practice in cases where a plaintiff resides out of Ontario, and the order is a stay of proceedings until the security is given.

(2) Where the alleged libel involves a criminal charge, the defendant is not entitled to security for costs under this section unless he satisfies the court that the action is trivial or frivolous, or that the circumstances which under section 5 entitle the defendant at the trial to have the damages restricted to actual damages appear to exist, except the circumstances that the matter complained of involves a criminal charge.

(3) For the purpose of this section, the plaintiff or the defendant or their agents may be examined upon oath at any time after the delivery of the statement of claim.

Section 13 states:

> An order made under section 12 by a judge of the Supreme Court is final and is not subject to appeal … .

Section 12 is restricted to actions stemming from statements made in a newspaper or in a broadcast.

Section 18 refers to slander actions:

(1) In an action for slander, the defendant may, at any time after the delivery of the statement of claim or the expiry of the time within which it should have been delivered, apply to the court for security for costs, upon notice and an affidavit by the defendant or the defendant's agent showing the nature of the action and of the defence, that the plaintiff is not possessed of property sufficient to answer the costs of the action in case judgment is given in favour of the defendant, that the defendant has a good defence on the merits, or that the grounds of action are trivial or frivolous, and the court may make an order for the plaintiff to give security for costs, which shall be given in accordance with the practice in cases where a plaintiff resides out of Ontario, and the order is a stay of proceedings until the security is given.

(2) For the purpose of this section, the plaintiff or the defendant may be examined upon oath at any time after the delivery of the statement of claim.

Sections 12 and 18 are identical, with the following exceptions:

i)   unlike section 12(1), section 18(1) does not contain the phrase "that the statements complained of were made in good faith;"

ii)   section 18 does not contain a subsection comparable to section 12(2), referring to criminal charges;

iii) section 12(3) and 18(2), both covering examination of parties, are identical except that section 18(2) is confined to "the plaintiff or the defendant" while section 12(3) refers to "the plaintiff or the defendant or their agents"; and

iv) section 18 has no counterpart to section 13, which states that "An order made under section 12 is final and not subject to appeal."

There are similar sections in the defamation legislation of British Columbia (sections 19 and 20), and Saskatchewan (section 12). However, the British Columbia provisions do not apply to slander, and the Saskatchewan libel provisions (unlike the British Columbia provisions) do not apply to libel in a broadcast, only in a newspaper.

The relationship between section 12 of the Ontario *Libel and Slander Act* and Rule 56 of the Ontario *Rules of Civil Procedure* was considered by the Divisional Court in *Khan* v. *Metroland Printing, Publishing and Distributing Ltd.*, [2003] O.J. No. 4261 where Linhares de Sousa J., speaking for the court, concluded at paragraph 85 that a motions and case management judge should have considered and applied section 12 to the question of posting of security for costs in the libel action before him, and not Rule 56, and that it was an error of law not to have done so. In reaching this conclusion, Linhares de Sousa stated at paragraph 70 that the "broad scope of the [*Libel and Slander Act*] supports the view that the Legislature intended the question of security for costs in libel and slander actions involving newspapers ... to be governed entirely by s. 12 ..." and (at paragraph 74) that section 12 "being specific legislation ... should prevail."

1) Intent of the Legislation

Chancellor Boyd in *Bennett* v. *Empire Printing & Publishing Co.* (1894), 16 P.R. 63 at 69 (Ont. C.A.), in referring to the security for costs sections in the Ontario *Libel and Slander Act*, held that:

> This legislation appears to be unique and the intention is to protect newspapers reasonably well conducted with a view to the information of the public.

B. CONTENTS OF THE AFFIDAVIT FILED BY THE DEFENDANT

The Ontario courts have held that the requirements for the contents of an affidavit are cumulative and not alternative, despite the use of the word "or" in section 12(1).

Gunn v. *North York Public Library Board* (1976), 2 C.P.C. 68 (Ont. H.C.J.) [material was presented to show a good defence to an action on the merits, but no material was presented to show the plaintiff was not possessed of sufficient property]. Per Robins J.:

> In my opinion an application for security for costs under s. 20(1) [slander] may not be founded on one or more of three possible grounds. Before a plaintiff can be ordered to give security for costs a defendant, as I read the section, is required to show by affidavit:
>
> (1) the nature of the action and the defence;
> (2) that the plaintiff is not possessed of property sufficient to answer the costs of the action in case judgment is given in favour of the defendant; and
> (3) either (a) that the defendant has a good defence on the merits, or (b) that the grounds of action are trivial or frivolous.
>
> This construction is the same as that which has been placed on s. 13(1) of the *Libel and Slander Act* [now s. 12], the section providing for security for costs in actions for libel in a newspaper or broadcast. While the wording of s. 13(1) varies slightly from s. 20(1), the sections are analogous, there is no distinction in principle between them and no reason to construe them differently.

See also *Nikolic* v. *Northern Life Publishing Co.*; *Bowgray Invt. Ltd.* v. *Northern Life Publishing Co.* (1976), 1 C.P.C. 335 (Ont. H.C.J.) .

Osahnek v. *Toronto Daily Star*, [1966] 1 O.R. 492 (S.C. (Mast.)).

Molina v. *Libman Manufacturing Ltd.* [1979] O.J. No. 3144 (S.C. (Mast.)).

The courts have held that an affidavit disclosing a *prima facie* good defence complied with section 12 of the Ontario *Libel and Slander Act*:

Swain v. *Mail Printing Co.* (1894), 16 P.R. 132 at 135 per Boyd C (Ont. H.C.):

> On applications for security for costs under R.S.O. ch. 57, sec. 9, the Judge is not to try the merits of the case or to pass upon disputed facts disclosed in conflicting affidavits filed against the application. The materials under oath used by the applicant are to be weighed, and if from these it appears that there is a good defence on the merits — that is, a *prima facie* case of justification or privilege — one which ought to succeed if it is not answered or explained away at trial, then the statute is satisfied and security should be ordered. Such is this case, the affidavits of the defendants shew a fair and accurate report of what

occurred in the open court of the police magistrate; that is sufficient for the obtaining of security. Whether the defence will be substantiated when tried before a jury is another matter not now pertinent.

See also *Feaster v. Cooney*, [1893] O.J. No. 215, 15 P.R. 290, per Ferguson J. at para. 12.

1) Inadequate Affidavits

The following affidavits filed in support of the application for security for costs were considered inadequate to enable the defendant to obtain the order:

(i)   where an affidavit baldly asserted that the libel was published in good faith without setting out the grounds;

Lancaster v. Ryckman (1893), 15 P.R. 199 [words imputing want of chastity to a plaintiff] per Street J. at para. 11 (Ont. H.C.):

> I agree with the learned local Judge that an affidavit merely stating that the defendant has a good defence on the merits is not sufficient under this section; and that a *prima facie* defence must be disclosed upon the affidavit: *Whiley v. Whiley*, 4 C.B.N.S. 633; and counter-affidavits should not be received, because the case will not be tried upon a summary application of this kind: *Warrington v. Leake*, 11 Ex. 304; so that I must decline to consider the affidavits on the part of the plaintiff produced on the appeal for the first time.

Nikolic v. Northern Life Publishing Co. [1976] O.J. No. 1436 at para. 8 (H.C.J.).

Greenhow v. Wesley (1910), 1 O.W.N. 1001–2 per Middleton J. (H.C.):

> The material filed by the defendants does not shew what is required by the statute. They state what they no doubt believe, that they have a good defence, but they must shew the nature of the defence. When they ask that it be found that the libel was published in good faith, they must condescend to give the facts surrounding the publication, so that their good faith may be ascertained by the Court. Different individuals may have different standards of "good faith," and to accept a defendant's own statement of his bona fides would be to make him judge in his own case.
>
> In the same way it is not enough for the defendants to say that there was reasonable ground for their belief that the publication was for the public benefit — they must say why they thought the pub-

lication was for the public benefit, and the Court will then ascertain if this was reasonable. The same considerations shew the worthlessness of the affidavit now sought to be filed, "that the publication took place in mistake or misapprehension of facts." This is an essential allegation if a defendant seeks security for costs after publishing a libel involving a criminal charge.

(ii)   where the affidavit failed to state the nature of the defence and only denied the allegations in the statement of claim;

Proniuk v. Petryk, [1933] 1 W.W.R. 648 (Alta. T.D.), aff'd [1933] 3 W.W.R. 223 (Alta. C.A.).

(iii)   where an affidavit only denies the innuendo;

Paladino v. Gustin (1897), 17 P.R. 553 (Ont. C.A.).

iv)   where an affidavit pleaded an apology and stated only that the defendant had a good defence on the merits;

Duval v. O'Beirne (1912), 3 O.W.N. 513 (H.C.).

(v)   where the only defence alleged was that the statement did not refer to the plaintiff;

Lennox v. Star Printing & Publishing Co. (1895), 16 P.R. 488 (Ont. Mast.).

(vi)   where an affidavit only swears to the truth of the charge.

MacDonald v. World Newspaper Co. (1894), 16 P.R. 324 (Ont. Mast.).

The defendant may seek to prove that the plaintiff is not possessed of property sufficient to answer an order for costs of the action either by the defendant's own affidavit or by an examination of the plaintiff.

Molina v. Libman Manufacturing Ltd. (1979), 15 C.P.C. 17 per Master Davidson at para. 9 (Ont. S.C. (Mast.)):

> ... it is my view that s. 20 of the *Libel and Slander Act* enables a defendant to seek to prove either by his own affidavit or by an examination of the plaintiff that the plaintiff is not possessed of property sufficient 4o answer the costs of the action.

On an application for security for costs under section 18 which refers to slander actions, the defendant may examine the plaintiff prior to the delivery of his affidavit, especially on those facts it is reasonable to believe the defendant will have little or no knowledge of. It is submitted that this decision ought to apply to applications under section 12(1).

Shewchun v. *McMaster University et al.* (1983), 33 C.P.C. 35 (Ont. S.C. (Mast.)).

C. PROCEDURE ON SECURITY FOR COSTS APPLICATIONS UNDER THE DEFAMATION STATUTES

The procedure for applications for security for costs is as follows:

(i)   In Ontario, the defendant must file an affidavit but is entitled to examine the plaintiff under oath before filing the affidavit at any time after the notice of motion for security has been delivered.

Shewchun v. *McMaster University et al.* (1983) 143 D.L.R. (3d) 238 at para. 7 (Ont. S.C. (Mast.)), applying *Nikolic* v. *Northern Life Publishing Co.* [1976] O.J. No. 1436 at para. 5 (Ont. H.C.J.).

Molina v. *Libman Mfg. Ltd.* (1979), 15 C.P.C. 17 (Ont. S.C. (Mast.)).

Hull v. *Deare* (1983), 40 C.P.C. 59 (Ont. S.C.) [it is a condition precedent to conducting the examination of the plaintiff that the defendant deliver a motion seeking security for costs].

(ii)   The defendant must file an affidavit establishing:

a. the nature of the action;

Ontario: sections 12 and 18.

British Columbia: section 19.

Saskatchewan: section 12 does not refer to describing the nature of the action.

b. the nature of the defence;

Ontario: section 12 and 18.

British Columbia: section 19 (2) reads simply "the defence," unlike the Ontario statute which uses the word "nature."

Saskatchewan: section 12 reads "showing the matter of the defence."

c. that the plaintiff is not possessed of property sufficient to answer the costs of the action should a judgment be given in favour of the defendant;

Ontario: sections 12 and 18.

British Columbia: section 19(1)(c) reads "in case a verdict or judgment is given."

Saskatchewan: section 12(1).

d. that the defendant has a good case on the merits ;

Ontario: sections 12 and 18: "the defendant has a good defence on the merits."

British Columbia: section 19: "the defendant has a good defence on the merits."

Saskatchewan: section 12(1): 'that he has a good defence on the merits to the action."

e. that the statements complained of were made in good faith;

Ontario: section 12 (1) requires that the statements complained of were made in good faith but section 18 (slander) does not have this requirement.

Oshanek v. *Toronto Daily Star*, [1966] 1 O.R. 492 per Senior Master Rodger (S.C. (Mast.)):

> As I read s. 13(1) of the *Libel and Slander Act*, the defendant, in order to succeed on an application of this kind, must show that the plaintiff is not possessed of property sufficient to answer the costs of the action in case judgment is given in favour of the defendant and either that the statements complained of were made in good faith or that the grounds of action are trivial or frivolous. Showing that the grounds of action are trivial or frivolous would appear to be an alternative to showing that the plaintiff is not possessed of property sufficient to answer the costs of the action in case judgment is given in favour of the defendant.
>
> If I am correct in this interpretation the defendant cannot succeed on this application unless he can show that the plaintiff is not possessed of property sufficient to answer the costs of the action in case judgment is given in favour of the defendant.

Following Riddell J. in *Robinson* v. *Mills* (1909), 19 O.C.R. 162 (K.B.).

See *Nikolic* v. *Northern Life Publishing Co.* [1976] O.J. No. 1436 at para. 7 (Ont. H.C.J.).

British Columbia: section 19(1)(c) reads "published in good faith."

Saskatchewan: section 12(1) does not have a "good faith" requirement.

f. that the grounds of action are trivial or frivolous;

Ontario *Libel and Slander Act*, s. 12(2)

Hill v. *Creed Furs Ltd.* [1972] 3 O.R. 827 (S.C.) [held that an examination under then section 20(1) of the *Libel and Slander Act* was premature until an application for security for costs was made].

(iii)   The plaintiff may examine the defendant or his agent.

Ontario *Libel and Slander Act*, s.12(3)

(iv)   The examination of the plaintiff or defendant may occur any time after the delivery of the statement of claim.

Ontario *Libel and Slander Act*, s.12(3)

D. HEARING AND APPEAL RIGHTS OF APPLICANT

The application is made before a Master, a local judge of the Supreme Court, or a judge of the Superior Court of Justice in Ontario.

Rules of Civil Procedure, r. 37.02(3).

In Ontario, if the matter is heard by the Master or local judge of the Supreme Court, an appeal lies to a judge of the Supreme Court whose order is final and is not subject to appeal. If the order is made by a judge of the Supreme Court, that order is final and not subject to appeal.

Libel and Slander Act, s. 12

No such limitation applies in applications under sections 19 or 20 of the British Columbia *Libel and Slander Act* or section 12 of the Saskatchewan *Libel and Slander Act*.

E. SECURITY FOR COSTS PROVISIONS IN THE LIBEL AND SLANDER ACTS

A defendant who was a correspondent to a newspaper was not entitled to the benefit of the security for costs provisions as they applied only to the publisher, editor, or proprietor of a newspaper.

> *Egan* v. *Miller* (1887), 7 C.L.T. 443 (Ont. Div. Ct.) [defendant wrote and signed a letter which was printed in the newspaper — discussed in *Robinson* v. *Mills*, below, at para. 32].

> *Axelrod* v. *Beth Jacob of Kitchener*, [1943] O.W.N. 169, rev'd in part, [1944] 1 D.L.R. 255.

> *Robinson* v. *Mills* (1909), 19 O.L.R. 162 (K.B.) [defendant a sporting editor of newspaper. Court held that "all who are concerned with the actual publication in the newspaper and all who are responsible for the acts of those" people are able to avail themselves of provision relating to security for costs]. Riddell J. held at 172–73 :

>> Were it not for the cases referred to, I should be prepared to hold that the statute means what it says; but, even with the said cases and giving full effect to them, I think the lest the statute did was to throw a mantle of protection over all who are concerned in the actual publication in the newspaper and all who are responsible for the acts of those.

>> The reason for the legislation we need not inquire; it is no concern of the Courts; but it would seem that the Legislature has, for some reason, decreed that different laws shall be applied to all connected with newspapers published at intervals of not less than 26 days between issues and to those — editors or what not — who write private letters, or publish circulars, or monthly magazines.

>> It seems to me that all within the favoured group, whether proprietor, publisher, editor, printer, sub-editor, or what you will, must receive the protection of the Act respecting actions of libel and slander.

A corporation is entitled to the benefits of the security for costs provisions.

> *Adcock* v. *Man. Free Press Co.* (1909), 12 W.L.R. 362 (Man. C.A.).

F. SPECIAL REQUIREMENT WHERE THE LIBEL INVOLVES A CRIMINAL CHARGE

The Ontario *Libel and Slander Act*, section 12(2) states as follows:

Where the alleged libel involves a criminal charge, the defendant is not entitled to security for costs under this section unless he satisfies the court that the action is trivial or frivolous, or that the circumstances which under section 5 entitle the defendant at the trial to have the damages restricted to actual damages appear to exist, except the circumstances that the matter complained of involves a criminal charge.

There is no equivalent qualification to Ontario's section 18 relating to security for costs for slander; there is a comparable requirement in British Columbia section 19(5) and Saskatchewan section 12(2).

This section applies not only where the imputations of the crime are clear, but also where an innuendo is required to give the words a defamatory sense. It is enough if the plaintiff alleges that the words are so used and they are capable of that meaning.

Smyth v. Stephenson (1897), 17 P.R. 374 (Ont. H.C.).

Duval v. O'Beirne (1912), 3 O.W.N. 513 (H.C.).

Wallace v. Lawson, [1919] 2 W.W.R. 408 (B.C.).

Section 12 applies even where a crime was imputed because of a misprint.

Kelly v. Ross (1909), 1 O.W.N. 48 (H.C.), leave to appeal to S.C.C. refused, 1 O.W.N. 116 (H.C.).

Where the matter is doubtful, it should only be determined at trial and therefore an order for security for costs ought to be refused.

Pringle v. Financial Post Co. (1908), 12 O.W.R. 912 (Master).

It is not a frivolous or trivial action where the photo and the caption imputed a more serious crime than the crime that the plaintiff was actually charged with.

Baird v. John Blunt Publications Ltd., [1955] O.W.N. 75 (Master).

In *Graeme v. Globe Printing Co.* (1890) 14 P.R. 72 (Ont. C.A.), the published article, which contained the words complained of, referred to "Graham" whereas the plaintiff's name was "Graeme." MacMahon J. held at paragraph 24.

It is clear that the plaintiff is not the person referred to, and it is impossible to conceive — having regard to all the facts of the case — how he could have imagined he was the person referred to.

G. REQUIREMENT OF NOTICE OF OWNERSHIP DOES NOT APPLY

Section 8 of the Ontario *Libel and Slander Act*, which requires that a statement of ownership of the newspaper be published on the editorial page, only applies to sections 5 and 6 of the Act, which state:

5.(1) No action for libel in a newspaper or in a broadcast lies unless the plaintiff has, within six weeks after the alleged libel has come to the plaintiff's knowledge, given to the defendant notice in writing, specifying the matter complained of, which shall be served in the same manner as a statement of claim or by delivering it to a grown-up person at the chief office of the defendant.

(2) The defendant shall recover only actual damages if it appears on the trial,

(a) that the alleged libel was published in good faith;

(b) that the alleged libel did not involve a criminal charge;

(c) that the publication of the alleged libel took place in mistake or misapprehension of the facts; and

(d) that a full and fair retraction of any matter therein alleged to be erroneous,

   (i) was published either in the next regular issue of the newspaper or in any regular issue thereof published within three days after the receipt of the notice mentioned in subsection (1) and was so published in as conspicuous a place and type as was the alleged libel, or

   (ii) was broadcast either within a reasonable time or within three days after the receipt of the notice mentioned in subsection (1) and was so broadcast as conspicuously as was the alleged libel.

(3) This section does not apply to the case of a libel against any candidate for public office unless the retraction of the charge is made in a conspicuous manner at least five days before the election.

6. An action for a libel in a newspaper or in a broadcast shall be commenced within three months after the libel has come to the knowledge of the person defamed, but, where such an action is brought within that period, the action may include a claim for any other libel against the plaintiff by the defendant in the same newspaper or the same broadcasting station within a period of one year before the commencement of the action.

Section 8 of the Ontario statue also makes no reference to section 12. Consequently, on a literal reading, a newspaper which does not comply with section 8 is still entitled to the security for costs provisions. There is a similar gap in the Saskatchewan legislation (section 16) and the British Columbia legislation (section 12).

H. SHIFT OF BURDEN OF PROOF

It has been held that once the defendant has stated in his affidavit that after a diligent inquiry he was satisfied that the plaintiff company was not possessed of certain property, the burden of proof shifts to the plaintiff.

Dinnard v. Moore (1907), 11 O.W.R. 61.

Augustine Automatic Rotary Engine Co. v. Saturday Night Ltd. (1915), 34 O.L.R. 166 (C.A.).

I. PLAINTIFF WITHIN THE PROVINCE

It has been held that section 12 of the Ontario *Libel and Slander Act* is not confined to plaintiffs who are not ordinarily resident in Ontario. Provided the requirements for security for costs set out in section 12(1) are otherwise made out, the defendant is *prima facie* entitled to an order for security for costs subject to a discretion in the court which should be judicially exercised.

Howard-Azzeh v. St. Catherines Standard Group Inc., [2003] O.J. No. 4990, per Then J. at paras. 12–15 (Div. Ct.).

CHAPTER ELEVEN:
Joinder

A. JOINDER OF CAUSES OF ACTION

There is no general rule that a defamation claim cannot be joined to another cause of action.

> *Caulfield Creative Arts Ltd.* v. *Cats Defence Support Systems Inc.* (1987), A.R. 172 (Q.B.).

> *Parisien* v. *Saskatchewan Economic Development Corp.*, [1997] S.J. No. 561 (Q.B.).

> *Kenaidan Contracting Ltd.* v. *Powell*, [2003] O.J. No. 5168, per Swinton J. at paras. 15–17 (S.C.J.).

> *Liao* v. *Griffioen*, [2003] O.J. No. 5321, per O'Neill J. at paras. 13–27 (S.C.J.).

The modern trend is to encourage joinder of causes of action. It is a false assumption that the jury must deal with all issues in an action just because a jury was mandatory for the trial of the issue of libel.

> *Someplace Else Restaurant Ltd.* v. *Calendar Magazines Ltd.*, (1979), 27 O.R. (2d) 760, 107 D.L.R. (3d) 636 (H.C.J.).

If there has been defamation by an individual, the issue of whether the individual's employer is legally responsible for the defamation will more conveniently be dealt with in defamation proceedings against both the employee and the employer in one proceeding.

> *Caulfield Creative Arts Ltd.* v. *Cats Defence Support Systems Inc.*, above.

> *Riddick* v. *Thames Board Mills Ltd.*, [1977] 1 Q.B. 881, 3 All E.R. 677 (C.A.).

A court may, in its discretion, join a claim for damages for wrongful dismissal with a claim for damages for defamation. It is desirable that claims arising from the same facts should be tried together.

Romanic v. Hartman, [1986] 5 W.W.R. 610 (Sask. Q.B.).

Stadler v. Terrace Corporation (Construction) Ltd. (1983), 41 A.R. 587 (Q.B.).

Tellier v. Bank of Montreal (1982), 32 C.P.C. 17 (Ont. S.C. (Mast.)).

Clough v. Greyhound Leasing & Financial of Can. Ltd. (1979), 26 O.R. (2d) 590, 103 D.L.R. (3d) 565 (H.C.J.).

Foley v. Signtech Inc. (1988), 66 O.R. (2d) 729, 55 D.L.R. (4th) 152 (Ont. H.C.J.).

There may be circumstances, however, where the court will conclude that joinder of other causes of action will be prejudicial to the fair determination of the libel action.

Accord Planners Insurance Agencies Ltd. v. *Wise/Riddell Insurance Agency Inc.*, [1997] O.J. No. 2423 (Gen. Div.).

Rotenberg v. Rosenberg, [1964] 1 O.R. 160 (S.C. (Mast.)), aff'd [1964] 1 O.R. 162n (H.C.J.).

Makkar v. City of Scarborough (1985), 48 C.P.C. 141 (Ont. H.C.J.).

Motruk v. Jeannot (1987), 16 C.P.C. (2d) 160 (Ont. H.C.J.).

Claims for libel arising from separate publications have been joined where the court concluded that joinder may promote the convenient administration of justice, where the claims for relief arose out of occurrences closely connected in time and subject-matter, and where common questions of fact and law arose with respect to the allegedly defamatory statements.

Gracey v. Thomson Newspapers Corp. (1991), 82 D.L.R. (4th) 244 (Ont. Gen. Div.).

Liao v. Griffioen, [2003] O.J. No. 5321, per O'Neill J. (S.C.J.).

B. JOINDER OF PARTIES

Whenever more persons than one are concerned in the same publication, the plaintiff may sue all or any of them in the same action. Thus, where the libel has appeared in a newspaper, he can always join as defendants in the same action the proprietor, the editor, the printer, and the publisher, or so many of them as he thinks fit.

Berry v. *Retail Merchants Ass'n*, [1924] 2 D.L.R. 916 (Sask. C.A.).

Dickhoff v. *Armadale Communications Ltd.* (1993), 108 D.L.R. (4th) 464 (Sask. C.A.).

If a plaintiff does not join in one action all potential defendants to the publication of one libel, it may not be possible to bring a separate action later. It may be considered an abuse of process to bring a subsequent action against other defamation defendants for damages after judgment has already been obtained against the first set of defendants.

Thomson v. *Lambert*, [1938] S.C.R. 253, 2 D.L.R. 545 .

The various provincial defamation statutes permit the court, on application by the defendants in two or more actions for the same or substantially the same libel, to make an order for the consolidation of the actions for trial together.

Dickhoff v. *Armadale Communications Ltd.* (1993), 108 D.L.R. (4th) 464 (Sask. C.A.).

Alberta, *Defamation Act*, R.S.A. 1980, c. D-6, ss.7(1), 7(2).

British Columbia, *Libel and Slander Act*, R.S.B.C. 1996, c. 263, ss.15(1), 15(2).

Manitoba, *Defamation Act*, R.S.M. 1987, c. D20, s.7.

New Brunswick, *Defamation Act*, R.S.N.B. 1973, s.7.

Newfoundland and Labrador, *Defamation Act*, S.N. 1983, c. 63, ss.9(1), 9(2).

Northwest Territories, *Defamation Act*, R.S.N.W.T. 1988, c.D-1, ss.8(1), 8(2).

Nova Scotia, *Defamation Act*, R.S.N.S. 1989, c. 122, s.11.

Ontario, *Libel and Slander Act*, R.S.O. 1990, c. L.12, s.11(1).

Prince Edward Island, *Defamation Act*, R.S.P.E.I. 1988, c. D-5, ss.8(1), 8(2).

Saskatchewan, *Libel and Slander Act*, R.S.S. 1978, c. L-14, s.6(1).

Yukon Territory, *Defamation Act*, R.S.Y.T. 1986, c.41, ss.7(1), 7(2).

Two actions for separate libels published by different newspapers but concerning the same subject matter can be tried successively by separate juries.

Lewis v. *Daily Telegraph Ltd.*, [1964] A.C. 234.

Separate actions for libel, trespass, and damages for breach of contract have also been ordered to be tried together: two with a jury, one without.

Iona Corporation v. *Rooney* (1987), 25 C.P.C. (2d) 174 (Ont. H.C.J.).

Claims against different defendants for separate publications which differ in material respects do not arise out of "the same transaction or occurrence" within the meaning of a statute permitting an amendment to pleadings notwithstanding the lapse of a limitation period. Accordingly, a court refused permission to join a second newspaper publication to an existing libel action.

Dickhoff v. *Armadale Communications Ltd.*, above.

The foregoing discussion is subject to the caveat that close attention must be paid to the rules of court of the jurisdiction where the action is brought. Case law from one province may not be applicable in another.

For example, Rule 5 of the *British Columbia Supreme Court Rules* provides that a person, whether claiming in the same or different capacities, may join several claims in the same proceeding and may bring the action against two or more persons where:

i)   if separate proceedings were brought by or against each of them, a common question of law or fact would arise in all the proceedings, or

ii)   a right to relief claimed in the proceedings, whether it is joint, several, or alternative, is in respect of or arises out of the same transaction or series of transactions, or

iii)   the court grants leave to do so.

Nevertheless, the British Columbia *Rules* also provide that where a joinder of several claims or parties in a proceeding may unduly complicate or delay the trial or hearing of the proceeding or is otherwise inconvenient, the court may order separate trials or hearings or make any other order it thinks just. See also:

Alberta, *Judicature Act*, R.S.A. 2000, c. J-1, Alberta *Rules of Court*, Alta. Reg. 390/68.

British Columbia, *Court Rules Act*, R.S.B.C. 1996, c. 80; *Supreme Court Rules*, B.C. Reg. 221/90, r.5.

Manitoba, *Court of Queen's Bench Act*, S.M. 1988-89, c. 4, *Court of Queen's Bench Rules*, Man. Reg. 553/88.

New Brunswick, *Judicature Act*, R.S.N.B. 1973, c. J-2, *Rules of Court*, N.B. Reg. 1973-82.

Newfoundland and Labrador, *Judicature Act*, R.S.N. 1990, c. J-4, *Rules of the Supreme Court*, 1986, S.N. 1986, c. 42, Sched. D.

Northwest Territories, *Judicature Act*, R.S.N.W.T. 1988, c. J-1, [Alberta *Rules of Court* apply].

Nova Scotia, *Judicature Act*, R.S.N.S. 1989, c. 240, *Civil Procedure Rules*.

Ontario, *Courts of Justice Act*, R.S.O. 1990, c.C-43, *Rules of Civil Procedure*, R.R.O. 1990, Reg. 194.

Prince Edward Island, *Supreme Court Act*, R.S.P.E.I. 1988, c. S-10, *Rules of Civil Procedure*.

Saskatchewan, *Queen's Bench Act*, R.S.S. 1978, c. Q-1, *Queen's Bench Rules*.

Yukon Territory, *Judicature Act*, R.S.Y. 1986, c. 96 [B.C. *Supreme Court Rules* apply].

CHAPTER TWELVE

Trial by Jury

A. INTRODUCTION

Statutes or court rules in certain provinces give a defamation litigant either an absolute or a qualified right to demand a jury trial.

Alberta, *Jury Act*, R.S.A. 2000, c. J-3,1 s.17(1).

British Columbia, *Supreme Court Rules*, r. 39(24), (26), (27).

Newfoundland and Labrador, *Jury Act*, S.N. 1991, c. 16, s.32(1) as amended by S.N. 1999, c. 13.

Nova Scotia, *Judicature Act*, R.S.N.S. 1989, c. 240, s.34.

Ontario, *Courts of Justice Act*, R.S.O. 1900, c.43, s.108 (2).

Saskatchewan, *Jury Act*, R.S.S. 1981, c. J.-4.1, s.16.

In *Mitchell* v. *Nanimo District Teachers Association* (1994), 94 B.C.L.R. (2d) 81 (C.A.), the majority judgment of the British Columbia Court of Appeal suggested that the question whether a publication defamed the plaintiff is best decided by a jury:

> Upon an issue "libel or no libel' [that is, the question of fact to be answered] eight opinions are better than one. Had it been, the jury could have returned a verdict for either plaintiff or defendants without being deserving of the epithet 'unreasonable.'

The importance of a jury in civil libel cases is discussed in *Rothermere* v. *Times Newspapers*, [1973] 1 W.L.R. 448, where Lord Denning M.R. stated at page 452 that the right to a jury trial "is of the highest importance, especially when the defendant has ventured to criticise the government of the day, or those who hold authority or power in the state." Writing one of the majority judgments of the Court of Appeal, which rejected Lord Rothermere's application to strike the jury on the ground that the trial would involve a prolonged examination of documents, Denning M.R. stated at page 454:

> It is true that a trial by judge alone would have many advantages. In particular, a judge could deal better with the mass of documents: and he would give reasons which could be reviewed by a Court of Appeal. But the result is not always better justice. As Lord Devlin points out in his *Trial by Jury*, at p. 159:
>
>> The malady that sooner or later affects most men of a profession is that they tend to construct a mystique that cuts them off from the common man.
>
> In no department is this mystique more pronounced than the law of libel. But a jury looks at a case more broadly. They give weight to factors which impress the lay mind more strongly than the legal. To achieve a just result, I do not think they should be set an examination paper containing many questions to answer. Only three or four at most. But it must always be remembered that they have an absolute right to give a general verdict; that is to say, whether they find for the plaintiff or the defendant: and, if for the plaintiff, how much damages. And since they have given a general verdict, that is the end of the matter: see *Barnes v. Hill*, [1967] 1 Q.B. 579.

The Canadian Broadcasting Corporation, although a Crown entity, does not have immunity from a civil jury trial.

Pierre v. Pacific Press Ltd., [1994] 1 W.W.R. 23 (B.C.C.A.), leave to appeal to S.C.C. denied, [1993] S.C.C.A. No. 466.

B. THE DIFFERENT PROVINCIAL REGULATIONS

In British Columbia, the right to deliver a notice requiring trial by a jury in a defamation action is absolute. Subrule 39(26) of the *Rules of Court* provides that a party may require that the trial of an action be heard by the court with a jury by filing and delivering to all parties of record, within twenty-one days after delivery of the notice of trial and not later than thirty days before trial, the form of notice prescribed in the appendix to the Rules, and by paying to the sheriff, not less than thirty days before trial, a sum sufficient to pay for the jury and the jury process.

In British Columbia, a civil jury consists of eight individuals. In cases involving defamation, false imprisonment, and malicious prosecution, the court has no discretion to order the trial to take place without a jury, although in other cases a party to civil litigation may apply under Rule 39(27) for a trial by judge alone on the grounds that the issues require a prolonged examination of documents or accounts or a scientific or local investigation which cannot be conveniently made with a jury, or that the issues are of an intricate or complicated nature.

Libel litigants in British Columbia occasionally sidestep the requirement for a jury trial by bringing summary judgment or summary trial proceedings. It seems, however, that this tactic is less likely to succeed where the claim is for libel. In *McLean v. Southam Inc.*, [2002] B.C.J. No. 700, 2002 BCCA 229, Saunders J.A. in chambers refused the plaintiff leave to appeal a lower court's refusal to try the libel claim under Rule 18A — British Columbia's "summary trial" rule where the evidence takes the form of affidavits. Saunders J.A. concluded that there was little likelihood the Court of Appeal would interfere with the lower court's decision, particularly given the "extra value" of a jury trial in cases of reputation, and the desirability of *viva voce* evidence on issues of credibility and reputation. The lower court judge had relied on *Rothermere v. Times Newspapers*, above, in concluding that the issue of malice in this defamation case was better suited to be tried by a jury.

In Nova Scotia, the *Rules* provide that juries are to hear defamation actions unless the parties waive that right.

> *Rajkhowa v. Watson* (2000), 1 C.P.C. (5th) 218 (N.S.C.A.) [interlocutory order severing liability and quantum set aside, impractical to recall jury or empanel new jury].

In Alberta, the mode of trial is by judge alone unless a civil jury is directed under Rules 224 and 234. The *Jury Act* in section 17(1)(a) however, provides a *prima facie* right to a jury in an action for defamation.

In Alberta, it appears that once a judge has made an order for trial by jury the other party cannot in effect circumvent a jury trial by making a summary trial application on affidavits in Chambers:

> *Hajjar v. Repetowski*, 2001 ABQB 432, [2001] 8 W.W.R. 539 [not a defamation case], but see *Elliott v. Amante*, 2001 ABQB 1080, [2002] 3 W.W.R. 735.

In Alberta, the court may dismiss an application for a jury trial if prolonged examination of exhibits cannot conveniently be made by a jury.

> *Voskoboinikova v. Calgary Herald* (2000), 5 C.P.C. (5th) 396, 2000 ABQB 50 [libel action, accounting records].

In Ontario, on application by a party the court may direct a trial by judge alone if highly technical evidence will be tendered at trial or if the case may involve prolonged examination of documents. On the motion, the court may order that issues of fact be tried or damages assessed, or both, without a jury.

Courts of Justice Act, R.S.O. 1990, c. 43, s.108(3).

Sussman v. *Eales* (1987), 61 O.R. (2d) 316 (H.C.J.) [court dismissed a motion to strike out a jury as being premature in advance of examinations for discovery since it could not be known whether highly technical and specialized damage evidence would be required].

Toronto-Dominion Bank v. *Berthin* (1994), 50 A.C.W.S. (3d) 470 (Ont. Gen. Div.) [jury dismissed during trial in part because of the complexity of the evidence].

Porter v. *York (Regional Municipality) Police*, [2001] O.J. No. 2657 (S.C.J.) [jury notice struck where plaintiff pleaded nine distinct causes of action making case too complex for a jury].

The right to a jury trial in a defamation action may be restricted in certain provinces if the plaintiff seeks damages within the monetary jurisdiction of the provincial small claims court. In New Brunswick, for example, actions for damages (including libel and slander) not exceeding $3,000 are required to be tried by a small claims judge.

Wilson v. *Maber* (1998), 198 N.B.R. (2d) 247 (C.A.); Rule 46.01(2) Rule 75.01.

Similarly, in Manitoba, Ontario, and Prince Edward Island, libel and slander actions within the monetary jurisdiction of the small claims court are tried in that court.

Suedfeld v. *Lancia*, [1993] O.J. No. 1693 (Ont. Ct. J. (Gen. Div. Sm. Cl.Ct.)).

Bhaduria v. *Standard Broadcasting Inc. (c.ob. CFRB)*, [1996] O.J. No. 2853 (Ont. Gen. Div. (Sm. Cl. Ct.)).

Hasnu v. *Deshe Bedeshe Inc.*, [1998] O.J. No. 3493.

On the other hand, in Alberta, British Columbia, Newfoundland and Labrador, Nova Scotia, Quebec, and Saskatchewan the provincial legislation specifically excludes libel and slander claims from the jurisdiction of the small claims courts.

Cohen v. *Wilder*, [1996] B.C.J. No. 856 (Prov. Ct. (Civ. Div.)) [court refused to consider defamation claim].

Dawe v. *Nova Collection Services (Nfld.) Ltd.* (1998), 160 Nfld. & P.E.I.R. 266 (Nfld. Prov. Ct. (Sm. Cl.)).

The jurisprudence in provinces where the right to a jury trial is not absolute is constantly evolving. Accordingly, legal counsel for defamation litigants are well-advised to keep abreast of the law.

See, for example, *Clarke* v. *Manufacturers Life Insurance Co.*, 2003 NLSCTD 40 [order that case be tried by a jury, not a defamation case].

CHAPTER THIRTEEN

Identification of the Plaintiff

A. OVERVIEW

Any defamatory expression must be about the plaintiff in order to be actionable. The burden is on the plaintiff to satisfy this requirement.

Although the requirement is obviously satisfied if the plaintiff is expressly named, the converse is not true. Merely omitting the name of a plaintiff from the defamatory expression will not necessarily insulate the defendant. Liability for defamatory expression may be imposed if the expression would reasonably lead persons acquainted with the plaintiff to the conclusion that it does refer to the plaintiff. It is irrelevant whether or not the defendant subjectively intended to refer to the plaintiff or was even aware of the plaintiff's existence.

The case law illustrates many different situations where liability has been imposed although the plaintiff was not expressly named, including the following:

i)   A defendant deliberately refrains from naming the plaintiff in the belief this will enable the defendant to avoid legal liability or in the belief the plaintiff will not sue and thereby risk revealing his or her identity to the world.

ii)   The defamatory expression concerns members of a group or class of individuals.

iii) The defamatory expression is ambiguous or confusing but nevertheless points to the plaintiff, whether or not the plaintiff is the actual target.

iv)   The defamatory expression is a work of fiction and no reference to the plaintiff is intended.

The leading authority on this topic is *Knupffer* v. *London Express Newspaper, Ltd.*, [1944] 1 All E.R. 495 (H.L.) which is invariably cited with approval in the Canadian jurisprudence and informs much of the discussion in this chapter.

B. ESSENTIAL ELEMENT OF CAUSE OF ACTION

[I]t is an essential element of the cause of action for defamation that the words complained of should be published "of the plaintiff." If the words are not so published the plaintiff cannot have any right to ask that the defendant should be held responsible to him.

Knupffer v. London Express Newspaper, Ltd., [1944] A.C. 116 at 118.

An essential element of such a cause of action is that the words complained of should be published "of the plaintiff" …

Arnott v. College of Physicians and Surgeons of Saskatchewan, [1954] S.C.R. 538 per Kellock J. at 554.

Booth v. British Columbia Television Broadcasting System (1982), 139 D.L.R. (3d) 88, per Lambert J.A. at 92 (B.C.C.A.).

Butler v. Southam Inc. (2001), 197 N.S.R. (2d) 97, per Cromwell J.A. at para. 29 (C.A.).

Grant v. Cormier-Grant (2001), 56 O.R. (3d) 215, per Borins J.A. at para. 19 (C.A.).

Aiken v. Police Review Publishing Co., [1995] E.W.J. No. 5681 per Lord Justice Hirst at para. 13 (C.A.).

Bai v. Sing Tao Daily Ltd., [2003] O.J. No. 917 per McMurtry C.J.O. at para. 10 (C.A.), leave to appeal to S.C.C. denied, [2003] S.C.C.A. No. 354.

1) A Two-part Test

To establish this element of the cause of action, the plaintiff must satisfy a two-part test:

1. as a question of law, can the expression be regarded as capable of referring to the plaintiff? and
2. as a question of fact, does the article in fact lead reasonable people who know that plaintiff to the conclusion that it does refer to him?

Knupffer v. London Express Newspaper, Ltd., [1944] 1 A.C. 116 per Viscount Simon at 121.

Arnott v. *College of Physicians and Surgeons of Saskatchewan*, above, at 555, citing with approval Viscount Simon at 119 in *Knupffer*, above:

> [The] test which decides whether the words used refer to him is the question whether the words are such as would reasonably lead persons acquainted with the plaintiff to believe that he was the person referred to.

Sykes v. *Fraser*, [1974] S.C.R. 526, per Ritchie J. for the majority at 541 and Laskin J. at 559 [for the minority who dissented but not on this point], both citing *Knupffer* with approval

Booth v. *British Columbia Television Broadcasting System* (1982), 139 D.L.R. (3rd) 88, per Lambert J.A. at 92 (B.C.C.A.).

Butler v. *Southam Inc.* (2001) 197 N.S.R. (2d) 97, per Cromwell J.A. at para. 21 (C.A.).

These tests must be satisfied whether the plaintiff is an individual or a corporation.

Shendish Manor Ltd. v. *Coleman*, [2001] E.W.C.A. Civ. 913, per Keene L.J. at paras. 33, 36–39.

2) Failure on First Part of Test

If the plaintiff cannot satisfy the first part of the test, the second question does not arise. A trial judge errs if she treats evidence in support of identification in fact as governing the matter if the plaintiff cannot show as a matter of law that the expression is capable of referring to the plaintiff.

Knupffer v. *London Express Newspaper, Ltd.*, [1944] 1 A.C. 116 at 121.

It has been held that the first part of the test is particularly appropriate to be decided by a judge in Chambers on an application to strike as it involves a question of law, not one of fact.

Boland v. *Probst*, [1954] O.J. No. 31 per Gale J. at para. 10 (H.C.).

For a statement of claim to fail the first part of the test, it must be "plain and obvious" that it is incapable of referring to the plaintiff. If that is not demonstrated, the claim should be permitted to proceed.

Raho v. *Craig Broadcasting Systems Inc.* (1999), 141 Man. R. (2d) 288 (Q.B.) citing *Reid* v. *Marr's Leisure Holdings Inc.*, [1994] 7 W.W.R. 542, per Scott C.J.M. at 544 (Man. C.A.), in turn citing *Dumont* v. *Canada (Attorney General)*, [1990] 1 S.C.R. 279.

3) Application of Test if No Jury

It has been held, however, that where a judge alone determines both questions, there is "no reason for any precise separation of the functions or decision of the two questions that have been raised by Viscount Simon" in *Knupffer*, above.

> *Booth v. British Columbia Television Broadcasting System* (1982), 139 D.L.R. (3d) 88, per Lambert J.A. at 94 (B.C.C.A.).

4) Test Is Objective

Although the second part of the test involves a finding of fact, it requires the application of an objective test whether the expression is libel or slander.

> *Morgan v. Odhams Press Ltd. et al.*, [1971] 2 All E.R. 1156 (H.C.).

> *Shendish Manor Ltd. v. Coleman*, [2001] E.W.C.A. Civ. 913, per Keene L.J. at para. 39:

>> A jury could not, in my judgment, properly conclude that the alleged statements refer to the [plaintiff] company. They were not words which, judged objectively, were capable of being understood by the ordinary, sensible person as referring to that corporate body.

> *Grant v. Cormier-Grant* (2001), 56 O.R. (3d) 215, per Borins J.A. at paras. 24, 25 (C.A.):

>> ¶24 It is clear from the decision of the House of Lords in *Morgan* [v. *Odhams Press Ltd.*, [1971] 2 All E.R. 1156] that the test is an objective one, whether on the evidence an ordinary sensible person would draw the inference that the words referred to the plaintiff....

>> ¶25 I would observe that although the cases to which I have referred considered the issue of identification in the context of a libel case, and, indeed the legal treatises also discuss the issue in that context, I can see no reason in principle why the test to be applied in determining whether a defamatory statement refers to the plaintiff should not be the same in slander cases.

The objective test with respect to identification of the plaintiff requires consideration of all of the circumstances.

> *Knupffer v. London Express Newspaper, Ltd.*, [1944] A.C. 116 at per Lord Porter at 124:

Each case must be considered according to its own circumstances. I can imagine it being said that each member of a body, however large, was defamed where the libel consisted in the assertion that no one of the members of a community was elected as a member unless he had committed a murder.

In *Booth v. British Columbia Television Broadcasting System* (1982), 139 D.L.R. (3d) 88 per Lambert J.A. at 93–94 (B.C.C.A.):

> ... we are not concerned with what the speaker subjectively meant to say; we are concerned with the meaning that reasonable men would take from what was said. But words, of course, are merely a mode of communication and all the circumstances of the communication must be considered as well as the mode that was used. The kind of person that the speaker was, and the kind of knowledge that people would anticipate that the speaker would have are relevant factors in determining the content of the communication. The circumstances in which the words are used are also relevant. So is the general audience to which the statements might be considered to be directed, and the special audience with special knowledge ... These too are relevant factors in deciding whether reasonable people generally, or whether reasonable people with special and particular knowledge, would find that the defamatory statement was published of and concerning the particular plaintiff.

Lord Pearson stated in *Morgan v. Odhams Press Ltd.*, [1971] 2 All E.R. 1156 (H.L.), 1 W.L.R. 1239 at 1269, in relation to a defamatory report in a Sunday newspaper:

> I do not think the reasonable man — who can also be described as an ordinary sensible man — should be envisaged as reading this article carefully. Regard should be had to the character of the article: it is vague, sensational and allusive: it is evidently designed for entertainment rather than instruction or accurate information. The ordinary, sensible man, if he read the article at all, would be likely to skim through it casually and not give it concentrated attention or a second reading. It is no part of his work to read this article, nor does he have to place any practical decision on what he reads there. The relevant impression is that which would be conveyed to an ordinary sensible man (in this case having knowledge of the relevant circumstances) reading the article casually and not expecting a high degree of accuracy.

C. PLEADING EXTRINSIC FACTS (LEGAL INNUENDO)

Defamatory expression may identify the plaintiff by virtue of extrinsic facts known to specific people or classes of people exposed to that expression. The plaintiff may therefore plead and prove the extrinsic facts which permit the identification of the plaintiff.

> *Aiken v. Police Review Publishing Co.*, [1995] E.W.J. No. 5681, per Hirst L.J. at para. 13 (C.A..):
>
>> ... When, as in the present case, each plaintiff relies on extrinsic facts to establish the identification, the test is accurately defined in *Duncan and Neil on Defamation*, second edition, paragraph 6.03, page 23:
>>
>>> Where identification is in issue the matter can sometimes be decided by construing the words themselves in their context. More often, however, the plaintiff will be seeking to show that the words would be understood to refer to him because of some facts and circumstances which are extrinsic to the words themselves. In these cases the plaintiff is required to plead and prove the extrinsic facts on which he relies to establish identification and if these facts are proved, the question becomes: would reasonable persons, knowing these facts or some of them, reasonably believe that the words referred to the plaintiff?
>
> *Fraser v. Sykes* (1971), 19 D.L.R. (3d) 75 (Alta. S.C. (A.D.)), aff'd (1973), 39 D.L.R. (3d) 321 (S.C.C.) per Clement J.A. at 81:
>
>> The allegations of the words complained of were preceded and followed by prefatory averments setting out the circumstances by which [the plaintiff] asserts those words point in his direction. This is a proper form of pleading and entitles the plaintiff to give evidence of those extrinsic circumstances.

Whether it is necessary or appropriate for the plaintiff to plead and establish extrinsic facts depends on all the circumstances. A helpful description of the spectrum of possibilities is found in the judgment of Isaacs J. in *David Syme & Co. v. Canavan* (1918), 25 C.L.R. 234 which is quoted with approval in *Grant v. Cormier-Grant* (2001), 56 O.R. (3d) 215 by Borins J.A. at paragraph 21 (C.A.):

> Where the plaintiff is referred to in an indirect way or by implication it will be a question of degree how far evidence will be required to connect the libel

with him. At one extreme, if there is a libel on "the Prime Minister" that officer does not need to produce witnesses to testify that they know who he is. At the other extreme, the plaintiff may only be identifiable by reason of extrinsic facts which are not generally known, in which case there is no actionable publication unless it is shown that the words were communicated to persons with such knowledge. Even in the latter type of case, however, it is not enough that the recipients of the statement did understand it to refer to the plaintiff: the issue is whether reasonable people with their knowledge would so understand it.

Even where extrinsic facts are alleged, the second part of the two-part test to determine whether the allegedly defamatory expression referred to the plaintiff must be addressed objectively. The court must determine the conclusion that would be reached by a hypothetical sensible reader who knew the special facts alleged.

> *Morgan v. Odhams Press Ltd.*, [1971] 2 All E.R. 1156 per Lord Reid at 1163c–e (H.L.):
>
>> What has to be decided is whether it would have been unreasonable for a hypothetical sensible reader who knew the special facts proved to infer that this article referred to the appellant. I shall not set out those facts because it appears to me that in the end it all depends on the way in which one is required to assume that a sensible reader will react on reading this kind of article in a daily newspaper. If one must assume that he thinks and acts cautiously as a lawyer would do in his professional capacity then I have no doubt that he would say that inference is not justified in this case. But if one is entitled to be more realistic and take account of the way in which ordinary sensible people do in fact read their newspapers and draw inferences then equally I have no doubt such people would quite probably draw this inference.

> *Dale's Trad'N Post Ltd. v. Rhodes* (1987), 19 B.C.L.R. (2d) 73, per Legg J. at 84–85 (S.C.).

Cases where the plaintiff established extrinsic facts to prove the element of identification include the following:

i)   prior communications between the plaintiff and City officials, prior attendance of plaintiff at City Council regular public meeting, and prior newspaper articles.

> *Fraser v. Sykes* (1971), 19 D.L.R. (3d) 75 (Alta. S.C. (A.D.)), aff'd (1973), 39 D.L.R. (3d) 321, [1974] S.C.R. 526. In a passage expressly approved

by Ritchie J. for the majority in the Supreme Court of Canada, Clement J.A. for the Court of Appeal stated at 85–86:

> ... All those attending the Council meeting of November 10th, both members of the public, alderman, city officials and reporters would have little difficulty concluding that [the plaintiff] was pointed to [in subsequent defamatory statements by the defendant on November 12]. Others would undoubtedly have in their minds the newspaper report of November 11th which specifically named Fraser: it was this report that caused [the defendant] himself to act as he did. Those who attended the two press conferences summoned by [the defendant] could have no doubt that he was implicating [the plaintiff]. In light of the surrounding circumstances, the words complained of were capable of being understood by a reasonable man as pointing to Fraser, and I am of the opinion that the learned trial judge was correct in finding as a fact that they did so.

ii) a later newspaper article which named the plaintiff.

Hayward v. Thompson, [1981] 3 All E.R. 450 (CA). A weekly paper published an article referring to "a wealthy benefactor of the Liberal party." The following week, an article dealing with the same subject-matter named the plaintiff, who was in fact wealthy and had made a substantial donation to the party. It was held that the jury was entitled to look at the second article to see to whom the first article referred. Per Lord Denning at 457e:

> The second article was admissible in evidence so as to show that [... the first article ...] aimed at Mr. Jack Hayward and intended to refer to him: and therefore that the first article was published "of and concerning" Mr. Hayward.

iii) a series of newspaper articles, the last of which named the plaintiff.

Misir v. Toronto Star Newspapers (1997), 105 O.A.C. 270 (C.A.). A dozen articles were published during the period from May to September. Only the last article named the plaintiff. Laskin J.A., speaking for the Court of Appeal, held [at paragraphs 15–16] that the jury would be entitled to find that the May articles were defamatory because of the publication of the last article in September:

> ¶16 Indeed, had the plaintiffs given notice within six weeks of the publication of the May articles and issued their statement of claim before September 30, 1995, the defendants would undoubtedly have moved

> to dismiss the action because the articles did not refer to the plaintiffs. Thus it seems to me that the trier of fact can look at the September 30 article to see to whom the previous eleven articles referred. A newspaper cannot avoid an action for libel by publishing a series of defamatory articles but only link the plaintiffs to the defamation by identifying them in the last article.

iv)   three newspaper articles, the first of which named the plaintiff.

> *Barcan v. Zorkin*, [1991] A.J. No. 271 (Q.B.) per Shannon J.

See also:

> *Butler v. Southam Inc.* (2001) 197 N.S.R. (2d) 97, per Cromwell J.A. at paras. 43–48 (C.A.), reversing a Chambers judge and concluding that it was an issue for the jury at trial whether publications prior to 21 November 1999, which did not name the plaintiffs, nevertheless referred to the plaintiffs by virtue of an article published on that date which did name them.

> *Thomas v. Canadian Broadcasting Corporation and Sanders*, [1981] 4 W.W.R. 289 (N.W.T.S.C.).

It appears that another approach open to the court is to treat two closely-related publications as one. For example, it has been held that a defamatory noon-hour radio broadcast (which did not name the plaintiff) promoting a defamatory evening television broadcast (which did) should be treated with the television program as one publication.

> *Yellowhead Investment Corp. (c.o.b. Yellowhead Honda) v. Canadian Broadcasting Corp.*, [1996] A.J. No. 689, per MacCallum J. at para. 99 (Q.B.).

D. CORPORATIONS AND THEIR AFFILIATES AND OFFICERS

It is trite law that each corporation is a separate legal entity. A plaintiff corporation may accordingly have difficulty satisfying the two-part objective test to establish that it has been identified in the defamatory expression if it shares elements of a common name with affiliated corporations which operate domestically or internationally.

The problems are conveniently illustrated by certain Canadian decisions involving "Scientology."

In *Church of Scientology of Toronto v. International News Distributing Co.* (1974), 4 O.R. (2d) 408 (H.C.J.), Lieff J. struck out a statement of claim and dismissed an action brought over a magazine published in France and referring to the activities of "the Society of Scientology" in Germany. In arriving at his decision, Lieff J. noted that nothing in the words complained of in the statement of claim referred expressly to the Ontario corporation, nor was there an allegation that the plaintiff was the "Society of Scientology" or of any connection between the plaintiff and the "Society of Scientology." Nor did the statement of claim allege that the Toronto organization was one of the world group of churches of "Scientology" and that it had suffered damage as a result.

On the other hand, in *Church of Scientology Mission of Calgary v. Levett* (1978), 12 A.R. 256 (S.C. (T.D.)), Master Bessemer declined to strike out the action although the impugned statements made by the defendant during the course of a television interview referred simply to Scientology and did not mention the specific corporation by name. He held that the uniqueness of the name enhanced the likelihood that it would be linked to the plaintiff churches even in the absence of extrinsic evidence, having regard to the names and the locale. The subject television broadcast had aired both in Canada and in the USA.

In the case of multinational enterprises that enjoy substantial goodwill associated with a global brand name, there may be cases where both the parent company and its subsidiary are defamed by a publication which employs that brand name.

> *McDonald's Corp. v. Steel*, [1999] E.W.J. No. 2173 (C.A.) where Pill L.J., after referring to *Habib Bank v. Habib Bank AG Zurich*, [1981] 1 W.L.R. 1265 [a passing-off case], stated at para. 81:
>
> > McDonald's generally is a well-known name. Its use in this jurisdiction would import to the ordinary reader both the U.S. corporation and (if they are different) whatever company runs the local restaurants. The first and second respondents each have a related but distinct reputation and each have related but distinct goodwill.

It appears clear that a corporate plaintiff cannot bring an action for libel based on words which reflect not upon itself but upon its individual officers or members. In such a situation the officers or members must bring the action themselves.

> *Church of Scientology of Toronto v. Globe and Mail Ltd.* (1978), 19 O.R. (2d) 62 per Cory J. at 65 (H.C.J.).

In certain situations, however, the court may permit a corporation to sue where expression containing imputations against the conduct of individual members may reflect upon the corporation.

Greenpeace Foundation of Canada v. *Toronto Sun Publishing Corp.* (1989), 69 O.R. (2d) 427 per O'Driscoll J. at V. Conclusions (H.C.).

Alternatively, it is sometimes the case that a court may permit individual officers to sue where only the corporation is named in the defamatory expression.

Accord Planners Insurance Agencies Ltd. v. *Wise/Riddell Insurance Agency Inc.*, [1997] O.J. No. 2423 per Spence J. at para. 9 [derogatory comments capable of referring to the three principals of the company].

It is well-settled law that unincorporated bodies cannot be defamed. Only their members can.

Stark et al. v. *Toronto Sun Publishing Corp.* (1983), 42 O.R. (2d) 791 (H.C.) per Smith J. at 794 g–h (H.C.J.):

> ... the unincorporated body "Operation Dismantle" cannot be defamed. Only its members can. The distinction is important because the danger is forever lurking in the background of actions being prosecuted superficially on behalf of members of a class when in reality they are suing for and on behalf of the unincorporated association or entity.... When defamatory words are spoken of the members of a small association comprising 10 members ... a representative action would lie, as long as the pleadings were satisfactory, even absent specific names in the offensive article.

E. EVIDENCE CONCERNING IDENTIFICATION

It has been held that there should be evidence upon which a jury could conclude that the plaintiff was the person referred to in the expression complained of.

Sykes v. *Fraser*, [1974] S.C.R. 526 per Laskin J. for the minority who dissented but not on this point, referring to *Knupffer*, stating at 559 that the requirement that the words complained of be capable of referring to the plaintiff means

> ... there is evidence upon which such a finding may be made ... [and] that this is a reasonable conclusion in the circumstances.

The plaintiff should show that at least one person to whom the defamatory expression was published did in fact conclude at the time that it referred to the plaintiff. If extrinsic facts are alleged, that publishee should testify that he or she had knowledge of those facts which led to that conclusion.

Masters v. Fox (1978), 85 D.L.R. (3d) 64 per MacFarlane J. at 68 (B.C.S.C.):

> Several witnesses have been called by the plaintiffs who have said that, upon reading the letter soon after its publication, they understood it to refer to the plaintiffs. I accept their evidence. It is clear from reading the article that a reasonable person in the community in which it was published would identify the plaintiffs as the objects of the criticism.

Shendish Manor Ltd. v. Coleman, [2001] E.W.C.A. Civ. 913, per Keene L.J. at para. 11.

The fact that the evidence of witnesses may vary does not mean the plaintiff must fail on the issue of identification. Such evidence may nevertheless support a finding that the expression is "of and concerning" the plaintiff.

Booth v. British Columbia Television Broadcasting System (1982), 139 D.L.R. (3d) 88 per Lambert J.A. at 93, 95 (B.C.C.A.).

It appears that courts are likely to discount, however, the value of testimony of persons closely related to the plaintiff:

Dale's Trad'N Post Ltd. v. Rhodes (1987), 19 B.C.L.R. (2d) 73 per Legg J. at 82 (S.C.):

> Thus the evidence upon which the plaintiffs ... rely to establish that reasonable persons who knew the plaintiffs considered that the advertisements referred to the plaintiffs is limited to the evidence of Mrs. Steward, the wife and business partner of [the individual plaintiff] and a shareholder in [the corporate plaintiff], and the evidence of Mr. Manz who was a business associate and friend of [the individual plaintiff] and a person who had business connections with [the corporate plaintiff].

Halprin v. The Sun Publishing Company Ltd., [1978] 4 W.W.R. 685 (B.C.S.C.) where the Court declined to rely on evidence of nine witnesses called by the plaintiff where three were close friends and the others were associates and former associates of the plaintiff. Per Anderson J. at 699:

> It is, I think, common for professional persons and their close friends to become so emotionally involved in matters of this kind that they infer from newspaper reports the very worst inferences that can be drawn from these reports. They see things through their eyes which do not even occur to the average reader.

A plaintiff may testify about comments received from friends, neighbours, relatives, acquaintances, and strangers which convinced the plaintiff that persons exposed to the defamatory expression identified the plaintiff with that expression. This testimony is not, of course, determinative.

> *A.U.P.E.* v. *Edmonton Sun* (1986), 39 C.C.L.T. 143 (Alta. Q.B.) per McFayden J.

There is some support for the view that testimony of witnesses who did not actually read, view or hear the defamatory expression when it was originally published is likely to be given less or no weight. In *Arnott* v. *College of Physicians and Surgeons of Saskatchewan*, [1954] S.C.R. 538, Locke J. concluded that there was no evidence that the article at issue contained a reference to the plaintiff, stating at page 562:

> Of the persons to whom publication was proven, only two were called by the plaintiff as witnesses … Neither of these witnesses were asked by counsel for the [plaintiff] as to what they understood from the language complained of and there is nothing in the evidence from either of them suggesting that they understood from it that the appellant was a quack doctor, or that the article reflected upon him in any way.

Locke J. noted the plaintiff called other witnesses to whom he was known but the article at issue had not been published to them. Although the witnesses testified at trial, in response to questions from the plaintiff's counsel, that the article referred to the plaintiff, Locke J. gave this little or no weight, noting [at page 563] that "[i]t was not shown that any of these witnesses had seen or read the report complained of."

A witness' evidence that she had an immediate suspicion is not necessarily an indication that the words are capable of being considered as published of and concerning the particular plaintiff.

> *Booth* v. *British Columbia Television Broadcasting System* (1982), 139 D.L.R. (3d) 88 per Lambert J.A. at 96 (B.C.C.A.):
>
> > It is true that the evidence indicates that there was immediate suspicion of all of the members of the narcotics squad and indeed there may well have been suspicion beyond that into the morality squad, into the vice squad as a whole, but that suspicion is more a matter of the mind of the person who heard the statement and his or her association with particular members of the police force. A neighbour who knows only one police officer, for example, and hears something about the police force would think immediately of that police officer, whether the words that are used have any real link to that police officer or not. So an immediate suspicion is not necessarily an indication that the words are

capable of being considered as published of and concerning the particular plaintiff.

A plaintiff may testify about telephone conversations with third parties
and statements made by third parties at meetings after the defamatory
expression was published. Similarly, it appears that third persons may testify about talk in the community concerning the plaintiff as being the person referred to in defamatory expression. Such evidence may be admissible
as an exception to the hearsay rule, or possibly as original evidence.

> *Jozwiak v. Sadek*, [1954] 1 W.L.R. 275 [persons present at meetings of Polish
> community in London testified to effect they identified plaintiff as person
> referred to in Polish newspaper article which purported to be fiction; anony-
> mous telephone messages accusing the plaintiff of being a murderer]

> *Steele v. Mirror Group Newspapers Ltd.*, [1974] 2 N.S.W.L.R. 348 per Hutley
> J.A. at 369–70:

>> A number of grounds of appeal were argued, based on the admission
>> of evidence as to the talk concerning [the plaintiff] in the town of
>> Parkes.... I presume that the evidence was admitted for the purpose of
>> establishing the extent of the identification of [the plaintiff] in the town
>> with the article. If the hearsay rule strictly applied, the evidence could
>> not be admitted to prove the identification and this kind of situation is
>> not in text-books of evidence listed as an exception to the hearsay rule.
>> However, Wallace P. referred to a number of cases of which *Jozwiak v.
>> Sadek* is the clearest in support for this exception.
>> Leading writers accept that declarations of the kind tendered are
>> admissible, thus *Cross on Evidence*, Australian edition by Gobbo, says:
>> "A person's declarations may likewise be proved in order to show his
>> belief that defamatory statements referred to the plaintiff."

> *Andrews v. John Fairfax & Sons Ltd.*, [1980] 2 N.S.W.L.R. 225 [plaintiff archi-
> tect called witnesses to establish that he was identified by readers with a new
> government building, which was the subject of derogatory comments]

> *Snider v. Calgary Herald* (1985), 57 A.R. 93, per Master Quinn at paras. 16–17
> (Q.B.):

>> ¶16 *Phipson on Evidence*, 11th ed., says at s. 1279: "... To prove that a
>> libel referred to the plaintiff, evidence that he was publicly jeered
>> at in consequence of the libel, or in the case of a caricature, excla-
>> mations of recognition by spectators in a public gallery, are admis-

sible." And *Wigmore on Evidence*, 3d ed., s. 1715, treats the assertion of a person to prove the state of his mind as an exception to the hearsay rule.

¶17 A different doctrine was advanced by *Taylor on Evidence*, 6th ed., p. 530, that such statements were original evidence and so admissible.

1) Pointers

A number of court decisions speak of "pointers" (or "keys" or "tags") which establish the identification of the plaintiff. The absence of such pointers is not conclusive against the identification of the plaintiff.

> *Morgan v. Odhams Press Ltd. et al.*, [1971] 2 All E.R. 1156 per Lord Reid at 1162c (H.L.), citing *Cassidy v. Daily Mirror Newspapers*, [1929] 2 K.B. 311 (C.A.) and *Hough v. London Express Newspaper Ltd.*, [1940] 2 K.B. 507:
>
> > I ... reject the argument that the appellant must fail because the respondent's article contained no pointer or peg for his identification.
>
> and per Lord Morris of Borth-y-Gest at 1170c–f
>
> *Aiken v. Police Review Publishing Co.*, [1995] E.W.J. No. 5681, per Hirst L.J. at para. 31 (C.A.).

A non-exhaustive list of "pointers" that have been held to be capable of contributing to the identification of a plaintiff include:

i) reference to the leader and second-in-command of a named organization.

> *Booth v. British Columbia Television Broadcasting System* (1982), 139 D.L.R. (3d) 88 (B.C.C.A.) ["two on the Narc Squad that are high up — right on top"].
>
> *Gordon v. Star Printing & Publishing Co.* (1905) 6 O.W.R. 887 (Master).

ii) reference to ethnic origin, city of residence, leadership status with provincial and national organization, boasts of past acts, past continent of residence, geographic location of contacts.

> *Mouammar v. Bruner* (1978), 84 D.L.R. (3d) 121 (Ont. H.C.J.) ["Toronto man ... believed to be PLO's top representative in Ontario.... close associate of and in frequent contact with a man in Ottawa ... considered to be a top PLO representative to Canada ... a Palestinian who has boasted of committing acts of terrorism in Israel before escaping into Lebanon ... contacts in South America, where he has lived ..."].

iii) reference to the activities or characteristics of the plaintiff.

> *Hayward* v. *Thompson*, [1981] 3 All E.R. 450 at 451, 456, 457 [wealthy, a major donor to a political party].

> *Halluk* v. *Brown* (1982), 41 A.R. 350 (Q.B.) [plaintiff supervisor of street construction for Calgary. Defamatory expression alleged "We just had an assistant superintendent put in from outside in the street paving which has caused nothing but problems ... he treats people like dogs ..."].

iv) reference to a former employee, and location of employment, published in letter issued on date of plaintiff's termination.

> *Weisenberger* v. *Johnson & Higgins Ltd.* (1998), 168 D.L.R. (4th) 298 (Man. C.A.) ["certain irregular and improper premium billing practices have taken place within the Winnipeg Branch Office. They were performed by some former employees"].

v) videotape close-up showing the plaintiff, voice also broadcast.

> *Johnston* v. *Australian Broadcasting Commission* (1993), 113 F.L.R. 307 (A.C.T.S.C.) [plaintiff, not named, portrayed along with fellow workers as shamelessly taking a break for lunch when not entitled]. Per Higgins J. at para. 129:

>> It seems to me ... that for publication in the States of Queensland, South Australia and Western Australia and the Northern Territory, it is not necessary (any more than for Victoria) to call a witness who saw the program there and recognized the plaintiff.

vi) reference to a product name.

> *Vulcan Industrial Packaging Ltd.* v. *Canadian Broadcasting Corporation*, [1983] O.J. No. 242 per R.E. Holland J. at para. 44 (H.C.):

>> It appears to me that with the mention of the product Explosafe, which a knowledgeable investor would know was Vulcan's product, as a matter of law the broadcast could be regarded as capable of referring to Vulcan and it appears clear to me that as a matter of fact the connection was made this being shown by the dramatic fall in stock and the increase in trading of the stock.

> See also an injurious falsehood case: *Church & Dwight Ltd.* v. *Sifto Canada Inc.* (1994), 20 O.R. (3d) 483 (Gen Div) where Jarvis J. held at 488 that although the plaintiff was not identified by name in the defendant's advertisement, it was identified by implication because its product (which was

impugned by the defendant) dominated the market and "for that reason the disparaging comments would fall upon them with virtually full force."

vii) naming a website.

> *Airline Seat Co. (c.o.b. Canadian Affair) v. 1396804 Ontario Inc.*, [2000] O.T.C. 481 (S.C.) per Mesbur J. [competitor of plaintiff travel company advertised "Canada's hottest, juiciest, wettest, most luscious girls girls girls" on its website www.canadianaffair.com. Plaintiff's website was www.canadian-affair.com].

viii) reference to business or other relationships with which the plaintiff may have been associated.

> *Owen Sound Bldg. & Savings Society v. Meir* (1893), 24 O.R. 109 (C.A.).

A misleading "pointer" may be ignored by the court if persons who knew the plaintiff would reasonably conclude the defamatory expression referred to the plaintiff despite the misinformation.

> *Re International Assn. of Bridge, Structural and Ornamental and Reinforcing Iron-workers (Local 97) and Campbell et al.* (1997), 152 D.L.R. (4th) 547 per Macdonald J. at paras.16–18 (B.C.S.C.) [inaccurate statements in news release and newspaper article said that BC's ex-Premier Glen Clark (not a party) was member of the plaintiff union whose activities were being questioned. In fact, Clark belonged to a different Local, not to plaintiff Local 97].

F. DEFENDANT'S INTENTION IRRELEVANT

The knowledge and intention of the defendant is irrelevant to the determination of whether the defamatory expression is capable of referring, or does in fact refer, to the plaintiff. The fact that the publication is fiction, or purports to be fiction, is also irrelevant.

> *E. Hulton & Company v. Jones*, [1910] A.C. 20, per Lord Loreburn L.C. at 23 (H.L. (Eng.)) [see also the judgment of Lord Shaw at 26]:
>
> > Just as the defendant could not excuse himself from malice [in law] by proving that he wrote it in the most benevolent spirit, so he cannot show that the libel was not of and concerning the plaintiff by proving that he never heard of the plaintiff.
>
> *Cassidy v. Daily Mirror*, [1929] 2 K.B. 331 per Scrutton L.J. at 341 (C.A.).
>
> *Newstead v. London Express Newspapers*, [1940] 1 K.B. 377, per Sir Wilfred Green M.R. at 387.

Morgan v. Odhams Press Ltd. et al., [1971] 2 All E.R. 1156 (H.L.), per Lord Reid at 1242, 1243.

O'Shea v. MGN Ltd., [2001] E.W.J. No. 4029, per Morland J. at para. 20 (Q.B.), citing the Faulks Report of 1975 at para. 121.

G. INDIVIDUAL CLAIMS BASED ON STATEMENTS ABOUT A GROUP

It has been held that there are no special legal rules concerning individual claims of defamation based on statements made about a group. The two-part objective test is applied to determine whether such a statement is "of and concerning" the plaintiff.

> *Butler v. Southam Inc.* (2001) 197 N.S.R. (2d) 97, per Cromwell J.A. at para. 53 (C.A.).

The leading case on this subject is *Knupffer v. London Express Newspaper, Ltd.*, [1944] 1 All E.R. 495, where Lord Atkin unequivocally rejected the proposition that statements about a group cannot give individual members of the group a cause of action, stating at pages 497–98:

> It is irrelevant that the words are published of two or more persons if they are proved to be published of [the plaintiff], and it is irrelevant that the two or more persons are called by some generic or class name. There can be no law that a defamatory statement made of a firm, or trustees, or the tenants of a particular building is not actionable, if the words would reasonably be understood as published of each member of the firm or each trustee or each tenant. The reason why a libel published of a large or indeterminate number of persons described by some general name generally fails to be actionable is the difficulty of establishing that the plaintiff was, in fact, included in the defamatory statement, for the habit of making unfounded generalizations is ingrained in ill-educated or vulgar minds, or the words are occasionally intended to be a facetious exaggeration. Even in such cases words may be used which enable the plaintiff to prove that the words complained of were intended to be published of each member of the group, or, at any rate, of himself.... It will be as well for the future for lawyers to concentrate on the question whether the words were published of the plaintiff rather than on the question whether they were spoken of a class.

Lord Simon agreed, stating in *Knupffer* at pages 496–97:

There are cases in which the language used in reference to a limited class may be reasonably understood to refer to every member of the class, in which case every member may have a cause of action. A good example is Browne v. Thomson & Co., [1912] SC 359, where a newspaper article stated in Queenstown 'Instructions were issued by the Roman Catholic religious authorities that all Protestant shop assistants were to be discharged', and … seven pursuers who averred that they were the sole persons who exercised religious authority in the name and on behalf of the Roman Catholic Church in Queenstown were held entitled to sue for libel as being individually defamed.

Lord Porter wrote a separate judgment in *Knupffer* in which he briefly discussed factors to be taken into account in determining whether a member of a named group would have an individual right to sue for defamation. He stated at page 499:

> In deciding [whether the words refer to the plaintiff or plaintiffs] the size of the class, the generality of the charge, and the extravagance of the accusation may all be elements to be taken into consideration, but none of them is conclusive. Each case must be considered according to its own circumstances. I can imagine it being said that each member of a body, however large, was defamed when the libel consisted in the assertion that no one of the members of a community was elected as a member unless he had committed a murder.

In Canadian jurisprudence, there are a number of reported cases where individual members of a group have failed to prove that a defamatory statement pointing to the group was "of and concerning" them. Examples include:

> *Aiken v. Ontario (Premier)* (1999), 177 D.L.R. (4th) 489 (Ont. S.C.) [defamation action by a number of teachers over politician's statements concerning teachers was struck out on the basis that it was plain and obvious the words were not capable of referring to one or more of the individual plaintiffs].

> *Booth v. British Columbia Television Broadcasting System* (1982), 139 D.L.R. (3d) 88 (B.C.C.A.) [allegations by prostitute that she knew two members of police narcotics squad "that are high up — right on the top that take payoffs" did not refer to nine police plaintiffs who were all members of the narcotics squad; only two other plaintiffs were identified].

> *Elliot v. Canadian Broadcasting Corporation* (1995), 125 D.L.R. (4th) 534 (Ont. C.A.), leave to appeal to S.C.C. denied, [1995] S.C.C.A. No. 393 [surviving airmen of World War II "Bomber Command" could not sue; defamatory alle-

gations held to refer only to the highest levels of the group's leadership, not to all members].

Roach v. *Random House of Canada Ltd.*, [2000] O.T.C. 526 (S.C.) per Nord-heimer J. at paras. 11–13 (S.C.J.) [sections of a book which referred to "blacks" or to "black activists" as a group held not capable of referring to the plaintiff although "the plaintiff is clearly both black and a black activist"].

Seafarers International Union of Canada v. *Lawrence* (1979), 24 O.R. (2d) 257 (C.A.) per MacKinnon A.C.J.O.

Bai v. *Sing Tao Daily Ltd.*, [2003] O.J. No. 1917 (C.A.), leave to appeal to S.C.C. refused, [2003] S.C.C.A. No. 354 [statements concerning Falun Gong did not attach to appellant plaintiffs as individuals].

Gauthier v. *Toronto Star Daily Newspapers Ltd.*, [2003] O.J. No. 2622 (S.C.J.).

Attempts in Ontario to certify certain defamation actions as a class action failed where the pleadings did not disclose a cause of action on behalf of each and every member of the class, group, or organization. Examples include:

Kenora (Town) Police Services Board v. *Savino* (1997), 20 C.P.C. (4th) 13 (Ont. Div. Ct.) at paras. 3, 5 [all members of a municipal police force attempted to sue over allegations some members of the force were racist].

McCann v. *Ottawa Sun* (1993), 16 O.R. (3d) 672 (Gen. Div.) per Chilcott J. [all residents of a city tried to sue over a sports column criticizing the behaviour of some fans at a hockey game].

Seafarers International Union of Canada v. *Lawrence*, above, at 263, 266, 267–68 [leave to appeal to S.C.C. refused 18 June 1979]:

> The alleged defamatory statement does not say that all members of the Seafarers International Union are thugs, but rather is directed at the union.... While one has a certain sympathy with a union which may find itself defamed in this Province, a union must accept the restrictions placed on it by s. 3(2) of the *Rights of Labour Act*. ... To allow an action under Rule 75 in the circumstances here pleaded (with payment to the union treasury of any damages awarded) would be to allow, in another guise, as already pointed out, the bringing of a derivative action.

Campbell et al v. *Toronto Star Newspapers Ltd.* (1990), 73 D.L.R. (4th) 190, per O'Leary J. at 191–92 (Ont. Div. Ct.):

> Here, no attempt has been made to plead facts that would show that the alleged defamation was published of, and concerning any particu-

lar member or members of the [Emmanuel Baptist] church. This means there have been no facts pleaded to support even the claim made by [plaintiff] Jones personally, and so it also has no foundation.

Stark v. *Toronto Sun Publishing Corporation.* (1983), 42 O.R. (2d) 791, per Smith J. at 794 (H.C.J.):

> ... my conclusion is that the individual plaintiffs have failed to establish the necessary link between themselves and the words used. They have pleaded membership in Operation Dismantle but they must go further. They must bring their personal reputations into play and they must as a minimum rely on pertinent facts in the pleadings that will raise the question of the tendency which the words have of lowering them in the estimation of others. ... There is nothing in the pleadings to indicate an identification on the part of these plaintiffs in the minds of the public with the organization ...

In *Lunney* v. *Agostini* (1983), 47 A.R. 385 (Q.B.), Purvis J. refused to strike out a claim advanced by Edmonton Chief of Police Robert Lunney "on behalf of the class known as Members of the City of Edmonton Police Department" over a cartoon in the *Edmonton Sun* depicting a "devilish ape-like creature in a black uniform with three badges affixed, namely: the skull and cross-bones, a Nazi swastika and the third bearing the inscription "Lunney's Dummies." The key to this decision was the finding [at paragraph 17] that "it is open for a court to hold, after hearing all the evidence, that the reference to "Lunney's dummies" can be taken to apply to all Members of the Edmonton Police Force and not just a portion thereof."

There are instances where a court has found after trial that individual members of a large group were defamed although not named individually. Examples include:

A.U.P.E. v. *Edmonton Sun* (1986), 39 C.C.L.T. 143 (Alta. Q.B.) where McFayden J. held that a group of approximately 200 guards employed at the Fort Saskatchewan Correctional Centre was each defamed, stating at 155:

> The author made no effort to limit his remarks to specific individuals or to the incident itself. I am satisfied that the ordinary, sensible reader would reasonably believe that comments were made generally of guards employed at the Fort Saskatchewan Correctional Centre. A reader who either knew one of the Plaintiffs or was aware that he performed such duties at the Fort Saskatchewan Correctional Centre or who identified one of the Plaintiffs by the distinctive uniform which he wore, would be of the opinion that this article referred to that individ-

ual ... The group (approximately 200 individuals) is not so large as to make it improbable that any ordinary reader would identify the Plaintiff as being referred to in the statements. Nor are the claims of such a generalized or exaggerated nature that no individual could reasonably identify them with the plaintiffs.

There are also instances where claims by members of a group have been allowed to proceed to trial. Examples of cases where interlocutory applications to strike brought by the defence (on the grounds of non-identification of the purported plaintiffs) were dismissed include:

Lennon v. Ontario (Premier) (1999), 45 O.R. (3d) 84 (S.C.J.) where MacDonald J. declined to strike out an action brought by several presidents of teacher's unions against the Ontario Premier stating at 90:

The words in issue referred repeatedly to what the bosses of teachers' unions want. Desire is often an individual's emotion. In their ordinary sense, the words in issue are capable of meaning that all the individual bosses of teachers' unions want certain specified things.

Butler v. Southam Inc. (2001) 197 N.S.R. (2d) 97, per Cromwell J.A. at paras. 86–88, 99–100, 102 (C.A.). See, for example, para. 88:

This article is not simply a sweeping and generalized critique of government action. It could reasonably be taken as alleging the existence of documents showing specific wrongdoing by each and every member of a finite, identifiable and prominent group of individuals of which the plaintiff Muinonen, by virtue of his positions, could be found to be one.

In *Butler v. Southam Inc., ibid.*, the Nova Scotia Court of Appeal developed a suggested, nonexhaustive list of factors to be taken into account when determining if the defamatory expression is "clearly incapable of being defamatory of the plaintiff" for the purposes of a defence motion to strike. The Court listed the factors under two headings:

i) Nature of the group (paragraphs 61–67):
    a. Size — generally, the larger the group the more difficult it will be for the plaintiffs to prove identification
    b. Identity — factors favouring the plaintiffs include clearly defined membership, organization, and hierarchy, members being highly visible in the community
    c. Clear organizational structure — positions or status of plaintiffs are potential pointers favouring some plaintiffs, not favouring others

      d. Restricted membership — if misconduct of a specific type is requirement for membership

ii)   Nature of the alleged defamatory statement (paragraphs 68–70)

      a. Generality — the more serious and inflammatory the allegation, the wider may be its sting

      b. Extravagance — certain types of allegations are understood not to be taken literally.

      c. Way in which allegations relate to the group — certain statements may clearly relate to each and every member of the group, other statements may not

      d. Free speech issues — balancing free speech and reputational interests may be sensitive where defamatory expression addresses, in broad and general terms, government institutions, actions, and decisions

H. STATUTORY GROUP LIBEL

Certain provincial human rights statutes confer a right to claim damages or an injunction from a human rights tribunal for what is loosely called "hate speech" or "discriminatory speech." The *Canadian Human Rights Act* also confers an analogous right with respect to facilities under federal jurisdiction.

In Manitoba, section 19(1) of the *Defamation Act*, D-20, provides:

> The publication of a libel against a race or religious creed likely to expose persons belonging to the race, or professing the religious creed, to hatred, contempt or ridicule, and tending to raise unrest or disorder among the people, entitles a person belonging to the race, or professing the religious creed, to sue for an injunction to prevent the continuation and circulation of the libel; and the Court of Queen's Bench may entertain the action.

It is beyond the scope of this book to address statutory group libel provisions.

CHAPTER FOURTEEN:
Publication and Republication

A. AN ESSENTIAL ELEMENT

Proof of publication by the defendant to a third party is an essential element in an action for defamation and the burden of proving this element rests on the plaintiff.

> *Gaskin* v. *Retail Credit Co.*, [1965] S.C.R. 297 per Ritchie J. at 1.
>
> *Arnott* v. *College of Physicians and Surgeons of Saskatchewan*, [1954] S.C.R. 538 per Locke J. at 555.
>
> *Dickhoff* v. *Armadale Communications* (1993), 108 D.L.R. (4th) 464, per Lane J.A. at 469 (Sask. C.A.).
>
> *Pressler* v. *Lethbridge* (2000), 86 B.C.L.R. (3d) 257, per Southin J.A. at para. 53 (C.A.).

B. PUBLICATION REQUIRES COMMUNICATION

There is a distinction between publication and simply creating or uttering defamatory expression. Publication requires an act on the part of the defendant which communicates the defamatory expression to a third party.

> *McNichol* v. *Grandy*, [1931] S.C.R. 696, where Anglin C.J.C. states at 699:

> The material part of the cause of action in dispute is not the uttering, but the publication, of the language used (*Hebditch* v. *MacIlwaince* [1894] 2 Q.B. 54, at 58, 61, 64, *O'Keefe* v. *Walsh* [1903] 2 Ir. R. 681, at 706).

and at the same page approves the following statement from Clement Gatley, *Gatley on Libel and Slander*, 2d ed. (London: Sweet & Maxwell, 1929) at 92:

… publication can be effected by any act on the part of the defendant which conveys the defamatory meaning of the matter to the person to whom it is communicated.

Newson (Chief Provincial Firearms Officer for B.C.) v. Kexco Publishing Co. (1995), 17 B.C.L.R. (3d) 176 per Lambert J.A. at para. 21 (C.A.):

> But publication for the purposes of libel means communication, not creation of the text for the purposes of printing.

Pullman v. Hill & Co., [1891] 1 Q.B. 524 per Lord Esher M.R. at 527:

> What is the meaning of 'publication'? The making known the defamatory matter after it has been written to some person other than the person of whom it is written.

C. ONE PERSON SUFFICIENT

Publication to one person other than the plaintiff is sufficient to constitute the cause of action for defamation.

McNichol v. Grandy, above at 699, approving *Duke of Brunswick v. Harmer* (1849), 14 Q.B. 185 at 188–89.

D. EACH PUBLICATION IS A SEPARATE CAUSE OF ACTION

Every sale or delivery of a written or printed copy of a libel is a fresh publication, for which an action lies.

Lambert v. Roberts Drug Stores Ltd., [1933] 4 D.L.R. 193, per Trueman J.A. at 195 (Man. C.A.).

Similarly, each slanderous statement is a distinct tort. Every person who repeats the slander becomes independently liable to the plaintiff.

Stewart v. Sterling (1918), 42 O.L.R. 477, per Clute J. at para. 16 (C.A.), citing W.B. Odgers & W.J. Tremecar, *Odgers on Libel and Slander*, (Canadian notes only), 5th ed. (London: Stevens, 1912) at 177.

Pootlass v. Pootlass (1999), 63 B.C.L.R. (3d) 305, per Burnyeat J. at para. 14 (S.C.), citing *Emmerton v. University of Sidney*, [1970] 2 N.S.W.R. 633 (N.S.W.C.A.) and *Thomas v. Canadian Broadcasting Corporation and Sanders*, [1981] 4 W.W.R. 289 (N.W.T.S.C.).

1) The U.S. "Single Publication Rule"

Many American courts and legislatures have modified the common law position with respect to libellous works by adopting the so-called "single publication rule" which provides that if only one work is involved, its distribution constitutes but a single publication on the date of first distribution of the work. (It appears this rule does not apply to private communications such as a series of identical defamatory statements made by an individual defendant to third parties).

> Robert D. Sack & Sandra S. Baron, *Michie's Libel, Slander and Related Problems on CD ROM*, 2d ed. (The Mitchie Company, a division of Reed Elsevier Inc.: 1995), at 6.2, "Statutes of Limitation and the Single Publication Rule," citing *Keeton v. Hustler Magazine Inc.*, 465 U.S. 770 (1984), citing RESTATEMENT (SECOND) OF TORTS, para. 577A(4)(1977):
>
> > The single publication rule has been summarized as follows: "As to any single publication, (a) only one action for damages can be maintained; (b) all damages suffered in all jurisdictions can be recovered in the one action; and (c) a judgment for or against the plaintiff upon the merits of any action for damages bars any other action for damages between the same parties in all jurisdictions."

Canadian courts and legislatures have not adopted the American form of a single publication rule.

This does not mean, however, that a plaintiff is entitled to bring separate lawsuits in Canadian courts over each publication of each copy of a newspaper. That would undoubtedly be considered an abuse of process. Further, it has been held that liability for a defamatory publication, whether of publisher, distributor, or vendor, is determinable in one action, and where litigation has been brought and recovery obtained by the plaintiff against the distributors and vendors of the newspaper containing the libel, no successive action can be maintained for the same publication against the publishers on the ground of separate publication of the libel by them to the distributors. Successive actions for the same libel constitute an abuse of the process of the court.

> *Thomson v. Lambert*, [1938] S.C.R. 253, per Davis JJ. at 560–61:
>
> > The respondents should not be permitted to go on suing one person after another ad infinitum where a complete remedy was available in one action. The law is well employed when it puts an end to just such actions as this.

Sir Lyman P. Duff, C.J.C., in his separate concurring judgment in *Thomson* v. *Lambert*, stated at page 556:

> It would, in my opinion, be an abuse of substantial justice to permit the respondents to proceed against the Imperial News Co. in another action in respect of the publication now sued upon. And since the Imperial News Co. were jointly liable with the publishers and the appellant for these publications, it follows, I think, that proceedings against the appellant must also fail.

Fry L.J., in *Macdougall* v. *Knight* (1890), 25 Q.B.D. 1 at 10 said:

> The injustice of allowing a litigant to select one portion of a libel as the ground for one action and another as the ground for a second action, and so on indefinitely, is obvious. The whole publication would be before the jury in each case, and it would be quite impossible for the jury in each case to separate the damages due to the particular part of the libel relied on in that case from the damages arising from other parts of the libel. I think, therefore, that a plea of *res judicata* would succeed, and that we are bound to stay the action. Suppose, however, this to be otherwise, still, in such a case, I do not hesitate to say that such successive actions in respect of the same libel would be an abuse of the process of the Court, and so, *quacunque via*, the application should succeed, and the action be stayed.

E. COMMUNICATIONS ADDRESSED TO PLAINTIFF

Publication solely to the plaintiff is not an actionable publication.

Hills v. *O'Bryan and O'Bryan*, [1949] 2 D.L.R. 716, per Manson J. at 718 (B.C.S.C.), citing *Powell* v. *Gelston*, [1916] 2 K.B. 615.

Symons v. *Toronto Dominion Bank*, [1997] S.J. No. 434, per Gunn J. at para. 21 (Q.B.).

Communications nominally addressed to the plaintiff, however, may be designed by the defendant to attract the attention of third persons and to be published to them. For example, defamatory postcards may be read by employees at a small community post office or letters sent to the plaintiff's place of employment may be opened and read in the ordinary course of business by the plaintiff's subordinates or superiors. In such circumstances, the court may determine that the defamatory expression has been published by the defendant.

Kohuch v. *Wilson* (1988), 71 Sask. R. 33, per McLellan J. at 57, para. 135 (Q.B.) [held that handmade postcards addressed directly to the plaintiffs designed to attract attention and to be read at the post office, school, and school board office, were published to third parties. Plaintiff was the school principal].

Where a letter was addressed to the plaintiff in his official capacity as a representative of a political organization to the address of that organization, it was held not to be a "personal letter." As it was reasonably foreseeable by the defendant that the letter would be opened by a third party at the organization's office, or that its contents would or could be communicated to other members of the organization, the letter was "published."

O'Malley v. *O'Callaghan* (1992), 89 D.L.R. (4th) 577, per Mason J. at 585 (Alta. Q.B.).

1) Communications Addressed to Agents of Plaintiff

A communication to a lawyer acting for an opposing party relative to proceedings handled by that lawyer does not constitute an actionable publication. It is equivalent to publication solely to the plaintiff.

Olson v. *Runciman* (2001), 291 A.R. 195, per Hart J. at para. 13 (Q.B.).

And see *Ward* v. *McIntyre* (1920), 56 D.L.R. 208 (N.B.C.A.) where Hazen C.J. at 217 distinguishes *Pullman* v. *Hill & Co.*, [1891] 1 Q.B. 524 [publication of letter to clerk at plaintiff's office] stating it "is not at all analogous to the receipt of a letter by an attorney who is an officer of the Court and who would not, if he respected his position, and who as a matter of fact did not, shew the letter to anyone except the plaintiff himself."

It also appears that delivery to the person defamed or to his agents of a defamatory communication relevant to negotiations taking place with the person defamed or his agents is not an actionable publication.

Industrial Ecology Inc. v. *Kayar Energy Systems Inc.*, [1997] O. J. No. 204, per Cameron J. at para. 12 (Gen. Div.).

F. PUBLICATION BROUGHT ABOUT BY PLAINTIFF'S CONTRIVANCE

It has been held that a publication brought about by the contrivance of the plaintiff with a view to the foundation of an action is an actionable publication.

Duke of Brunswick v. *Harmer* (1849), 14 Q.B. 185.

Rudd v. Cameron (1912), 26 O.L.R. 154 (Div. Ct.), aff'd (1912) 27 O.L.R. 327 (C.A.).

Modern courts are uncomfortable with this principle. See Chapter 22, "Consent," for a discussion of the limited Canadian jurisprudence.

G. CORPORATE COMMUNICATIONS

1) Communications Within a Corporation or Society

Whether or not a defamatory communication is kept within the confines of a corporation is generally irrelevant to the issue of publication.

Although many American jurisdictions hold that communications between officers and employees of the same corporation do not constitute publication to third parties for the purposes of defamation law, none of the Canadian common law provinces have enacted such a rule.

The general rule is that the communication of defamatory expression by one employee or officer to another constitutes publication. A distinction must be made, however, between the issue of publication (which is an essential element of the cause of action for defamation) and the availability of the defence of qualified privilege which is very likely to arise in a workplace setting where employees and officers frequently have a reciprocal duty and interest to communicate with one another. See Chapter 18, "Qualified and Statutory Privilege."

This principle has long been accepted as law. For example, where the plaintiff's superior delivered a letter to the plaintiff terminating his employment with a large energy corporation (their common employer), it was accepted by all parties at the trial, on appeal to the provincial appellate court, and in the Supreme Court of Canada that the distribution of the termination letter to four other individuals who headed other departments of the corporation constituted publication to those individuals.

Jerome v. Anderson (1963), 39 D.L.R. (2d) 641 (Sask. C.A.), rev'd on another point [1964] S.C.R. 291.

Dalrymple v. Sun Life Assurance Co. of Canada, [1966] 2 O.R. 227 (C.A.), aff'd (1967), 60 D.L.R. (2d) 192 (S.C.C.) [plaintiff at time of alleged slander was branch manager of defendant company, individual defendant A was a director of agencies of the defendant company — slander was allegedly published to another employee of defendant company].

The question of publication commonly arises with respect to communications by boards of nonprofit societies with the membership and vice versa. The same principle applies: in most instances, defamatory communications will be considered published if they reach anyone other than the plaintiff.

Tatum v. *Limbrick*, [1994] B.C.J. No. 1471, per Edwards J. at para. 41 (S.C.).

MacDonald v. *Tamitik Status of Women Assn.*, [1998] B.C.J. No. 2709, per Sigurdson J. at para. 94 (S.C.).

When an officer or employee of an enterprise authors a defamatory letter and arranges to have a typewritten version prepared by a secretary or clerk, dictation of that letter or delivery of a handwritten draft to the secretary or clerk constitutes "publication" of its contents.

Lawrence v. *Finch* (1930), 66 O.L.R. 451, per Masten J.A. at 455 (C.A.) [held that dictation is slander, not libel].

Greenan v. *Minneapolis Threshing Machine Co.*, [1929] 4 D.L.R. 501,per Harvey C.J.A. at 505 (Alta. C.A.), citing, *inter alia*, *Moran* v. *O'Regan* (1907), 38 N.B.R. 189 (C.A.), *Hall* v. *Geiger*, [1929] 4 D.L.R. 420 (B.C.S.C.), *Boxsius* v. *Goblet Freres*, [1894] 1 Q.B. 842 (C.A.), *Pullman* v. *Hill & Co.*, [1891] 1 Q.B. 524.

Puterbaugh v. *Gold Medal Furniture Manufacturing Co.* (1904), 7 O.L.R. 582 (C.A.) [handwritten letter given to clerk to type].

See also *Quillinan* v. *Stuart*, [1917] 38 O.L.R. 623, per Lennox J. at paras. 11–17, Rose J. at paras. 31–35 (C.A.).

There are few recent court decisions involving this restricted form of publication — perhaps because the difficulties presented by a likely defence of qualified privilege or the prospect of a miniscule damage award deter most potential litigants.

2) Vicarious Liability of Employer or Principal

An employer is vicariously liable to the plaintiff for the publication by an employee of defamatory expression when acting within the scope of her employment.

Murphy v. *Alexander*, [2001] O.J. No. 5465 where Belleghem J. states at paras. 150–51 (S.C.J.):

¶150 The next issue with respect to the defamation claim relates to the question whether Re/Max Professional Inc. is vicariously liable for Morris' defamation. The leading Canadian case on this issue is *Bazley* v.

> *Curry*, [1999] 2 S.C.R. 534. In that case Chief Justice McLachlin applies
> the Salmond test from *Salmond and Heuston on the Law of Tort*, 19th edi-
> tion 1987 at pages 521–22. Employers are vicariously liable for an
> employee's wrongful conduct falling within the "scope of employment."
>
> ¶151 The conduct for which the employer is vicariously liable is con-
> duct which consists of either (1) acts authorized by the employer or (2)
> unauthorized acts that are so connected with the acts that the employ-
> er has authorized that they may rightly be regarded as modes —
> although improper modes — of doing what has been authorized ...

Watson v. *Southam Inc. (c.o.b. Hamilton Spectator)* (1998), 52 O.T.C. 1, per
Crane J. at para. 178 (Gen. Div.) varied on other grounds (2000), 189 D.L.R.
(4th) 695 (Ont. C.A.).

Hiltz and Seamone Co. v. *Nova Scotia (Attorney General)* (1997), 164 N.S.R.
(2d) 161, per Stewart J. at paras. 4–9 (S.C.), aff'd without express discussion
of this point (1999), 172 D.L.R. (4th) 488 (N.S.C.A.) per Pugsley J.A.

Harrison v. *Joy Oil Co.*, [1938] 4 D.L.R. 360 per Middleton J.A. at 362–63
(Ont. C.A.).

A principal may be liable for defamatory statements made by her agent if
the agent was acting within the scope of the agency at the time of publication.

Lapointe v. *Summach*, [2001] B.C.J. No. 1322 (S.C.) per Beames J.

Harrison v. *Joy Oil Co.*, above, at 362–63.

Botiuk v. *Toronto Free Press Publications Ltd.*, [1995] 3 S.C.R. 3, per Cory J. at
paras. 89–90.

Dalrymple v. *Sun Life Assurance Co of Canada*, [1966] 2 O.R. 227 (C.A.), aff'd
(1967), 60 D.L.R. (2d) 192 (S.C.C.) per Evans J.:

> The vicarious liability of a principal for the defamatory words of an
> agent applies to attach liability to the principal for words spoken by the
> agent. This liability attaches not because the principal uttered defama-
> tory words but because the agent uttered them and the liability for the
> slander is imputed to the principal by virtue of their relationship.

A principal may also be liable if, knowing that the agent is publishing
defamatory expression and purporting to do so with the principal's authority, the principal does nothing to disavow the agent's authority or the defamatory expression.

Lapointe v. *Summach*, above.

3) Publication by "operating mind" of corporation

A corporate defendant will be held responsible for defamatory expression which has been published by an individual whose position as an "operating mind" of the corporation makes his defamatory publication the act of the corporation itself.

> *Hiltz and Seamone Co.* v. *Nova Scotia (Attorney General)* (1997), 164 N.S.R. (2d) 161, per Stewart J. at paras. 4–9 (S.C.), aff'd (1999), 172 D.L.R. (4th) 488 per Pugsley J.A. at paras. 143–50 (N.S.C.A.).

> *Botiuk* v. *Toronto Free Press Publications Ltd.*, [1995] 3 S.C.R. 3, per Cory J. at para. 90.

This basis of liability is distinct from vicarious liability of an employer for the acts of an employee.

Although a plaintiff should expressly plead an allegation of vicarious liability, it appears that a plaintiff is entitled to simply plead that defamatory expression was published by the corporation, without particularizing the identity of the operating mind of the corporation and his or her specific acts. A corporate defendant would seek such particulars when confronted with an allegation that it published defamatory expression.

> *Hiltz and Seamone Co.* v. *Nova Scotia (Attorney General)*, above.

F. JOINT LIABILITY

All persons who aid or participate in the publication of defamatory expression in furtherance of a common design may be held liable in damages to the plaintiff, whether or not at the time they realized they were committing the tort of libel or slander. The law regards them as joint tortfeasors.

> *Botiuk* v. *Toronto Free Press Publications Ltd.*, above, at paras. 73–77.

> *Dominion Telegraph Co.* v. *Silver (sub. nom. Silver* v. *Dominion Telegraph Co.)* (1882), 10 S.C.R. 238, per Ritchie C.J. at 257–59.

> *Hill* v. *Church of Scientology of Toronto*, [1995] 2 S.C.R. 1130, per Cory J. at para. 176:

>> It is a well-established principle that all persons who are involved in the commission of a joint tort are jointly and severally liable for the damages caused by that tort. If one person writes a libel, another repeats it, and a third approves what is written, they all have made the defamatory libel. Both the person who originally utters the defamato-

ry statement, and the individual who expresses agreement with it, are liable for the injury.

1) Books

Where the plaintiff complained of libel in a novel, he appropriately named as defendants the author, the publisher, and the printer of the novel as well as the printer of an illustrated advertising wrapper in which the book was sold.

> *Marchant* v. *Ford*, [1936] 2 All E.R. 1510, mentioned with apparent approval in *Thomson* v. *Lambert*, [1938] S.C.R. 253, per Davis J. at 272.

2) Newspapers

Where the libel has appeared in a newspaper, the plaintiff is entitled to sue in one action the publisher, the editor, the owner, the reporter, the printer, and every person at the newspaper involved in the preparation and distribution of its contents. The publisher and editor are liable whether or not they had actual knowledge of the specific defamatory content before publication.

> *Lambert* v. *Roberts Drug Stores Ltd.*, [1933] 4 D.L.R. 193 per Trueman J.A. at 195 (Man. C.A.), citing *Odgers on Libel & Slander*, 6th ed., p. 486.

> *Popovich* v. *Lobay*, [1937] 3 D.L.R. 713, per Trueman J.A. for the court at 718–19 (Man. C.A.) [although printer could not understand the publication, which was in a foreign language, he was liable as a joint tortfeasor with the publisher. Note: the claim was dismissed on the basis of a statutory defence.]

Where similar defamatory news stories are published by different newspapers, each constitutes a separate cause of action.

> *Dickhoff* v. *Armadale Communications* (1993), 108 D.L.R. (4th) 464, per Lane J.A. at 470 (Sask. C.A.).

3) Retail Vendors

A sale by a retail vendor of a publication prepared and distributed by others is a separate and distinct publication, with its own damages. A defendant retail vendor may escape liability for such publication if it establishes that it was ignorant of the contents of the publication and had no reason to suspect it was libellous [see section M below].

Lambert v. Roberts Drug Stores Ltd., [1933] 4 D.L.R. 193 per Trueman J.A. at 195 (Man. C.A.), citing *Emmens v. Pottle* (1885), 16 Q.B.D. 354 and *Vizetelly v. Mudie's Select Library, Ltd.*, [1900] 2 Q.B. 170 (C.A.).

4) Ad Hoc Groups

In the context of a dispute within an ethnic community, a number of prominent lawyers were held jointly and severally responsible for the publication of a defamatory "Declaration" they signed which confirmed a report prepared by another defendant, an engineer. At the latter's request, the Declaration was published in a community newspaper and was mailed to certain members of the ethnic community along with another document (the Reply) prepared by the engineer. In these circumstances, the Court treated the two defamatory publications (together with another) as a single libel. The lawyers and the engineer were held to be liable to the plaintiff as concurrent tortfeasors (persons whose torts concur, or run together, to produce the same damage).

Botiuk v. Toronto Free Press Publications Ltd., [1995] 3 S.C.R. 3, where Cory J. held at para. 76:

> The Lawyer's Declaration expressly adopted the contents of the Maksymec Report. It follows that the appellant lawyers must be jointly responsible with Maksymec for the publication of the Report. The appellant lawyers accepted and intended that Maksymec would use the Declaration extensively and publish it. They placed no restrictions on the use to which it might be put. The Declaration and the Report are by their terms inextricably interrelated. By their actions, the appellants became joint tortfeasors. Further, they as lawyers, signed the Declaration without undertaking any investigation. For lawyers to act in this way constituted reckless behaviour. Therefore, they must be as responsible as Maksymec, not only for its publication but also for its subsequent republication.

5) Members of Nonprofit Organizations

Members of political, social, or economic lobby groups may be held liable for defamatory expression published by such groups pursuant to their common purpose if they cause, procure, authorize, concur in, or approve such publications. In determining whether a group member did in fact participate in a common enterprise to publish defamatory expression, the court may consider whether or not the defendant:

i)   authored or co-authored the defamatory matter;

ii)   distributed it at demonstrations;

iii)   put it out for collection at meetings and events;

iv)   sent it through the mail, whether in response to requests for information or as an unsolicited mailing;

v)   encouraged other groups to distribute it, and that in fact occurred;

vi)   issued it in the form of a press release;

vii)   assisted in printing, reprinting, or photocopying the defamatory matter;

viii) encouraged the group in its campaign which employed the defamatory matter;

ix)   spoke in support of the group on occasions when it was distributed in such terms as to indicate express or implied approval of the defamatory matter available at the meeting; and/or

x)   actively participated in group meetings which approved the contents of defamatory matter.

> *McDonald's Corp.* v. *Steel*, [1999] E.W.J. No. 2173 per Pill L.J. at para. 204 (C.A.), applied in *Home Equity Development Inc.* v *Crow*, 2004 BCSC 124, per Quijano J. at paras. 133–38.

Mere membership in an informal and unincorporated group does not make an individual responsible in law for the actions of other members undertaken without members' general consent or authorization. The determination of liability of each member of such a group can only be made on the basis of the involvement, if any, of each defendant in the preparation or publication of the defamatory material.

> *Derrickson* v. *Tomat* (1992), 88 D.L.R. (4th) 401 at 422 (B.C.C.A.) per Hinds J.A., leave to appeal to S.C.C. denied (1992), 93 D.L.R. (4th) vii (S.C.C.).

In certain circumstances, group members may face a plea of conspiracy to defame. Where the plaintiffs alleged and proved that three defendants conspired together to defame them, the publication of certain defamatory letters was the joint publication of all three defendants. "[E]ach of the defendants was agent for each of the other defendants and … therefore all are guilty of each of the publications."

> *Paul* v. *Van Hull* (1962), 36 D.L.R. (2d) 639 per Maybank J. at 649–50, 654 (Man. Q.B.).

If a campaign involves the publication of a leaflet, then those who involve themselves in that campaign may be found to be responsible for that publication, and involvement in the campaign may be inferred from the various activities.

McDonald's Corp. v. *Steel*, above, at para. 204.

Approving a publication does not mean merely "approve" in the sense of regarding publication as a desirable event. It requires a defendant to have sanctioned the publication, so that he or she is shown to have acted with the intention that publication should occur.

McDonald's Corp. v. *Steel*, *ibid.* at para. 197, citing *R.* v. *Paine* (1696), 5 Mod. 163, at 167 and *Webb* v. *Bloch* (1928), 41 C.L.R. 331, at 364 (Isaacs J.).

In the case of an unincorporated association or other body lacking a corporate identity, a member will only be liable for defamatory material published in the name of the association or group if it can be shown that he was personally responsible for that publication, either by publishing it directly himself, or by producing it with a view to publication, or by causing, inciting, or authorizing its publication. Mere membership alone will not suffice.

McDonald's Corp. v. *Steel*, *ibid.* at paras. 201–4, citing *Mercantile Marine Service Association* v. *Toms*, [1916] 2 K.B. 243, *Ricci* v. *Chow* (1987), 3 All E.R. 534, expressly approving, *inter alia*, the following statement by the trial judge:

> One still has to look for evidence for or against actual participation in any particular activity, such as publication of a leaflet like the one complained of, or involvement in a campaign which in turn involves publication of a leaflet; but if a group appears to be promoting a particular campaign by particular means, it may be an easy inference that those who attend its meetings or events or contribute to them from a distance are actively encouraging campaigning by that means, unless there is evidence to the contrary such as evidence of an altogether different motive for being there.

Failure by group members to disassociate themselves from the activities of a group, however, may permit the court to draw an inference of their intention. This does not mean that the burden of proof is reversed and that the defendants have an onus to establish that they did not publish and were not responsible for publishing defamatory expression.

Home Equity Development Inc. v *Crow*, 2004 BCSC 124, per Quijano J. at para. 139, approving the following passage from *McDonald's Corp.* v. *Steel*, [1999] E.W.J. No. 2173 where Pill L.J. stated at paras. 222–23 (C.A.):

Intention is normally a matter of inference, and in drawing an inference a judge is entitled and required to look at all the relevant circumstances, including the absence of action on the part of the person concerned. The absence of evidence that [a defendant] had ever tried to stop publication of a leaflet which he had been found to have produced was a relevant consideration in this context. It went along with other evidence of positive actions on his part, such as the encouragement of the anti-McDonald's campaign, of which publication of the leaflet formed part.

G. REPUBLICATION

1) A Separate Tort

Every republication of a libel is a separate tort and each republisher is answerable to the plaintiff in damages for his own act of publication.

> *Basse v. Toronto Star Newspapers Ltd.* (1983), 44 O.R. (2d) 164, per Montgomery J. at 165 (H.C.J.), citing Philip Lewis, *Gatley on Libel and Slander*, 8th ed. (London: Sweet & Maxwell, 1981), paras. 261, 266.

> *Chinese Cultural Centre of Vancouver v. Holt* (1978), 87 D.L.R. (3d) 744 (B.C.S.C.) per van der Hoop, J., citing *Cutler et al. v. McPhail*, [1962] 2 Q.B. 292, *Eyre v. New Zealand Press Ass'n Ltd.*, [1968] N.Z.L.R. 736, Sir Robert McEwen & Philip Lewis, *Gatley on Libel and Slander*, 7th ed. (London: Sweet & Maxwell, 1974) at 123.

2) Liability of Initial Publisher

The initial publisher is *prima facie* not liable for damage caused by republication of her defamatory expression by another person.

There are certain exceptions, however, which are described by Lord Justice Lopes in *Speight v. Gosnay* (1891), 60 L.J. Q.B. 231 at 232, the leading case on the subject. The initial publisher will be jointly and severally liable with the republisher:

i)   where the initial publisher authorized or intended the publishee to repeat them to some third person;

ii)   where the republication to a third person was the natural and probable result of the initial publication; or

iii) where the publishee was under a moral duty to repeat the defamatory expression to a third person.

Cohl v. *Donovan* (1996), O.T.C. 18 per O'Driscoll J. at para. 22 (Gen. Div.), citing Philip Lewis, *Gatley on Libel and Slander*, 8th ed. (London: Sweet & Maxwell, 1981) at 119, and also citing *Jaffe* v. *Americans for International Justice Foundation* (1987), 22 C.P.C. (2d) 286 (Ont. S.C.), *Reichman* v. *Toronto Life Publishing Co.* (1988), 27 C.P.C. (2d) 37, 39–40 (Ont. H.C.J.).

Peters-Brown v. *Regina District Health Board*, [1996] 1 W.W.R. 337,per Halvorson J. at paras. 2–28 (Sask. Q.B.) , aff'd without discussion of this point, [1997] 1 W.W.R. 638 (Sask. C.A.).

Smith v. *Matsqui (District)*, [1986] 4 B.C.L.R. (2d) 342, per Davis J. at paras. 25–26 (S.C.).

Botiuk v. *Toronto Free Press Publications Ltd.*, [1995] 3 S.C.R. 3, where Cory J., at para. 77, expressed approval of the decision of Montgomery J. in *Basse* v. *Toronto Star Newspapers Ltd.* (1983) 44 O.R. (2d) 164 at 165 (Ont. H.C.J.) [natural and probable result].

Chinese Cultural Centre of Vancouver v. *Holt* (1978), 87 D.L.R. (3d) 744, per van der Hoop J., citing Sir Rovert McEwen & Philip Lewis, *Gatley on Libel and Slander*, 7th ed. (London: Sweet & Maxwell 1974), p. 122 [natural and probable result].

The defendant is entitled to have the precise exception relied upon by the plaintiff set out in the statement of claim.

Jordon v. *Talbot*, [1998] O.J. No. 1876 per Jennings J. at para. 3 (Gen Div), citing *Cohl* v. *Donovan*, above, and *Basse* v. *Toronto Star*, above.

Hiltz and Seamone Co. v. *Nova Scotia (Attorney General)* (1999), 172 D.L.R. (4th) 488, per Pugsley J.A. at para. 153 (N.S.C.A.), aff'g (1997), 164 N.S.R. (2d) 161 (S.C.) at paras. 22–25.

It has been held that the natural and probable result exception is not the same test as foreseeability (of consequences implicit in tort claims) because that test deals with possibilities. "Natural and probable results are in the realm of probabilities."

Peters-Brown v. *Regina District Health Board*, above, at para. 28.

If the natural and probable result exception applies, the initial publisher may be liable with subsequent publishers for all subsequent publications by other persons. Liability is not limited to republication by the person to whom the initial publication was made.

Brown v. *Cole* (1995), 14 B.C.L.R. (3d) 53 per Hollinrake J.A. at para. 9 (C.A.).

The British Columbia Court of Appeal has approved the following plea of authorized republication adapted from *Gatley on Libel and Slander*, 8th ed. (London: Sweet & Maxwell, 1981) at paragraph 1620:

> It was the natural and probable result of the said publication that the said words would be repeated by [the persons to whom they were originally published].
>
> The said words were in fact so repeated to [here insert names of persons to whom they were repeated].

Brown v. Cole (1998), 61 B.C.L.R. (3d) 1, per Southin J.A. at paras. 15–16 (C.A.), leave to appeal to S.C.C. denied, [1998] S.C.C.A. No. 614.

It has been held that the initial publisher may be liable even for republication by the plaintiff to third persons (as opposed to republication by a third party) if that was the natural and probable consequence of the initial publication. It appears, however, that a plaintiff may have greater difficulty convincing a court this test is satisfied than if the initial publication was republished by a third party.

Hills v. O'Bryan and O'Bryan, [1949] 2 D.L.R. 716, per Manson J. at 718 (B.C.S.C.) citing *Hedgpeth v. Coleman* (1922), 24 Am.L.R. 232 [plaintiff an immature youth — faced with threat of prosecution and imprisonment, necessary exposure of defendant's letter by the plaintiff was natural and probable result. However, Manson J. dismissed the claim that the plaintiff's publication of a defamatory letter to a friend, to her sister, to her son and to the Employment Service was the reasonable and probable consequence of plaintiff's foreseeable mental upset on receipt of letter.]

Pacheco (c.o.b. Pacheco Cleaners) v. DeRango, [2001] O.T.C. 669, per Swinton J. at para. 32 (S.C.J.).

In a more recent case it was suggested (but not finally determined) that there should be "some level of compulsion or necessity acting upon the plaintiff" before his or her republication of defamatory expression initially received from the defendant can impose liability on the defendant. Further, it was suggested, that the defendant should know of the circumstances which give rise to that necessity.

McNabb v. Equifax Canada Inc., [2000] 6 W.W.R. 562 per Beard J. at paras. 39, 43–44 (Man. Q.B.)

See also, *Kidder v. Healy* (2002), 215 Sask. R. 97 (Q.B.) where Allbright J. at paras. 32–36 appears to apply a test of "necessity" or "compulsion" or "duty" in deciding to strike a statement of claim.

There is no liability upon the original publisher of the libel when the repetition is the voluntary act of a free agent, over whom the original publisher had no control and for whose acts he is not responsible.

Basse v. *Toronto Star Newspapers Ltd.* (1983), 44 O.R. (2d) 164, per Montgomery J. at 165, citing *Ward* v. *Weeks* (1830), 7 Bing. 211 at 215, 131 E.R. 81, approved in *Weld-Blundell* v. *Stephens*, [1920] A.C. 956 at 999, *Eyre* v. *New Zealand Press Ass'n Ltd.*, [1968] N.Z.L.R. 736 at 744 (S.C.), *Macy* v. *New York World-Telegram Corp.*, 161 N.Y.S. 2d 55 at 60 (C.A., 1957).

Greenan v. *Minneapolis Threshing Machine Co. & Christiansen*, [1929] 4 D.L.R. 501, per Harvey C.J.A. at 502 (Alta. C.A.), citing *Huth* v. *Huth*, [1915] 3 K.B. 32.

It appears that the "duty" exception includes moral, legal, and social duties [see page 264 of this Chapter].

Cooper v. *Warburton* (1931), 44 B.C.R. 328 (S.C.).

Where the claim is based on republication by a third party, the words which are alleged to have been repeated must be examined to determine whether they convey the same defamatory meaning as the defendant's initial publication, whether or not that defamatory meaning is stated in verbatim quotes. If the alleged repetition varies substantially from the meaning of the initial publication, it is doubtful there is any liability on the initial publisher.

Anderson v. *Investors Group Financial Services Inc.*, [2001] M.J. No. 573, 2001 MBQB 295, per Master Harrison.

McNabb v. *Equifax Canada Inc.*, [2000] 6 W.W.R. 562 per Beard J. at 568 (Man. Q.B.).

Where the plaintiff elects to sue only over the initial publication, but seeks also to recover as a consequence the damage which he or she has suffered by its repetition by the news media, even a partial publication of the original sting can be causative of damage.

McManus v. *Beckham*, [2002] EWCA Civ 939 per Waller L.J. at para. 13.

3) Republication in the News Media

The law on this topic is complex.

Where a defendant's defamatory expression is republished by the news media, the plaintiff may sue:

i)   the initial publisher both for the initial publication and for the republication by the news media, which constitute two separate causes of action; or

ii)   the initial publisher solely for the initial publication, but seek to recover as a consequence of the initial publication the damage suffered by reason of the republication by the news media;

iii) the initial publisher solely for the republication by the news media; and/or

iv)   the news media for its republication of the initial publication.

> *McManus* v. *Beckham*, above, at para. 11, citing Patrick Milmo & W.V.H. Rogers, *Gatley on Libel and Slander*, 9th ed. (London: Sweet & Maxwell, 1998), para. 6.30.

Two principles come into apparent conflict where the news media republish all or part of defamatory expression initially published by someone else:

- The initial publisher is responsible where the republication was the natural consequence of the publication by the initial publisher

but

- The initial publisher is not liable where the republication was the voluntary act of a free agent over whom the initial publisher had no control.

It is submitted that this conflict may be conceptually resolved on the basis that there are circumstances where "the unauthorized act of an independent third party might be the natural and probable result of the defendant's conduct." In such circumstances, the initial publisher is liable for the republication.

> *Slipper* v. *BBC*, [1991] 1 QB 283, per Stocker L.J. at 296c, Bingham L.J. at 300c-e, Slade L.J. at 300f, 301c, 302d, 302g.

It has been held that the initial publisher may be held responsible for the damage caused by republication:

a)   if a defendant is actually aware (1) that what she says or does is likely to be reported, and (2) that if she slanders someone that slander is likely to be repeated in whole or in part (a subjective test); or

b)   if a reasonable person in the defendant's position would have appreciated that there was a significant risk that what she said would be repeated in whole or in part in the press, and that would increase the damage (an objective test).

> *McManus v. Beckham*, above, at para. 34, following an extensive analysis of *Slipper v. BBC*, [1991] 1 QB 283, and per Laws L.J. concurring in a separate judgment at paras. 43–44 [recommending avoidance of the term "forseeability" in directions to the jury for reasons of "clarity"].

It has also been held that a defendant may be held liable for the increased damage caused by republication of her slander in the news media.

> *McManus v. Beckham*, above, at para. 34, following an extensive analysis of *Slipper v. BBC*, [1991] 1 QB 283.

It is settled law that where a person speaks defamatory words to the press with the intention or knowledge that they will be republished, the speaker is responsible in libel rather than slander for the republication.

> *Stopforth v. Goyer* (1978), 87 D.L.R. (3d) 373, per Lieff J. at 375 (Ont. H.C.J.), rev'd on other grounds (1979), 97 D.L.R. (3d) 369 (Ont. C.A.).

> *St. Michael's Extended Care Society v. Frost*, [1994] 6 W.W.R 718, per Cawsey J. at para. 37 (Alta. Q.B.):

> > If a man hands a copy of a slanderous speech to a reporter to publish, or requests a reporter to take the speech down and publish it, or an outline or summary of it, he will be taken to constitute the reporter as an agent for the purpose of the publication and be answerable for the result. *Odgers on Libel and Slander* extends this statement of law at p. 141:

> > > Thus, it (a request to print or publish) may be inferred from the defendant's conduct in sending his manuscript to the editor of a magazine, or making a statement to the reporter of a newspaper, with the knowledge that they will be sure to publish it, and without any effort to restrain their so doing.

The complexity of the law on this topic was recently the subject of sharp criticism in the English Court of Appeal.

> *McManus v. Beckham*, above at paras. 41–44:

> > ¶42 The law needs to be simplified. The root question is whether D, who has slandered C, should justly be held responsible for the damage which has been occasioned, or directly occasioned, by a further publication by X. I think it plain that there will be cases where that will be entirely just. The observation of Bingham L.J. as he then was in *Slipper* at 300 that "[d]efamatory statements are objectionable not least because of their propensity to percolate through underground channels and contaminate hidden springs" states an ancient and persistent truth,

long ago vividly described in Virgil's account of Aeneas and Dido Queen of Carthage (*Aeneid* IV, 173–88).

A defendant may be held to have authorized publication of the defendant's statement in a newspaper if the defendant knew the listener was a journalist and the defendant made no explicit restriction on publication. The plaintiff need not demonstrate that the defendant made an express request of the journalist that his or her statement be published.

> *Hay v. Bingham*, [1905] 11 O.L.R. 148 per Osler J.A. at para. 17 (C.A.), citing William Blake Odgers & James Bromley Eames, *Odgers on Libel and Slander*, 4th ed. (London: Stevens, 1905) at 161 [approved in *Douglas v. Tucker*, [1952] 1 S.C.R. 275, per Cartwright J. at 289].

Where a defendant made defamatory remarks while addressing a public meeting in the course of an election campaign, and later reviewed and made several changes to a typewritten proposed story about his speech prepared by a journalist, it was open to a jury to decide that the defendant knew and intended the story to be published.

> *Douglas v. Tucker*, [1952] 1 S.C.R. 275 per Cartwright J. at 282, citing Richard O'Sullivan, *Gatley on Libel and Slander*, 3d ed. (London: Sweet & Maxwell, 1938), at 439–40; William Blake Odgers & Robert Ritson, *Odgers on Libel and Slander*, 6th ed. (London: Stevens, 1929), at 141; and *Hay v. Bingham*, [1905] 11 O.L.R. 148 at 153 (C.A.).

It has been held that an interviewee is liable for a publication on television if by his antecedent dealings with the broadcaster he has authorized the publication of its substance and its sting, and what is published by the broadcaster is that substance and that sting. Accordingly, the liability of a defendant interviewee is not limited to his specific words which are displayed on-camera or otherwise expressly quoted in the broadcast.

> *Pressler v. Lethbridge* (2000), 86 B.C.L.R. (3d) 257, per Southin J.A. at paras. 53, 55–57 and Esson J.A. at paras. 116–19 (C.A.), citing *Douglas v. Tucker*, [1952] 1 S.C.R. 275, and per Braidwood J.A. at paras. 124–28, citing *Douglas v. Tucker* and *Hay v. Bingham* (1905), 11 O.L.R. 148 (C.A.).

H. EVIDENCE OF PUBLICATION

The question of whether or not the plaintiff has satisfactorily proved publication should be left to the jury to determine, if there is any evidence from which it might reasonably be concluded to be more probable than not that a defamatory statement has been made known to a third party or parties.

> *Gaskin v. Retail Credit Co.*, [1965] S.C.R. 297 per Ritchie J. at 298–99, approving *Halsbury's Laws of England*, 3d ed., Lord Simonds, ed. (London: Butterworths, 1952–64) vol. 24 at 39:
>
> > If publication is disputed by the defendant and there is any evidence of publication by him, it must be left to the jury to decide whether there was in fact publication of the libel by him.

As on other issues, the onus of proof is on a balance of probabilities. It appears that circumstantial evidence of publication may suffice.

> *Royal Bank of Canada (c.o.b. Chargex) v. Battistella*, [1994] O.J. No. 1717 at para. 1 (C.A.):
>
> > … [W]e think that all of the circumstances of the case establish that the defamatory words were probably published by the Bank. It is highly unlikely that anyone else would have done so. Accordingly, we would not interfere with the trial judge's finding that the Bank published the defamatory words to Air Canada.

It is not always necessary for the plaintiff to call the alleged recipient of the defamatory expression to prove this essential element of publication. This element may be established by circumstantial evidence which permits a reasonable inference that publication occurred.

> *Gaskin v. Retail Credit Credit Co.*, above, at 300:
>
> > In my opinion … the general principle is correctly stated in *Gatley on Libel & Slander*, 5th ed., p. 89, where it is said:
> >
> > > It is not necessary for the plaintiff in every case to prove directly that the words complained of were brought to the actual knowledge of some third person. If he proves facts from which it can reasonably be inferred that the words were brought to the knowledge of some third person, he will establish a *prima facie* case.

In order to prove publication of a libel by a defendant, a plaintiff may rely on the defendant's failure to specifically deny publication in her statement of defence, depending on the rules of court applicable to the jurisdiction where the suit is brought.

Masters v. *Fox* (1978), 85 D.L.R. (3d) 64, per MacFarlane J. at 68, 75–76 (B.C.S.C.) ["… a review of the whole of the pleadings indicates that publication was not in issue"].

In the case of credit reporting companies which as part of their business routinely issue credit reports to subscribing clients, it is open to a jury to infer that publication occurred if there is evidence that some of those clients requested credit reports concerning the plaintiff and that such reports were sent by the respondent. The fact that there is no evidence that any particular individual read the reports is not necessarily fatal to the plaintiff's claim.

Gaskin v. *Retail Credit Co.*, [1965], above, at 300, approving the dissenting judgment of MacKay J.A. in *Gaskin* v. *Retail Credit Co.* (1963), 43 D.L.R. (2d) 120 at 12.

I. PLEADING PUBLICATION

The plaintiff must allege when, in what circumstances, by whom, and to whom the allegedly defamatory expression was published.

Wesson v. *Campbell River (District)* (1985), 63 B.C.L.R. 327, per Taggart J.A. at 331 (C.A.).

Allegations of libel in a statement of claim which fail to allege the material elements of publication may be struck out.

R.E.L. v. *J.G.* (2000), 191 Sask. R. 204, per Barclay J. at paras. 37–40, 42, 44 (Q.B.).

Lowenberg v. *Oderbien* (2000), 146 Man. R. (2d) 120 per Master Harrison at paras. 19–22 (Q.B.) [no particulars given of identity of persons to whom publication allegedly made].

Anderson v. *Investors Group Financial Services Inc.*, [2001] M.J. No. 573 per Master Harrison at paras. 17–18 (Q.B.).

In circumstances where the limitation period for a defamation claim has not expired, it is common for a defendant to bring a motion to compel the plaintiff to provide the requisite particulars of publication, failing which the claim will be struck. Alternatively, the court may exercise its discretion not to strike the claim but to require the plaintiff to provide the requisite particulars.

Hausman v. *Molson Canada*, [2000] O.J. No. 4451, per Cullity J. at para. 36 (S.C.J.).

Where the statement of claim simply alleged publication by the defendant to "divers persons," the plaintiff was ordered to provide the requisite particulars before examination for discovery of the defendant. The plaintiff was not entitled to embark on a "fishing expedition" to develop a concrete case of publication.

Wesson v. Campbell River (District), above, at 331, Esson J.A. concurring in separate reasons at 331.

The same principle applies when the defamation claim is made in a counterclaim.

B.K. v. V.K. Thapar Professional Corp., [1999] A.J. No. 28, per Burrows J. at para. 25 (Alta. Q.B.).

Similarly, a plaintiff was ordered to provide particulars of publication where the statement of claim merely alleged that the defamatory expression was sent to unnamed "judges, lawyers and decision makers." The plaintiff offered no evidence that the impugned document was ever published and did not allege that such particulars were peculiarly within the knowledge of the defendant.

Citizens for Foreign Aid Reform Inc. v. Canadian Jewish Congress, [2000] B.C.J. No. 957, 2000 BCSC 737, per McKinnon J. at para. 14.

See also *Walker v. C.R.O.S.* (1993), 18 C.C.L.T. (2d) 166 per Shabbits J. at 172 (B.C.S.C.) [plaintiff alleged defence sent information package to "member of C.R.O.S. … and other unknown persons in South Surrey"].

Testimony by the plaintiff that a third person told the plaintiff that the defendant had uttered the defamatory remarks is inadmissible to prove publication. Such testimony offends the hearsay rule.

Dalrymple v. Sun Life Assurance Co. of Canada, [1966] 2 O.R. 227, per Evans J.A. at 231 (C.A.), aff'd (1967), 60 D.L.R. (2d) 192 (S.C.C.), per Cartwright J.

The same particulars must be provided if the plaintiff sues over republication as a separate cause of action.

Brown v. Cole, [1994] B.C.J. No. 2356, per Master Doolan at paras. 8–10, 35 (S.C.).

1) Pleading Publication to Persons Unknown

The British Columbia Court of Appeal has approved the following plea of publication by the defendant to other persons not yet identified by the plaintiff adapted from *Gatley on Libel and Slander*, 8th ed. (London: Sweet & Maxwell, 1981) at paragraph 1619:

> The plaintiff believes that the said or similar words were also published to some other persons whom he cannot [at] present identify, but he will rely upon the publication thereof to each and every person to whom he may discover the same have been published.

> *Brown* v. *Cole* (1998), 61 B.C.L.R. (3d) 1, per Southin J.A. at paras. 15, 17 (C.A.), leave to appeal to S.C.C. denied, [1998] S.C.C.A. No. 614.

It has been held that the right to maintain a pleading of publication by the defendant to other persons not identified is restricted to cases where the plaintiff makes out a *prima facie* case of publication to a named person and produces some evidence of publication to other persons.

> *Gaskin* v. *Retail Credit Company*, [1961] O.W.N. 171 (H.C.) per Schatz J. upholding a decision of the Senior Master who summarized the law on this point at 173.

Where the plaintiff alleges publication to both named and unnamed persons, the plaintiff will be ordered to give particulars of the publications to unnamed persons unless the plaintiff files material on the motion establishing a *prima facie* case of such publication and deposing that she does not know the names or any other identifying information as to these other people. If the plaintiff has absolutely no information or knowledge about such publications, she will not be permitted to plead it in the hope that during examination for discovery or at trial such evidence will emerge.

> *Jaffe* v. *Americans for International Justice Foundation* (1987), 22 C.P.C. (2d) 286 at paras. 13–15 (Ont. S.C.).

It has been held, however, that where the plaintiff's pleadings identified the people who allegedly rejected the plaintiff's employment application as a result of a defamatory letter initially published by a defendant, the plaintiff was not required to provide particulars of how republication actually took place — there the plaintiff was claiming against the defendant solely for the initial publication, but seeking to recover as a consequence of the initial publication the damage suffered by reason of the republication by others.

> *Pacific Coast Savings Insurance Services Ltd.* v. *Strong* (1996), 4 C.P.C. (4th) 37 per Edwards J. at paras. 26–29 (B.C.S.C.).

J. VENUE OF PUBLICATION

See Chapter 8, "Jurisdictional Issues" for a discussion of this subject.

K. FORM OF PUBLICATION

Human ingenuity in devising new methods of communication ensures that there is no limit on the form that publication may take. A nonexhaustive list of the forms of publication which have inspired past defamation lawsuits includes:

Waxworks: *Monson v. Tussauds Ltd.*, [1894] 1 Q.B. 671.

Cartoons: *Vander Zalm v. Times Publishers Ltd.* (1979), 96 D.L.R. (3d) 172, rev'd on other grounds (1980), 18 B.C.L.R. 210 (C.A.), *Ross v. New Brunswick Teachers' Assn.* (2001), 201 D.L.R. (4th) 75 (N.B.C.A.).

Posters: *Sun Life Assurance Co. of Canada v. W.H. Smith & Sons Ltd.* (1933), 150 L.T. 211.

Motion pictures: *Yousouppoff v. M.G.M.* (1934), 50 T.L.R. 581 (C.A.).

Telegraph: *Dominion Telegraph Co. v. Silver (sub. nom. Silver v. Dominion Telegraph Co.)* (1882), 10 S.C.R. 238.

Radio: *Jenner v. Sun Oil Co. Ltd.*, [1952] 2 D.L.R. 526 (Ont. H.C.J.).

Open-line radio programs: *Kohuch v. Wilson*, [1988] S.J. No. 682 (Q.B.).

Television: *England v. Canadian Broadcasting Corporation*, [1979] 3 W.W.R. 193 (N.W.T.S.C.), *Grossman v. CFTO-TV Limited* (1982), 39 O.R. (2d) 498 (C.A.).

Hand-made postcards: *Kohuch v. Wilson*, above.

Greeting cards: *Kohuch v. Wilson, ibid.*

Banners: *McKerron v. Marshall*, [1999] O.J. No. 4048 (S.C.J.).

More recently, defamatory expression has taken the form of e-mails and website postings. See Chapter 32, "Related Causes of Action," section M.

1) Libraries

When a libellous book is located in a lending library, publication to library subscribers is presumed.

Vizetelly v. Mudie's Select Library Limited, [1900] 2 Q.B. 170 (C.A.).

Similarly, if a libellous document is placed in a library which is open to the public and controlled by the defendant, and the document is available to anyone without limitation, the court may find that publication has occurred even if the plaintiff does not call testimony to establish that any member of the public actually accessed the document.

> *Hiltz and Seamone Co.* v. *Nova Scotia (Attorney General)* (1999), 172 D.L.R. (4th) 488 per Pugsley J.A. at paras. 154–58 (N.S.C.A.).

L. UNINTENDED OR NEGLIGENT PUBLICATION

A defendant may be held liable for his negligent (that is, unintended) and direct publication of defamatory expression to a third party.

> *McNichol* v. *Grandy*, [1931] S.C.R. 696, per Anglin C.J.C. at 701.

It is not yet settled law whether the burden of proof rests on the plaintiff to establish such negligence, or whether the defendant has the onus to show she was not negligent. When this subject last came before the Supreme Court of Canada, the majority expressly declined to decide the point.

> *McNichol* v. *Grandy*, above, per Anglin C.J.C. at 704 [Lamont J., in separate reasons at 708, would have placed the onus on the defendant].

M. INNOCENT DISSEMINATION

A mere distributor may be able to rely on the common law defence of innocent dissemination. Pursuant to this defence, a defendant will be held not to have published the defamatory expression if it was disseminated in the ordinary course of business and:

i)   the defendant was innocent of any knowledge of the libel contained in the work the defendant disseminated,

ii) there was nothing in the work or the circumstances under which it came to the defendant or was disseminated by the defendant which ought to have led the defendant to suppose that it contained a libel, and

iii) when the work was disseminated by the defendant, it was not by any negligence on the defendant's part that the defendant did not know that it contained the libel.

> *Vizetelly* v. *Mudie's Select Library Limited*, [1900] 2 Q.B. 170 (C.A.).

Slack v. *Ad-Rite Associates Ltd.* (1998) 79 O.T.C. 46, per Fedak J. at paras. 17–22 (Gen. Div.), citing *Vizetelly* v. *Mudie's Select Library Limited*, [1900] 2 Q.B. 170 (C.A.).

Hays v. *Weiland* (1918), 42 O.L.R. 637, per Hodgins J.A. at para. 35 (C.A.) ["Innocence in circulating libelous matter may entirely absolve the person publishing if he shews that he was not negligent"] citing *Vizetelly* v. *Mudie's Select Library Limited*, [1900] 2 Q.B. 170; *Smith* v. *Streatfeild*, [1913] 3 K.B. 764; *Haynes* v. *DeBeck* (1914), 31 T.L.R. 115.

The burden of proving the facts essential to this defence rest on the defendant.

Menear v. *Miguna* (1997), 33 O.R. (3d) 223 at 223 (Ont. C.A.).

Slack v. *Ad-Rite Associates Ltd.*, above, at para. 22.

The rationale for this defence is that distributors do not have an opportunity to review the contents of all material that passes through their hands.

Slack v. *Ad-Rite Associates Ltd. ibid.* at para. 17, citing *Goldsmith* v. *Sperrings Ltd.*, [1977] 1 W.L.R. 478 (C.A.).

Other persons in the chain of distribution of defamatory expression who do only mechanical or menial acts may also be able to establish this defence.

Slack v. *Ad-Rite Associates Ltd.*, *ibid.* at para. 17, citing *Lobay* v. *Workers and Farmers Publishing Association Ltd.*, [1939] 2 D.L.R. 272 (Man. Q.B.).

A defendant does not satisfy the onus merely by stating that he or she did not have actual knowledge of the contents of the publication. A defendant who had an opportunity to read the libelous publication (but did not) and who thought it "might" be libellous does not establish this defence.

Slack v. *Ad-Rite Associates Ltd.*, *ibid.* at para. 22:

> To object on these grounds "goes for nothing," and would be an excuse for "all sorts of infamy," as Lord Mansfield observed in the case of *Anon.* (1774), Lofft. 544, 98 E.R. 791. It would be a licence for character assassination.

This defence is potentially applicable to Internet service providers, bulletin board service operators and other entities active in an electronic environment who may unwittingly disseminate defamatory material. Where a newsletter simply referred to a website, but the newsletter publisher had no knowledge of the defamatory comments on the website, the innocent dissemination defence was held to apply.

Carter v. *B.C. Federation of Foster Parents Assn.*, [2004] B.C.J. No. 192, 2004
BCSC 137, per Taylor J. at paras. 59–63.

The identity of the person to whom a libel was published is relevant to
the defence of innocent dissemination. The intent and knowledge of the
printer, when delivering copies of a libelous publication, is an element of
considerable weight in determining whether he was an innocent printer or
a participant in an attack. The name of the recipient to whom copies were
given may be illuminating and indicate the purpose known to the printer.

Hays v. *Weiland*, [1918] 42 O.L.R. 637, per Hodgins J.A. at paras. 34–35 (S.C.
(A.D.)) , referring to *Vizetelly* v. *Mudie's Select Library Limited*, [1900] 2 Q.B.
170 (C.A.), *Smith* v. *Streatfeild*, [1913] 3 K.B. 764, *Haynes* v. *DeBeck* (1914),
31 T.L.R. 115.

It has recently been doubted that a printer who merely prints a book and
delivers it to its author, and does not participate in their distribution, can
be considered a publisher. The decision, pronounced on a summary dismissal of a libel action, was reversed on appeal on the grounds there was
evidence on which a jury could find there was publication. That evidence
was not specified in the appeal judgment.

Menear v. *Miguna* (1996,) 30 O.R. (3d) 602, per J.B. Wright J. at 605 (Gen.
Div.), rev'd (1997), 33 O.R. (3d) 223 at 223 (C.A.).

It has been suggested that a book printer receiving defamatory content
in an electronic form should not be held liable simply by virtue of being the
printer, in light of changing technology which makes it unnecessary for the
printer or any of its employees to actually review the content word by word.
Electronic transmission of text from the editor to the printer may result in
a situation where the printer does not read the manuscript, has no editing
function, and is not aware of the allegedly libellous statements.

Menear v. *Miguna*, *ibid*. at 223, citing *Vizetelly* v. *Mudie's Select Library Ltd.*,
[1900] 2 Q.B. 170 (C.A.).

It has been held that the validity of a defence of innocent dissemination
should not be determined in summary proceedings. There are issues of fact
which should be decided at trial — on those issues, the onus is on the
defendant.

Menear v. *Miguna*, *ibid*. at 223.

N. THIRD PARTY PROCEEDINGS FOR CONTRIBUTION OR INDEMNITY

A commercial broadcaster, by virtue of the terms of its contract with a commercial news wire service, may be entitled to claim contribution or indemnity from the wire service if the latter supplied the broadcaster with defamatory matter.

> *Allan v. Bushnell T.V. Co. Ltd.; Broadcast News Ltd., Third Party,* [1968] 1 O.R. 720 at 722–23 (C.A.):
>
> What, in my view, is central to resort to third party proceedings is that the facts upon which the plaintiff relies against the defendant should issue out of the relations between the defendant and the third party.

It was held that a defendant in a Manitoba defamation action was not entitled to take third party proceedings in that action against someone else who allegedly defamed the defendant. Nor was the defendant entitled to seek contribution or indemnity for damages that might be assessed in favour of the plaintiff absent contractual liability or a claim that the third party supplied information to the defendant under an obligation to ensure that it was correct. The facts did not establish the necessary nexus required by the Manitoba *Rules of Court*.

> *Raymond v. Asper* (2001), 155 Man. R. (2d) 148 per Master Sharp at para. 22 (Q.B.), aff'd (2002), 161 Man. R. (2d) 309, per Jewers J. at paras. 5–14 (Q.B.).

In Saskatchewan, a third party notice by a defendant newspaper to a university student who authored a defamatory letter to the editor was struck out on the basis that the *Contributory Negligence Act* of that jurisdiction only applied to negligence, so that the common law rule that there was no right to contribution or indemnity between joint tortfeasors still applied respecting libel, an intentional tort.

> *Cherneksey v. Armadale Publishers Ltd.* (1974), 53 D.L.R. (3d) 79, per Brown J.A. at 84 (Sask. CA.):
>
> ... The third party, a university student, simply wrote a letter to the defendant newspaper. What happened to the letter after its receipt was solely a matter for determination by the responsible employee or employees of the defendant newspaper. It was solely for the defendant to decide whether or not the letter would be published, to determine whether or not it was libelous, or, if published, what heading, if any to

place thereon. The publication of the letter did not arise out of any relations between the defendant and the third party as there was none.

See also *Atkinson v. A.A. Murphy & Sons Ltd.*, [1974] 2 W.W.R. 367 (Sask. Q.B.) [radio commentator read over the air a letter to the editor originally published in a local newspaper].

Third party proceedings were permitted to proceed to trial where the plaintiff alleged that the defendants ought to have anticipated that an ethnic organization would republish their communication to that organization. In the third party claim against the ethnic organization, the defendants alleged that their communication was intended to be kept confidential, that the ethnic organization knew it was intended to be kept in confidence, and that the ethnic organization breached its duty of confidentiality and disseminated the communication in order to foment discord between the plaintiff and the defendant.

Slaby v. Godzisz, [1996] O.J. No. 3174 (C.A.).

It has been held that an "off the record" restriction is an example of a circumstance where the initial publisher may not have authorized or intended a republication by the news media and where republication may not be the natural and probable result of the initial publication to the journalist.

Thomas v. McMullan, [2002] B.C.J. No. 230, 2002 BCSC 22, per Ralph J. at paras. 101–2.

Under the British Columbia *Negligence Act* (formerly the *Contributory Negligence Act*), however, a defamation defendant may be entitled to contribution from third parties if the plaintiff proves at trial that the defendants knew or ought to have known that their slanderous rumours would be spread by the third parties to whom they initially published them. The defendants and third parties would be "independent concurrent tortfeasors." It was held that there is an arguable case that the defendant would be entitled to contribution in such circumstances.

Brown v. Cole (1995), 14 B.C.L.R. (3d) 53 per Hollinrake J.A. at para. 47 (C.A.).

In a recent British Columbia decision, a defamation lawsuit was brought by one municipal politician against another politician. The defendant third-partied several newspaper groups which had republished her initial defamatory statements. Relying on the apportionment of fault provision in section 4 of the *Negligence Act*, R.S.B.C. 1996, c. 333, the court held that the defendant and the newspapers were "several concurrent tortfeasors" and that the defendant's claim for contribution was properly before the court. The court therefore apportioned liability for the plaintiff's damages as follows: 80 percent to the individual politician, 10 percent to one newspaper group, and 5 percent to each of the other two newspaper groups.

Thomas v. McMullan, above, at paras. 96, 110–15.

O. INTERNET PUBLICATION

A British Columbia court disagreed with the proposition that a person who operates an Internet "chat room" or "bulletin board" is to be equated to a telephone company, which is not in law considered a publisher of defamatory communications it may transmit. The court held this analogy was flawed, at least where the chat room provided "a form of archiving comments which are accessible by those who use the chat room."

Carter v B.C. Federation of Foster Parents Assn., [2004] B.C.J. No. 192, 2004 BCSC 137 per Taylor J. at para. 100.

CHAPTER FIFTEEN:

Defamatory Meaning

A. A GENERAL DEFINITION

Expression which tends to lower a person's reputation in the estimation of ordinary, reasonable members of society generally, or to expose a person to hatred, contempt, or ridicule, is defamatory.

Cherneskey v. Armadale Publishers Ltd., [1979] 1 S.C.R. 1067 at 1079.

Expression which would cause a plaintiff to be shunned or avoided is also defamatory. The weight of authority appears to favour the view that such allegations are defamatory even if there is no implication that the plaintiff deserves blame for his or her condition.

Halls v. Mitchell (1926), 59 O.L.R. 590 (C.A.).

Gatley on Libel and Slander, 9th ed., Patrick Milmo & W.V.H. Rogers, eds. (London: Sweet & Maxwell, 1998) at 22–23.

Youssoupoff v. Metro-Goldwyn-Mayer (1934), 50 T.L.R. 581 (U.K.C.A.).

Peters-Brown v. Regina District Health Board, [1996] 1 W.W.R. 337 (Sask. Q.B.), aff'd (1996), 148 Sask. R. 248 (C.A.).

But see *Serdar v. Metroland Printing, Publishing and Distributing Ltd.*, [2001] O.J. No. 1596 (S.C.J.).

B. THE "STING" OF DEFAMATORY EXPRESSION

The case authorities often refer to the "sting" or "bite" or "gist" of the defamatory meaning of the expression. At the outset of a defamation complaint, a plaintiff or defendant who is uncertain whether the expression conveys particular stings may find it helpful to consult friends and acquaintances. In special circumstances, plaintiff's legal counsel may even empanel an unofficial "jury" of lay persons to help identify the "stings" before completing a statement of claim.

C. THREE BASIC FORMS OF DEFAMATORY EXPRESSION

The case law suggests that defamatory imputations arise in one of three ways:

i)   The literal meaning: for example, where the plaintiff has been called a thief or a murderer it is not necessary to go beyond the words themselves. This is called the "natural and ordinary" meaning in the case authorities.

ii)   An inferential meaning: Here the sting of the defamation lies not so much in the expression itself as in the meaning that the ordinary person, without special knowledge, will infer from it. This meaning is a matter of impression. This is also called a "natural and ordinary meaning." It is also sometimes referred to as "popular" or "false" innuendo.

iii) A "legal innuendo": ostensibly innocent expression may convey a defamatory meaning by virtue of extrinsic facts known to specific people or classes of people exposed to that expression. This is also referred to in the case law as a "true innuendo."

See also Chapter 23, "Pleadings." When a plaintiff chooses to rely on the literal meaning of expression, the statement of claim may simply quote the precise words and other expression in the publication or broadcast which are alleged to be defamatory.

However, in most defamation lawsuits, the plaintiff will not quote the precise words or other expression at issue, but will also plead one or more added inferential meanings. This is commonly done in a statement of claim by alleging that "The said words meant and were understood to mean that..."

Pressler v. Lethbridge (2000), 86 B.C.L.R. (3d) 257 at para. 36 (C.A.)

Hodgson v. Canadian Newspapers Co. (1998), 39 O.R. (3d) 235 per Lane J. at 250–51 (Gen. Div.), varied on appeal as to damages (2000), 49 O.R. (3d) 161 (C.A.).

1) Literal Meaning

A leading textbook suggests that it is only in a rare case that a plaintiff should rely solely on the literal meaning of expression in formulating his or her libel complaint. Philip Lewis, *Gatley on Libel and Slander*, 8th ed. (London: Sweet & Maxwell, 1981), states at paragraph 1075 on pages 446–47:

> Where the words complained of are defamatory in their natural and ordinary meaning and can reasonably only have one meaning, no innuendo is needed; such a case would be an allegation of a specific act of misconduct. Where the plain and obvious meaning of the words is defamatory, an innuendo (as to their meaning) is unnecessary, and, if made, negligible [citation omitted]. But this is only the rule in the plainest cases. Where there is any unclarity as to the natural and ordinary meaning, or any uncertainty as to the meaning for which the plaintiff will contend at the trial, or there is room for disagreement as to what inferences might reasonably be drawn from the words themselves in the light of the ordinary man's knowledge, the plaintiff must plead the meaning which he alleges the words to have. If he does so, he should make it clear that he is relying on the natural and ordinary meaning of the words, and is not seeking to plead a true innuendo without the support of extrinsic facts.

2) Inferential Meaning

An oft-quoted discussion of the nature of inferential meanings is contained in the judgment of Lord Reid in *Lewis v. Daily Telegraph Ltd.*, [1963] 2 All E.R. 151 at 154–55 (H.L.):

> What the ordinary man would infer without special knowledge has generally been called the natural and ordinary meaning of the words. But that expression is rather misleading in that it conceals the fact that there are two elements in it. Sometimes it is not necessary to go beyond the words themselves as where the plaintiff has been called a thief or a murderer. But more often the sting is not so much in the words themselves as in what the ordinary man will infer from them and that is also regarded as part of their natural and ordinary meaning. Here there would be nothing libelous in saying that an inquiry into the appellants' affairs was proceeding: the inquiry might be by a statistician or other expert. The sting is in inferences drawn from the fact that it is the fraud squad which is making the inquiry. What those inferences should be is ultimately a question for the jury but the trial judge has an important duty to perform.
>
> ...
>
> In this case it is, I think, sufficient to put the test this way. Ordinary men and women have different temperaments and outlooks. Some are unusually suspicious and some are unusually naïve. One must try to envisage people between these two extremes and see what is the most damaging meaning that they would

put on the words in question … What the ordinary man not avid for scandal, would read into the words complained of must be a matter of impression.

3) Legal Innuendo

A legal innuendo will need to be proved by the extrinsic facts which give the otherwise innocent expression its defamatory sting. The statement of claim must specifically allege those extrinsic facts.

It is another peculiar aspect of a legal innuendo that the law regards it as constituting a separate cause of action from any cause of action for defamatory natural and ordinary meanings which otherwise arise solely from the published expression itself.

> *Hodgson* v. *Canadian Newspapers Co.* (1998), 39 O.R. (3d) 235, per Lane J. at 250b (Gen. Div.), varied as to damages (2000), 49 O.R. (3d) 161 (C.A.), leave to appeal to S.C.C. denied, [2000] S.C.C.A. No. 465.

4) Determining the Natural and Ordinary Meaning

Where the plaintiff does not rely upon a pleaded legal innuendo, no evidence is admissible concerning the reasonable and ordinary meaning of the expression at issue, or the sense in which the expression was understood, or of any facts giving rise to the inferences to be drawn from the words used.

It is for the trier of fact to determine the sense in which the words would reasonably have been understood by an ordinary person in the light of generally known facts. The intention of the author and publisher is not relevant on the issue of meaning. Nor is the subjective opinion of the plaintiff as to the meaning of the expression any more relevant.

> *Hodgson* v. *Canadian Newspapers Co.*, above.

What is defamatory may be determined from the ordinary meaning of the published words or matter, or from the surrounding circumstances, as they would be understood by the ordinary, reasonable, and fair-minded reader. The test is an objective one.

> *Botiuk* v. *Toronto Free Press Publications Ltd.*, [1995] 3 S.C.R. 3 at para. 62.

It has been held that whether the expression complained of defames the plaintiff should be judged from the perspective of a "reasonably thoughtful and well-informed person" who has a degree of common sense.

> *Colour Your World Corp.* v. *Canadian Broadcasting Corporation* (1998), 38 O.R. (3d) 97 at 106, paras. d–g (C.A.), leave to appeal dismissed, [1998] S.C.C.A. No. 170.

The standard of what constitutes a reasonable person should not be so low as to stifle free expression unduly, nor so high as to imperil the ability to protect the integrity of a person's reputation.

Colour Your World Corp. v. Canadian Broadcasting Corporation, ibid.

The measure of what is defamatory is not determined by the standard of someone "avid for scandal." *Moon v. Sher*, [2003] O.J. No. 2464, per Hoilett J. at para. 9 (Ont. S.C.J.), citing *Lewis v. Daily Telegraph Ltd.*, [1963] 2 All E.R. 151 (H.L.). Nor are the impugned words to be construed according to what "persons setting themselves to work to deduce some unusal meaning might succeed in exacting from them." *Mantini v. Smith Lyons LLP*, [2003] O.J. No. 1830, per Catzman J.A. for the court at para. 14 (C.A.), leave to appeal to S.C.C. refused, [2003] S.C.C.A. No. 344.

In the case of a newspaper libel, a distinction must be drawn between the reader's objective understanding of what the newspaper is saying and judgments or conclusions which he may reach as a result of his own beliefs and prejudices. It is one thing to say that a statement is capable of bearing an imputation defamatory of the plaintiff because the ordinary reasonable reader would understand it in that sense, drawing on his own knowledge and experience of human affairs in order to reach that result. It is quite another thing to say that a statement is capable of bearing such an imputation merely because it excites in some readers a belief or prejudice from which they proceed to arrive at a conclusion unfavourable to the plaintiff. The defamatory quality of the published material is to be determined by the first, not by the second, proposition.

Mirror Newspapers Ltd. v. Harrison (1982), 149 C.L.R. 293 at 296, para. 17 (H.C.A.).

5) Determining Legal Innuendo Meaning

A legal innuendo, which requires that the plaintiff plead and prove certain extrinsic facts known to select categories of readers, often arises:

i)   where technical terms are used in the expression at issue;
ii)   where local words or slang are used;
iii) where the expression is in a foreign language; or
iv)   where certain other expressions, not in general use, are known and employed by persons in certain professions or occupations.

A classic example of a legal innuendo is a newspaper photograph of a man and a woman depicted together at a racetrack with a caption alleging that they are husband and wife. To readers who know that the man and woman are not married to each other, the photograph could be held to convey the defamatory imputation either that one of them is a bigamist or that they are carrying on a shameful affair.

6) The Importance of Pleadings

Where a plaintiff chooses to rely not on the natural and ordinary meaning of the words, but only on an extended meaning, he cannot go beyond the pleaded innuendo meaning at trial to allege other meanings.

Netupsky v. Craig, [1971] 1 O.R. 51 at 65–66 (C.A.).

Where a legal innuendo is pleaded, it will be necessary to call evidence from a witness with knowledge of the extrinsic facts which makes the expression defamatory.

Mosley v. Focus Magazin Verlag GmbH, [2001] EWCA Civ 1030.

Fulham v. Newcastle Chronicle and Journal Ltd., [1977] 1 W.L.R. 651.

Grappelli v. Derek Block Ltd., [1981] 1 W.L.R. 822, Dunn L.J., at 830.

Dwek v. Macmillan Publishers Ltd., [2000] E.M.L.R. 284.

A plaintiff may prove a defamatory meaning arising from legal innuendo in the following circumstances:

i) Where the pleaded facts or circumstances would lead a reasonable person to infer that ambiguous words conveyed the meaning alleged by the plaintiff.

   Knott v. Telegram Printing Co., [1917] 3 W.W.R. 335 (S.C.C).

ii) Where the meaning is conveyed by a cartoon, or pictures and a caption, in which event witnesses may testify as to the meaning ascribed to that expression.

   Vander Zalm v. Times Publishers, [1980] 4 W.W.R. 259 (B.C.C.A.).

   Hough v. London Express Newspapers Ltd., [1940] 2 K.B. 507 at 513–15 (C.A.).

However, in establishing the legal innuendo, the plaintiff is not entitled to introduce facts which were unknown to the person to whom the expression was published, or facts and circumstances which did not exist at or before the time the expression was published.

Capital & Counties Bank Limited v. George Henty & Sons (1880), 5 C.P.D. 514 at 539, 542, aff'd (1882) 7 A.C. 741 (H.L.).

D. JUDGE OR JURY?

1) The Gatekeeper Function of the Judge

Whether or not the expression is capable of bearing a defamatory meaning is a question of law for a judge. This authority permits a judge to withhold outrageous pleaded meanings from the jury's consideration or to dismiss an obviously frivolous lawsuit.

> *Laufer v. Bucklaschuk* (1999), 181 D.L.R. (4th) 83 at paras. 25–35 (Man. C.A.), leave to appeal to S.C.C. denied, [2003] S.C.C.A. No. 77, 189 D.L.R. (4th) vii.

> *Mantini* v. *Smith Lyons LLP*, [2003] O.J. No. 1830 per Catzman J.A. for the court at para. 11 (C.A.), leave to appeal to S.C.C. denied, [2003] S.C.C.A. No. 344.

Where the trial judge's finding of law on this issue is appealed, the appellate court may simply substitute its opinion for that of the trial judge, with no requirement to find that the lower court's finding was "palpably and manifestly wrong."

> *Mitchell v. Nanaimo District Teachers Association* (1994), 94 B.C.L.R. (2d) 81 (C.A.).

2) The Key Question of Fact Is for the Jury

Whether or not the expression is in fact defamatory is a question for the jury.

No Canadian legislature has defined what constitutes defamatory expression. The *Report of the Saskatchewan Commissioners to the Uniform Law Conference of Canada* in 1983 recommended a definition of "defamation" to be included in the *Uniform Defamation Act*. The Uniform Law Conference of Canada has since abandoned efforts at codification of a definition because of difficulties arriving at a satisfactory wording.

> ULCC, Proceedings of 65 Annual Meeting, August 1983, app. G, p. 96.

A jury ruling on this issue is normally given great respect by an appellate court unless there has been a significant misdirection by the trial judge.

There are many formulations in the case law concerning what constitutes defamatory expression. The gist of the tort being injury to reputation, however, a jury is well placed to make this determination of fact without undue complex legal instruction.

3) Where There Is No Jury

The approach taken by the court sitting without a jury is discussed in *Grassi v. WIC Radio Ltd. (c.o.b. CKNW/98)*, [2000] 5 W.W.R. 119 (B.C.S.C.), where Mr. Justice Lysyk stated:

> In a trial without a jury, where the judge will decide both issues, the questions of whether the words are capable of being defamatory and whether they are in fact so are likely to run together. Thus, in *Slim v. Daily Telegraph Ltd.*, [1968] 2 Q.B. 159 (C.A.) Diplock L.J. after discussing the respective roles of judge and jury, stated at 176:
>
> > But where a judge is sitting alone to try a libel action without a jury, the only questions he has to ask himself are: "Is the natural and ordinary meaning of the words that which is alleged in the statement of claim?" and: "If not, what, if any, less injurious defamatory meaning do they bear?"

E. CRITICISM AND INSULT DISTINGUISHED FROM DEFAMATION

Not all criticism is defamatory. It has long been held that people accepting or seeking public office can expect attack and criticism, on the grounds that the public interest requires that their conduct shall be open to the most searching critique.

> *Martin v. Manitoba Free Press Co.* (1892), 8 Man. L.R. 50 at 72 (Q.B.), aff'd (1892), 21 S.C.R. 518

Insults and vulgar abuse, or statements merely in bad taste, are not defamatory.

> *Vander Zalm v. Times Publishers Ltd.* (1980), 109 D.L.R. (3d) 531 (B.C.C.A.)

F. CONTEXT OF EXPRESSION

1) The Importance of Context and Mode of Publication

In order to determine the natural and ordinary meaning of the words of which the plaintiff complains, it is necessary to take into account both the context in which the words were used and the mode of publication. A plaintiff cannot select an isolated passage in an article and complain of that alone if other parts of the article throw a different light on that passage. The publication must be considered as a whole, even if the plaintiff only complains of part.

Charleston v. *News Group Newspapers Ltd.*, [1995] 2 A.C. 65 at 70–71, paras. F and G; 72, paras. D and G (H.L. (Eng.)).

2) Audio-visual Expression

A television broadcast may be defamatory by virtue of the overall impression created by the words and images in the broadcast, even if the words and narrative themselves, taken alone, are not false or defamatory.

Leenen v. *Canadian Broadcasting Corporation* (2000), 48 O.R. (3d) 656 (S.C.J.), aff'd (2001), 54 O.R. (3d) 612 (C.A.), leave to appeal to S.C.C. denied, [2001] S.C.C.A. No. 432.

The audio-visual dimension of a television broadcast can transform the impression one might otherwise get from a statement. Features such as voice intonation, visual background, facial expression, and gesture are brought into unique play, all of which can accompany the articulated facts to dramatic effect. Because of these distinguishing factors, the overall impression of the broadcast, in addition to the accuracy of the statements, is relevant.

Colour Your World Corp. v. *Canadian Broadcasting Corporation* (1998), 38 O.R. (3d) 97 at 106, paras. d–g (C.A.), leave to appeal to S.C.C. dismissed, [1998] S.C.C.A. No. 170.

Vogel v. *C.B.C.* (1982), 3 W.W.R. 97 (B.C.S.C.) at 155. Per Esson J. (as he then was): "I have made many references to the impression conveyed to viewers. This is a matter which must be considered in assessing television programs, which, by reason of their transitory nature, tend to leave the audience with an impression rather than a firm understanding of what was said. Images, facial expressions, tones of voice, symbols and the dramatic effect which can be achieved by juxtaposition of segments may be more important than the meaning derived from careful reading of the words of the script. Television is different from the printed word. The interested reader can reread and analyze. The emphasis in considering the defamatory impact of say, a newspaper story must therefore be upon the words used. Libel by television is, in this respect, more like slander. In slander cases, regard may be had to such things as gestures and intonations.

The visual and auditory components of a television broadcast do not render the words used irrelevant. When determining how a reasonable viewer might perceive the meaning of a broadcast, one must look not only to image, sound, and sequence; one must also look to the actual words used. A broadcast must be considered as a whole to determine whether it has a defamatory sting.

Pressler v. Lethbridge (2000), 86 B.C.L.R. (3d) 257 at para. 36 (B.C.C.A.)

G. BANE AND ANTIDOTE

If something disreputable to a plaintiff is stated in one part of a publication, but this stain is removed in another part of the same publication, the bane and antidote must be taken together when a court is asked to consider whether the publication is defamatory.

Chalmers v. Payne, [1835] 2 C.M. & R. 156.

Only in the rarest of cases may a judge consider that the alleged antidote so obviously extinguishes the alleged bane that there is no issue which can properly be left to a jury.

Cruise v. Express Newspapers, [1998] E.W.J. No. 935 (C.A.).

Morosi v. Broadcasting Station 2GB Pty Ltd., [1980] 2 N.S.W.L.R. 418(n) (N.S.W.C.A.).

Sergi v. Australian Broadcasting Commission, [1983] 2 N.S.W.L.R. 669.

This chapter will not attempt the impossible task of creating a catalogue of defamatory expression. Examples of words, phrases, or other expression held to be defamatory are found in other chapters, particularly those dealing with the substantive defences of justification, fair comment, qualified privilege, and absolute privilege. Examples of expressions held not to be defamatory are found in the other chapters, particularly Chapter 25, "Pre-Trial Disposition of Claims and Defences."

A catalogue — even if one could be attempted — might also be misleading. As society changes over time, expression which might be held to be libellous in one era may lose its stigma and cease to be actionable. Local differences may have the same effect.

CHAPTER SIXTEEN:

Express Malice

A. INTRODUCTION

A defendant is actuated by express malice if he or she publishes defamatory expression:

i)   knowing it is false; or
ii)   with reckless indifference whether it is true or false; or
iii) for the dominant purpose of injuring the plaintiff because of spite or animosity; or
iv)   for some other dominant purpose which is improper or indirect, or also, if the occasion is privileged, for a dominant purpose not related to the occasion.

More than one of these closely-related findings of express malice may be made by the court in a given case.

> *Hiltz and Seamone Co.* v. *Nova Scotia (Attorney General)* (1997), 164 N.S.R. (2d) 161, N.S.J. No. 530 per Stewart J. at paras. 92 [improper dominant purpose], 103 [reckless falsities], 108 [indirect or improper purpose and recklessness] (S.C.), aff'd (1999), 172 D.L.R. (4th) 488 at paras. 88, 91, 98 (N.S.C.A.).

> *Kelly* v. *Magnolo*, [1983] B.C.J. No. 376 per Callaghan J. at para. 36 (S.C.) [no positive belief in truth and dominant purpose a desire to injure].

Express malice is also referred to as actual malice and as malice in fact. Express malice is to be distinguished from the "malice in law" which is presumed upon proof of publication of defamatory expression.

> *Davies & Davies Ltd.* v. *Kott*, [1979] 2 S.C.R. 686, per McIntyre J. at 694:

... the word "malice" is used to connote malice in fact, actual malice, or express malice which goes beyond the malice ordinarily presumed upon the mere publication of libelous words.

Malice in law merely means that the defamatory expression was "published without lawful excuse."

Farrell v. St. John's Publishing Co. Ltd. (1986), 58 Nfld. & P.E.I.R. 66, per Morgan J.A. for the court at 76, para.45 (Nfld. C.A.).

Proof that a defendant was actuated by express malice at the time of publication of the defamatory expression defeats the defences of qualified privilege and fair comment.

Cherneskey v. Armadale Publishing Ltd., [1979] 1 S.C.R. 1067, per Ritchie J. (Laskin C.J. and Pigeon and Pratte JJ. concurring) at para. 21:

In cases where the essential ingredients of either the plea of "qualified privilege" or that of "fair comment" have been established by the defence, then if it can be proved that the statements complained of were made or written maliciously the plea must fail; ...

Taylor-Wright v. CHBC-TV, a Division of WIC Television Ltd. (2000), 194 D.L.R. (4th) 621, per Esson J.A. at 644, para. 57 (B.C.C.A.).

Leenen v. Canadian Broadcasting Corporation (2000), 48 O.R. (3d) 656, per Cunningham J. at 706 (S.C.J.), aff'd (2001), 54 O.R. (3d) 612 (C.A.), leave to appeal to S.C.C. denied [2001] S.C.C.A. No. 432.

Re International Assn. of Bridge, Structural and Ornamental and Reinforcing Inronworkers (Local 97) and Campbell (1997), 40 B.C.L.R. (3d) 1, per Macdonald J. at paras. 37–38 (S.C.).

It has been held that the authorities on malice regarding the two defences of fair comment and qualified privilege are essentially interchangeable.

Hodgson v. Canadian Newspapers Co. (1998), 39 O.R. (3d) 335 per Lane J. at 393 (Gen. Div.), approving the statement to this effect in Patrick Milmo & W.V.H. Rogers, *Gatley on Libel and Slander*, 9th ed. (London: Sweet & Maxwell, 1998) at para. 16.2, varied on other grounds (2000), 49 O.R. (3d) 161 (C.A.), leave to appeal to S.C.C. denied, [2000] S.C.C.A. 465.

Proof of express malice also supports a claim for aggravated damages and punitive damages.

Hill v. Church of Scientology of Toronto, [1995] 2 S.C.R. 1130 per Cory J. at para. 190, citing *Walker v. CFTO Ltd.* (1987), 37 D.L.R. (4th) 224 (Ont. C.A.),

Vogel v. *Canadian Broadcasting Corporation*, [1982] 3 W.W.R. 97 at 197–99 (B.C.S.C.), *Kerr* v. *Conlogue*, [1992] 4 W.W.R. 258 at 281–82 (B.C.S.C.), and *Broome* v. *Cassell & Co.*, [1972] 1 All E.R. 801 at 825–26 (H.L.).

[See also Chapter 30, "Damages," "Aggravated Damages" and "Punitive Damages."]

B. STATE OF MIND AT THE TIME OF PUBLICATION

Determining whether or not the defendant was actuated by express malice at the time of publication of the defamatory expression requires an inquiry into the state of mind of the defendant.

Jerome v. *Anderson*, [1964] S.C.R. 291 per Cartwright J. (Maitland, Ritchie, and Hall JJ. concurring) at p. 299:

> The difficulty of proving the state of a man's mind at a particular time was commented on by Bowen L.J. in his famous dictum in *Edgington* v. *Fitzmaurice* [(1885), 29 Ch.D. 459, 55 L.J. Ch. 650] at p. 483 ["… the state of a man's mind is as much as fact as the state of his digestion]; but as was said by Lord Wright in *Clayton* v. *Ramsden* [[1943] A.C. 320, 112 L.J. Ch. 22.] at p. 331: "States of mind are capable of proof like other matters of fact."

C. EXTRINSIC AND INTRINSIC EVIDENCE OF EXPRESS MALICE

Evidence of express malice may be extrinsic or intrinsic. Intrinsic evidence may found in the defamatory expression itself.

Davies & Davies Ltd. v. *Kott*, [1979] 2 S.C.R. 686 per McIntyre J. at 696.

Foran v. *Richman* (1975), 64 D.L.R. (3d) 230, per Arnup J.A. at 233 (Ont. C.A.).

Lawson v. *Thompson* (1968), 1 D.L.R. (3d) 270, per Seaton J. at 275 (B.C.S.C.), aff'd (1969), 5 D.L.R. (3d) 550 (B.C.C.A.).

Taylor v. *Despard*, [1956] O.R. 963, per Roach J.A. at 168–69 (C.A.).

Spill v. *Maule* (1869), L.R. Ex. 232, L.J. Exch. 138, 17 W.R. 805 (Ex. Ct.).

Where intrinsic evidence only is relied upon to show express malice (that is evidence provided by the defamatory expression itself) the plaintiff must show that (1) either the defendant did not believe that his or her statements were true; or (2) if he or she did so believe, it was unreasonable in the circumstances that he or she should so believe; or (3) the defamatory statements were so disproportionate to the occasion as to provide evidence of improper motive.

> *Taylor v. Despard*, [1956] 6 D.L.R. (2d) 161 per Roach J.A. at 168–69 (Ont. C.A.).

"Extrinsic evidence consists of evidence apart from the statements themselves from which the trier of fact can infer some improper motive and a court will look at the conduct of the defendant throughout the course of events both before and after the defamatory publication."

> *Leenen v. Canadian Broadcasting Corporation* (2000), 48 O.R. (3d) 656, per Cunningham J. at para. 143 (S.C.J.), aff'd (2001), 54 O.R. (3d) 612 (C.A.), leave to appeal to S.C.C. denied, [2001] S.C.C.A. No. 432.

> *Taylor v. Despard*, [1956] 6 D.L.R. (2d) 161, per Roach J.A. at 168 (Ont. C.A.).

The extrinsic evidence of the defendant's express malice at the time of publication of the defamatory expression may include the actions of the defendant preceding publication of the defamatory expression, the circumstances of its publication, and the defendant's subsequent actions including the conduct of the defence up to and including the trial as well as any subsequent appeals including a hearing in the Supreme Court of Canada.

> *Boland v. Globe and Mail* (1959), 17 D.L.R. (2d) 313, per Lebel J. at 317, 318 (Ont. C.A.).

> *Hill v. Church of Scientology of Toronto*, [1995] 2 S.C.R. 1130, per Cory J. at paras. 192–94.

D. OTHER PARTIES

1) Co-defendants

Express malice must be proven against each defendant. It is not the law that on a joint publication, the express malice of one defendant taints his or her codefendant.

> *Sun Life Assurance Co. of Canada v. Dalrymple*, [1965] S.C.R. 302, per Spence J. (Ritchie and Cartwright JJ. concurring) at 310:
>
> > It is a mistake to suppose that, on a joint publication, the malice of one defendant infects his co-defendant. Each defendant is answerable sev-

erally, as well as jointly, for the joint publication: and each is entitled to his several defence, whether he be sued jointly or separately from the others. If the plaintiff seeks to rely on malice to aggravate damages, or to rebut a defence of qualified privilege, or to cause a comment, otherwise fair, to become unfair, then he must prove malice against each person whom he charges with it.

Munro v. Toronto Sun Publishing Corporation (1982), 39 O.R. (2d) 100, per J. Holland J. at para. 76 (H.C.J.).

2) Responsibility of Employers for Employees or Agents

The relationship between a news agency and its independent subscribers such as a television station is not necessarily analogous to a principal and agent relationship such that the television station would be tainted by the express malice of the news agency. The nature of the arrangement between a news supplier and a broadcaster or publisher must therefore be closely scrutinized to determine whether the relationship is one of principal/agent or one of contract between independent entities.

Allan v. Bushnell T.V. Co. Ltd. (1969), 4 D.L.R. (3d) 212 per Schroeder J.A. at 214–15 (Ont. C.A.):

The news broadcasts in question were based upon news releases obtained from Broadcast News Ltd., a wholly owned subsidiary of Canadian Press. The latter organization is a co-operative news agency having as members approximately 103 newspaper publishers across Canada who have joined in an enterprise for the purpose of exchanging news for use of its constituent members ... The Canadian Press serves the Canadian Broadcasting Corporation only, but all private broadcasting companies such as the appellant are served under a contractual arrangement entered into between them and Broadcast News Ltd. under which the latter supplies news copy prepared in a manner appropriate for vocal dissemination by means of a single circuit operated out of Toronto. The copy is based on Canadian Press reports, and the service is paid for by the privately owned stations in the manner provided for by contract. The relationship between them is not that of principal and agent, but their dealings are entirely founded upon a contract for the service provided by the news gathering corporation.

If an employee is found to have been actuated by express malice when publishing defamatory expression during the course and scope of his or her employment, that malice will taint the employer. Accordingly, the employer will not be able to rely on a defence of qualified privilege or fair comment. A principal is also tainted by the express malice of his or her agent.

> *Sun Life Assurance Co. of Canada* v. *Dalrymple*, above, at 310, citing *Egger* v. *Viscount Chelmsford et al.*, [1964] 3 All E.R. 406 (C.A.), where Lord Denning M.R. stated at 412:
>
> > A defendant is only affected by express malice if he himself was actuated by it: or if his servant or agent concerned in the publication was actuated by malice in the course of his employment.

3) Findings of Express Malice

a) Knowledge of Falsity

Express malice may be established by proving that the defendant published the defamatory expression knowing it to be untrue.

> *Hill* v. *Church of Scientology of Toronto*, [1995] 2 S.C.R. 1130, per Cory J. at para. 145, citing *McLoughlin* v *Kutasy*, [1979] 2 S.C.R. 311 at 323–24, and *Netupsky* v. *Craig*, [1973] S.C.R. 55 at 61–62.

> *Botiuk* v. *Toronto Free Press Publications Ltd.*, [1995] 3 S.C.R. 3, per Cory J. at 29.

> *Horrocks* v. *Lowe*, [1974] 1 All E.R. 662, per Lord Diplock at 669 (H.L.):
>
> > The motive with which a person published defamatory matter can only be inferred from what he did or said or knew. If it be proved that he did not believe that what he published was true this is generally conclusive evidence of express malice, for no sense of duty or desire to protect his own legitimate interests can justify a man in telling deliberate and injurious falsehoods about another, save in the exceptional case where a person may be under a duty to pass on without endorsing, defamatory reports made by some other person.

A finding that the defendant knowingly published a defamatory falsehood is normally conclusive that he or she was actuated by express malice. In *Clark* v. *Molyneux* (1877), 3 Q.B.D. 237, Brett L.J. stated at 247:

> If a man is proved to have stated that which he knew to be false, no one need inquire further. Everybody assumes thenceforth that he was malicious, that he did do a wrong thing for some wrong motive.

In *Horrocks* v. *Lowe*, [1974] 1 All E.R. 662 (H.L.), Lord Diplock suggests at 669 that express malice may not exist if the defendant was under a duty to pass along information, whether it be true or false, at least with respect to information communicated on the occasion of such a duty.

It has been suggested that knowledge of untruth may be easier to prove in many instances than spite or animosity.

Hodgson v. *Canadian Newspapers Co.* (2000), 49 O.R. (3d) 161, per Sharpe J.A. at para. 35 (C.A.), leave to appeal to S.C.C. denied, [2000] S.C.C.A. 465.

Evidence of the defendant's intended meaning is admissible and relevant to express malice, although the defendant's testimony of subjective intent may well be regarded with skepticism by the court in many circumstances. It is an error to base a finding of express malice on a defendant's evidence that at the time of publication he or she did not believe in the truth of the defamatory meanings alleged by the plaintiff to be conveyed by the expression at issue, if the court accepts that the defendant honestly intended and believed that his or her expression conveyed a different meaning.

Hodgson v. *Canadian Newspapers Co.*, above, at paras. 40–44.

Green v. *Miller* (1901), 31 S.C.R. 177, per King J.:

> If the inquiry were as to the bare meaning of the words, as for instance whether the words were susceptible of a defamatory construction, I should think that the ordinary and natural sense would govern, as being the sense in which the words would be understood by a person receiving the letter; but, if the question upon the statement related to malice or not, then, inasmuch as the knowledge of the defendant of the falsity of the facts alleged is the material fact, the sense in which the defendant may have used the words becomes the governing consideration; and, notwithstanding that the receiver might suppose that a grave charge was made, the person using the language cannot be said to have knowingly stated a falsehood, if he honestly meant to use the words in any innocent sense.

If the defamatory expression is published in a foreign language not known to a printer or to a distributor, who testifies that he therefore did not understand its contents, actual malice will not be found against such a defendant.

Popovich v. *Lobay*, [1937] 3 D.L.R. 715, per Trueman J.A. at 717 and 720 (Man. C.A.).

[T]here may be cases where, after publication, a defendant obtains proof that what he or she said was untrue. In such circumstances, a failure to retract a serious charge may provide evidence that at the time of the original publication, he was actuated by malice.

Haas v. Davis (1998), 37 O.R. (3d) 528, per Doyle J. at 540–41 (Q.B.), finding strong evidence of express malice in the following circumstances:

i.   "repetition of the defamatory statement after it has been made clear that the facts on which the statement is based are false [citing Porter and Potts, *Canadian Libel Practice* (1982), p. 75, para. 671(iii)] or at least not proven as in the trial …";

ii. "the reiteration of the defamatory statement when it is clear that there is no basis for the statement in evidence" [para. 671(iv)]; and

iii. "the defendant's reassertion of their belief" at this trial after the charge had been disproved at a previous hearing before members of the union local. "This is in my view strong evidence of malice on the part of the defendants …".

If a plea of justification is made recklessly and the defendant persists at trial in an imputation that he knows to be unfounded or cross examines the plaintiff with a view to showing that he is guilty of that which he has been acquitted of, express malice can properly be inferred.

Farrell v. St. John's Publishing Co. Ltd., above, at 78, para. 53.

Although a failure on the part of the defendant to apologize combined with a persistence in a plea of justification may be evidence of malice, in certain circumstances such conduct may merely show the defendant's sincerity and belief in what had been said:

Broadway Approvals Ltd. v. Odhams Press Ltd., [1995] 2 All E.R. 523 at 533 per Sellars L.J., approved in *Farrell v. St. John's Publishing Co. Ltd.*, above.

An exaggeration or extreme statement is not necessarily proof of malice. A defendant may be protected, even if his language is violent or excessively strong, depending on all the circumstances.

Adam v. Ward, [1917] A.C. 309, per Lord Atkinson at 339 (H.L.):

[A] person making a communication on a privileged occasion is not restricted to the use of such language as merely as is reasonably necessary to protect the interest or discharge the duty which is the foundation of his privilege; but that, on the contrary, he will be protected, even though his language should be violent or excessively strong, if, having regard to all the circumstances of the case, he might have honestly and on reasonable grounds believed that what he wrote or said was true and necessary for the purpose of his vindication, though in fact it was not so.

McLoughlin v. *Kutasy*, [1979] 2 S.C.R. 311, per Ritchie J. at 323 and 325, approving the principle stated in *Adam* v. *Ward, ibid.*

Netupsky v. *Craig*, [1973] S.C.R. 55, per Ritchie J. at 62, approving the principle stated in *Adam* v. *Ward*, above.

Davies & Davies Ltd. v. *Kott*, [1979] 2 S.C.R. 686, per McIntyre J. at 697, approving the principle stated in *Adam* v. *Ward*, above.

O'Malley v. *O'Callaghan* (1992), 89 D.L.R. (4th) 577, per Mason J. at 590–91 (Alta. Q.B.).

MacArthur v. *Meuser* (1997), 146 D.L.R. (4th) 125, per Adams J. at paras. 36, 44 (Ont. Gen. Div.).

The wording may be so violent, outrageous, or disproportionate to the facts, however, that it furnishes strong evidence of malice.

Spill v. *Maule* (1869), L.R. Ex. 232, 38 L.J. Exch. 138, 17 W.R. 805 (Ex. Ct.).

The fact that statements may have been calculated to create a negative or a false impression through vehicles of misrepresentation or exaggeration may lead to a finding of express malice.

O'Malley v. *O'Callaghan*, above, at 589.

Lawson v. *Thompson* (1968), 1 D.L.R. (3d) 270 (B.C.S.C.), aff'd (1969), 5 D.L.R. (3d) 550 (B.C.C.A.) [illustrates a finding of express malice based on intrinsic evidence in the defamatory expression itself].

In *Lawson*, Seaton J. (later Seaton J.A.) found at 275 that the defendant union official said of the plaintiff union official: "As long as he lives on Teamster's dues he is taking money fraudulently. He should get his money from the employers for whom he works in my opinion." The defendant also described the plaintiff as a "labour faker," and referred to the plaintiff as one of the "Judases" in the labour movement. In a subsequent letter, the defendant stated, *inter alia*, "there is no use denying that within the labour movement there are deep sores that at times fester and run like a rotten sewer."

Seaton J., in arriving at his conclusion in *Lawson* that the defendant spoke such words maliciously, stated [page 275]:

> The most significant evidence of malice is that found in the words used and the manner of their use. It is difficult to describe them without using the word malicious.

Similarly, in *Slack* v. *Ad-Rite Associates Ltd.* (1998), 79 O.T.C. 46 (Gen. Div.), Fedak J. found intrinsic evidence of express malice in the words in an advertisement published by the defendant, who opposed the construction by the plaintiff of a large waste disposal plant [at para. 28]:

> However, the personal invective in the ad, such as "tell the Slacks they have bitten the hands that have been feeding them for years" and "hit the road Slack" is evidence of actual malice. [The defendant's] comments in her letter to Neil Slack that she did not give "a tinkers damn" for the Slack family and her flagrant breach of the injunction prohibiting her from coming within 500 feet of Slack's property provide corroboration of actual and express malice.

On the other hand, in *Silbernagel* v. *Empire Stevedoring Co.* (1979), 18 B.C.L.R. 384 (S.C.), aff'd [1981] B.C.J. No. 1439 (C.A.), Wallace J. held that ostensibly severe expression did not permit an inference of actual malice. In that case, the defendant said of the plaintiff that "He hardly knows what day it is, let alone mechanical work." Wallace J. found that expression would be interpreted by the reasonable man as slang meaning that the plaintiff was absolutely incompetent as a heavy-duty mechanic; an assertion in which he held the defendant had an honest belief [p. 392].

Wallace J. stated in *Silbernagel* at 394 that:

> use of such an idiom among the dockyard and union administrators could not be considered sufficiently extreme to support an inference of express malice or wrong-doing or rebut the presumption of bona fides. The words were used to impress the recipients with the author's opinion of the degree of the plaintiff's incompetence and thus prevent his being dispatched on future occasions to Empire Stevedoring as a heavy duty mechanic. ... The words were not used for any purpose other than that directly connected with the employment potential of the plaintiff, an object that clearly falls within the privilege.

It is open to the Court to make reasonable inferences from the nature of the expression if such reasonable inferences are logical probabilities arising out of the evidence.

RTC Engineering Consultants Ltd. v. *Ontario (Ministry of the Solicitor General and Correctional Services)*, [2000] O.T.C. 471 per Roberts J. at para. 75 (S.C.J.), aff'd (2002), 58 O.R. (3d) 726 (C.A.).

Boland v. *Globe & Mail Ltd.* (1959) 17 D.L.R. (2d) 313, per Lebel J.A. at 317 (Ont. C.A.):

> We do not consider it necessary or advisable to consider what has been addressed to us on the question of intrinsic evidence of malice in the article in question since there is to be a new trial. However, we wish to point out that when language is severe that kind of express malice may exist if there is an absence of grounds for the publisher's reasonable belief that what he wrote was true.

Decisions illustrating other circumstances where the court found that the defendant published defamatory expression knowing it to be untrue include:

i) *Lawson* v. *Thompson*, above.

   The defendant union official alleged the plaintiff union official was neither trustworthy, loyal, nor honest, and was unfit to be associated with or represent a trade union [p. 272]. On being examined for discovery in advance of trial, the defendant said: "I don't question [the plaintiff's honesty] and integrity, never have" and "Well, if you are implying in the question here whether I think [the plaintiff] worked for the employer or not, the answer is an emphatic no."

   Seaton J. concluded at page 275 the defendant knew that his words were false.

ii) *Slack* v. *Ad-Rite Associates*, [1998] 79 O.T.C. 46 (Gen. Div.).

   In opposition to the proposed construction of a large waste disposal plant, the defendant published an advertisement in a local newspaper describing the plaintiff as joining in a venture that would destroy the homes and injure the health of the area residents and their children. Fedak J. held at para. 28:

   > Attacks against a person where a dishonourable motive of destroying homes and the health of children for profit is alleged must be warranted by the facts. Since even the defendant did not believe the accusations in the ad, one can only conclude that this is evidence of malice. The defence of fair comment therefore fails.

Where an employee has voluntarily resigned, a letter written by his employer stating that he has been discharged and cautioning his customers against any dealings with him, thus by innuendo implying his dishonesty, is libellous, and evidence as to whether the severance of the relation of employer and employee was in fact a dismissal or resignation is admissible to show malice.

Lockington v. *Siegrist & Co.*, [1935] 3 D.L.R. 566 (Ont. C.A.).

There may be extreme cases in which the news media engage in deception for the purpose of producing a sensational story, either to enhance reputations or to attract viewers, ratings, and ultimately revenue. This constitutes express malice.

> *Pressler* v. *Lethbridge* (2000), 86 B.C.L.R. (3d) 257, per Esson J.A. at para. 113 (C.A.):

> > As Southin J.A. puts it in para. 98 of her reasons, the reporter "was blinded by Mrs. Pressler's avowed opinions and thus was unable to grasp that what he was doing was wrong." The reporter's motive was in large part to support [the defendant] Lethbridge in his campaign to expose the plaintiffs' hateful opinions. That state of mind led to the program being tainted by a certain amount of distortion of the facts as known to the reporter which was particularly apparent in the attempt to create an impression that the house being built was very large and intended to be used for some ominous purpose. An example of that is a shot of an unidentified workman on the property who, in answer to a shouted question from the reporter as to the size of the building, replies "16,000 feet." The reporter well knew from a reliable source that the square footage was something over 3,000 feet. I am unable to say that the trial judge, having heard and weighed all the evidence, erred in finding malice on the part of [the defendant] Westcom.

> *Vogel* v. *Canadian Broadcasting Corporation*, [1982] 3 W.W.R. 97 (B.C.S.C.) per Esson J., explained in *Pressler* v. *Lethbridge* (2000), 86 B.C.L.R. (3d) 257, per Esson J.A. at para. 112 (C.A.):

> > In Vogel's case, some of those who produced the programs did not believe what they published was true and others were indifferent to its truth or falsity. The story, as I said in my reasons, was not so much dug up as made up. It was a case in which the natural desire of reporters and producers to gain favourable attention led to a virtually complete loss of balance.

4) Reckless Indifference To Truth

Reckless indifference to the truth is express malice.

> *Botiuk* v. *Toronto Free Press Publications Ltd.*, [1995] 3 S.C.R. 3, per Cory J. at 29.

> *Kelly* v. *Magnolo*, [1983] B.C.J. No. 376, per Callaghan J. at para. 36 (S.C.):

Defence counsel submitted the allegations by the defendant Magnolo as to the plaintiff's dishonesty were untrue. But he submitted the defendant honestly believed them to be true. I have difficulty in accepting that submission. After it was suggested an audit be obtained the defendant indicated it wasn't necessary, that he already knew the plaintiff was dishonest, and thereafter referred to the plaintiff's alleged business practices in Dawson Creek and the alleged acceptance of a bribe from DuPont. He was not interested in seeking the truth. ... All of the evidence leads me to conclude he could not have had a positive belief in the truth of what he published and that the desire to injure was the dominant motive for the defamatory publication.

The leading case on the cause of action for deceit holds that reckless indifference to the truth is equivalent to a lack of honest belief in what has been stated.

Derry v. Peek (1889), 14 App. Cas. 337, per Lord Herschell at 374:

> ... fraud is proved when it is shown that a false representation has been made (1) knowingly, (2) without belief in its truth or (3) recklessly, careless whether it be true or false. Although I have treated the second and third as distinct cases, I think the third is but an instance of the second, for one who makes a statement under such circumstances can have no real belief in the truth of what he states. To prevent a false statement being fraudulent, there must, I think, always be an honest belief in its truth.

The law draws a line between reckless indifference to the truth of what has been published (which constitutes malice) and carelessness or irrationality in arriving at that belief (which does not). Lord Diplock explains the distinction in *Horrocks v. Lowe*, [1974] 1 All E.R. 662 at 669 (H.L.):

> [W]hat is required on the part of the defamer to entitle him to the protection of the privilege is positive belief in the truth of what he published or, as it is generally though tautologously termed, "honest belief." If he publishes untrue defamatory matter recklessly, without considering or caring whether it be true or not, he is in this, as in other branches of the law, treated as if he knew it to be false. But indifference to the truth of what he publishes is not to be equated with carelessness, impulsiveness or irrationality in arriving at a positive belief that it is true ... In ordinary life it is rare indeed for people to form their beliefs by a process of logical deduction from facts ascertained by a rigorous search for all available evidence and a judicious assessment of its

probative value. In greater or lesser degree according to their temperaments, their training, their intelligence, they are swayed by prejudice, rely on intuition instead of reasoning, leap to conclusions on inadequate evidence and fail to recognise the cogency of material which might cast doubt on the validity of the conclusions they reach. But despite the imperfection of the mental process by which the belief is arrived at it may still be "honest," that is, a positive belief that the conclusions they have reached are true. The law demands no more.

For example, in *Camporese* v. *Parton* (1983), 150 D.L.R. (3d) 208 (B.C.S.C.), Wallace J. held at page 227 that although the defendant consumer affairs columnist wrote the defamatory expression "without adequate research and with untimely haste in the circumstances," she honestly believed the facts and opinions expressed in her column. Accordingly, the plaintiffs failed to prove express malice.

The defendant's belief in the truth of the defamatory expression must be honestly held but generally it need not be reached on what, objectively viewed, are reasonable grounds. Mere carelessness or negligence or failure to inquire into the truthfulness of a defamatory allegation is not necessarily evidence of malice.

Korach v. *Moore* (1991), 76 D.L.R. (4th) 506, per Grange J.A. at 509–10 (Ont. C.A.):

> The question is not whether [the defendant's] belief was reasonable but whether it was honestly held. Of course, if there was no ground for the belief it might be that a court would conclude that the statement was made recklessly and that conclusion would have been more readily reached if the statement were made out of an improper motive but there is no such motive here as the trial judge properly found.

Loos v. *Robbins* (1987), 37 D.L.R. (4th) 418, per Gerwing J.A. for the Court at 428–29 (Sask. C.A.):

> Here the [defendant] Minister relied on sources within the Crown corporation that losses existed; that an investigation was taking place to attempt to alleviate this and other problems, and as a result of these investigations 13 employees were to be terminated. Based on this, can it be said there was a demonstration, that in probability, he did not honestly believe the statements he made? I think the learned [trial] judge was entitled to hold this demonstration had not been made out on the plaintiff's evidence.

Strutt v. Ahmed (1986), 54 Sask. R. 199 per Geatros J. at 203, para. 17 (Q.B.):

> The defendants say they had no "proof" that the plaintiff was instrumental in Ms. K's elopement [the defamatory allegation]. But it is apparent that they believed on reasonable grounds that their statements to Hunter were true.

Chrispen v. Novak, [1995] 5 W.W.R. 752, per Klebuc J. at para. 17 (Sask. Q.B.), citing *Horrocks v. Lowe*, [1974] 1 All E.R. 662 at 671 (H.L.).

In determining whether the defendant did in fact have an honest belief, however, the court is "entitled to take into consideration the ground on which it is founded."

Farrell v. St. John's Publishing Co. Ltd. (1986), 58 Nfld. & P.E.I.R. 66, per Morgan J.A. at 78, para. 55 (Nfld. C.A.).

Korach v. Moore, above, at 512:

> If it can be said that [the defendant] had no basis for believing that what the plaintiff had set out in the reports was false or exaggerated, then it can be inferred that his belief in the truth of his allegations of "discrepancy between what had been reported and what had actually occurred" was not honestly held.

MacDonald v. Poirier (1991), 120 N.B.R. (2d) 18 at 45–46 (Q.B.), per Russell J. adopting the following passage from Philip Lewis, *Gatley on Libel and Slander,* 8th ed. (London: Sweet & Maxwell) at para. 1341:

> Although the fact that the defendant had no reasonable grounds for believing his statement to be true is not in itself conclusive evidence of malice, yet 'honest belief must be founded on some sort of reasonable basis,' and therefore in determining whether such an honest belief did in fact exist, the jury are entitled to take into consideration the grounds on which it was founded. The defendant's belief may have been so groundless that the jury may come to the conclusion that he could not, and did not, honestly believe the statement he made to be true.

Amalgamated Transit Union v. Independent Canadian Transit Union, [1997] 5 W.W.R. 662, per Lutz J. at para. 88 (Alta. Q.B.):

> 88 I find that the Defendants' purported honest belief in their defamatory statements was so groundless that they could not and did not honestly believe the statements to be true.

Anderson v. *Kocsis*, [1998] 86 O.T.C. 107, per Kovacs J. at para. 37 (Gen. Div.):

> I am satisfied there was publication of the sign ["[The plaintiff] is a queer, steroid-using cop ..."] and there was a libel of the plaintiff. I am also satisfied that no defence has been established. The evidence the defendant knew nothing of the plaintiff's background when he prepared the sign leads me to find the defendant exhibited indifference or recklessness to the truth, so I find there was express malice by the defendant.

Hynes v. *Hayes* (1999), 179 N.S.R. (2d) 158 (S.C.).

Statements made to the defendant by others before publication, or documents relied upon by the defendant in formulating his or her belief, may demonstrate that the defendant had some ground for his or her belief and therefore was not actuated by express malice.

Korach v. *Moore* (1991), above at 510:

> The trial judge's failure to appreciate the true test is demonstrated by his refusal to permit counsel for the defendants to tender evidence of what had been said by others to [the defendant] Moore concerning the matter. That evidence was not tendered for its truth but to show Moore's state of mind. It was not hearsay; it was evidence going to the issue in the action — the honesty of Moore's belief in what he had written. The question is not whether his belief was reasonable but whether it was honestly held. Of course, if there was no ground for the belief it might be that a court would conclude that the statement was made recklessly and that conclusion would have been more readily reached if the statement were made out of an improper motive but there is no such motive here as the trial judge properly found.

Derrickson v. *Tomat* (1992), 88 D.L.R. (4th) 401, per Hinds J.A. at 423, (leave to appeal to S.C.C. denied (1992), 93 D.L.R. (4th) vii (S.C.C.)):

> At the conclusion of the hearing of the evidence and before the final submissions of counsel were presented, the trial judge gave a ruling against the admissibility of the Report [on the affairs of the Indian Band including the conduct of the plaintiffs]. In my respectful view, the Report was admissible because it formed the basis for some of the allegations contained in the [allegedly defamatory] Petition. Some of the defendants, when testifying, stated that they had seen the Report, that they were aware of its contents, and that it formed the basis of their

honest belief in the truth of some of the allegations contained in the Petition. That would be relevant to whether the plaintiffs had established malice against those defendants.

Where a plaintiff reads in the discovery evidence of a defendant to prove what little ground the defendant had for her statements, the court may nevertheless take that evidence as valid proof that she did have those particular grounds. At a minimum, the evidence may be relevant to the question of the defendant's honest belief.

W.Y. Carter, Burr Co. Ltd. v. *Harris* (1922), 70 D.L.R. 420, per Stuart J.A. at 433 (Alta C.A.).

Derrickson v. *Tomat*, above, at 423:

> "To prove belief, which is after all subjective and except to the individual himself a matter of inference, the existence of good grounds for a belief is evidence of belief." The existence of facts which would induce a reasonable person to believe a statement is true is relevant to the issue of express malice. The absence of such facts may be evidence of the non-existence of the alleged honest belief.

Robertson v. *Boddington and Robinson*, [1925] 2 D.L.R. 483, per Riddell J. at 487 (Ont. H.C.).

"Whether the reasons are good or not is for the jury — because a court might think them insufficient does not follow that they are not to be given." Any fact tending to prove or disprove honesty of belief is admissible on the issue of express malice.

Ibid.

Where there are a number of different false and defamatory allegations published on different occasions a court may more readily conclude the defendant knew that his or her statements were false or alternatively acted recklessly without caring whether they were true or not.

Kelly v. *Magnolo*, [1983] B.C.J. No. 376, per Callaghan J. at para. 38 (S.C.):

> The defendant published statements on four separate matters ... If there had been one mis-statement it might be reasonable to conclude that the individual making the statement was merely careless. Where, however, there are a number of statements as is here, one is led irresistibly to the conclusion that either the defendant knew the statements were false or alternatively that he acted recklessly without caring whether they were true or not.

Publication of defamatory information received from a source regarded by the defendant as dubious may be compelling evidence of express malice.

Olson v. Runciman (2001), 291 A.R. 195 per Hart J. at para. 18 (Q.B.):

> I find striking evidence of express malice in [the defendant's] startling admission alone that he had reason to doubt his informer's credibility yet used his "information" as a foundation for his complaint against the Plaintiff in any event.

The conduct of the defendant may be inconsistent with a belief in the truth of a defamatory accusation and contribute to a finding that the defendant was actuated by express malice.

Larsen v. A & B. Sound Ltd., [1996] 9 W.W.R. 253, per Shaw J. at para. 31 (B.C.S.C.):

> I infer from all the evidence that [the defendant] had no honest belief that [the plaintiff] was a thief or was dishonest. I find that [the defendant's] evidence and his actions are inconsistent with such a belief. As noted earlier, [the defendant] offered [the plaintiff] a move to another branch of A & B Sound. This offer and the arrangements he made with the manager of the other branch were made after [the defendant] was aware of most of [the plaintiff's] invoicing errors and his former practice of including free speaker wire with speaker sales. If [the defendant] truly considered [the plaintiff's] conduct as dishonest, surely he would not have tried to keep him in the employ of A & B Sound.

A plaintiff may succeed in establishing express malice where the evidence demonstrates that the defendant:

i)   relied on a source when he knew of the friction between the source and the plaintiff and knew the source to be partisan;

ii)   knew of evidence that supported the position of the plaintiff but suppressed it;

iii) failed to give the plaintiff a fair chance to explain his side of the story;

iv)   made no effort to present a balanced picture in the article; and/or

v)   made no attempt at trial to justify the defamatory sting of the defendant's expression.

> *Hodgson v. Canadian Newspapers Co.* (1998), 39 O.R. (3d) 235, per Lane J. at 384, 397 (Gen. Div.), varied on other grounds (2000), 49 O.R. (3d) 161 at para. 42 (C.A.), leave to appeal to S.C.C. denied [2000] S.C.C.A. No. 465.

In the case of a publication in the news media, a factor which may indicate express malice is a failure to provide the plaintiff with a fair opportunity to defend by contacting him or her before publication and providing a chance to make a meaningful and considered response.

Leenen v. Canadian Broadcasting Corporation (2000), 48 O.R. (3d) 656 at para. 143 (S.C.J.), aff'd (2001), 54 O.R. (3d) 612 (C.A.), leave to appeal to S.C.C. denied, [2001] S.C.C.A. No. 432.

The systematic reporting of only one side of the story, the deliberate refraining by a defendant from making important further inquiries, the omission of highly significant information contrary to the story's thesis – all these may lead to a conclusion of malice. A court may well find that such matters were done deliberately in order to slant the expression to the prejudice of the plaintiff.

Leenen v. Canadian Broadcasting Corporation, ibid. at para. 162.

There may be cases where the failure to make further investigation or inquiry is evidence of express malice.

Arnott v. College of Physicians and Surgeons of Saskatchewan, [1954] S.C.R. 538 per Estey J. at 551.

Ramsey v. Pacific Press, a Division of Southam Inc., [2000] B.C.J. No. 2422, 2000 BCSC 1551, per Taylor J. at para. 128 [journalist held to have acted recklessly rather than carelessly in failing to conduct a reasonable investigation to determine the veracity of the attribution of a quote to the plaintiff politician].

Munro v. Toronto Sun Publishing Corporation (1982), 39 O.R. (2d) 100 per Holland J. at para. 74 (H.C.J.):

> I have no difficulty on the evidence in finding that each of [the defendants] Ramsey and Reguly were motivated by actual malice ... Ramsay before and then Ramsay and Reguly together set out to "get" not only [the plaintiff] Mr. Munro but anyone attached to the government who benefited from the purchase and sale of Petrofina shares in the critical period. Having perceived the possibility of impropriety, they assumed it to be present and provable and went on from there. I accept that they misled senior management into believing that all had been done by obtaining documentation and investigation to ensure the truth and accuracy of the story. Ramsay, of course, knew that he did not have the verification necessary and Reguly, entrusted by senior management

with the responsibility for the investigation and development of this story, was so driven by a desire to destroy and gain notoriety that he did not even look at the documentation alleged to be available. ...

"When the defendants are lawyers who must be presumed to be reasonably familiar with both the law of libel and the legal consequences flowing from signing a document, their actions will be more closely scrutinized than would those of a lay person. That is to say, actions which might be characterized as careless behaviour in a lay person could well become reckless behaviour in a lawyer with all the resulting legal consequences of reckless behaviour."

Botiuk v. Toronto Free Press Publications Ltd., [1995] 3 S.C.R. 3, per Cory J. at 35, para. 98. [Malice was found in this case where the defendant lawyers, knowing their endorsement of a libelous allegation would have a devastating effect on the plaintiff, signed the document without undertaking a reasonable investigation to ensure it was correct.]

It appears that professional engineers, like lawyers, are more likely than a lay person of modest education or experience to be held recklessly indifferent to the truth. "As a professional engineer reasoning rather than intuition or assumptions is a way of life. Every day [the defendant] functions in circumstances where she cannot afford to reach conclusions on assumptions or inadequate evidence/information. [The defendant] constantly assesses the validity of her conclusions by weighing them against what other professionals know and in examining why they reached their own conclusions. I am struck by [the defendant's] lack of adequate inquiry into, or verification of, the accuracy of the subject matter" of the defamatory communication.

Hiltz and Seamone Co. v. Nova Scotia (Attorney General) (1997), 164 N.S.R. (2d) 161, per Stewart J at paras. 95, 103 (S.C.), aff'd (1999), 172 D.L.R. (4th) 488 per Pogsley J.A. at para. 98 (N.S.C.A.).

In *Amalgamated Transit Union v. Independent Canadian Transit Union*, [1997] 5 W.W.R. 662 (Alta. Q.B.), Lutz J. stated at paras. 84–85:

... the Court of Appeal in *Horrocks v. Lowe*, *supra*, implied that Defendants could be held to differing standards depending on their individual abilities and qualities:

... In greater or in lesser degree according to their temperaments, their training, their intelligence, they are swayed by prejudice, rely on intuition instead of reasoning, leap to conclusions on inadequate evidence and fail to recognize the cogency of material which might cast doubt on the validity of the conclusions they reach. But despite the imperfection of the mental process by which the belief is arrived at it may still be 'honest', that is, a positive belief that the conclusions they have reached are true. The law demands no more (p. 150).

I note that the Defendants here are a union and two of its officials. These are sophisticated parties who are experienced in such matters as reporting to members, recruiting new members, and conducting negotiations with members and management. They are well aware of the importance of reputation and public opinion, and well-informed about the issues and controversies at work in the union context.

A court may conclude that defamatory expression was published with reckless indifference to the truth if the contents of the expression conflict with unchallenged and unquestionable facts and the defendant does not give a comprehensible and logical explanation for the false accusation.

Platt v. Time International of Canada Ltd., [1964] 2 O.R. 21, per McRuer C.J.H.C. at 31–32 (H.C.J.):

> The defamatory part of the article cannot in any sense be attributed to a slip or an accident. Every word published was checked and vetted. It was written with full knowledge that there was no suggestion that the plaintiff was in any way involved in the opium traffic. No explanation was at any time given as to why his name was associated with those found guilty of trafficking in opium. ... The only reason I can see for associating the plaintiff's name with those who had been found guilty of smuggling opium was to add colour to the article by suggesting that a field officer in the Canadian Armed Services was charged with traffic in narcotics. I find that the publication, if not deliberate, was done with a reckless indifference to any injury that might be done to the good name of the plaintiff.

Defiance may be treated as essentially dishonest and therefore indicative of express malice where the defendant attempts to gloss over the real nature of the defamatory expression. "We are going to continue to fight the public's battle for a square deal irrespective of threatening letters we have received from Safeway Stores and in this respect we cannot be either bribed, bought or frightened and we want both the public and Safeways to know this." This statement was held to be proof of express malice.

Safeway Stores Ltd. v. Harris, [1948] 4 D.L.R. 187, per Williams C.J.K.B. at 195–96 (Man. K.B.), aff'd, [1948] 4 D.L.R. 187 at 188 (Man. C.A.).

Evidence of the defendant's intended meaning is admissible, and relevant to reckless indifference to the truth. See section D(3)(a) "Knowledge of Falsity" above, page 296.

In *Leenen v. Canadian Broadcasting Corporation* (2000), 48 O.R. (3d) 656 (S.C.J.), [aff'd (2001), 54 O.R. (3d) 612 (C.A.), leave to appeal to S.C.C. denied, [2001] S.C.C.A. No. 432], the factors which contributed to a finding of malice at trial were identified by Cunningham J. at paras. 144–86:

i)   Failure to provide the plaintiff with a fair opportunity to defend;

ii)   Deliberately refraining from making inquiries;

iii)   Systematic reporting of only one side of the story;

iv)   Omitting significant information that was contrary to the defendants' thesis;

v)   Reliance on an obviously biased source;

vi)   Conduct of the defendants following the defamatory broadcast, prior to, and during the trial;

vii)   A biased and disdainful attitude on the part of the defendants towards the plaintiff;

viii)   A malicious tone to the pleadings, alleging that the plaintiff was the author of his own misfortune;

ix)   Failure to present a fair portrayal of the plaintiff; and

x)   Use of ambush interview tactics.

There is a distinction to be made, however, between:

i)   carelessness in arriving at an honest belief that what has been published is true; and

ii)   carelessness in the publication of the defamatory expression so that it does not express the honest belief, or shows that the honest belief was never formed.

It was held in *Leverman v. Campbell Sharp Ltd.* (1987), 36 D.L.R. (4th) 401 (B.C.C.A), per Lambert J.A. (Taggart and McLachlin JJ.A. concurring) at page 404, that carelessness in the publication of the statement so that it does not express the honest belief, or shows that the honest belief was never formed, is equivalent to malice in relation to the defence of qualified privilege.

In *Leverman*, the defendant trustee of the estate of a bankrupt lawyer, Alexander Watt, published a notice to creditors which was headed "In the Matter of the Bankruptcy of Alexander Peter (Sandy) Watt (doing business as Leverman and Watt, Barristers and Solicitors)." The defendant trustee knew that the partnership between Watt and the plaintiff Leverman had been dissolved and that Leverman was not in bankruptcy. The trial judge found that the clear implication to readers was that the firm of Leverman and Watt was in bankruptcy, not just Watt, but dismissed the action on the basis the communication was privileged and made without malice.

On appeal, the British Columbia Court of Appeal held that the defence of qualified privilege did not apply because of carelessness in the expression of what the defendant wished to convey, which was equivalent to malice. In this connection, Lambert J.A. (Taggart and McLachlin JJ.A. concurring), referred to the judgements of Lord Diplock and Viscount Dilhorne in *Horrocks* v. *Lowe*, [1974] 1 All E.R. 662, and stated at 404:

> The question then centred on whether carelessness was to be equated with not holding an honest belief in the truth of the statement. That very point was addressed by Lord Diplock in the passage in Horrocks v. Lowe immediately following the passage which I have already quoted, at p. 669:
>
> > ...if he publishes untrue matter recklessly, without considering or caring whether it be true or not, he is in this, as in other branches of the law, treated as if he knew it to be false. But indifference to the truth of what he publishes is not to be equated with carelessness, impulsiveness, or irrationality in arriving at a positive belief that it is true. The freedom of speech protected by the law of qualified privilege may be applied by all sorts and conditions of men. In affording to them immunity from suit if they have acted in good faith in compliance with a legal or moral duty or in protection of a legitimate interest the law must take them as it finds them. In ordinary life, it is rare indeed for people to form their beliefs by a process of logical deduction from facts ascertained by a rigorous search for all available evidence and a judicious assessment of its probative value.

The reasons for judgment of Viscount Dilhorne, at p. 666, are to the same effect.

In summary, carelessness in forming an honest belief does not take away the defence of qualified privilege. The honest belief can be formed on the slimmest of evidence. The questions are whether it is honestly held and whether there is a duty to make the statement. But carelessness in the publication of the statement so that it does not express the honest belief, or shows that the honest belief was never formed, takes away the defence of qualified privilege.

On the facts of this case, I am satisfied that the trustee and Mr. Liebert did not have an honest belief that the firm of Leverman and Watt was in bankruptcy, and that the carelessness lies in the publication of the statement so that it does not express the honest belief. In those circumstance the careless-ness is equivalent to malice in its relationship to the defence of qualified priv-ilege, and it undermines that defence so that it is no longer available.

On this subject of carelessness in the expression, Clearwater J. of the Manitoba Court of Queen's Bench held in *McKinnon v. Dauphin (Rural Municipality)*, [1996] 3 W.W.R. 127 at paras. 56–57 that the defendant "could not have had an honest belief in the statement he made when he said that the plaintiffs were 'not reliable'," that the defendant "misspoke" him-self, but that such negligence in expressing his views "does not amount to the degree of recklessness from which the court could infer malice."

5) Spite or Animosity

An honest belief in the defamatory expression does not necessarily negate malice. A defendant can honestly believe a statement yet publish it with express malice for an improper reason or motive.

> *Christie v. Westcom Radio Group Ltd.* (1990), 75 D.L.R. (4th) 546 (B.C.C.A.), leave to appeal to S.C.C. denied, [1991] 1 S.C.R. vii.

> *Botiuk v. Toronto Free Press Publications Ltd.*, [1995] 3 S.C.R. 3, per Cory J. at para. 79.

Although express malice does not require the presence of a desire to injure the plaintiff, or any ill will towards him or her, the Court should find express malice if such an intention is the dominant motive of the defendant.

> *Hodgson v. Canadian Newspapers Co.* (1998), 39 O.R. (3d) 235, per Lane J. at 393 (Gen. Div.), citing *Horrocks v. Lowe*, above; varied on another issue (2000), 49 O.R. (3d) 161 (C.A.), leave to appeal to S.C.C. denied, [2000] S.C.C.A. 465.

Evidence tending to suggest the existence of such express malice should be balanced, however, with evidence of other motives. In *Horrocks v. Lowe*, [1974] 1 All E.R. 662, Lord Diplock states at 670:

> Judges and juries should, however, be very slow to draw the inference that a defendant was so far actuated by improper motives as to deprive him of the protection of the privilege unless they are satisfied that he did not believe that what he said or wrote was true or that he was indifferent to its truth or falsi-ty. The motives with which human beings act are mixed. They find it difficult to hate the sin but love the sinner. Qualified privilege would be illusory, and the public interest that it is meant to serve defeated, if the protection which

it affords were lost merely because a person, although acting in compliance with a duty or in protection of a legitimate interest, disliked the person whom he defamed or was indignant at what he believed to be that person's conduct and welcomed the opportunity of exposing it. It is only where his desire to comply with the relevant duty or to protect the relevant interest plays no significant part in his motives for publishing what he believes to be true that 'express malice' can properly be found.

The desire to injure must be the dominant motive. In the context of the defence of qualified privilege, Lord Diplock stated in *Horrocks* v. *Lowe*, above, at 669:

> "Express malice" is the term of art descriptive of such a motive. Broadly speaking it means malice in the popular sense of a desire to injure the person who was defamed and that generally is the motive which the Plaintiff sets out to prove. But to destroy the privilege the desire to injure must be the dominant motive for the defamatory publication: knowledge that it will have that effect is not enough if the defendant is nevertheless acting in accordance with a sense of duty or in bona fide protection of his own legitimate interests.

One view is that the animosity or spite which negates the defences of qualified privilege and fair comment must be directed towards the plaintiff, as opposed to a third party.

> *Re International Assn. of Bridge, Structural and Ornamental and Reinforcing Iron-workers Union (Local 97) and Campbell* (1997), 40 B.C.L.R. (3d) 1 per Macdonald J. at para. 46 (S.C.) [this issue was conceded by the plaintiff].

Mere dislike or indignation and welcoming the opportunity to expose the plaintiff does not constitute express malice, as long as the defendant otherwise spoke honestly.

> *Davies & Davies Ltd.* v. *Kott*, [1979] 2 S.C.R. 686, per McIntyre J. for the Court at 698, approving *Horrocks* v. *Lowe*, above at 670, d.

The law recognizes that there is a fine line to be drawn between anger on the one hand and hatred amounting to express malice on the other hand. Anger does not necessarily beget express malice.

> *Awood Air Ltd.* v. *Cowman*, [1997] B.C.J. No. 970 (S.C.).

"Honest anger surely is not evidence of malice; the anger spoken of in some of the cases as evidence of malice must mean unreasoning anger resulting in an intention to injure."

W.Y. Carter, Burr Co. Ltd. v. Harris (1922), 70 D.L.R. 420, per Beck J.A. at 448 (Alta. C.A.) [concurring in result with Stuart J.A. and Hyndman J.A. in allowing the appeal with respect to the libel claim and dismissing the action on the basis malice was not proven].

However, "[i]f a person from anger or some other wrong motive has allowed his mind to get into such a state as to make him cast aspersions on other people reckless whether they are true or false, it has been held …that a jury is justified in finding malice."

Royal Acquarium and Summer and Winter Garden Society Ltd. v. Parkinson, [1892] 1 Q.B. 431, per Lord Esher M.R. at 444 (C.A.), adopted in *W.Y. Carter, Burr Co. Ltd. v. Harris,* 70 D.L.R. 420, per Stuart J.A. (Hyndman J.A. concurring) at 434 (Alta. C.A.).

"If it be proved that out of anger, or for some other wrong motive, the defendant has stated as true that which he does not know to be true, and he has stated it not stopping or taking the trouble to ascertain whether it is true or not — stated it recklessly by reason of his anger or other indirect motive — the jury may infer that he used the occasion not for the reason which justifies it [i.e. the privilege] but for the gratification of his anger or other indirect motive."

Royal Aquarium and Summer and Winter Garden Society Ltd. v. Parkinson, above, at 454, adopted in *W.Y. Carter, Burr Co. Ltd. v. Harris,* above, at 434–35, 436:

> In this passage Lopes L.J., was quoting almost verbatim the words of Brett, L.J., in *Clark v. Molyneux,* 3 Q.B.D. 237 at p. 247, and this latter case received the direct approval of the Judicial Committee in *Jenoure v. Delmege,* [1891] A.C. 73…
>
> And in *Royal Aquarium etc. Society v. Parkinson,* [1892] 1 Q.B. 431, the Court did find evidence of a sort of fanatical prejudice against the plaintiff's entertainment halls.

In determining the question of express malice in a radio or television broadcast, the trier of fact is entitled to consider not only the contents of the publication, but the tone of voice of the commentator.

Christie v. Westcom Radio Group Ltd. (1990), 75 D.L.R. (4th) 546 (B.C.C.A.), leave to appeal to S.C.C. denied, [1991] 1 S.C.R. vii.

The modern use of recorded voice messaging services, tape recorders, and video recorders ensures that courts will now often be asked to consider the audio component of expression even if it has not been broadcast by the news media. "If a picture is worth a thousand words, then a tape recording is worth a thousand transcripts."

Fitzpatrick-Smith v. *Jacobson*, [2000] O.T.C. 142, per Low J. at para. 37 (S.C.J.):

> There is ample evidence of express malice, the most vivid of which is to be found in the tape recording of the defendant's telephone messages … which both pre-date and post-date the letters … The messages … reveal a campaign to visit punishment and revenge upon the plaintiffs. The messages are abusive, profane, insulting to both Don Crawford and to the plaintiffs, and threatening. They show a pattern of escalating hysteria as the days pass and the defendant does not succeed in attracting any attention or concessions to her demands. … The voice messages contain intrinsic evidence of malice and also constitute extrinsic evidence of an improper motive in making the written allegations of racism to the executive councillors.

A defendant may avoid a finding of express malice by establishing that his defamatory statement, although vigorous or inflammatory, was a means of defense to a written or verbal attack by the plaintiff. It is a very fine line to draw in the evidence because if the court finds that the libel defendant went on the offence or attack, a finding of express malice is open to the court.

Mallett v. *Clarke* (1968), 70 D.L.R. (2d) 67, per Gould J. at 73 (B.C.S.C), approving the following passage from the judgment of Lord Oaksey in *Turner* v. *M-G-M Pictures, Ltd.*, [1950] 1 All E.R. 449 at 470–71:

> There is, it seems to me, an analogy between the criminal law of self defence and a man's right to defend himself against written or verbal attacks. In both cases, he is entitled, if he can, to defend himself effectively, and he only loses the protection of the law if he goes beyond defence and proceeds to offence. That is to say, the circumstances in which he defends himself, either by acts or words, negative the malice which the law draws from violent acts or defamatory words. If you are attacked with a deadly weapon you can defend yourself with a deadly weapon or with any other weapon which may protect your life. The law does not concern itself with niceties in such matters. If you are attacked by a prize fighter you are not bound to adhere to the Queensberry rules in your defence.

Where the plaintiff can show any example of spite or indirect motive, whether before or after the publication, he may establish his case provided that the examples given are so connected with the state of mind of the defendant as to lead to the conclusion that she was malicious at the date when the libel was published.

> *Boland v. Globe and Mail Ltd.* (1961), 29 D.L.R. (2d) 401 (Ont. C.A.), per Porter C.J.O. dissenting on question of ordering a new trial, citing with approval *Turner v. M-G-M Pictures Ltd.*, [1950] 1 All E.R. 449, per Lord Porter at 454–55.

A deliberate omission by the defendant may be evidence of express malice in certain circumstances.

> *Boland v. Globe and Mail* (1959), 17 D.L.R. (2d) 313 per Lebel J. for the Court at 317, 318 (Ont. C.A.), citing Wilfred Alan Button, *Principles of the Law of Libel and Slander*, (London: Sweet & Maxwell, 1935) p. 191:

>> The second example of express malice lay, in our opinion, in what we think was another unexplained omission from the columns of the *Globe and Mail* … On the morning of the day of the election the paper published "for the convenience of its readers in the Toronto area" a list of candidates standing in the various ridings for election in the Metropolitan area, together with the locations and telephone numbers of their respective committee rooms. The names of, and the said information concerning, the C.C.F., the Liberal and the Progressive-Conservative candidates in the Parkdale riding were given but the appellant's name and the information with respect to this committee room were omitted. Why? We should think that an omission of that kind — appearing on the morning of the day the electors were to go to the polls and following upon the paper's severe criticism of the appellant's "disgusting" conduct during his campaign needed considerable explanation before it could be found to be unintentional.

>> The learned judge considered this omission might have been deliberate on the part of the respondent (thereby implying that if it were so, it could be evidence of malice), but he held that it might also have been merely accidental, and that in any event, the incident provided no more than a mere scintilla in the required proof of malice. With the greatest respect for his view, we entirely disagree. Whether the omission was deliberate or accidental, and what the real reason for the omission was, were matters solely within the knowledge of the respondent; and it was for the jury alone to say whether that omission … amounted to proof of express malice … .

See also *Hill v. Church of Scientology of Toronto*, [1995] 2 S.C.R. 1130, per Cory J. at para. 194.

The defendant's conduct after the libel trial and during the course of appeal proceedings through to and including the Supreme Court of Canada may permit a finding of "real and persistent malice."

Hill v. Church of Scientology of Toronto, ibid. at paras. 192–94:

> [192] In this case, there was ample evidence upon which the jury could properly base their finding of aggravated damages. The existence of the file on Casey Hill under the designation "Enemy Canada" was evidence of the malicious intention of Scientology to "neutralize" him. The press conference was organized in such a manner as to ensure the widest possible dissemination of the libel. Scientology continued with the contempt proceedings although it knew its allegations were false. In its motion to remove Hill from the search warrant proceedings, it implied that he was not trustworthy and might act in those proceedings in a manner that would benefit him in his libel action. It pleaded justification or truth of its statement when it knew it to be false. It subjected Hill to a demeaning cross-examination and, in its address to the jury, depicted Hill as a manipulative actor.

> [193] It is, as well, appropriate for an appellate court to consider the post-trial actions of the defendant. It will be recalled that Scientology, immediately after the verdict of the jury, repeated the libel, thus forcing the plaintiff to seek and obtain an injunction restraining Scientology from repeating the libel. It did not withdraw its plea of justification until the hearing of the appeal. All this indicates that the award of aggravated damages was strongly supported by the subsequent actions of Scientology.

> [194] In summary, every aspect of this case demonstrates the real and persistent malice of Scientology. Their actions preceding the publication of the libel, the circumstances of its publication and their subsequent actions in relation to both the search warrant proceedings and this action amply confirm and emphasize the insidious malice of Scientology. Much was made of their apology tendered at the time of the hearing in the Court of Appeal. There is a hollow ring to that submission when it is remembered that it was not until the fifth day of oral argument before the Court of Appeal that the apology was tendered.

Scientology can gain little comfort from such a late and meaningless apology.

Pre-existing unfriendliness on the part of the defendant, or any hard things said by the defendant to and concerning the plaintiff, or any quarrel that the defendant had with the plaintiff before publication of the defamatory expression, could lead to a finding of express malice.

Green v. Miller (1901), 31 S.C.R. 177 per King J. at 184–85.

Anderson v. Smythe, [1935] 4 D.L.R. 72, per MacDonald J.A. at 76 (B.C.C.A.):

Had the respondent [plaintiff] ... entered the witness box, not only to maintain his case but also, if possible, to testify to other incidents (e.g. a private quarrel) which might account for the [defendant] appellant's action ... some basis might be laid for a finding of malice.

The Court may look at the conduct of the defendant after receiving the libel complaint, particularly where the defendant goes public again and alleges that the plaintiff does not like his criticism. "Safeways, like the politicians, have started to squeal at my criticism and are making threats against me for doing so, which is the best proof of the value of my criticism to the public who are seeing the truth and saying so."

Safeway Stores Ltd. v. Harris, [1948] 4 D.L.R. 187 per Williams C.J.K.B. at 195–96 (Man. K.B.), aff'd [1948] 4 D.L.R. 187 (Man. C.A.).

The defendant's repetition and confirmation of his previous statement, which demonstrates a continuing train of thought, may be evidence of express malice.

Lawson v. Thompson (1968), 1 D.L.R. (3d) 270, per Seaton J. (later Seaton J.A.) at 275 (B.C.S.C.), approving *Defries v. Davis* (1835), 7 Car. & P. 112, 173 E.R. 50.

Similarly, where a defendant before trial has said that he would be delighted to appear in Court and repeat in open Court the defamatory expression, but then fails to testify at trial in defence of the defamation action, the Court may be influenced to find express malice.

Lawson v. Thompson above, at 276

Where the defendant union forged a document purporting to bear the signature of the plaintiff, with contents objectionable to union members purporting to be expressed by the plaintiff, its preparation and circulation was held to reflect the express malice of the defendant toward the plaintiff and confirmed the defendant's "improper and indirect motive" for publishing the false and defamatory statements.

> *Doyle v. International Association of Machinists & Aerospace Workers, Local 1681* (1991), 110 A.R. 222 per O'Leary J. at 232–33 (Q.B.), aff'd (1992), 131 A.R. 101 (C.A.).

Decisions involving findings of malice based on animosity towards the plaintiff include:

i)   *DeMoor v. Harvey*, (1989) 24 C.C.E.L. 293 (B.C.S.C.).

The defendant union president, writing about the plaintiff business representative in relation to his resignation, wrote that he "committed a series of misdemeanours involving union funds" and that "when the evidence was brought forward he admitted the misdemeanours." After determining that these statements were not justified, and reviewing all the circumstances, Paris J. concluded that "the defendant undoubtedly felt animosity towards the plaintiff and, whether it was due to a desire to eliminate him for political reasons or simply because he was being uncooperative and obstructive, or a combination of both, it is clear that when an opportunity presented itself, she was only too happy to move against him" and that "the only reasonable explanation why the defendant used the words she did ... was to put as bad a light as possible on the actions of the plaintiff in the eyes of the membership. Her predominant motive was malice towards him." Paris J. stated at p. 304 that "[i]t may well be that the defendant actually believed, and still believes, that the plaintiff's claims for car allowance were illicit. However, that does not relieve her from liability, given the findings ... that the statement was defamatory and false and that her predominant motive was malicious."

ii) *Doyle v. International Association of Machinists & Aerospace Workers, Local 1681*, above.

O'Leary J., after finding that union magazine articles describing the plaintiff and others as "new-hire scabs," as a "mean, contemptible person," and as a scab were defamatory [at 228, para. 30], concluded that the statements were not published to communicate information of common interest or mutual concern to the members of the Union "but to promote and encourage the harassment and intimidation of the Plaintiff to punish him for his conduct in working for the Airline during the strike." "Specifically, the imputations that the Plaintiff was dishonest, lacked integrity, was incompetent in his trade, was a thief and a mean, contemptible person had nothing to do with the dissemination of information of common interest or mutual concern ... but it was part of a conscious and deliberate campaign to discredit the Plaintiff and other rehired replacement workers and thereby to punish them and to dissuade others from working as scabs in the future ... to encourage their isolation and alienation from fellow workers." (at 232)

iii) *Amalgamated Transit Union* v. *Independent Canadian Transit Union*, [1997] 5 W.W.R. 662, per Montgomery J. at para. 79 (Alta. Q.B.):

> I find that the Defendants' purpose in publishing the defamatory and false statements was not to communicate that information, but rather to undermine, harass and pressure the Plaintiffs. Their dominant motive was to injure the Plaintiffs.

iv) *Olson* v. *Runciman* (2001), 291 A.R. 195, per Hart J. at para. 18 (Q.B.):

> ... I turn now to qualified privilege. On this issue I find that the letter of December 6, 1996 from [the defendant], the President of a regulated company, to Sherritt, the Acting Director of the regulator, complaining about the conduct of a subordinate employee of the regulator, was a communication made on an occasion of qualified privilege. I also find, however, that the dominant motive of the letter was not a legitimate attempt to protect Canadian Aero's interest but rather to vent spite and ill-will against [the plaintiff] who was seen by [the defendant], if not as the enemy, then at least as consorting with the enemy.

v) *Fitzpatrick-Smith* v. *Jacobson*, [2000] O.T.C. 142, per Low J. at para. 37 (S.C.):

> ... the allegations of racism and the alleged incidents of racial comments were an invention of the defendant's mind. I am of the view that the defendant's dominant motive in writing the letters was the improper one of seeking revenge and that she did not honestly believe the truth of her allegations.

6) Improper or Indirect Purpose

There are many reported and unreported decisions which involve findings of actual malice referable to an improper purpose on the part of the defendant. Such a finding is often coupled with a reference to the defendant's lack of a positive, honest belief in the truth of the defamatory expression.

In *Schultz* v. *Porter* (1979), 26 A.R. 61 (S.C. (T.D.)), for example, the defendant delivered a letter purporting to cancel a real estate transaction to the manager of a real estate agency which employed the plaintiff, alleging deliberate and fraudulent misrepresentation by the plaintiff as the ground for the cancellation.

After concluding that the communication was not made on an occasion of privilege, Waite J. found express malice [at para. 28]:

> The plaintiff has affirmatively established actual or express malice. There can be no doubt that the statements complained of by the plaintiff were false to the knowledge of [the defendant]. I am satisfied on a consideration of all of the evidence that [the defendant] did not — indeed could not – honestly believe that the plaintiff had been guilty of misrepresentation. I am satisfied that [the defendant] was motivated by a dishonest, improper or wrong motive, being the protection of himself and his principals against the consequences of what was clearly a negligent breach of duty by the defendants to their own client Feltham [the property vendor]. The offending letter ... was a calculated attempt to extricate the vendor from a transaction that was improvident and that had been entered into in such circumstances as would have entitled the vendor to an appropriate action for damages against the defendants.

There may be instances where a defendant's dominant motive has been to obtain some private advantage, unconnected with the duty or interest which constitutes the reason for finding that the defamatory expression was published on an occasion of qualified privilege. If so, the defendant loses the benefit of the privilege even if he or she has a positive belief that what he or she expressed was true. That is because the purpose of publication was improper or indirect.

> *Horrocks v. Lowe*, [1974] 1 All E.R. 662, per Lord Diplock at 669 (H.L.), cited with approval in *Leenen v. Canadian Broadcasting Corporation* (2000), 48 O.R. (3d) 656, per Cunningham J. at para. 139 (S.C.J.), aff'd (2001), 54 O.R. (3d) 612 (C.A.), leave to appeal to S.C.C. denied, [2001] S.C.C.A. No. 432.

> *Leenen v. Canadian Broadcasting Corporation*, above, at para. 139.

Testimony by the defendant that he or she acted under a sense of duty, although not relevant or admissible to prove whether or not the occasion is privileged, may be admissible and relevant to the question of malice. Such testimony goes to the purpose of the expression.

> *Wade and Wells Co. v. Laing* (1957), 11 D.L.R. (2d) 276 per Sheppard J.A. at 282–83 (B.C.C.A.), citing *Stuart v. Bell*, [1891] 2 Q.B. 341 per Lindley L.J. at 349:

But the question still remains whether the defendant was not under a moral or social duty to make such communication. Both the defendant and Stanley say that the defendant acted under a sense of duty, but this, though important on the question of malice, is not, I think, relevant to the question whether the occasion was or was not privileged. That question does not depend on the defendant's belief, but on whether he was right or mistaken in that belief.

There may be extreme cases in which the news media engage in deception for the purpose of producing a sensational story, either to enhance reputations or to attract viewers, ratings, and ultimately revenue. However, unless the publication occurred with knowledge of untruth or reckless indifference to the truth, the desire of a publisher, broadcaster, editor, or reporter to produce a sensational story does not constitute an improper purpose amounting to express malice.

Pressler v. *Lethbridge* (2000), 86 B.C.L.R. (3d) 257, per Esson J.A. at paras. 110–11 (C.A.):

> The desire of persons employed in the media to enhance their reputations by producing interesting and lively programs is not in itself a basis for finding malice. In particular, I agree with the statement in the speech of Lord Diplock in *Horrocks* v. *Lowe, supra*, that:
>
>> Judges and juries should, however, be very slow to draw the inference that a defendant was so far actuated by improper motives as to deprive him of the privilege unless they are satisfied that he did not believe that what he said or wrote was true or that he was indifferent to its truth or falsity.

E. TIMING OF SUBMISSION CONCERNING MALICE

In *Loos* v. *Robbins* (1987), 37 D.L.R. (4th) 418, Gerwing J. for the Saskatchewan Court of Appeal approved the following passage from Sir Robert McEwen & Philip Lewis, *Gatley on Libel and Slander*, 7th ed. (London: Sweet & Maxwell, 1974) at page 344:

> 794. Time of submission. The submission that there is no evidence of malice to go to the jury is invariably made at the close of the plaintiff's case. But the judge is not bound to give his ruling then; under the present practice he has a discretion whether he will rule at the close of the plaintiff's case, or whether he will defer ruling on the matter until after he has heard the evidence for the

defendant. Indeed, he can, if he wishes, defer his ruling until the jury have given their verdict. Such a course is often convenient, for if the Court of Appeal should think that the judge's ruling was erroneous the advantage is gained that it is unnecessary to send the case back for trial before another jury. If the judge allows the case to go to the jury, and the jury return a verdict for the plaintiff, the judge is nonetheless entitled to enter judgment for the defendant if he is then of the opinion that there is no evidence of malice, or that the evidence of malice is so weak that a verdict in the plaintiff's favour would be set aside by the Court of Appeal as unreasonable.

CHAPTER SEVENTEEN:

Fair Comment

A. A CORNERSTONE OF FREE SPEECH

The defence of fair comment is a cornerstone of free speech in Canada.

In *Cherneskey* v. *Armadale Publishers Ltd.*, [1979] 1 S.C.R. 1067, all nine Justices of the Supreme Court of Canada emphasized the importance of this defence to Canadian democracy. Although Dickson J. (Spence and Estey JJ. concurring) dissented on the specific question before the Court, he agreed with the majority on the vital role of fair comment, stating at page 1096:

> ... A free and general discussion of public matters is fundamental to a democratic society. The right of persons to make public their thoughts on the conduct of public officials, in terms usually critical and often caustic, goes back to earliest times in Greece and Rome. The Roman historian, Tacitus, spoke of the happiness of times when one could think as he wished and could speak as he thought (1 Tacitus, *History*, para. 1). Citizens, as decision-makers, cannot be expected to exercise wise and informed judgment unless they are exposed to the widest variety of ideas, from diverse and antagonistic sources. Full disclosure exposes, and protects against, false doctrine.

There were two majority judgments in *Cherneskey*; one written by Martland J. (Chief Justice Laskin and Beetz J. concurring) and the other written by Ritchie J. (Chief Justice Laskin and Pigeon and Pratte JJ. concurring). Both drew on English common law for their description of the importance of this defence. Martland J., quoting R.F.U. Heuston, *Salmon on the Law of Torts*, 17th ed. (London: Sweet & Maxwell, 1977) at 180, stated at page 1072:

> A fair comment on a matter which is of public interest or is submitted to public criticism is not actionable. This right is one of the aspects of the fundamental principle of freedom of expression, and the courts are zealous to

preserve it unimpaired. It must not be whittled down by legal refinements. The jury are the guardians of the freedom of public comment as well as of private character. It is only on the strongest grounds that a court will set aside a verdict for a defendant when fair comment is pleaded.

Ritchie J. adopted the following passage from the judgment of Lord Denning in *Slim* v. *Daily Telegraph Ltd.*, [1968] 1 All E.R. 497 at 503 (H.L.) [at S.C.R. 1086]:

> ... [T]he right of fair comment is one of the essential elements which go to make up our freedom of speech. We must ever maintain this right intact. It must not be whittled down by legal refinements. When a citizen is troubled by things going wrong, he should be free to "write to the newspaper": and the newspaper should be free to publish his letter. It is often the only way to get things put right. The matter must of course, be of public interest. The writer must get his facts right: and he must honestly state his real opinion. But that being done, both he and the newspaper should be clear of any liability. They should not be deterred by fear of libel actions.

Similar views about the importance of fair comment for freedom of expression have been expressed by every other appellate and trial court in Canada.

On the Atlantic coast, MacKeigan C.J.N.S., writing the judgment of the Nova Scotia Court of Appeal in *Barltrop* v. *Canadian Broadcasting Corp.* (1978), 86 D.L.R. (3d) 61 (N.S.S.C. (A.D.)), stressed the fundamental importance of this defence at page 73:

> The defence of fair comment on matters of public interest has been rightly termed "a basic safeguard against irresponsible political power" and "one of the foundations supporting our standards of personal liberty": Fleming on the Law of Torts, 4th ed. (1971), p. 511.

On the other side of the country, in British Columbia, Southin J.A. caught the essence of the defence in her dissent in *Baumann* v. *Turner* (1993), 105 D.L.R. (4th) 37 at page 52 (B.C.C.A.):

> The defence of fair comment provides wide scope for knock down, no holds barred, public debate. It does require, however, that he who relies upon it get his facts straight, and state his facts to his readers or listeners. Having done so, he can heap invective, assuming he has some command of the language, upon his opponent.

B. MATERIAL ELEMENTS OF THE DEFENCE

The defence of fair comment is available if the defamatory expression is:

- made honestly and fairly;
- without malice;
- on true facts (or facts stated on a privileged occasion) expressed or implied in the defamatory expression; and
- on a matter of public interest.

> *Vander Zalm* v. *Times Publishers* (1980) 109 D.L.R. (3d) 531, per Nemetz, C.J.B.C. at 535–36 (B.C.C.A.).

> *Ross* v. *New Brunswick Teachers' Association* (2001), 201 D.L.R. (4th) 75 at para. 63 (N.B.C.A.).

The burden is on the defendant to prove that the expression is:

- recognizable by the ordinary reasonable person as comment;
- on a matter of public interest;
- based upon facts that are true (or facts stated on a privileged occasion); and
- made honestly and fairly.

> *Cherneskey* v. *Armadale Publishers Ltd.*, [1979] 1 S.C.R. 1067 at 1099–1100, per Dickson J. citing Colin Duncan & Brian Neill, *Defamation* (London, Butterworths, 1978) at 62, para. 12.02.

> *Barltrop* v. *Canadian Broadcasting Corp*, above, at 73–75.

> *Jones* v. *Bennett*, [1969] S.C.R. 277 at 285, rev'g (1967), 66 D.L.R. (2d) 497 (B.C.C.A), and adopting the reasons of the trial judge at (1967), 59 W.W.R. 449.

The defence of fair comment will be defeated if the plaintiff satisfies the burden of proof, which rests on the plaintiff, of establishing on a balance of probabilities that the defendant was guilty of express malice in publishing the comment.

> *Cherneskey* v. *Armadale Publishers Ltd.*, above, at 1080–81 .

> *Myers* v. *Canadian Broadcasting Corp.* (1999), 47 C.C.L.T. (2d) 272 at 300, citing Patrick Milmo & W.V.H. Rogers, *Gatley on Libel and Slander*, 9th ed. (London: Sweet & Maxwell, 1998) at para. 12.21.

C. VERACITY OF COMMENT IS IRRELEVANT

The defence of fair comment is distinct from a plea of justification that the libel is true. The defendant who raises fair comment does not have the burden of proving that the comment is true.

> *Ross* v. *New Brunswick Teachers' Association* (2001), above at para. 50, citing *Sutherland* v. *Stopes*, [1925] A.C. 47,where Viscount Finlay states at 62 (H.L. Eng.):
>
> > It is clear that the truth of a libel affords a complete answer to civil proceedings. This defence is raised by plea of justification on the grounds that the libel is true not only in its allegations of fact but also in any comments made therein.
> >
> > The defence of fair comment on matters of public interest is totally different. The defendant who raises this defence does not take upon himself the burden of showing that the comments are true. If the facts are truly stated with regard to a matter of public interest, the defendant will succeed in his defence to an action of libel if the jury are satisfied that the comments are fairly and honestly made. To raise this defence there must, of course, be a basis of fact on which the comment is made.

D. THE DISTINCTION BETWEEN A COMMENT AND A STATEMENT OF FACT

The defendant has the onus of establishing, on a balance of probabilities, that the impugned expression is a comment. An assertion of fact can never be defended as fair comment.

> *Manitoba Free Press Co.* v. *Martin* (1892), 21 S.C.R. 518 at 528.

The expression must be recognizable to the ordinary reasonable person as a comment upon true facts and not as a bare statement of fact. The reader, viewer, or listener is then in a position to arrive at her own conclusion as to whether the defamatory expression is founded or unfounded.

> *Vander Zalm* v. *Times Publishers Ltd.* (1980), 18 B.C.L.R. 210 (C.A.).

> *Baxter* v. *Canadian Broadcasting Corporation and Malling* (1979), 28 N.B.R. (2d) 114 at 160 (Q.B. (T.D.)).

> *Ross* v. *New Brunswick Teachers' Association*, above, at para. 63.

The distinction between a statement of fact and a comment is explained in *Barltrop* v. *Canadian Broadcasting Corp.* (1978), 86 D.L.R. (3d) 61 (N.S.S.C. (A.D.)), leave to appeal to S.C.C denied (1978), 23 N.R. 447n, where MacKeigan C.J.N.S., speaking for a unanimous panel of the Nova Scotia Supreme Court Appeal Division, said at pages 73–74:

> To be comment, fair or unfair, a statement must be a statement of opinion and not a statement of fact. It must be an expression of opinion about facts which must have been presented to the readers or listeners, or be well known to them, and which must themselves be substantially true. Such comment, with such a base, may then be excused even though it is defamatory, if it was a fair and honest expression of opinion on a matter of public interest: see Fleming, pp. 512–13; *Gatley, supra,* paras. 711–14.
>
> The vital distinction [between comment and fact] is pointed up by Ferguson J., in *Myerson* v. *Smith's Weekly Publishing Co., Ltd.* (1923), 24 S.R. (N.S.W.) 20 at p. 26, quoting Fleming [on the Law of Torts, 4th ed. (1971)] at p. 512:

> > To say that a man's conduct was dishonourable is not comment, it is a statement of fact. To say that he did certain specific things and thus his conduct was dishonourable is a statement of fact coupled with a comment.

Gatley, para 713, quotes the following example, referring to and quoting from *Popham* v. *Pickburn* (1862), 7 H. & N. 891, 158 E.R. 730:

> Thus where the defendant published in his newspaper a report of a medical officer of health, which asserted that the plaintiff, a chemist and druggist, had given false medical certificates, and advised that he should be prosecuted for forgery, it was held that such report could not be justified as fair comment. It was contended that this libel might be justified as a matter of public discussion on a subject of public interest. The answer is this: This is not discussion or comment. It is a statement of fact. To charge a man incorrectly with a disgraceful act is very different from commenting on a fact relating to him truly stated — there, the writer may, by his opinion, libel himself rather than the subject of his remarks.

Applying the distinction expressed in *Barltrop, ibid.:* to say of an individual that she is a thief would be a defamatory statement of fact. To say of an individual that she is (i) a thief because (ii) she found a dollar lying on the sidewalk, (iii) put it in her pocket, and (iv) later spent it without reporting it to the police, would be a comment (i) coupled with statements of fact (ii), (iii), and (iv).

The defence of fair comment is not limited to opinions per se but can also apply to inferences of fact drawn by the commentator. In such circumstances, the reader, listener, or viewer is in a position to agree or disagree with the commentator's conclusions or deductions. To illustrate: whether or not a person has been negligent is a question of fact. In order to arrive at a conclusion that a person was negligent, one must draw inferences from other facts relating to his conduct. For example, in the case of a motor vehicle collision, the facts relevant to drawing an inference of fact that the individual was negligent may include:

- the speed at which the person was operating his vehicle,
- weather conditions,
- road surface conditions,
- the amount of traffic on the highway,
- visibility,
- the conduct of the other driver.

To publish a simple assertion that A was negligent is probably a statement of fact. To publish the assertion that A was negligent *because* ... and then go on to list all the objective facts from which negligence is to be inferred may be regarded as comment for the purposes of this defence.

> *Hodgson v. Canadian Newspapers Co.* (1998), 39 O.R. (3d) 235, per Lane J. at 385 (Gen. Div.), quoting *O'Brien v. Marquis of Salisbury* (1889), 6 T.L.R. 133 at 137 (Q.B.):
>
> > Comment may sometimes consist in the statement of fact, and may be held to be comment if the fact so stated appears to be a deduction or conclusion come to by the speaker from the facts stated or referred to by him, or in the common knowledge of the person speaking and those to whom the words are addressed and from which his conclusions can reasonably be inferred.
>
> *Ross v. New Brunswick Teachers' Association* (2001), 201 D.L.R. (4th) 75 per Daigle C.J.N.B. at para. 56 (N.B.C.A.)
>
> *Watson v. Southam Inc. (c.o.b. Hamilton Spectator)* (1998), 52 O.T.C. 1 at para. 171 (Gen. Div.), varied on other grounds (2000) 189 D.L.R. (4th) 695 (Ont. C.A.).
>
> *Bird v. York Condominium Corp. No. 340*, [2002] O.J. No. 1993 at para. 45 (S.C.J.).

Peckham v. *Mount Pearl (City)*, (1994) 122 Nfld. & P.E.I.R. 142 at paras. 35, 36 (Nfld. S.C. (T.D.)).

The test for determining whether expression is a comment or a statement of fact is objective. What is comment and what is fact must be determined from the perspective of a reasonable viewer, listener, or reader. Whether or not the defendant subjectively intended the expression to be a comment is irrelevant to the determination of this specific issue.

Ross v. *New Brunswick Teachers' Association*, above, at para. 62.

Re International Assn. of Bridge, Structural and Ornamental and Reinforcing Iron-workers (Local 97) and Campbell (1997), 40 B.C.L.R. (3d) 1 (S.C.).

Comment must appear as comment. It must not be so mixed up with statements of fact that the reader or listener is unable to distinguish between the reported facts and the comment. If that occurs, the defence of fair comment will not be available.

Leenen v. *Canadian Broadcasting Corp.* (2000), 48 O.R. (3d) 656 at 699–700, per Cunningham J., citing Peter F. Carter-Ruck, *Carter-Ruck on Libel and Slander*, 5th ed. (London: Butterworths, 1997) at 109, aff'd (2001), 54 O.R. (3d) 612 (C.A.), leave to appeal to S.C.C. denied, [2001] S.C.C.A. No. 432.

Jones v. *Bennett*, [1969] S.C.R. 277 at 285 adopting the reasons of the trial judge for rejecting this defence at (1967) 59 W.W.R. 449, where Ruttan J. stated at page 459 that:

> in the present case, if [the defendant's] remarks contain any element of comment, that comment is so bound up in false statements of fact that his allegations are essentially ones of fact and he cannot rely on the defence of fair comment.

Mitchell v. *Victoria Daily Times (No. 3)*, [1944] 1 W.W.R. 400, 60 B.C.R. 39 (S.C) where Bird J. complained at 406:

> The article, as I have said before, is a combination of comment and statements of fact, and I have experienced difficulty in determining which was intended as comment and which as statement of fact. I have no doubt that the reasonable man to whom reference is constantly made in actions of this nature would have as great difficulty. The defendant must take the consequences of the editor's failure to so frame the article as to show clearly what was intended as comment and what as statement of fact.

The difference between a comment and a statement of fact may be subtle. Opinions are often expressed more as facts than as personal views.

> *Myers* v. *Canadian Broadcasting Corporation* (1999), 47 C.C.L.T. (2d) 272, per Bellamy J. at 300, para. 89 (Ont. S.C.J.), aff'd (2001), 54 O.R. (3d) 626 (C.A.), leave to appeal to S.C.C. denied, [2001] S.C.C.A. 433:
>
> > The key lies in determining whether a defamatory statement or broadcast is presented as an objective fact which requires no support, or whether it is presented as a comment or opinion for which the supporting facts are included. Indeed, the differences can be a subtle one, since opinions are often expressed more as facts than as personal views. Regardless of how it is expressed, in order for the defence of fair comment to apply, the opinion must still be recognizable to the reasonable viewer as an opinion. To do this, the opinion must be supported by enough true facts for the viewer to see how the commentator could have reached this conclusion.

Cartoons, by their very nature, typically represent statements of opinion rather than statements of fact. They rely on devices of allegory, caricature, and analogy to convey subjective expressions of opinion. Accordingly, if they convey a defamatory meaning, a cartoon is more likely to be regarded by the reasonable viewer or reader as comment than as a statement of fact.

> *Ross* v. *New Brunswick Teachers' Association*, above, at paras. 63–66.

> *Vander Zalm* v. *Times Publishers* (1980), 109 D.L.R. (3d) 531 per Nemetz C.J.B.C. 538 (B.C.C.A.).

It has been held that the question whether the expression complained of is comment or a statement of fact is a question of construction for the judge. If, in the opinion of the judge, there is no reasonable doubt, the judge must direct the jury accordingly. However, if in the view of the judge there is reasonable doubt as to whether the words are statements of fact or expressions of opinion, the court must leave it to the jury to decide.

> *Telnikoff* v. *Matusevitch*, [1991] 3 W.L.R. 952, per Lord Kinkel at 956 (H.L.), citing F.M. Walter, *Halsbury's Laws of England*, 4th ed. (London: Butterworths, 1979) vol. 28, para. 228.

> *Scott* v. *Fulton* (2000), 73 B.C.L.R. (3d) 392, per Braidwood J.A. at 397 (C.A.) approving *Telnikoff*, *ibid.*

In reaching a determination whether defamatory expression is comment or fact, the court must have regard to the entire publication or broadcast. In the case of an audiotape or videotape, the court must view and listen to the tape before determining whether the expression is comment or fact.

Scott v. Fulton (2000), above, at 397, approving the course followed by Tallis J. in *England v. Canadian Broadcasting Corp.*, [1979] 3 W.W.R. 193 (N.W.T.S.C.) where at 210 Tallis J. noted:

> ... during the course of the trial I was able to view the program in its entirety. In my opinion an actual viewing of the program gives much more colour and meaning to the words used than if we were merely to read the transcript.

The amount of factual information accompanying defamatory expression may also be an important factor in determining whether it should be characterized as a comment or as a statement of fact. The absence of a detailed factual underpinning for a statement may make the statement less susceptible to characterization as comment.

Myers v. Canadian Broadcasting Corporation, above.

Hodgson v. Canadian Newspapers Co. (1998), 39 O.R. (3d) 235, per Lane J. at 385–86 (Gen.Div.), aff'd (2000), 189 D.L.R. (4th) 241 (C.A.), leave to appeal to S.C.C. denied, [2000] S.C.C.A. 465.

Murphy v. LaMarsh (1970), 18 D.L.R. (3d) 208 at 209–10 (B.C.C.A.), leave to appeal to S.C.C. denied, [1971] S.C.R. ix.

Barltrop v. Canadian Broadcasting Corporation (1978), 86 D.L.R. (3d) 61 (N.S.S.C. (A.D.)), leave to appeal to S.C.C denied (1978), 23 N.R. 447n.

McDonald's Corporation v. Steel, [1999] E.W.J. No. 2173 at para. 591 (C.A.), where Lord Justice Pill spoke for the Court of Appeal as follows:

> Some statements are obviously statements of fact: some are obviously capable only of being expressions of opinion amounting to comment. Others are capable of being either statements of fact or comment depending on their context. Bare statements, which are not obviously capable only of being expressions of opinion, will usually be statements of fact. The same such statements may be comment, if there are also facts stated or indicated upon which the statements are comment. The defence will fail if the facts upon which the statements are comment are not shown to be sufficiently true to support the comment as objectively fair. There may be difficulties if this requirement is applied formalistically to facts which may themselves contain elements of evaluation. On the other hand, a statement which might be regarded as comment

may be so intermingled with statements of fact that it must be regarded as a statement of fact for want of a sufficient separate identity.

A defamatory publication might more likely be regarded as a comment if it clearly is responsive to a public debate initiated by the plaintiff.

Pound v. Scott (1973), 37 D.L.R. (3d) 439 (B.C.S.C.).

E. COMMENT MUST BE BASED ON TRUE FACTS

The comment must be based on true facts, either stated in the communication or generally known.

Hodgson v. Canadian Newspapers Co. (1998), 39 O.R. (3d) 235 at 385, 391 (Gen. Div.), (2000), 49 O.R. (3d) 161, 189 D.L.R. (4th) 241 (C.A.), leave to appeal to S.C.C. denied, [2000] S.C.C.A. 465.

It is generally accepted that there must therefore be a sufficient substratum of fact to warrant the comment in the sense that on those facts a fair-minded person might honestly hold that opinion.

Ross v. New Brunswick Teachers' Association (2001), 201 D.L.R. (4th) 75 at para. 69 (N.B.C.A.) .

Kemsley v. Foot, [1952] A.C. 345 per Lord Porter at 356, 358 (H.L.).

At common law, the onus is on the defendant to prove, on a balance of probabilities, the truth of all the facts published with the comment. If a defamatory publication misstates the facts, the defence of fair comment will not be available.

Hodgson v. Canadian Newspapers Co., above.

Olsen v. Abbotsford, Clearbrook Free Press Ltd., [1981] B.C.J. No. 551 at paras. 8, 13–19, 28–29 (B.C.C.A.).

Thomas v. Canadian Broadcasting Corporation and Sanders, [1981] 4 W.W.R. 289 at 331 (N.W.T.S.C.).

Not all the facts need be published with the comment in order for a fair comment defence to apply. In a cartoon, it is often not practical to set out all the facts on which the cartoonist relies in support of the comment made in the cartoon. Facts that are in the public arena, that have gained public notoriety so as to become matters of common knowledge, do not have to be stated so long as they are clearly identified.

Ross v. New Brunswick Teachers' Association, above at para. 65.

The facts may be implied in the impugned publication and specified as particulars in the statement of defence. If the commentator sets out the facts with the published comment, he may rely on the defence of fair comment only if he proves every fact to be true. On the other hand, it seems that if the defendant merely implies the facts in the comment and gives the facts in the form of particulars in the statement of defence, he need to establish only the truth of one of the facts pleaded.

Vander Zalm v. Times Publishers Ltd. (1980), 109 D.L.R. (3d) 531 (B.C.C.A.).

Holt v. Sun Publishing Co. Ltd. (1979), 100 D.L.R. (3d) 447 (B.C.C.A.).

Olsen v. Abbotsford, Clearbrook Free Press Ltd., [1981] B.C.J. No. 551 per Craig J.A. at paras. 28–29 (B.C.C.A):

> ¶28 The defence of fair comment too must be distinguished from the defence of justification. *Kemsley v. Foot* (1952) A.C. 345 held that if a commentator sets out the facts in his comments and relies on the defence of fair comment he must prove every fact to be true. On the other hand, if he merely implies a fact, or facts, in the comment and later specifies the facts in the form of particulars he need establish proof of only one of these facts. In referring to this case, *Duncan and Neill on Defamation* at page 64 state:
>
> > If the facts on which the comment is based are stated by the commentator the general rule of common law is that all those facts must be proved to be true. "In a case where the facts are fully set out in the alleged libel, each fact must be justified and if the defendant fails to justify one, even if it be comparatively unimportant, he fails in his defence."
>
> ¶29 Here, the Judge said that he found the facts were "substantially" true. That word bothers me. My brother presiding has given his views as to the Judge's meaning. I think the word in this context is susceptible of the meaning that if nine out of ten facts are true that is sufficient. This, I think, is not the common law.

The common law relating to proof of the substratum of facts has been altered by statute in Ontario and Nova Scotia. In Ontario, the *Libel and Slander Act*, R.S.O. 1990, c. 1-12, s. 23 states:

> In an action for libel or slander for words consisting partly of allegations of fact and partly of expression of opinion, a defence of fair comment shall not fail by reason only that the truth of every allegation of fact is not proved if the

expression of opinion is fair comment having regard to such of the facts alleged or referred to in the words complained of as are proved.

A virtually identical provision is found in section 10 of the *Defamation Act*, R.S.N.S. 1989, c. 122.

The Law Reform Commission of British Columbia has recommended the abolition of the common law rule requiring the strict proof of the accuracy of all facts published by the defendant as the basis for the comment. This recommendation has not been implemented by the Legislature of British Columbia.

British Columbia Law Reform Commission, *Report on Defamation* (1985), at 51.

If the facts are not presented to the readers together with the defamatory expression, they must be well known to the readers or the defence fails.

Barltrop v. Canadian Broadcasting Corp. (1978), 86 D.L.R. (3d) 61 at 73 (N.S.S.C. (A.D.)), leave to appeal to S.C.C. denied (1978), 23 N.R. 447n.

The importance of the rule requiring the facts to be true is illustrated in *Holt v. Sun Publishing Co. Ltd.*, above, where Aikins J.A. held that an editorial did not enjoy a fair comment defence, stating at page 454:

The true facts were not stated with the result that the ordinary reader's understanding of what Mrs. Holt had been doing would be as I have set it out earlier in these reasons and be inaccurate. Thus, the ordinary reader, having an inaccurate factual base upon which to assess the virtue of the editorial opinion, would probably conclude that the imputation in the opinion that Mrs. Holt had, in the words of the trial judge, "disregarded and neglected her duties as a member of Parliament and as a member of the parliamentary subcommittee ... whilst in California at the public expense and engaged in improper activities for her own private purposes," was justified by fact. With true facts, the ordinary reader might well have concluded otherwise.

It has been held that comment cannot be fair if it is based on facts which are distorted or invented.

Leenen v. Canadian Broadcasting Corporation (2000), 48 O.R. (3d) 656 at 701–2 (S.C.J.), aff'd (2001), 54 O.R. (3d) 612 at 618 (C.A.), leave to appeal to S.C.C. denied, [2001] S.C.C.A. No. 432.

Myers v. Canadian Broadcasting Corporation (1999), 47 C.C.L.T. (2d) 272 (Ont. S.C.J.), aff'd (2001), 54 O.R. (3d) 626 (C.A.), leave to appeal to S.C.C denied, [2001] S.C.C.A. No. 433.

England v. *Canadian Broadcasting Corporation*, [1979] 3 W.W.R. 193 (N.W.T.S.C.).

Amalgamated Transit Union v. *Independent Canadian Transit Union*, [1997] 5 W.W.R. 662 (Alta. Q.B.).

Comment may be also be held to be unfair if the broadcaster defendant omits key information, thereby creating a slanted program, and in consequence much of what is presented is false. This type of selectivity may lead a court to conclude that a defendant never intended there to be fairness.

Leenen v. *Canadian Broadcasting Corporation*, above, per Cunningham J. at 48 O.R. (3d) 703, specifically approved the following passage from the judgment of Disbery J. in *Thomas* v. *Canadian Broadcasting Corporation and Sanders*, [1981] 4 W.W.R. 289 (N.W.T.S.C.), at 338:

> To only give the public a look at the side of the coin supportive of their comments and opinions and not show the facts to the contrary on the other side of the coin is to deal in half truths, and comments made in this way are neither fair nor made in good faith.

There must be a sufficient basis of truth in the facts to warrant the comment. Hence truth is material not to justify such allegations of fact as are defamatory (that being the function of the separate defence of justification), but as one step in establishing that the comment itself is fair.

Amalgamated Transit Union v. *Independent Canadian Transit Union*, above.

A rumour is not a fact for the purpose of the defence of fair comment.

Pressler v. *Lethbridge* (2000), 86 B.C.L.R. (3d) 257, per Southin J.A. at 298, para. 76 (C.A.):

> If a rumour is not true, it cannot protect him who publishes it and comments on its implications from an action for defamation.

Unlike the plea of justification, it is clear that the defendant who pleads fair comment cannot rely on facts which occurred after the publication of the defamatory expression.

Cohen v. *Daily Telegraph*, [1968] 2 All E.R. 407 at 409 (C.A.).

1) The Exception: Privilege

There is a well-recognized exception to the rule that the defence of fair comment is only available if the comment is based on accurate facts. This exception arises where the facts were stated on a privileged occasion, such as a statement in Parliament, or testimony in court, or proceedings at a public meeting.

British Columbia Law Reform Commission, *Report on Defamation*, (1985), p. 50, citing *Gatley*, para. 719; *Duncan & Neill*, para. 12.07.

London Artists Ltd. v. *Littler*, [1969] 2 Q.B. 375 at 395 (C.A.), per Edmund Davies L.J.

Magena v. *Wright*, [1909] 2 K.B. 958 (K.B.).

Thore v. *Mudry*, [1999] B.C.J. No. 1693 at para. 14 (S.C.).

Ager v. *Canjex Publishing Ltd. (c.o.b. Canada Stockwatch)*, 2003 BCSC 891, per Shaw J. at paras. 55–56, citing *Grech* v. *Odham's Press Ltd.*, [1958] 2 Q.B. 275 at 285 (C.A.) and *Brent Walker Group* v. *Time Out Ltd.*, [1991] 2 All E.R. 753 at 780 (C.A.).

If facts are incorrectly asserted on a privileged occasion, such as court proceedings, and if the commentator relies on these alleged but mistaken facts, there will be no liability, even though the facts are inaccurate. The only qualification in such a circumstance is that the comment be a fair one.

Taylor-Wright v. *CHBC-TV, a Division of WIC Television Ltd.*, [1999] B.C.J. No. 334 at para. 38 (S.C.), aff'd (2000), 194 D.L.R. (4th) 621 (B.C.C.A.), citing *Grech* v. *Odhams Press*, [1958] 2 Q.B. 275 (C.A.), *Brent Walker Group* v. *Time Out Ltd.*, [1991] 2 All E.R. 753 (C.A.).

The fairness of the comment requires the commentator to base the comment on a fair and accurate account of the privileged occasion. *Ager* v. *Canjex Publishing Ltd. (c.o.b. Canada Stockwatch)*, above, at paragraphs 58–59, citing *Brent Walker*, above, *Patterson* v. *Edmonton Bulletin Co. Ltd.* (1908), 1 Alta. L.R. 477 (S.C.), and *Sims* v. *Hickey* (1988), 71 Nfld. & P.E.I.R. 298 (Nfld. S.C.T.D.).

F. IMPUTATIONS OF CORRUPT OR DISHONOURABLE MOTIVES

There is authority for the proposition that to qualify as fair comment, the expression must not contain imputations of corrupt or dishonourable motives on the part of the person whose conduct is criticized unless such imputations are warranted by the facts.

Vogel v. *Canadian Broadcasting Corporation*, [1982] 3 W.W.R. 97, per Esson J. at 173 (S.C.).

If there is nothing left to justify the imputation that the plaintiff acted from improper motives after the false and misleading facts are stripped away, the defence of fair comment will not be available.

Vogel v. *Canadian Broadcasting Corporation*, above, at 173.

Masters v. *Fox*, (1978), 85 D.L.R. (3d) 64 (B.C.S.C.), citing Sir Robert McEwen & Philip Lewis, *Gatley on Libel and Slander*, 7th ed. (London: Sweet & Maxwell, 1974), para. 725.

In *Hodgson* v. *Canadian Newspapers Co.* (1998), 39 O.R. (3d) 235 at 390–91 (Gen. Div.), the trial judge, Lane J., discussed the special rule relating to imputations of dishonourable or corrupt motives on the part of the plaintiff and stated:

> ... it is clear that there is considerable authority for its existence, and [the rule] appears to me to be the law. An example is the comment by Esson J. in *Vogel* v. *Canadian Broadcasting Corp.*, [1982] 3 W.W.R. 97 at page 173:
>
>> To be fair, comment must be based on facts truly stated, and must not contain imputations of corrupt or dishonourable motives on the person whose conduct is criticized, save insofar as such imputations are warranted by the facts.
>
> It is not necessary for me to explore the matter further than I have, because in either case the defence depends on the facts having been truly stated, which did not happen here. It is enough for me to say that if there is such an added requirement, the defendants did not meet it, as the imputations of the base motive of making a gift of public money to his friend were not well founded and the articles were otherwise unfair in many ways particularized at length in these reasons.

The Court of Appeal in *Hodgson* did not consider issues relating to the imputation of corrupt or dishonourable motives in view of its conclusion that the trial judge's finding of malice, which the Court of Appeal affirmed, was fatal to the defence of fair comment.

189 D.L.R. (4th) 241 at 260 (Ont. C.A.), leave to appeal to S.C.C. denied, [2000] S.C.C.A. 465.

Cunningham J., the trial judge in *Leenen*, referred with apparent approval to the above-quoted passage in the judgment of Esson J. in *Vogel* v. *Canadian Broadcasting Corporation* concerning imputations of corrupt or dishonourable motives.

Leenen v. Canadian Broadcasting Corporation (2000), 48 O.R. (3d) 656 at 701 (S.C.J.).

The Court of Appeal in *Leenen* quoted from that portion of the trial judgment in which *Vogel* is mentioned by Cunningham J. but made no specific observations about the fair comment defence aside from noting that there was ample evidence to support the trial judge's conclusion that there was malice.

(2001), 54 O.R. (3d) 612 at 618–19, paras. 15–17 (C.A.), leave to appeal to S.C.C. denied, [2001] S.C.C.A. No. 432.

The Law Reform Commission of British Columbia recommended that the rule regarding allegations of corrupt or dishonourable motives should be abolished by including in a new defamation act the following section: "The defence of fair comment in an action for defamation shall not be limited or otherwise affected by reason only of the fact that dishonourable, corrupt, base or sordid motives have been attributed to the plaintiff." In arriving at this recommendation, the Law Reform Commission noted that the status of the rule had been doubted and the nature of this supposed exception from the defence of fair comment was ambiguous.

British Columbia Law Reform Commission, *Report on Defamation*, (1985), at 49–50.

Similarly, Patrick Milmo & W.V.H. Rogers *Gatley on Libel and Slander*, 9th ed. (London: Sweet & Maxwell, 1998), state at paragraph 12.26 that:

… the defence of fair comment is in any event complex and difficult to explain to a jury and a special rule for these cases will only increase this difficulty. On balance, therefore, it is thought that there should be no special rule for imputations of corrupt or dishonourable motives.

G. COMMENT MUST BE HONEST AND FAIR

The onus is on the defendant to prove honesty and fairness.

The weight of authority suggests that this element of the fair comment defence requires that the defendant satisfy both a subjective and an objective test:

i)   subjective honesty of belief in the defamatory comment; and

ii)   objective fairness in the sense that the comment is one which a person could honestly make on the basis of all the facts known to the defendant.

Hodgson v. *Canadian Newspapers Co.*, above, at 385, 389–90.

Cherneskey v. *Armadale Publishers Ltd.*, [1979] 1 S.C.R. 1067 at 1099–1100, per Dickson J., citing Colin Duncan & Brian Neill, *Defamation* (London: Butterworths, 1978) at 62, para. 12.02.

Myers v. *Canadian Broadcasting Corporation* (1999) 47 C.C.L.T. (2d) 272 at 303–4 (Ont. H.C.J.), aff'd (2001), 54 O.R. (3d) 626 (C.A.), leave to appeal to S.C.C. denied, [2001] S.C.C.A. No. 433,

Leenen v. *Canadian Broadcasting Corporation* (2000), 48 O.R. (3d) 656 at 701–4 (S.C.J.), aff'd (2001), 54 O.R. (3d) 612 (C.A.), leave to appeal to S.C.C. denied, [2001] S.C.C.A. No. 432.

In *Myers* v. *Canadian Broadcasting Corporation*, above, at 47 C.C.L.T. (2d) pages 303–4, Bellamy J. framed the objective test in the following terms:

> Is the comment one which a fair-minded person could honestly make on the facts proved?
>
> This final step in making out the defence requires that a person be able to honestly come to the defamatory conclusion, after looking at all the proved facts. It is not enough that one true fact may support the defamation. Looking at all the proved facts, the conclusion must fall within the realm of an honest possibility. It is at this point that one examines selectivity in reporting, since all the facts, whether or not they were included in the broadcast, become relevant.

In the result, Bellamy J. concluded in *Myers* that no fair-minded person, nor indeed any reasonable person, could have come to hold the views about the plaintiff which were conveyed in the television broadcast at issue, given all the facts (reported and unreported) available to the defendants.

It is settled law that the comment must be fair in that it must represent an honest expression of the real view of the person making the comment.

Vander Zalm v. *Times Publishers Ltd.* (1980), 109 D.L.R. (3d) 531 (B.C.C.A.).

Ross v. *New Brunswick Teachers' Association* (2001), 201 D.L.R. (4th) 75 at para. 75 (N.B.C.A.).

The comment need not be fair, in the sense of being reasonable by objective standards, as long as it was made honestly and without improper motives.

Sara's Pyrohy Hut v. *Brooker*, [1992] 1 W.W.R. 556, aff'd [1993] 3 W.W.R. 662 (Alta. C.A.).

Further, the comment need not be temperate. The opinions expressed can be couched in a language vividly reflecting a writer's emotions no matter how caustic, acerbic, or even extravagant and far-fetched the comments may be. Severity in the use of denunciatory language is not enough to vitiate the defence of fair comment.

> Re International Assn. of Bridge, Structural and Ornamental and Reinforcing Iron-workers (Local 97) and Campbell (1997), 40 B.C.L.R. (3d) 1 at 10–11 (S.C.).

A state of mind does not amount to a belief in the truth of the defamatory comment if the defendant simply hopes that the allegations will turn out to be true and considers that the benefits of publishing the expression are worth the risk of being proved wrong.

> Vogel v. Canadian Broadcasting Corporation, [1982] 3 W.W.R. 97, per Esson J. at 174 (B.C.S.C.).

In the case of a corporate defendant, the court may determine that the state of mind of one of the individual defendants is the mind of the corporate defendant.

> Vogel v. C.B.C., ibid.

There is some authority for the proposition that the latitude given to politically driven comment may be particularly broad.

> Boland v. Globe and Mail, [1961] O.R. 712 (C.A.), discussed in Re International Assn. of Bridge, Structural and Ornamental and Reinforcing Ironworkers (Local 97) and Campbell, above, at 11 per Macdonald J.:
>
>> … I have some sympathy with that argument insofar as it relates to otherwise defamatory statements directed toward a government, a political party or its leader, a minister of a government, or even a candidate in an election.

The defendant's purported honest belief in the defamatory expression may be so groundless that a court will find the defendant could not and did not honestly believe the expression to be true.

> Amalgamated Transit Union v. Independent Canadian Transit Union, [1997] 5 W.W.R. 662 at para. 88 (Alta. Q.B.).

In certain circumstances, a defendant may not be able to assert an honest belief in opinions expressed in a defamatory communication if that position is incompatible with a published clarification or correction.

Bains v. *Indo-Canadian Times Inc.* (1995), 38 C.P.C. (3d) 53 per Donald J.A. at paras. 25–26 (B.C.C.A.):

> ¶ 25 Turning to the ingredient of honest belief, I do not think that the defendant can assert that it held an honest belief in the opinions expressed in the letter given the "correction" it published on 3 August 1990. The correction stated in part:
>
> > That letter has no connection with Malkit Singh Bains. Readers are requested to note the above correction.
>
> ¶26 Having represented to the world that the letter did not refer to the plaintiff, the defendant cannot later claim to have had an honest belief that the opinions expressed in the letter regarding the plaintiff were true.

A determination of whether the comment represents the real views of the defendant involves an inquiry into the defendant's state of mind at the time of publication of the libel. It is difficult to determine the state of a person's mind at a particular time but it is capable of proof like other matters of fact.

Jerome v. *Anderson*, [1964] S.C.R. 291.

It is obvious that a court does not need to accept at face value a defendant's evidence that she had an honest belief in the defamatory comment. It is submitted that as in the case of other evidence, the court may subject the defendant's testimony concerning an honest belief in defamatory expression to an examination of its consistency with the probabilities that surround the currently existing conditions.

Faryna v. *Chorny*, [1952] 2 D.L.R. 354, per O'Halloran J.A. at 357 (B.C.C.A.):

> In short, the real test of the truth of the story of a witness in such a case must be its harmony with the preponderance of the probabilities which a practical and informed person would readily recognize as reasonable in that place and in those conditions.

1) *Cherneskey v. Armadale Publishers Ltd.*

In *Cherneskey* v. *Armadale Publishers Ltd.*, [1979] 1. S.C.R. 1067, the Supreme Court of Canada ruled that fair comment was not a defence available to a newspaper which published a letter to the editor, because the newspaper failed to prove that a defamatory comment in the letter also represented the newspaper's opinion or the letter writer's opinion.

The troubling implications of *Cherneskey* for the viability of the defence of fair comment led Alberta, Manitoba, New Brunswick, Newfoundland

and Labrador, the Northwest Territories, Ontario, Prince Edward Island, and the Yukon Territory to amend their defamation statutes.

Alberta's amended statute provides that a defence of fair comment does not fail merely because the defendant did not share the defamatory opinion expressed by another person.

Defamation Act, R.S.A. 2000, c. D-6, s.09(1).

The defamation acts of Manitoba, New Brunswick, Newfoundland and Labrador, the Northwest Territories, Ontario, Prince Edward Island, and the Yukon Territory are similar to Alberta's but each also requires proof that a person could honestly hold the defamatory opinion. Moreover, in those jurisdictions the defence fails (except in Ontario) if the defendant knew the opinion was dishonestly expressed by its originator. New Brunswick's statute requires that the person expressing the defamatory opinion be identified.

Manitoba, *Defamation Act*, R.S.M. 1970, c. D-20, s.9(1) .

New Brunswick, *Defamation Act*, R.S.N.B. 1973, c. D-5, s.8.1.

Newfoundland and Labrador, *Defamation Act*, R.S.N. 1990, c. D-3, s.11.

Northwest Territories, *Defamation Act*, R.S.N.W.T. 1988, c. D-1, s.10(1).

Ontario, *Defamation Act*, R.S.O. 1990, c.L-12, s.24.

Prince Edward Island, *Defamation Act*, R.S.P.E.I. 1988, c. D-5, s.9(1).

Yukon Territory, *Defamation Act*, R.S.Y.T. 1986, c. 41, s.8.

British Columbia, Nova Scotia, and Saskatchewan have not amended their defamation statues to override the decision in *Cherneskey*. This is one instance where a defendant's reliance on the guarantee of freedom of expression in section 2(b) of the *Canadian Charter of Rights and Freedoms* might result in an incremental change in the common law in British Columbia, Nova Scotia, and Saskatchewan so that it is harmonized with the statutory amendments made in the other Canadian jurisdictions.

H. MATTER OF PUBLIC INTEREST

The onus is on the defendant to persuade the court that the subject is a matter of public interest. This is a question of law for the judge.

Price v. Chicoutimi Pulp Co. (1915), 51 S.C.R. 179.

Governmental affairs and matters of public health and safety have been found to be matters of public interest.

Myers v. *Canadian Broadcasting Corporation* (1999), 47 C.C.L.T. (2d) 272, per Bellamy J. at 303 (Ont. S.C.J.), aff'd (2001), 54 O.R. (3d) 627 (C.A.), leave to appeal to S.C.C. denied, [2001] S.C.C.A. 433.

The jurisprudence can often be of help in answering this question. The phrase "public interest" has not been defined, but it is not to be confined within narrow limits.

London Artists Ltd. v. *Littler*, [1969] 2 All ER 193 at 198 per Lord Denning M.R. (C.A.):

> Whenever a matter is such as to affect people at large, so that they may be legitimately interested in, or concerned at, what is going on; or what may happen to them or others, then it is a matter of public interest on which everyone is entitled to make fair comment.

The status of the person who is the target of the defamatory comment is frequently of importance. A citizen's personal ethics are not a matter of public interest. Accordingly, the premier could not avail himself of the defence of fair comment for remarking that if the plaintiff was well enough to lead a protest against the provincial government's French-language policy, he was well enough to go back to his job as a government employee rather than drawing the taxpayer's money on sick leave.

Russell v. *Pawley* (1987), 36 D.L.R. (4th) 625 (Man. C.A.).

A private individual's health has been held not to constitute a matter of public interest.

McLoughlin v. *Kutasy*, [1979] 2 S.C.R. 331.

Although the general subject matter of the comment may be of public interest, it appears there must be a public nexus between that subject matter and the person who is the direct target of the comment.

Vander Zalm v. *Times Publishers Ltd.* (1980), 109 D.L.R. (3d) 531 (B.C.C.A.).

If the defamatory matter is a cartoon, the cartoonist may not intrude upon the private life of a public man, no matter how interesting such an intrusion may be to the public, nor may he expose a private person to unsought publicity.

Vander Zalm v. *Times Publishers Ltd.*, *ibid.*

There is support for the proposition, however, that a subject may be of public interest even if it directly concerns only one person or a limited number of persons.

Colin Duncan & Brian Neill, *Defamation* (London: Butterworths, 1987) at 63.

South Hetton Coal Co. v. North-Eastern News Association Ltd., [1893]1 Q.B. 133 (C.A.).

London Artists Ltd. v. Littler, above, at 198

I. MALICE DEFEATS FAIR COMMENT

The onus is on the plaintiff to prove malice on a balance of probabilities. Proof of malice is fatal to the defence of fair comment.

Johnson v. Joliffe (1981), 26 B.C.L.R. 176 (S.C.).

Leenen v. Canadian Broadcasting Corporation (2000), 48 O.R. (3d) 656 at 701, aff'd (2001) 54 O.R. (3d) 612 (C.A.), leave to appeal to S.C.C.denied, [2001] S.C.C.A. No. 432 .

The plaintiff may prove malice by showing that the defendant published the defamatory matter:

i) to satisfy a private spite or for some other dominant, indirect, or improper purpose; or
ii) knowing it was false, or with reckless indifference as to whether it was true or false.

Hill v. Church of Scientology of Toronto, [1995] 126 D.L.R. (4th) 129 at 171 (S.C.C).

Sun Life Assurance Company of Canada v. Dalrymple, [1965] S.C.R. 302 at 309.

Jerome v. Anderson, [1964] S.C.R. 291 at 299.

Anderson v. Smythe (1935), 50 B.C.R. 112 at 117 (C.A.).

Newton v. Vancouver (City) (1932), 46 B.C.R. 67 at 72–73 (S.C.).

Determining whether malice is involved requires close scrutiny of the defendant's motives.

Horrocks v. Lowe, [1974] 1 All E.R. 662 at 669–70 (H.L.).

The relevant time is when the defamation was published.

Jerome v. Anderson, [1964] S.C.R. 291 at 299.

If the plaintiff seeks to rely on malice to cause a comment, otherwise fair, to become unfair, then she must prove malice against each person whom she charges with it.

Sun Life Assurance Company of Canada v. *Dalrymple*, above, per Spence J. quoting Lord Denning in *Egger* v. *Viscount Chelmsford et. al.* [1964] 3 All E.R. 406 at 412 (C.A.):

> A defendant is only affected by express malice if he himself was actuated by it.

There is a significant burden on a plaintiff who alleges malice.

Re International Assn. of Bridge, Structural and Ornamental and Reinforcing Ironworkers (Local 97) and Campbell (1997), 40 B.C.L.R. (3d) 1 at 12 (S.C.).

Silbernagel v. *Empire Stevedoring Company Limited* (1979), 18 B.C.L.R. 384 at 389–95 (S.C.).

Evidence of malice is to be balanced with evidence of other motives. The leading decision on malice is the judgment of Lord Diplock in *Horrocks* v. *Lowe*, above, where he states at page 670:

> Judges and juries should, however, be very slow to draw the inference that a defendant was so far actuated by improper motives as to deprive him of the protection of the privilege unless they are satisfied that he did not believe that what he said or wrote was true or that he was indifferent to its truth or falsity. The motives with which human beings act are mixed. They find it difficult to hate the sin but love the sinner. Qualified privilege would be illusory, and the public interest that it is meant to serve defeated, if the protection which it affords were lost merely because a person, although acting in compliance with a duty or in protection of a legitimate interest, dislike the person whom he defamed or was indignant at what he believed to be that person's conduct and welcomed the opportunity of exposing it. It is only where his desire to comply with the relevant duty or to protect the relevant interest plays no significant part in his motives for publishing what he believes to be true that "express malice" can properly be found.

A trial judge should not direct a jury that honest belief in the impugned statement will negate malice. Honest belief is at the root of fair comment. Malice defeats fair comment. One can honestly believe a statement yet publish it for an improper reason or motive; this malice will defeat a defence of fair comment.

Christie v. *Westcom Radio Group Ltd.* (1990), 75 D.L.R. (4th) 546 (B.C.C.A.) leave to appeal to S.C.C. denied, [1991] 1 S.C.R. vii, per Macfarlane J.A. at 365–66:

Watt v. Longsdon, [1930] 1 K.B. 130 at 154–55 (C.A.) is cited by the plaintiff. This passage from the judgment of Greer L.J. draws the distinction between honest belief and malice, and emphasizes the importance of the language used in the defamatory statement:

> Malice is a state of mind: see the judgments in the case of *Neville v. Fine Arts and General Insurance Co., Ltd.* [[1895] 2 Q.B. 156] in the Court of Appeal. A man may believe in the truth of a defamatory statement, and yet when he publishes it be reckless whether his belief be well founded or not. His motive for publishing a libel on a privileged occasion may be an improper one, even though he believes the statement to be true. He may be moved by hatred or dislike, or a desire to injure the subject of the libel, and may be using the occasion for that purpose, and if he is doing so the publication will be maliciously made, even though he may believe the defamatory statements to be true. I agree with the statement of the law contained in the late Mr. Blake Odger's monumental book on libel and slander, which will be found at p. 354 of the 5th edition. It is as follows: "And even though it is clear that the defendant believed in the truth of the communication he made, and was acting under a sense of duty on the privileged occasion, the plaintiff may still rely upon the words employed, and the manner and mode of publication, as evidence of malice. An angry man may often be led away into exaggerated or unwarrantable expressions; or he may forget where and in whose presence he is speaking, or how and to whom his writing may be published. Clearly this is often but faint evidence of malice; the jury will generally pardon a slight excess of righteous zeal. In some cases, however (which we will proceed to examine) such excess has secured the plaintiff a verdict. But if the jury find there was no malice in the defendant, such excess becomes immaterial."

In certain circumstances, notwithstanding the substantial onus of proof which rests on the plaintiff seeking to prove malice, "the affirmative evidence of malice may be sufficiently cogent to require the defendant to answer it or stand condemned."

Amalgamated Transit Union v. Independent Canadian Transit Union, [1997] 5 W.W.R. 662, per Lutz J. at para. 72 (Alta. C.A.), citing *Jones v. Bennett* (1968), 63 W.W.R. 1 (B.C.C.A.) per Davey C.J.B.C at 15–16:

Then it is said that the appellant's failure to testify and prove his good faith is evidence of malice. Except perhaps in exceptional circumstances, which do not exist here, there is no onus on a defendant relying on qualified privilege to prove the absence of malice until a prima facie case of it has been made out. Then the affirmative evidence of malice may be sufficiently cogent to require the defendant to answer it or stand condemned. In my opinion the proof of malice was not advanced to that point in this case.

In determining the question of malice in a radio or television broadcast, the jury is entitled to consider not only the contents of the publication, but the tone of voice of the commentator.

Christie v. Westcom Radio Group Ltd., above.

The existing case law requires defendants to base their defence of fair comment on information available to them at the time of publication. The defendants cannot use discovery to learn facts necessary to justify the comment.

Stetson v. MacNeill (c.o.b. The Eastern Graphic) (1997), 152 Nfld. & P.E.I.R. 225 (P.E.I.S.C. (T.D.)).

1) Malice and News Media Defendants

The courts will look closely to determine whether the media defendant's purported motive of serving the public interest by publishing or broadcasting the defamatory expression is supported in the evidence.

In the case of media defendants, a court may find that the real motive of the defendants was to enhance their own reputations by producing a sensational program:

Vogel v. Canadian Broadcasting Corporation, [1982] 3 W.W.R. 97, per Esson J. at 174 (B.C.S.C.):

> Their concern was not as to whether the allegations were true or as to whether the public interest was served. It was rather to give to allegations of scandal the appearance of truth to the extent necessary to succeed in achieving their goal. That attitude, in law, is malice.

However, something more is required than mere desire to enhance reputations by producing lively and interesting programs.

Pressler v. Lethbridge (2000), 86 B.C.L.R. (3d) 257 per Esson J.A. at 307, paras. 111–12 (C.A.):

In Vogel's case, some of those who produced the programs did not believe that what they published was true and others were indifferent to its truth or falsity. The story, as I said in my reasons, was not so much dug up as made up. It was a case in which the natural desire of reporters and producers to gain favourable attention led to a virtually complete loss of balance.

J. "FAIR" COMMENT

The use of the word "fair" in the name of this defence is a source of confusion and is potentially misleading. It has been appropriately characterized as a "misnomer."

> *Vander Zalm* v. *Times Publishers Ltd.* (1980), 109 D.L.R. (3d) 531 (B.C.C.A.) per Craig J.A. at 551.

The comment need not be reasonable nor one with which the jury agrees. It need only be proven to be fair in the sense that the comment relates to the proven underlying facts on which the commentator relies, and represents an honest expression of the real view of the person making the comment.

> *Ross* v. *New Brunswick Teachers' Association* (2001), 201 D.L.R. (4th) 75, per Daigle C.J.N.B. at para. 78 (N.B.C.A.).

In *Vander Zalm* v. *Times Publishers Ltd.,* above, Nemetz C.J.B.C. at page 538 referred to *Silkin* v. *Beaverbrook Newspapers Ltd.,* [1958] 1 W.L.R. 743 where Lord Diplock charged the jury in the following terms at page 747:

> ... [T]he expression 'fair comment' is a little misleading. It may give you the impression that you, the jury, have to decide whether you agree with the comment, whether you think it is fair. If that were the question you had to decide, you realize that the limits of the freedom which the law allows would be greatly curtailed. People are entitled to hold and to express freely on matters of public interest strong views, views which some of you, or indeed all of you, may think are exaggerated, obstinate or prejudiced, provided — and this is the important thing — that they are views which they honestly hold. The basis of our public life is that the crank, the enthusiast, may say what he honestly thinks just as much as the reasonable man or woman who sits on a jury, and it would be a sad day for freedom of speech in this country if a jury were to apply the test of whether it agrees with the comment instead of apply-

ing the true test: was this an opinion, however exaggerated, obstinate or prejudiced, which was honestly held by the writer?

In *Cherneskey v. Armadale Publishers Ltd.*, [1979] 1 S.C.R. 1067, Martland J. expressed agreement at page 1073 with the above-quoted passage from Lord Diplock's charge to the jury in *Silkin*. In the other majority judgment in *Cherneskey*, Ritchie J. stated at page 1090 that:

> As honesty of belief is an essential component of the defence of fair comment, that defence involves at least some evidence that the material complained of was published in a spirit of fairness.

Courts have recently emphasized the wide latitude to be applied in determining whether comment is "fair."

In *Reynolds v. Times Newspapers*, [1999] 4 All E.R. 609 (H.L.), Lord Nicholls of Birkenhead stated at page 615:

> ... [T]he time has come to recognize that in this context the epithet 'fair' is now meaningless and misleading. Comment must be relevant to the facts to which it is addressed. It cannot be used as a cloak for mere invective. But the basis of our public life is that the crank, the enthusiast, may say what he honestly thinks as much as the reasonable person who sits on a jury. The true test is whether the opinion, however exaggerated, obstinate or prejudiced, was honestly held by the person expressing it. See Diplock J. in *Silkin v. Beaverbrook Newspapers Ltd.* [1958] 2 All ER 516 at 518, [1958] 1 W.L.R. 743 at 747

> This passage was cited with apparent approval by Daigle C.J.N.B. in *Ross v. New Brunswick Teachers' Association* (2001), 201 D.L.R. (4th) 75 at paras. 77–78 (N.B.C.A.).

Despite virtually universal agreement that a comment does not need to be "reasonable" to be "fair comment," Canadian courts continue to wrestle with concepts of fairness and unfairness in the context of issues relating to truth of the facts supporting the comment, honesty of belief, and malice.

For a discussion of the rolled-up plea, see Chapter 21, "Justification," H.6; Chapter 23, "Pleadings," C.1.a)i); and Chapter 27, "Examination for Discovery," C.8.

CHAPTER EIGHTEEN:

Qualified and Statutory Privilege

A. INTRODUCTION

At common law, there are privileged occasions when the public interest in free and candid speech trumps the public and private interest in protecting individual or corporate reputation. In addition, the federal Parliament, the provinces and the territories have enacted certain statutory privileges which codify or extend the common law.

A crucial feature of a privilege defence is that it protects defamatory errors of fact which are not excused under the defences of justification or fair comment.

Privilege defences, whether arising at common law or based on statute, generally fall into three categories:

i)   absolute;
ii)   qualified; and
iii) fair and accurate report.

When defamatory expression is protected by absolute privilege, the mind-set and purpose of the speaker are irrelevant. Qualified privilege, on the other hand, will not protect statements made with actual or express malice, or for an indirect or improper purpose. Fair and accurate report privilege is defeated if the content of the defamatory expression does not satisfy certain standards.

The parameters of absolute privilege are well defined in the jurisprudence. The defence is therefore relatively easy to recognize, plead, and adjudicate. See Chapter 20 "Absolute Privilege."

The jurisprudence concerning common law qualified privilege lays down general guidelines for determining whether expression on a given occasion will enjoy the protection of this defence. Certain categories of occasion are described but they are not exhaustive: the existence of a qualified privilege defence in a particular case depends on the facts. Recognizing, pleading and assessing a qualified privilege defence therefore often demands considerable care.

The circumstances giving rise to fair and accurate report privilege at common law are reasonably defined in the jurisprudence. The determination of fairness and accuracy may require rigorous scrutiny of the facts of the particular case. Many of these privileges have been codified.

There are instances where the expression of defamatory imputations is privileged under provincial, territorial, or federal statutes. This chapter will also discuss these provisions.

A separate chapter also addresses recent jurisprudence of courts in the United Kingdom, Australia, and New Zealand which is shaping the common law of qualified privilege in terms of the public interest. See Chapter 19, "Qualified Privilege and Publication to the World at Large: Developments in Australia, Britain and New Zealand."

B. QUALIFIED PRIVILEGE AT COMMON LAW

1) The Elements of The Defence: Duty and Interest

This defence applies to an occasion where the defendant has (i) an interest or (ii) a duty – legal, social, or moral – to communicate the defamatory expression and its recipients have a corresponding duty or interest to receive that communication.

> *Pressler v. Lethbridge* (2000), 86 B.C.L.R. (3d) 257, per Southin J.A. at 295 (C.A.).

> *Haight-Smith v. Neden* (2002), 211 D.L.R. (4th) 370, per Levine J.A. for the court at 383 (B.C.C.A.), citing Lord Atkinson in *Adam v. Ward*, [1917] A.C. 309 at 334 (H.L.) and *Mcloughlin v. Kutasy*, [1979] 2 S.C.R. 311 at 321.

> *Stopforth v. Goyer* (1979), 97 D.L.R. (3d) 369, per Jessop J.A. at 372 (Ont. C.A.), adopting the description of the defence contained in *Halsbury's Laws of England*, 3d ed., vol. 24 (London: Butterworths, 1952–64) at 56–57.

Reciprocity of duty and interest between the communicator and the recipient is essential to this defence.

> *Sapiro v. Leader Publishing Co.*, [1926] 3 D.L.R. 68, per Lamont J.A. for the court at 68–69 (Sask. C.A.), citing *Adam v. Ward*, [1917] A.C. 309 (H.L.).

The burden is on the defendant to prove each of the elements of the defence.

Although a communication occurred on an occasion of qualified privilege, the protection of this defence is lost if:

i) the plaintiff proves that the dominant motive for publishing the defamatory expression is actual or express malice; or

ii) the limits of the duty or interest have been exceeded. This occurs when:

    a. the speaker includes anything which is not relevant or pertinent, or in other words, not reasonably appropriate in the circumstances existing on the occasion when the information is given;

    b. the manner and extent of communication is excessive.

Hill v. Church of Scientology of Toronto, [1995] 2 S.C.R. 1130, per Cory J. at 1189–90.

Botiuk v. Toronto Free Press, [1995] 3 S.C.R. 29 at 29–30, per Cory J. (La Forest, L'Heureux-Dubé, Gonthier, McLachlin and Iacobucci JJ. concurring).

Wade and Wells Co. v. Laing (1957), 11 D.L.R. (2d) 276 at 279, 282–83 (B.C.C.A.), Per Sheppard J.A. (Sidney Smith J.A. concurring), citing *Clark v. Molyneux* (1877), 3 Q.B.D. 237 at 247.

Kelsie v. Canada (Attorney General), [2003] N.J. No. 232, 2003 NLSCTD 139 per Barry J. at para. 33.

The burden of proving actual or express malice rests on the plaintiff.

Netupsky v. Craig, [1973] S.C.R. 55 per Ritchie J. for the court at 61–63.

McLoughlin v. Kutasy, [1979] 2 S.C.R. 311 at 324–25.

2) Foundation in Public Policy

The defence of qualified privilege is intended to serve "the general interests of society" and "the common convenience and welfare of society" rather than the interests of individuals or a class.

Halls v. Mitchell, [1928] S.C.R. 125 at 147, per Duff J. (Anglin C.J.C., Mignault, and Lamont JJ. concurring).

Sapiro v. Leader Publishing Co. Ltd., above, at 70.

Macintosh v. Dun, [1908] A.C. 390 (P.C.) per Lord Macnaghten at 398 and 399, citing *Toogood v. Spyring* (1834), 1 C.M & R. 181 at 193 where Parke B. stated:

If fairly warranted by any reasonable occasion or exigency, and honestly made, such communications [injurious to the character of another] are protected for the common convenience and welfare of society, and the law has not restricted the right to make them within any narrow limits.

Macintosh v. *Dun*, above, and *Toogood* v. *Spyring*, above were expressly approved by Duff J., writing for the majority of the Supreme Court of Canada in *Halls* v. *Mitchell*, above, at 132–33:

The defamatory statement is … only protected when it is fairly warranted by some reasonable occasion or exigency, and when it is fairly made in discharge of some public or private duty, or in the conduct of the defendant's own affairs in matters in which his interests are concerned. The privilege rests not upon the interests of the persons entitled to invoke it, but upon the general interests of society, and protects only communications "fairly made" in the legitimate defence of a person's own interests, or plainly made under a sense of duty, such as would be recognized by "people of ordinary intelligence and moral principles.

C. THE PRIVILEGED OCCASION

1) The Occasion is Privileged, Not the Expression

Qualified privilege attaches to the occasion upon which the communication is made and not to the communication itself.

Hill v. *Church of Scientology of Toronto*, [1995] 2 S.C.R. 1130 per Cory J. at 1188, para. 142, citing *McLoughlin* v. *Kutasy*, above at 321, which approved *Adam* v. *Ward*, [1917] A.C. 309 (H.L.) where Lord Atkinson stated at 334:

… a privileged occasion is … an occasion where the person who makes a communication has an interest or a duty, legal, social, or moral, to make it to the person to whom it is made, and the person to whom it is so made has a corresponding interest or duty to receive it. This reciprocity is essential.

Botiuk v. *Toronto Free Press*, [1995] 3 S.C.R. 29, per Cory J. (La Forest, L'Heureux-Dubé, Gonthier, McLachlin, and Iacobucci JJ. concurring) at 29.

RTC Engineering Consultants Ltd. v. *Ontario (Ministry of the Solicitor General and Correctional Services)* (2002), 58 O.R. (3d) 726, per Laskin J.A. for the court at para. 14 (C.A.).

2) Whether Occasion is Privileged is a Question of Law

It is a question of law for the judge whether or not the facts and circumstances are sufficient to create an occasion of privilege. The burden of proof to establish such facts and circumstances rests on the defendant.

Globe & Mail Ltd. v. *Boland*, [1960] S.C.R. 203 at 209.

In determining whether the circumstances of a particular case give rise to a moral or social duty the court applies an objective test: whether it is a duty recognized by people of ordinary intelligence and moral principle.

Halls v. *Mitchell*, above, at 133.

To qualify as a moral or social duty, it need not be enforceable by civil or criminal legal proceedings.

Sapiro v. *Leader Publishing Co. Ltd.*, [1926] 3 D.L.R. 68, per Lamont J.A. for the court at 70 (Sask. C.A.), citing *Stuart* v. *Bell*, [1891] 2 Q.B. 341 at 350, where Lindley L.J. stated:

> I take moral or social duty to mean a duty recognized by English people of ordinary intelligence and moral principle, but at the same time not a duty enforceable by legal proceedings, whether civil or criminal.

To clothe an occasion with privilege on the ground of common interest, the common interest must be in the subject matter of the communication complained of.

Sapiro v. *Leader Publishing Co. Ltd.*, above, at 69, 74.

It is not sufficient that the defendant, honestly and with some reason, believed that the interest or duty existed. There must in fact be such an interest or such a duty as, when all the circumstances are considered, warranted the communication. The court must say whether it is for the welfare of society that such a communication honestly made should be protected by clothing the occasion of the publication with privilege.

Halls v. *Mitchell*, above, at 134

Wade & Wells Co. v. *Laing* (1957), 11 D.L.R. (2d) 276, per Sheppard J.A. (Sidney Smith J.A. concurring) at 282 (B.C.C.A.):

> In *Stuart* v. *Bell*, [[1891] 2 Q.B. 341] Lindley L.J. at p. 349 said: " …
> Both the defendant and Stanley say that the defendant acted under a
> sense of duty, but this, though important on the question of malice, is
> not, I think, relevant to the question whether the occasion was or was

not privileged. That question does not depend on the defendant's belief, but on whether he was right or mistaken in that belief."

A defendant does not prove that an occasion is privileged by calling witnesses to express an opinion that the subject of the defamatory communication was a matter of great public importance, or to express an opinion that the defendants and those who received the communication had a common interest.

> *Sapiro* v. *Leader Publishing Co. Ltd.*, above at 73–74.

3) Reasonably Germane and Appropriate

It is a question of law for the judge whether a defamatory publication went beyond what was germane and reasonably appropriate to the occasion so that the privilege was exceeded.

> *Douglas* v. *Tucker*, [1952] 1 S.C.R. 275, per Cartwright J. for the court at 286.

4) Express or Actual Malice

Express or actual malice is not the presumed malice which the law implies from the mere publication of defamatory words. Presumed malice is rebutted by finding the occasion is one of qualified privilege, at which point the onus shifts to the plaintiff to prove express or actual malice.

> *Taylor* v. *Despard*, [1956] O.R. 963, per Roach J.A. at 973–74 (C.A.).

Whether or not a defendant was actuated by malice is a question of fact for the jury, not a question of law for the trial judge. Whether there is any evidence of malice to go to the jury is a question of law for the judge. On the issue of malice, evidence of the belief or motive of the defendant is relevant.

> *Sun Life Assurance Co. of Canada et al.* v. *Dalrymple*, [1965] S.C.R. 302, per Spence J. at 309, citing *Adam* v. *Ward*, [1917] A.C. 309 (H.L.).

5) Multiple Defendants

Where there are multiple defendants the court must individually evaluate the position of each defendant. Each is entitled to allege that his or her communication occurred on an occasion of qualified privilege.

> *Derrickson* v. *Tomat* (1992), 88 D.L.R. (4th) 401, per Hinds J.A. at 423–24 (B.C.C.A.).

Where the occasion is held to be privileged, the plaintiff has the burden of proving malice against each of the defendants. Express malice found against one employee may make a corporate defendant liable if the defamatory expression was published by that employee in the course and scope of his or her employment.

Sun Life Assurance Co. of Canada v. *Dalrymple*, above, at 310.

If the plaintiff seeks to rely on malice to rebut a defence of qualified privilege, she must prove malice against each defendant. It is not the law that on a joint publication, the malice of one defendant taints the co-defendant. A defendant is only affected by express malice if that defendant was actuated by it, or if his servant or agent concerned in the publication was actuated by malice in the course of his employment.

Sun Life Assurance Co. of Canada et al. v. *Dalrymple*, *ibid.* at 310, approving *Egger* v. *Viscount Chelmsford*, [1964] 3 All E.R. 406, per Lord Denning M.R. at 412 (C.A.):

> It is a mistake to suppose that, on a joint publication, the malice of one defendant infects his co-defendant. Each defendant is answerable severally, as well as jointly, for the joint publication: and each is entitled to his several defence, whether he be sued jointly or separately from the others. If the plaintiff seeks to rely on malice to aggravate damages, or to rebut a defence of qualified privilege, or to cause a comment, otherwise fair, to become unfair, then he must prove malice against each person whom he charges with it. A defendant is only affected by express malice if he himself was actuated by it: or if his servant or agent concerned in the publication was actuated by malice in the course of his employment.

6) Onus of Proof

The onus rests on the defendant to allege and prove all of the circumstances which are alleged to give rise to the occasion of qualified privilege.

Globe and Mail Ltd. v. *Boland*, [1960] S.C.R. 203, per Cartwright J. at 206, citing Richard O'Sullivan & Roland G. Brown, *Gatley on Libel and Slander*, 4th ed., (London: Sweet & Maxwell, 1953) at 282.

Banks v. *Globe & Mail*, [1961] S.C.R. 747 per Cartwright at 481, citing Richard O'Sullivan & Robert L. McEwen, *Gatley on Libel and Slander*, 5th ed. (London: Sweet & Maxwell, 1960) at 270.

Toronto Star Ltd. v. *Drew*, [1948] 4 D.L.R. 465 at 467 (S.C.C.).

The defendant does not have an onus to prove that he honestly believed his statement to be true in order to avail himself of the defence of qualified privilege.

Arnott v. *College of Physicians and Surgeons of Saskatchewan*, [1954] S.C.R. 538 per Estey J. at 550, citing *Jenoure* v. *Delmege*, [1891] A.C. 73.

Wade & Wells Co. v. *Laing* (1957), 11 D.L.R. (2d) 276 per Sheppard J.A. at 282 (B.C.C.A.):

> In deciding whether there is a privileged occasion the learned trial judge is not concerned with the belief of the speaker.

When words are spoken or written on an occasion of qualified privilege, the *bona fides* of the defendant and his or her honesty of belief in the truth of the defamatory expression is presumed and the burden then lies on the plaintiff to rebut that presumption.

Netupsky v. *Craig*, [1973] S.C.R. 55 per Ritchie J. at 61–62, approving the judgment of Schroeder J.A. in the Ontario Court of Appeal at (1970) 14 D.L.R. (3d) 387 at 404.

Once the defendant has established that the occasion is privileged, the burden shifts to the plaintiff to show that the defendant was actuated by express malice.

Netupsky v. *Craig*, *ibid.* at 61–63 .

McLoughlin v. *Kutasy*, [1979] 2 S.C.R. 311, per Ritchie J. at 324–25.

Adam v. *Ward*, [1917] A.C. 309, per Lord Atkinson at 334 (H.L.), citing *Wright* v. *Woodgate*, [1891] A.C. 73 at 79.

In the process of determining whether statements made on an occasion of qualified privilege are relevant, the court must carefully define the nature and extent of the interest at stake.

Gibbs v. *Jalbert* (1996), 18 B.C.L.R. (3d) 351, per Prowse J.A. at 357–58 (C.A.).

7) Factors Relevant to Determining Whether an Occasion is Privileged

It has been held that the circumstances required to create an occasion of qualified privilege cannot be defined with any degree of accuracy. They "can never be catalogued and rendered exact."

Arnott v. *College of Physicians and Surgeons of Saskatchewan*, above, at 539, quoting Lord Buckmaster in *London Association for Protection of Trade* v. *Greenlands, Limited*, [1916] 2 A.C. 15 at 22.

In determining whether an occasion is privileged on the grounds of duty or interest, the court will consider every circumstance connected with the origin and publication of the defamatory expression, including:

i) the content of the alleged defamatory expression;

ii) who published it;

iii) why it was published;

iv) to whom it was published;

v) under what circumstances it was published;

vi) the nature of the duty which the defendant claims to discharge or the interest which the defendant claims to safeguard;

vii) whether there are any statutory duties imposed on the speaker;

viii) the urgency of the occasion;

ix) the manner in which the defendant conducted him- or herself;

x) whether or not the expression was published in breach of confidence;

xi) whether or not the defendant officiously volunteered the information or whether it was in answer to an inquiry; and

xii) whether or not what was published was germane and reasonably appropriate to the occasion.

Halls v. *Mitchell*, [1928] S.C.R. 125, per Duff J. at 136, 139 and 142, citing *inter alia*, *London Association for Protection of Trade* v. *Greenlands, Limited*, above, at 28–29, and Sir Frederick Pollock, *The Law of Torts: A Treatise on the Principles Arising From Civil Wrongs in the Common Law*, 12th ed., (London: Stevens and Sons, Limited, 1921) at 270.

Sapiro v. *Leader Publishing Co. Ltd.*, [1926] 3 D.L.R. 68, Lamont J.A. at 70–71 (Sask. C.A.), citing *inter alia*, *Stuart* v. *Bell*, [1891] 2 Q.B. 341 at 350.

Defamatory communications may be made in answer to inquiry or may be volunteered. In cases which are near the line, and in cases which may give rise to a difference of opinion, the circumstance that the defamatory information is volunteered, rather than brought out in answer to an inquiry, may be an important element for consideration.

Halls v. *Mitchell*, above, at 132–33, citing Lord Macnaghten in *Macintosh* v. *Dun*, [1908] A.C. 390 at 398 and 399 (P.C.).

The fact that defamatory matter has originated in breach of confidence, to the knowledge of the defamer, or that it was produced under a system which contemplated the violation of confidence as a source of information, may constitute a reason for rejecting the claim of privilege.

> *Halls* v. *Mitchell*, above, at 136, 139–40, citing *Macintosh* v. *Dun*, above, at 400.

A person making a communication on a privileged occasion is not restricted to the use of such language merely as is reasonably necessary to protect the interest or discharge the duty which is the foundation of his or her privilege.

> *Netupsky* v. *Craig* (1972), 28 D.L.R. (3d) 742 per Ritchie J. for the court at 746 (S.C.C.), citing *Adam* v. *Ward*, [1917] A.C. 309 where Lord Atkinson stated at 339 (H.L.):

> > ... [O]n the contrary, he will be protected, even though his language should be violent or excessively strong, if, having regard to all the circumstances of the case, he might have honestly and on reasonable grounds believed that what he wrote or said was true and necessary for the purpose of his vindication, though in fact it was not so.

> *Korach* v. *Moore* (1991), 76 D.L.R. (4th) 506 per Grange J.A. at 509 (Ont. C.A.) referring, *inter alia*, to *Horrocks* v. *Lowe*, [1975] A.C. 135 (H.L.). [Application for leave to appeal to the Supreme Court of Canada dismissed 13 June 1991, S.C.C. File No. 222.]

> *Arnott* v. *College of Physicians and Surgeons of Saskatchewan*, above, per Estey J. at 551 citing *Warren* v. *Warren*, 1 C.M. & R. 250, and *Adam* v. *Ward*, above:

> > The ... dictionary describes a quack as 'an ignorant pretender to medical skill; one who boasts to have a knowledge of wonderful remedies; an empiric or imposter in medicine." While, therefore, no one could properly suggest the appellant is ignorant of medical skill, it is possible that he may be in error, and those who honestly believe him to be so may find some similarity in his practices and methods in respect to the Koch treatment and the characteristic practices or methods of a quack. However that may be, the sentence here complained of was used to describe the prescription or administration of the treatment. It was, therefore, not an expression unconnected with or irrelevant to the performance of the duty which gives rise to qualified privilege. At the most it was an exaggeration, or an extreme statement, which could be evidence of malice, but, apart from an express finding that it did constitute malice, would not, of itself, remove the privilege.

Where an individual or corporation is subjected to a defamatory attack, a communication responding to the attack is made on an occasion of qualified privilege. Such responses are considered to be essential to protect one's own interests and reputation.

Botiuk v. Toronto Free Press, [1995] 3 S.C.R. 3 per Cory J. at 31, para. 86

Netupsky v. Craig, [1973] S.C.R. 55, (1972) 28 D.L.R. (3d) 742, per Ritchie J. for the Court at 28 D.L.R. (3d) 746 approving the reasons of Schroeder J.A. (14 D.L.R. (3d) 387 at 407 (Ont. C.A.)) where he stated:

> A more apposite and firmer basis for the privilege arises from the fact that the statements were made in the conduct of the defendants' own affairs in a manner in which their own interest was concerned. More specifically, they were replying to an unfair and unwarranted attack upon their professional integrity and competence which they were justified in repelling by a denial and explanation. This forms a more substantial and relevant foundation for the privilege, and entitles the defendants to considerably wider latitude than does the basis upon which the learned trial judge rested it.

Douglas v. Tucker, [1952] 1 S.C.R. 275 per Cartwright J. at 286, citing *Adam v. Ward*, [1917] A.C. 309 (H.L.).

Mallett v. Clarke (1968), 70 D.L.R. (2d) 67, per Gould J. at 72 (B.C.S.C.) [defendant principal of institute had duty to answer serious allegations made by the plaintiff, an expelled student, to journalists who contacted the defendant for comment].

O'Malley v. O'Callaghan (1992), 4 W.W.R. 81 at 91–92 (Alta. Q.B.) [personal dispute between plaintiff pro-life spokesperson and defendant newspaper publisher over news coverage and editorial policy of newspaper on the abortion issue. Defendant held entitled to respond to attacks on his newspaper.]

When determining whether the necessary reciprocity exists between the speaker and the listener, the court will consider whether the defamatory communication was restricted to a specific audience to which the defendant has a duty of information.

In *Upton v. Better Business Bureau of Mainland of B.C.* (1980), 114 D.L.R. (3d) 750 (B.C.S.C.), Gould J. held at 755 that a nonprofit society, incorporated for the purpose, *inter alia*, of "promoting honesty, truthfulness, and reliability in merchandising and advertising of all kinds" and discouraging "fraudulent and deceptive methods in business," published its monthly bulletin to members and to associate Better Business Bureaus across the country on an occasion of qualified privilege. "I hold that it is in the public interest that information from such an institution should be available and that pursuant to its objects the Bureau is under duty to supply such information."

If a publication is given a wider circulation than intended, and that did not occur by reason of any negligence on the part of the defendant, the fact of that wider circulation is not a breach of the privilege.

> *Gallant v. West,* [1955] 4 D.L.R. 209, per Walsh C.J. at 217 (Nfld. S.C.).

The British Columbia Supreme Court rejected a defence of qualified privilege pleaded by a union regarding a publication on its website which defamed a competing union. Although the defendant contended the expression was aimed only at its own members who would have an interest in receiving union news, the court noted the defendant did not restrict access to the portion of the site where the defamatory message was posted, although other parts of the site were password protected and accessible only to members. Rice J. concluded that any privilege was therefore defeated by excessive publication. He stated at paragraph 31:

> It is not that the internet and use of a website is to be discouraged, but if statements are to be made which are admittedly defamatory, and there is a risk of significant numbers of uninterested people seeing it, that can be excessive, and will be if restrictions are available but disregarded.

> *Christian Labour Association of Canada v. Retail Wholesale Union,* 2003 BCSC 2000.

The response should be in keeping with, and responsive to the original attack, and normally should be made in the same forum. In answering an attack, a person must not make countercharges or unnecessary imputations on the private life of the attacker which are wholly unconnected with the attack and irrelevant to the victim's vindication. The privilege extends only so far as to enable the victim to repel the charges brought against him, and not to bring fresh accusations against his adversary.

> *Douglas v. Tucker,* above, at 286:

> In my view the appellant was entitled to reply to such a charge and his reply would be protected by qualified privilege, but I think it clear that this protection would be lost if in making his reply the appellant went beyond matters that were reasonably germane to him. It is for the judge alone to rule as a matter of law not only whether the occasion is privileged but also whether the defendant published something beyond what was germane and reasonably appropriate to the occasion so that the privilege does not extend thereto.

O'Malley v. *O' Callaghan* (1992), 89 D.L.R. (4th) 577, per Mason J. at 587 (Alta Q.B.), citing Philip Lewis, *Gatley on Libel and Slander*, 8th ed. (London: Sweet & Maxwell, 1981) at 218:

> [A] person whose character has been attacked is entitled to answer such attack, and any defamatory statements he may make about the person who attacked him will be privileged, provided they are published *bona fide* and are fairly relevant to the accusations made.

Bennett v. *Stupich* (1981), 30 B.C.L.R. 57, per Mackoff J. at 62–63 (S.C.) [plea of qualified privilege that defamatory words were written by the defendant in defence of his own reputation and the reputation of other opposition members of the legislature rejected by the court on the basis of a finding of fact "there was here … not a word in defence of his reputation or that of the other N.D.P. M.L.A.s … The defamatory words of the defendant answer nothing, they only attack."].

Therefore where the original attack is made in the news media, the person attacked may respond in kind in the same or similar news media. The fact that the news media employed by the defendant may have a larger audience or circulation does not destroy the privilege, nor does the fact the defendant employed vigorous language.

Mallett v. *Clarke* (1968), 70 D.L.R. (2d) 67 (B.C.S.C.).

Ward v. *Clark*, [2002] 2 W.W.R. 238 per Esson J.A. at paras. 28–29 (B.C.C.A.).

Falk v. *Smith*, [1941] O.R. 17 at 19, per McFarland J. at 20 (C.A.).

Adam v. *Ward*, [1917] A.C. 309, per Lord Atkinson at 343 (H.L.) [Defendant, secretary to the Army Council, sent the press a copy of his letter to a General who had been attacked in Parliament by the plaintiff. The letter was published in the British and foreign press.]:

> It would be a disgrace and injury to the Service if a man, publicly accused of the shameful breach of duty of which General Scobell was accused, was allowed to continue in command of a brigade in the Army unless and until he had been cleared of the accusation made against him. Every subject, therefore, who had an interest in the Army had an interest in being by a public communication informed of General Scobell's acquital. But I go further. I think it may be laid down as a general proposition that where a man, through the medium of Hansard's reports of the proceedings in Parliament, publishes to the world vile slanders of a civil, naval or military servant of the Crown in relation to the discharge

by that servant of the duties of his office he selects the world as his audience, and that it is the duty of the heads of the service to which the servant belongs, if on investigation they find the imputation against him groundless, to publish his vindication to the same audience to which his traducer has addressed himself.

Ward v. *Clark*, above, at 252.

An exaggeration or extreme statement could be evidence of malice, but absent proof of malice, it does not defeat the privilege. A defendant may be protected, even if his language is violent or excessively strong.

Netupsky v. *Craig*, [1973] S.C.R. 55 at 61–62, citing *Adam* v. *Ward*, [1917] A.C. 309 (H.L.).

McLoughlin v. *Kutasy*, [1979] 2 S.C.R. 311 at 323 .

There is a distinction between disproportionate language, which does not destroy the privilege, and language which is not germane and reasonably appropriate to the occasion, which does.

Ward v. *Clark*, above, at 257–60:

> The law does not require either blandness, or accuracy as a condition of successfully invoking qualified privilege ... The phrase "germane and reasonably appropriate to the occasion is derived from the reasons of Cartwright J. (later C.J.C.) in *Tucker* v. *Douglas* [(1951),[1952] 1 S.C.R. 275 (S.C.C.)]. In using those words, Cartwright J. was not considering whether the statement was bland, or factually correct ...
>
> Nothing said by Mr. Clark to the Sun reporter was unconnected with the matters in controversy. Mr. Clark believed on reasonable grounds that Mr. Ward was "feeding misinformation" on the fast ferry issue. He knew Mr. Ward to be a disgruntled bidder. So it was germane and reasonably appropriate for him to suggest that as explaining why Ward would feed misinformation. It may not have been true, it may have been hurtful but it was germane and reasonably appropriate to the occasion. ... If a defamatory response meets that test, the law allows much leeway in the language used.

8) In The Public Interest

The mere fact that the defamatory expression "relates to matters of public interest" or is "addressed to matters of public interest" is not sufficient to create an occasion of qualified privilege.

Littleton v. Hamilton (1974), 4 O.R. (2d) 283, per Dubin J.A. at 285 (C.A.).

The statement of Dubin J.A. in *Littleton v. Hamilton* is in accord with the judgment of Southin J.A. in *Pressler v. Lethbridge* (2000), 86 B.C.L.R. (3d) 257 (C.A.), where at pages 295–97 she adopted the principles expressed by the English Court of Appeal in *Blackshaw v. Lord* (1984), [1983] 2 All E.R. 311, which rejected a claim for generic protection for a widely-stated category characterized by the defendants as "fair information on a matter of public interest."

> [63] In *Blackshaw v. Lord* (1984), [1983] 2 All E.R. 311 (Eng. C.A.), Stephenson L.J. summarized the principles in terms which I consider accurate, at 327:

>> The subject matter must be of public interest; its publication must be in the public interest. That nature of the matter published and its source and the position or status of the publisher distributing the information must be such as to create the duty to publish the information to the intended recipients, in this case the readers of the *Daily Telegraph*. Where damaging facts have been ascertained to be true, or been made the subject of a report, there may be a duty to report them (see *Cox v. Feeney* (1863) 4 F & F 13, 176 ER 445, *Perera v. Peiris*, [1949] A.C. 1 and *Dunford Publicity Studios Ltd. v. News Media Ownership Ltd.* [1971] N.Z.L.R. 961) provided the public interest is wide enough (*Chapman v. Lord Ellesmere*, [1932] 2 K.B. 431, [1932] All ER Rep 221). But where damaging allegations or charges have been made and are still under investigation (*Purcell v. Solwer* (1877) 2 CPD 215) or have been authoritatively refuted (*Adam v. Ward* (1915) 31 TLR 299; aff'd [1917] AC 308, [1916-17] All ER Rep 157), there can be no duty to report them to the public.

>> ...

>> There may be extreme cases where the urgency of communicating a warning is so great, or the source of the information is so reliable, that publication of suspicion or speculation is justified; for example where there is danger to the public from a suspected terrorist or the distribution of contaminated food or drugs; but there is nothing of that sort here. ...

Blackshaw v. Lord was recently considered by the House of Lords in *Reynolds v. Times Newspapers Ltd.*, [1999], 4 All ER 609 (H.L. (Eng.)), where Lord Nicholls stated at page 618:

Similarly, in *Blackshaw v. Lord*, [1983] 2 All E.R. 311, [1984] Q.B. 1, the Court of Appeal rejected a claim to generic protection for a widely stated category: 'fair information on a matter of public interest' (see [1984] Q.B. 1 at 6). A claim to privilege must be more precisely focused. In order to be privileged publication must be in the public interest. Whether a publication is in the public interest, or, in the conventional phraseology, whether there is a duty to publish to the intended recipients, there the readers of the Daily Telegraph, depends upon the circumstances, including the nature of the matter published and its source or status.

Reynolds v. Times Newspapers Ltd., above, was recently considered in *Leenen v. Canadian Broadcasting Corporation* (2000), 48 O.R. (3d) 656 (S.C.J.), where Cunningham J. held at page 694 that *Reynolds* had reaffirmed the principle of reciprocity and provided a "sound basis upon which the trier of fact may weigh [all the circumstances] and determine whether the reciprocal nature of the test has been met."

After reviewing all circumstances related to a CBC broadcast which he held defamed Dr. Leenen, Cunningham J. concluded that the impugned broadcast "was contrary to the public interest because of its potential for harm by inciting panic amongst patients suffering from high blood pressure." At page 697:

> As I look at what was actually broadcast, how can it be said that a reasonable person would have felt any duty to broadcast this sort of program. It had nothing to do with a duty to communicate important information. It had everything to do with sensationalizing an issue, with creating viewer interest through alarm and with providing a podium for its producer's long held views, capably assisted by the over-heated concerns of a disgruntled regulator.

Although the judgment of the Ontario Court of Appeal affirming the trial decision made reference to the trial judge's finding that the program was "of public interest" but not "in the public interest" [para. 11], it shed no further light on the meaning of "in the public interest." *Leenen v. Canadian Broadcasting Corporation* (2001), 54 O.R. (3d) 612 (C.A.), leave to appeal to S.C.C. denied, [2001] S.C.C.A. No. 432.

In *Leenen*, above, Cunningham J. did not expressly assert that "in the public interest" involves applying a new test to determine if an occasion is privileged. On the basis of Lord Nicholl's statement in *Reynolds*, it appears that determining whether a publication is "in the public interest" is equivalent to determining (as conventionally expressed) whether there is a duty to publish to the intended recipients in light of all the circumstances.

D. ILLUSTRATIONS OF PRIVILEGED OCCASIONS

Occasions of privilege arise in every sector of human endeavour. A random selection of court rulings relating to qualified privilege appears below organized into arbitrary categories. The categories are not comprehensive. Litigants assessing a potential defence of qualified privilege should thoroughly research the jurisprudence for authorities relevant to their particular circumstances.

1) Communications Relating to the Workplace

a) Employment Reference

The employment reference is a classic occasion of qualified privilege. In *Sapiro v. Leader Publishing Co. Ltd.*, [1926] 3 D.L.R. 68 (Sask. C.A.), Lamont J.A. held at 71 that "it is so manifestly for the advantage of society that one about to employ a servant should learn what his previous conduct has been that it may well be deemed the moral duty of the former master to tell what he knows and believes without fear of being confronted with an action for libel."

b) Employee Termination

Depending on all the circumstances, it may be an occasion of privilege for an employer to communicate to other employees or to its officers or directors the reason why an employee was dismissed.

> *Tench v. Great Western Railway* (1873), 33 U.C.Q.B. 8 at 17–18 [general manager of a railroad dismissed a conductor for alleged dishonesty and posted placards describing the offence and the dismissal in company's private offices (although visible there to 3 or 4 strangers) and in circular books of the conductors, to inform and warn the other employees. Occasion held to be privileged.].

> *Gilman v. Society for Information Children*, [2003] B.C.J. No. 2298, 2003 BCSC 1527, per Brooke J. at para. 9 [defendant had interest in providing a copy of the defamatory letter of termination to its directors].

> *Somerville v. Hawkins* (1851), 10 Q.B. 583 [when plaintiff, who was dismissed on suspicion of theft, attended to obtain wages, the defendant employer informed two other employees "I have dismissed that man for robbing me, do not speak to him any more in public or private or I shall think you as bad as him." Occasion held privileged as it was duty of the defendant and also in his interest to prevent his employees from associating with a person of such character].

Fisher v. *Rankin*, [1972] 4 W.W.R. 705 (B.C.S.C.) [company is entitled to inform its supervisory personnel of disciplinary action taken against employee, union may inform other employees who are parties to collective agreement of the resolution of grievance over such disciplinary action].

Costello v. *Bremner and Coles* (1961), 31 D.L.R. (2d) 537 (Nfld. S.C.) [plaintiff civilian employee was suspended from the naval base fire brigade for disciplinary reasons and denied entry to the base. To make the denial effective, the defendant naval officers issued an order to that effect and distributed two copies each to the main gate and fire station to be posted as a constant reminder. Two additional copies, six in all, were distributed to the Area Naval Commander and the Base Security Officer. Held the publications were privileged].

Hunt v. *Great Northern Railway Co.*, [1891] 2 Q.B. 189 (C.A.) [plaintiff security guard was dismissed by defendant for gross neglect of duty. The defendant published the plaintiff's name in a monthly circular addressed to all employees, stating the plaintiff had been dismissed and that he had been fired for gross abuse of duty. Held: employer had an interest in stating this to employees who had an interest in hearing the company treated certain things as misconduct.]

Litster v. *British Columbia Ferry Corporation*, 2003 BCSC 557, per Gray J. at paras. 124–28 [plaintiff terminal manager sued over letter of termination sent to five employees, all involved in administration; all had an interest in receiving the dismissal letter to discharge their employment duties].

Where rumours were circulating in the community and company directors were concerned that shareholders were becoming panicky, the company published an advertisement to correct the rumours. The advertisement, which mentioned the dismissal of the mine manager, was held to be privileged.

Robinson v. *Estella Mines Ltd.* (1953), 10 W.W.R. (N.S.) 374, per Clement J. at 337 (B.C.S.C.).

It has been held, in some circumstances, that an employer and its officers may claim qualified privilege for disclosure of information about an employee to the employee's parents.

Matheson v. *Brown*, [1915] 49 N.S.R. 198.

c) Complaints to Employers

Where a forestry company employee defamed the plaintiff union business agent in response to questions from a senior union official, her statements were made on a privileged occasion.

Cantelon v. Industrial Wood and Allied Workers of Canada, Local 1-71, [1999] B.C.J. No. 1620 (S.C.).

Where the defendant company sent a letter to a union hiring hall alleging a worker was incompetent, it was held that the employer and the union hiring hall had a common interest in the evaluation of the plaintiff's competence, both by reason of their respective obligations under the collective agreement and because of their relationship to each other in the providing and employing of competent stevedoring labour.

Silbernagel v. Empire Stevedoring Co. (1979), 18 B.C.L.R. 384 (S.C.).

d) Workplace Investigations

Statements by a school secretary, a support worker, and a custodian in response to specific inquiries by the assistant superintendent of schools were privileged.

Haight-Smith v. Neden (2002), 211 D.L.R. (4th) 370 at para. 55 (B.C.C.A.).

Statements contained in a report prepared by an Internal Affairs investigator concerning the plaintiff Customs Inspector were held to be privileged.

Bires v. Canada (Minister of National Revenue), [2001] N.B.R. (2d) (Supp.) No. 52 per McLellan J. at para. 9 (Q.B. (T.D.)).

Where the plaintiff union officer made unfounded complaints about the defendant's management to a meeting of a joint union/management standing committee, a letter subsequently issued by the defendant which defamed the union officer was held to be privileged. The plaintiff, as president of the Union local, had a duty to fairly represent all members. The defendant, as a member of the local, was held to have an interest in the conduct of the plaintiff and a right to complain if he thought the plaintiff's conduct inappropriate.

Masunda v. Johnson, [1999] B.C.J. No. 2570 (S.C.), aff'd (2002) 158 B.C.A.C. 196 (C.A.), per Donald J.A. at para. 5.

2) Complaints About Teachers

It has been held that parents are permitted to communicate their honestly held concerns about alleged mistreatment of students by their teachers to the proper authorities.

> *Gibbs v. Jalbert* (1996), 18 B.C.L.R. (3d) 351, per Prowse J.A at 357–58 (C.A.):

It was held that a professor was under a duty to disclose information he obtained from another academic to certain other professors, all of whom were either actively involved in the plaintiff's employment or were the professor's own direct supervisors. The information contained allegations of questionable academic behaviour and were of very serious nature in an academic context.

> *Lipczynska-Kochany v. Gillham* (2001), 14 C.C.E.L. (3d) 304, per Lissaman J.
> at para. 77 (Ont. S.C.J.), aff'd [2003] O.J. No. 789 (C.A.).

3) Communications With Parents

Where a mother asked a police officer why a police investigation was necessary, an occasion of qualified privilege was created and the police officer was entitled to inform her of allegations that had been made against her son. A parent of a suspected thief was a person who had a sufficient interest in receiving information regarding the actions of her child to create an occasion of qualified privilege.

> *Chrispen v. Novak*, [1995] 5 W.W.R. 752 (Sask. Q.B.).

4) Disclosure to Health Professionals

Disclosures made to therapists or to a parent may be protected by qualified privilege.

> *L.G.C. v. V.M.C.*, [1997] 1 W.W.R. 746 per Dorgan J. at 750 (B.C.S.C.):

> Surely it is the professional duty of a treating therapist to receive and hear information from patients whose emotional and psychological welfare they are looking after. Certainly the defendants have a real interest in communicating this information to those from whom they are seeking professional psychological assistance ... . Similarly it is not difficult to conclude that parents will be held to the highest moral, legal and social duty to receive information from their children regarding incidents or allegations of sexual abuse and that their interest in receiving communications of this nature are common with the interests

of children who make such communications. The fact that the alleged abuser is one of the parents, it seems to me, highlights the importance of legally recognizing this privilege.

5) Business and Commercial Life

If a business communication is made on a privileged occasion, the privilege covers all incidents of the transmission and treatment of that communication which are in accordance with the reasonable and usual course of business.

> *Lacarte v. Toronto Board of Education*, [1959] S.C.R. 465.

Accordingly, the defendant's dictation to his stenographer, in the ordinary method of dealing with his correspondence, of a letter containing defamatory matter, is a publication on an occasion of qualified privilege. Similarly, the privilege extends to publication to employed clerks, in the one case by the sender, and in the other by the receiver of the communication, when made in the usual and ordinary course of business.

> *Greenan v. Minneapolis Threshing Machine Co. & Christiansen*, [1929] 4 D.L.R. 501 (Alta. C.A.).

> *Toronto-Dominion Bank v. Berthin*, [1994] O.J. No. 2066 (Gen. Div.) per Winkler J. [pursuant to rights defined in a General Security Agreement, bank sent letters to other financial institutions which were in a position to assist it. Held that the recipients had an interest in receiving the letter, taking into account that the Municipal Trust applied the funds it held to its own mortgage.].

> *Puterbaugh v. Gold Medal Furniture Manufacturing Co.* (1904), 7 O.L.R. 582 (C.A.) [citing *Pullman v. Hill & Co.*, [1891] 1 Q.B. 524, manager gave secretary a draft letter to be typewritten in the interest of the company, but unconnected with its ordinary business, no privilege.].

6) Communications Made During Proceedings of a Public Organization

Communications made during the course of proceedings before municipal and town councils are considered to be protected by qualified privilege.

> *Edwards v. Gattmann* (1928), 40 B.C.R. 122 per McDonald J. at 123–24 (S.C.).

> *McKinnon v. Dauphin (Rural Municipality)*, [1996] 3 W.W.R. 127, per Clearwater J. at 148 (Man. Q.B.).

Savidant v. *Day* (1933), 5 M.P.R. 554 (P.E.I.T.D.), aff'd [1933] 4 D.L.R. 456 (P.E.I.C.A.) [meeting of Charlottetown City Council on occasion of application by the plaintiff for a position] per Saunders J. at 460:

> The alleged words were spoken at a meeting of Charlottetown city council. It was unquestionably a conditional or qualified privilege occasion ... the defendant's memory being refreshed by his son's statement, it seems to me it was his clear duty to have informed his fellow councilors of the true character and reputation of the applicant for a city position, otherwise what safety would the city have in respect to its appointees. I hold the words were spoken by the defendant in the *bona fide* discharge of his duty as a councillor to the mayor and fellow councillors.

Baumann v. *Turner* (1993), 105 D.L.R. (4th) 37 at 58–59 (B.C.C.A.).

Watson v. *Southam Inc.* (c.o.b. *Hamilton Spectator*) (1998), 52 O.T.C. 1 at para. 151 (Gen. Div.), varied on other grounds, (2000), 189 D.L.R. (4th) 695 (C.A.).

Edwards v. *Gattmann* (1928), 40 B.C.R. 122, per McDonald J. at 123 (S.C.).

McKinnon v. *Dauphin* (*Rural Municipality*), [1996] 3 W.W.R. 127 (Man. Q.B.).

Hopewell v. *Kennedy* (1904), 9 O.L.R. 43 (Div. Ct.).

The rationale for applying the defence of qualified privilege to communications before municipal councils has been explained by several courts. Riddell, J. in *Ward* v. *McBride* (1911), 24 O.L.R. 555 at 568 (C.A.), speaking with reference to the office of aldermen, said:

> Aldermen are legislators in as true and in many instances as important a sense as members of Parliament or of the Legislature – it is their right and their duty to speak their mind fully and clearly without evasion or equivocation – they should show no fear, favour, or affection; and it is their duty, as well as their right, to use all legitimate means, oratorical or otherwise to impress their fellow-legislators with the righteousness of their views – they have no need to be mealy-mouthed and should call a spade a spade.

Lord Diplock in *Horrocks* v. *Lowe*, [1974] 1 All E.R. 662 at 671 held:

> My Lords, what is said by members of a local council at meetings of the council or of any of its committees is spoken on a privileged occasion. The reason for the privilege is that those who represent the local government electors should be able to speak freely and frankly, boldly and bluntly, on any matter, which they believe affects the interest or welfare of the inhabitants. They may be swayed by strong political prejudice, they may be obstinate and pig-headed,

stupid and obtuse, but they were chosen by the electors to speak their minds on matters of local concern and so long as they do so honestly they run no risk of liability for defamation of those who are the subjects of their criticism.

Matheson C.J. instructing the jury in *Savidant* v. *Day*, above, said:

> as a City Councillor with his [the Defendant's] duty to protect and guard the property and interest of the public ... and if in that position he made statements which were made in the public interest and in pursuit of his duty and made them to those who are interested in the same matter then a privilege would arise and that although the words might otherwise be slanderous that privilege would be capable of safeguarding him from a prosecution for slander even although the words he spoke were untrue and even although they were slanderous and injurious except for this protection, he could wrap that cloak around him and it would protect him from attack — that cloak of privilege.

Mr. Justice Clearwater of the Manitoba Court of Queen's Bench stated in *McKinnon* v. *Dauphin (Rural Municipality)*, [1996] 3 W.W.R. 127 at 148:

> the law should be careful not to dampen a person's enthusiasm for participation in local politics. There should be and is a wide latitude for discussion and debate of issues properly before municipal council.

Statements made to municipal councils on an occasion of qualified privilege do not necessarily lose their privilege only because they are made in the presence of the press.

Pittard v. *Oliver*, [1891] 1 Q.B. 474, per Lord Esher at 478 (C.A.):

> If a person whose duty it is to make a statement to certain persons calls in other persons to whom he owes no duty to make the statement, in order that those other persons may hear it, I should be inclined to say (although it is not necessary to the decision of the present case), that it would not become his duty to refrain from making his statement to the proper persons, but that there would be evidence of malice in his making it in the presence of others who might promulgate it.

Bay Tower Homes v. *Illingworth*, April 1987, unreported decision of Ont. Div. Ct.

Baumann v. *Turner* (1993), 105 D.L.R. (4th) 37 (B.C.C.A.).

McKinnon v. *Dauphin (Rural Municipality)*, above, at 148, para. 50:

> Councillor Spencer, and all councillors, had an obligation and duty to debate and discuss the relative merits and abilities of all bidders being considered for the contract in question. I am satisfied that the defen-

dant has fulfilled the onus on it of establishing that these words were spoken during or on an occasion of qualified privilege (during the conduct of a public municipal council meeting).

Lawson v. *Thompson* (1968), 66 W.W.R. 427 at 432 (B.C.S.C.), aff'd (1969), 69 W.W.R. 304 (B.C.C.A.) per Seaton J. at 66 W.W.R. 432 [words spoken a meeting of the Vancouver and District Labour Council by the president of the Vancouver local of the I.W.A. about the president of the Teamster's Joint Council No. 36, the alleged sting being that he was a police informer]:

> It is suggested that the presence of the press and visitors so altered the character of the meeting as to take away the privilege. There is no evidence that the defendant either invited the visitors or the press or had the authority to remove them. I conclude that the presence of others left the defendant's duty untouched. ... *Parsons* v. *Surgery* (1864) 4 F & F 247, 176 ER 551, must be distinguished on the ground that there the defendant called the meeting and summoned reporters and the public.

In *Cardwell et al.* v. *Hutchison et al.*, [1995] B.C.J. No. 1656 (S.C.), aff'd (1997), 36 B.C.L.R. (3d) 86 (C.A.), the defendant councillor made a brief comment about the settlement of litigation at a meeting of the Council for West Vancouver sitting as a Committee. The court held, *inter alia*, that the defence of qualified privilege was available to the councillor (as well as the media defendants.) However, for reasons not explained in the Court of Appeal, a new trial was ordered in respect to the claim against the councillor.

Statements by other public officials reported in the press have been held to be protected by qualified privilege.

> *Re International Assn. of Bridge, Structural and Ornamental and Reinforcing Iron-workers (Local 97) and Campbell* (1997), 152 D.L.R. (4th) 547 (B.C.S.C.).

> *Stopforth* v. *Goyer* (1979), 23 O.R. (2d) 696 (C.A.).

> *Parlett* v. *Robinson* (1986), 30 D.L.R. (4th) 247 (B.C.C.A.).

> *Loos* v. *Robbins*, [1987] 4 W.W.R. 469 (Sask. C.A.).

If the defamatory statements have nothing to do with and are not relevant to the issues before the council, however, the qualified privilege will not apply.

> *Peckham* v. *Mount Pearl (City)* (1994), 122 Nfld. & P.E.I.R. 142 (Nfld. S.C. (T.D.)).

The trial judge in *Watson* v. *Southam Inc.* above, held at para. 144 that the statements by one of the defendants was not protected by qualified privilege because his purpose in making it was "character assassination."

Statements made at a public meeting by an alderman of a city, concerning the manner in which the defendant contractor was performing his contract, were *prima facie* privileged, despite the presence of newspaper reporters. In *Hopewell* v. *Kennedy*, above, Teetzel J. stated at 45:

> I take it to be well settled that where a person publishes in a newspaper statements reflecting on the conduct or character of another the aggrieved party is entitled to have recourse to the same paper for his defence and vindication and may at the same time retort upon the assailant when such retort is a necessary part of the defence, or fairly arises out of the charges made by the assailant, and in so doing if he reflects upon the conduct and character of the assailant it is for the jury to say whether he did so honestly and in self defence or was actuated by malice.

See also:

> *Savidant* v. *Day* (1933), 5 M.P.R. 554 (P.E.I.T.D.), aff'd [1933] 4 D.L.R. 456 (P.E.I.C.A.).
>
> *Baumann* v. *Turner* (1993), 105 D.L.R. (4th) 37 at 58–59 (B.C.C.A.).
>
> *Watson* v. *Southam Inc.* (*c.o.b. Hamilton Spectator*) (1998), 52 O.T.C. 1 (Gen. Div.), varied (2000), 189 D.L.R. (4th) 695 (Ont. C.A.).

See the discussion of qualified privilege at common law in *Prud'homme* v. *Prud'homme*, 2002 SCC 85, per L'Heureux-Dubé and Lebel JJ. at paras. 50–60.

7) Elected Private Bodies

A statutory annual meeting of an association directed to be held for the information of the membership is a privileged occasion. The presence of one nonmember will not destroy the privilege.

> *Robinson* v. *Estella Mines Ltd.* (1953), 10 W.W.R. (N.S.) 374 (B.C.S.C.).

A meeting of the residents' council of a nursing home was held to be a privileged occasion.

> *Creedan Valley Nursing Home Ltd.* v. *Van Klaveran*, [1996] O.J. No. 4475 (Gen. Div.).

A statement by a condominium unit owner in a notice distributed to other owners of the condominiums was held to be issued on a privileged occasion.

> *McCullough v. Cohen*, [2000] O.J. No. 3431 (S.C.J.).

Words spoken at a meeting of condominium unit owners to review a condominium budget were held to be privileged.

> *Bird v. York Condominium Corp. No. 340*, [2002] O.J. No. 1993 per O'Neill J. at para. 57 (S.C.J.).

8) Regulatory and Disciplinary Bodies

A statutory body such as a College of Physicians and Surgeons owes a duty not only to its members but to the public to make known information in its possession that a few of its members are prescribing a treatment that is considered to be without merit.

> *Arnott v. College of Physicians and Surgeons of Saskatchewan*, [1954] S.C.R. 538, per Estey J. at 543.

Similarly, a communication to the governing body of a profession may occur on a privileged occasion at common law.

> *Hung v. Gardiner* 2002 BCSC 1234, per Joyce J. at para. 84 [letter sent to law society and CGA association, investigative report, prepared in connection with a professional conduct inquiry which related in part to the plaintiff].

9) Law Enforcement

Citizens who make a statement to police about suspected crimes do so on an occasion of qualified privilege.

> *B.G. v. D.B.*, [2003] O.J. No. 2895 per Dunnet J. at paras. 27–31 (S.C.J.), citing *Corbett v. Jackson*, [1844] O.J. No. 53, 1 U.C.Q.B. 128 (C.A.), *Lee v. Jones*, [1954] 1 D.L.R. 520 (Man. Q.B.), *Crocker v. Inglis* (1889), 16 R. 778 (Ct. Sess.), *Bowles v. Armstrong* (1912), 32 N.Z.L.R. 409 at 425 (C.A.).

> *Brule v. Chmilar* (2000), 256 A.R. 168, per Gallant J. at paras. 61–62 (Q.B.), applying *Lightbody v. Gordon* (1882), 9 R. 934 (Ct. Sess.):

> > When it comes to the knowledge of any one that a crime has been committed, a duty is laid on that person, as a citizen of the country, to state to the authorities what he knows respecting the commission of the crime, and if he states only what he knows and honestly believes

he cannot be subjected to an action of damages merely because it turns out that the person as to whom he has given the information is, after all, not guilty of the crime.

Maher v. K Mart Canada Ltd. (1990), 84 Nfld. & P.E.I.R. 271 (Nfld. S.C. (T.D.)).

Mullins v. Beneteau, [1996] O.J. No. 2784. (Gen. Div.). At paras. 26–27, Quinn J. held that statements to police alleging a bribe attempt were not protected because they were made with malice; "a statement to a police officer is subject to a qualified and not an absolute privilege," citing Sir Robert McEwen & Philip Lewis, *Gatley on Libel and Slander*, 7th ed. (London: Sweet & Maxwell, 1974), c. 13, under heading "Qualified Privilege," and *Dijkstra v. Westerink*, 401 A.2d 1118, 168 N.J. Super. 128 (Super. Ct. App. Div. 1979); *Heggy v. Grutzner*, 456 N.W.2d 845 (Wis. Ct. App. 1990).

Lee v. Jones, [1954] 1 D.L.R. 520 (Man. Q.B.) per DuVal J., citing *Hebditch v. MacIlwaine*, [1894] 2 Q.B. 54 and *Harrison v. Bush*, 5 El. & Bl. 344, and *Padmore v. Lawrence*, (1840), 11 Ad. & El. 380 at 382, 113 E.R. 460, per Coleridge J.: "For the sake of public justice, charges and communications, which would otherwise be slanderous, are protected if made bona fide in the prosecution of an inquiry into a suspected crime."

Lupee v. Hogan (1920), 47 N.B.R. 492 at 499 (C.A.) [defendant missed a fur collar and sent for the police, intimating to officer that she suspected the plaintiff – who worked for the defendant shortly before — had stolen the collar. Held this was an occasion of qualified privilege.]

De Haas v. Mooney, [2003] O.J. No. 549, per Sachs J. at para. 15 (S.C.J.) [statement made to police held to be on an occasion of qualified privilege].

Where the defendant police officer showed the plaintiff's mug shot to a meeting of Loss Prevention Officers at a Cooperative Policing Program Meeting, which was a regular monthly meeting sponsored by Crime Prevention Service of Edmonton Police Force, it was held the occasion was privileged.

Chopra v. Hodson, 2001 ABQB 380, per Hembroff J.

Where a store issued a credit warning to its employees, which was poorly worded, and suggested that the plaintiff was dishonest and of poor character, and the warning was displayed at that store's tills and seen by, and caused concern for many customers, it was held the publication was protected by privilege. The need to prevent crime and protect merchandise created the privilege.

Pleau v. Simpson-Sears Ltd. (1977), 15 O.R. (2d) 436 (C.A.).

A complaint to the police about an alleged assault was held to be clearly privileged.

> *Brule v. Chmilar*, [2000] A.J. No. 39, 2000 ABQB, per Gallant J. at para. 60.

10) Complaints to Public Authorities

A qualified privilege may attach to communications by a constituent to his or her governmental representative or to the appropriate governmental authority concerning misconduct, neglect, or incompetency of public officials or others. A privilege may also attach to a communication by a private organization pursuant to a statutory duty to report.

> *Wood v. Nor-sham (Markham) Hotels Inc.*, [1988] O.J. No. 4765 (Gen. Div.). [Disclosure of information to the unemployment insurance commission an occasion of qualified privilege.]

> *Taylor v. Bank of Nova Scotia*, [1998] O.J. No. 2701, per W. Jenkins J. at paras. 78–80 (Gen. Div.). [Bank said the plaintiff was guilty of unprofessional conduct in its response to Unemployment Insurance Commission.]

> *Tremblay v. Goddard*, [1996] O.J. No. 2518 (Gen. Div.) [defendants under duty to report serious occurrences to the Ministry of Community and Social Services and the Children's Aid Society for Ottawa-Carlton (CAS)].

A member of an Indian Band has at least an interest in making known to the Minister of Indian Affairs complaints and allegations of wrongdoing in respect of the Chief and Councillors of a Band. The Minister has a duty to receive such complaints and allegations.

> *Derrickson v. Tomat* (1992), 88 D.L.R. (4th) 401 per Hinds J.A. at 423–24 (B.C.C.A.).

11) Government Officials

Government officials normally enjoy qualified privilege when communicating within the scope of their duties with other government officials or representatives, who have a corresponding interest.

> *Savidant v. Day*, [1933] 4 D.L.R. 456 (P.E.I.C.A.).

> *Horrocks v. Lowe*, [1975] A.C. 135 at 147 (H.L.).

> *Watson v. Southam Inc. (c.o.b. Hamilton Spectator)* (1998), 52 O.T.C. 1 at para. 67 (Gen. Div.), varied on other grounds (2000), 189 D.L.R. (4th) 695 (Ont. C.A.).

> *Wooding v. Little*, [1982] B.C.J. No. 1422 (S.C.).

Kelsie v. *Canada (Attorney General)*, [2003] N.J. No. 232, 2003 NSLCTD 139, per Barry J. at para. 32.

E. PUBLICATION "TO THE WORLD"

12) Supreme Court Decisions Deny Broad Privilege to News Media

As noted above, reciprocity is a key factor in the court's evaluation of the defence of qualified privilege. To succeed, the defendant must establish not only some public or private duty or interest, but also that the recipient had a corresponding interest in receiving the information.

Where an occasion might otherwise be privileged, the defendant may go outside its protection by communicating the defamatory expression to those who do not have a proper reciprocal interest in receiving it. A series of five judgments of the Supreme Court of Canada, all except the last written by Cartwright J. (later C.J.C.), continue to be cited as authority for the proposition that the news media cannot raise a defence of qualified privilege at common law because "publication to the world" is unduly broad:

i)   *Douglas* v. *Tucker*, [1952] 1 S.C.R. 275;

ii) *Globe and Mail Ltd.* v. *Boland*, [1960] S.C.R. 203;

iii) *Banks* v. *Globe and Mail Ltd.*, [1961] S.C.R. 474;

iv) *Jones* v. *Bennett*, [1969] S.C.R. 277;

v)   *Fraser* v. *Sykes*, [1974] S.C.R. 526.

In *Douglas* v. *Tucker*, above, Cartwright J. for the Court held that the defendant Premier of Saskatchewan made defamatory accusations at a public meeting during an election campaign that the plaintiff Leader of the Opposition was facing a charge of fraud. The Premier personally handed a newspaper reporter his notes summarizing his speech. The reporter spoke to the Premier before publication in the *Star-Phoenix* newspaper and showed him a copy of the story, which republished the Premier's allegation of fraud.

When the matter came before the trial court, one basis on which the Premier alleged the occasion was privileged was that "the defendant, as an elector, a candidate for election, and the leader of his party, had a duty to communicate to those having a legitimate interest in the result of such election, facts which he honestly believed to be true, relevant to the fitness, or otherwise, for office of other candidates offering themselves for election." [S.C.R. 287]

In the Supreme Court of Canada, Cartwright J. rejected this defence at pages 287–88, concluding that whatever its merits, "It is settled that whatever may be the extent of such privilege it is lost if the publication is made in a newspaper." Cartwright concluded that publication in a newspaper is publication to the world.

> Cartwight cited *Duncombe* v. *Danielle* (1837), 8 Car. & P. 222 (action for libel against voter over his letters published in a newspaper which reflected adversely on the character of a candidate for Parliament; per Lord Denham C.J.: "However large the privilege of electors may be, it is extravagant to suppose that it can justify the publication to all the world of facts injurious to a person who happens to stand in the situation of a candidate."); *De Crespigny* v. *Wellesly* (1829), 5 Bing. 392 and *Adam* v. *Ward*, [1917] A.C. 309 [held to be authority for proposition that "publication in a newspaper is publication to the world."]; *Gatley on Libel and Slander*, 3d ed., pp. 251 and 278; *Odgers on Libel and Slander*, 6th ed., at pp. 171 and 246; *Anderson* v. *Hunter* (1891), 18 R. 467; *Bethell* v. *Mann*, *The Times*, October 29, 1999; and *Lang* v. *Willis*, 52 C.L.R. 637 at 667, 672.

In *Globe and Mail Ltd.* v. *Boland*, above, Cartwright J. for the Court overturned a finding by the trial judge that a newspaper editorial concerning a candidate in a federal election was published on an occasion of privilege stating at pages 207–8:

> … [T]he learned trial judge has confused the right which the publisher of a newspaper has, in common with all Her Majesty's subjects, to report truthfully and comment fairly upon matters of public interest with a duty of the sort which gives rise to an occasion of qualified privilege.
>
> It is well to bear in mind the following passage from the judgment of Lord Shaw in *Arnold* v. *The King Emperor* (1914), 30 T.L.R. 462 at 468, quoted by Lebel J.A.:
>
> > The freedom of the journalist is an ordinary part of the freedom of the subject, and to whatever lengths the subject may go, so also may the journalist, but apart from statute law, his privilege is no other and no higher. The responsibilities which attach to his power in the dissemination of printed matter may, and in the case of a conscientious journalist do, make him more careful; but the range of his assertions, his criticisms, or his comments, is as wide as, and no wider than, that of any other subject. No privilege attaches to his position.

To hold that during a federal election campaign in Canada any defamatory statement published in the press relating to a candidate's fitness for office is to be taken as published on an occasion of qualified privilege would be, in my opinion, not only contrary to the great weight of authority in England and in this country but harmful to that "common convenience and welfare of society" which Baron Parke described as the underlying principle on which the rules as to qualified privilege are founded.

The matter of qualified privilege for publication in the news media again came before the Supreme Court of Canada in *Banks* v. *Globe & Mail Ltd.*, above, where the Court ruled that a newspaper editorial which defamed the vice-president of the Seafarer's International Union of North American was not published on an occasion of qualified privilege, overturning the finding of the trial judge and the Court of Appeal of Ontario in this regard. Cartwright J., again speaking for the Court, stated at pages 483–84, after expressly approving *Douglas* v. *Tucker*, above, and *Globe and Mail Ltd.* v. *Boland*, above:

> The decision of the learned trial judge in the case at bar, quoted above, appears to involve the proposition of law, which in my opinion is untenable, that given proof of the existence of a subject-matter of wide public interest throughout Canada without proof of any other special circumstances any newspaper in Canada (and semble therefore any individual) which sees fit to publish to the public at large statements of fact relevant to that subject-matter is to be held to be doing so on an occasion of qualified privilege.

Furthermore, as he had done earlier in *Globe and Mail Ltd.* v. *Boland*, above, Cartwright J. stated that, although newspapers enjoy the same right as all other citizens to report truthfully and comment fairly upon matters of public interest, that right must not be confused with the sort of duty that gives rise to an occasion of qualified privilege. In *Boland*, at page 209, Cartwright J. suggested that that the public interest and the interests of newspapers find adequate protection in the defence of fair comment.

The series of judgments authored by Cartwright J. on publication to the world is completed by *Jones* v. *Bennett*, above, where, speaking again for the Court, he rejected a defence of qualified privilege for statements made by the Premier of British Columbia about the plaintiff civil servant while addressing a meeting of political supporters at which the press were present. Cartwright J. stated at 284:

> I am satisfied that any privilege which the defendant would have had was lost by reason of the fact that, as found by the learned trial judge:

The Premier must have known that whatever he did say would be communicated to the general public. The two reporters sat at a press table in full view of the speaker's table.

...

In view of the unanimous judgments of this Court in *Douglas v. Tucker*, [[1952] 1 S.C.R. 275], particularly at pp. 287 and 288, and in *Globe and Mail v. Boland* [[1960] S.C.R. 203], it must regarded as settled that a plea of qualified privilege based on a ground of the sort relied on in the case at bar cannot be upheld where the words complained of are published to the public generally, or as it is sometimes expressed, "to the world."

Jones v. Bennett, above, was applied in *Fraser v. Sykes*, above, where the Supreme Court of Canada, with little discussion, held that a defence of qualified privilege did not apply either to statements made by the defendant mayor at a special press conference he called for all the news media to give his statements "the widest possible publicity" or to a subsequent regular press conference at which he answered media questions. The impugned statements, which alleged a "breach of faith," concerned the plaintiff lawyer who was chief negotiator for two companies in negotiations with a municipality concerning a land development plan [*Fraser v. Sykes*, above, at 532, 534].

13) Decisions Concerning Publication to the World

a) Politicians' Duty to Ventilate

Despite the Supreme Court of Canada decisions noted above, a number of appellate court decisions have subsequently recognized a qualified privilege defence where the court has found the politician had a duty to ventilate the subject matter and the electorate had an interest in knowing of the matter:

i)   *Stopforth v. Goyer* (1979), 23 O.R. 696 (C.A.).
ii) *Parlett v. Robinson* (1986), 30 D.L.R. (4th) 247 (B.C.C.A.).
iii) *Loos v. Robbins*, [1987] 4 W.W.R. 469 (Sask.C.A.).
iv) *Baumann v. Turner* (1993), 82 B.C.L.R. (2d) 362 (C.A.).

None of these four defamation lawsuits involved recognition of a qualified privilege defence for news media defendants.

In *Stopforth v. Goyer*, above, the Ontario Court of Appeal held, reversing the trial judge, that comments made to the news media by a federal government minister with respect to the dismissal of a senior civil servant were made on an occasion of qualified privilege. Per Jessup J.A. for the Court at pages 699–770:

In my opinion the electorate, as represented by the media, has a real and *bona fide* interest in the demotion of a senior civil servant for alleged dereliction of duty. It would want to know if the reasons given the House [of Commons in Ottawa] were the real and only reasons for demotion. The appellant had a corresponding public duty and interest in satisfying that interest of the electorate.

Neither the trial judge [20 O.R. (2d) 262] nor Jessup J.A. mentioned or made any attempt to distinguish the decisions of the Supreme Court of Canada in *Jones* v. *Bennett*, *Globe and Mail Ltd.* v. *Boland*, *Douglas* v. *Tucker*, or *Banks* v. *Globe and Mail Ltd.* Although the trial judgment in *Stopforth* did refer to *Littleton* v. *Hamilton* (1974), 4 O.R. (2d) 283 (C.A.), leave to appeal to S,C,C, refused (1979), 4 O.R. (2d) 283n, where Dubin J.A. considered the decision *Banks* v. *Globe and Mail Ltd.*, above, that decision involved the position of a news media defendant, which was not an issue in *Stopforth*.

The British Columbia Court of Appeal in *Parlett* v. *Robinson* (1986), 30 D.L.R. (4th) 247, held that a defence of qualified privilege applied to statements to the news media by a Member of Parliament, who was the New Democratic Party's spokesperson concerning the affairs of the Ministry of the Solicitor General. The subject matter of the communication was a demotion of the plaintiff, a senior civil servant, for alleged dereliction of duty, incompetence, and lack of integrity. The statements were published to the Canadian electorate in a news conference and on television.

In *Parlett*, above, Hinkson J.A. at page 257 distinguished *Jones* v. *Bennett* on the basis that in *Jones* "the defendant was under no duty to communicate the concern he had about the plaintiff to anyone." Referring to *Stopforth* v. *Goyer*, above, Hinkson J.A. concluded at pages 259–60 that if a Member of Parliament has a "duty to ventilate the subject matter and the electorate has a duty in knowing the matter" it cannot be said that publication to the world was too broad.

In *Loos* v. *Robbins*, [1987] 4 W.W.R. 469, the Saskatchewan Court of Appeal held that a communication by a Minister to the news media was made on an occasion of qualified privilege. The statement related to the dismissal of government employees by a crown corporation for which the Minister was responsible. In this judgment, Gerwing J.A. for the court distinguished the Supreme Court of Canada decisions in *Globe & Mail Ltd.* v. *Boland*, above, and *Jones* v. *Bennett*, above, in the following terms:

With respect to [*Globe & Mail Ltd.* v. *Boland*], at least one valid distinction is set out in the Law Society of Upper Canada Lectures (1983) at pp. 344–45 [C.R. Thompson, Q.B. and R. McCloskey, "Libel and Slander," p. 335]:

> ... It is submitted ... that the Stopforth case can be distinguished from the Boland case decided by the Supreme Court of Canada by reason of the fact that in *Stopforth* v. *Goyer* it was a Minister who had a duty to make a statement to the public about a matter of public interest regarding his department. The defence of qualified privilege is dependent on the duties of the speaker: not every member of the public would have been able to make the same statement and avail himself of the privilege accorded.

The British Columbia Court of Appeal in *Baumann* v. *Turner* (1993), 82 B.C.L.R. (2d) 362, concluded that a mayor was entitled to a defence of qualified privilege for communicating to a local newspaper a copy of his letter to the Provincial Member of the Environment in which he alleged that the plaintiff had misused his Professional Engineer's certificate in a political matter. In finding the occasion privileged, Legg J.A. concluded that the mayor was in a similar position to the defendant in *Parlett* v. *Robinson*, above, stating at page 386:

> When [the defendant mayor] learned that the newspaper had obtained a copy of the [Provincial Minister of the Environment's] statement of his opposition to the project, and support of the [plaintiff's] opposition to that project, his publication to the local newspaper of his answer to that opposition prior to a public meeting called to discuss that matter, cannot be said to have been "to the public generally" or "unduly wide." In my opinion, the privilege was not lost.

A number of trial level decisions have also recognized a qualified privilege where a politician has been held to have a duty to ventilate:

a)   *Re International Assn. of Bridge, Structural and Ornamental and Reinforcing Ironworkers (Local 97) and Campbell* (1997), 152 D.L.R. (4th) 547, 40 B.C.L.R. (3d) 1 (S.C.) [provincial opposition party leader issued news release on government deal allegedly benefitting governing party and plaintiff union]. Per Macdonald J. at 556–57:

> [25] The Official Opposition (indeed, any member of an opposition party) and its leader have both a duty and an interest to investigate and expose any impropriety or irregularity in the management of government monies by the government of the day, and to communicate their findings to the electorate. The electorate has a corresponding interest in receiving such information.

...

[26] I do not accept the proposition that the Province [newspaper] and Kieran [the columnist] can "huddle under the same umbrella" of qualified privilege. There is no direct authority for that proposition, and it is neither necessary or appropriate to extend the law on this defence. It may be that a news story reporting nothing more than the bare fact of the Liberal news release and its contents (as opposed to an editorial or a column such as Kieran's of May 10, 1994) would and should be considered part and parcel of an occasion of qualified privilege. But even that is doubtful in the light of *Globe and Mail Ltd.* v. *Boland*, [1960] S.C.R. 203, 22 D.L.R. (2d) 277, and that is not this case. The Kieran column of May 10, 1994 was more than a simple reporting of facts.

b)   Where a government minister, in response to public allegations by the plaintiff of criminal wrongdoing against a former attorney general and deputy attorney general of the province, made public statements critical of the plaintiff, it was held they were privileged. *Milgaard* v. *Mitchell*, [1997] 3 W.W.R. 82 per Barclay J. at 92 (Sask. Q.B.):

> In the case at bar, Mitchell was the Minister of the Crown responsible for the administration of justice within the province of Saskatchewan. ... After the Supreme Court refused to hold that [the plaintiff] Milgaard was not guilty, he continued to profess his innocence in the public forum. He also claimed compensation from the government which was denied. Milgaard then made public allegations of criminal wrongdoing against a former attorney general and deputy attorney general of the province.

And at page 94, paragraph 36:

> The foundation of all privilege is the public interest in the sense of a legitimate and proper interest as opposed to an interest due to idle curiosity or a desire for gossip. In *Webb* v. *Turner Publishing Co.*, [1960] 2 Q.B. 535, the court held that qualified privilege attached to a report of judicial proceedings of a foreign court where its subject matter was closely connected with the administration of justice in England, and therefore was of legitimate and proper interest to the English newspaper reading public.
>
> ...
>
> In my view, the electorate, as represented by the media, has a real and bona fide interest in the administration of justice in the Province of Saskatchewan, and in particular the alleged public wrongdoing concerning the manner in which certain senior officials of the Attorney General's

Department has handled Milgaard's case in 1971. However, Mitchell, as Minister of the Crown and as Attorney General, has a corresponding public duty and interest in satisfying the electorate. ... These allegations of wrongdoing with respect to the handling of the Milgaard case are such that there is a duty to communicate a response by the Minister of Justice. [Court refuses to strike plea of qualified privilege.]

In *Wade & Wells Co. Ltd.* v. *Laing* (1957), 11 D.L.R. (2d) 276 (B.C.C.A.), Sheppard J.A. at 281 distinguished *Douglas* v. *Tucker*, [1952] 1 D.L.R. 657 on the basis that in the case at bar, although the plaintiff alleged that the defendant intended his words to be published in newspapers by speaking at a meeting at which reporters were present and had published them, the plaintiff did not allege that there was in fact any publication by any newspaper.

b) Lawyers' Obligation to Speak Out Against Injustice

In *Campbell* v. *Jones* (2002), 220 D.L.R. (4th) 201, 2002 NSCA 128, the Nova Scotia Court of Appeal set aside a jury's $240,000 defamation verdict against two lawyers over statements they made at a press conference which allegedly conveyed the innuendo that the plaintiff police officer was racist, motivated by racism, or discriminated in the conduct of her duties on the basis of race, economic status and social status. The lawyers represented three twelve-year-old black schoolgirls from a poor neighbourhood. The Supreme Court of Canada denied an application for leave to appeal, [2002] S.C.C.A. No. 543.

Roscoe J.A. (Glube C.J.N.S. concurring), reversing the trial judge, held that the lawyers' statements had been made on an occasion of qualified privilege. The trial judge considered he was bound by the decision of the Supreme Court of Canada in *Jones* v. *Bennett* and that a broad publication "to the world at large" is not privileged. The trial judge had determined that the "integral importance of an individual's reputation" as explained in *Hill* v. *Scientology* required him to conclude that there should be "continued restraint where privilege is claimed over a defamatory statement made to the world at large." [See the trial judgment: (2001), 197 N.S.R. (2d) 212, per Moir J. at para. 28 (S.C.).]

The news media defendants had settled with the plaintiff before trial for $14,500 and were therefore not parties to the appeal. The judgment does not directly deal with the existence of a privilege for the media to report the lawyers' statements.

Applying the Supreme Court of Canada's decision in *R.* v. *Golden*, [2001] S.C.J. 81 (decided after the trial), the Court of Appeal held that the three girls had in fact been subjected to an unlawful "strip search" contrary to the *Charter*, as alleged by the lawyers in the complaint and at the press conference. [Paragraphs 23, 65, 72.] The trial judge had found that the search was "not technically a strip search."

The appeal decision did not address a defence of justification (truth) with respect to the imputations of racism.

Roscoe J.A. (Glube C.J.N.S. concurring) held that the two lawyers, who in advance of the press conference had filed complaints to the Police Commission on behalf of the three girls, had an ethical duty to speak out against injustice. Roscoe J.A. held that the press conference was an occasion of qualified privilege, stating *inter alia*:

> 59 ... [L]awyers, who are officers of the court with duties to improve the administration of justice and uphold the law, have a special relationship with and responsibility to the public to speak out when elements of the justice system itself have breached the fundamental rights of citizens and they have reason to believe that complaints pursuant to the *Police Act* will not provide an adequate remedy.
>
> ...
>
> 68 ... In determining whether the press conference was an occasion of qualified privilege, the trial judge had to consider all of the circumstances. Here, there was an intertwining of *Charter* rights; the right to counsel and the right not to be subjected to an unreasonable search, with *Charter* values; freedom of speech and equality rights. Freedom of speech was being exercised to promote equality rights and to draw attention to violations of *Charter* rights.
>
> ...
>
> 70 ... In a case such as this where freedom of expression is exercised not merely for its own sake, or to advance one's own self-interest, but to bring attention to and seek redress for multiple breaches of such important *Charter* rights as the right to counsel, the right to security of the person, including the right not to be subject to unreasonable search, and the right to equal protection and benefit of the law, one would expect it to be even more difficult to justifiy its curtailment. In any event, in my view, it was incumbent upon the trial judge to at least turn his mind to the myriad of *Charter* rights and values at issue in the case before him. If constitutional rights are to have any meaning, they must surely include the freedom of persons whose *Charter* guarantees have been deliberately violated by officials of state agencies to cry out loud and long against their transgressors in the public forum, and in

the case of children and others less capable of articulation of the issues, to have their advocates cry out on their behalf.

Roscoe J.A. noted the trial judge had found that the defendant lawyers were not actuated by express malice, either in the sense of personal animosity or in the sense of reckless indifference to the truth.

Notably, Roscoe J.A. observed that the Supreme Court of Canada's decision in *Jones v. Bennett*, [1969] S.C.R. 277, often cited as authority for the proposition that "publication to the world" via the news media is too broad to be an occasion of qualified privilege, "pre-dated the *Charter* by over 12 years" [para. 67] and stated that the common law should be modified incrementally to ensure that it conforms with *Charter* values [para. 69].

In dissent, Saunders J.A. rejected the defence submissions that the occasion of the press conference was privileged. He agreed with the assessment of the trial judge that *Jones v. Bennett*, above, was binding on the court, although the House of Lords in *Reynolds v. Times Newspapers Ltd.*, [1999] 4 All E.R. 609 at paras. 99–100, set a new approach for publication to the world which was markedly different from *Jones v. Bennett*. Saunders J.A. also held that *Reynolds* was distinguishable on its facts because *Reynolds* concerned press publications about politicians, whereas the case before the Nova Scotia Court of Appeal concerned the publication of statements by members of the bar about public officials who were not politicians. Saunders J.A. concluded his dissent on this particular issue by stating (at para. 129):

> The common law defences of qualified privilege, justification and fair comment are sufficient protection, whether to pro-active lawyers or ordinary citizens. While the categories of qualified privilege are not foreclosed, there is no special protection to be attached to occasions where activists or lawyers happen to be in attendance.

See also *Prud'homme v. Prud'homme*, 2002 SCC 85, per L'Heureux-Dubé and Lebel JJ. at para. 50 [although the decision involved Quebec civil law, the Court discussed the defence of qualified privilege available at common law].

c) False Charges

Where a false charge has been published to the world, the defendant is entitled to address the same audience when refuting it.

Adam v. Ward, [1917] A.C. 309 (H.L.).

Mallett v. Clarke (1968), 70 D.L.R. (2d) 67 (B.C.S.C.).

Falk v. Smith, [1941] O.R. 17 at 19 (C.A.).

d) News Media Defendants
i) *Where Qualified Privilege Defence Rejected*

Although courts have recognized that politicians have a "duty to ventilate" on certain occasions, it is not clear that the news media enjoy a qualified privilege if they convey such ventilated statements to their readers, viewers, or listeners.

In *Re International Assn. of Bridge, Structural and Ornamental and Reinforcing Ironworkers (Local 97) and Campbell* (1997), 152 D.L.R. (4th) 547, the defendant newspaper and its political columnist argued that "they could huddle under the same umbrella" of privilege that the defendant Leader of the Opposition enjoyed for his defamatory press release. That media defence was rejected, Macdonald J. stating at page 557:

> [27] I do not accept the proposition that the *Province* [newspaper] and Kieran [the columnist] can "huddle under the same umbrella" of qualified privilege. There is no direct authority for that proposition, and it is neither necessary or appropriate to extend the law on this defence.

More recently in *Thomas v. McMullan*, 2002 BCSC 22, Ralph J. rejected arguments that a newspaper had a legal, social, or moral duty to publish information about accusations made by one politician against another.

In British Columbia, the leading decision rejecting a defence of qualified privilege for the news media is *Moises v. Canadian Newspaper Co. (c.o.b. Times-Colonist)* (1996), 24 B.C.L.R. 211 (C.A.), where the court appeared to accept, however, that there may be occasions when publication "to the world" may be privileged. For example, Williams J.A., at page 221, appeared to approve *Camporese v. Parton* (1983), 47 B.C.L.R. 78 (S.C.), where it was held that a consumer columnist had a moral duty to pass on a health warning concerning a product she had previously recommended to the readers of her newspaper.

Nevertheless, in *Moises* the defence of qualified privilege was held not to apply to the defendant newspaper because although the Court of Appeal agreed the public had a legitimate interest in receiving the information published about the plaintiff, it did not agree that the newspaper was under a duty to publish that information. "This was not, after all, a situation where [the plaintiff] or [an organization he was reputed to belong to] presented any threat to Canada, or to anyone in Victoria" [page 221].

An earlier decision of the Ontario Court of Appeal in *Littleton v. Hamilton* (1974), 4 O.R. (2d) 283 held there is no general privilege available to the media at common law — special circumstances will be required before the public's interest in any given matter will be strong enough to impose a duty upon the news media to publish defamatory matter. Such special circumstances do not override the need for a reciprocal interest/duty relationship before qualified privilege will attach to the occasion.

In other instances, news media publications or broadcasts have failed to qualify as an occasion of qualified privilege:

> *Bordeleau* v. *Bonnyville Nouvelle Ltd.* (1992), 6 Alta L.R. (3d) 128, 97 D.L.R. (4th) 764 (Q.B.) [publication of an advertisement placed by an unknown person, congratulating an unmarried 18 year old female plaintiff, a resident of a small town, on the birth of a baby, a matter she wanted to keep confidential].

> *Pressler* v. *Lethbridge* (2000), 86 B.C.L.R. (3d) 257 (C.A.). [Southin J.A. at 297 rejected what she characterized as a defence "argument that every citizen has a right, protected by law, to publish to all and sundry, of and concerning persons who hold and publicly express objectionable opinions, defamatory statements. No authority was cited in support of such a broad concept of occasion of qualified privilege. If adopted, such a concept would enable every citizen to arrogate unto himself the right to decide, according to his view of the public good, when reputations may be ruined."]

In *Hodgson* v. *Canadian Newspapers Co.* (1998), 39 O.R. (3d) 235 (Gen. Div.), Lane J. reviewed the law relating to qualified privilege at pages 373–76 and stated at 376:

> Absent *Charter* considerations, which were not pursued before me, the Supreme Court of Canada's decision in *Boland* and in *Banks* remain the law in Canada with respect to the inability of a newspaper to raise the defence of qualified privilege at common law. I note the conclusion of Cory J. in *Hill*, that the law of defamation should not be modified by incorporating the *New York Times* v. *Sullivan* [376 U.S. 254, 11 L.Ed.2d 686 (1964)] actual malice standard (whereby public officials cannot succeed in libel unless they show that the publication was made with knowledge of untruth or recklessly) as stated at p. 1187 …

> The adoption of a common law qualified privilege defence for newspapers in their reporting on public officials and public matters would come unacceptably near to adopting the Sullivan rule.

The Ontario Court of Appeal, which varied the decision in *Hodgson* on other grounds, expressly agreed with Lane J's conclusion that qualified privilege could not apply because the defendants were guilty of express malice which defeats the privilege, and accordingly declined to express any view concerning whether the occasion was privileged. (2000) 189 D.L.R. (4th) 241 per Sharpe J.A. at 260, para. 46, leave to appeal to Supreme Court of Canada denied, [2000] S.C.C.A. 465

In *Leenen v. Canadian Broadcasting Corporation* (2000), 48 O.R. (3d) 656 (S.C.J.), Cunningham J. discussed the defence of qualified privilege raised by the Canadian Broadcasting Corporation at pages 693–98 and held at page 694, paragraph 110, that the recent decision of the House of Lords in *Reynolds v. Times Newspapers Ltd.*, above, reaffirmed the principle of reciprocity and provided a "sound basis upon which the trier of fact may weigh [all the circumstances] and determine whether the reciprocal nature of the test has been met."

Cunningham J. held at page 695, paragraph 113, that an essential element of the defence of qualified privilege is good faith, and it is important therefore that those publishing and broadcasting defamatory statements do so after a proper and thorough investigation of the facts. "Of course, it goes without saying that if what is broadcast deliberately omits information contrary to a thesis that may have been developed for the program, good faith cannot exist."

Cunningham J. continued at page 695, paragraph 114:

> Until recently, there was some doubt as to whether publication to the world at large could ever give rise to an occasion of qualified privilege. However, that issue was definitively resolved by the Court of Appeal in *Grenier v. Southam Inc.*, [1997] O.J. No. 12193 (Q.B.) In that case, the court upheld the finding at trial that qualified privilege can attach to a communication by the media published to the world at large if it is published in the context of a social or moral duty to raise the underlying issue. This principle was enunciated further by the House of Lords in *Reynolds v. Times Newspapers, supra*.

Reviewing the factors in the case before him, Cunningham J. noted at page 296 that there was no crisis which made it urgent to communicate the serious defamatory allegations, stating at page 687, paragraph 118:

> As I look at what was actually broadcast, how can it be said that a reasonable person would have felt any duty to broadcast this sort of program. It had nothing to do with a duty to communicate important information. It had everything to do with sensationalizing an issue, with creating viewer interest through alarm and with providing a podium for its producer's long held views, capably assisted by the over-heated concerns of a disgruntled regulator.

In *Leenen*, Cunningham J. specifically referred at page 698, paragraph 119 to the *Reynolds* decision of the House of Lords:

As a result of the decision of the House of Lords in *Reynolds* v. *Time Newspapers Ltd.* [1999] H.L.J. no 45, Canadian trial courts have recently considered the test for a finding of qualified privilege for news media defamation in the context of the factors discussed by Lord Nicholls in that case, namely:

a) The seriousness of the allegation. The more serious the charge the more the public is misinformed and the individual harmed, if the allegation is not true.

b) The nature of the information, and the extent to which the subject-matter is a matter of public concern.

c) The source of the information. Some informants have no direct knowledge of the events. Some have their own axes to grind, or are being paid for their stories.

d) The steps taken to verify the information.

e) The status of the information. The allegation may have already been the subject of an investigation which commands respect.

f) The urgency of the matter. News is often a perishable commodity.

g) Whether comment was sought from the [plaintiff]. He may have information others do not possess or have not disclosed. An approach to the [plaintiff] will not always be necessary.

h) Whether the article contained the gist of the plaintiff's side of the story.

i) The tone of the article. A newspaper can raise queries or call for an investigation. It need not adopt allegations as statements of fact.

j) The circumstances of the publication, including the timing.

In *Young* v. *Toronto Star Newspapers Ltd.*, [2003] O.J. No. 3100 (S.C.J.), Rouleau J. rejected a defence of qualified privilege used by the newspaper after applying, *inter alia*, the factors enumerated by Lord Nicholls in *Reynolds*. Rouleau J. stated at paras. 188–89:

> 188. The allegations made in this article were of a most serious nature … . Few steps were taken by the reporter to verify the information, and the debate which the information would inevitably create among members of the public would not be in the public interest as the allegations made had already been fairly and appropriately resolved [by a court ruling related to a publication ban].

> 189. The defendants were, in a sense, sensationalizing certain statements made in court, when the essence of the allegations had been demonstrated to be unfounded … .

ii) Where Qualified Privilege Defence Accepted

There are a number of instances, however, where publications in the Canadian news media were held to have occurred on an occasion of qualified privilege.

> *Camporese v. Parton* (1983), 150 D.L.R. (3d) 208 at 225–226 (B.C.S.C.). [consumer advice columnist],

> *Parsons v. Windsor Star* (1989), 71 O.R. (2d) 5 (H.C.J.) [report of news conference concerning claims of racial abuse against a police officer].

> *Grenier v. Southam Inc.*, [1997] O.J. No. 2193 (C.A.) [social and moral duty for newspaper to publish information in an article about an organization helping people obsessed by gospel preachers].

> *Kovlaske v. International Woodworkers of America – Canada, Local 1-217*, [1999] B.C.J. No. 2326 (S.C.) [Indo-Canadian newspaper which was devoted to matters of interest to Indo-Canadian community held to have a "legitimate common interest" with its readers in reporting allegations a mill manager was racist, majority of mill workers were Indo-Canadian].

In *Silva v. Toronto Star Newspapers Ltd.* (1998), 167 D.L.R. (4th) 554 (Ont. Gen. Div.), a newspaper successfully established a defence of qualified privilege for the publication of an investigative article, which concerned a public housing project where the tenants held a press conference to protest about conditions and alleged they lived in fear. An appeal from the trial verdict was dismissed with very brief reasons, [2002] O.J. No. 1960 (C.A.).

F. THE BOUNDARIES OF QUALIFIED PRIVILEGE

Once the judge has determined as a matter of law that the occasion is privileged, the burden of showing that the defendant did not act in respect of the reason of the privilege, but for some other indirect reason, is thrown on the plaintiff.

The protection of qualified privilege is lost if:

i) the plaintiff proves that the dominant motive for publishing the defamatory expression is actual or express malice. Actual or express malice includes
    a. spite or ill will;
    b. any indirect motive or ulterior purpose which conflicts with the occasion;

    c. speaking dishonestly, or in knowing or reckless disregard for the truth.

ii)   the limits of the duty or interest have been exceeded. This occurs when:

    a. the speaker includes anything which is not relevant or pertinent, or in other words, not reasonably appropriate in the circumstances existing on the occasion when the information is given;

    b. the manner and extent of communication is excessive.

Hill v. Church of Scientology of Toronto, [1995] 2 S.C.R. 1130, 126 D.L.R. (4th) 129 per Cory J. at paras. 144–48.

Gazette Printing Co. v. Shallow (1909), 41 S.C.R. 339

RTC Engineering Consultants Ltd. v. Ontario (Ministry of the Solicitor General and Correctional Services) (2002), 58 O.R. (3d) 726, per Laskin J.A. at para. 18 (C.A.).

Wade & Wells Co. v. Laing (1957), 11 D.L.R. (2d) 276 at 279, 282–83 (B.C.C.A.).

Testimony by the defendant that he or she acted under a sense of duty, although not relevant to the question of whether or not the occasion is privileged, may be relevant to the question of malice.

Wade & Wells Co. v. Laing, ibid.

Stuart v. Bell, [1891] 2 Q.B. 341.

Sun Life Assurance Co. of Canada et al. v. Dalrymple, [1965] S.C.R. 302.

There may be cases where the failure to make further investigation or inquiry is evidence of lack of honesty or even malice.

Arnott v. College of Physicians and Surgeons of Saskatchewan, [1954] S.C.R. 538.

The jury in a libel action is entitled to bring in a general verdict without making specific findings on questions propounded by the trial judge, including a question whether the defendant was actuated by malice.

Dennison v. Sanderson, [1946] 4 D.L.R. 314 (Ont. C.A.).

See Chapter 16, "Express Malice."

G. FAIR AND ACCURATE REPORT PRIVILEGE

At common law, a defence of privilege protects fair and accurate reports of the public proceedings of institutions such as Parliament, the legislative assemblies of the provinces, the courts, and quasi-judicial tribunals. This privilege defence extends not only to those participating directly in the work of such institutions but also to the news media. The rationale for the privilege is that the general advantage of having the proceedings made known to the public outweighs the harm to private reputation.

Perera v. Peiris, [1949] A.C. 1.

Fleming v. Newton (1848), 1 H.L.C. 353, 9 E.R. 797.

Wason v. Walter, [1868] L.R. 4 Q.B. 73.

Hill v. Church of Scientology of Toronto, [1995] 2 S.C.R. 1130.

1) Open Court Proceedings

It is in the public interest to have reports of judicial proceedings made available to the public. As a result, there is a common law privilege for persons to publish fair and accurate reports of judicial proceedings before a properly constituted judicial tribunal, exercising its jurisdiction in open court. The duty to make the report and the corresponding interest in receiving it is presumed by law.

Gazette Printing Co. v. Shallow (1909), 41 S.C.R. 339.

Douglas v. Tucker, [1952] 1 S.C.R. 275, per Cartwright J. for the Court at 285:

> … [T]here is no doubt that as stated by Lord Esher in *Kimber v. Press Association Ltd.* (1893), 1 Q.B. 65 at 68:
>
> > The rule of law is that, where there are judicial proceedings before a properly constituted judicial tribunal exercising its jurisdiction in open Court, then the publication, without malice, of a fair and accurate report of what takes place before that tribunal is privileged.

In *Campbell v. Jones* (2001), 197 N.S.R. (2d) 212, 2001 NSSC 139, a press conference had been called to publicize the filing of a complaint under the *Police Act*, and copies of the complaint were distributed. Moir J. held that this did not fall within the privilege afforded to fair and accurate reports of court proceedings, which under *Hill v. Scientology*, above, had been extended to reports upon the pleadings, notices of motions, and affidavits not yet read in open court. Although he concluded that the extension of privilege established by *Hill v. Scientology* logically applies to any document to be referred to in the public hearings of a tribunal, Moir J. stated at paragraph 77:

However, many legislative schemes for administrative regulation mix judicial functions with others. I believe that where privilege is claimed for publication of a document that involves a legislated scheme with a mixture of functions, care must be taken to determine when and how the public, judicial aspects of the scheme arise.

The Court noted at paragraphs 17–18 that the *Police Act* and regulations do not provide for a public, judicial hearing upon the making of a complaint.

The public interest in scrutinizing judicial proceedings is to be distinguished from the public interest in knowing about the details of such an investigation, and I think it would be dangerous to extend the license of qualified privilege to the publicizing of a document designed to launch an investigation, rather than solely to define the issues for a public hearing.

The decision of Moir J. in *Campbell* v. *Jones*, 2002 NSCA 128 was reversed by the Nova Scotia Court of Appeal on the basis that the defendant's statements were made on an occasion of qualified privilege: (2002), 220 D.L.R. (4th) 201, leave to appeal to S.C.C. denied, [2002] S.C.C.A. No. 543. Roscoe J.A., with Glube C.J.N.S. concurring, held that it was "therefore not necessary to discuss qualified reporting privilege or to deal with the other grounds of appeal or the notice of contention" [paragraph 73]. In his dissenting judgment in the Court of Appeal, Saunders J.A. would have held that Moir J. did not err on this issue or any other issue of significance [at paragraph 760].

The question in examining this defence of privilege is whether what transpired in the judicial proceedings was fairly and accurately reported. The defendant does not need to show that facts taken from the judicial proceedings are true.

Thore v. *Mudry*, [1999] B.C.J. No. 1693 (S.C.).

The report must be accurate. It must not misstate facts and must be a true account of the judicial proceedings.

Bennett v. *Sun Publishing Co.*, [1972] 4 W.W.R. 643 (B.C.S.C.).

The privilege applies to everyone, not just the new media.

Weslowski v. *Armadale Publishers Ltd.* (1980), 112 D.L.R. (3d) 378 (Sask. Q.B.).

In *Bennett* v. *Sun Publishing*, above, at 656, Anderson, J. held that the defendant is required to report a substantially fair or correct account of the proceedings that took place in open court because "[t]he failure to report all of the facts or a fair summary of all the facts may lead to an inference of unfairness or inaccuracy."

However, there is no requirement that the proceedings be reported verbatim or in their entirety.

Gazette Printing Co. v. *Shallow* (1909), 41 S.C.R. 339.

The mere fact that there is a discrepancy between the report and what occurred in the proceeding will not defeat the privilege if the difference is not of a substantial nature or does not produce a different effect. Only significant errors will deprive the reporter of the privilege. Journalists are not expected to be infallible and their reports are not to be judged by the standards of the legal profession.

Andrews v. *Chapman* (1853), 175 E.R. 558.

Taylor-Wright v. *CHBC-TV, a Division of WIC Television Ltd.*, [1999] B.C.J. No. 334 (S.C.) per Drossos J. at para. 496, citing *Cardwell* v. *Hutchinson*, [1995] B.C.J. No. 1656 (S.C.), aff'd (1997), 36 B.C.L.R. (3d) 86 (C.A.), varied on other grounds, (2000), 194 D.L.R. (4th) 621 (B.C.C.A.).

If facts are incorrectly asserted at a judicial proceeding and the reporter relies and reports on the alleged, but ultimately mistaken facts, so long as the report is fair and accurate as to what has transpired in court, there will be no liability, even though the facts are incorrect.

Cardwell v. *Hutchison*, above.

The report must also be fair and must reflect the events which it purports to report. In *Bennett* v. *Sun Publishing Co.*, above, at 655, Anderson J. held that the term "fair" includes such meanings as "free from moral stain; unblemished; free from bias, fraud or injustice; equitable; legitimate" and that the report should "not be coloured or garbled."

While the facts of an entire judicial proceeding need not be reported, i.e. the reporter is permitted to summarize, a reporter cannot pick and choose those facts which distort the true nature of the proceedings.

Bennett v. *Sun Publishing Co.*, above.

Taylor-Wright v. *CHBC-TV, a Division of WIC Ltd.*, above.

Tedlie v. *Southam Co.* (*No. 3*), [1950] 4 D.L.R. 415.

Headlines must themselves be fair and accurate or the report will not be protected by the privilege. An inaccurate or inflammatory headline can negate the privilege attaching to otherwise fair and accurate reports. Headlines are only privileged when they give a fair idea of the article which follows.

Bennett v. Sun Publishing Co., above, at 655.

Geary v. Alger (1925), 57 O.L.R. 218 (H.C.J.), aff'd 58 O.L.R. 39 (C.A.).

Tedlie v. Southam Co. (No. 3), [1950] 4 D.L.R. 415.

The privilege does not protect personal comments included in the report, which may destroy the privilege for the entire publication: the reporter must add nothing of her own. A voluntary statement and comment by the defendant will not constitute a fair and accurate report.

Tedlie v. Southam Co. (No. 3), above.

Lewis v. Levy (1858), E.B. & E. 537, 120 E.R. 610.

Andrews v. Chapman (1853), 3 Car. & K. 286, 175 E.R. 558.

Ager v. Canjex Publishing Ltd. (c.o.b. Canada Stockwatch), 2003 BCSC 891, per Shaw J. at paras. 34–38.

If a hearing lasts many days, it is permissible to report what occurred each day and not wait until all the evidence has been submitted:

Kimber v. Press Association Ltd., [1893] 1 Q.B. 65 (C.A.).

It is not fair, however, to give a one-sided account of the proceedings or to unduly emphasize the facts of one side of the case and not the other.

The privilege does not attach until the defendant proves the report is fair and accurate. Therefore, a defendant who is unable to prove that the report was fair and accurate, or who is shown by the plaintiff to have not been fair and accurate, does not lose the privilege; rather, the report was never privileged in the first place.

M.D. Mineralsearch Inc. v. East Kootenay Newspapers Ltd. (2002), 209 D.L.R. (4th) 375 (B.C.C.A.), where Levine J.A. considered the standard to be applied in determining whether a report of judicial proceedings is "fair":

2. The newspaper truthfully reported that the plaintiff dealer had been found guilty in Provincial Court of a "deceptive act or practice" under the B.C. *Trade Practice Act*, but did not report that the Provincial Court judge stated in his reasons for judgment that it was a minor error, in the nature of a clerical error, and not designed to deceive. The trial judge found the newspaper liable because the report was not complete and therefore created a false impression.

13. The trial judge then went on to discuss whether the report was privileged as a fair and accurate report of public court proceedings,

pursuant to section 3(1) of *Libel and Slander Act*, RSBC 1996, c. 263 which provides:

> "A fair and accurate report in a public newspaper or other periodical publication or in a broadcast of proceedings publicly heard before a court exercising judicial authority if published contemporaneously with the proceedings, is privileged."

28. In linking fairness to balanced reporting of the evidence, the trial judge correctly reflected the authorities which have considered the meaning of "fair and accurate," where the privilege extended to the public reporting of proceedings is claimed for reports of allegations or evidence.

29. In *Bennett v. Sun Publishing*, [1972] 4 W.W.R. 643 (B.C.S.C.), Anderson J. considered the meaning of "fair and accurate" in the context of s. 4 of the *Libel and Slander Act*, which provides qualified privilege for "fair and accurate" public reports of a public meeting, including a meeting of a select committee of the Legislature. In *Bennett*, a newspaper published a report of defamatory allegations made during a meeting of such a committee, although the newspaper knew, from its own prior investigations, that the allegations were untrue. The report was found to be unfair and inaccurate because the newspaper failed to publish the true facts.

30. Anderson J. noted (at pp. 654–5) that "the privilege extends to judicial proceedings as well as legislative proceedings: and this was of "some importance in looking at the earlier cases dealing with judicial proceedings to ascertain the meaning of 'fair and accurate' in a legal sense."

31. Anderson J. defined "fair" (at p. 655) as including the following meanings: "free from moral stain, unblemished; free from bias, fraud or injustice, equitable; legitimate." At p. 656, he said: "The failure to report all the facts or a fair summary of the facts may lead to an inference of unfairness or inaccuracy ..."

36. Thus the trial judge correctly reflected the authorities in suggesting that there is a higher standard imposed on the media when reporting on the evidence tendered in judicial proceedings. ...

38. In *Duncan v. Associated Scottish Newspapers Limited*, [1929] S.C. 14 (Ct. of Sess.), the court of appeal upheld the lower court's decision that "where the newspaper merely purports to report the result of a case

and does so with accuracy, it cannot be liable because it fails to narrate the steps which led up to the judgment" (headnote).

40. ... "It would impose too high a standard on the media to require it to explain that words used by the Legislature should not, in a particular case, be given their ordinary meaning."

2) Court Documents and Exhibits

At common law, the judicial reporting privilege applied only in the case of reporting "proceedings publicly heard before a court." As a result, if a document had not been filed with the court and referred to in open court then the reporter was not protected by the qualified privilege.

Gazette Printing Co. v. *Shallow* (1909), 41 S.C.R. 339.

However, the long-standing common law rule refusing to extend the privilege to reports on pleadings (before the proceedings were publicly heard before a court) was recently changed by the Supreme Court of Canada in *Hill* v. *Church of Scientology of Toronto*, [1995] 2 S.C.R. 1130, where Cory J., speaking for the majority of the court stated at paragraph 152:

> In [*Edmonton Journal* v. *Alberta* (A.G.), [1989] 2 S.C.R. 1326] I noted that the public scrutiny of our courts by the press was fundamentally important in our democratic society and that s. 2(b) [of the *Charter*] protected not only speakers but listeners as well. This right to report on court proceedings extended to pleadings and court documents filed before trial, since access to these documents served the same societal needs as the reporting on trials. Even in private actions ... the public may well have an interest in knowing the kinds of submissions which can be put forward. Both societal standards and the legislation have changed with regard to access to court documents. When the qualified privilege rule was set out in *Shallow*, supra, court documents were not open to the public. Today, the right of access is guaranteed by legislative provision ... . As well, s. 2(b) of the *Charter* may in some circumstances provide a basis for obtaining access to some court documents ... . It follows that the concept of qualified privilege should be modified accordingly.

The view that *Hill* v. *Scientology* changed the common law in this regard is confirmed by the decision of the British Columbia Court of Appeal in *Taylor-Wright* v. *CHBC-TV, a Division of WIC Ltd.* (2000), 194 D.L.R. (4th) 621.

The new rule expanding the ambit of privilege to reporting on aspects of judicial proceedings can be expressed as follows:

i)　the common law defence of qualified privilege protects those who report on court documents, including pleadings, affidavits, exhibits, and supporting material, filed (or about to be filed) in court before such have been referred to in open court;

ii)　if the publisher (or broadcaster) acts in a manner other than to present a substantially accurate and fair report of the judicial proceedings, the court may deny the protection of qualified privilege; and

iii)　even if the report of the judicial proceedings is fair and accurate, it may in the case of common law qualified privilege still be defeated by proof of malice by the defamed party.

Taylor-Wright v. CHBC-TV, a Division of WIC Ltd., above.

It has been held, however, that a high degree of care must be taken by the media to ensure fairness when reporting on documents filed in a court action.

Ager v. Canjex Publishing Ltd. (c.o.b. Canada Stockwatch), [2003] B.C.J. No. 1349, 2003 BCSC 891, per Shaw J. at paras. 35–36, citing *Taylor-Wright v. CHBC-TV, a Division of WIC Ltd.*, above, at paras. 44, 49, and *M.D. Mineralsearch v. East Kootenay Newspapers Ltd.* (2002), 209 D.L.R. (4th) 375, 2002 BCCA 42 at paras. 35–35.

This privilege is defeated, however, if a published report is not reasonably appropriate in the circumstances existing at the time of publication.

Hill v. Church of Scientology of Toronto, [1995] 2 S.C.R. 1130 at paras. 155–56.

3) Legislative Proceedings

A fair and accurate report in a newspaper or broadcast of any proceedings in the House of Commons or the Senate, or the proceedings of a provincial legislature, or any committees of those bodies, is privileged unless the plaintiff establishes the defendant published the report maliciously.

Wason v. Walter, [1868] L.R. 4 Q.B. 73

The requirements of fairness and accuracy are discussed above and below in connection with reports of court proceedings.

H. STATUTORY PRIVILEGES

In large measure, the statutory privileges are a codification and extension of the common law.

1) Reports of Government Proceedings

The federal *Parliament of Canada Act* requires that civil courts stay any proceedings based on the publication of any copy of a report, paper, votes, or proceedings originally published by or under the authority of the Senate or the House of Commons. In addition to that absolute privilege for publication of entire government documents, a defendant who publishes merely an extract or abstract enjoys a qualified privilege if he or she proves that it was published in good faith, and without malice.

R.S.C. 1985, c. P-1, ss. 7, 8, 9.

Federal legislation also creates a defence of qualified privilege for any fair and accurate report made in good faith, in a newspaper or any other periodical publication or in a broadcast: of an official report made by the federal Information Commissioner under the *Access to Information Act*, by a Corrections Investigator made under the *Corrections and Conditional Release Act*, by the Commissioner of Official Languages under the *Official Languages Act*, and by the Privacy Commissioner under the *Privacy Act*.

R.S.C. 1985, c. A-1, s.66(2).
R.S.C. 1985, c. C-44.6, s.190(b).
R.S.C. 1985, c. C. p-21, s.67(2).
R.S.C. 1985, c. 31 (4 Sup), s.75(2).
R.S.C. 1985, c. P-1, ss.7, 8, 9.

Each of the common law provinces and the Yukon and Northwest Territories have legislated, to varying degrees, privilege defences for reports in newspapers and broadcasts of the proceedings of government bodies. (Saskatchewan's statute only applies to newspapers). Nunavut Territory has adopted the Northwest Territories defamation statute. A list of those statutory provisions follows:

Defamation Act, R.S.A. 2000, c. D-6, s.10.
Libel and Slander Act, R.S.B.C. 1996, c. 263, s.4.
Defamation Act, R.S.M. 1987, c. D20, s.10.
Defamation Act, R.S.N.B. 1973, s.9.
Defamation Act, S.N. 1983, c.63, s.12.
Defamation Act, R.S.N.W.T. 1988, c. D-1, s.11.
Defamation Act, R.S.N.S. 1989, c. 122, s.13.
Libel and Slander Act, R.S.O. 1990, c. L.12, s.3.
Defamation Act, R.S.P.E.I. 1988, c. D-5, s.10.

Libel and Slander Act, R.S.S. 1978, c. L-14, s.10.

Defamation Act, R.S.Y.T. 1986, c. 41, s.10.

Except for British Columbia, each statute protects a fair and accurate report, published without malice in a newspaper or broadcast, of proceedings in the Senate or House of Commons of Canada, the Legislative Assembly of any province, or a committee of any of those bodies, except where neither the public nor any reporter was admitted.

Defamation Act, R.S.A. 2000, c. D-6, s.10(1)(b).

Defamation Act, R.S.M. 1987, c. D20, s.10(1).

Defamation Act, R.S.N.B. 1973, c. D-5, s.9(1).

Defamation Act, R.S.N. 1990, c. D-3, s.12(1).

Defamation Act, R.S.N.W.T. 1988, c. D-1, s.11(2).

Defamation Act, R.S.N.S. 1989, c. 122, s.13(1).

Defamation Act, R.S.P.E.I. 1988, c. D-5,10(1).

Libel and Slander Act, R.S.S. 1978, c. L-14, s.10(1).

Defamation Act, R.S.Y.T. 1986, c. 41, s.10(1).

Ontario's statute is somewhat more expansive as it protects a fair and accurate report in a newspaper or in a broadcast of the proceedings of any legislative body or any part or committee thereof "in the British Comonwealth that may exercise any sovereign power acquired by delegation or otherwise."

Libel and Slander Act, R.S.O. 1990, c. L.12, s.3(1).1.

The Northwest Territories and the Yukon Territory statutes also apply to their respective legislative assemblies and to committees of those assemblies.

Defamation Act, R.S.N.W.T. 1988, c. D-1, s.11(2).

Defamation Act, R.S.Y.T. 1986, c. 41, s.10(1).

Oddly, British Columbia's statute applies only to select committees of its own Legislative Assembly. It does not even apply to its own Legislative Assembly or to those of other jurisdictions.

Libel and Slander Act, R.S.B.C. 1996, c. 263, s.4(1).

In British Columbia, an action at law or other civil proceeding cannot be brought against a member of the legislature or any person because of the printing or publication of documents or papers printed or published by the order of the Legislative Assembly or the Speaker.

Constitution Act, R.S.B.C. 1996, c. 66, 51(3).

The defamation statutes of Alberta, Manitoba, New Brunswick, Nova Scotia, Prince Edward Island, Newfoundland and Labrador, the Northwest Territories, and Saskatchewan also recognize a privilege defence for fair and accurate, good faith reports of a public meeting, a meeting of a municipal council, school board, board of education, board of health, or of any other board or local authority formed or constituted under a federal or provincial statute, or of a committee appointed by any such board or local authority.

Defamation Act, R.S.A. 2000, c. D-6, s.10(1)(a), (d).
Defamation Act, R.S.M. 1987, c. D20, s.10(1)(e).
Defamation Act, R.S.N.B. 1973, s.9(1).
Defamation Act, S.N. 1983, c. 63, s.12(1)(e).
Defamation Act, R.S.N.W.T. 1988, c. D-1, s.10(1)(a), (d).
Defamation Act, R.S.N.S. 1989, c. 122, s.13(1)(b).
Defamation Act, R.S.P.E.I. 1988, c. D-5, s.10(1).
Libel and Slander Act, R.S.S. 1978, c. L-14, s.10(1).
Defamation Act, R.S.Y.T. 1986, c. 41, s.10(1)(d).

The meaning of "public meeting" is of vital importance in many cases. It is not clear whether a police press conference meets the statutory definition of a public meeting.

Cassidy v. Abbotsford (City) Police Department, [1999] B.C.J. No. 2961 (S.C.); leave to appeal granted, [2000] B.C.J. No. 878 (C.A.).

The statutes of the Northwest Territories and the Yukon Territory recognize an equivalent privilege but also extend it to boards constituted under statutes of the two territories.

Defamation Act, R.S.N.W.T. 1988, c.D-1, s.10(1)(a), (d).

In British Columbia, the statute protects a fair and accurate report of the proceedings of a public meeting, a meeting of a municipal council, school board, or local authority formed or constituted under any Act, or a francophone education authority as defined in the *School Act*, or a committee appointed by any of those bodies.

Libel and Slander Act, R.S.B.C. 1996, c. 263, s.4(1).

Ontario's legislation also extends a similar qualified privilege defence to the proceedings of "any administrative body that is constituted by any public authority in Canada" and to "any organization whose members, in whole or in part, represent any public authority in Canada."

Libel and Slander Act, R.S.O. 1990, c.L.12, s.3(1).2, 4.

The defamation statutes of the Northwest Territories and the Yukon Territory and the common law provinces (except Prince Edward Island, Saskatchewan, and Ontario) also expressly recognize a qualified privilege defence for fair and accurate, good faith reports of meetings of commissioners authorized to act by letters patent, statute, or other lawful warrant or authority.

Defamation Act, R.S.A. 2000, c. D-6, s.10(1)(c).
Libel and Slander Act, R.S.B.C. 1996, c. 263, s.4(1).
Defamation Act, R.S.M. 1987, c. D20, s.10(1)(d).
Defamation Act, R.S.N.B. 1973, s.9(1).
Defamation Act, S.N. 1983, c. 63, s.12(1)(d).
Defamation Act, R.S.N.W.T. 1988, c. D-1, s.11(2)(c).
Defamation Act, R.S.N.S. 1989, c. 122, s.13(1)(e).
Defamation Act, R.S.Y.T. 1986, c. 41, s.10(1)(c).

Nova Scotia and Ontario statutes protect fair and accurate reports of the proceedings of any commission of inquiry that is constituted by any public authority in the British Commonwealth.

Defamation Act, R.S.N.S. 1989, c. 122, s.13(1)(d).
Libel and Slander Act, R.S.O. 1990, c. L.12, s.3(1)3.

Nova Scotia's defamation statute also protects reports of "the proceedings of any administrative body that is constituted by any public authority in Canada."

Defamation Act, R.S.N.S. 1989, c. 122, s.13(1)(c).

The defamation statutes of each common law province and of the Yukon Territory provide that the privilege for reports of government bodies does not apply to the publication of any matter not of public concern, or the publication of which is not for the public benefit.

Defamation Act, R.S.A. 2000, c. D-6, s.10(5).
Libel and Slander Act, R.S.B.C. 1996, c. 263, s.4(4).
Defamation Act, R.S.M. 1987, c. D20, s.10(5).
Defamation Act, R.S.N.B. 1973, s.9(5).
Defamation Act, S.N. 1983, c. 63, s.12(5).
Defamation Act, R.S.N.W.T. 1988, c. D-1, s.11(1).
Defamation Act, R.S.N.S. 1989, c. 122, s.13(7).
Libel and Slander Act, R.S.O. 1990, c. L.12, s.3(6).
Defamation Act, R.S.P.E.I. 1988, c. D-5, s.11.

Libel and Slander Act, R.S.S. 1978, c. L-14, s.10(4).
Defamation Act, R.S.Y.T. 1986, c. 41, s.10(6).

2) Publication at Request of Government

The defamation statutes of each of the common law provinces and the territories provide that the publication in a newspaper or broadcast, at the request of a government department, bureau or office or public officer, of a report, bulletin, notice or other document issued for the information of the public, is privileged unless it is proved that the publication was made maliciously.

Defamation Act, R.S.A. 2000, c. D-6, s.10(2).
Libel and Slander Act, R.S.B.C. 1996, c. 263, s.4(4).
Defamation Act, R.S.M. 1987, c. D20, s.10(2).
Defamation Act, R.S.N.B. 1973, c. D-5, s.9(2).
Defamation Act, S.N. 1983, c. 63, s.12(2).
Defamation Act, R.S.N.W.T. 1988, c. D-1, s.11(3).
Defamation Act, R.S.N.S. 1989, c. 122, s.13(3).
Libel and Slander Act, R.S.O. 1990, c. L.12, s.3(3).
Defamation Act, R.S.P.E.I. 1988, c. D-5, s.10(2).
Libel and Slander Act, R.S.S. 1978, c. L-14, s.10(1).
Defamation Act, R.S.Y.T. 1986, c. 41, s.10(2).

The Northwest Territories expressly extends the protection to include requests by the council of a municipality.

Defamation Act, R.S.N.W.T. 1988, c. D-1, s.11(3).

Nova Scotia and Ontario expressly extend the protection to publication at the request of any government entity if reports of that entity's proceedings are protected by the defamation statute.

Defamation Act, R.S.N.S. 1989, c. 122, s.13(3).
Libel and Slander Act, R.S.O. 1990, c.L. 12, s.3(3).

Saskatchewan expressly protects publications requested by the commissioner of police or chief constable.

Libel and Slander Act, R.S.S. 1978, c. L-14, s.10(1).

The defamation statutes of each common law province except Ontario and the Yukon Territory provide that the privilege for reports at the request of government does not limit or abridge any privilege existing by law, nor does it apply to the publication of any matter not of public concern or the publication of which is not for the public benefit.

Defamation Act, R.S.A. 2000, c. D-6, s.10(5).
Libel and Slander Act, R.S.B.C. 1996, c. 263, s.4(4).
Defamation Act, R.S.M. 1987, c. D20, s.10(5).
Defamation Act, R.S.N.B. 1973, c. D-5. s.9(5).
Defamation Act, S.N. 1983, c. 63, s.12(5).
Defamation Act, R.S.N.W.T. 1988, c. D-1, s.11(1).
Defamation Act, R.S.N.S. 1989, c. 122, s.13(7).
Libel and Slander Act, R.S.O. 1990, c. L.12, s.3(6).
Defamation Act, R.S.P.E.I. 1988, c. D-5, s.11.
Libel and Slander Act, R.S.S. 1978, c. L-14, s.10(4).
Defamation Act, R.S.Y.T. 1986, c. 41, ss.10(5), (6).

None of the foregoing statutory provisions expressly creates a general privilege defence for news media reports of police press conferences or police information.

3) Reports of Court Proceedings

The defamation statutes of each of the common law provinces and the three territories enact an absolute privilege defence for fair and accurate reports, published without malice, of proceedings publicly heard before a court exercising judicial authority, if published contemporaneously with the proceedings, and if they contain no comment.

Defamation Act, R.S.A. 2000, c. D-6, s.11(1).
Libel and Slander Act, R.S.B.C. 1996, c. 263, s.4(4).
Defamation Act, R.S.M. 1987, c. D20, s.11(1).
Defamation Act, R.S.N.B. 1973, c. D-5, s.10(1).
Defamation Act, S.N. 1983, c. 63, s.13(1).
Defamation Act, R.S.N.W.T. 1988, c. D-1, s.12(1).
Defamation Act, R.S.N.S. 1989, c. 122, s.14(1).
Libel and Slander Act, R.S.O. 1990, c. L.12, s.12(4).
Defamation Act, R.S.P.E.I. 1988, c. D-5, s.12(1).
Libel and Slander Act, R.S.S. 1978, c. L-14, s.11(1).
Defamation Act, R.S.Y.T. 1986, c. 41, s.11(1).

Taylor-Wright v. *CHBC-TV, a Division of WIC Ltd.* (1999), B.C.J. No. 334 (S.C.), aff'd (2000), 194 D.L.R. (4th) 621 (B.C.C.A.).

Ager v. *Canjex Publishing Ltd.* (*c.o.b. Canada Stockwatch*), [2003] B.C.J. No. 1349, 2003 BCSC 891, per Shaw J. at paras. 35–37.

Fairness and accuracy are to be determnined by reference to a full day's proceedings.

Young v. *Toronto Star Newspapers Ltd.*, [2003] O.J. No. 3100, per Rouleau J. at paras. 153–53 (S.C.J.).

A report of in-camera proceedings is not protected nor is a report which contravenes a court publication ban. A report need not be verbatim, but any significant inaccuracies will defeat the privilege. A report must not be biased or garbled. A summary is acceptable provided there is "substantive" accuracy. Trivial inaccuracies will not defeat the privilege. It is necessary to consider all of the complaints about the report together and then determine whether it is fair or accurate.

Wenman v. *Pacific Press Ltd.*, 1991 BCSC C891725.

J.M.F. v. *Chappell and News Publishing Company Ltd.* (1998), 158 D.L.R. (4th) 430 (B.C.C.A.), leave to appeal to S.C.C denied, [1998] S.C.C.A. 154.

While the common law qualified privilege now clearly covers reports of publicly-filed court documents, there is some division as to whether the statutory absolute privilege does.

Taylor- Wright v. *CHBC-TV, a Division of WIC Television Ltd.*, above, at para. 34.

Dale v. *The Guardian* (1999), 30 C.P.C. (4th) 148 (P.E.I.S.C. (T.D.)).

4) Headlines and Captions

Most provinces make it clear that a headline and caption is deemed to be a "report" for purposes of the statutory privilege; or, alternatively, that they enjoy the protection of the "report" privilege.

Defamation Act, R.S.A. 2000, c. D-6, s.11(3).
Defamation Act, R.S.N.S. 1989, c. 122, s.15.
Defamation Act, R.S.M. 1987, c. D20, s.12.
Defamation Act, R.S.N.B. 1973, c. D-5, s.11.
Defamation Act, S.N. 1983, c. 63, s.14.
Defamation Act, R.S.N.W.T. 1988, c. D-1, s.14.
Defamation Act, R.S.P.E.I. 1988, c. D-5 s.12(2) [court proceedings only].
Defamation Act, R.S.Y.T. 1986, c. 41, s.12.

5) Miscellaneous Statutory Privileges

Nova Scotia and Ontario have enacted a qualified privilege defence for fair and accurate newspaper or broadcast reports of the decisions of associations for the promotion of art, science, religion, or learning, or for the promotion of trade, business, industry, or professional bodies, or for the promotion of sports, insofar as the decision relates to a member of the association.

> *Defamation Act*, R.S.N.S. 1989, c. 122, s.13(4)
> *Libel and Slander Act*, R.S.O. 1990, c. L.12, s.3(4).

6) Right of Contradiction or Explanation

In the common law provinces and the three northern territories, the above-noted statutory privileges concerning reports of court or legislative proceedings are defeated if the defendant newspaper or broadcaster fails, upon request, to publish or broadcast a reasonable statement by way of contradiction or explanation of the report or other publication.

> *Defamation Act*, R.S.A. 2000, c. D-6, ss.10(4), 11(2).
> *Libel and Slander Act*, R.S.B.C. 1996, c. 263, s.4(3).
> *Defamation Act*, R.S.M. 1987, c. D20, ss.10(4), 11(2).
> *Defamation Act*, R.S.N.B. 1973, c. D-5, ss.9(4), 10(2).
> *Defamation Act*, S.N. 1983, c.63, ss.12(4), 13(2).
> *Defamation Act*, R.S.N.W.T. 1988, c.D-1, ss.11(4), 12(2).
> *Defamation Act*, R.S.N.S. 1989, c.122, ss.13(6), 14(2).
> *Libel and Slander Act*, R.S.O. 1990, c.L.12, s.3(7).
> *Defamation Act*, R.S.P.E.I. 1988, c.D-5, ss.10(4), 12(2).
> *Libel and Slander Act*, R.S.S. 1978, c. L-14, ss.10(3), 11(1).
> *Defamation Act*, R.S.Y.T. 1986, c.41, ss.10(4), 11(2).

In British Columbia, however, this stipulation does not apply to reports of court proceedings.

> *Libel and Slander Act*, R.S.B.C. 1996, c. 263, s.3.

The obligation is on the plaintiff to prepare the contradiction or explanation to be inserted. A request by the plaintiff for a retraction or an apology does not trigger the application of this provision nor does a request for an apology.

> *Hansen* v. *Nugget Publishers Ltd.*, [1927] 4 D.L.R. 791, per Ridell J.A. at 795 (C.A.).

> *Khan* v. *Ahmed*, [1957] 2 Q.B. 149, per Linskey J. at 153.

> *Nowlan* v. *Moncton Publishing*, [1952] 4 D.L.R. 808, per Harrison J. at 810 (N.B.S.C. (A.D.)).

7) Exclusions

Each of the defamation statutes contains a number of exclusions. Nothing "blasphemous, seditious or indecent" is protected.

> *Defamation Act*, R.S.A. 2000, c. D-6, ss.9(3), 11(1)(c).
> *Libel and Slander Act*, R.S.B.C. 1996, c. 263, ss.3(2), 4(2).
> *Defamation Act*, R.S.M. 1987, c. D20, ss.10(3), 11(1)(c).
> *Defamation Act*, R.S.N.B. 1973, c. D-5, ss.9(3), 10(1)(c).
> *Defamation Act*, S.N. 1983, c. 63, ss. 2(3), 13(1)(c).
> *Defamation Act*, R.S.N.W.T. 1988, c. D-1, ss.11(1)(c), 12(1)(c).
> *Defamation Act*, R.S.N.S. 1989, c. 122, ss.13(5), 14(1)(c).
> *Libel and Slander Act*, R.S.O. 1990, c. L.12, ss.3(5), 4(2).
> *Defamation Act*, R.S.P.E.I. 1988, c. D-5, ss.10(3), 12(1)(c).
> *Libel and Slander Act*, R.S.S. 1978, c. L-14, ss.10(2), 11(2).
> *Defamation Act*, R.S.Y.T. 1986, c. 41, ss.10(3), 11(1)(c).

Nowlan v. Moncton Publishing Co., above.

8) Specific Provisions Relevant to Libel and Slander in Other Statutes

There are many provisions buried in provincial statutes which are relevant to a determination of liability for defamatory speech. Many statutes which protect public servants and others from liability for anything said or done or omitted to be done in the performance or purported performance of a duty specifically exclude libel or slander actions from the scope of the protection. Examples include:

> *Library Act*, R.S.B.C. 1996, c. 264, s.54 (3)(b).
> *Municipal Act*, R.S.B.C. 1996, c.323, s.755.1(3).
> *The Open Learning Agency Act*, R.S.B.C. 1996, c. 341, s.12(2)(b).
> *The School Act*, R.S.B.C., c. 412, s.112(2)(b).

Other statutes specifically confer a "fair and accurate" report privilege with respect to newspaper publications or broadcasts of proceedings before specialized tribunals, or the contents of records or reports of such proceedings. Example:

> *Forest Practices Code of British Columbia Act*, R.S.B.C. 1996, c. 159, s.161.

Other statutes confer a qualified privilege on reports of auditors of public or private bodies. Example:

Community Financial Services Act, R.S.B.C. 1996, c. 61, s.22.

Society Act, R.S.B.C. 1996, c. 433, s.55.

A province or territory may provide statutory privileges which either exempt public servants or others from liability for defamatory speech or codify a qualified or conditional privilege for defamatory communications. It is impossible in this book to catalogue them all.

CHAPTER NINETEEN:

Qualified Privilege and Publication to the World at Large:

Developments in Australia, the United Kingdom, and New Zealand

A. INTRODUCTION

The scope of a qualified privilege defence for publication to the world at large in the news media has significantly expanded in Australia, the United Kingdom, and New Zealand since the Supreme Court of Canada last discussed qualified privilege in *Hill* v. *Church of Scientology of Toronto*, [1995] 2 S.C.R. 1130.

The highest courts in those three foreign jurisdictions have extended the common law defence of qualified privilege as it applies to expression in the news media. The leading cases are:

Lange v. *Australian Broadcasting Corp.* (1997), 145 A.L.R. 96, where a unanimous High Court of Australia recognized an extended category of qualified privilege for expression concerning government and political matters that affect the people of Australia. As a constraint, a test of "reasonableness" must be satisfied by the publisher.

Reynolds v. *Times Newspapers Ltd.*, [1999] 4 All E.R. 609 (H.L. (Eng.)), where the House of Lords held that a publication to the world at large may attract the protection of qualified privilege, on a case-by-case basis, depending on all the circumstances, if the public interest is served. To obtain the benefit of "*Reynolds* privilege," a publisher must satisfy the requirements of "responsible journalism."

Lange v. *Atkinson*, [2000] 3 N.Z.L.R. 385, where the New Zealand Court of Appeal unanimously held that political expression concerning the actions and qualities of persons currently or formerly elected to Parliament and those with immediate aspirations to such office, so far as those actions and qualities directly affect or affected their capacity to meet their political responsibilities, was privileged. The constraint is that the privilege must be responsibly used, not misused. In some cases, the obligation to be responsible will come close to a requirement to take reasonable care; in others, a genuine belief after hasty and incomplete consideration may be adequate.

These decisions and subsequent foreign authorities which have interpreted or applied them warrant close scrutiny by Canadian judges who are now being asked by defendants, particularly the news media, to expand the scope of qualified privilege for publication to the world at large.

Lord Nicholls, speaking as a member of the Judicial Committee of the Privy Council in *Lange v. Atkinson*, [2000] 1 N.Z.L.R. 257, said (at pages 261–63):

> ... [S]triking a balance between freedom of expression and protection of reputation calls for a value judgment which depends on local political and social conditions. These conditions include matters such as the responsibility and vulnerability of the press ... Even on issues of public policy, every jurisdiction can benefit from examinations of an issue undertaken by others. Interaction between the jurisdictions can help to clarify and refine the issues and the available options, without prejudicing national autonomy.

A succinct explanation of the distinctions between the three decisions is given in the judgment of the New Zealand Court of Appeal in *Lange v. Atkinson*, [2000] 3 N.Z.L.R. 385:

> ¶8 Each country has recognized a new occasion or the potential for a new occasion may be one in which the communication is made to the public at large, thereby removing any capacity for the defence to be defeated by excess of publication. The compass of the subject-matter seen as giving rise or capable of giving rise to the privilege is not the same in the three countries. In the United Kingdom the subject-matter is widely defined, but the focus is directly particularly to the position of a national newspaper. In Australia the subject-matter relates essentially to the conduct of politicians, both in that country and elsewhere. In New Zealand, the subject-matter is tightly defined, but its application is to all manner of publications. It is primarily the definition of the controls governing the extension which has given rise to differences of approach.

The implications of the differing solutions adopted by the Australian, United Kingdom, and New Zealand courts cannot be understood without a detailed review of the facts and judicial reasoning underlying the decision in each jurisdiction. This chapter attempts such a review below.

B. *LANGE* v. *AUSTRALIAN BROADCASTING CORPORATION*

Plaintiff David Lange, a former Prime Minister of New Zealand, sued the Australian Broadcasting Corporation in the Supreme Court of New South Wales over a broadcast which occurred when he was a member of the New Zealand Parliament.

The broadcaster defended by pleading, among other defences, common law qualified privilege, alleging that the expression at issue concerned subjects of public interest and political matters and that the defendant had a duty to publish the material to viewers who had a legitimate interest therein, and a reciprocal interest in receiving information relating to those subjects because they related to political, social, and economic matters occurring in New Zealand.

The matter came before the High Court of Australia on a stated case from the Supreme Court of New South Wales [(1997), 145 A.L.R. 96]. At the hearing in the High Court, the plaintiff asked the Court to reconsider its decisions in *Theophanous* v. *Herald and Weekly Times Ltd.* (1994), 182 C.L.R. 104 (H.C.A.) and *Stephens* v. *West Australian Newspapers Ltd.* (1994), 182 C.L.R. 211 (H.C.A.), and to hold that those decisions did not, in any event, apply to the discussion in Australia of the conduct of a Member of Parliament for New Zealand.

On 8 July 1997, the High Court of Australia unanimously ruled (5-0) [paragraphs 62–63]:

¶62 ... each member of the Australian community has an interest in disseminating and receiving information, opinions and arguments concerning government and political matters that affect the people of Australia. The duty to disseminate such information is simply the correlative of the interest in receiving it. The common convenience and welfare of Australian society are advanced by discussion — the giving and receiving of information — about government and political matters. The interest that each member of the Australian community has in such a discussion extends the categories of qualified privilege. Consequently, those categories now must be recognised as protecting a communication made to the public on a government or political matter. Discussion of matters concerning the United Nations or other countries may be protected by the extended defence of qualified privilege, even if those discussions cannot illuminate the choice for electors at federal elections or in amending the Constitution or cannot throw light on the administration of federal government.

¶63 Similarly, discussion of government or politics at State or Territory level and even at local government level is amenable to protection by the extended category of qualified privilege, whether or not it bears on matters at the federal level.

The High Court noted that at common law, however, privileged occasions are ordinarily occasions of limited publication — often publication to a single person. The Court considered that although honesty of purpose in the publisher may be the appropriate protection for individual reputation in the context of limited publication, that test was not appropriate when the publication "is to tens of thousands, or more, of readers, listeners or viewers."

Accordingly, the High Court held that because the damage that can be done by publication to the world at large is likely to be much greater than the limited publications protected by established common law categories, there should be a requirement that the publisher satisfy a test of "reasonableness of conduct" which goes beyond mere honesty. This requirement only applies when a publication concerning a government or a political matter is made in circumstances that, under the English common law, would have failed to attract a defence of qualified privilege; namely, when the extended category of qualified privilege recognized in this judgment is invoked to protect a publication that would otherwise have been made to too wide an audience. The Court stated:

> ¶67 In all but exceptional cases, the proof of reasonableness will fail as a matter of fact unless the publisher establishes that it was unaware of the falsity of the matter and did not act recklessly in making the publication.

Further, the Court held that the extended category of qualified privilege for political expression will be defeated if the plaintiff proves that the publication was actuated by common law malice to the extent that the elements of malice are not covered under the rubric of reasonableness. In this context, expression "actuated by malice" is to be understood as "signifying a publication made not for the purpose of communicating government or political information or ideas, but for some improper purpose." The Court stated:

> ¶70 ... we see no reason why a publisher who has used the occasion to give vent to its ill will or other improper motive should escape liability for the publication of false and defamatory statements. As we have explained, the existence of ill will or other improper motive will not itself defeat the privilege. The plaintiff must prove that the publication of the defamatory matter was actuated by that ill will or other improper motive. Furthermore, having regard to the subject matter of government and politics, the motive of causing polit-

ical damage to the plaintiff or his or her party cannot be regarded as improper. Nor can the vigour of an attack or the pungency of a defamatory statement, without more, discharge the plaintiff's onus of proof of this issue.

The reasons of the Court for recognizing this new category of extended privilege included the following:

i)   Although not expressly mentioned in the Constitution, freedom of communication on matters of government and politics is an indispensable incident of the system of representative government created by the Constitution [paragraph 31].

ii)   Communications concerning political or governmental matters between electors and elected representatives, between electors and candidates for election, and between the electors themselves are central to the system of representative government [paragraph 32].

iii) The Constitution necessarily protects freedom of communication between people concerning political or governmental matters, which enables the people to exercise a free and informed choice as electors. This does not confer personal rights on individuals, but precludes the curtailment of the protected freedom by the exercise of legislative or executive power [paragraph 33].

iv)   If the freedom is to be effective, it cannot be confined to the election period because that would deprive the electors of the greater part of the information necessary to make an effective choice at the election [paragraph 34].

v)   The freedom of communication which the Constitution protects is not absolute. It may be restricted by a law enacted to satisfy some other legitimate end if the law is reasonably appropriate and adapted to the fulfillment of the legitimate purpose [paragraph 36].

vi)   One common law operates in the Australian federal system established by the Constitution and within that single system of jurisprudence, the Constitution may have effect on the content of the common law [paragraph 42].

vii) Conversely the Constitution itself is informed by the common law [paragraph 43].

viii) Since 1901 when the Constitution took effect, there has been an expansion of the franchise, an increase in literacy, the growth of modern political structures operating at both federal and state levels, and the development of mass communications, especially electronic media. These changes require the striking of a different balance between free-

dom of expression and the protection of reputation from that which
was struck in 1901 [paragraph 46].

ix) The common law of libel and slander cannot be developed inconsis-
     tently with the Constitution, which requires a qualified freedom to
     discuss government and politics [paragraph 48].

x)   The common law rights of persons defamed may be diminished by
     statute but they cannot be enlarged so as to restrict freedom of expres-
     sion [paragraph 50].

xi) The Constitutional requirement of freedom of communication is not
     a private "right of communication" and is therefore to be distin-
     guished from the private right conferred by the First Amendment to
     the United States Constitution [paragraph 53].

xii) Insofar as the law of defamation requires electors and others to pay
     damages for the publication of communications concerning govern-
     mental or political matters relating to the Commonwealth of Australia,
     it effectively burdens the freedom of communication about those mat-
     ters. "That being so, the critical question in the present case is whether
     the common law of defamation as it has traditionally been under-
     stood, and the New South Wales law of defamation in its statutory
     form, are reasonably appropriate and adapted to serving the legitimate
     end of preserving personal reputation without unnecessarily or unrea-
     sonably impairing the freedom of communication about government
     and political matters protected by the Constitution" [paragraph 56].

xiii) The constitutionally-prescribed system of government would be
      adversely affected by an unqualified freedom to publish defamatory
      matter damaging the reputations of individuals involved in govern-
      ment or politics [paragraph 57].

xiv) Only in exceptional cases has the common law of Australia recognized
      an interest or duty to publish defamatory expression to the general
      public. "However, the common law doctrine as espoused in Australia
      must now be seen as imposing an unreasonable restraint on that free-
      dom of communication, especially communication concerning govern-
      ment and political matters, which 'the common convenience and
      welfare of society' now requires. Equally, the system of government pre-
      scribed by the Constitution would be impaired if a wider freedom for
      members of the public to give and to receive information concerning
      government and political matters were not recognized" [paragraph 60].

xv)   The "quality of life and freedom of the ordinary individual in Australia
      are highly dependent on the exercise of functions and powers vested

in public representatives and officials by a vast legal and bureaucratic apparatus funded by public moneys." Information concerning those subjects is "of vital concern" to the community [paragraph 60, citing *Stephens*, above].

xvi) Before the decision of the High Court in *Theophanous*, the common law of defamation concerning qualified privilege failed to meet the requirements of the Constitution [paragraph 61].

Australian cases which have considered or applied *Lange* include:

Archer v. *Channel Seven Perth Pty. Ltd.*, [2002] W.A.S.C. 160.

McMullin v. *TCN Channel Nine Pty. Ltd.*, [2000] N.S.W.S.C. 925.

Chapman & Ors v. *Conservation Council of South Australia Inc.*, [2003] S.A.S.C. 4.

Marsden v. *Amalgamated Television Services Pty. Ltd.*, [2001] N.S.W.S.C. 510, [2002] N.S.W.C.A. 419.

Orion Pet Products Pty. Ltd. v. *Royal Society for the Prevention of Cruelty to Animals (Vic)*, [2002] F.C.A. 860.

Buddhist Society of Western Australia Inc. v. *Bristile Ltd.*, [2000] W.A.S.C. 210.

Nationwide News Pty. Ltd. v. *International Financing & Investment Pty. Ltd.*, [1999] W.A.S.C.A. 95.

Popovic v. *Herald & Weekly Times Ltd.*, [2002] V.S.C. 174.

Heytesbury Holdings Pty. Ltd. v. *City of Subiaco* (1998), 19 W.A.R. 440.

Moriarty and Wortley v. *Advertiser Newspapers Ltd.*, [1998] S.A.D.C. 3843.

Reynolds v. *Nationwide News Pty. Ltd. & Ors*, [2001] W.A.S.C. 116.

Brander v. *Ryan* (2000), S.A.S.C. 449.

C. *REYNOLDS* v. *TIMES NEWSPAPERS LTD.*

In *Reynolds* v. *Times Newspapers Ltd.*, the former Prime Minister of the Irish Republic (Eire) sued for libel, alleging that an article published by the Sunday Times newspaper meant that he had deliberately and dishonestly misled the Dail Eireann (the Irish Parliament) on 15 November 1994 by suppressing vital information, that he had similarly misled his coalition cabinet colleagues by delaying until 16 November the release of certain information concerning an extradition case, and that he had lied to the Dail and his coalition colleagues about when that information had come to his attention.

In its statement of defence, the defendant newspaper justified the article as meaning "that the collapse of the coalition Government led by the Plaintiff and his resignation as [Prime Minister] and leader of Fianna Fail were occasioned by the fact that he knowingly mislead the Dail and his coalition partners in relation to the appointment of Mr. Whelehan as President of the High Court."

Over the objections of his coalition partners, the Labour Party, the plaintiff had appointed Attorney General Harold Whelehan as President of the High Court before making the statements in the Dail which were germane to the libel claim. This occurred despite public controversy over the inaction of Whelehan's office in handling a request from Northern Ireland for the extradition of a Roman Catholic priest on charges of child sex abuse.

In the Dail, the leader of the Labour Party, Dick Spring, stated before publication of the *Sunday Times* article that the plaintiff:

> … should have included this vital information in the statement he made to the House yesterday, if he wished to give a full explanation of all these events. Had he done so, it would have completely altered the thrust of his speech, and had a profound effect on the subsequent debate and questioning.

Reynolds resigned as Prime Minister on the morning of 17 November and Whelehan also resigned as President of the High Court.

On 20 November 1994, the British mainland edition of the *Sunday Times* newspaper contained an article about the crisis and Reynolds' resignation headlined 'Goodbye, gombeen man'" with the sub-heading: "Why a fib too fair proved fatal for the political career of Ireland's peacemaker and Mr. Fixit."

The Court of First Instance

At the trial of the plaintiff's libel action, the jury returned a majority verdict (10-1) that the allegation made by the plaintiff was untrue but that the words complained of correctly reported Mr. Spring's reasons for withdrawing from the coalition government headed by the plaintiff. The jury awarded the plaintiff "zero damages."

After hearing submissions concerning the legal significance of the jury's verdict, the judge awarded the plaintiff damages in the amount of one pence. Subsequently, the judge heard and rejected submissions by the defendant contending for a wide qualified privilege at common law for "political speech."

Reynolds' Appeal to the English Court of Appeal

The plaintiff Reynolds appealed to the Court of Appeal seeking a new trial on the ground the trial judge had misdirected the jury by misstating the factual issues for decision. The defendants cross-appealed, *inter alia*, on the issue of qualified privilege for political speech.

On 8 July 1998, the Court of Appeal found there was mis-direction to the jury on the facts relating to the defence of justification, allowed the appeal, and ordered a new trial: [1998] 3 All E.R. 961.

On the cross-appeal relating to qualified privilege, the English Court of Appeal dismissed the appeal on the merits but gave extensive reasons concerning the availability of a defence of qualified privilege to the news media.

The English Court of Appeal considered but rejected the approach taken by the New Zealand Court of Appeal in *Lange* v. *Atkinson* [see section D below]. Instead, the court gave a broader scope to the qualified privilege.

Writing for the Court, Lord Chief Justice Bingham concluded that (at 1004–5):

- a defence of qualified privilege may apply to a publication by a newspaper to the public at large, as it may be the duty of the news media to inform the public and engage in public discussion on matters of public interest, and the public may have a corresponding interest in receiving information on such matters (as opposed to matters in which the public may be interested).

- in modern conditions, the duty of the media and the interest of the public should more readily be found to exist. However, assuming that a statement is defamatory and factually false although honestly believed to be true, the defence is not established unless the "circumstances of the publication are such as to make it proper, in the public interest, to afford the publisher immunity from liability in the absence of malice."

On the facts before the Court, it was held that the duty and interest tests were satisfied. The circumstances in which the Reynolds government fell from power were matters of "undoubted public interest" to the people of Great Britain. It was therefore clear the defendants had a duty to inform the public of those matters and the public had a corresponding interest to receive that information.

However, the "circumstantial test" was not satisfied and the qualified privilege defence therefore did not apply. The allegation that Reynolds had lied was attributed to an unidentified member of the staff of one of Reynolds' leading political opponents, who could "scarcely be judged an authoritative source for so serious a factual allegation." Reynolds was criticised in the Dail, but in terms consistent with an honest but mistaken impression on Reynolds' part. The defendant newspaper completely failed to report Reynolds' own account of his conduct, given while addressing the

Dail on 18 November, and thereafter did not alert Reynolds to their "highly damaging" conclusion that he had lied and obtain his comments before publication. In the edition published to readers in Ireland, the newspaper alleged Reynolds was a victim of circumstance, whereas the British edition conveyed the defamatory imputation to readers on the mainland of Britain. "It should have been obvious that he could not be both."

In the course of his reasons for recognizing the existence of a defence of qualified privilege for publication to the world at large by a newspaper defendant, Lord Justice Bingham stated the scope of the privilege in broad terms at 1004–5:

> We do not for an instant doubt that the common convenience and welfare of a modern plural democracy such as ours are best served by an ample flow of information to the public concerning, and by vigorous public discussion of, matters of public interest to the community. By that we mean matters relating to the public life of the community and those who take part in it, including within the expression "public life" activities such as the conduct of government and political life, elections … and public administration, but we use the expression more widely than that, to embrace matters such as (for instance) the governance of public bodies, institutions and companies which give rise to a public interest in disclosure, but excluding matters which are personal and private, such that there is no public interest in their disclosure. Recognition that the common convenience and welfare of society are best served in this way is a modern democratic imperative which the law must accept …
>
> As it is the task of the news media to inform the public and engage in public discussion of matters of public interest, so is that to be recognised as its duty. The cases cited show acceptance of such a duty, even where publication is by a newspaper to the public at large. In modern conditions what we have called the duty test should, in our view, be rather more readily held to be satisfied.
>
> Corresponding to the duty of the media to inform is the interest of the public to receive information.… We have no doubt that the public also have an interest to receive information on matters of public interest to the community (as opposed, of course, to information about matters in which the public may happen to be interested). The cases have accepted that the public generally may have an interest to receive information published in a newspaper, so satisfying that we have called the interest test. In modern conditions the interest test should also, in our view, be rather more readily held to be satisfied.
>
> It would, however, in our judgment, run counter to English authority and do nothing to promote the common convenience of our society to discard the circumstantial test. Assuming in each case that a statement is defamatory and

factually false although honestly believed to be true, it is one thing to publish a statement taken from a government press release, or the report of a public company chairman, or the speech of a university vice-chancellor, and quite another to publish the statement of a political opponent, or a business competitor or a disgruntled ex-employee; it is one thing to publish a statement which the person defamed has been given the opportunity to rebut, and quite another to publish a statement without any recourse to the person defamed where such recourse was possible; it is one thing to publish a statement which has been so far as possible checked, and quite another to publish it without such verification as was possible and as the significance of the statement called for. While those who engage in public life must expect and accept that their public conduct will be the subject of close scrutiny and robust criticism, they should not in our view be taken to expect or accept that their conduct should be the subject of false and defamatory statements of fact unless the circumstances of the publication are such as to make it proper, in the public interest, to afford the publisher immunity from liability in the absence of malice. We question whether in practice this is a test very different from the test of reasonableness upheld in Australia.

Lord Bingham rejected the defendant newspaper's submission that qualified privilege should exist unless the plaintiff proved the publisher lacked an honest belief in the truth of the statement. The newspaper unsuccessfully argued that such a rule would have the positive virtue of discouraging irresponsible journalism by imposing a salutary discipline on the editor and journalists involved since, absent a plea of justification, the focus of a trial would shift from the conduct of the plaintiff to the conduct of the newspaper, which in answer to a plea of malice would need to vindicate the conscientiousness of its investigation and of its conduct leading up to the publication. The Court of Appeal held that the application of its "circumstantial" test would exert the same beneficial influence.

Lord Bingham also noted that his description of the qualified privilege defence available to the news media was not limited to "political speech." He held that such a limitation would not serve the common convenience and welfare of society, because "there are many matters which affect the public interest and the health of society much more profoundly than the small change of political controversy."

The Times' Appeal to the House of Lords

On 28 October 1999, the House of Lords, by a narrow majority (3–2), dismissed an appeal by the newspaper from the decision of the Court of

Appeal which had rejected the defence of qualified privilege in the particular circumstances of the case: [1999] 4 All E.R. 609.

Although there was to be a new trial for reasons relating to the defence of justification, the majority declined to order that the availability of a defence of qualified privilege be reconsidered in the context of the evidence to be tendered at the new trial.

The principal majority judgment was delivered by Lord Nicholls (expressly approved by Lord Cooke and Lord Hobhouse in separate concurring speeches), who held that a publication to the world at large may attract a defence of qualified privilege at common law, if in all the circumstances of publication, the public interest is served by treating the occasion as one of qualified privilege, including consideration of the nature of the matter published and its source and status.

Lord Nicholls emphatically rejected the defence proposition that there should be a generic privilege for the news media extending to the publication of political information to the public at large, whatever its source and whatever the circumstances.

Discussing the conflicting interests of freedom of expression and protection of reputation, Lord Nicholls stated at 614:

> The common law has long recognised the 'chilling' effect of this rigorous, reputation-protective principle. There must be exceptions. At times people must be able to speak and write freely, uninhibited by the prospect of being sued for damages should they be mistaken or misinformed. In the wider public interest, protection of reputation must then give way to a higher priority.

Lord Nicholls continued his discussion of these conflicting interests at 621–22:

> ... At a pragmatic level, freedom to disseminate and receive information on political matters is essential to the proper functioning of the system of parliamentary democracy cherished in this country. This freedom enables those who elect representatives to Parliament to make an informed choice, regarding individuals as well as policies, and those elected to make informed decisions. Freedom of expression will shortly be buttressed by statutory requirements. Under section 12 of the Human Rights Act 1998, expected to come into force in October 2000, the court is required, in relevant cases, to have particular regard to the importance of the right to freedom of expression. The common law is to be developed and applied in a manner consistent with article 10 of the European Convention for the Protection of Human Rights and Fundamental Freedoms (Cmd. 8969), and the court must take into account relevant decisions of the European Court of Human Rights (sections

6 and 2). To be justified, any curtailment of freedom of expression must be convincingly established by a compelling countervailing consideration, and the means employed must be proportionate to the end sought to be achieved.

Likewise, there is no need to elaborate on the importance of the role discharged by the media in the expression and communication of information and comment on political matters. It is through the mass media that most people today obtain their information on political matters. Without freedom of expression by the media, freedom of expression would be a hollow concept. The interest of a democratic society in ensuring a free press weighs heavily in the balance in deciding whether any curtailment of this freedom bears a reasonable relationship to the purpose of the curtailment. In this regard it should be kept in mind that one of the contemporary functions of the media is investigative journalism. This activity, as much as the traditional activities of reporting and commenting, is part of the vital role of the press and the media generally.

Reputation is an integral and important part of the dignity of the individual. It also forms the basis of many decisions in a democratic society which are fundamental to its well-being: whom to employ or work for, whom to promote, whom to do business with or to vote for. Once besmirched by an unfounded allegation in a national newspaper, a reputation can be damaged for ever, especially if there is no opportunity to vindicate one's reputation. When this happens, society as well as the individual is the loser. For it should not be supposed that protection of reputation is a matter of importance only to the affected individual and his family. Protection of reputation is conducive to the public good. It is in the public interest that the reputation of public figures should not be debased falsely. In the political field, in order to make an informed choice, the electorate needs to be able to identify the good as well as the bad. Consistently with these considerations, human rights conventions recognise that freedom of expression is not an absolute right. Its exercise may be subject to such restrictions as are prescribed by law and are necessary in a democratic society for the protection of the reputations of others.

In his review of the prior jurisprudence concerning the scope of qualified privilege, Lord Nicholls stated:

The requirement that both the maker of the statement and the recipient must have an interest or duty draws attention to the need to have regard to the position of both parties when deciding whether an occasion is privileged. But this should not be allowed to obscure the rationale of the underlying public interest on which privilege is founded. The essence of this defence lies in the law's recognition of the need, in the public interest, for a particular recipient to receive frank and uninhibited communication of particular information from a particular source. That is the end the law is concerned to attain. The protection afforded to the maker of the statement is the means by which the law seeks to achieve that end. Thus the court has to assess whether, in the public interest, the publication should be protected in the absence of malice.

In determining whether an occasion is regarded as privileged the court has regard to all the circumstances: see, for example, the explicit statement of Lord Buckmaster L.C. in *London Association for Protection of Trade* v. *Greenlands Ltd.*, [1916] 2 A.C. 15, 23 ('every circumstance associated with the origin and publication of the defamatory matter'). And circumstances must be viewed with today's eyes. The circumstances in which the public interest requires a communication to be protected in the absence of malice depend upon current social conditions. The requirements at the close of the twentieth century may not be the same as those of earlier centuries or earlier decades of this century.

With respect to qualified privilege for publication to the world at large, Lord Nicholls held at 619 that the principles stated by the Court of Appeal required modification:

> In its valuable and forward-looking analysis of the common law the Court of Appeal in the present case highlighted that in deciding whether an occasion is privileged the court considers, among other matters, the nature, status and source of the material published and the circumstances of the publication. In stressing the importance of these particular factors, the court treated them as matters going to a question ('the circumstantial test') separate from, and additional to, the conventional duty-interest questions: see [1998] 3 W.L.R. 862, 899. With all respect to the Court of Appeal, this formulation of three questions gives rise to conceptual and practical difficulties and is better avoided. There is no separate or additional question. These factors are to be taken into account in determining whether the duty-interest test is satisfied or, as I would prefer to say in a simpler and more direct way, whether the public was entitled to know the particular information. The duty-interest test, or the right to know test, cannot be carried out in isolation from these factors and without regard to them. A claim to privilege stands or falls according to whether the claim passes or fails this test. There is no further requirement.

He went on to hold at 626 that a court should be slow to conclude that a publication is not in the public interest and that therefore the public had no right to know, especially when the information is in the field of political discussion:

... Any lingering doubts should be resolved in favour of publication.

In arriving at his conclusion that the particular circumstances of the *Reynolds* litigation did not justify the recognition of a privilege, Lord Nicholls stated at 625–26:

> My conclusion is that the established common law approach to misstatements of fact remains essentially sound. The common law should not develop 'political information' as a new 'subject-matter' category of qualified privilege, whereby the publication of all such information would attract qualified privilege, whatever the circumstances. That would not provide adequate protection for reputation. Moreover, it would be unsound in principle to distinguish political discussion from discussion of other matters of serious public concern. The elasticity of the common law principle enables interference with freedom of speech to be confined to what is necessary in the circumstances of the case. This elasticity enables the court to give appropriate weight, in today's conditions, to the importance of freedom of expression by the media on all matters of public concern.
>
> Depending on the circumstances, the matters to be taken into account include the following. The comments are illustrative only.
>
> 1. The seriousness of the allegation. The more serious the charge, the more the public is misinformed and the individual harmed, if the allegation is not true.
> 2. The nature of the information, and the extent to which the subject-matter is a matter of public concern.
> 3. The source of the information. Some informants have no direct knowledge of the events. Some have their own axes to grind, or are being paid for their stories.
> 4. The steps taken to verify the information.
> 5. The status of the information. The allegation may have already been the subject of an investigation which commands respect.
> 6. The urgency of the matter. News is often a perishable commodity.
> 7. Whether comment was sought from the defendant. He may have information others do not possess or have not disclosed. An approach to the defendant will not always be necessary.
> 8. Whether the article contained the gist of the plaintiff's side of the story.
> 9. The tone of the article. A newspaper can raise queries or call for an investigation. It need not adopt allegations as statements of fact.
> 10. The circumstances of the publication, including the timing.

This list is not exhaustive. The weight to be given to these and any other relevant factors will vary from case to case. Any disputes of primary fact will be a matter for the jury, if there is one. The decision on whether, having regard to the admitted or proved facts, the publication was subject to qualified privilege is a matter for the judge. This is the established practice and seems sound. A balancing operation is better carried out by a judge in a reasoned judgment than by a jury. Over time, a valuable corpus of case law will be built up.

The key circumstance in *Reynolds* was that the newspaper had failed to mention the plaintiff's own explanation to the Dail. This was held to be a deliberate omission by the newspaper because it rejected the plaintiff's version of events and concluded the plaintiff had been deliberately misleading. The press spokesperson had stated that the plaintiff would not be giving interviews but saying all he had to say in the Dail, per Lord Nicholls at 627:

> ... His statement in the Dail was his answer to the allegations. An article omitting all reference to this statement could not be a fair and accurate report of proceedings in the Dail. Such an article would be misleading as a report. By omitting Mr. Reynolds' explanation English readers were left to suppose that, so far, Mr. Reynolds had offered no explanation. ...

Lord Nicholls at 627 approved the proposition that a journalist is entitled and bound to reach her own conclusions and to express them honestly and fearlessly, and in this regard, is entitled to disbelieve and refute explanations given. However, this could not be a good reason for omitting, from a hard-hitting article making serious allegations against a named individual, all mention of that person's own explanation.

> ... Further, it is elementary fairness that, in the normal course, a serious charge should be accompanied by the gist of any explanation already given. An article which fails to do so faces an uphill task in claiming privilege if the allegations prove to be false and the unreported explanation proves to be true.

Lord Nicholls also concluded at 626 that a media defendant's unwillingness to disclose the identity of its sources should not weigh against it.

In his concurring judgment, Lord Hobhouse at 659 expressed his agreement with the circumstantial test described by Lord Nicholls, noting at 658 that the burden is on the publisher to show that the publication was in the public interest and that a publisher does not do this merely by showing that the subject matter was of public interest. To attract privilege, the report by the journalist must have qualitative content sufficient to justify the defence should the report turn out to have included some misstatement of fact (at 658).

Similarly, in his concurring judgment Cooke J. expressed agreement with the circumstantial test described by Lord Nicholls, but cautioned [at page 644 in [1999] 4 All E.R.:

> ... there is no room for any suggestion that the motive of increasing readership or audience is a sufficient interest [to publish defamatory material to the world at large].

And further at page 644 [1999] 4 ALL E.R.:

> It is undeniable that a privilege depending on particular circumstances may produce more uncertainty [than a generic privilege] and require more editorial discretion than a rule-of-thumb one. But in other professions and callings the law is content with the standard of reasonable care and skill in all the circumstances. The fourth estate should be as capable of operating within general standards.

The minority in the House of Lords — Lord Steyn and Lord Hope — agreed with Lord Nicholls that the court should not recognize a generic qualified privilege for the news media extending to the publication of political information to the public at large, whatever its source and whatever the circumstances.

Lord Steyn and Lord Hope also agreed that in order to attract a defence of qualified privilege, a publication to the world at large must be "in the public interest."

In his judgment dissenting on the result of the appeal, Lord Steyn would have rejected both a generic qualified privilege (at 631) for political speech *and* a circumstantial test (at 632–33), and held (at 633) that "the only sensible course is to go back to the traditional twofold test of duty and interest," stating that these tests "are flexible enough to embrace, depending on the occasion and the particular circumstances, a qualified privilege in respect of political speech published at large."

In Lord Steyn's view, if a newspaper stood on its right not to disclose its sources, it may "run the risk of what the judge and jury will make of the gap in the evidence" (at 634). Similarly, he would have held that a failure to report the other side

> ... will often be evidence tending to show that the occasion ought not to be protected by qualified privilege, but that will not always be so, such as when the victim's explanation is unintelligible or plain nonsense [at 634].

Lord Steyn stated (at 636) that "[i]n the result, I would uphold the qualified privilege of political speech, based on a weighing of the particular circumstances of the case."

Lord Hope disagreed with the "circumstantial test" prescribed by the Court of Appeal on the basis it tended to obscure the difference between questions which go to malice and the question whether the occasion is privileged. He criticized the circumstantial test at 656:

> ... It is too widely formulated. It includes "the nature, status and source of material and the circumstances of its publication" without any qualification as to the purpose of examining this evidence (see 3 All E.R. 961 at 995, [1998] 3 W.L.R. 862 at 899). It has the effect of introducing, at the stage of examining the question of law whether the occasion was privileged, assumptions which are relevant only to the question of fact as to the motive of the publisher. ... It has introduced questions as to the use of sources, failure to publish [the plaintiff's] own account of his conduct, failure to alert [the plaintiff] to [the newspaper's] conclusion that he had lied to his coalition colleagues and knowingly misled the Dail so as to obtain his observations on it. In my opinion, these considerations go the question of whether the [newspaper] abused the occasion. ... They do not go to the question whether the occasion itself is privileged.

Lord Hobhouse therefore held at 657 that the issue of privilege had not been properly addressed in the Court of Appeal.

1) United Kingdom Decisions Applying or Considering *Reynolds* privilege

The implications of the House of Lords' decision in *Reynolds* were canvassed in the unanimous judgment of the Court of Appeal on 5 December 2001 in *Loutchansky* v. *The Times Newspapers Ltd.*, [2001] E.W.J. No. 5622, E.W.C.A. Civ. 1805.

The Master of the Rolls, Lord Phillips, speaking for the Court of Appeal, held that *Reynolds* constituted a "striking departure" from the approach to the defence of qualified privilege which was adopted in the earlier jurisprudence and that "*Reynolds* privilege" should be recognized as "a different jurisprudential creature from the traditional form of privilege from which it sprang."

Reynolds privilege, said the Master of the Rolls, attaches to the publication itself whereas conventional qualified privilege attaches to the occasion of the publication.

Once *Reynolds* privilege attaches, there is little remaining scope for any subsequent finding of malice:

> ¶33 ... Actual malice in this context has traditionally been recognized to consist either of recklessness i.e. not believing the statement to be true or being indifferent as to its truth, or of making it with the dominant motive of injur-

ing the claimant. But the publisher's conduct in both regards must inevitably be explored when considering Lord Nicholls' ten factors i.e. in deciding whether the publication is covered by qualified privilege in the first place. As May LJ. observed in *G.R.K. Karate (UK) Limited v. Yorkshire Post Limited*, [2000] 1 WLR 2571, at 2580:

> If the judge decides that the occasion is not privileged, the issue of malice does not arise. If the judge decides that the occasion was privileged, he must have decided that, in all the circumstances, at the time of publication, including the extent of ... enquiries, the public was entitled to know the particular information available ... without [the journalist] making further enquiries. It is a little difficult to see how the same enquiries which objectively sustained the occasion as privileged would be capable of contributing to a conclusion that subjectively she was recklessly indifferent to the truth or falsity of her publication.

The Master of the Rolls expressed doubt whether *Reynolds* privilege could be vitiated by the plaintiff's proof that the publisher's dominant motive was to injure the plaintiff:

> ¶34 ... Once the publication of a particular article is held to be in the public interest on the basis of the public's right to know, can the privilege really be lost because the journalist (or editor) had the dominant motive of injuring the claimant rather than fulfilling his journalistic duty. It is a surprising thought.

The Court of Appeal in *Loutchansky* also suggested that in a case of neutral reportage, verification by the publisher may not be necessary or even appropriate, citing *Al-Fagih v. H.H. Saudi Research and Marketing (UK) Limited*, [2001] E.W.J. No. 4813 (C.A.).

With respect to the application of the circumstantial test to the news media, the Master of the Rolls stated:

> ¶36 ... The corresponding duty on the journalist (and equally his editor) is to play his proper role in discharging that function. His task is to behave as a responsible journalist. He can have no duty to publish unless he is acting responsible any more than the public has an interest in reading whatever may be published irresponsibly. That is why in this class of case the question of whether the publisher has behaved responsibly is necessarily and intimately bound up with the question whether the qualified privilege defence arises. That is not the case with regard to the more conventional situations in which qualified privilege arise. A person giving a reference or reporting a crime need not act responsibly: his communication will be privileged subject only to relevance and malice.

The Court of Appeal also expressed the view that *Reynolds* privilege could not arise in the circumstances in *Horrocks* v. *Lowe*, [1975] A.C. 135, 150:

> "Carelessness, impulsiveness and irrationality" would cost a journalist dear in the evaluation of his claim to privilege under several of the *Reynolds* factors, perhaps most notably factors 3, 4, 6,7 and 8.

This conclusion of the English Court of Appeal is echoed in the judgment of the New Zealand Court of Appeal in *Lange* v. *Atkinson*, [2000] 3 NZLR 385, where the judgment of that Court spoke at paragraph 24 of what it called the

> blurring, perhaps even the removal, of the line between the occasion and its abuse in Lord Nicholls of Birkenhead's non-exhaustive list …

In *Loutchansky*, the Master of the Rolls went on to conclude that the judge below had misstated the *Reynolds* test in the following terms:

> … the duty owed is such that a publisher would be open to legitimate criticism if he failed to publish the information in question.

The Master of the Rolls held:

> ¶49 To apply the test merely as a "cross-check" is unexceptionable where the test is satisfied. If, indeed, the publisher would have been open to legitimate criticism had he not published, his claim to privilege will be indisputable. But the converse is not true. That would be to impose too stringent a test. There will undoubtedly be occasions when one newspaper would decide to publish and quite properly so, yet a second newspaper, no less properly, would delay or abstain from publication. Not all journalists can be or should be expected to reach an identical view in every case. Responsible journalism will in certain circumstances permit equally of publication or non-publication.

> ¶50 We therefore conclude that Gray J. applied the wrong test to the question whether there was duty upon the appellants to publish these defamatory articles to the world at large. He was right to grant leave to clarify the standard. The standard required is that of responsible journalism in accordance with the principles earlier explained …

Reynolds v. *The Times Newspapers Ltd.* has also been interpreted as prescribing an objective test of "responsible journalism" which is a question for the judge, not a jury.

> *Bonnick* v. *Morris*, [2002] 3 W.L.R. 820 (P.C.), per Lord Nicholls at paras. 23–25:

¶23 Stated shortly, the *Reynolds* privilege is concerned to provide a proper degree of protection for responsible journalism when reporting matters of public concern. Responsible journalism is the point at which a fair balance is held between freedom of expression on matters of public concern and the reputations of individuals. Maintenance of this standard is in the public interest and in the interests of those whose reputations are involved. It can be regarded as the price journalists pay in return for the privilege. If they are to have the benefit of the privilege, journalists must exercise due professional care and skill.

¶24 To be meaningful this standard of conduct must be applied in a practical and flexible manner. The court must have regard to practical realities. Their Lordships consider it would be to introduce unnecessary and undesirable legalism and rigidity if this objective standard, of responsible journalism, had to be applied to all cases exclusively by reference to the "single meaning" of the words. Rather, a journalist should not be penalized for making a wrong decision on a question of meaning on which different people might reasonably take different views. ... If the words are ambiguous to such an extent that they may readily convey a different meaning to an ordinary reasonable reader, a court may take this other meaning into account when determining whether *Reynolds* privilege is available as a defence. In doing so the court will attribute to this feature of the case whatever weight it considers appropriate in all the circumstances.

¶25 This should not be pressed too far. Where questions of defamation arise ambiguity is best avoided as much as possible. It should not be a screen behind which a journalist is "willing to wound, and yet afraid to strike." In the normal course a responsible journalist can be expected to perceive the meaning an ordinary, reasonable reader is likely to give to his article. Moreover, even if the words are highly susceptible of another meaning, a responsible journalist will not disregard a defamatory meaning which is obviously one possible meaning of the article in question. Questions of degree arise here. The more obvious the defamatory meaning, and the more serious the defamation, the less weight will a court attach to other possible meanings when considering the conduct to be expected of a responsible journalist in the circumstances.

MacIntyre v. Chief Constable of Kent, [2002] All E.R. 338 per Brooke L.J. at para. 11(i) (C.A.):

Under *Reynolds* v. *Times Newspapers* [2001] A.C. 127 a journalist is not entitled to rely on the privilege unless he has acted responsibly.

Lukowiak v. *Unidad Editorial SA*, [2001] E.M.L.R. 1043 at para. 53:

It was, I believe, agreed on all sides that the test to apply is simply that of responsible journalism: see e.g. the remarks of Lord Nicholls in *Reynolds* at pp. 1024–1025.

For the purposes of *Reynolds* privilege, the defendant's state of mind is to be determined at the time of publication. The subsequently determined truth or falsity of the publication is not material.

A failure to make further or proper inquiries is capable of being an ingredient from which recklessness may be inferred. What the response to those inquiries might have been is not capable of being such an ingredient.

G.R.K. Karate Ltd. v. *Yorkshire Post Newspapers Ltd.*, [2000] 2 All E.R. 931, per May L.J. at para. 22 (C.A.):

The reliability of the source of the information is to be judged by how objectively it should have appeared to the defendant at the time. It is to be considered in conjunction with the inquiries which the defendant made at the time relevant to the reliability of the source. If the defendant made careful inquiries which, judged objectively, reasonably justified a conclusion that the source was apparently reliable, that will be a positive (though not determinative) indication in favour of the occasion being privileged. If the defendant made no, or only perfunctory, inquiries, a conclusion that the source was apparently reliable will be less likely. In neither instance is a subsequent investigation at trial into the actual reliability of the source relevant.

G.R.K. Karate Ltd. v. *Yorkshire Post Newspapers Ltd.*, *ibid.* at para. 19

See also:

Al-Fagih v. *H.H. Saudi Research and Marketing (UK) Limited*, [2002] E.M.L.R. 215 (C.A.).

Mark v. *Associated Newspapers*, [2002] E.M.L.R. 839 (C.A.).

Gilbert v. *Mirror Group Newspapers Ltd.*, [2000] E.M.L.R. 680 (Q.B.D.).

Grobbelaar v. *News Group*, [2001] E.W.C.A. Civ. 1213 (C.A.).

Sheikha Mouga Al-Misnad v. *Azzaman Ltd.*, [2003] E.W.H.C. 1783 (Q.B.).

D. *LANGE* v. *ATKINSON*

The Facts

The plaintiff Lange brought a libel suit against Australian Consolidated Press and a political scientist who authored an article in the October 1995 issue of *North and South* magazine. The article constituted a critical review of the plaintiff's performance as a politician, including his tenure as Prime Minister of New Zealand and as a Member of Parliament. It was accompanied by a cartoon which depicted the plaintiff at breakfast being served a packet labelled "Selective Memory Regression for Advanced Practitioners."

The plaintiff claimed the article and cartoon meant he was dishonest, lazy, insincere, and irresponsible.

The Court of First Instance: [1997] 2 N.Z.L.R. 22

The plaintiff brought an unsuccessful interlocutory application in the High Court at Auckland to strike out parts of the amended statement of defence filed on behalf of both defendants, which pleaded a "defence of political expression" and qualified privilege.

With respect to political expression, the defence pleaded that the article arose out of, or related to, matters which had previously been the subject of public comment by the plaintiff himself both as a Member of Parliament and/or as a Member of the New Zealand House of Representatives, Leader of the Parliamentary Labour Party and the Official Opposition, and the Prime Minister of New Zealand; that it dealt with his performance of his duties in respect of those capacities; and that it was written and published for the dominant purpose of bringing to the attention of readers various matters relevant to an informed consideration of that performance. Further, the article was published without malice and not recklessly, and it was reasonable in the circumstances having regard to the defendant author's belief that the article did not contain any matters that were false, and the steps the author had taken before publication. [These steps were detailed in the Court of Appeal's judgment, [1998] 3 N.Z.L.R. 424, namely, that the defendant had: (i) performed an extensive review of the "substantial public record regarding the plaintiff," (ii) interviewed on a confidential basis people closely associated with the plaintiff, (iii) followed "standard and well-accepted" research procedure, and (iv) become aware that the plaintiff had stated in the plaintiff's newspaper column that "a politician's life is spent rebutting criticism which makes it easy, or necessary, to dismiss criticism as misguided at best or deranged at worst." The author also observed that the plaintiff had suggested that politicians are particularly prone to "self-deception."]

With respect to the defence of qualified privilege, the defendants alleged the article was published in circumstances relating to the defence of political expression (see the penultimate paragraph); that the first defendant was on the faculty of the Political Studies Department at the University of Auckland, and had lectured and published on issues relating to the fourth Labour Government, including the matters dealt with in the article; he had a regular column in the defendant magazine, where he commented on various political issues relevant to New Zealand society; and he had a duty to write and publish the article. The defence also alleged that the New Zealand public, in particular the readers of the magazine, had a corresponding interest in receiving the information in the article.

On 14 February 1997, Elias J. dismissed Lange's application, but held that the two defences should be repleaded as one because the protection of political discussion does not require a stand alone defence. The chambers judge declined to strike out the pleadings, concluding that this was "largely a matter of form," [1997] 2 N.Z.L.R. 22.

The First Ruling of the Court of Appeal: [1998] 3 N.Z.L.R. 424

The plaintiff Lange appealed from his unsuccessful interlocutory application to strike the political expression defence and those portions of the qualified privilege defence which repeated the allegations in the political expression defence.

In its 25 May 1998 ruling ([1998] 3 N.Z.L.R. 424 (N.Z.C.A.)), the New Zealand Court of Appeal unanimously ruled that the defence of qualified privilege to a claim for damages for libel applies to generally published statements made about the actions and qualities of those currently or formerly elected to Parliament and those with immediate aspirations to be Members, so far as those actions and qualities directly affect or affected their capacity (including their personal ability and willingness) to meet their public responsibilities. The court held that the determination of the matters that bear on that capacity will depend on a consideration of what is properly a matter of public concern rather than of private concern.

The basis of the court's reasoning in its 1998 ruling was expressed in the following statement about representative democracy in New Zealand (at 463):

> In substance the people, rather than the (temporary) government, are to be seen as having ultimate power. Such an understanding of the constitution is not a new one — Dicey also expressed it over 100 years ago in his balancing of the (legal) sovereignty of Parliament by the (political) sovereignty of the

electors ... As well, simple majority rule within our national constitutional system is itself subject to critical limits. ... We are citizens of New Zealand rather than subjects of the Sovereign.

Proceeding from that fundamental principle, the Court of Appeal unanimously stated the following conclusions about the defence of qualified privilege as it applies to political statements which are published to the world at large in relation to those elected or seeking election to Parliament (at 467–468):

i)   The defence of qualified privilege may be available in respect of a statement which is published generally.

ii)   The nature of New Zealand's democracy means that the wider public may have a proper interest in respect of generally-published statements which directly concern the functioning of representative and responsible government, including statements about the performance or possible future performance of specific individuals in elected public office.

iii)   In particular, a proper interest does exist in respect of statements made about the actions and qualities of those currently or formerly elected to Parliament and those with immediate aspirations to such office, so far as those actions and qualities directly affect or affected their capacity (including their personal ability and willingness) to meet their public responsibilities.

iv)   The determination of the matters which bear on that capacity will depend on a consideration of what is properly a matter of public concern rather than of private concern.

v)   The width of the identified public concern justifies the extent of the publication.

Each of the above five elements was held to be necessary to the establishment of the qualified privilege defence.

The Court of Appeal held, however, that the defence of qualified privilege for publication to the world at large was subject to section 19 of the *Defamation Act 1992*, which stipulates that the defence of qualified privilege fails if the plaintiff proves that, in publishing the matter, the defendant was predominately motivated by ill will towards the plaintiff or otherwise took improper advantage of the occasion of publication.

In the 1998 ruling, the New Zealand Court of Appeal approached the meaning of section 19 by referring to (and paraphrasing) Lord Diplock's speech in *Horrocks v. Lowe*, [1975] A.C. 135 (H.L.), a leading English case on malice which stated three propositions relevant to the "ill will" part of section 19. The court held at 468–69 that the first and especially the second provided some protection to reputation:

1. If it be proved that [the defendant] did not believe that what he published was true, this is generally conclusive evidence of express malice, for no sense of duty or desire to protect his own legitimate interests can justify a man in telling deliberate or injurious falsehoods about another, save in the exceptional case where a person may be under a duty to pass on, without endorsing, defamatory reports made by some other person (*Horrocks* at 149–150).

2. If [the defendant] publishes untrue defamatory matter recklessly, without considering or caring whether it be true or not, he is in this, as in other branches of the law, treated as if he knew it to be false (*Horrocks* at 130).

3. But indifference to the truth of what he publishes is not to be equated with carelessness, impulsiveness or irrationality in arriving at a positive belief that it is true. The freedom of speech protected by the law of qualified privilege may be availed of by all sorts and conditions of men (*Horrocks* at 150).

With respect to the "improper advantage" element of section 19, the New Zealand Court of Appeal's 1998 judgment referred at 469 to the following passage from Lord Diplock's judgment in *Horrocks* v. *Lowe*, above, at page 150E-F:

Even a positive belief in the truth of what is published on a privileged occasion — which is presumed unless the contrary is proved — may not be sufficient to negative express malice if it can be proved that the defendant misused the occasion for some purpose other than that for which the privilege is accorded by the law. The commonest case is where the dominant motive which actuates the defendant is not a desire to perform the relevant duty or to protect the relevant interest, but to give vent to his personal spite or ill will towards the person he defames.

The Court of Appeal rejected the incorporation of a requirement of reasonableness into this expanded defence of qualified privilege.

Plaintiff's Appeal to the Judicial Committee of the Privy Council: [2000] 1 N.Z.L.R. 257

On the same day the House of Lords rendered its decision in *Reynolds* v. *The Times Newspapers Ltd.*, the same Law Lords constituted as the Judicial Committee of the Privy Council in *Lange* v. *Atkinson*, [2000] 1 N.Z.L.R. 257 set aside the decision of the New Zealand Court of Appeal reported at [1998] 3 N.Z.L.R. 424 (N.Z.C.A.).

In its 28 October 1999 ruling on the appeal from the 25 May 1998 decision of the New Zealand Court of Appeal, the Judicial Committee of the Privy Council noted that subsequently the English Court of Appeal had delivered its judgment in *Reynolds* on 8 July 1998.

The Judicial Committee of the Privy Council noted at 261–62:

> Their Lordships' Board heard the present appeal a few days before Their Lordships, in their capacity as members of the Appellate Committee of the House of Lords, heard oral argument in the *Reynolds* case … .
>
> … [O]ne feature of all the judgments, New Zealand, Australian and English, stands out with conspicuous clarity: the recognition that striking a balance between freedom of expression and protection of reputation calls for a value judgment which depends upon local political and social conditions. These conditions include matters such as the responsibility and vulnerability of the press. In Their Lordships' view, subject to one point mentioned later, this feature is determinative of the present appeal. For some years Their Lordships' Board has recognised the limitations on its role as an appellate tribunal in cases where the decision depends upon considerations of local public policy. The present case is a prime instance of such a case. As noted by Elias J. and the Court of Appeal, different countries have reached different conclusions on the issue arising on this appeal. The Courts of New Zealand are much better placed to assess the requirements of the public interest in New Zealand than Their Lordships' Board. Accordingly, on this issue the Board does not substitute its own views, if different, for those of the New Zealand Court of Appeal.

The Privy Council noted that the New Zealand Court of Appeal had previously rejected a requirement of "reasonableness" in the sense of taking reasonable care to ascertain the facts, as a condition of enjoying a qualified privilege defence for publication to the world at large. In effect, this decision of the Privy Council at 264 invited New Zealand's senior court to revisit that issue in light of the *Reynolds* privilege which requires "responsible" journalism. It also invited the New Zealand Court of Appeal to reconsider its 1998 ruling in light of *Reynolds'* rejection of a new generic privilege for political speech.

Remission to the Court of Appeal — Final Ruling: [2000] 3 N.Z.L.R. 385

On 21 June 2000, in *Lange* v. *Atkinson*, [2000] 3 N.Z.L.R. 385, the New Zealand Court of Appeal ruled unanimously that its 1998 decision struck the correct balance between freedom of expression and protection of reputation and therefore appropriately described the five conditions to be satisfied if the defence of qualified privilege were to apply to publications to the world at large. The five conditions are described on page 441 above.

Accordingly, the Court affirmed its earlier decision to dismiss the appeal brought by the plaintiff Lange and to allow the defence of qualified privilege to stand. (The Court conceded that amendments might be required to the statement of defence to reflect the law as now stated in this ruling.)

The Court concluded that there was a need for amplification of its earlier five-point conclusion in the 1998 judgment, however, because it might be read as suggesting that a communication within the category of the qualifying subject matter will always attract qualified privilege. The Court therefore stated (at paragraph 13):

> ¶13 Thirdly, it should be made clear that the five-point conclusion ... was not intended to remove from the assessment whether the occasion is privileged an inquiry into the circumstances or context of the publication. Conclusion no. (3) [a proper interest does exist in respect of statements made about the actions and qualities of those currently or formerly elected to Parliament and those with immediate aspirations to such office] confirmed that statements within those parameters are those in which the wider public has a legitimate interest. Ordinarily it can be expected such a statement will warrant protection, but it is still necessary to take into account the circumstances of publication. Those circumstances will include such matters as the identity of the publisher, the context in which the publication occurs, and the likely audience, as well as the actual content of the information. As an example of circumstances where the subject-matter may not be determinative, it is questionable whether a one-line reference to alleged misconduct of a grave nature on the part of a parliamentary candidate reflecting on his or her suitability, appearing in an article in a motoring magazine about that person's activities in motor sport, should receive protection. By contrast, the inclusion of such material in the course of a lengthy serious article on a coming election may justifiably attract the protection.

The Court of Appeal expressed approval for the reasoning of Lord Hope in Reynolds (who dissented in result) that it is the occasion (not the publication) which should attract the qualified privilege stating (at paragraph 23):

> ... That point is important. [Lord Hope] said that to make this identification it is necessary to examine "the nature of the material, the persons by whom and to whom it was published and in what circumstances." This in present circumstances represents an inquiry into whether the subject-matter qualifies in terms of conclusion (3) of our earlier formulation; and whether the maker

and recipients of the communication have the necessary shared interest on the occasion of publication — they usually will in relation to the defined subject-matter but not always. And, as His Lordship added, questions of occasion and misuse are separate inquiries.

The New Zealand Court of Appeal declined to follow the decision of the House of Lords in *Reynolds* for several reasons. First, the New Zealand Court held (at paragraph 24) that the uncertainties inherent in Lord Nicholls' case-by-case application of a circumstantial test would add significantly to the "chilling" effect of defamation law on freedom of expression. Second, the Court expressed concern [at paragraph 25] that *Reynolds* privilege reduces the role of the jury in freedom of speech cases because it is the judge rather than the jury who weighs the circumstances to determine the primary facts relevant to whether the privilege exists, leaving little scope for the jury to determine the existence of malice or whether the occasion of privilege has been abused by the defendant.

The court obviously considered that *Reynolds* reduced the role of the jury by failing to "keep conceptually separate the questions of whether the occasion is privileged and, if so, whether the occasion has been misused ..." (at paragraph 5).

The New Zealand Court of Appeal also concluded there were significant social and political differences between New Zealand and the United Kingdom which warranted a different solution to striking a balance between freedom of expression and protection of reputation (at paragraphs 26–35):

- The electoral system of New Zealand enables each voter to vote on an equal nationwide basis for the party which the voter wishes to see in the House of Representatives and in the government, whereas the general elections for the United Kingdom Parliament are still on a plurality, constituency-by-constituency basis.

- Freedom of information legislation is in force in New Zealand whereas United Kingdom law and practice relating to access to and release of information "has yet to emphasise ... the rights of citizens to participate in the process of policy and decision making and to call the government to account."

- The New Zealand *Bill of Rights Act* 1990 has a significantly narrower focus than the United Kingdom Act which gives effect to all the substantive provisions of the *European Convention for the Protection of Human Rights and Fundamental Freedoms* and certain of its protocols. The New Zealand Act emphasises the protection of political processes.

- The United Kingdom Act, in addition to protecting freedom of expression, unlike the New Zealand *Bill of Rights*, also expressly protects the right to privacy.
- The United Kingdom *Human Rights Act* gives a particular direction to the courts about how to approach freedom of expression matters. The United Kingdom courts are to have regard to the extent to which it is or would be in the public interest for journalistic material to be published and it may not be enough to determine that the material related to governmental or political matters. A more specific examination appears to be contemplated, which requires a balancing exercise in the light of the concrete facts of each case.
- New Zealand has repealed three criminal offences restricting public debate on political matters whereas the United Kingdom has not. The offences include criminal libel and publishing untrue matters calculated to influence votes during an election campaign or a local election or poll.
- Local political and social conditions, including the responsibility and vulnerability of the press, are different.
- New Zealand has a newer, smaller, closer, if increasingly diverse, society. The characteristics of the society, particularly the relationship of New Zealanders to their government, involve popular participation in the making and administration of laws and policies, the promotion of the accountability of those in office and the government's need for public understanding and support to get its policies carried out.
- New Zealand is a small country. The government has a pervasive involvement in everyday national life. This involvement is not only felt, but is also sought, by New Zealanders, who have tended to view successive governments as their agents, and have expected them to act as such. The government is a principal agency in deploying the resources required to undertake many large scale projects, and there is considerable pressure for it to sustain its role as a major developer, particularly as an alternative to overseas ownership and control. New Zealand social support systems also rely heavily on central government. History and circumstances give New Zealanders special reason for wanting to know what their government is doing and why.
- There are differences between the responsibility and vulnerability of the media in New Zealand and in the United Kingdom.
- It is possible to say that New Zealand has not encountered the worst excesses and irresponsibilities of the English national daily tabloids. Invasion of personal privacy, fabrication of interviews, and the obtaining

of information by dishonest means have become the norm in the English tabloid press. In New Zealand, media intrusion is tame by comparison.

- The combination of the smallness of the population with the fact that the New Zealand dailies are not national papers produces low circulation figures.
- Because of the regional character of the New Zealand dailies, there is not the same intense competition as has arisen between national papers in the United Kingdom.
- Some of the United Kingdom dailies have close associations with particular political parties whereas the opinion pages of New Zealand dailies and weeklies often publish competing viewpoints.

The New Zealand Court of Appeal reiterated the validity and importance of the constraint on the expanded qualified privilege defence represented by section 19 of the *Defamation Act 1992*, noting that "the purpose of the newly-recognised privilege is to facilitate responsible public discussion of the matters which it governs." The Court discussed the factors to be considered in addressing the issue whether publication was "responsible" (at paragraphs 42–43, 47–48):

¶42 … If the privilege is not responsibly used, its purpose is abused and improper advantage is taken of the occasion. [Section 19 of the *Defamation Act 1992*] is concerned with situations in which qualifed privilege is lost. Occasions of privilege are both fact-dependent and not limited by closed categories. Where the common law affords privilege to a particular occasion, s. 19 must be applied to that occasion in an appropriate way, without any reading down of its terms.

¶43 If a false and defamatory statement which qualifies for protection is made, and is disseminated to a wide audience, the motives of the publisher and whether the publisher had a genuine belief in the truth of the statement, will warrant close scrutiny. If the publisher is unable or unwilling to disclose any responsible basis for asserting a genuine belief in truth, the jury may well be entitled to draw the inference that no such belief existed. In *Reynolds* Lord Steyn adverted to this risk at p 103. Furthermore, a publisher who is reckless or indifferent to the truth of what is published cannot assert a genuine belief that it was true.

¶47 What constitutes recklessness is something which must take its colour from the nature of the occasion, and the nature of the publication. If it is reckless not "to consider or care" whether a statement be true or false, as Lord Diplock indicated, it must be open to the view that a perfunctory level of consideration (against the substance, gravity and width of the publication) can also be reckless. It is within the concept of misusing the occasion to say that the defendant may be regarded as reckless if there has been a failure to give such responsible consideration to the truth or falsity of the statement as the jury considers should have been given in all the circumstances. In essence the privilege may be lost if the defendant takes what in all the circumstances can fairly be described as a cavalier approach to the truth of the statement.

¶48 No consideration and insufficient consideration are equally capable of leading to an inference of misuse of the occasion. The rationale for loss of the privilege in such circumstances is that the privilege is granted on the basis that it will be responsibly used. There is no public interest in allowing defamatory statements to be made irresponsibly — recklessly — under the banner of freedom of expression. What amounts to a reckless statement must depend significantly on what is said and to whom and by whom. It must be accepted that to require the defendant to give such responsible consideration to the truth or falsity of the publication as is required by the nature of the allegation and the width of the intended dissemination, may in some circumstances come close to a need for the taking of reasonable care. In others, a genuine belief in truth after relatively hasty and incomplete consideration may be sufficient to satisfy the dictates of the occasion and to avoid any inference of taking improper advantage of the occasion.

The New Zealand Court of Appeal clearly suggests [at paragraph 49] that a greater degree of responsibility is generally required where there is publication to the world at large. This appears to represent a change in substance from its previous decision in 1998, [1998] 3 N.Z.L.R. 424, where the court rejected the incorporation of a requirement of reasonableness into the defence of qualified privilege, stating:

> The basis of qualified privilege is that the recipient has a legitimate interest to receive information assumed to be false. How can that interest differ simply because the author has failed to take care to ensure that the information is true?

New Zealand decisions which have considered *Lange v. Atkinson* include:

Midland Metals Overseas Pte & Anor v. Christchurch Press Company & ORS, [2001] N.Z.C.A. 321, where Gault J. stated at para. 23:

> [23] ... Reference was made to the recent decision of this Court in *Lange v. Atkinson*, [2000] 3 N.Z.L.R. 385 in which the Court recognised that absence of reasonable or responsible conduct might be a legitimate consideration in considering misuse of an occasion of privilege.

Ross Harold Vickey v. *Thomas McLean & ORS*, [2000] N.Z.C.A. 338, where
Tipping J. for the Court rejected the application of *Lange* v. *Atkinson* privilege
to allegations of serious criminality, which "cannot sensibly be regarded as
political discussion" (para. 17).

E. IMPLICATIONS FOR THE DEVELOPMENT OF CANADIAN JURISPRUDENCE RELATING TO QUALIFIED PRIVILEGE

The Supreme Court of Canada last surveyed the status of privilege defences
elsewhere in the Commonwealth in *Hill* v. *Church of Scientology of Toronto*,
[1995] 2 S.C.R. 1130. In that case, however, the defendant was not asking
the Court to import Commonwealth law but rather to modernize Canadian
law to provide defences analogous to those which have been available under
the First Amendment to the United States *Constitution* since the 1964 decision of the U.S. Supreme Court in *New York Times* v. *Sullivan*, 376 U.S. 254
(1964). In *Sullivan*, it was held that the First Amendment prevents politicians or public servants from suing for libellous statements made about
their conduct or fitness for office unless they can prove that the defendant
published the libel with malice; that is, "with knowledge that it was false or
with reckless disregard of whether it was false or not."

Cory J., noting that the "actual malice" rule in *New York Times* v. *Sullivan*
had been rejected in both the United Kingdom and Australia, similarly
declined to import the rule into Canadian law, stating:

> ¶137 The law of defamation is essentially aimed at the prohibition of the pub-
> lication of injurious false statements. It is the means by which the individual
> may protect his or her reputation which may well be the most distinguishing
> feature of his or her character, personality and perhaps identity. I simply can-
> not see that the law of defamation is unduly restrictive or inhibiting. Surely
> it is not requiring too much of individuals that they ascertain the truth of the
> allegations they publish. The law of defamation provides for the defences of
> fair comment and qualified privilege in appropriate cases. Those who publish
> statements should assume a reasonable level of responsibility.

Cory J. expressly noted however (at paragraphs 139–40) that:

> ¶139 None of the factors which prompted the United States Supreme Court
> to rewrite the law of defamation in America are present in the case at bar.
> First, this appeal does not involve the media or political commentary about
> government policies ...

¶140 Second, a review of jury verdicts in Canada reveals there is no danger of numerous large awards threatening the viability of media organizations. Finally, in Canada there is no broad privilege accorded to the public statements of government officials which needs to be counterbalanced by a similar right for private individuals.

These observations may open the door to future submissions by news media defendants that the common law of privilege should be modernized to apply more readily to defamatory expression published to the world at large in newspapers, broadcasts, or other mass media.

Issues to be considered by the Canadian courts may include the following:

i)   Is it appropriate, in the context of Canada's social and political environment, to import into Canadian common law the new form of qualified privilege represented by:
      a. *Reynolds* privilege,
      b. Australia *Lange* v. *Australian Broadcasting Corp.* privilege, or
      c. New Zealand *Lange* v. *Atkinson* privilege?

ii)   Should Canadian courts import the new form of qualified privilege contemplated by the dissenting judgments in the House of Lords in *Reynolds*?

iii) Should Canadian courts reconsider the requirement of reciprocity as a condition of establishing that an occasion is one of privilege? See the decision of the New Zealand Court of Appeal in *Lange* v. *Atkinson* where it is observed that Lord Atkinson's dictum in *Adam* v. *Ward* was only one decision. Justice Dixon of the Australian High Court has also suggested that reciprocity may not be required.

iv)   Should there be a generic privilege for subject matter which may be characterized as:
      a. "in the public interest," and/or
      b. "political"?

v)   Should there be any special limits to a new form of qualified privilege for publication to the world at large in terms of:
      a. geography,
      b. content,
      c. timing?

vi)   If a new form of privilege for publication to the world at large is to be recognized, should it be the occasion that is privileged (as in classical qualified privilege) or the publication that is privileged?

vii) In determining whether the new form of privilege applies, is the test to be:
   a. objective, or
   b. subjective?

viii) Is there to be a presumption of honest belief on the part of the defendant with respect to a new form of qualified privilege for publication to the world at large (as there is in classic common law qualified privilege)?

ix) Is honest belief of the defendant to be determined by an objective standard or by a subjective standard? (Compare *Korach* v. *Moore* and *Horrocks* v. *Lowe*.)

x) If there is to be a new form of qualified privilege defence for publication to the world at large, should the defendant be required to prove as a condition of the defence:
   a. that it conformed to the standards of responsible journalism,
   b. that its conduct was reasonable in all the circumstances, or
   c. that it acted responsibly?

xi) Should the Canadian courts import the ten point nonexhaustive "circumstantial test" checklist employed by Lord Nicholls in *Reynolds*? What weight should be given to each item? Or should Canadian courts develop a different checklist to address the particular context of:
   a. the Canadian media,
   b. Canadian values, and/or
   c. Canadian civil litigation procedure (for example, more extensive discovery rights including oral examinations for discovery of parties under oath before trial; summary judgment procedure)?
   Should the checklist be more precise or more general?

xii) Should a new defence of qualified privilege for publication to the world at large be defeated by malice? If so, what evidence should the court take into account?

xiii) In respect of a defence for publication to the world at large, is it appropriate to characterize it as a defence of "privilege"? Would it be more appropriate to characterize it as a "responsible reporting" defence?

1) Canadian decisions which have referred to *Reynolds*

There have been a number of interlocutory decisions concerning the right of media defendants to plead a defence of qualified privilege based on *Reynolds* v. *Times Newspapers*. Relying on the principle that a pleading should not be struck out unless it is plain and obvious that it cannot succeed, a number of courts have rejected such applications by plaintiffs. However, these decisions do not contain a searching analysis of the decision in *Reynolds*, nor do they appear to reflect an understanding that *Reynolds* privilege is quite different from the classical qualified privilege defence.

Lee v. The Globe and Mail (2001), 52 O.R. (3d) 652 (S.C.J.)

Dhami v. Canadian Broadcasting Corporation, [2001] B.C.J. No. 2773, 2001 BCSC 1811.

Khan v. Metroland Printing, Publishing & Distributing Ltd., [2000] O.J. No. 638 (S.C.J.).

In *Goddard v. Day*, [2001] 5 W.W.R. 651 (Alta. Q.B.), the court heard argument on a point of law concerning the availability of the generic defence of qualified privilege in relation to a letter to the editor which had been published in a newspaper. The defendant sought to plead a new category of qualified privilege for political speech and asked the Court to distinguish *Reynolds*, which had rejected a newspaper's submission supporting such a "generic defence." The Court held that the "defence of qualified privilege relating to political discussion does not exist in Canada" and stated its intention not to provide any directions to the jury relative to such a defence.

A number of Canadian decisions refer to *Reynolds v. Times Newspapers*, in each case without extensive analysis, but reject a defence of qualified privilege in the circumstances before the court.

Leenen v. Canadian Broadcasting Corporation (2000), 48 O.R. (3d) 656 (S.C.J.), aff'd (2001), 54 O.R. (3d) 612 (C.A.), leave to appeal to S.C.C. denied, [2001] S.C.C.A. No. 432.

Myers v. Canadian Broadcasting Corporation, (1999) 47 C.C.L.T. (2d) 272 (Ont. S.C.J.), varied (2001), C.C.L.T. (3d) 112 (Ont. C.A.), leave to appeal to S.C.C. denied, [2001] S.C.C.A. No. 433.

Ramsey v. Pacific Press, a Division of Southam, Inc., [2000] B.C.J. No. 2422, 2000 BCSC 1551.

Grassi v. WIC Radio Ltd. (c.o.b. CKNW/98), [2000] 5 W.W.R. 119 (B.C.S.C.).

P.G. Restaurant Ltd. (c.o.b. Mama Panda Restaurant) v. Northern Interior Regional Health Board, [2004] B.C.J. No. 424, 2004 BCSC 294.

Hodgson v. Canadian Newspapers Co. (1998), 39 O.R. (3d) 235 (Gen. Div.), varied as to damages (2000), 189 D.L.R. (4th) 241 (Ont. C.A.), leave to appeal to S.C.C. denied, [2000] S.C.C.A. No. 465.

Fiola v. LeBrun, 2002 MBQB 312.

Young v. *Toronto Star Newpapers Ltd.* (2003), O.J. No. 3100 (S.C.J.) per
Rouleau J. at paras. 176–190 [*Reynolds* applied].

None of the decisions mentioned above explore in depth the desirability of
importing *Reynolds* privilege, *Lange* v. *Australian Broadcasting Corp.* privilege, or New Zealand *Lange* v. *Atkinson* privilege into the Canadian law of
qualified privilege.

In *Campbell* v. *Jones* (2001), 197 N.S.R. (2d) 212 (S.C.), the trial judge
rejected a defence of qualified privilege for defamatory statements made by
the defendant lawyers at a press conference, concluding that the Court was
bound by the decisions of the Supreme Court of Canada in *Jones* v. *Bennett*,
[1969] S.C.R. 277. Moir J. referred at length to *Reynolds* v. *Times Newspapers Ltd.*, and clearly recognized that it represented a significant modification to the pre-existing law, stating:

> ¶23 Although Lord Nicholls did not consider this approach to involve any
> change in the principles of common law, it certainly marks a loosening of the
> restrained approach the common law has taken in extending qualified privi-
> lege to publications to the world at large.
>
> Lord Cooke of Thorndon, who would have adopted the position of the
> Court of Appeal "[s]ubject to the refinement that the circumstantial test
> should not be treated as something apart form the duty-interest test" (para.
> 116), had this to say in the course of his judgment:
>
>> Hitherto the only publications to the world at large to which English
>> courts have been willing to extend qualified privilege at common law
>> have been fair and accurate reports of certain proceedings or findings
>> of legitimate interest to the general public. In *Blackshaw* v. *Lord* [1984]
>> Q.B. 1, *Templeton* v. *Jones* [1984] 1 N.Z.L.R. 448, and now the present
>> case, the law is being developed to meet the reasonable demands of
>> freedom of speech in a modern democracy, by recognising that there
>> may be a wider privilege dependent on the particular circumstances.
>
> Lord Cooke mentions the qualified privilege protecting reports of judicial
> proceedings as exceptional to a reluctance to apply qualified privilege to pub-
> lications to the world at large. …

The trial judge in *Campbell* v. *Jones* conducted an extensive review of
Canadian jurisprudence since *Jones* v. *Bennett*, above, and then stated his
conclusion that it is still good law:

> ¶28 I am not suggesting that *Hill* v. *Church of Scientology* decides the present
> issue. Nor am I suggesting it necessarily conflicts with *Reynolds* v. *Times News-*

papers. After all, the speech of Lord Nicholls began with "My Lords, this appeal concerns the interaction between two fundamental rights: freedom of expression and protection of reputation," and he discussed expression and reputation in terms similar to those of Cory J. at para. 37 to 39. In principle, Lord Nicholls' conclusion is the same as that of Cory J.: "... the established common law approach to misstatements of fact remains essentially sound" (para. 53). Further, as Lord Nicholls observes, *Hill* v. *Church of Scientology* "did not concern political discussion" and "The Supreme Court has not had occasion to consider this issue in relation to political discussion." (para. 30). However, I read *Reynolds* as setting a new approach to publications for the world at large, an approach markedly different from that of *Jones* v. *Bennett*. I am bound by *Jones* v. *Bennett*. The Court of Appeal in this province has not, to my knowledge, protected such a broad publication as we see here by bringing anything like it within the shield of qualified privilege. Thus, I do not have the liberty to say, with the British Columbia Supreme Court, that the 'too broad' argument no longer has application. Further, the integral importance of an individual's reputation as explained in *Hill* v. *Church of Scientology* suggests to me continued restraint where privilege is claimed over a defamatory statement made to the world at large.

On the defendant's appeal to the Court of Appeal, 2002 NSCA 128, leave to appeal to S.C.C denied, [2002] S.C.C.A No. 543, the majority held the publication occurred on an occasion of qualified privilege (see Chapter 18, "Qualified and Statutory Privilege," page 398). Although the majority decision mentioned *Reynolds* v. *Times Newspapers Ltd.*, it devotes little space to a discussion of that decision. It does not appear from the decision that *Reynolds* privilege was actually applied.

In his dissent in *Campbell* v. *Jones*, Saunders J.A. held at paragraphs 100 and 128 that the trial judge did not err in declining to apply *Reynolds* and that the Court "need not endorse *Reynolds* as having any application to this case." Saunders J.A. distinguished *Reynolds* on its facts:

¶101 Before doing that, let me say concerning the Reynolds case, that I do not think it insignificant that the judgment concerned press publications about politicians; whereas, both Hill and this case concern the publication of statements by members of the bar about public officials who were not politicians. Thus, the circumstances involving Messrs. Morris Manning, Casey Hill and the Church of Scientology offer the closest parallel to Mr. Jones' and Ms. Derrick's defamation of Cst. Campbell.

There are also a number of Canadian decisions that simply refer to *Reynolds* v. *Times Newspapers* but do not consider the novelty of its conclusions concerning qualified privilege in any context.

Ross v. *New Brunswick Teachers' Assn.* (1998) 199 N.B.R. (2d) 245, rev'd (2001), 201 D.L.R. (4th) 75 (N.B.C.A.).

Johnston v. *Saint John Regional Hospital*, [2001] N.B.R. (2d) (Supp.) No. 71 (Q.B.).

Ward v. *Clark*, 2000 BCSC 979 (2000) 77 B.C.L.R. (3d) 364, rev'd 2001 BCCA 724, (2001), 95 B.C.L.R. (3d) 209, leave to appeal to S.C.C. denied, [2002] S.C.C.A. No. 73.

In *Goddard* v. *Day* (2000), 194 D.L.R. (4th) 559 (Alta. Q.B.), the court rejected a defence submission, which hinged on the meaning of "political information" discussed in *Reynolds* v. *Times Newspapers*, seeking an incremental deveopment of the common law "by creation of a new category of occasion when privilege derives from the subject matter alone: Political information." According to the defendant, political infomation would be "information, opinion and arguments concerning government and policical matters that affect citizens." Ritter J. (at paragraph 42), noted that *Reynolds* held that "the common law should not develop political information as a generic category of information whose publication attracted qualified privilege … ."

CHAPTER TWENTY

Absolute Privilege

A. OVERVIEW

The common law defence of absolute privilege provides complete immunity for defamatory expression even if it was published with actual malice.

This defence applies to expression that was made:

i)   in the course of a judicial proceeding;
ii) in the course of a quasi-judicial proceeding;
iii) in communications between officers of state about affairs of state; or
iv) in the course of parliamentary proceedings.

The onus is on the defendant to prove the circumstances giving rise to this defence. Whether the defence exists on particular facts is a question of law for the judge.

> *Ayangma* v. *NAV Canada* (2001), 203 D.L.R. (4th) 717 per McQuaid J.A. at 725 (P.E.I.S.C. (A.D.)), leave to appeal to S.C.C. denied, [2001] S.C.C.A. No. 76.

B. IN THE COURSE OF A JUDICIAL PROCEEDING

There is usually little difficulty in applying the defence of absolute privilege to proceedings of the civil or criminal courts of justice.

The determination whether a tribunal is a court of law is discussed in *A-G* v. *BBC*, [1981] A.C. 303 where Lord Scarman states at pages 359–60:

> I would identify a court in (or "of") law, i.e. a court of judicature, as a body established by law to exercise, either generally or subject to defined limits, the judicial power of the state. In this context judicial power is to be contrasted with legislative and executive (i.e. administrative) power. If the body under review is established for a purely legislative or administrative purpose,

it is part of the legislative or administrative system of the state, even though it has to perform duties which are judicial in character. Though the ubiquitous presence of the state makes itself felt in all sorts of situations never envisaged when our law was in its formative stage, the judicial power of the state exercised through judges appointed by the state remains an independent, and recognizably separate, function of government. Unless a body exercising judicial functions can be demonstrated to be part of this judicial system it is not, in my view, a court of law. I would add that the judicial system is not limited to the courts of the civil power. Courts-martial and consistory courts, (the latter since 1540) are as truly entrusted with the exercise of the judicial power of the state as are civil courts: *R. v. Daily Mail, ex p. Farnsworth* and *R. v. Daily Herald, ex p. Bishop of Norwich.*

No action for defamation lies against judges, counsel, parties, jury members, or witnesses for words spoken or written in the course of a judicial proceeding before a court recognized by law.

Munster v. Lamb (1883), 11 Q.B.D. 588, per Brett M.R. at 601, Fry L.J. concurring at 607–8 (C.A.).

Royal Aquarium and Summer & Winter Garden Society Ltd. v. Parkinson, [1892] 1 Q.B. 431, per Lopes L.J. at 451 (H.L.).

Geyer v. Merritt (1979), 16 B.C.L.R. 27, per Legg J. at 32 (S.C.), aff'd (1980), 26 B.C.L.R. 374 (C.A.).

Fabian v. Margulies (1985), 53 O.R. (2d) 380, per Labrosse J. at 381–83 (S.C.).

Lincoln v. Daniels, [1961] 3 All E.R. 740 at 384 (C.A.).

Halls v. Mitchell, [1928] 2 D.L.R. 97, S.C.R. 125 per Duff J. at 113–14.

Schwartz v. Smith (1964), 45 D.L.R. (2d) 316 (B.C.S.C.) per Verchere J. at 318

Stevens v. Oakes (1995), 104 Man. R. (2d) 229, per Master Bolton at paras. 5–6 (Q.B.), citing *Dawkins v. Lord Rokeby* (1875), L.R. 7 H.L. 744 (H.L. (Eng.)).

Mann v. O'Neill (1997), 191 C.L.R. 204, per Brennan C.J., Toohey and Gaudron JJ. at 211 (H.C.), citing [with respect to jury members] *Bushell's Case* (1670), 1 Freeman 1, 89 E.R. 2.

If the defamatory expression was uttered in the course of a judicial proceeding, it is irrelevant whether the defamatory expression was written or spoken maliciously, or without any justification or excuse, or from personal ill-will and anger against the person defamed.

Royal Aquarium and Summer and Winter Garden Society Ltd. v. *Parkinson,* above, at 451

Foran v. *Richman* (1975), 64 D.L.R. (3d) 230, per Arnup J.A. at 233 (Ont. C.A.), leave to appeal to S.C.C. dismissed (1976), 64 D.L.R. (3d) 230n (S.C.C.).

Dugas v. *Landry* (1997), 188 N.B.R. (2d) 21, per Savoie J. at para. 21 (Q.B. (T.D.)).

1) Rationale and Extent of Defence

The rationale for applying the protection of absolute privilege defence to judicial proceedings has been discussed by many judges, including:

i)   in *Royal Aquarium and Summer and Winter Garden Society Ltd.* v. *Parkinson,* above, at 451:

This "absolute privilege" has been conceded on the grounds of public pol-icy to ensure freedom of speech where it is essential that freedom of speech should exist, and with the knowledge that Courts of justice are presided over by those who from their high character are not likely to abuse the privilege, and who have the power and ought to have the will to check any abuse of it by those who appear before them.

ii)   in *Munster* v. *Lamb* (1883), 11 Q.B.D. 588, by Fry L.J. at 507 (C.A.):

Why should a witness be able to avail himself of his position in the box and make without fear of civil consequences a false statement, which in many cases is perjured, and which is malicious and affects the character of another? The rule exists, not because the conduct of those persons ought not of itself to be actionable, but because if their conduct was actionable, actions would be brought against judges and witnesses in cases in which they had not spoken with malice, in which they had not spoken with falsehood. ... It must always be borne in mind that it is not intend-ed to protect malicious and untruthful persons, but that it is intended to protect persons acting bona fide, who under a different rule would be liable, not perhaps to verdicts and judgments against them, but to the vex-ation of defending actions.

iii)   in *Cinapri* v. *Guettler* (1997), 33 B.L.R. (2d) 289, by Howden J. at 296, para. 16 (Ont. Gen. Div.):

If this were not so [i.e. absolute privilege did not apply], legal action would be grafted on legal action in an endless siege of litigation whereby each step in an action could be seen by someone as an attack or intrusion upon his or her reputation or economic interests.

iv)   in *Marrinan v. Vibert*, [1963] 1 Q.B. 234 by Salmon J. at 237:

> This immunity exists for the benefit of the public, since the administration
> of justice would be greatly impeded if witnesses were to be in fear that any
> disgruntled and possibly impecunious persons against whom they gave
> evidence might subsequently involve them in costly litigation.

v)   in *Crossan v. Mortgage and Appraisals Ltd.* (1998), 164 Nfld. & P.E.I.R.
319 (Nfld. S.C. (T.D.)) by Dunn J. at para. 33:

> ... the primary rationale for the retention of the witness immunity rule
> and its logical extension to reports, is to protect the integrity of the judi-
> cial process thus enabling expert or other witnesses to appear without fear
> of attracting liability.

The statement must be made "in the course of" the litigation, which
demands an inquiry into the particular facts surrounding the allegedly
defamatory statements.

> *Dechant v. Stevens*, [2001] 5 W.W.R. 405, per Conrad J.A. at 424, paras.
> 49–50 (Alta. C.A.); [application for leave to appeal to S.C.C. discontinued,
> [2001] S.C.C.A. No. 180]:
>
> > ¶49 ... The statement must be made within a step recognized as afford-
> > ing the privilege. ... [i]n judicial proceedings, the steps are more obvi-
> > ous than may be the case in many quasi-judicial settings.

There is ample case law concerning the application of absolute privilege to
both civil and criminal court proceedings.

In the context of court litigation between private parties, it has been held
that absolute privilege clearly applies to defamatory expression communicated or tendered in open court or contained in documents placed on the
court file. In this context, there is jurisprudence applying the privilege to
the following:

i)   the originating process and other pleadings:

> *Dooley v. C.N. Weber Ltd.* (1994), 19 O.R. (3d) 779, per Reilly J. at 788
> (Gen. Div.) [alleged libels contained in a statement of defence and related
> particulars], applying, *inter alia, Hall v. Baxter* (1922), 22 O.W.N. 207 per
> Orde J. at 208–9 (H.C.J.) [alleged libel contained in a writ and statement
> of claim] and *Razzell v. Edmonton Mint Ltd.* [1981] 4 W.W.R. 5, per Dea J.
> at 10 (Alta. Q.B.) [alleged libels contained in a statement of claim].
>
> *B.K. v. V.K. Thapar Professional Corp.*, [1999] A.J. No. 28, 1999 ABQB 33,
> per Burrows J. at para. 22.

Perry v. Heywood (1997), 154 Nfld. & P.E.I.R. 91, per Osborne J. at para. 80 (Nfld. S.C.(T.D.)), aff'd without discussion of this point (1998), 175 Nfld. & P.E.I.R. 253 (Nfld. C.A.).

Industrial Ecology Inc. v. Kayar Energy Systems Inc., [1997] O.J. No. 204 per Cameron J. at para. 11 (Gen. Div.).

Bottomly v. Brougham, [1908] 1 KB 584 at 588.

Lilley v. Roney (1892), 61 Law J. Rep QB 727 at 727–28.

Big Pond Communications 2000 Inc. v. Kennedy, [2004] O.J. No. 820 at para. 20 (S.C.J.).

ii)   affidavits:

Web Offset Publications Ltd. v. Vickery (1998), 40 O.R. (3d) 526 per Kruzick J. at 535 (Gen. Div.), appeal dismissed (1999), 43 O.R. (3d) 802 (C.A.), leave to appeal to S.C.C. dismissed (1999), 43 O.R. (3d) 802n (S.C.C.).

Kyser v. Bank of Montreal (1998), 72 O.T.C. 180, per Somers J. at paras. 6–8 (Gen. Div.), applying *Hall v. Baxter*, above, at 208–9, referring with approval to William Blake Odgers, *Odgers on Libel and Slander*, 5th ed. (London: Stevens, 1912) at 233; varied on other grounds (1999), 123 O.A.C. 119 (C.A.).

Samuel Manu-Tech Inc. v. Redipac Recycling Corp. (1998), 66 O.T.C. 16 (Gen. Div.), aff'd (1999), 38 C.P.C. (4th) 297 (Ont. C.A.) per Feldman J.A. for the Court of Appeal at 302, para. 19.

Martini v. Wrathall (1999), 179 D.L.R. (4th) 74 per Roscoe J.A. at 75–76 (N.S.C.A.).

iii) notices of motion and other records filed in relation to interlocutory applications:

Cinapri v. Guettler (1997), 33 B.L.R. (2d) 289 per Howden J. at 295–96 (Ont. Gen. Div.).

iv)   factums:

Fratesi v. Sims (1996), 7 O.T.C. 263 per Gravely J. at paras. 2–8 (Gen. Div.), applying *Dingwall v. Lax* (1988), 63 O.R. (2d) 336 (H.C.J.), *GWE Consulting Group Ltd. v. Schwarz* (1990), 72 O.R. (2d) 133 (H.C.J.).

v)   statements in court by counsel for a party:

Munster v. Lamb (1883), 11 Q.B.D. 588, per Brett M.R. at 603–4 (C.A.).

Edwards v. Kitely, [1987] O.J. No. 1190 (H.C.J.) per Montgomery J.

Boerner v. *Bruhaug* (1992), 17 B.C.A.C. 206, per McEachern C.J.B.C. at para. 6 (C.A.).

Piercey v. *Newfoundland (Attorney General)* (1999), 30 C.P.C. (4th) 324, per Wells J. at 330, para. 21 (Nfld. S.C.(T.D.)).

Hawkes v. *Mitchell*, [2003] P.E.I.J. No. 46, 2003 PESCAD 11, per Mitchell C.J.P.E.I. at para. 4.

vi) testimony of a witness in the witness-box at trial:

Watson v. *McEwan*, [1905] A.C. 480 per Earl of Halsbury L.C. at 486 (H.L.):

> By complete authority, including the authority of this House, it has been decided that the privilege of a witness, the immunity from responsibility when evidence has been given by him in a Court of justice, is too well established now to be shaken.

Kansa General Insurance Co. (Canadian Branch) v. *Morden & Helwig Ltd.* (2001), 208 D.L.R. (4th) 339, per Sutherland J. at 369, para. 57 (Ont. S.C.J.).

Mackenzie v. *Chilliwack (District)*, [1997] B.C.J. No. 2289 per Coultas J. at para. 18 (S.C.).

Presley v. *Canada (Royal Canadian Mounted Police)*, [1999] Y.J. No. 20 per Maddison J. at para. 10 (Y.S.C.).

Mayer v. *Mayer*, [1995] 2 W.W.R. 97 per Hutchinson J. at 101–2, paras. 13–17 (B.C.S.C.), applying, *inter alia*, *Cabassi* v. *Vila* (1940), 64 C.L.R. 130 (H.C.A.).

See however *Seaman* v. *Netherclift* (1876), 2 C.P.D. 53, where Cockburn C.J. stated at 56–57 (C.A.):

> ... I am very far from desiring to be considered as laying down as law that what a witness states altogether out of the character and sphere of a witness, or what he may say dehors the matter in hand, is necessarily protected. I quite agree that what he says before he enters or after he has left the witness-box is not privileged ... Or if a man when in the witness-box were to take advantage of his position to utter something having no reference to the cause or matter of inquiry in order to assail the character of another ... .

Electra Sign Ltd. v. *Gallagher*, (1995) 38 C.P.C. (3d) 141 (Man. Q.B.) [Master Ring held at para. 10 that the "turn of the century exception to absolute privilege when the words are not pertinent to the issues before the court is no longer an exception" and that absolute privilege protected the defendants' evidence with respect to a death threat against them by both of the plaintiffs].

M.S. v. K.S., [1995] M.J. No. 203 (Q.B.) per Master Goldberg [allegations of sexual assault made during a custody trial].

vii) an expert report prepared by a witness who testifies orally at the trial:

Fabian v. Margulies (1985), 53 O.R. (2d) 380 per Labrosse J. at 381–83 (S.C.).

viii) testimony of a witness at an assessment of costs following a trial:

Turner v. Cutler, [1997] B.C.J. No. 1014 (S.C.) per Collver J.

ix) documents placed in evidence at a hearing:

Lincoln v. Daniels, [1962] 1 Q.B. 237, per Devlin L.J. at 257 (C.A.).

x) an expert report prepared at the direction of the court :

Crossan v. Mortgage and Appraisals Ltd. (1998), 164 Nfld. & P.E.I.R. 319 per Dunn J. at para. 33 (Nfld. S.C.(T.D.)).

xi) anything said by a judge in her judgment:

Charman v. Canadian Newspapers Co., [1991] 6 W.W.R. 710, per Master Halbert at 714, para. 9 (B.C.S.C.), citing Philip Lewis, *Gatley on Libel and Slander*, 8th ed. (London: Sweet & Maxwell Ltd., 1981) at 385, para. 388.

Absolute privilege also protects communications made out of court which relate to a step taken in existing court litigation. In this context, it has been held that absolute privilege applies to:

i) out of court statements made by a witness to a party, to a party's legal counsel, or to a private investigator:

Lincoln v. Daniels, [1961] 3 All E.R. 740 (C.A.).

Watson v. McEwan, [1905] A.C. 480 per Lord Halsbury L.C. at 486 (H.L.).

Larche v. Middleton (1989), 69 O.R. (2d) 400, per Granger J. at 407g, h (H.C.J.):

> The immunity in the doctrine of absolute immunity must extend to all steps taken in contemplation of litigation including statements made by a potential witness even if he or she is never called upon to testify … It matters not whether a potential witness is interviewed by a lawyer or by an investigator hired to gather evidence in the course of judicial proceedings. [The party] could have repre-

sented themselves in the proceedings and it would be ludicrous to assert that the privilege did not extend to witnesses being interviewed by members of [the party] rather than a solicitor.

Web Offset Publications Ltd. v. *Vickery* (1998), 40 O.R. (3d) 526, per Kruzick J. at 535 (Gen. Div.), appeal dismissed (1999), 43 O.R. (3d) 802 (C.A.), leave to appeal to S.C.C. dismissed (1999), 43 O.R. (3d) 802n (S.C.C.):

> ... where a lawyer seeks out information from another person and that other person provides the information, then whether called as a witness or not, the information is absolutely privileged. See *Gatley on Libel and Slander*, 9th ed., pp. 289–90.

Horn Abbot Ltd. v. *Reeves* (2000), 189 D.L.R. (4th) 644, per Roscoe J.A. at 658 (N.S.C.A.).

ii) testimony by a witness on her pretrial examination for discovery:

Razzell v. *Edmonton Mint Ltd.*, [1981] 4 W.W.R. 5, per Dea J. at 10 (Alta. Q.B.).

Horn Abbot Ltd. v. *Reeves*, (2000) 189 D.L.R. (4th) 644, per Roscoe J.A. at 658 (N.S.C.A.).

iii) an expert report prepared at the request of counsel for a party:

Fabian v. *Margulies*, above, at 383.

Carnahan v. *Coates* (1990), 71 D.L.R. (4th) 464, per Huddart J. (as she then was) at 478e (B.C.S.C.):

> ... the protection of the integrity of the judicial process requires at least that an expert witness be immune from suit by any person with whom his only relationship derives from the judicial proceeding.

M.-A.(N.) *(Guardian ad litem of)* v. *M.-A* (I.A.S.) (1992), 93 D.L.R. (4th) 659, per Carrothers J.A. at 666, g (B.C.C.A.).

iv) a personal and confidential letter written by plaintiff's counsel in a fraudulent conveyance action to a list of suspected creditors of the defendant informing them of the status of the fraudulent conveyance action, the bankruptcy of the defendant, and requesting an exchange of information:

Fuss v. *Fidelity Electronics of Canada Ltd.*, [1996] O.J. No. 161, per MacKinnon J. at paras. 6–7 (Gen. Div.), reversed on the basis that it was not plain and obvious that the circumstances justified the application of absolute privilege without cross-examination, [1998] O.J. No. 2339, per endorsement at paras. 5–8 (C.A.).

v) a letter by a lawyer acting for a plaintiff in a lawsuit against an ex-employee and his new employer, sent to a supplier of the new employer, alleging use of information improperly taken by the ex-employee. (The supplier would likely be a required witness at the trial of that lawsuit against the ex-employee and his new employer.):

> *Construction Distribution Supply Co.* v. *Pearson*, [2001] O.J. No. 1848 (SCJ) per Somers J.

vi) statements contained in a certificate of pending litigation filed against the property stipulated in that certificate:

> *Geo. Cluthe Manufacturing Co.* v. *ZTW Properties Inc.* (1995), 23 O.R. (3d) 370, per Southey J. at 378, a–b (Div. Ct.), applying *Tersigni* v. *Fagan*, [1959] O.W.N. 94 (C.A.) and *Pete & Martys (Front) Ltd.* v. *Market Block Toronto Properties Ltd.* (1985), 5 C.P.C. (2d) 97 (Ont. H.C.J.).

2) Steps Prior to and Following Judicial Proceedings

It has been held that absolute privilege may apply to preparatory steps taken with a view to judicial proceedings but that the expression must be directly connected with such contemplated proceedings.

> *Dingwall* v. *Lax* (1988), 63 O.R. (2d) 336, per Potts J. at 339 (H.C.J.), approving John G. Fleming, *The Law of Torts*, 5th ed. (Sydney: Law Book Co., 1977), at 551–52.

In the context of steps preparatory to judicial proceedings, it has been held that absolute privilege applies to:

i) a letter written by a physician to the plaintiff's lawyer who sought information in preparation for a motor vehicle accident case:

> *Foran* v. *Richman* (1975) 64 D.L.R. (3d) 230, per Arnup J.A. at 233 (Ont. C.A.), leave to appeal to S.C.C. dismissed (1976), 64 D.L.R. (3d) 230n (S.C.C.).

ii) reports prepared by an expert witness in contemplation of using them for future hearings in Unified Family Court (but not the publication of such reports outside the boundaries of the court proceedings):

> *R.G.* v. *Christison*, [1997] 1 W.W.R. 641, per Wedge J. at 661, para. 66 (Sask Q.B.):
>
> > … necessary to do so in order to protect those who are to participate in the proceedings from a flank attack.

iii)   a courtesy letter and a draft statement of claim sent to solicitors personally involved in the action:

> *Fabian* v. *Margulies* (1985), 53 O.R. (2d) 380, per Labrosse J. at 381–83 (S.C.).

iv)   a letter written by a lawyer to nonparties seeking information and documents which, acting bona fide, he would have had good reason to believe were probably relevant to his own client's claims against the person allegedly defamed:

> *GWE Consulting Group Ltd.* v. *Schwartz* (1990), 72 O.R. (2d) 133, per Austin J. at 141–42 (H.C.J.), referring to *Hoover* v. *VanStone*, 540 F.Supp. 1118 (U.S. Dist. Ct. 1982).

v)   a letter written by a lawyer to a bank advising it that a transfer of funds by the defendant may have been fraudulent

> *Lubarevich* v. *Nurgitz* (1996), 1 O.T.C. 360, per G.D. Lane J. at paras. 22–24 (Gen. Div.).

It has also been held that steps taken subsequent to a judicial verdict may attract the protection of absolute privilege in certain circumstances. In this context, it has been held that absolute privilege protects correspondence from the plaintiff's legal counsel to the defendant's legal counsel concerning enforcement of the judgment.

> *Simons* v. *Carr & Co.*, [1996] 10 W.W.R. 64, per Nash J. at 72, para. 37 (Alta. Q.B.).

3) Where Absolute Privilege Does Not Apply

It has been held by one Canadian court, however, that statements made by a witness to a private investigator who was interviewing him as a potential witness in litigation already in progress between other parties did not enjoy the protection of absolute privilege because the statement was based on hearsay. This decision warrants further consideration in an appropriate case as it would appear to place an unwelcome restriction on the character of information which may be solicited from a prospective witness.

> *Larche* v. *Middleton* (1989), 69 O.R. (2d) 400, per Granger J. at 409, g–h (H.C.J.):
>
> > The doctrine should only protect statements which could be made in court, and which would be subject to cross-examination.

See also *Teskey v. Toronto Transit Commission*, [2003] O.J. No. 5314, per J. Wilson J. at para. 8 (S.C.J.) [absolute privilege does not apply to investigations by an employer into employee conduct that may later result in criminal proceedings].

Further, the mere fact that words are spoken in a courtroom or within the court precincts does not necessarily attract immunity. What a witness says before he enters or after he has entered the witness box is not protected by absolute privilege, although spoken in the room where the court is sitting.

Trotman v. Dunn (1815), 4 Camp. 211, 171 E.R. 67, per Lord Ellenborough.

It has been held that it is not plain and obvious that allegedly defamatory statements made off the record by a lawyer after adjournment of an examination for discovery enjoy the protection of absolute privilege. This point remains to be determined in a future case.

Gutstadt v. Reininger (1995), 27 O.R. (3d) 152, per McCombs J. at 156 (Gen. Div.):

> In the case at bar, the alleged defamatory statements were made following an adjournment of an examination for discovery, and were made off the record, not in the actual course of the examination. ... As the law of absolute privilege currently stands in Canada, I am unable to find that it is "plain and obvious" that remarks made after an adjournment of an examination are privileged.

It has been held that absolute privilege did not apply to a letter written by a solicitor to the Court Registrar objecting to the correctness of a Master's order where it was not in fact necessary to the action for the solicitor to send the subject letter or to make therein his libelous statement and innuendo, particularly where the letter did not ask for any remedy at law and did not ask for any court hearing, and the solicitor stated he was no longer on record for the party he previously represented.

Fabian & Kaye v. Iseman (1997), 50 O.T.C. 232, per Day J. at para. 5 (Gen. Div.), approving *R. v. Dyson*, [1972] 1 O.R. 744 where Haines J. stated at 752 (H.C.J.):

> [Absolute] privilege is, however, limited to statements which are necessary to the judicial proceeding as can be seen in the statement of Devlin L.J. in *Lincoln v. Daniels*, [1962] 1 Q.B. 237 at p. 263 (C.A.):
>
> > I have come to the conclusion that the privilege that covers proceedings in a court of justice ought not to be extended to matters outside those proceedings except where it is strictly necessary to

do so in order to protect those who are to participate in the proceedings from a flank attack.

Communications by or on behalf of potential plaintiffs have been excluded from the protection of absolute privilege where a solicitor wrote a letter to customers of the defendant alleging that the defendant had misappropriated certain files.

> *Dashtgard v. Blair* (1990), 4 C.C.L.T. (2d) 284, per McDonald J. at 285, 289–90 (Alta. Q.B.).

It seems that no Canadian court to date has definitively held that absolute privilege protects an irrelevant statement made against a non-party.

> *M.J.M. v. D.J.M.* (2000), 187 D.L.R. (4th) 473, per Jackson J.A. at 482, paras. 17–18 (Sask. C.A.).

The Saskatchewan Court of Appeal recently held that a statement ostensibly made in judicial or quasi-judicial proceedings that gratuitously defames a non-party and has no conceivable relevance or connection to the judicial or quasi-judicial proceedings at issue is not privileged.

> *Duke v. Puts*, [2004] S.J. No. 60, 2004 SKCA 12. Vancise J.A., speaking for the Court of Appeal, cited *Salmond and Heuston on the Law of Torts*, 18th ed. (London: Sweet & Maxwell 1981), *More v. Weaver*, [1928] 2 K.B. 520 at 525, and stated at para. 57:
>
> > … [T]here is authority for the proposition that although comments made in the context of judicial or quasi-judicial proceedings need not be relevant in the sense that they contribute to the resolution of the matter they must have some nexus or be connected to the proceedings.

4) Absolute Privilege in Criminal Proceedings

There is a considerable body of jurisprudence about the application of absolute privilege in the context of criminal court proceedings. As in the case of civil court proceedings, communications taking place during, incidental to, and in the processing of criminal judicial proceedings are subject to absolute privilege, sometimes referred to as immunity.

> *Kravit v. Dilli* (1998) 56 B.C.L.R. (3d) 150, per Baker J. at 155, para. 23 (S.C.).

Absolute privilege clearly applies to defamatory expression communicated or tendered in open court in criminal proceedings or contained in documents placed on the court file.

Mullins v. *Beneteau*, [1996] O.J. No. 2784, per Quinn J. at para. 24 (Gen. Div.) [testimony at a preliminary inquiry and at the subsequent criminal trial in relation to a charge of bribery held to be privileged].

Barber v. *Baird* (1993), 20 C.P.C. (3d) 15, per Master Quinn at 17, para. 14 (Alta. Q.B.) [duty counsel's statements about an accused in criminal court proceedings in relation to her background and present circumstances held to be privileged].

Kopyto v. *Ontario (Court of Justice (Provincial Division))*, [1995] O.J. No. 601, per Thomson J. at paras. 28–31(Gen. Div.) [suit against a judge, the Crown, and Legal Aid over statements made during an adjournment hearing in a criminal proceeding ordered dismissed on the grounds, inter alia, of absolute privilege].

Kravit v. *Dilli*, above, at 155, para. 23 [report prepared by psychiatrist for Crown Counsel].

Absolute privilege may also protect communications by an investigator to a third party which are relevant to the process of investigating the criminal charge.

Taylor v. *Director of the Serious Fraud Office*, [1998] 4 All E.R. 801, per Hoffman L.J. at 814, a (H.L.):

> At the time of the investigation it is often unclear whether any crime has been committed at all. Persons assisting the police with their inquiries may not be able to give any admissible evidence; for example, their information may be hearsay, but none the less valuable for the purposes of the investigation. But the proper administration of justice requires that such people should have the same inducement to speak freely as those whose information subsequently forms the basis of evidence at trial.

But see also *Darker* v. *Chief Constable of West Midlands Police* (2000), [2001] 1 A.C. 435 (H.L.), applied in *Teskey* v. *Toronto Transit Commission*, [2003] O.J. No. 5314, per J. Wilson J. at para. 9 (S.C.J.).

Communications by police to their superiors or to Crown counsel may be protected by absolute privilege.

Marrinan v. *Vibert*, [1962] 3 All E.R. 380 (C.A.).

Canadian decisions recognizing an absolute privilege for communications to police by the alleged victim include:

i)   *Kazas v. Peterson*, [1992] O.J. No. 1666 (Gen. Div.) where Adams J.
      held absolute privilege applied to a report by the female defendant
      Peterson to police that the plaintiff had assaulted her and subsequent-
      ly threatened her and her family if she testified in criminal proceed-
      ings arising from the reported assault. The report of the alleged assault
      (the plaintiff was later acquitted of the charge and charges of obstruc-
      tion of justice were withdrawn) was initially made orally in a call by
      Peterson to two police constables and was supplemented by her sub-
      sequent written statement to police.

ii)   *Canada v. Lukasik* (1985), 37 A.R. (2d) 170 (Q.B.), where a wholly
      false accusation of rape was made by the defendant against the plain-
      tiff in a written statement given to the police. Purvis J. held that
      absolute privilege protected the written statement given to the police.

iii) In *Lowenberg v. Oderbien* (2000), 146 Man. R. (2d) 120 (Q.B.), it was
      held that absolute privilege applied to certain statements made by the
      defendant to the Royal Canadian Mounted Police, which resulted in
      charges of uttering threats and mischief being laid against the plain-
      tiff. The court held that this communication "took place during and
      incidental to the investigation and processing of the criminal judicial
      proceedings."

Other Canadian courts have declined to recognize an absolute privilege
for statements volunteered to police officers about alleged criminal offences.
In *Mullins v. Beneteau*, [1996] O.J. No. 2754 (Gen. Div.), Quinn J. held that
absolute privilege did not apply to statements made by the defendant to
Ontario Provincial Police about a bribery incident. The statements resulted
in criminal charges against the plaintiff, who was eventually acquitted.
Quinn J., after considering the discussion of qualified privilege in Sir Robert
McEwen & Philip Lewis, *Gatley on Libel and Slander*, 7th ed. (London:
Sweet & Maxwell, 1974) and several U.S. cases, held that a statement to a
police officer is subject to a qualified and not an absolute privilege. Quinn
J. does not mention *Kazas v. Peterson*, above.

In *Rajkhowa v. Watson*, (1998) 23 C.P.C. (4th) 292 (N.S.S.C.), Hood J.
examined the authorities relating to absolute privilege and declined to follow *Kazas v. Peterson*, above, stating at page 298 that the

> … cases recognize that absolute privilege must be rare and apply only in
> exceptional cases, because it protects even where there is malice.

In his analysis, Hood J. [at page 299] rejected the defendant's submission
that absolute privilege should apply:

... back at the point where the information is given to the police for them to investigate.... A judicial or quasi-judicial proceeding does not commence each time the police commence an investigation. If the question is asked: Do the police exercise quasi-judicial or administrative functions? To ask the question is to answer it. The police investigate, they do not adjudicate.

Although there appears to be no recent Canadian appellate authority on the application of absolute privilege to criminal investigations, the subject was recently canvassed by the House of Lords in *Taylor* v. *Director of the Serious Fraud Office*, [1998] 4 All E.R. 801 (H.L.), where Lords Goff, Hoffman, Hope, and Hutton held that absolute immunity extended to a statement of conduct which could fairly be said to be part of the process of investigating a crime or a possible crime with a view to a prosecution or a possible prosecution in respect of the matter being investigated. In the case before the House of Lords, this absolute privilege was held to apply to:

i) A letter sent by a lawyer employed by the defendant Serious Fraud Office to the Attorney General of the Isle of Man, formally asking for his assistance in the investigation of a fraud by summoning a local solicitor Taylor for an interview about certain transactions. That letter suggested the Serious Fraud Office suspected Taylor of having been a party to the fraud.

ii) A file note prepared by the lawyer employed by the Serious Fraud Office of an interview with someone who worked for the Law Society in the administration of the solicitors' compensation fund, which was subject to a claim by the victim of the fraud, recording defamatory statements about Mr. Taylor.

Lord Hoffman discussed the novelty of the claim for absolute privilege which was considered by the House of Lords, and its resolution, at pages 813–14:

> There is no doubt that the claim for absolute immunity in respect of statements made by one investigator to another (as in the case of the letter from the SFO to the Attorney General of the Isle of Man), or by an investigator to a person helping with the inquiry (as in the statements of Ms. McKenzie recorded in the file note), or to an investigator by a person helping the inquiry who is not intended to be called as a witness (as in the remarks of Mr. Rogerson included in the file note), is a novel one. So far as I know, it is not a category of absolute immunity which has been considered before. But it should not for that reason be rejected. Again, I would imagine that the reason why this question now arises for the first time is that before the broaden-

ing of the prosecution's disclosure obligation, such letters and memoranda, internal to the investigation, would never have seen the light of day. At any rate, the question is now whether they fall within the underlying rationale for the existence of immunity from suit.

In *Mann v. O'Neill* (1997), 71 A.L.J.R. at 907 the judgment of Brennan CJ, Dawson, Toohey, and Gaudron JJ. describes the rationale as one of necessity:

> It may be that the various categories of absolute privilege are all properly to be seen as grounded in necessity, and not on broader grounds of public policy. Whether or not that is so, the general rule is that the extension of absolute privilege is "viewed with the most jealous suspicion, and resisted, unless its necessity is demonstrated." Certainly, absolute privilege should not be extended to statements which are said to be analogous to statements in judicial proceedings unless there is demonstrated some necessity of the kind that dictates that judicial proceedings are absolutely privileged.

Thus the test is a strict one; necessity must be shown, but the decision on whether immunity is necessary for the administration of justice must have regard to the cases in which immunity has been held necessary in the past, so as to form part of a coherent principle.

Approaching the matter on this basis, I find it impossible to identify any rational principle which would confine the immunity for out of court statements to persons who are subsequently called as witnesses. The policy of the immunity is to enable people to speak freely without fear of being sued, whether successfully or not. If this object is to be achieved, the person in question must know at the time he speaks whether or not the immunity will attach. If it depends upon the contingencies of whether he will be called as a witness, the value of the immunity is destroyed. At the time of the investigation it is often unclear whether any crime has been committed at all. Persons assisting the police with their inquiries may not be able to give any admissible evidence; for example, their information may be hearsay, but nonetheless valuable for the purposes of the investigation. But the proper administration of justice requires that such people should have the same inducement to speak freely as those whose information subsequently forms the basis of evidence at a trial. When one turns to the position of investigators, it seems to me that the same degree of necessity applies. It would be an incoherent rule which gave a potential witness immunity in respect of the statements which he made to an investigator but offered no similar immunity to the investigator if he passed that information to a colleague engaged in the investigation or put it to another potential witness. In my view it is necessary for the administration of justice that investigators should be able to exchange information, theories and hypotheses among themselves and to put them to other persons assisting in the inquiry without fear of being sued if such statements are disclosed in the course of the proceedings. I therefore agree with the test proposed by Drake J. in *Evans* v. *London Hospital Medical College (University of London)*, [1981] 1 W.L.R. 184, 192:

> ... the protection exists only where the statement or conduct is such that it can fairly be said to be part of the process of investigating a crime or a possible crime with a view to a prosecution or a possible prosecution in respect of the matter being investigated.

This formulation excludes statements which are wholly extraneous to the investigation — irrelevant and gratuitous libels — but applies equally to statements made by persons assisting the inquiry to investigators and by investigators to those persons or to each other.

See the extensive discussion of *Taylor* in *Teskey* v. *Toronto Transit Commission*, [2003] O.J. No. 5314 (S.C.J.), where J. Wilson J. held [at para. 8] that absolute privilege should not be extended to investigations conducted by employers into employee conduct that may later result in criminal proceedings. Documents not created in the context of a criminal investigation do not enjoy absolute privilege merely because they eventually find their way into a Crown brief [para. 87].

In a recent decision, a trial court held that "there is not a single Canadian authority which supports the suggestion that statements in a police investigation are absolutely privileged" and therefore decided to hold that an "Occurence Report," a "Report to Crown Counsel," or a "Continuation Report" were not absolutely privileged.

Hanisch v. *Canada*, [2003] B.C.J. No. 1518, 2003 BCSC 1000, per Harvey J. at paras. 142–43.

C. IN THE COURSE OF QUASI-JUDICIAL PROCEEDINGS

Absolute privilege has been extended to "tribunals exercising functions equivalent to those of an established court of justice."

O'Connor v. *Waldrin*, [1935] A.C. 76 at 81 (P.C.) per Lord Atkin.

Stark v. *Auerbach*, [1979] 3 W.W.R. 563 per Legg J. at 567 (B.C.S.C.).

Voratovic v. Law Society of Upper Canada (1978), 20 O.R. (2d) 214 at 217–18 (H.C.J.).

The distinction between a tribunal or board which is acting in a purely administrative function and one which is exercising a judicial function is determined by reference to certain factors, namely:

i)   under what authority the tribunal acts;
ii)   the nature of the question into which it is the duty of the tribunal to inquire;
iii)   the procedure adopted by the tribunal in carrying out the inquiry; and
iv)   the legal consequences of the conclusion reached by the tribunal as a result of the inquiry.

> *Trapp v. Mackie*, [1979] 1 All E.R. 489 per Lord Diplock at 491–92 (H.L.).

> *Boyachyk v. Dukes* (1982), 136 D.L.R. (3d) 28 per Quigley J. at 32 (Alta. Q.B.):

> The chief of police is saddled with the statutory duty of maintaining discipline within the force and to apply the procedures and penalties set out in the regulations. To accomplish this purpose witnesses may be required to appear and testify on oath. It is mandatory that all complaints be directed to the chief of police and he must cause each such complaint to be investigated. The chief of police must make a finding that the complaint was (a) non-justified; (b) not sustained, or (c) justified. If he finds the complaint to be justified he must then proceed to impose the appropriate sanction under the regulations. If he finds all or any of the portion of the complaint not to be justified he must inform the complainant of his right of appeal … The statutory powers, procedures and sanctions under the Police Act create a judicial proceeding in its broadest sense.

> *Kelly v. Low* (2000), 257 A.R. 279 per LoVecchio J. at paras. 182–94 (Q.B.).

To qualify for absolute privilege, the authority of the tribunal must be "recognized by law." Although the description "recognised by law" is not necessarily confined to tribunals constituted or recognized by statute, it potentially embraces all such tribunals.

> *Dechant v. Stevens*, [2001] 5 W.W.R. 405 (Alta. C.A.), approving *Trapp v. Mackie*, at para. 35.

> *Oliver v. Bryant Straton Management Pty Ltd.* (1997), 41 N.S.W.L.R. 514 at 519.

> *Ayangma v. NAV Canada* (2001), 197 Nfld. & P.E.I.R. 83 at 94 (P.E.I.S.C. (A.D.)).

Tertiary Institute Allied Staff Associates Inc. v. *Tahama*, [1998] 1 N.Z.L.R. 41 at 47 (C.A.).

It has been said that the occasions entitled to absolute privilege within a quasi-judicial context have not been extensively canvassed by the courts.

Dechant v. *Stevens*, above, at paras. 34, 53.

If a body merely carries out investigative functions, but does not determine rights, or the guilt or innocence of anyone, only a qualified privilege may be available.

Sussman v. *Eales* (1985), 33 C.C.L.T. 156 (Ont. H.C.), rev'd on other grounds (1986), 25 C.P.C. (2d) 7 (Ont. C.A.).

O'Connor v. *Waldron*, [1935] 1 D.L.R. 260, A.C. 76, per Lord Atkin at 262–63 (P.C.):

> It is only necessary to remember that the Commissioner [conducting an inquiry under the Combines Investigation Act, R.S.C. 1927, c. 26] by the Act is empowered to enter premises and examine the books, papers and records of suspected person to see how far his functions differ from those of a Judge. His conclusion is expressed in a report; it determines no rights, nor the guilt or innocence of anyone. It does not even initiate proceedings, which have to be left to the ordinary criminal procedure. While it is true that some tribunals are charged with the duty of inquiry whether a breach of duty has been committed have been held entitled to judicial immunity, such as a military Court of Inquiry (*Dawkins* v. *Rokeby* (1875), 45 L.J.Q.B. 8; 8 L.R. 7 H.L. 744), or an investigation by an ecclesiastical commission (*Barratt* v. *Kearns*, [1905] 1 K.B. 504) there were in those cases conditions as to the way in which the tribunal exercised its functions, and as to the effect of its decisions which led to the conclusion that such tribunals had attributes similar to those of a Court of justice.

It has been held that a sheriff carried out an administrative function (rather than a quasi-judicial function) under the Civil Enforcement Regulations in dealing with a request by an individual for an appointment as a bailiff. The Regulations did not obligate the sheriff to carry out an inquiry and the appointment provision was discretionary.

Kelly v. *Low* (2000), 257 A.R. 279, per LoVecchio J. at para. 191 (Q.B.):

> The individual whose application is denied may request that the initial decision be reviewed by the person who made it and is entitled to sub-

mit additional information. What is lacking in this process, and in my view, separates it from a judicial process, is the openness of the procedure, the right to be heard and the disclosure of the information or basis on which the decision was made.

D. DISCIPLINARY PROCESSES

It has been held that disciplinary proceedings of a Law Society may involve the exercise of "judicial" powers.

Harris v. Law Society of Alberta, [1936] 1 D.L.R. 401, per Rinfret J. at 414 (S.C.C.).

In Ontario, it has been held that the investigative functions of the Law Society, as well as the selection of a Discipline Committee, are quasi-judicial in nature, and that preparation and swearing of complaints against a solicitor are discretionary and quasi-judicial acts. [This decision, however, did not deal specifically with defamation, or the application of a defence of absolute privilege.]

French v. The Law Society of Upper Canada (1975), 61 D.L.R. (3d) 28, per Lacourciere J.A. at 32 (Ont. C.A.).

An Ontario court did apply a defence of absolute privilege to dismiss a defamation claim brought against the Law Society by a complainant over the Law Society's decision, following an investigation of the complaint, that there were no grounds to proceed against the solicitor complained of.

Voratovic v. Law Society of Upper Canada (1978), 20 O.R. (2d) 214, per Cromarty J. at 218 (H.C.J.).

See also, *Roach v. Long*, [2001] O.J. No. 70 (S.C.J.), affirmed 22 October 2002 (C.A.), leave to appeal to S.C.C. dismissed, [2002] S.C.C.A. No. 521.

In Ontario, it has been held that absolute privilege applied to a complaint in writing sent to the Royal College of Dental Surgeons alleging that a dentist was guilty of solicitation and harassment at the nursing home operated by the defendant. After investigation, the Complaints Committee of the Society had decided not to refer the matter to the Discipline Committee, choosing instead to gently chastise the plaintiff, which was within its statutory authority. The court declined to recognize a distinction between the Complaints Committee and the Discipline Committee, ruling that the legislature did not intend to break the machinery or the mechanism into discrete parts.

Sussman v. *Eales* (1985), 33 C.C.L.T. 156 (Ont. H.C.J.), rev'd on other grounds (1986), 25 C.P.C. (2d) 7 (Ont. C.A.), per Smith J. at 157, 159–160:

> … [t]he right to engage in professional activities must be the subject of rules governing them. These rules cannot be enforced without a corresponding right in the members of the public to complain uninhibited and without fear of being found wrong and as a result being subject to actions in defamation. Surely it is a small price for a professional person to pay.

It has been held that juries are capable of dealing with the defences of absolute privilege and qualified privilege.

Sussman v. *Eales* (1987), 61 O.R. (2d) 316 (H.C.J.) per Fanjoy D.C.J. (L.J.S.C.).

It has been held that the defence of absolute privilege may apply to a complaint by a citizen to the appropriate authorities about the conduct of a police officer.

Boyachyk v. *Dukes* (1982), 136 D.L.R. (3d) 28, per Quigley J. at 32–33 (Alta. Q.B.), aff'd 4 May 1983, docket no. 15812 (Alta. C.A.) [complaint to the chief of police of City of Edmonton Police Force].

Poland v. *Maitland* (1994), 27 C.P.C. (3d) 334, per Richards J. at 336 (N.W.T.S.C.) [complaint under the *Royal Canadian Mounted Police Act* and regulations about conduct of an RCMP officer].

But see *Forster* v. *Gross* (1999), 182 Sask. R. 294, per Kreuger J. at para. 22 (Q.B) [declining to strike a claim for defamation arising from a utterances made to the RCMP Public Complaints Commission]:

> … The issue of whether the utterances occurred in a quasi-judicial proceeding and accordingly whether absolute privilege applies are, subject to ascertaining the facts, questions of law.

In British Columbia, it has been held following summary trial that absolute privilege protected a report delivered by a complainant to the Law Society and to the Certified General Accountant's Association because they are quasi-judicial bodies, empowered by statute, and each has a duty to investigate complaints and hold disciplinary proceedings. At the summary trial, the plaintiff unsuccessfully argued that the absolute privilege relied on by the defendants, "witness immunity," was not available to the defendants.

Hung v. *Gardiner* (2002), 45 Admin. L.R. (3d) 243, per Joyce J. at 259–60, para. 69 (B.C.S.C.), aff'd 2003 B.C.C.A. 257 per Levine J.A.(Ryan and Hall JJ.A. concurring).

In the summary trial judgment, Joyce J. stated [at paras. 68–69]:

¶68 The plaintiff submits that the absolute privilege relied on by the defendants, the "witness immunity," is not available to these defendants. She says the defendants could not be witnesses in any discipline proceedings under the *Legal Profession Act* or the *Accountants (Certified General) Act* because s. 22(2) of the *Accountants (Chartered) Act* expressly makes them non-compellable in civil proceedings other than under that Act. Therefore, she argues, they cannot claim witness immunity.

¶69 It is my view that the absolute privilege is not lost because of the statutory provision that makes the defendants non-compellable witnesses. The privilege was created by common law so that persons would not be deterred by "fear of proceedings and the vexation of defending actions" (*Sussman* v. *Eales*, supra, at p. 8) from bringing questionable conduct to the attention of the appropriate authorities. That underlying rationale for the protection remains notwithstanding s. 22(2) of the *Accountants (Chartered) Act*.

In British Columbia, a charge or complaint under section 53(1) of the *Medical Practitioners Act*, R.S.B.C. 1996, c. 285 constitutes a first step in the institution of a disciplinary inquiry, even if an inquiry does not proceed in every instance. Accordingly, such communications are absolutely privileged.

Schut v. *Magee*, 2003 BCSC 36, per Kirkpatrick J. at para. 18 [distinguishing *Dechant* v. *Stevens*, [2001] 5 W.W.R. 405 (Alta. C.A.)], aff'd 2003 BCCA 417 per Rowles J.A.

It has been held that a statutory regime providing for the cancellation by a hospital board of a doctor's hospital privileges creates a quasi-judicial process. *Cimolai* v. *Hall*, [2004] B.C.J. No. 187, 2004 BCSC 153 at para. 28.

In Alberta, however, it has been held the requirement of "good faith" for statutory immunity with respect to a conduct complaint against a lawyer is a legislated safeguard for the lawyer (or law student). Accordingly, such communications cannot be regarded as absolutely privileged, as that would nullify the conditions for the statutory protection.

Dechant v. *Stevens*, [2001] 5 W.W.R. 405, per Conrad J.A. at para. 27 (Alta. C.A.) [in relation to ss.112(2) of the *Legal Professions Act*, S.A. 1990, c. L-9.1, which provides that "No action for defamation may be founded on a communication regarding the conduct of a member or student-at-law if the communication is published to or by a person within any of the classes of persons enumerated in subsection (1), in good faith and in the course of any proceedings under this Act or the rules relating to that conduct."]

Assuming that absolute privilege may extend to disciplinary proceedings by the Law Society, there may be strict boundaries on the availability of that privilege. For example, it has been held that it is not plain and obvious that a defamatory statement made about a third party, who is not the subject of the complaint, will attract the privilege.

M.J.M. v. D.J.M. (2000), 187 D.L.R. (4th) 473 (Sask. C.A.), discussed in *Dechant v. Stevens*, above, at paras. 46–47.

Where a defendant pleads a defence of absolute privilege in relation to the proceedings of a disciplinary tribunal, the court will need to consider relevant evidence as to the procedures and protocol employed by the tribunal for processing a claim.

Dechant v. Stevens, above, at para. 55:

> If absolute privilege does not extend to malicious statements that are unrelated to the subject-matter of the inquiry then, although an occasion may be absolutely privileged, certain statements made on that occasion might not enjoy that absolute privilege. The law is, at best, unsettled on issues such as this and, in my view, should not be decided in a vacuum. It would have been a simple matter to set out the procedures and the circumstances surrounding the comments. A court could then weigh the competing objectives to determine whether the occasion is privileged.

E. ARBITRATION PROCEEDINGS

Statements by a lawyer in defence of an employer at a labour grievance proceeding following the dismissal of the employee plaintiff are protected by absolute privilege if the arbitrator and the Council perform quasi-judicial functions.

Kosendiak v. Parsons, [1993] B.C.J. No. 1579 (S.C.), per Cashman J.

Arbitration proceedings under residential tenancy legislation are quasi-judicial and the publication of reports during the course of such hearings is therefore protected by absolute privilege.

Zanetti v. Bonniehon Enterprises Ltd., 2002 BCSC 1203, per E.R.A. Edwards J. at paras. 26–27 [aff'd 2003 BCCA 507 per Mackenzie J.A.]:

> I understand [the argument of the plaintiff] to be that since the arbitrators did not have authority to grant a remedy for introducing false doc-

uments, such as finding the defendants in contempt, the proceedings were not quasi-judicial in nature.

I reject that submission. Many arbitrators and administrative tribunals lack the full powers of a court, such as to powers to punish for contempt or to enforce their own rules. That does not mean that their proceedings are not quasi-judicial.

A letter published by the defendants to a solicitor in response to his request for information in contemplation of possible mediation of a dispute, on the basis the defendants might be called as witnesses, either at an arbitration or in other litigation, is subject to absolute privilege.

> *Gursikh Sabha Canada v. Jauhal* [2001] O.T.C. 788 per Swinton J. at paras. 15–16 (S.C.J.), aff'd, [2002] O.J. No. 2005 (C.A.).

Publication of defamatory material to the arbitration board of a grievance under a collective agreement is protected by absolute privilege.

> *Venneri v. Bascom* (1996), 28 O.R. (3d) 281, per D. Lane J. at 285 (Gen. Div.):
>
> In my view, the act of putting a document into evidence is indistinguishable in principle from the act of speaking the same words to the court and hence must also be absolutely protected.
>
> The board of arbitration has similar attributes to a court and is therefore within the privilege: it proceeds in a manner similar to a court; its object is to arrive at a judicial determination and it is recognized by law ...

A formal response by a union with respect to a complaint made against the union by one of its members, clearly sent in the context of quasi-judicial proceedings before the Canada Labour Relations Board, is entitled to absolute privilege.

> *Penedo v. Fane*, [2000] O.J. No. 3950, per MacPherson J.A. at para. 3 (C.A.).

F. OTHER TRIBUNALS

It has been held that absolute privilege applies to a complaint to the Canadian Human Rights Commission and an investigator appointed by it, as they are part of an overall quasi-judicial process established under the *Canadian Human Rights Act*, 1976–77, c. 33.

> *Ayangma v. NAV Canada* (2001), 203 D.L.R. (4th) 717, per McQuaid J.A. at paras. 36–37 (P.E.I.S.C. (A.D.)), leave to appeal to S.C.C. denied, [2001] S.C.C.A. No. 76.

Upon receiving a complaint of discrimination contrary to the Act, the Commission appoints an investigator who has the responsibility of investigating and preparing a report of her findings for the Commission (section 43 and sections 44(1)). After receiving the report, the Commission requests comments from the parties involved, and after receiving any comments it may request the chair of the tribunal to institute an inquiry into the complaint pursuant to section 49, if it is of the opinion an inquiry is warranted (sections 44(3)(a)). The Commission may also dismiss the complaint, or refer it to a conciliator or to the appropriate authority (sections 44(3)(b), 47(1), and 44(2) respectively). Although the Commission is not an adjudicative body itself, when deciding whether or not a complaint should proceed to be inquired into by a tribunal, the Commission fulfils a screening/analysis role somewhat analogous to that of a judge at a preliminary inquiry. The central component of the Commission's role is that of assessing the sufficiency of the evidence before it.

> *Ayangma* v. *NAV Canada*, above, at paras. 36–37 [citing *Cooper* v. *Canada (Human Rights Commission)* (*sub. nom. Bell.* v. *Canada (Human Rights Commission)*), [1996] 3 S.C.R. 854 (per LaForest J. at para. 52)], leave to appeal to S.C.C. denied, [2001] S.C.C.A. No. 70.

It has been held that just as a complainant should not be inhibited in bringing forth a complaint by the threat of a defamation suit, neither should a witness or prospective witness who is obligated by the provisions of the Act to answer an investigator's inquiries be so inhibited.

> *Ayangma* v. *NAV Canada*, above, at paras. 44, 53, citing *Taylor* v. *Director of the Serious Fraud Office*, [1998] 4 All E.R. 801 (H.L.).

It has been held that a hearing before a court of revision is a quasi-judicial proceeding, and that a statement made by a ratepayer who defamed the plaintiff during a public hearing was protected by absolute privilege.

> *Perry* v. *Heatherington* (1971), 24 D.L.R. (3d) 127 at 128 (B.C.S.C.) per Munroe J.

>> The law is clear that the privilege applies wherever there is an authorized inquiry, which, though not before a Court of Justice, is before a tribunal which has similar attributes, or which acts in a manner similar to that in which Courts of Justice act.

A Worker's Compensation Board exercises a judicial function when it determines a claimant's right to compensation.

Halls v. *Mitchell*, [1928] S.C.R. 125.

Nixon v. *O'Callaghan*, [1927] 1 D.L.R. 1152 at 1159 (Ont. C.A.).

Battaglia v. *Workmen's Compensation Board* (1960), 24 D.L.R. (2d) 21 at 31–33 (B.C.C.A.).

R. v. *Workmen's Compensation Board, ex parte Chenoweth* (1963), 41 D.L.R. (2d) 360 (B.C.S.C.).

Re Canadian Forest Products Ltd. (1960), 24 D.L.R. (2d) 753 (B.C.S.C.).

Accordingly, it has been held that proceedings before a board of review constituted under the British Columbia *Workmen's Compensation Act* enjoy the protection of absolute privilege.

Stark v. *Auerbach* (1979), 98 D.L.R. (3d) 583 (B.C.S.C.) per Legg J. at 587:

> ... public policy and convenience require that absolute immunity be extended to members of a judicial or quasi-judicial tribunal from action for any statement appearing in a decision made pursuant to a statutory duty imposed on the tribunal.

The Nova Scotia Occupational Health and Safety Division, in dealing with a complaint by an ex-employee following her termination by the plaintiff, was exercising its judicial function and not its administrative function. Accordingly, absolute privilege applied from the commencement of the complaint before an officer of the Division through to the completion of the appeals process, as contemplated by the statute.

Keung v. *Sheehan* (2001), 193 N.S.R. (2d) 237, per Robertson J. at 239–40 (S.C.).

It has been held that complaints under the Ontario New Home Warranty Plan are protected by absolute privilege.

Gala Homes Inc. v. *Flisar* (2000), 48 O.R. (3d) 470, per Nordheimer J. at para. 16 (S.C.), aff'd (on other grounds), [2000] O.J. No. 3743 (C.A.).

An appeal to an appeal board pursuant to the provisions of section 21 of the *Public Service Employment Act*, R.S.C. 1970, c. P-32, against the results of a competition for promotion, constitutes an occasion of qualified privilege only. The appeal board proceedings are not sufficiently similar to court proceedings for defamatory publications to that tribunal to enjoy the protection of absolute privilege.

Duquette v. *Belanger* (1973), 38 D.L.R. (3d) 613 per Collier J. at 614 (F.C.T.D.).

A defence of statutory privilege may not apply if the defamatory communication was not published within the specific circumstances defined in the statute. For example, the *Insurance Act* of British Columbia provided that absolute privilege applied to information furnished to the superintendent of insurance pursuant to section 338(1) of that statute, which provided:

> Where an insurer appoints or terminates the appointment of a person as its agent, it shall immediately notify the superintendent, and in case of a termination state the reason.

It was held that absolute privilege did not apply where the agent submitted a letter of resignation before the insurer purported to reject the resignation and instead terminate the agent's employment.

Connor Financial Corp. v. Margetts, [1990] B.C.J. No. 832, per MacKinnon J. (S.C.).

G. FORFEITING ABSOLUTE PRIVILEGE

A defence of absolute privilege which protects a document filed in court may be forfeited if a defendant has published the document outside the context of the judicial or quasi-judicial proceedings.

R.G. v. Christison, [1997] 1 W.W.R. 641, per Wedge J. at para. 70 (Sask. Q.B.) [defendant published her expert report to various social workers at the provincial Department of Social Services, to police, and to doctors, for purposes other than the court proceedings].

In Alberta, absolute privilege will not protect the publication, outside the context of quasi-judicial proceedings taking place before the Alberta Human Rights Commission, of copies of defamatory communications originally published to that Commission.

Wagner v. Lim (1994), 158 A.R. 241 per Egbert J. at 264, para. 75 (Q.B.).

Absolute privilege does not apply to comments made by a lawyer at a public meeting with regard to contemplated legal proceedings.

Ridge Pine Park Inc. v. Schwisberg (1998), 65 O.T.C. 73, per Glass J. (Gen. Div.).

It also appears that dissemination of defamatory pleadings to the news media may not be protected by absolute privilege.

Hains Marketing Associates Ltd. v. Canadian Olympic Association, [2000] O.J. No. 973, per Pepall J. at paras. 19–20 (S.C.J.), referring to the following statement by Reilly J. in *Dooley v. C.N. Weber Ltd.* (1994), 19 O.R. (3d) 779 at 789, f–g (Gen. Div.):

> As a note of caution to the unscrupulous counsel or litigant who may be tempted to pursue his action beyond the courthouse door, I would emphasize the privilege applies only to the extent that the words or documents complained of are used in the ordinary course of the administration of justice. In my view (although I know of no jurisprudence directly on point), if counsel, or indeed any person, chooses to read the pleadings on the courthouse lawn to the media, or in any way publish or disseminate the pleadings outside the ambit of a normal legal proceeding, such conduct may well render that person liable to damages in a subsequent tort action.

Absolute privilege did not protect a party who mailed a statement of claim to certain customers owing money to either the plaintiff or the defendant.

Stevic v. Lefort, [1996] O.J. 999 per Cameron J. at paras. 1–3 (Gen. Div.).

H. COMMUNICATIONS BETWEEN OFFICERS OF STATE ABOUT AFFAIRS OF STATE

Absolute privilege protects a defamatory communication relating to a state matter made by one state official to another in the course of her official duty.

Chatterton v. Secretary of State of India in Council, [1895] 2 Q.B. 189 (C.A.).

For this absolute privilege to apply, three conditions must be satisfied:

i)   the statement must have been made by one officer of state to another officer of state;
ii) it must relate to state matters; and
iii) it must be made by an officer of state in the course of her duty.

> *Dowson v. The Queen (Canada)* (1981), 124 D.L.R. (3d) 260 (F.C.A.), per Le Dain J. for the Court of Appeal at 269, para. 28, leave to appeal to S.C.C. denied (1981), 124 D.L.R. (3d) 260n (S.C.C.).

A person who makes a statement as the agent of an officer of state should be regarded as having the benefit of this privilege. Accordingly, it was held the privilege applied to a statement by a Chief Superintendent of the R.C.M.P., made to the acting assistant deputy Attorney General of Ontario, at the request of the Solicitor General of Canada, in order to provide the Attorney General for Ontario with information that would permit the latter to give an answer in the Ontario Legislature to a question asked by the Leader of the Opposition.

Dowson v. The Queen (Canada), ibid., at 271, para. 24.

It is not entirely clear which officers of state may enjoy this privilege.

This form of absolute privilege has been held to apply in the following circumstances:

i) to a statement made by the Secretary of State for India to the Parliamentary Under-Secretary for India to enable the latter to answer a question in the House of Commons concerning the treatment of the plaintiff, as an officer in the Indian Army, by the Indian military authorities and government.

    Chatterton v. Secretary of State of India in Council, above, at 190–91.

ii) to a report made by the High Commissioner for Australia in the United Kingdom to the Prime Minister of Australia.

    M. Isaacs and Sons, Limited v. Cook, [1925] 2 K.B. 391.

iii) to reports made by naval or military officers in the course of their duties to their superior officers.

    Dawkins v. Lord Paulet (1869), L.R. 5 Q.B. 94.

It has been held that absolute privilege does not apply in the following circumstances:

i) to a report made by an inspector of police to his superior with reference to an application for transfer by a police officer under his authority.

    Gibbons v. Duffell (1932), 47 C.L.R. 520 (H.C.A.).

ii) to a report by an Assistant Commissioner of Police to the Commissioner of Police.

    Merricks v. Nott-Bower, [1964] 1 All E.R. 717 (C.A.).

iii) to a letter written by a senior Czechoslovakian officer in England to his government.

    Szalatnay-Stacho v. Fink, [1946] 2 All E.R. 231.

In certain instances, it may be necessary to fully establish the facts before the existence of the privilege can be determined. Accordingly, a request for a preliminary determination before trial was refused with respect to a report and letter from a Colonel in the United States Air Force with reference to a civilian employee of the Air Force in the United Kingdom.

Richards v. Naum, [1966] 3 All E.R. 812, per Lord Denning, M.R. at 814 (C.A.).

I. PARLIAMENTARY PRIVILEGE

Defamatory statements made during parliamentary proceedings are protected by absolute privilege. Malice does not defeat the privilege.

Ex parte Wason (1869), L.R. 4 Q.B. 573 per Cockburn C.J. at 576.

Clement v. McGuinty, [2000] O.J. No. 2466 per Somers J. at para. 32 (S.C.).

Sommers v. Sturdy (1956), 6 D.L.R. (2d) 642, per Wilson J. at 645 (B.C.S.C.).

The privilege extends to the proceedings of committees of either House.

Goffin v. Donnelly (1881), 6 Q.B.D. 307.

Witnesses who testify before select committees of the House of Commons are also entitled to the protection of absolute privilege.

Goffin v. Donnelly, ibid.

This privilege is rooted in the privileges, immunities, and powers of the members of the Canadian House of Commons, which include those conferred by the *Bill of Rights, 1689*, 1 Wm. & Mr. sess. 2, s. c. 2, art. 9, under the heading of "Freedom of Speech" as follows:

¶9 That the Freedom of Speech, and Debates or Proceedings in Parliament, ought not to be impeached or questioned in any Court or Place out of Parliament.

Roman Corp. Ltd. v. Hudson's Bay Oil & Gas Co. Ltd., [1971] 2 O.R. 418, per Houlden J. at 422 (H.C.J.), aff'd (1973), 23 D.L.R. (3d) 292 (Ont. C.A.), aff'd (1973), 36 D.L.R. (3d) 413 (S.C.C.):

The *Senate and House of Commons Act*, R.S.C. 1952, c. 249, s. 4 (a), provides that members of the House of Commons shall hold, enjoy and exercise the like privileges, immunities and powers as at the time of the passing of the *B.N.A. Act 1867* were held, enjoyed and exercised by the Commons House of Parliament of the United Kingdom and by the members thereof. The Government of Canada was given authority to pass this legislation by the *B.N.A. Act 1867*, s. 18, as amended by the *Parliament of Canada Act*, 1875 (U.K.), c. 38, s. 1.

It is clear that statements made by members of either House of Parliament in their places in the House, though they might be untrue to their knowledge, could not be made the foundation of civil or criminal proceedings however injurious they might be to the interests of a third person.

> *Ex parte Wason* (1869), L.R. 4 Q.B. 573 per Cockburn C.J. at 576.

The Court has no power to inquire into what statements were made in Parliament, why they were made, who made them, what was the motive for making them, or anything about them.

> *Roman Corp. Ltd.* v. *Hudson's Bay Oil & Gas Co. Ltd.*, above, at 423:
>
> > ... it seems to be well established that no person can have a judgment awarded against him in civil proceedings arising out of a speech made in the House of Commons ...

It has been held that a telegram sent by a defendant Prime Minister in which he quoted at length from a statement made in the House of Commons by a defendant Minister the same day were only extensions of statements made by those defendants in the House of Commons and were therefore privileged. The privilege was also held to apply to a press release in which the defendant Prime Minister announced publicly, and for the benefit of the public, certain guidelines implementing Government policy as previously announced in the House of Commons.

> *Roman Corp. Ltd.* v. *Hudson's Bay Oil & Gas Co. Ltd.*, above, at 426. Per Houlden J. citing *A.-G. Ceylon* v. *de Livera*, [1963] A.C. 103, *Halsbury's Laws of England*, 3d ed., vol. 28,(London: Butterworths, 1952–64) at 457–58, referring to the words "Proceedings in Parliament" in art. 9 of the *Bill of Rights, 1689*, and per Aylesworth J.A. for the Court of Appeal at page 299:
>
> > The object of the privilege is, of course, not to further the selfish interests of the Member of Parliament but to protect him from harassment in and out of the House in his legitimate activities in carrying on the business of the House; consideration of the interest of the public in this regard overbears the usual solicitude in our law for the private individual. Viewed in this manner, and that approach, I think, is historically correct, it becomes abundantly clear to me that the sending of the telegram and the issuing of the press release, were no more and no less than the legitimate and lawful discharge by the respondents of their duties in the course of parliamentary proceedings as Ministers of the Crown and Members of the House.

A recent explanation of the rationale for absolute privilege is found in the judgment of McLachlin J. (as she then was) in *New Brunswick Broadcasting*

Co. v. Nova Scotia (Speaker of the House of Assembly), [1993] 1 S.C.R. 319 at 378–79:

> I turn first to the historical tradition of parliamentary privilege. "Privilege" in this context denotes the legal exemption from some duty, burden, attendance or liability to which others are subject. It has long been accepted that in order to perform their functions, legislative bodies require certain privileges relating to the conduct of their business. It has also long been accepted that those privileges must be held absolutely and constitutionally if they are to be effective. The legislative branch of our government must enjoy a certain autonomy which even the crown and the courts cannot touch.

All reports, papers, notes, and proceedings ordered to be published by either the House of Commons or the Senate are absolutely privileged.

Bill of Rights, 1688, 1 Wm. & Mr., sess. 2, c. 2, art.9.

Parliament of Canada Act, R.S.C. 1985, c. P-1, s.4.

J. NO ABSOLUTE PRIVILEGE FOR DOMESTIC TRIBUNALS OF PRIVATE CLUBS

The defence of absolute privilege does not apply to domestic tribunals of private clubs or private organizations, regardless of the procedure of those tribunals.

Trapp v. Mackie, [1979] 1 W.L.R. 377 per Diplock L.J. at 379.

Lincoln v. Daniels, [1962] 1 Q.B. 237 per Devlin L.J. at 255.

CHAPTER TWENTY-ONE:

Justification

A. DEFINITION

Justification is the technical name for the defence of truth. In *Govenlock* v. *Free Press Co. Limited* (1915), 35 O.L.R. 79 (C.A.), Hodgins J.A. defined the defence at page 83:

Justification means one thing, and one thing only: i.e. that the libel is true as printed.

A plea of justification alleges that the defamatory expression at issue "is true in substance and in fact."

Douglas v. *Tucker*, [1952] 1 S.C.R. 275 at 285.

Hare & Grolier Society v. *Better Business Bureau*, [1947] 1 D.L.R. 280 at 284 (B.C.C.A.).

B. JUSTIFICATION MUST BE SPECIFICALLY PLEADED

Justification is an affirmative defence which must be expressly and specifically pleaded. A denial that the expression is defamatory does not constitute a defence of justification.

Stetson v. *MacNeill (c.o.b. The Eastern Graphic)* (1997), 152 Nfld. & P.E.I.R. 225 per Matheson J. at para. 15 (P.E.I.S.C. (T.D.)):

The case law is clear that the defendant cannot rely on particulars to raise the plea. In summary, the defendant cannot rely on the defence of justification unless it is specifically pleaded and he has not yet done so.

C. EFFECT OF THE DEFENCE

Justification is a complete defence to a defamation action. If the expression at issue is true, the plaintiff's defamation claim concerning that expression must be dismissed.

> *Leenen v. Canadian Broadcasting Corporation* (2000), 48 O.R. (3d) 656, per Cunningham J. at 689 (S.C.J.), aff'd (2001), 54 O.R. (3d) 612 at 617, para. 9 (C.A.), leave to to S.C.C. appeal denied, [2001] S.C.C.A. No. 432.

> *Hodgson v. Canadian Newspapers Co.* (1998), 39 O.R. (3d) 235 per Lane J. at 368–69 (Gen. Div.), aff'd on this issue, varied on other grounds (2000), 189 D.L.R. (4th) 241 at 256, para. 32 (C.A.), leave to appeal to S.C.C. denied, [2000] S.C.C.A. 465

> *Sutherland v. Stopes*, [1925] A.C. 47 per Viscount Finlay at 62 (H.L.):

>> It is clear that the truth of a libel affords a complete answer to civil proceedings. This defence is raised by a plea of justification on the ground that the words are true in substance and in fact. Such a plea in justification means that the libel is true not only in its allegations of fact but also any comments made therein.

The law presumes that defamatory expression is false. Therefore the plaintiff need only establish that the allegedly defamatory expression was published. The onus is not upon the plaintiff to prove that the defamatory expression is untrue but rather upon the defendant who pleads justification to prove on a balance of probabilities that it is true.

> *Kent v. Kehoe* (2000), 183 D.L.R. (4th) 503 at 512, para. 20 (N.S.C.A.).

> *Littleton v. Hamilton* (1974), 4 O.R. (2d) 283, per Dubin J.A. at 286 (C.A.), leave to appeal to S.C.C. denied (1974), 4 O.R. (2d) 283n (S.C.C.).

> *Jean v. Slyman*, [1990] B.C.J. No. 2044 (S.C.) per Cohen J.

> *Caldwell v. McBride* (1988), 45 C.C.L.T. 150 per Southin J. at 156 (B.C.S.C.), citing Philip Lewis, *Gatley on Libel and Slander*, 8th ed. (London: Sweet & Maxwell, 1981) at 150:

>> 351: Truth of the imputation. The plaintiff establishes a prima facie cause of action as soon as he has proved the publication of the defamatory words. It is no part of the plaintiff's case in an action of defamation to prove that the defamatory words are false, for the law presumes this in his favour.

Coates v. *The Citizen*, [1988] 44 C.C.L.T. 286 at 296–97 (N.S.S.C. (T.D.)).

Elliott v. *Freisen* (1982), 37 O.R. (2d) 409 (H.C.J.), aff'd (1984) 45 O.R. (2d) 285 at 287 (C.A.), leave to appeal to S.C.C. denied (1984), 45 O.R. (2d) 285n (S.C.C.). Per Steele J. at 37 O.R. (2d) 409 at 413:

> Once the statements are made or published that lower the reputation of the plaintiff, a defamation exists whether or not the statements are true. The element of falsity is only a legal presumption which arises after the defamation already exists.

Macdonald v. *Mail Printing Co.* (1901), 2 O.L.R. 278 per Ferguson J. at 283 and Boyd J. at 280–81 (Div. Ct.), the latter stating:

> Now, it does not lie upon the plaintiff to prove the falsity of the charge; it is, for the purposes of the trial, presumed in his favour, and the onus is on the defendant to prove it to be true if he pleads justification: *Belt* v. *Lawes* (1882), 51 L.J.Q.B. at p, 361

In *McPherson* v. *Daniel* (1829), 10 B. & C. 263 at 272, E.R. 109 at 451, Littledale J. explained the defence of justification in the following terms:

> To constitute a good defence, therefore, to such an action, where the publication of the slander is not intended to be denied, the defendant must negative the charge of malice (which in a legal sense denotes a wrongful act done intentionally without just cause or excuse) or shew that the plaintiff is not entitled to damages … [I]f the defendant relies upon the truth as an answer to the action, he must plead that matter specially: because the truth is an answer to the action, not because it negatives the charge of malice, (for a person may wrongfully or maliciously utter slanderous matter though true, and thereby subject himself to an indictment), but because it shews that the plaintiff is not entitled to recover damages. For the law will not permit a man to recover damages in respect of an injury to a character which he does not possess.

The defendant's state of mind is not relevant to the defence of justification. If the defamatory expression is true in substance and in fact, the defendant will not be liable even if he was not sure of the accuracy of the words at the time of publication.

Hodgson v. *Canadian Newspapers Co.*, [1998] 39 O.R. (3d) 235 per Lane J. at 368 (Gen. Div.), aff'd on the issue of justification, varied on other grounds (2000), 189 D.L.R. (4th) 241 at 256, para. 32 (C.A.), leave to appeal to S.C.C denied, [2000] S.C.C.A. 465.

Truth is a defence even if the defendant spoke maliciously with the intention of ruining the plaintiff's reputation.

Taylor-Wright v. CHBC-TV, a Division of WIC Television Ltd., [1999] B.C.J. No. 334 per Drossos J. at para. 34 (C.A.), aff'd without discussion of this point (2000), 194 D.L.R. (4th) 621 (B.C.C.A.).

It is no defence that the defendant honestly believed that the defamatory expression was true or that someone other than the defendant had in fact made such allegations.

Price v. Chicoutimi Pulp Co. (1915), 51 S.C.R. 179, per Duff J. at 199.

Caldwell v. McBride (1988), 45 C.C.L.T. 150 per Southin J. at 156 (B.C.S.C.), citing Philip Lewis, *Gatley on Libel and Slander*, 8th ed. (London: Sweet & Maxwell, 1981) at 150:

> 352. Proof of imputation. To establish a plea of justification, the defendant must prove that the defamatory imputation is true. It is not enough for him to prove that he believed that the imputation was true, even though it was published as belief only. "If I say of a man that I believe he committed murder, I cannot justify by saying and proving that I did believe it. I can only justify by proving the fact of the murder."

Douglas v. Tucker, [1952] S.C.R. 275, per Cartwright J at 285, citing *Watkin v. Hall* (1868), L.R. 3 Q.B. 396, where Blackburn J. explains the rationale for this principle at 401:

> As great an injury may accrue from the wrongful repetition as from the first publication of slander; the first utterer may have been a person insane, or of bad character. The person who repeats it gives greater weight to the slander. A party is not the less entitled to recover damages in a court of law for injurious matter published concerning him, because another person previously published it.

X. v. Y., [1947] 2 W.W.R. 1011 (Sask. K.B.).

Trafton v. Deschene (1917), 36 D.L.R. 433 at 434 (C.A.).

In *Lewis v. The Daily Telegraph*, [1964] A.C. 234, Lord Devlin explained at 283–84 why a defendant cannot insulate himself or herself from liability merely by publishing that the defamatory information was supplied by someone else:

> I agree of course, that one cannot escape liability for defamation by putting the libel behind a prefix such as "I have been told that ..." or

"it is rumoured that ... ," and then asserting that it was true that you had been told or that it was in fact being rumoured. You have, as Horridge J., said in a passage that was quoted with approval by Greer, L.J., in *Cookson v. Harewood*, "to prove that the subject matter of the rumour was true" ... For the purpose of the law of libel a hearsay statement is the same as a direct statement, and that is all there is to it.

D. DECISION TO PLEAD JUSTIFICATION

A decision to plead justification should not be made lightly. An unsuccessful plea of justification may be taken into account by the court when assessing damages. Depending on the circumstances, a failed plea of truth may aggravate the plaintiff's damages or underpin an award of exemplary damages. It may also lead to a more substantial award of costs against a defendant. See Chapter 30, "Damages."

In *Price v. Chicoutimi Pulp Co.*, [1915] 51 S.C.R. 179, Idington J. warned at 193–94:

> A defence of justification involving the truth in substance and in fact of an alleged libel is often a perilous sort of proceeding.

Lord Denning, M.R. recorded a warning to defendants in *Associated Leisure Ltd. v. Associated Newspapers Ltd.* (1970), 2 Q.B. 450, where he states at 456:

> ...I am sure Devlin J. did not wish in any way to detract from the rule, well settled, which I will read from *Gatley on Libel and Slander*, 6th ed. (1967), p. 462, para. 1046:
>
> > ... A defendant should never place a plea of justification on the record unless he has clear and sufficient evidence of the truth of the imputation, for failure to establish this defence at the trial may properly be taken in aggravation of damages ...
>
> I have always understood such to be the duty of counsel. Like a charge of fraud, he must not put a plea of justification on the record unless he has clear and sufficient evidence to support it.

On the other hand, if a defendant decides not to plead justification in the first instance, he or she should act with due diligence to investigate whether such a defence is available and if so, make the application to amend the defence at the earliest opportunity. It has been held that when the defendant seeks to plead justification at a late stage of a libel lawsuit, his or her conduct will be closely scrutinized. The court will expect the defendant to have shown diligence in making inquiries and investigations. The court may well refuse the application if the defendant has been guilty of delay or has not made proper inquiries earlier.

> *Associated Leisure Ltd.* v. *Associated Newspapers Ltd.*, above, at 456.

The defendant cannot use discovery procedures in libel litigation to investigate whether or not he or she should plead justification. Where a defamatory imputation is general (as opposed to specific), the defendant is not entitled to insert an ambiguous plea of justification in the statement of defence and then question the plaintiff on discovery or seek production of the plaintiff's documents to determine what particulars might support that plea. The onus is on the defendant in the first instance to supply such particulars either in the statement of defence or in a statement of particulars.

> *Care Canada* v. *Canadian Broadcasting Corporation* (1998), 65 O.T.C. 237, per Benotto J. at para. 3 (Gen Div).

> *Fletcher-Gordon* v. *Southam Inc.*, [1997] B.C.J. No. 107 per Dillon J. at paras. 6–8 (S.C.) [aff'd, [1997] B.C.J. No. 369 (C.A.)], citing, *inter alia*, *Arnold & Butler* v. *Bottomley*, [1908] 1 K.B. 151; *Metropolitan Saloon Omnibus Co.* v. *Hawkins*, (1859), 4 H.& N. 87 (Ex. Ct.); *Zierenberg* v. *Labouchere*, [1893] 2 Q.B. 183 (C.A.); *Yorkshire Provident Life Assurance Company* v. *Gilbert*, [1895] 2 Q.B. 148.

> *Drake* v. *Overland*, [1980] 2 W.W.R. 193 (Alta. C.A.).

E. THE SCOPE OF THE DEFENCE

The defendant has the option of pleading the defence of justification in relation to:

i)   The plain and obvious meaning of the defamatory expression in a literal sense;

ii) The natural and ordinary meaning of the defamatory expression in terms of its inferential meanings, also known as "popular" or "false" innuendo meanings; and/or

iii) The legal innuendo pleaded by a plaintiff.

> *Walkinshaw* v. *Drew*, [1936] 4 D.L.R. 685, per Roweall C.J.O. at 686 (Ont. C.A.).

See also Chapter 24, "*Polly Peck* and *Pizza Pizza*: Alleging the Defendant's Defamatory Meaning and Pleading That Meaning is True."

An unqualified plea in a statement of defence that the expression complained of in the statement of claim is "true in substance and in fact" will, as a matter of pleading, raise a defence of truth not only in relation to the plain and obvious (literal) meaning but also to any inferential meaning ("popular" or "false" innuendo) conveyed by the expression to the ordinary, reasonable reader, listener, or viewer.

> *Hare & Grolier Society* v. *Better Business Bureau*, [1947] 1 D.L.R. 280, per Sidney Smith J.A. at 284 (B.C.C.A.), adopting *Digby* v. *Financial News Ltd.*, [1907] 1 K.B. 502 at 507:

> > When a plea of justification is pleaded it involves the justification of every injurious imputation which a jury may think is to be found in the alleged libel.

A defendant may elect to plead justification only with respect to the plain and obvious (literal) meaning.

> *Walkinshaw* v. *Drew*, [1936] 4 D.L.R. 685, per Roweall C.J.O. at 686 (Ont. C.A.). The statement of defence alleged:

> > 3. The defendant denies that he meant, or was understood to mean by the said words that the plaintiff had committed the criminal offence of failing to account for trust moneys received in payment of insurance premiums, or that the plaintiff was dishonest in the management and operation of the Queen City Insurance Agencies Ltd. or that the insurance licence of the plaintiff had been suspended for cause or that during the last four years the plaintiff could not obtain the necessary insurance licence to enable him to engage in the insurance business.

> > 4. The said words in their natural and ordinary meaning and without the alleged meanings referred to in para. 3 hereof are true in substance and in fact.

Alternatively, a defendant may decide not to plead justification in relation to the plain and obvious (literal) meaning of the allegedly defamatory expression but instead to limit his or her plea of justification to one or more of the inferential meanings (popular or false innuendo) alleged by the plaintiff (or by the defendant in his or her defence; see Chapter 24, "*Polly Peck* and *Pizza Pizza*: Alleging the Defendant's Defamatory Meaning and Pleading That Meaning is True").

> *Hodgson* v. *Canadian Newspapers Co.* (1998), 39 O.R. (3d) 235 (Gen. Div.), aff'd on this issue, varied on other grounds (2000), 189 D.L.R. (4th) 241

(Ont. C.A.), leave to appeal to S.C.C. denied, [2000] S.C.C.A. 465. Per Lane J. at 39 O.R. (3d) 235 at 361–62:

> Many pages ago, I dealt with the question of whether the words complained of meant or were understood to bear any defamatory meaning of the plaintiff, including the meanings pleaded in para. 16 of the amended statement of claim. I held that the words were defamatory of the plaintiff in their plain and obvious meaning, both in the general sense as pleaded in the opening portion of para. 16, and also in the specific false innuendoes pleaded in paras. 16(a),(b),(e), and (f). The defendants pleaded that (b) and (f) were true in substance. However, they did not seek to justify (a) or (e). Because the defendants took the position that the only meanings open to the plaintiff were the inferential meanings in the subparas., there is no plea that the words in their plain and obvious meaning in the literal sense were true. Nevertheless, I will deal with the truth or falsity of the words in that sense on the assumption that the defendants had amended to justify those meanings.
>
> … In the result, the defendant's efforts to justify the imputations in paras. 16(b) and (f) have failed. …
>
> … Had the defendants pleaded justification of the natural and ordinary, plain and obvious meaning in the literal sense, they would have failed.

In order to obtain a complete dismissal of the defamation action, the defendant must prove the truth of all the defamatory imputations contained in the expression complained of by the plaintiff.

Boys v. Star Ptg. & Pub. Co., [1927] 3 D.L.R. 847 (Ont C.A.). Riddle, J.A. speaking for the court noted at 848 that the statement of claim, after pleading the words complained of in a newspaper article, alleged that certain words accused the plaintiff of a criminal offence and corrupt, improper, and discreditable conduct both in the practice of his profession as a lawyer and as an Member of Parliament. Other words allegedly charge the plaintiff with using his influence to prevent a criminal prosecution.

Per Riddle at 854:

> To succeed in a plea of justification, the defendant must prove the truth of all the material allegations contained in the words complained of – if any material part is not proved, the plaintiff is entitled (subject to our *Libel and Slander Act*, R.S.O. 1914, c. 71, s. 3, as to which see *Wilson v. London Free Press Ptg. Co.* (1918), 45 D.L.R. 503, 44 O.L.R. 12) to damages in respect of such part if by itself if would form a "substantial

ground of an action for libel" (*Clarke* v. *Taylor* (1836), 2 Bing. N.C. 654, per Tindal, C.J. at p. 665, 132 E.R. 252). Or, being doubtful of success in proving the truth of every material allegation, he divides his allegations into two classes, "statements of fact," which he thinks he can prove true, and "comment," about which he is not so certain.

Further, for the entire action to be dismissed on the basis of justification, a libellous headline in newspaper article must be justified as well as the facts stated in body of the newspaper article. A plea of justification which justifies all of the imputations except a distinct defamatory imputation conveyed by the headline or a photograph caption will not result in dismissal of the action.

Manitoba Free Press Company v. *Martin* (1892), 21 S.C.R. 518, per Patterson J. at 528, citing *Odgers on Libel and Slander*, 2d ed., at 539, which in turn cites *Lewis* v. *Clement*, 3 B. & Ald. 702, *Bishop* v. *Latimer*, 4 L.T. 775.

If the plaintiff has pleaded what he or she says are the inferential meanings of the literal words complained of in the statement of claim, the defendant must prove the truth of each of the defamatory meanings which are, in fact, conveyed by the expression at issue, if the entire action is to be dismissed.

Bank of British Columbia v. *Canadian Broadcasting Corporation* (1995), 126 D.L.R. (4th) 644, per Prowse J.A. (Hollinrake J.A. concurring) at 661 (B.C.C.A.):

> The issue of truth, as with all other issues, must be defined by the pleadings. As noted earlier in these reasons, it is not so much the literal truth of the statements contained in the broadcast which must be considered in relation to the issue of truth, but, rather, the truth of the alleged defamatory meaning attributed to those statements. It is the truth as the words would reasonably be understand in light of the particular circumstances that must be proved.

If the defendant choses to justify the words in the meaning attached to them by the plaintiff, the defendant must be held strictly to the innuendo which the plaintiff has asserted and which the defendant has accepted.

Sommers v. *Sturdy* (1956), 7 D.L.R. (2d) 30 (B.C.S.C.), aff'd (1957), 10 D.L.R. (2d) 269 (B.C.C.A.), leave to appeal to S.C.C. denied, [1957] S.C.R. x. Per Clyne J. at 7 D.L.R. (2d) 30 at 34–35, 36, citing Richard O'Sullivan & Roland G. Brown, *Gatley on Libel and Slander*, 4th ed. (London: Sweet & Maxwell, 1953) at 34–35.

> The innuendo asserted by the plaintiff is contained in para. 4 of the statement of claim which reads in part as follows: "By the said words

the defendant meant and intended and was understood to mean that the plaintiff, when acting as Minister of Lands & Forests as a member of the Government of British Columbia had received bribes in respect of the issuance and awarding of Forest Management licences and that the plaintiff had been guilty of a criminal offence."

In order to succeed the defendant must prove that the plaintiff received bribes and that he committed a criminal offence ... In pleading the [corrupt] agreement and giving the names of those who he says are parties to the agreement the defendant is setting out particulars which he ought to give to the plaintiff and which the plaintiff is entitled to receive.

The first step in determining the validity of a defence of justification is for the court to determine whether the expression complained of conveys one or more of the inferential meanings attributed to it by the plaintiff. A jury will only be asked to consider meanings which the judge rules are capable of being conveyed by the expression complained of. Only those meanings held, as a matter of fact, to be conveyed by the expression complained of need to be justified by the defendant.

Bank of British Columbia v. Canadian Broadcasting Corporation, above, at 662.

Lewis v. Daily Telegraph, [1964] A.C. 234 at 267, per Lord Morris of Borth-y-Gest:

... [T]he learned judge asked the jury whether, if the words bore the very limited meaning contended for by the newspaper, they considered that the words were justifiable as being true: the necessity to consider the defence of justification would only arise on the basis that the words were defamatory ... .

1) True in Substance

The defendant is not required to prove the literal truth of every word of the libel. If the defendant proves the sting, or main charge, of the libel, it is not necessary for her to prove the truth of statements or comments which do not add to the sting of the charge or introduce any matter by itself actionable. The onus on the defendant is to prove the substance of the allegations, not the literal truth of each separate word.

Hodgson v. Canadian Newspapers Co., [1998] 39 O.R. (3d) 235 (Gen. Div.), varied 49 O.R. (3d) 161 (C.A.), leave to appeal to S.C.C. denied, [2000] S.C.C.A. 465. Per Lane J. at 39 O.R. (3d) 235 at 368, citing *Hare & Grolier*

Society v. *Better Business Bureau*, [1948] 1 W.W.R. 569 at 571 (B.C.S.C.), where Macfarlane J. noted:

> The words alleged to be defamatory of the plaintiff Hare were so because of the innuendo they bore. The real complaint is, to use the words of the statement of claim, that "the plaintiff was acting in a fraudulent and dishonest manner in attempting to sell the "Book of Knowledge'" and (which is simply repetition) "was attempting to sell the 'Book of Knowledge' by making fraudulent misrepresentations."
>
> The defence is primarily justification, i.e. that the allegations were substantially true.
>
> *Gatley on Libel and Slander*, 3rd. ed., at p. 179, on the authority of *Edwards* v. *Bell* (1824) 1 Bing 403, 130 E.R. 162, and subsequent cases, states the duty of the party pleading substantial justification thus:
>
>> 'It is not necessary to prove the truth of every word of the libel. If the defendant succeeds in proving that 'the main charge or gist of the libel' is true, he need not justify statements or comments which do not add to the sting of the libel or introduce any matter by itself actionable. 'It is sufficient if the substance of the libelous statement be justified; it is unnecessary to repeat every word which might have been the subject of the original comment. As much must be justified as meets the sting of the charge and if anything be contained in a charge which does not add to the sting of it, that need not be justified.'

Minors v. *Toronto Sun Publishing Corp.* (1996), 21 O.T.C. 325 (H.C.), aff'd [1999] 122 O.A.C. 43 (C.A.), leave to appeal to S.C.C. denied, [1999] S.C.C.A. No. 472.

Courts frequently speak of the "charge" or the "sting" of defamatory expression. The term "charge" is also found in certain defamation statutes. In order to succeed on a justification defence, the truth of the charge or sting must be demonstrated by the defendant on a balance of probabilities.

Hodgson v. *Canadian Newspapers Co.*, above, at 368 ("sting").

Bank of British Columbia v. *Canadian Broadcasting Corporation*, above, at 661.

Re International Assn. of Bridge, Structural and Ornamental and Reinforcing Iron-workers (Local 97) and Campbell (1997), 40 B.C.L.R. (3d) 1, per Macdonald J. at 7, paras. 7, 9 (S.C.) ("sting," "bite").

Peddie v. *Kerr*, [1996] O.J. No. 2551, per Taliano J. at para. 60 (Gen. Div.) ("sting").

Lewis v. *Daily Telegraph Ltd.*, [1964] A.C. 234, per Lord Reid at 258 (H.L.) ("sting").

Hare & Grolier Society v. *Better Business Bureau*, [1947] 1 D.L.R. 280 at 284 (B.C.C.A.) ("sting of the charge").

Libel and Slander Act, R.S.O. 1990, c. L.15, s. 22 ("charge").

A slight inaccuracy in one or more of its details will not prevent a defence of justification from succeeding.

Hodgson v. *Canadian Newspapers Co.*, above, at 369 citing Philip Lewis, *Gatley on Libel and Slander*, 8th ed. (London: Sweet & Mawell, 1981) at para. 364.

Peddie v. *Kerr*, above, at para. 60, citing *Gatley on Libel and Slander*, 8th ed., *ibid.*, at 155:

> The sting of the article was that the plaintiff had been discharged for his shortcomings in his performance on the Centara project. The fact that historical shortcomings (i.e. that the plaintiff was unable to get along with other department heads and that his approach and attitude were objectionable) were also factors and yet were not mentioned in the article scarcely justifies the complaint that the article was inaccurate. Does the fact that the article that proclaimed his discharge preceded the release of the final report to council that detailed his deficiencies deprive The Star of its defence? I think not. The decision to discharge was driven by the draft report not the final report plus the discharge was executed by Burns, not council. What transpired at Council after the discharge can have little bearing on the earlier events. For these reasons, the defence of justification must prevail with respect to this passage in the article.

If a defendant pleads justification but does not plead fair comment in relation to defamatory opinions in the expression at issue, he or she must prove that the statements of opinion are true. Some opinions are, by their nature, incapable of being proven true.

Upton v. *Better Business Bureau of the Mainland of B.C.* (1980), 114 D.L.R. (3d) 750, per Gould J. at 752–53 (B.C.S.C.):

> The burden upon a defendant in a plea of justification is that the impugned allegations are substantially true. The complained-of words

contain statements of fact in the first paragraph and a statement of opinion in the second paragraph, namely, that without competitive quotations, a prospective customer is in danger of being overcharged. As to when there is both fact and opinion contained in the alleged libel, *Gatley on Libel and Slander*, 7th ed. (1974), at p. 155, para. 358, says: "If the libel contains defamatory statements both of fact and of opinion, the defendant, under a plea of justification, must prove that the statements of fact are true and that the statements of opinion are correct."

... It is not every opinion that is capable of being proven "correct" or otherwise. A statement such as "we do not think the Jones Tractor Repair Company has or ever has had facilities for repairing diesel-powered tractors" is an opinion capable, upon inquiry, of being shown to be either correct or incorrect. But a statement such as "we do not think the architect William Jones has ever designed or ever will design a public building in the least pleasing to any taste other than his own" cannot be capable upon any practical amount of inquiry of being shown to be correct or otherwise. A statement such as the latter is usually defended by the plea of fair comment. There is no such plea in this case, nor a rolled-up plea, which includes a fair comment defence as to opinion. From the whole of the evidence I am unable to find that the prospective customers of the plaintiff are generally speaking, exposed to being overcharged. Therefore the plea of justification cannot succeed.

Fast v. Cowling (c.o.b. Fast & Co.) (1996), 24 B.C.L.R. (3d) 82, per Harvey J. at 91 (S.C.).

Makow v. Winnipeg Sun, [2003] M.J. No. 79, 2003 MBQB 56, per Monnin J. at para. 54.

However, it is not always necessary to prove the correctness of all comments because where the facts are proven as true and the inference is fair, then the comment is necessarily correct.

Hodgson v. Canadian Newspapers Co., above, at 368, citing *Gatley on Libel and Slander*, 8th ed., above, *Cooper v. Lawson* (1838), 8 Ad. & El. 746 at 753, 1 Per. & Dav. (Q.B.).

2) Multiple Stings

If several distinct libels are alleged by the plaintiff, the trial judge should direct the jury that the truth of each defamatory imputation must be considered separately and that they should not award damages in respect of any imputation proven by the defendant to be true.

Leonard v. Wharton (1921), 65 D.L.R. 323, per Idington J. at 325 (S.C.C).

If an article contains two separate and distinct stings and a plaintiff complains only about one of the stings, the defendants are not allowed to plead the truth of the sting in respect of which the plaintiff has not sued.

Cruise v. Express Newspapers, [1998] E.W.J. No. 935, per Lord Justice Brooke at paras. 55 and 58 (C.A.):

> [55] It is no defence to a charge that "you called me A" to say "Yes, but I also called you B on the same occasion, and that was true," if the second charge was separate and distinct from the first. It may in any given case be difficult to decide whether the two charges are indeed separate and distinct (for rival approaches to the published words in the New Zealand case of *Templeton v. Jones*, [1984] NZLR 448, see O'Connor LJ. in *Polly Peck* at pp. 1030–1031), but whether they are or not is a question of law which can conveniently be determined on an interlocutory application of this kind. A good example on the other side of the line is *Thompson v. Bernard* (1807) 1 Camp 47, cited in *Polly Peck* at p. 1023, where the words "Thompson is a damned thief" were clearly not severable from the words that followed, which were to the effect that he had received the proceeds of the ship and failed to pay the wages.
>
> …
>
> [58] … The judge was in my judgment correct to hold that this libel action should not be permitted to get out of control by allowing the defendants to justify or plead fair comment in respect of a quite separate and distinct sting, if indeed it be a sting at all, of which the plaintiffs make no complaint

F. PARTIAL JUSTIFICATION

1) At Common Law

At common law, if the plaintiff complains of more than one defamatory sting, the defendant is entitled to choose to justify only one of the stings. In other words, the defendant may elect not to plead justification with respect to certain distinct imputations pleaded by the plaintiff. However, the defendant remains liable for damages in respect of any defamatory imputation which is not justified (or otherwise defensible).

Hodgson v. Canadian Newspapers Co., above, citing Colin Duncan & Brian Neil, *Defamation*, (London: Butterworths, 1978) at para. 11.07.

One court recently held that where a defendant justified a number (but not all) of the defamatory imputations complained of by the plaintiff, the assessment of damages should take place on the basis that the plaintiff should not be viewed as a person of unimpeachable character, but one whose reputation has been partially blemished.

Makow v. Winnipeg Sun, [2003] M.J. No. 79, 2003 MBQB 56, per Monnin J. at para. 146.

2) Statute Law

The Ontario *Libel and Slander Act*, R.S.O. 1990, c. L.12, provides in section 22:

22. In an action for libel or slander for words containing two or more distinct charges against the plaintiff, a defence of justification shall not fail by reason only that the truth of every charge is not proved if the words not proved to be true do not materially injure the plaintiff's reputation having regard to the truth of the remaining charges.

Hodgson v. Canadian Newspapers Co., above, at 373:

In terms of s. 22, the defendants would have proved one of their charges, that the plaintiff misled Council; but not another, that he had done so deliberately. Even assuming that the mis-leading was negligent, proof of that charge does not invoke the section's protection because the words not proved to be true do nevertheless, materially affect the plaintiff's reputation. Proof of negligence is not even a partial answer to a charge of dishonesty or deliberate misconduct.

Young v. Toronto Star Newpapers Ltd., [2003] O.J. No. 3100 (S.C.J.) per Rouleau J. [s.22 held to have no application where defamatory meanings alleged were proven by plaintiff and not shown to be true by defendant].

The only other province with a statutory provision concerning partial justification is Nova Scotia. Section 9 of that province's *Defamation Act*, R.S.N.S. 1989, c. 122, is virtually identical to the Ontario statute.

G. GENERAL AND SPECIFIC IMPUTATIONS

Defamation law makes a distinction between charges of a "general" nature and charges of a specific nature.

Loos v. Leader-Post Ltd., [1982] 2 W.W.R. 459, per Cameron J.A. at 466 (Sask. C.A.):

(2) The charges pleaded in the statement of claim – that the plaintiffs were fired on account of their incompetence, financial and administrative mismangement and dereliction of duty – are charges of a general, as opposed to a specific nature. *Gatley*, at p. 433, discusses the distinction between general as opposed to a specific charge and gives these examples: if the plaintiff is charged as being a "charity swindler" or "imposter," that will be a general charge; if it is said that on a given day and at a place named he stole a specific article, that will be a specific charge: see also *Wismer v. Maclean-Hunter Publishing Co.*, 10 W.W.R. (N.S.) 625, [154] 1 D.L.R. 481, 501 (B.C.C.A.) and *Drake v. Overland*, [1980] 2 W.W.R. 193, 12 C.P.C. 303, 107 D.L.R. (3d) 323, 19 A.R. 472 (Alta. C.A.).

Per Cameron J.A. at 469:

> If one party levels a defamatory charge of a general nature against another and proposes at trial to prove that it is true, he must furnish particulars of that charge to the other in order to enable him to prepare adequately for trial.

If the expression complained of is precise and conveys a specific charge in full detail, it is sufficient for the defendant to plead that it is "true in substance and in fact" and the plaintiff is under no obligation to supply further particulars of fact.

Reid v. Albertan Publishing Company, Ltd. (1913), 10 D.L.R. 495 per Stuart J. at 496, citing William Blake Odgers, *Odgers on Libel and Slander*, 5th ed. (London: Stevens, 1912) at 190. The words complained of in the defendant's newspaper article were: "there is no disguising the fact that the effort to stampede the members of the council is not above suspicion. The first move to secure Sergt. Nuff's appointment to the police force was made by Johnny Reid (the plaintiff) of the notorious cafeteria and the later the pioneer of the still more notorious South Coulee" The plaintiff alleged the imputation conveyed by these words was that that the plaintiff was endeavouring unduly to influence members of Calgary city council to obtain the appointment of a police officer to the position of chief of police and that the plaintiff was the founder and was financially interested in a district inhabited by prostitutes.

Per Stuart at p. 496–97: In the present case the libel alleged does not, in my opinion, state any specific facts. The words, "of the notorious cafeteria" do not allege specific facts. Nor do the words "pioneer of the still more notorious South Coulee." ... There is no specific allegation of fact there at all ... The libel itself is only insinuation and the plaintiff has a right to know by particulars what is insinuated as a matter of fact before evidence is given.

Where the allegedly libellous statements are general in nature, however, the defendant must furnish the plaintiff with particulars of the facts relied upon as a justification.

Wismer v. Maclean-Hunter Publishing Co. Ltd. and Fraser (No. 1), [1954] 1 D.L.R. 481 per Robertson J.A. (Sloan, C.J.B.C. concurring) at 492–93 (B.C.C.A.):

> Where the libel is general in its nature and the defendant pleads justification the defendant must give particulars — see *Wooton v. Sievier*, [1913] 3 K.B. 499 at p. 503 — because in every case in which the defence raises an imputation of misconduct against him, a plaintiff ought to be enabled to go to trial with knowledge not only of the general case he has to meet, but also of the acts which it is alleged that he has committed and upon which the defendant intends to rely as justifying the imputation; see also *Zierenberg v. Labourchere*, [1893] 2 Q.B. 183.
>
> ... But in this case the allegations in the libel in the statement of claim are not general, but in my opinion, with respect, are specific. The appellants pleaded "the said words (i.e. in the libel) were true in substance and in fact." The respondent knows exactly what he has to meet.

Toronto Star Ltd. v. *Globe Printing Co.*, [1941] 113 per Master Barlow at 114, affirmed by Hope J. at 118.

In *Wismer* v. *MacLean-Hunter Publishing*, above, the British Columbia Court of Appeal held that the words complained of by the plaintiff were specific rather than general. The impugned text of the article at issue reads as follows [at 486–87]:

> B.C. liquor laws forbid the sale of spirits by the glass. A legal way around this is the establishment of 'private clubs' for the thirsty. In one such the annual membership fee is a dime; others run as high as two dollars. Most of the club licenses are held by friends of Wismer, several of whom worked their way up from humble beginnings by diligent service in the Vancouver Centre Liberal Association.
>
> Three years ago the Federal Government bought land for a new Vancouver customs building. Two holding companies got $140,000.00 for lots that had been bought for $85,000.00 (more than a year earlier, a director explained, though by some oversight the sale wasn't registered until a month before Ottawa bought them out). Anyway, the profit on the deal was sixty-five percent. Both these farsighted holding companies were owned by about fifteen shareholders. Among them were one club proprietor, one club director, two club stewards and Attorney-General Gordon Wismer.

H. JUSTIFICATION BASED ON POST-PUBLICATION FACTS

The basic principle is that a defamatory imputation must be true at the time it is published. In certain circumstances, however, the defendant may allege facts which have occurred within a reasonable time of the publication of the defamation to establish that the imputation was true when it was published or broadcast.

> *Hiltz and Seamone Co.* v. *Nova Scotia (Attorney General)* (1997), 164 N.S.R. (2d) 161 at paras. 125–27 (S.C.), aff'd (1999), 172 D.L.R. (4th) 488 at paras. 99–103 (N.S.C.A.). Stewart J. states at 164 N.S.R. (2d) 161 at paras. 126–27:
>
>> 126. Pickford, L.J. in *Maisel* v. *Financial Times Limited,* [1915], 3 K.B. 336 at p. 341 stated:
>>
>>> I wish to guard myself against being supposed to say that, if you want to prove a libel on a man alleging something at a particular date, you may always prove anything that happened afterwards in order to show that he was likely to have done it. I do not think such a proposition can be maintained for a moment. But where, as here, the allegation complained of is that he is a person of a character likely to do a certain act and that he would to the certain act if he got the opportunity, then it seems to be that it cannot be said to be irrelevant to prove that as soon as he got the opportunity, a short time after the libel, he did it. It may be that the act which he did was so long after the libel that it would have no relevance at all having regard to the time of the libel. If that were so, it would not be admissible.
>>
>> 127. Similarly, the Master of the Rolls, Lord Denning, in *Cohen* v. *Daily Telegraph Limited,* [1968] 2 All E.R. 407 at 409 referred to *Maisel* v. *Financial Times Limited, supra,* and the principle "…that on a plea of justification the pleader can rely on facts which happened subsequently."
>
> *Hare and Grolier Society* v. *Better Business Bureau,* [1947] 1 D.L.R. 280, at 285–86 (B.C.C.A.), citing *Maisel* v. *Financial Times Limited,* above.
>
> See also, *Makow* v. *Winnipeg Sun,* [2003] M.J. No. 79, 2003 MBQB 56, per Monnin J. at paras. 56–58 [evidence not in existence at time of libel, namely Web sites and writings of plaintiff, admitted at trial on issue of justification].

Unlike the defence of fair comment, the defence of justification entitles a defendant to allege facts in existence at the time of publication but not referred to in the defamatory expression and even unknown to the defendant at the time of publication.

> *Hodgson v. Canadian Newspapers Co.*, (1998) 39 O.R. (3d) 235 (Gen. Div.), varied (2000), 49 O.R. (3d) 161 (C.A.).

I. RELATED ISSUES

1) Alternative Defamatory Meanings

See Chapter 24, "*Polly Peck* and *Pizza Pizza*: Alleging the Defendant's Defamatory Meaning and Pleading That Meaning is True."

If a defendant alleges in the statement of defence that the expression complained of by the plaintiff conveyed a different popular or false innuendo meaning than alleged by the plaintiff, any defence of justification relating to that defamatory meaning alleged by the defendant will be subject to the ordinary obligation to deliver particulars of defamatory imputations.

2) Rumours and Hearsay

Where the defendant repeats a rumour, he or she cannot establish justification by proving that in fact the rumour existed. The defendant must prove that the subject-matter of the rumour was true. It is no defence that the defendant did not originate the rumour, but heard it from another, even if he or she names the source of the rumour.

> *Tucker v. Douglas*, [1950] 2 D.L.R. 827 (Sask. C.A.), aff'd, [1952] 1 S.C.R. 275.

> *Trafton v. Deschene* (1917), 36 D.L.R. 433, per Grimmer J. at 434 (N.S.C.A.):

> > "Tale bearers are as bad as tale makers," is a well established maxim. It is no defence that the speaker did not originate the scandal, but heard it from another, even though it was a current rumour and he believed it to be true: *Watkin v. Hall* (1868), L.R. 3 Q.B. 396

> *Pressler v. Lethbridge* (2000), 86 B.C.L.R. (3d) 257 per Southin J.A. at para. 57 (C.A.):

> > To say, "there are rumours to a certain effect but I do not believe them" is to speak words which, if the sting of the rumour would hold the person of whom the words are spoken up to odium, are capable of a defamatory meaning.

The circumstance that a libel, which a defendant has repeated rather than originated, was first published in some legal proceeding can have no effect on the plea of justification although it may become relevant to a plea that the publication by the defendant was protected by privilege.

Douglas v. Tucker, [1952] 1 S.C.R. 275 per Cartwright J. at 285.

Farrell v. St. John's Publishing Co. Ltd. (1986), 58 Nfld. & P.E.I.R. 66, per Morgan J.A. (Nfld. C.A.) The defendant newspaper's article at issue stated, *inter alia*:

> A Newfoundland Constabulary report that was forwarded to the provincial justice department June 9 concludes that the April 26 fire at the Elizabeth Towers apartment of Dr. Tom Farrell was deliberately set and that it was set by Farrell.

The plaintiff Farrell was subsequently charged with the arson. Following a preliminary inquiry, the charge against Farrell was dropped.

Morgan J.A. noted:

> At the commencement of the trial, however, counsel for the defendants (appellants) explained that he did not intend to adduce evidence of guilt but submitted that the plea of justification could be sustained by proof that the republications of the report were accurate. In my opinion [that plea] … is not a plea of justification at all. The sting of the words complained of being that the respondent deliberately set fire to his apartment, those words could be justified only by pleading and proving that he did in fact set the fire deliberately.

3) Allegations of Criminal Conduct

Expression concerning an individual and his or her relation to criminal activity may take a variety of forms:

i) A statement of suspicion short of guilt which does not impute that reasonable grounds for that suspicion exists.

ii) A statement of suspicion short of guilt that imputes that reasonable ground for that suspicion exists.

iii) A statement of suspicion imputing guilt.

iv) A statement that there is a police inquiry into the conduct of the plaintiff which does not impute that there are reasonable grounds for such an inquiry.

v) A statement that there is a police inquiry into the conduct of the plaintiff which does impute that there are reasonable grounds for such an inquiry.

vi) A statement that the plaintiff has been charged or accused of criminal conduct.

vii)   A statement imputing that the plaintiff is facing a trial on criminal charges.

viii) A statement that the plaintiff has been convicted of criminal conduct.

> *Grassi* v. *WIC Radio Ltd. 9c.o.b. CKNW/98*, [2000] 5 W.W.R. 119, per Lysyk at 135–38 (B.C.S.C.).

> *Bennett* v. *News Group Newspapers Ltd.*, [2002] E.M.L.R. 39.

> *Chase* v. *News Group Newspapers Ltd.*, [2003] E.M.L.R. 218.

Faced with an allegation by a plaintiff that the impugned expression alleges guilt, in appropriate circumstances a defendant may chose to plead an alternative defamatory meaning that the expression merely imputes suspicion, and plead justification of that meaning. See Chapter 24, "*Polly Peck* and *Pizza Pizza*: Alleging the Defendant's Defamatory Meaning and Pleading That Meaning is True."

> *Jameel* v. *The Wall Street Journal Europe*, [2003] E.W.C.A. Civ. 1694.

To say that a person is suspected of an offence does not necessarily convey the imputation that he or she is guilty of that offence.

> *Grassi* v. *WIC Radio Ltd. (c.o.b. CKNW/98)*, above, at 136–67, citing *Lewis* v. *Daily Telegraph Ltd.*, [1964] A.C. 234, per Lord Devlin at 284–85 (H.L. (Eng.)):
>
> > A man who wants to talk at large about smoke may have to pick his words very carefully if he wants to exclude the suggestion that there is also a fire; but it can be done.

It may be defamatory to state that the plaintiff's conduct is the subject of an inquiry if the expression conveys the allegation there are good grounds for the inquiry. In these circumstances, a defence of justification would allege there were in fact good grounds for the inquiry.

> *Lewis* v. *Daily Telegraph Ltd.*, above, at 284–85.

To say that a person is suspected of an offence may, and usually will, itself be defamatory even if it does not convey the further imputation of guilt. Where guilt is not insinuated, justification may be easy to establish if the defendant can prove that the plaintiff was in fact under suspicion.

> *Grassi* v. *WIC Radio Ltd.*, above, at 138.

Where a newspaper article stated that the plaintiff faced trial on "charges" that he owed a substantial sum of money to a credit card company, a defendant did not succeed in establishing justification by proving the existence of civil proceedings against the plaintiff. It was held that the average reasonable reader would gain the impression that the plaintiff faced trial on criminal charges.

> *Lenox Hewitt v. Queensland Newspapers Pty Limited* (5 June 1995), No. S.C. 283 of 1993 (AC.T.S.C.), cited in *Grassi v. WIC Radio Ltd. (c.o.b. CKNW/98)*, above, at 138.

It has been held that a statement that a person has been charged with a criminal offence does not necessarily bear the imputation that he or she is guilty or probably guilty of that offence. The ordinary reader is mindful of the principle that a person charged with a crime is presumed innocent until proven guilty. Although the reader knows that many persons charged with criminal offences are ultimately convicted, he or she is also aware that guilt or innocence is a question to be determined by a court.

> *Lang v. Australian Consolidated Press Ltd.*, [1970] 2 N.S.W.R. 408 (C.A.).
>
> *Lewis v. Daily Telegraph*, [1964] A.C. 234 (H.L. (Eng)).
>
> *Mirror Newspapers Ltd. v. Harrison* (1982), 149 C.L.R. 293 (H.C.A.).

Where the defamatory allegation is that the plaintiff committed a crime involving a corrupt agreement, the defendant may plead the conspiracy in pursuance of which the crime was committed.

> *Sommers v. Sturdy* (1956), 7 D.L.R. (2d) 30 (B.C.S.C.), aff'd (1957), 10 D.L.R. (2d) 269 (B.C.C.A.), leave to appeal to S.C.C. refused, [1957] S.C.R. x.

Where defamatory expression imputes guilt, a defendant may plead the plaintiff's conviction for the alleged misconduct. In certain provinces, the conviction will be conclusive proof the plaintiff committed the offence. In other provinces, a conviction constitutes *prima facie* proof. See Chapter 29, "The Defendant's Evidence," "Justification," "Criminal Conduct."

4) Negligence

Proof of negligence is not even a partial answer to a charge of dishonesty or deliberate misconduct.

> *Hodgson v. Canadian Newspapers Co.* [1998] 39 O.R. (3d) 235 (Gen. Div.), varied, (2000), 49 O.R. (3d) 161 (C.A.), leave to appeal to S.C.C. denied, [2000] S.C.C.A. No. 465.

5) Effect of an Apology

It is not beyond doubt that a defendant is unable to plead both apology and justification. The first decision must always be whether to apologize or not, and the practice is to do so where there is any doubt. If doing so was a bar to a later plea of justification, apologies would be fewer and this sort of litigation more frequent. That is a result to be avoided.

> *Dowding* v. *Pacific West Equities Ltd.* (1992), 63 B.C.L.R. (2d) 300 per Macdonald J. at paras. 19–20 (S.C.).

> See also *Camporese* v. *Parton* (1983), 150 D.L.R. (3d) 208 at 211 (B.C.S.C.) [defendant newspaper pleaded *inter alia* justification and mitigation of damages based on publication of apology for the alleged libel].

6) Rolled-up Plea

The "rolled-up" plea is only a plea of fair comment and does not raise a defence of justification. The rolled-up plea alleges that "in so far as the words consist of allegations of fact, they are true in substance and in fact, and in so far as they consist of expressions of opinion, they are fair comments made in good faith and without malice on a subject of public interest."

> *Boys* v. *Star Ptg. & Pub. Co.*, [1927] 3 D.L.R. 847 at 854–55 (Ont. C.A.).

> *Sutherland* v. *Stopes*, [1925] A.C. 47 at 62–63 (H.L. (Eng.)).

CHAPTER TWENTY-TWO:

Consent

A. DEFINITION

This defence is aptly described in Philip Lewis, *Gatley on Libel and Slander*, 8th ed. (London: Sweet & Maxwell, 1981) at paragraph 851:

> It is a defence to an action for defamation that the plaintiff consented to the publication of which he now complains by participating in or authorizing it. Thus, if the plaintiff has consented, expressly or impliedly or by conduct, to the publication of the words substantially as they were used, or to the findings of a tribunal in a specified newspaper, whatever the findings might be, there is a good defence to the action. But the proof of consent must be clear and unequivocal.

> See also, *Burnett* v. *Canadian Broadcasting Corporation (No. 2)* (1981), 48 N.S.R. (2d) 181, per Grant J. at paras. 159–62 (S.C.).

B. AN UNSUCCESSFUL DEFENCE

Peter F. Carter-Ruck & Harvey N.A. Starte, *Carter-Ruck on Libel and Slander*, 5th ed. (Butterworths: London, 1997) at 188:

> A man who provides a newspaper with false information about himself will not be able to sue that newspaper when it publishes the information. On the other hand the fact that in a lighter moment a man has told an anecdote against himself will not excuse a newspaper repeating that anecdote in its columns. [*Cook v. Ward* (1830), 6 Bing 409]. It is one thing to make oneself a laughing stock in an after-dinner speech; to be made to look ridiculous in a newspaper is quite a different matter. Because one consents to the former it does not follow that one has no objection to the latter.

A classic illustration of an unsuccessful defence of consent is *Moore* v. *News of the World*, [1972] 1 Q.B. 441, where the defendant newspaper interviewed the plaintiff ex-wife of Roger Moore (TV's "The Saint") and subsequently published a front page article "How Love Turned Sour by Dorothy Squires" and a page 10 article "How My Love For The Saint Went Sour by Dorothy Squires." The plaintiff Edna May Moore was known professionally as Dorothy Squires.

The matter at issue in *Moore* was described in the judgment of Lord Denning M.R. at pages 447–48:

> At the trial Dorothy Squires did not complain of any particular words in the first article itself. Her complaint was that people thought she had written it for money: and also that she was "washing her dirty linen" in public. These two complaints were put by the lawyers in the pleadings in the shape of what is called a "false innuendo." They alleged that:
>
>> "the said words ... by reason of the context in which they were published bore the natural and ordinary inferential meaning that the plaintiff was an embittered and unprincipled woman who had deliberately prepared and sold for a substantial sum of money a series of articles for publication in the said newspaper in a sensational form and manner revealing private and confidential details of her private life with the said Mr. Roger Moore."
>
> That allegation contains two distinct meanings. The first is that Dorothy Squires was a woman who was ready to "wash her dirty linen in public." The second is that she was a woman who would lend herself to articles like this for money.
>
> The "News of the World" said the first meaning was true. They sought to justify it. The second one they did not seek to justify. It is quite clear she did not give the interview for money. In addition to the defence of justification to the first meaning, they also pleaded that she assented.
>
> In the course of discussion in this court, it was recognized that the real question was whether Dorothy Squires consented expressly or impliedly or by her conduct to the publication of these words substantially as they were in the "News of the World." If she did, then the first meaning was also true; and also she assented to the publication.

The appeal was from a jury verdict in favour of Mrs. Moore, who had testified at trial that 90 percent of the article was not what she had told the *News of the World* reporter and that he must have gathered the information from someone else. The judge in his charge to the jury told them that the really important issue was whether the plaintiff had consented to the journalist publishing the information about her and her former husband [page 444].

Lord Denning M.R. found no error in the judge's charge, nor did Stephenson L.J. who stated at pages 452–53:

> ... The jury were entitled to believe the plaintiff and disbelieve the second defendant on the one crucial issue whether she consented to publication of the information contained in the article of April 20, 1969. Mr. Kempster [counsel for the newspaper] has failed to persuade me that there was any material misdirection of fact or law in a full and fair summing up.

Moore suggests the obvious: a journalist armed with a tape recorder or video-recorder may be better prepared to raise of defence of consent than a journalist armed with a note-book and a pen, at least with respect to proving that the plaintiff actually said the words attributed to her. That will still leave open, of course, the question whether the plaintiff consented to publication of the information conveyed to the reporter.

Similarly, in *Burnett v. Canadian Broadcasting Corporation (No. 2)* (1981), 48 N.S.R. (2d) 181, the Nova Scotia Supreme Court Trial Division rejected a defence of consent based primarily on a letter received by the CBC from the plaintiff's solicitors which stated in part "We have no objection to C.B.C. personnel conducting interviews or investigations to gather information with respect to [the plaintiff]." Grant J. held [at para. 170] that in all the circumstances, the plaintiff "had every right to anticipate that the interviews would be conducted within the framework of the law, including the law of defamation."

C. A SUCCESSFUL DEFENCE

A plaintiff has been held to consent to publication of defamatory matter when, fully aware of the defamatory topic to be discussed on a radio program, and that the defamatory matter would be repeated during that conversation and therefore published to the listening audience, he agreed to appear on the radio program for the purpose of denying the truth of the defamatory matter.

Syms v. Warren (1976), 71 D.L.R. (3d) 558 (Man. Q.B.) per Hamilton J.

See also *Burnett v. Canadian Broadcasting Corporation (No. 2)* (1981), 48 N.S.R. (2d) 181 per Grant J. at paras. 165–72 (S.C.).

D. SCOPE OF APPLICATION

Consent will be narrowly construed. Initial assent will not necessarily imply a consent to any and all subsequent discussion of defamatory material.

> Consent is a narrow defence to defamation, one not often seen and one where the consent must be clearly established. Consent must be given or able to be inferred with respect to each publication of defamatory material.
>
> *Syms v. Warren*, above, at 562–63.

An application by newspaper defendants to strike a statement of claim on the ground of consent was dismissed where the court was not satisfied that the plaintiffs' consent to being interviewed on a national television program owned and operated by a different company constituted consent to subsequent publication of a defamatory newspaper article by the defendant newspaper.

> *Butler v. Southam Inc.*, [2002] N.S.J. No. 505, per Scanlan J. at paras. 13–17 (N.S.S.C.), aff'd (2002), 210 N.S.R. (2d) 210, 2002 NSCA 149.

E. RELATED ISSUES

1) Failure to Sue Is Not Consent

A plaintiff will not be held to consent to publication of defamatory expression merely because he or she does not sue when the defendant's course of defamatory conduct begins. It is not necessary for a plaintiff to commence legal proceedings to demonstrate a lack of consent to defamatory expression. Nor is it reasonable to infer consent from the mere absence of a lawsuit.

> *Amalgamated Transit Union v. Independent Canadian Transit Union*, [1997] 5 W.W.R. 662 per Lutz J. at paras. 113, 117 (Alta. Q.B.).

2) Initial Publication by Plaintiff

Initially placing the words into circulation does not necessarily constitute consent to their further publication. It would be particularly unreasonable to infer consent or waiver after a plaintiff expressed opposition to the defendant's statements.

> *Amalgamated Transit Union v. Independent Canadian Transit Union*, ibid.

If the plaintiffs publish certain statements about themselves that are later repeated by the defendants, the statements will nevertheless be actionable if the plaintiffs published the statements under circumstances where the audience would understand them in an innocent sense but the recipients of the defendants' expression would not.

> *Amalgamated Transit Union* v. *Independent Canadian Transit Union, ibid.*, at para. 115.

3) Consent by a Corporation

Whether or not a corporate plaintiff put the defamatory expression into circulation will turn on whether the alleged corporate spokesperson was in fact speaking for the plaintiff at the time.

> *Amalgamated Transit Union* v. *Independent Canadian Transit Union, ibid.*, at para. 116.

4) Disciplinary Proceedings

It has been held that where an employee accepts a disciplinary code as part of a contract of employment, he or she thereby consents to the republication of the accusation or complaint as part of that process, otherwise there is no way in which the truth or falsity of the accusation or complaint can be fairly established.

> *Friend* v. *Civil Aviation Authority*, [1998] E.W.J. No. 87 at para. 43 (C.A. (Eng.)). Hirst L.J. for the Court of Appeal explained the leading case on consent in this context:
>
> > ¶36 So far as the authorities are concerned, Mr. Moloney drew our attention to the universal recognition in the text books of the applicability of the principle of *volenti*, or leave and licence, in the defamation context (see *Clerk and Lindsell* 17th Edn. paragraph 3.23, *Gatley* 9th Edn. paragraph 18/17, *Duncan and Neill* 2nd Edn. paragraph 16.01). The *locus classicus* on the topic, cited in all three textbooks, is the judgment of Slesser L.J. in *Chapman* v. *Ellesmere* [1932] 2 KB 431 at page 463–65.
> >
> > ¶37 In that case the plaintiff was the trainer of a racehorse which ran in a race at a meeting held under the Jockey Club rules. After the race the acting stewards of the meeting ordered an examination of the horse, and on receiving a report of that examination they referred the matter to the Stewards of the Jockey Club who held an inquiry, the outcome of which was reported inter alia in the Racing Calendar, stating that after further investigation the Stewards were satisfied that a drug

had been administered to the horse for the purpose of the race in question. One of the many defences maintained by the defendant was that the publication of the Stewards' decision in the Racing Calendar had been assented to by the plaintiff, with the consequence that the principle of *volenti* applied, so that no claim for damages in respect of that publication would lie.

¶38 This submission was upheld by Slesser L.J., who, having analysed the principles, held that the plaintiff must fail in respect of the publication in the Racing Calendar by reason of his assent thereto, pursuant to Rule 17 of the rules of racing....

¶39 Romer L.J. briefly expressed a similar view at page 474, and the conclusion was also in line with a similar Court of Appeal decision in *Cookson* v. *Harewood* which is reported as a note to *Chapman* v. *Ellesmere* at [1932] 2 KB 478. (see per Scrutton L.J. at p. 482 and per Greer L.J. at p. 485).

F. PROVOKING OR PROCURING DEFAMATORY EXPRESSION

In certain circumstances, it has been held that if publication of the defamatory expression was "brought about by the plaintiff's own contrivance, the action must fail."

> *Rudd* v. *Cameron* (1912), 4 D.L.R. 567 (Ont. Div. Ct.), aff'd (1912), 8 D.L.R. 662, per Meredith C.J. at 4 D.L.R. 573, citing William Blake Odgers, *Odgers on Libel and Slander*, 5th ed. (London: Stevens, 1912) at 179.

A plaintiff is not to be allowed to entrap people into making statements to him on which he can take proceedings.

> If the only publication that can be proved is one made by the defendant in answer to an application from the plaintiff, or some agent of the plaintiff, demanding explanation, such answer, if fair and relevant, will be held *privileged*, for the plaintiff brought it upon himself.

> *Rudd* v. *Cameron, ibid.* at 574.

If the plaintiff engages a private investigator to determine whether the defendant is publishing defamatory expression, the availability of a defence of consent concerning defamatory expression published to the investigator is not clear.

It has been held that if defamatory rumours are circulating, which the plaintiff seeks to trace to their source, all defamatory statements made by the defendant to the plaintiff's agent (typically a private investigator) in the course of their investigation are "protected by the privilege."

Rudd v. Cameron, ibid. at 574.

On the other hand, if the plaintiff is able to demonstrate that the defamatory rumours originated with the defendant, so that what the defendant himself previously said resulted in the plaintiff's inquiry, and the defendant repeats the words in the presence of a third person, stating his belief in the accusation, the defence of consent will not apply.

Rudd v. Cameron, ibid. at 574, citing *Griffiths v. Lewis,* 7 Q.B. 61, 14 L.J.Q.B. 199.

From the plaintiff's perspective, it is therefore important for the investigator to obtain an admission from the defendant that he or she published the defamatory allegations on previous occasions. If in answer to the plaintiff's inquiry, the defendant acknowledges uttering the defamatory expression on a previous occasion, the plaintiff may use the acknowledgement as proof of the earlier defamation and sue over the earlier publication.

Rudd v. Cameron, ibid.

The defence of consent in a defamation context has been sometimes cited in the older jurisprudence as "privilege" and sometimes as an instance of the maxim *volenti non fit injuria.*

Rudd v. Cameron, ibid., citing Lord Ellenborough in *Smith v. Wood,* 3 Camp. 323; *Duke of Brunswick v. Harmer,* 14 Q.B. 185; *Warr v. Jolly,* 6 Car. & P. 497; *Griffins v. Lewis,* 7 Q.B. 67, 14 L.J.Q.B. 199, 9 Jut. 370; *Richards v. Richards,* 2 Moo. & Rob. 557.

Rudd v. Cameron was not discussed in a reported Canadian case until 1974, when the question of consent in the context of statements made to private detectives employed by the plaintiff came before the Saskatchewan Court of Queens Bench in *Jones v. Brooks* (1974), 45 D.L.R. (3d) 413.

In *Jones v. Brooks,* where the plaintiff lawyer sued the defendant mayor for slander, MacPherson J. described the genisis of the defamatory expression as follows at pages 417–18:

As 1971 progressed, the plaintiff observed that his practice at Hudson Bay was falling off dramatically. His earnings there were down by two-thirds. He heard rumors of what was being said about him and in April he consulted solicitors and soon afterwards instructed private detectives, Flaman from Saskatoon and Poley from Winnipeg. These two went to Hudson Bay independently. Each was equipped with a hidden tape recorder. Flaman interviewed Brooks and Bracken but did not tape Bracken. Poley interviewed Kondra and Brooks and taped both. ...

Each detective had a cover story. He was investigating the plaintiff on behalf of national corporations who proposed to invest in West Bay, that the inquiry was confidential and the source would not be reported to anyone. In his interview with Flaman, Brooks said of the plaintiff that he was unethical, that he had no character, that he was a shyster, that he had no scruples. To Poley, Brooks referred to the plaintiff as a crooked son-of-a-bitch and as a real shyster.

MacPherson J. accepted that the defendants said the defamatory words recorded on the tapes but noted at page 418 that much of what was said of a defamatory nature by Brooks and Kondra to the detectives was provoked and cajoled and indeed invited by the words and manner of the detectives, particularly Poley.

After reviewing the authorities including *Rudd* v. *Cameron*, McPherson J. [at page 419] approved and applied *Teichner* v. *Bellan*, 181 N.Y.S. 2d 842 (N.Y. App. Div, 1959), a decision of the Appellate Division of the Supreme Court of the State of New York, where Justice Halpern for the Court of five said at pages 845–46:

> There are decisions in some States that a communication of defamatory matter to an agent of the person defamed in response to an inquiry does not constitute a publication to a third person ...
>
> But the better view seems to us to be that taken in another line of cases, holding that the communication to the plaintiff's agent is a publication, even though the plaintiff's action may ultimately be defeated for other reasons. The agent is, in fact, a different entity from the principal; the communication to the agent is, in fact, a publication to a third person ...
>
> Consent is a bar to a recovery for defamation under the general principle of *volenti non fit injuria* or, as it is sometimes put, the plaintiff's consent to the publication of the defamation confers an absolute immunity or an absolute privilege upon the defendant ... . However, a plaintiff who had authorized an agent to make an inquiry on his behalf is not to be charged with consent to a defamatory statement made in reply to the inquiry, unless he had reason to anticipate that the response might be a defamatory one ... . Only in such a case can it be said that he had impliedly agreed to assume the risk of a defamatory communication to his agent ...

Applying *Teichner*, McPherson J. held that what the defendants said to the detectives constituted publication to third parties notwithstanding that the detectives were agents for the plaintiff. Arriving at his conclusion that the statements were not actionable, however, McPherson J. stated at page 420:

> Unquestionably the plaintiff knew when he dispatched the detectives that he had been defamed. The plaintiff testified that he instructed Flaman to learn the nature of the statements Brooks was making about him. Flaman said that the plaintiff felt he was being slandered and he was to find out what was being said. Poley said that his purpose was "to check out the slanders." When the plaintiff instructed Poley the plaintiff knew what Brooks had said to Flaman. ...
>
> The plaintiff therefore had good reason when he sent his detectives to anticipate that the response by the defendants to the inquiries might be defamatory.
>
> This is the very essence of *volenti non fit injuria* — the knowing consent of the plaintiff to the defendant's wrong which the plaintiff expected.

To the same effect, where a plaintiff asked her union to inquire why the defendant had not hired her, it was held the plaintiff's action for defamation based on the defendant's response was barred by the defence of consent and by the defence of privilege. On her examination for discovery in the libel action, the plaintiff stated that she expected some negative and ill-founded comments about herself.

Hanly v. Pisces Productions Inc., [1981] 1 W.W.R. 369 at 376–79 (B.C.S.C.).

CHAPTER TWENTY-THREE:
Pleadings

A. VITAL IMPORTANCE

Pleadings are of vital importance in a defamation action and should be prepared with great care and scrutinized closely. A century of jurisprudence is replete with observations about the special role of defamation pleadings. Examples include:

Lieberman J.A. in *Lougheed* v. *Canadian Broadcasting Corporation* (1979), 98 D.L.R. (3d) 264 at 273 (Alta. S.C. (A.D.)):

The pleadings in defamation are of extreme importance.

Cunningham J. in *Leenen* v. *Canadian Broadcasting Corp.*, [2000] O.T.C. 672 at para. 2 (S.C.J.), affirmed (2001), 147 O.A.C. 317 (C.A.), leave to appeal refused, [2001] S.C.C.A. No. 432:

The prosecution of a television libel action is, in my view, especially difficult given the voluminous material involved in the production of a single one hour program ... but the pleadings in such an action, unlike so many other actions, are more than a simple road map; they are the essence of the claim and must be prepared with precision and diligence.

William Blake Odgers, *Odgers on Libel and Slander*, 6th ed. (London: Stevens, 1929):

The pleadings in an action of libel or slander are more important, perhaps, than in any other class of actions usually brought in the King's Bench Division.

Riddell J. in *Foster* v. *Maclean* (1916) 37 O.L.R. 68 at 76 (C.A.):

I confess to great sympathy with a solicitor called upon to draw a statement of defence in a libel action — in the general debacle of pleadings, this remains an action in which it is not safe to treat pleadings as a mere exercise in English composition for the junior articled clerk and the typist; there is still some art in libel pleadings.

Scarth J. in *Finnamore v. Sun Publishing Company* (1993), 77 B.C.L.R. (2d) 293 at 298 (S.C.):

> The action is clearly not a labour relations proceeding; it is a libel action. And although the tendency of the Courts in England has been to apply the ordinary rules of pleading to libel actions: see *Lucas-Box v. News Group Newspapers Ltd.*, [1986] 1 All E.R. 177, at 181, where Ackner L.J. (as he then was) states:
>
> > Although to some it may be seen as a startling observation, we can see no reason why libel litigation should be immune from ordinary pleading rules.
>
> Courts in Canada continue to take what has been characterized in the cases as the "classic approach" to libel pleadings and to apply long recognized principles of defamation law: *Turner v. Toronto Sun Publishing Corp.* (1990), 5 C.C.L.T. (2d) 184 (Ont H.C.J.); *Loos v. The Leader-Post Limited* (1982), 26 C.P.C. 30 (Sask. C.A.).

Master McCallum in *Meyer v. Chouhan*, [2001] B.C.J. No. 2218 (S.C.), 2001 BCSC 1446 at para. 7:

> Defamation proceedings are technical in nature and "pleading-dependent."

Hodgins J.A. in *Govenlock v. London Free Press* (1915), 35 O.L.R. 79 at 83 (C.A.):

> The pleadings in a libel action must define the issue which is being tried. Justification means one thing, and one thing only: i.e., that the libel is true as printed. If the parties can shift their ground during the trial, and evidence can be given, not under the limitations imposed by such a plea, upon the theory that the pleadings do not bind the parties, utter confusion may be caused and a general verdict one way or the other may mean a mistrial. Examples of this may be found in many cases. See *Brown v. Moyer* (1893), 20 O.R. 509; *Manitoba Free Press Co. v. Martin* (1892), 21 S.C.R. 518; *Jackes v. Mail Printing Co.* (1915), 7 O.W.N. 677.
>
> The defendant upon such a plea is limited to proving the truth of his assertion, and ought not to be allowed, to the prejudice of the

plaintiff, to adduce evidence which may raise a totally different issue. The right to amend is one thing, but the binding effect of an admission or a plea in a libel action should not be frittered away.

Dubin J.A. in *Littleton* v. *Hamilton* (1974), 4 O.R. (2d) 283 (C.A.), leave to appeal to S.C.C. denied (1974), 4 O.R. (2d) 283n (S.C.C.):

> I pause to observe that the defence of fair comment was not pleaded, and it has been said many times in actions of libel the parties are bound by their pleadings and careful regard must be given to the pleadings before matters are left for the consideration of the jury.

Deficiencies in defamation pleadings may provoke severe judicial criticism. For example:

Southin J.A. in *Baumann* v. *Turner* (1993), 82 B.C.L.R. (2d) 362 at 364 (C.A.):

> Not the least of the problems in this appeal is that the pleadings are incomplete, the appellant not having delivered a reply, although he relies on express malice to defeat a defence of publication on occasions of privilege. ...
>
> Lest I be thought unduly harsh to the appellant, I say that the statement of defence also leaves a good deal to be desired. ... The learned trial judge could not have been faulted had he refused to hear a case so ill pleaded.

Southin J.A. in *Brown* v. *Cole* (1998), 61 B.C.L.R. (3d) 1 at 9 (C.A.):

> Counsel for the respondent, in drafting the statement of claim in this action, might better have followed the time-honoured pleas to be found in *Gatley on Libel and Slander*, rather than inventing his own ... [h]ad this case been tried with a jury, and had the trial judge permitted, over the objection of the defendants, the case to go to the jury on this statement of claim, the court might well have found, unless the jury had been required to deliver a lengthy special verdict, the trial unsatisfactory.

In a recent case, a court held that a statement of claim was so deficient it could not even support an assessment of defamation damages after the plaintiff obtained judgment in default of defence. Of his own motion, McEwan J. set aside the default judgment, referring to the pleadings as "gibberish."

Poznekoff v. *Binning* (1998), 19 C.P.C. (4th) 347, per McEwen J. at 351 (B.C.S.C.), varied, 2000 BCCA 155.

This chapter cannot address every nuance of the rules of court in force in the nine common law provinces and three northern territories as they relate to the content of defamation pleadings. Further, the content of defamation pleadings is influenced to some extent by the defamation statutes in each jurisdiction, which also vary. Accordingly, when considering the application to one province of jurisprudence decided in another jurisdiction, careful attention should be given to differences in the wording of the relevant rules or statutes.

See Chapter 26, "Discovery of Documents," section A, "Rules of Court" for citations to the provincial rules of court, and Chapter 6, "Notice of Intended Action and Limitation Defences," at 62, for citations to the provincial and territorial defamation statutes.

1) Statement of Material Facts, not Evidence

It is a basic principle of practice found in the rules of court of most provinces that a pleading should contain only a statement in summary form of the material facts on which a party relies for her claim or defence, but not the evidence by which those facts are to be proved.

The application of this basic principle in a defamation context is supplemented by the principle that a court may order a party to provide particulars of her pleading to clarify the issues, so that the opposite party may be able to prepare for trial, by examination for discovery and otherwise, and to facilitate the trial.

Scammel v. *Koessler*, [1994] B.C.J. No. 2013, per Master Bishop at para. 22 (S.C.).

London College v. *Sun Media*, [1999] O.J. No. 3133, per Master Haberman at para. 10 (S.C.).

B. THE STATEMENT OF CLAIM

Generally, the statement of claim in a defamation action should plead the following:

- the precise contents of the expression complained of;
- any natural and ordinary meaning (popular innuendo) attributed to that expression;
- if the expression is innocent on its face, or has some special meaning, the extrinsic facts and circumstances which give it a defamatory sting (legal innuendo);
- an allegation that the expression was of and concerning the plaintiff;

- an allegation that the expression was published;
- if applicable, an allegation of republication for which the defendant is responsible;
- the identity of the defendant who published the allegedly defamatory expression;
- if applicable, the circumstances making a defendant vicariously liable for a defamatory publication by another person (such as an employee);
- the date, time, and place of publication;
- the medium of publication (such as a letter, an oral statement, or a television broadcast);
- if slander is alleged, whether it is actionable *per se;*
- if slander is alleged, and is not actionable *per se*, an allegation that the plaintiff has suffered special damages, and particulars of such special damages (except in provinces where the defamation statute makes this unnecessary);
- the identity of the persons (other than the plaintiff) to whom the defamatory expression was published;
- a claim for general damages;
- if applicable, a claim for aggravated damages and particulars supporting it, including particulars of malice;
- if applicable, a claim for punitive damages and particulars supporting it, including particulars of malice;
- if applicable, a claim for special damages;
- if applicable, a claim for an interlocutory and/or permanent injunction
- a claim for costs on an appropriate scale;
- a claim for pre-judgment and/or post-judgment interest;
- any other material facts;
- any other special relief.

The authorities relating to the elements of a defamation statement of claim are discussed below.

1) The Precise Contents of the Expression Complained Of

a) Oral or Written Words

The general rule is that the statement of claim must set out verbatim the precise words published by the defendant of which the plaintiff complains. This fundamental requirement applies to both libel and slander. The words alleged to be defamatory are material facts.

Hay v. *Bingham* (1902), 5 O.L.R. 224 at 226 (K.B.) per Falconbridge C.J.:

> ... in an action of defamation ... the very words complained of must
> be set out by the plaintiff "in order that the Court may judge whether
> they constitute a cause of action": *Wright* v. *Clements* (1820), 3 B. &
> Ald. 503, at 506

Berry v. *Retail Merchant's Ass'n.*, [1924] 2 D.L.R. 916, per Haultain C.J.S. at
916 (Sask. C.A.), citing *Harris* v. *Warre* (1879), 4 C.P.D. 125, 48 L.J.C.P. 310.

Shannon v. *King*, [1931] 4 D.L.R. 438, per Macdonald C.J.B.C. at 439 (B.C.C.A.):

> The law of libel and slander is definitely settled, that the libelous and
> slanderous words must be set out, and that practice has existed for a
> long time.

Paquette v. *Cruji* (1979), 26 O.R. (2d) 294, per Grange J. at 296 (H.C.J.).

> It is true and has been said over and over again — see, for example,
> *Odgers' Digest of the Law of Libel and Slander*, 6th ed. (1929), at p. 504,
> that pleadings in a defamation action are more important than in any
> other class of action. It is also generally true as put by *Gatley on Libel
> and Slander*, 7th ed. (1974), p. 422, para. 1015, that "... the defendant
> is entitled to particulars of the date or dates on which, and of the per-
> son or persons to whom the slander was uttered ...," and that the
> Court will not permit the plaintiff to proceed to use discovery as a
> "fishing expedition" to seek out a cause of action: see *Gaskin* v. *Retail
> Credit Co.*, [1916] O.W.N. 171; *Collins* v. *Jones*, [1955] 2 All E.R. 145.
> There are, however, limitations to the strictness of pleading. Our
> Courts have always refused to strike out a claim where the plaintiff has
> revealed all the particulars in his possession and has set forth a prima
> facie case in his pleading: see *Winnett* v. *Appelbe et ux.* (1894), 16 P.R.
> (Ont.) 57 and *Lynford* v. *United States Cigar Stores Ltd.* (1917), 12
> O.W.N. 68. In the latter case Falconbridge, C.J.K.B., refused to strike
> out a statement of claim wherein the plaintiff had been unable to set
> forth the exact words of an allegedly defamatory letter which had
> resulted in the loss of employment, quoting with approval [at p. 69]
> the words of *Odgers*, 5th ed. (1912), at p. 624:
>
> > If the plaintiff does not know the exact words uttered, and can-
> > not obtain leave to interrogate before the statement of claim, he
> > must draft his pleading as best he can and subsequently apply
> > for leave to administer interrogatories, and, after obtaining
> > answers, amend his statement of claim, if necessary.

Pennington v. *Smith* (1980), 16 C.P.C. 151, per Master Donkin at 154 (Ont. S.C. (Mast.)).

Olsen v. *St. Martin* (1981), 32 A.R. 51, per Master Funduk at 53 (Q.B.):

> ... Defamation actions are one of the few forms of action where strictness in pleading is still insisted on. In a slander action the exact words uttered are a material fact, and accordingly, the exact words alleged to have been uttered must be pleaded. It is the utterance of the words which gives rise to the action. In the present action the words allegedly uttered, to be actionable, must impute to the plaintiff the commission of a criminal offence. Whether any words uttered do make such an imputation is a conclusion, which conclusion is for the trier of fact to decide. The opinion of the plaintiff that any words uttered by the defendant imputed to the plaintiff the commission of a criminal offence is irrelevant.

Shinkaruk v. *Saskatoon (City)* (1985), 41 Sask R. 187, per Noble J. at para. 8 (Q.B.).

Canmar Grain Inc. v. *Ferguson* (1986) 16 C.P.C. (2d) 169, per Barclay J. at 173–74 (Sask. Q.B.), citing *The Capital & Countries Bank Limited* v. *George Henty & Sons* (1882), 7 A.C. 741 at 771 (H.L.) and *Collins* v. *Jones* (1955), Q.B.D. 564, where Denning L.J. states at 571:

> In a libel action it is essential to know the very words on which the plaintiff founds his claim. As Lord Coleridge C.J. said in *Harris* v. *Warre* (1879), 4 C.P.D. 12 Sat 128:
>
> > In libel and slander everything may turn on the form of words, and in olden days plaintiffs constantly failed from small and even unimportant variance between the words of the libel or slander set out in the declaration and the proof of them ...In libel and slander the very words complained of are the facts on which the action is grounded. It is not the fact of the defendant having used defamatory expressions, but the fact of his having used the defamatory expressions alleged, which is the fact on which the case depends.

Pylot v. *Cariou* (1987), 60 Sask. R. 116, per Hrabinksy J. at 122 (Q.B.).

Mergen v. *Berrns* (1988), 71 Sask. R. 93, per Gerien J. at 95 (Q.B.).

Moss v. *Boisvert* (1990), 74 Alta. L.R. (2d) 344 per Master Funduk at 349 (Q.B.).

MacKay v. *Stomp*, [1992] 5 W.W.R. 475, per Dielschneider J. at 478 (Sask. Q.B.).

Voutsinos v. New Brunswick (Research and Productivity Council) (1993), 136 N.B.R. (2d) 364 (Q.B. (T.D.)).

Rosen v. Alberta Motor Assn. Insurance Co., [1994] 1 W.W.R. 719, per Fruman J. at 722 (Alta. Q.B.).

Chaput v. Finley, [1995] N.W.T.J. No. 83, per Schuler J. at para. 8 (N.W.T.S.C.).

Pootlass v. Pootlass (1999), 63 B.C.L.R. (3d) 305 per Burnyeat J. at 319 (S.C.):

> "It is clear that the actual words complained of must be set out verbatim so that the defendant will know with certainty the words which are alleged to be defamatory," citing, *inter alia, Cook v. Cox* (1814), 3 M. & S. 110, 105 E.R. 552 (K.B.); *Pirie v. Carroll* (1931), 4 M.P.R. 127 (N.B.C.A.); *MacKay v. Stomp*, [1992] 5 W.W.R. 475 (Sask.Q.B.); *Barkhouse v. Steele* (1995), 142 N.S.R. (2d) 397 (C.A.); *Masunda v. Johnson*, New Westminster Registry No. S020697, [1995] B.C.J. No. 182 (S.C. (Mast.)); *Rosen v. Alberta Motor Assn. Insurance Co.*, [1994] 1 W.W.R. 719 (Alta. Q.B.); *Voutsinos v. New Brunswick (Research & Productivity Council)* (1993), 136 N.B.R. (2d) 364 (Q.B. (T.D.)).

Chopra v. T. Eaton Co., [1999] A.J. No. 277, per Brooker J. at paras. 202–5 (Q.B.).

Jackson v. Canada (Customs and Revenue Agency), 2001 SKQB 377, per McIntyre J. at para. 26.

MacRae v. Santa, [2002] O.J. No. 3000, per Pierce J. at para. 15 (S.C.J.).

Lawrence v. Wallace (2002), 203 N.S.R. (2d) 197, per Cromwall J.A. at paras. 6–8 (C.A.).

b) Words to the Effect

It is not sufficient for a statement of claim to allege that the defendant published words to a certain "effect" or that the defendant published words which were "calculated to mean" something or to "convey a certain impression."

Berry v. Retail Merchant's Ass'n., [1924] 2 D.L.R. 916, per Haultain C.J.S. at 916 (Sask. C.A.).

Pylot v. Cariou (1987), 60 Sask. R. 116 (Q.B.) per Hrabinksy J. [striking counterclaim allegation that the defendant "slandered (the Plaintiff by Counterclaim) by making statements to third parties to the effect that the Plaintiff by Counterclaim was acting illegally, fraudulently, unlawfully and maliciously and such further statements as are within the knowledge of Olga Pylot will become known upon discovery."]

Voutsinos v. New Brunswick (Research and Productivity Council), above, at para. 11.

Rosen v. Alberta Motor Assn. Insurance Co., above, at 722:

> The defamatory statements are said to be words to the effect that the Plaintiffs are liars, arsonists, have committed perjury, have committed arson, have attempted to defraud, are poor risks … . It is defamatory words which are to be pleaded. The inferences from the words are to be made as conclusions by the trier of fact.

M.J.S. v. W.M., [1996] A.J. No. 981 per Andrekson J. at para. 25 (Q.B.) [striking the phrase "or words to that effect"].

Symons v. Toronto Dominion Bank, [1997] 9 W.W.R. 132, per Gunn J. at 137 (Sask. Q.B.):

> In the case at bar, Mr. Symons has failed to plead the precise words said to constitute the "character assassination." At best, Mr. Symons' claim alleges that the bank manager said words to the effect that no financial institution would want him as a client. On either line of authority cited above, this would not assert a reasonable cause of action.

c) Substance or Purport

It is not sufficient for the statement of claim to simply set out the "substance" or the "purport" of allegedly defamatory expression.

Davis v. Côté (2000), 157 Man. R. (2d) 1 (Q.B.), per Master Sharp at para. 16, citing *Bullen & Leake & Jacob's Precedents of Pleading*, 13th ed. (London: Sweet & Maxwell, 1990) at 623.

B.E. v. J.E.M. (1995), 133 Sask. R. 175 (Q.B.) per MacLeod J., approving *Canadian Encyclopedic Digest*, West. 3d ed., Vol. 11A, title 47, para. 220.

d) Conclusions

A statement of claim is not sufficient if it merely pleads a general conclusion that the plaintiff has been defamed.

Lougheed v. Canadian Broadcasting Corporation (1978), 86 D.L.R. (3d) 229, per Millar J. at 245 (Alta. Q.B.), varied (1979), 98 D.L.R. (3d) 264 (Alta. S.C. (A.D.)).

e) Paraphrasing

Pleadings which constitute only paraphrasings (not an exact replication) of a broadcast are insufficient.

> *Raho* v. *Craig Broadcasting Systems Inc.* (1999), 141 Man. R. (2d) 288, per Master Sharp at paras. 16–18 (Q.B.).

f) Fishing Expeditions

A plaintiff is not entitled to commence a defamation lawsuit without knowing whether or not the defendant has published any defamatory words or what the nature of those words might be. Such a lawsuit will be considered an unlawful "fishing expedition" or "action for discovery," constitutes an abuse of process and will be struck out.

> *Bremer* v. *Barrett* (1975), 59 DLR (3d) 618, per Meredith J. at 619 (B.C.S.C.), citing *Somers* v. *Kingsbury*, [1924] 2 D.L.R. 195, (1923), 54 O.L.R. 166 (C.A.).

> *Paquette* v. *Cruji* (1979), 26 O.R. (2d) 294, per Grange J. at 296 (H.C.J.):

> > … the Court will not permit the plaintiff to proceed to use discovery as a "fishing expedition" to seek out a cause of action: see *Gaskin* v. *Retail Credit Co.*, [1916] O.W.N. 171; *Collins* v. *Jones*, [1955] 2 All E.R. 145.

> *Rosen* v. *Alberta Motor Assn. Insurance Co.*, above, at paras. 16 and 17:

> > ¶16 … I agree that the law must be fluid and must change and adapt to the times. However, I find the policy reasons behind the requirement for specificity in defamation pleadings to be sound. I think it would be a sad day if an individual who felt that another person had said something unflattering about him could issue a Statement of Claim and thereby commence a fishing expedition, placing the onus on the Defendant to disgorge all that might have been said.

> > ¶17 I am also mindful of the Plaintiff's problems in confronting as intimidating an opponent as the insurance industry. I think I would have been willing to go some way to ease their burden if there had been something in the pleadings that indicated to me that the Plaintiffs were acting in good faith, were not on a fishing expedition and that the defamatory words had actually been published. I might have been prepared to relax the strict rules if a summary of the words had been specified with an indication of the dates or times or people by and to whom the communications were made. However, the Amended Statement of claim provides no specifics and deals only with inferences. I therefore

allow the motion to strike out the Statement of Claim as against the Insurance Crime Prevention Bureau.

If the actual words alleged to constitute the libel or slander are not pleaded, the court may order the defamation claim struck out or may order that it be amended to include the words actually written or spoken.

Bulkley Nechako Cable Vision Ltd. v. CKPO Television Limited (1982), 37 B.C.L.R. 23, per Hardinge L.J.S.C. at 27 (S.C.).

Lapointe v. Summach, [1999] B.C.J. No. 1459, per Master Bishop at para. 58 (S.C.).

Frost v. Fox Insurance Brokers Ltd. (c.o.b. Demara Insurance Brokers), [1999] B.C.J. No. 2562 per Master Bishop at para. 11 (S.C.), varied on other grounds [2000] B.C.J. No. 176, per Drossos J. (S.C.).

2) Deferral of Pleading the Precise Defamatory Words

a) Traditional Solution

In a case of slander, if the exact words are not known to the plaintiff at the time legal process is issued, older authority suggests that the plaintiff should plead some words verbatim, allege those words to be the precise words uttered, and then conduct discovery to determine the actual words uttered.

Berry v. Retail Merchant's Ass'n., [1924] 2 D.L.R. 916, per Haultain C.J.S. at 918 (Sask. C.A.), interpreting William Blake Odgers, *Odgers on Libel and Slander*, 5th ed. (London: Stevens, 1912) at 623–24.

b) Special Circumstances

It has been held in Ontario that in a limited set of circumstances the court may permit a plaintiff to proceed with a defamation action without pleading the precise words allegedly published by the defendant.

To obtain this special permission, which only defers (but does not remove) the obligation to plead the precise words complained of, the plaintiff must show:

a) that he has pleaded all of the particulars available to him with the exercise of reasonable diligence;

b) that he is proceeding in good faith with a *prima facie* case and is not on a fishing expedition; normally this will require at least the pleading of a coherent body of fact surrounding the incident such as time, place, speaker and audience;

c) that the coherent body of fact of which he does have knowledge shows not only that there was an utterance or a writing emanating from the defendant, but also that the emanation contained defamatory material of a defined character of and concerning the plaintiff;

d) that the exact words are not in his knowledge but are known to the defendants and will become available to be pleaded by discovery of the defendant, production of a document, or by other defined means, pending which the plaintiff has pleaded words consistent with the information then at his disposal.

> *Magnotta Winery Limited* v. *Ziraldo* (1995), 25 O.R. (3d) 375, per D. Lane J. at 583–84 (Gen. Div.).

Saskatchewan courts have approved the approach prescribed in *Magnotta, ibid.*

> *Duke* v. *Puts*, [1998] 6 W.W.R. 510, per Zarzeczny J. at 515 (Sask. Q.B.).

> *R.E.L.* v. *J.G.* (2000), 191 Sask. R. 204 (Q.B.) per Barclay J.

If a defective defamation claim does not plead "a coherent body of fact surrounding the incident such as time, place, speaker, and audience," a court may nevertheless decline to strike the pleading and instead order the plaintiff to provide further and better particulars which satisfy the *Magnotta* conditions.

> *Hausman* v. *Molson Canada*, [2000] O.J. No. 4451, per Cullity J. at para. 36 (S.C.J.).

It has been suggested by a British Columbia court that the obligation to plead the precise words may be deferred in special circumstances where the plaintiff "does not know and has no means of ascertaining the exact terms of the allegedly defamatory words except by extracting them from the defendant." In such circumstances, the court may allow the plaintiff to serve interrogatories or to examine the defendant for discovery. The plaintiff must subsequently amend the statement of claim to plead the exact words based on the information obtained through such discovery. In the interim pending discovery, the plaintiff must set out in the statement of claim as nearly as possible the defamatory words allegedly published by the defendant.

> *Bulkley Nechako Cable Vision Ltd.* v. *CKPO Television Limited,* above, at 25–26.

In order to qualify for such a deferral, the plaintiff must show that the particulars of the precise words are beyond the reach of the plaintiff except through the defendant.

Bulkley Nechako Cable Vision Ltd. v. *CKPO Television Limited*, above, at 26, citing *Wall* v. *Lalonde* (1974), 7 O.R. (2d) 129, per Vannini L.J.S.C. at 133 (H.C.J.).

Where the plaintiff did not merely have a suspicion that he had been slandered but had in fact been told by the defendant that he was going to defame the plaintiff, a British Columbia court held that the plaintiff's defamation lawsuit was not merely a "fishing expedition." The court also held that it would be unrealistic to require the plaintiff to make inquiries among representatives of the industry in which the plaintiff worked to determine the precise words. The court therefore refused to strike out the statement of claim, stating that the plaintiff had revealed all the particulars in his possession and had set forth a *prima facie* case.

Richardson v. *Norton Lilly International (Canada) Ltd.*, [1993] B.C.J. No. 1890 (S.C.) per Allan J., citing *Paquette* v. *Cruji* (1979), 26 O.R. (2d) 294 (H.C.J.).

See also, *Benson* v. *Versa Services Ltd.*, [1997] B.C.J. No. 2648, per Master Powers at para. 19 (S.C.).

A British Columbia court declined to strike out a counterclaim for purported defamation where the particulars of the words complained of set out "an approximation of the words spoken." The court accepted that such a pleading was equivalent to employing the phrase "substantially to the same effect." The court ruled this interim form of pleading was permissible because the counterclaimants did not merely have a suspicion that the alleged defamatory statements occurred, but, to the extent of the information and knowledge available to them, had set out the words spoken by the defendants by counterclaim. The court further ordered that on the completion of discoveries, the counterclaimants would be at liberty to amend their counterclaim and to supply further particulars (presumably of the defamatory expression).

Central Minera Corp. v. *Lavarack* (2001), 6 C.P.C. (5th) 260 per Drossos J. at 265–68 (B.C.S.C.).

In Nova Scotia, it has been accepted that in cases of slander in which the plaintiff is not aware of the specific words or precise occasions on which defamatory words were published, the requirement for very precise pleading of the claim may be somewhat relaxed.

Lawrence v. *Wallace* (2002), 203 N.S.R. (2d) 197, per Cromwall J.A. at para. 6 (C.A.).

c) Pleading an Entire Document Alleged to Be Defamatory

In appropriate circumstances, a plaintiff may plead an entire document either by attaching to the statement of claim:

i) a typewritten schedule which contains all of the words published in the document, or

ii) an original copy of the document, or

iii) a photocopy of the document;

or, by setting out the content of the entire document (including graphics) in the body of the statement of claim itself.

In some instances, in addition to pleading the entire document, the plaintiff will simultaneously plead particulars in the statement of claim which identify the specific words or phrases or other specified elements of the document alleged to be defamatory.

In other instances, the statement of claim will expressly or impliedly make it clear that the plaintiff intends to simply rely on the entire document; that the plaintiff will resist confining her claim to specific words, phrases, or other elements of the publication. In such circumstances, a defendant may apply to strike the statement of claim, or in the alternative seek an order for particulars.

Considerable jurisprudence has been generated by defence challenges to a statement of claim which does not furnish particulars limiting the plaintiff's complaint to specific words, phrases, or other specified elements of a document. There is also a great deal of case law concerning defence challenges to the adequacy of particulars pleaded voluntarily by a plaintiff.

In circumstances where the plaintiff's reliance on the entire document (or the adequacy of particulars) is challenged by a defendant, a court hearing an interlocutory application may:

- strike the statement of claim, with or without leave to amend;
- require the plaintiff to deliver further and better particulars of the expression complained of, or to amend the statement of claim; or
- dismiss the defendant's application.

Court decisions which have sustained a plaintiff's right to plead the entire article without supplying particulars frequently rely on the principles expressed in *Churchill Forest Industries (Manitoba) Limited* v. *Finkel*, [1971] 1 W.W.R. 745 (Man. C.A.) where Guy J.A. stated at page 749:

> The plaintiff says "Here is the whole matter alleged to be defamatory. Read as a whole, and not out of context, I aver that it is defamatory of me. Look at

the three schedules [to the statement of claim]. You published them. I didn't. It does not lie in your mouth to ask me to pin myself down to some little point and to exclude the rest." I cannot see where the defendant is taken by surprise, or can pretend to be taken by surprise.

Court decisions which strike the statement of claim, or require the plaintiff to deliver particulars (or to amend) frequently rely on the principles expressed in another leading case: *Gouzenko v. Doubleday Canada Ltd.* (1981), 32 O.R. (2d) 216 (H.C.J.) (involving a chapter from a book consisting of 18 pages and approximately 6,600 words), where O'Driscoll J. at page 224, approved the following passages from *DDSA Pharmaceuticals Ltd. v. Times Newspapers*, [1972] 3 All E.R. 417 at 419 (C.A.), where Lord Denning M.R. stated:

> In the second place, the pleading is defective because it throws — and I use that word deliberately — on to the defendants a long article without picking out the parts said to be defamatory. Some of the article is not defamatory of anyone at all. It describes only the method of importing drugs. Other parts of the article are defamatory of some unnamed chemists, but not of the plaintiffs at all. Yet other parts may be defamatory of the plaintiffs. To throw an article of that kind at the defendants and indeed at the court — without picking out the particular passages, is highly embarrassing. Master Bickford put it very sensibly:
>
> > It is tremendously embarrassing to claim the whole of the article as a libel. There is a tremendous amount of the article which is not defamatory of [the plaintiffs]. You must pick out the particular bits and rely on the rest as extrinsic or surrounding facts giving a defamatory meaning to the words.

That ruling is in accord with the practice, as it has been known for many years. The plaintiffs must specify the particular parts defamatory of them.

Decisions which have applied the approach taken in *Gouzenko* include, *inter alia*:

> *Fletcher-Gordon v. Southam Inc.*, [1995] B.C.J. No. 253 (S.C.), where the statement of claim set out in thirteen pages the complete text of seven newspaper articles and twenty-five pages of a transcript alleged to be published by the radio media. Master Horn ordered particulars of the matters complained about as being defamatory, and of which plaintiff the words were defamatory, noting that "there is a great deal of material set out in those articles and transcripts which is in no way defamatory of either plaintiff." Master Horn stated:
>
> > ¶12 That the plaintiffs should put the alleged defamatory words in their proper context is desirable. ... But what the plaintiffs have done

here is not to place the defamatory words in their context but to plead the entire context as being defamatory.

¶15 There is authority for the proposition that the shorter and more succinct the statement the less necessity there is for particulars. ... The proposition has been applied in Manitoba, (see *Churchill Forest Industries (Manitoba) Ltd.* v. *Finkle, Bodie, et al*, [1971] 1 W.W.R. 745 (Man. C.A.))

¶18 Murray, J. in *Bank of British Columbia* v. *C.B.C.* [(1986) 5 B.C.L.R. (2d) 131 (S.C.), leave to appeal refused (1986), 6 B.C.L.R. (2d) 215 (C.A.)] at page 140 thought each case must be decided on its own facts and that it was a matter of degree whether, when an entire article was set out as being defamatory, particulars were needed. I respectfully agree.

The authorities which have applied the approach taken in *Churchill Forest Industries* include:

* *London College* v. *Sun Media*, [1999] O.J. No. 3133 (S.C.J.), where the words of two newspaper articles were fully set out in an amended statement of claim. Master Haberman held at paragraph 20 that the articles were short and uncomplicated. Accordingly, she dismissed a defence motion seeking to have the plaintiffs identify which words are not true, which are defamatory, and which gave rise to each of eight natural and ordinary meanings, stating at paragraph 11:

   The current state of the law in Ontario with respect to the degree of particularity required in a libel case appears to depend on the length of the alleged publication and the complexity of the issues with which it deals.

* *Lightfoot* v. *Southon*, (1983) 33 C.P.C. 89 (Ont. H.C.J.), where a 3½ page single-spaced typewritten "brief" allegedly read orally by the defendant to a municipal council was attached to the statement of claim. Fitzgerald L.J.S.C. held at page 93 that it is not objectionable to set out the whole article where the publication meets the criteria of conciseness and relevance, and where the plaintiff put the document in issue by pleading the entire document as being "defamatory in both meaning and innuendo of the plaintiff."

* *Boyer* v. *Toronto Life Publishing Co.* (1997), 51 O.T.C. 302 (Gen. Div.), where the plaintiff reproduced and attached an entire magazine article as a schedule to the statement of claim. Cumming J. declined to order that the plaintiff provide particulars, stating that "it is clear from the statement of claim as a whole that the plaintiff is relying upon the entire article, together with the cover, the index, the headline prefacing the article,

and the location of the photographs, in support of the specific innnuendos pleaded ..."

Where the statement of claim pleaded that "the Plaintiff intends to rely upon the whole of the Article, in its text, context and tone at the trial of this matter to support his claims" and "without limiting the generality" of the foregoing, specifically quoted 330 of the 750 words of the "Article," the defendant was entitled to particulars of "which passages defame, which words defame, and in which way they defame."

Keating v. Southam Inc. (c.o.b. Halifax Daily News Publishing), [1999] N.S.J. No. 351, per Kennedy C.J.S.C. at paras. 2–4, 9–12 (S.C.).

Churchill Forest Industries and *Gouzenko* can be reconciled on the basis that each represents an end of the spectrum: at one extreme, no particulars are necessary because the publication is short, clear, and obviously defamatory of the plaintiff alone; at the other extreme, the publication is very long, much of it does not relate to the plaintiff, and none of it is obviously defamatory of the plaintiff. *Keating* falls somewhere along the middle of this spectrum.

Churchill Forest Industries and *Gouzenko* are also frequently cited and applied in the context of audio-visual libel. See section (B)(2)(e), "Pleading audio-visual defamation," below.

d) Pleading to Tender the Entire Article in Evidence at Trial

This situation is not equivalent to attaching the entire article to the statement of claim.

It has been held that it is proper for a plaintiff to pick out the parts of a newspaper article that he relies on as defamatory, plead those specific words, plead the plain and ordinary meaning of the words, and also plead the false innuendos or implications or inferences. Where that is done, the plaintiff may also properly plead as follows:

The plaintiff further pleads that he will give in evidence the entire content of the article in support of the inferences pleaded in paragraph [__ of this statement of claim] and, aside from the inferences in paragraph 7, does not plead any other inferences.

Code v. Toronto Star Newpapers, Ltd. (1983), 48 C.P.C. 64 (Ont. S.C.), where Master Sandler stated at 68:

If the defendant is entitled to have read as part of the plaintiff's case, the whole of the publication from which an alleged libel is extracted, to make clear the meaning of the alleged defamatory words, I see no reason why a plaintiff cannot plead that he intends to do just that.

Similarly, where the plaintiff has set out in the statement of claim the specific words of an article which are alleged to be defamatory, it is permissible for the statement of claim to allege that those words "in the context of the entire article" convey certain natural and ordinary meanings. The plaintiff is not required to give particulars of "the context." This is to be distinguished from a situation where a plaintiff alleges that an entire article is libellous.

> *Reichmann* v. *Toronto Life Publishing Co.* (1988), 27 C.P.C. (2d) 37 (Ont. H.C.J.), where after referring to *Code* v. *Toronto Star Newspaper Ltd.*, above, Anderson J. states at page 50:
>
> > Given the nature and quality of the article which gives rise to this action, I do not see how the statement of claim could well have been framed without the words "in the context of the whole article" or some words of similar import, or how any portions of the article could well have been set out as comprising the only relevant portions of the context.

See Chapter 15, "Defamatory Meaning."

e) Pleading Audio-Visual Defamation

In *Lougheed* v. *Canadian Broadcasting Corporation* (1978), 86 D.L.R. (3d) 229 (Alta. Q.B.), the plaintiff incorporated (by reference) a copy of an alleged defamatory broadcast into his statement of claim and pleaded that "the defamation was achieved and crafted by the Defendant combining images and scenes, statements falsely attributed to [the Plaintiff] and to others, music and narration, and the combination of all those elements, which in their totality were calculated to convey and did convey falsely to the viewing public" certain defamatory imputations.

In his trial judgment, Miller J. noted the paucity of Canadian or English authority dealing with the problem of defamation in audio-visual presentations and resorted to American jurisprudence, including *Brown* v. *Paramount Publix Corp.* (1934), 270 N.Y.S. 544, (N.Y. App. Div. 1934), where the complaint incorporated a television broadcast in almost exactly the same language as Mr. Lougheed employed in his statement of claim against the Canadian Broadcasting Corporation.

Miller J. described the key problem of pleading defamation in the context of a fifty-minute television play with many characters and scenes [*Lougheed*, above, at pages 235–36]:

In this medium [a television play] it is quite possible that the words themselves spoken by the actors or actor do not convey a defamatory meaning but the manner in which the words are spoken or the gestures of the actor speaking them may convey an entirely different impression to the viewing audience. An actor skilled in mime can create an impression of the person being portrayed by the use of facial expressions and body movement without saying a single word and such an impression might well be perceived by the audience to be defamatory of the person being portrayed. The combinations and permutations available to an audio-visual type of presentation are endless. How, then, should the established legal principles which have stood the test of time respond to a broadcast of a television play? Are they appropriate or adequate or must we now develop modifications or even entirely new principles to be fair to all sides?

Miller J. rejected the plaintiff's contention that it was entitled to plead that the whole television play constitutes the defamation, but did rule [at page 245]:

The plaintiff in a defamation case involving an audio-visual presentation should not be bound by the same strict rules as apply to particulars which apply to a written document or verbal statement. However, this privilege … should not be extended to permit the pleading merely of general conclusions that the plaintiff has been defamed. The plaintiff must, through his pleadings, clearly indicate to the plaintiff which portions of the television play give rise to allegations of defamation in order to delineate properly the issues of the case and to inform the defendant of the case he must meet.

In the particular circumstances before the court, Miller J. directed [at pages 244–45]:

i) that the plaintiff must indicate to the defendant which parts of the television play defame him;

ii) that if the plaintiff is relying upon the method of portrayal of him by the actor in the play as being defamatory or contributing to the alleged defamatory image, he should specify what specific methods are involved;

iii) that if the plaintiff relies upon an innuendo arising out of the play, he should specify what, in his opinion, is the alleged innuendo. For example, throughout the play there are references to the Watergate incident in the United States which was unfolding before the public at the time when the Syncrude negotiations were going on in Canada. The plaintiff should be able to specify whether he intends to rely, or not rely, on any innuendo that these references may or may not imply; and

iv)   If the plaintiff intends to rely upon any impression created by the background music, as alleged in the statement of claim, he should be able to specify what there is about the music that creates or helps create the alleged defamation.

On appeal by the plaintiff in *Lougheed* v. *Canadian Broadcasting Corporation* [(1980), 98 D.L.R. (3d) 264 (Alta. S.C. (T.D.))], Clement J.A. noted at page 268 that the:

> … transcript of the audio part of the presentation is keyed to the visual part by a time frame recorded in intervals of 10 seconds: for example, the introductory statement is shown to commence at (0:00) and to conclude at (2:10) which is to say, it is presented within a readily identifiable time frame of two minutes and 10 seconds.

Clement J.A. held [at page 268]:

> By means of this identification device the plaintiff is enabled to designate with particularity each episode alleged to be defamatory and to assign to such episode the nature of the defamation and the manner in which it is said to be communicated. It may be by an innuendo to be drawn from words spoken during a specified time interval, and in that case particulars of the words used and the innuendo assigned to them, should be given. Or, within another specified time interval the gestures or facial expressions of a character may convey an innuendo, both of which should be particularized. In many instances the matter complained of as defamatory may consist in the combination of several factors. It is to be taken, of course, that this particularity will have as its background the totality of the production in the context of which the particular matters of complaint are to be judged. Accordingly, I would order that the plaintiff deliver particulars by designating episodes identified by reference to the time frame, and in respect of each stating the nature and manner of the alleged defamation. This course, in my view, is no more than an adaptation to the techniques of television communication of the method of particularization required in respect of books and articles where the page, the paragraph and, if necessary, the lines are designated in order to bring the matter of complaint into focus.

The plaintiff may find it difficult or impossible to meet the standards of pleadings set forth in *Lougheed* if the plaintiff is not given access to a tape of the subject program by a defendant. In that situation, the court is unlikely to strike a statement of claim and more likely to defer the obligation to plead precisely. For example, in one such case, the plaintiff was given liberty to move to amend the statement of claim at a later date when it was in a position to do so.

> *Davis v. Côté* (2000), 157 Man. R. (2d) 1, per Master Sharp at paras. 23–24 (Q.B.).

In *Vulcan Industrial Packaging Ltd.* v. *Canadian Broadcasting Corporation* (1979), 94 D.L.R. (3d) 729 (Ont. S.C. (Mast.)), the plaintiff sued over three television programs which the defendant broadcast in April 1977. Transcripts of two of the programs were attached to the statement of claim, which alleged in part:

> ¶7 The plaintiff complains of the whole of the said programs aforesaid, both as to the words and pictures by television and will refer to the whole of the said programs both as to words and pictures by television at the trial of this action. Delivered herewith as Schedule "A" to this Statement of Claim is a transcript of the "Fifth Estate" program aforesaid. Delivered herewith as Schedule "B" to this Statement of Claim is a transcript of part of the "90 Minutes Live with Peter Gzowski" as referred to aforesaid. The plaintiff will deliver particulars of part of the transcript of the "National News" aforesaid as referred to after examinations for discovery.

> ¶8 By the said words and pictures by television aforesaid in their natural and ordinary meaning and/or by way of innuendo, the defendants meant and were understood to mean: [twenty-three sub-paragraphs set out the alleged meaning]

> ¶11 The plaintiff will rely on the juxtaposition of the said words and pictures by television aforesaid and all of the words and pictures broadcast and the entire broadcasts aforesaid.

In his ruling on an interlocutory application in *Vulcan*, above, Master Sandler concentrated on the thirty-minute investigative journalism television program known as *The Fifth Estate*. After noting that the trial decision in *Lougheed*, above, was the only Canadian authority cited to him concerning pleading the libellous content of a television program, the Master ruled at pages 741–42 that an investigative journalism program is subject to the same considerations as apply to a television play:

> This type of programme is still an audio-visual presentation and can rely on the visual element to communicate the desired message relying on the old adage "a picture is worth a thousand words." In my view, the same type of considerations apply to this type of television programme as apply to a tele-

vision play, since they both have the vast potential for presenting a message from elements in the programme, other than the spoken words themselves.

The Master therefore ordered that the plaintiff "indicate to the defendant which portions of the 'words and pictures' give rise to the allegations of defamation."

In *Vogel v. Canadian Broadcasting Corporation*, [1982] 3 W.W.R. 97 (B.C.S.C.), the plaintiff Deputy Attorney General for British Columbia sued over three television broadcasts which he alleged falsely asserted that he influenced, or tried to influence, the course of justice in certain criminal proceedings for the purpose of protecting his friend. Esson J. (as he then was) awarded the plaintiff $125,000 damages, and described in his judgment the special feature of audio-visual programs [at page 155]:

> I have made many references to the impression conveyed to viewers. That is a matter which must be considered in assessing television programs, which, by reason of their transitory nature, tend to leave the audience with an impression rather than a firm understanding of what was said. Images, facial expressions, tones of voice, symbols, and the dramatic effect which can be achieved by the juxtaposition of segments may be more important than the meaning derived from careful reading of the words of the script. Television is different from the printed word. The interested reader can reread and analyze. The emphasis in considering the defamatory impact of, say a newspaper story, must therefore be upon the words used. Libel by television is, in this respect, more like slander. In slander cases, regard may be had to such things as gestures and intonations: see *Gatley on Libel and Slander*, 7th ed. (1974), p. 500, para. 1225. Here, regard must be had to the devices used to create an impression that what was being reported was a serious scandal.

After setting out in the text of his trial judgment in Vogel the entire transcripts of the principal broadcast, Esson J. gave a detailed explanation [pages 143–53] how the impact of the words used on the program was

> immeasurably increased by photographs and other visual devices and by deceptive methods which were employed to give the accusations the appearance of being very much more serious than, in print, they are seen to be.

In *Moffat v. British Columbia Television System Ltd.*, [1985] 1 W.W.R. 271 (B.C.S.C.), the plaintiff sued over eight television broadcasts which had occurred over a seventeen-day period. The statement of claim appended a full transcript of the broadcasts and pleaded "that the words of the broadcasts together with the video portion, including graphs, charts, and other visual aids and sounds, and the innuendoes arising therefrom, are false and libelous of him" [page 272]. The statement of claim did not identify which portion or portions of the broadcasts were libellous. The plaintiff contended that the broadcasts as a whole were defamatory; no particular aspect of them could be pleaded to be defamatory except in the context of the ongoing theme of the whole series [page 272].

Low L.J.S.C., hearing an interlocutory application in *Moffat*, held that there was "nothing wrong in making the full transcript of the broadcasts part of the plaintiff's pleadings" but that was not sufficient, stating at 277–78:

> In my opinion, the statement of claim identifies the publications and pleads the defamatory meanings without specifically identifying those portions of the publication which, separately and collectively, give rise to the defamatory meanings. In their present state the pleadings raise and do not answer these questions: What words of themselves are false? What false innuendoes arise from the words? What words taken together with what pictures, graphs, charts and sounds give rise to false innuendoes? The plaintiff must isolate those portions, as numerous as they may be, of the broadcasts which the plaintiff says answer those questions. The remainder would be background which would be considered in determining whether the isolated portions have the defamatory meaning ascribed to them by the plaintiff in … the statement of claim. Particulars are necessary to define the issues of fact at trial.
>
> … There will be an order requiring the plaintiff to provide particulars as to what words in the broadcast are themselves false; what false innuendoes arise from what words; and what words taken together with what pictures, graphs, charts and sounds give rise to what false innuendoes.

In *Bank of British Columbia* v. *Canadian Broadcasting Corporation* (1986), 5 B.C.L.R. (2d) 131 (S.C.) [leave to appeal denied (1986), 6 B.C.L.R. (2d) 215 (C.A.)], the plaintiff set out in the statement of claim the "spoken component" of a television news broadcast and pleaded that the "videotape of this Broadcast will be shown at the trial of this action, and will include the visual images and film which formed part of the Broadcast …" [page 134]. Noting that the broadcast relating to the plaintiff occupied a time segment of only two minutes and ten seconds out of a much longer national news broadcast, Murray J. distinguished *Lougheed* and *Moffatt*, and stated at page 140:

> … in all of the cases relied upon by the defendant there are extraneous matters and persons other than the plaintiffs referred to in the articles or broadcasts. The broadcast in the case at bar deals with only one subject, namely, the financial position of the plaintiff bank. Each case must be decided on its own facts. At one end of the spectrum is the type of case where a plaintiff alleges

that an entire book or hour-long documentary on radio or television defames him. At the other end is the type of case where only one sentence in a book or one line of a radio television broadcast is alleged to be defamatory. In the first case particulars will be ordered. In the second case they cannot be ordered. Other cases such as the present fall in between the two foregoing extremes and a decision must be made as to which side of the line the case falls. My decision in the case at bar is that it falls on the plaintiff's side of the line.

In *137240 Assn. Canada Inc. v. Ontario Medical Assn.*, [1989] O.J. 1625 (H.C.J.), the plaintiff sued for damages with respect to a video cassette recording and slide reproduction thereof and alleged that they were in their entirety defamatory. However, the defamation was not alleged to be by reason of the nature of the video, but by reason of the words spoken on the video. Those words were attached to the statement of claim and the specific pleading of their natural and ordinary meanings directed attention to each section of the article and the pleaded meanings arose from those words and from the facts otherwise pleaded. Van Camp J. held that this was a sufficient pleading:

> The test is set out in my opinion in *Fairbairn v. Sage* (1925), 29 O.W.N. 48, cited by Guy J.A. in *Churchill Forest Indust. (Man) Ltd. v. Finkel et al.*, [1971] 1 W.W.R. 745, namely that the pleading must (1) define the issues (2) prevent surprise (3) enable the parties to prepare for trial (4) facilitate the hearing.

In *Colour Your World Corp. v. Canadian Broadcasting Corp.* (1994), 17 O.R. (3d) 308 (Gen. Div.), rev'd (1998), 38 O.R. (3d) 97, 156 D.L.R. (4th) 27 (C.A.), the plaintiff sued for libel over a television consumer affairs program. Somers J., the trial judge, described the statement of claim in the following terms [pages 310–11]:

> In para. 9 of its statement of claim the plaintiff pleads not so much that the words in the impugned segment of the defendant CBC's show are untrue, but that taken as a whole and bearing in mind the nature and contents of the various matters described during the segment and their juxtaposition in the overall presentation, a libel was created and published.

> Paragraph 9 of the statement of claim reads as follows:

> > The Plaintiff pleads that the combination of the words and pictures and their arrangement resulted in a defamatory broadcast that meant and was understood to mean that: [various meanings are then set out]

> Given the nature of the plea it is necessary to review the television item complained of in its entirety.

The trial judgment then set out the text of the program together with a description of what appeared on screen at the time the words were spoken [at pages 311–18].

Somers J. made a finding that "[I]f one were to have regard only to the words that were spoken during the show, one would be hard-pressed to find statements that are untrue" [page 334]. He nevertheless concluded that the television program was defamatory stating that "the method of presenting particular words which in themselves are strictly speaking true can shade or even alter the meanings of those words to the point where what has been said has been given a defamatory meaning" [page 336], citing *Grossman* v. *CFTO-TV Ltd.* (1982), 39 O.R. (2d) 498 (C.A.), where Cory J.A. said at pages 502–3:

> … television or radio broadcasts can be ephemeral and fleeting. Ephemeral though it may be, the impact of a broadcast may be far greater than that of a newspaper article. The audio-visual effect can be devastating. The words used in the broadcast may be of secondary importance to a number of other features. The intonation, tone of voice and inflexion can make innocent words defamatory. A voice combined with background effects, scenery, music or images can still more readily lead to an insidious result where, although innocent words are used, a person is held up to the most flagrant ridicule and contempt.

On appeal, Abella J.A., speaking for the Court of Appeal, described the content of the scenes in the twelve-minute segment of the television program which was the subject of the libel action at pages 98–103. She described the plaintiff's complaint in the following terms at page 104:

> Other than a few introductory remarks, the entire program was impugned. The statements of fact were not, on the whole, said to be false; rather, it was the overall impression, created by the combination of words and images, that was alleged to be defamatory.

Addressing the audio-visual dimension of a television broadcast, Abella J.A. stated at page 107:

> There is no doubt that the audio-visual dimension of a television broadcast can transform the impression one might otherwise get from a statement. The audio-visual aspects of a broadcast bring into play unique features such as voice intonation, visual background, facial expression, and gestures, all of which can accompany the articulated facts to dramatic effect. Because of these distinguishing factors in a broadcast, the overall impression, in addition to the accuracy of the statements, is relevant.

She qualified those remarks as follows at page 107:

> There may well be circumstances where the impact of what the viewer sees and hears so dramatically contradicts the words used, that the meaning of those words attributed by a viewer is distorted. But one cannot ignore the content of the statements made. The fact that there are both visual and auditory components to a television broadcast does not render the words used irrelevant. When determining how a reasonable viewer might perceive the meaning of a broadcast, we must look not only to image, sound and sequence, we must also look to the actual words used. If the content of those words is not distorted by the audio-visual aspects of the broadcast, they should be deemed the primary conveyor of a program's meaning.

On the basis of her very detailed review of the program, Abella J.A. concluded that it was not defamatory, allowed the defendants' appeal, and dismissed the action.

In *Leenen v. Canadian Broadcasting Corporation* (2000), 48 O.R. (3d) 656 (S.C.J.), the plaintiff sued over an hour-long television documentary. The trial judge, Cunningham J., described the plaintiff's complaint in the following terms at page 666:

> ¶19 It is Dr. Leenen's position that he was defamed by this program and that the innuendoes arising from the broadcast have libeled him personally and professionally. In advancing this position, Dr. Leenen relies upon the entirety of the broadcast, including its introduction, text, visualizations, context and tone.

The trial judgment describes the hour-long broadcast in detail, and records, *inter alia*, the trial judge's criticism [at pages 668–72] of a "sensationalized introduction," "highly dramatized" presentations with "eerie music and frightening visual scenes," and "a tasteless and insulting interview."

Cunningham J. held the program was defamatory of the plaintiff, stating at pages 674–75:

> ¶45 Television, as compared with print media, has the potential of a far greater impact and, because of its audio-visual nature, the words used may be of less importance than other aspects of the broadcast. Thus, in the present case, as in all cases of television libel, it is important to consider not only context but also the manner in which the program is presented. This issue has been considered in a number of cases, including *Colour Your World Corp.* v. *Canadian Broadcasting Corp.* (1998), 38 O.R. (3d) 97, 156 D.L.R. (4th) 27 (C.A.) ...

While I must accept that the words, so long as they are not distorted, should be deemed the primary conveyor of a program's meaning, they are not the only conveyor.

In *Dhami v. Canadian Broadcasting Corporation*, [2001] B.C.J. No. 2773 (S.C.), the plaintiffs sued over statements in a television program and set out a transcript of the words complained of as a schedule to their statement of claim. Slade J., hearing an interlocutory application, stated, *inter alia*, at paragraph 8:

> The force of the allegations, and their tenor, is said to be amplified by the tone of voice and facial expressions of the defendant Kevin Evans ... .

Slade J. ordered the plaintiffs to provide particulars "identifying the photographic images on which they rely in support of their claim of defamatory meaning" and that such particulars specify, in relation to each such image, the basis for such reliance [paragraph 116].

3) Pleading the Defamatory Meaning

See Chapter 15, "Defamatory Meaning." As stated in that Chapter at page 192, the plaintiff may choose to plead:

i)   The literal meaning: Here it is not necessary to go beyond the words themselves, as where the plaintiff has been called a thief or a murderer. This is called a "natural and ordinary" meaning in the case authorities; and/or

ii)   An inferential meaning: Here the sting of the defamation lies not so much in the expression itself as in the meaning that the ordinary person, without special knowledge, will infer from it. This meaning is a matter of impression. This is also called a "natural and ordinary meaning." It is also sometimes referred to as "popular" or "false" innuendo; and/or

iii) A "legal innuendo": Expression, ostensibly innocent on its face, which conveys a defamatory meaning only by virtue of extrinsic facts known to specific people or classes of people exposed to that expression. This meaning is also referred to in the case law as a "true innuendo."

When a plaintiff chooses to rely on the literal meaning of words, the statement of claim may simply quote the precise words in the publication or broadcast which are alleged to be defamatory. However, in most defamation lawsuits, a plaintiff will not merely quote the precise words or any other expression at issue, but will also plead one or more added inferential meanings. This is commonly done in a statement of claim by alleging that "The said words meant and were understood to mean that …".

Pressler v. Lethbridge (2000), 86 B.C.L.R. (3d) 257 at para. 36 (B.C.C.A.)

Hodgson v. Canadian Newspapers Co. (1998), 39 O.R. (3d) 235 at 248 (Gen. Div.), varied as to damages on appeal (2000), 49 O.R. (3d) 161 (C.A.).

The distinction between a false and a legal innuendo was discussed by Somers J. in *Clement v. McGuinty*, [2000] O.T.C. 438 (S.C.J.) [varied on other grounds (2001), 143 O.A.C. 328 (C.A.)] at paragraph 23:

> The position taken by the plaintiff is that by pleading in paragraph 13 of his Statement of Defence, that the words complained of, have a separate and distinct meaning the defendant has raised a separate issue by way of legal innuendo. Much of the law of libel concerns itself with secondary meanings arising out of the words complained of. These secondary meanings are covered by the word "innuendo" which signifies pointing out what and who is meant by the words complained of. The so-called false innuendo has been described by the House of Lords in the case of *Lewis v. Daily Telegraph Ltd.* [1963] 2 All E.R. 151 where Lord Morris of Borthy-y-Gest said at p. 165:
>
> > the first sub-division of the innuendo has lately been called false innuendo as it is no more than an elaboration or embroidering of the words used without proof of extraneous facts. The true innuendo is that which depends on extraneous facts which the plaintiff has to prove in order to give the words the secondary meaning of which he complains.

Certain courts have held that a plea that "the defendant meant" (as opposed to what the words meant) is not relevant and offends the rules of pleading.

Toronto Star Ltd. v. Globe Printing Co., [1941] 3 D.L.R. 376, per Roach J. at 378–79 (Ont. H.C.):

> It is immaterial what the defendant meant. He may have meant something that was not discernible to any other person having regard to the language used. The issue is not what the defendant meant or was understood to mean, but rather what do the words mean and what were they understood by the public to mean.

Mengarelli v. Forrest, [1972] 2 O.R. 397, per Master Davidson at 398 (S.C. (Mast.)), citing *Tisdall v. Sowdon*, [1942] O.W.N. 383 (H.C.J.), *Toronto Star Ltd. v. Globe Printing Co.*, above.

Church of Scientology of Toronto v. Sun Publishing Ltd. (1977), 4 C.P.C. 207, per Master Garfield at paras. 4–6 (Ont. S.C.), citing Richard O'Sullivan & Roland G. Brown, *Gatley on Libel and Slander*, 4th ed. (London: Sweet & Maxwell, 1953) at 44.

Pennington v. Smith (1980), 16 C.P.C. 151, per Master Donkin at para. 8 (Ont. S.C. (Mast.)).

a) Pleading a Literal Meaning

A leading textbook suggests that rarely should a plaintiff rely solely on the literal meaning of the expression in formulating her libel complaint. Philip Lewis, *Gatley on Libel and Slander*, 8th ed. (London: Sweet & Maxwell, 1981) states at 446–47, para. 1075:

> Where the words complained of are defamatory in their natural and ordinary meaning and can reasonably only have one meaning, no innuendo is needed; such a case would be an allegation of a specific act of misconduct. Where the plain and obvious meaning of the words is defamatory, an innuendo (as to their meaning) is unnecessary, and, if made, negligible [citation omitted]. But this is only the rule in the plainest cases. Where there is any unclarity as to the natural and ordinary meaning, or any uncertainty as to the meaning for which the plaintiff will contend at the trial, or there is room for disagreement as to what inferences might reasonably be drawn from the words themselves in the light of the ordinary man's knowledge, the plaintiff must plead the meaning which he alleges the words to have. If he does so, he should make it clear that he is relying on the natural and ordinary meaning of the words, and is not seeking to plead a true innuendo without the support of extrinsic facts.

In *Hodgson v. Canadian Newspapers Co.*, above, Lane J. stated at 250–51:

> It is open to the plaintiff in a libel case to rely upon the natural and ordinary meaning of the words in both senses: that is in the plain and obvious, or literal, meaning, and in one or more added inferential meanings. In my view that is what the pleader did in para. 16 of the statement of claim, "in particular, but without limiting the generality of their natural and ordinary meanings," being careful to preserve the right to rely upon the literal meaning while adding the extended or inferential meanings in the sub-paragraphs as innuendoes."

b) Pleading an Inferential Meaning

See Chapter 15, "Defamatory Meaning."

The purpose of pleading an inferential meaning (also known as a "popular" or "false" innuendo) is to make clear to the opposing party and the court the meaning that the plaintiff seeks to have placed upon the words complained of.

> *Silva* v. *Toronto Star Newspapers Ltd.* (1998), 167 D.L.R. (4th) 554, per Somers J. at 558, 561 (Ont. Gen. Div.), aff'd (2002), 215 D.L.R. (4th) 77 (Ont. C.A.).

In England, courts have held that unless the meanings of the words are clear and explicit, it is desirable that the plaintiff plead inferential meanings.

> *Lewis* v. *Daily Telegraph Ltd.*, [1963] 2 All E.R. 151, per Lord Hodson at 166 (H.L.):
>
> > A pleader is entitled to allege in his statement of claim what the words in their natural and ordinary meaning convey, provided he makes it clear that he is not relying on a true innuendo, which gives a separate cause of action and requires a separate verdict from the jury. It is desirable that he should do so, for where there is no true innuendo, the judge should define the limits of the natural and ordinary meaning of the libel and leave to the jury only those meanings which he rules are capable of being defamatory. If the natural and ordinary meaning is pleaded the defence will know what the contentions of the plaintiff are, and the judge will not have to analyse the submissions of counsel in his charge to the jury without having the benefit of a pleading setting out what those submissions are.

> *London Computer Operators Training* v. *B.B.C.*, [1973] 2 All E.R. 170 per Lord Denning M.R. at 172f.

Similarly, it has been held by Canadian courts that unless the literal meaning of the words complained of is plain and obvious, the plaintiff should plead what he alleges the words were intended to mean.

> *Laufer* v. *Bucklaschuk* (1999), 181 D.L.R. (4th) 83, per Scott C.J.M. and Helper J.A. at 92, para. 23 (Man. C.A.), leave to appeal to S.C.C. denied, [2000] S.C.C.A. No. 77.

> *Wharton* v. *Vopni Press Ltd.* (1982), 30 C.P.C. 243, per Referee Cantlie at 249 (Man. Q.B.).

One court recently stated that it is unnecessary but not improper to plead a false or popular innuendo.

> *Fletcher-Gordon* v. *Southam Inc.*, [1995] B.C.J. No. 253, per Master Horn at para. 7 (S.C.), aff'd, [1995] B.C.J. No. 879 (S.C.) [The Master's decision relies

in part on *Wharton v. Vopni Press Ltd.*, above, which, it is respectfully submitted, may have been misinterpreted].

Where a false or popular innuendo is pleaded, the statement of claim may plead as follows:

Fletcher-Gordon v. Southam Inc., above, at paras. 6–7:

> The said words in their natural and ordinary meaning meant and were understood to mean that...

Wharton v. Vopni Press Ltd., above, at 247:

> The allegation that the defendants "meant and were understood to mean" is not two alternative allegations. It is a single allegation and is the standard, indeed required, way of pleading an innuendo.

An alternative form of pleading that has been held to allege a popular or false innuendo is as follows:

Silva v. Toronto Star Newspapers, above, at 558, 561:

> The plaintiff states that the words in the article in their plain and ordinary meaning and by way of innuendo imply that ... .

A decision to plead a popular or false innuendo should be taken only after a careful assessment of the potential defences. For example, if a very general false innuendo is pleaded (for example, the plaintiff is "dishonest"), the defendant may be able to justify that broad meaning, but not a more narrow meaning (for example, "the plaintiff robbed a bank of $1,500 on 10 May 2003").

Maisel v. Financial Times Ltd. (1915), 84 LJKB 2145 (C.A.).

London Computer Operators Training Ltd. v. B.B.C., [1973] 2 All E.R. 170, per Lord Denning MR at 173a (C.A.):

> The greater the conceivable width [of the innuendo], the greater the scope of the particulars of justification].

The following pleas have been held to constitute an allegation of a popular or false innuendo:

i)   the words complained of "were defamatory in that they meant and were understood to mean ..."

> *Dhami v. Canadian Broadcasting Corporation*, 2001 BCSC 1811, per Slade J at paras. 26–28.

ii)   "The said words are defamatory in their natural and ordinary meaning. In the alternative, the said lines are defamatory in their natural and ordinary meaning in that the words meant and were understood to mean that the Plaintiff ..."

> *Campbell* v. *Jones* (2002), 220 D.L.R. (4th) 201, per Saunders J.A. at 286, para. 222 (N.S.C.A.).

iii)   "The words concerning the plaintiff quoted in paragraph 7 above and the headline under which they appeared in the *Vancouver Sun* quoted in paragraph 9 above are defamatory in their natural and ordinary meaning in that the words meant and were understood to mean that ..."

> *Coutts* v. *Fotheringham* (1980), 19 C.P.C. 270, per Master Sandler at paras. 13–14 (Ont. S.C.).

iv)   "The plaintiff complains of false and defamatory innuendo created by the cumulative effect" of the words complained of.

> *Eagleson* v. *Dowbiggan*, [1996] O.J. No. 322, per E.M. Macdonald J. at paras. 20, 33 (Gen. Div.).

i)   A Defective Plea

One court ordered a portion [italicized] of the following plea to be struck out, apparently on the ground that it does not constitute a plea of a popular or false innuendo, but rather an inadequate legal innuendo.

> The words complained of are defamatory of each of the plaintiffs in their natural and ordinary meaning *as well as by innuendo.* The words imply that: ...
>
> *Lennon* v. *Ontario (Premier)* (1999), 45 O.R. (3d) 84, per J. Macdonald J. at paras. 14–18 (S.C.J.).

It has also been held that a statement of claim is deficient if it simply pleads the word "innuendo" without setting out whether it is a false or true innuendo which is being alleged.

> *Keating* v. *Southam Inc. (c.o.b. Halifax Daily News Publishing)*, [1999] N.S.J. No. 351, per Kennedy C.J.S.C. at para. 13 (S.C.).

Where a plaintiff pleads only "false" meanings, and does not plead reliance on the literal meaning, it appears that the only meanings the court may be entitled to consider at trial are the false innuendo meanings pleaded by the plaintiff.

> *Netupsky* v. *Craig*, [1971] 1 O.R. 51, per Schroeder J.A. at 65–66 (C.A.).

On the other hand, where a plaintiff has pleaded the literal meaning of the words, the plaintiff will be entitled to rely at trial not only on any inferential meanings also pleaded, but on the literal meanings.

Hodgson v. Canadian Newspapers Co. (1998), 39 O.R. (3d) 235, per Lane J. at 252 (Gen. Div.):

> In my view, the position is well expressed in Colin Duncan and A.T. Hoolahan, *A Guide to Defamation Practice*, 2nd ed. (London: Sweet & Maxwell, 1958) at pp. 26–27:
>
>> But even where the words are *prima facie* defamatory, an innuendo may be needed to allege additional and perhaps more serious meanings. A plaintiff can always rely upon the natural and ordinary meanings of the words, but only upon such innuendo meanings as he has pleaded and not upon any others which may occur to him or his legal advisers at trial.

It has been held that even in the absence of a plea of a legal innuendo, the court has a discretion under the British Columbia Supreme Court Rules to make an order for particulars of facts relating to an innuendo.

Dhami v. Canadian Broadcasting Corporation, 2001 BCSC 1811, per Slade J. at paras. 32–35.

c) Pleading a "Legal Innuendo"

Sir Brian Neill & Richard Rampton, *Duncan & Neill on Defamation*, 2d ed. (London: Butterworths, 1983), a leading English textbook, aptly explained the concept of legal innuendo as follows at page 17:

> 4.17 The law of defamation recognizes —
>
> (a) that some words have technical or slang meanings or meanings which depend on some special knowledge possessed not by the general public but by a limited number of persons; and
> (b) that ordinary words may on occasions bear some special meaning other than their natural and ordinary meaning because of some extrinsic facts or circumstances.

These special meanings are called innuendoes, or, more strictly, legal or true innuendoes to distinguish them from popular or false innuendoes.

See also *Lewis v. Daily Telegraph Ltd.*, [1963] 2 All E.R. 151, per Lord Devlin at 171F–G (H.L.):

It is said that it may not always be easy to decide whether an extrinsic factor relied on is a matter of special knowledge, or whether it is just general knowledge in the light of which the ordinary though indirect meaning of the words has to be ascertained. The pleader must ask himself whether he contemplates that evidence will be called in support of the allegation: if he does, it is a legal innuendo and if he does not, it is not. If he is in doubt, he can plead in two paragraphs; and then if at trial his opponent agrees or the judge rules that it is a matter of general knowledge, the legal innuendo can be dropped.

A legal innuendo creates a separate cause of action from any cause of action arising from the natural and ordinary meaning of the expression complained of.

> *Stumpf* v. *Globe Holdings Ltd.*, [1982] A.J. No. 638, per Master Funduk at para. 14 (Q.B.), citing *Lewis* v. *Daily Telegraph*, above, at 166–67, approving *Grubb* v. *Bristol United Press Ltd.*, [1963] 1 Q.B. 309.

> *Grubb* v. *Bristol United Press Ltd.*, [1963] 1 Q.B. 309 per Holroyd-Pearce L.J. at 327:

> > Thus there is one cause of action for the libel itself, based on whatever imputations or implications can reasonably be derived from the words themselves, and there is another different cause of action, namely, the innuendo, based not merely on the libel itself but on an extended meaning created by a conjunction of the words with something outside them. The latter cause of action cannot come into existence unless there is some extrinsic fact to create the extended meaning. This view is simple and accords with common sense. Unless, therefore, the alleged innuendo has the support of such a fact, it cannot go to the jury, and in the interlocutory stages of the action it may be struck out.

Where the words complained of are not defamatory in their natural and ordinary meaning, but depend for their defamatory meaning upon extrinsic facts or circumstances, the plaintiff must plead in his statement of claim a legal innuendo and full particulars of all the special facts or circumstances relied on.

> *Laufer* v. *Bucklaschuk* (1999), 181 D.L.R. (4th) 83, per Scott C.J.M. and Helper J.A. at 92, para. 24 (Man. C.A.), leave to appeal to S.C.C. denied, [2000] S.C.C.A. No. 77.

> *Hodgson* v. *Canadian Newspapers Co.*, above, at 250b.

Lightfoot v. *Southon* (1983), 33 C.P.C. 89, per Fitzgerald L.J.S.C. at 94–95, paras. 19–21 (Ont. H.C.J.).

Eagleson v. *Dowbiggan*, [1996] O.J. No. 322, per E.M. Macdonald J. at para. 32 (Gen. Div.).

Dhami v. *Canadian Broadcasting Corporation*, 2001 BCSC 1811 per Slade J. at para. 16, citing Allen M. Linden, *Canadian Tort Law*, 5th ed. (Toronto: Butterworths, 1993) at 644.

To the extent that the plaintiff alleges defamation by means of a legal innuendo, the words complained of which create the legal innuendo meaning must be identified in the statement of claim.

Keating v. *Southam Inc. (c.o.b. Halifax Daily News Publishing)*, [1999] N.S.J. No. 351, per Kennedy C.J.S.C. at para. 14 (S.C.).

The plaintiff must also plead the identities of those persons who it is alleged possess knowledge of the extrinsic facts and to whom it is alleged that the words complained of were published.

Aboutown Transportation Ltd. v. *London Free Press Printing Co.* (1993), 14 O.R. (3d) 19, per McDermid J. at 23 c–e (Gen. Div.):

> Rule 25.06(1) requires the plaintiffs to plead a concise statement of the material facts on which they rely for their claim. The pleadings should define the issues to be tried and will bind the parties with respect to the evidence that may be called at trial. Without proof at trial of the extrinsic facts relied upon by the plaintiffs to support the legal innuendoes pleaded and the identities of those who possessed knowledge of the extrinsic facts and to whom the words complained of were published, the cause of action must fail.

In British Columbia, the *Rules of Court* require that a plea of a legal innuendo must be particularized. Rule 19(12)(a) of the British Columbia Supreme Court *Rules* provides:

> (12) In an action for libel or slander, (a) where the plaintiff alleges that the words or matter complained of were used in a derogatory sense other than their ordinary meaning, the plaintiff shall give particulars of the facts and matters on which the plaintiff relies in support of that sense …

Dhami v. *Canadian Broadcasting Corporation*, above, at paras. 15, 30–31. [This Rule has no application to a "popular" or "false innuendo."]

"[I]f the meanings alleged in the statement of claim are no more than the meanings expressed or conveyed by or to be implied from the words themselves," there is no need to plead a legal innuendo.

> *Eagleson* v. *Dowbiggan*, above, at paras. 34–36, approving Lord Morris of Borth-y-Gest in *Lewis* v. *Daily Telegraph Ltd.*, [1963] 2 All E.R. 151 at 159–60 (H.L.).

A plaintiff should consider the effect on the scope of the action of pleading extrinsic facts. The statement of claim may unnecessarily put in issue certain facts which will entitle the defendant to conduct examinations for discovery which will be embarrassing or otherwise disadvantageous to a plaintiff, or to plead a justification defence which has the same result.

> *Jay* v. *Hollinger Canadian Newspapers Limited Partnership*, 2002 BCSC 23, per McEwan J. at paras. 1–9.

Expression in a technical language or slang may give rise to a legal innuendo. A legal innuendo must be pleaded where the words complained of are "not ordinary English, but local, technical, provincial, or obsolete expressions, or slang or cant terms."

> *Meier* v. *Klotz*, [1928] 1 D.L.R. 91, per Macdonald J. at 92 (Sask. K.B.), rev'd on other grounds, [1928] 4 D.L.R. 4 (Sask. C.A.). At 1 D.L.R. 91 at 92, Macdonald J. quotes from William Blake Odgers, *Odgers on Libel and Slander*, 5th ed. (London: Stevens, 1912) at 125:
>
> > It is always prudent to explain by an innuendo "slang" words and expressions, words with a local meaning, words used by particular classes of persons, words which have no meaning at all in the ordinary acceptation, novel combinations of words, provincial expressions, historical and literary allusions, and the like. It is necessary or unnecessary so to do, according as ordinary persons at the present day would understand them, without explanation of the surrounding circumstances or extrinsic facts, to be defamatory or actionable *per se*, as the case may be: 18 Hals., pp. 649.51, para. 1209.

4) Defamation in a Foreign Language

The statement of claim must plead the words actually spoken or written in the foreign language; identify that foreign language; plead that the listeners, readers, or viewers understood that foreign language; plead the English translation of those foreign words; and plead that the translation is complete and accurate.

Dickman v. Gordon (1912), 23 O.W.R. 512.

Pirie v. Carroll (1931), 4 M.P.R. 127 (N.B.C.A.).

Polehyki v. Chromik, [1920] 15 Alta. L.R. 274, per Stuart J. at 348 (C.A), citing *Jenkins v. Phillips* (1841), 9 C. & P. 766, 25 Cyc. 448; 18 Hals. 648.

Skorski v. Sajur, [1998] O.J. No. 6285, per Dandie J. at para. 8 (Gen. Div.).

5) Of and Concerning the Plaintiff

The statement of claim must plead that the expression complained of is "of and concerning" the plaintiff, or equivalent words alleging that the expression is about the plaintiff.

Mount Cook Group Ltd. v. Johnstone Motors Ltd., [1990] 2 N.Z.L.R. 488.

Where it is not clear on the face of the allegedly defamatory expression that it refers to the plaintiff, the statement of claim should plead a legal innuendo stating that the plaintiff is the person referred to, and also give particulars of any facts the plaintiff relies on to show that the expression refers to the plaintiff.

Vulcan Industrial Packaging Ltd. v. Canadian Broadcasting Corporation (1979), 94 D.L.R. (3d) 729, per Master Sandler at 735 (Ont. S.C. (Mast.)), citing Sir Robert McEwen & Philip Lewis, *Gatley on Libel and Slander,* 7th ed. (London: Sweet & Maxwell, 1974) at 411–12, para. 989.

Church of Scientology of Toronto v. International News Distributing Co. (1974), 48 D.L.R. (3d) 176, per Lieff J. at 181 (Ont. H.C.J.), citing W.B. Williston & R.J. Rolles, *The Law of Civil Procedure* (Toronto: Butterworths, 1970), vol. 2, at 678, and *Bruce v. Odhams Press, Ltd.,* [1936] 1 K.B. 697 (C.A.).

Arnott v. College of Physicians and Surgeons of Saskatchewan, [1954] 1 D.L.R. 529, per Gordon J. at 557 (Sask. C.A.), citing *Knuppfer v. London Express Newspaper Ltd.,* [1944] A.C. 116 (H.L.). Gordon J. stated:

> It is beyond argument that such an allegation was necessary in the statement of claim when the plaintiff was not named in the alleged libel.

6) Slander — Additional Requirement

If slander is alleged, the statement of claim must specify whether the slander is actionable *per se*.

Lawrence v. Wallace (2002), 203 N.S.R. (2d) 197, per Cromwall J.A. at para. 8 (C.A.).

The statement of claim must also plead that the plaintiff suffered actual pecuniary loss if the slander is not actionable *per se* (unless the provincial defamation statute makes ordinary slander actionable without proof of such loss.)

> *Pootlass v. Pootlass* (1999), 63 B.C.L.R. (3d) 305 per Burnyeat J. at 327, para. 63 (S.C.).

> *Symons v. Toronto Dominion Bank*, [1997] 9 W.W.R. 132 per Gunn J. at paras. 23–24 (Sask. Q.B.).

> *Knox v. Spencer*, [1923] 1 D.L.R. 162, per White J. at 168–69 (N.S.C.A.) [in the context of slander and malicious falsehood].

Section 16 of the *Libel and Slander Act* of Ontario provides:

> In an action for slander for words calculated to disparage the plaintiff in any office, profession, calling, trade or business held or carried on by the plaintiff at the time of the publication thereof, it is not necessary to allege or prove special damage, whether or not the words are spoken of the plaintiff in the way of the plaintiff's office, profession, calling, trade or business, and the plaintiff may recover damages without averment or proof of special damage.

> R.S.O. 1990, c. L.12, s.16.

A plaintiff seeking to rely on the provisions of section 16 may plead it in the statement of claim.

7) Identity of Publishees

A statement of claim should allege publication of the defamatory expression to at least one named or identifiable person other than the plaintiff.

> *Hall v. Geiger*, [1930] 3 D.L.R. 644 (B.C.C.A.).

> *Kidder v. Healy*, 2002 SKQB 6, per Allbright J. at para. 34.

> *Symons v. Toronto Dominion Bank*, above, at paras. 21–22.

> *Seaton v. Autocars North (1983) Inc. (c.o.b. North Toronto Mazda)*, [2000] O.T.C. 348 per Lamek J. at paras. 27–28 (S.C.J.).

It is no objection to this requirement that a rule of court provides that a party should not plead the "evidence" by which the material fact of publication is to be proved, or that a rule of court provides that a party is not obliged to name witnesses.

> *Meredith v. Dalton*, [1944] O.J. No. 288 (Ont. H.C.J.), per Rose C.J.O.

Except in the case of publication in the mass media, the names of identified individuals to whom the defamatory expression was published should be pleaded.

Lowenberg v. Oderbien, [2000] M.J. No. 139 (Q.B.), applying *Shinkaruk v. Saskatoon*, [1985] 41 Sask. R. 187 (Q.B.).

MacRae v. Santa, [2002] O.J. No. 3000, per Pierce J. at para. 15 (S.C.J.).

Menasco Aerospace Limited (1996), 28 O.R. (3d) 343, per Greer J. at 350–51 (Gen. Div.).

Bankten Communication Services Ltd. v. General Motors of Canada Ltd., [1996] O.J. No. 2931 (Gen. Div.) per Dambrot J. at para. 5.

Ferguson v. McBee Technographics Inc., [1988] 6 W.W.R. 716, per Jewers J. at 720 (Man. Q.B.) [giving the plaintiff leave to amend the statement of claim to plead " … either the names of, or some means of identifying, the person or persons to whom publication was made"].

Peck v. La Valley, [1929] 2 D.L.R. 370, per Simmons C. J. at 371 (Alta. S.C. (T.D.)), citing William Blake Odgers, *Odgers on Libel and Slander*, 5th ed. (London: Stevens, 1912) at 674, *Davey v. Bentinck*, [1893] 1 Q.B. 185 (C.A.); *Br. Legal & United Provident Ass'ce Co. v. Sheffield*, [1911] 1 I.R. 69.

In the case of news media defendants, it is sufficient for the plaintiff to plead facts from which publication to third persons may be inferred, without identifying those persons by name.

Gaskin v. Retail Credit Co., [1965] S.C.R. 297, per Ritchie J. at 300.

Re McCain Foods Ltd. v. Agricultural Publishing Co. Ltd. (1979), 103 D.L.R. (3d) 724 per Cromarty J. at 731–33 (Ont. H.C.J.), appeal dismissed (1979), 103 D.L.R. 724 at 734 (Ont. C.A.), leave to appeal to S.C.C. denied (1980), 31 N.R. 449n.

Publication of a newspaper "in its legal sense in a libel action" occurs on the date it is received by the publishee.

Re McCain Foods Ltd. and Agricultural Publishing Co. Ltd. (1979), above, at 733.

Although in general there is a wide discretion to order that particulars of a claim be postponed until after examination for discovery of the defendants, the scope of that discretion is narrower in a defamation action than in most, if not all other classes of action. A plaintiff should therefore provide particulars before discovery of when, in what circumstances, by whom, and to whom the allegedly defamatory words were published.

Wesson v. Campbell River (District) (1985), 63 B.C.L.R. 327, per Taggart J.A. at 330 (C.A.), citing Philip Lewis, *Gatley on Libel and Slander*, 8th ed. (London: Sweet & Maxwell, 1981), at para. 1067.

Jaffe v. Americans for International Justice Foundation (1987), 22 C.P.C. (2d) 286, per Master Peppiatt at paras. 13, 18, 24 (Ont. S.C.).

Accordingly, where the plaintiff can raise no more than a speculation of publication by one or more of the defendants to persons unknown, of words complained of in the statement of claim, it is an error to defer such particulars until after the discovery of the defendants has been completed.

Wesson v. Campbell River (District), above, at 331.

Walker v. C.R.O.S., [1993] B.C.J. No. 2834, per Shabbits J. (S.C.):

> Paragraph 6 of the statement of claim alleges that the libelous material was distributed to members of C.R.O.S. and other unknown persons in South Surrey. The pleadings allege that C.R.O.S. is no more than an unorganized "group of residents who have printed letterhead." The defendant is entitled to particulars as to the plaintiffs' case on the issue of publication before he is discovered.

It has been held that where a statement of claim alleges the publication of a libel or slander to a named person, it may also allege publication to other unnamed persons, provided the plaintiff is able to produce uncontradicted evidence of publication to other persons.

137240 Assn. Canada Inc. v. Ontario Medical Assn., [1989] O.J. 1625, per Van Camp J. (H.C.J.), citing *Gaskin v. Retail Credit Company*, [1961] O.W.N. 171 per Schatz J.

But see *Paquette v. Cruji* (1979), 103 D.L.R. (3d) 141, per Grange J. at 145 (Ont. H.C.J.):

> I cannot believe that case [*Gaskin*] stands for the proposition that a plaintiff must establish his case by affidavit evidence before a pleading will stand.

And *Jaffe v. Americans for International Justice Foundation*, above, at para. 17:

> With respect I do not think that that case [*Gaskin*] stands for that proposition either; however, I do think that it stands for the proposition that the plaintiff must produce some evidence to justify his pleading, although he is not required to establish his case at that stage.

It has been held, however, that the discretion to defer particulars of the identities of everyone to whom defamatory expression was published may be greater where it is libel than where it is slander.

> The defendant is entitled to be told the names of the person to whom a slander was uttered in order that he may investigate and support his denial.

> *137240 Assn. Canada Inc.* v. *Ontario Medical Assn.*, above.

In one case, however, an Ontario court refused to strike out a statement of claim which pleaded the following particulars identifying persons to whom an alleged slander had been uttered:

> Thomas Prue, Theresa Houston, and others, the names of whom are not known to the Plaintiff, but known to the Defendant, but particulars of the identity of whom are that they were an employee or agent of the following corporations or institutions from each of which the Plaintiff sought employment during the periods set out after each, and during said periods, each made an inquiry of the Defendant concerning the Plaintiff's suitability for employment for the corporation or institution in question.

> *Paquette* v. *Cruji*, above, at 144:

> The plaintiff maintains he was slandered by the defendant by communication to persons unknown (but associated with particular institutions) at times unknown (though within a specified time span). He sets forth the words used. He has stated everything he knows. If he proves the facts pleaded he will have established a *prima facie* case. The law will always protect a defendant from a frivolous action but it should not deprive a plaintiff of his cause of action, ostensibly valid, where the particulars are not within his knowledge and are well within those of the defendant. If the plaintiff should fail to prove any of the 16 slanders specifically alleged there is always a remedy in costs.

A plaintiff resisting an application to strike a plea of publication to other individuals not named, or resisting an order to deliver particulars of those names, should make reasonable efforts to obtain that information and describe those efforts in an affidavit.

> *Richter* v. *Richter* (1995), 133 Sask R. 254, per MacPherson C.J.Q.B. at paras. 5–7 (Q.B.), citing *Winnett* v. *Appelbe*, [1894] Pr. 57 (Div. Ct.), *Mergen* v. *Brad Berrns* (1988), 71 Sask R. 93 (Q.B.), and Sir Robert McEwen & Philip Lewis, *Gatley on Libel and Slander*, 7th ed. (London: Sweet & Maxwell, 1974) at 422, para. 1015.

An Alberta court held that where the plaintiff had established a *prima facie* case (that is, the details of the dates, and places, and speakers, and words used to defame it) this was sufficient to permit the plaintiff to ask the defendants if they have made similar statements to other people.

> *550433 Alberta Ltd.* v. *Stealth Alarm Systems Inc. (c.o.b. Castle Security and Surveillance)* (1998), 40 C.P.C. (4th) 279, per Veit J. at 287 (Alta. Q.B.).

8) The Identity of the Defendant

See Chapter 14, "Publication and Republication."

In a defamation action against seventeen defendants concerning a posting on a website and the circulation of a flyer, a plaintiff has been ordered to provide particulars of the involvement of each defendant in the publications.

> *Craig* v. *Langley Citizen's Coalition*, 2003 BCSC 124, per Henderson J., at paras. 15–17:
>
> ... the plaintiff alleges, in the broadest possible terms, that each of these 17 named defendants printed certain material, published certain material, authorized it, incited them, and encouraged them. There is no particularization whatsoever as to who did what. To take one example, there is no particularization as to who controlled the website, in the sense of being the registered owner of the domain name and possessing, through the means of a password, the right to access that website. I think it highly unlikely that each of these 17 named defendants had that power.
>
> In essence, the case as it is presently constituted amounts to a fishing expedition. The plaintiff in effect says that, through the discovery process, he will determine from the mouths of the individual named defendants who did what. In many circumstances that would be permissible. Conspiracy cases, for example, have been permitted by this court to proceed on precisely that basis.
>
> However, in my view, defamation is different. The law and the Rules of Court require a greater degree of specificity in defamation pleadings than is required in most other causes of action.

The plaintiff must plead what each defendant is alleged to have published.

It is not sufficient to simply lump a number of defendants together in one paragraph of the pleading.

> *Cassagnol* v. *Pickering Automobiles Inc. (c.o.b. Pickering Honda)*, [2001] O.J. No. 4117, per Sheppard J. at para. 7 (S.C.), citing *Lana International Ltd.* v. *Menasco Aerospace Ltd.* (1996), 28 O.R. (3d) 343 at 351 (Gen. Div.).

9) Date, Time, and Place of Publication

The statement of claim must contain sufficient particulars of the time and place of publication.

Stevens v. Oakes, [1995] M.J. No. 304, per Master Bolton at para. 10 (Q.B.).

Lana International Ltd.v. Menasco Aerospace Ltd., above, at 350–51.

Bankten Communication Services Ltd. v. General Motors of Canada Ltd., [1996] O.J. No. 2931, per Dambrot J. at para. 5 (Gen. Div.).

Lawrence v. Wallace (2002), 203 N.S.R. (2d) 197, per Cromwall J.A. at paras. 6–8 (C.A.).

Ferguson v. McBee Technographics Inc., [1988] 6 W.W.R. 716. per Jewers J. at 720 (Man. Q.B.).

What constitutes sufficient particulars is a matter for determination in the specific circumstances of each case.

Peck v. La Valley, [1929] 2 D.L.R. 370 (Alta. S.C.) per Simmons C.J., holding at 372 that an allegation that four defendants published the defamatory expression in the months of November and December was adequate, and that particulars stipulating the precise dates within those months need not be delivered.

10) Republication

See Chapter 14, "Publication and Republication."

The statement of claim must specifically plead the precise exception(s) to the general rule that a defendant is not liable for republication by others.

Jordon v. Talbot, [1998] O.J. No. 1876, per Jennings J. at para. 3 (Gen. Div.).

The statement of claim should provide particulars with respect to the time, place, and circumstances of any republication, including the names of the persons who republished the defamatory expression and the persons to whom it was republished.

Brown v. Cole, [1994] B.C.J. No. 2356, per Master Doolan at para. 8 (S.C.).

It has been held, however, that further particulars were unnecessary where the statement of claim adequately particularized the original publication and sought aggravation of damages only based on the allegation that the defendants were the original publishers and that republication was a natural and probable result of the original publication.

Pacific Savings Insurance Services Ltd. v. Strong (1996), 4 C.P.C. (4th) 37 per Edwards J. at 43 (B.C.S.C.):

I conclude the details of how republication took place, which are necessarily outside the plaintiff's means of knowledge, need not be particularized where the plaintiff properly pleads an exception to the normal rule that the original publisher is not liable for unauthorized or unintended republication.

Similarly, an Ontario court ruled that the following pleading provides adequate particulars of republication.

The Plaintiff alleges and the fact is that the Defendants intended that the letter set out in paragraph 14 would be circulated widely, and its defamatory content spoken of widely, and that the Defendants knew or ought to have known that this re-publication was a natural and probable result of the letter complained of for which they are responsible.

Jaffe v. Americans for International Justice Foundation (1987), 22 C.P.C. (2d) 286, per Master Peppiatt at paras. 26–28 (Ont. S.C.).

11) Damages

a) Claim for General Damages

At common law, a plaintiff is entitled to plead general damages without providing particulars.

William P. Crooks Consultants Ltd. v. Cantree Plywood Corp. (1985), 62 B.C.L.R. 281, per Wallace J. at paras. 5–7 (S.C.), citing, *inter alia,* D.B. Casson & I.H. Dennis, *Odgers' Principles of Pleading and Practice*, 21st ed. (London: Stevens & Sons, 1975) at 165:

> ... General damages such as the law will presume to be the natural and probable consequence of the defendant's act need not be specifically pleaded. It arises by inference of law, and need not, therefore, be proved by evidence and may be averred generally.

An application for particulars of general damages will therefore be dismissed.

Meredith v. Dalton, [1944] O.J. No. 288 (H.C.J.) per Rose C.J.O.

Court decisions have described the following as pleadings of general damages.

i)   The plaintiff further says that the said heading and letter as a whole would tend to lower the plaintiff in the estimation of right-thinking members of society generally and the citizens of Saskatoon in particular and that the words are defamatory.

Cherneskey v. Armadale Publishers Ltd., [1979] 1 S.C.R. 1067.

ii)   The plaintiff was in consequence seriously injured in his character and in his reputation and in the way of his occupation, employment and office and has been brought into public scandal, odium and contempt.

> *Mengarelli v. Forrest*, [1972] 2 O.R. 397, per Master Davidson at 398 (S.C. (Mast.)).

As the law presumes that some damage will flow from the mere publication of the defamatory statement, courts have held that a general allegation that the plaintiff has suffered damage is sufficient.

> *Ratcliffe v. Evans* (1892), 2 Q.B. 524, per Brown L.J. at 528 (C.A.).

> *Waterhouse v. Australian Broadcasting Corp.* (1987), 87 L.R. 369.

If the plaintiff pleads diminution of profits, he must provide particulars.

> *Blanchford v. Green* (1892), 14 P.R. 424 (Ont. H.C.).

b) Special Damages

The general rule is that special damages must be specifically pleaded.

> *Botiuk v. Toronto Free Press Publications Ltd.* (1995), 126 D.L.R. (4th) 609, per Cory J. at para. 109 (S.C.C.).

> *Pootlass v. Pootlass*, (1999) 63 B.C.L.R. (3d) 305, per Burnyeat J. at 327, para. 64 (S.C.):

>> This is the case no matter how certain it is that the words will injure the reputation of the plaintiff: *Jones v. Jones*, [1916] 1 K.B. 351. Actual pecuniary damage or loss is not presumed, must be included in the Statement of Claim and set out specifically in order to be recovered: *Dom. Telegraph Co. v. Silver* (1882), 10 S.C.R. 238; *Knox v. Spencer* (1922), 50 N.B.R. 69 (N.B.C.A.).

> *Klein v. Kaip* (1989), 37 C.P.C. (2d) 245 at 246 (Sask. Q.B.), affirmed (1989), 37 C.P.C. (2d) 245 at 250 (Sask. C.A.), leave to appeal to S.C.C. refused (1990), 83 Sask. R. 160n (S.C.C.).

> *Civil Service Assn. of Ontario Inc. v. Little*, [1970] O.J. No. 704, per Wright J. at para. 14 (S.C.).

> *Mathews v. Cameron* (1964), 48 W.W.R. 162, per Sirois J. at paras. 26–27 (Sask. Q.B.), citing *Ratcliffe v. Evans*, above; *Ashdown v. The Manitoba Free Press Co.* (1891), 20 S.C.R. 43.

Special damages for the purposes of the law of defamation have been defined as any material or temporal loss which is either a pecuniary loss or is capable of being estimated in money. Special damages are not confined to business loss or loss of employment income. Rather, losses such as the loss of hospitality from friends, providing such loss is capable of being estimated in money, are also recoverable as special damages.

> *Pootlass* v. *Pootlass*, above, at 327, para. 64.

To qualify as special damage, the loss must be the natural and reasonable result of the publication of the words complained of.

> *Ludlow* v. *Batson* (1903), 5 O.L.R. 309 (Div. Ct.) per Falconbridge C.J. citing *Ratcliffe* v. *Evans*, above at 527, and Britton J. citing *Lynch* v. *Knight* (1861), 9 H.L. 577 at 600 (H.L. (Eng.)).

Where loss of custom and similar damages are claimed as special, exact monetary damages and full details with regard to the losses must be set forth in the plaintiff's pleadings, including the names of the lost customers, traders, or others.

> *Civil Service Assn. of Ontario Inc.* v. *Little*, above, at para. 14, citing, *inter alia*, *Dojcman* v. *St. Marie*, [1969] 2 O.R. 745 (C.A.), *Blachford* v. *Green* (1892), 14 P.R. 424 at 426–27 (Ont. H.C.); *Berscht* v. *The Toronto Star Limited*, [1945] O.W.N. 8 (Ont. Master).

> *Botiuk* v. *Toronto Free Press Publication*, above, at 633.

> *Ashdown* v. *Manitoba Free Press Co.* (1891), 20 S.C.R. 43, per Strong J. at 50:

> > I take it to be clear that where special damages are sought to be recovered in an action for libel, or in an action for verbal slander where the words are actionable *per se*, such special damages, must be alleged and pleaded with particularity, and that in the case of special damage by reason of loss of custom the names of the customers must be given or otherwise evidence of the special damage is not admissible, and that this rule is not confined to cases of verbal slander where the words are not actionable *per se*, cases in which special damage is a necessary ingredient in the cause of action.

> *Berscht* v. *The Toronto Star Limited*, [1944] O.J. No. 351, per Urquhart J. at para. 4 (Master).

> *Symons* v. *Toronto Dominion Bank*, [1997] 9 W.W.R. 132, per Gunn J. at paras. 23–24 (Sask. Q.B.).

It has been held that the following plea is not an allegation of special damages:

Whereby the plaintiff has been greatly injured in his credit and reputation, and also has been greatly injured in his credit and reputation as a hardware merchant and in his said business, and has experienced and sustained sensible and material dimunition and loss in the custom and profits of his said trade and business by divers persons, whose names are to the plaintiff unknown, having in consequence of the committing of the said grievances by the defendants avoided the plaintiff's said shops, stores and warehouses, and abstained from being customers of the plaintiff as such merchant as aforesaid, as they otherwise would have been but for the committing of the said grievances by the defendants.

Ashdown v. Manitoba Free Press Co. (1891), 20 S.C.R. 43 per Strong J. at 50, citing *Odgers on Libel*, 2d ed., at 302:

> … Loss of custom is special damage and must be specifically alleged and the customer's names stated in the record. If that be done the consequent reduction in plaintiff's annual income can easily be reckoned. But if no names be given, it is impossible to connect the alleged diminution in the general profits of plaintiff's business with defendant's words; it may be due to fluctuations in prices, to change of management, to a new shop being opened in opposition, or to many other causes. Hence, such an indefinite loss of business is considered general damage and can only be proved when the words are spoken of the plaintiff in the way of his trade and so are actionable *per se*. For there the law presumes that such words must injure the plaintiff's business and therefore attributes to those words the diminution it finds in plaintiff's profits. See *Harrison v. Pearce*, 1 F. & F. 567.

A loss of general custom flowing directly and in the ordinary course of things may be alleged and proved generally.

Berscht v. The Toronto Star Limited, above, at para. 6, citing *Halsbury*. Vol. 20 p. 524, *Ratcliffe v. Evans*, above, at 529.

The degree of specificity in pleading special damages will vary with the circumstances of the case. If particulars of specific customers are impossible to ascertain because of the nature of the business, the court will not require specific names. It has been held that a loss of business was sufficiently pleaded to warrant an award of special damages where a plaintiff pleaded that, by reason of the defamatory statements made against him, he suffered, among other things, a "loss in his practice of his profession as a barrister and solicitor" and "suffered injury to his career." A lump sum for damages was claimed to compensate for these injuries.

Botiuk v. Toronto Free Press Publications Ltd., above, at para. 110.

Particulars of special damages must also be pleaded in a statement of claim for slander of title.

Cross v. Bain, Pooler & Co. et al., [1937] O.W.N. 220 per Greene J. at 221–22 (H.C.J.):

> Dealing with slander of title, in *Fraser on the Law of Libel and Slander*, 5th ed., p. 62, is the following:
>
> …
>
>> To support such an action [slander of title] it is necessary for the plaintiff to prove —
>> (1) That the statements complained of were untrue;
>> (2) That they were made maliciously;
>> (3) That the plaintiffs have suffered special damage thereby.
>
> … Where the plaintiff is confined to special damage, the defendant is entitled to know what claim he has to meet.

c) Aggravated Damages

The statement of claim should contain particulars of the acts of the defendant on which the plaintiff intends to rely at trial in support of her claim for aggravated damages.

Milligan v. Jamieson (1902), 4 O.L.R. 650, per Meredith C.J. at 652 (C.A.):

> It would be a highly inconvenient practice to require a defendant to go to trial at the risk of being met with a number of circumstances which the other side was permitted to give evidence of without setting them forth in his pleading, and which might, if unanswered, seriously affect the damages.

But see *Toronto Star Ltd. v. Globe Printing Co.*, [1941] 3 D.L.R. 376 (Ont. H.C.J.), where Roach J. stated at 378:

> The plaintiff need not allege matters on which he proposes to rely in the aggravation of damages but if he does plead them the Court will not strike them out as embarrassing or tending to prejudice the fair trial of the action. See *Millington v. Loring* (1880), 6 Q.B.D. 190.

Pleading such particulars in the statement of claim is permissible even though it has the effect of anticipating a plea of privilege by the defendant.

Berscht v. Toronto Sun, [1945] O.W.N. 8 at 10 (H.C. Mast.) per the Master, aff'd, [1945] O.W.N. 10, per Urquhart J. at 10–11 (H.C.).

The defendant's conduct before or after the publication of the defamatory statement may be pleaded in aggravation of damages.

Reichmann v. *Toronto Life Publishing Co.* (1988), 27 C.P.C. (2d) 37, per Anderson J. at 46 (Ont. H.C.J.).

Hallren v. *Holden* (1914), 20 D.L.R. 336, per Macdonald C.J.A. at 337 (B.C.C.A.), citing *Millington* v. *Loring* (1880), 6 Q.B.D. 190, per Irving J.A. at 339 (C.A.), citing William Blake Odgers, *Odgers Principles of Pleading and Practice*, 7th ed. (London: Stevens, 1912) at 103, and Galliher J.A. at 341.

Although the defendant's intention is not relevant to interpret the meaning of the defamatory expression, it is relevant on the question of express malice and material to the quantum of damages. The plaintiff is therefore entitled to plead such intent.

Toronto Star Ltd. v. *Globe Printing Co.*, above, at 378:

> It is one thing to accidentally libel a plaintiff but another to do so intentionally. It is well established that a jury in determining the injury done to the plaintiff may consider the spirit, the intention and the conduct of the defendant.

Kenora (Town) Police Services Board v. *Savino* (1995), 36 C.P.C. (3d) 46, per Stach J. at para. 22 (Ont. Gen. Div.), citing *Reichmann* v. *Toronto Life Publishing Co.*, above, at 42–43.

Reichmann v. *Toronto Life Publishing Co.*, *ibid.*, where Anderson J. held at 42–43 that the motive of the author was relevant to damages and a plea concerning that motive should not be struck out.

A plea that damages have been aggravated by republication in other publications may be appropriate, depending on the circumstances of the case.

Reichmann v. *Toronto Life Publishing Co.*, *ibid.*, where Anderson J. at 41–42 sustained certain pleas of republication of the libel or alleged republication of the libel in other periodicals.

d) Punitive Damages

If appropriate, punitive damages should be specifically claimed in the prayer for relief and the material facts alleged to justify punitive damages should be pleaded with some particularity.

Whiten v. *Pilot Insurance Company*, [2002] 1 S.C.R. 595, 2002 SCC 18, per Binnie J. at paras. 86–87:

¶87   One of the purposes of a statement of claim is to alert the defendant to the case it has to meet, and if at the end of the day the defendant is surprised by an award against it that is a multiple of what it thought was the amount in issue, there is an obvious unfairness. Moreover, the facts said to justify punitive damages should be pleaded with some particularity. The time-honoured adjectives describing conduct as "harsh, vindictive, reprehensible and malicious (per McIntyre J. in *Vorvis*, supra, p. 1108) or their pejorative equivalent, however apt to capture the essence of the remedy, are conclusory rather than explanatory.

Whether a defendant has been taken by surprise at trial by an inadequate pleading of punitive damages will be decided in the circumstances of the specific case.

Whiten v. Pilot Insurance Company, ibid., at para. 88.

A statement of claim should specifically relate the plea for punitive damages in the prayer for relief to the material facts alleged in the body of statement of claim to support that relief.

Whiten v. Pilot Insurance Company, ibid., at para. 91.

e)   Actual Malice

The relevant rules of court and related jurisprudence should be carefully considered when actual malice is relevant to a potential claim for aggravated or punitive damages, or to overcome a defence of fair comment or qualified privilege.

Pleading actual malice is discussed below in section D, "Reply."

12) Prayer for Relief

As a general principle, a prayer for relief does not contain allegations of fact but an indication of the various causes of action that the plaintiff proposes to raise on the facts otherwise alleged in the body of the statement of claim. Particulars will not be ordered of a prayer for relief.

The prayer for relief is for legal argument after the facts have been established.

Chaput v. Finley, [1995] N.W.T.J. No. 83, per Schuler J. at para. 9 (S.C.).

The court rules vary from province to province regarding what is permissible or required in a prayer for relief.

For example, in British Columbia, Rule 19(29) of the *Rules of Court* specifically prohibits a plaintiff from stating the amount to be claimed for general damages.

Where general damages are claimed, the amount of the general damages claimed shall not be stated in the originating process or in any pleading.

The converse is true in other provinces. For example, Ontario Rule 25.06(9) requires that the prayer for relief in the statement of claim set out "the amount claimed for each claimant in respect of each claim."

A plaintiff's failure to comply with the Ontario rule entitles the defendant to seek an order compelling the plaintiff to plead a specific figure.

Pennington v. Smith (1980), 16 C.P.C. 151, per Master Donkin at 154 (Ont. S.C. (Mast.)) [plaintiff consented to provide a figure].

In the context of a defamation claim, it has been held in Alberta that a statement of claim is not fatally insufficient if it omits from the prayer for relief a specific claim for defamation damages. There is no specific reference to a "prayer for relief" in the Alberta *Rules of Court*.

Temple v. Edmonton (City) (1990), 105 A.R. 77, per Master Quinn at 79 (Q.B.), approved the following passage from Basil Antony Harwood, *Odgers on Pleadings and Practice,* 15th ed. (London: Stevens, 1955) at 132:

> Damages and their amount are always in issue unless expressly admitted; do not therefore plead to them unless you wish to make some admission. Nor should you plead to the prayer or claim for relief at the end of your opponent's pleading.

C. STATEMENT OF DEFENCE

It is a basic principle, articulated in the rules of court in most provinces, that in a statement of defence a defendant shall plead specifically any matter of fact or point of law that

i) the defendant alleges makes a claim of the plaintiff not maintainable,
ii) if not specifically pleaded might take the plaintiff by surprise, or
iii) raises issues of fact not arising out of the plaintiff's pleadings.

1) Defences that May Be Pleaded

The principal defamation defences are discussed elsewhere in this book. The defamation defences which are available to be raised by a defendant will of course depend on the specific circumstances of the claim. The range of defences that may be pleaded include (but are not necessarily limited to) the following:

- A denial that the defendant published (or republished) the expression complained of. [See Chapter 14, "Publication and Republication."]
- A denial that the defendant was vicariously responsible for expression published by another person. [See Chapter 6, "Parties."]
- A denial that the expression was defamatory. [See Chapter 15, "Defamatory Meaning."]
- A *Pizza Pizza/Polly Peck* defence (alleging the defendant's defamatory meaning). [See Chapter 24, "*Polly Peck* and *Pizza Pizza*: Alleging the Defendant's Defamatory Meaning and Pleading That Meaning is True."]
- An allegation that the expression was jest or vulgar abuse. [See Chapter 15, "Defamatory Meaning."]
- A denial that the expression conveyed the popular or false innuendo meanings pleaded by the plaintiff. [See Chapter 15, "Defamatory Meaning."]
- A denial of the extrinsic facts and circumstances pleaded by a plaintiff in support of a legal innuendo. [See Chapter 15, "Defamatory Meaning."]
- A denial that the expression was of and concerning the plaintiff. [See Chapter 13, "Identification of the Plaintiff."]
- If slander is alleged:
  i) a denial that it is actionable per se
  ii) an allegation that the alleged special damage was not incurred or is too remote.
  [See Chapter 1, "Libel and Slander."]
- Consent. [See Chapter 22, "Consent."]
- Justification [See Chapter 21, "Justification."]
- Partial justification. [See Chapter 21, "Justification."]
- Fair comment. [See Chapter 17, "Fair Comment."]
- Qualified privilege. [See Chapter 19, "Qualified Privilege and Publication to the World at Large."]
- Absolute privilege. [See Chapter 20, "Absolute Privilege."]
- Statutory report privilege. [See Chapter 18, "Qualified and Statutory Privilege."]
- Innocent dissemination. [See Chapter 14 "Publication and Republication" at 186.]
- Other statutory defences. [See Chapter 9, "Apologies, Retractions and Clarifications."]
- Mitigation of damages at common law. [See Chapter 30, "Damages."]
- Mitigation of damages pursuant to statute. [See Chapter 30, "Damages," G. Statutory Provisions, (1) Mitigation.]

- Expiry of a limitation period. [See Chapter 6, "Notice of Intended Action and Limitation Defences."]
- Failure to serve libel notices prescribed by a defamation statute. [See Chapter 6, "Notice of Intended Action and Limitation Defences."]
- Miscellaneous other defences to liability or damages.

The jurisprudence concerning the requirements of pleading certain defamation defences is discussed below.

a) Fair Comment

See Chapter 16, "Fair Comment."

The customary form of pleading this defence is to state that the expression complained of was "fair comment made in good faith and without malice upon a matter of public interest."

McLoughlin v. Kutasy, [1979] 2 S.C.R. 311, per Ritchie J. at 320:

> An essential ingredient of [the defence of fair comment] is that the comment was made on a matter of public interest and the customary form of pleading in this regard is to state that the words complained of "were fair comment made in good faith and without malice upon a matter of public interest" (see Bullen and Leake, *Precedents of Pleadings*, 12th ed., at p. 1176).

In addition, the plea should set forth particulars of the facts expressed or generally understood upon which the comment was based, and identify the public interest.

A decision to abandon a plea of fair comment does not necessarily constitute a judicial admission that the words complained of are statements of fact which precludes a defendant from subsequently seeking to amend to plead fair comment again. The characterization of impugned statements may be seen as a matter of argument.

Ager v. Canjex Publishing Ltd. (c.o.b. Canada Stockwatch), 2003 BCSC 305, per Lowry J. at paras. 6–8.

The plaintiff is entitled to plead facts in support of the comment in the statement of defence even if those facts were not all referred to in the publication or broadcast at issue. The defence may be available even if the facts are not expressly stated in the publication or broadcast.

Scott v. Fulton, [1998] B.C.J. No. 2786 (S.C.), per R.D. Wilson J., citing, *inter alia*, *Kemsley v. Foot*, [1952] A.C. 345 (H.L.).

i) The Rolled-up Plea

The "rolled-up" plea raises the defence of fair comment, not justification. Typically, this plea alleges that insofar as the words complained of consist of statements of fact, they are true in substance and in fact, and insofar as they consist of an expression of opinion, they are fair comment made in good faith and without malice, upon the said facts which are matters of public interest.

> British Columbia Law Reform Commission, *Report on Defamation,* (1985), at 55.

> *Foster* v. *Maclean* (1916), 37 O.L.R. 68, per Riddell at 74–75, (C.A.) citing *Augustine Rotary Engine Co.* v. *S* *'urday Night Limited* (1916), 36 O.L.R. 551 (Div. Ct.), *Peter Walker & Son Limited* v. *Hodgson,* [1909] 1 K.B. 239 at 243–47.

> *Perini Pacific Ltd.* v. *The Citizen* (1962), 32 D.L.R. (2d) 244, per Collins J. at 245–46 (B.C.S.C.).

> *Boys* v. *Star Ptg. & Pub. Co.,* [1927] 3 D.L.R. 847 per Riddell J.A. at 854–55 (Ont. C.A.).

> *Sutherland* v. *Stopes,* [1925] A.C. 47, per Viscount Finlay at 62–63, Lord Shaw of Dunfermline at 77–78 (H.L. (Eng.))

> *Khurana* v. *Jouhal (c.o.b. Ranjeet),* [1982] B.C.J. No. 819, at paras. 6–7 (S.C.).

The defendant must prove that the opinion is fair comment and that the statements of fact are true.

> *Khurana* v. *Jouhal (c.o.b. Ranjeet), ibid.,* at para. 8.

As a result of amendments to the British Columbia *Rules of Court,* under the rolled-up plea the defendant must state which of the words complained of are statements of fact and which are opinion, and give particulars of the facts relied on.

> *Vogel* v. *Canadian Broadcasting Corporation* (1981), 26 B.C.L.R. 340 (S.C.), adopting the following language from *Stredwick* v. *Wiseman* (1966), N.Z.L.R. 263 at 264 (S.C.):

>> First, it should be recorded that the following words are statements of fact, and these should be set out *seriatum* and numbered. Then there should follow a second paragraph under the heading: "The facts and matters relied on in support of the allegation that the words set out above are true, are as follows," and the fact and matters should then be set forth and numbered.

British Columbia rule 19(12)(b) is essentially the same as the English Rule, O. 82, r. 3 — an "obligation to give particulars," discussed in *Lord* v. *Sunday Telegraph* (1971), 1 Q.B. 235 (C.A.). It is a rule specifically designed to require certain particulars where the defendant pleads the rolled-up plea, and requires the defendant to make the same distinction between fact and opinion and to give the facts he relies on to support the allegation that the words are true.

> *Khurana* v. *Jouhal (c.o.b. Ranjeet)*, above, at para. 12.

Rule 19(12)(b) of the British Columbia *Rules of Court* provides:

> Where the defendant alleges that, in so far as the words complained of consist of statements of fact, they are true in substance and in fact, and that in so far as they consist of expressions of opinion, they are fair comment on a matter of public interest, the defendant shall give particulars stating which of the words complained of the defendant alleges are statements of fact and of the facts and matters relied on in support of the allegation that the words are true.

In Ontario, it has been held that where the allegedly defamatory expression is general in nature and the facts relied upon for the comments are not specifically stated in the alleged libel, the defendant is required to deliver particulars of the facts supporting the comment, even where a rolled-up plea is used.

> *Gouzenko* v. *Doubleday Canada Ltd. et al. (No.2)* (1981), 34 O.R. (2d) 306 at 308–10 (H.C.J.), aff'd (1982), 142 D.L.R. (3d) 192 (Ont. C.A.). Per Reid J. at 34 O.R. (2d) 306 at 310:

> > ... the interpretation of [*Aga Khan* v. *Times Publishing Co.*, [1924] 1 K.B. 675] to the effect that particulars may not be obtained of a rolled-up plea is entirely contrary to the general tenor of practice in the courts of this province and the principles governing that practice. ... I am not bound by Aga Khan. But beyond that, if Aga Khan is offered for the proposition that by way of a rolled-up plea a defendant can escape the obligation to frame a statement of defence in such a way as to disclose the case the defendant proposes to show against him at trial; an obligation that lies on defendants in all other kinds of action, I say unhesitatingly that would, in my opinion, contravene both principle and practice and I see no justification for it.

> > The argument that the defendant should not be required to distinguish between fact and comment because that would pre-empt the

jury's authority is, in my respectful opinion, specious. If that argument were to succeed it would obviate the need for particulars in any action.

Where particulars of a rolled-up plea allege that all of the words in the impugned publication are statements of fact, leaving no room for a plea of fair comment, the defence of fair comment will be struck out.

Savein v. CJOR 600 Radio Station, [1989] B.C.J. No. 376 (S.C.).

A plea of justification is not included in a rolled-up plea. Accordingly, if the defendant wants to rely on justification, it must be specifically pleaded.

Stetson v. MacNeill (c.o.b. The Eastern Graphic) (1997), 152 Nfld. & P.E.I.R. 225 (P.E.I.S.C. (T.D.)).

Drake v. Overland (1979), 107 D.L.R. (3d) 323 at 328 (Alta. C.A.).

Where a plaintiff sued for libel over ten precise verbatim statements contained in two separate issues of a newspaper published twenty-five days apart (five statements in each edition), the court struck out a plea by the defendant that "insofar as the said articles, statements and words consist of allegations of fact, they are true in substance and in fact; insofar as they consist of expressions of opinion, they are fair comments made in good faith and without malice upon the said facts, which are matters of public interest." The use of the plural "articles" was embarrassing because it improperly amounted to a pleading that every statement of fact in either article is true and every expression of opinion in either article is a fair comment on the statements of fact appearing in either or both articles. That is to say, an expression of opinion in the second article may be a fair comment on a statement of fact in the first article. Moreover, it might be that neither the expression of opinion nor the statement of fact, in a given instance, would be found at all among the specific words complained of by the plaintiff. The defendant's pleading introduced an immaterial issue, namely whether expressions of opinion in the articles not among the words complained of constitute fair comment on statements of fact which may or may not be found among the words complained of.

Robinson v. Pearce Northern Ltd., [1942] 2 D.L.R. 384, per Kelly J. at 386–87 (Ont. H.C.J.).

The Law Reform Commission of British Columbia recommended the abolition of the rolled-up plea on the basis it creates confusion, noting that it is now in general disuse in England.

British Columbia, Law Reform Commission, *Report on Defamation*, (1985), at 56.

ii) *Particulars of Facts Relied Upon*

If the defendant has pleaded fair comment, the plaintiff is entitled to particulars of the facts on which the comment is based if they are not pleaded in the statement of defence.

Stetson v. MacNeill (c.o.b. The Eastern Graphic), above.

Rotstein v. Globe and Mail (1997), 18 C.P.C. (4th) 144 (Ont. Gen. Div.).

Cunningham-Howie v. F.W. Dimbleby & Sons Ltd., [1951] 1K.B. 360 at 363, [1950] 2 All E.R. at 882 (C.A.).

Lehoux v. Riehl, [1997] B.C.J. No. 1736 (S.C.).

Firestone v. Smith, [1991] B.C.J. No. 2660 at 4 (Master).

Ontario Society for the Prevention of Cruelty to Animals et al. v. Toronto Sun Publishing Corporation et al. (1982), 31 C.P.C. 252 (Ont. S.C. (Mast.)).

Archer International Developments Ltd. v. Pacific Press Ltd., [1989] B.C.J. No. 1198 at 2.

Failure to provide particulars of the facts on which the comment is based may result in the fair comment defence being struck out.

Stetson v. MacNeill (c.o.b. The Eastern Graphic), above.

Citing *Gouzenko v. Doubleday Canada Ltd. (No.2)* (1981), above, an Ontario Master ordered a defendant to state which of the allegedly defamatory words were "put forward as fact and which were put forward as opinion."

Rotstein v. Globe and Mail, above, at 150. Master Clark held at 149 that the statement of defence did not incorporate a rolled-up plea. The statement of defence, which the Master characterized as "simply misbegotten, in the sense of being poorly conceived," stated in part:

7. In the alternative, if the words complained of are found to bear any of the meanings ascribed to them by the plaintiffs in paragraph 14 of the statement of claim, the defendants plead:

(a) with respect to sub-paragraph (a), insofar as the meaning ascribed to the words complained of by the plaintiff are fact, they are true in substance and in fact, and insofar as they are comment, they represent fair comment on a matter of public interest, namely criticism of a literary work which was admitted for public scrutiny by the plaintiff; ...

If the defendant takes the position that certain facts are "implied" in the defamatory publication, the preferred practice is to particularize such facts in the statement of defence. This is done, for example, where a cartoon is alleged to constitute fair comment.

Vander Zalm v. *Times Publishers Ltd.* (1980), 109 D.L.R. (3d) 531 (B.C.C.A.), Craig J.A. at 547–48 set out the statement of defence which pleaded, in part: "Particulars of the facts upon which the Defendants plead fair comment are: ..." and then alleged certain facts in sixteen sub-paragraphs.

Ross v. *New Brunswick Teachers' Assn* (2001), 201 D.L.R. (4th) 75, per Daigle C.J.N.B. at 103 (N.B.C.A.):

> [70] In oral argument before this Court, Beutel [the defendant cartoonist] relied on three sets of underlying facts in support of the plea of fair comment: first, the facts set out in the cartoon itself by specific reference to Ross' writings, Web of Deceit and Spectre of Power; second the quotations read by Beutel as commentary accompanying the presentation of the Goebbels cartoon; third, the approximately 45 particulars pleaded in para. 8 of the Statement of Defence as the basic facts upon which the comment was made as they are specifically referenced in the Amended Statement of Better and Further Particulars. These facts consist mainly of specific views on and beliefs in the conspiracy theory expressed in Ross' writings, as well as Ross' association with other notorious anti-Semites from across this country and elsewhere.

There is a distinction between particulars of facts and the evidence by which those facts may be proved. The plaintiff is entitled to know what facts the defendant intends to prove. However, the manner in which the defendant intends to prove those facts is a matter of evidence.

Lehoux v. *Riehl*, above.

Although the weight of authority supports the proposition that the defendant should plead, either in the statement of defence or by way of particulars, the facts which are the alleged substratum for the defence of fair comment, there has been a suggestion in recent jurisprudence that some deviation from this approach may be permitted by a court in certain circumstances.

Siddon v. *Mair* [1997] B.C.J. No. 17, per Fraser J. (S.C.):

> ... the defendant is required to set out facts, known to him or her at the time the words complained of were spoken, and then allege that, on

the basis of these facts, the words amounted to fair comment ... Like any other rule of pleading, it is not absolute. The ultimate goal of pleadings is to present a comprehensible statement to the jury. In the present Statement of Defence, the defendants plead fair comment no less than 14 times and one can see that requiring the defendants to plead the facts they contend justify each comment might well lead to a cluttered and confusing document. Just how cluttered, however, may be affected by my future ruling on whether the environmental implications of the project are relevant to the case. If they are not, then it is conceivable that it would not be too onerous to ask the defendants to set out the facts relied upon, and that that might generate a Statement of Defence which was not too confusing. Thus, the form of the pleas of fair comment will await submissions as to the relevance of the environmental implications.

It appears that at common law, a defendant is not required to give particulars setting out which of the words were expressions of opinion and which of the words were statements of fact. The defendant is only required to give particulars of the facts, unless he has pleaded the rolled-up plea in which case rule 19(12)(b) of the British Columbia *Rules of Court* requires the defendant to stipulate which expression is comment.

> *Archer International Developments Ltd.* v. *Pacific Press Ltd.*, [1989] B.C.J. No. 1198 at 4, citing *Aga Khan* v. *Times Publishing Co.* [1924] L.J.K.B. 361, per Bankes L.J. at 363 and Sargant L.J. at 365, and *Lord* v. *Sunday Telegraph Ltd.* (1970) 3 All E.R. 504 at 506, line h, per Lord Denning.

> *Gouzenko* v. *Doubleday Canada Ltd.* (1981), 23 C.P.C. 45 (Ont. S.C. (Mast.)).

b) Qualified Privilege

In determining the words to complain of in the statement of claim, a plaintiff should consider a potential defence of privilege. It has been held that a plaintiff's failure to include the inflammatory caption or heading of an article in the words complained of deprived a plaintiff of the right to argue at trial that the article did not constitute a "fair and accurate report" within the meaning of the statutory privilege.

> *Hansen* v. *Nugget Publishers Ltd.*, [1927] 4 D.L.R. 791, per Riddell J.A. at 795–96 (Ont. C.A.).

The law is unsettled as to whether the statement of defence must expressly plead "qualified privilege."

A number of courts have stated that it is not necessary that qualified privilege be expressly pleaded, provided the facts supporting the existence of a qualified privilege are set out.

Day v. Day (1980), 29 Nfld. and P.E.I.R. 487, per Goodridge J. at 501 (Nfld. S.C. (T.D.)).

Lambe (Next Friend of) v. Walsh (1986), 61 Nfld. & P.E.I.R. 193 (Nfld. T.D.) where Cummings J., after referring to *Day v. Day*, *ibid.*, stated at 197:

> Counsel for the plaintiff said no facts were pleaded to support qualified privilege and, consequently, he was taken by surprise and the defendant should not be permitted to raise that defence. I agree with counsel for the plaintiff.

Moores v. Salter (1982), 37 Nfld. & P.E.I.R. 128 (Nfld. Dist. Ct.).

MacArthur v. Meuser (1997), 146 D.L.R. (4th) 125, per Adams J. at 137 (Ont. Gen. Div.), applying *Day v. Day*, above.

In *Blagden v. Bennett* (1885), 9 O.R. 593 (C.A.), it was held that a defendant was entitled to rely on a defence of qualified privilege although it had not been pleaded. One member of the panel, Cameron J., stated at page 601:

> It remains to be considered whether the defendant, by not setting up the privilege of the occasion, has forfeited or lost the defence that would otherwise have been open to him. I do not think he has.
>
> It would have been better and more correct as a matter of precise statement if he had alleged the occasion was privileged. But the plaintiff is bound to make out his case. In his endeavour to do so his evidence discloses that the occasion was privileged, and therefore he should have known it and been prepared with evidence to establish express malice. The Court is not to give judgment according to the matter alleged but to what the facts established by the evidence in law demand. The pleadings should if necessary be amended; but as the gist of the action of slander is malice, and by what is made to appear in evidence, there was no malice on the defendant's part, but on the contrary the inference of malice that in the absence of privilege would arise, is rebutted, and the action fails.

In *Wells v. Lindhop* (1887), 13 O.R. 434 (C.A.), both members of the panel accepted that *Blagden v. Bennett* could not be regarded as authority for the proposition that a defendant is generally not required to plead privilege. Ordering a new trial, Proudfoot J. stated at page 437:

> It was contended by the defendant that the communication was privileged, and leave was asked to amend the record by pleading it, if necessary to do so.

As to the latter point, the case of *Blagden v. Bennett*, 9 O.R. 593, 601, appears to establish that if the plaintiff, in his endeavour to make out his case, discloses in his evidence that the occasion was privileged, there is no need for the defendant to plead the privilege; and that is the case here. All the facts upon which the privilege is claimed were extracted from the plaintiff's witnesses.

Also ordering a new trial, although on different grounds, Boyd C. stated at page 440:

> It is my opinion that this case has not been satisfactorily tried, and that the application for a new trial should be granted. The difficulties have arisen from the state of the pleadings and the inapplicability of much of the evidence to those pleadings. ... If *Blagden v. Bennett*, 9 O.R. 593 is to be taken as laying down as a general proposition that the omission to plead privilege does not preclude a defendant from setting it up, without amending the record, at the trial, I am not prepared to adopt that view of the law. ...

and at page 441:

> The judge, if the objection had been made, should have ruled out such a line of investigation because it was not in issue, as the defendant had not placed his defence on the ground of privilege: *Scott v. Sampson*, 8 Q.B.D. 491, *Bell v. Parke*, 11 Ir. C. L. Rep. 413 (1860).

On balance, it is suggested that "qualified privilege" should be expressly pleaded. This will assist in discovery of documents, examination for discovery, and preparation for and conduct of the trial.

The defendant should plead all of the circumstances which are alleged to give rise to the occasion of qualified privilege.

Globe and Mail Ltd. v. Boland, [1960] S.C.R. 203 per Cartwright J. at 206, citing Richard O'Sullivan & Roland G. Brown, *Gatley on Libel and Slander*, 4th ed. (London: Sweet & Maxwell, 1953) at 282.

Banks v. Globe & Mail, [1961] S.C.R. 747 per Cartwright J. at 481, citing Richard O'Sullivan & Robert L. McEwen, *Gatley on Libel and Slander*, 5th ed. (London: Sweeet & Maxwell, 1960) at 270.

Toronto Star Ltd. v. Drew, [1948] 4 D.L.R. 465 at 467 (S.C.C.).

Wismer v. Maclean-Hunter Publishing Co. Ltd. and Fraser (No. 1), [1954] 1 D.L.R. 481 per Robertson J.A. at 493 (B.C.C.A.):

As for Fraser's defence of privilege, it was necessary for him to set out the facts to show the occasion was privileged: see *Gatley on Libel and Slander*, 3rd ed., p. 530.

A defendant is permitted to plead the facts giving rise to the defendant's honest belief in the truth of the words he or she published.

Robertson v. Boddington, [1925] 2 D.L.R. 483, per Riddell J. at 486–87 (Ont. H.C.).

c) Absolute Privilege

The law is divided as to whether "absolute privilege" must be expressly pleaded. An early decision of the Ontario Court of Appeal held that it should be specifically pleaded.

Wills v. Lindoff (1887), 13 O.R. 434 at 440–42 per Boyd C.

More recently, two decisions in Newfoundland held that it was sufficient to merely set out the facts upon which the privilege is claimed without precisely or expressly pleading the privilege itself.

Day v. Day (1980), 29 Nfld. & P.E.I.R. 487 (Nfld. S.C. (T.D.)).

Moores v. Salter (1982), 37 Nfld. & P.E.I.R. 128 (Nfld. Dist. Ct.).

The prudent course is to expressly plead the defence of absolute privilege.

d) Pleading the Defamation Acts

A court in Newfoundland held that it was sufficient to plead "all sections" of the *Libel and Slander Act*.

Stetson v. MacNeill (c.o.b. The Eastern Graphic) (1997), 152 Nfld. & P.E.I.R. 225 (P.E.I.S.C. (T.D.)).

It has been held in Alberta that a defendant must plead that the plaintiff failed to satisfy a condition precedent by virtue of rule 108 of the Alberta *Rules of Court*. Accordingly, the defendant must expressly plead a plaintiff's failure to serve a notice required by Alberta's *Libel and Slander Act*. Where a defendant sought to amend to plead the condition precedent, the amendment was denied on the grounds of prejudice in the unusual circumstances of that case. The proposed plea read as follows:

The Defendants state that the Plaintiff has failed to comply with s.13 of the *Defamation Act*, R.S.A. 1980, as amended, in that the Plaintiff has:

a)   failed to set out the matter complained of;

b)   failed to serve notice upon the Defendant, Horst Heise;

c) failed to notify the Defendants of his intention to sue for his reputation as a private citizen.

The Defendants state that the name of the proprietor, publisher and the address of publication was published in a conspicuous place in the Calgary Herald and plead and rely upon s.17 of the *Defamation Act*, R.S.A. 1980. The Defendants state that the Plaintiff has failed to comply with a condition precedent and the limitations set out in the said Act.

Getty v. Calgary Herald, [1990] A.J. No. 237, per Master Funduk (Q.B.).

e) Mitigation

The British Columbia *Supreme Court Rules* require that a defendant plead mitigation.

Jay v. Hollinger Canadian Newspapers Limited Partnership, 2002 BCSC 23, per McEwan J. at para. 30.

f) Mitigation of Damages at Common Law

See Chapter 9, "Apologies, Retractions and Clarifications" and Chapter 31, "Evidence."

Facts intended to be given in evidence in mitigation of damages should be specifically pleaded.

Beaton v. The Intelligencer Printing & Publishing, etc. (1895), 22 O.A.R. 97 at 101.

Fulford v. Wallace (1901), 1 O.L.R. 278, per Meredith C.J. at para. 9 (Master).

Grant v. McRae (1906), O.W.R. 204 at 205.

Foster v. McLean (1916), 37 O.L.R. 68 at 74 (C.A.).

It is a matter for the trial judge to determine whether facts set out in a pleading in mitigation of damages should be admitted in evidence at trial.

Sentinel-Review Co. v. Robinson (1927), 60 O.L.R. 93, per Meredith C.J.C.P. (Master).

The defendant cannot plead a defence of justification under the guise of mitigation of damages.

Moore v. Mitchell (1886), 11 O.R. 21 (H.C.J.), per Wilson C.J. (Armour J. concurring) at 25.

One court in British Columbia has held that pleading an apology in mitigation of damages does not prevent a defendant from pleading justification.

Dowding v. *Pacific West Equities Ltd.* (1992), 63 B.C.L.R. (2d) 300, per Mac-
Donald J. at 305 (S.C.):

> With respect to the apparent inconsistency between the apology (on
> which the defendants still rely ...) and the new plea of substantial accu-
> racy or substantial justification, the defendants say that their apology is a
> fact. It cannot be withdrawn; it happened, and they cannot make it go
> away. The first decision must always be whether to apologize or not, and
> the practice is to do so where there is any doubt. If doing so was a bar to
> a later plea of justification, apologies would be fewer and this sort of liti-
> gation more frequent. Surely that is a result to be avoided. ...
>
> The refusal of the plaintiff to accept that apology and his insistence
> on continuing with this action, in my opinion, enables the defendants
> to now establish if they can that, despite their decision to apologize
> because no "formal" disbarment occurred, that the article in question
> can be substantially justified. I am not prepared to put the defendants
> to their election in that regard.

One court in Ontario held that a defendant should be entitled to plead,
in the alternative, the defence of justification and the defence of mitigation
of damages by apology.

New Era Home Appliances Ltd. v. *Toronto Star Ltd.*, [1963] 1 O.R. 339 (H.C.J.)
per Senior Master Marriott at 342 (S.C. (Mast.)):

> It appears that a defendant may plead in [sic] apology as a material fact
> upon which he relies: Odgers, *Libel & Slander*, 6th ed., p. 524, rule 143.
> ...
>
> Counsel for the defendants points out the quandary in which a
> newspaper finds itself when given notice under s. 5(1) of the *Libel &
> Slander Act*, in that in order to obtain the benefit of the statute it must
> publish a retraction within three days of receipt of the said notice giv-
> ing it only that very limited time to investigate the facts, and therefore
> it would be unfair to deprive it of the alternative plea of justification if
> subsequently such a plea was found to be available.
>
> Sufficient has been shown to indicate that the weight of authority is
> in favour of permitting this plea to stand along with the plea of justifi-
> cation. ...

It has been held by a British Columbia court that a simple denial of damages, whether expressed in a statement of defence or deemed by the Rules
of Court, does not raise a positive allegation of a failure to mitigate. Accord-

ingly, a defendant should expressly plead material facts that relate to mitigation of damages.

Petersen v. Bannon (1993), 107 D.L.R. (4th) 616, [leave to appeal to S.C.C. denied, [1994] S.C.C.A. No. 39], per Finch J.A. at 622 (B.C.C.A.):

> *Odgers' Principles of Pleading and Practice*, 23rd ed. (London: Sweet & Maxwell, 1991) at pp. 142–43 says this:
>
>> A "material fact" has been defined … as a fact essential to the plaintiff's cause of action or to the defendant's defence. But there are many facts which are not material on the main issue whether the plaintiff ought to succeed or not, and which will yet be proved and discussed at the trial because they affect the amount of damages which he will be entitled to recover. Such facts are called "matters in aggravation of damages" or "matters in mitigation of damages."
>>
>> Much learning has in the past been displayed in discussing whether the plaintiff and defendant respectively should state such facts in their pleading. In light of the rules in their present form and the decision in *Plato Films Ltd.* v. *Speidel* it seems clear that they should. Lord Denning says so expressly in relation to evidence of the plaintiff's bad character; moreover, Order 18, r. 8(1)(b) requires matter which might take the opposite party by surprise to be specially pleaded. Order 82, r. 7 prohibits a defendant in an action for libel or slander, who does not justify, from giving evidence in chief with a view to mitigation of damages, as to the circumstances under which the libel or slander was published, or as to the character of the plaintiff, without leave of the judge, unless seven days at least before the trial he furnishes particulars to the plaintiff of the matters as to which he intends to give evidence. This rule was not in force when *Scott* v. *Sampson* decided that facts in mitigation of damages should be pleaded; and the corresponding rule of 1883 was probably made in order to settle certain doubts which had arisen from other decisions.

Rule 19(15) of the British Columbia *Supreme Court Rules* states:

(15) In a pleading subsequent to a statement of claim a party shall plead specifically any matter of fact or point of law that:
a) the party alleges makes a claim or defence of the opposite party not maintainable;
b) if not specifically pleaded, might take the other party by surprise; or
c) raises issues of fact arising out of the preceding pleading.

g) Mitigation of Damages Pursuant to Statute

See also Chapter 30, "Damages," G. Statutory Provisions, (1) Mitigation. Section 21 of the Ontario *Libel and Slander Act* states as follows:

> In an action for libel or slander, where the statement of defence does not assert the truth of the statement complained of, the defendant may not give evidence in chief at trial, in mitigation of damages, concerning the plaintiff's character or the circumstances of publication of the statement, except,
>
> (a) where the defendant provides particulars to the plaintiff of the matters on which the defendant intends to give evidence, in the statement of defence or in a notice served at least seven days before trial; or
>
> (b) with leave of the court. R.S.O. 1990, c. L.12, s. 21.

There is a similar provision in the rules of court in several other provinces and territories.

Alberta, Rule 254 provides:

> In actions for defamation in which the defendant does not by his defence assert the truth of the statement complained of, the defendant is not entitled on the trial to give evidence in chief (with a view to mitigation of damages) as to the character of the plaintiff without the leave of the judge, unless seven days at least before the trial he furnishes particulars to the plaintiff of the matters as to which he intends to give evidence.

Saskatchewan, Rule 276 provides:

> In actions for libel or slander, in which the defendant does not by his defence assert the truth of the statement complained of, the defendant shall not be entitled on the trial to give evidence in chief, with a view to mitigation of damages, as to the circumstances under which the libel or slander was published, or as to the character of the plaintiff, without the leave of the judge, unless seven days at least before the trial, he furnishes particulars to the plaintiff of the matters as to which he intends to give evidence.

Manitoba, Rules 53.08–53.09 provide:

> 53.08 Where, in an action for libel or slander, a defendant fails to assert in the statement of defence the truth of the statement complained of, the defendant shall not be entitled to call evidence in chief at trial with a view to mitigation of damages, as to,
>
> (a) the circumstances under which the statement was published; or
>
> (b) the character of the plaintiff;

without the leave of the trial judge, unless particulars of the evidence are given to the plaintiff at least seven days before the trial.

53.09 Where evidence is admissible only with leave of the trial judge under,

(a) subrule 30.08(1) [failure to disclose document];

(b) rule 30.09 [failure to abandon claim of privilege];

(c) rule 31.07 [refusal to disclose information on discovery];

(d) subrule 31.09(3) [failure to correct answers on discovery];

(e) subrule 53.03(3) [failure to serve expert's report]; or

(f) rule 53.08 [libel or slander];

leave shall be granted on such terms as are just and with an adjournment if necessary, unless to do so will cause prejudice to the opposite party or will cause undue delay in the conduct of the trial.

Section 21 of the Ontario *Libel and Slander Act* has been referred to by courts in Ontario but there has been little discussion of its scope or application.

Bennett v. *Gage Educational Publishing Ltd.* (1980), 16 C.P.C. 241, per Master Sandler at para. 9 (Ont. S.C.):

... without such a plea [by the defendant of a lack of intention to refer to the plaintiff] ... the intention of the defendant would be irrelevant and R. 160 [the predecessor to s. 21 of the *Libel and Slander Act*] would protect the plaintiff from having this evidence tendered at the trial.

One court held that

The effect of Rule 158 [the predecessor of Rule 160 and section 21 of the *Libel and Slander Act*] is not that facts in mitigation of damages may be pleaded in certain cases but that they must be pleaded or notice given before trial if evidence in mitigation of damages is to be admitted at trial.

Siopiolosz v. *Taylor*, [1943] O.W.N. 69, per The Assistant Master at 71 [an action for slander of title].

The "circumstances of publication of the statement" may include a mistaken belief on the part of the defendant in the truth of facts relating to the defamatory imputation.

Lumsden v. *Spectator Printing Co.* (1913), 29 O.L.R. 293 (C.A.) per Meredith C.J.O. at para. 16 (C.A.).

h) Expiry of a Limitation Period

A plaintiff is not required in the statement of claim to plead compliance with a libel notice requirement of a provincial defamation statute. That is a condition precedent and need not be pleaded by the plaintiff.

> *Canadian Plasmapheresis Centres Ltd.* v. *Canadian Broadcasting Corporation* (1975), 8 O.R. (2d) 55, per Lieff J. at 56 (H.C.J.), citing *Sentinel Review Co.* v. *Robertson Estate*, [1928] S.C.R. 258 per Duff J. at 261–62:
>
> > … and the distinction is an old one, well recognized in the rules of pleading, between the substantive elements of a cause of action, and conditions precedent which a plaintiff must observe in order to entitle him to sue.
> >
> > The distinction (between a condition precedent in this sense, and a condition which is one of the constitutive elements of the plaintiff's right), is perhaps not easily capable of statement in abstract form; and differences of opinion will arise as to the category to which a particular fact belongs. But, as Mr. Justice Magee points out, statutory notices of action, which presuppose the existence of a completely constituted cause of action at common law independently of the notice, have commonly been held to be conditions precedent in this sense.

A defendant who wishes to rely upon a plaintiff's failure to comply with the notice requirements under the *Libel and Slander Act* must specifically plead it.

> *Sentinel Review Co.* v. *Robertson Estate*, above, at 261–62.

> *Canadian Plasmapheresis Centres Ltd.* v. *Canadian Broadcasting Corporation*, above, at 58.

> *Lear Sales & Investment Corp.* v. *F.P. Publications Ltd.*, [1976] A.J. No. 214, per Master Hyndman at paras. 8–12 (S.C. (T.D.)), applying *Canadian Plasmapheresis Centres Ltd.* v. *Canadian Broadcasting Corporation, ibid.*

A limitation defence must be specifically pleaded by a defendant.

> *Bloomfield* v. *Rosthern Union Hospital Ambulance Board* (1990), 40 C.P.C. (2d) 38, per Sherstobitoff J.A. at 39 (Sask C.A.).

A defendant may waive a substantive limitation defence by failing to plead it.

> *Tolofson* v. *Jensen*, [1994] 3 S.C.R. 1022, per La Forest J. (Gonthier, Cory, McLachlin, and Iacobucci JJ. concurring) at para. 88.

Compliance with the requirement in a provincial defamation statute to publish the name of the proprietor or editor at the head of the editorials or on the front page of the newspaper is a material fact (see Chapter 6, "Notice of Intended Action and Limitation Defences," at 88–90) which should be pleaded in the statement of defence. Nevertheless, it was held in Ontario that a plaintiff's failure to deny in his reply that a newspaper had complied with this requirement would not amount to an admission the newspaper had in fact done so under Con. R. 144.

> *Dingle v. World Newspaper Companies* (1918), 57 S.C.R. 573, per Anglin J. at 575–76.

D. REPLY

As noted above, it is a basic principle, articulated in the court rules of most provinces, that in a reply to a statement of defence, a plaintiff shall plead specifically any matter of fact or point of law that:

- the party alleges makes a defence not maintainable, or
- if not specifically pleaded might take the defendant by surprise .

Whether or not a plaintiff is required to deliver a reply alleging actual or express malice in response to defences of qualified privilege or fair comment will depend on the Rules of Court in force in the jurisdiction where the suit is brought.

In British Columbia, the *Supreme Court Rules* provide in subrule 19(23):

> It is sufficient to allege malice, fraudulent intention, knowledge or other condition of the mind of a person as a fact, without setting out the circumstances from which it is to be inferred.

The British Columbia Supreme Court dismissed an application by a defendant to compel the plaintiff to particularize the specific passages from seventy-five radio broadcasts to be relied upon by the plaintiff at trial in support of an allegation of malice, concluding that the issue was "not to be determined solely from the four corners of the words mouthed by a defendant, but by an examination of other matters and circumstances." Accordingly, the order sought by the defendant would unduly limit the plaintiff's case.

> *Siddon v. Mair*, [1997] B.C.J. No. 17, per Master Doolan at paras. 44–55 (S.C.).

> See also *Citizens for Foreign Aid Reform Inc. v. Canadian Jewish Congress* (1999), 36 C.P.C. (4th) 266, per Romilly J. at paras. 56–57 (B.C.S.C.), holding [without reference to Rule 19(23)] that an allegation of malice is sufficient without pleading the circumstances from which it is to be inferred.

Dhami v. *Canadian Broadcasting Corporation*, [2001] B.C.J. No. 2773 per Slade J. at para. 123 (S.C.):

> At the pleadings stage, a plaintiff may plead malice without specific knowledge of all or any of the facts from which it may ultimately be inferred. As malice is a state of mind attributed to the defendants, the plaintiffs could hardly be called upon to particularize, and thus limit the scope of discovery.

In Ontario, a plaintiff is required by Rule 25.06(8) to plead "full particulars" in support of an allegation of malice in the statement of claim.

Lennon v. *Ontario (Premier)* (1999), 45 O.R. (3d) 84 per J. Macdonald J. at 92, para. 19 (S.C.J.):

> ... Paragraph 16 of the Amended Statement of Claim pleads that the malice alleged is "evidenced" by the fact that "the defendants have deliberately misstated the position of the plaintiffs and broadcast the words complained of knowing that they are false and defamatory or with a reckless disregard for the truth." The defendant's Factum states that no facts are pleaded in support of the malice allegation. Facts have been pleaded succinctly in the Amended Statement of Claim. There is no basis for presuming that the plaintiffs have failed to plead all of the material facts relied upon in support of the malice allegation.

Orme v. *Law Society of Upper Canada*, [2003] O.J. No. 887, per Greer J. at para. 12 (S.C.J.):

> Rule 25.06(8) was changed in 1996 to ensure that full particulars of malice and malicious prosecution are pled. The rationale behind the amendments is to provide a defendant with full particulars of the allegation in view of its seriousness.

Bird v. *Public Guardian and Trustee*, [2002] O.T.C. 74, per Smith J. at para. 46 (S.C.J.).

Ontario cases decided before the amendments to Rule 25.06(8) must therefore be read with caution. For example, see *Lana International Ltd.* v. *Menasco Aerospace Ltd.* (1996), 28 O.R. (3d) 343, Greer J. at pages 347–48 (Gen. Div.).

The British Columbia *Supreme Court Rules* require that actual malice be expressly pleaded by a plaintiff if evidence of such malice is to be adduced to overcome an otherwise valid defence of fair comment or qualified privilege.

McConachy v. Times Publishers Limited (1964), 49 D.L.R. (2d) 349, per Sheppard J.A. at 353 (B.C.C.A.), citing *Dawson v. Dover and County Chronicle Ltd.* (1913), 108 L.T. 481 at 484, and BC Supreme Court M.R. 218.

Dashtgard v. Blair (1990), 4 C.C.L.T. (2d) 284, per McDonald J. at 293, para. 17 (Alta. Q.B.).

Masters v. Fox (1978), 85 D.L.R. (3d) 64 per Macfarlane J. at 68 (B.C.S.C.).

It is clear that in Ontario actual malice must be alleged either in the statement of claim or in a reply if the plaintiff intends to rely on such malice to overcome a statement which is otherwise privileged.

MacRae v. Santa, [2002] O.J. No. 3000, per Pierce J. at para. 14 (S.C.J.).

It is unnecessary for a plaintiff in British Columbia, in reply to a plea of fair comment, having adequately alleged malice, to also specifically join issue with the defendants on the plea "that the words complained of are expressions of opinion and are fair comment made in good faith … on a matter of public interest." There is no allegation of fact in such a defence plea. Supreme Court Rules 19(19) and 23(6),(7), read together, make that unnecessary.

Masters v. Fox (1978), above, at 68–69.

See also, *Winnipeg Steel Grainary and Culvert Co. v. Canadian Ingot Iron Culvert Co.* (1912), 22 Man. R. 576 at 580 (C.A.).

The Saskatchewan Court of Queen's Bench in *Cherneskey v. Armadale Publishers Limited*, [1974] 3 W.W.R. 10, held (at page 15) that although it was unnecessary to deliver a reply since the allegation will be deemed to have been denied, it would be safest for the plaintiff to deliver a reply alleging malice.

A plea of "falsely and maliciously publishing" in the statement of claim is not a plea of actual malice.

Clark v. Molyneux (1877), 3 Q.B.D. 237 at 246–47, discussed in *Baumann v. Turner* (1993), 105 D.L.R. (4th) 37 per Southin J.A. at 38 (B.C.C.A.).

1) Necessity to Plead Particulars of Malice in Reply

In Alberta, Rule 113 of the *Rules of Court* provides that particulars of malice need not be pleaded.

Dechant v. Stevens, [2001] 5 W.W.R. 405, per Conrad J.A. at para. 19 (Alta. C.A.), leave to appeal to S.C.C. denied, [2001] S.C.C.A. No. 180.

An old decision of the Manitoba Court of Appeal held that the defendant was not entitled to particulars of express malice.

> *Timmons v. National Life Assurance Co.* (1909) 19 Man. R. 227 at 232–33 (C.A.).

Recently, a British Columbia court did not require a plaintiff to provide particulars of malice. The court stated:

> At the pleading stage a plaintiff may plead malice without specific knowledge of all or any of the facts from which it may ultimately be inferred. As malice is a state of mind attributed to the defendants, the plaintiffs can hardly be called upon to particularize and thus limit the scope of discovery.

> *Dhami v. Canadian Broadcasting Corporation*, [2001] B.C.J. No. 2773, per Slade J. at para. 23 (S.C.).

2) Reply to a Statement of Defence Alleging Fair Comment

The better practice is for the plaintiff to plead express or actual malice in reply to a statement of defence which raises a plea of fair comment.

There is authority for the proposition that, in order for it to be an issue at trial, express malice must be explicitly pleaded in reply and a plaintiff who fails to do so cannot rely upon malice to defeat the defence of fair comment (or qualified privilege).

> *Lougheed v. Canadian Broadcasting Corporation* (1979), 15 A.R. 201 at 210, 98 D.L.R. (3d) 264 (S.C. (A.D.)).

> *Dashtgard v. Blair* (1990), 4 C.C.L.T. (2d) 284 (Alta. Q.B.).

In Nova Scotia, however, there is no provision in the Civil Procedure Rules for a reply. Accordingly, actual malice need not be explicitly alleged by a plaintiff in that jurisdiction in order to overcome a defence of fair comment or a defence of qualified privilege.

> *Hiltz and Seamone Co. v. Nova Scotia (Attorney General)* (1997), 164 N.S.R. (2d) 161, per Stewart J. at paras. 12–13 (S.C.), varied on other grounds (1999), 172 D.L.R. (4th) 488 (N.S.C.A.).

Polly Peck and Pizza Pizza: Alleging the Defendant's Defamatory Meaning and Pleading That Meaning is True

A. THE TRADITIONAL CANADIAN POSITION

The traditional rule in Canada (as well as England) was that in a defamation action where the plaintiff had pleaded a "popular" or "false" innuendo meaning, a defendant could plead justification or fair comment only in respect of that meaning.

A popular or false innuendo is a meaning that the ordinary person, without special knowledge, will infer from the expression itself. This meaning is a matter of impression and is also called a "natural and ordinary meaning." (See Chapter 15, "Defamatory Meaning," at 192.)

Under the traditional rule the defendant was not entitled to allege in her statement of defence that the expression at issue conveyed a different popular or false innuendo meaning than that complained of by the plaintiff, and then plead truth or fair comment with respect to her defamatory meaning.

This long-standing rule was reiterated in a series of Ontario cases during the period from 1980 to 1990 when it came under attack from defendants seeking to rely on certain changes taking place in English law. (See section B(1) below.)

In *Coutts v. Fotheringham* (1980), 19 C.P.C. 270 (Ont. S.C.), for example, the plaintiff civil servant, who was the principal secretary to Pierre Elliott Trudeau, then the Leader of the Opposition in Parliament, complained that the following words defamed him:

> … Coutts is now regarded generally by the press as an artful sneak.
>
> … He has become famous for his spurious election bet, papering the Liberal campaign jet each election with hundreds of dollars and scattering bottles of Scotch in bets on his man.

The press has little doubt that the bets, always outrageously optimistic, on his party's chances so as to hype the speculation, are written off in the legitimate expense accounts on behalf of the party.

Even Coutts' losses at the Monday night poker games with the campaign press are under suspicion, such is his reputation now.

It's an old advertising-row joke, but the most common line on Trudeau's chief aide is that you can tell when he's lying — his lips are moving.

The statement of claim filed on behalf of Mr. Coutts alleged that the above words:

> are defamatory in their natural and ordinary meaning. Further, they were understood to mean that:
> a) The plaintiff is a dishonest and despicable person;
> b) The plaintiff is a generally untrustworthy person;
> c) The plaintiff has been guilty of fraudulent or improper acts;
> d) The plaintiff has misappropriated funds to cover his gambling losses;
> e) The plaintiff is a habitual liar and never speaks the truth.

Master Sandler considered these "false" innuendos pleaded in the statement of claim and stated (at page 271):

> Clearly, it cannot be reasonably said that the words have only one meaning. There is a lack of clarity and uncertainty as to the natural and ordinary meaning and thus the plaintiff, quite rightly, further pleads the meanings for which the plaintiff will contend at the trial. This is generally known as a "false" innuendo as distinct from a "legal" or "true" innuendo.
>
> Also, the plaintiff has pleaded very general meanings for the words, especially innuendos (a), (b) and (e).

Master Sandler then referred to the following paragraph in the statement of defence (at page 272):

> In respect to paragraph 11 of the Statement of Claim the defendants plead that the words bear a different meaning than pleaded by the plaintiff and that the defendants justify the meaning that the words deserve in respect to all but the aforementioned apology in paragraph 12 herein.

Master Sandler ordered that this paragraph in the statement of defence be struck out. He accepted the plaintiff's submissions, *inter alia*, that the defendant "cannot allege that the words have some natural and ordinary meaning other than as contended for in sub-paras. (a) through (e) of para. 11 of the statement of claim" and that, in any event, the defendant would not be permitted to justify his alleged meanings at trial. In this connection, Master

Sandler rejected certain defence arguments which were based on the 1978 edition of Colin Duncan & Brian Neil, *Defamation* (London: Butterworths, 1978) at 57–58, para. 11.11:

> Where the plaintiff contends that the words complained of bear some extended meaning or meanings other than their literal meaning, the meaning or meanings put forward should be set out in the statement of claim. It is to be remembered, however, that the question for the jury in each case where justification is set up by way of defence is whether the words are true in the meaning which the jury find the words to bear. The defendant may therefore wish to contend that the words bear some different meaning from that put forward by the plaintiff and that in the meaning contended for by the defendant the words are true. It is submitted that the defendant is able to take this course and that the older authorities to the contrary would not now be followed. A defendant is not allowed, however, to set out in his defence what he says the words mean, though it is submitted that this rule needs re-examination; in many cases one of the crucial issues at the trial is the meaning of the words and it would clearly be convenient if the precise issue between the parties was placed on the record in the pleadings before the hearing.

Instead of accepting *Duncan and Neill's* submission concerning the need for change, Master Sandler in *Coutts* chose to apply the traditional rule expressed in Sir Robert McEwen & Philip Lewis *Gatley on Libel and Slander*, 7th ed. (London: Sweet & Maxwell, 1974) at para.1038, where the last sentence reads as follows:

> The defendant may, however, never place on the words a meaning of his own which differs from the natural and ordinary meaning of the words, and from the meaning (if any) assigned to them by the innuendo, and plead that, taken in such meaning, they are true, for that would be justifying a meaning of which the plaintiff does not complain.

Master Sandler stated that he preferred to follow "the Gatley text as this book has been cited in many Ontario cases as an authoritative and leading text in this field" and ruled (at page 275):

> I wish to make it clear that I am holding that the defendants cannot, even with the utmost particularity, plead that the words in para. 7 and 9 of the statement of claim mean something different from what the plaintiff has contended they mean in sub-paras. (a) through (e) of para. 11, and then justify them in such meaning.

Master Sandler's decision in *Coutts* was followed and applied by Master Peppiatt in *Cohl* v. *Toronto Star Newspapers Ltd.* (1986), 16 C.P.C. (2d) 296 (On. S.C.). In that case, the plaintiffs complained they were libeled in an article in the *Sunday Star* newspaper. Their statement of claim stated, *inter alia*, (at page 297):

> 16. The Plaintiffs plead that the words in their natural and ordinary meaning meant and were understood to mean that:
> a)   The Plaintiffs are engaged in a large scale scalping operation of their own tickets which is being investigated by the police; and
> b)   The Plaintiffs are engaging in a large scale operation of selling bogus tickets.
>
> 17. In the alternative, the plaintiffs plead by way of innuendo that the use of the word "scalp" in the article meant, and was understood to mean that the plaintiffs individually and as a corporation engaged in a large scale operation reselling tickets at greatly increased prices. The word "scalp" is a slang expression connoting the resale of tickets at greatly increased prices.

At issue in *Cohl* v. *Toronto Star Newspapers Ltd.*, above, was the validity of paragraphs 16 and 21 of the statement of defence, which read (at page 298):

> 16. In the further alternative, if the words complained of bore the meaning alleged in subparagraph 16(a) of the amended statement of claim, which is denied, then in such meaning, the defendants plead that the words complained of were true in substance and fact insofar as the words in subparagraph 16(a) of the amended statement of claim bear the following meanings:
> a)   The plaintiffs were involved in the sale of tickets, at prices greater than their face value, for concerts that they produced or promoted, including the Bruce Springsteen concerts, to persons chosen by or through senior officers and employees of Concert Productions International ("C.P.I.");
> b)   In doing so, the plaintiffs were involved in an offence under the *Ticket Speculation Act*, R.S.O. 1980, c. 499; and
> c)   The police were informed of such activities and investigated the information regarding them.
>
> 21. In the further alternative, the defendants propose at the trial of this action to give, with a view to mitigation of damages, evidence that the words complained of bore and were understood to bear the meanings referred to above in subparagraphs 16(a), (b) and (c), particulars of which are those set out above in subparagraphs 16(1) through (vi).

Master Peppiat (at page 299) ordered these paragraphs in the statement of defence struck out, relying on the traditional rule which prohibited a defendant from pleading an alternative defamatory meaning and seeking to justify that meaning. As Master Sandler had done in *Coutts*, Master Peppiat in *Cohl* rejected defence arguments based on *Duncan and Neill* that there was a need to reform the law relating to pleading a defendant's alternative meaning. Master Peppiat stated at page 300:

> If the plaintiffs cannot persuade the jury that the words complained of mean what they alleged them to mean, then they have failed to get over one of the hurdles which they must surmount in order to succeed in the action. The plaintiffs must prove their case and they have the right to describe what that case will be; it is not for the defendants to repel an attack which is not being made upon them.

Subsequently, in *Turner v. Toronto Sun Publishing Corporation*, (1990) 50 C.P.C. (2d) 73 (Ont. H.C.J.), the leader of the federal Liberal Party complained of certain words in the defendants' newspaper article. His statement of claim alleged, *inter alia* (at page 75):

> 6. The said words in their natural and ordinary meaning conveyed to readers of the aforesaid papers:
> a)   That the plaintiff was abusing his office as leader of the Liberal Party by setting out financial pre-conditions to retirement;
> b)   That the plaintiff was negotiating such financial pre-conditions with the Liberal Party;
> c)   In short, that the plaintiff was holding the Liberal Party to ransom.

Haley J. held (at page 76) that the false innuendos alleged by the plaintiff Turner in paragraph 6 of the statement of claim constituted one charge: "In my view they encompass a sting that the plaintiff was holding the Liberal Party to ransom."

At issue in *Turner*, however, was the propriety of paragraph 22 of the statement of defence which read (at page 77):

> The words complained of by the Plaintiff were substantially true in that prior to making his announcement regarding his resignation, and furthermore in deciding the timing of the announcement of his resignation, the Plaintiff was motivated in whole or in part by self-interest, rather than the best interests of the party, in order that he could obtain or arrange income and benefits of between $300,000.00 and $500,000.00 upon his return to private life.

Haley J. held (at page 77) that the course that the defendants sought to follow in paragraph 22, namely, pleading a lesser defamatory meaning of the words and then seeking to justify that meaning, was not open to the defendant under the classic approach to libel pleadings.

Following an extensive and detailed review of developments in English jurisprudence, including the decision of the Court of Appeal in *Polly Peck (Holdings) plc* v. *Trelford*, [1986] 2 All E.R. 84, Haley J. concluded in *Turner* (at pages 83–84) that the classic approach was still the law of Ontario:

> There is nothing in the classic approach as it has developed to prevent the defendant from pleading that the words have some natural and ordinary meaning other than that pleaded by the plaintiff. That can be done by referring to the whole of the article complained of. What the defendant cannot do is go on to plead that such other meaning, if it is defamatory, is true. This would produce the situation to which Master Peppiatt referred in *Cohl* v. *Toronto Star Newspaper Ltd.* (1986), 16 C.P.C. (2d) 296 at p. 300:
>
> > The plaintiffs must prove their case and they have the right to describe what that case will be: it is not for the defendants to repel an attack which is not being made upon them.
>
> The English Court of Appeal in rejecting the classic view now seems to be concerned that the defendant should inform the plaintiff what case the plaintiff has to meet and therefore wishes (if not requires) the defendant to plead what it thinks is the meaning to be ascribed to the words and then, if it chooses, how it would justify those words. This seems to me to be opening the door to the situation referred to in the *Cohl* case and by allowing the defendant to plead justification to some lesser defamation to enlarge the scope of the action both for discovery and trial.
>
> While the strictness which formerly applied to matters of pleading generally has now been relaxed so that issues may more readily be determined on their merits and not on the technicalities of pleading I do not think the general rules of pleading should apply to every type of case only for the sake of uniformity.
>
> Libel actions are a special case. It is very much in the interests of the parties to narrow the issues as much as possible and prevent extensive discovery into matters which affect the personal affairs of the plaintiff, thereby creating stress and discomfort over matters which are only tangentially relevant. It would be wrong in this case, where the plaintiff says the sting of the defamatory remarks is that he held the Liberal party to ransom, to allow the defendant to plead by way of justification to lesser defamatory remarks the financial position of the plaintiff and to allow the defendant to embark on extensive discovery into the plaintiff's financial affairs. The court has always been concerned about oppression and unfairness in libel actions for just those reasons.

B. *POLLY PECK* AND RELATED ENGLISH DECISIONS

1) *Polly Peck*

The decision of the English Court of Appeal in *Polly Peck (Holdings) plc* v. *Trelford*, [1986] 2 All E.R. 84 (C.A.) overturned the traditional English rule against pleading and justifying a defendant's defamatory meaning.

English decisions which have referred to or applied *Polly Peck* include:

Khashoggi v. *I.P.C. Magazines*, [1986] 1 W.L.R. 1412 (C.A.).

Prager v. *Times Newspapers Ltd.*, [1988] 1 All E.R. 300.

Aspro Travel Ltd. v. *Owners Abroad Group plc*, [1995] 4 All E.R. 728 (C.A.).

Viscount De L'Isle v. *Times Newspapers Ltd.*, [1987] 3 All E.R. 499 (C.A.).

Gaddafi v. *Telegraph Group Ltd.* [1998] E.W.J. No. 2876 (C.A.).

United States Tobacco International Inc. & Another v. *British Broadcasting Corporation*, [1988] E.M.L.R. 816, *The Independent* 15 March 1988 (C.A.).

McPhilemy v. *Times Newspapers Ltd.*, [1999] E.M.L.R. 751 (C.A.).

Cruise v. *Express Newspapers plc*, [1999] Q.B. 931 (C.A.).

McDonald's Corp. v. *Steel*, [1999] E.W.J. No. 2173 (C.A.).

Tancic v. *Times Newspapers Ltd.*, [1999] E.W.J. No. 6510 (C.A.).

In *Polly Peck*, the plaintiff individual and three companies he controlled sued for libel over the whole of one article and parts of two other articles about their business affairs which appeared in the *Observer* newspaper. The defendants plead justification and fair comment.

The plaintiff companies (Polly Peck, Uni-Pac, and Weaverwill) were engaged in the production of a variety of products in Turkish Cyprus and in Turkey and marketed them worldwide, particularly clothing, citrus fruit, and cartons for packaging.

With respect to the first article, the plaintiffs complained about three paragraphs and one photograph with its caption — the article contained thrity-two paragraphs of print of varying length and three photographs with captions. With respect to the second article, the plaintiffs complained of five paragraphs and part of a sixth paragraph — the article contained sixteen paragraphs of print of varying length and a photograph of the individual plaintiff, Mr. Nadir, captioned "Polly's chief."

The defendants in *Polly Peck* pleaded fifty-four paragraphs of particulars of justification. The plaintiffs applied to strike out those particulars of justification which purported to relate in part to statements in the two articles of which the plaintiffs did not complain. The major assertions that the plaintiffs had not complained about were:

i)   relating to the profitability of Uni-Pac;
ii) relating to the profitability of Wearwell's citrus fruit exports;
iii) the prospects for Polly Peck's television project in Turkey;
iv) the commercial prospects for Niksar;
v)   the completeness and reliability of the Polly Peck accounts.

Based on a detailed review of the two articles, Lord Justice O'Connor held (at page 94) that the sting of the libel relating to the individual plaintiff Nadir was that "he deceived or negligently misled shareholders, investors and members of the general public as to the operation of [the three plaintiff companies which were] his business enterprises" and that if the action succeeded, the jury would be asked to assess a single sum by way of damages.

Lord Justice O'Connor described the dispute between the plaintiff Nadir and the defendants over the pleadings in the following terms [at page 94]:

> It is the "sting" of the libel to which the defences of justification and fair comment are directed. The plaintiff says that he is entitled to pick the allegations of fact and comment on the Niksar project in the first article as proving the sting alleged, but that the defendants are not entitled to rely on any other allegations of fact and comment in the article which justify that sting or are alternatively fair comment.

Following an extensive review of the authorities, Lord Justice O'Connor stated the following principles (at page 102):

a)   In cases where the plaintiff selects words from a publication, pleads that in their natural and ordinary meaning the words are defamatory of him and pleads the meanings which he asserts they bear by way of false innuendo, the defendant is entitled to look at the whole publication in order to aver that in their context the words bear a different meaning to that alleged by the plaintiff. The defendant is entitled to plead that in that meaning the words are true and give particulars of the facts and matters on which he relies in support of his plea.

b)   Where a publication contains two or more separate and distinct defamatory statements, the plaintiff is entitled to select one for complaint, and the defendant is not entitled to assert the truth of others by way of justification.

c) Whether a defamatory statement is separate and distinct from other defamatory statements contained in the publication is a question of fact and degree in each case. The several defamatory allegations in their context may have a common sting, in which event they are not to be regarded as separate and distinct allegations. The defendant is entitled to justify the sting.

d) The foregoing can be applied by a parity of reasoning to fair comment, subject to certain limitations.

e) In all cases it is the duty of the court to see that the defendant, in particularizing a plea of justification or fair comment, does not act oppressively. Whether the particularization of the plea is oppressive depends not merely on the facts of each case, but also on the attitude of the plaintiff. I say this because a plaintiff can limit the extent and cost of inquiry at trial by making timely admissions of fact.

f) While this judgment has been under preparation, another division of this court has ruled in *Lucas-Box* v. *News Group Newspapers Ltd.*, [1986] 1 All E.R. 177 that the practice which dictated that a defendant does not state in his defence what he alleges is the natural and ordinary meaning of the words complained of is ill-founded and should not be followed. That case has decided that a defendant who pleads justification must state the meaning which he seeks to justify. It follows from that case and this that in future, where differences of meaning are proposed by the parties, the issue as to the possible meanings of the words will be confined to those pleaded.

In the circumstances before the Court of Appeal in *Polly Peck*, Lord Justice O'Connor held that the particulars to which the plaintiff objected were not separate and distinct allegations but particulars relating to the sting of the libel complained of. Accordingly, the defendants' pleadings were not struck out.

2) *Gaddafi v. Telegraph Group Ltd.*

In *Gaddafi* v. *Telegraph Group Ltd.*, [1998] E.W.J. No. 2876 (C.A.), the son of Libyan leader Colonel Gaddafi sued over two newspaper articles, one of which contained the following words alleged to be defamatory (at paragraphs 2–3):

> Saif Gaddafi, 23-year-old son of the Libyan leader, has been linked to a plan to flood Iran with fake currency. The scheme involving black market oil deals was foiled by Egyptian authorities.

The real sting: Saif Gaddafi in Tripoli. Egyptian bankers were wary of his name behind a plan to convert billions of dinars into US dollars.

This article was alleged by the plaintiff to convey the following natural and ordinary meanings [at paragraph 4]:

That the plaintiff:

a) had masterminded or alternatively had actively participated in an outrageous international criminal conspiracy to defraud Iran and to flood that country with fake currency; and

b) had thereby shown himself to be a thoroughly dishonest unscrupulous and untrustworthy maverick against whom the international banking community had been warned to be on its guard.

The second article "referred to an alleged invitation to the author of the article, Mr. Don Coughlin, to fly to Tripoli and meet the plaintiff, hinting that there was a much more sinister plan such as stringing him up from the nearest Tripoli lamp post" (at paragraph 5). The plaintiff attributed the same two meanings to this second article, adding the meaning that the plaintiff, through his henchman, had attempted to lure Mr. Coughlin to Libya with the object or at least the probable object of murdering him in revenge for an article published in the previous week's *Sunday Telegraph*.

Lord Justice Hirst, speaking for the Court of Appeal, described the defences pleaded by the newspaper as follows:

7 By its defence the defendant first of all, somewhat optimistically, contends that neither article bears the meanings complained of or any defamatory meaning. It then puts forward the following substantive defences:

A. In relation to the first article:

(1) Justification of the following Lucas-Box meanings:

(a) that the plaintiff was involved in a plan to evade the UN sanctions imposed on Libya because of its terrorist activities by arranging for Libyan currency to be laundered through Egyptian banks. The plaintiff's intention was to defy the international community by obtaining tradeable foreign currency needed by the regime to which he belongs for its purposes (which include the support and/or protection of terrorism);

(b) that the plaintiff was a loyal servant of a thoroughly dishonest, unscrupulous, untrustworthy and maverick regime against which the international banking community and the international community in general would be well advised to be on its guard.

B. In relation to the second article:

(1) Justification in the same *Lucas-Box* meanings by way of innuendo, coupled with the meaning that the plaintiff was a leading member of a regime which brutally and lawlessly murders and/or intimidates its opponents in Libya and in the UK and elsewhere, and is a person capable of inviting Mr. Coughlin to Libya in order that the revenge might be taken upon him there such revenge possibly taking the form of murder.

On application by the plaintiff, Butterfield J. in the Court of Queen's Bench had struck out parts of the defendant's *Lucas-Box* meanings and of their particulars of justification. Hirst L.J. commented:

> The plaintiff did not apply to strike out particulars of justification relating to U.N. sanction busting, nor the biographical details. He did however apply to strike out both in the Lucas-Box particulars and in the particulars of justification more general references to terrorist activity by Libyans who were said to have been sponsored by the regime and to the generally oppressive nature of the regime, together with specific allegations against third parties in which the plaintiff was not alleged to have been involved. (at paragraph 23).

Hirst L.J., speaking for the Court of Appeal, disagreed with the conclusion of Butterfield J. that the particulars were oppressive and allowed them to stand, stating at paragraphs 33 and 35–36:

> ¶33 The main thrust of [the plaintiff's] argument is that his objective is to ensure that the trial is not diverted from the plaintiff's own activities, and he concedes that if the plaintiff is indeed a top official in the Libyan government his case will be blown out of the water: what he wants to avoid is the diversion of the trial into controversial areas relating to the activities of the Libyan government generally, which he submits will prejudice the plaintiff in the eyes of the jury.

> ¶35 Most particularly, [the plaintiff] objects to any reference to the plaintiff involving himself in terrorism, which, he submits, reflects a meaning which the article is not capable of bearing. I cannot accept this submission, since I am quite satisfied that, in the light of recent history, any jury would inevitably associate the Libyan regime led by Colonel Gaddafi with terrorism, not least because of the very well known terms of the two UN resolutions which I have just quoted. Furthermore, the article itself in paragraph 13 specifically mentions the Lockerbie bombing.

> ¶36 If indeed the article is right in implicating the plaintiff in the activities of the Libyan regime (NB for example the opening words of the article "Like

father like son"), it seems to me quite unrealistic to suggest that he can be entirely dissociated from its general conduct.

3) *Cruise v. Express Newspapers plc.*

In *Cruise v. Express Newspapers plc.*, [1999] Q.B. 931, plaintiffs Tom Cruise and his wife, Nicole Kidman, complained that an article in the *Express on Sunday* conveyed, *inter alia*, the following meanings:

 i)   their marriage was a hypocritical sham, being a cover for the homosexuality of one or both of them, and/or a cynical business arrangement and/or a marriage ordered by the Church of Scientology so that Scientologists might dishonestly hold up the plaintiffs as an example to the young;

 ii) that Tom Cruise's failure to father children is attributable to impotence and/or sterility and his denial of sterility is probably a lie;

 iii) that the plaintiffs adopted some poor children because it was the fashion in uptown L.A.;

 iv) that the plaintiffs are hypocrites, frauds, and liars.

The newspaper's defence pleaded, *inter alia*:

6. Further or in the alternative, as to the references in the article complained of to Scientology, those are true of the plaintiffs in the following natural and ordinary meanings: (a) that the plaintiffs are active members of the Church of Scientology, a dangerous cult which combines ridiculous doctrines with a policy of exploiting gullible believers for the financial gain of the church's leaders; (b) that they are themselves instruments of that church, who by allowing it to exploit them and their fame contribute to the ensnaring by the church of other gullible converts; and are fair comment on a matters of public interest (namely, the plaintiffs, their public careers, the Church of Scientology and their role within it), the comment being: (c) that because the plaintiffs believe in and by their public example assist the Church of Scientology, they are themselves fit subjects for ridicule in that respect.

6A. So far as may be necessary, the defendants will rely in support of their case that the words complained of bear the meanings set out at 6 above on the contention that it is a matter of general knowledge among the British public as a whole and the readers of the *Sunday Express Magazine* in particular that the Church of Scientology is a dangerous cult, notorious for: (a) its ridiculous doctrines; (b) its policy and practice of ensnaring and exploiting gullible believers for the financial gain of its leaders.

These provisions in the statement of defence were struck out on an interlocutory application before the Court of Queen's Bench. On appeal by the defendants to the Court of Appeal, the defendant newspaper argued unsuccessfully that where an article contains two separate and distinct stings, a defendant may justify the sting not complained of if the words containing the sting complained of are inextricably mixed up with words containing that not complained of.

Brooke J.A. (Sir John Knox and Stuart-Smith L.J. concurring) rejected that submission, stating (at pages 954–55):

> [that he was unwilling] to accept that the length and cost of a libel action must be greatly extended simply because it is not easy for a pleader to extricate the sting or stings of which his client complains from the words surrounding them, which may contain a quite separate and distinct sting. The leading judgments of this court from *Allsop* v. *Church of England Newspaper Ltd.*, [1972] 2 Q.B. 161 onwards have been concerned to control the scope of this type of litigation, and I can see no logical basis for the supposed rule for which [counsel for the newspaper] contended. It is no defence to a charge that "You called me A" to say "Yes, but I also called you B on the same occasion, and that was true," if the second charge was separate and distinct from the first. It may in any given case be difficult to decide whether the two charges are indeed separate and distinct (for rival approaches to the published words in the New Zealand case of *Templeton* v. *Jones*, [1984] 1 N.Z.L.R. 448, see O'Connor L.J. in *Polly Peck (Holdings) Plc.* v. *Trelford*, [1986] Q.B. 1000, 1030–1031) but whether they are or not is a question of law which can conveniently be determined on an interlocutory application. A good example on the other side of the line is *Thompson* v. *Bernard* (1807) 1 Camp. 48, cited in the *Polly Peck* case [1986] Q.B. 1000, 1023, where the words "Thompson is a damned thief" were clearly not severable from the words that followed, which were to the effect that he had received the proceeds of the ship and failed to pay the wages.

In the circumstances, Brooke J.A. sustained the lower court's ruling striking out two paragraphs in the statement of defence in the following terms at [page 955]:

> This is not a case in which [the plaintiffs] are seeking to use a blue pencil upon the words published of them so as to change their meaning, and then prevent the defendant from justifying the words in their unexpurgated form (for which see O'Connor L.J. in the *Polly Peck* case, at p. 1023G). Their case is that the stings about their characters of which they complain are totally dis-

tinct from any sting the article may convey about their adherence to the Church of Scientology. The idea that they were ordered to marry is equally offensive whoever may have given the order, and their complaint about the innuendo that nobody should believe anything they say unless they are seen performing a lie-detector test is offensive in itself, and once again has nothing to do with their adherence to the Church of Scientology.

... The stings contained in the meanings pleaded in paragraph 4 of the statement of claim are freestanding charges. If anybody thought it was defamatory to say of the plaintiffs that they were members of the Church of Scientology, the plaintiffs do not complain of it, and this allegation, if defamatory, is unconnected with the matters of which they do complain, which relate to their arrogance, their perfidiou ess about the true state of their marriage, and so on. The judge was in my judgment correct to hold that this libel action should not be permitted to get out of control by allowing the defendants to justify or plead fair comment in respect of a quite separate and distinct sting, if indeed it be a sting at all, of which the plaintiffs make no complaint.

4) *Tancic v. Times Newspapers Ltd.*

The principle that a defendant should not be permitted to justify a different defamatory statement than the one complained of applies:

> even if the area of enquiry related to the same sector of the claimant's life or activities.

> *Tancic v. Times Newspapers Ltd.*, [1999] E.W.J. No. 6510 (C.A.), per Lord Justice Brooke at para. 18, referring with apparent approval to this statement by the judge in chambers.

In *Tancic*, the defendant newspaper appealed a refusal of a judge in chambers to grant a fifth amendment to their further particulars of justification. The plaintiff alleged he was defamed by an article which meant:

i)   he was a close associate and supporter of Radovan Karadzic, the Bosnian Serb leader responsible for the commission of war crimes; and/or

ii) he had improperly made donations to the Conservative Party from the assets of his London-based companies at a time when those assets were frozen under UN sanctions because he and/or his companies were so closely associated with Radovan Karadzic and the Serbian side in the Bosnian war.

In their statement of defence, the defendants had pleaded the following meanings:

1) That [Mr. Tancic] was linked to or connected with and happy to be associated with Radovan Karadzic, the Bosnian Serb leader, and to Slobodan Milosevic, the Yugoslav President, through a London public relations advisor, John Kennedy, at a time when Yugoslavia and the Bosnian Serbs were acting in a manner hostile to British interests and Karadzic was associated with war crimes, as [Mr. Tancic] well knew and:

2) That [Mr. Tancic] secured a donation to be made by [Metalchem] to the Conservative Party in January 1993 whose purpose was to secure favourable treatment from any British government for Serbian interests and which, in the light of the conduct of the Serbian side of the conflict in Bosnia at that time (of which [Mr. Tancic] was aware) was inappropriate and improper, and

3) [That] accordingly [Mr. Tancic] was a person whose financial support of the Conservative party was improper, embarrassing and should have been refused.

The defendants sought an amendment to insert into their plea of justification, without amending the above meanings, a plea to the effect that the claimant attempted to secure the assistance of Prince Idris of Libya to import oil to Yugoslavia in breach of United Nations sanctions. Prince Idris is said to be an heir to the Libyan throne who lives in exile in London.

Sustaining the lower court ruling refusing the amendment on the alternative ground that the defendant's particulars of justification and libel cases generally should be strictly confined to those matters which are essential to the proper disposal of the real issues between the parties, Brooke L.J. stated at paragraphs 27–28:

¶ 27 The recent judgments in this court in *McPhilemy* v. *Times Newspapers Ltd.*, [1999] EMLR 751 show the different factors that have to be balanced on an application of this kind. May L.J. described at pp. 770–71 how a defendant is entitled to seek to justify any meaning defamatory of the claimant which the words complained of are reasonably capable of bearing, and how he must then give proper particulars of the facts on which he relies to justify the meaning for which he contends. He stressed, however, that the defendants' particulars of justification and libel cases generally should be strictly confined to those matters which are essential to the proper disposal of the real issues between the parties.

¶28 He observed that this might mean cutting out peripheral matters the burden of whose investigation was disproportionate to their importance. On the other hand, he said (relying on *Basham* v. *Gregory*) that the action should be so structured that the defendant is not prevented from deploying his full essential defence and so that the claimant, if he wins, will obtain proper vindication upon a proper basis. He returned to the same theme at p. 773 when he said:

> As with all actions, libel actions should by proper case management be confined within manageable and economic bounds. They should not descend into uncontrolled and wide-ranging investigations akin to public inquiries, where that is not necessary to determine the real issues between the parties. The court will ... strive to manage the case so as to minimize the burden on litigants of slender means. This includes excluding all peripheral material which is not essential to the just determination of the real issues between the parties, and whose examination would be disproportionate to the importance of those issues. It does not ... extend ... to excluding the potentially important evidence which is central to a legitimate substantial defence.

Brooke J.A. held (at paragraph 30) that the question of whether an addition to a substantial plea of justification raises matters which are essential or central to a defence, or are merely peripheral, is:

> pre-eminently one for the discretion of the judge who hears the application.

C. AUSTRALIA

In Australia, the *Polly Peck* principles have been adopted in the states of Victoria, New South Wales, and Western Australia.

Kennett v. Farmer, [1988] V.R. 991.

Kelly v. Special Broadcasting Service Group, [1990] V.R. 69 at 72.

Gununa v. Williams (1990), 3 W.A.R. 351.

Curran v. The Herald and Weekly Times Ltd., 1993 VIC LEXIS 720; BC 9300747.

Hart v. Wrenn and the Australian Broadcasting Corporation (1995), 5 N.T.L.R. 17 (N.T.S.C.).

Watt v. General Television Corporation Limited, [1998] 3 V.R. 501.

Woodger v. Federal Capital Press of Australia PTY Ltd. (1992) 107 A.C.T.R. 1 (A.C.T.S.C.).

Kelly v. Nationwide News Pty. Limited, [1998] S.C.A.C.T. 117 (A.C.T.S.C.).

Carnell v. Speir, No. SC355 of 1995.

But see *Manobendro Chakravarti* v. *Advertiser Newspapers Limited* (1998), 154 A.L.R. 294 (H.C.A.), dissents by Brennan C.J. and McHugh J., rejecting *Polly Peck.*

D. NEW ZEALAND

The traditional rule prohibiting the defendant from pleading a different defamatory meaning and then seeking to justify that meaning has in the past been supported by authorities in New Zealand.

> *Isbey* v. *New Zealand Broadcasting Corp.*, [1975] 1 N.Z.L.R. 721 at 723.

> *Templeton* v. *Jones* (1984), 1 N.Z.L.R. 448.

> *Broadcasting Corp. of New Zealand* v. *Crush*, [1988] 2 N.Z.L.R. 234 (C.A.).

In *Manning* v. *TV3 Network Services Ltd.* (unreported, 31 August 2001), however, the Full Court of the High Court permitted the defendant to re-plead its defence of justification to allege that the plaintiff was guilty of "theft by destruction" in response to the plaintiff's allegation that a broadcast alleged he had stolen rimu trees in a manner that amounted to "tree rustling." The Court considered that the *Defamation Act 1992* had relaxed the law in relation to justification but held the defendant could only plead a meaning that was alleged in the television program.

> Ursula Cheer, "Recent Developments in Defamation Law: New Zealand Media Law Update," vol. 7.3 Media & Arts Law Review 223 at 224–25:

> > In between the *Manning* decisions, the Court of Appeal was asked to review its decision in *Broadcasting Corporation of New Zealand* v. *Crush*, [[1988] 2 N.Z.L.R. 234] that alternative and lesser meanings asserted by a defendant in a case that was not a "pick and choose" case cannot be the subject of a plea of truth. In *Television New Zealand* v. *Ah Koy*, [unreported, Court of Appeal, CA 64/01, 26 November 2001) the appellant had broadcast words suggesting the respondent had bankrolled the attempted Fijian coup and may therefore have committed the crimes of treason and kidnapping. TVNZ argued it had a right to assert lesser meanings and prove the truth of them. However, the Court found it did not have to decide that the law had changed because the lesser meanings asserted by TVNZ were not materially different from the meanings asserted by Mr. Ah Koy. On the assumption that a lesser defamatory meaning can be pleaded and proved, but not expressing a view either way, the Court held this should only be permitted if the alternative

meaning asserted by the defendant is one which is reasonably capable of material distinction from that asserted by the plaintiff.

E. ONTARIO DECISIONS

Influenced by the decisions of the English Court of Appeal in the *Polly Peck* line of cases, the law of Ontario has changed. A defendant is now entitled to plead his own meaning and justify it.

1) *Pizza Pizza Ltd. v. Toronto Star Newspapers Ltd.*

The leading case is the judgment of Sharpe J. for the Divisional Court in *Pizza Pizza Ltd. v. Toronto Star Newspapers Ltd.* (1998), 167 D.L.R. (4th) 748 (Ont. Div. Ct.). This ruling was affirmed by the Ontario Court of Appeal: [2000] O.J. No. 228. The Court of Appeal simply adopted the language of Mr. Justice Sharpe.

(It should be noted that the Divisional Court's decision in *Pizza Pizza* was anticipated by *Rumack v. Gatt*, [1997] O.J. No. 4075 (Gen. Div.), where Ground J. of the Ontario Court of Justice (General Division), chose to follow Cameron J.'s *Pizza Pizza* trial decision and adopt the *Polly Peck* approach in preference to *Turner v. Toronto Sun Publishing Corporation* (1990), 50 C.P.C. (2d) 730 (Ont. H.C.J.).)

In *Pizza Pizza* the plaintiff sued over an article which contained 1,330 words and described a number of complaints made by Pizza Pizza franchisees in relation to rent, territory, supplies, order processing, and advertising issues, and also referred to allegations that Pizza Pizza took certain steps to intimidate the complaining franchises. The article appeared under the headline "Pizza Pizza franchisees claim company exploits them" and continued on a separate page under the headline "Pizza franchisees form group to get a fairer deal from firm."

Justice Sharpe described the plaintiff's pleadings as follows (at page 751):

> [3] In its statement of claim, Pizza Pizza complains of the following 77 words contained in the article:
>
>> "Pizza Pizza franchisees claim company exploits them" and "the recession hasn't helped but Rafati says his major problem was a head office decision two years ago to award almost half his market to other franchisees. At the stroke of a pen with no recourse his dreams of financial security turned into a nightmare … why, in a recession, did head office raise rents to 10 per cent of sales? Rafati said at current sales levels, this year's rent will be $14,000 more than Pizza Pizza will pay his landlord."

Pizza Pizza asserts a false innuendo plea, pleading that the natural and ordinary meanings of the words complained of are as follows:

a) the plaintiff cheated Rafati by arbitrarily taking half of his market away from him contrary to the franchise agreement;

b) the plaintiff cheated Rafati by charging him excessive rent and using the excess for the plaintiff's own benefit.

The defendant's pleadings were described by Justice Sharpe as follows at page 751:

> [4] The defendants are separately represented. In their statement of defence, the *Star* defendants (all the defendants except Rafati) deny the meaning ascribed by Pizza Pizza and go on to plead in paragraph 8 that the article and the specific words complained of have a different meaning and that the meaning they ascribed to the article is true:
>
> > The *Star* defendants say that, to the extent the Article, including the words complained of, in its plain and ordinary meaning, meant and was understood to mean that the plaintiff exploits, takes advantage of, abuses and/or treats unfairly its franchises, then in such meaning the Article, including the words complained of, is true in substance and in fact.
>
> Extensive particulars are provided of the plea of justification. The *Star* defendants further plead in paragraph 11 that the meanings of the words complained of are what those words literally say and that those meanings are true. Again, extensive particulars are pleaded in support of this plea of justification.
>
> [5] In his statement of defence, the defendant Rafati adopts the above-mentioned defences pleaded by the Star defendants and adds his own list of particulars in support.

Pizza Pizza failed in its motion before Cameron J. of the Ontario Court (General Division) to strike out paragraphs 8 and 11 of the *Star* defendants' statement of defence and a portion of the Rafati statement of defence adopting those paragraphs. *Pizza Pizza* argued the traditional rule that a defendant to a libel action may not plead a lesser meaning of the words complained of and then seek to justify that lesser meaning. Cameron J., however, adopted the English rule enunciated in *Polly Peck (Holdings) plc* v. *Trelford*, [1986] 2 All E.R. 84 (C.A.) [see section B(1) above], stating, *inter alia*:

> It is unfair and prejudicial to the defendant that while a jury in a libel action may find a plain and ordinary meaning defamatory of the plaintiff but less so than alleged by the plaintiff, according to current Ontario precedents the defendant cannot plead or lead evidence respecting its justification for such

lesser meaning. It is unfair for the defendant to be deprived of pleading or presenting evidence on a relevant issue.

On the appeal to the Divisional Court, Sharpe J. concluded that Ontario should adopt the *Polly Peck* approach, which he described at page 755, paragraph 15:

> In *Polly Peck*, supra at p. 102, O'Connor L.J. concluded by formulating the following rule:
>
>> In cases where the plaintiff selects words from a publication, pleads that in their natural and ordinary meaning the words are defamatory of him and pleads the meaning which he asserts they bear by way of false innuendo, the defendant is entitled to look at the whole publication in order to aver that in their context the words bear a meaning different to that alleged by the plaintiff. The defendant is entitled to plead that in that meaning the words are true and give particulars of the facts and matters on which he relies in support of his plea.

Sharpe J. concluded, however, that the *Polly Peck* defence should be subject to certain qualifications, stating at page 755, paragraph 16:

> It is important to note that in *Polly Peck*, in order to protect the plaintiff from unfairness or oppression, the English Court of Appeal qualified the right of the defendant to plead justification to a different meaning. First, where a publication contains separate and distinct libels, the plaintiff is entitled to select one and sue on it, and the defendant is not permitted to assert the truth of the other defamatory statements. The defendant's right to plead justification only arises where it can reasonably be claimed that the article from which the offending words are taken has a "common sting" and does not make a separate and distinct allegation. *Polly Peck*, supra, at 102; see also *Khashoggi v. IPC Magazines Ltd.*, [1986] 3 All E.R. 577 (C.A.) at 581. Second, as explained in *Polly Peck*, supra, at p. 102, "[i]n all cases, it is the duty of the court to see that the defendant, in particularizing a plea of justification or fair comment, does not act oppressively."

The Divisional Court therefore sustained the decision of Cameron J. Sharpe J. stated the reasons of the Divisional Court at pages 756–59:

> ¶18 In my view, the approach taken by the English Court of Appeal in *Polly Peck*, supra is preferable to the traditional position reflected by *Turner v. Toronto Sun* for several reasons. First of all, I do not think it is possible to limit the plaintiff to the particular meaning pleaded. As already noted, the English

authorities are to the contrary. In Ontario, account must also be taken of the *Libel and Slander Act*, R.S.O. 1990, c. L-12, s. 14:

> On the trial of an action for libel, the jury may give a general verdict upon the whole matter in issue in the action and shall not be required or directed to find for the plaintiff merely on proof of publication by the defendant of the alleged libel and of the sense ascribed to it in the action, but the court shall, according to its discretion, give its opinion and directions to the jury on the matter as in other cases, and the jury may on such issue find a special verdict, if they think fit to do so …

It is submitted by counsel for Pizza Pizza that the trial judge could overcome the possibility of a verdict on a different meaning by directing the jury that it is only entitled to find in the plaintiff's favour if it finds the words complained of to have the meaning attributed to them by the plaintiff. However, it is impossible to ignore the statutory right of the jury to render a general verdict. The jury must be told of that right and cannot be required to give a special verdict by answering specific questions.

¶19 Second, even if the plaintiff could be limited to the meaning it pleads, I do not accept the submission that it is appropriate to give the plaintiff the exclusive right to define the issue for trial. It would, in my view, be fundamentally unfair to the defendants in this case to preclude them from justifying their version of the libel. Simply put, if the plaintiff is entitled to present its side of the case by selecting certain words as being offensive and claiming that the defendant has called it "a cheat," the defendant should be allowed to respond fully to the allegations made against it. There is no question but that the defendant is entitled to insist that the jury see the article in its entirety. The defendant who does not accept the meaning pleaded by the plaintiff cannot, as a practical or tactical matter, simply deny that meaning. Such a denial would ring hollow if the defendant did not offer a different meaning. Where, as in the present case, the defendant asserts a different but also defamatory meaning, its position becomes scarcely tenable before the trier of fact if it is precluded from pleading and proving the truth of that meaning. How can it be fair to these defendants who say "we did not call you a cheat, but we do say that you exploit, take advantage of and treat your franchisees unfairly" to preclude them from pleading and proving the truth of those very serious allegations. By curtailing the right of the defendant to explain fully what it said and why it said it, the traditional rule places the defendant in an awkward and unfair tactical position. It seems to me that in a case such as the present, the defendant can only explain its position adequately if allowed to say not only: "read this article as a whole — this is what it means" but also "and this meaning is true."

¶20 The unfairness of the traditional rule goes beyond placing the defendant in an unfair tactical position. By preventing the defendant from offering a full explanation of its position, the traditional rule is also substantively unfair and constitutes an unacceptable limitation on freedom of expression and freedom of the press. A defamation suit such as the present one represents a direct challenge to the right of a newspaper to publish an account of the concerns expressed by a particular group of people. It is important, in the interests of freedom of expression and freedom of the press, for the newspaper to be allowed to defend itself fully by presenting its entire case to the court for consideration. From this perspective, it is difficult to see why the newspaper should not be able to defend itself by saying "this is what we meant and what we meant is true."

...

¶22 Counsel for Pizza Pizza placed heavy reliance on the proposition that the defendant should be restricted in the interest of streamlining the issues for discovery and trial. There can be no doubt that simplifying issues and making discovery and trial more efficient represents a laudable goal. It is also clear that if the modern English rule is adopted, the issues for both discovery and trial are broader. However, the interests of efficiency of discovery and trial carry little weight if achieved at the price of curtailing the right of a party from presenting its entire case, particularly where fundamental rights are at issue. If it takes longer to try the whole case, so be it.

The Divisional Court in *Pizza Pizza* itself laid down certain qualifications to the right to plead and justify a different meaning. Sharpe J. stated for the Court at page 759:

¶ 23 Finally, I would emphasize that the Polly Peck approach is a balanced one that does take into account the interests of the plaintiff. The court retains a discretion to protect the defendant from unfairness or oppression. The right of the defendant to plead and prove the truth of a different meaning is not unfettered. The defendant is not permitted to plead justification to a separate or distinct libel. To that extent, the plaintiff is entitled to plead and rely on one libel without risking the embarrassment of the defendant attempting to justify another.

In the circumstances before the Court in *Pizza Pizza Ltd.*, Sharpe J. held that the defendant's pleadings were acceptable.

2) *Asper v. Lantos*

The *Polly Peck* approach was again considered by the Ontario Superior Court of Justice in *Asper v. Lantos* (1999), 46 O.R. (3d) 238, where the plaintiffs alleged that they had been defamed in a speech given by the defendant Lantos at Ryerson Polytechnic University in Toronto. Nordheimer J. noted that the plaintiffs alleged in paragraph 8 of their statement of claim that Lantos' words were false and defamatory in their ordinary meaning and by virtue of the innuendoes arising therefrom. Judge Nordheimer describes the statement of claim as follows, at page 240:

The plaintiffs then continue in that paragraph [8] to say:

Without limiting the generality of the foregoing, the said words meant and were understood to mean, *inter alia*,

(1) the Plaintiffs are dishonest in their scheduling, promotion and sale of Canadian programming;

(2) the Plaintiffs are guilty of employing fraudulent accounting techniques;

(3) the Plaintiffs have deliberately mislead [sic] the press and the Canadian public as to the realities of Canadian broadcasting and the realities of their own business practices;

(4) the Plaintiffs have reaped benefits from Canadian taxpayers while contributing nothing to Canadians, Canadian broadcasting and Canadian Culture;

(5) the Plaintiffs have participated in a cynical strategy to mislead the Canadian public and the Canadian Radio-television and Telecommunications Commission ("CRTC") for their own profit;

(6) the Plaintiffs use their position and power to suppress free speech and con, bribe and coerce agreement or silence from those in the Canadian broadcast industry;

(7) the Plaintiffs are nothing more than greedy middlemen and rebroadcasters who are lacking in talent and skill;

(8) the Plaintiffs are hypocritical in their public and private dealings;

(9) the Plaintiffs are disloyal to Canadian culture; and

(10) Mr. Asper is dishonest, insincere and hypocritical in his dealings in the broadcast industry and is undeserving of the Order of Canada.

[4] The plaintiffs then go on to allege that the speech has been reproduced in various newspapers and that the plaintiffs have suffered economic damage and damage to reputation.

The defendants' plea of justification was the subject matter of the plaintiff's motion to strike before Nordheimer J. That plea is described at pages 240–41:

> [6] In para. 17 of the statement of defence, the defendants plead:
>
> In the further alternative, in their plain and ordinary meaning and insofar as the Speech and any subsequent republications for which the defendants are responsible at law, including the words complained of, meant or were understood to mean that:
>
> (1) The plaintiffs have benefitted from governmental regulation while contributing significantly less than they could to the stated objectives and goals of the Canadian broadcasting system, namely providing a public service essential to the maintenance and enhancement of national identity and cultural sovereignty and contributing to the creation and presentation of Canadian programming, maximizing the use of Canadian creative and other resources;
>
> (2) The plaintiffs seek to give the impression of supporting distinctively Canadian drama programming but do significantly less than they could to broadcast such programming and attract the largest possible audience to it;
>
> (3) The audience and revenue levels obtained by Global and CanWest from the broadcast of distinctively Canadian drama programming have been lower than they might have been, in part, because of the scheduling and sales tactics used by them;
>
> (4) Historically, Global and CanWest have more extensively broadcast U.S.-produced programming, on a simulcast basis, during peak-viewing periods, than other Canadian networks, and revenues from such broadcasting are significant in making them the most profitable of major Canadian broadcasters; and
>
> (5) Despite their professed commitment to distinctively Canadian drama programming, Global and CanWest historically have given higher priority to their profitability, financial strength and growth than to maintaining and enhancing Canadian national identity and cultural sovereignty through the broadcast of such programming during peak-viewing periods.
>
> They are true in substance and in fact; particulars in addition to those set out in the speech itself are appended hereto in Schedule A.
>
> Schedule A then sets out in almost seven full pages, a list of 51 different particulars for the plea of justification set out in para. 17. That Schedule A detailing the particulars is attached to these reasons [at p. 251 post].

Nordheimer J. accepted (at page 246) the plaintiff's submission that a defendant, even under *Polly Peck*, can only assert a different meaning for the words complained of if that different meaning is also defamatory. In the case before him, Nordheimer J. concluded that paragraph 17 of the statement of defence and particulars of that paragraph, set out in Schedule A should be struck because the alleged meaning was not defamatory. He stated at pages 246–47:

> [20] ... I have considerable difficulty accepting that the meaning asserted by the defendants is sufficient to constitute defamation of the plaintiffs. That meaning is now so massaged and so anaemic in its thrust, that if the defendant's meaning is accepted, I am not satisfied that any jury properly instructed would find that such a meaning tended to lower or adversely affect the plaintiffs in the estimation of others. Relative comments are not generally considered to be defamatory and virtually every meaning contended for in para. 17 of the statement of defence is of a relative nature. Fairly read, the meaning asserted by the defendant could be reduced to the simple assertion that the plaintiffs "could do more" or "could do better." I would not consider such a meaning, in this day and age, spoken of the plaintiffs to be defamatory .... .

Nordheimer J. also held (at page 250) that permitting the defendants to plead their asserted meanings would be oppressive to the plaintiffs.

In *Asper*, Nordheimer J. also held that the *Polly Peck* defence is not limited to "pick and choose" cases, explaining this terminology at page 244:

> ¶13 A "pick and choose" case, as I understand it, is a case where there are two or more libels within the piece and the plaintiff complains of only one. If the two libels are clearly distinct or severable, then the plaintiff may choose which libel he will sue on. For example, if the plaintiff is accused of being a thief and an adulterer, he may sue only with respect to the accusation of adultery. However, if the libels are not distinct and severable, then the plaintiff cannot, by choosing one, prevent the defendant from having reference to the others and proving same in order to justify the statement on which the plaintiff sues.

After giving this definition, Nordheimer J. concluded that the *Polly Peck* defence is not restricted to such "pick and choose" cases, stating at page 245:

> ¶15 I say that because I do not consider that the modern approach [*sic*] to be restricted to pick and choose cases. My reading of the decisions of the English Court of Appeal in *Polly Peck* and of the decisions of Cameron J. and the Divisional Court in *Pizza Pizza* does not lead me to the conclusion that any such restriction was either stated or intended. The modern approach simply says that if the plaintiff alleges that the words complained of have one plain and

ordinary meaning, the defendant is entitled to allege that the words have a different plain and ordinary meaning and then to seek to justify that meaning.

Although the ruling of Nordheimer J. in *Asper v. Lantos* (1999), 46 O.R. (3d) 238 was not appealed, the finding he made about oppression came under the scrutiny of the Ontario Divisional Court in *Asper v. Lantos* (2000), 3 C.P.C. (5th) 330. This occurred after the defendants had amended paragraph 17 of their statement of defence by replacing it with a new paragraph 17. The new pleading is described by MacFarland J. for the Divisional Court at page 332:

> ... the defendants amended the Statement of Defence deleting paragraph 17 in the form it had been when the motion was brought before Nordheimer J. and replacing it with a new paragraph 17 and paragraphs 17(a) and 17(b). Paragraphs 17 and 17(a) do not plead any alternative meaning; they seek to justify the meaning which the plaintiffs attribute to the language. Paragraph 17(b) pleads alternative meanings.
>
> Schedule A was amended only slightly so that the particulars of paragraph 17, 17(a) and 17(b) in the Amended Statement of Defence were largely identical to the particulars delivered in relation to the original paragraph 17.

The court in *Asper v. Lantos* (2000), 3 C.P.C. (5th) 330 (Ont. Div. Ct.) was hearing an appeal from an order made by Lamek J. which struck out the defendants' Schedule A on the ground that it was oppressive. Lamek J. held that the notion of oppression (as described in *Pizza Pizza* and *Polly Peck*) can arise even where the defendant seeks to justify the words in the very meaning asserted by the plaintiff.

In the course of his judgment setting aside the order of Lamek J., MacFarland J. stated [at page 333] that the Divisional Court in *Pizza Pizza* was aware that adopting *Polly Peck* would broaden issues for both discovery and trial. The court took the opportunity to discuss the approach to be taken by the courts to a claim by a plaintiff that a defendant's pleading was oppressive. MacFarland J. held at page 334:

> ¶17 In our view, the *Pizza Pizza Ltd.* case did not add anything new in terms of the ability of a court to limit a pleading or particulars thereof on the basis of it being oppressive to a Plaintiff ... In all cases, the court has said it retains jurisdiction "to protect the Plaintiff from unfairness or oppression." We do not interpret this language as meaning anything more than a reiteration of a jurisdiction, which the court has always had, to strike pleadings where they are unfair or prejudicial. We do not accept [the defendant's] submission that where a Defendant pleads no alternative meaning but seeks to justify the

meaning alleged by the Plaintiff that his right to do so and to provide particulars thereof is unfettered, provided they are relevant.

¶18 In our view, the court has had and continues to have jurisdiction to strike a pleading even where it is relevant, where its probative value is outweighed by its prejudicial effect....

¶19 In our view, the principles that are brought to bear on a motion of this nature are those found in Rules 25.06, 25.10 and 25.11. The overall underlying theme of *Pizza Pizza Ltd.* is one of fairness, fairness to both sides. If a Plaintiff is of the view that particulars pleaded are unfair and offend the pleadings rules, a motion will be brought to strike. On the return of that motion, it is the duty of the court to consider not only whether the plea offends Rule 25.11 and is, thereby, unfair to a Plaintiff, but also whether it is relevant and necessary to the defendant's effort to justify the meaning it has alleged. It is an exercise in balancing the rights of the parties on the particular facts before the court.

[20] *Pizza Pizza Ltd.* does not stand for the proposition that it is open to a court to strike a pleading or particulars in a libel action where they are relevant, necessary and of reasonable probative value to the Defendant on the ground that such a plea is "oppressive." On the other hand, where a plea is strictly speaking relevant, but of marginal probative value, and would be onerous for a Plaintiff, it may well be found to offend the Rules.

In the circumstances before the Divisional Court, MacFarland J. held, at page 335, that Lamek J. had failed to conduct the necessary "balancing exercise" and therefore his order should be set aside.

3) Other Ontario Cases

A further example of the concept of balancing where a plaintiff alleges oppression is found in the judgment of Swinton J. in *Lee* v. *Globe and Mail* (2001), 52 O.R. (3d) 652 (S.C.J.), where the plaintiff, a former Prime Minister of the Republic of Singapore, sued the *Globe and Mail* newspaper over an article reporting an interview with the former President of Singapore concerning the alleged suppression of legitimate dissent in that country. The words complained of read:

SINGAPORE SAGE

1) Then, in 1985 came a shocking break. Mr. Lee told Singapore's parliament that Mr. Nair had resigned because he was an alcoholic, a charge Mr. Nair now calls a baseless slur.

2)   But before he could speak out, Mr. Nair found himself at the center of a rumour-mongering campaign that labeled him a drinker and a womanizer. He says he was neither, and he suspects that Mr. Lee had government doctors slip him hallucinatory drugs to make him appear befuddled. "Lee Kuan Yew decided: This man is going to be a threat, so I'd better begin a total demolishment of his character. He's very good at that."

Paragraph 9 of the plaintiff's statement of claim (at pages 654–55):

9. The Plaintiff pleads that the words in their natural and ordinary meaning meant and were understood to mean the following:

1)   The plaintiff, as the Prime Minister of Singapore, invented false allegations that Mr. Nair was an alcoholic for the purpose of destroying Mr. Nair's good character;

2)   The Plaintiff, as the Prime Minister of Singapore, invented false allegations concerning alcohol for the purpose of destroying Mr. Nair's good character;

3)   The Plaintiff, as the Prime Minister of Singapore, invented false allegations that Mr. Nair was a womanizer for the purpose of destroying Mr. Nair's good character;

4)   The Plaintiff, as the Prime Minister of Singapore, maliciously directed government doctors to slip Mr. Nair hallucinatory drugs in order to make him appear to be befuddled as part of a scheme to destroy his good character.

The issue before Swinton J. was the propriety of the plea of justification contained in the defence filed by the newspaper defendants, which he described as follows (at page 655):

[5] Paragraph 6 of the Statement of Defence of the Thomson defendants states that the words in para. 8 of the Statement of Claim are, to the extent that they are statements of fact, true. In subparas. (a) through (q), the facts relied on are set out. The two impugned subparagraphs read:

6(p) Mr. Nair is not an alcoholic or in any event he believes he is not an alcoholic and has received medical advice to that effect; and

6(q) Under Mr. Lee's leadership and direction the government of Singapore has on a number of occasions used its substantial resources to prosecute, imprison or otherwise discourage those who have expressed opinions critical of and therefore potentially threatening to Mr. Lee or his government, to the detriment of those who express those views and their personal standing.

The plaintiff argued that paragraph 6(q) was irrelevant and, in addition, oppressive, in that it was designed to embarrass the plaintiff and would lead to a complex and lengthy production and discovery process. Swinton J. rejected this argument, stating at paragraph 14:

> It is true that the facts alleged in this paragraph will entail a wide ranging factual inquiry. Nevertheless as MacFarland J. has observed in *Asper*, a pleading should not be struck just because it is oppressive to the plaintiff; rather, there must be a consideration of both prejudice and relevance. Here, given the relevance to a number of aspects of the defendant's case, the pleading should not be struck, even if it appears burdensome to the plaintiff.

In *Clement v. McGuinty* (2001), 18 C.P.C. (5th) 267 (Ont. C.A.), the plaintiff, an Ontario Cabinet Minister, sued the leader of the Official Opposition over statements broadcast by the news media which the plaintiff alleged meant he was corrupt because he had intervened on behalf of a developer on a matter concerning the "moraine lands" north of the city of Toronto, a subject that was before the Ontario Municipal Board.

The plaintiff had applied successfully to the Ontario Superior Court to strike out, *inter alia*, paragraphs 13 and 14 of the statement of defence, which read (at page 274–75):

> ¶ 13 Further and in the alternative, by way of legal innuendo the words meant and were understood to mean that the plaintiff had acted improperly and had failed in his public duty to the detriment of the public.

> ¶ 14 The particulars are:

> a. in the political argot "corruption" is used in the legislature as a form of attack covering a wide range of misdeed [*sic*] as indicated by one Michael Harris, the member from Nipissing on 21 June 1995 who said without censure the argot "corruption waste and mismanagement in the affordable housing industry have tainted ministers from Chaviva Hosek to Evelyn Gigantes" and Mr. Runciman on 21 June 1993 saying a minister had been corrupted even though he had respect for him.

> b. The tenor of the word corruption in political argument in Ontario is that the systems have deteriorated beyond functional good use and their foundations have suffered extreme sclerosis and in such innuendo the words are substantially true and fair comments, based on the particulars in paragraph 9 herein.

Such meaning and connotations were familiar to the audience hearing the broadcasts.

The cross-reference to paragraph 14(b) of the statement of defence in paragraph 9 of the particulars included (at 272):

h. Developers and their companies interested in developing the Oak Ridges Moraine for residential sites have contributed 209 separate political donations totalling $335,000 to the Progressive Conservative Party between 1995 and 1997 as stated in the Legislature on November 3, 1999;

i. One of these aforesaid companies, Fernbrook Homes, proposed by advertisement a private gated community overlooking the Oak Ridge Moraine;

j. The Cortellucci and Montemarano companies, who were interested in development of the Moraine, contributed $8,840 in 1998 to the plaintiff's riding association, which the plaintiff admitted in the Legislature on November 4, 1999;

Speaking for the Ontario Court of Appeal in allowing the defendant's appeal from the Superior Court's order, Austin J. held (at pages 276–77) that the judge below had erred:

On this point it is clear that the judge below did not consider to what extent the particulars attacked are necessary to enable the defendant to prove its case, nor their probative value in establishing that case. Nor can it be said from the nature of the particulars in issue that the oppression would clearly outweigh that probative value. For these reasons, the order below striking out paragraph 9(h)(i) and (j) must be set aside.

Other Ontario decisions on the subject of oppression include:

Mills v. MacFarlane (2000), 49 C.P.C. (4th) 184 (Ont. S.C.J.) [defendant pleaded justification to the meaning alleged by the plaintiff; did not plead an alternative defendant's defamatory meaning; no oppression established on the facts; plea proper].

Vella v. Schuller, [2002] O.J. No. 2027 (Ont. S.C.J.) [defendant pleaded an alternative defamatory meaning, which the court held was not unfair to the plaintiff; a reasonable individual would find the meaning of the words complained of to be broader than the meaning ascribed by the plaintiff].

F. THE STATUS OF *POLLY PECK* AND *PIZZA PIZZA* IN OTHER PROVINCES

There is jurisprudence in several other provinces on the subject of the defendant's entitlement to plead and justify an alternative defamatory meaning.

1) British Columbia

Predating *Pizza Pizza*, the decision of the British Columbia Supreme Court in *Finnamore v. Sun Publishing Company* (1993), 77 B.C.L.R. (2d) 293 (S.C.) concerned a libel claim against a newspaper. The plaintiff Finnamore complained about the following words:

> CAIMAW vice-president Roger Crowther said Finnamore "represents employers as far was (*sic*) we can tell. We say that from experience, because he led the raid on White Spot."

The plaintiff did not plead a false innuendo. In certain amendments to his statement of defence, which had been allowed by a Master, the defendant Crowther pleaded:

3. The words "represents employers as far as we can tell," attributed to this Defendant in paragraph 10 of the Statement of Claim, meant and were understood to mean that the Plaintiff Finnamore's conduct on behalf of the Teamsters Union in helping to organize a raid on White Spot employees in the months of September through to November 1988, while those employees were on a legal strike pursuant to the *Industrial Relations Act* of British Columbia, had the effect of impairing the effectiveness of the strike and of assisting the employer White Spot in that dispute.

4. Those words further meant and were understood to mean that the contract negotiated by Local 777 of United Food and Commercial Workers' Union, of which the Plaintiff Finnamore was a representative, was a substandard collective agreement, and had the effect of strengthening the hand of industry employers in collective bargaining with their employees.

5. Those words further meant and were understood to mean that after creating a one-man union local in 1983, the Plaintiff Finnamore accepted an invitation from an employer representative, negotiated a collective agreement on his own, in one day, with an employer, and then signed up the employer's employees into the Plaintiff Finnamore's union local. This course of conduct also had the effect of strengthening the hand of the employer and employers in collective bargaining with their employees.

6. These meanings are true in substance and in fact. There were no other meanings understood by those words. The Defendant Crowther relies on the entire article published by the Defendants Sun Publishing Company Limited and Pacific Press Limited.

Scarth J. considered *Turner v. Toronto Sun Publishing Corporation* (1990), 5 C.C.L.T. (2d) 184 (Ont. S.C.J.) and *Loos v. Leader-Post Limited* (1982), 26

C.P.C. 30 (Sask. C.A.), and *Slim* v. *Daily Telegraph Ltd.*, [1968] 1 All E.R. 497 (C.A.), all of which he described as expressing the traditional or classic approach to libel pleadings.

After referring to *Lucas-Box* v. *Associated Newspapers Group plc*, [1986] 1 All E.R. 177, Scarth J. stated [at page 302]:

> As in England, there is not, in the Rules of Court, a rule prohibiting the defendant from stating in his defence what he alleges was the natural and ordinary meaning of the words complained of. Any such prohibition, if it in fact now exists, is founded on conventional practice.

Scarth J. then examined the rationale for the convention to determine whether it should be applied in the particular circumstances before him in *Finnamore*. The crucial factor, from his point of view, was that "the plaintiff does not allege in his statement of claim what the natural and ordinary meaning of the words is. Nor does he plead they are defamatory of him by reason of an innuendo." Scarth J. therefore held [at page 303]:

> I think in this situation the defendant ought to be able to plead what he alleges the natural and ordinary meaning of the words is, although I confess to having some difficulty understanding why he should wish to confine his defence of justification to a particular meaning of the words, given the possibility the plaintiff's assertion of what the words mean, whatever that may be, may be accepted by the trier of fact. What is critical here, in my view, is that the defendant, at the pleadings stage, is not seeking to justify a different or lesser meaning than that alleged by the plaintiff, because the plaintiff has not alleged any specific meaning or stated what he says the natural and ordinary meaning is.

In *Dhami* v. *Canadian Broadcasting Corporation*, [2001] B.C.J. No. 2773, 2001 BCSC 1811, the plaintiffs claimed over a CBC television broadcast and certain Indo-Canadian newspaper articles concerning the International Sikh Youth Federation. The plaintiffs applied, *inter alia*, to strike the CBC's plea of justification, and particulars delivered by the CBC relating, among other things, to justification.

Slade J. recited the relevant plea of justification in the CBC's statement of defence, at paragraph 56:

> Paragraph 7(a) of the Amended Statement of Defence says as follows:

> > In the further alternative, if the words are capable in their plain and ordinary meaning of the meaning ascribed to them by the Plaintiffs, which is denied, then the words complained of in paragraph 13 of the

Statement of Claim were true in substance and in fact the particulars of which are set out in the Defendant's Statement of Further and Better Particulars dated November 23, 1999.

This plea, that the statements of fact were true, is the defendants' plea of justification.

The plaintiff's objection to this plea is explained by the court at paragraph 57:

The plaintiffs seek to strike this plea on the ground that it is confined to the words stated in the broadcast, and not to the meaning ascribed by the plaintiffs to those words having regard for the accompanying tone of voice and facial expression of the defendant Kevin Evans. The plaintiffs say that by this plea the defendants have pled a lesser meaning, and that they seek to justify that lesser meaning as the truth.

Slade J. held that if the defendants wished to rely generally on a plea of justification, they must plead in relation to the inference set out in the meaning ascribed to the words complained of by the plaintiffs. However, he then went on to consider whether the defendant could plead a lesser defamatory meaning, and stated at paragraphs 61–63:

¶61 In *Siddon v. Mair et al*, [1997] B.C.J. No. 280 (B.C.S.C.), Fraser J. held that the defendants were not entitled to plead a "lesser meaning" than that alleged by the plaintiffs. Reasons were not given, and this decision cannot be said to be determinative of the principle asserted by the plaintiffs. It may well be that, because the issue arose at trial, Fraser J. based his decision on oppression.

¶62 In *Pizza Pizza*, the court held that a defendant is not prevented from pleading a lesser defamatory meaning. *Pizza Pizza* was cited in passing on this point in *Grassi v. WIC Radio Ltd. (c.o.b.) CKNW/98*, [2000] 5 W.W.R. 119, 2000 BCSC 185; (reversed on the issue of costs) (2001), 89 B.C.L.R. (3d) 198, 2001 BCCA 376.

¶63 If a lesser defamatory meaning is possible, then a defendant is entitled to plead justification in relation to that meaning.

In the circumstances before the court, however, Slade J. concluded, at paragraph 66, that the defendant's plea of justification was improper because no lesser defamatory meaning had been ascribed by the defendant to the words complained of by the plaintiff or to any portion of them.

If the defendants wish to plead a lesser defamatory meaning, and plead justification in relation to that lesser meaning, they must identify that portion or
those portions of the broadcast which they contend are capable of the lesser
defamatory meaning.

That was not done, and accordingly paragraph 7(a) was struck.

See also, *Home Equity Development Inc. v. Crow*, 2002 BCSC 1688, per Quijano J. at paras. 11–18.

Miller v. Canadian Broadcasting Corp., 2003 BCSC 258, per Satanove J. at
paras. 4, 13–19.

2) Alberta

In *Goddard v. Day*, [2001] 5 W.W.R. 501, 2000 ABQB 820, the plaintiff, a
criminal lawyer, sued an Alberta politician over his letter to an Alberta daily
newspaper. In the statement of defence, the defendant purported to allege a
lesser defamatory meaning. Ritter J. concluded that *Polly Peck* and *Pizza Pizza*
would entitle the defendant to plead a lesser defamatory meaning, but stated
(at page 505), applying *Asper v. Lantos* (1999), 46 O.R. (3d) 238 (S.C.J.):

... a Defendant is not permitted to so massage and distort the statements
complained of that the allegedly defamatory statements take on a meaning
that is not at all defamatory. In those situations, the Defendant should simply
defend on the basis that what was said was not defamatory.

On the facts before him in *Goddard v. Day*, Ritter J. concluded (at page 505)
that the meaning pleaded by the defendant was not defamatory. He therefore struck out the plea.

3) Saskatchewan

A number of Canadian authorities, including *Turner v. Toronto Sun Publishing Corporation*, (1990) 50 C.P.C. (2d) 73 (Ont. H.C.J.), assert that the traditional approach was approved by the Saskatchewan Court of Appeal in
Loos v. The Leader-Post Ltd., [1982] 2 W.W.R. 459 (Sask. C.A.) (leave to
appeal denied). It is not clear that is the actual basis of the decision in *Loos*.

Although the Saskatchewan Court of Appeal did strike out portions of
the statement of defence which pleaded defendant's meanings, Cameron
J.A., writing for the Court, stated (at page 468) that the defendants' allegedly defamatory meanings were in fact "harmless" meanings and noted that
"innocent words need no justification." Cameron J.A. explained the con-

cerns which actually lead to the defence plea being struck in the case before him (at 469):

> A plea of justification amounts to a defendant saying, in effect, that if the challenged words should bear the plaintiffs' meaning and that meaning is defamatory, which is not admitted but denied, then the words are true. The defendants have not done this, and in my view, their pleas of justification are fraught with more difficulty than merely appearing to set up a meaning different than that pleaded by the plaintiffs and then seeking to justify that other meaning. The pleas fail adequately to engage the issue which is this: If the news stories bear the meaning ascribed to them by the plaintiffs, is it the defendants' contention that, in such sense, the stories are true, that the plaintiffs were remiss in their work and caused their employer millions of dollars in losses? It is critically important for the plaintiffs to know what the defendants are saying and will seek to prove at trial. I think the pleas, as drawn, leave the plaintiffs uncertain and confused. Moreover, the pleas weave in additional allegations of fact, as opposed to the sense of the words, allegations that appear, in part, at least, to go to context, and perhaps to what the defendants intended the words to mean.

To date, no Saskatchewan court has followed *Polly Peck* or *Pizza Pizza* or explicitly modified the traditional rule against pleading a defendant's defamatory meaning and justifying that meaning.

G. SUMMARY OF *POLLY PECK/PIZZA PIZZA* PRINCIPLES

The following principles emerge from a review of the cases involving the *Polly Peck/Pizza Pizza* defence:

i) The defendant is not permitted to plead a meaning that is not defamatory.

   Asper v. Lantos (1999), 46 O.R. (3d) 238, per Nordheimer J. at 246 (S.C.J.).

   Goddard v. Day, [2001] 5 W.W.R. 501, per Ritter J. at 505 (Alta. Q.B.).

   Cruise v. Express Newspapers plc, [1999] Q.B. 931, per Brooke J.A. at 948 (C.A.).

ii) The defendant is not permitted to plead a meaning which the publication at issue is not capable of conveying. This is a question of law for the judge.

   Prager v. Times Newspapers Ltd., [1988] 1 All E.R. 300 (C.A.), per Purchas L.J. at 308d, Nicholls L.J. at 310a–d, 312b–c.

United States Tobacco International Inc. & Another v. British Broadcasting Corporation, [1988] E.M.L.R. 816, *The Independent*, 15 March 1988 (C.A.), per Purchas L.J.

iii)   The defendant is not permitted to plead justification to a separate and distinct libel that the plaintiff does not complain of in the statement of claim. Expressed another way, if an allegedly defamatory publication contains two separate and distinct stings, and a plaintiff complains of only one of the stings, the defendant may not rely on a plea of justification or fair comment in relation to the other sting.

Polly Peck (Holdings) plc v. Trelford, [1986] 2 All E.R. 84, per O'Connor L.J. at 102 (C.A.).

Cruise v. Express Newspapers plc, [1999] Q.B. 931, per Brooke J.A. at 955 (C.A.).

Pizza Pizza Ltd. v. Toronto Star Newspapers Ltd. (1998), 167 D.L.R. (4th) 748, per Sharpe J. at 759 (Ont. Div. Ct.).

McDonald's Corp. v. Steel, [1999] E.W.J. No. 2173 (C.A.), per Pill L.J. at para. 419.

a.   Whether a defamatory statement is separate and distinct from other defamatory statements contained in the same publication is a question of degree in each case.

Polly Peck (Holdings) plc v. Trelford, above, at 102.

McDonald's Corp. v. Steel, above, at para. 419.

b.   The several defamatory allegations in a publication may have a common sting, in which event they are not to be regarded as separate and distinct allegations. The defendant is entitled to justify the common sting.

Polly Peck (Holdings) plc v. Trelford, above, at 102.

Khashoggi v. I.P.C. Magazines, [1986] 1 W.L.R. 1412 (C.A.), per Sir John Donaldson M.R. at 1417.

c.   "Separate and distinct" means that the one imputation defamatory of the plaintiff's character is different from the other; not that there are two passages in the text which are separate and distinct.

United States Tobacco International Inc. & Another v. British Broadcasting Corporation, [1988] E.M.L.R. 816, *The Independent*, 15 March 1988 (C.A.), per Purchas L.J.

McDonald's Corp v. *Steel*, above, at para. 419.

d. The principle that a defendant should not be permitted to justify a libel different than the one complained of, applies even if the area of enquiry related to the same sector of the claimant's life or activities.

Tancic v. *Times Newspapers Ltd.*, [1999] E.W.J. No. 6510, per Brooke L.J. at para. 18 (C.A.).

e. Even if the words conveying the two allegations are textually severable, so that it can be demonstrated that the draftsperson need not have included in the statement of claim any words conveying the allegation which the plaintiff is not complaining of, it does not follow that this in itself determines whether the allegations are separate and distinct.

United States Tobacco International Inc. & Another v. *British Broadcasting Corporation*, above.

f. If there are two separate and distinct defamatory allegations, and the statement of claim contains lengthy extracts from the publication or broadcast which include another allegation (which the plaintiff does not complain of) this does not mean the defendant is entitled to justify that other allegation.

United States Tobacco International Inc. & Another v. *British Broadcasting Corporation*, ibid.

g. Where an article contains two separate and distinct stings, the fact that words containing a sting which the plaintiff does not complain of are inextricably mixed up with words containing a separate sting of which the plaintiff does complain will not entitle a defendant to justify the sting not complained of.

Cruise v. *Express Newspapers plc*, above, at 954–55.

iv) The determination whether defamatory allegations are separate and distinct is a question of law which can conveniently be determined on an interlocutory application.

Cruise v. *Express Newspapers plc*, ibid., at 954–55.

v) In cases where the plaintiff selects words from a publication, pleads that in their natural and ordinary meaning the words are defamatory of him, and pleads the meanings which he asserts they bear by way of false or popular innuendo, the defendant is entitled to look at the whole publication in order to aver that in their context the words bear a different meaning to that alleged by the plaintiff. The defendant is entitled to plead that in that meaning the words are true and to give particulars of the facts and matters on which he relies in support of his plea.

Polly Peck (Holdings) plc v. Trelford, [1986] 2 All E.R. 84, per Connor L.J. at 102 (C.A.).

vi) The foregoing principles are applicable by a parity of reasoning to fair comment, subject to certain limitations.

Polly Peck (Holdings) plc v. Trelford, ibid., at 102

vii) In all cases, the court retains jurisdiction to see that the defendant, in particularizing a plea of justification or fair comment, does not act oppressively.

Polly Peck (Holdings) plc v. Trelford, ibid.

Asper v. Lantos (2000), 3 C.P.C. (5th) 330, per MacFarland J. at 334 (Ont. Div. Ct.).

a. Whether the particularization of the plea is oppressive depends not merely on the facts of the case, but also on the attitude of the plaintiff. A plaintiff can limit the extent and cost of inquiry at trial by making timely admissions of fact.

Polly Peck (Holdings) plc v. Trelford, above, at 102.

b. The jurisdiction of the court to protect against oppression is merely the jurisdiction to strike pleadings where they are unfair and prejudicial.

Polly Peck (Holdings) plc v. Trelford, ibid., at 102.

c. Even if the defendant pleads no alternative meaning but merely seeks to justify the meaning alleged by the plaintiff, his right to do so is not unfettered, simply because the particulars are relevant.

Polly Peck (Holdings) plc v. Trelford, ibid., at 102.

d. The court has jurisdiction to strike a pleading even where it is relevant, where its probative value is outweighed by its prejudicial effect.

Polly Peck (Holdings) plc v. Trelford, ibid., at 102.

e. In determining whether particulars of justification or fair comment should be struck, the court will consider not only whether a plea is unfair to the plaintiff (because it may prejudice or delay the fair trial of the action; or is scandalous, frivolous, or vexatious; or is an abuse of the process of the court) but also whether it is relevant and necessary to the defendant's effort to justify the meaning he or she has alleged. This is an exercise in balancing the rights of the parties on the particular facts before the court.

Asper v. Lantos, above, at 334.

Lee v. The Globe and Mail (2001), 52 O.R. (3d) 652, per Swinton J. at para. 14 (S.C.J.).

Clement v. McGuinty (2001), 18 C.P.C. (5th) 267, per Austin J. at 276–77 (C.A.).

i.   The court may not strike a pleading or particulars in a libel action where they are relevant, necessary, and of reasonable probative value.

Asper v. Lantos, above, at 334.

ii.   Where a plea is relevant, but of marginal probative value, it may well be found to offend the rules of practice and be struck out.

Asper v. Lantos, ibid., at 334.

viii) The *Polly Peck/Pizza Pizza* defence is not restricted to "pick and choose" cases.

Asper v. Lantos (1999), 46 O.R. (3d) 238, per Nordheimer J. at 244–45 (S.C.J.).

a.   A pick and choose case is a case where there are two or more distinct and separate libels within the publication and the plaintiff only complains of one.

Asper v. Lantos, ibid., at 244.

b.   In other cases, the libels are not separate and distinct but the plaintiff has complained of certain statements and not others, and pleaded an extremely narrow defamatory meaning.

Cruise v. Express Newspapers plc, [1999] Q.B. 931 (C.A.) per Brooke J.A. at 955.

ix)   Although this issue has not been decided in *Polly Peck*, *Pizza Pizza*, or any related cases, it would appear to follow that if the words at issue require the plaintiff to plead a legal innuendo, the defendant should be entitled to plead an alternative defamatory meaning to that legal innuendo.

Clement v. *McGuinty* (2000), O.J. No. 2466 at para. 23 (S.C.J.), rev'd on other grounds (2001), 18 C.P.C. (5th) 267 (Ont. C.A.).

x) If the plaintiff has not pleaded a legal innuendo, which is a separate cause of action, a defendant is not entitled to force the plaintiff to proceed on a separate and unpleaded cause of action by pleading his or her own legal innuendo.

Clement v. *McGuinty, ibid.*

xi) The defendant's particulars of justification in libel cases generally should be confined to those matters which are essential to the proper disposal of the real issues between the parties. This may mean cutting out peripheral matters, the burden of whose investigation is disproportionate to their importance.

Rechem International v. *Express Newspapers*, [1992] E.W.J. No. 329 at 19 (C.A.).

McPhilemy v. *Times Newspapers Ltd.*, [1999] E.M.L.R. 751 (C.A.).

Tancic v. *Times Newspapers Ltd.*, [1999] E.W.J. No. 6510, per Brooke L.J. at para. 27 (C.A.).

xii) On the other hand, the action should not be so structured that the defendant is prevented from deploying his or her full essential defence so that the plaintiff obtains vindication upon an improper basis.

Tancic v. *Times Newspapers Ltd, ibid.*, at para. 18.

Basham v. *Gregory*, C.A.T. 21 February 1996 at 10 and 11 (C.A.).

H. POTENTIAL FUTURE ISSUES

The *Polly Peck/Pizza Pizza* principles raise numerous procedural, evidentiary and substantive issues which may have to be addressed by courts in the future. The following matters are raised for the consideration of judges and lawyers.

Situation A

What if:

i)　the plaintiff's meaning is accepted by the jury;

ii)　the defendant does not plead to that meaning or plead that the plaintiff's meaning is true. Rather, the defendant pleads her own meaning and pleads that her meaning is true.

iii)　the jury also accepts the defendant's meaning and accepts that the defendant's meaning is true.

What happens?

- Does the jury's verdict that the defendant's meaning is true constitute a complete defence?
- Does it constitute mitigation of damages?
- If such a verdict would mitigate damages, what direction does the court give in charging the jury on this subject?
- Can the jury simply ignore the different meanings and give a general verdict for either the plaintiff or the defendant pursuant to section 14 of the *Libel and Slander Act*, R.S.O. 1990, c. L.12, and comparable provisions in other provinces? If it is able to render a general verdict, what impact does this have on the utility of *Polly Peck/Pizza Pizza* pleadings?

Situation B

What if the defendant:

i)　pleads to the plaintiff's meaning and attempts to justify that meaning; and

ii)　pleads in the alternative her own meaning; and

iii)　fails in her attempt to justify the plaintiff's meaning; but

iv)　succeeds in her attempt to justify her own meaning.

What happens?

- Would this result require a dismissal of the action?
- Will the adverse result on the plaintiff's meaning potentially aggravate damages, despite the positive result on the defendant's meaning?
- Will this result mitigate damages overall?

CHAPTER TWENTY-FIVE:
Pre-trial Disposition of Claims and Defences

The court rules in each province and territory authorize a judge to dispose of claims and defences before trial on a variety of grounds.

This chapter focuses on the defamation jurisprudence relating to pre-trial motions:

i)   to strike pleadings,
ii) for summary judgment, and
iii) for a summary trial verdict.

The rules of court governing these particular motions differ from jurisdiction to jurisdiction. For example, not all provinces have a "summary trial" rule. The jurisprudence reflects the differences in the rules as well as nuances in the common law relating to procedure. Accordingly, litigants must be cautious when considering case law from other jurisdictions and give very close consideration to the specific provisions of the rules in force where the defamation litigation is brought.

The rules relating to summary judgment and summary trial are particularly complex. It is beyond the scope of this chapter to examine each aspect of those rules in detail.

A. STRIKING PLEADINGS

Defamation claims and defences may be impeached pursuant to court rules in each jurisdiction which authorize a judge to strike out the whole or part of a pleading on the ground that:

(a)   it discloses no reasonable claim or defence,
(b)   it is scandalous, frivolous, or vexatious,
(c)   it may prejudice, embarrass or delay the fair trial of the action, or

(d)   it is otherwise an abuse of process of the court.

Alberta, *Judicature Act*, R.S.A. 1980, c. J-1, Alberta *Rules of Court*, Alta. Reg. 390/68, r. 129(1).

British Columbia, *Court Rules Act*, R.S.B.C. 1996, c. 80; *Supreme Court Rules*, B.C. Reg. 221/90, r. 19(24).

Manitoba, *Court of Queen's Bench Act*, S.M. 1988-89, c. 4, *Court of Queen's Bench Rules*, Man. Reg. 553/88, r. 25.11.

New Brunswick, *Judicature Act*, R.S.N.B. 1973, c. J-2, *Rules of Court*, N.B. Reg. 82/73, r. 27.09.

Newfoundland, *Judicature Act*, R.S.N. 1990, c. J-4, *Rules of the Supreme Court, 1986*, S.N. 1986, c. 42, Sched. D, r. 14.24(1).

Northwest Territories, *Judicature Act*, R.S.N.W.T. 1988, c. J-1, (Alberta *Rules of Court* apply).

Nova Scotia, *Judicature Act*, R.S.N.S. 1989, c. 240, *Civil Procedure Rules*, RR. r. 14.25.

Ontario, *Courts of Justice Act*, R.S.O. 1990, c. C-43; *Rules of Civil Procedure*, R.R.O. 1990, Reg. 194, r. 21.

Prince Edward Island, *Supreme Court Act*, R.S.P.E.I. 1988, c. S-10, *Rules of Civil Procedure*, r. 25.11.

Saskatchewan, *Queen's Bench Act*, R.S.S. 1978, c. Q-1, *Queen's Bench Rules*, r. 173.

Yukon, *Judicature Act*, R.S.Y. 1986, c. 96 (British Columbia *Supreme Court Rules* apply).

Federal Court Rules (1998), r. 419.

See Chapter 22, "Pleadings," for a discussion of the substantive law concerning deficiencies in defamation pleadings. Many of the decisions cited in that chapter involve applications to strike claims or defences.

1) Discloses No Reasonable Claim or Defence

The test to be applied in determining whether to strike out a pleading is whether it is "plain and obvious" that the statement of claim or statement of defence, as the case may be, discloses no reasonable claim or defence.

Hunt v. Carey Canada Inc., [1990] 2 S.C.R. 959, per Wilson J. at 980, citing *Dumont v. Canada (Attorney General)*, [1990] 1 S.C.R. 279 at 280 and *Attorney General of Canada v. Inuit Tapirisat of Canada*, [1980] 2 S.C.R. 735 at 740

The application of this stringent test to defamation pleadings is evidenced by a large body of case law, including:

Mantini v. Smith Lyons LLP, [2003] O.J. No. 1830, per Catzman J.A. for the court at para. 5 (C.A.), leave to appeal to S.C.C. denied, [2003] S.C.C.A. No. 344.

M.J.M. v. D.J.M. (2000), 187 D.L.R. (4th) 473, per Jackson J.A. at 476–77 (Sask. C.A.).

Future Inns Canada Inc. v. Nova Scotia (Labour Relations Board) (1999), 178 D.L.R. (4th) 202, per Pugsley J.A. at para. 28 (N.S.C.A.).

Fuss v. Fidelity Electronics of Canada Ltd., [1998] O.J. No. 2339, at para. 5 (C.A.).

Ridge Pine Park Inc. v. Schwisberg (1998), 65 O.T.C. 73, per Glass J. at para. 4 (Gen. Div.).

Misir v. Toronto Star Newspapers Ltd. (1997), 105 O.A.C. 270, per Laskin J.A. at para. 23 (C.A.).

Voutsinos v. New Brunswick (Research and Productivity Council) (1993), 136 N.B.R. (2d) 364, per Dickson J. at 374 (Q.B. (T.D.)).

Gustadt v. Reinninger (1993), 27 O.R. (3d) 152, per McCombs J. at 1576 (Gen Div).

The facts alleged in the pleading under attack are presumed to be true for purposes of a motion to strike.

Hunt v. Carey Canada Inc., [1990] 2 S.C.R. 959, per Wilson J. at 980, para. 33.

Bird v. Public Guardian and Trustee, [2002] O.J. No. 408, per G.P. Smith J. at para. 16 (S.C.J.).

Serdar v. Metroland Printing, Publishing and Distributing Ltd., [2001] O.J. No. 1596, per Goodman J. at para. 6 (S.C.J.).

Aiken v. Ontario (Premier) (1999), 177 D.L.R. (4th) 489, per J. Macdonald J. at 494 (Ont. S.C.J.).

Dowson v. The Queen (Canada) (1981), 124 D.L.R. (3d) 260, per Le Dain J. at 261, para. 2 (F.C.A.), leave to appeal to S.C.C. denied (1981), 124 D.L.R. (3d) 260n (S.C.C.).

Amendt v. *Canada Life Assurance Company*, [1999] S.J. No. 157, per Golden-
berg J. at para. 12 (Q.B.), citing *Saskatchewan Provincial Court Judges Assn.
(Saskatchewan)* v. *Saskatchewan (Minister of Justice)*, [1996] 2 W.W.R. 129 at
131 (Sask. C.A.).

Raho v. *Craig Broadcasting Systems Inc.*, (1999), 141 Man. R. (2d) 288, per
Master Sharp at para. 11 (Q.B.), citing *Reid* v. *Marr's Leisure Holdings Inc.*,
[1994] 7 W.W.R. 542, at 544 (Man. C.A.).

The rationale for the "plain and obvious" test is explained in many cases,
including *Hunt* v. *Carey Canada Inc.*, where Wilson J. stated at page 980,
paragraph 33:

> If there is a chance that the plaintiff might succeed, then the plaintiff should
> not be "driven from the judgment seat." Neither the length and complexity of
> the issues, the novelty of the cause of action, nor the potential for the defen-
> dant to present a strong defence should prevent the plaintiff from proceeding
> with his or her case. Only if the action is certain to fail because it contains a
> radical defect … should the relevant portions of a plaintiff's statement of
> claim be struck out …

The rules of court may provide that evidence is not admissible if the
ground for striking a pleading is that it does not disclose a reasonable claim
or defence. See for example:

British Columbia r. 19(27):

> No evidence is admissible on an application under subrule (24)(a).

Alberta r. 129(2).

Ontario r. 21.01(2)(b).

Alternatively, the rules may provide that evidence is not admissible without leave of the court or consent of the parties. See for example:

Nova Scotia r. 14.25(2).

Newfoundland and Labrador r. 14.24(2).

In Ontario, there is an exception to the general prohibition against
receiving evidence. A court may receive and examine documents which are
incorporated by reference and which form an integral part of the pleading.

Bird v. *Public Guardian and Trustee*, [2002] O.J. No. 408, per G.P. Smith J. at
paras. 20–31 (S.C.J.), citing *Montreal Trust Company of Canada* v. *Toronto-
Dominion Bank* (1992), 40 C.P.C. (3d) 389 (Ont. Gen. Div.); *Web Offset Publications Limited* v. *Vickery* (1998), 40 O.R. (3d) 526 (Gen. Div.).

The exception does not apply if the party is pleading evidence as opposed to a material fact.

Bird v. *Public Guardian and Trustee*, [2002] O.J. No. 408, per G.P. Smith J. at paras. 27–31 (S.C.J.), citing *Scott* v. *Ontario*, [2001] O.J. No. 3956 (S.C.J.).

2) Scandalous, Frivolous, or Vexatious/May Prejudice, Embarrass, or Delay Fair Trial /Is Otherwise an Abuse of Court Process

A pleading that demonstrates a complete absence of material facts will be declared frivolous or vexatious.

Senechal v. *Muskoka (District Municipality)*, [2003] O.J. No. 885, per Cameron J. at para. 52 (S.C.J.).

Pleadings that are irrelevant, argumentative, or inserted for colour, or that constitute bare allegations, should be struck out as scandalous.

Senechal v. *Muskoka (District Municipality)*, *ibid.*, at para. 52.

A pleading that contains only argument and includes unfounded and inflammatory attacks on the integrity of a party and speculative, unsupported allegations of defamation, should be struck out as scandalous and vexatious.

Senechal v. *Muskoka (District Municipality)*, above, at para. 52, citing *George* v. *Harris*, [2000] O.J. No. 1762, at para. 20 (S.C.J.).

DeHaas v. *Mooney*, [2003] O.J. No. 549, per Sachs J. at para. 10 (S.C.J.) ["smear campaign" struck].

Vexatious proceedings also include an action brought to determine an issue which has already been determined by a court of competent jurisdiction, or an action whose grounds and issues have been raised in previous proceedings and are rolled forward into subsequent actions and repeated and supplemented.

Crosby v. *Fisher*, 2003 NSSC 57, per LeBlanc J. at para. 39.

It has been held that a vexatious proceeding is one that is brought for an improper purpose, including the harassment or oppression of the other party.

Technovision Systems Inc. v. *Urquhart*, 2003 BCSC 427, per Barrow J. at para. 20, citing *Re Lang Michener and Fabian* (1987), 59 O.R. (2d) 253 (H.C.J.), adopted in *Ebrahim* v. *Ebrahim*, [2002] B.C.J. No. 638 (S.C.).

The intention to silence a defendant through a libel suit is not, by itself, an improper purpose.

> *Metropolitan Separate School Board* v. *Taylor* (1994), 21 C.C.L.T. (2d) 316, per Spence J. at 318 (Ont. Gen. Div.).

> *Home Equity Development* v. *Crow*, 2002 BCSC 1688, per Quijano J. at paras. 21–29.

Where it is alleged that a pleading should be struck on these grounds, the application to strike may be supported by affidavit evidence in most jurisdictions.

> *Dowson* v. *The Queen (Canada)* (1981), 124 D.L.R. (3d) 260, per Le Dain J. at para. 5 (F.C.A.), leave to appeal to S.C.C. denied (1981), 124 D.L.R. (3d) 260n (S.C.C.).

> Also see for example: Rule 19 (27) of the British Columbia *Supreme Court Rules*.

It has been held that no pleading can be said to be "embarrassing" if it alleges only facts that may be proved.

> The opposite party may be perplexed, astonished, startled, confused, troubled, annoyed, taken aback, and worried by such a pleading but the pleading should not be struck.

> *Bird* v. *Public Guardian and Trustee*, [2002] O.J. No. 408, per G.P. Smith J. at para. 57 (S.C.J.), citing *Duryea* v. *Koffman* (1910), 21 O.L.R. 161 (Div. Ct.).

3) Absolute Privilege

Defence applications to strike a statement of claim may succeed where it is clear from the facts alleged in the statement of claim that the impugned publication is absolutely privileged. See Chapter 18, "Absolute Privilege."

Statements of claim have been struck on this basis in many cases, including:

> *Schwartz* v. *Smith* (1964), 45 D.L.R. (2d) 316, per Verchere J. at 320 (B.C.S.C.).

> *Geyer* v. *Merritt* (1979), 16 B.C.L.R. 27, per Legg J. at 32 (S.C.), aff'd (1980), 26 B.C.L.R. 374 per Hinkson J.A. at 375 (C.A.).

> *Dowson* v. *The Queen (Canada)* (1981), 124 D.L.R. (3d) 260, per Le Dain J.A. at 273 (F.C.A.), leave to appeal to S.C.C. denied (1981), 124 D.L.R. (3d) 260n (S.C.C.).

> *Alkasabi* v. *Ontario* (1994), O.J. No. 1503, per Chapnik J. at paras. 16–17 (Gen. Div.).

> *Simons* v. *Carr & Co.*, [1996] 10 W.W.R. 64, per Nash J. at 72 (Alta. Q.B.).

Kyser v. *Bank of Montreal* (1998), 72 O.T.C. 180, per Somers J. at para. 8 (Gen. Div.), aff'd (1999), 123 O.A.C. 119 at paras. 9–10 (C.A.).

Web Offset Publications Ltd. v. *Vickery* (1999), 43 O.R. (3d) 802 at 803g (C.A.), leave to appeal to S.C.C. refused, [1999] S.C.C.A. No. 460.

Penedo v. *Fane*, [2000] O.J. No. 3950, per MacPherson J.A. at para. 3 (C.A.).

Lowenberg v. *Oderbien* (2000), 146 Man. R. (2d) 120 (Q.B.).

Construction Distribution and Supply Co. v. *Pearson*, [2001] O.J. No. 1848, per Somers J. at para. 16 (S.C.J.).

Keung v. *Sheehan* (2001), 193 N.S.R. (2d) 237, per Robertson J. at para. 17 (S.C.).

Hawkes v. *Mitchell*, 2002 PESCTD 73, appeal quashed 2003 PESCAD 1, per Mitchell C.J.P.E.I. at para. 4.

Kyles v. *Toronto-Dominion Bank*, [2003] O.J. No. 1282, per Sanderson J. at para. 1 (S.C.).

DeHaas v. *Mooney*, [2003] O.J. No. 549, per Sachs J. at para. 12 (S.C.J.).

Big Pond Communications 2000 Inc v. *Kennedy*, [2004] O.J. No. 820, per Pierce J. at para. 20 (S.C.J.).

The assertion of an absolute privilege defence may not lead to an order striking a claim, however, if the defendant cannot show that there is an existing bar in the form of a decided case directly on point from the same jurisdiction demonstrating that the same type of claim has been squarely dealt with and rejected by the court on the ground of privilege.

Fabian & Kaye v. *Iseman* (1997), 50 O.T.C. 232, per Day J at para. 8 (Gen. Div.), citing *Dalex Co.* v. *Schwartz Levitsky Feldman* (1994), 19 O.R. (3d) 463 at 466 (Gen. Div.).

4) Qualified Privilege

It has been held that a statement of claim generally should not be struck out if the defence is qualified privilege, because this defence requires a trial to examine all of the facts allegedly giving rise to the occasion of privilege, and/or the facts alleged to constitute express malice which would defeat the privilege.

George Cluthe Manufacturing Company Limited v. *ZTW Properties* (1995), 23 O.R. (3d) 370 (Gen. Div.).

Lennon v. *Ontario (Premier)* (1999), 45 O.R. (3d) 84, per J. MacDonald J. at para. 27 (S.C.J.):

This is an interlocutory motion respecting the sufficiency of a pleading. The question of whether the plaintiffs' plea of malice or the defendants' denial of malice will prevail cannot and should not be determined at this juncture. Consequently, it cannot be said now whether the plea of qualified privilege will be defeated by a finding of malice, or will be available to the defendants. This conclusion is sufficient to rule that determination of any issue of law which relates to the defence of qualified privilege will not dispose of all or part of the action, or substantially shorten the trial or result in a substantial savings of costs. Since these components of Rule 21.01(1)(a) have not been met, this aspect of the motion is dismissed.

Dashtgard v. Blair (1990), 4 C.C.L.T. (2d) 284, per McDonald J. at 293, paras. 18–19 (Alta. Q.B.):

What is, nevertheless, apparent is that in the defamation action the defence of qualified privilege cannot arise, like an absolute privilege, on the face of the situation. Two questions of fact, or at best of mixed law and fact, are involved. The first is whether the defendant solicitors owed a duty to protect the interest of their client by writing the letter. The second, even if it is proved that the solicitors had an interest in making the communication to the third parties, is whether those third parties had an interest in receiving it. In deciding the second question it will be important to decide whether each of those third parties in fact had an interest in receiving the communication, or whether any of the third parties did not in fact have such an interest. If any of the third parties did not in fact have such an interest, the solicitors may be held liable however much they may have believed the third party to have such an interest and however honestly or reasonably the solicitors entertained that belief.

These are issues that cannot be decided on a motion such as this. The Statement of Claim should not be struck out on the ground that on the face of the pleadings there is a qualified privilege. These issues should be decided at trial. They should not be decided at the hearing of a preliminary issue.

But see *DeHaas v. Mooney*, [2003] O.J. No. 549, per Sachs J. (S.C.J.) [statement of claim struck in part because no allegation of malice].

5) "Of and Concerning" the Plaintiff

Defence motions to strike a statement of claim may be granted where the court is satisfied that the defamatory expression is not "of and concerning" the plaintiff. See Chapter 13, "Identification of the Plaintiff."

Bai v. Sing Tao Daily Ltd., [2003] O.J. No. 1917, per McMurtry C.J.O., at paras. 15–16 (C.A.), leave to appeal to S.C.C. denied, [2003] S.C.C.A. No. 354:

¶15 I agree with the respondent that where a matter is allegedly libelous of a substantially large and indeterminate group of persons, it does not give rise to a cause of action for any specific member of that group or class unless it can be shown that the libel complained of points to a particular member or particular members of the group.

¶16 I am also of the opinion that a reasonable reader of the respondent's Article would likely interpret the reference to "Falun Gong" as referring to Falun Gong practitioners living in China.

Aiken v. Ontario (Premier) (1999), 177 D.L.R. (4th) 489, per J. Macdonald J. at 501, para. 21 (Ont. S.C.J.).

Elliott v. Canadian Broadcasting Corporation (1993), 16 O.R. (3d) 677, per Montgomery J. at 688 (Gen. Div.), aff'd (1995), 125 D.L.R. (4th) 534, per Grange J.A. at 541 (C.A.), leave to appeal to S.C.C. refused, [2001] S.C.C.A. No. 393.

Jordon v. Talbot, [1998] O.J. No. 1876, per Jennings J. at para. 2 (Gen. Div.).

Gauthier v. Toronto Star Daily Newspapers Ltd., [2003] O.J. No. 2622, per Cullity J. at paras. 23–25 (S.C.J.).

6) Not Capable of Being Defamatory

Where the words complained of in the statement of claim are clearly not capable in law of being defamatory, the action may be struck out.

Roth v. Aubichon (1998), 171 Sask. R. 271 (Q.B.) per Noble J. at paras. 6–7.

Mantini v. Smith Lyons, [2003] O.J. No. 1830, per Catzman J.A. for the court at paras. 12–18 (C.A.), leave to appeal to S.C.C denied, [2003] S.C.C.A. No. 344.

Moon v. Sher, [2003] O.J. No. 2464, per Hoilett J. at para. 20 (S.C.J.).

7) Failure to Allege Publication

A statement of claim may be struck out where it does not allege publication by the defendant.

Kidder v. Healy, 2002 SKQB 6, per Allbright J. at paras. 23–36.

8) Failure to Serve Libel Notice

See Chapter 6, "Notice of Intended Action and Limitation Defences."

A failure to deliver the notice required by section 5(1) of Ontario's *Libel and Slander Act* was held to be a basis for dismissing an action pursuant to Rules 19.01 and 19.02.

Sieger v. Boctor, [2002] O.J. No. 1371, per P. Thomson J. (S.C.J.).

Although a plaintiff fails to give the notice required by a defamation statute, if no trial efficiency is achieved by striking out paragraphs of the statement of claim relating to defamation in the media, the court may decline to strike the defective pleading.

St. Elizabeth Home Society v. Hamilton (City) (2002), 162 O.A.C. 284 at paras. 14–16 (S.C.J.)

Delay in bringing the application to strike on this ground may also be fatal to the application and result in the issue being deferred to trial.

Hill v. Hamilton-Wentworth Regional Police Services Board, [2003] O.J. No. 1208, per Himel J. at paras. 45–49 (S.C.J.).

9) Pleading Other Publications

A plea in a statement of claim which refers to other publications may be struck out as embarrassing if it is plain and obvious that the repetition of the libel is not the natural and probable consequence of the original publication. A jury should not take into account, in assessing damages against the original publisher, any damage done to the plaintiff by republications for which the original publisher is not responsible.

Basse v. Toronto Star Newspaper Ltd. (1983), 4 D.L.R. (4th) 381, per Montgomery J. at 383 (Ont. H.C.J.).

It has been held, however, that whether republication is a natural and probable result of the original publication is a difficult question of law which it is inappropriate to decide on an interlocutory motion to strike.

Reichmann v. Toronto Life Publishing Co. (1988), 27 C.P.C. (2d) 37, per Anderson J. at 41 (Ont. H.C.J.).

10) Amendments to Correct Deficiencies

Even in circumstances where the statement of claim is grossly deficient, the court may permit the plaintiff to amend, rather than simply dismiss the action on a motion to strike.

MacRae v. Santa, [2002] O.J. No. 3000, per Pierce J. at para. 17 (S.C.J.).

Swyers v. Peninsulas Health Corp., [2001] N.J. No. 278 (Nfld. S.C. (T.D.)).

Alternatively, the court may order a party to deliver particulars to remedy a deficiency in the pleadings. Frequently, a party applying to strike will move in the alternative for particulars of the opposing party's pleading.

Keating v. Southam Inc. (c.o.b. Halifax Daily News Publishing) (1999), 179 N.S.R. (2d) 208, per Kennedy C.J.S.C. at para. 17 (S.C.).

Citizens for Foreign Aid Reform Inc. v. Canadian Jewish Congress, 2000 BCSC 737, per McKinnon J. at para. 31.

Dhami v. Canadian Broadcasting Corporation, 2001 BCSC 1811, per Slade J.

B. SUMMARY JUDGMENT

1) General Rules

The court rules in most provinces provide for summary judgment proceedings to dispose of all or some of the issues in an action prior to trial.

Alberta, *Judicature Act*, R.S.A. 1980, c. J-1, Alberta *Rules of Court*, Alta. Reg. 390/68, r. 159.

British Columbia, *Court Rules Act*, R.S.B.C. 1996, c. 80; *Supreme Court Rules*, B.C. Reg. 221/90, r. 18.

Manitoba, *Court of Queen's Bench Act*, S.M. 1988-89, c. 4, *Court of Queen's Bench Rules*, Man. Reg. 553/88, r. 20.01.

New Brunswick, *Judicature Act*, R.S.N.B. 1973, c. J-2, *Rules of Court*, N.B. Reg. 82/73, r. 22.

Northwest Territories, *Judicature Act*, R.S.N.W.T. 1988, c. J-1, (Alberta *Rules of Court* apply).

Nova Scotia, *Judicature Act*, R.S.N.S. 1989, c. 240, *Civil Procedure Rules*, RR. Rule 13.01.

Ontario, *Courts of Justice Act*, R.S.O. 1990, c. C-43; *Rules of Civil Procedure*, R.R.O. 1990, Reg. 194, r. 20.

Prince Edward Island, *Supreme Court Act*, R.S.P.E.I. 1988, c.S-10, *Rules of Civil Procedure*, r. 20.

Saskatchewan, *Queen's Bench Act*, R.S.S. 1978, c. Q-1, *Queen's Bench Rules*, r. 485.

Yukon, *Judicature Act*, R.S.Y. 1986, c. 96 (British Columbia *Supreme Court Rules* apply).

Federal Court Rules (1998), rr. 213–18.

In Newfoundland, the summary judgment rule expressly excludes actions for libel.

Newfoundland, *Judicature Act*, R.S.N. 1990, c. J-4, *Rules of the Supreme Court, 1986*, S.N. 1986, c. 42, Sched. D, r. 17.01.

The summary judgment rules generally entitle a party to obtain judgment only where there is no genuine issue for trial.

Black v. Canadian Newspapers Co. (1991), 6 C.P.C. (3d) 324, per Chapnik J. at 326 (Ont. Gen. Div.).

Schreiber v. Lavoie, [2002] O.J. No. 2308 per Cameron J. at para. 6 (S.C.J.), citing *Aguonie v. Galion Solid Waste Material Inc.* (1998), 38 O.R. (3d) 161 (C.A.).

Canadian Community Reading Plan Inc. v. *Quality Service Programs Inc.* (2001), 141 O.A.C. 289, per MacPherson J.A. at para. 10 (C.A.):

> In my view, at a general level the motions judge had a proper understanding of her role on a Rule 10 motion. She said, correctly in my view:
>
> > My role as a motions judge is narrow: to assess the threshold issue of whether a genuine issue exists as to material facts requiring a trial.

Newton v. Merritt, [1996] N.B.J. No. 253, per Riordan J. (Q.B. (T.D.)).

Tsang v. Asia Dragon News Ltd., [1988] B.C.J. No. 1764, per Taylor J. (S.C.).

Lake v. Demb (1998), 70 O.T.C. 314, per Epstein J. at paras. 20–23 (Gen. Div.).

Bahaduria v. City-TV, a Division of Chum Television Group, [1998] O.J. No. 5118 (C.A.), leave to appeal to S.C.C. refused, [1999] S.C.C.A. No. 34.

Ayangma v. Canada (2000), 188 Nfld. & P.E.I.R. 65 (P.E.S.C. (T.D.)), rev'd (2001), 203 D.L.R. (4th) 717 (P.E.S.C. (A.D.)), leave to appeal to S.C.C. refused, [2001] S.C.C.A. No. 76 (P.E.I. *Civil Procedure* Rule 20).

The onus of establishing that there is no triable issue is on the moving party.

Levin v. Dubourg, [1998] O.J. No. 324, per Aitken J. at para. 18 (Gen. Div.) [plaintiff's motion for summary judgment on issue of liability with a reference to assess damages dismissed — factual issues raised by defences of fair comment, qualified privilege, and denial of causation of certain heads of damage].

Cannon v. Lange (1998), 163 D.L.R. (4th) 520 (N.B.C.A.) per Drapeau J.A. at 526:

It is up to the moving party to satisfy the court that an apparent factual controversy or credibility conflict is a sham. If material facts remain genuinely in dispute after the court has taken a hard look at the evidence and the pleadings, it is not appropriate to grant summary judgment. ... Like, where there is an unresolved genuine credibility conflict relating to a material question, it is not appropriate to grant summary judgment.

The requirement that the court be satisfied there is no genuine issue for trial is sometimes expressly stated in the relevant rule. For example, in Ontario, Rule 20.04(2) provides:

Where the court is satisfied that there is no genuine issue for trial with respect to a claim or defence, the court shall grant summary judgment accordingly.

Bhaduria v. Persaud (1998), 40 O.R. (3d) 140 at 141 (Gen. Div.).

See also Prince Edward Island r. 20.04(2):

The court shall grant summary judgment if
a) The court is satisfied there is no genuine issue for trial with respect to a claim or defence; or
b) The parties agree to have all or part of the claim determined by a summary judgment and the court is satisfied it is appropriate to grant summary judgment.

The test in Ontario is not whether the plaintiff cannot possibly succeed at trial but:

whether the court reaches the conclusion that the case is so doubtful that it does not deserve consideration by the trier of fact at a future trial.

Black v. Canadian Newspapers Co. (1991) 6 C.P.C. (3d) 324 (Gen. Div.) per Chapnik J. at 335, quoting with approval the judgment of Farley J. in *Avery v. Value Investment Corp.*, [1990] O.J. No. 843 (H.C.J.).

In New Brunswick, the rules of court provide that summary judgment may be granted only where

there is no defence or merit to a claim or part thereof, and ... the applicant is entitled to judgment.

It has been held that this is a very stringent test and sets the standard at a high level.

Cannon v. Lange (1998), 163 D.L.R. (4th) 520, per Drapeau J.A. at 525 (N.B.C.A.), quoting from *Ripulone v. Pontecorvo* (1989), 104 N.B.R. (2d) 56 at 63 (C.A.), where Stratton C.J.N.B. stated:

… Summary judgment should be granted only when there is no reason for doubt as to what the judgment of the court should be if the matter proceeds to trial. The moving party's case must be unanswerable.

It has been held that a New Brunswick court has:

an obligation to consider not only the pleadings, but also any admissible evidence, namely statements of fact within the personal knowledge of the deponents, presented by way of affidavits and of any cross-examination on those affidavits.

Cannon v. Lange (1998), 163 D.L.R. (4th) 520 (N.B.C.A.) per Drapeau J.A. at 525.

It has been held in New Brunswick that it is particularly important for a respondent to "put their best foot forward" on a summary judgment motion "since he or she has the most to lose." "In a vernacular expression, the respondent 'must lead trump or risk losing.'"

Cannon v. Lange, above, at 526, citing *1061590 Ontario Ltd. v. Ontario Jockey Club* (1995), 21 O.R. (3d) 547 at 557 (C.A.) ["… this power can only be exercised where the question of law is the only outstanding issue between the parties"].

In Alberta, the test has been stated various ways. In *Blackburn v. Bailey*, 2002 ABQB 78, Slatter J. referred to the jurisprudence in that province and stated the various formulations of the test as follows at paragraph 24:

(a) Is it plain and obvious that the action cannot succeed? *German v. Major* (1985), 39 Alta. L.R. (2d) 270 at 276, 20 D.L.R. (4th) 703, 62 A.R. 2 (C.A.);

(b) Does the material clearly demonstrate that the action is bound to fail or is it clear that the action has no prospect of success? *Zebroski v. Jehovah's Witnesses* (1988), 87 A.R. 229, 30 C.P.C. (2d) 197 (C.A.);

(c) Is it established that there is no merit to the claim, in the sense that it does not raise a genuine issue for trial? *Allied Signal Inc. v. Dome Petroleum Ltd.* (1991), 81 Alta. L.R. (2d) 307 at 319, rev'd other grounds (1992), 3 Alta. L.R. (3d) 155 (C.A.).

The test is a strict one, and if the affidavits raise any genuine issue for trial, then summary judgment cannot be granted. It is not appropriate to attempt to resolve conflicting allegations in the affidavits unless it is clear that the claim is truly hopeless.

It has been held in Alberta that the following factors are relevant to a determination of an application by a plaintiff for summary judgment pursuant to Rule 159:

a) Where a Respondent to a summary judgment application has made admissions which establish the applicant's cause of action or defence, the burden of proof shifts to the Respondent, who must then adduce some evidence, as opposed to mere allegations, to establish a triable issue;

b) It is not open to a Respondent on a summary judgment application to argue that a triable issue exists based on facts or evidence not currently available but which "may" emerge at discovery or trial;

c) Where an Applicant has shown there are no facts in issue for trial, it is incumbent upon the Respondent to adduce evidence that it has a reasonable chance of success at trial;

d) It is insufficient for a Respondent who resists summary judgment to present only bare allegations of fact; the Respondent must present evidence which lends some support to the claims it advances; and

e) A summary judgment application may be made at any time.

> *732311 Alberta Ltd. v. Paradise Bay Spa Tub Warehouse Inc.*, 2003 ABQB, 228 per Johnstone J. at para. 55.

The New Brunswick Court of Appeal has urged motion judges "not to be unduly timid where the circumstances demonstrate a clear lack of merit" of claims or defences.

> *Cannon v. Lange* (1998), 163 D.L.R. (4th) 520, per Drapeau J.A. at 523–24 (N.B.C.A.), citing *RCL Operators Ltd. v. National Bank of Canada* (1994), 144 N.B.R. (2d) 207 at 211, para. 6 (C.A.).

In Prince Edward Island, the law concerning summary judgment was enunciated in the following terms in *Dale v. The Guardian* (1999), 30 C.P.C. (4th) 148 by MacDonald C.J.T.D. at page 150 (P.E.I.S.C. (T.D.)):

> … In *Stewart v. Keith MacLeod & Fox Run Pet Supply Inc.*, [1997] 2 P.E.I.R. 239 (P.E.I.S.C.T.D.) at p. 241, I summarized the approach to be followed:
>
> (1) The objective to Rule 20 is to screen out claims that in the opinion of the court, based on the evidence presented to the court as required by the rule, ought not to proceed at trial because they cannot survive a good hard look.
>
> (2) Each case is to be decided on its own, based on the law and the facts available to the court through affidavit evidence or otherwise.

(3) The respondent must set out on the motion for summary judgment the specific facts and evidence on which it relies to show there is a genuine issue for trial.

(4) Apparent factual conflict in evidence does not end the inquiry and the court may draw inferences from the evidence.

(5) The court may look at the overall credibility of the plaintiff's action. Matters of credibility requiring resolution in the case of conflicting evidence ought to go to trial. However, the court in taking a hard look at the merits of the case may decide whether such conflict is more apparent than real.

(6) Finally, the responding party has a duty to enter specific facts to show there is a genuine issue for trial.

2) Nominal Damages

In Ontario, where the summary judgment application has been brought by the plaintiff, a defendant is not entitled to ask the court hearing that motion to grant judgment to the plaintiff for only nominal damages on the basis the defamatory meaning is not as serious as the plaintiff alleges.

Black v. *Canadian Newspapers Co.* (1991), 6 C.P.C. (3d) 324, per Chapnik J. at 336 (Ont. Gen. Div.):

> In my opinion, there is a genuine issue for trial. I have found that the words published in the article are capable of being viewed as defamatory. What better issue to be determined either by a jury or a judge as the trier of fact than whether the words used are indeed, within the context in which they were expressed, defamatory to the plaintiff; and if so, to assess damages.

3) Trial of a Question of Law

When a New Brunswick, Ontario, or Prince Edward Island court is satisfied that the only genuine issue is a question of law, it may determine the question and grant judgment accordingly.

Ontario r. 20.04(4).

New Brunswick r. 22.04(3).

Stevenson v. National Bank of Canada, [2000] 184 Nfld. & P.E.I.R. 95 at para. 1 (P.E.I. S.C. (A.D.)).

Ayangma v. NAV Canada (2000), 188 Nfld. & P.E.I.R. 65 (P.E.I.S.C. (T.D.)), rev'd (2001), 203 D.L.R. (4th) 717 (P.E.I.S.C. (A.D.)), leave to appeal to S.C.C. refused, [2001] S.C.C.A. No. 76.

4) Specifying Nondisputed Material Facts

In New Brunswick, the court may specify the material facts which are not in dispute and define the remaining issues if a trial is found to be necessary.

New Brunswick r. 22.05, discussed in *Cannon v. Lange* (1998), 163 D.L.R. (4th) 520 per Drapeau J.A. at 524 (N.B.C.A.).

5) Summary Judgment Granted

Summary judgment motions have succeeded in the following circumstances where it was held there was no genuine issue for trial in relation to a defamation claim or defence.

i)   The specific words complained of were not alleged to have been published to anyone other than the plaintiff and there was no allegation of specific words published by the defendant to third parties.

     Moss v. Forsyth, [1999] M.J. No. 89 per Master Lee at para. 9 (Q.B.).

ii)   The statement of claim alleging defamation did not set out the defamatory words used, nor the persons by whom and to whom the words were said, nor the occasion of the alleged publications, and the claims were also statute-barred based on the dates given at the examination for discovery.

     Zebroski v. Jehovah's Witnesses (1988), 87 A.R. 229 (C.A.), leave to appeal to S.C.C. refused (1989), 94 A.R. 320n (S.C.C.).

iii)   The statutory condition precedent of a notice of intention to bring an action was not satisfied.

     Pitre v. Jeffery (1994), 119 Nfld. & P.E.I.R. 335 (P.E.I.T.D.).

     Weiss v. Sawyer (2002), 217 D.L.R. (4th) 129, per Armstrong J.A. at 137 (Ont. C.A.).

iv)   The claim was statute-barred by virtue of the limitations period under section 6 of the *Libel and Slander Act*, R.S.O. 1990 c. L12. The court held that the limitation periods must be read as importing an objective component, in that the plaintiff could reasonably have had knowledge of the impugned statement.

     Bhaduria v. Persaud (1998), 40 O.R. (3d) 140 at 141 (Gen. Div.).

v)   The publication occurred on an occasion of qualified privilege.

     Simmonds v. Murphy (1996), 137 Nfld. & P.E.I.R. 332 (P.E.I.S.C. (T.D.)).

Hall v. Puchniak (1998), 42 C.P.C. (4th) 267, per Goodman J. at paras. 3–4 (Man. Q.B.).

Blackburn v. Bailey, 2002 ABQB 78, per Slatter J. at para. 89 [doctor had a duty to convey his true diagnosis to the plaintiff's family].

A.M.N. v. O'Halpin (1996), 16 O.T.C. 59 (Gen. Div.) per Thompson J. at paras. 20–23

Goldenburg v. Cohen, [1995] O.J. No. 2348 per Haines J. at para. 6 (Gen. Div.).

vi)   The publication was a privileged report of court proceedings pursuant to a defamation statute.

Dale v. The Guardian (1999), 30 C.P.C. (4th) 148, per MacDonald C.J.T.D. at 155 (P.E.I.S.C. (T.D.)).

vii) The words complained of did not bear any defamatory meaning.

Pollock v. Winnipeg Free Press, [1997] 2 W.W.R. 216, per Krindle J. at 221 (Man. Q.B.).

A.M.N. v. O'Halpin (1996), 16 O.T.C. 59, per Thompson J. at para. 14 (Gen. Div.).

viii) The statement of claim, in relation to its allegations of defamation, did not set out the defamatory statements.

Blackburn v. Bailey, 2002 ABQB 78, per Slatter J. at para. 33.

ix)   The words were not capable of bearing the defamatory meanings alleged by the plaintiff in the statement of claim.

Mantini v. Smith Lyons LLP, [2003] O.J. No. 1830, per Catzman J.A. at para. 12 (C.A.), leave to appeal to S.C.C. denied, [2003] S.C.C.A. No. 344.

x)   The libel was true.

Moharib v. Seven Oaks General Hospital (1999), 136 Man. R. (2d) 157, per Master Lee at para. 14 (Q.B.).

xi)   The publication was absolutely privileged.

Schut v. Magee, 2003 BCSC 36, per Kirkpatrick J., aff'd, 2003 BCCA 418, per Rowles J.A.for the court at paras. 14–20.

xii) The defendant denied making the impugned statement, he was not cross-examined on his affidavit to that extent, and his evidence to that extent was unchallenged.

Hoeppner v. *Linden* 2002, MBQB 270, per Master Sharp at paras. 20–21:

> ¶20 … the plaintiff relies on his own affidavit, which, in my view, is of no assistance to the plaintiff's case whatsoever. The plaintiff's affidavit is seriously deficient, as, although consisting more or less entirely of hearsay, it does not comply with Rules 39.01(4) or 20.02(3). …
>
> ¶21 As noted above, the court is entitled to draw an adverse inference from the failure of a party to provide evidence or persons having personal knowledge of contested facts, and in my view, this inference is particularly appropriate in a defamation action such as this.

James v. *Stonehocker*, [2002] O.J. No. 3204, per Nordheimer J. at para. 14 (S.C.J.).

xiii) None of the pleaded defences was established.

Ralston v. *Fomich*, [1991] 66 B.C.L.R. (2d) 166, per Spencer J. at 170 (S.C.).

6) Summary Judgment Denied

Applications for summary judgment have failed in the following circumstances:

i)   The court found that where, as a matter of law, the words are capable of being viewed as defamatory, the question of whether the words are in fact defamatory should be left to the trier of fact:

> In my opinion, there is a genuine issue for trial. I have found that the words published in the article are capable of being viewed as defamatory. What better issue to be determined either by a jury or a judge as the trier of fact than whether the words used are indeed within the context in which they were expressed, defamatory to the plaintiff and if so, to assess damages.

Black v. *Canadian Newspapers Co.* (1991), 6 C.P.C. (3d) 324, per Chapnik J. at 333, para. 26 (Ont. Gen. Div.).

ii)   When a defendant pleads qualified privilege, and the plaintiff pleads actual malice in reply, a motion for summary judgment may be denied as this will require a finding of fact based on the testimony of witnesses.

Roach v. *Long* (1998), 108 O.A.C. 241, at para. 3 (C.A.), followed in *McRae* v. *Santa*, [2004] O.J. No. 833, per G.P. Smith J. at paras. 27–29.

Lennon v. Ontario (Premier) (1999), 45 O.R. (3d) 84 (S.C.J.).

Nelles v. Canada (Royal Canadian Mounted Police), [1997] Y.J. No. 145 (S.C.) per Haines J.

iii) Defences of fair comment and justification were pleaded, requiring an evaluation of conflicting evidence and issues of credibility.

Lennon v. Ontario (Premier), above, per J. MacDonald J. at 96.

iv) Where the vicarious liability of corporate defendants for statements by their employees remained a live issue, the judge held:

> although one defendant made admissions extinguishing his plea of justification, it would be of little assistance to the plaintiff to grant summary judgment on this admission alone as it would result in fragmentation of the proceedings against the corporate defendants and make an assessment of damages virtually impossible.

732311 Alberta Ltd. v. Paradise Spa Tub Warehouse Inc., 2003 ABQB 228, per Johnstone J. at paras. 59–60.

v) The evidence did not establish a defence of qualified privilege or a defence of justification, and the plaintiff filed evidence to raise an issue as to whether the defendant had acted in good faith.

Okun v. Gawiuk, 2003 MBQB 21, per Master Lee at paras. 11–15.

vi) *Weber v. Ontario Hydro*, [1995] 2 S.C.R. 929, did not apply to deprive the court of jurisdiction [the dispute, in its essential character, arose from the interpretation, application, administration, or violation of a collective agreement].

Santamaria v. James, [2003] O.J. No. 472, per Snowie J. at paras. 13–14 (S.C.J.).

vii) The statutory requirement to serve notice of intention to sue for libel did not apply.

Fortomaris v. Mantini-Atkinson, [2002] O.J. No. 3203, per LaForme J. at paras. 15–23 (S.C.J.).

viii) There was conflicting evidence as to whether a university professor, speaking to her class made statements about the plaintiff student which were alleged to be defamatory.

Jackson v. University of Western Ontario, [2002] O.J. No. 1471, per Browne J. at paras. 12, 32 (S.C.J.).

ix) The facts raised a concern as to the fairness of the third party broad-caster's position that it was not bound by an agreement between the plaintiff and a co-defendant concerning an extension of the three-month limitation period prescribed by section 6 of the *Libel and Slander Act* of Ontario.

> *Schreiber v. Lavoie*, [2002] O.J. No. 2308, per Cameron J. at paras. 12–14 (S.C.J.)[refusing leave to appeal to the Divisional Court from an order of Lane J. dismissing motions for summary judgment].

x) Granting summary judgment against one individual on an untenable defence of justification with respect to one defamatory imputation would fragment the proceedings as against the corporate defendants, complicate the court's consideration of other allegations, and likely render an assessment of damages impossible.

> *732311 Alberta Ltd. v. Paradise Bay Spa Tub Warehouse Inc.*, [2003] A.J. No. 338, 2003 ABQB 228, per Johnstone J. at para. 60.

7) Avoidance of Jury Trial

It has been held that a summary trial may be granted despite the fact that a party's ordinary right to a jury trial is thereby displaced.

> *Weisenberger v. Johnson & Higgins* (1998), 131 Man. R. (2d) 274, per Kroft J.A. at 277 (C.A.).

8) Jurisdiction of a Master

In Manitoba, a Master has jurisdiction under the summary trial rule.

> *Hall v. Puchniak* (1997), 122 Man. R. (2d) 256 (Q.B.), affirmed (1998), 42 C.P.C. (4th) 267 (Man. C.A.), leave to appeal to S.C.C. refused, [1999] S.C.C.A. No. 7.
>
> *Hoeppner v. Linden*, [2002] M.J. No. 461 (Q.B.).

9) Setting Aside a Summary Judgment

In Manitoba, the standard for setting aside a summary judgment on the basis of fresh evidence is lower than the standard which applies after a full trial on the merits.

> *Weisenberger v. Johnson & Higgins Ltd,*. 2002 MBCA 33, per Monnin J.A. at para. 4, applying *Whitehall Development Corp. Ltd. v. Walker* (1977), 15 O.R. (2d) 130 (H.C.J.), aff'd (1977), 17 O.R. (2d) 241 (C.A.).

C. SUMMARY TRIAL

In Alberta, British Columbia, Manitoba, Ontario, Newfoundland, Saskatchewan, the Northwest Territories, and the Yukon Territory, a party is entitled to seek a "summary trial" pursuant to a distinct rule which permits the court to determine cases expeditiously even where there may be disputed issues of fact or law.

> *Inspiration Management Ltd. v. McDermid St. Lawrence Ltd.* (1989), 36 B.C.L.R. (2d) 202, per McEachern C.J.B.C. at 214 (C.A.):
>
> > Chambers judges should be careful but not timid in using R. 18A for the purpose for which it was intended.
>
> *U.B.'s Autobody Ltd. v. Reid's Welding (1981) Inc.*, 1999 ABQB 956.
>
> *Tsang v. Asia Dragon News Ltd.*, [1988] B.C.J. No. 1764 (S.C.) per Taylor J.
>
> *Christian Labour Assn. Of Canada v. U.F.C.W., Local 1518* (1993), B.C.J. No. 140 (S.C.) per Blair J.
>
> Alberta, *Judicature Act*, R.S.A. 1980, c. J-1, Alberta *Rules of Court*, Alta. Reg. 390/68, r. 158.1.
>
> British Columbia, *Court Rules Act*, R.S.B.C., 1996, c. 80; *Supreme Court Rules*, B.C. Reg. 221/90, r. 18A.
>
> Manitoba, *Court of Queen's Bench Act*, S.M. 1988–89, c. 4, *Court of Queen's Bench Rules*, r. 20.03(4).
>
> Newfoundland, *Judicature Act*, R.S.N. 1990, c. J-4, *Rules of the Supreme Court, 1986*, S.N. 1986, c. 42, Sched. D, r. 17A.01.
>
> Northwest Territories, *Judicature Act*, R.S.N.W.T. 1988, c. J-1 (Alberta *Rules of Court* apply).
>
> Ontario, *Rules of Court Procedure*, R.R.O. 1990, Reg. 194, amended by O.Reg. 284/01, Simplified Procedures, r. 76.12.
>
> Saskatchewan, *Queen's Bench Act*, R.S.S. 1978, c. Q-1, *Queen's Bench Rules*, r. 485.
>
> Yukon, *Judicature Act*, R.S.Y. 1986, c. 96 (British Columbia *Supreme Court Rules* apply).

Evidence on a summary trial may be adduced by affidavit, by admissions made on examination for discovery, admissions made in responses to written interrogatories, or by responses to a formal demand for admissions.

In British Columbia, the principles governing the application of Rule 18A were described by Joyce J. in *Hung* v. *Gardiner*, 2002 BCSC 781 as follows at paragraph 20:

> The plaintiff made a number of arguments in support of her position that the case is not appropriate for determination under Rule 18A. Before dealing with them, I refer to some of the principles laid down in the leading authority on the subject, *Inspiration Mgmt. Ltd.* v. *McDermid St. Lawrence Ltd.* (1989), 36 B.C.L.R. (2d) 202 (C.A.).

> (a) While every effort must be made to ensure a just result, the cost of litigation will not always permit the luxury of a full trial if a just result can be achieved by a less expensive and more expeditious procedure (p. 213);

> (b) A chambers judge cannot give judgment unless he can find the facts necessary to decide issues of fact or law (p. 214);

> (c) Even if a chambers judge can decide the necessary factual and legal issues he may nevertheless decline to give judgment if he thinks it would be unjust to do so (p. 214);

> (d) In deciding whether it would be unjust to give judgment the chambers judge is entitled to consider, inter alia, the amount involved, the complexity of the matter, its urgency, any prejudice likely to arise by reason of delay, the cost of taking the case forward to a conventional trial in relation to the amount involved, the course of the proceedings and any other matters which arise for consideration on this question (p. 214);

> (e) It is not necessary that both parties agree as to the appropriateness of a summary trial (p. 214);

> (f) If the chambers judge can find the facts, then he must give judgment as he would upon a trial unless for any proper judicial reason he has the opinion that it would be unjust to do so (p. 215);

> (g) A chambers judge is not necessarily obliged to remit a case to the trial list just because there are conflicting affidavits. While the chambers judge should not decide an issue solely on the basis of conflicting affidavits, there may be other admissible evidence that make it possible to find the facts necessary for judgment to be given. The chambers judge may also adjourn to permit cross-examination in order to resolve conflicts on the affidavit evidence (pp. 215–16).

A plaintiff's defamation claim has been dismissed in whole or in part on a summary trial:

i)   where only vague hearsay evidence was tendered by the plaintiff, and there was no evidence that any statements made by the defendant were untrue.

   Christensen v. *Kondratiuk*, [1999] A.J. No. 500, per Clarke J. at paras. 18–22 (Q.B.).

ii) on the basis that a newspaper article was fair comment, published without malice, on a subject of public interest.

   Thore v. *Mudry*, [1999] B.C.J. No. 1693, per McEwan J. at paras. 18–24 (S.C.).

iii) where there was no evidence of any defamatory remarks.

   Wilk v. *Kelowna and District Boys & Girls Club*, [1997] B.C.J. No. 220, per Lambert J.A. (in Chambers) at paras. 4, 12 (C.A.) [dismissing an application for leave to extend the time for perfecting an appeal].

iv) where there was uncontroverted evidence that the defendant did not make any defamatory statements.

   Macovei v. *Atmore*, 2001 BCSC 1017, per Slade J. at para. 33.

v)   where the impugned emails were ruled not to be defamatory.

   Burns v. *Pollock*, 2001 BCSC 986 per Ralph J. at para. 25.

vi) where the statements were absolutely privileged as having been made in the course of judicial proceedings, or alternatively, were published on an occasion of qualified privilege.

   Hung v. *Gardiner*, 2002 BCSC 1234, per Joyce J, aff'd 2003 BCCA 257, per Levine J.A. at paras. 57–58.

   Zanetti v. *Bonniehon Enterprises Ltd.*, 2002 BCSC 1203, per Edwards J. at paras. 28–30.

vii) where the defamatory report, prepared by an expert witness to assist a Crown prosecutor, was held to be protected by absolute privilege, or alternatively, by qualified privilege.

   Kravit v. *Dilli* (1998), 56 B.C.L.R. (3d) 150, per Baker J. (S.C.).

viii) where defences of justification or alternatively statutory privilege for a fair and accurate report of court proceedings in a public newspaper were established.

M.D. Mineralsearch Inc. v. East Kootenay Newspapers Ltd. (2002), 209 D.L.R. (4th) 375 (B.C.C.A.).

ix) where the court lacked jurisdiction on the principle in *Weber v. Ontario Hydro*, [1995] 2 S.C.R. 929, on the ground that the dispute, including a defamation claim, arose from and had to be dealt with under a collective agreement.

Haight-Smith v. Neden, 2002 BCCA 132, per Levine J.A. at paras. 44–45.

x) where the defamation claims were commenced after expiry of the limitation period prescribed by statute.

Safty v. Carey, [1996] B.C.J. No. 2652, per Braidwood J. at para. 30 (S.C.), aff'd (1998), 110 B.C.A.C. 242, per Hollinrake J.A. at para. 38 (C.A.).

Griffith v. Cox, [2003] B.C.J. No. 1586, 2003 BCSC 1039, per Crawford J. at para. 29.

Plaintiffs have recovered summary trial verdicts for defamation damages or defeated defences where:

i) the defendant was unable to substantiate the vast majority of allegations he made about the plaintiff, including allegations of fraud, theft, perjury, extortion, and forgery — defences of justification, fair comment, and qualified privilege were therefore rejected, the court making findings of express malice on the part of the defendant.

Fung v. Lu, [1997] B.C.J. No. 238, per Callaghan J. at para. 16 (S.C.).

ii) liability had been admitted, and an apology mitigated damages; the award was $6,000.

Kothlow v. Olsen, [1994] B.C.J. No. 1431, per Drost J. (S.C.).

iii) oral statements imputing unprofessional conduct were intended to dissuade prospective purchasers from dealing with the plaintiff real estate agent; the award was $10,000 general damages and $2,000 aggravated damages.

Tymofievich v. Miros, [1993] B.C.J. No. 1893, per Cooper J. at paras. 24–25 (S.C.), aff'd, [1994] B.C.J. No. 2606, per Cumming J.A. (C.A.).

iv) articles published by the defendant union alleged the plaintiff was not a union but an arm of the American-based Christian Reform Church; that the plaintiff lobbied the government to pass laws benefiting employers; and that the plaintiff held and promoted racist views: the award was $2,500.

Christian Labour Assn. Of Canada v. U.F.C.W., Local 1518 (1993), B.C.J. No. 140, per Blair J. at para. 30 (S.C.).

v)   defences of truth and fair comment failed.

U.B.'s Autobody Ltd. v. Reid's Welding (1981) Inc, 1999 ABQB 956.

vi)   a defence of justification of outrageous defamatory statements was not established by the evidence.

Ferguson v. Ferstay, 2000 BCCA 592, (2000), 81 B.C.L.R. (3d) 90 (S.C.).

See also *Webster v. Webster,* [1997] B.C.J. No. 1952 (C.A.), where Rowles J.A., hearing an application in Chambers for a stay of execution, noted at para. 2 that defamation damages of $25,000 had been awarded to the plaintiff following a summary trial.

Defence applications for judgment have been dismissed:

i)   where defamatory expression in a magazine was not justified and fair comment did not apply. [However, the court held there was sufficient evidence to proceed separately with an assessment of the plaintiff's damages.]

NR Developments Ltd. v. Thomas, 2002 BCSC 697, per Melnick J. at para. 80.

ii)   where circumstantial evidence of the defence of justification, albeit weak, required testing by cross-examination at trial.

Karabotsos v. Canwest Television Inc., [1998] B.C.J. No. 1753, per Grist J. at paras. 19–21 (S.C.).

iii)   where the defence of qualified privilege was not established on the evidence.

Campbell v. Finlayson, [1998] B.C.J. No 1922, per Harvey J. at paras. 14–15 (S.C.).

A plaintiff's application for judgment was dismissed where the court held it would be unjust to determine the issue of whether or not the words complained of were defamatory of the plaintiff at a summary trial, where there would in any event be a trial to assess damages.

I also believe that a trial judge in the case of defamation would be in a better position to assess damages under the various heads and to consider all of the defences that may be available if the trial was not bifurcated.

Remington v. Rahall, 2000 ABQB 196, per LoVecchio J. at paras. 27–28.

A plaintiff may apply for an assessment of damages on a summary trial basis following a summary trial ruling that the defendants made defamatory statements.

Lee v. Lee, 2000 BCSC 1770, per Pitfield J. awarding general damages of $100,000 and punitive damages of $50,000.

Alternatively, the plaintiff may apply for such an assessment on a summary trial basis after obtaining default judgment against the defendants.

Gracey v. Scott (Guardian ad litem of), 2002 BCSC 1209, per Gray J. awarding each of the two plaintiffs $75,000 damages.

Where express malice was pleaded in reply to a defence of qualified privilege, it was held that summary trial was not an appropriate vehicle for its resolution.

Bowering v. International Union of Operating Engineers, Local 882, 2002 BCSC 830, per Holmes J. at para. 6.

Campbell v. Finlayson, [1998] B.C.J. No 1922, per Harvey J. at paras. 14–15 (S.C.).

In a defamation case where the meaning of expression is at issue, in the context of a fair comment defence, the summary trial rule should not be used to accomplish a piecemeal determination of the defences. The parties should instead be afforded a full hearing on all issues at one time.

Scott v. Fulton, [2000] B.C.J. No. 367, per Braidwood J.A. at para. 20 (C.A.), quoting Lambert J. in *North Vancouver (District) v. Lunde* (1998), 162 D.L.R. (4th) 402 at 413–414 (B.C.C.A.):

> ¶33 With respect, it seems to me that if the answer to an issue sought to be tried under Rule 18A will only resolve the whole proceeding if one answer is given, but not if a different answer is given, then the applicant should be required to demonstrate and the judge should be expected to decide, that the administration of justice, as it affects not just the parties to the motion, but also the orderly use of court time, will be enhanced by dealing with the issue as a separate issue. It cannot be enough simply that the parties have agreed to a summary trial of one or more issues, but not all of the issues, raised in the proceeding, without any consideration for the effective use of court time, or the efficient resolution of the proceeding.

A summary trial was refused on the grounds that the availability of a jury trial holds an extra value in cases of defamation, and a jury was well-suited to determining defamatory meaning and damages.

> *McLean v. Southam Inc.*, 2002 BCCA 229, per Saunders J.A. (in Chambers) at paras. 10–11 [leave to appeal from decision of chambers judge refused]:
>
> > ¶11 ... On the suitability of the case for jury determination, the judge noted that Rule 39(27) supports the view that the availability of trial by jury holds an extra value in cases of defamation, that a jury was well suited to determining the use of the word pedophile in ordinary parlance and how it would be construed by the general reader, and whether the plaintiff suffered damage by reason of the libel, if libel is found ...

The British Columbia Court of Appeal is unlikely to interfere with the exercise of discretion by a trial judge to proceed, or not proceed, to dispose of the claims or defences under rule 18A.

> *McLean v. Southam Inc.*, 2002 BCCA 229, per Saunders J.A. (in Chambers) at para. 13 [leave to appeal from decision of chambers judge refused].

The fact that a summary trial under British Columbia Rule 18A will deprive a party of a jury trial need not be determinative. The court must also consider the rights of the opposing litigant to have the matter resolved as expeditiously and inexpensively as possible.

> *Hung v. Gardiner*, 2002 BCSC 781 per Joyce J. at para. 25, aff'd (2003), 13 B.C.L.R. (4th) 298, per Levine J.A. (Ryan and Hall JJ.A. concurring) at paras. 57–60 (C.A.).

It has been held that an order dismissing certain causes of action is a final order. Leave to appeal such dismissal orders is therefore not required.

> *Zanetti v. Bonniehon Enterprises Ltd.*, 2002 BCCA 555, per Ryan J.A. in Chambers.

On the other hand, an order declining an application by the defendant to have a defamation action against him dismissed is an interlocutory decision and leave to appeal is required.

> *Cassidy v. Abbotsford (City) Police Department*, 2000 BCCA 286, per Saunders J.A. (in Chambers) at para. 2.

CHAPTER TWENTY-SIX:

Discovery of Documents

A. RULES OF COURT

In defamation actions, discovery of documents presents certain distinctive features. To some extent, these mirror the special limitations on rights of discovery which apply in defamation cases to oral examinations under oath of the parties before trial. See Chapter 27, "Examination for Discovery."

Although rights of documentary discovery are governed by provincial rules of court, the wording of which may vary somewhat depending on the jurisdiction, courts across the country have taken a fairly consistent approach. The current statutory instruments are as follows:

Alberta, *Judicature Act*, R.S.A. 2000, c. J-2, Alberta *Rules of Court*, Alta. Reg. 390/68, rr. 186–99.

British Columbia, *Court Rules Act*, R.S.B.C., 1996, c. 80; *Supreme Court Rules*, B.C. Reg. 221/90, r. 26.

Manitoba, *Court of Queen's Bench Act*, S.M. 1988-89, c.4, *Court of Queen's Bench Rules*, Man. Reg. 553/88, r. 30.

New Brunswick, *Judicature Act*, R.S.N.B. 1973, c. J-2, *Rules of Court*, N.B. Reg. 82/73, r. 31.

Newfoundland and Labrador, *Judicature Act*, R.S.N. 1990, c. J-4, *Rules of the Supreme Court*, 1986, S.N. 1986, c. 42, Sched. D, r. 32.

Northwest Territories, *Judicature Act*, R.S.N.W.T. 1988, c. J-1 (Alberta *Rules of Court* apply).

Nova Scotia, *Judicature Act*, R.S.N.S. 1989, c. 240, *Civil Procedure Rules*, RR. r. 20.

Ontario, *Courts of Justice Act*, R.S.O. 1990, c. C-43; *Rules of Civil Procedure*, R.R.O. 1990, Reg. 194, r. 30.

Prince Edward Island, *Supreme Court Act*, R.S.P.E.I. 1988, c. S-10, *Rules of Civil Procedure*, r. 30.

Saskatchewan, *Queen's Bench Act*, R.S.S. 1978, c. Q-1, *Queen's Bench Rules*, rr. 212–21.

Yukon Territory, *Judicature Act*, R.S.Y. 1986, c. 96 (British Columbia *Supreme Court Rules* apply).

Federal Court Rules (1998), r. 240.

This chapter addresses discovery issues that are discussed in the defamation jurisprudence. It is not intended as a checklist of categories of documents to be sought in the discovery process.

1) Ontario: Simplified Procedure

In Ontario, if the matter is proceeding under the Simplified Procedure (Rule 76), discovery of documents is not permitted whether or not the action involves a defamation claim.

> *Mills* v. *MacFarlane* (2000), 49 C.P.C. (4th) 184, per Lax J. at 192 (Ont. S.C.J.).

B. PRODUCTION OF THE DEFAMATORY EXPRESSION

The plaintiff may be entitled to production by a news media defendant of any notes, tapes, and documents used in preparing an article or broadcast.

> *Del Zotto* v. *Canadian Newspapers Co. Ltd.* (1988), 65 O.R. (2d) 594 at 598 (S.C. (Mast.)).

The conduct, intention, and knowledge of the defendants, both before and after publication, and the care taken by the defendants prior to publication, may be relevant to issues of express malice and therefore material to the assessment of damages.

> *Getty* v. *Calgary Herald* (1991) 47 C.P.C. (2d) 42, per McFadyen J. at 44 (Alta. Q.B.).

A defendant may be ordered to produce a manuscript of a book concerning the plaintiff which has yet to be published, if the book is an extension or elaboration of an article which gave rise to the action before the court.

Reichmann v. Toronto Life Publishing Co. (1988), 28 C.P.C. (2d) 11 (Ont. H.C.J.), leave to appeal denied (1988), 29 C.P.C. (2d) 66, per Chilcott J. at 68–69 (Ont. H.C.J.):

> [The defendants] argue that the manuscript is not relevant to constitutional or actual malice because the state of mind relevant to such malice must be determined at the time of the writing and publishing of the complained of material .... I cannot agree that the manuscript and its earlier versions are not relevant. ... On the issue of actual malice ... the manuscript may indicate the state of mind of the defendant, Dewar, and her knowledge of, and views as to the conduct and character of the plaintiffs both before and after the publication of the article [which is the subject of this litigation] Southey J. in *Boushy v. Sarnia Gazette Publishing Co. Ltd. et al* (1980), 30 O.R. (2d) 667, by quoting from *Odgers on Libel and Slander* (1929), 6th ed., at 286, dealt with the issue of actual malice, as follows:
>
> > ...The plaintiff has to show what was in the defendant's mind at the time of publication, and of that no doubt the defendant's acts and words on that occasion are the best evidence. But if the plaintiff can prove that at any other time, before or after, the defendants had any ill-feeling against him that is some evidence that the ill-feeling existed also at the date of publication.

It appears that a court will not order the defendant to prepare a typewritten transcript of handwritten notes even if they are illegible to anyone except their author.

Reichmann v. Toronto Life Publishing Co. (1988), 28 C.P.C. (2d) 11, per Anderson J. at 13–14 (Ont. H.C.J.).

A computer disk containing a manuscript falls within the common law meaning of "document" and must be produced. The Ontario High Court has rejected a defence submission that a plaintiff is only entitled to production of the information recorded or stored by means of the disk. The defendants had supplied the plaintiffs with a copy of the manuscript of the book at issue, but unsuccessfully resisted production of the computer disk itself, on the grounds that information would be made available to the plaintiffs by possession of the disk which was not obtainable from a review of the hard copy transcript.

Reichmann v. Toronto Life Publishing Co. (1988), 30 C.P.C. (2d) 280, per Anderson J. at 282–83 (Ont. H.C.J.).

The disk which is in issue contains or carries the manuscript of the book which is referred to in para. 5. The plaintiffs have been provided with a copy of the manuscript produced from the disk but the defendants have resisted production of the disk itself. I do not at all understand the technology involved but it appears to be the position of the plaintiffs that information would be made available to them by the possession of the disk which is not obtainable from the product of the disk with which they have been provided ...

It seems fair to conclude that the definition contained in the rule was drafted to meet the problems created by the use of computers to store information. It may be that there is a lacuna. That would appear to be so if information can be derived from possession of the disk which is not provided by the product [*sic*] of the disk. On that assumption I think that the disk is comprehended in the wider definition of document referred to in the earlier authorities, however remote computer technology was from the contemplation of those who created those authorities. It would be inconsistent with the current trend in production and discovery to hold otherwise.

The disk should be produced.

If they are relevant, a court may order production of documents constituting the work product of the defendant in producing and televising a news program, including video tapes not broadcast (known as "outtakes") and any notes used to prepare the script and report. Where it is alleged that statements made in an interview have been taken out of context in the broadcast, production of the entire interview may be relevant to a defence of truth.

> *Bank of British Columbia* v. *Canadian Broadcasting Corporation* (1993), 23 C.P.C. (3d) 219 (B.C.S.C.), aff'd (1995), 40 C.P.C. (3d) 355 (B.C.C.A.), leave to appeal to S.C.C. refused, [1995] S.C.C.A. No. 429.

Submissions by a media defendant that reporters' work demands a special privilege so as to encourage courageous reporting on matters of public interest have been rejected by the British Columbia Supreme Court.

> *Bank of British Columbia* v. *Canadian Broadcasting Corporation* (1993), 23 C.P.C. (3d) 219, per Maczko J. at paras. 17, 51–52 (B.C.S.C.):
>
> ¶17 The defendants argue that reporters will hesitate to pursue valuable stories and will be inhibited from reporting the news as their honest editorial judgment would otherwise dictate. There is no historical evidence to support such a proposition and there is no persuasive evi-

dence to indicate that anything has changed in our society that would require the implementation of this new protection.

¶51 The plaintiff needs to know the state of mind or state of knowledge of the reporter to determine whether the opinion was honestly held or whether there was malice. In this case that can only be done by looking at the work product of the defendants.

¶52 In particular the plaintiff says that Mr. Palmer was interviewed for approximately thirty minutes and that only a few minutes of that interview was shown. Mr. Palmer says in an affidavit that the part of the interview that was shown was taken out of context and did not fairly represent what he said. If that is so, it may well reflect on what the reporter knew when the decision was made to broadcast. Her notes may reveal similar information.

An alternative submission by a media defendant that discovery of its journalists' work product should be deferred pending a trial of the issue of a broadcast's meaning and of the issue of truth was also rejected where the documents were relevant to the issue of truth. If the Chambers judge had not ordered disclosure in such circumstances, it would have been an abuse of discretion. The guarantee of freedom of expression contained in section 2(b) of the *Canadian Charter of Rights and Freedoms* has not altered a media defendant's obligation to give discovery.

Bank of British Columbia v. *Canadian Broadcasting Corporation* (1995), 40 C.P.C. (3d) 353 (B.C.C.A.), leave to appeal to S.C.C. refused, [1995] S.C.C.A. No. 429. Per Prowse J.:

¶65 A party cannot simply say that a document is not relevant and thereby preclude its discovery, particularly where, as here, the CBC has acknowledged the potential relevance of these documents by including them on its list of documents. In this case, all of the documents sought by the Bank are related to the broadcast in question. I am satisfied that all of them either are, or may be, related to the issue of truth and discoverable based on the passages from [*Boxer and Boxer Holdings Ltd.* v *Reesor, Gillespie et al.* (1983), 43 B.C.L.R. 352 (B.C.S.C. in Chambers) at 538].

There are other instances of news media defendants being asked to produce a journalist's work product or notes developed in connection with the preparation of a story or broadcast. Example:

Baxter v. *Canadian Broadcasting Corporation and Malling* (1978), 24 N.B.R. (2d) 308 (S.C. (Q.B. Div.)) [media defendant ordered to produce a pocket diary].

C. IDENTIFICATION OF SOURCES

The "newspaper rule" protects a news media defendant in certain provinces and in certain circumstances from being required to disclose the identity of a confidential source before trial. See Chapter 27, "Examination for Discovery," section C(13).

Notwithstanding the newspaper rule, a newspaper was ordered to produce documents of public record which did not contain any writing or marking that would show the source or identity of the person from whom they came, as well as three newspaper articles showing the name of the newspaper which published them but not the name of the reporter who wrote them.

> *Hatfield* v. *Globe and Mail Division of Canadian Newspapers* (1983), 41 O.R. (2d) 218 (S.C.).

However, even where the newspaper rule applies, the court may require the defendant to produce versions of relevant documents that have been edited to delete any reference to a source.

> *McInnis* v. *University Students Council, University of Western Ontario* (1984), 14 D.L.R. (4th) 126 (Ont. H.C.J.), varying (1984), 12 D.L.R. (4th) 457 (Ont. H.C.J.), leave to appeal denied, 14 D.L.R. (4th) at 127 (Ont. Div. Ct.). Per J. Holland J.:
>
> > The order below is varied by adding at the end of para. 1 thereof the following words: "after first deleting therefrom or blacking out any reference to the identification of the source of the information contained therein.
>
> *Reichmann* v. *Toronto Life Publishing Co.* (1988), 28 C.P.C. (2d) 11, per Anderson J. at 18 (Ont. H.C.J.):
>
> > If there is a serious concern on the part of the defendants that the production of any particular document or documents would have the effect of disclosing its source, by reason of the form or content of the document, the defendants may move for relief from the scope of this order to the limited extent of such document or documents. Any motion for relief would call for disclosure to the court of the document in question.

A "reference to a source" means material which is directly referable, such as a name, an address, or the name of a relative, employer, or association. In certain circumstances material may indicate the source, as for example by a quotation that only the confidential source could have made. In those circumstances, it appears that the defendant may apply to court for relief from the obligation to disclose such material.

> *Reichmann* v. *Toronto Life Publishing Co.* (1988), 30 C.P.C. (2d) 280, per Anderson J. at 284 (Ont. H.C.J.).

1) Confidential Sources

The court may, in an appropriate case, exercise its discretion and order disclosure of documents with information severed which would otherwise disclose confidential sources. It may be the case that the applicant for disclosure is agreeable to such severance.

> *Bank of British Columbia* v. *Canadian Broadcasting Corporation* (1995), 40 C.P.C. (3d) 353, per Prowse J. at para. 73 (B.C.C.A.), leave to appeal to S.C.C. refused, [1995] S.C.C.A. No. 429.

2) Young Offenders

When ordering documentary discovery, the court may protect the identities of alleged young offenders to preserve the anonymity they enjoy under federal criminal legislation.

> *Campbell* v. *Jones* (1998), 168 N.S.R. (2d) 1 at para. 45 (S.C.).

D. DISCOVERY WHERE JUSTIFICATION PLEADED

See Chapter 27, "Examination for Discovery," C.5.

As in the case of oral examination for discovery, where the defamatory expression is general the defendant can only obtain discovery of documents relating to matters referred to in her particulars of justification. The defendant may not use discovery to find a defence of which it was not aware at the time of pleading.

> *Yorkshire Provident Life Assurance Company* v. *Gilbert & Rivington*, [1895] 2 Q.B.C. 148 (C.A.).

> *Care Canada* v. *Canadian Broadcasting Corporation* (1998), 65 O.T.C. 237, per Benotto J. at para. 3 (Ont. Gen. Div.).

> *Fletcher-Gordon* v. *Southam Inc.* (1997), 28 B.C.L.R. (3d) 87 (S.C.), aff'd (1997) 29 B.C.L.R. (3d) 197 (C.A.).

> *I.B.E.W., Local No. 213* v. *Pacific Newspaper Group Ltd. Inc.*, [2004] B.C.J. No. 439, 2004 BCSC 310 per Boyd J. at paras. 8–11.

There may be differences of opinion about whether a defamatory accusation is "general," requiring the defendant to provide particulars before being entitled to discovery of documents, or "specific," in which case further particulars are not required.

For example, in one case, the plaintiff alleged that the words complained of meant, *inter alia*, that money raised by Care Canada from the public was not used in the Somalia relief effort but rather was misappropriated for unrelated purposes. The Master held that a defendant broadcaster was not permitted access to the plaintiff's entire donation history for Somalia and what happened to funds donated to the plaintiff where the statement of defence simply alleged that "the money never got there." The Master stated: "This is no different from the oi. quoted example of the statement. He is a thief. In the latter you need specifics ..."

> *Care Canada v. Canadian Broadcasting Corporation* (1998), 61 O.T.C. 216, per
> Master Polika at para. 10 (Gen. Div.).

In the same case, when the Master's decision was reviewed, Benotto J. concluded that the defamatory statements were not general in nature but specific. "The main, although not only criticism of CARE Canada is that, out of the $400,000 said to be raised for Somali relief, not a penny got to Somalia." Accordingly, the defence was entitled to certain documentary discovery from the plaintiff charity.

> *Care Canada v. Canadian Broadcasting Corporation* (1998), 65 O.T.C. 237 per
> Benotto J. (Gen. Div.), leave to appeal dismissed, [1998] O.J. No. 4271 (C.A.).

Where the defendant was sued over allegations that the plaintiff's motorized valves were defective, the court allowed the defendant access to the plaintiff's repair records, albeit for a shorter time frame than sought by the defendant. The court held that the defendant had given sufficient particulars.

> *Marrello Valve Ltd. v. Orbit Valve Canada Ltd.*, [1988] O.J. No. 2710 per
> Sutherland J. (S.C. (Mast.)).

E. DISCOVERY AND DAMAGES

Incorporated companies whose business character or reputation is injuriously affected are entitled without proof of special damages to a compensatory award representing the sum necessary to publicly vindicate their business reputation.

The authorities are not entirely consistent about the obligation of a plaintiff corporation to give disclosure to the defence of financial statements where special damages are not sought.

One Ontario court held that although a limited company did not seek special damages, or claim a general loss of business or diminution of profits, it should nevertheless produce financial documents for certain years.

Reichmann v. Toronto Life Publishing Company, [1990] 66 D.L.R. (4th) 162, per Anderson J. at 174 (Ont. H.C.J.):

> In a case where general damages are at large, where the only damage which Olympia & York can recover is damage to its pocket, I should find it difficult to conclude that its financial statements are not relevant …. I recognize that a fact, though relevant, may be of such scant probative value that it should be excluded, but that is a test more suited for the discretion of a trial judge than for application by a judge dealing with the interlocutory questions of production and discovery.

Another Ontario Court expressed concern about the implications of such disclosure, even where the plaintiff corporation did claim special damages. It suggested the court may have a residual discretion to withhold disclosure in certain circumstances.

Marrello Valve Ltd. v. Orbit Valve Canada Ltd., [1988] O.J. No. 2710 per Sutherland J. (S.C. (Mast.)):

> ¶21 The question that caused me the most difficulty is … the request for records as to servicing and repairs to the plaintiff's valves over the past six or seven years. There would appear to be something wrong with a rule that would enable a competitor to defame the plaintiff's products, perhaps maliciously, and then plead the defence of truth and then, through the discovery process, obtain detailed information as to every customer of the plaintiff who has required special servicing or repairs over a long period. There could be cases in which the prejudice that would result from an obligation to provide such information would clearly outweigh the legitimate value of the information gained. Here the plaintiff has a dominant position in its industry, and the nature of the oil and gas business — and the related valve business — is such that the defendant would already have a very good idea of who the customers of the plaintiff are. Answering the question would not lead to a knowledge of who the plaintiff's customers are but only to a record of which ones have required servicing and repairs and how often. That is relevant to the defence plea of the truth of the statement complained of.

¶22 If the plaintiff were merely asserting the defamatory nature of the statement and were claiming only general damages on the basis that the statement per se was defamatory, there would be no justification for such an invasion of the secrets of the plaintiff's business. But here the plaintiff is claiming special damages in this action and I really do not know what all in the other proceedings.

In the particular circumstances before the court in *Marrello Valve*, Sutherland J. concluded that there was sufficient pleading by the defendant to justify access to service and repair records for one year, but not the six to seven years ordered by the Master. Accordingly, the ambit of permissible discovery was considerably less than had been sought by the defence.

To some degree, these concerns by the disclosing party may be addressed by the "Implied Undertaking Rule" (see section F below).

It does appear clear, however, that where the court requires a plaintiff corporation to disclose financial documents to a defendant, it may impose safeguards to protect the privacy of the plaintiff before trial. In *Reichmann v. Toronto Life Publishing Co.* (1990), 44 C.P.C. (2d) 206 (Ont. H.C.J.), Anderson J. imposed the following terms:

1) Access shall be permitted to [certain specified lawyers] of the solicitors to the defendants.

2) Access shall be permitted to a chartered accountant, selected by the defendants, and one associate of such accountant. Prior to such access, each shall sign an agreement not to disclose any information obtained as a result of such access, the agreement to be in form satisfactory to the solicitors for the plaintiffs, or approved by the court.

3) The solicitors for the defendants shall within seven days of the date of this order advise the solicitors for the plaintiffs, in writing, of the name of the accountant, and the associate, if any, and the form of agreement proposed. The solicitors for the plaintiffs shall within seven days of receipt of such notice advise the solicitors for the defendants whether they object to the intervention of the proposed accountant or to the proposed agreement. If the parties are unable to agree on an accountant or an agreement, selection shall be made and the agreement settled by the court.

4) Access shall be provided at the offices [of the lawyers for the plaintiffs] where suitable and private facilities shall be provided for the purpose.

5) No copies of the statements shall be taken. Any notes made of their contents shall be kept in a secure and private place and shall be destroyed upon final disposition of this action.

6) If the solicitors for the defendants deem it necessary that any defendant have access, and are unable to arrange such access with the solicitors for the plaintiffs, they may seek leave of the court. Save pursuant to such an agreement or approval of the court, the defendants shall have no access and no information concerning the statements shall be communicated to them by any person who has access.

7) No part of the statements or any information derived from them shall be led in the court in any form without prior leave of the court.

See also *Agentis Information Services Inc.* v. *West Coast Title Search Ltd.*, [1997] B.C.J. No. 2780 (S.C.).

An individual plaintiff in a defamation action, who had pleaded a claim for loss of income, was excused by a court from complying with an undertaking he had given on his examination for discovery to produce financial information about his claim where, after discovery, he amended his statement of claim to abandon the income loss claim.

Fortunato v. *The Toronto Sun* (2001), 55 O.R. (3d) 371 (S.C.J.).

F. IMPLIED UNDERTAKING RULE

In Canada, some degree of privacy protection is provided by an implied undertaking to the court to preserve the confidentiality of documents obtained from an opposing party in civil litigation.

Pursuant to this undertaking, a party obtaining discovery of documents is *prima facie* under a general obligation in most cases to keep such documents confidential, whether or not they actually appear to disclose private or confidential information. In appropriate cases, the party which obtained disclosure may obtain either the owner's permission or leave of the court to use the documents in other proceedings or for purposes other than the litigation in which they were produced.

Hunt v. *Atlas Turner Inc.*, [1995] 5 W.W.R. 518 (B.C.C.A.).

Kyuquot Logging Ltd. v. *British Columbia Forest Products Ltd.*, [1986] 5 W.W.R. 481 (B.C.C.A.).

Where a party considers that its information is particularly sensitive, it may seek the added protection of an explicit court order limiting disclosure and requiring persons having access to the documents to execute special covenants of confidentiality. In *Agentis Information Services Inc.* v. *West Coast Title Search Ltd.*, [1997] B.C.J. No. 2780, for example, Kirkpatrick J. made such a special order in a defamation lawsuit to protect sensitive business information, administration, pricing, and advertising strategies of the plaintiff, and required all persons other than counsel to sign a confidentiality agreement.

In Ontario, in a defamation lawsuit, the Ontario Court of Appeal held that there was an "implied undertaking" to the court by a party not to use documents obtained in the discovery of documents process for a purpose other than the proceeding in which they were disclosed. Relief from such an undertaking may be granted by the court, however, in the interests of justice.

Goodman v. Rossi (1995), 125 D.L.R. (4th) 613 (Ont. C.A.), per Morden A.C.J.O.

Lacure Corporate and Leisure Inc. v. Coast Paper Ltd., [1997] O.J. No. 2963 (Gen Div.).

In Ontario, there is now a "deemed undertaking" rule contained in Rule 30.1.01 of the *Rules of Civil Procedure*. Relief from such an undertaking may be granted by the court in the interests of justice, but the circumstances warranting relief, and the basis of exercising the discretion, have not been precisely defined.

Unless the court has given relief from the implied undertaking, a document disclosed on discovery may not become the subject of an action for defamation. If such an action is brought, it may be stayed by the court.

Sezerman v. Youle (1996), 135 D.L.R. (4th) 266 (N.S.C.A.).

Goodman v. Rossi (1995), 125 D.L.R. (4th) 613, per Morden A.C.J.O. at 631 (Ont. C.A.):

> It is a necessary and appropriate part of the implied undertaking rule that the court have the power to grant relief from its application. ...
>
> The criteria for granting relief from the implied undertaking rule are an important part of the rule itself. In *Crest Homes plc v. Marks*, [1987] 2 All E.R. 1074, Lord Oliver said at p. 1085, on behalf of the House of Lords, that the authorities on the question illustrate no general principle beyond this, that the court will not release or modify the implied undertaking given on discovery save in special circumstances and where the release or modification will not occasion injustice to the person giving discovery.

Carbone v. De La Rocha, [1993] 13 O.R. (3d) 355 (Gen. Div.), per Whalen J.

Patterson v. Johnston, [1998] 7 W.W.R. 78 (Man. Q.B.).

In Alberta, it was held that the court has discretion to relieve a party to civil litigation from the implied undertaking. Upon application, the court will determine whether such relief is in the public interest. In one case, the court granted a plaintiff retroactive leave to sue for defamation where the defendant's identity had been disclosed to the plaintiff in the discovery process in an earlier action she had brought for wrongful dismissal.

Ochitwa v. *Bombino* (1997), 153 D.L.R. (4th) 555 (Alta. Q.B.).

A Nova Scotia court stayed a defamation action brought by the plaintiff based on documents that had been produced in a previous action involving the same defendant, where the plaintiff had not asked the court to be relieved of the implied undertaking before filing the defamation lawsuit.

Sezerman v. *Youle* (1996), 135 D.L.R. (4th) 266 at 283 (N.S.C.A.).

In *Discovery Enterprises Inc.* v *Ebco Industries Ltd.*, [1997] B.C.J. No. 2614 (S.C.), the British Columbia Supreme Court held that the implied undertaking on a party not to publicly disclose documents obtained by discovery procedures in civil lawsuits continues even if the documents are filed and read in open court. The Court specifically noted that a non-party spectator in the courtroom may record details of the materials read out in open court and use them for collateral purposes. The court warned, however, that a party should not be able to avoid the effect of its implied undertaking by simply filing an affidavit (attaching the documents) in some interlocutory matter in court as a device to make such information publicly available (coupled in some cases with an anonymous tip to the news media or other potentially interested nonparties).

See also:

Duke v. *Vervaeck*, 2000 SKQB 414.

Drabinsky v. *KPMG*, [1999] O.J. No. 3630 (S.C.J.).

Duffy v. *Great Central Publishing Co. Ltd.* [1995] O.J. No. 4057 (Gen. Div.).

LiszKay v. *Brouwer & Company General Insurance Adjusters Ltd.* (1978), 99 D.L.R. (3d) 266 (B.C.C.A.), aff'g (1978), 86 D.L.R. (3d) 546 (B.C.S.C.).

See also *Cheyne* v. *Alberta*, 2003 ABQB 244 [not a defamation case], concerning circumstances justifying a court order that a party disclose discovery materials generated in different litigation.

See *Taylor* v. *Director of Services Fraud Office*, [1998] H.L.H. No. 38 for a recent discussion of the implied undertaking rule in England.

G. COMPULSORY PRE-PLEADING DISCLOSURE

In *Hogan v. Great Central Publishing Limited* (1994), 16 O.R. (3d) 808 (Gen. Div.), the plaintiff was granted an order before the statement of defence was filed, directing the defendant company to disclose the names and addresses of persons who wrote certain articles published in *FRANK* magazine as well as the names and addresses of anyone involved in the editing, publishing, distributing, and printing of the articles. The masthead did not disclose that information.

MacDonald J. held, at page 808, that concerns regarding an unjustified "fishing expedition" or "premature discovery" did not arise because the plaintiff was "simply seeking the identification of the individuals involved in order to properly and expeditiously pursue her action." She noted that the plaintiff had expended a great deal of effort trying to obtain the information.

In making the order, the court prescribed certain guidelines for making such an order in future cases, stating :

1. the order should not be granted if the motion was brought in order to conduct a "fishing expedition or premature discovery"; in this case, given the unique facts and the unique nature of *FRANK*, I do not consider that this is a fishing expedition or premature discovery;

2. the identities sought must be specified as well as possible and they must be relevant; on this point, the plaintiff has been specific and the information is clearly relevant;

3. the plaintiff must have tried many different routes before seeking the court's assistance in obtaining the identifies; this, too, is clearly established by the plaintiff;

4. it should be a situation where the person or corporation's name is very difficult to obtain because of their own desire to remain anonymous; *FRANK* magazine appears to wish to remain anonymous;

5. the names will inevitably be revealed and the order to disclose will likely eliminate another motion on the same point;

6. there must be no prejudice to the responding party.

In British Columbia, it has been held that a judge has the jurisdiction to order that a defendant broadcaster turn documents in its possession over to the plaintiff prior to the close of pleadings. However, this is a very unusual order and consequently should only be granted in the most unusual circumstances. Such an order is to be distinguished from an order which simply protects the evidence by requiring a defendant to preserve pending trial documents such as videotapes, films, or other recordings or notes relating to broadcast or non-broadcast interviews.

> *Bank of British Columbia* v. *Canadian Broadcasting Corporation* (1986), 2 B.C.L.R. (2d) 80 (C.A.), referring to the order of the Chambers judge which the broadcaster appealed with respect to sub-para. 3, per Seaton J.A. at 85.

H. DISCOVERY OF NON-PARTY DOCUMENTS

Court rules in most provinces allow for the inspection and copying of documents of non-parties although they vary to some degree in their scope and timing. Such provisions typically apply in circumstances analogous to those where a non-party may be examined under oath before trial. See Chapter 27, "Examination for Discovery," section C.11.

For example, in Ontario the *Rules of Court* permit a party to obtain inspection of non-party documents which would be producible in evidence at trial.

> 30.10(1) The court may, on motion by a party, order production for inspection of a document that is in the possession, control or power of a person not a party and is not privileged where the court is satisfied that,
>
> a)   the document is relevant to a material issue in the action; and
> b)   it would be unfair to require the moving party to proceed to trial without having discovery of the document.

> *Ontario (Attorney General)* v. *Ballard Estate* (1995), 129 D.L.R. (4th) 52 (Ont. C.A.).

> *Care Canada* v. *Canadian Publishing Broadcasting Corp.* (1999), 175 D.L.R. (4th) 743 (Ont. Div. Ct.) [an order for production under r. 30.10(1) can only be made where it would be unfair to require the moving party to proceed to trial without having discovery of the document].

Ontario Rule 30.10(1) has been relied upon by a plaintiff to obtain an order compelling a television station to provide a certified copy of a videotape recording of a television broadcast which contained allegedly defamatory expression by the non-media individual defendant.

> *Hockenhull* v. *Laskin* (1987), 59 O.R. (2d) 157, per Fitzgerald D.C.J.(L.J.S.C.) at 159 (Dist. Ct.):

> > The tape shows not only the place of delivery but also the manner of presentation of the alleged defamation which may well assist the trial judge in appreciating the evidence as a whole.

The Court further held in *Hockenhull* that where, as in this case, the broadcaster had freely and voluntarily permitted the moving party to view and audit the tape, the copy should be produced at the expense of the moving party, such expense to include a reasonable component of overhead cost.

In British Columbia, the rules similarly authorize the court to order production by nonparties if the party applicant satisfies the court that the application is not in the nature of a fishing application and the documents sought may relate to a matter in issue.

Rule 26(11) provides:

> (11) Where a document is in the possession or control of a person who is not a party, the court, on notice to the person and all other parties, may order production and inspection of the document or preparation of a certified copy that may be used instead of the original. An order under Rule 41(16) in respect of an order under this subrule may be made if that order is endorsed with an acknowledgment by the person in possession or control of the document that the person has no objection to the terms of the proposed order.

The British Columbia rule and comparable provisions in other British Columbia statutes have been relied upon by parties to defamation litigation.

> *Ho v. Ming Pao Newspapers (Western Canada) Ltd.*, [1997] B.C.J. No. 2539 (S.C.).

> *Sommers v. Sturdy* (1957), 10 D.L.R. (2d) 269 (B.C.C.A.), aff'g (1956), 6 D.L.R. (2d) 642 (B.C.S.C.), leave to appeal to S.C.C. refused, [1957] S.C.R. x. [application of s. 36(5) of the *Evidence Act*, R.S.B.C. 1948, c. 113, authorizing a court to make an order permitting a party to inspect and take copies of entries in the books or records of a bank].

In Nova Scotia, Civil Procedure Rule 20 permits a party to obtain production of documents in the possession or control of a non-party if they are relevant or reasonably calculated to lead to the discovery of relevant and admissible evidence. Where a police officer brought libel proceedings over accusations about her investigative techniques, the court directed the Chief of Police to provide the defendants with certain standards, material, policies and procedures relating to the conduct of investigations, which were available to the plaintiff before she conducted the investigation which became the subject of the allegedly libelous expression.

> *Campbell v. Jones* (1998), 168 N.S.R. (2d) 1, per Macadam J. at paras. 34, 36, 41 (S.C.).

In Manitoba a court ordered the federal Department of Health and Welfare to produce documentation relating to certain flights where the plaintiff complained of a news broadcast stating the plaintiff was misleading its customers as to the qualifications of its pilots. The plaintiff had no documentation relating to those flights, and accordingly the defendants were held to be entitled to obtain them from the government.

Ministic Air Ltd. v. *Canadian Broadcasting Corp.*, [1995] 8 W.W.R. 31, per Oliphant A.C.J.Q.B. (Man. Q.B.).

The scope of documentary discovery is often contentious when a defendant pleads the libel is true. Historically, where the alleged libel is general in nature and no particulars are given, the courts have not permitted a defendant to use the discovery process to find a defence of which it was not aware at the time of pleading.

Earle v. *Coltsfoot Publishing Co.* (1998), 171 N.S.R. (2d) 110 (S.C.).

See Chapter 27, "Examination for Discovery," section C.5, for a discussion of this principle, which applies equally to documentary discovery.

I. SOLICITOR-CLIENT PRIVILEGE

Defamation counsel and their clients will be particularly sensitive to issues of privilege in view of the principle that the entire conduct of the defendants before, during, and after publication may be scrutinized by the court in the assessment of malice and damages.

It may be particularly important, therefore, that a defendant exercise great care to ensure that an otherwise lawful claim of solicitor/client privilege is not vitiated.

In certain circumstances, a legitimate claim of privilege may also forestall libel litigation by a person defamed in the privileged communication.

Solicitor/client privilege is a fundamental right which only yields in certain clearly defined circumstances.

R. v. *McClure*, [2001] 1 S.C.R. 445 at 455.

Lavallee, Rackel & Heintz v. *Canada (Attorney General)*, *White Ottenheimer & Baker* v. *Canada (Attorney General)*, *R.* v. *Fink* (2002), 216 D.L.R. (4th) 257, 2002 SCC 61, at para. 61.

At common law, the privilege attaches to confidential communications between solicitor and client for the purpose of obtaining and giving legal advice ("legal advice privilege") and to documents gathered and prepared by a solicitor for the dominant purpose of litigation ("litigation privilege").

Descôteaux v. Mierzwinski (1982), 141 D.L.R. (3d) 590 (S.C.C.).

Hodgkinson v. Simms (1988), 33 B.C.L.R. (2d) 129 at 136 (C.A.).

Because legal advice privilege protects the relationship of confidence between solicitor and client, the key question to consider is whether the communication is made for the purpose of seeking or providing legal advice, opinion, or analysis. Because litigation privilege facilitates the adversarial process of litigation, the key question to consider is whether the communication was created for the dominant purpose of litigation, actual or contemplated.

Legal advice privilege arises only where a solicitor is acting as a lawyer; that is, when giving legal advice to the client. Where a lawyer acts only as an investigator, no privilege protects communications to or from her. If, however, she is conducting an investigation for the purposes of giving legal advice to her client, legal advice privilege will attach to the communications between the lawyer and her client.

College of Physicians of British Columbia v. British Columbia (Information and Privacy Commissioner), 2002 BCCA 665 at para. 32.

Litigation privilege, on the other hand, arises where litigation is in reasonable prospect or in progress. It applies to communications between the lawyer and the client, and also between the lawyer and third parties, where the dominant purpose for the communication is litigation.

College of Physicians of British Columbia v. British Columbia (Information and Privacy Commissioner), 2002 BCCA 665 at para. 33.

In *General Accident Assurance Co. v. Chrusz* (1999), 180 D.L.R. (4th) 241 (Ont. C.A.), the owner of fire-damaged premises sued an ex-employee for libel over allegations that the owner had inflated his claim. An insurance adjuster retained by the insurance company to investigate the claim provided reports to the lawyer retained by the insurer to advise on the claim. The owner sought production of the adjuster's reports. Evaluating the insurer's claim for privilege, Doherty J.A. stated that the existence of the privilege depended on whether the adjuster had the authority to obtain legal services or to act on legal advice on behalf of the client. Where the third party, such as an adjuster, is empowered by the client to perform a function on the client's behalf which is integral to the solicitor/client function, privilege may be found to apply. In the circumstances before the court, reports prior to the allegation of inflation were not privileged; reports after were [at paragraph 125].

Another material form of privilege is the "common interest" or "joint defence" privilege. This permits litigation privilege to be preserved even where the information is shared with a third party. However, this privilege protects only against disclosure to the adversary and only until the termination of the litigation. The third party must have a common interest in the litigation or its prospect.

General Accident Assurance Co. v. Chrusz (1999), 180 D.L.R. (4th) 241 (Ont. C.A.).

CHAPTER TWENTY-SEVEN:
Examination for Discovery

A. DISTINCTIVE FEATURES

Discoveries in defamation actions, while fundamentally the same as discoveries in other actions, have certain distinctive features.

The extent of the discovery conducted by the defendant is governed very strictly by the pleadings. If the defendant has not pleaded a defence of justification, he or she is not entitled to question the plaintiff about the truth of the defamatory expression at issue. Moreover, if the defamatory accusation is general as opposed to specific, the defendant's questions relating to a plea of justification will be strictly confined to the facts alleged in the defendant's particulars of justification.

An unduly prolonged and hostile cross-examination of the plaintiff on discovery, which increases the mental distress and humiliation of the plaintiff, may support a finding of malice which aggravates the plaintiff's damages or supports an award of punitive damages.

The plaintiff is allowed considerable latitude in exploring the state of mind of the defendant if the latter pleads fair comment or qualified privilege, or if the plaintiff pleads express malice and seeks aggravated or punitive damages. The defendant's entire conduct before, during, and after publication may be explored by the plaintiff on discovery.

Although the identity of newspaper sources may be relevant, in certain provinces the court may defer until trial a decision whether or not the defendant should disclose those sources to the plaintiff pursuant to the newspaper rule.

This chapter addresses discovery issues that are discussed in the defamation jurisprudence. It is not, however, a checklist of topics to be covered by examining counsel on a defamation discovery. The specific issues of fact and law applicable to a particular defamation lawsuit will govern the conduct of discovery by plaintiff and by defendant.

Counsel must also give close consideration both to the general jurisprudence in their jurisdiction and to the specific discovery rights and obligations created by statutes or the rules of court in their jurisdiction.

The scope and nature of the right of oral examination for discovery under oath before trial varies to some degree from province to province, and older case law which predates amendments must be regarded with caution. Examination for discovery rights are currently defined in the following statutory instruments:

Alberta, *Judicature Act*, R.S.A. 2000, c. J-2, Alberta *Rules of Court*, Alta. Reg. 390/68, rr. 186-217, 468.

British Columbia, *Court Rules Act*, R.S.B.C., 1996, c. 80; *Supreme Court Rules*, B.C. Reg. 221/90, rr. 26, 27, 29, 30.

Manitoba, *Court of Queen's Bench Act*, S.M. 1988-89, c. 4, *Court of Queen's Bench Rules*, Man. Reg. 553/88, rr. 30–35.

New Brunswick, *Judicature Act*, R.S.N.B. 1973, c. J-2, *Rules of Court*, N.B. Reg. 82/73, rr. 31–36.

Newfoundland and Labrador, *Judicature Act*, R.S.N. 1990, c. J-4, *Rules of the Supreme Court, 1986*, S.N. 1986, c. 42, Sched. D, rr. 30–32, 34, 36.

Northwest Territories, *Judicature Act*, R.S.N.W.T. 1988, c. J-1 (Alberta *Rules of Court* apply).

Nova Scotia, *Judicature Act*, R.S.N.S. 1989, c. 240, *Civil Procedure Rules*, rr. 18–20, 22, 24.

Ontario, *Courts of Justice Act*, R.S.O. 1990, c. C-43; *Rules of Civil Procedure*, R.R.O. 1990, Reg. 194, rr. 30–35.

Prince Edward Island, *Supreme Court Act*, R.S.P.E.I. 1988, c. S-10, *Rules of Civil Procedure*, rr. 30–35.

Saskatchewan, *Queen's Bench Act*, R.S.S. 1978, c. Q-1, *Queen's Bench Rules*, rr. 212–40.

Yukon Territory, *Judicature Act*, R.S.Y. 1986, c. 96 (British Columbia *Supreme Court Rules* apply).

Federal Court Rules (1998), r. 240.

Generally, as in other actions, a defamation examination for discovery is a cross-examination in the true sense. The examining party is not confined to asking questions which merely go to proving the examining party's claim or defence (as the case may be) but may ask questions calculated to obtain statements or admissions which tend to impair the opposing party's case. As noted above, however, this general rule is subject to limiting features defined in the defamation jurisprudence, particularly with respect to the defence of truth where the quality of the defendant's pleadings are vital to issues of relevance.

The entitlement to cross-examine on an examination for discovery is explicitly stated in the rules of court in certain jurisdictions. For example, British Columbia Rule 27 (21) states:

> The examination of a person for discovery shall be in the nature of a cross-examination ...

The rules of court may, on their face confer wider discovery rights in some provinces than in others. For example, it has been held in a defamation context that the Nova Scotia discovery rule is somewhat wider than similar rules in force in some of the other provinces.

> *King v. King* (1975), 20 N.S.R. (2d) 260, per Cowan C.J.T.D. at 263 (S.C. (T.D.)), cited in *Campbell v. Jones* (1998), 168 N.S.R. (2d) 1, per MacAdam J. at paras. 8, 11 (S.C.).

> *McCrea v. Canada Newspapers Co.* (1993), 122 N.S.R. (2d) 411 (S.C.), aff'd (1993), 109 D.L.R. (4th) 396, per Hallett J.A. at 398–99 (N.S.S.C. (A.D.)).

The Nova Scotia discovery rights are found in Rule 18 which provides in material part:

> 18.09(1) Unless it is otherwise ordered, a person, being examined upon an examination for discovery, shall answer any question within his knowledge or means of knowledge concerning any matter, not privileged, that is relevant to the subject matter of the proceeding, *even though it is not within the scope of the pleadings* (emphasis added).

> 18.12(2) No objection to any question shall be valid if made solely upon the ground that any answer thereto will disclose the name of a witness, or that the question will be inadmissible at the trial or hearing if the answer sought appears reasonably calculated to lead to the discovery of admissible evidence.

The counterpart provision in British Columbia is Rule 27 (22) which simply provides:

(22) Unless the court otherwise orders, a person being examined for discovery shall answer any question within his or her knowledge or means of knowledge regarding any matter, not privileged, relating to a matter in question in the action, and is compellable to give the names and addresses of all persons who reasonably might be expected to have knowledge relating to any matter in question in the action.

In some measure, the differences between the Nova Scotia discovery rule and the British Columbia discovery rule are narrowed by the jurisprudence which has interpreted the latter rule fairly liberally. However, the distinctions between the wording of the two rules illustrates why defamation counsel must be careful when seeking to rely on case law from provinces other than the jurisdiction of the defamation lawsuit.

Moreover, discovery rights may widen or narrow with amendments. In Alberta, for example, it was held in a recent defamation case that the permissible scope of discovery questions had recently been narrowed by amendments to the *Rules of Court* in that jurisdiction.

> *Finning International Inc.* v. *Cormack*, [2001] A.J. No. 1092, 2001 ABQB 723, per Clarke J. at para. 49.

1) Two Points to Consider

a) Ontario: Simplified Procedure

In Ontario, under the Simplified Procedure (Rule 76), an oral examination for discovery is not permitted regardless of whether the action involves a defamation claim.

> *Mills* v. *MacFarlane* (2000), 49 C.P.C. (4th) 184 (Ont. S.C.J.), per Lax J. quoting Rule 76.05, which states:
>
> > An examination for discovery under Rule 31.03 or 31.10, a cross-examination for a deponent on an affidavit under Rule 39.02 and an examination of a witness on a motion under Rule 39.03 are not permitted in an action under the simplified procedure.

b) Examining Legal Counsel

Libel plaintiffs who have communicated with the defendant through legal counsel before or after publication should consider the implications of the decision of the British Columbia Supreme Court in *Canadian Free Speech League* v. *Canadian Broadcasting Corp.*, [1990] 1 W.W.R. 339 (B.C.S.C.), where a defendant was ordered to answer relevant questions on discovery notwithstanding that examining counsel might become a witness at trial. Hutchison L.J.S.C. stated at page 345:

> Were I to rule in favour of the defendants and hold that Mr. Christie, a member of the Law Society of British Columbia, could not appear and ask questions on the discovery of the defendants because he might later become an essential and necessary witness for the defence I would create a precedent by which difficult and obstreperous counsel could be deprived of a brief by the defence merely stating they propose to call plaintiff's counsel as witness at trial. The defendants have fortunately failed to establish such a rule exists.

B. THE PLAINTIFF'S EXAMINATION OF THE DEFENDANT

1) Identification of the Plaintiff

The plaintiff is entitled to question the defendant as to whom he intended the defamatory expression to refer if it does not mention any person by name but makes a reference to the plaintiff that can only be understood by connecting it to extraneous circumstances. The question is also proper when a defence of privilege has been pleaded, because the plaintiff is entitled to show that the defendant intended to strike at the plaintiff.

Morley v. Patrick (1910), 21 O.L.R. 240 at 244 (Divisional Court) per Meredith C.J.C.P. at 244, para. 20:

> ¶ 20 ... Now, might it not be a most cogent argument, if there was evidence gyro and con, to lead the jury to a conclusion as to which view to take, that the defendant had admitted when interrogated, "I intended to refer to the plaintiff"? It would tend to strengthen the view that the plaintiff was the person who would be understood by the associates of the plaintiff or persons acquainted with the circumstances, to have been referred to.

Clarke v. Stewart (1916), 32 D.L.R. 366, 10 Alta. L.R. 393 (C.A.) per Beck J. at 371:

> Whether or not in a civil case — for it certainly would be so in criminal libel — the plaintiff could support his case by proving merely that the mind of the defendant directed his words against the plaintiff without proof that any one so understood them or would be likely to so understand them, I need not, I think, attempt to solve; for it is not, I think, possible to contend that the real intention of the defendant with

relation to the whole affair is not admissible in evidence either in aggravation or in mitigation of damages. *Bray on Discovery*, p. 21, *Odgers' Libel and Slander*, p. 688. Ann. Prac. 1917, p. 522.

Now, all this I have said without regard to the special defence of fair comment. It seems to me that the plaintiff's right to put the contested questions to the defendant is much less open to argument in view of this plea. The plea assumes that the defamatory words apply to the plaintiff and gives the plaintiff the right to inquire fully into the sources of information and the grounds of belief of the defendant. It would, I think, be the height of absurdity that the defendant should be permitted to answer all such questions merely hypothetically.

There is good direct authority that the questions are proper. *Wilton v. Brignell* (W.N.), 1875, 239; 20 Sol. Jo. 121. *Morley v. Patrick*, 21 O.L.R. 240

Cherneskey v. Armadale Publishers Ltd. (1974) 45 D.L.R. (3d) 433 (Sask. Q.B.), rev'd on other grounds (1974), 53 D.L.R. (3d) 79 (C.A.), per Bence C.J.Q.B. [1974] 45 D.L.R. (3d) at paras. 14–32.

2) Extent of Publication

a) Non-media

A non-media defendant is required to disclose the names and addresses of the persons to whom the statement was published since the extent of publication is relevant on the issue of damages.

Massey-Harris Co. v. Delaval Separator Co. (1906), 11 O.L.R. 227 (H.C.), aff'd 11 O.L.R. 591, per Meredith C.J. at 593, para. 12 (Div. Ct.) [circular advising the plaintiff had decided to discontinue its business]:

> … the number and class of persons to whom the alleged libel was published may be most important, not merely on the question of damages but also on the question whether the defendants are entitled to succeed on their defence of qualified privilege, for it may be that the information sought may disclose the fact that the alleged libel was published to person to whom the appellants were not justified in communicating it, even though the occasion of its publication to some of them may be protected under the defence set up.

Hays v. Weiland (1918), 14 O.W.N. 146, per Hodgins J.A. at paras. 34–41 (C.A.).

550433 Alberta Ltd. v. *Stealth Alarms Systems Inc.* (1998), 40 C.P.C. (4th) 279, per Veit J. at para. 26 (Alta. Q.B.):

> Moreover, the plaintiff, having established a prima facie case, i.e. the existence of the defamatory statements made on specified dates to identified recipients by identified makers, the plaintiff is entitled, on discovery, to ask the defendants if they made similar statements to other people. This would not be a fishing expedition because the plaintiff would have established reasonable grounds — a prima facie case — for inferring that other such similar statements had in fact been made.

If publication of the alleged slander is not admitted, the plaintiff may ask the defendant whether he spoke the words set out in the statement of claim, or spoke words to that effect.

Brown v. *Orde* (1912), 2 D.L.R. 562 (O.H.C.J.) per Middleton J., citing *Dalgleish* v. *Lowther*, [1899] 2 Q.B. 590, 68 L.J.Q.B. 956, 81 L.T. 161:

> "Did you on or before the ___ day of ___ speak the following words to the plaintiff (here insert the words complained of) or words to that effect?" "Were such words spoken in the presence of (here insert names of the parties as set forth in the statement of claim or particulars) or some, and which of them?"

b) Media

The extent of publication of an alleged libel is relevant to the issue of damages. An officer of the defendant daily newspaper was therefore compelled to answer questions on examination for discovery about the number, extent, mode, and particular areas of distribution of the subject newspaper.

Cherneskey v. *Armadale Publishers Ltd.* (1974), 45 D.L.R. (3d) 433, per Bence C.J.Q.B. at paras. 9–12 (Sask. Q.B.), [rev'd on other grounds (1974), 53 D.L.R. (3d) 79 (C.A.)], citing *Platt* v. *Time International of Canada Ltd.* (1964), 44 D.L.R. (2d), 17 (Ont. H.C.J.) [specifically the judgment of McRuer, C.J.H.C.], [*Platt* aff'd (1964), 48 D.L.R. (2d) 508 (Ont. C.A.) without written reasons].

It appears that the court may not require a newspaper defendant to produce the mailing list of all subscribers, although it must divulge the number of copies printed and distributed and the methods of distribution, and answer questions dealing with the circulation in the community where the plaintiff resides and among the people on whose goodwill the plaintiff depends.

Popovich v. *Lobay*, [1937] 2 W.W.R. 64, per Haines J. at 65 (Man. K.B.).

c) Republication

If it is alleged in the statement of claim that the defendant is liable for republication of the defamatory expression by other persons, the plaintiff is entitled to ask the defendant whether or not he or she expected that such other persons would republish the defamatory expression in whole or in part.

> *Agnew v. O'Callaghan* (1980), 18 C.P.C. 258, per O'Leary J. at 263 (Ont. H.C.J.).

3) Meaning of the Defamatory Expression

Questions about the meaning of the expression at issue are usually improper unless the state of mind of the defendant is in issue, as where the defendant has pleaded fair comment or qualified privilege, or where the plaintiff has alleged actual malice on the part of the defendant.

The determination of the meaning of defamatory expression is a matter solely for the trier of fact. The test is objective and the opinion of the defendant is therefore irrelevant. The plaintiff is therefore not entitled to ask the defendant what meaning is conveyed by the expression at issue for the purpose of proving its actual meaning.

> *Morley v. Patrick* (1910), 21 O.L.R. 240, per Meredith C.J.C.P. at 244–45 (Div. Ct.):
>
> > ¶22 The question in the other case which has been referred to, *Heaton v. Goldney*, [1910] 1 K.B. 754, was an entirely different question. There the interrogatory was directed to ascertaining from the defendant what he meant by the words used. It seems to me that there is a plain distinction between the two cases. It was immaterial what the defendant meant. The question was, what meaning would be conveyed by the words to ordinary persons who heard or read them.
>
> *Popovich v. Lobay*, [1937] 2 W.W.R. 64, per Dysart J. at 65–66 (Man. K.B.).
>
> *Heaton v. Goldney*, [1910] 1 K.B. 754.
>
> *Clarke v. Stewart* (1916), 32 D.L.R. 366, per Stuart J. at 367 (Alta. S.C. (A.D.)), citing, *inter alia*, *Gibson v. Evans*, 23 Q.B.D. 384, *Heaton v. Goldney*, [1910] 1 K.B. 754.
>
> *Brown v. Orde* (1912), 2 D.L.R. 562 (Ont. H.C.J.), per Middleton J. citing *Heaton v. Goldney*, [1910] 1 K.B. 754, 79 L.J.K.B. 541, 26 Times L.R. 383.

Several appellate decisions from British Columbia, however, support the view that in that jurisdiction a plaintiff may ask a defendant journalist about her intended meaning if the statement of defence denies the meaning alleged in the statement of claim.

Wismer v. *Maclean-Hunter Publishing Co. Ltd. and Fraser (No. 2)*, [1954] 1 D.L.R. 501, [aff'g, [1953] 4 D.L.R. 349 (B.C.S.C.)], per Robertson J.A. at 519–20 (B.C.C.A.):

> ... para. 7 of the statement of claim sets up that the words complained of in para. 6 of the statement of claim meant and were intended and understood to mean certain things set out in paras. (a) and (b) of para. 7. Paragraph 4 of the amended statement of defence of the company denies each and every allegation of fact contained in para. 7 of the statement of claim. There is therefore a direct issue as to what was meant and intended by the words complained of. I can see no reason why there should not be cross-examination upon those points.

It should be noted however that in his dissenting judgment in *Wismer*, O'Halloran J.A. stated at page 513:

> Then regarding the seven questions directed to appellant's intention or opinion. In short they amount to "What did you mean when you wrote such and such a statement?" or "What meaning do you attach to these words when you say you believe them to be true?" In my judgment it is immaterial what meaning appellant intended his words to carry: cf. *Heaton* v. *Goldney*, [1910] 1 K.B. 754; *Stubbs* v. *Mazure*, [1920] A.C. 66, and *E. Hulton & Co.* v. *Jones*, [1910] A.C. 20. Whether the words are capable of a libelous meaning is a question of law for the Judge at the trial; but what meaning they did in fact convey to those who read them is a question of fact for the jury.

McConachy v. *Times Publishers Ltd.* (1964), 49 D.L.R. (2d) 349, per Norris J.A. at 356–64 (B.C.C.A.):

> Questions objected to as being questions as to the meaning of the innuendo
>
> ...
>
> Q. 28. By admitting that you intended to refer to him as a trade union boss, did you not intend to mean of him that he managed the affairs of his union in an undemocratic way?
>
> Q.33. Well, now, the defendants have admitted that they meant that the plaintiff was a trade union boss. Now, is it your contention that by

those words you meant that the plaintiff interfered with the democratic running of his trade union local?

Q. 37. Turning again to page 2 of the Statement of Claim, by the words "time to get rid of some people," did your paper mean to suggest that it was time to get ride of James McConachy, the plaintiff in this action?

...

Before this Court counsel for the plaintiff disavowed any intention of alleging that the defendants were actuated by express malice. However, in this Province the law with respect to the onus on defendants pleading fair comment or (as here) the rolled-up plea is the same as it was before the *Defamation Act*, passed in England in 1952, viz. that at the trial it is incumbent on the defendants to prove:

(1) that each and every statement of fact complained of was true, and
(2) that the comment on the facts so proved was bona fide and fair comment on a matter of public interest.

Gatley on Libel and Slander, 5th ed., pp. 331–32.

As of the date of the examination for discovery this burden still rested on the defendants in spite of the fact that express malice on the part of the defendants is not relied on by the plaintiff.... That which is to be considered is as to whether the questions may raise matters which are relevant to the issues raised on the pleadings. In my respectful opinion, these questions — save question 19 as to the politics of the reporter Sinclair — may raise such matters ... .

As to the questions which are objected to as being questions as to the meaning of the innuendo, counsel for the defendants argues in effect that these questions being in form questions as to what Tobin intended the words to mean are not relevant questions as that which is material is "would reasonable people acquainted with the circumstances give the words the meaning which the plaintiff imputes to them." He cites English authorities.

Again the wide latitude in cross-examination on examination for discovery as distinct from discovery by way of interrogatories is to be borne in mind. It is my opinion that these questions, as stated in *Hopper* v. *Dunsmuir (No. 2)*, and *Tisman* v. *Rae*, supra, may raise matters relevant to issues on the pleadings. Cross-examining counsel was doubtless embarking on one of the "circuitous routes" to establish the proposition essential to his case that reasonable people acquainted with the circumstances would understand the words to have the meanings which the plaintiff intended they had. At that, the route may not have been very circuitous for it is not conceivable that Tobin would not consider that he was a reasonable man or that he, as a newspaper editor, did not have a working knowledge of the meanings of words and their implications as accepted by members of the public ... . The judgment of this Court in *Wismer v. Maclean-Hunter Publishing Co. Ltd. and Fraser (No. 1)*, [1954] 1 D.L.R. 481, 10 W.W.R. (N.S.) 646 as to the innuendo is to be distinguished because the question at issue in that case was whether or not "particulars" of the defendant's state of mind might properly be demanded. Here the questions were asked on cross-examination on discovery — a very different matter as has been already indicated.

Wismer v. Maclean-Hunter was considered by the Nova Scotia Supreme Court in *McCrea v. Canada Newspapers Co.* (1993), 122 N.S.R. (2d) 411 (S.C. (T.D.)), where MacAdam J. appeared to agree with the British Columbia Court of Appeal and held that a defendant may be examined as to what he intended the words to mean if he denies the meanings placed on the words by the plaintiffs. MacAdam J stated at paragraphs 51–57:

¶51 We concur with the views of Robertson J.A. [in *Wismer v. Maclean-Hunter Publishing Company Ltd. and Fraser (No. 2)*, above] that by virtue of the denial of the meaning attributed to the words by the plaintiff, the defendant has put the meaning intended by the author of these words in issue and therefore the plaintiff is entitled to examine the author as to what she intended or meant.

¶52 In the alternative, the defendant has pleaded "fair comment" and therefore the defendant's state of mind is in issue, including whether the comment represented the honest opinion of the author and whether the comment was published without actual malice. (*Kolewaski v. Island Properties Ltd.* (1983), 56 N.S.R. (2d) 475 at 512). Counsel for the defendant does not dispute that where "fair comment" is pleaded that malice is in issue, although he submits that the nature of the malice is different than where "express malice" is pleaded. However, malice being in issue, even the malice inferred by virtue of the plea of fair comment, it is open for the plaintiff to examine the motives of the defendant in writing the article and the series of articles. The plaintiff is entitled to test the credibility of the witness as to her belief in the statements made and therefore is of necessity entitled to examine the defendant as to what she intended by the words that are complained of....

¶55 Although, the plaintiff has not pleaded actual malice, he has claimed exemplary damage. Counsel acknowledges that as a result the defendant's state of mind is relevant. In order to understand the defendant's state of mind it is necessary to know what the defendant intended by the words she used. This is not to require the defendant to interpret her own words, but rather to indicate what she intended and her basis or foundation for the comments and statements she made in the article. If is, of course, for the Jury to determine what the words actually mean.

¶56 Counsel for the defendant submits that if the words constitute comment, "then the defendant's state of mind as to whether they believe the comment is relevant, but only to that extent." In our view, the plaintiff is entitled to test the defendant's statement of belief by asking what was meant or intended by the defendant as well as the facts and circumstances on which the comment, and therefore the belief, is founded. As submitted by counsel for the plaintiff, "It is difficult to conceive how one can question the state of mind of the defendant without dealing with her intention."

¶57 To permit less and to restrict the scope of the examination would be to disentitle the plaintiff to test the plea of "fair comment" as well as the denial by the defendant of the meaning attributed to the words by the plaintiff in his amended Statement of Claim and to preclude the plaintiff from examining and testing the state of mind of the defendant in light of the plaintiff's claim for exemplary damages.

Although the Nova Scotia Court of Appeal affirmed the decision of MacAdam J. to order the defendant to answer the plaintiff's discovery questions concerning meaning, it did so on the basis that what the defendant meant "could be relevant to the punitive damage claim which is founded on the assertion that the appellants bore malice towards [the plaintiff] and could be relevant to the defence of fair comment." The decision of the Court of Appeal does not appear to approve of the British Columbia decisions.

McCrea v. Canada Newspapers Co. (1993), 109 D.L.R. (4th) 396, per Hallett J.A. at 398–99 (N.S.S.C. (A.D.)), stating in part at 399:

> The alleged defamatory statements having been made in the context of the series on political patronage in Nova Scotia Cameron is required to answer questions as to the meaning she intended to convey by use of relevant words in each of the articles.

In Alberta, the Court of Queen's Bench ordered a defendant journalist to answer discovery questions relating to his intended meaning of the word "green" to describe the plaintiff in the allegedly defamatory article and later communications. The court held that the issue of malice was relevant to the defences and that questions going to the defendant's state of mind should therefore be answered.

> *O'Callaghan v. Edmonton Sun Publishing Ltd.* (1981), 34 A.R. 207 (Q.B.).

> See also *Red Deer Nursing Home Ltd. v. Taylor* (1968), 1 D.L.R. (3d) 491, per MacDonald J. at 500 (Alta. S.C. (T.D.)).

In addition to *O'Callaghan, McCrea,* and *Red Deer Nursing Home,* the other authorities discussed below make it clear that the defendant may be questioned about her intended meaning where fair comment or qualified privilege is raised in the defence or malice is in issue.

4) Preparation of the Defamatory Expression

In an action against a newspaper where the plaintiff claimed substantial general damages (including aggravated damages) and exemplary damages, the Ontario High Court held that the plaintiff was entitled to ask what the defendants knew at the time of publication, what material they had, and what they decided to omit and what to include, as material to the issue. Such questioning could legitimately canvass the following issues:

- the reporter's notes, tapes, and documents used in preparation for the article;
- who the reporter made inquiries of, including details of all interviews;
- notes of all interviews with persons mentioned in the stories, as well as others not mentioned;
- whether the reporter saw any people off the record and details of such conversations;
- what the reporter said to the persons interviewed;
- whether the reporter or people interviewed conducted any surveillance;
- motivation in writing the story;
- whether the reporter worked on the story alone or had any assistance from other people at the news media organization which employed him, or from outsiders, and if so, whether they had notes;
- whether the story was amended before printing, whether parts were taken out or added — in other words, the evolution of the story, including computer printouts or earlier drafts;
- who was responsible for the story, whose idea it was, and whether the reporter consulted with the other defendants; and
- who arranged the layout of the stories, the cut lines, and the photographs.

Del Zotto v. *Canadian Newspapers Co. Ltd.* (1988), 65 O.R. (2d) 594 at 597–98 (S.C. (Mast.)).

The Court in *Del Zotto* reasoned that the plaintiffs would have to establish that the defendants acted in knowing disregard of the plaintiff's rights. The Court accepted the statement of Lord Reid in *Broome* v. *Cassell & Co. Ltd.*, [1972] A.C. 1027 at 1088:

> ... the jury were fully entitled to hold that the appellants knew when they committed this tort that passages in this book were highly defamatory of the respondent and could not be justified as true and that it could properly be inferred that they thought that it would pay them to publish the book and risk the consequences of any action the respondent might take.
>
> It matters not whether they thought they could escape with moderate damages or that the enormous expense involved in fighting an action of this kind would prevent the respondent from pressing his claim.

5) Post-publication Communications from the Defendant to the Plaintiff

The Ontario High Court held that a plaintiff was entitled to question a defendant editor, who was a representative of the defendant publisher, about the editor's letter to the plaintiff which expressed dismay about the article which became the subject of the litigation. The letter indicated that the editor held the plaintiff in high regard and that the article had been truncated to save space, and concluded: " I realize an article like the one we published may cause some unintended professional harm to your endeavours, but I hope that you realize, in turn, that as the editor of the magazine, I must stand behind what we have published." The court rejected the defendant's submission that the letter constituted, expressly or impliedly, a proposition for settlement between the parties and was therefore subject to privilege.

Drabinsky v. *Maclean-Hunter Ltd.* (1980), 108 D.L.R. (3d) 390, per Callaghan J. at 392–93 (Ont. H.C.J.).

Generally, the conduct of the defendant following the publication of the expression at issue is relevant to the assessment of damages, and questions bearing on that subject must therefore be answered.

O'Callaghan v. *Edmonton Sun Publishing Ltd.* (1981), 34 A.R. 207 (Master)

6) Questions that May Be Asked

a) Whether the Defendant Sought Pre-publication Legal Advice

It is submitted that such questions would be prohibited by solicitor/client privilege.

A British Columbia court has held, in a case where malice was alleged against the defendant radio hotline host, that whether the defendant ever consulted a lawyer for advice with respect to what he proposed to say and whether his proposed comments would be defamatory was simply not relevant.

Siddon v. Mair, [1997] B.C.J. No. 17 at para. 36 (S.C.).

b) Whether the Defendant Has Been Sued By Others for Libel

It has been held that no negative inference can be drawn about a defamation defendant from the fact that a number of other defamation lawsuits may have been filed against him or her. Accordingly, a hotline radio host was not required to answer questions about other lawsuits commenced against him for defamation while he was employed by the defendant radio station.

Siddon v. Mair, ibid., at para. 43.

c) Questions Relevant to the Defendant's State Of Mind

The defendant's state of mind is relevant and may therefore be the subject of examination for discovery in the following situations.

* The defence of fair comment has been pleaded and the defendant's honest belief is at issue.

  Drake v. Overland (1979), 107 D.L.R. (3d) 323, per Laycraft J.A. at 332 (Alta. C.A.):

  > [A]ny facts which show a defendant had no honest belief in the truth of his statement tends to show malice and thus is within the scope of the examination for discovery. Facts tending to show previous ill-will or intemperate statements made on other occasions may show malice.

  McConachy v. Times Publishers Ltd. (1964), 50 W.W.R. 389, per Norris J.A. at 364 (B.C.C.A.).

* The plaintiff pleads actual malice in reply to the defendant's plea of statutory or common law qualified privilege.

Wismer v. Maclean-Hunter Publishing Co. and Fraser (No. 2), [1954] 1 D.L.R. 501, per Robertson J.A. at 519 (B.C.C.A.).

- The plaintiff pleads that the defendant has been actuated by express malice in support of a claim for aggravated or exemplary damages.

  McKenzie v. McLaughlin (1902), 1 O.W.R. 58, leave to appeal to S.C.C. refused, 1 O.W.R. 80.

  O'Callaghan v. Edmonton Sun Publishing Ltd. (1981), 34 A.R. 207 (Q.B.).

  Teskey v. Canadian Newspapers Co. Ltd. (1985), 29 A.C.W.S. (2d) 295 (Ont. M.C.).

- Where damages are at large because the motives of the defendant may aggravate the injury done to the plaintiff.

  Getty v. Calgary Herald (1991), 47 C.P.C. (2d) 42 per McFadyen J. at 45 (Alta. Q.B.), citing Philip Lewis, *Gatley on Libel and Slander*, 8th ed. (London: Sweet & Maxwell, 1981) at 1452.

The meaning intended by the defendant is relevant to the issue of malice and therefore a defendant may be asked what he or she intended by the expression at issue.

O'Callaghan v. Edmonton Sun Publishing Ltd. (1981), 34 A.R. 207 (Q.B.).

McCrae v. Canada Newspapers Co. (1993) 122 N.S.R. (2d) 411 (S.C. (T.D.)), aff'd (1993) 109 D.L.R. (4th) 396 (N.S.S.C. (A.D.)).

Red Deer Nursing Home Ltd. v. Taylor (1968), 1 D.L.R. (3d) 491, per MacDonald J. at 500 (Alta. S.C. (T.D.)).

Getty v. Calgary Herald (1991), 47 C.P.C. (2d) 42 per McFadyen J. at 45 (Alta. Q.B.), citing *Toronto Star v. Globe Printing Co.*, [1941] O.W.N. 157 at 161 (H.C.J.).

The following decisions illustrate the scope of questioning of a defendant that has been allowed by the courts where the matter of honest belief or reckless indifference to the truth is in issue:

(i) Questions about whether the defendant had any differences with the plaintiff before publication of the defamatory expression, or whether he bore any animosity or malice towards the plaintiff about the time of publication.

   Popovich v. Lobay, [1937] 2 W.W.R. 64, per Dysart J. at 66 (Man. K.B.).

(ii) Questions concerning the foundation of particular statements.

Cherneskey v. *Armadale Publishers Ltd.* (1974), 45 D.L.R. (3d) 433 at 435–39 (Sask. Q.B.), rev'd on other grounds (1974), 53 D.L.R. (3d) 79 (Sask. CA) [the plaintiff sought information relating to the selection of the heading "Racist attitude" and the policy of the defendant corporation generally with respect to the selection of such headings].

Dennison v. *Sanderson*, [1944] O.W.N. 606 (M.C.).

Burford v. *Globe Printing Co.*, [1949] O.W.N. 510 (H.C.).

Red Deer Nursing Home Ltd. v. *Taylor* (1968), 1 D.L.R. (3d) 491, per MacDonald J. at 500 (Alta. S.C. (T.D.)).

Fink v. *Wagner* (1983) 30 Sask R. 170 (Q.B.).

(iii) Questions regarding the defendant's "education, training, or experience might be very material in the matter of judging whether or not malice existed on the part of the defendant."

Red Deer Nursing Home v. *Taylor* (1968), 1 D.L.R. (3d) 491, per MacDonald J. at 500 (Alta. S.C. (T.D.)).

(iv) Questions as to whether there are in the notes the defendant made at the time of his interview with the plaintiff prior to publication, any opinions which the defendant now says are based on false facts, or which he does not post-publication now hold or believe to be true.

Agnew v. *O'Callaghan* (1981), 18 C.P.C. 258, per O'Leary J. at 264 (Ont. H.C.J.), ruling that the question seeks

> to obtain information that will throw light on the issue of whether [the defendant] sincerely believed the opinions expressed in the statements complained of by the plaintiffs.

(v) Questions concerning thirty similar articles referring to the plaintiff that had been published in the defendant newspaper, some of which were written by the defendant journalist.

Boushy v. *Sarnia Gazette Publishing Co.* (1980), 30 O.R. (2d) 667, per Southey J. at 173 (H.C.J.):

> The questions being relevant to the matters in issue, they should not be denied because they will result in lengthy discoveries. If Saddy followed a systematic practice of libeling the plaintiff over a period of several years, the plaintiff is entitled to establish that fact in evidence and to ask about it on discovery. Furthermore, if the questions are put to Saddy on discovery, the proceedings may be

shortened. The answers given by Saddy may satisfy the plaintiff that some or all of the prior articles were perfectly innocent, or are not worth putting before the jury as evidence of malice. In that event, the discovery will shorten the trial, thus achieving one of the principal purposes of examinations for discovery.

Meyer v. Clarke (1912), 3 O.W.N. 893, (1912) 1 D.L.R. 927 (O.H.C.) citing *Odgers on Libel and Slander*, 8th Eng. ed., pp. 348, 390

(vi) Questions concerning a repetition by the defendant of the defamatory statement.

Klenman v. Schmidt (1911), 4 Sask. L.R. 366

(vii) Questions probing whether the defendant honestly believed the statements to be true at the time of publication.

Agnew v. O'Callaghan (1980), 18 C.P.C. 258, per O'Leary J. at 263 (Ont. H.C.J.). The court ordered the defendant to answer whether at the time of publishing the articles he considered the plaintiffs were immoral or dishonest; had carried out an illegal transaction or one that was in any way improper, dishonest, or immoral; had breached any public trust arising out of their position as senior officials in the City of Windsor; were in conflict with their public duties; or were unfit to hold their positions as officials of the City of Windsor:

> In my view, a jury might reasonably conclude that the words complained of either explicitly or by imputation are defamatory of the plaintiffs in any or all of the ways canvassed in QQ. 549 to 55, and so it is relevant to know just what was the belief of the defendant in that regard.

Getty v. Calgary Herald (1991), 47 C.P.C. (2d) 42 per McFadyen J. at 45 (Alta. Q.B) [plaintiff sought to ask questions relating, *inter alia*, to the knowledge of the defendant reporter and the publishers of the newspaper and to the care taken by them before publication to check the accuracy of the defamatory statements made by them].

(viii) Questions about the reason defamatory advertisements were published.

Dennison v. Sanderson, [1944] O.W.N. 606 (M.C.).

(ix) Questions about why the defendant chose particular words in the defamatory expression.

O'Callaghan v. *Edmonton Sun Publishing Ltd.* (1981) 34 Alta. R. 207 (Q.B.) [the word "green"].

Red Deer Nursing Home Ltd. v. *Taylor* (1968), 1 D.L.R. (3d) 491 at 500 (Alta. S.C.) [the words "questionable," "chain development companies"].

Hatfield v. *Globe and Mail Division of Canadian Newspapers Co.* (1983), 41 O.R. (2d) 218 per Master Sandler at 223 (S.C.):

> Questions 95, 96 and 97 seek Mr. Doyle's knowledge on why a particular sentence in the second article was written; whether he had any knowledge of the truth of that sentence prior to publication and whether he discussed the sentence with the managing editor, Mr. Moser, prior to publication. It is argued that these questions go to the issue of bona fides and malice under the fair comment and qualified privilege defences, and to damages. The objection to the questions is that the questions relate to pre-publication matters which are not relevant. These questions are proper in my view: *Agnew* v. *O'Callaghan*, supra.

(x)   Where the defendant had written thirty articles that referred to the plaintiff over a three-year period, the plaintiff was entitled to ask the following questions as they were considered to be relevant to the issue of malice:
   a. whether in some of the articles the reference to the person designated by pseudonyms was in fact the plaintiff;
   b. whether the fair comment was on a matter of public interest;
   c. whether the statements were true in fact;
   d. whether the defendant honestly believed the statements in the articles to be true at the time of publication.

Boushy v. *Sarnia Gazette Publishing Co.* (1980), 117 D.L.R. (3d) 171 (H.C.) per Southey J. at 174 (Ont. H.C.J.).

(xi)   Questions concerning what the journalist considered the main issue of his proposed story at the time he interviewed the plaintiff.

Agnew v. *O'Callaghan* (1980), 18 C.P.C. 258 per O'Leary J. at 263–64 (Ont. H.C.J.).

(xii) Questions concerning contracts confirming the financial capacity of the defendant broadcaster to pay a reasonable award of punitive damages.

Siddon v. *Mair*, [1997] B.C.J. No. 17 at para. 27 (S.C.):

> I wish to make it clear that if the contracts [between the defendant hotline host and his employer] show the defendant Mair or his companies were induced to improve ratings and that their inducement would result in a financial benefit to Mair or his companies, I would have made the order sought [for production of those contracts].

Among many other matters, counsel for a plaintiff may wish to examine a defendant for discovery to obtain admissions that she:

i) relied on a source knowing of the friction between the source and the plaintiff and knowing the source to be partisan;

ii) knew of information that supported the position of the plaintiff but suppressed it;

iii) failed to give the plaintiff a fair chance to explain his or her side of the story; or

iv) made no effort to present a balanced picture in the article.

> *Leenen v. Canadian Broadcasting Corporation* (2000), 48 O.R. (3d) 656 (S.C.J.), aff'd (2001), 54 O.R. (3d) 612 (C.A.), leave to appeal to S.C.C. denied ,[2001] S.C.C.A. No. 432.

See chapter 16 for a complete discussion of the subject of express malice.

Correspondence from the defendant's lawyer to the plaintiff's lawyer may be the subject of the plaintiff's questioning of the defendant on examination for discovery, under the principle that the conduct of the defendant from the publication of the libel to the very moment of the verdict may be considered by the jury. Such correspondence may be evidence of a refusal to apologize, of malice, or of motive and may therefore be relevant to aggravation of damages.

> *Kirschbaum v. "Our Voices" Publishing Co.*, [1972] 1 O.R. 737, per Haines J. at 738–39 (H.C.J.):
>
> > … [I]t is my opinion that the parties should have discovery on this correspondence and discovery whether the admissions were hypothetical or a statement of facts intended to represent the real position of the litigant.

7) Fair Comment

The defendant must say whether or not the facts on which he has commented are true.

> *Augustine Automatic Engine Co. v. Saturday Night* (1916), 30 D.L.R. 613 per Riddell J. at 618–19.

See also, the discussion above concerning questions regarding the state of mind of the defendant.

8) Qualified Privilege

The defendant may be required to answer questions about the identity of all persons to whom an allegedly slanderous statement was made if qualified privilege is raised as a defence. See Chapter 18, "Qualified and Statutory Privilege," section B.1.

In *Loftus* v. *Almec Leisure Group Ltd.*, [1999] B.C.J. No. 1785 (S.C.), a British Columbia Supreme Court Master declined to order the defendant to answer a question about the scope of publication although qualified privilege was pleaded as a defence. This decision appears to be wrongly decided, perhaps because (as the Master pointed out) neither counsel provided case authorities to the court.

See also, the discussion above concerning questions regarding the state of mind of the defendant.

9) Fair and Accurate Report

Where the defendant pleaded that the defamatory expression constituted a fair and accurate report of proceedings in a police court, it was held that the defendant should answer questions about a former action brought by the plaintiff against the defendant as they went to the issue of malice on the part of the defendant.

Bateman v. *Mail Printing Company* (1903), 2 O.W.R. 242.

10) Apology

It has been held that the efficacy of an apology does not depend on what the defendant intended his words to mean but rather on the jury's finding as to what his readers have taken them to mean. Accordingly, a defendant journalist was not required to answer questions on discovery which invited him to identify the expression covered by the apology.

Boushy v. *Sarnia Gazette Publishing Co. Ltd.* (1980), 117 D.L.R. (3d) 171 per Southey J. at 175 (Ont. H.C.J.).

C. THE DEFENDANT'S EXAMINATION OF THE PLAINTIFF

1) Identification of the Plaintiff

It has been held that a plaintiff is required to reveal the names of people at his workplace who associated him with the words in the allegedly defamatory article before he publicly proclaimed that he was the person referred to in the article.

> *Mouammar v. Bruner* (1978), 19 O.R. (2d) 59, per Steele J. at 62 (H.C.J.).

2) Meaning of the Defamatory Expression

The determination of the meaning of the defamatory expression is a matter for the trier of fact alone. The test is objective and the opinion of the plaintiff is therefore irrelevant. The defendant is not entitled to ask the plaintiff what portion of the expression at issue conveys a specific meaning pleadied as a false or popular innuendo.

> *Stumpf v. Globe Holdings Ltd.* (1982), 22 Alta. L.R. (2d) 55 per Master Funduk at para. 17 (Q.B.):
>
> > ¶17 ... [A] defendant cannot, on examinations for discovery, ask a plaintiff to point to any particular words as sustaining an alleged ordinary and natural meaning which is libelous. If the plaintiff had merely alleged, in paragraph 6, that the published words were defamatory the plaintiffs could not require the plaintiff to point to particular words. Merely because the plaintiff to his credit chosen [sic] at the inception of the action, to advise the defendants of how the words are libelous in their ordinary and natural meaning cannot change the situation.

3) Choice of Defendants

Decisions concerning who or how many persons to name as defendants are matters involving discussions between the plaintiff and her legal counsel. Accordingly, in the absence of evidence to substantiate an allegation that the claim as against the named defendants is an abuse of process, the plaintiff need not answer questions relating to these subjects.

> *Campbell v. Jones* (1998), 168 N.S.R. (2d) 1 per MacAdam J. at para. 23 (S.C.).

4) Fee Arrangements between Plaintiff and Legal Counsel

Whether a plaintiff is paying legal fees, or whether the plaintiff's lawyer is acting on a contingency or being paid by other persons are matters between the plaintiff and her legal counsel. The plaintiff need not respond to such a question, at least absent evidence to substantiate an allegation that the claim is an abuse of process.

> *Campbell v. Jones* (1998), 168 N.S.R. (2d) 1, per MacAdam J. at paras. 24–26 (S.C.).

> *Ilic v. Calgary Sun, a division of the Toronto Sun Publishing Corp.*, [1999] 1 W.W.R. 539 per Bielby J. at para. 1, 540 (Alta. Q.B.).

5) Justification

The pleadings play a crucial role in defining the scope of permissible discovery of the plaintiff concerning a defence of justification. The old rules of pleading and discovery in defamation cases have not been supplanted by the modern trend to wide discovery.

> *Kent v. Kehoe* (2000), 183 D.L.R. (4th) 503, 2000 NSCA 3, per Bateman J.A. at para. 5, citing *Care Canada v. Canadian Broadcasting Corp.*, [1998] O.J. No. 1532, (1998) 61 O.T.C. 216 (Gen. Div.). At para. 6, Bateman J.A. approved the following statement at para. 10 of the decision by the Chambers judge:

>> ¶10 I reject the defendant's arguments that in defamation proceedings generally, this rule is archaic [sic] and that Civil Procedure Rule 20 prevails. I am of the view that the rule applies to prevent an abuse of the discovery process in defamation proceedings. For good policy reasons, pre-trial disclosure should not be available to gather facts to prove a plea of justification and fair comment.

Rejecting defence arguments that it was sufficient to show that the plaintiff knows the case that must be met with respect to justification, Bateman J.A. stated in *Kent v. Kehoe* (2000), 183 D.L.R. (4th) 503 at paragraph 22 (N.S.C.A.):

> ¶22 When ... the issue before the court is the entitlement of the defendant to discovery, the court must consider the pleadings, not from the perspective of whether the plaintiff knows the case that must be met, but whether they are sufficiently specific to entitle the defendants to the discovery sought. As has already been said, the defendant is only entitled to discovery if he has set out what parts of the allegedly defamatory statements are facts, the truth of which is relied upon. (*Arnold & Butler v. Bottomley*, [1908] 2 K.B. 151 (C.A.)).

This derives from the longstanding policy which discourages persons from making defamatory statements about others when not possessed of facts which would support such statements.

The defendant therefore cannot ask the plaintiff questions about the truth of the defamatory expression if he or she has not pleaded a defence of justification.

Fletcher-Gordon v. *Southam Inc.* (1997), 28 B.C.L.R. (3d) 187, per Dillon J. at para. 9, 191 (S.C.) [aff'd (1997), 29 B.C.L.R. (3d) 197 (C.A.)]:

> ¶9 These old cases on the law of defamation are still good law in British Columbia. They have not been overtaken by the general rule of disclosure based on relevancy which is itself based upon the 1882 case of *Compagnie Financiere du Pacifique* v. *Peruvian Guano Co.* (1882), 11 Q.B.D. 55.

Savein v. *Green*, [1989] B.C.J. No. 1862 (S.C.).

A defendant who has pleaded justification to a defamatory accusation which is general as opposed to specific must furnish the plaintiff with particulars of the facts relied on as a justification before he can obtain discovery from the plaintiff. The defendant can only obtain discovery in respect of such facts so stated.

732311 Alberta Ltd v. *Paradise Bay Spa Tub Warehouse Inc.*, 2003 ABQB 228 per Johnstone J. at paras. 34–35.

The purpose of requiring particulars of a general defamatory imputation is to prevent a defendant from setting out on a fishing expedition to build up a case for justification, when he has no facts in his possession to justify his remarks at the time he published the libel or slander complained of.

Parkland Chapel Ltd. v. *Edmonton Broadcasting Co. Ltd.* (1964), 45 D.L.R. (2d) 752, per Riley J. at 758–59 (Alta. S.C. (T.D.)):

> The defendants in the present case, in my opinion cannot embark on an effort to ferret out items of truth, something that will "justify" their statements but they, on the strength of their pleadings, must be held to have made statements based on certain information — best known to themselves — and must prove it by their own evidence and not from the plaintiff.

Wismer v. *Maclean-Hunter Publishing Co. Ltd. & Fraser (No. 1)*, [1954] 1 D.L.R. 481, per Robertson J.A. at 492 (B.C.C.A.).

Beaton v. *Globe Printing Co.* (1894), 16 P.R. (Ont.) 281, per Osler J.A. at 288 (C.A.).

In *Gourley* v. *Plimsoll*, L.R. 8 C.P. 362, 373, ruling on a defence application for leave to deliver interrogatories before pleading in support of a plea of justification, Bovill C.J., said:

> What the defendant is endeavouring by this motion to do is, not to rely upon information which he possessed at the time of the publication of the alleged libel, but to ascertain what further facts he can extract from the plaintiff by way of defence. It seems to me that is not a legitimate course for the defendant to adopt … We ought not to compel the plaintiff to give him a case of which he has at the present time no notion.

Arnold & Butler v. *Bottomley* (1908), 77 L.J.K.B. 584, per Farwell L.J. at 587 (C.A.):

> A defendant in a libel action who pleads justification must state in his defence or particulars the facts on which he relies to prove such justification, and he can obtain discovery in respect only of such facts so stated.

And per Vaughn Williams L.J. at page 587:

> It is plain that the defendant Bottomley in this case is not entitled to inspection unless and until he has by his particulars precisely stated the facts on which he relies in support of his justification.

And per Kennedy L.J. at page 589:

> A merchant, who is libelled by a statement that he is insolvent, has a right to maintain an action; and the defendant has no right to say: "Let me examine all his affairs, for if you do I have some chance of proving that he is insolvent."

Goldschmidt v. *Constable & Co.*, [1937] 4 All E.R. 293, per Greer L.J. at 294:

> … in a libel action the party who alleges that the defamatory statements are true must make out his case on the information which he had in his possession at the time when the defence was delivered.

Zierenberg v. *Labouchere* (1893), 63 L.J.Q.B. 89, per Kay L.J. at 93 (C.A.):

> If the defendant says that he is unable to state any such facts without discovery, the answer is simple and conclusive: he ought not to have published the libel, and cannot plead any justification for having done so.

Yorkshire Provident Life Assurance Co. v. *Gilbert & Rivington* (1895), 64 L.J.Q.B.
578, per Lindsay L.J. at 580:

> I think it would be a very bad precedent to suggest that a person can,
> simply by libeling another, obtain access to all his books and see
> whether he can justify what he has said or not. I think it would be very
> lamentable if we should say that when a person has libeled another,
> and he has justified and has given particulars, he then is entitled to
> more than discovery of that which relates to those particulars.

Bullen v. *Templeton* (1896), 5 B.C.R. 43 (Full Ct.) per McCreight J. at 43–44,
approving *Zierenberg* v. *Labouchere* (1893), 2 Q.B. 183 (C.A.).

Nelson v. *Bradstreet*, [1917] 2 W.W.R. 1191 (B.C.S.C.), per Murphy J., approving *Yorkshire Provident Assurance Co.* v. *Gilbert*, [1895] 2 Q.B. 148, *Arnold* v. *Bottomley*, [1908] 2 K. B. 151 (C.A.), and applying *Bullen* v. *Templeton*, 5 B.C.R. 43.

Lebans v. *New Brunswick Publishing Co.* (1996), 50 C.P.C. (3d) 285, per Miller
J. at 288 (N.B.Q.B. (T.D.)).

On the other hand, if the defamatory accusation is specific as opposed to
general, it is sufficient for the defendant to plead simply that it was true in
substance and in fact in order to be entitled to examine the plaintiff about
the veracity of the accusation.

Wismer v. *Maclean-Hunter Publishing Co. Ltd. & Fraser (No. 1)*, [1954] 1 D.L.R.
481, per Robertson J.A. at 493 (B.C.C.A.):

> … in this case the allegations in the libel in the statement of claim are
> not general, but in my opinion, with respect, are specific. The appel-
> lants pleaded "the said words (i.e. in the libel) were true in substance
> and in fact." The respondent knows exactly what he has to meet.

See Chapter 21, "Justification," F.

Reid v. *Albertan Publishing Co., Ltd.* (1913), 10 D.L.R. 495, per Stuart J. at 497
(Alta. S.C.):

> It is of no advantage to the defendants to say that the innuendo alleged
> contains certain statements of facts to which therefore discovery may be
> sought because the defendants deny the innuendo. They cannot blow
> hot and cold. For myself, I not only do not see what defendant [sic] can
> examine upon, but I really do not see what they will be able to claim
> the right to prove at the trial. The libel itself is only insinuation and the
> plaintiff has a right to know by particulars what is insinuated as a mat-
> ter of fact before evidence can be given.

In *Wilson v. Toronto Sun Publishing Corp.*, [2000] A.J. No. 996, 2000 ABQB 584, per Master Breitkreuz, at paragraph 3, it was held that the above principles:

> [do] not mean that a statement of defence will become as bulky as a transcript of an examination for discovery. Even bearing in mind the specificity required of a defendant in a defamation action where the defence is justification, this does not completely override the general rule of pleadings which dictates that they are to be a short summary of the facts relied on by the defendant to justify the alleged defamatory publication.

The rule that discovery of the plaintiff is limited by the particulars of justification applies even if the plaintiff does not make a demand for particulars of a defence of justification.

Gnys v. Stansfield (1975), 11 O.R. (2d) 642, per Master Davidson at 643–44 (S.C.).

Drake v. Overland (1980), 107 D.L.R. (3d) 323, per Laycraft J.A. at 329 (Alta. C.A.).

When a defendant alleged the plaintiff was involved in specific bribery transactions and applied for an order to inspect the records of the parties involved, the court, to prevent the defendant in engaging in a fishing expedition, limited the defendant's inspection to records as of the dates alleged and allowed one day leeway before and after the date.

Sommers v. Sturdy (1956), 6 D.L.R. (2d) 653, Sullivan J. at 656 (B.C.S.C.), aff'd (1957), 10 D.L.R. (2d) 269 per Davey J.A. at 274 Sheppard J.A. at 276–79 (B.C.C.A.).

It was held that the defendant was not entitled to question the plaintiff about a statement he made to a police officer after the publications complained of.

Lebans v. New Brunswick Publishing Co. (1996), 50 C.P.C. (2d) 285, per Miller J. at 289 (N.B.Q.B. (T.D.)):

> ¶23 But my opinion is that the defence must succeed or fail on the basis of a state of facts which existed at the time of publication of the articles. They could not have had any foundation in disclosures made by the plaintiff in his statement to the police for no such statement had been made at that time.

The defendant is entitled to use information which came to his knowledge after publication of the libel to justify the defamatory statement. However, it must be pleaded.

Bowgray Invts. Ltd. v. Gordon, (1980), 3 A.C.W.S. (2d) 439.

It is clear that the long-established principles limiting examination for discovery of the plaintiff with respect to a defence of justification remain valid today.

> *Care Canada v. Canadian Broadcasting Corporation* (1998), 20 C.P.C. (4th) 149, per Benotto J. at 150 (Ont. Div. Ct.), discussing the "the interface between current discovery rules and the historical limitations placed on discovery in libel actions":

>> For well over a century, the scope of the examination of a plaintiff in a libel action has been limited. Where the defendant pleads justification, it bears an onus to prove that the words are substantially true. Where the alleged libel is general in nature and no particulars are given, a defendant may not use the discovery to find a defence of which it was not aware at the time of pleading. The rationale for this rule was to prevent a person from defaming another and then obtain [*sic*] access to all his books to see whether what was said can be justified. Once a defendant has particularized the defence, it is limited at discovery and trial to the issues that have been defined by the particulars furnished. (See: *Gatley on Libel and Slander,* 9th ed. (London: Sweet & Maxwell, 1998) pp. 233–35; *Yorkshire Provident Life Assurance Co. v. Gilbert,* [1895] 2 Q.B. 148 (Eng. C.A.): *Law of Defamation in Canada,* 2nd Edition, Volume II, Raymond D. Brown pp. 20–25).

>> Discovery has become broader in recent years. The test of "semblance of relevancy" recognizes that the purpose of discovery is not just to procure admissions, dispense with proof, and undermine the opponent's case, it is also to enable the examining party to know the case that must be met.

Marrello Valve Ltd. v. Orbit Valve Canada Ltd., [1988] O.J. No. 2710 (S.C.).

Pindling v. National Broadcasting Co., [1989] O.J. No. 263 (H.C.).

Lebans v. New Brunswick Publishing Co. (1996), 50 C.P.C. (3d) 285, per Miller J. at 288 (N.B.Q.B. (T.D.)).

Doucett v. Crowther (1992), 129 N.B.R. (2d) 1, 10 C.P.C. (3d) 322, per McLellan J. at 326 (Q.B.T.D.).

6) Opinions

Where the legality of the plaintiff's conduct is in issue, the defendant may cross-examine the plaintiff on her version of the facts. However, the plaintiff is not required to state whether or not the conduct was legal, as that involves a question of law and is not within the scope of examination of a non-expert witness. Accordingly, a police officer was not required to answer questions as to whether or not she believed her search of several school children was illegal.

> *Campbell v. Jones* (1998), 168 N.S.R. (2d) 1 per MacAdam J. at paras. 27–28 (S.C.).

Similarly, the defendant police officer was not required to provide opinion evidence concerning the quality of the investigative techniques displayed by another police officer who looked into complaints about the plaintiff's conduct.

> *Campbell v. Jones* (1998), *ibid.*, at paras. 31–32.

The Alberta Court of Queen's Bench held that a plaintiff was not required to express an opinion about patronage and cronyism alleged by the defendant.

> *Wilson v. Toronto Sun Publishing Corp.*, [2000] A.J. No. 996, 2000 ABQB 584, per Master Breitkreuz:
>
> ¶19 The second line of questioning in this group relates to the defendants' accusation in the various published materials of the plaintiff's patronage and cronyism in placing friends on the board rather than advertising the position so that it can be fairly filled in a competitive way. The questions relate to the witness's opinion of the alleged patronage and cronyism.
>
> ¶20 I think the answer to that is properly the domain of the trial judge, and I agree that the plaintiff's opinion on this matter is irrelevant....

7) Fair Comment

Where the defendant has pleaded fair comment, but not justification, he is not entitled on discovery to question the plaintiff regarding the truth of facts upon which he relies in support of the comment unless particulars of such facts have been set out in the statement of defence in advance.

> *Ministic Air Limited v. Canadian Broadcasting Corp.*, [1995] 8 W.W.R. 31 (Man. Q.B.).

Doucett v. *Crowther* (1992) 10 C.P.C. (3d) 322, per McLellan J. at 326–27 (N.B.Q.B. (T.D.)).

Parkland Chapel v. *Edmonton Broadcasting Co. Ltd.* (1964), 45 D.L.R. (2d) 752, per Riley J. at 758 (Alta. S.C. (T.D.)).

See, however, *Meyer* v. *Chouhan* (2001), 14 C.P.C. (5th) 81 (B.C.S.C.), where Master McCallum stated at paras. 12–13, 18:

> ¶12 The scope of examinations for discovery is determined by refer- ence to the pleadings. The Defendants have plead the allegations of fact in the documents incorporated by reference and ought to be able to question the plaintiff about those allegations unless the law prevents them from doing so.

> ¶13 The Plaintiff concedes that the Defendants are entitled to prove the facts on which the alleged defamatory comment was made unless those facts are themselves defamatory. If those facts are defamatory the Plain- tiff says the Defendant is not entitled to prove them (and, by inference, examine upon them) in the absence of a defence of justification or truth. That leaves open the question of how the determination of whether the facts are or are not defamatory would be made. That test would be of little assistance in the conduct of the examination for discovery.

> ¶18 The Plaintiff must answer questions at her discovery about the allegations in the statement of claim including those incorporated by reference. It will be up to the trial judge to determine whether that evi- dence is admissible in the context of the case each party has to make.

8) Rolled-up Plea

Prior to discovery, a defendant who pleads a rolled-up plea (which is not a defence of justification but a defence of fair comment) is obligated to give particulars of the truth of the facts upon which he or she relies.

Drake v. *Overland* (1979), 107 D.L.R. (3d) 323, per Laycroft J.A. at 328–29 (Alta. C.A.).

No questions as to the truth of the facts upon which the comment is based will be allowed unless the defendant has provided particulars.

Drake v. *Overland, ibid.,* per Laycroft J.A. at 329.

The failure of the plaintiff to demand such particulars will not prevent the plaintiff from objecting to such questions at the examination for discovery.

Drake v. *Overland, ibid.,* per Laycroft J.A. at 329.

9) Malice Rebuttal

The defendant is entitled to rebut an allegation of malice and is entitled to ask the plaintiff questions about the basis of the allegations.

> *Buford v. Globe Printing Co.*, [1949] O.W.N. 510 (H.C.J.).

10) Damages

If the plaintiff alleges diminution of profits, particulars should be given and questions allowed; but if there is no such claim there should be no discovery as to general damage in that regard.

> *Augustine Automatic Rotary Engine Co. v. Saturday Night Ltd.* (1916), 36 O.L.R. 551, per Boyd J. in Chambers at 552, aff'd (1916), 36 O.L.R. 551 (C.A.) [appeal did not relate to this specific issue].

To the extent that a plaintiff claims actual loss of profits, a defendant may seek information on examination for discovery to show that losses of profits arose from other causes. A defendant may seek detailed information, for example, about the pricing of the plaintiff's products and their quality.

> *Marrello Valve Ltd. v. Orbit Valve Canada Ltd.* [1988] O.J. No. 2710, per Sutherland J. at paras. 18, 21–22 (S.C. (Mast.)):
>
> > If the plaintiff were merely asserting the defamatory nature of the statement and were claiming only general damages on the basis that the statement was per se defamatory, there would be no justification for such an invasion of privacy of the secrets of the plaintiff's business. But here the plaintiff is claiming special damages in this action and I really do not know what all in the other proceedings. The defendant is not "fishing" in the gross sense of trying to find itself some sort of defence. It has settled upon its defence and claims to have, and has shown, some examples of cases tending to support its position: This is thus not a case where the defendant is seeking information which might enable him to make a case, or defence, of which he has no knowledge at present.

A defendant is entitled to cross-examine the plaintiff as to matters which have come to his or her attention which suggest that the plaintiff's reputation has been damaged before publication of the expression at issue, if such damage is alleged in the statement of defence.

> *Cherneskey v. Armadale Publishers Ltd.*, [1974] 45 D.L.R. (3d) 433, per Bence C.J.Q.B. at paras. 33–34 (Sask. Q.B.), rev'd on other grounds (1974), 53 D.L.R. (3d) 79 (C.A.).

A plaintiff may be ordered to answer questions concerning his character, competence, capacity, and ability where the defendant has alleged that he is unfit to occupy a public office.

Brown v. *Orde* (1912), 2 D.L.R. 562, per Middleton J. at 562–63 (Ont. H.C.J.).

Questions regarding the plaintiff's reaction to the alleged defamatory expression are relevant to damages. Presumably the answers to such questions would assist the trier of fact in determining the emotional impact of the expression on the plaintiff and the extent of the plaintiff's embarrassment or anxiety.

Wilson v. *Toronto Sun Publishing Corp.*, [2000] A.J. No. 996, 2000 ABQB 584 per Master Breitkreuz at para. 12.

It was held that the thickness of the plaintiff's skin cannot be measured, however, by asking her what the published words mean. Accordingly, such a question does not go to damages as it is not relevant to the grief and distress which the plaintiff felt at having been spoken of in defamatory terms.

Stumpf v. *Globe Holdings Ltd.*, [1982] A.J. No. 638, per Master Funduk at paras. 22–26 (Q.B.).

Where the plaintiff was not specifically named in a newspaper article alleged to be defamatory, but he subsequently proclaimed at a press conference that the article referred to him, the court ordered that the plaintiff re-attend at a continued discovery and there listen to and identify the voices of non-parties on a tape referred to at his previous examination for discovery. The tape showed who suggested the expression at issue identified the plaintiff.

Mouammar v. *Bruner* (1978), 19 O.R. (2d) 59, per Steele J. at 60–61 (H.C.J.).

D. NON-PARTY DISCOVERY

In 1985, the *Rules of Civil Procedure* introduced the concept of discovery of non-parties in Ontario.

Re Mulroney and Coates (1986), 54 O.R. (2d) 353, per Catzman J. at 360 (H.C.J.).

Ontario Rule 31.10 relating to examination of non-parties requires a party seeking such an order to satisfy the court that he has been unable to obtain the relevant information from other persons whom he is entitled to examine for discovery or from the person he seeks to examine (Rule 31.10(2)(a)); that it would be unfair to require him to proceed to trial without having the opportunity of examining that person (Rule 31.10(2)(b));

and that the proposed examination will not result in unfairness to the person the moving party seeks to examine (Rule 31.10(2)(c)).

Re Mulroney and Coates, above, per Catzman J. at 360.

Ontario Rule 31.10 has been applied to permit a defendant to examine an investigator employed by the plaintiff to determine the validity of libelous accusations, notwithstanding the investigator's assurances to employees of the plaintiff that statements made to him would be treated in confidence.

Care Canada v. *Canadian Broadcasting Corp.* (1999), 175 D.L.R. (4th) 743, per Southey J. at 749, paras. 12–13, 16–17 (Div. Ct.):

¶12 ... The purpose of Allen's interviews was to determine the validity of the allegations respecting Somalia relief that were contained in the report entitled "In the Matter of Management." The subject matter of the interviews was the same as the alleged libel.

¶13 I can see no merit in the argument that the communications between Allen and the employees whom he interviewed were not relevant to the plea of justification. I would expect them to be directly relevant.

¶16 Allen had been hired by Care to interview the employees of Care. Care then chose to commence an action in which Care alleges that statements made by the defendants on the same subject as the interviews are libellous. Those statements are relevant to the plea of justification for the reasons given above. I cannot accept that the confidence in which the communications arose was essential to the relationship of employer and employee between Care and the employees making the statements to Allen. Nor was the confidence essential to the relationship between Allen and the employees of Care. Unlike the relationship between a priest and a penitent, or a psychiatrist and a patient, Allen could not confer any blessing, advice or other benefit upon the interviewees which was dependent upon them making full and truthful disclosure to him. There was, of course, no continuing relationship between Allen and the persons interviewed by him.

¶17 Allen was not a solicitor. Care does not claim any litigation or solicitor-and-client privilege for the communications between him and the interviewees. The purpose of the interviews was supposed to be the determination of the truth. It should have been known by Care, Allen and the interviewees that any assurances of confidentiality could not displace the legal duty to give evidence if that truth became an issue in legal proceedings. That is especially so, in my judgment, when the legal proceedings are an action commenced by the employer at whose behest the inquiries were made.

In *Care Canada*, the Divisional Court took into account the fact that the defendants would be entitled to call the investigator at the trial and require him to produce the notes of his interviews, having regard to the general duty of everyone to give evidence. It was accordingly held to be unfair to the defendants to require them to proceed to trial without having discovery of the investigator and his documents.

In Nova Scotia, Rule 18 provides for discovery of non-parties without leave and without precondition.

> Nova Scotia, *Judicature Act*, R.S.N.S. 1989, c. 240, *Civil Procedure Rules*, rr. 18–20, 22, 24.

Rules concerning pre-trial discovery of non-parties are also found in other provinces.

E. DISCOVERY OUTSIDE THE PROVINCE

As noted above, in 1985, the *Rules of Civil Procedure* introduced the concept of discovery of non-parties in Ontario. An amendment to section 60(1) of the Ontario *Evidence Act* removed the basis on which earlier case law had refused to enforce foreign letters of request for such discovery.

> *Re Mulroney and Coates* (1986), 54 O.R. (2d) 353 per Catzman J. at 360 (H.C.J.).

Where the Nova Scotia Supreme Court granted letters of request for the examination for discovery of potential witnesses in Ontario, however, and the potential witness claimed immunity, the Nova Scotia court did not have jurisdiction to compel their re-attendance and testimony. Only the Ontario court had such jurisdiction.

> *Coates* v. *The Citizen*, [1987] N.S.J. No. 458 per Richard J. (N.S.S.C. (T.D.)).

F. IDENTIFICATION

1) Identification of Potential Defendants

A plaintiff who does not know the identity of the person who defamed her has several ways of obtaining that information, depending on the circumstances:

i)　Bring an action against a John Doe defendant and seek to examine a third party under the rules of court who may have knowledge of the identity of John Doe.

ii) Bring an action in the nature of a bill of discovery against a named defendant solely for the purpose of learning the identity of the defamer, so that a subsequent lawsuit may be filed against the defamer; or

iii) In Nova Scotia, obtain that information under special rules which provide for pre-action discovery.

If the third option is not available, the John Doe option is likely to present the lowest hurdle to success.

In *Irwin Toy Ltd.* v. *Doe*, (2000) 12 C.P.C. (5th) 103, [2000] O.T.C. 561 (S.C.J.), the court made an order pursuant to Ontario Rule 31.10 entitling the plaintiff to examine a non-party Internet service provider to determine the identity of the John Doe defendant. Wilkins J. stated at paragraphs 17–18:

¶17 Rule 31.10 contemplates that the moving party will demonstrate that there is reason to believe that the person sought to be examined has information relevant to a material issue in the action. Presumably, the true identity and appropriate address for service for a defendant could arguably always be something of such importance as to require its disclosure. Such disclosure, however, in my view, should not be automatic upon the issuance of the Statement of Claim. If such were to be the case, the fact of the anonymity of the internet could be shattered for the price of the issuance of a spurious Statement of Claim and benefits obtained by the anonymity lost in inappropriate circumstances.

¶18 In the circumstances of the case at bar, the moving party has demonstrated on the affidavit material filed before me that it has a prima facie case as against Joe Doe in respect to the allegations of claim made in the Statement of Claim. In my view, that is the appropriate test for the court to apply in determining whether or not to order a non-party internet service provider to disclose the identity of an internet protocol address.

The "bill of discovery" process requires the plaintiff to satisfy a stringent set of circumstances.

In *Kenney* v. *Loewen* (1999), 64 B.C.L.R. (3d) 346 (S.C.), Saunders J. (as she then was) held that in certain circumstances a plaintiff may bring an action in British Columbia solely for the purpose of discovery in order to facilitate an action against an unknown party where there is no allegation of actionable conduct by the named defendants, citing the following cases:

Norwich Pharmacal Co. and Others v. *Commissioners of Customs and Excise*, [1973] 2 All E.R. 943, [1974] A.C. 133.

P. v. *T. Limited*, [1997] 4 All E.R. 200 [defamation].

Bankers Trust v. Shapira and Others, [1980] 3 All E.R. 353.

Mercantile Group (Europe) AG v. Aiyela and Others, [1994] 1 All E.R. 110 (C.A.).

CHC Software Care Ltd. v. Hopkins and Wood, Chancery Division, [1993] F.S.R. 241 [defamation].

Coca Cola Co. and Others v. Gilbey and Others, [1995] All E.R. 711.

Societe Romanaise De La Chaussure SA v. British Shoe Corporation Limited, Chancery Division, [1991] F.S.R. 1.

Saunders J. held in *Kenney*, however, that the plaintiff had failed to establish the circumstances in which the extraordinary remedy of discovery should be granted, namely (at paragraph 33):

(a) the plaintiff must show that a *bona fide* claim exists against the unknown wrongdoer;

(b) the [plaintiff] must establish that the information is required in order to commence an action against the unknown wrongdoer, that is, the plaintiff must establish that disclosure will facilitate rectification of the wrong;

(c) the defendant must be the only practicable source of the information;

(d) there is no immunity from disclosure;

(e) the plaintiff must establish a relationship with the defendant in which the defendant is mixed up in the wrongdoing. Without connoting impropriety, this requires some active involvement in the transactions underlying the intended cause of action.

(f) disclosure by the defendant will not cause the defendant irreparable harm; and

(g) the interests of justice favour granting the relief.

Although the plaintiff in *Kenney* had established a valid claim of defamation, he failed to bring an action against one Watts when he could have done so within the limitation period under New York state law when he learned that an individual named Watts had passed the harmful misinformation to the defendant Loewen Group. In that action, Watts would have been a practicable source of the name of the originator of the defamatory expression.

In *Straka v. Humber River Regional Hospital* (2000), 51 O.R. (3d) 1 (C.A.), the court unanimously held that a prospective libel plaintiff had a free-standing right of action to obtain an order compelling a hospital to produce reference letters that were critical of his competence or character. After referring to *Kenny v. Loewen* (1999), 64 B.C.L.R. (3d) 346 (S.C.) and *Interclaim Holdings Ltd. v. Down* (2000), 16 C.B.R. (4th) 84 (Alta. Q.B.), Morden

J.A. concluded (at paragraph 32) the equitable action for discovery coexists with the Ontario *Rules of Practice*:

> The proceeding may be brought by way of application if there are no material facts in dispute (Rule 14.05(3)(h)).

Discussing the circumstances in which an action solely for discovery may lie, Morden J.A. concluded:

i) the person seeking discovery must have a *bona fide* claim against the alleged wrongdoer [page 12, paragraph 37];

ii) the person seeking discovery must share some sort of relationship with the person from whom discovery is sought, or expressed another way, a person against whom discovery is sought must be "mixed up in the tortious acts of others so as to facilitate their wrongdoing" [page 12, paragraphs 37, 40]:

> Humber requested the reference letters in question and, if they are defamatory, Humber is "mixed up" or "involved" in the commission of the alleged tort, albeit entirely innocently. In other words, Humber is not a "mere witness."

iii) the person from whom discovery is sought must be the only practical source of information available to the person seeking discovery.

With respect to the requirement that the person seeking discovery have a *bona fide* claim, Morden J.A. stated [at page 16]:

> ¶52 ... The appellant does not know whether he has a cause of action against the reference-givers. It could be said that he is "fishing" to find out if he has a case. I do not think, however, that he is engaged in "mere fishing." ... He does know that the letters damaged his opportunity of being appointed to the active medical staff at Humber. Although it is nowhere expressly stated in the material, it is obviously implicit in the appellant's position that he is unaware of what facts could have given rise to these letters. He would like to find out so that he may take steps to clear his name through legal proceedings if this should prove necessary.

> ¶53 On these facts, I do not think that the appellant should be "non-suited" because his claim is not a bona fide one, i.e. that his claim should fail because the threshold requirement of a bona fide claim has not been shown. As I have said, we are concerned with an equitable remedy the granting of which involves the exercise of a discretion. The general object is to do justice. Accordingly, I do not think that a rigid view should be taken of the elements

of the claim. With this approach in mind, I think that it is reasonable to accept that sufficient bona fides has been shown to justify consideration of the case as a whole. The nature and apparent strength of the appellant's case is a factor to be weighed together with the other relevant factors in arriving at the final determination of the claim.

In the particular circumstances before it in *Straka*, however, the Court concluded the documents sought were protected from disclosure by privilege, applying *Slavutych v. Baker*, [1976] 1 S.C.R. 254 and the *Wigmore* conditions.

> John H. Wigmore, *Wigmore on Evidence* (Boston: Little, Brown, 1961), vol. 8 at para. 2285.

In Nova Scotia, the right of pre-action discovery is conferred in the *Rules of Court*.

> *Leahy v. A.B.* (1992), 113 N.S.R. (2d) 417 (S.C. (T.D.)).

b) Identification of Sources

Discovery relating to the identity of the source of defamatory expression published by the defendant may be relevant to the issue of actual malice in several ways:

i)   The source may confirm or deny that he or she provided the information allegedly relied upon by the defendant;
ii) Whether the source is real or fictitious may be tested;
iii) The precautions taken by the defendant to verify the reliability of the information provided by the source may be explored.

> *Wismer v. Maclean-Hunter Publishing Co. Ltd. and Fraser (No. 2)*, [1954] 1 D.L.R. 501, per Robertson J. at 516, 519 (B.C.C.A.), citing with approval the following passage of Scott L.J. in *South Suburban Co-Operative Soc. v. Orum*, [1937] 2 K.B. 690 at 700–1:
>
> > In the ordinary case of a libelous statement made upon the faith of information gathered from third parties, it is relevant to the issue of malice … for the jury to know, not only what the information was, but also any facts affecting the propriety of the defendant's action in accepting the information at face value to the extent of making a defamatory statement about the plaintiff upon the credit of it. The whole of the circumstances in which the defendant obtained the information are or may be relevant; and of these circumstances not the least relevant will be the position, standing, character and oppor-

tunities of knowledge of the particular person upon whom the defendant says he relied for his information. If the defendant is in a position to give those particulars about his informants, the plaintiff is entitled to know them in order that he may criticize the defendant's conduct and also in order that he may make his own inquiries about the persons named, with a view to attacking the defendant's alleged reliance upon the information so received. If the defendant is not in a position to say from whom he got his information, this admission may in itself be a valuable piece of evidence for the plaintiff.

Massey-Harris Co. v. *DeLaval Separator Co.* (1906), 11 O.L.R. 227, per Mabee J. at 228–29 (H.C.J.), aff'd (1906), 11 O.L.R. 591 (C.A.), both courts approving and applying *White & Co.* v. *Credit Reform Association*, [1905] 1 K.B. 653.

Waslyshen v. *Canadian Broadcasting Corporation* (1989), 48 C.C.L.T. 1, *per curiam* at 21 (Sask. C.A.):

> In light of the pleadings, the questions asked [about sources] go to the heart of the plaintiff's case. Since there will likely be testimonial conflict between Mr. Barclay and Ms. Neil, her assertion that a thorough investigation preceded publication supports the plaintiff's entitlement to her evidence as to the identity of her sources and to answers to all relevant questions arising therefrom. In cases such as this, one reasonable method to pass upon recklessness may be to examine the reliability of the sources and have them called as witnesses at trial.

The Citizen v. *Coates* (1986), 29 D.L.R. (4th) 523, per MacKeigan J.A. at 524 (N.S.S.C. (A.D.)).

In addition, the plaintiff may wish to interview or investigate the source before trial concerning matters relevant to a defence of justification.

Price v. *Richmond Review et al.* (1965), 54 W.W.R. 378, per Nemetz J. at 380 (B.C.S.C.):

> In this case the defence is justification. It may be that in certain circumstances answers will not be ordered to questions arising in examinations-for-discovery where the plea of justification alone is made. However, in the circumstances before me there is no doubt in my mind that the questions concerning the defendant, Carlton's, source of information in so far as they relate to the material contained in the newspaper article are relevant and must be answered ... The ... questions

[which must be answered] probe the sources of the writer's information for the relevant purpose of ascertaining whether the story is, in the words of Lord Denning, M.R., "a pure invention" or "the gossip of some idler" or "mere rumour."

Bouaziz v. Ouston, 2002 BCSC 1297, per Brown J. at para. 27.

The inquiry as to the identity of a source may also be relevant where the defence is innocent dissemination.

Hays v. Weiland (1918), 42 O.L.R. 637, per Hodgins J.A. at 643–44 (C.A.).

The inquiry may also be relevant to bad faith on the part of the defendant and the question of aggravated damages.

Hays v. Weiland., ibid., at 644.

Nevertheless, the court should normally decline to order the defendant to identify the sources of non-defamatory expression in the publication complained of which has been neither pleaded nor particularized, because such information is usually irrelevant to matters in issue in the proceedings.

Siddon v. Mair, [1997] B.C.J. No. 17, per Master Doolan at paras. 37–39 (S.C.).

The fact that disclosing the name of a source will mean revealing the name of a potential witness is no bar to disclosure if the information is otherwise relevant.

Hays v. Weiland, above, at 643.

If the name of an individual who created a document relied upon as a source of information is not relevant, however, a court may decline to order a defendant to inform himself concerning that person's identity or to disclose it to the plaintiff.

Baxter v. Canadian Broadcasting Corporation (1978), 22 N.B.R. (2d) 308 (S.C. (Q.B. Div.)).

3) "Newspaper Rule"

In some provinces, the courts have made a distinction between an action for libel published in a newspaper and other actions for defamation. This distinction is expressed in the so-called newspaper rule.

For example, Ontario courts have held that the newspaper rule applies to a libel action against a newspaper reporter and her newspaper. This is a rule of practice which requires the court, on public policy grounds, to refuse to order newspaper defendants to disclose before trial the source of information for the defamatory expression, "in the absence of any special reason to the contrary."

> *Reid v. Telegram Publishing Co.* (1961), 28 D.L.R. (2d) 6, per Wells J. at 10–11 (Ont. H.C.J.), citing *Hope v. Brash*, [1897] 2 Q.B. 188, *Hennessy v. Wright* (1890), 24 Q.B.D. 445n, *Marsh v. McKay*, 3 O.W.R. 48, *Sangster v. Aikenhead*, 5 O.W.R. 438, and *Hays v. Weiland* (1918), 43 D.L.R. 137 at 139 (Ont. C.A.).

> *Drabinsky v. Maclean-Hunter Ltd.* (1980), 108 D.L.R. (3d) 390 (Ont. H.C.J.).

> *Hatfield v. Globe and Mail Div. of Canadian Newspapers Co. Ltd.* (1983), 41 O.R. (2d) 218 (S.C.).

The purpose of the newspaper rule is to protect the source of the information, not the information itself.

> *McInnis v. University Students' Council of University of Western Ontario* (1984), 48 O.R. (2d) 542 (H.C.J.) per Holland J., leave to appeal refused (1984), 48 O.R. (2d) 542 (Div. Ct.).

> *Reichmann v. Toronto Life Publishing Co.* (1988), 28 C.P.C. (2d) 11 (Ont. H.C.J.).

Pursuant to the newspaper rule, the court will not order the defendant to disclose a document, including tapes or transcripts, if that would reveal the identity of the human source.

> *Reid v. Telegram Publishing Co.* (1961), 28 D.L.R. (2d) 6, per Wells J. at 14 (Ont. H.C.J.).

On the other hand, if disclosure of documents will not reveal the identity of the source, they should be produced even if they were obtained from that source. Documents may be produced to the plaintiff in edited form to avoid identifying the source before trial.

> *Hatfield v. Globe and Mail Div. of Canadian Newspapers, Co. Ltd.* (1983), 41 O.R. (2d) 218 (S.C.) per Master Sandler:

> > I have satisfied myself that one class of documents are copies of documents of public record, do not contain on them any writing or marking which would show the "source" or identity of the person from whom they came and thus should be ordered to be produced for inspection. A second class of documents are three newspaper articles and they do show the name of the newspaper who published the articles but not the name of the reporter who wrote the articles.

> > I thus order the defendants to produce for inspection the documents in BMY 1 that are identified in the content list envelope as Items 1 to 10. I further order the defendants to produce for inspection the

documents shown as Nos. 11, 12, and 13 on the content list (the newspaper articles) by omitting any material therein pointing to the identity of the newspaper from which these articles were obtained.

The newspaper rule does not constitute a privilege such as solicitor-
client privilege, nor does it entitle a journalist to withhold disclosure at trial.
It merely permits the court, in the exercise of a discretion, to defer the question of source disclosure until trial. At trial, disclosure will be ordered if the
judge considers the identity of the source to be relevant.

Crown Trust Co. v. *Rosenberg* (1983), 38 C.P.C. 109, per Saunders J. at 117
(Ont. H.C.J.) [not a libel case].

Atty.-Gen. v. *Mulholland and Foster*, [1963] 2 Q.B. 477, per Lord Denning
M.R. at 491–92 (C.A.):

> There is no privilege known to the law by which a journalist can refuse
> to answer a question which is relevant to the inquiry and is one which,
> in the opinion of the judge, it is proper for him to be asked. I think it
> plain that in this particular case it is in the public interest for the tribu-
> nal to inquire as to the sources of information. How is anyone to know
> that this story is not a pure invention, if the journalist will not tell the
> tribunal its source? Even if it is not invention, how is anyone to know
> it was not the gossip of some idler seeking to impress? It may be mere
> rumour unless the journalist shows he got it from a trustworthy source.
> And if he has got it from a trustworthy source (as I take it on his state-
> ment he has, which I fully accept), then however much he may desire
> to keep it secret, he must remember that he has been directed by the
> tribunal to disclose it as a matter of public duty, and that is justifica-
> tion enough.

The refusal by a journalist to identify her source may be considered by
the court when assessing damages.

In *Hayward* v. *Thompson*, [1981] 3 All E.R. 450 (C.A.) at page 459, Lord
Denning M.R. stated:

> The problem arises, of course, because of the settled rule that there can only
> be one judgment for one sum against all the defendants. I must say that I
> think that, in newspaper cases, it is impossible to draw a distinction between
> one defendant and another, either as to exemplary damages or aggravated
> damages or any damages. Suppose the unknown "informant" had been a
> defendant, he might have been a wicked inventor of lies. Or he might have
> been paid money for his story by a more wicked journalist. Again, the jour-

nalist may have written a comparatively innocuous story but it was "doctored" by the sub-editor, just as Mr. House says his story was. So long as journalists insist on keeping secret their sources of information (for which they are now to get statutory authority in cl 11 of the Contempt of Court Bill [now s. 10 of the *Contempt of Court Act* 1981] now passing through Parliament) I think they must take the rough with the smooth. They cannot expect the jury to believe that they got their information from a trustworthy informant on whom they were entitled to rely, when they refuse to give his name. They cannot expect the jury to believe that it was not solicited or not paid for or not rewarded by them when they will not disclose how they got it. They cannot expect the jury to be sympathetic to them when they "lose" their notebooks, so they cannot be disclosed to the court. The assessment of damages is peculiarly the province of the jury in an action of libel. If they take a poor view of the conduct of any of the defendants, be it journalist, sub-editor, editor or proprietor, they are entitled to fix whatever sum they think fit in aggravation of damages without distinguishing between them, so long as they do not wander off into the forbidden territory of exemplary damages. That was made plain by Lord Devlin in *Rookes* v. *Barnard*, [1964] 1 All ER 367, [1964] AC 1129.

One Alberta Court has applied the newspaper rule to a non-media defendant. In *Red Deer Nursing Home Ltd.* v. *Taylor* (1968), 1 D.L.R. (3d) 491 (Alta. S.C. (T.D.)), MacDonald J. of the Alberta Supreme Court held that the defendant, who was a member of Red Deer municipal council and a candidate in the provincial election, was not required to answer questions about the sources she relied on, stating at pages 500–1:

> I feel that the defendant in participating as a candidate in an election campaign should be allowed as much freedom of comment as would be given to a newspaper and that it would not only be impractical but unfair to ask a candidate or expect a candidate to disclose or to be able to disclose the precise sources of all of the information respecting all the matters of public interest which would be discussed by her formally or informally during an election campaign.

It has been held that a novelist is not entitled to the protection of the newspaper rule. Accordingly, the Ontario Superior Court ordered the defendant novelist to answer discovery questions about the identity of his sources where that information was relevant to his plea that he had not intended to refer to the plaintiff.

Bennett v. *Gage Educational Publishing Ltd.* (1980), 16 C.P.C. 241 (Ont. S.C.).

The New Brunswick Court of Queen's Bench ordered the defendant newspaper to disclose on discovery its sources of information for an article where the plaintiff alleged express malice and the defendant pleaded fair comment. The court held that information provided to the individual defendant by his sources may be relevant to establish ill intent on the part of the defendant and noted that the discovery rules in New Brunswick were much broader than the rules in England, where the newspaper rule originated.

Rocca Enterprises Ltd. v. *University Press of New Brunswick Ltd.* (1989), 103 N.B.R. (2d) 224 (Q.B. (T.D.)) per Russell J.

The newspaper rule has been rejected in British Columbia and Saskatchewan.

McConachy v. *Times Publishers Ltd.* (1964), 49 D.L.R. (2d) 349, per Norris J.A. at 361–62 (B.C.C.A.).

> To restrict an examination for discovery by applying the English rule of practice that no interrogatories as to a defendant's sources of information shall be allowed is to deny a party a right given by our Rules to conduct a searching cross-examination of the other party.

Charman v. *Canadian Newspapers Co.*, [1991] B.C.J. No. 2625 (S.C.).

Waslyshen v. *Canadian Broadcasting Corporation* (1989), 48 C.C.L.T. 1, *per curiam* at 19 (Sask. C.A.).

In Nova Scotia, the Court of Appeal has ordered the disclosure, at examination for discovery of the defendant, of the identity of sources who did not have a special confidential relationship with a press defendant. It appears, however, that the newspaper rule has not been rejected outright in Nova Scotia but will only be applied if, after balancing the plaintiff's right to obtain full disclosure against free press rights, the latter outweighs the former.

The Citizen et al v. *Coates* (1986), 29 D.L.R. (4th) 523, per MacKeigan J.A. at 527 (N.S.S.C. (A.D.)):

> Relevancy is the first and paramount requirement for an order compelling a witness to testify.... Our discovery rules are very broad and "are designed to ensure the fullest possible disclosure of the facts and issues before trial.... Despite the breadth of our rules, the acid test for compellability, the test which must be applied before entering upon any balancing of public interest, is whether the answer sought is relevant at all (Rule 18.09(1)) and appears "reasonably calculated to lead to the discovery of admissible evidence."

In Manitoba, lower courts have declined to apply the "newspaper rule" in certain cases, but have not clearly rejected its potential application on appropriate facts.

Leslie v. Sterling Land Development Corp. (c.o.b. Sterling Real Estate Investment Services), [1993] M.J. No. 107 (Man. Q.B.), per Master Goldberg:

> In the case before me, the defence plea is not confined to justification. The defendants have pled qualified privilege and absence of malice. I am persuaded that the sources of the statements made to the appraiser are relevant in the circumstances.

Mackness v. University of Manitoba Faculty Assn., [1995] 8 W.W.R. 163, per Master Bolton at 167 (Man. Q.B.):

> This decision cannot constitute a blanket denial of the invocation of "the newspaper rule" in Manitoba. It is simply a finding that full discovery is appropriate in this case.

English authorities should be considered with caution by Canadian ligitants. None of the defamation statutes of the common law provinces or territories has a counterpart to the English Rule 0.82, r. 6, which provides:

> In an action for libel or slander where the defendant pleads that the words or matters complained of are fair comment on a matter of public interest or were published on a privileged occasion, no interrogatories as to the defendant's sources of information or grounds of belief shall be allowed.

Adams v. Sunday Pictorial Newspapers (1920) Ltd. and Champion, [1951] 1 K.B. 354, per Lord Denning at 358.

A plaintiff may also resist disclosure of a source. Taylor J.A. of the British Columbia Court of Appeal recently refused a plaintiff leave to appeal a decision of a Supreme Court Master in Chambers ordering the plaintiff, a university professor, to disclose the identity of the person who gave him the allegedly defamatory draft letter which the defendant faculty member allegedly prepared for consideration by a faculty committee. The plaintiff had promised confidentiality to his source and suggested he might have to abandon his claim rather than compromise his source.

Taylor J.A. held that discretion will not be exercised in favour of protecting confidences if the result will be significantly to hamper the other party in preparing or presenting their case, citing *Belzberg v. British Columbia Television Broadcasting Systems Ltd. and Jackson* (1981), 31 B.C.L.R. 140 (B.C.C.A.), varying, [1981] 3 W.W.R. 85 (B.C.S.C.).

Although Taylor J. observed that a "factor which might cause the courts to give special consideration in such cases is the assertion that the public interest is served by ensuring that the media maintain access to sources of information of public importance," he noted it did not arise for consideration in this case. Further, he held the case was "not at all analogous to those [cases] in which disclosure has been sought of a defendant's source of information," the case did not involve an issue of general importance, and the applicant had no prospect of persuading a panel of the Court of Appeal that the Master had erred in exercising his discretion.

> *Tatum* v. *Limbrick* (1992), 64 B.C.L.R. (2d) 252 (C.A.), aff'g, [1991] B.C.J. No. 2789 (S.C.), aff'g, [1990] B.C.J. No. 2717 (S.C. (Mast.)).

Confidential sources present special issues for future consideration by the court. The Supreme Court of Canada has not yet specifically ruled whether the constitutional guarantee of freedom of expression and freedom of the press contained in section 2(b) of the Canadian *Charter of Rights and Freedoms* protects journalists generally from being compelled to reveal their sources.

In *Moysa* v. *Alberta (Labour Relations Board)*, [1989] 1 S.C.R. 1572, the only case on the issue of source identification which has come before the Court, it was held that the evidence of the reporter did not demonstrate that the element of confidence was part of the continuing or any confidential relationship between the reporter and the reporter's sources. The Court declined to deal with the constitutional question in the abstract.

In *Dudley* v. *Doe* (1997), 151 D.L.R. (4th) 303 (Alta. Q.B.), the court ordered a non-party college to disclose an unsolicited letter it received from the Jane Doe defendant which was critical of the plaintiff's fitness as a social worker. The court rejected a claim by the Jane Doe defendant that she should enjoy a privilege analogous to a police informer. The court ordered that the allegedly defamatory letter be produced to the plaintiff although it would thereby identify the defendant.

Submissions by a newspaper's alleged confidential source that she should enjoy a privilege from disclosure within *Slavutych* v. *Baker*, [1976] 1 S.C.R. 254, or alternatively, that the newspaper rule should bar disclosure of her identity before trial, were recently rejected by the British Columbia Supreme Court in *Bouaziz* v. *Ouston*, 2002 BCSC 1297.

Even outside the context of *Charter* rights Canadian courts have recognized the existence of an overriding discretion not to compel journalists to identify their confidential sources.

Belzberg v. *British Columbia Television Broadcasting Systems Ltd. and Jackson*, [1981] 3 W.W.R. 85 (B.C.S.C.), varied (1981), 6 W.W.R. 273 (B.C.C.A.) [on the issue that the pleadings before the chambers judge did not raise an issue making source identification relevant]. Per Berger J. at 3 W.W.R. 85 at 89:

> ... while in the case of confidences entrusted to journalists there is a public interest in seeing that the media have the fullest access to sources of information that will enable them to be vigilant in their scrutiny of all of our institutions, and while litigants may be said to be seeking merely to vindicate private rights, there is nevertheless an over-riding public interest in seeing that justice is done in any suit before the courts. To that overriding interest confidences entrusted to journalists may have to give way.

R. v. *Hughes*, [1998] B.C.J. No. No. 1694 (S.C.).

Fullowka v. *Royal Oak Mines Inc.*, [2001] N.W.T.J. No. 4 (S.C.) [media non-defendant not required to produce video outtakes].

Alternatively, the court has jurisdiction to limit disclosure of the identity of a confidential source to the plaintiff and his or her counsel and to require an undertaking from the plaintiff to the court that he or she will not direct-ly or indirectly disclose the name or other particulars of the informant or source to any person.

Bouaziz v. *Ouston*, 2002 BCSC 1297, per Brown J. at para. 43 [the plaintiff did not object to this condition].

English decisions concerning protection of news media confidential sources should be treated with particular caution because legislation in the United Kingdom has shifted the balance on the side of non-disclosure.

Bouaziz v. *Ouston, ibid.*, per Brown J. at para. 37.

Libel litigants should also consider the implications of *National Post* v. *Canada*, [2004] O.J. 178, where Benotto J. of the Ontario Superior Court of Justice set aside a criminal search warrant and assistance order aimed at identifying a journalist's confidential source. The source information was held to be protected by privilege in the very specific circumstances of the case. The court refused to recognize a generic privilege or to develop guide-lines for source protection, stating that the existence of privilege must be determined on a case-by-case basis.

4) Statutory Source Protection

Certain provincial statutes insulate sources and information from the court discovery process. For example, the Nova Scotia *Evidence Act*, R.S.N.S. 1989, c. 154, provides in section 60 that a witness is excused from answering any question, or producing any report, statement, memorandum, recommendation, document, or information of, or made by, a research committee of a hospital, a hospital committee established for the purpose or studying or evaluating medical or hospital care or practices of a hospital, or a research committee recognized by the Minister of Health and Fitness and approved for the purposes of the section. This provision has been held to bar discovery in an action alleging, *inter alia*, defamation.

> *MacKenzie v. Kutcher*, 2003 NSSC 76, per Boudreau J. at para. 24, appeal dismissed, [2004] N.S.J. No. 6, 2004 NSCA 4.

CHAPTER TWENTY-EIGHT

Evidence at Trial

A. INTRODUCTION

This chapter should be read with the chapters concerning substantive defences. Court decisions which discuss the admissibility of certain types of evidence in defamation proceedings, or the weight to be given it, are the principal topic of discussion below. However, a number of court rulings are included because they illustrate how certain forms of evidence may be employed at trial.

B. THE PLAINTIFF'S EVIDENCE

1) Libel

The plaintiff must lead evidence to establish the following material facts, unless there have been formal admissions making such proof unnecessary:

1. the content of the allegedly defamatory expression;
2. if the expression is innocent on its face, or has some special meaning, proof of the extrinsic facts and circumstances which give that expression a defamatory sting;
3. if the expression does not identify the plaintiff, proof of the extrinsic facts and circumstances which establish that it is of and concerning the plaintiff to a select audience knowing those facts and circumstances; and
4. publication by the defendant.

2) Slander

Where the claim is for slander, the plaintiff must also prove special damage unless the slander is actionable *per se* or is deemed by a provincial defamation statute to cause damage.

C. PUBLICATION

1) Introduction

Publication is the essence of defamation. The plaintiff must introduce evidence that the statement was read, seen, heard, or otherwise communicated to a third party.

> *McNichol v. Grandy*, [1931] S.C.R. 696.

It has been held that embarking on calling defence evidence is to be taken as a virtual admission of publication by the defendant.

> *Patching v. Howarth*, [1930] 4 D.L.R. 489, per MacDonald C.J.B.C. at 490 (B.C.C.A.), affirming [1930] 2 D.L.R. 776.

Certain presumptions can assist a plaintiff to prove publication:

i)   a printed copy of a newspaper or other periodical publication is proof, in the absence of evidence to the contrary, of the publication of the printed copy and of the truth of the statements in that newspaper identifying the proprietor and publisher;

> *Libel and Slander Act*, R.S.B.C. 1996, c. 263, s.12(2).

ii)   when a libelous book or magazine is located in a lending library, publication to library subscribers is presumed;

> *Vizetelly v. Mudie's Select Library Limited*, [1900] 2 Q.B. 170 (C.A.).

iii) the sale of a book, magazine, or pamphlet in the public, open shop of a known bookseller is presumed to be a publication by the owner of the bookshop.

> *Rex v. Almon* (1770), 5 Burr. 2686, 98 E.R. 411.

iv)   where the expression is contained on a website, there is presumed publication to one or more persons unknown.

> Patrick Milmo & W.V.H. Rogers, *Gatley on Libel and Slander*, First Supplement to the 9th ed. (London: Sweet & Maxwell) at 6.24, citing *Bristile v. Buddhist Society of Western Australia Inc.*, [1999] WASC 259.

2) Slander

Where slander is alleged, the accuracy and authenticity of notes or tape or video recordings may be called into question by either of the parties. The author of purported notes of conversations should of course be called to prove their contents. A party's failure to challenge the accuracy of notes or other records, if testimony is offered to substantiate their accuracy, may weigh against that party.

Kelly v. *Low* (2000), 257 A.R. 279 (Q.B.) at paras. 107–111.

Where the answers given by a defendant on his examination for discovery are read into the record by the plaintiff at trial, and one of the answers by the defendant is a denial that he spoke the slander alleged, that answer must be taken as against the plaintiff regarding the defendant's denial that he used those words.

Robertson v. *McBride*, [1931] 4 D.L.R. 132, per Duff J. at 136 (S.C.C.).

When the defamatory expression is intended only to be communicated to the plaintiff but is unintentionally communicated by the defendant to a third party, the burden is on the defendant to show that the communication to the third party could not have been anticipated and did not occur through his negligence. A defendant may not be liable for a purely accidental communication to a third person who hears him utter a slander — the defendant not knowing, nor having any reason to suppose, that any person other than the plaintiff is within earshot, and being free from any fault leading to the communication to the third person.

McNichol v. *Grandy*, [1931] S.C.R. 696 per Duff J. at 704 [eavesdropper overheard loud, angry tones of defendant speaking to plaintiff in an adjoining room].

Dictating a letter to a stenographer in the ordinary course of business without further publication other than the typing by her and mailing to the plaintiff is probably slander, not libel.

Lawrence v. *Finch*, [1931] 1 D.L.R. 689, per Masten J.A. at 692 (Ont. S.C. (A.D.)) [nominal damages awarded].

A defendant who denies making allegedly slanderous remarks may cross-examine the plaintiff on his conversations with others to whom he might reasonably have been expected to refer to the slanderous remark, to establish that no reference to it was made. Furthermore, a defendant may testify that he would not have wanted to say anything to the effect of the alleged slander.

James J. Zelazo Professional Corp. v. *Daviduk Montgomery*, [1998] A.J. No. 445, per Moreau J. at paras. 73–75 (Q.B.).

In slander actions, the court must determine whether the alleged expression was published by the defendant, or whether anything to the like effect was said or mentioned by the defendant, and if so, whether it was mentioned as an allegation of fact or simply as a matter which had been reported to him or her.

Shapiro v. *Vancouver*, [1979] B.C.J. No. 577 per Fulton J. at paras. 24–25, 30.

3) Libel

An expert's evidence comparing 'ne writing in a certain allegedly defamatory letter with certain other writing may not be admissible unless both the letter and the specimen of writing are produced.

Morin v. *Walter*, [1924] 4 D.L.R. 140, per Mignault J. at 149 (S.C.C.).

4) Statements Made by a Source

A police source, sued as a defendant, may admit to making certain statements attributed to him by the news media but deny making other statements attributed to him by the news media, or alternatively may allege that his statements were taken out of context. If accepted, this exculpatory testimony may well exonerate him of liability.

Grassi v. *WIC Radio (c.o.b. CKNW/98)*, [2000] 5 W.W.R. 119 at paras. 59, 68, 69 (B.C.S.C.) [police source denied statement attributed to him in a radio broadcast].

5) Vicarious Liability

A corporation is liable for the defamatory expression made by its servants or agents while performing a duty under its orders. Where the statement has been made by an individual defendant who is employed by the corporate defendant, the latter may in appropriate circumstances lead evidence that the statement would not have been made by the employee within the scope of his employment.

Harrison v. *Joy Oil Co.*, [1938] 4 D.L.R. 360 (Ont. C.A.) [corporation nevertheless held liable].

Newlands v. *Sanwa McCarthy Securities Ltd.* (1996), 12 O.T.C. 81 at para. 28 (Gen. Div.).

The vicarious liability of a principal for the defamatory words of an agent applies to attach liability to the principal for slanderous words spoken by the agent.

> *Dalrymple v. Sun Life Assurance Co. of Canada*, [1966] 2 O.R. 227 per Evans J.A. at 232 (C.A.), aff'd (1967), 60 D.L.R. (2d) 192 (S.C.C.).

Defendants may attempt to demonstrate that they had no knowledge of and did not authorize the publication of defamatory material. Where a defendant printing company at first denied printing libellous material, but when confronted with expert evidence agreed its presses had been so employed, a judge rejected evidence by the company manager offered through the testimony of several employees that the latter had been on a frolic of their own, printing defamatory material without management's knowledge.

> *Lobay v. Workers & Farmers Publishing Assn. Ltd.*, [1939] 2 D.L.R. 272 (Man. K.B.) per Taylor J. at 275.

A defendant is responsible for a publication by virtue of an office held on a volunteer basis.

> *Bal v. Kular*, [2000] B.C.J. No. 1941, 2000 BCSC 1424 at para. 73.

6) Foreign Language

It must be shown by the plaintiff that a third party who understood that foreign language was present and heard the slanders when they were uttered.

> *Hahn v. Gettel* (1915), 9 W.W.R. 686, per McKay J. at 686–87 (Sask. S.C. (T.D.)).

> *Reilander v. Bengert* (1908), 7 W.L.R. 891, per Wetmore C.J. at 893 (Sask. C.A.):

> > Now it is unquestionably necessary, if words are spoken in a foreign language, that they must be spoken to persons who understood them, and that that must be proved. For instance, if slanderous words are spoken in the presence of the person slandered and other persons, and they are in a foreign language, and no person present understood each language except the person alleged to have been slandered, they would not be actionable. But in this case the slander was spoken to a man who, I must assume, understood German, because he states and swears what the German words were, and then he states what they mean in English. I am of the opinion that this is *prima facie* evidence that the man to whom they were spoken understood these German words, and it was not questioned that the words used were in the German language.

It has been urged that an interpreter should have been called, who, it was almost contended, must be proficient in German: that an ordinary German person would not be sufficient. I cannot appreciate this argument.

The plaintiff should consider, however, calling evidence from a professionally qualified interpreter to establish that the English translation of the foreign words, as pleaded in the statement of claim, is correct. This is particularly important where there may be a dispute about the meaning of the foreign words.

Hahn v. Gettel (1915), 9 W.W.R. 686, per McKay J. at 686–87 (Sask. S.C. (T.D.)).

Bal v. Kular, [2000] B.C.J. No. 1941, 2000 BCSC 1424 at paras. 8, 42.

The plaintiff himself may give evidence concerning the appropriate translation of expression in a foreign language.

Ho v. Ming Pao Newspapers (Western Canada) Ltd., [2000] B.C.J. No. 7, 2000 BCSC 8 at paras. 13–14.

Where slander in a foreign language is alleged, the foreign words set out in the claim must be translated into English at the trial, and evidence must be given that these particular words were in fact uttered by the defendant.

Polehyki v. Chromik, [1920] 51 D.L.R. 345, per Stuart J. at 350 (Alta. C.A.).

7) *Novus Actus Interveniens*

The defendant will not be liable where the defamatory matter is made known by the act of a third person for which the defendant can in no way be held responsible. This defence, *novus actus interveniens*, must be established by the defendant.

Hall v. Balkind, [1918] N.Z.L.R. 740 [butler opened letter out of mere curiously, having no right to do so].

Powell v. Gelston, [1916] 2 K.B. 615 [letter addressed to son opened by his father, at whose request the son had written — a fact unknown to the defendant — asking for information, which turned out to be libellous].

Gatley on Libel and Slander, 2d ed. (London: Sweet & Maxwell) at 98, cited in *McNichol v. Grandy*, [1931] S.C.R. 696.

A defendant who establishes that a letter was read by someone other than the person to whom it was addressed and that he was unaware that could occur, may succeed in disproving responsibility for publication. However, the defendant would be responsible for publication if he intended the letter to be opened by a clerk or some other third person, or if the defendant knew it would be opened by a clerk.

> *McNichol v. Grandy*, [1931] S.C.R. 696, per Lamont J. at 706, citing *Keogh v. Dental Hospital*, [1910] 2 I.R., K.B., 577 at 587; *Delacroix v. Thevenot* (1817), 2 Starkie, 63; and *Gomersall v. Davies* (1898), 14 Times L.R. 430.

Where a letter containing defamatory matter concerning the plaintiff has been negligently dropped by the defendant and picked up and read by a third person, the defendant will be held responsible for publication to the person picking it up and reading it.

> *McNichol v. Grandy*, [1931] S.C.R. 696, per Duff J. citing *Weld-Blundell v. Stephens*, [1920] A.C. 956 (H.L. (Eng.)).

8) Hearsay

Where the plaintiff seeks to prove publication by the defendant to a third party by testifying that the third party told him the defendant had uttered the defamatory words, such testimony offends the hearsay rule and is inadmissible because the truth of the statement by the third party is at issue and the third party is neither under oath nor subject to cross-examination. That the third party may be an agent of the defendant is irrelevant except where it is alleged in the pleadings that the third party has defamed the plaintiff and the defendant is vicariously liable, or where the third party was authorized by the defendant to make the statement to the plaintiff.

> *Dalrymple v. Sun Life Assurance Co. of Canada*, [1966] 2 O.R. 227 (C.A.), aff'd (1967), 60 D.L.R. (2d) 192 (S.C.C.).

9) Evidence of Circumstances Surrounding Publication

Other articles which are not intimately connected with the subject matter of the alleged libel are not admissible.

> *Brown v. Marron*, [2001] WASC 100.

> *McCann v. Scottish Media Newspapers Ltd.*, 2000 S.L.T. 256.

> *Pilcher v. Knowles* (1900), 19 N.Z.L.R. 368.

> *English and Scottish Co-op Properties Mtge. And Invt. Soc. Ltd. v. Odhams Press Ltd.* [1940] 1 K.B. 440 at 454 (C.A.).

D. IDENTIFICATION OF PLAINTIFF

Where a legal innuendo is pleaded, the plaintiff should lead evidence to establish the extrinsic facts relied upon to show the defamatory publication was of and concerning the plaintiff.

> *Fraser v. Sykes* (1971), 19 D.L.R. (3d) 75 (Alta. S.C. (A.D.)), aff'd (1973), 39 D.L.R. (3d) 321, aff'd [1974] S.C.R. 526.

The plaintiff should call testimony from at least one person to whom the derogatory expression was published to show that that person did conclude at the time that it referred to the plaintiff, on the basis of his or her knowledge of the extrinsic facts relied upon by the plaintiff.

> *Masters v. Fox* (1978), 85 D.L.R. (3d) 64, per MacFarlane J. at 68 (B.C.S.C.).

> *Booth v. British Columbia Television Broadcasting System* (1983), 139 D.L.R. (3d) 88, per Lambert J.A. at 93, 95 (B.C.C.A.).

> *A.U.P.E. v. Edmonton Sun* (1986), 39 C.C.L.T. 143 (Q.B.).

> *Taylor v. Massey*, [1891] 20 O.R. 429 (C.A.).

> *Jozwiak v. Sadek*, [1954] 1 W.L.R. 275.

> *Snider v. Calgary Herald* (1985), 65 A.R. 99 (Q.B.).

The plaintiff may present testimony from witnesses that they understood from reading the statement in the context of the circumstances outlined and from their knowledge of the plaintiff that the plaintiff was the person referred to in the defamatory expression.

> *Journal Printing Co. of Ottawa v. Maclean (sub nom. Journal Printing Co. v. MacLean)* (1896), 23 O.A.R. 324, per Osler J. at para. 37 (C.A.):
>
> > Then as to the improper reception of evidence as to the application of the libel — as to whom it was aimed at. It was strongly argued that this was nothing but evidence of opinion and ought not to have been admitted. I think the evidence went much further than this and that facts and circumstances were proved quite sufficient for the jury to find as they did. But even as to the opinion of the witness, nothing was admitted which has not been admitted in hundreds of cases, or that had not its warrant in the long and, so far as I know, unbroken course of practice adopted and followed almost from the necessity of the case. The writer of a libel is often careful to frame it, as, though the person attacked is not actually named, to enable any one who knows anything of the circumstances to identify him as easily and readily as if he were.

Abraham v. *Advocate Co.*, [1946] 2 W.W.R. 181, per Lord Goddard for the Privy Council at 182 (P.C.):

> All the witnesses were asked not only to whom they understood the words [in an article] to refer but also what meaning they attached to them. Where a plaintiff alleges that though he is not mentioned by name he is the person at whom an alleged libel is aimed, or, where a name is mentioned, that it would be understood by those who know him to refer to him, witnesses can be called to prove that they understood the words to refer to the plaintiff.

Atkinson and Atkinson v. *Canadian Broadcasting Corporation* (1981), 49 N.S.R. (2d) 381 (S.C.) per Glube J. [witnesses identified a child of the plaintiffs upon viewing a television broadcast; plaintiffs pleaded a legal innuendo that viewers would conclude the child had been removed from their custody to prevent abuse].

Where there is no direct evidence that the defendant spoke of the plaintiff by name, the court may infer from the fact that other persons knew of certain information and mentioned it to the plaintiff that the defendant had in fact referred to the plaintiff by name when uttering the defamatory statement.

Treitz v. *Suvila*, [1996] O.J. No. 4579 at para. 28 (Gen. Div.).

E. DEFAMATORY MEANING

Evidence is not admissible to show how a witness understood the allegedly defamatory expression unless it is first shown that the words were used in some other sense than their ordinary sense and had some meaning different from their ordinary meaning.

Green v. *Miller* (1903), 33 S.C.R. 193.

Damages may be reduced if the court finds that the plaintiff exaggerated the defamatory meaning of the expression.

Bal v. *Kular*, [2000] B.C.J. No. 1941, 2000 BCSC 1424 at para. 65.

It is for the judge to rule as a matter of law whether words are capable of having a defamatory meaning.

Lefolii v. *Gouzenko*, [1969] 3 S.C.R. 3.

In certain circumstances, outrageous statements will not be characterized as defamatory. If no factual details were uttered by the defendant, the court may conclude that the words are not defamatory.

968703 Ontario Ltd. (c.o.b. Headline Industries) v. *Vernon*, [1998] O.J. No. 2525, per MacKinnon J. at para. 26 (Gen. Div.), varied on other grounds (2002), 155 O.A.C. 386 (C.A.).

F. EXPRESS MALICE

[See Chapter 16, "Express Malice."]

An editorial witness for the defence may be called upon to candidly accept the grave nature of the defamatory allegations raised by the expression at issue, to acknowledge the error of senior management in failing to follow the fundamental requirement of examining the documentary proof, and even to concede that an internal document impresses him as showing malice on the part of an individual involved in the preparation of the story. This candour may insulate the editorial witness and other senior managers from malice.

Munro v. *Toronto Sun Publishing Corp.* (1982) 39 O.R. (2d) 100 at para. 55 (H.C.J.).

1) Defendant's Subjective Intent

The intention of the author and publisher is relevant and admissible on the issue of malice.

Hodgson v. *Canadian Newspapers Co.* (1998), 39 O.R. (3d) 235 (Gen. Div.), varied (2000), 49 O.R. (3d) 161 at paras. 37–42 (C.A.), citing *Fraser* v. *Mirza*, [1993] S.L.T. 527 (H.L.). [In *Fraser*, the House of Lords held that the defendant's intentions in respect of what he was trying to convey … are properly taken into account for the purpose of ascertaining what was the dominant motive operating on his mind at the time he wrote it."] Leave to appeal to S.C.C. denied, [2000] S.C.C.A. No. 465 .

It is an error of law for a judge to make a finding of malice on the basis that the defendant did not believe in the truth of the imputed meanings, if the defendant did not intend those imputed meanings.

Hodgson v. *Canadian Newspapers Co.* (1998), 39 O.R. (3d) 235 (Gen. Div.), varied (2000) 49 O.R. (3d) 161 at para. 42 (C.A.), leave to appeal to S.C.C. denied, [2000] S.C.C.A. No. 465.

Although the burden of proving malice rests on the plaintiff, the defendant must give close consideration to the desirability of testifying to his or her honest belief and legitimate motives. Evidence of due diligence, and attention to what was learned in the exercise of that due diligence, is admissible. This is particularly true where the defendant is a professional person who could be expected to satisfy a higher standard of care before making defamatory allegations.

Kelly v. *Low* (2000), 257 A.R. 279 (Q.B.) .

A media defendant may be cross-examined on her intended meaning, by being asked as to whether or not she accepts a dictionary definition of the word contained in the expression at issue, and whether she was aware of that definition at the time she wrote the article.

Ungaro v. *Toronto Star Newspapers Ltd.* (1997), 144 D.L.R. (4th) 84 at para. 15 (Ont. Gen. Div.).

2) Defendant's Post-publication Conduct

The plaintiff may lead evidence through cross-examination of the defendant about conduct — including an unrepentant attitude — displayed in post-libel interviews given to other news media.

Minors v. *Toronto Sun Publishing Corp.* (1997), 21 O.T.C. 325 at para. 94 (Gen. Div.), aff'd (1999), 122 O.A.C. 43 (C.A.), leave to appeal to S.C.C. dismissed, [1999] S.C.C.A. No. 472.

If the defendant appears on the witness stand to be demonstrating self-righteous arrogance, either in his testimony at trial or in the testimony from his examination for discovery which is read in at trial by the plaintiff, this may be evidence of malice.

Leenen v. *Canadian Broadcasting Corporation* (2000), 48 O.R. (3d) 656 at paras. 164–165 (S.C.J.), aff'd (2001), 54 O.R. (3d) 612 (C.A.), leave to appeal to S.C.C. denied, [2001] S.C.C.A. No. 432.

If the defendant claims source protection at trial when it is not appropriate, the court may conclude that it was done simply to sidetrack the plaintiff and cause delay.

Leenen v. *Canadian Broadcasting Corporation* (2000), 48 O.R. (3d) 656 at para. 165 (S.C.J.), affirmed (2001) 54 O.R. (3d) 612 (C.A.), leave to appeal to S.C.C. denied, [2001] S.C.C.A. No. 432.

The plaintiff may introduce tape, video recordings, or voice mail messages of the defendant concerning the plaintiff which pre-date or post-date the defamatory expression complained of in the litigation. If there is a substantial volume of such records, the court may conclude that the defendant was actuated by a desire to harm the plaintiff. This is particularly true if the communications are abusive, profane, insulting, or threatening. These records may contain intrinsic evidence of malice by virtue of their tone and contents and may also constitute admissions against the defendant that he or she was actuated by an improper motive in making the allegations at issue.

> *Fitzpatrick-Smith* v. *Jacobson*, [2000] O.T.C. 142 at para. 37 (S.C.J.).

In one case, a defendant condemned himself out of his own mouth, stating in his trial testimony that only a malicious or foolish person could read his articles complained of as making any charges against the plaintiff.

> *Safeway Stores Ltd.* v. *Harris*, [1948] 4 D.L.R. 187 (Man. K.B.).

Where one of the plaintiff's witnesses testifies that the defendant made a statement indicative of malice, the court may find that such a statement was made if the defendant does not take the witness stand to deny having done so, and call other persons who were also present as witnesses to support his denial.

> *Jerome* v. *Anderson*, [1964] S.C.R. 291.

3) Foreign Language

If the defamatory expression was published in a language not known to the defendant, he or she should give evidence of that fact. If a defendant who participated in the publication process testifies that he or she did not understand the contents of the impugned expression at the time of publication, and that evidence is accepted by the court, actual malice will not be found.

> *Popovich* v. *Lobay*, [1937] 3 D.L.R. 713 (Man. C.A.).

4) Warnings

Where a defendant has been warned in advance of publication of the dangers of publishing defamatory expression, a decision to ignore such warnings and to refuse or neglect to do further research may be held to constitute a clear case of actual malice.

> *Snider* v. *Calgary Herald* (1985), 65 A.R. 99 (Q.B.).

A court found that a defendant who repeated defamatory statements at trial after it had been made clear that the facts on which the statement was based were false, was acting with malice.

> *Haas* v. *Davis* (1998), 37 O.R. (3d) 528 at 540–41 (Gen. Div.).

A defendant may admit to being "hot under the collar" when drafting a response to a complaint filed by a plaintiff with a better business bureau, without this necessarily leading to a conclusion that malice was his dominant motive for publishing the defamatory expression. In these circumstances, the defendant may tender in evidence the plaintiff's communication which prompted his response in order to demonstrate the gravity of the plaintiff's accusation and the need for a vigorous response, so as to show why the court should give him "some degree of latitude."

> *Ibrajev v. 100278 Canada Ltd. (c.o.b. Canuck Door Systems Co.)*, [2000] O.J. No. 4049 at para. 9 (S.C.J.).

G. DAMAGES AND COSTS

1) Evidence of Damages

Although damages are presumed upon publication of a libel, a plaintiff who is seeking an award of substantial damages will normally call evidence of damages.

A plaintiff is unlikely to obtain significant damages unless she takes the witness box and submits to cross-examination.

> The [plaintiff] did not give evidence although his conduct, if not his honesty, was impugned. I would be better satisfied if, under such circumstances, one seeking damages for injury to his reputation would at least allow the trial judge to see him in the witness box, and also submit to cross-examination.
>
> *Anderson v. Smythe*, [1935] 4 D.L.R. 72 per Macdonald J.A. at 75 (B.C.C.A.).

The defendant will not be subject to the same criticism if he or she does not testify, particularly where practically all, if not all, of his or her examination for discovery is placed in evidence by the plaintiff as part of his case, and it covers the whole ground. In many cases, direct and positive statements in such discovery evidence may go to negative malice.

> *Anderson v. Smythe, ibid.*

In addition, evidence must be tendered to support a claim for aggravated damages, punitive damages, or special damages.

2) General Damages

The plaintiff is entitled to lead evidence as to his position and standing in the community in order to show that very many people who read the matter complained of would actually know him or know of him.

Bickel v. John Fairfax and Sons Limited, [1981] 2 N.S.W.L.R. 474 at 482, per Hunt, J.

It has been held that the plaintiff may not lead evidence of his or her general good reputation unless it is first attacked by the defence.

Wiley v. Toronto Star Newspapers Ltd. (1988), 65 O.R. (2d) 31 [varied on other grounds: (1990), 74 O.R. (2d) 100 (C.A.)] per MacFarland J. at 37 (H.C.J.):

> In an action for libel the law presumes that the plaintiff's character is good until the contrary is proved and the plaintiff can safely rest on that presumption: see *Gatley on Libel and Slander*, 8th ed., p. 548.
>
> Counsel for the plaintiff intended to call a number of persons prominent in the legal profession to attest to [the plaintiff] Mr. Wiley's good character and professional competence. As the defence challenged neither the plaintiff's character nor his professional competence, I did not allow such evidence to be called. The exception was the witness Michael Wadsworth who I permitted to testify only because he was very shortly leaving the jurisdiction. As I explained, I allowed Mr. Wadsworth to testify in order that his evidence would be available in the event there was some evidence led by the defence to challenge the plaintiff's reputation or character — in a sense reply evidence out of turn.
>
> As there was no such evidence led by the defence, I have disregarded Mr. Wadsworth's evidence in its entirety.

An opposing view expressed in certain Australian decisions is that evidence of good reputation may be tendered in the plaintiff's case in chief.

Bickel v. John Fairfax and Sons Limited, above, at 482–83, per Hunt J. at 483:

> All this means, as I understand it, is that a plaintiff need not lead evidence of injury to his reputation to establish his cause of action because some such injury is presumed. It does not mean that the plaintiff's reputation is necessarily presumed to be good, only that whatever his reputation is, it has suffered some injury.
>
> But whether the presumption be that the plaintiff's reputation was good or merely that it received some injury there is, in my opinion, neither logic nor principle to support the further step which the defendants take, that the evidence of good reputation is not only unnecessary but also "irrelevant" (as Gatley puts it) or inadmissible, as the defendants argue. Whichever presumption it is, it is clearly not an irrebuttable one. All that it does is to relieve a plaintiff of proof of an element of his cause of action so that if no evidence is led on that issue he

has nevertheless discharged his burden of proof and the jury must conclude that his reputation is good (or has been injured) unless the contrary is proved. ...

So far as I have been able to discover, a party is never prevented from leading evidence to establish an issue upon which he has a rebuttable presumption in his favour. ...

Moreover, in defamation litigation a question must arise in many cases as to the quality of the reputation which is presumed. A necessary consequence of the defendants' argument and one from which they do not shrink, is that a jury is obliged to treat a plaintiff with the highest reputation in the relevant sector upon exactly the same basis as a plaintiff with an indifferent reputation. To take an example, a bishop in charge of the church finances who is accused of embezzlement (who may not be widely known in the community) must, if the defendants are correct, be treated upon the same basis as a mere clerk who is similarly accused, so far as ordinary compensatory damages are concerned. In my view, this cannot be the law and I propose to admit the evidence of good reputation.

See also *Anderson v. Mirror Newspapers (2)* (1986), N.S.W.L.R. 735 at 737.

It is clear that a plaintiff may lead evidence of general good reputation only in the sector of his or her life which is relevant to the libel. Moreover, even in Australia, the plaintiff is not entitled to give evidence of particular facts in support of his or her claim to have such a general good reputation.

Anderson v. Mirror Newspapers (1986) N.S.W.L.R. 735 at 737.

The plaintiff is entitled to lead evidence of all the consequences of the defamatory expression.

McCarey v. Associated Newspapers Ltd. (No. 2), [1965] 2 Q.B. 86, per Pearson L.J. at 103 (C.A.):

> It must be remembered that in many cases of tort damages are at large, that is to say, the award is not limited to the pecuniary loss that can be specifically proved. In the present case, for example, and leaving aside any question of exemplary or aggravated damages, the appellant's damages would not necessarily be confined to those which he would obtain in an action for wrongful dismissal. He can invite the jury to look at all the circumstances, the inconveniences caused to him by the change of job and the unhappiness maybe by a change of livelihood.

Evidence of the plaintiff's own reaction upon learning of the libel or slander is clearly admissible.

John v. M.G.N. Ltd., [1996] Q.B. 596, per Sir Thomas Bingham M.R. at 605 (C.A.):

> On 1 November the plaintiff himself gave evidence, followed by Mr. Presland, Mr. Reid, and a number of representatives of the firm to whom, it was alleged, Mr. Scott tried to speak just before Christmas.
>
> The kernel of Mr. John's evidence, concerning the effect the article had upon him, was well summarized by the judge in his summing up:
>
> > ... he [Elton John] told you of the circumstances in which the article came to his attention. He was at his home in Atlanta in America when his mother who had got the newspaper in England telephoned him. "She read the article out in full at my request" he said, "I was incensed, absolutely outraged. The most satisfactory thing I have done in my life is to admit my problems, the drugs and food and face up to it and this article seems to say I had problems ... ." In other words, that he had failed to cure himself. I do take that into account in assessing the appropriate damages to award him as compensation for distress.

Hill v. Church of Scientology of Toronto, [1995] 2 S.C.R. 1130, per Cory J. at 1202:

> Hill movingly described the effect the reading of the press reports of the press conference had upon him and of viewing the television broadcast. He put it in this way:
>
> > I was sick. I was shocked. I understood from reading it that it related to access to the documents. The type of thing that Mr. Ruby and I had been dealing with over many months, and I was just incredulous.
> >
> > I was horrified when I saw it. I had had a long history of dealing with counsel for the Church of Scientology. Small problems, medium-sized problems and very serious problems had been raised between us.
> >
> > Every effort was made to answer those issues as they came up. When I saw the newscast, I realized that there was really nothing I could do to stop the information from getting out. I thought it was false. I thought it was a very dramatic representa-

tion. A well-known lawyer as Mr. Manning was — and he was gowned.

And he was standing before the High Court. The indication that I had been involved in opening sealed documents and giving permission was totally false. For me, in seeing it, it was equivalent to saying I was a cheat and that I had obstructed the course of justice. It was an attack on my professional reputation and I had no way of stopping it.

I also have no way of knowing whether there are people in the community who would be in a position to place some reliance on the fact that regardless of the outcome of the criminal case, Manning, a prominent lawyer, and the Church of Scientology of Toronto, had still expressed a view on September 17th.

Leenen v. Canadian Broadcasting Corporation (2000), 48 O.R. (3rd) 656, per Cunningham J. at 723–25 (S.C.J.):

> ¶191 It wasn't until Dr. Leenen returned to Ottawa that he first had an opportunity to review a videotape of this program. This was how Dr. Leenen described his reaction to what he watched:
>
> > Well, it's very difficult to describe and part of that does relate to the language barrier for which I have difficulties in expressing emotions, but at that moment I felt totally empty. The only previous time that I ever had that feeling so extensively was when I was a graduate student and I got a phone call that my sister had been in a very bad car accident and actually died an hour later at the age of 23. She was very close to me and it still creates emotions for me. That's the way I felt. I felt that something very dear had been taken away from me. I was gone. I was like in a black hole. After the foundation of your life has been taken away, you go down. I was sitting there. I didn't speak. I don't know for how long, maybe five, ten, fifteen minutes, speechless, number, like frozen for a time. It was a very weird feeling. A very feeling of hurt, that the essence for which I stood for, I felt, had been destroyed by this program. It was a disaster for me. Like a nightmare. That your reputation, your integrity that is so crucial for a scientist, is suddenly gone.
>
> ¶192 The impact of this program upon Dr. Leenen was devastating. It affected his relationships with his wife and children. He stated:

I was just there physically, but I wasn't there as a person. I was just like a ghost in the house. It was a very eerie feeling.

¶193 Dr. Leenen became withdrawn and non-responsive to the outside world. He felt his reputation as a scientist, the essence of what he was, had been destroyed by this program. When Dr. Leenen returned to work on the following Monday morning, he was greeted by a colleague who stated:

I saw the program. You have my sympathies.

Embarrassed, Dr. Leenen, usually a rather gregarious person, shunned the cafeteria preferring to take his lunch in his office. He felt that if one more person offered sympathy, he would have cried.

¶194 The very next day, in his clinic, one of his patients came into his office and stated point-blank:

Dr. Leenen, you wrongly prescribed nifedipine for me and you did it for personal gain, to make money.

To Dr. Leenen this was the worst accusation a patient could make because it went to the essence of being a physician. To Dr. Leenen, patient trust in his interaction with those he was treating for hypertension was essential. To be accused of placing a patient's safety at risk for personal gain was anathema to Dr. Leenen, something he had never experienced before. In Dr. Leenen's words when asked how important patient trust was, he stated:

Oh, it's absolutely crucial. Obviously they expect that I am knowledgeable and I have no doubts that anybody doesn't think that I am not knowledgeable. But the second component that is as important as knowledge is that the patient feels that you do the best possible for that particular patient and that no other loyalties, and certainly not money, would come into the reasons for prescribing something or doing something for an individual. Once that perception is there, that can never be taken away anymore. The trust is crucial for the patient-doctor relationship and if that trust, for whatever reason, is broken down, then one should really give up the doctor-patient relationship. And that is actually what this patient did. At that moment he said, well I can't come back to you anymore. And he didn't come back anymore.

...

¶196 While all of this was going on, Dr. Leenen had become quite withdrawn within the Institute, afraid that somebody would make a wisecrack about some element of the program. He stayed away from grand rounds and according to his nurse, Frances Allen, during grand rounds when CCB's were discussed, there was much joking amongst the residents about whether they would get a trip down the Nile if they prescribed the right medicine. When Ms. Allen informed Dr. Leenen about this, he described his reaction as being one of embarrassment, sadness and hurt. His nurse also heard many comments from patients about what they perceived to be Dr. Leenen's behaviour as depicted by the fifth estate. One very angry male patient told her that Dr. Leenen was prescribing Norvasc because he was getting a benefit. Another stated that during the program Dr. Leenen looked gullible and that he performed badly. Patients were either discontinuing or altering their medications and all of this, when it was relayed to Dr. Leenen, upset him greatly. These hurtful comments, especially from his patients, were devastating to Dr. Leenen and caused him great anxiety.

¶197 In addition to the observations of his nurse, we heard from Mindy Leenen, Dr. Leenen's wife. While he watched the program and for the next 24 hours she described him as being numb, shocked, devastated, and horrified. She said he was speechless, depressed, and physically pale. That night he was restless, agitated and withdrawn. The next day he was short-tempered and unable to interact either with her or the children, something which was totally unlike him. She stated this condition lasted for six to nine months.

[See also paragraphs 198–202 at pp. 725–726.]

Grassi v. WIC Radio Ltd. (2000) 5 W.W.R. 119, per Lysyk J. at 153 (B.C.S.C.):

Grassi testified that he first learned of the CKNW reports through a telephone call from a friend on Friday, April 18, 1997. He testified that the telephone call did not supply context or detail and it was only later that day, when he heard a CKNW broadcast on his car radio, that he realized his name had been linked with children. According to his testimony, the effect upon him was devastating, to the point of causing him to contemplate suicide. He testified to the effect that that Friday was one of the most distressing days of his life and that the subsequent news reports in The Province had a comparable impact. Among his concerns then and afterward, according to his testimony, were: the health of his wife, whose recent medical history involved a panic disorder; relationships within the family and with others, including those of their two school-age children; his relationships in the workplace and possible loss of his job; and the placing in jeopardy of his hockey coaching and related activities involving young people.

Evidence of the plaintiff's concern about the impact of the defamatory expression on his or her public image at the time of publication or afterwards is plainly admissible.

Hughes v. *Mirror Newspapers Ltd.* (1985), 3 N.S.W.L.R. 504, per Hunt J. at 508:

> During the course of his examination in chief, the plaintiff in this defamation action, who is a professional footballer, was asked what effect the publication of the matter complained of had had upon him. He answered:
>
> > It affected me as a player in that I was worried about my reputation and image to the general public.

Thomas v. *McMullan*, 2002 BCSC 22, per Ralph J. at para. 82:

> Mr. Thomas is a 40-year-old businessman who has lived in Langley since 1973. He has been active for many years in political organizations at the municipal, provincial and national level. In the mid-1980s he worked in Ottawa as an assistant to two cabinet ministers. He has also participated in a number of community organizations in the Langley area. It is Mr. Thomas' belief that future political activity has been wiped out because he is now seen as a liability to those he may wish to assist and support.

Prodor v. *Canwest Publishers Ltd.*, [1996] B.C.J. No. 2504, per Collver J. at paras. 23–24 (S.C.):

> He was devastated when he read the *Langley Times* articles. Essentially, he thought that it made him out to be a criminal, and that readers would think "another crook has fled the country."
>
> I will return to the emotional impact of the libel later in these reasons. However, I think it important to emphasize that Mr. Prodor's initial reaction was that fifteen years of hard work had "evaporated." In short, he considered that he had been "destroyed."

See also, *Young* v. *Toronto Star Newspapers Ltd.*, [2003] O.J. No. 3100, per Rouleau J. at paras. 214–24 (S.C.J.) [reviewing factors relevant to damages].

In order to establish the context for the plaintiff's reaction to the libel and concern for her reputation, the plaintiff may explain the meaning she gave to the words complained of. This testimony is not admissible on the issue of the actual meaning of the expression at issue, which must be determined by the application of an objective test.

Garbett v. *Hazell, Watson,* [1943] 2 All E.R. 359 (C.A.) per Scott L.J. at 359:

> The plaintiff gave evidence that that [publication] affected his position, as anybody would expect if you looked at those two photographs put together in that way in that magazine. He felt that the photograph meant that something very definitely wrong was being done by him, even though one person might put one meaning on it and another person a different one....

Hughes v. *Mirror Newspapers Ltd.* (1985) 3 N.S.W.L.R. 504 per Hunt J. at 509–10:

> Objection was taken by the defendant to the plaintiff identifying in his answer the imputations which he believed had been conveyed by the matter complained of.
>
> The defendant's objection was based upon the discussion of principle — but not the final ruling — in *Toomey* v. *John Fairfax & Sons Ltd.* (1985) 1 NSWLR 291. That discussion of principle was, however, very carefully and very deliberately restricted to the admissibility of evidence from witnesses called by the plaintiff as to the meaning which they understood the matter complained of to convey. It did not purport to deal with the evidence of the plaintiff himself as to the imputations which he believed had been conveyed. ...
>
> None of those propositions requires the rejection of the plaintiff's own evidence as to the meaning which was conveyed to him. That evidence from the plaintiff is led in relation to an entirely different issue. The evidence of his witnesses is led to establish the nature of the injury to the plaintiff's reputation — the effect which the matter complained of has had upon others. The plaintiff's evidence is led to establish the nature of the injury to the plaintiff's feelings — the effect which the publication has had on the plaintiff himself. That has nothing to do with the issue of reputation.
>
>   ...
>
> Similarly, the plaintiff has always been permitted to give evidence as to the natural grief and distress which he may have felt in having been spoken of in defamatory terms: *McCarey* v. *Associated Newspapers Ltd.* (*No. 2*), [1965] 2 QB 86 at 104. I can see no reason in either principle or common sense why the hurt to the plaintiff's feelings should not

include the embarrassment which he suffers concerning the nature of the imputations which he believes were conveyed to others. Once a person is entitled to establish a particular state of mind on his part concerning a publication, his specific beliefs and his specific assumptions relating to that publication must necessarily become admissible when those beliefs or assumptions induce that state of mind: cf. *Allied Pastoral Holdings Pty Ltd.* v. *Commissioner of Taxation*, [1983] 1 NSWLR 1 at 7.

As Lord Diplock said in *Cassell & Co Ltd.* v. *Broome*, [1972] AC 1027 at 1125, the harm caused to a plaintiff by the publication of a libel upon him often lies more in his own feelings, what he believes other people are thinking of him, than in any actual change made manifest in their attitude towards him. What the plaintiff believes other people are thinking of him necessarily includes the nature of the imputations which the plaintiff believes were conveyed to them.

There is, therefore, a clear basis both in principle and in precedent, quite apart from commonsense, for the admissibility of the plaintiff's evidence identifying the imputations which he believes were conveyed by the matter complained of. The jury will of course have to be told that they are not bound by the plaintiff's formulation of those imputations, and that it remains a question for them to determine how the ordinary reasonable reader would have interpreted the matter complained of — however the plaintiff may himself have interpreted it. ...

Testimony of other witnesses such as family members and business associates about their observations of the impact of the libel on the plaintiff is also admissible.

Thomas v. *McMullan*, 2002 BCSC 22, per Ralph J. at para. 82:

Mr. Thomas' wife described her observations of the effect of the publication upon her husband. She said that Mr. Thomas had become stressed, withdrawn and short tempered and it affected his relationship with his wife and children. Mr. Thomas' reduced income has had a financial impact upon the family. In addition, Mrs. Thomas testified that friends who were initially supportive appeared to change their opinions over time.

Vogel v. *Canadian Broadcasting Corporation*, [1982] 3 W.W.R. 97, per Esson J. at 161 (B.C.S.C.):

The evidence is clear that the impact upon the plaintiff of the programs, the ensuing controversy and the action itself was serious and lasting. He appeared to others to be depressed and to be getting no pleasure out of his job or other aspects of life, and I accept his evidence that that was the case. He resumed his duties after 20th March, but had to carry on in difficult and embarrassing circumstances. He was conscious that the staff of the ministry and others which whom he had to deal were suspicious of him, and that the level of trust and confidence existing prior to 20th March had been seriously damaged. Little was said to him to indicate the existence of such an attitude, but he could sense it in the reserve and formality with which others dealt with him. The overt indications of depression largely cleared about a year after the program and a few months before trial. That resulted in part from the efforts of his wife and family to "bring him around" and in part from his own realization, based on the evidence which came to light in the discoveries, of the weakness of the defendants' case. Nevertheless, the pressure on him continued and in some way increased in the months before trial. At one point, his senior subordinates came to him and asked him to drop his action because of the adverse effect which it was having on morale within the ministry.

Grassi v. WIC Radio Ltd. (c.o.b. CKNW/98), [2000] 5 W.W.R. 119, per Lysyk J. at 153 (B.C.S.C.):

> Grassi's wife testified about the extreme distress she observed in her husband after the initial news coverage and the depressive mode that manifested itself afterward. She and [a family friend] Ms. Woods contrasted his previously relaxed and easy-going manner with his subsequent guarded and withdrawn attitude.

The conduct of other persons towards the plaintiff following the publication of the defamatory expression is admissible. The plaintiff may testify that he was immediately shunned, called hurtful names, or suffered a decline in business revenue after the publication of the defamatory statement.

Garbett v. Hazell, Watson and Viney Ltd., [1943] 2 All E.R. 359 (C.A.) per Scott L.J. at 360:

> The plaintiff was … a perfectly decent man carrying on a perfectly innocuous business in an honourable way. The immediate result was that he was shunned by those who knew him. They used to call him by his Christian name and then they changed within a week of the publication and called him "Smutty," a word of obvious meaning. [The libel was that the plaintiff took indecent photographs of nude women]. He goes to Tooting, a place where he had carried on a flower shop in

previous years and had lived, and instead of doing a trade, as he said, of about £3 per week, during the time he went there he did nothing as a result of the libel. The place where he was then living saluted him in the same way. Counsel for the defendants, in the Court of Appeal, took the point that the evidence that the plaintiff was addressed as "Smutty" instead of "Sydney" was inadmissible. I reject that submission; it was admissible because it was evidence of the measure of damage done.

Ramsey v. Pacific Press, a Division of Southam Inc., 2000 BCSC 1551, per Taylor J. at paras. 44–45:

> The evidence of Ramsay is that he was upset by the attribution of the constituent's comments to himself for two reasons.
>
> The first is that it reflected poorly upon him because it could be perceived as an expression of his attitude as an MLA towards his constituents. Second, Ramsey was concerned about how his friends and neighbours, also voters, would view him in light of the words about them. This concern was highlighted by a threat of a long-time supporter and campaign worker who threatened to withdraw his support if in fact Ramsey had used such words.

Grassi v. WIC Radio Ltd. (c.o.b. CKNW/98), [2000] 5 W.W.R. 119, per Lysyk J. at 133 (B.C.S.C.):

> The consequences that Grassi says flowed from publication of the statements complained of are more conveniently reviewed later in these reasons in the context of assessment of damages. It may be noted in a preliminary way, however, that evidence was led about the impact of the statements upon his personal and family life, upon his activities involving contact with young people (notably, in coaching junior hockey and other sports), and upon his situation in the workplace. Grassi says that at work, in a wordplay on his first name, he was called "Paedophilia Phil," or "Paedo-Phil," or a variant of such nicknames. He asserts that it also affected his career to some extent, but he does not advance a claim for income loss.

Prodor v. Canwest Publishers Ltd., [1996] B.C.J. No. 2504, per Collver J. at para. 37 (S.C.):

> Stating that the tarnish will never go away, Mr. Prodor commented that people in Langley are no longer friendly, and even seem surprised to see him on the street. He does not feel trusted. The significance of that

is reflected in his stated belief that, "because a lawyer's reputation is the cornerstone of his existence, that has been taken away."

Testimony from witnesses other than the plaintiff relating incidents unfavourable to the plaintiff which appear to have been precipitated by the alleged libel may be received in evidence.

Cook v. *Ward* (1830), 6 Bing. 409 [public laughter at the plaintiff in a local church vestry was admitted "as identifying the subject of the libel, and as a proof of the consequences necessarily resulting from its publication."] at 1340.

Hughes v. *Mirror Newspapers Ltd.*, [1985] 3 N.S.W.L.R. 504 per Hunt J. at 510:

> The plaintiff in this action for defamation sought to lead evidence from his witness, Mr. Peter Peters (who conducts a radio talk back programme), that a number of listeners called his program following the publication of the matter complained of in the defendant's newspaper and expressed statements which demonstrated a hostile view of the plaintiff on their part as a result of having read the matter complained of.
>
> The objection taken by the defendant was that such evidence is mere hearsay and is not made admissible by the recent decision of the Court of Appeal in *Mirror Newspapers Ltd.* v. *Fitzpatrick*, [1984] 1 NSWLR 643. I disagree. What was held in that case was that a person's reaction to the matter complained of amounts to a state of mind or to an emotion, and that the existence of that reaction may be proved by giving evidence of statements made by that person out of court of his contemporaneous state of mind or emotion. Such statements, Samuels J.A. held (at 657), are admissible in principle. They are not hearsay but original evidence of that person's reaction to the matter complained of. Priestley J.A. also held (at 665) that such a statement made out of court (which he described as "the primary fact") was direct evidence of damage to the plaintiff's reputation caused by the defendant.

And per Hunt J. at page 511:

> What the plaintiff has sought to do in the present case is exactly the same. Mr. Peters was called to give evidence of statements made to him by other persons which demonstrated on their part a hostile view of the plaintiff as a result of having read the matter complained of. Such statements demonstrate the existence of a contemporaneous state of mind or emotion in those other persons, so that evidence of their statements out of court is original evidence of the existence of their reactions.

And per Hunt J. at page 512:

> The plaintiff also sought to lead from Mr. Peters evidence that the plaintiff's reputation after the publication of the matter complained of was bad in the relevant sector. A plaintiff is always entitled to lead evidence from witnesses that, as a result of the publication of the matter complained of, they subjectively thought the worse of the plaintiff. He is also entitled to lead evidence of the objective actions of others from which the jury can infer that those others had the same subjective reaction arising from the same source. As discussed earlier, the Court of Appeal has now held in *Mirror Newspapers Ltd.* v. *Fitzpatrick* that evidence from the plaintiff or from other witnesses of statements made to them out of court by others as to their contemporaneous reaction to the matter complained of is original evidence of that reaction itself.

Vogel v. *Canadian Broadcasting Corporation*, [1982] 3 W.W.R. 97, per Esson J. at 105 (B.C.S.C.):

> I will refer throughout these reasons to the first program, that broadcast at 6:00 p.m. on 6th March, as "the program." Its immediate consequences upon the plaintiff and his family were dramatic. On the same evening, the opposition demanded in the house that the offices of the Attorney General be "padlocked" and that the Chief Justice of British Columbia take immediate control of that ministry. There was a flood of publicity on television, on radio and in the newspapers. The plaintiff's house in Vancouver was besieged by reporters, including those dispatched by C.B.C., with their attendant personnel, equipped with cameras and microphones.
>
> On the morning of 7th March, the Attorney General suspended the plaintiff with pay, pending an investigation into the allegations. By the end of the weekend, both of the major Vancouver newspapers had, in leading editorials, demanded his resignation. The barrage of publicity was almost entirely adverse to the plaintiff and to the government for its failure, in the view of the media, to deal with the matter with adequate promptness and firmness.

And per Esson J. at pages 106–7:

> The Attorney General, with the assistance of a lawyer retained for that purpose, immediately embarked upon an investigation. On 19th March, having completed that investigation, he made a lengthy and detailed statement in the house, reviewing each of the three cases

referred to in the program and stating that his review disclosed no basis for the allegations of impropriety against the plaintiff.

...

That report, far from abating the storm of criticism, tended to increase it. Most of the comment in the media was to the effect that the report was a "whitewash."

And per Esson J. at page 156:

In the aftermath of the broadcasts, the plaintiff immediately went on leave of absence from his position and, after getting over the initial shock, sought ways to contain the libel. It was a hopeless endeavour. The allegations were too complex for a simple denial to be of any use. The storm of hostile criticism was so violent and continuous as to overwhelm any effort at reasoned rebuttal.

The plaintiff may also testify, in relation to his damages, concerning the effect upon the plaintiff of the damage done to others.

Vogel v. Canadian Broadcasting Corporation, [1982] 3 W.W.R. 97, per Esson J. at 161 (B.C.S.C.).

It is relevant to consider, in relation to damages, the effect upon the plaintiff of the damage done to others. He was the primary target of the program, but he was not the only victim. The damage done to the character of others is most obvious in relation to the Moran case. The imputation was Moran, his lawyer, and the Kootenay prosecutors had all participated in a plot to interfere with the course of justice, and it was implied that the Chief Judge of the Provincial Court had, at least, allowed himself to be used. It was also imputed to the prosecutors that they took part in a cover-up for the benefit of the plaintiff. Not only were Dr. Rigg and his family exposed to unpleasant publicity about a painful event, but Dr. Rigg was put in the position, quite unfairly, of appearing to have abused a friendship to gain an improper advantage.

And per Esson J. at page 162:

The former Attorney General, it was implied, had not done his duty, and in the uproar which ensued from the program Mr. Williams, Mr. Gardom and other members of the government were exposed to weeks of loud criticism. Other examples could be given. The knowledge of the hurts gratuitously inflicted on others because of their dealings, real or imaginary, with the plaintiff was a source of distress to him ...

Hodgson v. Canadian Newspapers Company Limited (1998), 39 O.R. (3d) 235, per Lane J. at 302 (Gen. Div.):

> Mr. Hodgson and his family were devastated by the article. He was distraught. His brother called him to try to get him to come over to talk about the article, but he just wanted to stay at home.

The defendant may testify that he received no support whatsoever from anyone to whom the defamatory expression was published, and that he and his wife felt obliged to leave their home town and move to another city.

Varga v. VanPanhuis (2000) 269 A.R. 211, 2000 ABQB 538, at para. 43.

Where a plaintiff testifies at trial that his reputation for honesty and integrity had never been called into question before the publication of the libel, he may be cross-examined to reveal that he had earlier sued for libel over similar allegations, and the pleadings in the earlier action may be filed as an exhibit. His attention may also be drawn to other public scandals in which his name was mentioned. The court may take this information into account in assessing the plaintiff's ability to evaluate the possible adverse effect which the publication in issue had on his reputation.

Munro v. Toronto Sun Publishing Corp. (1982), 39 O.R. (2d) 100 at paras. 50–52 (H.C.J.).

In assessing damages, the court may take into account that although the plaintiff has an unblemished and praiseworthy reputation, the underlying facts out of which the defamatory expression arose may be "such as to affect his complaint as to his reputation."

Per Macfarlane J. in *Stieb v. The Vernon News*, [1947] 4 D.L.R. 397 (B.C.S.C.):

> [The plaintiff's] statement that after one drink of beer, he fell into a deep sleep, leaving two girls and another man whom he had just met in that other man's room, is to me difficult of complete acceptance. I suppose any man may fall in with an evil companion by the way but when he does, it is not necessary that he sleep on his bed until the day breaks. He may do so perhaps without condemnation, but when he complains that the damage to his reputation is great, one may, I think consider these things in attempting to determine the real injury his reputation has suffered. I think here that considering the conduct of the defendants, which I hold to be free from malice, the facts regarding the publication, particularly the small number of its readers, who are not necessarily regular subscribers and the fact that the publication was simply an error arising through confusion or inattention and not in any other

respect condemnatory, that the sum of $350 is sufficient damage to allow the plaintiff.

The court may consider the plaintiff's behaviour, including his treatment of other persons, his position, and his standing in the community, as well as the limited scope of the publication and the harm actually caused by the libel, in awarding nominal rather than substantial damages.

Kelly v. Low (2000), 257 A.R. 279 at paras. 202, 204, 205, 218 (Q.B.).

3) Other Relevant Factors

a) No Request for Apology

It may be to the advantage of a defendant to demonstrate that the lawsuit was brought without any request for an apology from the plaintiff. This may support an argument that the plaintiff has brought the action to obtain the remedy of money as opposed to the immediate restoration of his good name. However, the court will have regard to all the circumstances before arriving at any such conclusion.

Grabarevic v. Northwest Publications Ltd. (1968), 67 D.L.R. (2d) 748 (B.C.C.A.).

In such circumstances, if the defendant would have apologized before the action, he or she should call evidence to affirm that it would have done so. It may otherwise be difficult for the court to draw an inference that the defendants are reasonable persons who would have given an appropriate apology and retraction had the plaintiff asked for one.

Grabarevic v. Northwest Publications Ltd., *ibid.*

b) Defendant's Financial Position

Evidence that the defendant is in a precarious financial position may influence the size of an award of punitive damages.

Fung v. Lu, [1997] B.C.J. No. 1316 at para. 14 (S.C.).

4) Aggravated Damages

The comportment and conduct of witnesses during the trial may come under judicial scrutiny. In *Leenen v. CBC*, the court remarked upon the fact that one of the defendants, knowing that the plaintiff had placed a mortgage on his home to prosecute his defamation action, said something to the plaintiff during a break in parallel proceedings to the effect that "somebody is going to lose his shirt" and "how's the mortgage going." This was held to be aggravating conduct.

Leenen v. Canadian Broadcasting Corporation (2000), 48 O.R. (3d) 656 at para. 213 (S.C.J.), aff'd (2001), 54 O.R. (3d) 612 (C.A.), leave to appeal to S.C.C. denied, [2001] S.C.C.A. No. 432.

A court will not lightly draw an inference that the defendant has been guilty of aggravating conduct on other occasions. For example, even where a plaintiff demonstrated that he was subject to "strange treatment ... by formerly loyal clients," the court held that other explanations were as probable, including the fact that the defendant may have spoken harshly about the plaintiff without crossing the line into defamation.

Musgrave v. Levesque Securities Inc., [2000] N.S.J. No. 109 (S.C.).

5) Punitive Damages

Where a defendant on cross-examination is compelled to admit knowing that statements published by him concerning the plaintiff were untrue, the jury will be entitled to consider that factor as justifying an award of punitive damages, particularly if the defendant has pleaded justification of his statements.

Ross v. Lamport (1957), 9 D.L.R. (2d) 585 (Ont. C.A.).

Defendants will be in a particularly dangerous position where the facts tend to indicate that he or she had a clear motive for heaping abuse and infamy on the plaintiff, such as revenge.

Ross v. Lamport (1957), 9 D.L.R. (2d) 585 (Ont. C.A.).

6) Special Damages

A defendant may lead evidence to establish that the cause of business losses was earlier adverse publicity arising from the dismissal of a previous libel lawsuit brought by the plaintiff.

Ward v. Clark (2000), 77 B.C.L.R. (3d) 364 (S.C.), rev'd, [2002] 2 W.W.R. 238 at para. 31 (B.C.C.A.), leave to appeal to S.C.C. denied, [2002] S.C.C.A. No. 73.

If possible, a defendant should seek to demonstrate that the body responsible for terminating a contract with the plaintiff, allegedly lost due to the defamation, independently reached a conclusion that the plaintiff was guilty of the wrongdoing attributed to him by the defamatory expression.

Hodgson v. Canadian Newspapers Co. (2000), 49 O.R. (3d) 161, per Sharpe J.A. at para. 50 (C.A.) [leave to appeal to S.C.C. denied, [2000] S.C.C.A. No. 465]:

> In my view, there was evidence to support the trial judge's finding that there was a sufficient causal link between the defamatory articles and the respondent's termination to justify an award of damages. ... Despite the fact that he was not guilty of any wrongdoing, the defamatory article rendered the respondent a liability that had to be disposed of. Had the Regional Council arrived at an independent conclusion that the respondent was guilty of the wrongdoing attributed to him by the article, the situation might well be different.

Evidence of repetitions of the defamatory expression is admissible in aggravation of damages, even though proof of malice is not essential to the plaintiff's case. However, such evidence cannot be considered for the purpose of allowing damages for the subsequent injury done by the repetitions.

Mercereau v. Hock, [1930] 3 D.L.R. 159 (Sask. K.B.).

With respect to damages, where the plaintiff has settled with another defendant who was a joint tortfeasor, the defence will want to tender mitigating evidence under the *Libel and Slander Act*, R.S.B.C. 1996, c. 263, that the plaintiff has already recovered or brought an action for damages, or has received or agreed to receive compensation in respect of a libel or libels to the same purport or effect as the libel for which this present action has been brought. That section clearly entitles a defendant to lead evidence of such a settlement in his defence.

Lawson v. Burns (No. 2) (1976), 70 D.L.R. (3d) 735 (B.C.S.C.).

7) Costs

A defendant who succeeds in demonstrating that the plaintiff has perjured himself at trial may succeed in persuading the court not to award costs to the plaintiff.

J.C. v. V.R. and C.A, 2000 SKQB 83 at para. 19.

8) Special Costs

In determining the amount to be awarded for special costs, the court will consider whether the defendant's conduct lengthened or shortened the proceeding and its impact on the plaintiff. Although it is the defendant's right to take every opportunity to thwart the plaintiff with the hope he will simply give up, if those tactics and that attitude do not produce a successful result and have made the plaintiff's work much more difficult, the plaintiff's allowable costs may significantly increase.

> *Leenen v. Canadian Broadcasting Corporation*, [2000] O.J. No. 3435 at para. 4 (S.C.J.), aff'd (2001), 54 O.R. (3d) 612 (C.A.), leave to appeal to S.C.C. denied, [2001] S.C.C.A. No. 432.

9) Justification

The court has discretion to direct that the plaintiff's evidence on justification be deferred to rebuttal, after the defence has presented its evidence.

> *Jeronme v. Anderson*, [1964] S.C.R. 291, per Cartwright J., citing *Beevis v. Dawson*, [1957] 1 Q.B. 195 (C.A.).

> *Makow v. Winnipeg Sun*, [2003] M.J. No. 79, 2003 MBQB 56, per Monnin J. at paras. 3–5 [discretion not exercised on grounds of difficulty in dealing with proper areas of cross-examination and possibly of splitting plaintiff's case].

H. NON-SUIT MOTIONS

A defendant is occasionally in a position at the close of the plaintiff's case to apply to dismiss the action on the basis there is no evidence relating to a material fact essential to the cause of action for defamation.

A non-suit application should be given particularly close consideration:

i) where it is questionable that the expression is defamatory of the plaintiff; or
ii) where it appears that a privilege defence is available.

For example in *Eagleson v. Dowbiggan*, [1996] O.J. No. 322 (Gen. Div.), the trial judge dismissed the defamation action upon the defendant's application for a non-suit. The judge concluded that the words in issue, including the pleaded legal innuendo, were not capable of a defamatory meaning in respect of the plaintiff. This non-suit ruling was sustained on appeal. [*Eagleson,* (1998), 113 O.A.C. 195.]

The non-suit motion is to be distinguished from an insufficient evidence motion.

Other instances where a defamation defendant has made a successful non-suit motion include:

> *Kelly v. Magnolo*, [1983] B.C.J. No. 376 at para. 4 [action dismissed against six of seven defendants].

Thomson v. Lambert, [1938] S.C.R. 253 [allowing an appeal from the Ontario Court of Appeal and restoring a trial judge's dismissal of the defamation action on a non-suit motion. The action had been barred because judgments had been recovered in the Manitoba courts against other defendants, who were joint tortfeasors in the publication of the newspaper libel at issue.]

Lacarte v. Toronto Board of Education, [1959] S.C.R. 465, dismissing an appeal from the Ontario Court of Appeal [1956] O.W.N. 844, which had dismissed an appeal from the trial judge's ruling on a non-suit motion. After the defendant's motion for a non-suit, the judge ruled that the communication was privileged, there was no evidence of malice to defeat the privilege, and directed the jury to find a verdict for the defendant.

In certain provinces, a defendant may be asked by the court to elect whether or not to call defence evidence as a condition of bringing a non-suit motion. That is not the case in British Columbia, where the *Rules of Court* specifically provide that a defendant is not required to elect whether or not to call evidence on a no evidence motion. Rule 40(8)(9) states:

No Evidence Motion

(8) At the close of the plaintiff's case, the defendant may apply to have the action dismissed on the ground that there is no evidence to support the plaintiff's case.

idem

(9) A defendant is entitled to make an application under sub-Rule (8) without being called upon to elect whether or not to call evidence.

The position is not clear in Ontario. The Ontario Court of Appeal recently declined to decide the point in *Eagleson v. Dowbiggan* (1998), 113 O.A.C. 195 at paragraph 10 (C.A.). The trial judge had more boldly concluded that a defamation defendant should not be put to his or her election whether or not to call evidence as part of the non-suit motion process, citing Sopinka, Lederman, and Bryant, *The Law of Evidence in Canada*, (Toronto: Butterworths, 1992) at 135, which in turn cited *M.V. "Polar Star" v. Louis Denker Inc.*, (1965), 53 D.L.R. (2d) 181 (P.E.I.S.C.).

1) Joint Liability

All those who participate in publishing and circulating a libel are liable as joint tortfeasors. Accordingly, defence counsel should investigate whether the plaintiff has already taken judgment against another person jointly responsible for the same libel. If so, a motion for a non-suit on the grounds the current action is an abuse of process may be successful.

Thomson v. Lambert, [1938] 2 D.L.R. 545, per Duff C.J.C. at 556 (S.C.C.).

I. THE DEFENDANT'S EVIDENCE

1) Fair Comment

For the essential ingredients of this defence, see Chapter 17, "Fair Comment."

a) Proof of facts

The defendant must prove that the facts on which he or she relies as the basis of the defamatory comment were present in his or her mind at the time of making the comment. Moreover, those facts must have been true at that time. However, it is not necessary for the defendant to prove he or she had direct personal knowledge that such facts were true, or was acquainted with the evidence by which their truth could be displayed.

> *Meyer v. Chouhan* (2001), 14 C.P.C. (5th) 81 at para. 10 (B.C.S.C.), citing Philip Lewis, *Gatley on Libel & Slander*, 8th ed. (London: Sweet & Maxwell, 1981) at 302.

Alternatively, the defendant must either prove that the facts on which the comment is based were asserted on a privileged occasion, such as court proceedings, and that the commentator relied on those facts.

> *Taylor-Wright v. CHBC-TV, a Division of WIC Television Ltd.*, [1999] B.C.J. No. 334 at paras. 34, 46 (C.A.) [citing *Grech v. Odhams Press*, [1958] 2 Q.B. 275 (C.A.)] varied (2000), 194 D.L.R. (4th) 621 (B.C.C.A.).

> *Cardwell v. Hutchison*, [1995] B.C.J. No. 1656 (S.C.), aff'd (1997), 36 B.C.L.R. (3d) 86 (C.A.).

Where the defence is fair comment in an editorial, a defendant may call evidence to prove the facts explicitly stated in the editorial. If the editorial is in effect a comment on other news stories, the defendant may put those news stories into evidence, prove that they were published, and that the facts reported in those stories were true.

> *Holt v. Sun Publishing Co. Ltd.* (1979), 100 D.L.R. (3d) 447 (B.C.C.A.), aff'g (1978), 83 D.L.R. (3d) 761 (B.C.S.C.).

It is an error for the court to exclude evidence of the truth of stated facts said to underpin defamatory expression if fair comment is pleaded.

> *Axelrod v. Beth Jacob of Kitchener*, [1943] O.W.N. 708 (C.A.).

The defendants have the right, without pleading justification, to adduce evidence to establish the truth of the allegations of fact upon which the comment is based as distinguished from the comment itself.

> *Boys v. Star Printing and Publishing Co.*, [1927] 60 O.L.R. 592, 3 D.L.R. 847 (C.A.).

The defendant who provides particulars of the facts on which his or her plea of fair comment is based will be confined to evidence of the truth of such facts at trial.

> *Augustine Automatic Rotary Engine Co. v. Saturday Night Ltd.* (1917), 38 O.L.R. 609, 34 D.L.R. 439 (C.A.).

> *Aga Kahn v. Times Publishing Co.*, [1924] 1 K.B. 675 at 680 (C.A.).

> *Tudor-Hart v. British Union for the Abolition of Vivisection*, [1937] 54 T.L.R. 154 (C.A.).

A defendant who pleads fair comment cannot rely on facts which occurred after the publication of the defamatory expression to support that expression as fair comment.

> *Cohen v. Daily Telegraph*, [1968] 2 All E.R. 407, 409 (C.A.).

b) Proof of Honest Belief

Because the expression at issue must represent the real view of the person making the comment, he or she should testify to that effect (except where this obligation is altered by statute; for example, publication of the opinions of others, *Libel and Slander Act*, R.S.O. 1990, C. L-12, s.24).

> *Cherneskey v. Armadale Publishers*, [1979] 1 S.C.R. 1067.

The defendant may be cross-examined as to the meaning of his or her expression at issue, and may testify as to the intended meaning and to his or her belief in that meaning.

> *Vander Zalm v. Times Publishers* (1980), 109 D.L.R. (3d) 531, per Nemetz C.J.B.C. at 537–38 (B.C.C.A.), [referring to the evidence of the defendant cartoonist concerning the meaning of the cartoon alleged to be defamatory].

2) Qualified Privilege

See Chapter 18, "Qualified and Statutory Privilege," for a discussion of the specific factors which have been addressed by courts in determining whether an occasion is privileged.

a) Belief in Expression

Where a statement is made on an occasion of qualified privilege, the law presumes that the person making it had a positive belief in its truth. Accordingly, it is unnecessary for the defendant to testify to a subjective, honest belief in the truth of expression to establish the elements of this defence.

> *McKearney* v. *Petro-Canada* (1994), 25 C.P.C. (3d) 218 at para. 6 (B.C.S.C.).

> *Arnott* v. *College of Physicians and Surgeons of Saskatchewan*, [1954] S.C.R. 538.

b) Every Circumstance Associated with Publication

Every circumstance associated with the origin and publication of the defamatory statement should be consiuered in determining whether or not the necessary conditions for the privilege exist.

> *Halls* v. *Mitchell*, [1928] S.C.R. 125, per Duff J. at 133, citing *London Assn. for Protection of Trade* v. *Greenlands Ltd.*, [[1916] 2 A.C. 15, at 22–23], where Lord Buckmaster stated [at 19]:

> > Indeed, the circumstances that constitute a privileged occasion can themselves never be catalogued and rendered exact … It is, I think, essential to consider every circumstance associated with the origin and publication of the defamatory matter in order to be able to ascertain whether the necessary conditions are satisfied by which alone protection can be obtained.

Although the burden of proving that the occasion was privileged is on the defendant, the evidence necessary to establish the privilege can often be brought out from the plaintiff or the plaintiff's witnesses. This may occur either on direct examination by the plaintiff's counsel or on cross-examination by defence counsel. A defendant may choose to call no witnesses of his own but simply to rely on the evidence of the plaintiff's witnesses.

> *Fisher* v. *Kinney* (1920) 51 D.L.R. 396, per Drysdale J. at 402 (N.S.S.C.):

> > While the burden of proving that the occasion was privileged is on the defendant, usually the evidence with regard to the whole matter is brought out from the plaintiff or his witnesses. It may very well be that the defendant calls no witnesses but relies on the facts brought out from plaintiff's witnesses to shew that the occasion was privileged. Can the plaintiff in such a case start over again to prove malice. I do not suggest that a trial Judge may not in a proper case allow further evidence to be taken at any stage, but of course the defendant must have

the opportunity of calling evidence to shew want of malice after the plaintiff has closed his case.

Where a defendant calls no evidence in support of the defence of qualified privilege to establish the facts and circumstances, the defence cannot succeed unless an admission in the plaintiff's pleadings supports such a defence.

Toronto Star Ltd. v. Drew, [1948] 4 D.L.R. 465 (S.C.C), aff'g, [1947] 4 D.L.R. 221 (Ont. C.A.).

A defendant cannot establish a defence of qualified privilege simply by putting in copies of the defamatory expression containing the editorials complained of, even though such editorials may contain statements of alleged facts. The documents cannot be used by the defendants to prove the truth of what is alleged in other parts of the publication.

Toronto Star Ltd. v. Drew, ibid.

The facts on which the claim of privilege is based must be proved before the judge can rule whether the occasion is privileged or not. If at the conclusion of the plaintiff's case, facts sufficient to support the plea of privilege have been clearly established, and no evidence of malice has been given, the judge should enter judgment for the defendant and not let the case go to a jury.

Bancroft v. Canadian Pacific Railway, [1920] 53 D.L.R. 272 (Man. C.A.).

c) Court Proceedings

A defendant who intends to rely on the common law privilege attaching to a fair and accurate report of a judicial proceeding need not show that he based his report directly on what was actually said in court, either by attending the proceeding himself or reading transcripts before publishing his report. It is sufficient for the defendant to prove that the information he or she used is found in the court proceedings and that, when a comparison is made, the report of those proceedings is fair and accurate.

Weslowksi v. Armadale Publishers Ltd. (1980), 112 D.L.R (3d) 378 (Sask. Q.B.).

d) Occasions of Privilege Arising from Legislation

An occasion of privilege may be proven by showing that the publication occurred pursuant to legislation and related regulations. To the extent the court is not entitled to take judicial notice of relevant regulations, rules, or codes, they must be proven in evidence.

Shapiro v. Vancouver, [1979] B.C.J. No. 577 at paras. 76–77, 91.

A finding that a statement of fact believed to be true by the defendant was in fact true constitutes a sustaining factor in establishing the defence of qualified privilege and negating malice.

McLoughlin v. Kutasy, [1979] 2 S.C.R. 311.

A legal duty exists where there is a statutory requirement for a person to report cases of abuse or neglect — persons having responsibility for the care of children, for example. The defendant should call factual evidence to bring himself within the terms of such statutory privilege.

Creedan Valley Nursing Home Ltd. v. Van Klaveren (1996), 20 O.T.C. 227 (Gen. Div.), aff'd (1999), 126 O.A.C. 163 (Div. Ct.).

The defendant should lead evidence of and refer to a statutory duty which creates the occasion of qualified privilege. The defendant's evidence should bring the facts of the situation within the terms of the statute.

Lacarte v. Toronto Board of Education, [1959] S.C.R. 465.

e) Attack Privilege

The defendant introduced evidence proving that prior publications by the plaintiff provoked the defamatory response. The defendant also led evidence that if the plaintiff's accusations had gone unchallenged, he or she would have sustained losses such as expenses, interference with business operations, or the costs associated with countering the effects of the attack.

RTC Engineering Consultants Ltd. v. Ontario (Ministry of the Solicitor General and Correctional Services), [2000] O.T.C. 471 at paras. 46–49 (S.C.J.), aff'd (2002), 58 O.R. (3d) 726 (C.A.).

Lawrence v. Barker (1968), 68 D.L.R. (2nd) 597 (B.C.S.C.).

A defendant may tender evidence of an interchange of abusive articles between the two parties over several years, in which each sought to provoke the other, to establish the occasion of this privilege.

Falk v. Smith, [1941] 1 D.L.R. 156 (Ont. C.A.), aff'g, [1940] 4 D.L.R. 765 (Ont. S.C.J.).

Although the court will not weigh the defendant's response too delicately, the defendant would be wise to establish that his or her defamatory response was proportionate in view of the serious nature of the misstatements or half-truths in the plaintiff's publication.

RTC Engineering Consultants Ltd. v. *Ontario (Ministry of the Solicitor General and Correctional Services),* [2000] O.T.C. 471 (S.C.J.) at paras. 46–49, aff'd (2002), 58 O.R. (3d) 726 (C.A.).

A defendant may testify to his or her honest belief in the defamatory expression, the grounds for that belief, the scope and nature of any investigation, and that the expression was considered necessary to protect the defendant's interest. If the plaintiff fails to cross-examine on such evidence, that point may be emphasized to the court. Where the defendant's response to the plaintiff's attack was published only to the recipients of the plaintiff's prior communication, the defendant may testify to this effect.

RTC Engineering Consultants Ltd. v. *Ontario (Ministry of the Solicitor General and Correctional Services),* [2000] O.T.C. 471 at paras. 64, 74 (S.C.J.), aff'd (2002), 58 O.R. (3d) 726 (C.A.)

Although evidence may be given of a previous publication by the plaintiff which allegedly provoked the defendant to vindicate his character. However, any article published by the plaintiff after the publication of the alleged libel is not admissible in evidence on any ground. Since it postdated the libel at issue, it cannot be considered provocation for it. In *Downey* v. *Armstrong* (1901), O.R. 237 (Div. Ct.), where such a letter had been improperly admitted and might have influenced the jury against the plaintiff, a new trial was ordered.

f) Subjective Belief in Duty to Publish

The defendant's testimony that he believed he was under a duty to communicate the defamatory expression to the recipient does not prove the occasion is privileged because that is determined from applying an objective test; however, that testimony is admissible on the issue of malice.

Fairview Management Services Ltd. v. *Ryeburn,* 2000 BCSC 930, at paras. 28, 31.

Similarly, it is open to the defence, on cross-examination of the plaintiff, to seek to extract an opinion that the recipient of the defamatory expression would be very interested to learn about it. That evidence is admissible (although it may not be decisive) as to whether the occasion was privileged.

Norman v. *Westcomm International Sharing Corp.* (1997), 46 O.T.C. 321 at paras. 96–98 (Gen. Div.).

If a defamatory publication had wider circulation than was intended by the defendant, the defence may lead evidence of that fact. If that evidence is accepted and there is no evidence the wider circulation was caused by the defendant's negligence, the protection of qualified privilege may apply notwithstanding that the defamatory expression may have reached persons who did not have the necessary reciprocity of interest.

> *Gallant v. West*, [1955] 4 D.L.R. 209, per Walsh C.J. at 216 (Nfld. S.C.):

> > I hold … that, insofar as there was publication to service personnel, the occasion was privileged and that there is no evidence or presumption of publication outside service ranks. Indeed, whatever evidence there is respecting publication to civilians is to the contrary. There is no evidence of negligence on the part of the defendant or of anyone for whose acts or omissions he, as an officer of the United States Air Force, can be held responsible, and unintentional publication due to no such negligence is not actionable against him.

g) State of Mind

As an exception to the hearsay rule, a defendant may testify about his or her conversations with third parties to illustrate the defendant's state of mind relative to the defence of qualified privilege.

> *Norman v. Westcomm International Sharing Corp.* (1997), 46 O.T.C. 321 (Gen. Div.).

h) Warnings

A defendant may testify he or she acted honestly and had a real concern for the wellbeing of another person out of concern she might be harmed, and had no other motive and therefore acted in good faith. They may testify they felt it was their duty to communicate the information to the person who received it as they had an honest fear something might happen to her.

> *J.C. v. V.R. and C.A.* (2000), 191 Sask. R. 295 at para. 14 (Q.B.).

Where a defendant is intending to rely on a defence of qualified privilege, he may give evidence that he never uttered the defamatory expression to anyone until he was contacted by persons with whom he had a reciprocal interest and was invited to make a statement under conditions of confidentiality.

> *Knorr v. Ibrahim* (1998), 169 N.S.R. (2d) 34 at paras. 21, 31 (S.C.).

3) Absolute Privilege

Judicial privilege applies wherever there is an authorized inquiry: either before a court of justice, or a tribunal with similar attributes. A commissioner conducting an inquiry under the *Combines Investigation Act*, R.S.C. 1927,

c. 26, was held to be merely part of the administrative machinery set up for inquiring whether offences have been committed; because the inquiry did not have the attributes of a court of justice, he could not claim absolute privilege.

O'Connor v. *Waldron*, [1935] 1 D.L.R. 260 (P.C.), aff'g, [1930] 4 D.L.R. 22 (Ont. S.C.), aff'g, [1931] 4 D.L.R. 147 (Ont. S.C. (A.D.)), rev'g, [1932] 1 D.L.R. 166 (S.C.C.).

4) Justification

The elements of this defence are discussed in Chapter 21, "Justification."

The burden is on the defendant to plead and prove the truth of the expression on the balance of probabilities.

Upton v. *Better Business Bureau of the Mainland of British Columbia* (1980), 23 B.C.L.R. 228 (S.C.).

Evidence in support of the truth of defamatory allegations may consist of

i)   the oral testimony of witnesses;
ii)   documents;
iii) other real evidence; and
iv)   statements by the person allegedly defamed.

The evidence that may be introduced at trial is limited to the pleaded particulars of justification.

Yorkshire Provident Life Ins. Co. v. *Gilbert and Rivington*, [1895] 2 Q.B. 148, per Lindley L.J. at 152, A.L. Smith L.J. at 154 (C.A.).

Parkland Chapel Ltd. v. *Edmonton Broadcasting Co.* (1964), 45 D.L.R. (2d) 752 (Alta. S.C. (T.D.)).

The general rule is that if the defendant pleads justification then he must prove the truth of the statement. If he does not plead justification then he cannot adduce evidence of truth to mitigate damages.

Capitanescu v. *Universal Weld Overlays Inc.*, [1997] 10 W.W.R. 666 at para. 18 (Alta. Q.B.) [referring to *Watt* v. *Watt*, [1905] AC 115 (H.L.)], varied (1999) 232 A.R. 334 (C.A.).

Absent a plea of justification, the court rejected evidence tending to show the truth of the defendant's allegation. Where the defendant contended that it would be less damaging to say of the plaintiff that he admitted something which was true than to say that he had asserted something which was false, the court decided such evidence was not admissable to prove the truth of the assertion. "The issue here is not whether the fluoridation of water supplies is harmful or beneficial but whether the plaintiff said that fluoridation was harmful to some people. Holding as I have that he did not so say and that to say he did was in the circumstances of this case libellous, the plaintiff must succeed."

Bonham v. Pure Water Association (1970), 14 D.L.R. (3d) 749 (B.C.S.C.).

Although the words may be literally true, the inferences and implications that would reasonably be drawn from them by their audience may be false. To establish a defence of justification, the defendant must prove the truth of the inferences and implications.

Norman v. New Westminster (City), [1999] B.C.J. No. 433 at paras. 17, 22 (S.C.).

Justification cannot be proved by evidence that the defendant relied upon information supplied by someone else. Nor is it relevant to this defence that the defendant honestly believed the truth of the statements.

Finning International Inc. v. Cormack, [2001] A.J. No. 1092, 2001 ABQB 723, at para 35.4.

Price v. Chicoutimi Pulp Co. (1915), 51 S.C.R. 179.

A defendant cannot be certain that she will be able to prove justification by the plaintiff's own testimony at trial. That is because a trial judge has the discretion to permit a plaintiff to postpone his evidence in rebuttal of a plea of justification until after the defendant has closed her case. There is no hard and fast rule, and the practice is based on general convenience. Where the court has ruled that the plaintiff may reserve his evidence, it rests in the discretion to rule that the defendant's right to cross-examine the plaintiff's witnesses in support of the plea of justification be postponed until after the defendant has presented her evidence. Alternately, if counsel for the defence is allowed in cross-examination to elicit facts in support of the plea of justification, the court may rule that such cross-examination does not deprive the plaintiff of the benefit of the court's ruling that he may reserve his general evidence in rebuttal until after the defendant has given her evidence.

Jerome v. Anderson, [1964] S.C.R. 291 at 306–7.

Generally speaking, defamatory accusations cannot be justified merely by evidence that the plaintiff engaged in other types of conduct equally or more reprehensible in character.

Finning International Inc. v. Cormack, [2001] A.J. No. 1092, 2001 ABQB 723, at para. 35.

In a libel action involving a charge that the plaintiff acted in a fraudulent and dishonest manner in attempting to make a particular sale, evidence of the plaintiff's acts subsequent to the event in issue is admissible in support of a plea of justification, where it is shown that a systematic method was pursued by the plaintiff in every attempted sale, aimed at the making of the same type of contract in each case.

Hare and Grolier Society v. Better Business Bureau, [1947] 1 D.L.R. 280 (B.C.C.A.).

Where it is shown that the plaintiff employed the same system or method before and after the publication of the libel, there is no good ground for excluding evidence of the latter.

Hare and Grolier Society v. Better Business Bureau, ibid.

Maisel v. Financial Times Ltd., [1915] 3 K.B. 336 (C.A.).

If the defamatory expression alleges that the plaintiff's character and reputation is such that he would be likely to do a certain act if he had the opportunity, evidence that the plaintiff committed such an act shortly after the date of the publication is admissible.

Maisel v. Financial Times Ltd., ibid.

a) Criminal Conduct

An allegation of criminality or the like on the plaintiff's part, with its associated stigma, should be strictly and precisely alleged and proven "to a more contextually sensitive variant of the standard of proof of balance of probabilities."

Beaver First National Band v. A.T.N. Farms Ltd., 2001 ABQB 748, at para. 16.

Smith v. Smith, [1952] 2 S.C.R. 312 at 331.

b) Criminal Charges

Evidence that a criminal charge had been laid should be established. If the arresting officer had reasonable grounds for suspicion, the defamatory imputation that the police suspected the plaintiff could be justified by the officer detailing the grounds for suspicion in evidence.

Grassi v. WIC Radio (c.o.b. CKNW/98), [2000] 5 W.W.R. 119 at para. 48 (B.C.S.C.).

c) Criminal Conviction

The defendant may adduce in evidence a certificate of conviction showing that the plaintiff was convicted of a criminal offence. Evidence of a conviction is admissible in subsequent civil proceedings of the facts which support the conviction.

> Re Del Core v. Ontario College of Pharmacists (1985), 51 O.R. (2d) 1 (C.A.), leave to appeal to S.C.C. dismissed (1986), 57 O.R. (2d) 296 (S.C.C.).

In Ontario, evidence of a criminal conviction constitutes *prima facie* but not conclusive proof of the fact of guilt in civil proceedings. The prior conviction must, of course, be relevant to the subsequent proceedings. Its weight and significance will depend on the circumstances of each case. The effect of a prior conviction may be countered in a variety of ways: for example, the conviction may be challenged or its effect mitigated by an explanation of the circumstances surrounding the conviction. The right to challenge a conviction is subject to an important qualification — a convicted person cannot attempt to prove that the conviction was wrong in circumstances where it would constitute an abuse of process to do so. The courts have rejected attempts to re-litigate the issues dealt with at a criminal trial where the civil proceedings were perceived to be a collateral attack on the criminal conviction.

> Re Del Core v. Ontario College of Pharmacists, ibid.

The relevant Ontario statute is the *Evidence Act*, S.O. 1993, c. 27, which provides in section 22(1) that proof of conviction anywhere in Canada, absent evidence to the contrary, is proof that the crime was committed by that person.

The British Columbia *Evidence Act*, R.S.B.C. 1996, c. 124, section 71, specifically addresses the use of a criminal conviction in a defamation action. If a person has been convicted or found guilty of any offence anywhere in Canada, and the commission of that offence is relevant to any issue in an action, proof of the conviction or finding of guilt is evidence to prove that person committed the offence, whether or not that person is a party to the defamation action (section 71(2)). There is an absolute right to tender the evidence of the conviction, and proof of the conviction or finding of guilt is conclusive proof in a defamation action that the person committed that offence (section 71(6)).

The Alberta *Evidence Act*, R.S.A. 2000, c. A-18, section 26(2), provides that when a person has been convicted or found guilty of an offence anywhere in Canada, and the commission of that offence is relevant to an issue in an action, proof of the conviction may be tendered in evidence and is conclusive proof that the individual committed the crime.

d) Interpretation of Documents

Where the defence of justification hinges on the interpretation of a contractual or statutory condition, the defendant has the onus of proving the correct interpretation. Where the wording is ambiguous, this task may require calling extrinsic evidence to establish the correct interpretation.

> *Hodgson v. Canadian Newspapers Co.* (1998), 39 O.R. (3d) 235 (Gen. Div.), varied (2000), 49 O.R. (3d) 161 at paras. 30–32 (C.A.), leave to appeal to S.C.C. denied, [2000] S.C.C.A. No. 465.

e) Complaints

Where a defendant referred to complaints he received from irate citizens regarding the treatment they have been receiving from the plaintiff, the court will expect the defendant to produce one or more of such complainants, to testify they made the complaints, or that they were true. Failure on the defendant's part to investigate the complaints assisted the court in finding actual malice.

> *Safeway Stores Ltd. v. Harris*, [1948] 4 D.L.R. 187 at 191, 197 (Man. K.B.), aff'g, [1948] 4 D.L.R. 187 at 188 (Man. C.A.).

f) Incompetence

The defendant may have difficulty proving that accusations of incompetence as a builder or developer are true if it cannot establish that the builder or developer failed to comply with government standards.

> *Morgenstern v. Oakville Record Star*, [1962] O.R. 638 (H.C.J.)

5) Consent

The defence of consent is a narrow one, and must be clearly established. Consent must be given or be able to be inferred with respect to each publication of defamatory material. However, damages may be somewhat mitigated if the plaintiff can be shown to have consented to part of a broadcast.

> *Syms v. Warren* (1976), 71 D.L.R. (3d) 558 (Man. Q.B.).

6) Innocent Dissemination

A defendant will be required to call evidence to show that he disseminated the material in the ordinary course of business; he did not know and had no reason to know that the material was defamatory; and his lack of knowledge in this respect did not result from any negligence on his part. The defendant will wish to lead evidence concerning the nature of its business and on whether he would, in the ordinary course of that business or by virtue of a particular undertaking, be expected to review or otherwise supervise or control the material he disseminates to the public. The court will consider whether the medium in question is one which would arouse the defendant's suspicion that it had been or would likely be used for the publication of defamatory material.

> *Vizetelly* v. *Mudie's Select Library Ltd.*, [1900] 2 Q.B. 170 at 180 (C.A.), per Romer J.

J. MITIGATION OF DAMAGES

1) Apology and Retraction

An apology should clearly state that there was no factual basis for making the defamatory allegation, otherwise the court may find that it has done little or nothing to erase the imprint on most readers' minds. The apology should also adequately identify the original story that it related to, as well as the nature of that story.

> *Snider* v. *Calgary Herald* (1985), 65 A.R. 99 at para. 106 (Q.B.).

Section 5 of the *Libel and Slander Act*, concerning retractions and apologies, requires only that the retraction be as conspicuous as the libel, not that it should be as conspicuous as the entire original article.

> *Murray Alter's Talent Associates Ltd.* v. *Toronto Star Newspapers Ltd.* (1985), 124 D.L.R. (4th) 105 (Ont. Div. Ct.).

To bring a defendant within section 7 of the *Libel and Slander Act*, R.S.B.C. 1996, c. 263, the defendant must prove that the article was published in good faith. Where a defendant admits in his evidence that he could not rely upon his source, this requirement will not be established.

> *Ramsey* v. *Pacific Press, a Division of Southam, Inc.*, 2000 BCSC 1551 at paras. 62–64.

To prove good faith, the defendant must establish not mere belief in the truth of the defamatory expression but also that he exercised "the care and vigilance of a prudent and conscientious man, wielding as he does, the great power of the public press." There must be an absence both of improper motive and negligence on his part. It is his duty to take all reasonable precautions to verify the truth of the statement and to prevent untrue and injurious publications against others.

> *Allan v. Pioneer Company*, 41 N.W. 936 (Minn. Sup. Ct. 1889), per Mitchell J. at 939, quoted with approval by the Ontario Court of Appeal in *Teskey v. Canadian Newspapers Co.* (1989), 59 D.L.R. (4th) 709, per Blair J.A. at 718 (Ont. C.A.).

It may be necessary for the defendant to take the witness stand and testify to his good faith, where that is a requirement of the statutory defence of qualified privilege.

> *MacArthur v. Meuser*, [1997] O.J. No. 1377 at paras. 43–44 (Ont. Gen. Div.).

> *Teskey v. Canadian Newspapers Co.* (1989), 59 D.L.R. (4th) 709 (Ont. C.A.), adopting the decision of the Supreme Court of Minnesota in *Allan v. Pioneer Company*, 41 N.W. 936 (Minn. Sup. Ct. 1889).

Even if the defendant cannot bring him- or herself within the apology provisions of the *Libel and Slander Act*, evidence of a timely apology may nevertheless be taken into account in mitigation of damages. The conduct, character, and circumstances of the defendant can be factors that go to mitigation of damages.

> *Tait v. New Westminster Radio Ltd.* (1984), 15 D.L.R. (4th) 115 (B.C.C.A.).

The defendant who apologizes but at the same time attempts to blame the plaintiff for his or her predicament will not succeed in proving a true apology.

> *Ramsey v. Pacific Press, a Division of Southam, Inc.*, 2000 BCSC 1551 at paras. 131–32.

An investigation launched by defence lawyers after the initiation of the defamation lawsuit need not detract from a published apology in any way. One would expect a law firm, properly approaching its responsibilities to its client, to institute such an inquiry.

> *Munro v. Toronto Sun Publishing Corp.* (1982), 39 O.R. (2d) 100 at para. 44 (H.C.J.).

2) Evidence of Defendant's *Bona Fides*

A defendant seeking to rely on the mitigation of damages provisions of section 9(2) of the *Libel and Slander Act*, may lead evidence to prove that they bona fide acted in reliance upon a report made to it under a contractual arrangement with a wire service, even if the original authors of the report were guilty of malice or gross negligence. The defendant, however, must not himself be personally guilty of actual malice or gross negligence in making the publication giving rise to the proceedings. Where there is nothing analogous to the principal and agent relationship between the defendant and the wire service, the statutory defence may be available.

Allan v. Bushnell T.V. Co. Ltd., Broadcast News Ltd., Third Party (1969), 4 D.L.R. (3d) 212 (Ont. C.A.).

3) General Bad Reputation of the Plaintiff

a) The General Rule

The leading case on the admissibility of evidence to attack the plaintiff's reputation is *Scott v. Sampson* (1882), 8 Q.B.D. 491, per Cave J. at page 503, which laid down the following three basic principles:

i)   general evidence of the plaintiff's bad reputation is admissible;

ii)   however, evidence of rumours in general circulation that the plaintiff committed either the specific acts of misconduct alleged in the defamatory expression, or that he or she committed other acts of misconduct, is irrelevant and inadmissible; and

iii)   evidence of specific acts or misconduct (aside from those pleaded in support of the defences of justification and fair comment) tending to show the plaintiff's disposition is inadmissible.

> … Speaking generally the law recognizes in every man a right to have the estimation in which he stands in the opinion of others unaffected by false statements to his discredit; and if such false statements are made without lawful excuse, and damage results to the person of whom they are made, he has a right of action. The damage, however, which he has sustained must depend almost entirely on the estimation in which he was previously held. He complains of an injury to his reputation and seeks to recover damages for that injury; and it seems most material that the jury who have to award those damages should know if the fact is so that he is a man of no reputation. …

> *Scott v. Sampson* (1882), 8 Q.B.D. 491 per Cave J. at 503.

The rationale for the principles laid down in *Scott v. Sampson, ibid.,* is found in the following statement of Cave J. at 503–5:

> As to the second head of evidence of rumours and suspicions to the same effect as the defamatory matter complained of, it would seem that on princi-

ple such evidence is not admissible, as only indirectly tending to affect the plaintiff's reputation. If these rumours and suspicions have, in fact, affected the plaintiff's reputation, that may be proved by general evidence of reputation. If they have not affected it they are not relevant to the issue. To admit evidence of rumours and suspicions is to given any one who knows nothing whatever of the plaintiff, or who may even have a grudge against him, an opportunity of spreading through the means of the publicity attending judicial proceedings what he may have picked up from the most disreputable sources, and what no man of sense, who knows the plaintiff's character, would for a moment believe in. Unlike evidence of general reputation, it is particularly difficult for the plaintiff to meet and rebut such evidence; for all that those who know him and can best say is that they have not heard anything of these rumours. Moreover, it may be that it is the defendant himself who has started them ... .

As to the third head or evidence of facts and circumstances tending to show the disposition of the plaintiff, both principle and authority seem equally against its admission. At the most it tends to prove not that the plaintiff has not, but that he ought not to have, a good reputation, and to admit evidence of this kind is in effect as was said in *Jones* v. *Stevens* [(1) 11 Price, 235] to throw upon the plaintiff the difficulty of shewing an uniform propriety of conduct during his whole life. It would give rise to interminable issues which would have but a very remote bearing on the question in dispute, which is to what extent the reputation which he actually possesses has been damaged by the defamatory matter complained of.

These principles were affirmed in 1929 by the Court of Appeal in *Hobbs* v. *Tinling, Hobbs* v. *Nottingham Journal*, [1929] All E.R. Rep. 33 again in 1961 by the Court of Appeal in *Dingle* v. *Associated Newspapers Ltd.* [1961] 1 All E.R. 897 (C.A.); and by the House of Lords in *Plato Films, Ltd.* v. *Speidel*, [1961] 1 All E.R. 876 (H.L.) See also *D. & L. Caterers, Ltd.* v. *D'Anjou*, [1945] 1 All E.R. 563 at page 565.

The defendant is entitled to plead and tender general evidence of bad reputation of the plaintiff whether or not he or she has pleaded justification.

Hobbs v. *C.T. Tinling & Co. Ltd.*, [1929] 2 K.B. 1 (C.A.). Scrutton L.J., after noting that the defendants did not plead justification, stated at pages 9, 11:

The worst of criminals is entitled to a fair hearing according to rules of law. I am not expressing any opinion whether [the plaintiff] Hobbs will ultimately be proved, as the defendants contend, though they do not assert their libel to be true, to be of the character I have referred to; ...

and lastly there was the allegation, in my opinion the only allegation properly included in the particulars [of the defendant's notice of mitigation of damages], which … is para 10. Para. 10 is: "That the plaintiff is a man of worthless reputation and character, being known to the police and in the profession of the law as such."

The nature of the evidence of general bad reputation of the plaintiff which may be admissible is discussed by Lord Denning in *Plato Films Ltd.* v. *Speidel*, [1961] 1 All E.R. 876 at pages 889–90:

My Lords, up till this point I have spoken of "general evidence of character" because that is how it was usually referred to before *Scott* v. *Sampson* [fn. 47 (1882) 8 Q.B.D. 491]. But Cave J. seems to prefer the expression "general evidence of reputation." The reason is, no doubt, because the words "character" and "reputation" have various meanings and he wished to make clear what he meant. A man's "character," it is sometimes said, is what he in fact is, whereas his "reputation" is what other people think he is. If this be the sense in which the words are being used, then a libel action is concerned only with a man's reputation, that is, with what people think of him; and it is for damage to his reputation, that is, to his esteem in the eyes of others, that he can sue, and not for damage to his own personality or disposition. That is why Cave J. spoke of "reputation" rather than "character."

But there is another sense in which the word "character" is used, and quite properly used, when it overlaps with the word "reputation." Thus, when I say of a man that "He has always borne a good character," I mean that he has always been thought well of by others; and when I want to know what his "character" is, I write, not to him, but to others who know something about him. In short, his "character" is the esteem in which he is held by others who know him and are in a position to judge his worth. A man can sue for damage to his character in this sense, even though he is so little known to the outside world that he has no "reputation" in the ordinary sense of that word. … But a man's "character," so understood, may become known to others beyond his immediate circle. In so far as this estimate spreads outwards from those who know him and circulates among people generally in an increasing range, it becomes his "reputation" which is entitled to the protection of the law just as much as his character. No other reputation is of any worth. The law can take no notice of a reputation which has no foundation except the gossip and rumour of busybodies who do not know the man. Test it this way. Suppose an honourable man becomes the victim of groundless rumour. He should be entitled to damages without having this wounding gossip dragged up against him. He can call people who know him to give evidence of his good character. On the other hand, suppose a "notorious rogue" manages to conceal his dishonesty from the world at large. He should not be entitled to damages on the basis that he is a man of unblemished reputation. There must, one would think, be people who know him and can come and speak to his bad character.

This leads me to the conclusion that, in order to arrive at a man's character and reputation, one should call those who know him and have had dealings with him; for they provide the only sound foundation on which to build. And in actual practice it is only such persons who are called. I have looked into many of the cases where evidence of good or bad character has been given, and I have been engaged in quite a number myself. It usually takes this form: If it is evidence of good character, a witness of good standing is called, such as a clergyman, a schoolmaster or an employer, and is asked such questions as these:

"What are you? How long have you known him? Have you known him well? Have you had an opportunity of observing his conduct? What character has he borne during that time for honesty, morality or loyalty [according to the nature of the case]? As far as you know, has he deserved that character?"

A good instance is *King v. Waring* [fn 49: (1803), 5 Esp. 13; 170 E.R. 721]. A servant girl was given a reference accusing her of dishonesty. In support of her claim for damages, Lord Alvanley C.J. allowed a former employer to come and give evidence of her general character for honesty. But the witness cannot be asked questions in examination-in-chief about particular facts so as to illustrate the plaintiff's good behaviour on particular occasions. In cross-examination, however, he may be asked what are the grounds of his belief and he may be asked as to particular facts known to him tending to shake it. If it is evidence of bad character which is given (such as that a man is a reputed thief or a woman is a common prostitute), the evidence often takes the form of a police officer who knows him being called and saying: "I know the defendant and have known him (or her) for some time. He is a well-known pickpocket," or "She is a common prostitute," or as the case may be. In such cases, the witness usually speaks from his own observation and knowledge. The greater his personal knowledge, the more valuable his evidence. A good illustration is *Wood v. Cox* [fn. 50: (1888), 4 T.L.R. 652] There a jockey had been accused of "pulling" a horse called Success. It was said that "he nearly pulled his head off." He sued for damages. Lord Coleridge C.J. admitted evidence of four officials of the Jockey Club who gave evidence of the plaintiff's bad character for foul riding and not trying to win. (Incidentally, his employer, the Duke of Portland, gave evidence in the jockey's favour, though he seems to have been cross-examined to some effect.) The jockey only got one farthing damages. When general evidence of bad character is given, the witness cannot in chief give particular instances; though he can, of course, in cross-examination be asked the grounds of his belief and on what it is based. When evidence of good or bad character is given, it should be directed to that sector of a man's character which is relevant. Thus, if the libel imputes theft, the relevant sector is his character for honesty, not his character as a motorist. And so forth. It is for the judge to rule what is the relevant sector.

b) Limits on Admissible Evidence

There are a number of limits on the general evidence of the plaintiff's bad reputation that the defendant can introduce:

i)   What may be taken into account is the plaintiff's general reputation in that sector of his or her life which has relevance to the libel complained of. Relevance is a question of law for the judge at trial.

   Pressler v. Lethbridge, (2000), 86 B.C.L.R. (3d) 257, per Southin J.A. at 302 (C.A.), citing Lord Radcliffe in *Plato Films Ltd. v. Speidel*, [1961] 1 All E.R. 876 at 885 (H.L.):

   > ... general evidence of reputation ... must mean reputation in that sector of a plaintiff's life that has relevance to the libel complained of ...

   Plato Films Ltd. v. Speidel, [1961] 1 All E.R. 876 (H.L.) per Lord Denning at 890:

   > When evidence of good or bad character is given, it should be directed to that sector of a man's character which is relevant. Thus, if the libel imputes theft, the relevant sector is his character for honesty, not his character as a motorist. And so forth. It is for the judge to rule what is the relevant sector.

   Williston v. Smith (1847), 5 N.B.R. 443 (C.A.).

ii) The evidence must be confined to the reputation of the plaintiff prior to or at the time of the publication of the libel. Evidence of the plaintiff's general bad reputation after the publication of the libel is not admissible.

   Associated Newspapers, Ltd. v. Dingle, [1962] 2 All E.R. 737, per Lord Radcliffe at 747 (H.L.):

   > When one speaks of a plaintiff's "actual" reputation or "current" reputation (to quote my own adjective) one means his reputation as

accumulated from one source or another over the period of time that precedes the occasion of the libel that is in suit.

iii) The evidence of general bad reputation may not include evidence of other publications to the same effect as the libel.

Amalgamated Transit Union v. *Independent Canadian Transit Union*, [1997] A.J. No. 191, at para. 63 (Q.B.).

Associated Newspapers, Ltd. v. *Dingle*, [1962] 2 All E.R. 737, per Lord Radcliffe at 745 (H.L.):

> A libel action is fundamentally an action to vindicate a man's reputation on some point as to which he has been falsely defamed and the damages awarded have to be regarded as the demonstrative mark of that vindication. If they could be whittled away by a defendant calling attention to the fact that other people had already been saying the same thing as he had said and pleading that for this reason alone the plaintiff had the less reputation to lose, the libeled man would never get his full vindication. It is, I think a well understood rule of law that a defendant who has not justified his defamatory statements cannot mitigate the damages for which he is liable by producing evidence of other publications to the same effect as his; and it seems to me that it would involve an impossible conflict between this rule and the suggested proof of tarnished reputation to admit into consideration other contemporary publications about the same incident. A defamed man would only qualify for his full damages if he managed to sue the first defamer who set the ball rolling: and that, I think, is not and ought not to be the law.

And Lord Denning at page 754:

> Our English law does not love tale-bearers. If the report or rumour was true, let him justify it. If it was not true, he ought not to have repeated it or added to its circulation. He must answer for it just as if he had started it himself. Newspapers in particular must not speak ill of people for the spice that it gives their readers. It does a newspaper no good to say that other newspapers did the same. They must answer for the effect of their own circulation without reference to the damage done by others. They may not even refer to other newspapers in mitigation of damages. Such has been the law ever since 1829 (*Saunders* v. *Mills* [fn 36: (1819), 6 Bing. 213]) and it cannot be called in question now. It is but a particular instance of

the general rule which excludes rumours or reports to the same effect as the libel ...

But here comes the question: Suppose that the reports in other newspapers were privileged, as they were in this case, cannot they be referred to in order to mitigate damage? I think that the answer must be "No." If a newspaper seeks to rely on the privilege attaching to a parliamentary paper, it can print an extract from the parliamentary paper and can make any fair comment on it.

c) Applications of *Scott v. Sampson*

A number of Canadian decisions have applied *Scott v. Sampson*.

Moore v. Mitchell (1886), 11 O.R. 21 (C.A.).

Redmond v. Stacey (1917), 13 O.W.N. 206, per Middleton J. at 207 (H.C.).

DePalma v. P.F. Collier & Son Limited, [1946] O.W.N. 316 (H.C.J.).

Bennett v. Gage Educational Publishing Ltd. (1980), 16 C.P.C. 241 (Ont S.C.).

Perhaps the most outrageous facts were found in *Fong Young v. Shing Wah* (1928), O.L.R. 370, where Middleton J.A. noted that the defendant had admitted the untruth of their defamatory publication but adopted the tactic of seeking to avoid payment of damages by alleging the plaintiff was guilty of many other misdeeds, including bootlegging, opium smuggling, consorting with women of low character, and having once been convicted of a criminal offence. At page 373 Middleton J.A. stated:

What the defendants now seek, although [default] judgment has passed against them, is an examination for discovery of the plaintiff, to enable them to rake over the plaintiff's entire life-history and so to furnish them with ammunition which may be used to reduce the damages. The suggestion is that by the time the plaintiff has revealed his true character the article published will, under the circumstances, be regarded as rather complimentary. ...

Futhermore, what is being sought here is clearly a gross abuse of the right to examine for discovery. The plaintiff in an action of libel cannot properly be examined for discovery as to his character. In cases where there is justification there may be much to examine the plaintiff about; but in the absence of a plea of justification, it is hard to conceive anything concerning which the plaintiff can properly be interrogated.

In *Hobbs v. CT Tinling & Co. Ltd.*, [1929] 2 K.B. 1 (C.A.), the plaintiff had the unusual handicap of having been convicted of a criminal conspiracy to blackmail an Indian prince called "Mr. A." A number of newspapers published stories on the day of his conviction which alleged other crimes and misconduct not connected with that conviction. When sued, the defendant newspaper did not plead justification or fair comment but simply gave notice of their intention to tender evidence in mitigation of damages. At trial, the plaintiff presented himself as a person of unblemished reputation before his conviction. Cross-examined by defence counsel, the plaintiff was asked about specific incidents not mentioned in the libel or in particulars previously delivered by the defendants. On the second day of the trial, the jury made a "tentative intimation" to the court, and found for the plaintiff in the smallest possible amount of damages. In the circumstances, the trial judge entered judgment for the defendants.

When the plaintiff appealed, Scrutton L.J. observed at page 11 that:

> ... the defendant's statement of defence alleged the plaintiff is a man of worthless reputation and character, being known to the police, and in the profession of the law as such. Paragraph 9 may possibly have some relevance, though I doubt it. It reads: "That immediately following the result of the plaintiff's trial there was published in a great number of newspapers and journals throughout the country articles purporting to give the story of the life of the plaintiff similar to that complained of by the plaintiff in this action, and the defendants had no reason to believe that the said articles were untrue." That appears to be a statement of rumours which has been excluded by *Scott v. Sampson* as inadmissible.

[At page 12]:

> I am not clear that plaintiff's counsel was entitled on the pleadings to give evidence of specific facts from which good character or reputation might be inferred, as distinguished from general evidence of good reputation.

[At page 16]:

> The defence asserted at trial that as the plaintiff had put his good character in issue by affirmative evidence the defendant's counsel was entitled to cross-examine on credit on specific incidents for the purpose of negativing that good reputation, to mitigate damages.

[at pages 17–18]:

> It follows that a defendant may reduce damages for libel by proving that the plaintiff already had a bad reputation. To do this the jury must take the view that his reputation is so bad that the defamatory statement complained of would reasonably and ordinarily cause much less damage than would be caused to a man of good reputation by the same statement. They may con-

ceivably take the view that his reputation was so bad before the defamatory statement was published that no further defamatory allegation could make it worse. But they would have to consider, before taking such a view, the undoubted fact that the worse a man's character is the more ready are people to believe such reports about him, and to face the question whether it is lawful or desirable that because a man's character is bad any one should be at liberty to make any defamatory statements they liked about him, regardless of their untruth. I am not aware of, and counsel was unable to refer me to, any reported case where it was held that, in the case of any prima facie defamatory statement, proof that the plaintiff had a bad reputation which could not be made worse was an answer to the action.

The defendant may mitigate damages by giving evidence to prove that the plaintiff is a man of bad general reputation, and the plaintiff may rebut it by coming prepared with friends who have known him to prove that his reputation had been good. On the other hand, the defendant may not give evidence of rumours at the time of publication to the same effect as the libel, nor may the defendant give evidence of specific facts and circumstances to show the disposition of the plaintiff, as distinct from general evidence that he has that reputation.

[At page 18]:

If those specific facts are to the same effect as the libel, which he has not justified, he cannot justify under the plea of mitigation of damages. If those facts are different from the libel they do not prove actual reputation, which can be proved under the first head, but that he ought not to have such a reputation. Cave J. says of the evidence that it would throw upon the plaintiff the difficulty of showing a uniform propriety of conduct during his whole life.

In my opinion, just as you cannot prove in chief specific instances of misconduct, as distinguished from general reputation, whether involved in the libel or not, in order to mitigate damages, so also you cannot achieve that purpose by cross-examination as to such specific instances.

The law is clear that a defendant cannot seek to mitigate the plaintiff's damages by proving that some other specific incident of misconduct by the plaintiff tends to show bad character.

Finning International Inc. v. Cormack, 2001 ABQB 723, at para. 29.

As noted above, the law is also clear that a defendant is not entitled to plead or introduce evidence of rumours to the same effect as the defamatory expression complained of.

Kelly v. *Ross* (1909), 14 O.W.R. 1078 at 108.

Plato Films v. *Speidel*, [1961] 1 All E.R. 876, per Lord Radcliffe at 884 (H.L.):

> If a man cannot justify the libel that he has actually published, it would be too confusing to the jury to allow him nevertheless to put in evidence on the mitigation issue evidence of rumours or suspicions to the same effect, the more so as the two issues, justification and mitigation, are often not tried in successive stages. Such evidence is a poor sort of evidence at best; and, although it is not irrelevant on the question of a defendant's express malice in issuing the libel and, originally, was probably admitted on this basis, I think that the better rule of practice is not to allow it at all ...

Per Lord Denning at 888:

> ... The rest of the rejected evidence related to rumours to the same effect as the libel. Sampson sought to call a witness to say that, before the article appeared in "The Referee," he had heard the same story in a London club. It seems perfectly obvious to us today that such evidence was not admissible. But at that time there was a considerable body of authority in support of it. Rumours were admissible, it was said, to the same effect as the libel so long as they were in existence before the publication. The point had been left open in *Thompson* v. *Nye* ... I need add nothing to the forceful remarks made by Cave J. [fn 44 (1882), 8 Q.B.D. at pp. 503,504)] in rejecting it. Was the court to receive the gossip of some idler in a club? Rumour is a lying jade, begotten by gossip out of hearsay, and is not fit to be admitted to an audience in a court of law.

Associated Newspapers Ltd. v. *Dingle*, [1962] 2 All E.R. 737, per Lord Denning at 754:

> At one time in our law it was permissible for a defendant to prove, in mitigation of damages, that, previously to his publication, there were reports and rumours in circulation to the same effect as the libel. That has long since ceased to be allowed, and for a good reason. Our English law does not love tale-bearers. If the report or rumour was true, let him justify it. If it was not true, he ought not to have repeated it or aided its circulation.

In Alberta, general evidence of bad character is admissible in mitigation of damages. Evidence of particular misconduct is not, at least in the absence of particulars as required by Rule 254. The reason is no one can be prepared to justify the actions of an entire lifetime — or business career — without notice.

Capitanescu v. *Universal Weld Overlays Inc.* [1997] A.J. No. 740 at para. 34 (Q.B.), citing *Plato Films* v. *Speidel; Scott* v. *Sampson* (1882), 8 Q.B.D. 491.

If general evidence of the plaintiff's bad character is given, the witness can be cross-examined on the grounds for that belief and asked particular questions of fact to contradict it.

Capitanescu v. *Universal Weld Overlays Inc., ibid.* at para. 36.

Where a defendant is obviously mentally unstable, his or her counsel may seek to lead evidence of that fact and that it was generally known to the community of people to whom the defamatory expression was published. That is because it is open to the court to find, in the assessment of damages, that where reasonable business people who constitute the most important source of potential clientele for the plaintiff would be unlikely to be affected by the defamatory matter as emanating from such a defendant, that factor should be taken into account as a mitigating circumstance negating an award of punitive or exemplary damages. Evidence that the appellant was temperamentally unstable and given to making unreasoned and extravagant statements about the plaintiff would also be admissible and relevant.

McElroy v. *Cowper-Smith and Woodman* (1967), 62 D.L.R. (2d) 65 (S.C.C.).

Where a newspaper was sued for libel one court held that the defendant could introduce into evidence earlier newspaper clippings as evidence of the bad reputation of the plaintiff, at least so far as those clippings showed that the words which are the subject of the law suit had been previously published of the plaintiff.

Leonhard (otherwise known as Leonard) v. *Sun Publishing Co. Ltd.* (1956), 4 D.L.R. (2d) 514 (B.C.S.C.).

The facts in *Leonhard* were very unusual. The defendant newspaper, in a year-end roundup of news stories, republished information about a drug war which the plaintiff alleged portrayed him as the head of an illegal drug syndicate. The newspaper did not seek to justifiy the publication, but printed an apology. In mitigation of damages, the newspaper tendered several news clippings from each of the three daily newspapers, including the defendant *Vancouver Sun*, not to prove anything contained therein but as proof of evidence of the general bad reputation of the plaintiff. Some clippings had headlines such as "Leonhard Named City Drug King," "Bomb

Blast Broke Up City Drug Ring." Plaintiff's counsel objected to their reception in evidence. Per Lord J. at page 417:

> In *Wigmore on Evidence*, vol. 1, page 492, the learned author says:
>
> > Whether in an action for defamation, the defendant may use the plaintiff's poor reputation (or lack of reputation) to mitigate the damages has been one of the most controverted questions in the whole law.

Lord J. continued at page 418:

> I think that the clipping are admissible in evidence in this sense — that the words of the libel complained of, or words of similar import referred to the plaintiff as "drug king Jacob Leonard" had been published some few months before by all the Vancouver daily newspapers. If the plaintiff had been damaged in his character and reputation by the libel sued upon then surely his character and reputation had already been damaged by the earlier publications, accompanied as they were with large headlines, as compared with a single line contained in an article dealing with other news items. It transpired during the course of the trial that no proceedings were taken by the plaintiff respecting such publications. He gave no evidence at the trial — he did not see fit to come into court and seek to protect his name and reputation. But he admitted on examination for discovery that he had suffered damage in this respect before the publication of the libel.

The conventional view, however, is that evidence of prior publication of the libel complained of is inadmissible to show the plaintiff's poor reputation.

> *Amalgamated Transit Union v. Independent Canadian Transit Union*, [1997] A.J. No. 191 at para. 63. (Q.B.).

Further, the defendants cannot use their own defamatory statements to establish the poor reputation of the plaintiff.

> *Amalgamated Transit Union v. Independent Canadian Transit Union*, [1997] A.J. No. 191 at para. 65 (Q.B.), applying *Associated Newspapers Ltd. v. Dingle*, [1962] 2 All E.R. 737, per Lord Morris of Borth-y-Gest at 758 (H.L.).

In certain circumstances, the rules of the court may require the defendant to give particulars to the plaintiff of the matters intended to be given in evidence in mitigation of damages. These rules should be meticulously complied with.

> *Leonhard (otherwise known as Leonard) v. Sun Publishing Co. Ltd.* (1956), 4 D.L.R. (2d) 514 (B.C.S.C.).

The defendant may be able to mitigate damages substantially by proving that the plaintiff has perjured himself in the defamation trial, or that he is a convicted criminal, to the point where the court may conclude he had little or no reputation to lose.

J.C. v. V.R. and C.A., 2000 SKQB 83 at para. 19.

In mitigation of damages, a defendant may not give evidence of facts which, if proved, would constitute justification. It is not an objection, however, that evidence directed to showing the defendant's honest belief in defamatory expression will tend to establish the truth of the charge.

McKergow v. Comstock (1906), 11 O.L.R. 637 (C.A.), cited with approval in *Arnott v. College of Physicians and Surgeons of Saskatchewan*, [1954] 1 D.L.R. 529 at 558 (Sask. C.A.).

Where the plaintiff calls sympathetic witnesses, the defence may cross-examine to show that the plaintiff's reputation was not injured, at least *vis à vis* those witnesses, by establishing that they did not believe the defamatory allegations.

Atkinson and Atkinson v. Canadian Broadcasting Corporation (1981), 49 N.S.R. (2d) 381 (S.C.).

In appropriate circumstances, the defendant may be anxious to show the court that the plaintiff, in the witness box, is not lacking in self-esteem and that the trial of the libel action is to him a trivial affair.

Neeld v. Western Broadcasting Co. Ltd. (1976), 65 D.L.R. (3d) 574 (B.C.S.C.).

However, a defendant's attempt to give such evidence in examination in chief or to elicit such evidence by cross-examination of the plaintiff or any of the plaintiff's witnesses may be counterproductive, is certain circumstances, and be regarded by the court as a reason for aggravated damages.

Watt v. Watt, [1905] A.C. 115 at 118 (H.L.)

d) Cross-examination as to Credibility

If the plaintiff testifies, defence counsel may of course cross-examine him or her as to credit in relation to testimony about general reputation, about specific acts of misconduct other than those alleged in the libel, but the plaintiff's answers to such questions will not mitigate damages. It has been suggested that the court should control the scope of such cross-examination.

Plato Films Ltd. v. Speidel, [1961] 1 All E.R. 876, per Lord Denning at 892 (H.L.):

The only legitimate purpose of cross-examination as to credit is to damage or destroy the plaintiff's credibility; but as often as not, the plaintiff will have said nothing to warrant it. The plaintiff cannot speak as to his own character and reputation because he does not know what other people think of him, or at any rate, he cannot give evidence as to what they think of him. And if the purpose of the cross-examination is to introduce illegitimately specific instances of misconduct — which cannot legitimately be put in evidence — then it should be discouraged. It is not good for the law that a judge should admit a "roving" cross-examination to credit and then go on to tell the jury to ignore when they come to assess damages, knowing that it is an impossible thing to ask them to do. Better not to have it introduced at all. Better to keep to general evidence of bad character which, when given by people who know the plaintiff and can judge his worth, it worth more than many instances and does not embarrass the trial as they would do.

If the plaintiff on cross-examination does not make the admissions of specific instances of misconduct which are sought by counsel, the defendant may not call evidence to contradict the plaintiff's answers.

Hobbs v. Tinling & Co. Ltd., Hobbs v. Nottingham Journal, [1929] 2 K.B. 1, per Scrutton J. at 18–19 (H.L.):

When a witness has given evidence material to the issues in the case, you can cross-examine him on matters not directly material to the case in order to ask the jury to infer from his answers that he is not worthy of belief, not a credible person, and therefore that they should not accept his answers on questions material to the case as true. This is cross-examination as to his credibility, commonly called cross-examination as to credit. But as it is on matters not directly material to the case, the party cross-examining is not allowed to call evidence in chief to contradict his answers. To permit this would involve the Court in an interminable series of controversies not directly material to the case on alleged facts of which the witness had no notice when he came into Court, and which he or the party calling him might not be prepared without notice to meet.

And at page 21:

It was argued that when counsel for the plaintiff opened and called evidence as to his client's actual life, as distinguished from the version put forward in the libel, he let loose cross-examination as to every fact of his past life. I think he did entitle the defendants to endeavour to destroy his evidence by cross-examination to credit to show that his evidence should not be accepted because he was not a credible witness, but I do not think (1.) that it entitled the defendants to justify when they had not pleaded justification, nor do I think (2) that it entitled the defendants to cross-examine as to other specific facts in the plaintiff's life to mitigate damages, contrary to the ruling in *Scott v. Sampson*. The defendants would, however, be entitled to cross-examine on such facts to prove that the witness was not a credible person and to employ that proof of his unreliability to the evidence he had given in chief. But by destroying that evidence you do not prove its opposite. If by cross-examination to credit you prove that a man's oath cannot be relied on, and he has sworn he did not go to Rome on May 1, you do not, therefore, prove that he did go to Rome on May 1; there is simply no evidence on the subject.

e) Deception

Where the defamatory expression alleges that the plaintiff made misleading statements, the court will not expect the defence witnesses to remember the exact words used by the plaintiff. In fact, the deception may have been accomplished less by the actual words the plaintiff used than by the impression the plaintiff conveyed to the witnesses.

Hare and Grolier Society v. Better Business Bureau, [1947] 1 D.L.R. 280 (B.C.C.A.).

f) Criminal Convictions: *Goody v. Odhams Press*

Evidence of a criminal conviction is the most cogent evidence of a bad reputation.

Goody v. Odhams Press Ltd. ,[1966] 3 All E.R. 370, approved in *Dennis v. Malone*, [1976] O.J. No. 814 (Master).

In *Goody v. Odhams Press Ltd.*, [1966] 3 All E.R. 370, the plaintiff had been convicted of conspiracy to stop a mail train, being armed with offensive weapons, and robbery, and was sentenced to thirty years. The conviction was not admissible as evidence of the truth of the facts found in his criminal trial. The defamation defendants had first pleaded justification of their entire article, then amended to plead partial justification, in that he had been convicted. In mitigation of damages, the defendants pleaded he already had a bad reputation as a thief and a robber and other relevant previous convictions. The Court of Appeal held that the plaintiff's previous convictions were admissible in mitigation of damages. Per Lord Denning at page 372:

> The previous convictions ... stand in a class by themselves. They are the raw material on which bad reputation is built up. They have taken place in open court. They are matters of public knowledge. They are accepted by people generally as giving the best guide to his reputation and standing. They must of course, be relevant, in this sense, they must be convictions in the relevant sector of his life and have taken place within a relevant period such as to affect his current reputation. But being relevant, they are admissible. They are very different from previous instances of misconduct, for those have not been tried out or resulted in convictions or come before a court of law. To introduce those might lead to endless disputes. Whereas previous convictions are virtually indisputable.

The defendant can properly adduce evidence that a plaintiff admits being in prison and associating with underworld characters.

Leonhard (otherwise known as Leonard) v. Sun Publishing Co. Ltd. (1956), 4 D.L.R. (2d) 514 (B.C.S.C.).

4) Evidence Negating Malice

In *Pearson v. Lemaitre* (1843), 5 Man. & G. 700 at 719-720, 134 E.R. 742 at 749–50, Tindal C. J. stated for the Court of Common Pleas:

> ... a defendant has been allowed to give evidence palliating, though not justifying, his act in publishing a libel, ex. gr. that he copied it from a newspaper; *Saunders v. Mills* [6 Bingh. 213, 3 M. & P. 520]. And this appears to us to be the correct rule, viz. that either party may, with a view to the damages, give evidence to prove or disprove the existence of a malicious motive in the mind of the publisher of defamatory matter; ... upon principle, we think that the spirit and intention of the party publishing a libel, are fit to be considered by a jury, in estimating the injury done to the plaintiff ...

This passage from the judgment in *Pearson v. Lemaitre* has been considered in a number of Canadian decisions:

McKergow v. Comstock (1906), 11 O.L.R. 637 (C.A.).

Hays v. Weiland, [1918] 42 O.L.R. 637, per Hodgins J.A. at 643–44 (C.A.).

Baxter v. Canadian Broadcasting Corporation and Malling (1979), 28 N.B.R. (2d) 114, per Stratton J. at 162 (Q.B. (T.D.)).

Klein v. *Jenoves*, [1932] O.R. 504, per Riddell J.A. at 511 (C.A.) [inducing breach of contract].

In *McKergow* v. *Comstock* the principle stated in *Pearson* v. *Lemaitre* was expressly approved by Anglin J. who stated at 643–44:

> Apart from any question of privilege bona fides is always material upon the question of damages. A plaintiff may offer evidence to prove lack of good faith — absence of honest belief on the part of a defendant — in order to aggravate his damages; a defendant may, in like manner, give evidence to shew that he acted in good faith to mitigate the damages: *Pearson* v. *Lemaitre* (1843), 5 M. & G. 700, 719. The existence or absence of express malice is the issue to which such evidence is relevant and, as the lack of honest belief is cogent evidence of such malice, the existence of such belief goes far to negative it.

In the fourth edition of his work on libel and slander (William Blake Odgers & J. Bromley Eaves, *Odgers on Libel and Slander*, 4th ed. (London, Stevens, 1905)), Ogders cites *Manning* v. *Clement* (1831), 7 Bing. 362, 365, and says at page 645:

> Where no justification is pleaded, the defendant can give no evidence of the truth of his words, not even in mitigation of damages. ... But evidence admissible and pertinent under another issue cannot be excluded merely because it happens incidentally to prove the truth of the libel. ... Thus, if the defendant had pleaded privilege, he may shew that he reasonably and bona fide believed in the truth of the charge he made, and it is no objection that the grounds of his belief are so forcible as to convince every reasonable man of the plaintiff's guilt: *Huson* v. *Dale* (1869), 19 Mich. 17.

Similarly, in *Baxter* v. *Canadian Broadcasting Corporation and Malling*, Stratton J. expressly applied the principle in *Pearson* v. *Lemaitre* in arriving at a modest award of libel damages to the plaintiff. He referred to the evidence mitigating damages in the following terms at 162-163:

> ¶61 I am also satisfied upon the evidence that there was here no malicious motive or intention on the part of the C.B.C. or Mr. Malling and that Mr. Malling had a bona fide belief in the truth of what was stated. It seems clear that what occurred is that the author of the words complained of drew an incorrect conclusion of fact from the material available to him and that the publication occurred in mistake or misapprehension of the facts. Taking into account all of the factors to which I have referred, including the fact that Mr. Baxter [the plaintiff] did not hold the office of Minister of Justice when the telecast took place as well as my impression of him that he seeks principally the

vindication of his reputation, I am of the opinion that a modest award will meet the ends of justice, notwithstanding the absence of any retraction or apology.

Hays v. *Weiland* and *Klein* v. *Jenoves* also refer to *Pearson* v. *Lemaitre* with apparent approval. It is clear from a reading of many other libel decisions that the principle that a defendant may tender evidence of his or her lack of malice to mitigate damages is uniformly accepted by Canadian courts.

5) Provocation

If there is an appropriate defence plea, the assessment of damages may take into account the behavior of the plaintiff.

Hill v. *Church of Scientology of Toronto*, [1995] 2 S.C.R. 1130, per Cory J. at para. 182:

> The factors which should be taken into account in assessing general damages are clearly and concisely set out in *Gatley on Libel and Slander* (8th ed.), supra, at pp. 592–93, in these words:
>
> SECTION 1. ASSESSMENT OF DAMAGES
>
> 1451. Province of the jury. In an action of libel "the assessment of damages does not depend on any legal rule." The amount of damages "is peculiarly the province of the jury," who in assessing them will naturally be governed by all the circumstances of the particular case. *They are entitled to take into their consideration the conduct of the plaintiff,* his position and standing, the nature of the libel, the mode and extent of publication, the absence or refusal of any retraction or apology, and "the whole conduct of the defendant from the time when the libel was published down to the very moment of their verdict...."[emphasis added]

Dingle v. *Associated Newspapers*, [1964] A.C. 371, per Lord Radcliffe at 395 (H.L.):

> Damages for defamation are an expression of many contributing factors, and, as we know, they can be affected one way or the other by a defendant's conduct, by his pleadings, by his counsel's handling of his case, just as, occasionally, even a plaintiff may find his damages affected by the way he has behaved.

Broome v. *Cassell & Co.*, [1972] A.C. 1027, per Lord Hailsham at 1071–72 (H.L.):

The bad conduct of the plaintiff himself may also enter into the matter, where he has provoked the libel, or where perhaps he has libeled the plaintiff in reply.... In a sense, too, these damages [general damages] are of their nature punitive or exemplary in the loose sense in which the terms were used before 1964, because they inflict an added burden on the defendant proportionate to his conduct, just as they can be reduced if the defendant has behaved well — as for instance by a handsome apology — or the plaintiff badly, as for instance by provoking the defendant, or defaming him in return. In all such cases it must be appropriate to say with Lord Esher M.R. in *Praed* v. *Graham*, 24 Q.B.D. 53, 55:

> "... in actions of libel ... the jury in assessing damages are entitled to look at the whole conduct of the defendant" (I would personally add "of the plaintiff") from the time the libel was published down to the time they give their verdict. They may consider what his conduct has been before the action, after action and in court during the trial.

Where the defence pleads mitigation of damages, a defendant may lead evidence that his defamatory expression was provoked by the plaintiff.

Hayer v. *Chardi Kala Punjabi Newspaper Society*, [1996] B.C.J. No. 1426, per Shaw J. at paras. 43–44 (S.C.):

> ¶43 I mentioned earlier [the defendant's] motive. He was provoked by an anonymous letter published in the *Indo-Canadian Times* in its November 12–24, 1993 edition. [In that letter the defendant was accused of misconduct] ... I also find that [the defendant] was justified in assuming [the plaintiff], as editor of the *Indo-Canadian Times*, had a hand in either writing the letter or at least approving it for publication.

> ¶44 I find that [the defendant's] responses were out of all proportion to the attacks upon him. While I take the provocation into account as a mitigating factor, I will also take into account the lack of proportionality of [the defendant's] responses into account [*sic*] as an exacerbating factor.

Stirton v. *Gummer* (1899), 31 O.R. 227, per Meredith C.J. at 235–36 (Div. Ct.):

> The provocation which is admissible in evidence ... must be not only matter relevant to the defamatory statements complained of, but the publication must have been made in a moment of heat and passion induced by the immediately preceding acts of the plaintiff: *Townshend*

on Slander and Libel, 4th ed., par. 4124; *Sheffill v. VanDeusen* (1860), 15 Gray (81 Mass.) 485; *Heiser v. Loomis* (1881), 47 Mich. 16; *Keiser v. Smith* (1882), 71 Ala. 481; 46 Am. Rep. 342; *Quimby v. Minnesota Tribune Co.* (1888), 38 Minn. 528

The principle upon which such evidence is admissible is stated to be the same as that upon which evidence of provocation is received in cases of homicide, and it follows, it is said, that if there has been time and opportunity for "hot blood to cool" and calm reason to resume its ordinary control, a mere provocation not connected with the wrong complained of cannot be shewn.

Dojacek v. West Canada Publishing Co. (1916), 34 W.L.R. 645 (Man. K.B.), per Mathers C.J.K.B.

Burstein v. Times Newspapers, [2001] 1 W.L.R. 579 per May L.J. at 590b:

It seems to me that it is intrinsically just that a court assessing libel damages should receive evidence to the effect that the claimant's conduct has directly provoked the publication of which he complains. Typically, if there were [*sic*] heated slanging match between the claimant and the defendant, and the publication complained of was in retaliation to a publication by the claimant defamatory of the defendant, there would be no sense of justice in excluding evidence of the claimant's publication. It would be part of the context in which the publication complained of was made and should normally, depending on the facts, be admitted whether or not it would be likely to reduce the claimant's award of damages. It may be supposed that a claimant who brings a defamatory publication on himself will normally receive a lower award of damages than a claimant who has been defamed without provocation. There is ample support in decided cases for admitting evidence of this kind of direct provocation — see for example *Cassell and Co Ltd. v. Broome*, [1972] AC 1027 and 1071.

It is not necessary that the defamatory publication of the plaintiff, offered in evidence by the defendant in mitigation of damages, should deal with the same subject matter as the defendant's libel.

Stirton v. Gummer (1899), 31 O.R. 227, per Meredith C.J. at 241 (Div. Ct.):

¶53 *Percy v. Glasco* (1873), 22 C. P. 521, is the only reported case I have been able to find in which the question for decision has been considered by the Courts of this Province.

¶54 The action was for assault, and it was held that evidence of libellous and abusive articles reflecting on the defendant published on the day of and preceding the assault in a newspaper of which the plaintiff was the proprietor, were admissible in evidence in mitigation of damages. That conclusion was reached upon the broad general principle that a defendant may in order to mitigate damages for an act which he is unable to justify give in evidence the recent conduct of the plaintiff towards him in order to shew that his act was not wholly unprovoked but was committed while he was smarting under the provocation he had recently received at the hands of the plaintiff. [31 O.R. at 241]

¶55 Notwithstanding the varving and somewhat conflicting cases and opinions which I have quoteu, we are, I think, bound to follow *Percy v. Glasco*, which seems to me to have been rightly decided both upon principle and authority.

¶56 To require that the defamatory matter offered in evidence by a defendant in mitigation of damages, to be admissible, should deal with the same subject matter as that dealt with by the libel of which the plaintiff complains would be inconsistent with the principle of the decision in *Percy v. Glasco*, and I can see no good reason why the right should be so limited. I can understand that the act of the plaintiff sought to be given in evidence ought to appear to be the inducing cause of or provocation for the wrongful act of the defendant, and that in that way the matter complained of and that urged in mitigation ought to be connected, but beyond that, as it seems to me, the limitation ought not to be extended.

In one case, where the court found that the plaintiff in large part provoked one defendant's libels by publishing libels himself about the defendant, damages with respect to libels by that defendant were assessed in a nominal amount.

Hayer v. Chardi Kala Punjabi Newspaper Society, [1996] B.C.J. No. 1426, per Shaw J. at para. 72 (S.C.).

Where the reaction of the defendant in publishing the libel is wholly out of proportion to the provocation, it may form little basis for diminution of damages.

Hayer v. Chardi Kala Punjabi Newspaper Society, ibid. at para. 75.

A defendant's disproportionate reaction to provocation may exacerbate the plaintiff's damages.

Hayer v. Chardi Kala Punjabi Newspaper Society, ibid. at para. 44:

> I find that [the defendant's] responses were out of all proportion to the attacks upon him. While I will take the provocation into account as a mitigating factor, I will also take into account the lack of proportionality of [the defendant's] response as an exacerbating factor.

The conduct of the plaintiff must be sufficiently close in time to the publication of the defendant's libels to qualify as provocation.

Hayer v. Chardi Kala Punjabi Newspaper Society, ibid. at paras. 75, 96.

An Ontario court held that evidence that the plaintiff attacked the reputation of someone other than defendant following publication of the defendant's libel was not admissible to mitigate the plaintiff's damages.

Downey v. Stirton (1901), 1 O.L.R. 186, per MacMahon J. at 191 (C.A.).

See also *Downey v. Armstrong* (1901), 1 O.L.R. 237, per Falconbridge C.J. at 238 and Street J. at 239 (C.A.).

And see *Burstein v. Times Newspapers,* [2001] 1 W.L.R. 579 where May L.J. at 590–91 approved a decision of Morland J. in *Godfrey v. Demon Internet* in the following terms:

> ¶26 *Gatley on Libel and SLander,* p. 820, para. 33.40 [9th edition] suggests that admissible conduct of the plaintiff might include more broadly provocative actions by the claimant. Mr. Rushbrooke on behalf of the defendants in the present case based his initial submissions on this possibility. He submitted that the claimant's conduct as pleaded in the particulars should be seen as generally provocative and offensive and that evidence in support of it should be admitted on those grounds. He suggested that Morland J.'s decision in *Godfrey v. Demon Internet Inc.* could be seen, if necessary as an example of proper controlled enlargement of the scope of conduct by the claimant admissible in reduction of damages. If it were necessary, as I think it is not, to confine the question in the present case to provocation by the claimant or conduct which is causally connected to the publication of the libel, I am inclined to think that the ambit of this class of admissible conduct should be confined to exceptional cases in which the provocative conduct of the claimant would be admissible even though it did not directly or exclusively provoke the defendant. *Godfrey v. Demon Internet (No. 2)* was, I think, such an exceptional case. It concerned allegedly defamatory postings on the Internet. The particulars on which the defendant

wished to rely in reduction of damages described the Internet news-group in which the postings were made. There was an understanding that those who participated would exercise self-restraint with regard to the content of the postings. It was alleged in the particulars that the plaintiff had cynically pursued the tactic of posting deliberately provocative, offensive, obnoxious and frequently puerile comments about other countries, their citizens and cultures; and had done so with a view to provoking others to trade insults which he could then claim were defamatory and seek to use them as a basis for bringing vexatious libel proceedings against them and against access or service providers such as the defendant. The postings relied on were very numerous and those to which Morland J. referred in his judgment jus-tified the description of them in the proposed particulars. In addition, the particulars gave details of six libel actions brought by the plaintiff against a variety of defendants in a number of countries who had responded to his postings. The defendant's case was that the postings were designed to tempt people to overstep the mark and defame the plaintiff so that he could sue. Morland J said that, untrammelled by authority, he would have no hesitation in allowing the proposed amendment. If he did not, he would be assessing damages in blinkers. In deciding that the particulars should be permitted, he said:

> I accept the argument of Mr. Barca that the proposed amend-ments do not offend the principle in *Scott* v. *Sampson*. They are not introduced to establish that the plaintiff should not be awarded damages because he has a bad or undeserved reputa-tion but to establish that the plaintiff should only receive deriso-ry or small damages because of his bad conduct which is causally connected to the libel sued upon. In my judgment, the plaintiff's postings are germane to the defamatory posting the subject of his claim.

¶27 It will be seen that the decision was based on causative provoca-tion in exceptional circumstances, even though some or all of the plaintiff's provocative publications were not directed specifically against the defendant. The decision was also based — correctly, in my view — on the fact that the plaintiff's postings were germane to the defamatory posting the subject of his claim.

It was stated in *Downey* v. *Stirton*, above, that evidence that the plaintiff attacked the reputation of the defendant after the defendant's libel was inadmissible.

> *Downey* v. *Stirton* (1901), 1 O.L.R. 186, per MacMahon J. at 191 (Div. Ct.):
>
> It is, I think, clear beyond question on the authorities that the defendant in order to mitigate the plaintiff's damages must shew that he was provoke to libel the plaintiff because the plaintiff had previously libeled him; no subsequent libel or slander by the plaintiff can be given in evidence.

A contrary conclusion was recently expressed by a British Columbia court, which held that damages may be mitigated if the plaintiff takes revenge upon a defendant after the latter has published her defamatory expression.

> *Hayer* v. *Chardi Kala Punjabi Newspaper Society*, [1996] B.C.J. No. 1426 per Shaw J. at paras. 24–28 (S.C.), referring to *Kelly* v. *Sherlock* (1866), L.R. 1 Q.B.D. 686, but preferring and adopting the dissenting judgment of Rose J. in *Downey* v. *Stirton* (1901), 1 O.L.R. 186 at 193–94 (C.A.), where Rose J. stated, *inter alia*:
>
> ... It seems to me equally should the defendant be permitted to shew that after he had used defamatory words, either oral or written, concerning the plaintiff, the plaintiff punished him by words, either written or spoken, or both written and spoken, defending himself and attacking the defendant with a vigour and force that largely, if not completely, redressed any injury that the plaintiff had suffered. ...

On the subject of the plaintiff's conduct post-libel, see Patrick Milmo & W.V.H. Rogers, *Gatley on Libel and Slander*, 9th ed. (London: Sweet & Maxwell, 1997) at para. 33.46:

> Limits of this area of mitigation. Whether the limits of this area of mitigation should be defined narrowly is uncertain.... It has been suggested that the fact that the plaintiff had libelled the defendant in reply might be conduct which could be taken into account in the assessment of damages. [per Lord Hailsham in *Broome* v. *Cassell*, above, at 1071].

Gatley also cites *Kelly* v. *Sherlock* as support for the suggestion that the limits of mitigation may be broader than thought. Note however that in *Burstein* v. *Times Newspapers*, [2001] 1 W.L.R. 579 (C.A.), where May L.J. at page 590, paragraph 24, expressed doubt about the authority of *Kelly* v. *Sherlock* (1866), L.R. 1 Q.B. 686:

... I do not consider this particular old case helpful in the procedural context. It was decided before the *Judicature Acts* 1873 and 1875, let alone the *Civil Procedure Act* 1997. There was no issue about whether the evidence in question was admissible: it had already been admitted. Blackburn J's remarks were not centrally relevant to the point in issue which was whether the one farthing damages awarded by the jury was so palpably little that the court should order a new trial.

See Chapter 23, "Pleadings," section C(1)(f), Mitigation of Damages at Common Law, page 585. Provocation, which is a matter of mitigation, must be specifically pleaded with particulars in the statement of defence.

Beaton v. Intelligencer Printing & Publishing etc. (1895), 22 O.A.R. 97.

Hopewell v. Kennedy (1904), 9 O.L.R. 43 at 48 (Div. Ct.).

Dojackek v. West Canada Publishing Co. (1916), 34 W.L.R. 645 (Man. K.B.), per Mathers C.J.K.B.

6) Statutory Provisions Concerning Mitigation of Damages

The defamation statutes provide that in certain circumstances, damages are mitigated if the defendant proves that the plaintiff has already brought action for, or has recovered damages, or has received or agreed to receive compensation in respect of defamation to the same purport or effect as that for which the action is brought. See Chapter 32, "Damages," page 874.

The application of these provisions differs from province to province.

For example, section 11 of the British Columbia *Libel and Slander Act*, R.S.B.C. 1996, c. 263 only applies to libel contained in a "newspaper or other periodical publication or broadcast" as defined in the statute. Section 11 reads as follows:

Damages recovered in another action, or compromise

At the trial of an action for a libel contained in a newspaper or other periodical publication or in a broadcast, the defendant may give in evidence in mitigation of damages that the plaintiff has already recovered, or has brought action for, damages, or has received or agreed to receive compensation in respect of a libel to the same effect as the libel for which the action has been brought.

The Ontario provision is similarly limited to libels contained in a "newspaper or in a broadcast" as defined in the statute. The *Libel and Slander Act*, R.S.O. 1990, c. L.12, reads in section 10:

> In an action for a libel in a newspaper or in a broadcast, the defendant may prove in mitigation of damages that the plaintiff has already brought action for, or has recovered damages, or has received or agreed to receive compensation in respect of a libel or libels to the same purport or effect as that for which such action is brought.

> See *Young v. Toronto Star Newspapers Ltd.*, [2003] O.J. No. 3100 (S.C.J.), per Rouleau J. [discussion of s.10 at paras. 225, 242; 10 percent reduction applied to general damage award in recognition that a portion of damages was jointly caused by the defendant and other publications].

In order to rely on the Ontario provision in section 10 of the *Libel and Slander Act*, a defendant should prove not only the existence of the other libel lawsuits, but also that the other publications overlap with the defendant's market. If on the evidence, there is a low likelihood of overlap, the mitigating impact of the other publications will be negligible.

> *Young v. Toronto Star Newspapers Ltd.*, [2003] O.J. No. 3100, per Rouleau J. at paras. 234–35, 237 (S.C.J.).

The Saskatchewan provision is limited to libel in a newspaper.

> *Libel and Slander Act*, R.S.S. 1978, c. L-14, s.17 .

The New Brunswick provision, contained in section 16(2) of the *Defamation Act*, R.S.N.B. 1973, c. D-5, is not so limited. It reads:

> 16(2) The defendant may prove in mitigation of damages that the plaintiff has already brought action for, or has recovered damages, or has received or agreed to receive compensation in respect of defamation to the same purport or effect as that for which action is brought.

Like the New Brunswick statute, the corresponding mitigation provisions in the defamation statutes of Manitoba, Nova Scotia, and Prince Edward Island are not limited to libels in the news media.

> Manitoba *Defamation Act*, R.S.M. 1987, c. D-20, s.1 6(2).

> Nova Scotia *Defamation Act*, R.S.N.S. 1989, c.122, s.6.

> Prince Edward Island *Defamation Act*, R.S.P.E.I. 1988, c. D-5, s.17(2).

> Alberta's *Defamation Act*, R.S.A. 2000, c. D-6, s. 15(2) provides:

The defendant may also prove in mitigation of damages that the plaintiff has already brought action for, or has recovered damages, or has received or agreed to receive compensation in respect of defamation to the same purport or effect as that for which the action is brought.

The defamation statutes of Newfoundland and Labrador, the Yukon, and the Northwest Territories contain a mitigation provision which is virtually identical to the Alberta provision.

Newfoundland and Labrador *Defamation Act*, R.S.N. 1990, c. D-3, c. 63, s. 18(2).

Yukon *Defamation Act*, R.S.Y.T. 1986, c. 41, s.17(2).

Northwest Territories *Defamation Act*, R.S.N.W.T. 1988, c. D-1, s.18(2).

At common law, evidence that the plaintiff had already recovered damages in a separate action against other persons for the publication of the same libel is inadmissible.

Tucker v. Lawson (1886), 2 T.L.R. 593 (Q.B.):

> Mr. Justice Denman said … he did not think that these interrogatories could be allowed. As to other publications of the alleged libel, the plaintiff ought not to be interrogated on oath about them, and as to other actions for the libel, they were legally irrelevant in the present action except as to cross-examination, and the plaintiff ought not to be interrogated about these other actions or the sums of money received or recovered in them.

K. EXPERT EVIDENCE OF EDITORIAL AND JOURNALISTIC STANDARDS

Expert evidence may be called, perhaps from academics who formerly worked in journalism, to testify to the separation of functions between the reporter and the editor. One such witness testified: it is the responsibility of the editor to confirm the accuracy of the contents of a story before publication and, where important documentation has been obtained, to put it in a safe place and thereafter work from a copy. The editor must maintain constant supervision over the reporter, with a regular reporting requirement, and it is the editor's responsibility to know in detail, before publication, the documentation to support the story, and the reliability of the sources, and so ensure its accuracy. When the story is prepared, it is basic and necessary that the person be confronted with it so that he or she may give their reaction. This could cause the story to be discarded or could also enable the newspaper to add those comments should publication take place. This prevents a newspaper from publishing an inaccurate story.

Munro v. Toronto Sun Publishing Corp. (1982) 39 O.R. (2d) 100 at para. 57 (H.C.J.).

Defence evidence that a newspaper must place trust in its reporter or else no story would ever be published is not likely to impress the court as conforming to sound journalistic practice. The court will expect there to be a marked difference between the functions and responsibilities of the investigative reporter and those of senior management of a newspaper prior to publication of any article or news story.

Munro v. Toronto Sun Publishing Corp., ibid. at para. 57.

The plaintiff may tender an expert witness who is qualified to give opinion evidence on the proper standards of journalism in reporting and research. An individual might be asked to give evidence about what would constitute an appropriate response by a news media defendant to a letter of complaint from the plaintiff.

Ungaro v. Toronto Star Newspapers Ltd., [1997] O.J. No. 201 at paras. 27–29 (Gen. Div.).

It has been held that in order to justify a finding of good faith, a newspaper must establish that it was following a standard of reasonable care to bring itself within the provisions of the Ontario *Libel and Slander Act.*

Ungaro v. Toronto Star Newspapers Ltd., ibid.

Where a defendant is contacted by telephone by a plaintiff requesting the retraction of an article or a warning against the publication of a defamatory article, the defendant should locate and produce in evidence copies of any memos which might support the argument that the defendant acted reasonably in the circumstances. A defendant may properly testify that after receipt of a notice of intention to sue, he immediately sought to investigate the complaint, and referred the matter to his solicitors and travelled and did other things to conduct an investigation. The defendant may then testify when and how he realised that the expression contained inaccurate statements about the plaintiff, and the events which followed leading up to the decision to publish an apology. The defendant may also properly testify that his solicitors assisted in the drafting of the apology, and testify where it was placed and why. The defendant may testify that a journalist would regard a story on page A2 to be more prominent than one elsewhere, because it is closer to the front page, and about the addition of a border to attract attention to make it even more visible. He should also state, if it is the case, that this was his first opportunity to publish the apology after he had verified the errors and received legal advice.

Snider v. *Calgary Herald* (1985), 65 A.R. 99 at para. 43 (Q.B.).

In testimony, a defendant may confirm that he or she does not now allege the truth of the allegations contained in the defamatory communication, and may testify that he or she was willing to make any further apologies requested by the plaintiff.

Snider v. *Calgary Herald*, *ibid.* at paras. 44–45.

CHAPTER TWENTY-NINE:

Charge and Questions to the Jury

As in other actions, the trial judge gives the charge to the jury in a defamation action after the speeches by counsel.

The elements of the jury charge generally have been thoroughly discussed and analyzed in John Sopinka, Donald B. Houston, & Melanie Sopinka, *The Trial of an Action*, 2d ed. (Toronto: Butterworths, 1998), P. VI, c. 6 and in *The Law Society of Upper Canada Special Lectures 1959: Jury Trials* (Toronto: Richard De Boo, 1959) in the chapter entitled: "The Charge to the Jury" by the Honourable Mr. Justice Schroeder.

Useful examples of jury charges in defamation actions may be found in the following cases:

Willows v. Williams (1950), 2 W.W.R. (N.S.) 657 (Alta. S.C. (T.D.)).

Ross v. Lamport, [1957] O.R. 402 (C.A.).

Paletta v. Lethbridge Herald Company Limited (No. 2) (1976), 4 Alta. L.R. (2d) 97 (S.C. (T.D.)).

The following sample charge may be of some assistance to judges and lawyers.

A. CHARGE TO THE JURY

1) Introduction

Members of the jury, it now becomes my duty to instruct you on the law in this case, and to show you how that law should be applied to the facts as you find them.

You and I have quite different functions in this case. It is my duty to instruct you in the law that applies to the case and you must follow that law as I state it to you. You must discard any notions or opinions of your own about the law, or the views which counsel may have expressed about the law insofar as those views contradict what I say to you concerning the law applicable to this case. But while I am the judge so far as the law is concerned, you have the sole and exclusive authority to determine the facts. As jurors it is your exclusive duty to decide all questions of facts submitted to you, and for that purpose to determine the effect and value of the evidence that you have heard.

Under our system of law I have the right to comment upon the evidence of the witnesses, their truthfulness, or the inferences to be drawn from the evidence. If I do that, I emphasize that you are in no way bound to follow my opinion so far as the facts are concerned. It is your duty to place your own interpretation on the evidence and if your views are at variance with mine, or if you disagree with my comments, it is your duty to disregard my views or opinions on the facts and to give effect to your own. I repeat, while I may comment to some extent on the evidence, it is for you to decide whether my comments are consistent with your own views because you are the sole judge of the facts, not I.

When you retire to your jury room I would suggest that you first select a forelady or foreman to preside over your discussions. Ultimately, your forelady or foreman will announce to the court the verdict you have arrived at.

The attitude and conduct of the jurors at the outset of their deliberations are of the greatest importance. I suggest that you avoid expressing too definite an opinion in the early stages of your deliberation. If you listen calmly to the arguments of your fellow jurors and put forward your own views in a calm and reasonable way, you will arrive at a just and proper verdict.

Deal with this case in the same manner, as you would expect an honest and impartial judge to decide it. Set aside all feelings of sympathy, prejudice, or passion.

During the course of this charge I will from time to time be mentioning the onus of proof; that is, I will say that the onus of proof is on the plaintiff in respect of certain matters, or the onus of proof is on the defendant in respect of others. When I refer to onus of proof, this means that the plaintiff or the defendant must prove that proposition by a preponderance of evidence. The term "preponderance of evidence" means such evidence as, when considered and compared with that opposed to it, has more convincing force and a greater probability of proof.

In the event that the evidence is evenly balanced so that you are unable to say that the evidence on either side of an issue preponderates, then your finding upon that issue must be against the party who has the burden of proving it. In a criminal trial the guilt of an accused must be proven beyond a reasonable doubt. But that heavy burden does not exist in civil proceedings such as these. It is only necessary in this type of action for the party who has the burden to establish the matter by a preponderance of evidence. If you can say in respect of a particular issue "we think it more probable than not," then the burden of proof has been met.

Let me illustrate this with an analogy. Imagine if you will a scale with two pans, one on each side. If the evidence in favour of a proposition is put in one pan and the evidence against it is put in the other, and the two pans remain evenly balanced in the sense that the evidence does not preponderate on one side or the other, then the person who has the burden of proof has failed. Or, if the scale is tipped the wrong way, that is, the evidence weighs in favour of the person who does not have the onus of proof, again, that person fails. The scale must be tipped in favour of the person who has the burden of proof in order for the onus to be satisfied.

Now it is very important for you to bear in mind that in determining whether an issue has been proven by a preponderance of the evidence, you should consider all of the evidence bearing upon the issue, and not just the evidence called by the plaintiff or defendant upon whom the burden of proof rests in respect to that issue. You should consider all of the evidence regardless of which party has adduced it.

2) How to Weigh Testimony

In weighing the testimony of witnesses you are not obliged to decide an issue in conformity with the majority of the witnesses. Just because a certain number of witnesses have testified in a certain way does not necessarily mean that you must accept their evidence as being valid. You may, if you see fit, believe one witness against many. The test is not in the relative number of witnesses, but in the relative force or strength of the witnesses. And, with respect to the testimony of any particular witness, you may believe everything that witness has said or part of what that witness has said, or you may reject what that witness has said entirely.

Discrepancies in a witness' testimony or between his testimony and that of others do not necessarily mean that the witness should be discredited. Failure of recollection is a common experience and inaccurate recollection is not uncommon. It is also a fact that two persons witnessing or hearing an incident or event often will see it or hear it differently. Discrepancies on trivial detail may be unimportant but a falsehood is always serious.

In determining the credit to be given to the evidence of a witness you should use your good common sense and your knowledge of human nature. You may in assessing credibility consider the following [go to original notes if necessary]. In this case the plaintiff sues for defamation of her character, or I should more properly say she sues for libel. I should perhaps at the outset explain briefly the difference to you between libel and slander. Libel occurs when the defamatory material is contained in writing or is printed, and there is a permanent record of it. An action for slander is one in which the words are spoken and have not been reduced to writing. This is an action for libel.

3) The Defamation Action

Libel is the publication in writing or print of a false statement or statements about a person to her discredit, or statements which tend to lower a person in the minds of right-thinking members of society.

Our law recognizes in every person a right to have the estimation in which he or she stands in the opinion of others, unaffected by any false statement which discredits that person. Our law protects every person against damage to his or her character, and that is what this case is all about. Our rules require that libel or slander actions be tried by judge and jury on the theory that members of the community are best equipped to determine whether a person's character has been damaged, and if so, what award of damages would be appropriate.

There are four main elements to be considered in a libel or slander case, namely:

i)   publication;
ii)   whether the statement is "of or concerning" the plaintiff;
iii)   whether the statement is defamatory;
iv)   causing damage to the plaintiff. [If the statement is oral and not slander *per se*].

a) Publication

The first requirement in a civil action for libel is to prove publication of the defamatory words to a third person. By publication I mean communication. There must be proof that the defamatory words were communicated to a third person. A man does not publish a libel by sending it to himself. For example, if a defendant wrote a terribly scurrilous article about the plaintiff accusing her of all sorts of vile and untrue things, but sent the letter to the plaintiff only and the plaintiff was the only one who saw it, or if after preparing the document the defendant destroyed it, then there would be no libel because there would be no publication or communication to a third person.

Now in this case there is no dispute about publication. That is admitted by the defendant, so you will not have to concern yourselves with that. Here the defendant admitted that the report in question was circulated to [name of persons to be inserted by judge].

b) The Statement Must Be About the Plaintiff

In order to maintain an action for defamation (libel) it is essential that the words complained of refer to an ascertained individual, and the plaintiff must establish by evidence that that individual is herself. It does not matter if the plaintiff is not named provided she is sufficiently identified by designation or description. Here again there is no issue on that and it is clear that the person referred to in the statement in question was the plaintiff.

In answering this question, you have to answer the question "are the words about the plaintiff?"

[Please note that generally speaking quoting law to a jury is not helpful. It is preferable to distill the statements of law into your own language. The following extracts from the decisions are simply included for the assistance and convenience of judges and lawyers.]

Where plaintiff is not referred to, see *Knupffer v. London Express Newspaper Ltd.*, [1944] 1 All E.R. 495 at 499 (H.L.):

A court in deciding whether a reasonable person would understand the words to refer to the plaintiff does not expect such a person to consider the matter in detail.

In *Morgan v. Odhams Press*, [1971] 2 All E.R. 1156 at 1184 (H.L.) Lord Pearson stated the position as follows:

... I do not think the reasonable man — who can also be described as an ordinary sensible man — should be envisaged as reading this article carefully. Regard should be had to the character of the article; it is vague, sensational and allusive; it is evidently designed for entertainment rather than instruction or accurate information. The ordinary, sensible man, if he read the article at all, would be likely to skim through it casually and not give it concentrated attention or a second reading. It is no part of his work to read this article, nor does he have to base any practical decision on what he reads there. The relevant impression is that which would be conveyed to an ordinary sensible man (in this case having knowledge of the relevant circumstances) reading the article casually and not expecting a high degree of accuracy.

Lord Reid in *Morgan* v. *Odhams Press Ltd., ibid.,* referred to *Rubber Improvement* v. *Daily Telegraph*:

> If we … take the ordinary man as our guide then we must accept a certain amount of loose thinking. The ordinary reader does not formulate reasons in his own mind; he gets a general impression and no one can expect him to look again before coming to a conclusion and acting on it. But formulated reasons are very often an afterthought. The publishers of newspapers must know the habits of mind of their readers and I see no injustice in holding them liable if readers, behaving as they normally do, honestly reach conclusions which they might be expected to reach. If one were to adopt a stricter standard, it would be too easy for purveyors of gossip to disguise their defamatory matter so that the judge would have to say that there is insufficient to entitle the plaintiff to go to trial on the question whether that matter refers to him, but the ordinary reader with perhaps more worldly wisdom would see the connection and identify the plaintiff with consequent damage to his reputation for which the law would have to refuse him reparation.

See *Rubber Improvement* v. *Daily Telegraph*, [1964] A.C. 234.

The defendant's intention to refer to the plaintiff is irrelevant as to whether the words do refer to the plaintiff.

E. Hulton & Co. v. *Jones*, [1910] A.C. 20 (H.L. (Eng.)).

c) The Statement Must Be Defamatory

My duty as a judge in an action of this kind is to first decide as a matter of law whether the words complained of are capable of being defamatory of the plaintiff.

I have decided that they are. It is now for you to say whether in fact they are defamatory of the plaintiff. The result of my decision that the words are capable of bearing a defamatory meaning is that the words complained of are in law presumed to be false; that is, the plaintiff does not have to prove they are false but they are presumed so in her favour.

It is your duty to decide whether the words complained of are in fact defamatory of the plaintiff, or were defamatory of the plaintiff in the sense alleged in the innuendo. I want again to assure you that merely because I have said as a matter of law that they are capable of being defamatory does not remove from you the responsibility of deciding whether they were or were not defamatory. You must say whether the words are defamatory of the plaintiff or are not defamatory of the plaintiff.

Now we come to the test what is defamatory. The test of what is defamatory of a person is whether under the circumstances reasonable people in the community to whom the publication was made, that is to whom the statement was communicated, would be likely to understand it in a defamatory sense; would reasonable men and women on reading this article understand the words to convey a meaning to the plaintiff's discredit? In ascertaining whether the words are defamatory or not, certain principles must be borne in mind. You should consider the whole writing. You should read the whole article again and satisfy yourselves whether or not the words in the publication would discredit the plaintiff in the eyes of reasonable men or women reading that article for the first time. The interpretation that the defendant puts on his writing is quite irrelevant. The meaning the plaintiff places on the article is irrelevant. It is what reasonable men and women reading the article for the first time would understand.

i) *False Innuendo*
In this case the words are alleged to bear an innuendo. What is an innuendo? Let me give you an example. Supposing the defendant had written an article in which he said that the plaintiff in carrying out his business transactions was always a very "sharp" person. Now, describing the plaintiff as "sharp" might in some quarters be considered a compliment. Where the plaintiff alleges the word "sharp" is not to be taken in its ordinary meaning but the innuendo was that he was crafty and a little dishonest, and lacking in some integrity. That would be the innuendo the plaintiff says is to be drawn from the use of the word "sharp," in this case.

The innuendo must be a reasonable, natural inference to be drawn from the words used. Ordinary readers of newspapers or similar articles may be expected to apply their general knowledge of the world to what they read: to read between the lines, as it is sometimes called. Readers cannot be expected to draw fine lines between possible meanings of what is written and often the true sting of the libel is found not so much in the very words, but in the implied meaning that ordinary people will draw from them. In this action, the plaintiff asks you to find that these words would be likely to be understood by ordinary readers as having such a meaning. Let me read to you the innuendo suggested here.

A helpful statement of the law is made by Lord Reid in *Lewis* v. *Daily Telegraph*, [1964] A.C. 234 at 258:

> There is no doubt that in actions for libel the question is what the words would convey to the ordinary man: it is not one of construction in the legal

sense. The ordinary man does not live in an ivory tower and he is not inhibited by a knowledge of the rules of construction. So he can and does read between the lines in the light of his general knowledge and experience of worldly affairs ... .

What the ordinary man would infer without special knowledge has generally been called the natural and ordinary meaning of the words. But that expression is rather misleading in that it conceals the fact that there are two elements in it. Sometimes it is not necessary to go beyond the words themselves, as where the plaintiff has been called a thief or a murderer. But more often the sting is not so much in the words themselves as in what the ordinary man will infer from them, and that is also regarded as part of their natural and ordinary meaning.

See also a statement of Lord Devlin at pages 277 and 284 in the same case:

The proposition that ordinary words are the same for the lawyer as for the layman is as a matter of pure construction undoubtedly true. But it is very difficult to draw the line between pure construction and implication, and the layman's capacity for implication is much greater than the lawyer's. The lawyer's rule is that the implication must be necessary as well as reasonable. The layman reads in an implication much more freely; and unfortunately, as the law of defamation has to take into account, is especially prone to do so when it is derogatory.

When an imputation is made in a general way, the ordinary man is not likely to distinguish between hints and allegations, suspicion and guilt. It is the broad effect that counts and it is no use submitting to a judge that he ought to dissect the statement before he submits it to the jury.

In this action, the plaintiff has pleaded that the words of which she complains have certain meanings, which are defamatory of her, namely **[set out plaintiff's meanings]**. The defendant has denied that the words actually bear those meanings and has said that, in their context, they actually would mean something else to the reader, namely **[set out defendant's meanings]**. In each case, it is my duty to decide whether the words are capable of bearing the meanings alleged. I have already advised you that I have found that the words will bear the meaning alleged by the plaintiff. I have applied the same test to the meanings alleged by the defendant and I

[ALTERNATIVE 1] have found that they will not bear those meanings [or some of them]. Accordingly, you will not consider any of those meanings in your deliberations.

[ALTERNATIVE 2] have found that they are capable of bearing those meanings and that those meanings [or some of them] are defamatory. Accordingly you will consider whether those words, in those alleged meanings were likely to have been understood by the readers as defaming the plaintiff.

[ALTERNATIVE 3] have found that in their ordinary meaning these words are not capable of bearing the meaning alleged by the defendant, but that if the readers happened to be aware of certain facts alleged by the defendants, then such readers might understand those words in the meaning attributed to them by the defendant. That will make it necessary for me to instruct you further on the law of innuendo.

The onus is on the plaintiff to satisfy you that words in their natural and ordinary meaning or as alleged by innuendo are defamatory of her. And if she succeeds in establishing that any of the meanings of the innuendo, or that the words in their natural ordinary meaning, are defamatory in the sense that I have mentioned, then that is sufficient.

ii) Legal Innuendo

The law of defamation recognises:

- that some words have technical or slang meanings or meanings which depend on some special knowledge not possessed by the general public but only by a limited number of persons. For example, the statement that "Parson Smith is frequently at Madam Rosa's" is not of itself defamatory nor would ordinary people draw adverse inferences about the Parson, unless they had the special knowledge that Madam Rosa was a bootlegger or operated a brothel; and
- that ordinary words may on occasions bear some special meaning other than their natural and ordinary meaning because of some external facts or circumstances.

In this action the plaintiff has pleaded that there are certain special facts which were known to the community in which she moves, although not to the general public, which facts alter the apparent meaning of the words and make the words complained of defamatory of her. It is the burden of the plaintiff to establish for you that there are such special facts and that they were in fact known to some of the readers to whom this article was published. She must establish this on the test of the balance of probability, which I have already discussed with you. [Review the special facts alleged and the evidence pro and con]. If you are satisfied that the plaintiff has shown that it is more probable than not that some of the readers knew these special facts and that the words, in the light of those facts, were defamatory of the plaintiff in the eyes of the readers, then you will answer Question 1 "Yes."

[Add where the defendant has pleaded his own meaning]. The same process is to be applied to the special facts which the defendant has pleaded give rise to the meaning which he alleges. [Review the evidence as to the special facts]. If you are satisfied that the defendant has shown that the special facts on which he relies actually existed, and that it is more probable than not that some of the readers knew these special facts and that the words, in the light of those facts, bore to those readers the meaning alleged by the defendant, then you will answer Question 2 "Yes."

[If the meanings are not mutually exclusive, say so]. It is possible that you may think that for some readers the words would actually have been understood to mean what the plaintiff alleges, whereas for others they would actually have been understood to mean what the defendant alleges. In that case you will find that you answer both Question 1 and Question 2 "Yes." That is not contradictory, and I will give you instructions dealing with that possibility later when we discuss the defences raised by the defendant.

These special meanings are called innuendoes or, more strictly, legal or true innuendoes to distinguish them from popular or false innuendoes.

> See, for example, *Rubber Improvement Ltd.* v. *Daily Telegraph*, [1964] A.C. 234 at 280, [1963] 2 All ER 151 at 170 per Lord Devlin
>
> Colin Duncan & Brian Neill, *Defamation* (London: Butterworths, 1978) at para 4.17.

A legal innuendo constitutes a separate cause of action from the false innuendo.

d) Damage to the Plaintiff

The law presumes there will be damage to the plaintiff upon proof of publication. More will be said on this later.

4) Defences

The defendant raises three defences to this action. First, that the words were in fact true — that is, a defence of justification or truth; second, the defence of fair comment; and third, that the words were then published to the people in question on an occasion of qualified privilege.

a) Justification

Proving the truth of the alleged defamatory statement is always a complete defence in a libel action. To succeed in this defence, the defendant must establish the substantial truth of the whole of the libel. Justification means proving the truth of the words used; it means proving the truth of the gist and substance of the defamatory words.

The burden of proving this defence lies with the defendant because as I explained to you earlier, once the plaintiff has established publication by the defendant of words which refer to her and which are reasonably capable of bearing a defamatory meaning, the presumption of their falsity arises. The defendant must then rebut the falsity and prove the truth of the words complained of.

The standard of proof is the balance of probabilities.

The plea of justification is sometimes a dangerous plea to place upon the record, for by repeating the defamation and persisting in it at the trial, the defendant gives it a greater publicity. An unsuccessful attempt to justify a defamation which is entirely untrue may, and almost certainly will, aggravate the damages. I will have more to say to you about this when I deal with the subject of damages.

I have one more point on the subject of justification. Suppose a defendant had said, "John Smith told me that George Brown stole a motor car." Now if a libel action were brought as a result of that statement, the defendant, in order to prove justification, would have to prove that George Brown stole a motor car, not merely that John Smith had said he had. It is the very charge that has to be proved to be true. It is no defence to say somebody else said it; you have to prove that the charge made is true.

Lord Devlin stated as follows in *Lewis v. Daily Telegraph Ltd.*, [1963] 2 All E.R. 151 at 173:

> I agree, of course, that one cannot escape liability for defamation by putting the libel behind a prefix such as "I have been told that ..." or "It is rumoured that ...", and then asserting that it was true that one had been told or that it was in fact being rumoured ... For the purpose of the law of libel, the hearsay statement is the same as a direct statement, and that is all there is to it.

The following remarks may be made if section 22 of the *Libel and Slander Act* applies.

Finally on this defence, a provision in Ontario's *Libel and Slander Act* (R.S.O. 1990, c. L.12, s. 22) has application. In an action for libel or slander for words containing two or more distinct charges against the plaintiff, the defence of justification shall not fail only because the truth of every charge is not proved if the words not proved, to be true do not materially injure the plaintiff's reputation, having regard to the truth of the remaining charges. So if you conclude here (on the two or more distinct charges of libel and slander) that the defence of justification has been established on one or more of these charges, and that although the remaining charges against the plaintiff have not been proved by the defendant to be true, if they are relatively unimportant, bearing in mind the facts that have been proved true, then you can still find that the defence of justification has been made out by the defendant and your answer to Question will be "Yes."

[This is an alternative explanation of section 22 for judges and lawyers to consider.]

Section 22 of the *Libel and Slander Act* applies in this case.

There are two or more distinct charges.

The plaintiff is complaining about both charges.

The following illustrations may assist you. Assume that the statement distinctly says that the plaintiff was (a) a murderer, (b) a thief, (c) slept in church. Assume the plaintiff sued on all three charges. If the defendant was able to prove that the plaintiff was a murderer and a thief but not that she slept in church, the defendant would succeed in his defence of justification because the remaining unproven charge did not materially affect her reputation.

b) Fair Comment

The defence of fair comment requires the defendant to establish that:

i) the words complained of are recognizable by the ordinary reader as comment, although the comment may consist of, or include inferences from, facts;

ii) the comment is based on true facts set out in the article or clearly indicated therein;

iii) the comment is on a matter of public interest;

iv) the comment is one which a person could honestly make on the facts proved; and (some authorities indicate) must, at least where dishonourable motives are imputed, be fair, in the sense that a fair-minded person could believe it;

v) the defence will fail if the plaintiff shows that the defendant was actuated by express malice; it is here that the question of actual belief in the comments made becomes an issue.

There is a good statement of this principle in the old case of *Davis* v. *Shepstone* (1886), 11 App. Cas. 187 at 190 (P.C.), in the following terms:

> There is no doubt that the public acts of a public man may be lawfully made the subject of fair comment or criticism, not only by the press, but by all members of the public. But the distinction cannot be too closely borne in mind between comment or criticism and allegations of fact, such as, that disgraceful acts have been committed. It is one thing to comment upon or criticize, even with severity, the acknowledged or proved acts of a public man, and quite another to assert that he has been guilty of particular acts of misconduct.

The jury's attention should be drawn to the problem about whether there is a requirement for the comment to be objectively fair:

Hodgson v. *Canadian Newspapers Co.* (1998), 39 O.R. (3d) 235, as per Lane J.:

> The defendants assert that there is no additional fairness requirement. A comment is fair, to the extent required to establish the defence, if it is one that an honest person could hold, and this was the law even before the statute, which was enacted to restore the earlier law which had been confused by the majority decision in *Cherneskey.* Any additional need for fairness is taken care of by the malice test. The citation from the speech of Lord Diplock in *Horrocks* v. *Lowe,* set out below in the discussion of malice, lends strong support to this position.
>
> The plaintiffs say that there is an additional requirement. The comment must not only be one which an honest person could hold, it must be objectively fair, and in the case of imputations of dishonourable conduct or motives, as here, it must also be warranted on the facts.
>
> The difference in the two positions is of fundamental importance in this area of defamation law. It is for the defendant to establish each of the constituent elements of the defence of fair comment; but it is for the plaintiff to establish malice. Furthermore, malice and unfairness are far removed from each other. Malice is much more than mere unfairness. So the result of the defendants' submissions would be to remove from the defendant any burden of proving fairness, beyond the light standard of honest believability; and thereby force the plaintiff into reliance upon being able to prove malice.
>
> In *Telnikoff,* supra, Lord Keith, for the majority in the House of Lords, said that he agreed with the reasons of Lloyd L.J. in the Court of Appeal. Those reasons included, at p. 878, this citation from 24 Halsbury's Laws, (3rd ed.) para. 131.

In the case of a defence of fair comment on a matter of public interest the burden is on the defendant to show that the facts are true and, if there is any evidence of unfairness, that the comment is objectively fair, and it is then open to the plaintiff to prove that the defendant made the comment maliciously, for example from a motive of spite or ill-will.

Lloyd L.J. then continued at page 878:

My conclusion is that the law is correctly stated in *Duncan and Neill on Defamation* (2d ed., 1983) para. 12.02 as follows:

(d) the comment must satisfy the following objective test: could any fair-minded man honestly express that opinion on the proved facts?

c) Privilege

Now let me discuss with you the law relating to the defence of privilege. The law has through the years recognized that on a limited number of occasions public policy and convenience require that a person should be free from any legal responsibility for publishing defamatory words.

i) Absolute Privilege

The occasion may be one of absolute privilege or qualified privilege. For example, members of parliament are given the protection of privilege while speaking in the legislature, and nothing said by them on those occasions can be the subject matter of a libel action. There are also occasions when the person making the defamatory statement has a qualified privilege.

ii) Qualified privilege

If the defendant made a statement which was defamatory of the plaintiff, he still may not incur any legal liability for that statement if it was made on an occasion of qualified privilege. Qualified privilege attaches to certain statements such as those made in the discharge of a public or private duty, or those made with reference to a subject in which both the defendant and the person to whom the statements are made have a legitimate common interest. Whether or not the statements here were published on an occasion of qualified privilege is a matter of law for me to decide. I have decided in that respect that the statements that were complained of were in fact communicated on an occasion of qualified privilege. But the protection given by law to statements made on an occasion of qualified privilege is not absolute. On an occasion of qualified privilege, a person may make untrue and defamatory statements about another person without incurring any liability, provided the statements are made in good faith, honestly and for the purpose for which the privilege exists. But if they were made in circumstances which constitute an abuse to that occasion — that is, prompted by some improper motive — the protection afforded by the law is lost. Put another way, if the statement was prompted by malice, the protection of qualified privilege is lost.

Where the defence of qualified privilege is pleaded, the judge decides as a matter of law if the qualified privilege exists. For an extended discussion of the law of qualified privilege, see R.E. Brown, *The Law of Defamation in Canada*, 2d ed. (Scarborough, ON: Carswell, 1994).

iii) Express Malice

Any statement made on an occasion of qualified privilege is not protected if it is made maliciously. The onus of proving by a preponderance of evidence that the words complained of were published maliciously is on the plaintiff. Before charging a jury on express malice, the judge should keep the following statements in mind.

The law is well-settled that in order to enable the plaintiff to have the question of malice submitted to the jury, it is necessary that the evidence should *raise a probability of malice* and be more consistent with its existence than with its nonexistence and that there must be more than a mere scintilla of evidence.

In exercising the function of gatekeeper, the question for the judge is whether there is sufficient evidence to raise a probability of malice. Where express malice is in issue, the trial judge is required to undertake an advance screening of the weight of the evidence and to determine whether there is sufficient evidence to raise a probability of malice before the case is submitted to the jury. To meet this test, the evidence must be more than a "mere scintilla of evidence of malice," more than a "possibility" of malice, more than "some" evidence of malice and "more consistent with the existence of malice" than with its nonexistence.

I have decided that the occasion on which these statements were made is privileged. But it is your duty to make a finding whether or not there was express malice on the part of the defendant. Any statement made on an occasion of qualified privilege is not protected if it is made maliciously, and the onus of proving by a preponderance of evidence that the words complained of were published maliciously is on the plaintiff. Malice has a very wide meaning. It includes

- spite or ill will,
- every unjustifiable intent to inflict injury,

- stating what the defendant knows to be untrue,
- in anger or from wrong motives stating what he does not know to be true, recklessly for the gratification of his anger or other wrong motive,
- using language stronger than the circumstances of the case warrant.

In summary then, malice includes any motive other than the honest fulfillment of the purpose for which the occasion is privileged, and is fatal to a claim of qualified privilege.

Generally speaking, evidence of malice may be divided under two heads: intrinsic evidence and extrinsic evidence. Intrinsic arises from the terms of the statement itself, and includes everything which can be gathered from its language to indicate the state of the mind of the writer. You have heard defence counsel put to you that the statements were not disproportionate, and counsel for the plaintiff arguing that they were violent and far beyond the occasion. If you are satisfied that the language was excessive and strong, having in mind the particular occasion, and out of proportion to the facts or containing gross irrelevancies, that would be evidence of malice. If you conclude that the language falls within that classification, you will find that there was express malice. If you do not, you will find there is no express malice arising from the words themselves.

As to extrinsic evidence: honest belief in the truth of the statement will generally be conclusive evidence that the defendant acted without malice. He may not have acted reasonably, provided that he acted honestly. Knowledge that the statement was false, on the other hand, will generally be conclusive evidence that the defendant was actuated by malice.

Failure of the defendant to make enquiries that were reasonable in the circumstances before he made the statement may be evidence of malice. Lack of inquiry may be evidence of indifference whether the statement was true or false, or it may be evidence of prejudice or bias that you may consider to be evidence of malice.

Korach v. Moore (1991), 1 O.R. (3d) 275 (C.A.).

Evidence that he was reckless or indifferent whether what he stated was true or false would be evidence that he had abused the occasion.

To find malice, you must be satisfied on the preponderance of the evidence that the dominant purpose of the defendant's words was to injure the plaintiff's reputation. You must start by presuming the good faith and honest belief of the defendant in the truth of the statement. The burden of rebutting that presumption and proving malice is on the plaintiff. This onus on the plaintiff can not be lightly satisfied. The defendant loses his qualified privilege if the limits of the defendant's duty or interest are exceeded. You should be very slow to draw the inference that a defendant was so far actuated by improper motives as to deprive him of the protection of privilege, unless you are satisfied that he did not believe what he said or wrote was true, or that he was indifferent to its truth or falsity.

The test of honest belief is subjective not objective. This means that the belief does not have to be reached on reasonable grounds. The test is whether the defendant honestly believed the words to be true — if you so find, there is no malice.

Korach v. Moore (1991), 1 O.R. (3d) 275 at 278

[Review evidence for and against a finding of malice].

5) Damages

In all libel cases there is a presumption in favour of the plaintiff that she has suffered damages, which relieves her of the necessity of proving them. The result is that in actions for libel, if the plaintiff proves that the defendant published a defamatory statement about her, the words are presumed to have caused her damage.

The damages in an action for libel are always peculiarly within the province of the jury. The damages which a jury may award, are classified as follows: special, general, and punitive.

a) Special Damages
Special damages are the actual out-of-pocket expenses lost by the plaintiff as a result of the libel or slander. The onus is on the plaintiff to prove these.

b) General Damages
General damages are awarded when the jury honestly endeavour as representatives of the community to arrive at a figure which will clearly compensate the plaintiff for the injury which she has in fact received. In assessing such damages, you should as nearly as possible award that sum of money which will compensate the plaintiff for the injury she has suffered. Because perfect compensation or exact mathematical compensation is not realistically possible, you must bring your reasonable common sense to bear so that your award will be fair to all parties — fair both to the plaintiff and to the defendant.

You should remember that this is the only occasion on which an award of damages can be given. Under our law the plaintiff must sue in this one action for all her loss, and no subsequent action may be brought to increase or decrease the award made by you. You should strive to fix an amount of money that will reasonably and fairly compensate the plaintiff for the damage which she has suffered. The amount of award should be reasonable, and not extravagant or oppressive. Your aim should be to reach a fair balance, neither too much nor too little.

> *Hill* v. *Church of Scientology of Toronto* (1995), 126 D.L.R. (4th) 129 at 175, on general damages, paras. 164–165, pp. 176, 181, 182 (S.C.C.).

In assessing these damages you are entitled to take into consideration the conduct of the plaintiff, his position and standing, the nature of the libel, the mode and extent of the publication, the absence or refusal of any retraction or apology and the whole conduct of the defendant from the time when the libel was published down to the very moment of your verdict. You may take into consideration the conduct of the defendant before the action, after the action, and in court at the trial of the action. You should also allow for the sad truth that no apology or retraction or withdrawal at this stage can ever be guaranteed completely to undo the harm that has been done or the hurt it has caused. You should take into consideration the evidence as to loss of employment, ... **[add in any other relevant factors]**.

i) Evidence of the plaintiff's reputation

Evidence of general bad reputation is admissible. However, there are several limits on evidence of general bad reputation:

- The evidence must be directed to the particular area of reputation that is relevant. The trial judge will rule what is the relevant sector.

> *Williston* v. *Smith* (1847), 5 N.B.R. 443 (C.A.).

> *Plato Films Ltd.* v. *Speidel*, [1961] All E.R. 876 at 889–90 (H.L.).

- Evidence of rumors that the plaintiff has committed either the specific acts of misconduct alleged in the words complained of or any other acts of misconduct is irrelevant and inadmissible.
- Evidence of specific acts of misconduct in the absence of a plea of justification is inadmissible, with the exception of evidence of a criminal conviction.

> *Scott* v. *Sampson*, [1881-5] All E.R. 628.

> Approved in *Plato Films* v. *Speidel*, [1961] 1 All E.R. 876.

> *Goody* v. *Odhams Press*, [1966] 3 All E.R. 369 (C.A.).

- The evidence must be confined to the general bad reputation of the plaintiff prior to or at the time of the publication of the libel. Evidence of character after publication is not admissible in mitigation of damages as "a person might slander another and then call some of the neighbours to say that they had heard the imputations which he had himself set afloat."

Thompson v. Nye (1850), 16 Q.B. 175.

In the House of Lords in *Associated Newspapers* v. *Dingle*, [1962] 2 All E.R. 737 at 747, Lord Radcliffe put the matter as follows:

> When one speaks of a plaintiff's "actual" reputation or "current" reputation (to quote my own adjective) one means his reputation as accumulated from one source or another over the period of time that precedes the occasion of the libel that is in suit.

c) Contemptuous Damages

Contemptuous damages are awarded where the jury considers that the action should never have been brought. That is, the jury finds that what was complained of was defamatory but they find the action should not have been brought. The plaintiff was being overly sensitive, and although he was technically libelled there was no need to bring the matter to court. In the case of contemptuous damages, a very small amount, one cent or five cents, is awarded.

d) Nominal Damages

The next type of damage is nominal damage. Nominal damages would be awarded if you conclude that the action was properly brought, but the plaintiff has suffered no particular or special damage — she has cleared her character as a result of this hearing, but no substantial damage has been suffered. In such a case, it would be appropriate to award a small amount by way of damages.

e) Aggravated Damages

Hill v. Church of Scientology of Toronto, above, at paras. 183, 184, 188, 189, 190.

Aggravated damages may be awarded in circumstances where the defendants' conduct has been particularly high-handed or oppressive, thereby increasing the plaintiff's humiliation and anxiety arising from the libellous statement.

The nature of aggravated damages was aptly described by Robins J.A. in *Walker* v. *CFTO Ltd.*, (1987) 37 D.L.R. (4th) 224, in these words at page 231 (Ont. C.A.):

> Where the defendant is guilty of insulting, high-handed, spiteful, malicious or oppressive conduct which increases the mental distress — the humiliation, indignation, anxiety, grief, fear and the like — suffered by the plaintiff as a result of being defamed, the plaintiff may be entitled to what has come to be known as "aggravated damages."

These damages take into account the additional harm caused to the plaintiff's feelings by the defendant's outrageous and malicious conduct. Like general or special damages, they are compensatory in nature. Their assessment requires consideration by the jury of the entire conduct of the defendant prior to the publication of the libel and continuing through to the conclusion of the trial. They represent the expression of natural indignation of right-thinking people arising from the malicious conduct of the defendant.

If aggravated damages are to be awarded, there must be a finding that the defendant was motivated by actual malice, which increased the injury to the plaintiff, either by spreading further afield the damage to the reputation of the plaintiff, or by increasing the mental distress and humiliation of the plaintiff.

There are a number of factors that a jury may properly take into account in assessing aggravated damages. For example, was there a withdrawal of the libellous statement made by the defendants and an apology tendered? If there was, this may go far to establishing that there was no malicious conduct on the part of the defendant warranting an award of aggravated damages. The jury may also consider whether there was a repetition of the libel; conduct that was calculated to deter the plaintiff from proceeding with the libel action; a prolonged and hostile cross-examination of the plaintiff; or a plea of justification, which the defendant knew was bound to fail. The general manner in which the defendant presented its case is also relevant. Further, it is appropriate for a jury to consider the conduct of the defendant at the time of the publication of the libel. For example, was it clearly aimed at obtaining the widest possible publicity in circumstances that were the most adverse possible to the plaintiff?

> *Hill* v. *Church of Scientology of Toronto* (1995), 126 D.L.R. (4th) 129 at 183–184 (S.C.C.).

f) Punitive Damages

Punitive damages may be awarded in situations where the defendant's misconduct is so malicious, oppressive, and high-handed that it offends the court's sense of decency. Punitive damages bear no relation to what the plaintiff should receive by way of compensation. Their aim is not to compensate the plaintiff, but rather to punish the defendant. It is the means by which the jury or judge expresses its outrage at the egregious conduct of the defendant. They are in the nature of a fine, which is meant to act as a deterrent to the defendant and to others from acting in this manner. It is important to emphasize that punitive damages should only be awarded in those circumstances where the combined award of general and aggravated damages would be insufficient to achieve the goal of punishment and deterrence.

Punitive damages can and do serve a useful purpose. But for them, it would be all too easy for the large, wealthy, and powerful to persist in libelling vulnerable victims. Awards of general and aggravated damages alone might simply be regarded as a license fee for continuing a character assassination. The protection of a person's reputation arising from the publication of false and injurious statements must be effective. The most effective means of protection will be supplied by the knowledge that fines in the form of punitive damages may be awarded in cases where the defendant's conduct is truly outrageous.

Hill v. Church of Scientology of Toronto, above, at 185–186.

Whiten v. Pilot Insurance Co. (2002), S.C.J. No. 19.

If you have found _____[THE DEFENDANT] responsible for the damages allegedly suffered by _____ [THE PLAINTIFF], you will have assessed the compensatory damages to which the plaintiff is entitled.

Only after fixing the plaintiff's compensatory damages, in accordance with my previous instructions, may you then consider whether the plaintiff is entitled to punitive damages, and if so, in what amount.

The purpose of punitive damages is not to compensate the plaintiff, but to punish the defendant by giving the defendant his just desert, to deter the defendant and others from similar misconduct in the future, and to emphasize the community's collective denunciation of what the defendant did.

Punitive damages are very much the exception rather than the rule. You may award punitive damages only if you have found, in answer to the question, that the defendant [for example: defamed the plaintiff] and the defendant's misconduct in doing so has been so high-handed or malicious or arbitrary or highly reprehensible that it departs to a marked degree from ordinary standards of decent behaviour.

You may award punitive damages only where the compensatory damages you have already awarded are insufficient to accomplish the purposes of retribution, deterrence, and denunciation. This is because compensatory damages may, to some extent, serve to punish.

Punitive damages are generally given only where the misconduct of the defendant would otherwise go unpunished or where other penalties are, or are likely to be, inadequate to achieve the objectives of retribution, deterrence, and denunciation.

While normally the state would receive any fine or penalty for misconduct, the plaintiff keeps any award of punitive damages as a windfall, in addition to compensatory damages.

If you find the defendant defamed the plaintiff, your task, members of the jury, is first to decide whether the plaintiff should be awarded punitive damages, and second, if you have decided to award punitive damages, to assess them in accordance with my instructions.

Remember, you may award punitive damages only if the defendant's misconduct has been so high-handed or malicious or arbitrary or highly reprehensible, that it departs to a marked degree from ordinary standards of decent behaviour.

[Review evidence of defendant's conduct.]

Remember, you may award punitive damages only where the compensatory damages you have already awarded are insufficient to accomplish the purposes of retribution, deterrence, and denunciation.

Remember, punitive damages are generally given only where the misconduct of the defendant would otherwise go unpunished or where other penalties are, or are likely to be, inadequate to achieve the objects of retribution, deterrence and denunciation.

[Review evidence of any fines or punishment already imposed on the defendant]

If you decide to award punitive damages, you must then decide on the appropriate amount. In assessing punitive damages, the amount awarded must be reasonably proportionate to the objectives of retribution, deterrence, and denunciation. In arriving at the appropriate amount, you must consider the following factors:

- the award should be proportionate to the blameworthiness of the defendant's misconduct.

[Review evidence as to whether the misconduct was planned or deliberate; the intent and motive of the defendant; the duration of the misconduct; whether the defendant admitted or attempted to hide the misconduct; the defendant's awareness of wrongdoing; whether the defendant profited from the misconduct.]

- the award should be proportionate to the relative vulnerability of the plaintiff.

[Review evidence of financial vulnerability; and of personal vulnerability, such as age, disability, education, experience.]

- the award should be proportionate to the harm or potential harm directed specifically at the plaintiff.

[Review any evidence of defendant's conduct which shows the conduct could be expected to cause severe injury specifically to the plaintiff.]

- the award should be proportionate to the need for deterrence.

[Review any evidence showing that defendant's conduct towards the plaintiff was consistent with the defendant's conduct towards other, similarly-situated customers, policy holders, etc.]

- the award should be proportionate, even after taking into account the other penalties, both civil and criminal, which have been or are likely to be inflicted on the defendant for the same misconduct. Punitive damages are awarded "if, but only if," all other penalties, including compensatory damages, have been taken into account and found to be inadequate.

[Review any evidence of fines, imprisonment, compensatory damages, etc. bearing on "other penalties."]

- the award must be proportionate to any advantage or profit gained by the defendant.

[Review evidence.]

In assessing punitive damages, the amount awarded should be no more than necessary to effect reasonable retribution, deterrence, and denunciation. It is for you to decide.

Whiten v. Pilot Insurance Co., [2002] S.C.J. No. 19 at paras. 97 and 167.

[If counsel have agreed on the appropriate range of punitive damages, add:]

Counsel in this case have agreed that, if you determine you should award punitive damages, the appropriate range is between $____ and $ ____. This range is put forward for your guidance only and you are not bound to accept it. You must remember you are the sole judges of the facts in this case. In addition, you should not simply take the range suggested by counsel and choose the middle ground between the two suggested figures. If you did that, you would be avoiding your responsibilities to decide the matter fairly. You are entitled to know the views of counsel but you must exercise your own independent judgment.

- As in any civil case, *Whiten* e~ ~hasizes the judge's obligation to be satisfied that the pleadings support an award of punitive damages. See paras. 84 to 92.
- *Whiten* requires the judge to put a range of punitive damages to the jury if counsel agree. Failing agreement, specific figures should not be mentioned. See paras. 97 and 167.

6) Actions Against a Newspaper

In an action against a newspaper, sections 5, 6, 7, 9, and 10 of the *Libel and Slander Act*, R.S.O. 1990, c. L.12 should be covered where appropriate. If the alleged libel was published in good faith; did not involve a criminal charge; was published in mistake or apprehension of the facts; and a full and fair retraction of the erroneous matter was published, the plaintiff shall recover only actual damages. See *Teskey* v. *Canadian Newspapers Co.* (1989), 68 O.R. (2d) 737 (C.A.).

a) Evidence in Mitigation of Damages

In an action for libel in a newspaper, the defendant may plead in mitigation of damages that the libel was inserted without actual malice and without gross negligence and that before the commencement of the action, or at the earliest opportunity afterwards, he inserted in such newspaper a full apology for the libel or, if the newspaper in which the libel appeared is one ordinarily published at intervals exceeding one week, that he offered to publish the apology in any newspaper to be selected by the plaintiff.

In an action for a libel in a broadcast, the defendant may plead in mitigation of damages that the libel was broadcast without actual malice and without gross negligence and that before the commencement of the action, or at the earliest opportunity afterwards, he broadcast a full apology for the libel.

7) Final Instructions

Members of the jury, may I first thank you for the conscientious way in which you have performed your duties during the course of this trial. I appreciate the disruption of your lives that has been caused by your coming to this court to perform your civic duty as jurors. You can have the satisfaction of knowing, however, that you have performed an essential role in the administration of justice in this province.

In this case you have been given certain questions to answer which have been prepared with the approval of counsel. However, I should point out that you have discretion. Instead of answering the questions you may return what is described as a "general verdict." That is, you may deliver a verdict "We find for the plaintiff," followed by the amount of damages, or "We find for the defendant." In this case I would hope that you would see fit to answer the questions because in that way we will be able to determine the basis upon which you arrived at your verdict. Only five out of six of you need agree on the answer to any one question, or if you decide to deliver a general verdict, only five out of six of you need agree to do that. There is no need to be unanimous, but at least five of you must agree. If you decide to answer the questions it is not necessary that the same five agree on each question, as long as five of you are in agreement.

This is the end of my charge to you and I would like to conclude again by mentioning your duty as jurors in the jury room. When you go to the jury room it is your duty to consult with one another and to deliberate with a view to reaching a just verdict based on the facts as you find them and on the law as I have explained it for you. You will be given the exhibits, which you may consider, in your room.

Do not take a dogmatic position. Keep an open mind. Listen in a calm and impartial manner to what is said by your fellow jurors, and put your own views forward in a reasonable way.

I would remind you that your first task would be to select your foreman or forelady. He or she will preside over your deliberations and will record your answers to the questions.

As I have told you, any five of you may agree on one answer. It need not be the same five in all answers. Any five can agree on one answer and a different five on another answer.

After you have retired to consider the verdict, it is the practice of the court to invite counsel to make their submissions as to any additional charge they consider necessary. If I accept their submissions and recall you after you have commenced your deliberation, there is always the danger of placing undue emphasis on what I may say to you at that time. You must not do that. You should consider what I may say then with what I am saying now as one complete instruction.

If after you retire you require any further instructions from me on any point, you need only indicate to the Sheriff's officer who will be waiting beside your jury room. We will reconvene the court so that you can have any such questions answered in court. I ask you now to retire to your jury room to consider your answers to the questions that have been posed.

[If you see fit, comment on the jury's verdict. Or, state that it is not your practice to comment on the verdict of a jury. Or say nothing.]

This completes your duties as jurors and you are now discharged.

or

The jury panel will be returning at • o'clock tomorrow, and I ask that you rejoin the panel at that time.

B. QUESTIONS TO THE JURY

1) Libel

1. Did the defendant, on the 14th July 1937, make the following statement: "Have you been throwing away five dollar bills? If you are not throwing them away you must be putting them in your pocket."?

ANSWER: Yes or No

2. If your answer to Question 1 is "Yes," then was this statement heard by persons other than the plaintiff?

ANSWER: Yes or No

3. If the answers to Questions 1 and 2 are both "Yes," would the words uttered be understood in a defamatory sense by persons of ordinary reason in the position of those who heard the statement?

ANSWER: Yes or No

4. If your answers to Questions 1 and 2 are "Yes," were there facts known to the hearers which would lead them to reasonably impute to the plaintiff that he was stealing money of the defendant's company and committing a crime punishable by imprisonment?

ANSWER: Yes or No

5. Did the defendant speak the words complained of with malice?

ANSWER: Yes or No

6. Are the words complained of true in substance and in fact?

ANSWER: Yes or No

7. Did the defendant honestly believe the statement made by him was true?

ANSWER: Yes or No

8. If your answer to Question 3 is "Yes," are the words in ordinary and literal meaning defamatory of the plaintiff in relation to his calling trade or employment?

ANSWER: Yes or No

9. At what amount do you assess damages?

ANSWER: $_____

2) Slander

1. Did the defendant, on the 15th day of October, 1937, make the following statement or substantially the following statement: "You stole pipes and fittings and used them on your other jobs."

ANSWER: Yes or No

2. If your answer to Question 1 is "Yes," was this statement heard by persons other than the plaintiff and defendant?

ANSWER: Yes or No

3. If the answers to Questions 1 and 2 are both "Yes," would the words be understood in a defamatory sense by persons of ordinary reason in the position of those whom you find heard the statement?

ANSWER: Yes or No

4. If the answers to Questions 1 and 2 are "Yes," would the words spoken lead the hearers thereof reasonably to impute that the plaintiff had stolen chattels of the defendant?

ANSWER: Yes or No

5. Did the defendant, on the said day make the following statement or substantially the following statement: "Mr. Taner, I want you to please leave

my stuff alone, you know what I mean. Just leave my stuff alone, that is all I am asking you."?

ANSWER: Yes or No

6. If your answer to Question 5 is "Yes," was this statement heard by persons other than the plaintiff and defendant?

ANSWER: Yes or No

7. If the answers to Questions 5 and 6 are both "Yes," would the words be understood in a defamatory sense by persons of ordinary reason in the position of those whom you find heard the statement?

ANSWER: Yes or No

8. If the answers to Questions 5 and 6 are "Yes," would the words spoken lead the hearers thereof reasonably to impute that the plaintiff had stolen chattels of the defendant?

ANSWER: Yes or No

9. Are the words complained of in Question 5 true in substance and in fact?

ANSWER: Yes or No

10. At what amount do you assess the plaintiff's damages for slander?

ANSWER: $_____

CHAPTER THIRTY:
Damages

A. GENERAL PRINCIPLES

The plaintiff in a defamation action may be awarded damages in four general categories:

i)   compensatory;
ii)   punitive or exemplary;
iii) nominal; or
iv)   contemptuous.

Within the category of compensatory damages, a plaintiff may seek awards under the following heads of damage:

a. general;
b. aggravated;
c. specific pecuniary loss (special damages) including but not limited to loss of income or capacity to earn income (past, present, and future), loss of business opportunities, out-of-pocket expenses, and amounts incurred to mitigate damages.

The distinction between general and special damages is discussed in Harvey McGregor, *McGregor on Damages*, 15th ed. (London: Sweet & Maxwell, 1988) at page 1119 where the author says:

> General damage consists in all items of loss which the plaintiff is not required to specify in his pleadings in order to permit proof and recovery in respect of them at trial. Special damage consists in all items of loss which must be specified by him before they may be proved and recovery granted.

In the context of a defamation claim, Bowen L.J. in *Ratcliffe* v. *Evans* (1892), 2 Q.B. 524 at page 528 (C.A.) explained special damage as follows:

... [I]t is desirable to recollect that the term "special damage," which is found for centuries in the books, is not always used with reference to similar subject-matter, nor in the same context. At times (both in the law of tort and of contract) it is employed to denote that damage arising out of the special circumstances of the case which, if properly pleaded, may be superadded to the general damage which the law implies in every breach of contract and every infringement of an absolute right: see *Ashby v. White*. (1) In all such cases the law presumes that some damage will flow in the ordinary course of things from the mere invasion of the plaintiff's rights, and calls it general damage. Special damage in such a context means the particular damage (beyond the general damage), which results from the particular circumstances of the case, and of the plaintiff's claim to be compensated, for which he ought to give warning in his pleadings in order that there may be no surprise at the trial.

Special damages must be pleaded in detail. [See chapter 23, "Pleadings," section B(11)(b), Special Damages.]

Ratcliffe v. Evans (1892), 2 Q.B. 524 (C.A.).

Ashdown v. The Manitoba Free Press Co. (1891), 20 S.C.R. 43 at 50, 51.

Instead of awarding substantial damages, a court may choose to award nominal or contemptuous damages. Of course, no plaintiff will seek contemptuous damages — these are typically awarded where the court wishes to express its disapproval of the plaintiff because the plaintiff's reputation was worthless before the libel or because the lawsuit is considered trivial. It is open to a plaintiff to seek nominal rather than substantial damages where the plaintiff simply wishes to make the point that she has been defamed.

Daishowa Inc. v. Friends of the Lubicon (1998), 39 O.R. (3d) 620 at 665 (Gen. Div.), where McPherson J. stated:

Daishowa is entitled to the $1 damage award it seeks. The Friends' defamation of Daishowa with respect to the March 7, 1988 meeting and genocide deserves to be sanctioned by the nominal amount Daishowa seeks.

In an action for libel or for slander *per se*, the plaintiff does not need to prove damage in order to recover a verdict for damages. Damage is presumed.

Ratcliffe v. Evans (1892), 2 Q.B. 524 at 528, per Bowen L.J. at 529 (C.A.):

Every libel is of itself a wrong in regard to which the law implies general damage ... Akin to actions of libel are those actions which are brought for oral slander, where such slander consists of words actionable in themselves, and the mere use of which constitutes the infringement of the plaintiff's right. The very speaking of such words, apart from all damage, constitutes a wrong and gives rise to a cause of action. The law in such a case presumes, and in theory allows proof of, general damages.

Halls v. *Mitchell*, [1926] 59 O.L.R. 590, per Riddell J.A. at para. 54 (C.A.) [citing *Ratcliffe* v. *Evans*, [1892] 2 Q.B. 524]:

> As to the libels alleged — written defamation does not require special damage to support an action, for "the law presumes that some damage will flow in the ordinary course of things from the mere invasion of the plaintiff's rights."

On the other hand, in an action for slander only, the plaintiff must prove actual damages (special damages) unless the relevant defamation statute provides that damages are presumed or that proof of special damage is not required:

Pootlas v. *Pootlas* (1999), 63 B.C.L.R. (3d) 305 (S.C.), citing *Gibson* v. *McDougal* (1919), 17 O.W.N. 157 (H.C.).

Merkoff v. *Pawluk*, [1931] 1 W.W.R. 669 (Alta. S.C. (T.D.)).

Brockley v. *Maxwell*, [1949] 1 W.W.R. 1039 (B.C.S.C.).

Mengarelli v. *Forrest*, [1972] 2 O.R. 397 (S.C. (Mast.)).

Johnson v. *Jolliffe* (1981), 26 B.C.L.R. 176 (S.C.).

Robertson v. *Robertson* (1932), 45 B.C.R. 460 (S.C.).

Ratcliffe v. *Evans* (1892), 2 Q.B. 524 (C.A.).

Damages in defamation cases are not always amenable to precise determination. Often, as in other cases, the evidence will not permit the court to make an exact assessment. However, it is clear on the authorities that where a reasonable estimate of the loss can be made from the evidence, the plaintiff cannot be deprived of damages because of difficulty in measuring them.

Wilson v. *Rowswell*, [1970] S.C.R. 865 at 872.

Tai Hing Cotton Mill Ltd. v. *Kansas Knitting Factory*, [1979] A.C. 91 at 106.

B. COMPENSATORY DAMAGES

Compensatory damage awards will invariably include general damages, and may also include aggravated or special damages.

At common law, as noted above, damages are presumed to flow from publication of a libel. This principle is codified by the defamation statutes of all common law provinces except Nova Scotia, Saskatchewan, and British Columbia:

Alberta, *Defamation Act*, R.S.A. 2000, c. D-6, s.2.
Manitoba, *The Defamation Act*, R.S.M. 1987, c. D20, s.2.
New Brunswick, *Defamation Act*, R.S.N.B. 1973, c. D-5, s.2.
Newfoundland and Labrador, *Defamation Act*, S.N. 1983, c. 63, s.3.
Ontario, *Libel and Slander Act*, R.S.O. 1990, c. L.12.
Prince Edward Island, *Defamation Act*, R.S.P.E.I. 1988, c. D-5, s.2.

Those statutes define defamation to mean libel or slander. In consequence, the common law distinction between slander actionable *per se* and ordinary slander no longer applies in those jurisdictions. Damages are therefore presumed even in the case of slander which is not actionable *per se* except in Nova Scotia, Saskatchewan, and British Columbia.

Similarly, the defamation statutes of the Northwest Territories and the Yukon Territory provide that a defamation action may be commenced without alleging or proving special damage, that is, actual pecuniary loss. Those statutes also define defamation to include libel or slander, eliminating the common law distinction between slander and slander actionable *per se*.

Northwest Territories, *Defamation Act*, R.S.N.W.T. 1988, c. D-1, ss.1, 2.
Yukon, *Defamation Act*, R.S.Y.T. 1986, c. 41, ss.1, 2.

See Chapter 1, "Distinction between Libel and Slander" for a detailed discussion of the distinction at common law between slander and slander actionable *per se*.

The *Libel and Slander Act* of Ontario provides in section 16 that in an action for slander for words calculated to disparage the plaintiff in any office, profession, calling, trade, or business held or carried on by the plaintiff at the time of publication, it is not necessary to allege or prove special damage, whether or not the words are spoken of the plaintiff in the way of the plaintiff's office, profession, calling, trade, or business.

Libel and Slander Act, R.S.O. 1990, c. L.12, s.16.

1) General Damages

General damages for libel are at large, meaning that the court is entitled to make a subjective assessment without requiring proof of specific financial loss.

Munro v. *Toronto Sun Publishing Corp.* (1982), 21 C.C.L.T. 261 at 296 (Ont. H.C.J.).

The expression "at large" was explained by Lord Hailsham in *Broome* v. *Cassell & Co.*, [1972] 1 All E.R. 801 at 824 (H.L.):

> In actions of defamation and in any other actions where damages for loss of reputation are involved, the principle of *restitutio in integrum* has necessarily an even more highly subjective element. Such actions involve a money award which may put the plaintiff in a purely financial sense in a much stronger position than he was before the wrong. Not merely can he recover the estimated sum of his past and future losses, but, in case the libel, driven underground, emerges from its lurking place at some future date, he must be able to point to a sum awarded by a jury sufficient to convince a bystander of the baselessness of the charge. As Windeyer J. well said in *Uren* v. *John Fairfax & Sons Pty Ltd.*:
>
> > It seems to me that, properly speaking, a man defamed does not get compensation for his damaged reputation. He gets damages because he was injured in his reputation, that is simply because he was publicly defamed. For this reason, compensation by damages operates in two ways — as a vindication of the plaintiff to the public, and as consolation to him for a wrong done. Compensation is here a solatium rather than a monetary recompense for harm measurable in money.
>
> This is why it is not necessarily fair to compare awards of damages in this field with damages for personal injuries. Quite obviously, the award must include factors for injury to the feelings, the anxiety and uncertainty undergone in the litigation, the absence of apology, or the reaffirmation of the truth of the matters complained of, or the malice of the defendant. The bad conduct of the plaintiff himself may also enter into the matter, where he was provoked to the libel, or where perhaps he has libelled the defendant in reply. What is awarded is thus a figure which cannot be arrived at by any purely objective computation. This is what is meant when the damages in defamation are described as being 'at large.' In a sense, too, these damages are of their nature punitive or exemplary in the loose sense in which the terms were used before 1964, because they inflict an added burden on the defendant proportionate to his conduct, just as they can be reduced if the defendant has behaved well — as for instance by a handsome apology or the plaintiff badly, as for instance by provoking the defendant, or defaming him in return. In all such cases it must be appropriate to say with Lord Esher MR in *Praed* v. *Graham*:

> ... in actions of libel ... the jury in assessing damages are entitled to look at the whole conduct of the defendant [I would personally add "and of the plaintiff"] from the time the libel was published down to the time they give their verdict. They may consider what his conduct has been before action, after action, and in court during the trial.

Lord Hailsham continued at page 826:

> The expression "at large" should be used in general to cover all cases where awards of damages may include elements for loss of reputation, injured feelings, bad or good conduct by either party, or punishment, and where in consequence no precise limit can be set in extent. It would be convenient if, as the appellant's counsel did at the hearing, it could be extended to include damages for pain and suffering or loss of amenity. Lord Devlin uses the term in this sense in *Rookes* v. *Barnard*, when he defines the phrase as meaning all cases where "the award is not limited to the pecuniary loss that can be specifically proved." But I suspect he was there guilty of a neologism. If I am wrong, it is a convenient use and should be repeated.

Each libel case is unique. Accordingly, there is no formula for determining general compensatory damages. However, the court will usually consider the confluence of the following elements: the nature and circumstances of the publication of the libel, the nature and position of the victim of the libel, the possible effects of the libel upon the life of the plaintiff, and the actions and motivations of the defendants.

Hill v. Church of Scientology of Toronto, [1995] 2. S.C.R. 1130 at 1205

Some of the factors taken into account by the courts were enumerated in *Leenen* v. *Canadian Broadcasting Corp.* (2000), 48 O.R. (3d) 656 at para. 205 (S.C.J.), aff'd (2001), 54 O.R. (3d) 612 (C.A.), leave to appeal to S.C.C. refused, [2001] S.C.C.A. No. 432, by Cunningham J.:

a) the seriousness of the defamatory statement;
b) the identity of the accuser;
c) the breadth of distribution of the publication of the libel;
d) republication of the libel;
e) the failure to give the audience both sides of the picture and not presenting a balanced review;
f) the desire to increase one's professional reputation or to increase ratings of a particular program;
g) the conduct of the defendant and defendant's counsel through to the end of trial;

h)   the absence or refusal of any retraction or apology; and

i)   the failure to establish a plea of justification.

The matter of compensatory damages has also been addressed by Southin J.A. in *Brown v. Cole* (1998), 61 B.C.L.R. 1 at paragraph 107 (C.A.), [leave to appeal to S.C.C. refused, [1998] S.C.C.A. 614] as follows:

> Compensatory damages — I put aside for the moment aggravating circumstances — in actions for defamation have many aspects:
>
> 1.   the compensation for "insult offered and pain given";
> 2.   vindication of reputation;
> 3.   injury to pride and self-confidence — this may just be another way of saying "insult offered and pain given";
> 4.   social damage and possible economic damage which may result but which cannot be expressly proven — this is particularly important, in my opinion, in defamation in the mass media.

Liability for general damages arising from a publication is joint and several. All persons involved in the commission of the tort are jointly and severally liable for the damages caused by that tort.

> *Hill v. Church of Scientology of Toronto*, [1995] 2. S.C.R. 1130 at paras. 174–75.

2) Aggravated Damages

Aggravated damages may be awarded in circumstances where conduct of the defendant or his or her counsel has been particularly high-handed or oppressive, thereby increasing the plaintiff's humiliation and anxiety arising from the defamatory statement. Like general or special damages, aggravated damages are compensatory in nature. Their assessment requires that the court consider the entire conduct of the defendant prior to the publication of the libel and continuing through to the conclusion of the trial. They represent the expression of natural indignation of right-thinking people arising from the malicious conduct of the defendant.

> *Hill v. Church of Scientology of Toronto, ibid.* at paras. 188, 189.

In order for aggravated damages to be awarded, there must be a finding that the defendant was motivated by actual malice which increased the injury to the plaintiff, either by spreading the damage to the plaintiff's reputation further afield or by increasing the mental distress and humiliation of the plaintiff. Malice may be established by extrinsic evidence derived from the libellous statement itself and the circumstances of its publication, or pertaining to the surrounding circumstances which demonstrate that the defendant was motivated by an unjustifiable intention to injure the plaintiff.

Hill v. Church of Scientology of Toronto, ibid. at para. 190.

In assessing aggravated damages, the court may take into account whether there was a retraction and apology. If so, this may negate malice. Aggravated damages are more likely to be awarded if there was a repetition of the libel, or if the defendant's conduct was calculated to deter the plaintiff from proceeding with the libel action, or if the defendant engaged in a prolonged and hostile cross-examination of the plaintiff for a plea of justification which the defendant knew was bound to fail.

Hill v. Church of Scientology of Toronto, ibid. at para. 191.

Although a corporate plaintiff cannot recover aggravated damages for injury to hurt feelings, it may be able to recover aggravated damages arising from the conduct of a defendant, both within and outside court.

Hiltz and Seamone Co. v. Nova Scotia (Attorney General) (1999), 172 D.L.R. (4th) 488 at paras. 233–38 (N.S.C.A.).

Liability for aggravated damages is to be determined defendant by defendant. It is not joint and several.

Hill v. Church of Scientology of Toronto, above, per Cory J. at para. 195:

> … there cannot be joint and several responsibility for either aggravated or punitive damages since they arise from the misconduct of the particular defendant against whom they are awarded.

Reichmann v. Berlin, [2002] O.J. No. 2732 per Sachs J. at para. 15 (S.C.J.), applying *Hill,* above, in making separate awards of $50,000 aggravated damages against each of two defendants.

3) Avoiding Overlap between General and Aggravated Damages

Appellate courts have suggested that a trial judge is not obligated to break an assessment of compensatory damages into general damages and aggravated damages where there is only one defendant. Where there are two defendants, however, the position of each defendant with respect to liability for aggravated damages may be different. Liability for aggravated damages is not joint and several. Therefore in cases of two or more defendants, it is appropriate to break the compensatory damage award into the two components.

Brown v. Cole (1998), 61 B.C.L.R. (3d) 1 at para. 80 (C.A.), leave to appeal refused, [1998] S.C.C.A. 614.

Hill v. Church of Scientology of Toronto (1994), 18 O.R. (3d) 385 at 434 (C.A.).

Where a trial judge makes separate awards of general and aggravated damages, it has been suggested that there is a "very great danger in fixing damages for defamation of double counting" the factors relating to general damages and those said to relate to aggravated damages.

Brown v. Cole (1998), 61 B.C.L.R. (3d) 1, per Southin J.A. at paras. 78, 97, 98, 107 (C.A.), leave to appeal refused, [1998] S.C.C.A. 614.

This danger of double counting does not exist with respect to punitive damages. "[T]he authorities have excavated a sufficient chasm between punitive (exemplary) damages and compensatory damages — general and aggravated."

Brown v. Cole (1998), 61 B.C.L.R. (3d) 1, *ibid.* at para. 97.

It has been held that the factors to consider in determining whether aggravated damages should be awarded overlap to some extent with the factors relevant to general damages.

The court may consider the entire conduct of the defendant toward the plaintiff from before publication through the end of the proceeding.

Reichmann v. Berlin, [2002] O.J. No. 2732 per Sachs J. at para. 15

It is an error of law to "double count" the factors relating to the two categories of compensatory damages — general and aggravated.

Brown v. Cole (1998), 61 B.C.L.R. (3d) 1 at para. 100 (C.A.), leave to appeal refused, [1998] S.C.C.A. 614.

4) Special Damages

Special damages involve actual pecuniary loss. They must be specifically pleaded and proven by the plaintiff to have been caused by the defamatory expression. They include, among other things, loss of income and profits and other financial benefits, past and future.

Botuik v. Toronto Free Press Publications Ltd., [1995] 3 S.C.R. 3.

Significant awards for special damages are the exception rather than the rule for defamation claims. Where the circumstances of a libel allow for full compensation for pecuniary damages in the form of a special damage award, the trial judge should take that factor into account when fixing the sum to be awarded for general damages. In the ordinary case, where special damages are not proven, the trial judge normally makes an allowance for actual and anticipated pecuniary loss in the general damage award. Accordingly, where special damages are awarded, the award of general damages might be moderated.

> *Hodgson v. Canadian Newspapers Co.* (1998), 39 O.R. (3d) 235 (Gen. Div.), aff'd (2000), 49 O.R. (3d) 161 (C.A.), leave to appeal to S.C.C. refused, [2000] S.C.C.A. No. 465.

> *P.G. Restaurant Ltd. (c.o.b. Mama Panda Restaurant) v. Northern Interior Regional Health Board*, [2004] B.C.J. No. 424, 2004 BCSC 294 (award consisted solely of special damages, general damages were not claimed).

C. PUNITIVE DAMAGES

Punitive damages are not at large.

> *Whiten v. Pilot Insurance Co.* (2002), 209 D.L.R. (4th) 257 at para. 133 (S.C.C).

At common law, punitive damages are awarded only in rare and exceptional cases, in situations where the defendant's conduct is so malicious, oppressive, and high handed that it offends the court's sense of decency.

> *Hill v. Church of Scientology of Toronto*, [1995] 2 S.C.R. 1130, per Cory J. at 1208:

> > Punitive damages bear no relation to what the plaintiff should receive by way of compensation. Their aim is not to compensate the plaintiff, but rather to punish the defendant. It is the means by which the jury or judge expresses outrage at the egregious conduct of the defendant. They are of the nature of a fine, which is meant to act as a deterrent to the defendant and to others from acting in this manner.

Punitive damages are only to be awarded in those circumstances

> ... where the combined award of general and aggravated damages would be insufficient to achieve the goal of punishment and deterrence....

> Unlike compensatory damages, punitive damages are not at large. Consequently, courts have a much greater scope and discretion on appeal. The appellate review should be based upon the court's estimation as to whether punitive damages serve a rational purpose. In other words, was the misconduct of the plaintiff so outrageous that punitive damages were rationally required to act as deterrence.

Hill v. *Church of Scientology of Toronto, ibid.* at paras 197–98.

The subject of punitive damages was exhaustively reviewed by the Supreme Court of Canada in *Whiten* v. *Pilot Insurance Co.* (2002), 209 D.L.R. (4th) 257 (S.C.C.), where the Court upheld a jury award of $1,000,000 punitive damages against an insurance company for its bad faith in contesting coverage on a fire insurance policy, reversing the Ontario Court of Appeal which had reduced the punitive damages award to $100,000. Binnie J. (McLachlin C.J. and L'Heureux-Dubé, Gonthier, Major, and Arbour JJ. concurring) held:

i)   The test defined in *Hill* v. *Church of Scientology of Toronto* limits the award to misconduct that represents a marked departure from ordinary standards of reasonable behaviour" [paragraph 36].

ii) Punishment is a legitimate objective not only of the criminal law but of the civil law as well. Punitive damages serve a need that is not met either by the pure civil law or the pure criminal law. Over-compensation of a plaintiff is given in exchange for this socially useful service [paragraph 37].

iii) Jury awards of punitive damages in civil actions have a long and important history in Anglo-Canadian jurisprudence. They defy modern attempts at neat classification of remedies. The jury is invited to treat a plaintiff as a public interest enforcer as well as a private interest claimant [paragraph 40].

iv) The three objectives identified in prior jurisprudence — punishment, deterrence, and denunciation — are still in use although they might be more appropriately referred to as retribution, deterrence, and denunciation [paragraph 43].

Further to the Supreme Court of Canada's decision to uphold the $800,000 punitive damages award in *Hill* v. *Church of Scientology of Toronto*, above, Binnie J. held in *Whiten* that the Court should further clarify the rules governing whether an award of punitive damages ought to be made, and if so, the assessment of a quantum that is fair to all parties [paragraph 45]. He stated at paragraph 94 that the trial judge's charge to the jury should convey the following points:

(1) Punitive damages are very much the exception rather than the rule,

(2) imposed only if there has been high-handed, malicious, arbitrary or highly reprehensible misconduct that departs to a marked degree from ordinary standards of decent behaviour.

(3) Where they are awarded, punitive damages should be assessed in an amount reasonably proportionate to such factors as the harm caused, the degree of the misconduct, the relative vulnerability of the plaintiff and any advantage or profit gained by the defendant, and

(4) having regard to any other fines or penalties suffered by the defendant for the misconduct in question.

(5) Punitive damages are generally given only where the misconduct would otherwise be unpunished or where other penalties are or are likely to be inadequate to achieve the objectives of retribution, deterrence and denunciation.

(6) Their purpose is not to compensate the plaintiff, but

(7) to give a defendant his or her just dessert (retribution), to deter the defendant and others from similar misconduct in the future (deterrence), and to mark the community's collective condemnation (denunciation) of what has happened.

(8) Punitive damages are awarded only where compensatory damages, which to some extent are punitive, are insufficient to accomplish these objectives, and

(9) they are given in an amount that is no greater than necessary to rationally accomplish their purpose.

(10) While normally the state would be the recipient of any fine or penalty for misconduct, the plaintiff will keep punitive damages as a "windfall" in addition to compensatory damages.

(11) Judges and juries in our system have usually found that moderate awards of punitive damages, which inevitably carry a stigma in the broader community, are generally sufficient.

Binnie J. in *Whiten* went on to state at paragraph 97 that "if counsel can agree on a 'bracket' or 'range' of an appropriate award, the trial judge should convey these figures to the jury, but at the present time specific figures should not be mentioned in the absence of such an agreement," citing *Hill v. Church of Scientology of Toronto*, above, at paragraphs 162–63. He warned that this prohibition may have to be re-examined in the future, based on further experience. "Counsel should also consider the desirability of asking the trial judge to advise the jury of awards of punitive damages made in comparable circumstances that have been sustained on appeal" [paragraph 97].

In *Whiten* it was also held [at paragraphs 111 to 126] that a proper award of punitive damages must be rationally proportionate in several dimensions:

i)   The blameworthiness of the defendant's conduct; including

   a.   whether the misconduct was planned and deliberate;

   b.   the defendant's intent and motive;

   c.   whether the defendant persisted in the outrageous conduct over time;

   d.   whether the defendant concealed or attempted to cover up his or her misconduct;

   e.   the defendant's awareness that what he or she was doing was wrong;

   f.   whether the defendant profited from his or her misconduct; and

   g.   whether the misconduct violated something integral to the plaintiff, such as professional reputation as in *Hill v. Church of Scientology of Toronto.*

ii)   The degree of vulnerability of the plaintiff.

iii)   The harm or potential harm specifically directed at the plaintiff.

iv)   The need for deterrence.

v)   Taking into account the other penalties, both civil and criminal, which have been or are likely to be inflicted on the defendant for the same misconduct.

vi)   The advantage wrongfully gained by the defendant from the misconduct.

It was also suggested in *Whiten* [at paragraph 122] that where a trial judge is concerned that the claim for punitive damages may affect the fairness of the liability trial, bifurcated proceedings may be appropriate.

As proportionality is a broader concept than the relationship between punitive damages and compensatory damages, adoption of a ratio between the two types of damages would be inappropriate [*Whiten*, paragraph 127]. Per Binnie J. at paragraph 132:

> While, as stated, I do not consider the "ratio" test to be an appropriate indicator of rationality, the ratio of punitive damages to compensatory damages in the present case would be either a multiple of three ... or a multiple of less than two.... Either way, the ratio is well within what has been considered "rational" in decided cases.

Punitive damages might not be appropriate where the defendant was previously convicted and punished by a criminal court for defamatory libel in relation to the same publication.

Anderson v. Kocsis, [1998] 86 O.T.C. 107 at paras. 50–56 (Gen. Div).

D. NOMINAL DAMAGES

The purpose of nominal damages is to vindicate the plaintiff's rights even where no sum of money is necessary.

> Nominal damages are a small sum of money, awarded when the plaintiff is able to establish a cause of action but has suffered no substantial loss or is unable to prove what that loss is.

Langille v. McGrath (2001), 243 N.B.R. (2d) 360 at para. 18 (C.A.), per Deschenes J.A., adopting the following passage from J. Cassels, *Remedies: The Law of Damages* (Toronto: Irwin Law, 2000) at 281 and 285:

> McGregor describes the purpose of nominal damages as "establishing, determining or protecting a legal right." [Note 1: H. McGregor, *McGregor on Damages*, 15th ed. (London: Sweet & Maxwell Ltd., 1988) at 403]. He states that they are available in two situations. The first is where the plaintiff proves that she has suffered some wrong, but no loss (or a trifling loss) has arisen from that wrong. The other, less important, situation is when the plaintiff has shown there was a loss, but the "necessary evidence as to its amount is not given." An ancillary reason for awarding nominal damages is that they may be a "peg on which to hang costs." [Note 2: Maule J. in *Beaumont v. Greathead* (1846), 2 C.B. 494 at 499, 135 E.R. 1039]

The Mediana, [1900] A.C. 113, per Lord Halsbury L.C. at 116:

> "Nominal damages" is a technical phrase which means that you have negatived anything like real damage, but that you are affirming by your nominal damages that there is an infraction of a legal right which, though it gives no right to any real damages at all, yet gives you a right to the verdict or judgment because your legal right has been infringed.

A jury is not limited to awarding nominal damages merely because the plaintiff leads no evidence concerning damages.

Munro v. Toronto Sun Publishing Corp., (1982), 39 O.R. (2d) 100 at 119 (H.C.), adopting WIlliam Blake Odgers, *Odgers on the Law of Libel and Slander*, 5th ed. (London: Stevens, 1912) at 373:

> … Even if no evidence be offered by the plaintiff as to damages, the jury are in no way bound to give nominal damages only; they may read the libel and give substantial damages as will compensate the plaintiff for such defamation.

Reichmann v. Toronto Life Publishing Co. (1990), 71 O.R. (2d) 719 (H.C.J.) per Anderson J., approving *Blachford v. Green* (1892), 14 P.R. 424 (Ont. H.C.).

The primary remedy for defamation is an award of damages. Accordingly, the verdict in a defamation action should not normally be limited to nominal damages.

Langille v. McGrath (2001), 243 N.B.R. (2d) 360, per Deschenes J.A. at para. 21 (C.A.), citing P.H. Osborne, *The Law of Torts* (Toronto: Irwin Law, 2000) at 368–69.

Although no amount of substantial damages can be adequate where a conscientious plaintiff carrying out public duties has been defamed, and the injury is not easily capable of monetary compensation, it is normally inappropriate for the court to limit its award to nominal damages.

MacKay v. Southam Co. Ltd. (1955), 1 D.L.R. (2d) 1 (B.C.C.A.), applied in *McCullough v. Cohen*, [2000] O.T.C. 671 at para. 30 (S.C.J.).

Nominal damages may be awarded where the judge or jury considers that there has been no real damage to the plaintiff even in the case of a malicious libel.

Dennison v. Sanderson, [1946] O.R. 601 (C.A.), per Robertson C.J.O., citing *Cooke v. Brogden and Co.* (1885), 1 T.L.R. 497 at 499

It is not the usual practice to order a new trial to enable a plaintiff to recover merely nominal damages.

Dennison v. Sanderson, [1946] O.R. 601 (S.C.A.D.), per Robertson C.J.O. citing *Milligan v. Jamieson* (1902), 4 O.L.R. 650 (C.A.); *Scammell v. Clarke* (1894), 23 S.C.R. 307; *Simons v. Chesley* (1891), 21 S.C.R. 174.

In some instances, it has been held that an award of nominal damages may constitute a reflection of the jury's conclusion that although the action was properly brought by the plaintiff, the plaintiff was able to clear his or her reputation through the proceedings and did not suffer substantial damages.

GWE Consulting Group Ltd. v. Kant, [1993] B.C.J. No. 1282, per Hutchison J. at para. 13 (S.C.).

Nominal damages may also be awarded where there is extremely limited publication, there has been no real diminution in the plaintiff's reputation, and the defendant apologizes.

Fisher v. Richardson, [2002] B.C.J. No. 1017, 2002 BCSC 653 [nominal damages: $100].

Even where there is no apology, if the injury to the plaintiff's reputation is slight, the award may be limited to nominal damages.

Woldu v. Desta (1998), 170 Sask. R. 18, per Wimmer J. at paras. 8–10 (Q.B.) [nominal damages: $1,000].

Singh v. Doad, [1990] A.J. No. 240 [nominal damages: one plaintiff $1,000; the other $500].

Even where defamatory words are spoken at a public meeting, where the main relief sought by plaintiff's counsel was a judgment that amounted to a vindication of her reputation, the award was limited to nominal damages because no one who heard the statements believed that they were true and the plaintiff cleared her name with no substantial damages.

Willes v. Duce, [1993] O.J. No. 3169 per Woods J. at paras. 24–28 (Gen. Div.) [nominal damages: $500].

It is not unusual for only very nominal damages to be awarded in slander actions because so often no great harm has been done.

Colliar v. Robinson Diesel Injection Ltd. (1988), 72 Sask. R. 81 (Q.B.) per Wimmer J.

1) What Constitutes a Nominal Award?

There is no clear consensus in the jurisprudence about what sum or range of sums constitutes a merely nominal award. For example:

- $1,000 damages was held to be "not merely nominal" in a case where a court found evidence of injury to a corporate plaintiff's reputation.

  Ascot Holdings Ltd. v. Wilkie (1993), 49 C.P.R. (3d) 188 (B.C.S.C.) per Tysoe J.

- $1,000 was held to be nominal damages.

  Woldu v. Desta (1998), 170 Sask. R. 18 (Q.B.).

  Singh v. Doad, [1990] A.J. No. 240.

  Slack v. Ad-Rite Associates Ltd., [1998] O.J. No. 5446 (Gen. Div.).

  Kelsie v. Canada (Attorney General), [2003] N.J. No. 232, 2003 NLSCTD 139, per Barry J. at para. 38.

- $500 was held to be nominal damages.

  Singh v. Doad, [1990] A.J. No. 420.

  Willes v. Duce, [1993] O.J. No. 3169 (Gen. Div.).

- $100 held not to be a nominal award.

  Maietta v. Bennett (1988), 72 Nfld. & P.E.I.R. 185 (Nfld. S.C. (T.D.)).

- $100 was held to be a nominal award.

  Fisher v. Richardson, [2002] B.C.J. No. 1017, 2002 BCSC 653.

- $1 was held to be a nominal award.

  Frier v. Lambert, [1961] O.J. No. 362.

In *Wilson v. Taylor*, [1980] O.J. No. 229 (H.C.J.), Hollingworth J. charged the jury that nominal damages would be somewhere between $1 and $150 [paragraph 35].

Molloy J., in her judgment addressing issues arising from the jury's verdict in *Gouveia v. Toronto Star Newspapers Ltd.* (1998), 75 O.T.C. 186 (Gen. Div.), discussed the jury's award of $5,000 damages at paragraphs 45–46:

> ... the jury in this case was given no guidance as to the range of general compensatory damages except that counsel for the plaintiffs submitted that the damages should be "substantial" and counsel for the defendants submitted that if damages were awarded they should be "nominal." Many people would consider $5000.00 to be a lot of money. I have no way of determining whether this jury considered a $5000.00 award to be nominal or substantial. Further, if the jury meant to award nominal damages, I have no way of knowing whether this might have been because they considered that the injury to the plaintiff was minimal or that the libel itself was minimal, or both, or neither.

The boundary between a sum of money representing a contemptuous award and nominal damages is not clearly defined in the authorities. In *Doyle v. Sparrow* (1979), 106 D.L.R. (3d) 551 (Ont. C.A.), MacKinnon A.C.J.O. agreed that it was not clear whether the $2 damages awarded by the jury was nominal damages or contemptuous damages.

E. CONTEMPTUOUS DAMAGES

Contemptuous damages are described in Peter F. Carter-Ruck & Harvey Starte, *Carter-Ruck on Libel and Slander*, 5th ed. (Butterworths: London, 1997) where the authors state:

> Contemptuous damages, usually the award of "the smallest coin in the realm," originally a farthing, more recently a half-penny, and presumably now a penny, are traditionally awarded when in the opinion of the jury the action ought never to have been brought [Note 4: *Newstead v. London Express News-*

papers Ltd. [1940] 1 K.B. 377, [1939] 4 All E.R. 319; *Dering v. Uris* [1964] 2 Q.B. 669, [1964] 2 All E.R. 660n; *Brooks v. IPC Newspapers Ltd.* (1974), Times 26 November; *Pamplin v. Express Newspapers Ltd. (No. 2)* [1988] 1 All E.R. 282, [1988] 1 W.L.R. 116n, C.A.], perhaps because the plaintiff's reputation is already so bad that the publication cannot have done him any harm, or because the libel or slander complained of, though technically actionable, was nevertheless utterly trivial.

J. Cassels, *Remedies: The Law of Damages* (Toronto: Irwin Law, 2000) at 281 and 285, adopted in *Langille v. McGrath* (2001) 243 N.B.R. (2d) 360 at para. 18 (C.A.), per Deschenes J.A.:

> Contemptuous damages are awarded when the plaintiff is entitled to judgment but the judge or jury disapproves of the plaintiff's conduct. To signal this disapproval, the award will be of the smallest amount of money possible. In these cases, the plaintiff is technically successful in the lawsuit, but the judge or jury is of the opinion the action should never have been brought.

A judge or jury may award contemptuous damages if they consider the action should never have been brought.

> *Dennison v. Sanderson,* [1946] O.R. 601 (C.A.), referring to the trial judge's charge to the jury.

However, it has been held that it is inappropriate to award only contemptuous damages where a serious defamatory allegation was admittedly made by the defendant, it was disseminated to a large audience during a televised meeting of a municipal council, it was repeated to a television reporter for broadcasting, there was no apology, and justification was pleaded.

> *Langille v. McGrath* (2001), 243 N.B.R. (2d) 360 (C.A.).

F. RELEVANT ISSUES

1) Appellate Intervention Limited

There is no cap for general damages in libel cases similar to the $100,000 level (adjusted for inflation) imposed by the so-called trilogy of 1978 decisions of the Supreme Court of Canada with respect to damages for non-pecuniary loss for pain and suffering in personal injury cases.

> *Hill v. Church of Scientology of Toronto,* [1995] 2 S.C.R. 1130 at 1197.

> *Botiuk v. Toronto Free Press Publications Ltd.,* [1995] 3 S.C.R. 3 at 37.

The test for appellate interference with sums awarded for general or aggravated damages is whether they shock the conscience of the court.

> *Hill v. Church of Scientology of Toronto*, [1995] 2 S.C.R. 1130 at 1194, adopting the reasons of Robins J.A. in *Walker v. CFTO Ltd.* (1987), 59 O.R. (2d) 104 at 110 (C.A.), describing the task of the court as to consider:
>
> > … whether the verdict is so inordinately large as obviously to exceed the maximum limit of a reasonable range within which the jury may properly operate or, put another way, whether the verdict is so exorbitant or so grossly out of proportion to the libel as to shock the court's conscience and sense of justice.

Unlike compensatory damages, punitive damages are more susceptible to appellate review, which should be based on the court's estimation as to whether they were rationally required to serve the purpose of deterrence.

> *Hill v. Church of Scientology of Toronto*, above, at paras 196–99.
>
> *Hodgson v. Canadian Newspapers Co.*, (1998), 39 O.R. (3d) 235 (Gen. Div.), aff'd (2000), 49 O.R. (3d) 161 (C.A.), leave to appeal to S.C.C. denied, [2000] SCCA 465.

In *Whiten v. Pilot Insurance Co.* (2002), 209 D.L.R. (4th) 257, the Supreme Court of Canada held that the "rationality" test prescribed in *Hill v. Church of Scientology of Toronto* applies to the question of whether an award of punitive damages should be made at all, as well as to the question of its quantum [paragraph 102].

The jury must be given some latitude with respect to punitive damages. The test is whether a reasonable jury, properly instructed, could have concluded that an award in that amount and no less was rationally required to punish the defendant's misconduct.

> *Whiten v. Pilot Insurance Co.* (2002), 209 D.L.R. (4th) 257, per Binnie J. at para. 107 (S.C.C.).

2) Personal Injury Awards Not Comparable

The Supreme Court of Canada in 1995 unequivocally rejected the argument that a comparison should be made between defamation and personal injury cases in determining the amount to be awarded for damages.

> "[T]he injury suffered by a plaintiff as a result of injurious statements is entirely different from the non-pecuniary damages suffered by a plaintiff in a personal injury case. In the latter case, the plaintiff is compensated for every

aspect of the injury suffered: past lost of income and estimated future loss of income, past medical care and estimated cost of future medical care, as well as non-pecuniary damages." "A very different situation is presented with respect to libel actions. In these cases, special damages for pecuniary loss are rarely claimed and often exceedingly difficult to prove."

Hill v. Church of Scientology of Toronto, [1995] 2 S.C.R. 1130 at paras. 168–69.

Less than six months after *Hill v. Church of Scientology of Toronto* was decided, however, the English Court of Appeal unanimously ruled in *John v. MGN Ltd.*, [1995] N.L.O.R. No. 510, [1996] 2 All. E.R. 35 (C.A.) that judges and lawyers, in their remarks to the jury in a defamation case, may:

(i)   refer to the conventional levels of damages awarded in personal injury cases;

(ii)   refer to previous libel awards made or approved by the Court of Appeal (but not by other juries); and

(iii)   indicate the level of award they consider appropriate.

John expressly overruled *Rantzen v. MGN (1986) Ltd.*, [1994] Q.B. 670, which had been relied upon by the Supreme Court of Canada in its assertion that English law had rejected the proposition that juries should be referred to conventional awards for personal injuries as a check on the reasonableness of proposed awards for defamation.

The Supreme Court of Canada referred to *John v. MGN Ltd*, above, in *Whiten v. Pilot Insurance Co.* (2002), 209 D.L.R. (4th) 257 (S.C.C.) in the context of an appeal concerning punitive damages. Although *Whiten* (see discussion above, section C) may impact the practice with respect to charging the jury concerning the punitive damages component of a potential verdict, the Supreme Court of Canada gave no hint that it may be rethinking its position with respect to a comparison between personal injury and defamation verdicts.

See *Gleaner Co. v. Abrahams*, [2003] J.C.J. No. 55 (P.C.), where the Judicial Committee of the Privy Council explains the current English practice since *John v. MGN Ltd.* Although expressly declining to approve or disapprove *John v. MGN Ltd.*, the Judicial Committee at paragraphs 49–56, 61–63 articulates certain significant differences between libel and personal injury cases, particularly the influence of "society's views on the need to use private litigation as a means of controlling the irresponsible behaviour by the media."

3) Awards

Defamation verdicts fall into a very wide range. At the top end of the scale in the common law provinces is the award of an Ontario jury in *Hill v. Church of Scientology of Toronto*, [1995] 2 S.C.R. 1130, which consisted of $300,000 general damages, $500,000 aggravated damages, and $800,000 punitive damages.

Prior to *Hill*, the largest Canadian trial verdict for defamation sustained on appeal was $135,000, awarded by a Quebec jury as non-pecuniary damages against a Montreal daily newspaper.

Snyder v. Montreal Gazette, [1988] 1 S.C.R. 494.

In *Hill*, Canada's highest court unanimously upheld an award more than ten times higher, rendered by an Ontario jury in favour of a lawyer employed by the provincial Ministry of the Attorney General which funded his libel action through all stages of the litigation. Before the defendant Scientology's appeal was heard by the Supreme Court of Canada, the plaintiff was appointed a judge of the Ontario High Court. This unprecedented $1.6 million award did not include special damages as none were proven.

In the years since *Hill v. Scientology*, the median value of defamation damage awards has increased significantly. The top ten Canadian judgments from the Canadian common law jurisdictions as of 1 April 2004 (in terms of aggregate awards to all plaintiffs in the lawsuit) are in order of descending magnitude (including *Hill*):

i) **$1,600,000:** consisting of $300,000 general damages, $500,000 aggravated damages, and $800,000 punitive damages.

    Hill v. Church of Scientology of Toronto, [1995] 2 S.C.R. 1130.

ii) **$950,000:** consisting of $400,000 general damages, $350,000 aggravated damages, and $200,000 punitive damages. In addition, the Court awarded trial costs of $836,178.94.

    Leenen v. Canadian Broadcasting Corporation (2000), 48 O.R. (3d) 356 (S.C.J.), aff'd (2001), 54 O.R. (3d) 612 (C.A.), leave to appeal to S.C.C. refused, [2001] S.C.C.A. No. 432.

iii) **$875,000:** consisting of general damages totalling $675,000, aggravated damages of $100,000, and punitive damages of $100,000 against a number of defendants in relation to various related libels and slander.

    Southam Inc. v. Chelekis (2000), 133 B.C.A.C. 253 (C.A.), leave to appeal refused, [2000] S.C.C.A. No. 177.

iv) **$780,000:** consisting of $400,000 general damages and $380,000 special damages.

Hodgson v. Canadian Newspapers Co. (1998), 39 O.R. (3d) 235 (Gen. Div.), aff'd (2000), 49 O.R. (3d) 161 (C.A.), leave to appeal to S.C.C. denied, [2000] S.C.C.A. No. 465.

v) **$705,000:** consisting of $500,000 general damages and $205,000 punitive damages in favour of a number of individual and corporate plaintiffs against a number of defendants.

Amalgamated Transit Union v. Independent Canadian Transit Union, [1997] 5 W.W.R. 662 (Alta. Q.B.).

vi) **$663,423:** consisting solely of pecuniary damages. $400,000 for the value of a destroyed business; $133,423 for loss of profit; $100,000 for expenses to mitigate damages.

P.G. Restaurants Ltd. (c.o.b. Mama Panda Restaurant) v. Northern Interior Regional Health Board, [2004] B.C.J. No. 424, 2004 BCSC 294.

vii) **$475,665:** consisting of $250,000 general damages, $100 aggravated damages, and $125,665 pecuniary damages for net loss of income.

Fiola v. LeBrun, [2003] 2 W.W.R. 700 (Man. Q.B.).

viii) **$465,000:** consisting of $140,000 general and aggravated damages including the present value of future pecuniary loss, and $325,000 pecuniary damages for loss of income.

Botiuk v. Toronto Free Press Publications Ltd., [1995] 3 S.C.R. 3

ix) **$400,000:** consisting of $200,000 general damages, $100,000 aggravated damages, and $100,000 punitive damages.

Reichmann v. Berlin, [2002] O.J. No. 2732 (S.C.)

x) **$350,000:** consisting of $200,000 general damages and $150,000 aggravated damages.

Myers v. Canadian Broadcasting Corp. (1999), 47 C.C.L.T. (2d) 272, varied (2001) 6 C.C.L.T. (2nd) 112 (C.A.), leave to appeal to the Supreme Court of Canada denied [2001]

This top ten list excludes the 1996 verdict of an Ontario jury which awarded $700,000 to Toronto lawyer T. Allen Eagleson against *The Globe and Mail* newspaper. That jury award of $600,000 general damages and $100,000 aggravated damages was settled for an undisclosed sum before the defendants' appeal was heard by the Ontario Court of Appeal.

4) Jury Trials

Where the trial is heard with a jury, no reference to the amount of damages awarded by juries or judges in other cases may be made by the parties, their counsel, or the judge. The jury is to be completely insulated from such information.

Brisson v. Brisson (2002), 213 D.L.R. (4th) 428 (B.C.C.A.).

Gray v. Alanco Developments, [1967] 1 O.R. 597 (C.A.).

See *Hill v. Church of Scientology of Toronto*, [1995] 2 S.C.R. 1130 at 1194, where Cory J. stated that jurors speak for their community and are uniquely qualified to assess damages, approving the principle that the "assessment of damages is peculiarly the province of the jury."

The Supreme Court of Canada has ruled that it is a matter for the legislature to decide whether the court should provide juries with guidelines for damage awards in libel actions.

Hill v. Church of Scientology of Toronto, ibid. at para. 163.

The only exception is that the trial judge should convey a range of damages for punitive damages if counsel for the plaintiff and defendant agree upon the range of an appropriate award.

Whiten v. Pilot Insurance Co. (2002), 209 D.L.R. (4th) 257, per Binnie J. at para. 97 (S.C.C.).

5) Non-Jury Trials

Trial judges, sitting without a jury, routinely permit legal counsel to make submissions with reference to prior awards in other cases.

The British Columbia Court of Appeal has concluded that it may have regard to libel awards approved by trial and appellate courts in British Columbia and elsewhere in Canada, and compare the circumstances in those to the case on appeal.

Brown v. Cole (1998), 114 B.C.A.C. 73, 61 B.C.L.R. (3d) 1 (C.A.), leave to appeal to S.C.C. denied, [1998] S.C.C.A. No. 614.

The Ontario Court of Appeal in *Hill v. Church of Scientology* (1994) 18 O.R. (3d) 385 at 431 has stated, however:

… each libel case is unique and it is virtually impossible to categorize them or compare them. The personality and character of the defamed person, the nature of the libel and the circumstances surrounding its publication, the motivation and persistence of the person who defames, and the effect of the defamation upon the injured person depend upon many variables which are rarely duplicated. No two cases are the same, indeed, they rarely resemble one another. An award in one case is rarely, if ever, a useful guide in another.

6) Corporate Damages

The law of defamation protects not only the reputation of an individual but also the reputation of a corporation.

Hiltz and Seamone Co. v. Nova Scotia (Attorney General) (1997), 164 N.S.R. (2d) 161 (S.C.), aff'd (1999), 172 D.L.R. (4th) 488 (N.S.C.A.).

Ascot Holdings Ltd. v. Wilkie (1993), 49 C.P.R. (3d) 188 (B.C.S.C.) per Tysoe J.

Walker v. CFTO Ltd. (1987), 37 D.L.R. (4th) 224, per Robins J.A. at 233 (Ont. C.A.).

South Hetton Coal Co. Ltd. v. North-Eastern News Ass'n Ltd., [1893] 1 Q.B. 133 (C.A.), approved, Derbyshire County Council v. Herald and Times Newspapers Ltd., [1993] A.C. 534 (H.L. (Eng.)).

McDonalds Corp. v. Steel, [1999] E.W.J. No. 2173, per Pill L.J. at paras. 39–87 (Eng. C.A.), cited in Home Equity Development Inc. v Crow, 2004 BCSC 124, per Quijano J. at paras. 84–185.

A trading corporation is entitled to sue in respect of defamatory matters which can be seen as having a tendency to damage it in the way of business.

McDonalds Corp. v. Steel, ibid. at paras. 39–87.

Metropolitan Saloon Omnibus Co. Ltd. v. Hawkins (1859), 4 H.&N. 87 (Ex. Ct.).

South Hetton Coal Co. Ltd. v. North-Eastern News Ass'n Ltd., [1893] 1 Q.B. 133 (C.A.), approved, Derbyshire County Council v. Herald and Times Newspapers Ltd., [1993] A.C. 534 (H.L. (Eng.)).

The law presumes damages from the publication of a libel and, as in the case of an individual, the action is maintainable without proof of special damages.

Walker v. CFTO Ltd. (1987), 37 D.L.R. (4th) 224, per Robins J.A. at 233 (Ont. C.A.), approving South Hetton Coal Co., Ltd. v. North-Eastern News Ass'n Ltd., [1893] 1 Q.B. 133 at 139 (C.A.):

> With regard to a firm or company, it is impossible to lay down an exhaustive rule as to what would be a libel on them. But the same rule is applicable to a statement made with regard to them. Statements may be made with regard to their mode of carrying on business, such as lead people of

ordinary sense to the opinion that the conduct their business badly or inefficiently. If so, the law will be the same in their case as in that of an individual and the statement will be libelous. Then, if the case be one of libel — whether on a person, a firm, or a company — the law is that damages are at large. It is not necessary to prove any particular damage; the jury may give such damages as they think fit, having regard to the conduct of the parties respectively, and all the circumstances of the case.

Ascot Holdings Ltd. v. Wilkie (1993), 49 C.P.R. (3d) 188 (B.C.S.C.) per Tysoe J.

McDonalds Corp. v. Steel, [1999] E.W.J. No. 2173 per Pill L.J. at para. 74 (C.A.):

A company whose business character or reputation (as distinct from the character or reputation of the persons who compose it) is injuriously affected by a defamatory publication is entitled, without proof of damage, to a compensatory award representing the sum necessary to publicly vindicate the company's business reputation.

Walker v. CFTO Ltd. (1987), 37 D.L.R. (4th) 224, per Robins J.A. at 233 (Ont. C.A.).

In *Broome v. Cassell & Co.*, [1972] 1 All E.R. 801 at 824 (H.L.), Lord Hailsham observed that:

in case the libel, driven underground, emerges from its lurking place at some future date, [the plaintiff] must be able to point to a sum awarded by a jury sufficient to convince a bystander of the baselessness of the charge.

In certain provinces, including Alberta, the statutory presumption that "when defamation is proved, damage shall be presumed," buttresses the common law principle.

Defamation Act, R.S.A. 2000, c. D-6, s.2.

In *Hiltz and Seamone Co. v. Nova Scotia (Attorney General)* (1997), 164 N.S.R. (2d) 161 (S.C.), the trial judge, in her decision awarding general damages of $200,000 and punitive damages of $100,000 to the corporate plaintiff, stated at paragraph 137:

Similarly, [the corporate plaintiff] exists on its reputation and no less than the plaintiff Union and the local, "its reputation is its lifeblood". Professional organizations survive on the confidence and trust generated in those that deal with them and the integrity and the character of the work they provide to their clients. Defamatory statements, such as in the present case, strike at the foundation of the reputation and erode the confidence of the public in the defamed party, no less when it's a corporation than when it's an individual.

Similarly, other non-individual plaintiffs such as unions have recovered substantial libel damages.

Amalgamated Transit Union v. *Independent Canadian Transit Union*, [1997] 5 W.W.R. 662 (Alta. Q.B.).

A company is not entitled, however, to compensation for damages which can only be sustained by an individual, such as hurt feelings.

Walker v. *CFTO Ltd.* (1987), 37 D.L.R. (4th) 224, per Robins J.A. at 233 (Ont. C.A.).

It has been held that a corporation is not entitled to aggravated damages for injury to feelings as those can only be sustained by an individual.

Hiltz and Seamone Co. v. *Nova Scotia (Attorney General)* (1997),164 N.S.R. (2d) 161 (S.C.), aff'd, [1999] 172 D.L.R. (4th) 488 (N.S.C.A.).

Walker v. *CFTO Ltd.* (1987), 37 D.L.R. (4th) 224, per Robins J.A. at 233 (Ont. C.A.), approving *Lewis* v. *Daily Telegraph, Ltd.*, [1963] 2 All E.R. 151, per Lord Reid at 156 (H.L.):

> [a] company cannot be injured in its feelings, it can only be injured in its pocket.

Ascot Holdings Ltd. v. *Wilkie* (1993), 49 C.P.R. (3d) 204 (B.C.S.C.) per Tysoe J.

Contrary to suggestions occasionally made by defendants, a plaintiff corporation is not restricted to recovering only nominal damages if it cannot prove a specific pecuniary loss resulting from the libel:

English and Scottish Co-operative Properties v. *Odhams Press*, [1940] 1 K.B. 440 per Lord Goddard at 461:

> There is no obligation on the plaintiffs to show that they have suffered actual damage. A plaintiff may, if he can, by way of aggravating damages, prove that he has suffered actual damage. But in every case he is perfectly entitled to say that there has been a serious libel upon him; that the law assumes that he must have suffered damage; and that he is entitled to substantial damages.

McDonalds Corp. v. *Steel*, [1999] E.W.J. No. 2173 per Pill L.J. at paras. 39–87 (Eng. C.A.).

Although there is no irrebuttable presumption of substantial damages in the case of a corporate plaintiff, if it shows that it has a reputation within the jurisdiction and that the defamatory publication is likely to damage its goodwill, the court is entitled to make an award of substantial damages.

McDonald's Corp. v. *Steel, ibid.* at paras. 75–77.

Lewis v. *Daily Telegraph, Ltd.,* [1963] 2 All E.R. 151 per Lord Reid at 156 (H.L.):

> [a company's] reputation can be injured by a libel but that injury must sound in money. The injury need not necessarily be confined to loss of income. Its goodwill may be injured.

A corporation does not have to trade within the jurisdiction where it brings the libel action provided that it has a reputation within the jurisdiction.

McDonalds Corp. v. *Steel,* above, at paras. 76–81.

A corporation may recover punitive damages.

Hiltz and Seamone Co. v. *Nova Scotia (Attorney General)* (1997) 164 N.S.R. (2d) 161 (S.C.), aff'd, [1999] 172 D.L.R. (4th) 488 (N.S.C.A.).

7) Politically Motivated Defamation

It has been suggested that courts should exercise restraint in awarding damages to a politician for politically motivated defamation generated in the heat of political controversy.

Derrickson v. *Tomat* (1992), 10 C.C.L.T. (2d) 1, leave to appeal to S.C.C. denied (1992), 93 D.L.RL. (4th) vii (S.C.C.).

However, it has been held that such restraint does not apply to defamation of civil servants, who are not allowed to explain their actions and who have not entered a public arena in such a way as to invite public discussion.

Newson (Chief Provincial Firearms Officer for B.C.) v. *Kexco Publishing Co.* (1995), 17 B.C.L.R. (3d) 176 (C.A.).

8) Impact of an Apology

At common law, a full retraction and apology may reduce the damages otherwise payable to the plaintiff. This defence is available even if the requirements of the statutory provisions noted below cannot be satisfied.

Tait v. *New Westminster Radio Ltd.* (1984), 58 B.C.L.R. 194 (C.A.).

Thompson v. *NL Broadcasting Ltd.* (1976), 1 C.C.L.T. 278 (B.C.S.C.).

Newson v. *Kexco Publishing Co.* (1995), 17 B.C.L.R. (3d) 176 (C.A.).

Hunter v. *Fotheringham* (20 January 1986), Vancouver C843668 (B.C.S.C.).

At common law, damages may also be mitigated by permitting the plaintiff to publish or broadcast a rebuttal.

Thompson v. NL Broadcasting Ltd. (1976), 1 C.C.L.T. 278 (B.C.S.C.).

It is questionable whether the court has jurisdiction to order a defendant to apologize to a plaintiff who has succeeded in obtaining a libel damages verdict.

Hasnu v. Deshe Bedeshe Inc,. [1998] O.J. No. 3493 at para. 39 (Gen. Div. (Sm. Cl.)).

Laufer v. Bucklaschuk (1998) 128 Man. R. (2d) 156 (Q.B.), rev'd on unrelated grounds (1999), 181 D.L.R. (4th) 83, (2000) W.W.R. 462 (Man. C.A.) [jury ordered apology; formal, entered order of court did not include apology, as statement of claim did not request one].

Vancouver Industrial Electric Ltd. v. Leone Industries Inc. [1999] B.C.J. No. 2444 (S.C.) [court held it had no authority to order defamer to write letter of retraction].

It is questionable whether the publication of an apology by the defendant, which retracts allegations made against another person, ought to be grounds for increasing the damages awarded to a plaintiff who has not been given an apology.

Hodgson v. Canadian Newspapers Company Limited (1998), 39 O.R. (3d) 235, per Lane J. at 405g (Gen. Div.), varied (2000), 49 O.R. (3d) 161 (C.A.), leave to appeal to S.C.C. denied, [2000] S.C.C.A. No. 465.

A false or insincere apology may aggravate damages.

Wiley v. Toronto Star Newspapers Ltd. (1988) 51 D.L.R. (4th) 439 at 449–50 (Ont. H.C.J.).

Brannigan v. Seafarers International Union of Canada (1963), 42 D.L.R. (2d) 249 at 258 (B.C.S.C.).

Hoste v. Victoria Times Publishing Co. (1889), 1 B.C.R. 365 at 366 (S.C.).

G. STATUTORY PROVISIONS

1) Mitigation

The defamation statutes of Alberta, British Columbia, the Northwest Territories, Ontario, Saskatchewan, and the Yukon Territory provide that in an action for libel in a newspaper or other periodical publication, or in a broadcast, the defendant may plead in mitigation of damages that the libel was published or broadcast without actual malice and without gross negligence, and that before the commencement of the action, or at the earliest opportunity afterwards, the defendant published or broadcast a full apology. If the newspaper or periodical publication in which the libel appeared is ordinarily published at intervals exceeding one week, the defendant may plead that it offered to publish an apology in another newspaper or periodical publication to be selected by the plaintiff. (Saskatchewan's defamation statute only applies to libel contained in a newspaper).

Alberta, *Defamation Act*, R.S.A. 2000, c. D-6, s.15.
British Columbia, *Libel and Slander Act*, R.S.B.C. 1996, c. 263, s.6.
Northwest Territories, *Defamation Act*, R.S.N.W.T. 1988, c. D-1, s.18(1).
Ontario, *Libel and Slander Act*, R.S.O. 1990, c..L.12, s.9.
Saskatchewan, *Libel and Slander Act*, R.S.S. 1978, c. L-14, s.7.
Yukon, *Defamation Act*, R.S.Y.T. 1986, c. 41, s.17(1).

In Alberta, the Northwest Territories, and the Yukon, this mitigation provision applies only to actions for defamation against the proprietor or publisher of a newspaper, the owner or operator of a broadcasting station, or an officer, servant, or employee thereof in respect of defamatory matter published in that newspaper or broadcast from that station.

Alberta, *Defamation Act*, R.S.A. 2000, c. D-6, s.12.
Northwest Territories, *Defamation Act*, R.S.N.W.T. 1988, c. D-1, s.14.
Yukon, *Defamation Act*, R.S.Y.T. 1986, c. 41, s.13.

The defamation statutes of Manitoba, New Brunswick, Newfoundland and Labrador, Nova Scotia, and Prince Edward Island contain a somewhat different mitigation of damages provision concerning apologies. In each of those jurisdictions, the statutory provision is not limited to publications in a newspaper or periodical or broadcast. Where the defendant has only pleaded a denial of the alleged defamation, or has suffered judgment by default, or judgment has been given against her on a motion for judgment on the pleadings, she may give in evidence, in mitigation of damages, that she made or offered a written or printed apology before commencement of the action, or, if the action was commenced before there was an opportunity of making or offering the apology, that she did so as soon afterwards as she had an opportunity.

Manitoba, *Defamation Act*, R.S.M. 1987, c. D-20, s.4.
New Brunswick, *Defamation Act*, R.S.N.B. 1973, c. D-5, s. 4.

Nova Scotia, *Defamation Act*, R.S.N.S. 1989, c .122, s.5.

Newfoundland and Labrador, *Defamation Act*, R.S.N. 1990, c. D-3, s.5.

Prince Edward Island, *Defamation Act*, R.S.P.E.I. 1988, c.D-5, s.4.

Damages are also mitigated if the defendant proves that the plaintiff has already brought an action for, or has recovered damages, or has received or agreed to receive compensation in respect of, defamation to the same purport or effect as that for which the action is brought.

Alberta, *Defamation Act*, R.S.A. 2000, c. D-6, s.15(2).

British Columbia, *Libel and Slander Act*, R.S.B.C. 1996, c. 263, s.7.

Manitoba, *Defamation Act*, R.S.M. 1987, c. D-20, s.16(2).

New Brunswick, *Defamation Act*, R.S.N.B. 1973, c. D-5, s.16(2).

Newfoundland and Labrador, *Defamation Act*, R.S.N. 1990, c. D-3, c. 63, s.18(2).

Northwest Territories, *Defamation Act*, R.S.N.W.T. 1988, c. D-1, s.18(2).

Nova Scotia, *Defamation Act*, R.S.N.S. 1989, c. 122, s.6.

Ontario, *Libel and Slander Act*, R.S.O. 1990, c. L.12, s.10.

Prince Edward Island, *Defamation Act*, R.S.P.E.I. 1988, c.D-5, s.17(2).

Saskatchewan, *Libel and Slander Act*, R.S.S. 1978, c. L-14, s.17 [newspaper libel only].

Yukon, *Defamation Act*, R.S.Y.T. 1986, c. 41, s.17(2).

2) Special Damages Limitations

The defamation statutes also provide that a plaintiff shall recover only special damages (referred to in British Columbia and Ontario as "actual damages") if:

- the defamatory matter was published in good faith,
- there was reasonable ground to believe that it was for the public benefit,
- it did not involve a criminal charge,
- the publication took place in mistake or misapprehension of the facts, and
- a full and fair retraction was published, in as conspicuous a place and type as the defamatory matter. The full and fair retraction must be published within a specified time after service of the writ [Saskatchewan's statute limits this defence to newspapers].

Alberta, Manitoba, New Brunswick, the Northwest Territories, Nova Scotia, Prince Edward Island, and the Yukon also require that a full apology accompany the retraction. This defence does not apply to defamation of a candidate for public office published or broadcast within five days of the election (fifteen days in Saskatchewan).

Alberta, *Defamation Act*, R.S.A. 2000, c. D-6, s.16(1).

British Columbia, *Libel and Slander Act*, R.S.B.C. 1996, c. 263, s.7.

Manitoba, *Defamation Act*, R.S.M. 1987, c. D-20, s.17.

New Brunswick, *Defamation Act*, R.S.N.B. 1973, c. D-5, s.17(1).

Newfoundland and Labrador, *Defamation Act*, R.S.N. 1990, c. D-3, s.19(1).

Northwest Territories, *Defamation Act*, R.S.N.W.T. 1988, c. D-1, s. 19(1).

Nova Scotia, *Defamation Act*, R.S.N.S. 1989, c. 122, s.22(1).

Ontario, *Libel and Slander Act*, R.S.O. 1990, c. L.12, s.5(2).

Prince Edward Island, *Defamation Act*, R.S.P.E.I. 1988, c. D-5, s.18(1).

Saskatchewan, *Libel and Slander Act*, R.S.S. 1978, c. L-14.

Yukon, *Defamation Act*, R.S.Y.T. 1986, c. 41, s.18(1).

In British Columbia, it was held that a retraction was not "full and fair" where a newspaper defendant did not make reasonable efforts to contact the plaintiff and obtain his input to the retraction, and where the newspaper did not contact knowledgeable, independent sources to obtain correct information about the plaintiff before the retraction.

Fulton v. West End Times Ltd. (1998), 45 B.C.L.R. (3d) 288 (S.C.)

A poorly drafted apology may aggravate the plaintiff's damages.

Turco v. Dunlop, [1998] B.C.J. No. 2711 at para. 81 (S.C.).

3) Offer of Amends

Nova Scotia's *Defamation Act*, unique to the common law jurisdictions in Canada, provides that a defendant who has innocently published defamatory words may make an "offer of amends" to publish or join in the publication of a suitable correction of the words complained of, and a sufficient apology to the plaintiff. Where copies of a document or record containing the defamatory words have been distributed by or with the knowledge of the defendant, the latter must also offer to take such steps as are reasonably practicable on his part for notifying persons to whom copies have been so distributed that the words are alleged to be defamatory of the plaintiff. If the offer of amends is accepted by the plaintiff, the court is empowered to determine any dispute relating to fulfilment of the offer, and to order the defendant to pay the full legal costs of the plaintiff and any expenses reasonably incurred by the plaintiff in consequence of the defamatory publication.

> Nova Scotia, *Defamation Act*, R.S.N.S. 1989, c. 122, s.16.

To establish that the words were published "innocently," the defendant must show either that he or she did not intend to publish them of and concerning the plaintiff and did not know of circumstances by virtue of which they might be understood to refer to the plaintiff, or that the words were not defamatory on their face, and that the defendant did not know of circumstances by virtue of which they might be understood to be defamatory of the plaintiff. The defendant must also show that he or she exercised all reasonable care in relation to the publication.

> Nova Scotia, *Defamation Act*, R.S.N.S. 1989, c. 122, s.16.

4) Rebuttal

The defamation statutes create an incentive for defendants to publish or broadcast a rebuttal by the plaintiff in certain instances. Defendants will not be able to rely upon the statutory defence of qualified privilege for fair and accurate reports published in a newspaper or by broadcasting of reports of public meetings or legislative proceedings if the defendant has failed to comply with the plaintiffs request to publish or broadcast a "reasonable letter or statement of explanation or contradiction."

> Alberta, *Defamation Act*, R.S.A. 2000, c. D-6, s.10(4).
> British Columbia, *Libel and Slander Act*, R.S.B.C. 1996, c. 263, s.4.
> Manitoba, *Defamation Act*, R.S.M. 1987, c. D-20, s.10(4).
> New Brunswick, *Defamation Act*, R.S.N.B. 1973, c. D-5, s.9(4).
> Newfoundland and Labrador, *Defamation Act*, R.S.N. 1990, c. D-3, c. 63, s.12(4).
> Nova Scotia, *Defamation Act*, R.S.N.S. 1989, c. 122, s.13(6).
> Northwest Territories, *Defamation Act*, R.S.N.W.T. 1988, c. D-1, s.11(4).
> Ontario, *Libel and Slander Act*, R.S.O. 1990, c. L.12, s.3(7).
> Prince Edward Island, *Defamation Act*, R.S.P.E.I. 1988, c. D-5, s.10(4).
> Saskatchewan, *Libel and Slander Act*, R.S.S. 1978, c. L-14, s.10(3).
> Yukon, *Defamation Act*, R.S.Y.T. 1986, c. 41, s.10(4).

CHAPTER THIRTY-ONE:
Appeals

A. GENERAL

1) Appeals within the Province

An appeal in a defamation lawsuit from a trial-level superior court to a provincial appellate court is governed by the general law contained in provincial statutes and rules of court. No province has legislated special laws for appeals in defamation cases.

The statutes and rules differ from province to province. A defamation litigant should therefore be alert to identify and diarize relevant limitation periods peculiar to the jurisdiction in which the appeal will take place.

A defamation litigant has a right of appeal to the provincial appellate court from a final order of the trial court.

> *Brown v. Cole* (1998), 114 B.C.A.C. 73, 61 B.C.L.R. (2d) 1, per Southin J.A.
> for the Court at para. 50 (C.A.); leave to appeal to S.C.C. denied, [1998]
> S.C.C.A. No. 614.

Normally, the court of appeal rules require the parties to submit written argument (called a "factum") summarizing the facts and law to be argued on the appeal. Most provincial appeal courts sit as a panel of three to hear an appeal. The parties are usually entitled to present oral argument although appeal courts may set strict time limits for the hearing. In British Columbia, the appeal court may sit as a panel of five if a party intends to ask the court to overrule a prior decision on a point of law or if such a course is warranted by the significance of the issues.

There is a significant distinction between an appeal based on an error of law and an appeal based on an error of fact. In the case of an error of law, the standard of review on appeal is correctness. Nevertheless, even if the lower court has erred in law, the court of appeal must still determine whether the error of law has affected the result so as to merit overturning or varying the lower court's verdict.

On appeal on facts alone the standard of review is much narrower. Generally, in the absence of a palpable and overriding error on the part of the trial judge which affected her assessment of the facts, the findings of fact at trial must be accepted by the appellate court. A trial judge is in a privileged position in particular on issues of credibility where the demeanour of a witness may be of critical importance.

> Ross v. New Brunswick Teachers' Association (2001), 201 D.L.R. (4th) 75 per Daigle C.J.N.B. (Turnbull and Larlee JJ.A. concurring) at para. 44 (N.B.C.A.).

Even when credibility of a witness is not at issue, reasons of policy suggest deference to the trial judge to ensure that the autonomy and integrity of the trial process is preserved.

> Ross v. New Brunswick Teachers' Association, ibid.

In the absence of a palpable and overriding error, it is not the function of the appellate court to substitute its assessment on the balance of probabilities for the findings of fact made by the judge who presided at trial.

> Stein v. The Kathy K, [1976] 2 S.C.R. 802, per Ritchie J. for the Court at 808.
>
> Lewis v. Todd, [1980] 2 S.C.R. 694, per Dickson J. for the Court at 700.
>
> Beaudoin-Daigneault v. Richard, [1984] 1 S.C.R. 2, per Lamer J. at 11.
>
> Royal Bank of Canada v. First Pioneer Inv. Ltd., [1984] 2 S.C.R. 125, per Wilson J. for the Court at 131.
>
> Ontario (Attorney General) v. Bear Island Foundation, [1991] 2 S.C.R. 570, per the Court at para. 5.
>
> Lapointe v. Hôpital Le Gardeur, [1992] 1 S.C.R. 351, per L'Heureux-Dubé J. for the Court at 358–59.
>
> Hodgkinson v. Simms, [1994] 3 S.C.R. 377, per La Forest, L'Heureux-Dubé, and Gonthier JJ. at 425–26.
>
> Schwartz v. Canada, [1996] 1 S.C.R. 254 at paras. 32–35.
>
> Quebec (Public Curator) v. Syndicat national des employés d l'hôpital St Ferdinand, [1996] 3 S.C.R. 211, per L'Heureux-Dubé for the Court at para. 46.

Sidorsky v. CFCN Communications Ltd. (1997), 40 C.C.L.T. (2d) 94, per the Court at para. 23 (Alta. C.A.).

Hiltz and Seamone Co. v. Nova Scotia (Attorney General) (1999), 172 D.L.R. (4th) 488, per Pugsley J.A. (Hart and Freeman JJ.A. concurring) at para. 33 (N.S.C.A.).

It has been said that only in exceptional circumstances is an appellate court justified in accepting and acting upon the evidence of a witness whom the trial judge has expressly disbelieved.

Jerome v. Anderson, [1964] S.C.R. 291, per Cartwright J. (Maitland, Ritchie, and Hall JJ. concurring) at 301.

Where the trial judge's conclusions concerning credibility are not based on his observations of a witness, the appellate court has greater latitude to consider whether his conclusions are supported in the evidence.

Hiltz and Seamone Co. v. Nova Scotia (Attorney General), above, per Pugsley J.A. (Hart and Freeman JJ.A. concurring) at para. 40.

An appellate court is not fettered in considering whether a trial judge erred in answering a question of law.

Pressler v. Lethbridge (2000), 86 B.C.L.R. (3d) 257, 2000 BCCA 639, per Southin J.A. at para. 38.

2) Appeals to the Supreme Court of Canada

An appeal from a provincial appellate court to the Supreme Court of Canada is governed by the *Supreme Court Act*, R.S.C. 1985, c. 5-26, which requires leave either:

i)   from the provincial appeal court, on the ground that the question is one that ought to be submitted to the Supreme Court for decision [section 37] [Note: This jurisdiction is rarely exercised.]; or

ii) from the Supreme Court of Canada, on the ground that any question involved on the appeal is, by reason of its public importance or the importance of any issue of law or any issue of fact involved in that question, one that ought to be decided by the Supreme Court or is, for any other reason, of such a nature or significance as to warrant decision by it [section 40].

Since the landmark decisions of the Supreme Court of Canada in *Hill v. Church of Scientology of Toronto*, [1995] 2 S.C.R. 1130 and *Botiuk v. Toronto Free Press*, [1995] 3 S.C.R. 3, no civil defamation litigant has been granted leave to appeal in a common law province to the Supreme Court of Canada.

Chief Justice Dickson, as he then was, stated in "Operations and Practice, a Comparison, the Supreme Court" (1980) 3 Can.-U.S.L.J. 86 at page 90:

> It is, however, fair to say that the type of case standing the best chance of success when leave to appeal is sought is one which raises a constitutional issue, or a question of native rights or civil liberties, or an important question of criminal law or labour law or administrative law, or one which involves conflicting decisions of two provincial appellate courts. The chances are less than propitious when the issue is interlocutory or largely factual, or one which involves interpretation of a contract or procedure within a provincial court system, or one which calls for construction of a local by-law or a provincial statute, the wording of which is peculiar to the locality or province.

Defamation litigants seeking leave to appeal in a defamation matter may choose to develop their submission along one or more of the following lines:

i)   asserting that a *Charter* or other constitutional issue affecting the balance between freedom of expression and protection of reputation is involved, and that a decision of the Supreme Court would be of value, particularly because the correct resolution of the issue is unclear;

ii) asserting that there are conflicting decisions of appellate courts on the issue involved;

iii) asserting that an important provision of a provincial defamation statute, which has counterparts in one or more other provinces, is involved;

iv) asserting that the issues are of national or interprovincial scope;

v)   asserting that the present law requires reconsideration or revision;

vi) asserting that the appeal will give the court an opportunity to develop important common law principles of general application which, for any reason, require updating, revision, elaboration, or clarification.

3) Motion to Admit New Evidence

Where evidence of publication was available at the time of the proceedings in the trial court, the appellate court will not admit fresh evidence.

> *Ayangma v. NAV Canada* (2001), 203 D.L.R. (4th) 717, per McQuaid J.A. for the court at para. 12 (P.E.I.S.C. (A.D.)).

4) Application for Security for Costs or Security for Judgment

In British Columbia, the authority to order security for costs is expressly provided for in section 24 of the *Court of Appeal Act*, R.S.B.C. 1996, c. 77. The factors that have been considered in various cases in which orders for security for costs have been sought are set out in *Southeast Toyota Distributors Inc. v. Branch* (1997), 45 B.C.L.R. (3d) 163 (C.A.), and include the financial means of the appellant, the merits of the appeal, the timeliness of the application, and whether or not the cost will be fully recoverable.

The power of the British Columbia Court of Appeal to require a defendant appellant to stay execution is found in section 18 of the *Court of Appeal Act*, R.S.B.C. 1996, c. 7. The power to order the defendant appellant to post security for the trial judgment as a condition of such a stay is found in section 18(3)(h). Further, in British Columbia the trial court has jurisdiction under Supreme Court Rule 42(21) to grant a stay. It has recently been held that although section 18 does not necessarily require the Court of Appeal to order that the entire amount be secured, generally there should be full security. The successful party should not have to run the risk of the other party fleeing or becoming bankrupt.

> *Ager v. Canjex Publishing Ltd.*, 2003 BCCA 613, per Southin J.A. (Huddart and Low JJ.A. concurring) at paras 18–20, 23–24 [security of $316,500 ordered, varying 2003 BCCA 511, where security of $275,000 had been ordered by Hall J.A. in Chambers].

> See also, *Ferguson v. Ferstay* (2000), 81 B.C.L.R. (3d) 90, (2000), 147 B.C.A.C. 61, per Rowles J.A. at paras. 14–21 (C.A.) reviewing the cases concerning posting security for judgment.

Where the respondents were concerned not about the defendants' appeal impairing their ability to execute on the judgment as much as they were concerned about the potential prejudice they may suffer should the appellants continue to make defamatory statements about them while the appeal was pending, security for the judgment was not ordered where a permanent injunction was in place.

> *Ferguson v. Ferstay*, above.

B. APPEALS FROM INTERLOCUTORY ORDERS

In most of the common law provinces and territories, leave is required to appeal an interlocutory order in a defamation lawsuit.

In British Columbia, the criteria for giving leave to appeal are as follows:

i)   whether the appeal is *prima facie* meritorious or whether it is frivolous;
ii)   whether the point on appeal is of significance to the practice or of general importance to the public;
iii) whether the point raised is of significance to the action itself; and
iv)   whether the appeal will unduly hinder the progress of the action.

> *Cassidy v. Abbotsford (City) Police Department*, 2000 BCCA 286, per Saunders J.A. at para. 7.

> *Tatum v. Limbrick* (1992), 64 B.C.L.R. (2d) 252 (C.A.) per Taylor J.A.

If leave is not granted by a single judge of the Court of Appeal, the disappointed applicant may seek review by a division of the Court of Appeal.

> *Ward v. Clark* (2000), 77 B.C.L.R. (3d) 364, 50 C.C.L.T. (2d) 288, per Donald J.A. (MacKenzie and Low JJ.A. concurring) at paras. 4–5 (S.C.).

The test to be applied when a division of the Court of Appeal reviews an order of a single Court of Appeal judge in chambers is as follows:

> … the review hearing is not a hearing of the original application as if it were a new application brought to a division of the court rather than to a chambers judge, but is instead a review of what the chambers judge did against the test encompassed by asking: was the chambers judge wrong in law, or wrong in principle, or did the chambers judge misconceive the facts. If the chambers judge did not commit any of those errors, then the division of the court should not change the order of the chambers judge.

> *Ward v. Clark* (2000), 77 B.C.L.R. (3d) 364, per Donald J.A. (MacKenzie and Low JJ.A. concurring) at para. 4 (S.C.), citing *Haldorson v. Coquitlam (City)*, 2000 BCCA 672.

> … The court will not intervene unless it is satisfied that the chambers judge was wrong in the legal sense and not merely that he or she exercised discretion incorrectly.

> *Frew v. Roberts* (1990), 44 C.P.C. (2d) 34 (B.C.C.A.), per McEachern C.J.B.C. (Proudfoot J.A. concurring).

Ward v. *Clark* (2000), 77 B.C.L.R. (3d) 364, per Donald J.A. (MacKenzie and Low JJ.A. concurring) at para. 5 (S.C.).

In Ontario, an application for leave to appeal an interlocutory order is governed by Rule 62.02(4)(a) and (b). The issues are:

i)   Is there a good reason to doubt the correctness of the order sought to be appealed?

ii)   Does that appeal involve matters of importance such that leave to appeal should be granted?

> *MacRae* v. *Santa*, [2004] O.J. No. 833, per G.P. Smith J. at para. 2 (Div. Ct.).

Both criteria must be met.

> *Pizza Pizza Ltd.* v. *Toronto Star Newspapers Ltd.*, [2002] O.J. No. 184, per McCombs J. (S.C.J.).

> *Schreiber* v. *Lavoie*, [2002] O.J. No. 2308, per Cameron J. at para. 3 (S.C.J.).

> *Monaghan* v. *Ontario (Attorney General)*, [2002] O.J. No. 907, per Cavarzan J. at para 12 (S.C.J.):

> Insofar as he held, as I understand his reasons, that because the plaintiff's claim is for damages for breach of his *Charter* rights, a pleading in response to the plaintiff's allegations of defamation is irrelevant, the proposed appeal involves a matter of general importance. In such circumstances, the issue transcends the immediate interests of parties to the litigation and leave to appeal should be granted.

1) Standard of Review

A provincial appellate court will not intervene unless the chambers judge applied wrong principles of law, the result of the order is a patent injustice, or the chambers judge made a palpable and overriding error respecting findings of fact..

> *Fraser* v. *Westminer Canada Limited* (1998), 171 N.S.R. (2d) 123, per Cromwell J.A. (Hallett and Freeman JJ.A. concurring) at para. 2 (C.A.).

> *Mitsui & Co. (Point Aconi) Ltd.* v. *Jones Power Co. et al.* (1999), 173 N.S.R. (2d) 159, per Flinn J.A. (Glube C.J.N.S. and Freeman J.A. concurring) (C.A.).

> *Rajkhowa* v. *Watson* (2000), 1 C.P.C. (5th) 218, per Pugsley J.A. at 224 (N.S.C.A.).

> *MacKenzie* v. *Kutcher*, [2004] N.S.J. No. 6, 2004 NSCA 4, per Hamilton J.A. for the court at para. 10.

C. APPEALS FROM FINAL ORDERS

1) Stay of Execution Pending Appeal

An unsuccessful defamation defendant may seek a stay or partial stay of execution pursuant to a statute or a rule of court. The test that has been applied in Nova Scotia is set out in *Fulton Insurance Agencies Ltd.* v. *Purdy* (1990), 100 N.S.R. (2d) 341 (S.C. (A.D.)), where Hallett J.A. said at page 346:

> A review of the cases indicates there is a trend towards applying what is in effect the *American Cyanamid* test for an interlocutory injunction in considering applications for stays of execution pending appeal. In my opinion, it is a proper test as it puts a fairly heavy burden on the appellant which is warranted on a stay application considering the nature of the remedy which prevents a litigant from realizing the fruits of his litigation pending the hearing of the appeal.
>
> In my opinion, stays of execution of judgment pending disposition of the appeal should only be granted if the appellant can either:
>
> (1) satisfy the Court on each of the following:
>> (i) that there is an arguable issue raised on the appeal;
>> (ii) that if the stay is not granted and the appeal is successful, the appellant will have suffered irreparable harm that it is difficult to, or cannot be compensated for by a damage award. This involves not only the theoretical consideration whether the harm is susceptible of being compensated in damages but also whether if the successful party at trial has executed on the appellant's property, whether or not the appellant if successful on appeal will be able to collect, and
>> (iii) that the appellant will suffer greater harm if the stay is not granted than the respondent would suffer if the stay is granted; the so-called balance of convenience or:
>
> (2) Failing to meet the primary test, satisfy the Court that there are exceptional circumstances that would make it fit and just that the stay be granted in the case.

This principle was applied in *Campbell* v. *Jones* (2001), 197 N.S.R. (2d) 196 (C.A.) per Roscoe J.A. (Application for a partial stay of execution of a libel judgment).

The test in British Columbia is different. Counsel must have regard to the particular rule or principle in force in each province.

An application that a judgment of a provincial appellate court be stayed pending determination of an application for leave to appeal to the Supreme Court of Canada is governed by s. 65.1(2) of the *Supreme Court Act*, R.S.C. 1985, c. S-26.

> *Pelley v. Pelley*, 2003 NLCA 12, per Wells C.J.N. at para. 1.

D. APPEALS FROM JURY VERDICTS

As in other actions, a judgment of a jury on an issue relating to liability may be attacked in a defamation case on the following grounds:

i)   the judge erred in leaving a question to the jury;
ii) there was a misdirection to the jury;
iii) there was misconduct by counsel which influenced the jury;
iv) the verdict was perverse.

1) Error in Leaving a Question to the Jury

The question whether the expression is capable of being regarded as statements of fact or comment is a question of construction for the judge. If in her opinion there is no reasonable doubt, she must direct the jury accordingly, but if, in her view, there is reasonable doubt as to whether the words are statements of facts or expressions of opinion, she must leave it to the jury to decide.

> *Scott v. Fulton* (2000), 73 B.C.L.R. (3d) 392, per Braidwood J.A. for the court at para. 19 (C.A.), approving *Telnikoff v. Matusevitch*, [1991] 3 W.L.R. 952 at 956 (H.L.), adopting *Halsbury's Laws of England*, 4th ed., (1979) vol. 28, para. 228 [held that the determination as to whether the statements of the defendant should be characterized as fact or comment was not made according to the appropriate principle of law].

Where a new trial is sought on the ground of misdirection of the jury it is sufficient, under section 28(1) of the *Ontario Judicature Act*, to show that the misdirection *may* have affected the verdict; the appellant is not required to show that it actually did so. If the appellate court is in doubt, it is for the respondent to show it did not.

> *Leslie v. Canadian Press*, [1956] S.C.R. 871 per Kerwin C.J. (Fauteux, Abbott, and Nolan JJ. concurring) at 874.

The trial judge plays a gatekeeper role in determining whether a particular statement is capable of bearing the defamatory meaning alleged by a plaintiff.

Jones v. Skelton, [1963] 1 W.L.R. 1362 at 1370–71 (P.C.) per Lord Morris of Borth-y-Gest.

Laufer v. Bucklaschuck (1999), 181 D.L.R. (4th) 83, [2000] 2 W.W.R. 462, per Scott C.J.M. and Helper J.A. at para. 25 (Man. C.A.), leave to appeal to S.C.C. denied, [2000] S.C.C.A. No. 47.

See *Jameel v. The Wall Street Journal Europe SprL*, [2003] E.W.C.A. Civ. 1694,per Lord Justice Simon Brown at paras. 9–14, stating at para. 14: "The judge's function is no more and no less than to pre-empt perversity."

In a defamation trial, the trial judge is required to engage in a two-stage process. She must first determine as a question of law whether the challenged words are capable of bearing the meaning or meanings set forth in the pleadings. She must also determine whether the alleged defamatory meaning or meanings relate to the plaintiff. The threshold question in every defamation action is whether the words cited are reasonably capable of a defamatory meaning in relation to the plaintiff.

Laufer v. Bucklaschuck, ibid.

It is an error of law for a trial judge to defer ruling on these questions of law until after the jury has rendered its verdict. A statement which is not capable of being defamatory should not be left with the jury.

Further, the trial judge must make this determination as a matter of law with respect to each publication complained of by the plaintiff.

It is an error of law for a trial judge to submit *en bloc* the innuendoes pleaded by the plaintiff for the jury's consideration.

Allan v. Bushnell T.V. Co. Ltd. (1969), 4 D.L.R. (3d) 212, per Schroeder J.A. at 221–22 (Ont. C.A.).

Before submitting the innuendo to a jury, the trial judge must go through the various alleged meanings to determine which meaning or meanings, as pleaded, each statement is capable of bearing.

Laufer v. Bucklaschuck, above, at para. 47.

The trial judge should identify on the record how she reached her decision, the test she applied, and must identify to the jury the particular meaning or meanings that she finds each statement is reasonably capable of bearing.

Laufer v. Bucklaschuck, ibid. at paras. 46, 47.

Ross v. Lamport, [1955] 4 D.L.R. 826, per Pickup C.J.O. at 831 (Ont. C.A.), rev'd, [1956] S.C.R. 366, per Cartwright (Locke and Abbott JJ. concurring) at 380.

If the jury is presented by the trial judge with the alleged defamatory statements *en bloc*, and is never instructed on the meanings that each is capable of bearing, no one except the jury members themselves know the meaning or meanings which have actually been attributed to the statements at issue.

It would thus be impossible for an appellate court to ascertain the basis of the damage award.

Laufer v. Bucklaschuck, above, at para. 52:

> It is important to distinguish between the role of the judge deciding this question of law and the role of the jury at trial. The judge is entrusted with the task of setting the outer limits of potential liability; the jury with deciding whether to attach liability, within these limits, in the particular case. In fixing these outer limits, the judge must be mindful of the fundamental objective of the law of defamation, and acutely sensitive to the delicate balance required to protect both individual reputation and free speech.
>
> A judge at first instance may be required to rule on these outer limits in two situations. The first arises where ... the defendant applies by preliminary application to strike out the statement of claim as disclosing no reasonable cause of action. The second ... arises at trial when the defendant applies to the trial judge at the end of the plaintiff's case for a directed verdict on the basis there is no case to answer.

Butler v. Southam Inc. (2001), 197 N.S.R. (2d) 97, per Cromwell J.A. (Chipman and Moscoe JJ.A. concurring) at paras. 24–25 (C.A.).

The trial judge should not permit the jury to consider a defence of qualified privilege unless there is evidence to establish the facts and circumstances pleaded as giving rise to the qualified privilege. Similarly, if there is no evidence to establish the truth of the facts upon which the alleged libel is claimed to be fair comment, that defence should not be left to the jury.

Toronto Star Ltd. v. Drew, [1948] 4 D.L.R. 465, per Kerwin J. (Rinfret C.J.C. and Tashereau JJ. concurring) at 446 (S.C.C.).

Similarly, a jury verdict will be set aside where the trial judge incorrectly failed to rule, before the case went to the jury, that no case of qualified privilege had been made out.

Douglas v. Tucker, [1952] 1 S.C.R. 275, per Cartwright J. for the Court at 288.

Banks v. Globe and Mail Ltd., [1961] S.C.R. 474, per Cartwright J. for the Court at 485.

On the issue of malice, the trial judge's role prior to her charge to the jury is to properly analyze the evidence to determine whether it raises "a probability of malice."

Sun Life Assurance Co. of Canada v. Dalrymple, [1965] S.C.R. 302, per Spence J. at 309.

In order to enable a plaintiff to have a question of malice submitted to the jury, it is necessary that the evidence should raise a probability of malice and be more consistent with its existence than its nonexistence and there must be more than a mere scintilla of evidence.

Tavlor v. Despard, [1956] O.R. 963, per Roach J.A. at 978 (C.A.).

It has been suggested that applying this test necessitates "a weighing of the evidence," a function usually reserved for the jury.

Silbernagle v. Empire Stevedoring Company (1979), 18 B.C.L.R. 384 at 391 per Wallace J. (S.C.).

Laufer v. Bucklaschuck (1999), 181 D.L.R. (4th) 83, [2000] 2 W.W.R. 462, per Scott C.J.M. and Helper J.A. for the Court at para. 88 (Man. C.A.), leave to appeal to S.C.C. denied, [2000] S.C.C.A. No. 47.

The failure to properly instruct the jury with respect to the onus upon the plaintiff where malice is in issue constitutes a serious misdirection.

Netupsky v. Craig, [1973] S.C.R. 55, per Ritchie J. at 61.

Where a plaintiff has given no evidence of malice, and the defamatory statement was made on an occasion of qualified privilege, it is the duty of the trial judge to say there is no question for the jury and to direct a non-suit or verdict for the defendant.

Dewe v. Waterbury (1881), 6 S.C.R. 143, per Ritchie C.J. at 155.

2) Misdirection to Jury

The whole of the charge to the jury should be looked at in order to see whether, upon the whole, it afforded the jury a fair guide.

Morton v. Dean (1921), 14 Sask. L.R. 328, per Turgeon J.A. at 330 (C.A.).

Doyle v. Sparrow (1979), 27 O.R. (2d) 206, per MacKinnon A.C.J.O. at 207–8 (C.A.).

Bligh v. Warren (1912), 46 N.S.R. 440, per Turgeon J.A. for the Court at 527 (C.A.):

> The defendant is not called upon to shew that he acted in good faith; this is presumed in his favour. In this important particular I think the trial Judge did not make the position of the parties clear in his charge.
>
> In the course of his charge the trial Judge told the jury that the defendant would be justified, "if as a reasonable man he had a right to think that it was true." This is clearly a misdirection in view of the rules to which I have referred. The question to be determined is, not whether an ordinary reasonable man would have believed the charge under the circumstances, but whether the defendant did in fact believe it, regardless of his degree of intelligence, or credulity. The only thing to be considered is the state of the defendant's mind.

a) On Defamatory Meaning

A judge is permitted to express her own views to a jury on whether the statement is defamatory, but is not bound to do so. She should make it clear that it is a question of fact for the jury to decide. The judge cannot disclose to the jury the existence of a motion for non-suit.

Knott v. Telegram Printing Company Limited (1916), 27 Man. R. 336 (C.A.), aff'd (1917), 55 S.C.R. 631.

Where a judge goes further than this, there will be a mistrial on the grounds of misdirection.

Quillinan v. Stuart, [1917] 38 O.L.R. 623 at 635, 35 D.L.R. 35 (C.A.)

> A judge is not entitled to say to the jury: I direct you that the words are defamatory and your duty is to assess damages.

Broome v. Agar (1928) 138 L.T. 698 at 702 per Sankey L.J. at 702.

A new trial may be ordered on grounds of misdirection if the trial judge left to the jury a possible meaning which the words are not capable of bearing.

b) Re: Reference to Plaintiff

There will be a new trial if the trial court directed the jury that the defendant's intention to refer to the plaintiff was essential to a verdict.

Godhard v. James Inglis & Co. Ltd. (1904), 2 C.L.R. 78, per Griffith C.J. at 88 (H.C.A.).

c) Re: Fair Comment

It is a misdirection to tell the jury that if the comment tended to charge the plaintiff with improper conduct, then it could not be fair comment.

d) Re: Defence of Qualified Privilege

There was a misdirection because the trial judge failed to make it clear that the plaintiff must prove malice; the defendant does not have the burden of showing he acted in good faith.

> *Morton v. Dean*, [1921] 2 W.W.R 847, per Turgeon J.A. at 527 (Sask. C.A.).

Failure to tell the jury about the presumed *bona fides* of the defendant is a misdirection.

> See *Netupsky v. Craig,* in *Gatley* footnote 49 at p. 855.

e) Re: Damages

There is a duty to direct the jury to any rule of law which governs in the assessment of damages. If there has been a failure to do so, the court may grant a new trial even if the damages are not excessive.

> *Edmondson v. Allen* (1910), 40 N.B.R. 299 (C.A.).

f) Re: Personal Injury Damages Awards

It is a misdirection to refer a jury to a probable range of damage awards.

> *Hill v. Church of Scientology of Toronto*, [1995] 2 S.C.R. 1130 .

> *Brisson v. Brisson* (2002), 213 D.L.R. (4th) 428 (B.C.C.A.) .

g) Miscellaneous Misdirections

A judge may express her views of the facts to the jury but should not confuse and mislead the jury on compensation so that its assessment of damages may be suspect.

> *Lefoli v. Gouzenko*, [1969] S.C.R. 3, per Hall J. (Maitland and Ritchie JJ. concurring) at 7.

If the jury raises the issue of costs, they should be told not to concern themselves with costs.

> *Pamplin v. Express Newspapers*, [1988] 1 W.L.R. 116, per Neill L.J. at 122–23 (C.A.).

The appellant must make any objections at the time an issue arises. Failure to do so may result in a finding that any objections have been waived — the appellant cannot then complain of these errors on appeal.

Neville v. *Fine Art and General Insurance Company Limited* (1897), A.C. 68, per Halsbury L.C at 76 (H.L.):

> That would, but for what I am about to say, give the appellant only a right to ask for a new trial, which, though he has not asked for it, it is no doubt within your Lordships' competence to give him; but what puts him out of court in that respect is this, that where you are complaining of non-direction of the judge, or that he did not leave a question to the jury, if you had an opportunity of asking him to do it and you abstained from asking for it, no Court would ever have granted you a new trial; for the obvious reason that if you thought you had got enough you were not allowed to stand aside and let all the expense be incurred and a new trial ordered simply because of your own neglect.

Thompson v. *Fraser Cos.*, [1930] S.C.R. 109, per Newcombe J. at 117–18.

However, see *Quillinan* v. *Stuart* (1916), 36 O.L.R. 474, per Meredith C.J.O. (Gareau, Maclaren and Hodgers J.A. concurring) at para. 38 (C.A.):

> ¶38 It was contended by Mr. Nesbitt that, as no objection was taken to the charge to the jury, it was not open to the appellant to object to it on the ground of this misdirection, but I am not of that opinion; and *St. Denis* v. *Shoultz* (1898), 25 A.R. 131, is a clear authority against the contention.

3) Misconduct by Counsel

Appellate intervention with respect to the assessment of damages will more readily be warranted where counsel have been permitted to make misleading or inflammatory submissions to the jury.

Laufer v. *Bucklaschuck* (1999), 181 D.L.R. (4th) 83, [2000] 2 W.W.R. 462, per Scott C.J.M. and Helper J.A. at para. 11 (Man. C.A.), leave to appeal to S.C.C. denied, [2000] S.C.C.A. No. 47.

Ross v. *Lamport*, [1955] 4 D.L.R. 826, per Pickup C.J.O. at 836 (Ont. C.A.).

Counsel's address to the jury may legitimately employ rhetoric but it must not cause the jury to lose a sense of the proper relationship between the alleged wrong and the remedy to be applied. An inflammatory address is sufficient to call for a reassessment of damages unless the amount awarded demonstrates that the jury could not have been influenced by it.

Ross v. *Lamport, ibid.* at 836.

It is an error for counsel to tell the jury that in considering punitive damages they could consider an amount sufficient to deter not only the defendant specifically but others generally from similar conduct in the future.

Laufer v. Bucklaschuck, above, at para. 117.

4) Unreasonable Verdict

The court will only set aside a verdict or grant a new trial on grounds that the verdict is unreasonable or perverse if there is very good reason to do so.

E. CONSIDERATIONS APPLICABLE TO ALL VERDICTS

1) Improper Rejection of Evidence

Where a defendant is faced with an allegation of express malice, it is unfair to deny the defendant a full opportunity to explain his or her state of mind. Evidence may be admissible on malice which is not admissible on meaning.

Hodgson v. Canadian Newspapers Co. (1998), 39 O.R. (3d) 235 per Lane J. at para. 40 (2000) 49 O.R. (3d) 161, 189 D.L.R. (4th) 241 (Ont. C.A.), leave to appeal to SCC denied [2000] SCCA 465

2) Improper Admission of Evidence

A new trial was ordered when evidence of special damages was improperly admitted because it had not been pleaded.

Dominion Telegraph Co. v. Silver (sub nom. Silver v. Dominion Telegraph Co.) (1882), 10 S.C.R. 238 [evidence of special damage not admissible unless special damage pleaded].

3) Natural and Ordinary Meaning of Expression at Issue

A finding of fact as to the natural and ordinary meaning of the expression at issue is not one which depends on the trial judge's assessment of the credibility of witnesses or the evidence they gave. An appellate court may justify its decision to reverse a trial judge on this issue on the basis that the appellate court is in as good a position as the trial judge to draw the proper inference from the evidence.

Ross v. New Brunswick Teachers' Association (2001), 201 D.L.R. (4th) 75, per Daigle C.J.N.B. at paras. 44–45 (N.B.C.A.).

Carter v. *Gair*, 1999 BCCA 132.

Colour Your World Corp. v. *Canadian Broadcasting Corp.* (1998), 156 D.L.R. (4th) 27, per Abella J.A. at para. 39 (Ont. C.A.), leave to appeal to S.C.C. denied, [S.C.C.A. No. 170].

The appellate court has a duty to intervene where an inference is improperly drawn and is unreasonable.

Ross v. *New Brunswick Teachers' Association*, above, at para. 44.

4) Publication

The question of whether or not the burden of proving publication had been discharged was one which should be left for the jury to determine, if there was any evidence from which it might reasonably be concluded to be more probable than not that a defamatory statement concerning the plaintiff had been made known to a third party.

Gaskin v. *Retail Credit Co.*, [1965] S.C.R. 297, per Ritchie J. (Cartwright, Maitland, and Spence JJ. concurring) at 298–99.

5) Review of Assessment of Damages

An appellate court should not intervene with an award of general damages at trial merely because it would have arrived at a different figure. The appellate court can only intervene where the verdict is:

> ... so inordinately large as obviously to exceed the maximum limit of a reasonable range within which the jury may properly operate or, put another way, whether the verdict is so exorbitant or so grossly out of proportion to the libel as to shock the court's conscience and sense of justice.

Walker v. *CFTO Ltd.* (1987), 58 O.R. (2d) 104, per Noluns J.A. at 111 (C.A.).

Hill v. *Church of Scientology of Toronto*, [1995] 2 S.C.R. 1130 per Cory J.

Accordingly, jury libel awards for general and aggravated damages where there is evidence of malice are almost immune to appellate review. In *Hill* v. *Church of Scientology of Toronto*, the Supreme Court of Canada stated at paragraph 158 that juries are:

> uniquely qualified to assess the damages suffered by the plaintiff ... when properly instructed.

Adopting the reasons of Robins J.A. in *Walker* v. *CFTO Ltd.* (1987), 59 O.R. (2d) 104 (C.A.), the Supreme Court of Canada in *Hill* v. *Church of Sci-*

entology of Toronto, at page 1194, affirmed that the sole task of an appellate court in such circumstances is to consider:

> ... whether the verdict is so inordinately large as obviously to exceed the maximum limit of a reasonable range within which the jury may properly operate or, put another way, whether the verdict is so exorbitant or so grossly out of proportion to the libel as to shock the court's conscience and sense of justice.

Even awards for general and aggravated damages made by judges sitting without a jury appear to be substantially insulated from appellate intervention.

Hodgson v. Canadian Newspapers Co. (1998), 39 O.R. (3d) 235, per Lane J. at para. 40 (Gen. Div.), varied (2000), 49 O.R. (3d) 161 (C.A.), leave to appeal to S.C.C. denied, [2000] S.C.C.A. No. 465.

Southam Inc. v. Chelekis (2000), 133 B.C.A.C. 253, leave to appeal to S.C.C. denied, [2000] S.C.C.A. No. 465.

There is little Canadian authority on the standard of review by a provincial appellate court of damage awards in defamation made by judges sitting without a jury.

Brown v. Cole (1998), 114 B.C.A.C. 73, 61 B.C.L.R. (3d) 1, per Southin J.A. at para. 47 (C.A.), leave to appeal to S.C.C. denied, [1998] S.C.C.A. No. 614.

Neither the Ontario Court of Appeal nor the Supreme Court of Canada in *Hill v. Church of Scientology of Toronto* (1994), 18 O.R. (3d) 385 (C.A.), addressed the standard, although the Ontario Court of Appeal did remark at page 430:

> The English courts have held that an appellate court might more readily overturn an award by a judge sitting alone than an award by a jury: see *Blackshaw v. Lord*, [1984] Q.B. 1 at p. 27, [1983] 2 All E.R. 311.

The Supreme Court of Canada made no direct comment on the question. The remarks of Justice Cory, who rejected the application of a cap to defamation awards are, however, some indication that appellate tribunals do have some obligation to keep damage awards in tort within reasonable bounds.

Brown v. Cole (1998), 114 B.C.A.C. 73, 61 B.C.L.R. (3d) 1 at para. 49 (C.A.), leave to appeal to S.C.C. denied, [1998] S.C.C.A. No. 614:

> ¶49 The Supreme Court of Canada made no direct comment on the question. The remarks of Mr. Justice Cory on the imposing of the "cap"

in personal injury cases are, however, some indication that appellate tribunals do have some obligation to keep damage awards in tort within reasonable grounds.

In determining whether an award is either inadequate or overly generous in personal injury cases, judges do have regard to awards in cases of injury similar to that of the particular plaintiff.

In *Vogel v. Canadian Broadcasting Corporation.*, [1982] 3 W.W.R. 97 (B.C.S.C.), Esson J., as he then was, referred to other awards to assist him in making his assessment.

> Trial judges, in seeking a standard by which to assess damages for other than provable pecuniary loss, should appreciate that the judgment of the jury in *Hill v. Church of Scientology of Toronto* is not a benchmark in ordinary cases of defamation. One does not start with the award in *Hill v. Church of Scientology of Toronto* and work down.

> See also, *Brown v. Cole* (1998), 114 B.C.A.C. 73, 61 B.C.L.R. (3d) 1, per Southin J.A. at para. 61 (C.A.), leave to appeal to S.C.C. denied, [1998] S.C.C.A. No. 614.

With respect to aggravated damages, an appellate court is entitled to consider the post-trial actions of the defendant. If an unsuccessful libel defendant repeats the libel after the verdict, and maintains a plea of justification, these factors will weigh in favour of aggravated damages.

> *Hill v. Church of Scientology of Toronto*, [1995] 2 S.C.R. 1130, at paras. 196–99.

Punitive damages are only to be awarded in those circumstances where the combined award of general and aggravated damages will be insufficient to achieve the goal of punishment and deterrence. Unlike compensatory damages, punitive damages are not at large. Consequently, courts have a much greater scope and discretion on appeal. The appellate review should be based upon the court's estimation as to whether punitive damages serve the purpose of deterrence.

> *Hill v. Church of Scientology of Toronto*, *ibid.*

Where a trial judge erred in law by awarding damages for a libel which was not pleaded in the statement of claim, an appellate court correspondingly reduced the award of damages.

> *Proenca v. Squires Home Improvements and Total Renovations Ltd.*, 2001 NBCA 45.

a) Relevance of Conduct on Appeal

The quantum of damages awarded can be increased by conduct of the defendant during the hearing of an appeal.

6) Remedies on Appeal

The appellate court has no power to strike out portions of the text of a trial judgment.

> *Pressler v. Lethbridge* (2000), 86 B.C.L.R. (3d) 257, 2000 BCCA 639, per Southin J.A. at para. 101.

7) Order for a New Trial

The court may set aside a jury verdict as perverse and unreasonable and order a new trial:

> *Sydney Post Publishing v. Kendall* (1910), 43 S.C.R. 461 [where the jury gave a verdict for the defendants but the article complained of was libellous upon its face] per Anglin J. at 474 (Girouard J. concurring).

> *Lumsden v. Spectator Printing Co.* (1913) 29 O.L.R. 293 (C.A.) [jury held that a publication was not a libel although it plainly was a libel].

a) Limited to Specified Issues

An appeal may be allowed and a new trial ordered solely concerning the amount of damages.

> *Ross v. Lamport*, [1956] S.C.R. 366 at 367.

Where a new trial is ordered, the appellate court should not discuss the evidence or contested issues of fact but may discuss the law at length so the law is stated correctly to the new jury.

> *Douglas v. Tucker*, [1952] 1 S.C.R. 275, per Cartwright J. at 288.

b) Variation of "Judgement"

Where the conduct of the trial judge has not resulted in a miscarriage of justice, and to order a new trial would be a denial of justice to the plaintiff in all the circumstances, the appellate court may vary the trial judgment rather than remit the case for a new trial.

> *Jerome v. Anderson*, [1964] S.C.R. 291 per Cartwright J. (Maitland, Ritchie, and Hall JJ. concurring) at 308–9.

8) Other Orders

a) Reference Back to Trial Judge

Although an appellate court has the jurisdiction to order a reference back to the trial judge to determine specific factual issues, it will not do so unless that is required by the interests of justice. Where the court was in a position to draw required inferences of fact on appeal, the issues are not sent back to the trial judge for determination.

> *Ross v. New Brunswick Teachers Association* (2001), 201 D.L.R. (4th) 75, per Daigle C.J.N.B. at para. 98 (N.B.C.A.).

b) Dismissal of Action

Where the occasion of publication was privileged, and there was no evidence of malice, the plaintiff was non-suited.

> *Dewe v. Waterbury* (1881), 6 S.C.R. 143.

The general principle is that a new trial should not be ordered unless the interests of justice plainly require it. "The interests of justice" is a very broad notion which includes considerations of cost to the parties.

> *Ross v. New Brunswick Teachers Association*, above, at para. 98.

c) Order for Judgment for the Plaintiff

Where the defense of qualified privilege failed on appeal and the answers of the jury negatived the other available defences of fair comment, the Supreme Court of Canada set aside the judgments of the Court of Appeal and the trial judge and entered judgment for the plaintiff for $3,500 damages.

> *Banks v. Globe and Mail Ltd.*, [1961] S.C.R. 474 per Cartwright J. at 485.

Where the answers of the jury necessarily negatived all defences, the court varied the damages awarded by the trial judge to account for a sum which the trial judge improperly deducted.

> *Jerome v. Anderson*, [1964] S.C.R. 291 per Cartwright J. at 308–9.

A court of appeal may add an award of punitive damages.

> *Pressler v. Lethbridge* (2000), 86 B.C.L.R. (3d) 257 at para. 100 (C.A.) [on a cross-appeal by a plaintiff from a trial judge's refusal to award punitive damages].

d) Ontario Rule 52.09 — Record Jury Verdict

The verdict of the jury shall be endorsed on the trial record.

A trial judge does not have the authority to declare a jury verdict to be perverse.

Baboi v. Gregory (1986), 56 O.R. (2nd) 175 (Dist. Ct.).

Segreti v. Toronto (City) (1981), 20 C.P.C. 110 (Ont. H.C.J.).

Loffredi v. Simonetti (1985), 29 C.P.C. (2nd) 10 (Ont. Dist. Ct.).

e) Substituting an Appellate Assessment of Damages

The assessment of damages is clearly within the jury's power to decide.

Dennison v. Sanderson, [1946] O.R. 601 at 616 (C.A.).

Lawson v. Thompson (1969), 69 W.W.R. 304 (B.C.C.A.).

Knott v. Telegraph Printing Company (1916), 27 Man. R. 336 (C.A.), aff'd (1917), 55 S.C.R. 631.

Littleton v. Hamilton (1974) 4 O.R. (2d) 283 (C.A.).

Hill v. Church of Scientology of Toronto, [1995] 2 S.C.R. 1130 at para. 184.

In general terms, the court will only intervene when the verdict is considered shocking. Examples of such intervention:

Netupsky v. Craig, [1971] 1 O.R. 51 (C.A.) [court set aside an award of $240,000].

Walker v. CFTO Ltd. (1987), 59 O.R. (2d) 104 (C.A.) [jury award of $41.00 per viewer was considered to be perverse].

Lefoli v. Gouzenko, [1969] S.C.R. 3 [held: the summing-up must have confused the jury].

9) *Stare Decisis*

An appellate court is not strictly bound by its earlier decisions.

Schreiber v. Canada (Attorney General) (2001), 196 D.L.R. (4th) 281, at para. 44 (Ont. C.A.), aff'd 2002 SCC 62.

CHAPTER THIRTY-TWO:

Related Causes of Action

A. INJURIOUS FALSEHOOD

The tort of injurious falsehood consists of the malicious publication of a falsehood concerning the plaintiff that leads other persons to act in a manner that causes actual loss, damage, or expense to the plaintiff. Injury to reputation is not a necessary element to this tort.

Manitoba Free Press v. Nagy (1907), 39 S.C.R. 340.

NR Developments Ltd. v. Thomas, [2002] B.C.J. No. 971, per Melnick J. at para. 62 (S.C.).

Renger v. Vancouver (City), 2003 BCSC 31,2 per Romilly J. at paras. 54–59.

Janssen-Ortho Inc. v. Amgen Canada Inc., [2003] O.J. No. 2158, per Nordheimer J. at para. 57 (S.C.J.).

Claims for injurious falsehood often arise in the context of comparative advertising. However, courts are reluctant to interfere in the marketplace unless comparative advertising is clearly unfair.

Purolator Couriers Ltd. v. United Parcel Service Canada Ltd. (1995), 60 C.P.R. (3d) 473 (Ont. Gen. Div.).

Proof of malice is crucial.

Boehringer Ingelheim (Canada) Ltd. v. Bristol-Myers Squibb Canada Inc. (1998), 81 C.P.R. (3d) 114, 83 C.P.R. (3d) 51 (Ont. Gen. Div.).

Proof of malice is satisfied by proof of reckless indifference to the truth. Willful blindness amounts to malice. Actual malice in the sense of a predetermined intention to injure the plaintiff or his property need not be proved.

Manitoba Free Press v. *Nagy* (1907), 39 S.C.R. 340.

The tort may also be characterized as trade libel, commercial disparagement, slander of title, or malicious falsehood, depending on the context of the publication.

George Cluthe Manufacturing Co. v. *ZTW Properties Inc.* (1995), 23 O.R. (3d) 370 (Gen. Div.), leave to appeal to Ontario Court of Appeal granted; by consent endorsement of Court of Appeal, appeal was deemed abandoned as moot (1997), 38 O.R. (3d) 319 (C.A.).

Frank Flaman Wholesale Ltd. v. *Firman* (1982), 20 C.C.L.T. 246 (Sask. Q.B.).

The plaintiff may sue for interference with any potential advantage, including those of a non-commercial nature. A common claim, however, is that the injurious falsehood amounts to a disparagement of the plaintiff's property, products, business, or services which affects their marketability. The plaintiff has the onus of proving that the statements were false; that the defendant acted maliciously with intent to cause injury without lawful excuse; and that actual economic loss has occurred or will occur as a result. A plaintiff or its products must normally be identified by name in the impugned publication, but identification by implication may be sufficient, such as where the plaintiff enjoys almost exclusive dominance of the market.

Church & Dwight Ltd. v. *Sifto Canada Inc.* (1994), 22 C.C.L.T. (2d) 304 (Ont. Gen. Div.).

In Ontario, the common law tort has been modified somewhat by the *Libel and Slander Act*, R.S.O. 1990, c. L.12, section 17, which provides that in an action for slander of title, slander of goods, or other malicious falsehood, it is not necessary to allege or prove special damage if the falsehood is calculated to cause pecuniary damage to the plaintiff and is published in writing or some other permanent form or if the falsehood is calculated to cause pecuniary damage to the plaintiff in respect of any office, profession, calling, trade, or business. In this particular context (that is, proof of damages) the meaning of "calculated" is "fitted, suited, apt; proper or likely to."

Hudson Bay Co. v. *Beaumark Mirror Products Inc.* (1987), 13 C.I.P.R. 86 at 91, 15 C.P.R. (3d) 38 (F.C.T.D.).

R. v. *Hill* (1976), 33 C.C.C. (2d) 60 (B.C.C.A.).

Alberta (Attorney General) v. *Interwest Publications Ltd.* (1990), 73 D.L.R. (4th) 83 at 98, [1990] 5 W.W.R. 498, 58 C.C.C. (3rd) 114 (Alta. Q.B.).

Subjective intent to cause pecuniary damage is not a required ingredient of the tort under the *Libel and Slander Act* of Ontario.

A person is entitled to make general, unfavourable comparisons of competitive merchandise or services with their own.

> *Future Shop Ltd.* v. *A & B Sound Ltd.* (1994), 93 B.C.L.R. (2d) 40, [1994] 8 W.W.R. 376 (S.C.).

However, a person is not entitled to make specific, false comparisons between their goods and the plaintiff's goods, or to make false, disparaging statements regarding particular aspects of the plaintiff's goods or services.

> *B.C. Tel Mobility Cellular Inc.* v. *Rogers Cantel Inc.* (1995), 63 C.P.R. (3d) 464 (B.C.S.C.), appeal dismissed (1995), 66 B.C.A.C. 62 (C.A.) [interim injunction granted against advertisement].

> *Unitel Communications Inc.* v. *Bell Canada* (1994), 29 C.P.C. (3d) 159 (Ont. Gen. Div.) [interim injunction to restrain defendant's advertisement refused as it did not identify plaintiff].

> *Rust Check Canada Inc.* v. *Young* (1988), 47 C.C.L.T. 279 (Ont. H.C.J.) [interim injunction to restrain competitor's advertisement refused where no evidence of damage].

> *Mead Johnson Canada* v. *Ross Pediatrics* (1996), 70 C.P.R. (3d) 189, 31 O.R. (3d) 237 (Gen. Div.), leave to appeal refused (1996), 70 C.P.R. (3d) 417 (Ont. Gen. Div.) [interim injunction granted where Similac Advance infant formula promotion contained exaggerated claims to unique superiority over competitor's product, based on alleged but nonexistent scientific breakthrough].

> *Johnson & Johnson Inc.* v. *Bristol-Myers Squibb Canada Inc.* (1995), 62 C.P.R. (3d) 347 (Ont. Gen. Div.) [interim injunction dismissed where federal Health Protection Board had approved superiority claims in advertisement].

> *Cooke* v. *Maxwell* (1997), 24 O.T.C. 8 (Gen. Div.) [interim injunction granted where aspersions cast in news release about competing sports magazine].

> *UL Canada Inc.* v. *Proctor & Gamble Inc.* (1996), 65 C.P.R. (3d) 534 (Ont. Gen. Div.) [interim injunction denied, defendant's product in fact superior].

> *Effem Foods Ltd.* v. *H.J. Heinz Co. of Canada* (1997), 75 C.P.R. (3d) 331 (F.C.T.D.) [interim injunction denied, applicant failed to provide adequate evidence of harm to restrain an imminent television commercial comparing dog foods].

Claims in malicious falsehood are occasionally brought against the news media.

Sheppard Publishing Co. v. *Press Publishing Co.* (1905), 10 O.L.R. 243 (Div. Ct.) [newspaper falsely and maliciously published a story that the plaintiff had discontinued business].

Deli Holdings Ltd. v. *Central Broadcasting Co.* (1996), 149 Sask. R. 138 (Q.B.) [broadcast news item correctly reported young girl had been sexually assaulted outside a roller rink].

B. PRIVACY

Defamation claims are occasionally joined with claims for invasion of privacy, either based on the statutory tort created by legislation in British Columbia, Manitoba, Newfoundland and Labrador, and Saskatchewan or based on an alleged right to privacy at common law.

British Columbia, *Privacy Act*, R.S.B.C. 1996, c. 373.

Manitoba, *Privacy Act*, R.S.M. 1987, c. P125.

Newfoundland and Labrador, *Privacy Act*, R.S.N. 1990, c. P-22, R.S.N. 1990, c. P-22.

Saskatchewan, *Privacy Act*, R.S.S. 1978, c. P-24.

Whether the courts in those provinces without legislation will recognize the existence of the common law tort is questionable.

In British Columbia, the *Privacy Act* provides that "It is a tort, actionable without proof of damage, for a person, wilfully and without a claim of right, to violate the privacy of another." The statute further provides that the "nature and degree of privacy to which a person is entitled in a situation or in relation to a matter is that which is reasonable in the circumstances, giving due regard to the lawful interests of others." The Act directs that in determining whether the act or conduct of a person is a violation of another's privacy, regard must be given to "the nature, incidence and occasion of the act or conduct and to any domestic or other relationship between the parties."

British Columbia's *Privacy Act* recognizes certain defences analogous to those available in defamation law. For example, the Act provides that publication is not a violation of privacy if the matter published was of public interest or was fair comment on a matter of public interest, or if the publication was privileged in accordance with the rules of law relating to defamation [section 2(3)]. The privilege defence does not apply to publication of portions of court proceedings which are subject to a publication ban.

> *J.M.F. v. Chappell and News Publishing Company Ltd.* (1995), B.C.J. No. 1438, (S.C.), varied (1998), 158 D.L.R. (4th) 430 (B.C.C.A.), leave to appeal to S.C.C. dismissed, [1998] S.C.C.A. No. 154.

A defendant is not guilty under the British Columbia statute of "willfully" invading the plaintiff's privacy merely because he or she committed an intentional act that had the effect of violating privacy. The plaintiff must prove an intention to do an act which the defendant knew or should have known would violate the plaintiff's privacy.

> *Hollinsworth v. BCTV, a division of Westcom TV Group Ltd.*, [1999] 6 W.W.R. 54 (B.C.C.A.), aff'g (1996), 34 C.C.L.T. (2d) 95 (B.C.S.C.)

In British Columbia the tort is also not complete unless the defendant violated the plaintiff's privacy "without a claim of right," which means an honest belief in a state of facts which, if it existed, would be a legal justification or excuse. It is unclear yet whether the honest belief must be a reasonable one.

> *Davis v. McArthur* (1969), 10 D.L.R. (3d) 250 (B.C.S.C.)..

> *Hollinsworth v. BCTV*, above, per Lambert J.A. at para. 31.

Acts or conduct that are "… consented to by some person entitled to consent" or that are "… authorized or required by or under a law in force in the Province …" are not actionable violations of privacy in British Columbia.

> *Privacy Act*, ss. 2(2)(a) & (c).

> *Walker v. British Columbia (College of Dental Surgeons)*, [1997] B.C.J. No. 433 (S.C.).

Damages have been awarded over a schoolmaster's surreptitious entry into a student's home.

> *Getejanc v. Brentwood College Assn.* (2001), 6 C.C.L.T. (2d) 261 (B.C.S.C.).

> See also *Lee v. Jacobson* (1992), 87 D.L.R. (4th) 401 (B.C.S.C.), rev'd (YEAR) 99 B.C.L.R. (2d) 144 (C.A.) [peephole into washroom].

> *Milton v. Savinkoff* (1993), 18 C.C.L.T. (2d) 288 (B.C.S.C.) [nude photos released by boyfriend].

The statutory tort created by section 2 of Saskatchewan's *Privacy Act* is virtually identical in terms to the British Columbia tort.

It has been held that a negligent breach of privacy is not actionable in Saskatchewan.

Peters-Brown v. Regina District Health Board (1996), 1 W.W.R. 337 (Sask. Q.B.), aff'd without discussion of privacy tort, [1997] 1 W.W.R. 638 (Sask. C.A.).

As in British Columbia, the cause of action for invasion of privacy under the Saskatchewan statute is subject to certain defences analogous to those available in defamation. A publication is not a violation of privacy where there were reasonable grounds to believe the matter was of public interest, was fair comment on a matter of public interest, or was privileged in accordance with defamation law [sec᾽ ᴐn 4(2)].

The Saskatchewan statute directs the courts to take into account, among other things, the conduct of the plaintiff and of the defendant both before and after the alleged invasion of privacy, including "any apology or offer of amends made by the defendant" [section 6(2)].

If no reasonable person would regard an investigation by a public officer within the scope of his duty as breaching the plaintiff's privacy, the court may strike out such a claim as failing to disclose a reasonable cause of action.

Kish v. Chapple, [1999] S.J. No. 186 (Sask. Q.B.).

In Manitoba, the tort of invasion of privacy is defined slightly differently that in British Columbia and Saskatchewan. The *Privacy Act*, R.S.M. 1987, c. P125 provides that a "person who substantially, unreasonably and without a claim of right, violates the privacy of another person, commits a tort against that other person" [section 2(1)]. Proof of damage is not required [section 2(2)].

Manitoba's *Privacy Act* also protects publication of any matter if there were reasonable grounds to believe that publication was in the public interest, was privileged under defamation law, or was fair comment on a matter of public interest [section 5 (f)].

Newfoundland and Labrador's *Privacy Act* creates a tort of invasion of privacy in almost the same terms as the British Columbia and Saskatchewan legislation [section 3].

Like the other three provinces, Newfoundland and Labrador has enacted defamation-style defences. A publication is not a violation of privacy if the matter published was of public interest, fair comment on a matter of public interest, or privileged in accordance with defamation law [section 5(2)].

It has been held that video surveillance of a plaintiff personal injury claimant did not violate the Newfoundland statute where the defendants recorded information which could have been and was being observed by members of the public as it occurred. The plaintiff could not reasonably have expected any degree of privacy relating to her actions in public.

> *Druken v. R.G. Fewer and Associates Inc.* (1998), 171 Nfld. & P.E.I.R. 312 (Nfld. S.C. (T.D.)).

In Ontario, where recognition of a common law privacy tort has only been tested at an interlocutory level, plaintiffs have occasionally sought to side-step limitations or notice requirements under defamation law by alleging a breach of privacy.

> *Graye v. Filliter* (1995), 25 O.R. (3d) 57 (Gen. Div.).

C. COMPETITION ACT

The federal *Competition Act*, R.S. 1985, c. 34, section 52(1), prohibits a representation to the public that is false or misleading in a material respect, for the purpose of promoting, directly or indirectly, the supply or use of a product or for the purpose of promoting, directly or indirectly, any business interest, by any means whatever. This prohibition applies only where the representor knowingly or recklessly made the false or misleading representation.

It is not clear whether a breach of this section gives a person who has suffered loss or damage a civil cause of action for general damages.

> *137240 Assn. Canada Inc. v. Ontario Medical Assn.*, [1989] 29 C.P.R. (3d) 63 (Ont. H.C.J.).

> *Canadian Community Reading Plan Inc. v. Quality Service Programs Inc.* (1999), 107 O.T.C. 18 (S.C.), varied (2001), 141 O.A.C. 289 (C.A.).

In *137240 Assn. Canada Inc. c.o.b. Canadian Drugs Manufacturers Ass'n. v. Ontario Medical Ass'n.* [1989], 29 C.P.R. (3d) 63, the court rejected a defence motion to strike a claim that "the defendants have made false and misleading representations to the public" in a video cassette recording and slides which constituted a presentation on the clinical effects of drug product substitution. The plaintiff was incorporated to represent generic drug manufacturers and alleged that the video and slides were for the purpose of undermining the viability of generic drug manufacturers. Although Van Camp J. struck out a claim for slander of goods, he stated [at page 65]:

> To bring an action under s. 311 [now s. 52(1)] a person must have suffered loss or damage as a result of that offence. The French version of loss or damage is "*une perte ou un prejudice.*" It may well be that s. 31.1 which is a rela-

tively new section is intended to cover only economic loss and not general damages, that it is in effect a provision for restitution, but I am not persuaded that [the plaintiff] could not succeed in asserting a claim thereunder if the matter were to go to trial.

See also *Janssen-Ortho Inc.* v. *AmgeN Canada Inc.* [2003] O.J. No. 2158 (S.C.J.) where the plaintiff pleaded five causes of action, including a breach of section 52 of the *Competition Act*, in relation to a letter by the defendant to health care professionals concerning the plaintiff's product, a drug called EPREX, a subsequent letter-writing campaign to the Ontario government, and a media campaign.

D. PASSING-OFF

A cause of action for passing-off may be alleged where the plaintiff has suffered injury to business reputation or goodwill caused by a defendant's promotion of her own product or business in such a way as to create the false impression that her product or business is in some way approved, authorized, or endorsed by the plaintiff or that there is some business connection between the defendant and the plaintiff. By these means a defendant may hope to cash in on the goodwill of the plaintiff.

> *British Columbia Automobile Assn.* v. *Office and Professional Employees' International Union Local 378*, [2001] 4 W.W.R. 95, per Sigurdson at para. 55 (B.C.S.C.).

> *National Hockey League* v. *Pepsi-Cola Canada Ltd.* (1992), 42 C.P.R. (3d) 390 (B.C.S.C.), aff'd (1995) 59 C.P.R. (3d) 216 (B.C.C.A.).

> *Greystone Capital Management* v. *Greystone Properties Ltd.* (1999), 87 C.P.R. (3d) 43 (B.C.S.C.).

The tort of passing-off may also occur where competitors are engaged in a common field of activity and the plaintiff has alleged that the defendant has named, packaged, or described its product or business in a manner likely to lead the public to believe the defendant's product or business is that of the plaintiff.

The plaintiff must allege and prove:

(i) the existence of reputation or goodwill at the relevant time (whether the plaintiff was recognized by the trade name and whether the trade name was distinctive within the relevant field of activity);

(ii) a misrepresentation leading the relevant public to believe there is a business association or connection between the parties (whether the defendants' use of the trade name is likely to deceive the relevant public).

The misrepresentation need not be deliberate, and proof of intent is not necessary. Evidence of likelihood of confusion, leading to the possibility of lost business opportunity, is relevant. However, the establishment of actual confusion is not required. Damage or potential damage flowing to the plaintiff as a result of any misrepresentation due to loss of control over its reputation is presumed.

Ciba-Geigy Canada Ltd. v. Apotex Inc. (1992), 44 C.P.R. (3d) 289 (S.C.C.).

Draper v. Trist, [1939] 3 All E.R. 513 (C.A.).

Visa International Service Assn. v. Visa Motel Corp. (1984), 1 C.P.R. (3d) 109 (B.C.C.A.).

The element of deceit on the part of the defendant is essential.

Westfair Foods Ltd. v. Jim Pattison Industries Ltd. (1990), 30 C.P.R. (3d) 174 (B.C.C.A.).

E. NEGLIGENT MISREPRESENTATION

A cause of action for negligent misrepresentation may be alleged where:

- there is a duty of care based on a "special relationship" between the representor and the representee;
- the representation in question is untrue, inaccurate, or misleading;
- the representor acted negligently in making the alleged misrepresentation;
- the representee relied, in a reasonable manner, on the alleged misrepresentation; and
- the reliance was detrimental to the representee in the sense that damages resulted.

Queen v. Cognos Inc. (1993), 99 D.L.R. (4th) 626 at 643 (S.C.C.).

Haskett v. Equifax Canada Inc., [2003] O.J. No. 77, per Feldman J.A.for the court at paras. 53–56 (C.A.)

F. *TRADEMARKS ACT*

Under the federal *Trademarks Act*, R.S. 1985, c. t-15, section 22, a plaintiff may bring a civil action for depreciation of the value of the goodwill attaching to a trademark. Section 22(1) prohibits the use of a registered trademark by another person in a manner that is likely to have the effect of depreciating the value of the goodwill attaching thereto.

The defendant's use of the trademark must be in relation to goods or services. It appears that it is not necessary for the infringing defendant to be in commercial competition with the trademark owner before the latter may have recourse to section 22.

Rotisseries St- Hubert Ltée v. Syndicat des Travailleurs(euses) de la Rotisserie St-Hubert de Drummondville (C.S.N.) (1986), 17 C.P.R. (3d) 461 (Qc. S.C.).

A parody of a registered trademark which is likely to create confusion in the minds of the plaintiff's customers falls within the scope of section 22. The defendant's intention to create a spoof is not a defence to infringement.

Source Perrier (SA) v. Fira-Less Marketing Co. Ltd. (1983), 70 C.P.R. (2d) 61 (F.C. (T.D.)).

G. CONSPIRACY TO DEFAME

Although conspiracy to defame is occasionally alleged by a plaintiff where there are multiple defendants, it is questionable whether such a pleading adds anything of substance to the claim.

The tort of civil conspiracy requires a plaintiff to allege and prove either:

(i) an agreement among the defendants, with the predominant purpose of causing injury to the plaintiff (as opposed to pursuing legitimate interests of their own) whether the means used by the defendants are lawful or unlawful; or

(ii) that there is an agreement among the defendants to carry out unlawful conduct directed towards the plaintiff which the defendants know or ought to know is likely to result in injury and which does, in fact, cause the plaintiff harm.

Damages are an essential ingredient of this cause of action.

Canada Cement LaFarge Ltd. v. British Columbia Lightweight Aggregate Ltd., [1983] 1 S.C.R. 452, 145 D.L.R. (3d) 385.

Nicholls v. Richmond (Township) (1984), 52 B.C.L.R. 302 (S.C.).

Merling v. Southam Inc., [2001] O.J. No. 4227 (S.C.J.).

Where conduct is libellous, the concept of a conspiracy may be redundant because of the principle that all those who participate in publishing and circulating a libel, or who authorize, incite, or encourage such publication, are liable as joint tortfeasors.

Thomson v. Lambert, [1938] S.C.R. 253, 2 D.L.R. 545.

Further, where republication occurs, the original publisher of the defamatory expression and the republisher (assuming the original publisher is liable) are considered to be several concurrent tortfeasors and are responsible for the same damage.

Brown v. Cole, [1996] 2 W.W.R. 567 (B.C.C.A.).

It may be that a plaintiff cannot plead both conspiracy and the substantive tort of defamation. It is arguable that where the conspiracy is to injure reputation, the conspiracy claim merges in the defamation claim.

Elliott v. Canadian Broadcasting Corporation (1994), 24 C.P.C. (3d) 143 (Ont. Gen. Div.), aff'd (1995), 38 C.P.C. (3d) 332 (Ont. C.A.).

Sun Life Assurance Co. of Canada v. 401700 Ontario Ltd. (1991), 3 O.R. (3d) 684 (Gen. Div.).

Ahluwalia v. Varma, [1991] O.J. No. 2335 (Gen. Div.).

Magnotta Winery Ltd. v. Ziraldo (1995), 25 O.R. (3d) 575 (Gen. Div.).

Guccione v. Bell, [1998] 229 A.R. 365, 239 A.R. 277 (Q.B.).

Ward v. Bosveld (1983), 40 C.P.C. 24 (Ont. H.C.J.).

Ward v. Lewis, [1955] 1 All E.R. 55.

In England, it appears that the tort of conspiracy does not allow for the recovery of injury to reputation or injury to feelings.

Lonhro plc v. Fayed (No. 5), (1993) 1 W.L.R. 1489 (C.A.).

Gregory v. Portsmouth City Council, [2000] H.L.J. No. 4.

In Canada, actions for conspiracy to defame have been dismissed on the basis that they were merely an attempt to dress up in the guise of conspiracy what was properly a libel claim that was statute-barred by the expiry of a limitation period.

Elliott v. Canadian Broadcasting Corporation (1994), 24 C.P.C. (3d) 143 (Ont. Gen. Div.), aff'd (1995), 38 C.P.C. (3d) 332 (Ont C.A.).

Ward v. Bosveld (1983), 40 C.P.C. 24 (Ont. H.C.J.).

At a minimum, if the plaintiff pleads a conspiracy to defame, particulars of the overt acts and of the alleged agreements or other combinations, including particulars such as their objects and purposes, must be supplied.

Industrial Ecology Inc. v. Kayar Energy Systems Inc., [1997] O.J. No. 204 (Gen. Div.).

H.V.K. v. *Children's Aid Society of Haldimand-Norfolk*, [2003] O.J. No. 1572, per Himel J. at paras. 21, 34 (S.C.J.).

It is submitted that the particulars of the overt acts should include the ordinary particulars of publication which must be pleaded in a defamation action. A plaintiff cannot sidestep those requirements by pleading conspiracy.

It has been suggested that a plea of conspiracy may in some instances extend the scope of the litigation and temper the general rule requiring specificity in pleadings relating to defamation. This would not apply, however, where a plea of conspiracy relates only to the alleged defamation.

550433 Alberta Ltd. v. *Stealth Alarm Systems Inc.*, [1998] A.J. No. 1421 (Q.B.).

Guccione v. *Bell* (1998), 239 A.R. 277 (Q.B.).

Fulton v. *Globe and Mail*, [1997], 3 W.W.R. 200 (Alta. Q.B.).

It has also been suggested that if the conspiracy had been to libel the plaintiff, damages could be recovered in such a case without proof of actual loss, but if the conspiracy was to slander by speaking and publishing something which was not actionable without proof of special damage, then the plaintiff's action for conspiracy would fail.

Varner v. *Morton* (1919), 46 D.L.R. 597 (N.S.C.A.).

Kovlaske v. *International Woodworkers of America-Canada Local 1-217*, [1999] B.C.J. No. 2326 (S.C.).

L.N.Klar, *Remedies in Tort*, Vol. 1 (Toronto: Carswell, 1987) at 3–21.

Canadian Community Reading Plan Inc. v. *Quality Service Programs Inc.* (1999), 50 B.L.R. (2d) 303 (Ont. S.C.J.), varied (2001), 141 O.A.C. 289 (C.A.).

In any event, a corporate entity can act only by its officers, employees, or agents. Consequently it is not open to a plaintiff to allege that a corporation has conspired to defame the plaintiff through its individual officers, employees, or agents.

Citizens for Foreign Aid Reform Inc. v. *Canadian Jewish Congress* (1999), 36 C.P.C. (4th) 266 (B.C.S.C.).

H. NEGLIGENT INFLICTION OF EMOTIONAL DISTRESS

It has been held that a claim for loss of reputation is properly the subject of a claim in defamation and should not be brought in negligence.

Fulton v. *Globe and Mail* (1997), 152 D.L.R. (3d) 212 (Alta. Q.B.); see also, Master's decision (1997), 3 W.W.R. 200 (Alta. Q.B.).

Guccione v. *Bell* (1998), 229 A.R. 365 (Q.B.).

P.G. Restaurant Ltd. (c.o.b. Mama Panda Restaurant) v. *Northern Interior Regional Health Board*, [2004] B.C.J. No. 424, 2004 BCSC 294, per Goepel J. at paras. 182–206 [no duty of care on municipal officers concerning statement about restaurant].

But see *Haskett* v. *Equifax Canada Inc.*, [2003] O.J. No. 771, per Feldman J.A. at paras. 53–53 (C.A.) [whether the law of defamation precludes recognition of a relationship of proximity between credit reporting agencies and consumers who are the subject of credit reports, held not suitable for determination on a motion to strike]. Leave to appeal to S.C.C. denied, [2003] S.C.C.A. No. 208.

Further, it is arguable that there is no common law duty of care not to expose a person to humiliation or emotional distress by publication of true statements.

Roed v. *Association of Professional Engineers of British Columbia* (1988), 29 B.C.L.R. 59 (C.A.).

In any event, absent any physical symptoms or recognizable psychiatric illness (as opposed to mere emotional upset or distress) and some degree of foreseeability of the injury, the courts have not recognized a claim in negligence for infliction of emotional distress in defamation cases. Even erroneous media reports do not necessarily give rise to a cause of action, where there is no malice and no actual physical or psychiatric illness involved.

Guay v. *Sun Publishing Co. Ltd.*, [1953] 2 S.C.R. 216.

It has been held that embarrassment caused by news media publicity entitled a plaintiff to damages where the police violated their own procedures by giving the media advance notice to have television cameras cover the execution of a search warrant.

Uni-Jet Industrial Pipe Ltd. v *Canada (Attorney General)*, [2000] 6 W.W.R. 753 (Man. Q.B.), varied (2001), 198 D.L.R. (4th) 577 (Man. C.A.).

See also, *Ms. R.* v *W.A.*, 2002 ABQB 201.

One court held that it has not been determined whether the publication of false statements to third parties may be the wrongful act which caused the distress.

Refco Futures (Canada) Ltd. v. Keuroghlian, [2002] O.J. No. 2981, per Master Dash at para. 36 (S.C.J.).

I. INTERFERENCE WITH ECONOMIC RELATIONSHIPS

The tort of unlawful interference with economic interests requires the plaintiff to prove three components:

i)   the intent of the defendant to injure the plaintiff;

ii) economic loss by the plaintiff; and

iii) that the means employed by the defendants to interfere with the plaintiff's living or business were unlawful.

> *Janssen-Ortho Inc. v. Amgen Canada Inc.* [2003] O.J. No. 2158, per Nordheimer J. at para. 58 (S.C.J.).

> *Canadian Community Reading Plan v. Quality Service Programs Inc.* (2001), 141 O.A.C. 289 at para. 30 (C.A.).

> *Lineal Group Inc. (c.o.b. Samsonite Furniture) v. Atlantis Canada Distributors Inc.* (1998), 42 O.R. (3d) 157 (C.A.), leave to appeal to S.C.C. denied, [1998] S.C.C.A. No. 608.

> *Mintuck v. Valley River Bend No. 63A*, [1977] 2 W.W.R. 309 (Man. C.A.)

> *Industrial Ecology Inc. v. Kayar Energy Systems Inc.*, [1997] O.J. No. 204 (Gen. Div.).

> *Daishowa Inc. v. Friends of the Lubicon* (1996), 27 O.R (3d) 215 (Div. Ct.), leave to appeal to Ont. C.A. refused 24 April 1996, Doc. CAM 17675.

The defendant's actions must be targeted at the plaintiff for the intention required by the tort of economic interference to be made out.

> *Cheticamp Fisheries Co-operative Ltd. v. Canada* (1995), 26 C.C.L.T. (2d) 40 at 50 (N.S.C.A.).

J. INTIMIDATION

The tort of intimidation requires the plaintiff to prove:

(i)   coercion of another to do or refrain from doing an act;

(ii) the use of a threat as a means of compulsion;

(iii) that the threat was to use unlawful means;

(iv) that the person so threatened complied with the demand;

(v)   the defendant intended to injure the person threatened; and

(vi)   the person threatened suffered damage.

> *Daishowa Inc.* v. *Friends of the Lubicon* (1996), 27 O.R (3d) 215 (Div. Ct.).

The tort is committed if the defendant intimidates other persons to the injury of the plaintiff.

> *Rookes* v. *Barnard*, [1964] 1 All E.R. 367 at 397, [1964] A.C. 1129 (H.L.), per Lord Devlin.

K. INDUCING BREACH OF CONTRACT

The tort of inducing breach of contract requires the plaintiff to prove:

i)   the defendant's knowledge of the contract and its terms;
ii)   the intention to procure a breach of the contract;
iii) conduct by which the defendant directly persuades or induces a third party to break a contract with the plaintiff;
iv)   a breach of contract; and
v)   damage.

> *Daishowa Inc.* v. *Friends of the Lubicon* (1996), 27 O.R (3d) 215 (Div. Ct.).
>
> *Great West Marketing Inc.* v. *Connell*, 2002 ABQB 677, per Lee J. at paras. 47–50.
>
> *DeHaas* v. *Mooney*, [2003] O.J. No. 549, per Sachs J. at paras. 21–22 (S.C.J.), citing *Chaplin* v. *Logix Systems Inc.*, [1998] O.J. No. 1775, per Aitken J. at para. 8 (Gen. Div.); *Ontario Store Fixtures Inc.* v. *Mmmuffins* (1989), 700 O.R. (2d) 42, per MacFarland J. at 44 (H.C.J.).

Direct influence involves immediate pressure on one of the contracting parties.

> *Great West Marketing Inc.* v. *Connell, ibid.*

In *Great West Marketing Inc.* v. *Connell, ibid*, Lee J. states:

¶ 49 In *369413 Alberta Ltd.* v. *Pocklington* (2000), 271 A.R. 280 (C.A.) it was noted at 293 that in some cases a distinction is drawn between direct interference, for which the breach must be a foreseeable or reasonable consequence of the conduct, and indirect interference, for which the breach must be a necessary or substantially certain consequence.

¶ 50 A further distinction has been drawn between direct and indirect interference in that some Canadian authorities hold that indirect means must be lawful in themselves (L. Klar, *Tort Law*, 2nd ed. (Toronto: Carswell, 1996) at

508; Ed Miller supra; *Retail, Wholesale and Department Store Union Local 558 v. Pepsi-Cola Canada Beverages (West) Ltd.*, [1999] 8 W.W.R. 429 (Sask. C.A.), affirmed on other grounds (2002), 208 D.L.R. (4th) 385 (S.C.C.); *Mark Fishing Co. v. United Fishermen and Allied Workers' Union*, [1972] 3 W.W.R. 641 (B.C.C.A.), appeal dismissed [1973] 3 W.W.R. 13 (S.C.C.); *Waryk v. Bank of Montreal* (1991), 6 BCAC 81, leave denied [1992] 1 S.C.R. xii; and *Unisys Canada Inc. v. York Three Associates Inc.* (1999), 39 R.P.R. (3d) 220 (Ont. Sup. Ct. J.) varied (2001), 150 O.A.C. 49. It appears from a review of the case law that this requirement has not been seriously disputed.

L. PERSONAL INFORMATION PROTECTION ACT

In a situation where the defamatory expression involves the publication of personal information, a plaintiff may on appropriate facts allege a breach of personal information protection legislation of general application to the private sector:

i)   the federal *Personal Information Protection and Electronic Documents Act*, S.C. 2000, c. 5, Part 1, which came into force for the federally-regulated private sector on 1 January 2001. All private sector organizations involved in commercial activities in the Saskatchewan, Manitoba, Ontario, New Brunswick, Nova Scotia, Prince Edward Island and Newfound and Labrador became subject to this federal law on 1 January 2004;

ii) British Columbia's *Personal Information Protection Act*, S.B.C. 2003, c. 63, which applies to the provincially-regulated private sector including non-profit organizations; or

iii) Alberta's *Personal Information Protection Act*, S.A. 2003, c. P-6.5, which applies to the provincially-regulated private sector including non-profit organizations.

Where the federal statute applies, the federal Privacy Commissioner has broad powers to investigate complaints, including the right to enter business premises without a warrant and review and make copies of documents, to compel testimony under oath, and generally to carry out any interviews and inquiries he or she considers necessary [section 12(1)].

The Commissioner has the authority to shame an organization by publicizing any information concerning the personal information management practices of that organization [section 20(2)].

In relation to a complaint, the Commissioner must prepare a report containing his or her findings and recommendations, any settlement reached by the parties, a request that the organization notify the Commissioner of any action taken to be taken to implement the recommendations, and the recourse available to the individual if the complaint is eventually referred to the Court [section 13(1)].

After receiving the Privacy Commissioner's report, a complainant may apply to the Trial Division of the Federal Court, within forty-five days, for a hearing in respect of the complaint (except complaints concerning recommendations) or any matter referred to in the report [section 14(1), 14(2)]. The Federal Court may conduct a summary hearing and award general damages to the complainant, including damages for "humiliation" [section 16(c)].

The personal information protection statutes of Alberta and British Columbia each confer responsibility for monitoring compliance on their respective provincially-appointed Information and Privacy Commissioner, who has order-making power to require an organization to stop collecting, using or disclosing personal information in violation of the statute.

In British Columbia and Alberta, if the Commissioner makes an order under the statute, or if a person has been convicted of an offence under the statute, an individual affected by the order or by the conduct that gave rise to the offence has a cause of action for damages. In British Columbia, the claim is limited to damages for "actual harm" [s.57(1)] whereas the Alberta statute speaks of "damages for loss or injury." [s. 60(1)].

The statutory restrictions, and the cause of action for their breach, do not apply in respect of personal information that an organization collects, uses or discloses solely for journalistic, artistic or literary purposes or to any individual in respect of personal information that the individual collects, uses or discloses solely for personal or domestic purposes [federal, ss. 4(2)(b), 4(2)(c); British Columbia, ss. 3(2)(a), 3(2)(b); Alberta, ss.4(3)(a), 4(3)(b), 4(3)(c).]

In England, model Naomi Campbell recovered a modest award of damages, including aggravated damages, plus substantial costs following a trial of an action under section 13 of the United Kingdom's *Data Protection Act* and for breach of confidentiality. The violation, according to the English High Court, consisted of the newspaper's publication of details of the plaintiff's drug therapy, which was sensitive personal data, in circumstances where the method used to obtain the data (surreptitiously photographing the plaintiff as she left a Narcotics Anonymous meeting) was not fair, and the information was obtained unlawfully because it was obtained in breach of confidence.

Campbell v. Mirror Group Newspapers, [2002] E.W.J. No. 1901, [2002] EWHC 499 (Q.B.).

On appeal to the Court of Appeal, Lord Phillips M.R. noted [at paragraph 8] that lawsuit was the first proceeding in which the interpretation of the *Data Protection Act* had fallen for determination. In his ruling that there had been no infringement of the statute by the defendant newspaper, Lord Phillips M.R. held that the defendant fell within the exemption contained in section 32 relating to the processing of personal information "undertaken with a view to the publication by any person of any journalistic, literary, or artistic material."

> *Campbell v. Mirror Newsgroup Newspapers Ltd.*, [2002] EWCA Civ 1373, appeal heard by House of Lord, judgment reserved February 2004..

A somewhat similar exemption in respect of personal information collected, used, or disclosed for journalistic or literary purposes is contained in the *Personal Information Protection and Electronic Documents Act*, section 4(2).

Naomi Campbell has been granted leave to appeal to the House of Lords.

M. CYBERLIBEL

1) Introduction

Unlike injurious falsehood, cyberlibel is not an independent tort but merely a form of libel. The case law relating to Internet defamation is discussed in the other chapters of this book under appropriate topic headings.

Nevertheless, it may be useful to consider here those special features of electronic expression via the Internet which add to the factual matrix in a cyberlibel lawsuit.

Cyberlibel demonstrates, in a stark fashion, the conflict between those who advocate uninhibited freedom of expression and others including e-business which seek order, predictability, and the protection of their valuable goodwill and reputation.

Those who favour unlimited freedom of expression encountered a perfect medium when the Internet became popular. The ease of access, opportunity for anonymity, and global scope of publication enable and encourage unfettered discussion. Yet those same characteristics came to be viewed as a threat by individuals and corporations worried about protecting an international reputation.

2) Libel and the Internet

A number of features unique to the Internet distinguish it from other communications media.

a) Global Nature

Internet expression is oblivious to international boundaries and accessible to anyone with access to a linked computer in numerous countries. Although Canadian courts have grappled with difficult issues of jurisdiction, venue, and choice of law in the context of cross-border radio and television broadcasts, international telex, telephone, and telegraph messages; and multi-country distribution of books, magazines, and newspapers, Internet libel has exponentially complicated the task of addressing those issues.

i) The global nature of potential access to defamatory expression raises perplexing questions which courts have recently begun to address, such as:

 a. Where did the publication of the defamation occur?

 • theoretically, every time a third party accesses a defamatory posting on the Internet, publication has occurred.

 b. Where should the plaintiff sue?

 • where the plaintiff resides?

 • where the defendant resides?

 • wherever publication has occurred?

 • defamation laws vary from country to country and in countries such as Canada, Australia, and the United States, laws can vary from province to province and state to state. Therefore, plaintiffs may seek to "forum shop" to sue in the jurisdiction with the most favourable procedural or substantive law.

 c. Whose laws should apply?

 • for example, should the public figure defence available in the United States pursuant to the First Amendment be applied by a Canadian court hearing a case of cyberlibel on a bulletin board located on a server in California? Or should the Canadian court apply domestic law?

 P.F. Carter-Ruck on Libel and Slander, 4th ed. (London: Butterworths, 1992).

 d. Will it be possible to enforce any judgment obtained?

 • courts in the United States appear to be unwilling to enforce defamation judgments from other jurisdictions which have not recognized an otherwise-applicable First Amendment protection for the defendant.

Bachchan v. *India Abroad Publications Inc.* 585 N.Y.S. (2d) 661 (1992), cited in M. Linda Dragos, "Curing a Bad Reputation: Reforming Defamation Law" 17 U. Haw. L.Rev. 113 at 161 (1995).

e. What is the quantum of damages?
    - in theory, damages may be increased by publication to potentially millions of people around the world. On the other hand, some sites which contain libellous expression may never receive a "hit." How is the measure of damages to be calculated?

ii) The global reach of Internet libel also raises procedural questions. In traditional libel law, there are three different types of defamatory statements:

a. Literal libel: expression which clearly and obviously defamatory on its face;

b. Inferential libel: expression which conveys a defamatory inferential meaning to "ordinary reasonable" readers. But the ordinary reader in Europe draws different reasonable inferences from a reader in Australia, depending on the specific cultural context in which he or she interprets the expression at issue; and

c. Legal innuendo: expression which is only defamatory by virtue of extrinsic facts known to a special category of reader. Clearly, there is an increased risk that contextual knowledge will render a statement defamatory in one jurisdiction but not in another.

Julian Porter & David A. Potts, *Canadian Libel Practice* (Toronto: Butterworths, 1986) at 46–51.

b) Interactive Nature

Another key feature of the Internet is its highly interactive nature. The ease with which users of the Internet may access bulletin boards and usenets and communicate with each other has engendered in its users a false sense of freedom in their communications. This is exemplified by the prevalence of activities such as "spamming" (mass mailings of unwanted information) and "flaming" (aggressive language). As a result, the Internet is qualitatively different from any other medium, other than perhaps a talk show or village townhall session. According to Mike Godwin, who has acted as counsel for the Electronic Frontier Foundation, the First Amendment public figure defence should apply to statements made on the Internet because a plaintiff has the ability to reply immediately to a worldwide audience, which Godwin claims is more gratifying and potent than launching a libel action.

Mike Godwin, "Libel Law: Let It Die" *Wired Magazine* (March 1996) 116.

Other American commentators have argued that "libel Plaintiffs who have been defamed by bulletin board speech and who have both access to the bulletin board on which the defamatory material appeared and a history of participation on the bulletin board are functionally equivalent to public figures."

Jeremy Weber, "Defining Cyberlibel: A First Amendment Limit for Libel Suits Against Individuals Arising From Computer Bulletin Board Speech" (1995) 46 Case W. Res. L.Rev. 235 at 237.

These American proposals raise a number of related questions:

i) Should American courts recognize a special defence, anchored to First Amendment principles, based on the ease of reply on the Internet?
ii) Would courts outside the United States recognize a special "First Amendment" type defence for Internet expression?
iii) What would be the material elements of such a defence?
    a. access to the Internet?
    b. access to the Internet to a particular bulletin board system where the defamatory statement was published?
    c. participation in the discussion?
    d. a previous history of participation and discussions in that particular bulletin board system?
iv) What subject matters should be covered?
v) How do you define issues of public interest on a global medium of communication?
vi) Is this defence only available to the operators of bulletin board systems, or to the original publishers?
vii) What type of malice ought to defeat this defence? Should it be the test set out by *New York Times* v. *Sullivan*, or the tests set out under Canadian common law?
viii) Should this concept be a defence or simply a mitigation of damages?

Few of these issues have been fully addressed by the courts to date.

c) Accessibility

Accessibility is another feature of the Internet which distinguishes it from traditional print or broadcast media. The relatively low cost of connecting to the Internet and even of establishing one's own website means that the opportunity for defamation has increased exponentially. Now, on the Internet, everyone can be a publisher and can be sued as a publisher.

d) Anonymity

Users do not have to reveal their true identity in order to send email or post messages on bulletin boards. Users can assume false names and identities. This tends to provoke uninhibited speech and increase the likelihood that the content of communications will be deliberately or negligently false.

e) Further Characteristics

i)   The Internet is a multimedia forum in that it can transmit images and information by means of sound, pictures, and words.

ii) By the use of hypertext, there can be links to many different sites, and defamatory juxtapositions can occur in a way never intended by the author.

iii) Statements are permanently stored and can be easily searched by computer and located by persons conducting due diligence or other inquiries.

iv) Republication is cheap, instantaneous, and hard for a plaintiff to track.

CHAPTER THIRTY-THREE:
Charter Issues

Sections 1 and 2(b) of the *Canadian Charter of Rights and Freedoms*, R.S.C. 1985, Appendix II, No. 44 provide:

1. The Canadian Charter of Rights and Freedoms guarantees the rights and freedoms set out in it subject only to such reasonable limits prescribed by law as can be demonstrably justified in a free and democratic society.

2. Everyone has the following fundamental freedoms: ...
   (b) freedom of thought, belief, opinion and expression, including freedom of the press and other media of communication;

Section 24(1) of the *Charter* provides:

Anyone whose rights or freedoms, as guaranteed by this Charter, have been infringed or denied may apply to a court of competent jurisdiction to obtain such remedy as the court considers appropriate and just in the circumstances.

Section 52(1) of the *Constitution Act, 1982* provides:

The Constitution of Canada is the supreme law of Canada, and any law that is inconsistent with the provisions of the Constitution is, to the extent of the inconsistency, of no force or effect.

Section 33 of the *Charter* provides for legislative override of the section 2(b) rights and freedoms:

(1) Parliament or the legislature of a province may expressly declare in an Act of Parliament or of the legislature, as the case may be, that the Act or a provision thereof shall operate notwithstanding a provision included in section 2 or sections 7 to 15 of this Charter.

(2) An Act or a provision of an Act in respect of which a declaration made under this section is in effect shall have such operation as it would have but for the provision of this Charter referred to in the declaration.

(3) A declaration made under subsection (1) shall cease to have effect five years after it comes into force or in such earlier date as may be specified in the declaration.

(4) Parliament or the legislature of a province may re-enact a declaration made under subsection (1).

(5) Subsection (3) applies in respect of a re-enactment made under subsection (4).

The leading case on the application of the *Charter* to the law of defamation is the Supreme Court decision in *Hill* v. *Church of Scientology of Toronto*, [1995] 2 S.C.R. 1130. In the course of rejecting defence arguments that the actual malice defence recognized in the United States Supreme Court's landmark decision in *New York Times* v. *Sullivan*, 376 U.S. 254 (1964) should be imported into Canadian law, Cory J. reasoned that defamatory statements are "very tenuously related to the core values which underlie section 2(b)" as they are inimical to the search for truth. He discussed the correct approach to be followed when a court faces a *Charter* argument from a defendant in a libel case at paragraphs 91–99 inclusive:

i)   The common law must be interpreted in a manner which is consistent with *Charter* principles, which are the fundamental values which guide and shape our democratic society and our legal system. Accordingly, it is appropriate for the courts to make such incremental revisions to the common law as may be necessary to have it comply with the values enunciated in the *Charter*.

ii)   When government action is challenged, whether it is based on legislation or the common law, and a claimant alleges that the state has breached its constitutional duty, the state must justify that breach.

iii)   Private parties owe each other no constitutional duties and cannot found their cause of action upon a *Charter* right, which does not exist in the absence of state action. However, a private litigant can argue that the common law is inconsistent with *Charter* values.

iv)   Courts must be cautious in amending the common law, and must not go further than is necessary when taking *Charter* values into account. Far-reaching changes to the common law must be left to the legislature.

v)   When the common law is in conflict with *Charter* values, a traditional section 1 framework for justification of the infringement when government action is involved is not appropriate. Instead, the balancing must be more flexible, and *Charter* values, framed in general terms, should be weighed against the principles which underlie the common law.

vi) The party who is alleging that the common law is inconsistent with the *Charter* should bear the onus of proving both that the common law fails to comply with *Charter* values and that, when these values are balanced, the common law should be modified. In the ordinary situation, where government action is said to violate a *Charter* right, it is appropriate that the government undertake the justification for the impugned statute or common law rule.

Cory J. ruled that the libel litigation brought by a Crown prosecutor did not involve the requisite "government action" and therefore the *Charter* had no direct application. However, the Court did expand the common law defence of qualified privilege for reporting on court proceedings, ruling that the privilege should apply even to documents, including pleadings, that were accessible to the public even if not yet filed.

In a number of subsequent defamation rulings by lower courts, defences based on section 2(b) of the *Charter* have failed:

Pressler v. Lethbridge (1997), 41 B.C.L.R. (3d) 350 (S.C.) [common law presumptions of falsity and damage upheld, varied on other grounds: 2000 BCCA 639].

Ironworkers Local 97 of the Internaional Assn. of Bridge, Structutal and Ornamental and Reinforcing Irwonworkers v. Liberal Party of British Columbia (1998), 152 D.L.R. (4th) 547, 40 B.C.L.R. (3d) 1 (S.C.) [in *obiter dicta*, the court rejected constitutional privilege based on *Charter*] .

Goddard v. Day (2000), 194 D.L.R. (4th) 559 (Alta. Q.B.) [special qualified privilege for political discussion and comment in the absence of malice rejected].

Ross v. New Brunswick Teachers' Assn. (2001), 201 D.L.R. (4th) 75 at para. 84 (N.B.C.A.) [as traditional defence of fair comment succeeded, the court declined to consider submissions "modulating the common law of defamation to accord with *Charter* values"].

Clement v. McGuinty (2001), 143 O.A.C. 328 (C.A.) [defence struck alleging the "hurly burly" of political debate protected by section 2(b) of the *Charter*].

Dhami v. Canadian Broadcasting Corp., [2001] B.C.J. No. 2773, BCSC 1181 [defence pleaded that if statements were defamatory, it was protected speech under section 2(b) of the *Charter* which allegedly expanded the common law defence of qualified privilege. Court rejected defence arguments this novel plea should be permitted to go to trial. *Charter* plea struck out].

However, in *Pizza Pizza Ltd.* v. *Toronto Star Newspapers Ltd.* (1998), 42 O.R. (3d) 36 (Div. Ct), aff'd (2000), 187 D.L.R. (4th) 761 (Ont. C.A.), the Ontario court modified the common law of libel to permit a defendant newspaper to plead a lesser meaning of the words complained of and then seek to justify that lesser meaning. [See Chapter 24, "*Polly Peck* and *Pizza Pizza*," E. Ontario Decisions, (1) *Pizza Pizza Ltd.* v. *Toronto Star Newspapers Ltd.*] The trial judge, sustained by the Divisional Court and by the Court of Appeal, held that it "is important, in the interests of freedom of expression and freedom of the press, for the newspaper to be allowed to defend itself fully by presenting its entire case to the court for consideration," relying on *Hill* v. *Church of Scientology of Toronto*, [1995] 2 S.C.R. 1130 to employ *Charter* values for this purpose.

In *Campbell* v. *Jones* (2002), 220 D.L.R. (4th) 201 (N.S.C.A.), the court reversed the trial judge and held that two lawyer defendants in a defamation action spoke on an occasion of qualified privilege when they held a press conference to complain about alleged infringements by the plaintiff police officer of their clients' *Charter* rights. Roscoe J.A. (Glube C.J.N.S. concurring) stated at paragraph 70 that it would be difficult to justify curtailing expression which was designed to:

> ... bring attention to and seek redress for multiple breaches of such important *Charter* rights as the right to counsel, the right to security of the person, including the right not to be subject to unreasonable search, and the right to equal protection and benefit of the law.

Accordingly, she held that the common law of qualified privilege should be modified incrementally to ensure that it conforms to *Charter* values by protecting a "publication to the world" via the news media in such circumstances. Leave to appeal to the Supreme Court of Canada was denied: [2002] S.C.C.A. No. 543. See a more detailed discussion of *Campbell* v. *Jones* in Chapter 18, "Qualified and Statutory Privilege."

In *Derrickson* v. *Tomat* (1992), 88 D.L.R. (4th) 401 (B.C.C.A.), Wood J.A. expressed the view at page 411 that the Court must define the limits of non-pecuniary damages in cases of politically-motivated defamation in such a way as to afford reasonable protection to reputation without endangering the fundamental freedom of expression on which the survival of our governmental system depends.

[T]he non-pecuniary damages awarded ought to be limited to an amount to bring sufficiently clearly to public attention the fact that the allegations were unwarranted, and that no lawful excuse of making them existed. But beyond that, the courts must be careful not to award damages which may tend more to stifle freedom of expression of opinion than to rehabilitate the reputation of the defamed.

It remains to be seen whether section 2(b) of the *Charter* protects journalists generally from being compelled to reveal their sources. In *Moysa* v. *Alberta (Labour Relations Board)*, [1989] 1 S.C.R. 1572, the issue was the right of the appellant, a journalist, to refuse to answer relevant questions in a proceeding before the Alberta Labour Relations Board in part on the basis of an alleged right to protect sources of information. The Supreme Court of Canada held there was an inadequate evidentiary basis to decide the point.

CHAPTER THIRTY-FOUR:

Insurance Issues

A. OVERVIEW

Coverage for liability for defamation is often provided under commercial and homeowners insurance policies. A person who is served with legal process or who is notified of a potential defamation claim should immediately investigate whether insurance coverage is available, identify each potentially relevant policy of insurance, and give notice of claim to the insurer as required by each policy.

A libelled plaintiff should also consider whether he or she is entitled to indemnity under a policy they have purchased from their own insurer in respect of damages inflicted by the tortfeasor.

B. INSURANCE POLICY CONTENTS

An insurance policy ordinarily contains:

- the declarations of insurance,
- the description of the coverages,
- the limits of insurance for the various coverages,
- the policy conditions,
- any special conditions, and
- the exceptions or exclusions with respect to coverage.

Policies of insurance written in Canada are typically prepared by the insurer and employ preprinted, standardized forms adopted by the Insurance Bureau of Canada. On occasion, however, a manuscript policy will be prepared to address the specific needs of an insured. A manuscript policy is normally assembled by an insurance broker.

E.M. v. *Reed* (2000), 24 C.C.L.I. (3d) 229, per Wilkins J. at para. 60 (Ont. S.C.J.) [discusses the essential ingredients of a policy].

C. POLICIES PROVIDING DEFAMATION COVERAGE

1) Comprehensive General Liability Policies

A common form of comprehensive general liability (CGL) insurance policy may provide coverage for liability for defamation in the description of coverage for liability imposed by law for "personal injury," "bodily injury," or "advertising injury." In certain policies, defamation coverage may also apply to liability for "property damage."

For example, a comprehensive general liability policy available to commercial enterprises contains a clause related to "personal injury" or "bodily injury" providing coverage for liability arising from defamatory expression:

> "Personal injury" means injury sustained by any person or organization and arising out of one or more of the following offences committed during the policy period in the conduct of the Named Insured's business designated in the Declaration Page(s):
>
> > the publication or utterance of a libel or slander or of other defamatory or disparaging material or a publication or utterance in violation of an individual's right of privacy, except publications or utterances in the course of or related to advertising, publishing, broadcasting or telecasting activities, conducted by or on behalf of the Named Insured

Compare the policy described in *Neiman* v. *CGU Insurance Co.*, [2002] O.J. No. 2215 at para. 4 (S.C.J.) and in *Hanis* v. *University of Western Ontario*, [2003] O.J. No. 4167 at paras. 13–15, 23–26 (S.C.J.).

Advertising activities are often excluded from personal injury coverage. Accordingly, a potential defamation defendant may wish to ensure that it obtains explicit coverage for liability for advertising injury. A commonly used definition of advertising injury reads as follows:

> "Advertising injury" means injury arising out of an offence committed during the policy period occurring in the course of the Named Insured's advertising activities, if such injury arises out of libel, slander, defamation, violation of right of privacy, piracy, unfair competition, or infringement of copyright, title or slogan.

One court held that injury for defamation was not included under a policy which provided liability coverage for claims alleging personal injury or property damage where the policy definitions did not define such losses to include damage to reputation caused by defamatory expression.

> *Maillett v. Halifax Insurance ING Canada*, 2003 NBQB 7, per Guerette J.:
>
> ¶30 The policy covers damages arising from personal injuries or property damage. It would be stretching the ordinary terms of the policy to find that damages arising from injury to reputation falls within the category of "bodily injuries."

2) Homeowner Policies

A homeowner's policy may also provide coverage for defamation liability but it will also often contain a clause excluding from coverage any liability which arises in relation to services rendered in the insured's occupation or from the business activities of the insured. A common definition of "business" in such a policy reads as follows:

> "Business" means any continuous or regular pursuit undertaken for financial gain, including a trade, profession, or occupation.

3) Miscellaneous Policies

Many insurance policies which provide liability for professional errors and omissions may include coverage for liability for defamation. The same is true of policies which apply to corporate officers and directors. In each case, it is a question of examining the available coverage, with the assistance of the broker and/or legal counsel, to determine whether an insurer will be responsible for defence costs or for payment of a judgment.

D. BASIC PRINCIPLES OF INTERPRETATION

A policy of insurance should be interpreted in accordance with certain general principles, including but not limited to the following:

i)   any ambiguity in a policy written by the insurer should be resolved in favour of the insured (the "*contraproferentum* rule");

ii) coverage provisions should be construed broadly;

iii) exclusion clauses should be construed narrowly; and

iv) at least where the policy is ambiguous, effect should be given to the reasonable expectations of the parties.

> *Brissette Estate v. Westbury Life Insurance Co.*, [1992] 3 S.C.R. 87.

Reid Crowther Ltd. v. *Simcoe & Erie General Ins. Co.*, [1993] 1 S.C.R. 252 at 268–69.

Non-Marine Underwriters, Lloyd's of London v. *Scalera*, [2000] 1 S.C.R. 551, per Iacobucci J. at 591.

Hodgkinson v. *Economical Mutual Insurance Co.*, [2003] I.L.R. I-4168, per Pitt J. at para. 5 (Ont. S.C.J.).

C. Brown and J. Menezes, *Insurance Law in Canada* (2d ed. 1991), at 123–31.

1) Construing an Endorsement

In construing an endorsement to an insurance policy, the endorsement and policy must be read together, and the policy remains in full force and effect except as altered by the words of the endorsement; conversely, the endorsement modifies the terms and conditions of the original insurance contract. Where the endorsement expressly provides that it is subject to all terms, limitations, and conditions of the policy, it does not abrogate or nullify any provision of the policy unless it is so stated in the endorsement.

Ben's Ltd. v. *Royal Insurance Co. of Canada*, [1985] N.S.J. No. 47 (S.C. (T.D.)).

2) Duties of the Insurer

Where the insured is named as a defendant in a lawsuit, two distinct issues arise:

i)   whether the insurer has a duty to defend the insured; and
ii) whether the insurer has a duty to indemnify the insured in the event the latter is found liable to pay damages or costs to the plaintiff.

The duty to defend is broader than and independent of the duty to indemnify, in the sense that the duty to defend arises where the claim alleges acts or omissions falling within the policy coverage, while the duty to indemnify arises only where such allegations are proven at trial.

Non-Marine Underwriters, Lloyd's of London v. *Scalera* (2000), 185 D.L.R. (4th) 1 (S.C.C.).

Nichols v. *American Home Assurance Co.* (1990), 68 D.L.R. (4th) 321 (S.C.C.).

Reform Party of Canada v. *Western Union Insurance Co.*, [2001] 5 W.W.R. 245 at para. 274 (B.C.C.A.).

The duty to defend is not triggered when it is clear and unambiguous that a claim falls outside the coverage provided by the policy.

Hodgkinson v. *Economical Mutual Insurance Co.,* [2003] O.J. No. 5125, per Morden J.A. at para. 18 (C.A.), citing *Nichols* v. *American Home Assurance Co.,* [1990] 1 S.C.R. 801 at 810–11 and 812.

3) The Pleadings Govern

Where it is clear from the pleadings that the lawsuit falls outside of the coverage of the policy, the duty to defend does not arise. However, the court will look beyond the labels used by the plaintiff to determine the true nature of the claim pleaded. In determining whether the duty to defend exists, the court simply assumes the truth of the plaintiff's factual allegations and decides whether the pleadings could reasonably support the plaintiff's legal allegations. The mere possibility that a claim within the policy may succeed is sufficient.

Nichols v. *American Home Assurance Co.* (1990), 68 D.L.R. (4th) 321 (S.C.C.).

Hodgkinson v. *Economical Mutual Insurance Co.,* [2003] O.J. No. 5125, per Morden J.A. at paras. 18–19 (C.A.), citing *Nichols* v. *American Home Assurance Co.,* [1990] 1 S.C.R. 801 at 810–11 and 812.

Reform Party of Canada v. *Western Union Insurance Co.,* [2001] 5 W.W.R. 245 at para. 9 (B.C.C.A.).

Bacon v. *McBride* (1984), 6 D.L.R. (4th) 96 at 99 (B.C.S.C.).

Opron Maritimes Construction Ltd. v. *Canadian Indemnity Co.* (1986), 19 C.C.L.I. 168, 73 N.B.R. (2d) 389 (C.A.), leave to appeal to S.C.C denied, [1987] 1 S.C.R. xi.

The widest latitude is to be given to the allegations in the pleadings in determining whether they raise a claim within the policy and any doubt as to whether the claim falls within the policy is to be resolved in favour of the insured.

Dyne Holdings Ltd. v. *Royal Insurance Co. of Canada,* [1996] P.E.I.J. No. 28 (C.A.).

Nichols v. *American Home Assurance Co.* (1990), 68 D.L.R. (4th) 321 (S.C.C.).

Nevertheless, the plaintiff cannot attract insurance coverage for his or her claim by crafting a pleading which changes an intentional tort into an unintentional tort. The court will examine the substance of the allegations when determining whether the plaintiff's legal allegations are properly pleaded.

Non-Marine Underwriters, Lloyd's of London v. *Scalera,* [2000] 1 S.C.R. 551, per Iacobucci J. at 596

Where it is clear from the pleadings that a lawsuit falls outside the coverage of the policy by reason of an exclusion clause, the duty to defend has been held not to arise.

Nichols v. American Home Assurance Co. (1990), 68 D.L.R. (4th) 321 at 327 (S.C.C.).

4) Breach by Insurer

Where an insurer refuses to defend, in breach of its obligation, it must bear the insured's legal costs to defend the lawsuit.

Wilkinson v. Security National Insurance Co., [2000] 9 W.W.R. 127 at para. 38 (Alta. Q.B.).

In such circumstances, the insured has the right to carry on his defence through a solicitor of his choosing at the expense of the insurer.

Wilkinson v. Security National Insurance Co., *ibid.* at para. 38.

5) Property Damage

Where property damage is not defined in the relevant legislation or the policy, one court held that it included economic loss and reduction in the value of the plaintiff corporation's goodwill arising from an alleged defamatory statement. Accordingly it was held that coverage was provided to an injured plaintiff for damages arising from defamatory expression published by others.

Blanchard v. Halifax Insurance Co. (1996) 40 C.C.L.I. (2d) 258 at para. 16 (N.B.Q.B. (T.D.)).

A policy of insurance may, however, specifically limit coverage for "property damage" to injury to tangible property.

G.B. Catering Services Limited v. Beckley (1994), 18 O.R. (3d) 135 (Gen. Div.).

Bird Construction Co. v. Allstate Insurance Co. of Canada, [1996] 7 W.W.R. 609 (Man. C.A.).

Alternatively, the policy may explicitly exclude coverage for liability for defamation by excluding libel, slander, and defamation from the meaning of property damage or personal injury as used in the policy.

Wood Buffalo (Regional Municipality) v. Scottish & York Insurance Co., 2001 ABQB 1109.

6) Advertising Injury

Coverage litigation relating to the meaning of "advertising injury" in the context of a defamation claim has recently clarified the nature of such insurance. Advertising, which is typically excluded from personal injury coverage, suggests a broad distribution of a message as opposed to a one-on-one oral statement or communication directed to only one person.

> *Reform Party of Canada* v. *Western Union Insurance Co.*, [2001] 5 W.W.R. 245 at para. 274 (B.C.C.A.).

The coverage for advertising injury may extend not merely to commercial insureds but to political parties and other non-commercial organizations. A necessary element of an advertising activity is a promotional message. A political website which was part of a promotional website actively seeking public support for an elected senate was an advertising activity. Although it denigrated those who benefit from the existing Senate policy, it reinforced the positive comments about an elected Senate contained on another page of the political party's website.

> *Reform Party of Canada* v. *Western Union Insurance Co.*, *ibid.* at para. 274 .

A publication of a message in 130 letters delivered to specific recipients was not a communication in the sense of advertising, broadcasting, and telecasting. All denote delivery of the message to a broad audience.

> *P.C.S. Investments Ltd.* *(c.o.b. Property Claims Service)* v. *Dominion of Canada General Insurance Co.* (1994), 18 Alta. L.R. (3d) 270 (Q.B.), varied (1996) 34 C.C.L.I. (2d) 113 (Alta. C.A.).

A defamatory posting on the World Wide Web is publication to a potentially broad audience of unknown recipients and therefore may constitute an "advertising injury."

> *Reform Party of Canada* v. *Western Union Insurance Co.*, above, at para. 4.

7) Business Exclusion

A homeowner's policy containing a "business exclusion" does not provide coverage where the defamatory statement arises in relation to services rendered in the insured's occupation.

> *Blanchard* v. *Halifax Insurance Co.* (1996), 40 C.C.L.I. (2d) 258 at para. 16 (N.B.Q.B. (T.D.)).

8) Coverage Disputes

Where a coverage dispute arises between insurer and insured, the court may in certain circumstances authorize the insured to name and instruct defence counsel. However, to protect the interest of the insurer, who has also has a contractual right to defend and therefore a right to raise defences that best suit its interest, at least one court has permitted the insurer to name its own counsel to participate in the defence.

> P.C.S. Investments Ltd. (c.o.b. Property Claims Service) v. Dominion of Canada General Insurance Co. (1994), 25 C.C.L.I. (2d) 119 (Alta. Q.B.), varied (1996), 34 C.C.L.I. (2d) 113 (Alta. C.A.).

E. INSURED'S DUTY TO CO-OPERATE

Typically, a policy will contain a clause imposing a general duty of co-operation on the insured. As part of the duty to cooperate, there may be an obligation to convey material information concerning significant developments in the litigation to the insurer.

> Canadian Newspapers Company Limited v. Kansa General Insurance Company Ltd. (1996), 30 O.R. (3d) 257 (C.A.), leave to appeal to S.C.C dismissed, [1996] S.C.C.A. No. 553.

1) Reporting during Litigation

Where new information comes to light concerning the plaintiff's position as regards malice and lack of good faith, the greatly increased legal fees for an anticipated lengthy trial may significantly affect the risk to the insurer. Accordingly, the insured is under an obligation to report such information to the insurer.

> Canadian Newspapers Company Limited v. Kansa General Insurance Company Ltd., ibid.

An offer to settle by the plaintiff may be a material development requiring notice to the insurer. The insurer may be entitled to invoke a settlement clause in the policy.

> Canadian Newspapers Company Limited v. Kansa General Insurance Company Ltd., ibid.

The insured is not obliged to disclose facts which the insurer is presumed to know from their public character and notoriety.

Canadian Indemnity Co. v. Johns-Manville Co., [1990] 2 S.C.R. 549, 72 D.L.R. (4th) 478.

Where the information is not in the public domain, the insured is not entitled to withhold information simply because the insurer fails to ask questions.

Canadian Indemnity Co. v. Johns-Manville Co., *ibid*.

Where there is an infringement of the insurer's right to defend a defamation action, the insurer is absolved from liability to indemnify the insured under the policy.

Mallett v. Lumbermen's Mutual Casualty Co., [1928] 3 DLR 150 (Ont. C.A.).

Canadian Newspapers Company Limited v. Kansa General Insurance Company Ltd., above.

Typically, the insurance policy will contain a clause to the following effect:

No action shall lie against the Company for the enforcement of any claim under this Policy unless the insured has complied with all the terms and conditions set out in this Policy.

Although insurance statutes in the various common law provinces typically authorize the court to relieve the insured against forfeiture of coverage under a policy of insurance, insurance contracts are contracts of good faith. It is well-settled that conduct amounting to a breach of good faith by an insured will disentitle the insured to relief against forfeiture.

Canadian Newspapers Company Limited v. Kansa General Insurance Company Ltd., above.

Where an insured seeks relief against forfeiture, the onus is on the insured to show that the insurer suffered no prejudice.

Canadian Newspapers Company Limited v. Kansa General Insurance Company Ltd., above.

On rare occasions, an insured may refuse to agree to a settlement proposed by an insurance company, thereby putting the company in the position of deciding whether or not to invoke the clause.

Canadian Newspapers Company Limited v. Kansa General Insurance Company Ltd., above.

F. NEWS MEDIA DEFENDANTS

In the case of news media defendants, there may be special arrangements with the insurer that permit the media insured to protect non-economic interests such as journalistic integrity.

This may afford the defendant greater control than usual over the conduct of the defence and the settlement of the litigation.

G. EXCLUSION FOR INTENTIONAL ACTS

Policies of insurance typically exclude liability for an intentional act. The meaning of intentional act in the context of a defamation claim has been considered in a number of recent decisions.

A New Brunswick court has made a distinction between:

i) intending to speak in a way that allegedly defamed, and
ii) intending to defame.

In that case, the court held that statements made accidentally in the nature of a "slip of the tongue" or a "poor choice of words" would not fall within the exclusion for intentional acts.

> *Blanchard v. Halifax Insurance Co.* (1996), 40 C.C.L.I. (2d) 258, per McLellan J. at paras. 19–22 (N.B.Q.B. (T.D.)) [a duty to defend was denied, however, based on a business exclusion clause].

An Alberta court considered the following exclusionary wording in the context of an insured's application for a declaration that the insurer had a duty to defend a defamation claim:

> Exclusions — This Policy does not Apply Under Coverages F and H
>
> 6.(a) to Bodily Injury or Property Damage caused intentionally by or at the direction of an Insured; ...
>
> *Wilkinson v. Security National Insurance Co.* (1999), 15 C.C.L.I. (3d) 80, per McMahon J. at para. 28 (Alta. Q.B.).

In that case, the court held:

i)   that it is the injury which must have been intentional for the exclusion to apply [at para. 28];
ii)   a comment can be erroneous or incorrect without this being the intended result [at para. 20];

iii)   the allegation in the statement of claim that the defendant "falsely" published the words complained of contemplates both unintentional and intentionally incorrect statements. As the statement of claim did not specify which meaning of the word "false" was intended, it should be taken to include both [at paras. 29–32];

iv)   the allegation in the statement of claim that the defendant "maliciously" published the words complained of does not necessarily incorporate an element of intention, as actual intention is not necessary to prove malice. Reckless disregard for the truth will suffice (at paras. 33–34);

v)   the defendant's intention will be a finding of fact for the trial judge (at para. 36); and

vi)   accordingly, the insurer had a duty to defend although it could not be determined until after trial whether the insurer had a duty to indemnify the defendant for a libel judgment awarded to the plaintiff (at para. 36).

Wilkinson v. Security National Insurance Co., ibid.

See also, *P.C.S. Investments Ltd. (c.o.b. Property Claims Service) v. Dominion of Canada General Insurance Co.* (1996), 178 A.R. 274 (C.A.).

Distinguishing both *Blanchard* and *Wilkinson*, above, the Ontario Court of Appeal recently held, however, that the intentional act exclusion applied to claims for defamation over the publication by the defendant of electronic messages on the Internet portraying the plaintiff's business ethics in a negative light and questioning the viability of the plaintiff corporation. The Court of Appeal reached this conclusion in the particular circumstances of the case, including the allegations made not only in the statement of claim, but also in the statement of defence. Accordingly, the insurer had no duty to defend.

Hodgkinson v. Economical Mutual Insurance Co., [2003] O.J. No. 5125 (C.A.) per Morden J.A. for the court.

The judgment of Morden J.A. for the unanimous Court of Appeal in *Hodgkinson* makes it clear that the application of the "intentional act" exclusion will depend on the unique circumstances of each defamation case. Morden J.A. held:

i)   The exclusion requires more than an intentional act that causes injury. It requires, on the part of the insured, "*the intent not only to do the act but also, in doing the act, the intent to injure*" [para. 20];

ii)   In the context of a defamation action, the intent to injure requires an intent to injure a person by injuring his or her reputation [para. 21];

iii)   Where a defendant did not intend either that his or her statement be defamatory or where he or she did not intend in the statement to refer to the plaintiff at all, there is no intention to injure the reputation of the plaintiff [para. 24];

iv)   A plea in a statement of claim that the insured acted *"falsely and maliciously"* in publishing the defamatory expression is not necessarily determinative of coverage, despite its allegation of intentional conduct on the part of the defendant, because *"liability in the defamation action is not legally dependant on a finding of intent"* [para. 28];

v)   In the particular circumstances of Hodgkinson, there was no room for a conclusion that the defendant did not intend to injure the plaintiff:

     a. It was *"clear from the statement of defence … that it negates the possibility that the publication was accidental — that is not intended — and that the insurer did not have the plaintiffs in mind in making his statements"* [para. 31]

     b. The statement of defence pleaded truth which in the circumstances in Hodgkinson was *"consistent only with the view [the statements] were made with the intention of warning others of the plaintiff's unethical behaviour and lack of financial viability"* [para 31].

vi)   The "intentional act" exclusion may apply even if the insured genuinely believes that what he or she is publishing is true. That is because truth may be defamatory. *"[A]lthough the falsity of the defendant's statements is an element of the cause of action for defamation, it is not an element of the defamation itself. Defamation exists once a statement has been published lowering the plaintiff's reputation whether it is true or not."* [para. 33]

See also, *Lee v. Townsend* (2002), 43 C.C.L.I. (3d) 261 (Ont. S.C.J.) where Killeen J. held that an action for malicious prosecution clearly fell within the policy exclusion for intentional acts, stating at para. 41 that "reckless indifference" was

> either fully tantamount to intentional conduct within the policy exception or, optionally, to use Iacobucci J.'s analysis [in *Non-Marine Underwriters, Lloyd's of London v. Scalera*, [2000] 1 S.C.R. 551], a derivative claim within an intentional tort which must be subsumed into the intentional tort for the purposes of the exclusion clause analysis.

An Ontario court recently held that where the extended definition of "bodily injury" in the Additional Coverages portion of a policy included, *inter alia*, "the publication or utterance of a libel or slander or of other defamatory or disparaging material," a general exclusion that the insurance did not apply to "bodily injury caused intentionally by or at the direction of the insured" was inoperative. The court refused to apply the exclusion "as it would basically nullify coverage." In the alternative, the court held it had "real doubt" whether the exclusion applied and resolved that doubt in favour of the insureds.

> *Hanis v. University of Western Ontario*, [2003] O.J. No. 4167, per Power J. at para. 91 (S.C.J.), citing *Weston Ornamental Iron Works Ltd. v. Continental Insurance Co.*, [1981] I.L.R. 1-1430 (Ont. C.A.).

H. ANALOGOUS INDEMNITIES

A defamation defendant should also investigate the possibility of indemnity for defence costs or liability for the payment of damages under arrangements analogous to insurance, which are typically offered by governments. In Alberta, for example, legislators enjoyed protection under the regulations to the *Financial Administration Act*, R.S.A. 1980, c. F-9, for defamatory expression which occurred during the course and scope of their activities as a member of the legislature.

> *Carter v. Alberta* (2001), 290 A.R. 127, 2001 ABQB 429, aff'd (2002) 222 D.L.R. (4th) 40, application for leave to appeal to S.C.C. dismissed, [2003] S.C.C.A. No. 58.

Table of Cases

Index

About the Authors

Roger D. McConchie

Member of the Bars of British Columbia and Alberta

Roger D. McConchie is a civil litigator in Vancouver with a practice focused on defamation, privacy, media, trade libel and Internet law. He has advised and represented domestic and international clients at all levels of the court system for more than 25 years. He has written extensively and spoken frequently on the subjects of libel and slander to academic, journalism, and professional audiences and his comments about legal developments are often reported in the news media.

David A. Potts

Member of the Ontario Bar

David Potts is a member of the Ontario bar and Counsel to Deacon, Spears, Fedson & Montizambert in Toronto. He has acted for both plaintiffs and defendants in libel actions including: major corporations, government, notable Canadian publications, as well as influential individuals and politicians. He is a frequent speaker on the subject of libel in Canada and abroad and is the co-author, with Julian Porter, of *Canadian Libel Practice*.